LITERATURE
A WORLD OF WRITING
STORIES • POEMS • PLAYS • ESSAYS

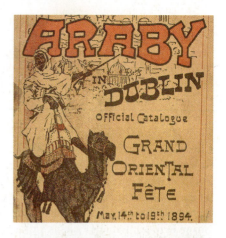

DAVID L. PIKE
AMERICAN UNIVERSITY

ANA M. ACOSTA
BROOKLYN COLLEGE,
CITY UNIVERSITY OF NEW YORK

Longman

Boston   Columbus   Indianapolis   New York   San Francisco   Upper Saddle River
Amsterdam   Cape Town   Dubai   London   Madrid   Milan   Munich   Paris   Montreal   Toronto
Delhi   Mexico City   Sao Paulo   Sydney   Hong Kong   Seoul   Singapore   Taipei   Tokyo

Vice President and Editor in Chief: Joseph Terry
Senior Development Editor: Katharine Glynn
Senior Supplements Editor: Donna Campion
Marketing Manager: Joyce Nilsen
Production Manager: Ellen MacElree
Project Coordination, Text Design, and Electronic Page Makeup: GGS Higher Education
    Resources, a Division of PreMedia Global, Inc.
Cover Design Manager: John Callahan
Cover Designer: Maria Ilardi
Cover Photo: *Front cover:* The Granger Collection, New York; *Back cover:* iStockphoto.
Photo Researcher: Jody Potter
Senior Manufacturing Buyer: Dennis J. Para
Printer and Binder: Worldcolor/Dubuque
Cover Printer: Lehigh/Phoenix Color/Hagerstown

For permission to use copyrighted material, grateful acknowledgment is made to the
copyright holders on pp. C-1–C-4, which are hereby made part of this copyright page.

Library of Congress Cataloging-in-Publication Data
Pike, David L. (David Lawrence), (date)
  Literature : a world of writing : poems, stories, plays, and essays / David L. Pike, Ana M. Acosta.
    p. cm.
  Includes index.
  ISBN-13: 978-0-321-36489-0
  ISBN-10: 0-321-36489-9
  1. College readers.   2. English language—Composition and exercises—Study and teaching
(Higher)   3. English literature—Study and teaching (Higher)   4. Literature—Study and teaching
(Higher)   5. Academic writing—Study and teaching (Higher)   6. Literature—Collections.
I. Acosta, Ana M.   II. Title.
  PE1417.P474 2009
  808'.0427—dc22

                        2009046492

2 4 5 6 7 8 9 10—WCD—13 12 11 10

Longman
is an imprint of

www.pearsonhighered.com

ISBN-10: 0-321-36489-9
ISBN-13: 978-0-321-36489-0

CONTENTS

2 WRITING IN THE WORLD: ARGUMENT, CRITICAL THINKING, AND THE PROCESS OF WRITING 38

3 INVESTIGATING THE WORLD: PLANNING, WRITING, AND REVISING A RESEARCH PAPER 82

4 ORGANIZING THE WORLD OF LITERATURE: THE CONVENTIONS OF GENRE   114

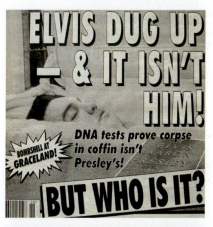

PART 2 THE WRITER'S WORLD: GENRES AND THE CRAFT OF LITERATURE

5 READING THE WORLD: EXPLORING THE FORMS OF LITERATURE   174

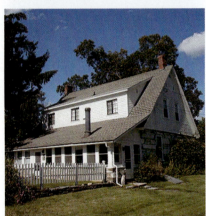

6 WRITING THE WORLD: WORKING WITH LITERARY DEVICES   210

11 THE WORLD WE SHARE: NATURE, CITIES, AND THE ENVIRONMENT 622

READING GLOBALLY, WRITING LOCALLY
GABRIEL GARCÍA MÁRQUEZ AND
THE LITERATURE OF THE AMERICAS 667

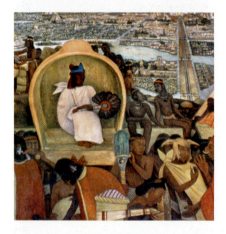

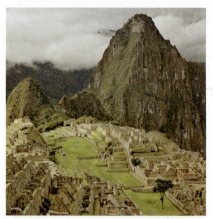

CONTENTS BY GENRE

We wrote this book because we believe that students learn best when they apply the skills that they use in their everyday lives to the worlds of literature and academic writing. Most students already think critically and have powerful, if imperfect, argument skills. They now enter a world in which they are expected to read reflectively, to think critically, and to construct and sustain an academic conversation, and this poses a serious challenge to many students working at the college level for the first time.

Literature: A World of Writing provides them with the tools they need to respond to that challenge on their own terms. We begin by recognizing that, in order to write anything about literature, students first need to be able to recognize how writers use language, and then need to be able to explain what they—the students—are doing with it. That is, they need to start with a degree of comfort and proficiency with the most basic of building blocks—words. To achieve this, *Literature: A World of Writing* employs the best of several theories and strategies in a design that allows you—the instructor—a choice of paths through a rich selection of stories, poems, plays, and essays. Additionally, students will find a comprehensive and unique guide to critical thinking, argument, and academic writing.

Students will find readings that are accessible, diverse, and compelling; they will find a guide to writing that addresses them as peers, expecting them to succeed and providing them with all of the tools they need to do so. They will find timeless masterpieces, exciting contemporary works, and fresh and accessible writing from around the world. They will discover that reading and writing are not nearly as forbidding as they may first appear to be, nor as deadly serious, and that rigor and humor, work and pleasure are complementary rather than mutually exclusive terms.

A new approach calls for a new design, and you will already have noticed that *Literature: A World of Writing* does not look like your typical textbook. Consistent with our goal to develop a book that makes YOUR teaching experience more fruitful, we've worked hard to design a book that students will WANT to carry and read. By opening up the layout, we have been able to make visual connections between the different components of each chapter in the same way that Web pages use links to make sense of the overwhelming mass of information available on the Internet. In designing *Literature: A World of Writing* our primary goal was to use illustrations that intelligently inform the work. We wanted a visual program that truly complements the written word, and we think we have achieved that goal.

We have also responded to requests for a shorter book by halving the page count of standard writing and literature textbooks, though we have done so without sacrificing coverage of either the classic works you expect or the fresh ones you look forward to.

We hope you enjoy reading *Literature: A World of Writing* as much as we enjoyed writing it.

Features of the Book

- A truly rich blend of *classic and contemporary selections* offers the comfort of the *known* for instructors who prefer teaching from the canon with the energy of the *new* for instructors who are more inclined to vary what they teach.
- *Dynamic writing instruction* is covered in the first six chapters of the book followed by a four-themed anthology. Each theme is broken down into easy-to-teach clusters.
- *Interactive Annotations* from both first and second readings of a selection show how to approach critical thinking about writing. In addition, some annotated examples include comments from the authors which help students understand how to apply their critical reading to other selections.

You cannot open a book without learning something.
—CONFUCIUS

- *Guides to Reading and Writing* give key information in chartlike format allowing students to readily grasp the concepts and definitions being presented.
- *Idea Maps* show students how to visually approach a mental process like generating ideas and finding topics to write about.
- *Writer @ Work* sections trace the process followed by a student from analyzing a selection to writing about it. Through these detailed examples, students learn how to **break down their assignments into manageable steps.**
- Nearly *20 examples of student writing* are given and many include instructor annotations.
- *Writing Exercises* throughout Chapters 1 through 6 give brief writing assignments to prompt students to apply what they have learned.
- *Questions for Reading and Discussion* follow every reading selection and a good number of images.
- *"Looking Back," a chapter summary box,* ends each chapter.
- *Chapter titles* all employ the "world" metaphor, reinforcing the book's story.
- *Four thematic chapters*—The World Closest to Us: Me and You; The Worlds Around Us: Beliefs and Ethics; The World We Live In: Spaces and Places; and The World We Share: Nature, Cities, and the Environment—conclude the book. Each theme is divided into subthemes that give instructors the option of assigning these as complete teaching units.
- **Four casebooks,** "Reading Globally, Writing Locally," ease students into reading some diverse texts by giving them a brief but colorful tour of the region's culture and history. Casebooks include: *Orhan Pamuk and the Literature of Europe; Naguib Mahfouz and the Literature of Africa; Jhumpa Lahiri and the Literature of Asia;* and *Gabriel*

García Márquez and the Literature of the Americas. Lesser-known writers from each region are also represented. Research writing assignments conclude each casebook and offer a choice of projects from writing about the literature of the region to exploring more fully the region's culture and history.

- **Pike Plus!** Since *Literature: A World of Writing* is, by design, a briefer, less expensive book, instructors who wish to customize it may do so through our Pike Plus! program. We offer a wide array of stories, poetry clusters, plays, and essays that can be bound into *Literature: A World of Writing* for less than the cost of a cup of coffee.

Organization

Part 1: A Reader's Guide to the World of Writing

takes the student step by step through the world of critical thinking, argument, and academic writing. From reading to summary, from argument and critical thinking to paper-writing and genre, students master the processing and writing skills they need to succeed academically and in the workplace. A liberal selection of *student papers* provides students with examples of writing by their peers on all of the major topics in the writing handbook. The *Writer @ Work* feature in each chapter traces one student's process from beginning reading to final paper. *Cognitive maps* render the process of each chapter visually; *question sets* promote reflection and discussion, beginning with questions of form and comprehension before moving on to questions of theme, content, and broader context; *writing exercises* develop a comprehensive range of paper genres and writing styles; *concluding features* review, reinforce, and extend the topic of each chapter.

Although grounded in the essential structures of logic and rhetoric, *Literature: A World of Writing* is also invested in connecting those structures with the dominant forms of today's cultures. Relevant examples drawn from popular culture make connections with student interests without pandering or sacrificing rigor. Visual material is smoothly and thoughtfully incorporated throughout the book; it is also highlighted

in specific sections. Each chapter concludes with a unit on visual culture that builds on and extends its literary topic:

- In Chapter 1, students learn about the visual assumptions we make, and how to write a summary of an image.
- In Chapter 2, they work on thinking critically about visual culture through examples from advertising.
- In Chapter 3, they discover how to incorporate visual material effectively into a research paper.
- In Chapter 4, they identify the genre conventions used by a variety of visual media, including movies and the Internet.

Part 2: The Writer's World: Genres and the Craft of Literature

approaches writing and literature the way writers and artists would be likely to group them: according to their use of genre and their dominant literary devices. Clear and expert exposition neatly summarized in tables link to examples in classic and contemporary texts in Part 3 to demonstrate how the materials and tools of literature actually work to create thematic meaning. Rather than having to grasp the tools of critical thinking and literary analysis abstractly, students master them inductively by working directly with stories, poems, plays, and essays as in these examples:

- Under "Describing the World: Stories," readers are asked to discuss the use of description in a brief story, shown a student's descriptive essay, and prompted to write a descriptive essay.
- Under "Staging the World: Plays," readers will read a play, study a guide to writing about a live or taped performance, and encounter *student notes* and a *student paper* written in response to a filmed version of the play they have read.
- Under "Patterns of Repetition," readers will find classic and contemporary selections categorized by alliteration and by assonance, among others.
- Under "Imagery," readers will find classic and contemporary selections categorized by simile, metaphor, allegory, and symbol.

Chapter 5 provides *student papers* that work with each of the four genres anthologized in Part 3. Chapter 6 supplements

exposition of the primary forms of literary devices with a wide variety of *writing exercises* to assist students in learning for themselves how these devices function in everyday life and their own writing as well as in literary texts. Chapter 7 reinforces the book's global theme with a collection of readings that introduce issues of translation and bilingualism and alert students to the presence of these issues in their own lives.

Part 3: The Reader's World: Exploring the Themes of Literature

provides essential texts and pleasant surprises in thematic groupings that help students to find new meaning in classic texts and to find classic issues in new texts: *The World Closest to Us: Me and You; The Worlds Around Us: Beliefs and Ethics; The World We Live In: Spaces and Places; The World We Share: Nature, Cities, and the Environment*. Each thematic grouping is divided into two or three units focused around different facets of the theme; readings within each unit are grouped according to genre. Between each thematic chapter is a "Reading Globally, Writing Locally" casebook focused on a specific region of the world. Each casebook begins with a selection of fictional and nonfiction writings by a major world author: *Orhan Pamuk and the Literature of Europe; Naguib Mahfouz and the Literature of Africa; Jhumpa Lahiri and the Literature of Asia; Gabriel García Márquez and the Literature of the Americas*. Each chapter unit and each casebook concludes with suggested topics for essays extending work on the readings and the thematic issues and with further readings on the same theme or region elsewhere in *Literature: A World of Writing*. The questions and essay topics at the end of each chapter encourage students to make further connections between the different issues raised.

Appendix A provides a succinct, accessible, and reliable introduction to the major trends of literary criticism, with suitable applications of different schools of criticism to college writing. **Appendix B** provides coverage of MLA documentation and includes a literary research paper. A **Glossary of Literary Terms** ends the book.

Flexible Structure

Every instructor has the same goal of teaching students to write, but each of us has a different way of getting there. Rather than dictate a specific program and specific pedagogy, we designed this book with a flexible and adaptable modular structure to allow each instructor the freedom either to follow a built-in sequence or to craft his or her own curriculum. If you desire a highly structured introduction to the fundamentals of reading, writing, and thinking critically about literature, you can follow the given sequence of Part 1. If you then prefer further work based on form and structure, you can continue with Part 2. If you prefer to move directly to the thematically oriented readings, you can skip Part 2 and begin with Part 3, incorporating the readings you want with reference to the "Further Readings" feature in Part 3 and suggestions in the Instructor's Manual. If you want to feature world literature, you can focus on the four casebooks in Part 3 and draw from the rich diversity of cross-referenced selections elsewhere in the anthology. If you prefer a more geographically delimited selection of literature, all of the must-have classics are here, too.

If you prefer to construct your own units of reading and use the writing handbook components as reference, the contents by genre provides ready access to the capacious and varied readings included in *Literature: A World of Writing,* ranging from a core of canonical texts to contemporary selections from around the world. Rather than promoting a particular theoretical or pedagogical viewpoint, *Literature: A World of Writing* provides everything you need to teach a course the way you want to teach it. It's your world.

RESOURCES

MyLiteratureLab.com

MyLiteratureLab empowers student writers and facilitates writing instruction by uniquely integrating a composing space and assessment tools with market-leading instruction, rich literary resources, multimedia tutorials, and exercises for writing, grammar, and research.

MyLiteratureLab adds a new dimension to the study of literature by offering several dynamic tools. Writers on Writing, produced exclusively for MyLiteratureLab, includes 23 video interviews of prominent contemporary authors who discuss their writing careers and inspire students to explore their creativity. Longman Lectures are evocative, richly illustrated audio readings, given by our roster of Longman authors (including one of the authors of this book), that offer students advice on how to read, interpret, and write about literary works. This powerful program also features Diagnostic Tests, Interactive Readings with clickable prompts, film clips of popular stories and plays, sample student papers, a media-based Literature Timeline, and Avoiding Plagiarism guidance. A new, searchable eAnthology offers direct links to dozens of poems, essays, short stories, and plays, in which students can take notes and highlight selections while they read.

MyLiteratureLab is an eminently flexible application that instructors can use in ways that best complement their course and teaching style. They can recommend it to students for self-study, set up courses to track student progress, or leverage the power of administrative features to help manage their time and the course more effectively. The assignment builder and commenting tools, developed specifically for writing instruction, bring instructors closer to their student writers, make managing assignments and evaluating papers more efficient, and put powerful assessment within reach. Students receive feedback within the context of their own writing, which encourages critical thinking and revision and helps them to develop skills based on their individual needs. Learn more at **www.myliteraturelab.com.**

Pike Plus!

Literature: A World of Writing was designed to offer you and your students maximum flexibility. Through our Pike Plus! custom program, you can choose from a wide selection of stories, poems, plays, and essays that can be custom bound into this text for less than the cost of a cup of coffee. To see a complete list of available selections, go to **www.pearsoncustom.com,** keyword search: introlit. For more information, contact your Pearson sales representative **(www.pearsonhighered.com/replocator).**

Instructor's Manual

Written exclusively by David L. Pike and Ana M. Acosta and based on their years of classroom teaching experience, the Instructor's Manual is an integral part of the book's conception. Comprehensive and detailed entries devoted to every selection in the book summarize useful criticism, propose strategies for teaching customized for different levels of student, offer class-by-class outlines for longer texts and suggest alternate groupings to respond to specific instructor interests and needs.

ACKNOWLEDGMENTS

We would like to thank the 43 students who gave us their deep and sustained involvement in this project. We are especially grateful to the members of the Pearson Student Advisory Board including Rachel Brickner, University of Pittsburgh; Alexis Fabrizio, University of Florida; Dustin Farivar, University of Colorado, Boulder; Christopher Gast, Arizona State University; Dianna He, University of Pennsylvania; Jason Hustedt, University of Nebraska, Lincoln; Laura Morel, Miami Dade Community College; Meghana Reddy, University of California at Los Angeles; Drew Rudebusch, University of Washington; and Evan Skinner, Oklahoma State University.

We would like to extend our sincere appreciation to the many reviewers who gave us advice and guidance on every aspect of this textbook.

Gabriela Adler
   Bristol Community College
Julie Amberg
   York College of Pennsylvania
Audrey Antee
   Florida Community College—
      Jacksonville
Joe Antinarella
   Tidewater Community College
Sydney Bartman
   Mount San Antonio College, CA
Cynthia Baw
   Tarrant County College
Dr. Kristina Bechman-Brito
   Pima College
Evelyn Beck
   Piedmont Technical College
Barbara Bengels
   Hofstra University
Wyatt Bonikowski
   Suffolk University
Cynthia Bowden
   Las Positas College
Pennie Boyett
   Tarrant County College
Harry Brown
   DePauw University
Dona Cady
   Middlesex Community College
Evelyn Cartright
   Barry University
Alexandria Casey
   Graceland University
Dean R. Cooledge, PhD
   University of Maryland, Eastern Shore
Sheilah Craft
   University of Indianapolis
Jerry DeNuccio
   Graceland University
Josh Dickinson
   Jefferson Community College
Douglas Dowland
   The University of Iowa
Mary Dutterer
   Howard Community College

Cynthia Eisen
   Nazareth College
Tom Ernster
   Kirkwood Community College—
      Marion Center Campus
Mary Evans
   Hudson Valley Community College
Rob Franciosi
   Grand Valley State University
Ruth Ann Gambino
   Palo Alto College
Joseph Gawel
   University of North Florida
David Glaesemann
   Cy-Fair College, TX
Esther Godfrey
   University of South Carolina Upstate
J. Bartholomay Grier
   Wilkes University
Jerry Hamby
   Lee College
Tamara Harvey
   George Mason University, VA
Katie Heid
   Baker College of Owosso
Shawn Hellman
   Pima Community College, AZ
Eric Hibbison
   J. Sargeant Reynolds Comm.
      College, VA
Ed Higgins
   George Fox University
Gerry Himmelreich
   San Juan College
Catherine Holmes
   College of Charleston
M L Horn
   Middlesex Community
      College
Dr. Elizabeth Howells
   Armstrong Atlantic State University, GA
Willis Humiston
   Palo Alto College, TX
Amy Hundley
   Merced College, CA

Elizabeth Joseph
   Tarrant County College—SE
Catherine Keohane
   Montclair State University
Howard Kerner
   Polk State College
Millie M. Kidd
   Mount St. Mary's College, CA
Lynn Kostoff
   Francis Marion University
Jennifer Lane
   Glendale Community College, AZ
Shanie Latham
   Jefferson College
Andrea Leavey
   Collin College, TX
Jonathan Lewis
   Columbus State University
Patricia Lonchar
   University of the Incarnate World
Dr. Robert Lunday
   Houston Community College—
      Southeast Campus
Kelly Martin
   Collin College, TX
Vickie Melograno
   Atlantic Cape Community College
Fred Mench
   Richard Stockton College of NJ
Rhea Mendoza
   Hartnell College
Christian Michener
   Saint Mary's University of Minnesota
Joyce Marie Miller
   Collin County Community College, TX
Dorothy Minor
   Tulsa Community College
Danielle Mitchell
   Penn State, Fayette
Lyle Morgan
   Pittsburgh State University, KS
Michael Morris
   Eastfield College
David Mulry
   Schreiner University

Dana Nichols
    Gainesville State College
Diana Nystedt
    Palo Alto College
Elizabeth Oness
    Winona State University
Dr. Daniel Payne
    SUNY Oneonta
Ben Railton
    Fitchburg State College
Henriette Recney
    SUNY Buffalo
Jane E. Rosencrans
    J. Sargeant Reynolds Community
    College, VA
Laura Rotunno
    Penn State Altoona
Dr. Lisa Roy-Davis
    Collin County Community
    College, TX
Gloria Santrucek
    Baker College of Owosso

Judith Schmitt
    Macon State College
Mary Simpson
    Central Texas College
Carissa Smith
    Charleston Southern University
James R. Sodon
    St. Louis Community College at
    Florissant Valley, MO
Robert Soza
    Mesa Community College
Henry Spann
    Anderson College, SC
Laura Steinert
    South Texas College
Dr. Pam Stinson
    Northern Oklahoma College, OK
Jeniffer Strong
    Central New Mexico Community
    College
Karl Terryberry
    Daemen College

Andrew Tomko
    Bergen Community College
Chris Twiggs
    Florida State College at
    Jacksonville
April Van Camp
    Indian River State College
Bente Videbaek
    SBU
Marianna Vieira
    Quinnipiac University
Janice Vierk
    Metropolitan Community
    College
Joyce Wexler
    Loyola University Chicago
Christopher Wixson
    Eastern Illinois University
Judy Young
    University of West Florida
Beth Younger
    Drake University

In the extended process of planning and preparing this textbook, we have been fortunate to have the support, advice, and assistance of many people. Our publisher, Roth Wilkofsky, has supported our project in every possible way. Our editor, Joseph Terry, has unfailingly worked to help us realize the potential of a rapidly evolving field. Mary Ellen Curley, Director of Development, English, was a stabilizing force throughout the project. We want to thank Joseph Terry's assistant, Rosie Ellis, and Mary Ellen Curley's assistant, Annie England, for their help in keeping all of the details in order. We thank our first development editor, Lai Moy, for her creativity and encouragement in getting the project underway. We are grateful to her successor, the indefatigable Katharine Glynn, for her sound judgment, painstaking attention to detail, and unflappable humor in the long and hard but ultimately rewarding work of producing the beautiful volume you now hold in your hands. Teresa Ward's patience and persistence gave us the time and energy we needed to produce an Instructor's Manual that would live

up to its parent text. Lisa Yakmalian worked diligently to clear the myriad text permissions. Jody Potter brought acumen, personal vision, and lightning-fast responses to the daunting task of knowing what images we wanted, finding them, and clearing permissions for them. John Callahan and Maria Ilardi found the outer image and design to match the story inside the cover. Laura Coaty, Director, Market Research & Development, Megan Galvin-Fak, Executive Marketing Manager, and Joyce Nielsen, Executive Marketing Manager helped smooth the book's entry into the marketplace. Once the manuscript was complete, Ellen MacElree, the production manager, shepherded the project to and monitored the staff at PreMedia Global, Inc., where textbook designer, Amy Musto, coordinated the effort to put all of the content together visually. Doug Bell, the senior production editor, our copyeditor, Stephanie Magean, and Susan Bogle carefully reviewed the manuscript and oversaw the complex production of a challenging design and worked, it seemed, around the clock to keep us, and the book, on schedule. We wish to

thank our students and colleagues at Brooklyn College and American University for generously sharing their writing and their experience with us. David L. Pike expresses his gratitude to successive research assistants for their help in tracking down texts and information: Mark Stein, Mickie Tencza, Joelle Tybon, Mary Sweeney, and Tara Schupner. He also wishes to recognize his inspirational colleagues in the College Writing Program at American University, especially the program director, John Hyman, the Writing Center director, Janet Auten, and veteran instructors Cynthia Bair van Dam, Glenn Moomau, and Lacey Wooton-Don. Their wisdom, savvy, and dedication remind us every day that our profession, in spite of institutional constraints, can still remain a vocation. But this book will not be finished until it has opened up a dialogue with the teachers and readers for whom we wrote it. We warmly welcome your reactions and suggestions at dpike@american.edu and aacosta@brooklyn.cuny.edu.

David L. Pike and Ana M. Acosta

A WORLD OF MEANING

READING AND THINKING

ABOUT LITERATURE

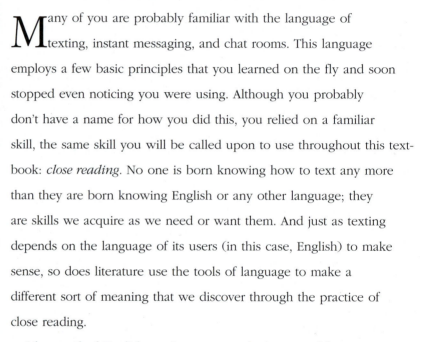

Many of you are probably familiar with the language of texting, instant messaging, and chat rooms. This language employs a few basic principles that you learned on the fly and soon stopped even noticing you were using. Although you probably don't have a name for how you did this, you relied on a familiar skill, the same skill you will be called upon to use throughout this text-book: *close reading*. No one is born knowing how to text any more than they are born knowing English or any other language; they are skills we acquire as we need or want them. And just as texting depends on the language of its users (in this case, English) to make sense, so does literature use the tools of language to make a different sort of meaning that we discover through the practice of close reading.

Like standard English, texting assumes that we are able to distinguish between a number of possible choices in order to make an informed decision about what each term means. No matter what you are reading, there will be parts you recognize immediately, parts you can figure out based on context and past experience, and parts you have to look up in a dictionary or ask about. Consequently, the first step in reading is to divide up the different components of what you are reading into three categories: what you know, what you can figure out on your own, and what you need help with.

It is also important to consider who wrote the message you are read-ing, for what purpose, and for whom. When you receive a message from a friend, you are probably able to decipher the meaning even if you haven't understood every abbreviation in it. That is the sort of work literature requires from you. As the publisher Charles Scribner, Jr., put it, "Reading is a means of thinking with another person's mind; it forces you to stretch your own." Many of the things that literary writing asks you to think about will be new to you, but the tools you use to stretch your mind to accommodate those thoughts may be surprisingly familiar—you already rely on them every day, and usually without even noticing you are using them. The difference with literature lies in the act of noticing. We called this book *Literature: A World of Writing* because of the extraordinarily rich world that becomes available to you once you take notice of it. Learning to read and write effectively opens up this world to you, from the culture of texting to the graded research paper, from Egyptian hieroglyphs to Hollywood blockbusters, from poems written across the globe to stories set in your hometown.

In this chapter, you will rediscover the basic tools you use to interact with the world around you, and learn how to apply them to reading and thinking about the world of literature. It has been said that reading is an art form, and that every person can be an artist. This chapter will help you move step by step through the skills necessary for mastering the art of reading: ways of understanding how literary writing creates meaning; techniques for understanding, enjoying, and working productively with what you read; and strategies for organizing your thoughts by summarizing the meaning of what you have read.

The principles of texting are as old as writing itself. Egyptian hieroglyphs, as in this 3,500-year-old example from the Valley of the Kings in Luxor, abbreviated ideas into picture-images rather than letters and words. During the Middle Ages, monks trying to save time and space when copying manuscripts by hand would substitute letters or signs for common words and run all the words together in a line.

MEANINGLESS WORDS AND THE WORLD OF MEANING

An effective way to heighten your awareness of the tools you already possess is to focus on **literary form,** the way in which a writer has chosen to organize thoughts and words. Here, too, you will be surprised how much you already recognize of the different forms writing can take. Consider the following letter, sent in 1862 by the English poet Edward Lear to his good friend Evelyn Baring, the 1st Earl of Cromer:

> Thrippsy pillivinx,
>
> Inky tinky pobblebockle abblesquabs?—Flosky! Beebul trimble flosky!—Okul scratchabibblebongibo, viddle squibble tog-a-tog, ferrymoyassity amsky flamsky ramsky damsky crocklefether squiggs,
>
> Flinkywisty pomm,
> Slushypipp

Recognizing the form taken by a piece of writing is a crucial step in the process of reading. In this case, it is the only thing we are able to recognize: there is a **salutation,** or greeting ("Thrippsy pillivinx"); a **body** that, from its punctuation marks, includes a question, several exclamations, and a descriptive phrase; and a **closing** ("Flinkywisty pomm"); followed by a **signature** ("Slushypipp"). If you have ever written or received a letter, you will have understood these as the **conventions,** or typical components, of a letter. We might have thought that we would need the words ("Dear Evelyn") in order to recognize these conventions, but Lear demonstrates here that specific writing mechanics (capitalization, punctuation) are all that he needs to help his reader distinguish the different parts of the letter (assuming, that is, that his reader is willing to stretch his mind enough to notice those parts). A period or an exclamation point shows the reader where one sentence might end and another might begin. It is because we recognize the letter form, not because we know anything about what the words mean, that we can begin to make some sense out of what Lear has written. Thus, when you want to determine what a text means, start by asking questions about its form.

Literary Form and Assumptions about Meaning

Thinking about literary form can help us answer questions about literary meaning. Let's review again Lear's text. Looking at each expression in isolation reveals very little. Looking at each expression in relation to the others, however, allows you to determine that Lear has written a letter. The next natural question would then be, what **genre,** or type, of letter is it supposed to be? At this point, you can begin to make assumptions about meaning.

Several questions may be asked about Lear's composition:

- Are the letters grouped into recognizable patterns—that is, into words?
- Are these words comprehensible to the general public?
- Were they comprehensible to Baring, his intended audience?
- What is it about Lear's tone or attitude that enables you to assume that he was probably not writing a business or an official letter?

While these questions will not help you to translate Lear's nonsense word for word, they do allow you safely to assume that the letter was intended for a friend. Why? First, would it make sense to fill a business

letter with nonsense words? Second, would a serious correspondence permit a signature as casual and affectionate as "Slushypipp"? By answering these questions, you can conclude that Lear's letter was likely a personal one, just as the txtspk above was appropriate for a personal communication but inappropriate for a classroom essay.

If you wanted to verify the hypothesis derived from your close reading and undertook a bit of research on Lear and Baring, you would discover that Lear (1812–1888) was a poet and illustrator famous for his nonsense verse, and that he wrote many personal letters to his younger friend Baring. In fact, he was still sending nonsense poems and pictures to his friend's son many years later. This detail would still not tell you what the letter you just read is about, but it would confirm the hypothesis that it is a communication between close friends. See the illustration on page 5 to read another letter from Lear.

The Point of Literary Meaning

What is the function of literary form? According to the Caribbean novelist Jean Rhys, "Reading makes immigrants of us all. It takes us away from home, but more important, it finds homes for us everywhere." Writers of literature strive to introduce us to situations we have probably never before encountered; at the same time, as Rhys suggests, they also want to make us identify with

Another letter from Edward Lear to Evelyn Baring. The text, wrapped around the spirals of a snail's shell, reads: "Feb. 19. 1864 Dear Baring Please give the enclosed noat to Sir Henry—(which I had just written:-& say that I shall have great pleasure in coming on Sunday. I have sent your 2 vols of Hood to Wade Brown. Many thanks for lending them to me—which they have delighted me eggstreamly Yours sincerely" Note how Lear uses his own version of texting ("enclosed noat," "eggstreamly") to personalize the snail-mail message.

and understand that unfamiliar situation. Combining the unfamiliar with the familiar is a hallmark of literary writing that you will encounter again and again in the pages of this book. Few people, for example, are members of a royal family or suffer unconscionable tragedies or have mystical experiences; yet such has been the fate of countless characters in countless plays and novels, from Sophocles' Antigone in ancient Greece (p. 465), to Shakespeare's Hamlet in an imagined Denmark (p. 286), to the characters in the Egyptian writer Naguib Mahfouz's short stories (p. 488). Few people find themselves transformed into an exotic amphibian, as in the Argentinean writer Julio Cortázar's short story, "Axolotl" (p. 416), or hearing voices within the walls of their bedroom, as in the late nineteenth-century American writer Charlotte Perkins Gilman's story, "The Yellow Wallpaper" (p. 541). Nevertheless, as you travel great distances in these extraordinary works of literature, you will find yourselves immersed, and, eventually, at home, in the strange worlds they create within their pages.

At the same time, literature can also make what we thought was familiar suddenly seem utterly unfamiliar. Opening a letter, few people would expect it to be composed of utter nonsense, or its words wrapped around the spirals of a snail's shell, as happened to Lear's friend Evelyn Baring. Few people would have thought to portray the relationship between a mother and a daughter in the terms chosen by the contemporary American poet Sharon Olds in "The Possessive" (p. 16), or think about food the way Japanese-American poet Garrett Hongo does in "Who Among You Knows the Essence of Garlic?" (p. 618). Rather than transport us to a foreign place, as many older literary works do, many works of contemporary literature will ask us to view our own world in a new way. This kind of strangeness may shock us, as in Olds's poem; it may illuminate us, as in Hongo's poem; or it may be a sign of friendship, as Baring surely came to understand the nonsense Lear sent him. Often, it will elicit many different emotions at once—this is another way in which literature stretches our minds.

Whether making the unfamiliar familiar or the familiar seem strange, and whether living nearly 2,000 years ago, like the South Indian poet Uruttiran (p. 382), or in the present day, like the Indian-American author Jhumpa Lahiri (p. 602), writers have a single means at their disposal with which to perform their magic: words. What we take for granted in everyday life—that we know what the words we say actually mean—writers do not. There are many ways in which writers encourage their readers to pay attention to the words on the page. The simplest way—as we have already observed—is with nonsense. We understand what words mean only in comparison with what they do not mean and what they do not say.

Forming Literary Meaning

As we learned earlier by close attention to the patterns made by the words of Lear's letter to his friend Baring, in order for nonsense to make sense it must take a form we can recognize. Consider this sentence, composed by the linguist Noam Chomsky: "Sleep colorless furiously green ideas." Unlike Lear's imagined nonsense, Chomsky's five words are indeed familiar to us, yet in their current order, they make no more sense than do Lear's. But if we rearrange the words, as Chomsky went on to do, they suddenly sound as if they should make sense: "Colorless green ideas sleep furiously." The words sound sensible because they are in perfectly grammatical order—a subject ("ideas") modified by two adjectives ("colorless" and "green"), and a predicate ("sleep") modified by an adverb ("furiously")—but it is a statement that has no meaning in the real world. Like Edward Lear's letter, it sounds as if it means something because it is presented in a recognizable form—that is, because it is a complete sentence.

Chomsky composed his nonsense to make a point about how language works; literature uses the same strategy to affect the way we see the world. Consider this beautiful poem by the twentieth-century Spanish poet Federico García Lorca. The poem begins:

Green how I want you green

Green wind. Green branches.

The ship on the sea

And the horse in the mountains.

Further along in the poem, Lorca introduces us to a gypsy whose skin and hair are also green. What does "green" mean here? How can a wind be green? How can skin and hair be green? Clearly the speaker wants to say *something*, but what? In order to understand the speaker's meaning, we as readers must search for the **figurative meaning** of the color, rather than what the words say **literally,** which makes no more sense than Chomsky's phrase above.

That is, what else can "green" represent in addition to what we usually understand as its color? To discover figurative meaning, it is not enough to be a passive reader, to read literally, as we would a newspaper. Instead, we must, as the philosopher Arthur Schopenhauer phrased it, "think with someone else's head instead of with our own." To be aware of the possibility of figurative meaning is part of the practice of close reading: how are the words put together, what choices

has the writer made, what mood do the words evoke, how do the words make us feel? If you reread the lines from Lorca's poem closely, you can sense that the speaker is longing for something that he does not have. But rather than spelling out at length what he wants, the poet uses the single word "green" to bind together all of the different things he is longing for, because that is the way he experiences them, and that is the way he wants us to experience them.

WRITING EXERCISE: Making Your Own Nonsense

1. Using Edward Lear's letter as your model, write a letter to a friend or a family member without using any of Lear's words, any words in English, or any words in any other language with which you are familiar. A third party reading your letter should be able to judge the mood of the letter (happy, sad, angry, pleading, etc.) and get a sense of its message. Be sure to pay close attention to the punctuation and the form of the letter. Test your letter on a classmate, family member, or friend. How successful were you in communicating your message?

2. Write a short paragraph reflecting on the process of composing nonsense. Which part was most difficult? Which part was easiest? What strategies did you use to impart mood, and how did you get across the sense of the message? How pleased are you with the result? If you were to do it again, is there anything you would do differently?

MAKING SENSE

Reading literature requires us to be tentative and exploratory, hypothesizing, testing, and revising our hypotheses as we go along, and then once again as we go back and reread. This is not to say that anything goes—that would result in pure nonsense. Instead, **reading critically** is a process of constantly judging between greater and lesser degrees of certainty. In the same way, reading is a constant balance between comprehension and incomprehension, between knowing what we know; knowing what we don't know but can easily find out in a dictionary or reference work; and knowing what we cannot know for certain and will require us to collect evidence supporting what we consider the likeliest meaning or possible meanings. An important part of close reading is reducing our uncertainty as far as it can go; the kernels of puzzlement that remain will usually be the most exciting and engaging moments of the text, and they

will provide the key to all of the further work we will do with it.

Once we can distinguish sense from nonsense and know that a text does indeed mean something, the next step to understanding literature is to make sense of the confusion between possible meanings of words that we think we recognize. A case in point is Ramona Quimby, the eight-year-old protagonist of Beverly Cleary's popular book series. She understands the end of the first line of "The Star-Spangled Banner" as "the donzer lee light," and asks her teacher what a "lee light" is. (Do you know the actual words to this line of the song? Do you know the words that follow?) Have you had the experience of hearing something said or sung over and over again and then realizing after seeing the words in print that what you thought you heard was completely different from what was actually written? Or, have you read a word, or series of words, to yourself and thought you knew

The evolution of sense is, in a sense, the evolution of nonsense.
—VLADIMIR NABOKOV

the correct pronunciation, only to discover it was completely different from what you thought it sounded like in your head? Many jokes are based on such confusions, as are all manner of wordplay and poetic effects, not to mention everyday misunderstandings over how a word is used or what it means. The English, for example, call an elevator a "lift," a cookie a "biscuit," a French fry a "chip," and a cigarette a "fag." The effect of **ambiguity,** or uncertain meaning, can be derived from something as simple as a difference in accent. In everyday life, this may create a bit of confusion, but in the world of literature it can be the cause of tragedy or, just as frequently, the basis for comedy.

The meeting of different cultures has long resulted in confusion and misunderstanding;

the more we live in a global society, the more important it is to know how to speak and write clearly and to be able to resolve ambiguity. In person-to-person communication, we tend to rely on body language and tone of voice to help us understood the words we hear—think of the range of meaning, from pleading to disgust, that can be injected into a simple word such as "please." None of these aids are available to us when we read or when we communicate electronically. Even with the range of emoticons now available for chatting, e-mail, and text messaging, it remains extremely difficult to express complex emotions or to make sure that our jokes are understood when we have only words and typewritten symbols at our disposal.

Making Meaning out of Misunderstanding

Cross-cultural ambiguity is subject to the same potential for misunderstanding, as the Cuban American writer Roberto Fernández demonstrates in the following short story, first published in 1996. For an immigrant like the character Barbarita, whose permanent residency in the United States depends upon the success of her medical examination, effective communication is very nearly a matter of life and death. The author certainly wants the reader of "Wrong Channel" to appreciate the difficulty of her predicament, but he makes his point through comedy, underlining the absurdity of a situation in which a disease, "TB," can be confused with a television. There is more to this story than simply an

invitation to laugh at an example of cultural misunderstanding, however; notice how carefully Fernández has chosen the details of the story to suggest the cultural assumptions that help create the misunderstanding.

Notice how Fernández binds together these concerns and assumptions through a key choice of words: through **homophones,** or sound-alike, words "TB" and "TV" (in spoken Spanish "B" and "V" *do* sound exactly alike). Without this play on words, the misunderstanding would not have occurred, and Fernández would not have been able either to make us laugh or to demonstrate the ease with which cross-cultural misunderstandings can occur. Within the world of the story, language causes ambiguity; however, in its conversation with the reader, that same ambiguity helps us to grasp the story's meaning.

ROBERTO FERNÁNDEZ
WRONG CHANNEL

BARBARITA WAITED IMPATIENTLY FOR her ride as beads of sweat dripped from her eyebrows into her third cup of cold syrupy espresso. She was headed for the toilet when she heard the knocking sounds of Mima's old Impala. "About time you got here," yelled Barbarita from the Florida room.

"It wouldn't start this morning."

Barbarita got in, tilted the rearview mirror, and applied enough rouge to her face for a healthier look. She wanted to make a good impression on the doctor who would approve her medical records for her green card. On the way to Jackson Memorial, Mima talked about her grandchildren.

Barbarita knocked down all the Bibles and *Reader's Digests* on the table when the nurse finally called her name.

"Sorry Ma'am, but you can't come in," the nurse said to Mima.

"I'm her interpreter," replied the polyglot.

> The fact that the doctor speaks Spanish poorly and that the narrator refers to Mima with the exaggerated term "polyglot" signals to us that neither is as much in control of the situation as he or she believes.

"*No bueno,*" said the doctor grimly as he walked in with Barbarita's X-rays. He told Mima, "Ask her if she had TB."

Mima turned to Barbarita. "He says, if you have a television?"

"Tell him yes, but in Havana. Not in Miami. But my daughter has a television here."

Mima told the doctor, "She says she has TV in Cuba, not in Miami, but her daughter has TV here."

"In that case we need to test her daughter for TB too."

Mima translated, "He says he needs to test your daughter's television to make sure it works, otherwise you cannot get your green card."

"Why the television?" asked a puzzled Barbarita.

"How many times did I tell you you needed to buy one? Don't you know, Barbarita? This is America."

> Both Mima and the doctor are well intentioned and both believe that they are being perfectly clear. His first words to the two women are in Spanish ("No bueno"); she introduces herself as an "interpreter."

> The doctor's primary concern is health, and he assumes that Barbarita, being a poor immigrant, has health problems (in fact, Cuba has universal health care).

> Like most Americans, the doctor uses an abbreviation ("TB") for efficiency rather than the complete word ("tuberculosis"), which would have avoided the misunderstanding.

> Nervous and eager to please, Mima and Barbarita don't stop to consider the context of the doctor's question or ask him to explain why he is interested in their televisions.

There are many ways in which words that look or sound different can have the same meaning, or words that look or sound the same can have different meanings. Here are some exercises to start thinking about the multiplicity and ambiguity of language.

1. Make a list of as many words as you can with which you have had personal experience of multiple pronunciations. When you write them down, try to render the different pronunciations visually, in the way in which you spell the words, as in *tomayto / tomahto.* Don't worry, for this exercise at least, about your spelling. It will not be evaluated!

2. If you are having a difficult time thinking of words with multiple pronunciations, try instead to make a list of **homonyms** (words with the *same sound and the same spelling*, but with different meanings, such as the *bow* you tie and the *bow* that shoots an

arrow), **homophones** (words with the *same sound, but with different spellings* and different meanings, such as *bow* and *beau*), and/or **homographs** (words with the same spelling *but different pronunciations and different meanings*, such as the *bow* you tie and the *bow* of a ship).

3. If you are familiar with a second language besides English, try instead to make a list of **cognates**, words that have the same meaning in two languages, or of **false cognates,** words that look like cognates but have a different meaning in one language than in the other (for example, *embarazada* in Spanish means "pregnant"). Alternatively, add to the list on page 6 of words that have different meanings for different speakers of the English language (as a car trunk in American English becomes a "boot" in British English).

DECIPHERING MEANING: THE RIDDLE GAME

As "Wrong Channel" demonstrates so well, confusion and contradiction are inescapable occurrences in social interactions. In our everyday lives, however, we do not always recognize confusion and contradiction, because we have learned to accept them in the same way that automobile drivers stop on red and go on green automatically, without even noticing or considering why. Change the rules and conventions, and we quickly start paying attention. Say you find yourself behind the wheel of a car in England or Japan, but the wheel is on the right-hand side and you are driving on the left-hand side of the road. You would be thoroughly disoriented, and acutely aware of every move you are making, conscious of the ingrained physical and mental habits urging you to do exactly the opposite of what the situation required, and adapting your familiar knowledge to survive an unfamiliar situation.

Confusion works by making us compare what is unfamiliar with what is familiar, what is nonsense with what makes sense. Literature in particular uses our confusion and sense of contradiction to prompt us to decipher its meanings. Just as texting poses puzzles to the unititiated, literary images pose enigmas, or

riddles, that we must resolve by close attention to the details of the riddle's form. But we will find those details only if we recognize what is unfamiliar instead of assuming we know what it means right off the bat. Becoming a critical thinker and writer about literature means learning to recognize when we are confused by what we read and to use that confusion as a tool for discovering meaning.

In J. R. R. Tolkien's fantasy novel *The Hobbit,* the title character Bilbo takes a journey in which he discovers a ring of immense power. Bilbo wins the ring from the creature Gollum through a game of riddles. Nearly all of the riddles are conventional

> *A writer is someone who can make a riddle out of an answer.*
>
> —KARL KRAUS

enigmas, such as this elegant description of a common food source: "A box without hinges, key, or lid, / Yet golden treasure inside is hid." In the last of the series of riddles that Bilbo asks Gollum, Bilbo in desperation breaks the rules and asks a direct question, "What have I got in my pocket?" This resembles a riddle in that it has a single correct answer, but the answer depends on what a hobbit put in his pocket that morning

Bilbo and Gollum play the riddle game. Tim Kirk, *The Riddle Game* (1975).

instead of a mystery decipherable through proper attention to the clues. Unlike a proper riddle, there is no way to respond to Bilbo's question with any hope of success. It does not, in other words, follow the conventions of riddling, and Gollum justifiably gets very angry and never forgives Bilbo's transgression of the rules.

The riddle is one of the most ancient forms of wordplay. Traditionally, it works on the same principle as the game show *Jeopardy:* the riddle gives the answer, and you must provide the question. Take, for example, the famous riddle that the ancient Greek hero Oedipus answered to break the Sphinx's curse on the city of Thebes: "What is that animal which in the morning goes on four feet, at noon goes on two, and in the evening goes on three feet?" The solution is "man"; the elegance of the riddle lies in the thought process that leads from question to answer. As a scholar of riddles explains, "we must have a perfectly true description of a thing: every term used must be as scrupulously appropriate as in a logical definition; but it must be so ingeniously phrased and worded that the sense is not obvious, and the interpreter is baffled." Nearly all riddles use the literary device called **metaphor,** which equates one thing with another to which it bears no obvious connection (for more on metaphor, see p. 218). In the riddle Oedipus solved, the metaphor equates the time of day with the age of a man: morning equals infancy (babies crawl on all fours); midday equals adulthood (walking on two legs); evening equals old age (walking with the help of a stick). Before you figure out the solution, a good riddle seems impossible; after you know the solution it seems obvious. The same holds true for a good explanation of the meaning of a literary text.

We need to decipher the meaning of literary writing because it does not follow the same rules as other forms of writing, where the goal is to make oneself understood as clearly as possible. Why can literary meaning be so difficult to grasp at first glance?

Writers of literature want to make us understand something that cannot be expressed directly, something so new and unusual that we don't know how to talk about it yet, or something clichéd and familiar that they have nevertheless discovered a new way to talk about. There would be no reason to write a riddle if it didn't take an elegant, yet enigmatic, form: the word "Man" is not a work of literature, but the Sphinx's riddle, which means the same thing as "Man," is. Moreover, riddles have a stricter set of rules than most genres of literature, and they remind us how much meaning and communication depend on following the rules. When Bilbo breaks the rules, his riddling competition with Gollum ceases to be a game between two equals (albeit a game with serious stakes; Gollum will eat Bilbo if he loses). Once Bilbo breaks the rules of the competition, his encounter becomes a free-for-all from which he barely escapes.

Here are two traditional riddles with the same answer as the proper one that Bilbo asked Gollum. See if you can decipher them solely by attention to the way their imagery correlates to the unnamed object they are describing.

1. In a marble hall white as milk
   Lined with skin as soft as silk
   Within a fountain crystal-clear
   A golden apple doth appear.
   No doors there are to this stronghold,
   Yet thieves break in to steal its gold.
2. Humpty Dumpty sat on a wall.
   Humpty Dumpty had a great fall.
   All the king's horses and all the king's men
   Couldn't put Humpty together again.

Work through the imagery. Nearly every part makes perfect sense: a hall, a fountain, an apple; a wall, a fall, men and horses. Yet in each riddle, one element doesn't fit, and this element is what creates the **enigma,** or mystery, that defines these as riddles and not simple descriptions: "No doors there are

to this stronghold"; "Couldn't put Humpty together again." If we read them literally, these two phrases don't make sense, but if we can guess their figurative meaning, we will have solved the riddle: an egg.

The Riddle as a Literary Device

The riddle is a specific form that makes us newly imagine an unnamed object by making it unfamiliar, describing it in terms of the qualities of something else. Literary writing in general uses this strategy in several different ways. In detective fiction, we will often find an explanation at the story's conclusion explaining how words we had read without realizing their significance were in fact hidden clues allowing us to solve the mystery on our own. Following the plot of a love story or an adventure story, we often find ourselves trying to imagine how the author is going to find a way to resolve the seemingly impossible obstacles to a happy ending: to bring the lovers together or to disentangle the hero or heroine from cliff-hanging perils.

Thinking about riddles can also help us to understand how literary images work. As the American poet Sylvia Plath (1932–1963) suggests in her short poem "Metaphors," the best way to approach literary images is to remember that they are riddles and to puzzle through their meanings. Best-known for the disturbing and often autobiographical poems collected posthumously in *Ariel* (1965), Plath was married to the English poet Ted Hughes. As you read, make a list of the different images she uses to describe the hidden subject of her poem. (Whenever you are reading closely, keep something at hand to write with. A pencil is best, since it allows you to erase, and to make neater changes. Underline or circle key words or passages, jot down questions, makes notes to yourself in the margins.) To get you started, we have annotated "Metaphors" with some initial questions we asked when reading the poem.

Sylvia Plath

Metaphors

I'm a riddle in nine syllables,
An elephant, a ponderous house,
A melon strolling on two tendrils.
O red fruit, ivory, fine timbers!
This loaf's big with its yeasty rising.   5
Money's new-minted in this fat purse.
I'm a means, a stage, a cow in calf.
I've eaten a bag of green apples,
Boarded the train there's no getting off.

What in the poem has nine syllables?

What do the different images in lines 2–3 have in common?

And what do the different images in lines 4–7 have in common? Do these images make us revise our answer to the previous question?

How are the final two images (8–9) different from the previous ones?

Readers of Plath's poem generally agree upon the answer to her riddle; like most riddles, the answer is obvious once you know it, but not necessarily beforehand. When she was writing "Metaphors," Plath believed she was pregnant. If we make a chart of the images and initial associations that go with them, the clues to her riddle's meaning begin to emerge. We will then be prepared to move on to the Questions for Reflection and Discussion on page 11.

WRITER'S GUIDE

Making Sense of "Metaphors"

"IMAGES"	"IMAGES"
I'm a riddle in nine syllables,	Each line of the poem has nine syllables (and the word "metaphors" has nine letters); a normal pregnancy lasts nine months
An elephant,	Big, heavy
a ponderous house,	Big, with someone living inside, a home
A melon strolling on two tendrils.	Round, and much bigger than what supports it (legs?)
This loaf's big with its yeasty rising.	Womb as loaf, stomach rising from the yeast inside it; life and growth; a conventionally "female" image (baking)
Money's new-minted in this fat purse.	Same terms as the previous image: a swelling container, but a new tone and context (not in the house, not necessarily female)—why equate a baby to money in a purse?
I'm a means, a stage, a cow in calf.	The images are almost the same as what she is describing: a means (pregnancy) to an end (baby); a stage in a process. A cow in calf describes an actual pregnancy, but provides associations a literal statement would not—of being subject to a farmer, of being an animal, of a wholly physical experience
I've eaten a bag of green apples,	Why would you eat a bag of green apples (probably only if you were a horse, a cow, or a pig)? The result is extreme indigestion. What extra associations does this add to the nausea of morning sickness?
Boarded the train there's no getting off.	Like the image of money in the purse, a human, civilized image in contrast to others focused on animals. Like the previous image, a sense of inability to take back what one has done.

Now that you have thought about the associations of the poem and answered its riddle, you are ready to reflect on and discuss some further questions. Once you know the riddle's solution, you are in fact faced with more questions rather than simply an answer; for the poem's images don't just describe pregnancy, they make you think about what it means to be pregnant and how the speaker is responding to her experience.

1. Using the different metaphors and their associations as evidence, how would you characterize the speaker's attitude toward her suspected pregnancy? What about the associations is positive? What about them is negative? What about them is ambivalent?

2. Why do you think Plath chose to use metaphors from both nature (elephant, cow, yeast) and from commerce and industry (money, trains)? Do the images complement each other? Contrast with each other?

3. Choose a single metaphor from the poem and imagine how the poem would be different if this were the only metaphor Plath used to describe pregnancy. What is the effect of having so many different metaphors instead of just one?

4. In what way does the poem reach a conclusion about its subject? In what ways does it not reach a conclusion?

WRITING EXERCISE: A Riddle

1. Choose a person, place, or thing, something or someone that would be well known to most readers. Next, find a way to describe this person, place, or thing that suits it metaphorically but also makes sense on its own terms without obviously giving away its secret. Use the riddles above as your model. The test of a good riddle will be that it can stump almost anyone you show it to, but that same person will understand it immediately after being told the answer.

2. Once you have found your riddle, write a few sentences explaining the terms of the comparison between the riddle and the solution, the way the Sphinx's riddle is explained, or the way you would explain the comparison between a box, a marble hall, or Humpty Dumpty and an egg in the riddles above.

MAKING AND BREAKING THE RULES

Every language and every literary form has its own set of **constraints**—rules or conventions that determine what is and is not permitted. Although often artificial, these rules are important in limiting what we can expect, allowing us to make sense of what we read. We expect a writer in English to use the twenty-six letters of the alphabet in his or her writing, and are surprised when, as in the contemporary American writer Jonathan Safran Foer's short story, "Primer for the Punctuation of Heart Disease" (p. 274), other symbols appear. Just to attempt to put thoughts into words is already to accept a constraint on the imagination and to stretch the limits of our powers of expression. How many times have you tried to write something that sounded absolutely perfect in your mind, only to have it come out all wrong when you put it onto the page or the computer screen?

As the English filmmaker Nicholas Roeg suggests, rules are made to be broken, and if literary writing did not break rules it would not be literature. But, as Roeg also tells us, it is only because there are rules that we can know when they are being broken. Because rhyme is still the rule in poetry, we are aware even when reading unrhymed verse such as Plath's "Metaphors" that it is *not* rhyming. Many works of literature choose to follow a set of constraints most of the time, and to confound our expectations at crucial moments. A poem written without rhyme will suddenly include a few lines that do rhyme; a rhyming poem will break its rhyme scheme. Breaking our expectations is a subtle way to make us stop and pay more attention to what we are reading.

In "Absence," the short story by American-born Canadian writer Carol Shields that you are about to read, there are four moments in which the protagonist begins typing a sentence, only to stop at the crucial point when she reaches for the letter that is broken on her computer keyboard. The story is about this broken key, but it is also about a crisis within the protagonist that is being expressed figuratively through the image of that letter on the key. As you read

The rules are learnt in order to be broken, but if you don't know them, then something is missing.
—NICHOLAS ROEG

"Absence," watch for these four sentences, stop yourself each time you reach one, and think about the letter and word that is to follow, and what it might mean to the protagonist at this point. Best known for her prize-winning novel, *The Stone Diaries*, Shields (1935–2003) was adept at finding meaning, as here, in the everyday, domestic lives of female protagonists.

CAROL SHIELDS
ABSENCE

SHE WOKE UP EARLY, DRANK A CUP OF STRONG unsugared coffee, then sat down at her word processor. She knew more or less what she wanted to do, and that was to create a story that possessed a granddaughter, a Boston fern, a golden apple, and a small blue cradle. But after she had typed half a dozen words, she found that one of the letters of the keyboard was broken, and, to make matters worse, a vowel, the very letter that attaches to the hungry self.

Of course she had no money and no house-handy mate to prod the key free. Many a woman would have shrugged good-naturedly, conceded defeat, and left the small stones of thought unclothed, but not our woman; our woman rolled up her sleeves, to use that thready old metaphor, and began afresh. She would work *around* the faulty letter. She would force her story, however awkwardly, toward a detour. She would be resourceful, look for other ways, and make an artefact out of absence. She would, to put the matter bluntly, make do.

She started—slowly, ponderously—to tap out words. "Several thousand years ago there—"

But where her hands had once danced, they now trudged. She stopped and scratched her head, her busy, normally useful head, that had begun, suddenly, to thrum and echo; where could she go from here? she asked herself sharply. Because the flabby but dependable gerund had dropped through language's trapdoor, gone. Whole parcels of grammar, for that matter, seemed all at once out of reach, and so were those bulky doorstop words that connect and announce and allow a sentence to pause for a moment and take on fresh loads of oxygen. Vocabulary, her well-loved garden, as broad and taken-for-granted as an acre of goldenrod, had shrunk to a square yard, and she was, as never before, forced to choose her words, much as her adored great-aunt, seated at a tea table, had selected sugar lumps by means of a carefully executed set of tongs.

5   She was tempted, of course, to seek out synonyms, and who could blame her? But words, she knew, held formal levels of sense and shades of deference that were untransferable one to the other, though thousands of deluded souls hunch each day over crossword puzzles and try. The glue of resonance makes austere demands. Memory barks, and context, that absolute old cow, glowers and chews up what's less than acceptable.

The woman grew, as the day wore on, more and more frustrated. Always the word she sought, the only word, teased and taunted from the top row of the broken keyboard, a word that spun around the center of a slender, one-legged vowel, erect but humble, whose dot of amazement had never before mattered.

Furthermore, to have to pause and pry an obscure phrase from the dusty pages of her old thesaurus threw her off balance and altered the melody of her prose. Between stutters and starts, the sheen was somehow lost; the small watery pleasures of accent and stress were roughed up as though translated from some coarse sub-Balkan folk tale and rammed through the nozzle of a too-clever-by-half, space-larky computer.

Her head-bone ached; her arms-bones froze; she wanted only to make, as she had done before, sentences that melted at the center and branched at the ends, that threatened to grow unruly and run away, but that clause for clause adhered to one another as though stuck down by Velcro tabs.

She suffered too over the *sounds* that evaded her and was forced to settle for those other, less seemly vowels whose open mouths and unsubtle throats yawned and groaned and showed altogether too much teeth. She preferred small slanted breakable tones that scarcely made themselves known unless you pressed an ear closely to the curled end of the tongue or the spout of a kettle. The thump of heartbeat was what she wanted, but also the small urgent jumps lodged between the beats. (She was thankful, though, for the sly *y* that now and then leapt forward and pulled a sentence taut as a cord.)

10   "Several thousand years ago a woman sat down at a table and began to—"

Hours passed, but the work went badly. She thought to herself: to make a pot of bean soup would produce more pleasure. To vacuum the hall rug would be of more use.

Both sense and grace eluded her, but hardest to bear was the fact that the broken key seemed to demand of her a parallel surrender, a correspondence of economy subtracted from the alphabet of her very self. But how? A story had to come from somewhere. Some hand must move the pen along or press the keys and steer, somehow, the granddaughter toward the Boston fern or place the golden apple at the foot of the blue cradle. "A woman sat down at a table and—"

She felt her arm fall heavy on the table and she wondered, oddly, whether or not the table objected. And was the lamp, clamped there to the table's edge, exhausted after so long a day? Were the floorboards reasonably cheerful or the door numb with lack of movement, and was the broken letter on her keyboard appeased at last by her cast-off self?

Because now her thoughts flowed through every object and every corner of the room, and a moment later she *became* the walls and also the clean roof overhead and the powerful black sky. Why, she wondered aloud, had she stayed so long enclosed by the tough, lonely pronoun of her body when the whole world beckoned?

15   But the words she actually set down came from the dark eye of her eye, the stubborn self that refused at the last moment to let go. "A woman sat down—"

Everyone knew who the woman was. Even when she put a red hat on her head or changed her name or turned the clock back a thousand years or restored to wobbly fables about granddaughters and Boston ferns, everyone knew the woman had been there from the start, seated at a table, object and subject sternly fused. No one, not even the very young, pretends that the person who brought forth words was any other than the arabesque of the unfolded self. There was no escape and scarcely any sorrow.

"A woman sat down and wrote," she wrote.

[2000]

Architect's rendering of the Carol Shields Memorial Labyrinth in King's Park, in Winnipeg, Manitoba, where the writer lived for twenty years and wrote her major books. The labyrinth suggests a visual image of the riddling construction of her fiction.

QUESTIONS FOR REFLECTION AND DISCUSSION

1. Why do you think the author entitled this story "Absence"?

2. What is the answer to the riddle: Which key is missing? Would the absence of a different letter have the same effect as the absence of this letter? Why or why not?

3. What is the relation between the unnamed protagonist of the story, who sits down one day with a cup of strong unsugared coffee to find a key on her word processor broken, and the story's author, who we can imagine might have done the same thing while writing this story?

4. How would you characterize the difference between the constraints the protagonist sets herself before starting ("a granddaughter, a Boston fern, a golden apple, and a small blue cradle") and the constraint set by the failure of her keyboard to function correctly?

5. In the final analysis, do you think the story the protagonist will write will be better or worse for being written without the benefit of the missing letter? Explain your reasoning with arguments based on the language of the story.

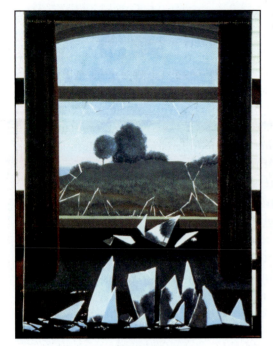

René Magritte, *The Key to the Fields* (1936. Oil on canvas. Thyssen-Bornemisza Collection, Madrid, Spain). Like the missing letter in "Absence," the picture painted on the broken glass within this painting by René Magritte at first seems the same as the view outside despite the broken window. It is only when we examine the edges of the painting or the details of the story that we begin to notice what is different. The picture on the floor *is* the same, but because it is broken into fragments, and because we expect to see transparent glass, it defies our expectations. Magritte challenges us to rethink the assumptions we make when we look at a painting. We expect a painting to behave like reality, but there is no actual reason it has to do so. Painters can follow the constraints and rules that make paintings look real, or they can ignore them, or they can draw attention by making them the focus of the painting, as Magritte does here.

WRITING EXERCISE: Something's Missing

1. Write a paragraph describing in detail something you did in the past few days, or something that you witnessed someone else do.

2. Choose a formal constraint. You could, like Shields, choose to eliminate a common vowel from your paragraph. You could eliminate an important consonant (*s*, for example). Or you could forbid yourself to use pronouns (*I, you, he, she, it*, etc.) or definite articles (*the*), or adjectives. Or you could constrain yourself to words beginning with a particular letter or letters. Your constraint should be difficult enough to be noticeable to a classmate or instructor, but not so difficult as to make your task impossible (probably not a good idea to try eliminating verbs, unless you are feeling extremely ambitious). If you are stumped, ask your instructor for ideas.

3. Rewrite your paragraph using the constraint you have chosen. Make sure that your sentences remain as grammatically correct and stylistically polished as in any other paper.

4. Write a paragraph reflecting on the process of what you have just accomplished. What was the most difficult part of the assignment and what was the easiest? Are you satisfied with the results? If you exchanged paragraphs with a classmate, was he or she able to recognize the constraint you had chosen? Did anything change in the paragraph as a result of your rewriting? Did you have to leave out anything important from your first version? Did you add anything new?

READING FOR WHAT DOES NOT MAKE SENSE

When we read a book for fun, we often find ourselves "reading for the plot" to find out what happened. This is an important and highly pleasurable form of reading, but it is not an effective way of drawing meaning out of many of the texts included in this book, or of reading for class work in general. First of all, few of the selections included here are long enough to sustain the sort of suspense that would make you skim the pages of a novel to find out what happened. Furthermore, most poems are unconcerned with stringing together events to make a plot, and most short stories emphasize a particular incident or event rather than the accumulation of a chain of events characteristic of the novel. Nevertheless, there are plenty of stories, poems, and essays that for various reasons you will find quite gripping to read and will speed through to find out what happens in them. There is, for example, something quite satisfying in discovering the answer to the riddle in Sylvia Plath's

A man does not know what he is saying until he knows what he is not saying.

—G. K. CHESTERTON

"Metaphors," or figuring out which letter is missing in Carol Shields's "Absence." Literature draws us in with riddles and mysteries, fascinating places and compelling characters. But no good mystery is exhausted by its solution, and places and people worth knowing only get better the more you know about them. Moreover, like some friends, there are readings that you may not hit it off with immediately but whose qualities you will come to appreciate slowly, with a longer acquaintance. When you find that you have skimmed over your first reading of a text to get to the end, either because you had to find out or because constraints on your time obliged you to do so, be sure to set aside time to reread, either before the class or after, and this time, read for what does not make sense rather than for what does.

Reading for what does not make sense is one of the best ways to appreciate further something you love immediately and to come to appreciate something you were not so sure about to begin with. "Strategies for Reading Critically," the flowchart shown here, outlines key strategies to help you read for what does not make sense.

Strategies for Reading Critically

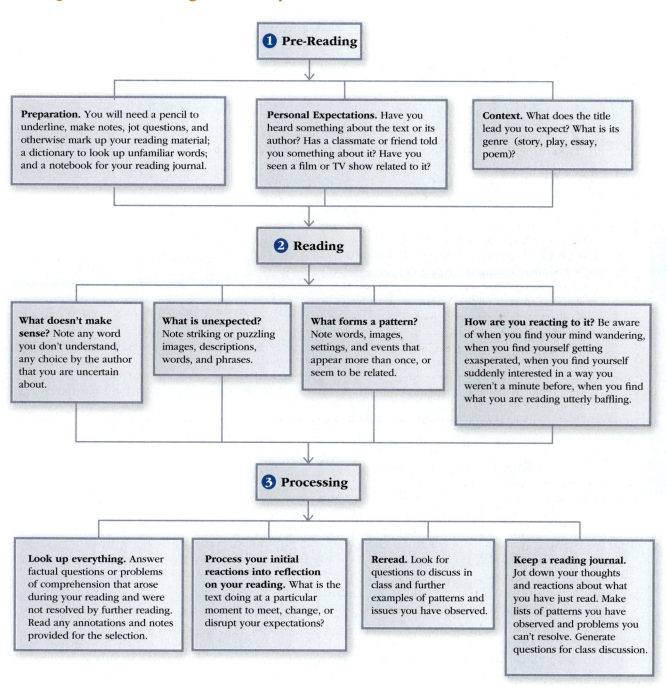

❶ Pre-Reading

Preparation. You will need a pencil to underline, make notes, jot questions, and otherwise mark up your reading material; a dictionary to look up unfamiliar words; and a notebook for your reading journal.

Personal Expectations. Have you heard something about the text or its author? Has a classmate or friend told you something about it? Have you seen a film or TV show related to it?

Context. What does the title lead you to expect? What is its genre (story, play, essay, poem)?

❷ Reading

What doesn't make sense? Note any word you don't understand, any choice by the author that you are uncertain about.

What is unexpected? Note striking or puzzling images, descriptions, words, and phrases.

What forms a pattern? Note words, images, settings, and events that appear more than once, or seem to be related.

How are you reacting to it? Be aware of when you find your mind wandering, when you find yourself getting exasperated, when you find yourself suddenly interested in a way you weren't a minute before, when you find what you are reading utterly baffling.

❸ Processing

Look up everything. Answer factual questions or problems of comprehension that arose during your reading and were not resolved by further reading. Read any annotations and notes provided for the selection.

Process your initial reactions into reflection on your reading. What is the text doing at a particular moment to meet, change, or disrupt your expectations?

Reread. Look for questions to discuss in class and further examples of patterns and issues you have observed.

Keep a reading journal. Jot down your thoughts and reactions about what you have just read. Make lists of patterns you have observed and problems you can't resolve. Generate questions for class discussion.

THE READING PROCESS

Let's watch the process of reading for what doesn't make sense as one student put it into practice in an assignment for class. As you read "The Possessive," a poem by the contemporary American poet Sharon Olds (p. 16), observe the steps, Justin Schiel took in pre-reading, reading, and processing it for his writing class. First, Justin prepared himself to read. Then he read through the poem once quickly, to get a general sense of it, and then he read it again, slowly, highlighting text with pencil (shown here in yellow), and noting his expectations, reactions, observations, and questions in the margins (shown here in blue).

Justin Schiel's Reading Annotations

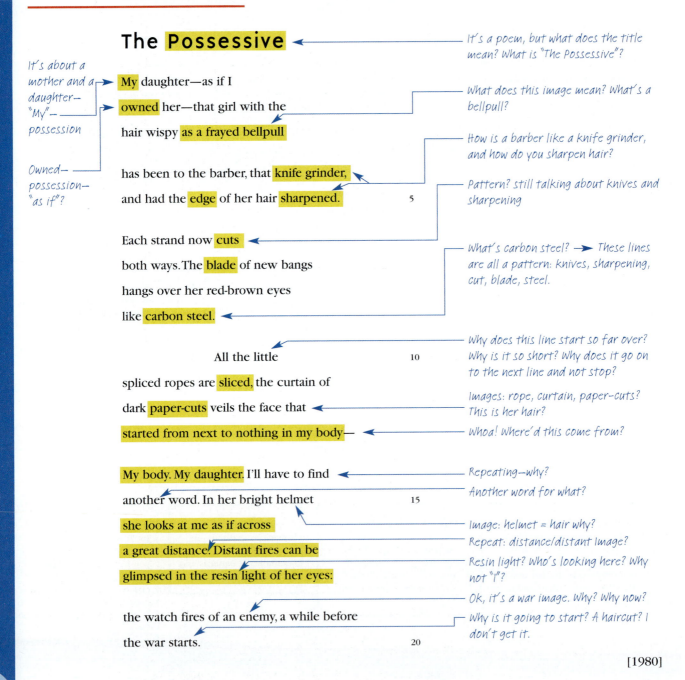

Sharon Olds

The Possessive

It's a poem, but what does the title mean? What is "The Possessive"?

It's about a mother and a daughter— "My"— possession

My daughter—as if I

owned her—that girl with the

hair wispy as a frayed bellpull

What does this image mean? What's a bellpull?

Owned— possession— "as if"?

has been to the barber, that knife grinder,

and had the edge of her hair sharpened.   5

How is a barber like a knife grinder, and how do you sharpen hair?

Pattern? still talking about knives and sharpening

Each strand now cuts

both ways. The blade of new bangs

hangs over her red-brown eyes

like carbon steel.

What's carbon steel? → These lines are all a pattern: knives, sharpening, cut, blade, steel.

                    All the little   10

spliced ropes are sliced, the curtain of

dark paper-cuts veils the face that

started from next to nothing in my body—

Why does this line start so far over? Why is it so short? Why does it go on to the next line and not stop?

Images: rope, curtain, paper-cuts? This is her hair?

Whoa! Where'd this come from?

My body. My daughter. I'll have to find

another word. In her bright helmet   15

she looks at me as if across

a great distance. Distant fires can be

glimpsed in the resin light of her eyes:

Repeating—why?

Another word for what?

Image: helmet = hair why?

Repeat: distance/distant image?

Resin light? Who's looking here? Why not "I"?

the watch fires of an enemy, a while before

the war starts.   20

Ok, it's a war image. Why? Why now?

Why is it going to start? A haircut? I don't get it.

[1980]

CHAPTER 1 | A WORLD OF MEANING: READING AND THINKING ABOUT LITERATURE

Next, Justin began processing his first reading. He looked up the words and terms he was unsure about. He copied the meanings into his notebook along with his comments shown below, so that he could refer back to them if later in the semester he decided to write about the poem.

Noticing that his reaction to the poem had changed at line 13 and again at line 18, he returned to his notes and thought about these lines in the context of the poem as a whole.

Having resolved uncertainties about dictionary meaning and processed his initial reaction to the poem, Justin read back through it another time, adding further annotations shown in orange on page 18.

The goal of the critical reading assignment was to produce a reading journal entry on "The Possessive" that summarized and reflected informally on Justin's initial response to the reading in the form of an initial reflection followed by notes and questions. Justin's response is shown on page 19.

"Possessive" – "a possessive word or word group" – like "my" – or a
 possessive person? – still sounds strange
"frayed" – "worn away or tattered along the edges"
"bellpull" – "a handle or knob attached to a cord by which one rings
 a bell; also: the cord itself" So her hair is like a worn cord?
 Split ends? But why use the image?
"carbon steel" – "a strong hard steel that derives its physical properties from the presence of carbon and is used in hand tools
 and kitchen utensils." Her eyes are sharp and hard and like
 metal (and so is her hair)
"resin" – "any of various solid or semisolid amorphous fusible flam-
 mable natural organic substances that are usually transparent
 or translucent and yellowish to brown." "Red-brown" like line 8,
 but also see-through and burning—part of the war image

Notes on lines 13 and 18

""Started from next to nothing in my body"—it's a new thought, but
 the same sentence. What makes her think of being pregnant here?
""Distant fires can be glimpsed in the resin light of her eyes" –
 The "I" changed, it's passive. Looking back, the image changed
 before, when she says "bright helmet," but I didn't notice. But
 what does the image have to do with the "I"?

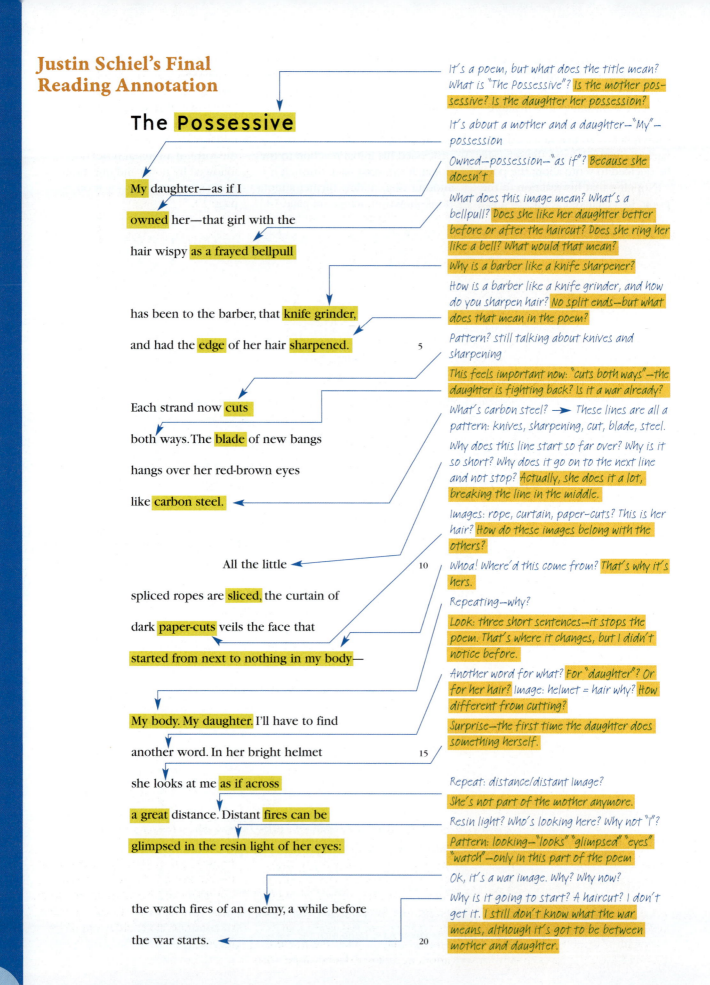

The Possessive

My daughter—as if I

owned her—that girl with the

hair wispy as a frayed bellpull

has been to the barber, that knife grinder,

and had the edge of her hair sharpened.   5

Each strand now cuts

both ways. The blade of new bangs

hangs over her red-brown eyes

like carbon steel.

                    All the little   10

spliced ropes are sliced, the curtain of

dark paper-cuts veils the face that

started from next to nothing in my body—

My body. My daughter. I'll have to find

another word. In her bright helmet   15

she looks at me as if across

a great distance. Distant fires can be

glimpsed in the resin light of her eyes:

the watch fires of an enemy, a while before

the war starts.   20

It's a poem, but what does the title mean? What is "The Possessive"? Is the mother possessive? Is the daughter her possession?

It's about a mother and a daughter—"My"—possession

Owned—possession—"as if"? Because she doesn't

What does this image mean? What's a bellpull? Does she like her daughter better before or after the haircut? Does she ring her like a bell? What would that mean?

Why is a barber like a knife sharpener?

How is a barber like a knife grinder, and how do you sharpen hair? No split ends—but what does that mean in the poem?

Pattern? still talking about knives and sharpening

This feels important now: "cuts both ways"—the daughter is fighting back? Is it a war already?

What's carbon steel? → These lines are all a pattern: knives, sharpening, cut, blade, steel.

Why does this line start so far over? Why is it so short? Why does it go on to the next line and not stop? Actually, she does it a lot, breaking the line in the middle.

Images: rope, curtain, paper-cuts? This is her hair? How do these images belong with the others?

Whoa! Where'd this come from? That's why it's hers.

Repeating—why?

Look: three short sentences—it stops the poem. That's where it changes, but I didn't notice before.

Another word for what? For "daughter"? Or for her hair? Image: helmet = hair why? How different from cutting?

Surprise—the first time the daughter does something herself.

Repeat: distance/distant Image?

She's not part of the mother anymore.

Resin light? Who's looking here? Why not "I"?

Pattern: looking—"looks" "glimpsed" "eyes" "watch"—only in this part of the poem

Ok, it's a war image. Why? Why now?

Why is it going to start? A haircut? I don't get it. I still don't know what the war means, although it's got to be between mother and daughter.

Justin's response

"The Possessive" is a poem about a mother looking at her daughter while she gets her hair cut. I found two main images. One is in lines 4–12, words like: knife, edge, sharpened, cuts, blade, carbon steel, sliced, paper-cuts. One is at the end: helmet, fires, enemy, war. When I read it again, I found another kind of image in the end, about looking: looks, glimpsed, light, eyes, watch. I think this must go with the war images—to be on guard. I noticed two shifts in how I was reading the poem, but now I think they are really about the same thing, when she says "My body. My daughter. I'll have to find another word" (14–15). "Body" and "daughter" are repeated, and they always have the word "my" with them, which is a "possessive," like the title.

What changes?
The mother remembers when her daughter was inside her.
The girl's split ends are cut.
The girl does something for the first time.
She looks (or the mother notices she is looking?)
She is distant, which I don't think she was before.
The speaker doesn't use "I" anymore.
Does the mother change?
"The war starts."

Questions:
What changes between the mother and daughter and why?
Who or what makes the change happen?
Why do you need "another word" and what is it?
Why does Olds use images of knives and cutting to describe the daughter at the barber's?
What is so significant about getting a haircut?
How do the two parts of the poem fit together?
When will the war start, and why does the mother notice it now?

Things I'm still pretty confused about:
What exactly does the title refer to?
What's going on in lines 10–13? Why the image of "curtain" and "veil" and what do these have to do with the images of cutting and of war? What is their connection to the two parts of the poem?

A number of good observations have emerged from working through Justin's initial responses in his reading notes. Processing the results of his reading has provided him with several lists of images that can form the basis of further work on the poem. He has also generated some fruitful questions for class discussion and for his own reflection. Reading for what does not make sense has given him a strong grasp of what the poem is about and how it works. It has also helped him to identify clearly what he still has not figured out about the poem and has shown him what questions he needs to ask in order to continue his exploration of its meanings.

CLARITY AND AMBIGUITY OF LANGUAGE

How can we characterize the point Justin has reached in his work with Sharon Olds' poem "The Possessive"? He has clarified every technical question he had about the poem: the events it describes; the dictionary meanings of its words; the images it is using; its patterns of repetition; the way the structure breaks into two parts. He has also clarified for himself exactly what in the poem he is still unsure about: the meaning of the title; the figurative meaning of the imagery he has identified; the function of the images in lines 10–13. In other words, he has nearly concluded his **analysis** of the poem and is ready to begin his **interpretation** of it.

It is impossible to speak in such a way that you cannot be misunderstood.

—KARL POPPER, PHILOSOPHER

I guess I should warn you, if I turn out to be particularly clear, you've probably misunderstood what I've said.

—ALAN GREENSPAN, FORMER CHAIR OF THE FEDERAL RESERVE BOARD

Working with Ambiguity in Literary Writing

Like the answer to a riddle, a good analysis may not have been obvious before you started, but can be agreed upon generally by the rest of the class. An interpretation is, by definition, debatable. Its goal is to offer a plausible explanation of everything your analysis has identified as important but cannot resolve. An analysis tries to explain everything that is clear about a text; an interpretation tries to explain everything that is ambiguous about it, to answer questions like those Justin raises at the end of his journal entry. Let's work back through Justin's close reading of "The Possessive" and discuss one by one the analytical steps he took intuitively by following the strategies on page 15.

Clarifying Grammar   Although Justin was not consciously aware of it, his reading of "The Possessive" was guided by its grammatical structure: the way its sentences are put together. Each time he stopped, it was because Olds had ended one

sentence and begun another. In his rereading of the poem, he had the insight that the three short sentences "My body. My daughter. I'll have to find another word." signaled a change in the poem. Writers use form to guide our understanding of theme and content, and, here, Olds uses short sharp sentences to make us notice her thematic point: "I'll have to find another word." Many instances of ambiguity in literary writing derive from different possible grammatical possibilities of reading a sentence; this is known as **ambiguity of syntax.** Remember that Justin noticed how sentences did not always end when the lines ended? This technique, called **enjambment** in poetry, often makes us think one thing about a sentence (what it means at the end of the line) before coming to another (what it means when it continues). When we read, we intuitively scan the grammar of, or **parse,** the sentences. All sentences divide into **clauses,** or individual units of subjects, predicates, and their modifiers (adjectives, adverbs, and longer phrases that function as adjectives and adverbs). There are **independent clauses,** which can make sense on their own, and **dependent clauses,** which depend on the context of the sentence for their meaning. For example, in the sentence you just finished reading, there are two dependent clauses (the ones that begin with "which" and are set off by commas) and one independent clause (the rest of the sentence, including the bit before the first comma and "and

dependent clauses," which is the remainder of the same clause). When the sentences we are reading do not parse easily, we pause, confused.

Let's see what happens when we parse the sentences of "The Possessive" in a chart (see page 21).

What does our breakdown tell us? Remember Justin's analysis of the "three short sentences" in lines 14–15? It turns out that Olds's use of enjambment creates such a strong effect that Justin overlooked the fact that "My body" was actually the end of the previous sentence, and that, like "My daughter," it is an exclamation or interjection, rather than an independent sentence. Part of what made Justin pause at this moment was the ambiguity of the grammar: does "My body" belong with the previous sentence and the previous line or on its own? Note how this ambiguity mirrors the poem's theme, which Justin identified as the moment of change in the mother's attitude toward the daughter. While mostly grammatical, and easy to follow even when it is not, the **syntax,** or grammatical construction, of Olds's poem becomes ambiguous at the same moments in which Justin in his close reading located ambiguity in its meaning.

Types of Ambiguity   There are a number of ways in which writing can be ambiguous, and it is often important for your analysis and interpretation to be able to distinguish between them. We can single out three types of ambiguity that help to draw out the themes with

Parsing a Poem

"THE POSSESSIVE"	PARSED	INSTRUCTOR'S COMMENTS
1. My daughter—as if I owned her—that girl with the hair wispy as a frayed bellpull has been to the barber, that knife grinder, and had the edge of her hair sharpened.	Subj (*daughter*) + predicate (*has been*) + object (*barber*) + second predicate (*had + sharpened*) + object (*edge*)	The first half of the sentence (up to "has been") is so full of images of the daughter that it doesn't scan: "—as if I owned her—that girl with the hair wispy as a frayed bellpull" is ungrammatical
2. Each strand now cuts both ways.	Subj (*strand*) + predicate (*cuts*) + adverb	A simple sentence
3. The blade of new bangs hangs over her red-brown eyes like carbon steel.	Subj (*blade*) + predicate (*hangs*) + adverbial phrases	Another simple sentence
4. All the little spliced ropes are sliced, the curtain of dark paper-cuts veils the face that started from next to nothing in my body—My body.	Subj (*ropes*) + predicate (*are sliced*) Subj (*curtain*) + predicate (*veils*) + object (*face*) + dependent clause (*that ...*) with predicate (*started*) + adverbial phrases + ??? (*My body*)	A long sentence introducing the first (and only) dependent clause of the poem, but it is grammatical until the final dash ("—My body")
5. My daughter.	Possessive adjective + noun	Not a grammatical sentence, since there's no predicate
6. I'll have to find another word.	Subj + predicate + object	Another simple sentence
7. In her bright helmet she looks at me as if across a great distance.	Adverbial phrase + subj (*she*) + predicate (*looks at*) + object (*me*) + adverbial phrase	Just like sentence no. 3
8. Distant fires can be glimpsed in the resin light of her eyes: the watch fires of an enemy, a while before the war starts.	Subj (*fires*) + predicate (*can be glimpsed*) + adverbial phrases + appositional phrase (*watch fires ...*) modifying initial subj	Grammatical until the colon (":"), but the long adjectival phrase that follows needs a new subject and predicate to be truly grammatical

which the speaker is primarily concerned in "The Possessive." Note how they draw out the themes without letting us know exactly what the speaker thinks about them. Ambiguity is how literature contextualizes the questions it wants us to ask of it.

- **Ambiguity of syntax** depends on the **syntax,** the way the parts of the sentence fit together grammatically. Does "My body" belong to the previous sentence and the imagery it contains or does it belong with "My daughter" in line 14? Can you find any

other ambiguities of syntax in the poem?

- **Ambiguity of diction** refers to a difficulty in understanding the way words are put together within a particular clause. The poem begins and ends with phrases that add information about the daughter but don't tell us exactly how they relate to her: "—as if I owned her—that girl with the hair wispy as a frayed bellpull"; "the watch fires of an enemy, a while before the war starts." The ambiguity of diction helps to express the speaker's confusion

over her relationship with her daughter.

- **Ambiguity of words** refers to multiple meanings of a particular word or group of words. Does Olds's title, "The Possessive," refer in general to the possessive adjective ("my") that is central to the poem's meaning? Or does it refer to the mother herself? Although the meanings are related, they are quite different, and there is nothing in the word itself to decide for certain which one we are supposed to choose.

Reading versus Writing

Reading literature requires a different balance of focus than writing about literature. When you read literature, you need to be open to every sort of ambiguity and wordplay, and to try to pinpoint the key moments where they occur. When you write, you have to make constant decisions to clarify and to limit the possible meanings of what you have read. It is a hard balance to maintain, since it is as impossible to figure out everything about a literary text as it is to control entirely what the words you write down on the page will mean to someone else reading them. Nevertheless, there are proven techniques for doing both as well as possible. The more you follow these techniques, the better you will grasp the two sides of the process of interpretation: the opening up of a text that makes a good analysis and the honing down of an argument that makes a good interpretation.

In your own writing for class, your goal is to raise questions and to frame in particular ways the questions you want to raise. Why, then, when you commit ambiguities of syntax, diction, and meaning, does your instructor correct them and ask you to rewrite them rather than praise your use of them? When we are reading any sort of text, ambiguities halt the flow of ideas and confuse us, usually momentarily, and sometimes even permanently. This is essential to a work of literature, but disastrous when you are making a critical argument, since you will have no chance of persuading the readers of your argument if you confuse them and bring their concentration on your writing to a grinding halt.

When you write an essay for class, you are generally making a single, linear argument, and you want the reader to know where you are going and how you are going to get there. You want each step in the essay to lead to the next step clearly and smoothly. In contrast, confused pauses are often exactly what writers of literature want to prompt in us, for this is how they control the twists and turns of our thinking as we read, and call our attention to nuances and details of argument without having to spell them out for us. Critical writing wants us to move in a single direction from start to finish; literature wants us thinking in many different directions at once, and is often unconcerned if we ever reach an endpoint, as long as we are thinking and enjoying ourselves wherever in the reading process we happen to be.

How do you shift from the infinite process of reading into the finite process of writing? The answer is: you don't. You simply pause periodically to notice where you are before returning to the process again. This is true of many literary writers as well. Some of the greatest works of literature, including Shakespeare's plays, have been published in one form and then revised into radically different versions. Each piece of formal writing you produce should feel finished to you, the way Shakespeare's first versions must have felt when they were performed, but once your teacher and peers have read, commented on, and discussed your work, you will discover that it needs to be finished all over again, sometimes in quite a different form. What seemed clear before will have become murky, and you will go back to the texts again, and revisit what you had written about them, and find something new, and discover different ways to express what you had already written.

Working with Clarity in Nonliterary Writing: The Summary

Before you can write about any text, you need to be clear about what it is about. An important tool for preparing to write about any text, literary or nonliterary, is the **summary.** As you will see below, there are different types of summaries. But all of them have the same goal: clarification. Your summary should be able to provide someone who has not read the text with a clear and concise idea of its purpose and what happens in it. The summary is also an important tool for understanding the basic meaning of a text before you complete your critical analysis and begin your interpretation. Although it may take a slightly different form, understanding the basic meaning of a text is equally important whether you are dealing with literary writing or with nonliterary texts, such as the secondary sources for a research paper. We concentrate here on summarizing literary texts; Chapter 3 will present a discussion of summarizing a work of criticism for a research paper.

- The first part of a summary is the *title,* which should include the author, title, and initial date of publication of the work you are summarizing. If your source is not in this textbook, you should provide a full bibliographical reference (see Appendix B, p. APP B–2); if it is here, page numbers will suffice.
- The *body paragraph* of the summary contains at least three sentences:
  - The *opening sentence* expresses the main idea of the text. For example, here's a way to summarize the main idea of "The Possessive": "In this poem, the speaker realizes that her relationship with her daughter has changed."
  - The *second sentence* identifies the text's principal formal features (you will read more about these in Chapter 2): What genre is it? Is it narrated in the first, second, or third person? Is its point of view limited or omniscient? Are there any prominent images and literary devices, such as metaphors? If it is a poem, does it have a particular rhythm or rhyme scheme?
  - The *rest of the paragraph* states what happens in the text. The number of sentences in this part will depend upon the length of the text you are summarizing. The rule of thumb for short pieces should be no more than one sentence

per stanza of a poem or one sentence per scene in a short story (see the discussion of "Before the Law" on page 27 for more on dividing up a short story). For longer pieces, you will have to be thriftier, as a good summary should never be longer than a single paragraph, and not more than a page in total. Your summary of a text should be as brief as you can make it without omitting anything that is essential to understanding what happens in it.

Here are four examples of summaries of "The Possessive":

1. Sharon Olds, "The Possessive" (1980)

   In this poem, the speaker wonders about her daughter. The daughter gets a haircut at the barber. The speaker thinks a war is going to start soon with her.

2. Sharon Olds, "The Possessive" (1980)

   Sharon Olds is an American poet who was born in San Francisco in 1942 and lives in New York City. The poem has 20 lines and 6 stanzas. There are no rhymes and the lines have a different number of syllables. In the first three lines, she compares her daughter's hair to "a frayed bellpull." In Lines 4–5, she describes the barber as a "knife grinder" sharpening the edges of her daughter's hair. In the third stanza, she describes her daughter's cut hair like a knife. In Lines 10–13, she remembers carrying the girl inside her body before she was born. In the fifth stanza, which is the longest, she repeats the words "My body. My daughter" and imagines her daughter wearing a helmet and having "distant fires" in her eyes. In the last stanza, which is the shortest, Sharon Olds says a war is going to start with her daughter.

3. Sharon Olds, "The Possessive" (1980)

   In this poem, the speaker tries to understand her changing relationship with her daughter. The daughter was her possession, but then she grew up and fought with her. Now the mother is frightened of her. She doesn't feel like part of her anymore.

4. Sharon Olds, "The Possessive" (1980)

   The speaker reflects on how her relationship with her daughter is changing. The poem is composed of twenty unrhymed lines of irregular length divided into five brief stanzas. In the first three stanzas, a mother describes her daughter getting a haircut with a series of images related to knives and cutting. In the fourth stanza, she connects this moment with a memory of the daughter in her womb, but then immediately states that she needs a new way to describe the situation. The poem concludes by describing the daughter as an enemy guard, watching her mother from a distance as if a war is about to begin between them.

1. Make a list of the strengths and weaknesses of the four summaries. What does each one include and what does it leave out? Has it included the required parts of a summary? Has it included material that does not need to be there? How well has it observed the list of dos and don'ts? Which summary is the more effective, and why?

2. Revise the summary you found the more effective in order to make it even better.

Clarity and Ambiguity in Storytelling

Both poems and stories employ ambiguity of syntax, diction, and words, but they tend to employ them to different ends. Because most poems are not focused on telling a story, they tend to withhold clarity in order to focus our attention on the dense interrelationship of its themes. In contrast, fiction withholds information to hold and focus our attention on particular aspects of the events of a story. The art of storytelling lies in knowing what to include and what to leave out of a narrative that unfolds over time, as opposed to most poems, which focus on moods and particular moments. Consequently, in fiction you will also find another sort of ambiguity based on the situations in which characters find themselves. For starters, you may not even be sure exactly what is happening. You may also be unclear about the **setting:** the location (*where* a story is taking place) and the time frame (*when* a story is taking place). You may not be sure about the relation of different events to one another (*how* a story is taking place). You may be uncertain about a particular character's motivation: *why* has he or she acted a particular way or done a particular thing?

Short story narratives vary widely in style; some attempt to give every detail about a situation and others restrict themselves to reporting an enigmatic encounter, as in the example of "Before the Law," a short story by Franz Kafka that you will read below. But because words are fundamentally incapable of duplicating the full spectrum of the world we experience through our five senses, much will have to be left out of even the most obsessively comprehensive description. Try it yourself as an experiment: Can you describe everything you are seeing, hearing, touching, smelling, tasting, and thinking at this moment? Don't forget the room around you, and the world outside, and don't leave out all the tangents your mind has wandered onto while reading the last two paragraphs. Where do you draw the line? At what point can you say you have described everything? The answer is never: there is always something else you could add.

Storytelling requires endless choices, and the **genre,** or type of story being told, often guides the choices an author makes. If you are a real-life detective describing the scene of a crime, you will try to include every detail possible, since you never know what seemingly inconsequential bit of dust or scrap of paper might turn out to be a clue. If you are a writer telling the story of a detective at the scene of a crime, you will already know which details are clues, so you will also know what you can leave out. If you describe the scene of the crime too clearly in terms of the clues, however, you will give away the mystery. So you have to work in some ambiguity. You throw in a few red herrings, leads that look promising but go nowhere. You describe clues in such a way that readers will assume they mean one thing but will discover later that they meant something else entirely. Other types of stories have other conventions, but there are few stories indeed that do not make use of the element of surprise, and surprise in narrative depends on temporarily fooling the readers, making us expect something other than what is coming. Storytellers create surprise through **ambiguity of situations,** or uncertainty about the basic meaning of what is happening, which we will examine now, and through **ambiguity of plot,** or surprises about the events we thought we had understood, which we will discuss later.

Parables and the Ambiguity of Situations
"Before the Law," the brief narrative that you are about to read is part of *The Trial,* a novel by the influential Jewish-Czech writer Franz Kafka (1884–1924). *The Trial* tells the story of a bank official, Josef K., who is arrested at night, tried, and eventually executed in spite of a long struggle to prove his innocence of a charge—the substance of which he never discovers. Kafka specialized in the nightmare depiction of hapless figures trapped in a bureaucratic web they cannot understand. His stories and novels were so distinctive that we now refer to such a situation as "Kafkaesque."

"Before the Law" offers a possible explanation for Josef K.'s predicament through the use of an ancient literary genre known as the **parable**—a story, usually quite brief, that describes a series of events with an ambiguous moral at the end. The facts of what happen in a parable are not in doubt, but everything else is, especially what the facts are supposed to mean. When you read a parable, it sounds as if it is giving you a lesson, but to figure out what the lesson is usually requires quite a bit of thought. Because it is enigmatic, the parable resembles a riddle. There is always a single correct answer to a riddle; however, with a parable, you are never sure if you have completely understood it.

Like Olds's poem "The Possessive," "Before the Law" contains a play on words in its title. The preposition "before" has two possible meanings here. One is spatial: in a courtroom, for example, you stand before, or in front of, the law (or its human representative). The other meaning is temporal, as in the phrase, "before the law existed." As you read, think about which usage better applies to the situation being described. Also recall the strategies for reading critically introduced above (p. 15); as you process your reading, make a list for yourself of what is clear in the story and what is ambiguous, and a list of questions about what you, like the man from the country trying to enter the gate, don't know.

FRANZ KAFKA
BEFORE THE LAW

BEFORE THE LAW SITS A GATEKEEPER. TO THIS gatekeeper comes a man from the country who asks to gain entry into the law. But the gatekeeper says that he cannot grant him entry at the moment. The man thinks about it and then asks if he will be allowed to come in later on. "It is possible," says the gatekeeper, "but not now." At the moment the gate to the law stands open, as always, and the gatekeeper walks to the side, so the man bends over in order to see through the gate into the inside. When the gatekeeper notices that, he laughs and says: "If it tempts you so much, try it in spite of my prohibition. But take note: I am powerful. And I am only the most lowly gatekeeper. But from room to room stand gatekeepers, each more powerful than the other. I can't endure even one glimpse of the third." The man from the country has not expected such difficulties: the law should always be accessible for everyone, he thinks, but as he now looks more closely at the gatekeeper in his fur coat, at his large pointed nose and his long, thin, black Tartar's beard, he decides that it would be better to wait until he gets permission to go inside. The gatekeeper gives him a stool and allows him to sit down at the side in front of the gate. There he sits for days and years. He makes many attempts to be let in, and he wears the gatekeeper out with his requests. The gatekeeper often interrogates him briefly, questioning him about his homeland and many other things, but they are indifferent questions, the kind great men put, and at the end he always tells him once more that he cannot let him inside yet. The man, who has equipped himself with many things for his journey, spends everything, no matter how valuable, to win over the gatekeeper. The latter takes it all but, as he does so, says, "I am taking this only so that you do not think you have failed to do anything." During the many years the man observes the gatekeeper almost continuously. He forgets the other gatekeepers, and this one seems to him the only obstacle for entry into the law. He curses the unlucky circumstance, in the first years thoughtlessly and out loud, later, as he grows old, he still mumbles to himself. He becomes childish and, since in the long years studying the gatekeeper he has come to know the fleas in his fur collar, he even asks the fleas to help him persuade the gatekeeper. Finally his eyesight grows weak, and he does not know whether things are really darker around him or whether his eyes are merely deceiving him. But he recognizes now in the darkness an illumination which breaks inextinguishably out of the gateway to the law. Now he no longer has much time to live. Before his death he gathers in his head all his experiences of the entire time up into one question which he has not yet put to the gatekeeper. He waves to him, since he can no longer lift up his stiffening body. The gatekeeper has to bend way down to him, for the great difference has changed things to the disadvantage of the man. "What do you still want to know, then?" asks the gatekeeper. "You are insatiable." "Everyone strives after the law," says the man, "so how is it that in these many years no one except me has requested entry?" The gatekeeper sees that the man is already dying and, in order to reach his diminishing sense of hearing, he shouts at him, "Here no one else can gain entry, since this entrance was assigned only to you. I'm going now to close it."

[1915]

1. What is the effect of Kafka's choice to withhold all details about the place or time in which this encounter occurs?

2. There are two sentences of physical description in the story. What are they and what is their role in the story?

3. What is the source of the gatekeeper's authority? Why is he referred to in the second segment as a "great man"?

4. Why doesn't the man from the country go home when he fails in his initial attempt to gain entry?

5. The final line is supposed to explain the parable, but the explanation creates as many new puzzles as it solves. What is the meaning of the gatekeeper's final speech, and what does it tell us about the meaning of the parable?

6. Who would you rather be, the man from the country or the gatekeeper? Explain your choice.

The situation of the story is clear on a very basic level: A man is trying to persuade the gatekeeper to let him in to see the law. But that is all we know for certain. We do not know who the man is, why he is here, or what the law is. Nor do we know where this takes place, or when. Before trying to resolve these ambiguities through interpretation, however, we need to analyze the form of the text. Just as it was helpful to parse the sentences of "The Possessive" in order to summarize and discuss its meaning, we can analyze "Before the Law" much better if we take the time to examine it part by part.

Clarifying Narrative: The Segmentation   When reading a poem, you will often find that you need to parse the sentences before analyzing and then writing a summary. Not only are stories generally much longer, but sentence-level comprehension is generally not an issue; instead, before writing a summary you will find it helpful to divide a story into segments, one for each narrative unit. When you break down a story into individual narrative units—self-contained scenes or sequences of actions—the result is called a **segmentation.**

There are a number of possible principles to use for dividing narrative units, but the most common is by setting, either by place or by time. As in a play or a movie, a scene change in a story often implies a shift in action and the beginning of a new segment of the narrative.

"Before the Law" uses a single location, but its three separate temporal moments allow us to divide the story into three segments:

"Before the Law": A Sample Segmentation

1. The initial encounter between the man from the country and the gatekeeper, which extends from the beginning of the story to the sentence, "There he sits for days and years," which marks the beginning of segment 2.
2. The man from the country makes many attempts to gain entry to the law. These attempts continue to the sentence that begins, "Finally his eyesight grows weak," and initiates segment 3.
3. Now dying, the man from the country discovers the meaning of the gate.

There is always room for discussion about exactly where to break a segmentation, and whether to subdivide the larger segments (for example, segment 1 could be subdivided into four parts: the initial arrival, the first conversation, the gatekeeper's warning, and the man's acceptance of a chair). As with other questions of interpretation, you will discover that the moments in a story that elicit discussion over how to segment it will raise important questions about its meaning. Moreover, if your segmentation cannot withstand outside scrutiny, it is probably not consistent enough, and needs more work. The Writer's Guide below gives a couple of rules of thumb about segmenting narratives.

These rules will not apply to all stories; however, knowing that they do not apply will tell you that you are dealing with an unconventional story, a fact that will also help you in discovering its meaning.

The following summaries of "Before the Law" are based on the segmentation above. As you will see, the process of writing a segmentation greatly simplifies the process of writing a summary.

WRITER'S GUIDE

Segmenting Narratives

- Most stories follow a consistent principle for dividing their segments. If you cannot find a principle (such as setting or time), the lack of a principle constitutes a significant aspect of the story's meaning.

- The narrative segments of most stories are of roughly equivalent length. If there is a great divergence in length, the segment that breaks the pattern (that is, the segment much longer or much shorter than the others) is often especially important.

1. Franz Kafka, "Before the Law" (1915)

"Before the Law" describes the unsuccessful efforts of a man to persuade a gatekeeper to let him in to see the law. It is a parable, narrated in the third person from a limited point of view. A man from the country arrives at the gate and is refused entry. He waits for many years, makes many attempts to be admitted, but the gatekeeper refuses. Just before the man dies, the gatekeeper tells him that the gate was made for the man alone.

2. Franz Kafka, "Before the Law" (1915)

"Before the Law" is a parable about life. It is narrated in the third person from the point of view of a man from the country who wants to be admitted before the law for an unknown reason. An imposing gatekeeper refuses to let him enter, and the man waits for many years. He becomes obsessed with his quest, and questions and pleads with the gatekeeper, but to no avail. As he is dying, he asks the gatekeeper why no one else has come to this gate, and the gatekeeper answers that the gate was made for this man only. We do not discover why this is the case, nor what the man wanted from the law, but only that he has spent his life unable to get it.

WRITING EXERCISE: Summarizing "Before the Law"

1. Make a list of the strengths and weaknesses of the two summaries. What does each one include and what does it leave out? Has it included the required parts of a summary? Has it included material that does not need to be there? How well has it observed the list of dos and don'ts on page 23? Which summary is the more effective, and why?

2. Revise the summary you found the more effective in order to make it even better.

WRITING EXERCISE: Summarizing a Work of Fiction

1. Choose a short story from anywhere in *A World of Writing* and write a one-paragraph summary of it.

2. Write a brief paragraph reflecting on the process of writing your summary. What was most difficult about writing the summary? What do you feel you left out of your summary? How was summarizing a work of fiction different from summarizing a poem?

Clarity and Ambiguity of Plot   In addition to withholding information about the how, when, and where of the action, fiction can also surprise us through the use of **ambiguity of plot.** When the climax of a story throws us a plot twist—say, the trusted advisor turns out to be a traitor—it not only creates suspense but also compels us to reevaluate all of the judgments we had made on the basis of our assumptions about prior events. The short story you are about to read was written by the esteemed American fantasy and science-fiction writer Ursula K. Le Guin. The daughter of anthropologists, Le Guin writes fiction that explores the structures of human society from an anthropological perspective to raise profound ethical questions. In this story, she uses our expectations about ways in which horror stories withhold information to create an ambiguity of plot and question the assumptions we make about our world. Read the story carefully; after you finish, it will be your turn to do a segmentation and summary.

URSULA K. LE GUIN
THE WIFE'S STORY

HE WAS A GOOD HUSBAND, A GOOD FATHER. I don't understand it. I don't believe in it. I don't believe that it happened. I saw it happen but it isn't true. It can't be. He was always gentle. If you'd have seen him playing with the children, anybody who saw him with the children would have known that there wasn't any bad in him, not one mean bone. When I first met him he was still living with his mother over near Spring Lake, and I used to see them together, the mother and the sons, and think that any young fellow that was that nice with his family must be one worth knowing. Then one time when I was walking in the woods I met him by himself coming back from a hunting trip. He hadn't got any game at all, not so much as a field mouse, but he wasn't cast down about it. He was just larking along enjoying the morning air. That's one of the things I first loved about him. He didn't take things hard, he didn't grouch and whine when things didn't go his way. So we got to talking that day. And I guess things moved right along after that, because pretty soon he was over here pretty near all the time. And my sister said—see, my parents had moved out the year before and gone South, leaving us the place—my sister said, kind of teasing but serious, "Well! If he's going to be here every day and half the night, I guess there isn't room for me!" And she moved out—just down the way. We've always been real close, her and me. That's the sort of thing doesn't ever change. I couldn't ever have got through this bad time without my sis.

Well, so he came to live here. And all I can say is, it was the happy year of my life. He was just purely good to me. A hard worker and never lazy, and so big and fine-looking. Everybody looked up to him, you know, young as he was. Lodge Meeting nights, more and more often they had him to lead the singing. He had such a beautiful voice, and he'd lead off strong, and the others following and joining in, high voices and low. It brings the shivers on me now to think of it, hearing it, nights when I'd stayed home from meeting when the children was babies—the singing coming up through the trees there, and the moonlight, summer nights, the full moon shining. I'll never hear anything so beautiful. I'll never know a joy like that again.

It was the moon, that's what they say. It's the moon's fault, and the blood. It was in his father's blood. I never knew his father, and now I wonder what become of him. He was from up Whitewater way, and had no kin around here. I always thought he went back there, but now I don't know. There was some talk about him, tales, that come out after what happened to my husband. It's something runs in the blood, they say, and it may never come out, but if it does, it's the change of the moon that does it. Always it happens in the dark of the moon. When everybody's home asleep. Something comes over the one that's got the curse in his blood, they say, and he gets up because he can't sleep, and goes out into the glaring sun, and goes off all alone—drawn to find those like him. And it may be so, because my husband would do that. I'd half rouse and say, "Where you going to?" and he'd say, "Oh, hunting, be back this evening," and it wasn't like him, even his voice was different. But I'd be so sleepy, and not wanting to wake the kids, and he was so good and responsible, it was no call of mine to go asking "Why?" and "Where?" and all like that.

So it happened that way maybe three times or four. He'd come back late, and worn out, and pretty near cross for one so sweet-tempered—not wanting to talk about it. I figured everybody got to bust out now and then, and nagging never helped anything. But it did begin to worry me. No so much that he went, but that he come back so tired and strange. Even, he smelled strange. It made my hair stand up on end. I could not endure it and I said, "What is that—those smells on you? All over you!" And he said, "I don't know," real short, and made like he was sleeping. But he went down when he thought I wasn't noticing and washed and washed himself. But those smells stayed in his hair, and in our bed, for days.

5   And then the awful thing. I don't find it easy to tell about this. I want to cry when I have to bring it to my mind. Our youngest, the little one, my baby, she turned from her father. Just overnight. He come in and she got scared-looking, stiff, with her eyes wide, and then she begun to cry and try to hide behind me. She didn't yet talk plain but she was saying over and over, "Make it go away! Make it go away!"

The look in his eyes, just for one moment, when he heard that. That's what I don't want ever to remember. That's what I can't forget. The look in his eyes looking at his own child.

I said to the child, "Shame on you, what's got into you?"—scolding, but keeping her right up close to me at the same time, because I was frightened too. Frightened to shaking.

He looked away then and said something like, "Guess she just waked up dreaming," and passed it off that way. Or tried to. And so did I. And I got real mad with my baby when she kept on acting crazy scared of her own dad. But she couldn't help it and I couldn't change it.

He kept away that whole day. Because he knew, I guess. It was just beginning dark of the moon.

10   It was hot and close inside, and dark, and we'd all been asleep some while, when something woke me up. He wasn't there beside me. I heard a little stir in the passage, when I listened. So I got up, because I could bear it no longer. I went out into the passage, and it was light there, hard sunlight coming in from the door. And I saw him standing just outside, in the tall grass by the entrance. His head was hanging. Presently he sat down, like he felt weary, and looked down at his feet. I held still, inside, and watched—I didn't know what for.

And I saw what he saw. I saw the changing. In his feet, it was, first. They got long, each foot got longer, stretching out, the toes stretching out and the foot getting long, and fleshy, and white. And no hair on them.

The hair begun to come away all over his body. It was like his hair fried away in the sunlight and was gone. He was white all over, then, like a worm's skin. And he turned his face. It was changing while I looked. It got flatter and flatter, the mouth flat and wide, and the teeth grinning flat and dull, and the nose just a knob of flesh with nostril holes, and the ears gone, and the eyes gone blue—blue, with white rims around the blue—staring at me out of that flat, soft, white face.

He stood up then on two legs.

I saw him, I had to see him, my own dear love, turned into the hateful one.

15   I couldn't move, but as I crouched there in the passage staring out into the day I was trembling and shaking with a growl that burst out into a crazy, awful howling. A grief howl and a terror howl and a calling howl. And the others heard it, even sleeping, and woke up.

It stared and peered, that thing my husband had turned into, and shoved its face up to the entrance of our house. I was still bound by mortal fear, but behind me the children had waked up, and the baby was whimpering. The mother anger come into me then, and I snarled and crept forward.

The man thing looked around. It had no gun, like the ones from the man places do. But it picked up a heavy fallen tree-branch in its long white foot, and shoved the end of that down into our house, at me. I snapped the end of it in my teeth and started to force my way out, because I knew the man would kill our children if it could. But my sister was already coming. I saw her running at the man with her head low and her mane high and her eyes yellow as the winter sun. It turned on her and raised up that branch to hit her. But I come out of the doorway, mad with the mother anger, and the others all were coming answering my call, the whole pack gathering, there in that blind glare and heat of the sun at noon.

The man looked round at us and yelled out loud, and brandished the branch it held. Then it broke and ran, heading for the cleared fields and plowlands, down the mountainside. It ran, on two legs, leaping and weaving, and we followed it.

I was last, because love still bound the anger and the fear in me. I was running when I saw them pull it down. My sister's teeth were in its throat. I got there and it was dead. The others were drawing back from the kill, because of the taste of the blood, and the smell. The younger ones were cowering and some crying, and my sister rubbed her mouth against her forelegs over and over to get rid of the taste. I went up close because I thought if the thing was dead the spell, the curse must be done, and my husband could come back—alive, or even dead, if I could only see him, my true love, in his true form, beautiful. But only the dead man lay there white and bloody. We drew back and back from it, and turned and ran, back up into the hills, back to the woods of the shadows and the twilight and the blessed dark.

[1979]

QUESTIONS FOR REFLECTION AND DISCUSSION

1. What clues does the text provide about the narrator's identity? How does Le Guin use our expectations to surprise us about that identity?

2. In what ways does the story follow the usual werewolf formula? In what ways does it diverge from that formula?

3. How is the ending different from what you had expected? What does that difference suggest about the meaning of this short story?

4. How does the final twist compare with the final twist at the end of Kafka's parable?

WRITING EXERCISE: Segmentation and Summary of "The Wife's Story"

1. Divide "The Wife's Story" into narrative segments. Because this is a longer story, each segment will include a greater amount of material than your segmentation of "Before the Law." Nevertheless, you shouldn't have more than half a dozen segments total. Feel free to add subsegments if this makes it easier for you to keep within this limit.

2. Based on your segmentation, write a summary of "The Wife's Story" in two introductory sentences, plus one sentence for each narrative segment.

3. Write a brief paragraph reflecting on the process of writing your segmentation and your summary. What was most difficult about writing the segmentation? What do you feel you left out of your summary? How was summarizing a longer short story different from summarizing a shorter one like "Before the Law"?

Clarity and Ambiguity of Argument: Summarizing an Essay

When summarizing fiction or poetry, your challenge will be to condense the ambiguities of the words and events into a single meaning. Essays will sometimes employ ambiguity, but as part of their argument, rather than the events they are relating or discussing. Consequently, when summarizing an essay, your greatest challenge will be to condense a complex and detailed argument without sacrificing the clarity of the original. You should use the template provided on page 23, but your opening sentence should include a statement of the essay's thesis or main idea, and you should add a final sentence summarizing the essay's conclusion about the significance of its thesis.

The title of essayist Rosa Ehrenreich Brooks' short piece "I Hate Trees" both surprises us and prepares us for the ambiguities of the argument she will make about her subject. Born in 1970, Brooks is a law professor and essayist specializing in human rights, international law, and national security issues. As you read "I Hate Trees," annotate it with notes relating to summarizing it. Then read Melissa Kim's summary of the essay to see how it compares with your notes.

ROSA EHRENREICH BROOKS
I HATE TREES

YES, IT'S TRUE. I DETEST, LOATHE AND DESPISE trees. Here's why: Yesterday, I went out to buy stationery, and every kind I found was not only made of recycled paper but had something printed on it, like "earth friendly!" in childlike writing.

I went into a fit of rage so uncontrollable that I had to leave the store before I flipped out and flung my newspaper into the trash can instead of the recycling bin. After all, what have trees ever done for us? They don't work on assembly lines. They don't write poems. And when was the last time you saw a tree rush into a burning building to save a child or air-drop food into a famine-ridden country?

Trees have every right to hang out unmolested. But recall Dr. Seuss's Lorax, who spoke for the trees, "for the trees have no tongues." This isn't true today—every tree has a tongue. In fact, they have protectors running around in natural cotton T-shirts. A recent *Times Mirror* poll showed that 56 percent of Americans believe that improving the global environment should be a top priority for the nation. The U.S. has spent $2 trillion on environmental protection. Hell, trees have recycling laws; they even have Rainforest Crunch ice cream.

But what about people? You know, all 5.3 billion of us. What about the 15.7 million American children who live below the poverty line? Or the 1.5 million Sudanese who were killed in the recent civil war? Or the 5 million African children who die each year from treatable or preventable illnesses? Who speaks for them? Who has even heard of them?

5   You don't see 56 percent of Americans campaigning for human rights. Nah, we're too busy sipping cappuccino from our refillable plastic mugs. That's the danger of environmentalism. For many of us, it's an easy way to feel good: "Look at me, I'm recycling!"

There's nothing wrong with recycling. I recycle (so I lied about hating it; shoot me.) And it's okay to buy Rainforest Crunch. Just don't let caring about trees become a substitute for what's harder—caring about people.

The next time you buy earth-friendly paper, use it to write to your senator, or write a letter to Amnesty International. Use a recycled envelope to send a check to a cause you care about. Speak for the trees—but speak for people too.

[1995]

A Summary of Rosa Ehrenreich Brooks, "I Hate Trees" (1995)

by Melissa Kim

In this short essay, Rosa Ehrenreich Brooks says that she hates worrying about trees because they distract us from worrying about people. Recycling makes her mad because trees have never done anything to help us. Trees are incredibly well protected, but people aren't, because we don't worry nearly as much about poverty and war. Recycling makes us feel good. That's alright, but it's more important to protect people.

WRITING EXERCISE: Summarizing "I Hate Trees"

1. Make a list of the strengths and weaknesses of Melissa's summary. What does she include and what does she leave out? Has she included each required part of the summary? Has she included material that does not need to be there? How well has she observed the list of dos and don'ts?

2. Revise Melissa's summary in light of your comments and evaluation of it.

QUESTIONS FOR REFLECTION AND DISCUSSION

1. Why is Brooks's title surprising?

2. Why do you think the author "lies" about hating recycling? Why do you think she then tells us that she lied?

3. Do you agree with Brooks that trees have never done anything for us? Why or why not?

4. Does the author change her mind about trees by the end of the essay, or does she still hate them?

5. Is it possible to "speak for" both trees and people?

WRITING EXERCISE: Summarizing an Essay

1. Choose an essay from anywhere in this book and write a one-paragraph summary of it.

2. Write a brief paragraph reflecting on the process of writing your summary. What was most difficult about writing the summary? What do you feel you left out of your summary? How was summarizing an essay different from summarizing a short story or a poem?

CLARITY AND AMBIGUITY IN VISUAL CULTURE

Just as our brains must resolve millions of ambiguities daily in order to make sense of the languages we read and hear, so must they resolve millions more ambiguities in order for us to understand what we are looking at. We spend every waking hour of our lives processing complex visual information and transforming it into a form that makes sense to us. Beyond interpreting the physical world itself, we are also constantly processing the cultural information presented by that physical world. Traffic signals tell us to stop or to go, how quickly or how slowly to do so, and what possible obstacles we may encounter along the way. We make constant assumptions about the people around us from the clothing they wear, their hairstyles, and their movements and facial expressions. We can walk into a cinema, turn on the television, or click on a video and know within a couple of minutes what we are watching and, quite often, when it was made and what is going to happen in it. With only the faintest effort, we recognize many of the actors, the genres, the settings, the styles, the situations.

Because visual recognition seems so instantaneous and because we take it so much for granted, we tend to forget how much we rely on it. We also tend to forget the degree to which how we interpret what we see depends on the world we know: our origins and upbringing, our social situation, our geographic and ethnic background, our cultural expectations. Recall what it feels like to enter a strange place with unfamiliar faces, codes, and visual signals: the first day in a new school, a new job, an unknown city, a foreign country. Your perceptions are suddenly confused: you barely trust what you see before your eyes, much less all the other ways of making sense of what is going on around you that you know so well in your home ground. Like learning to think critically about language, learning to think critically about visual culture means learning to reflect and discuss the questions raised by what you see around you.

Visual Assumptions

Because we need to process images so quickly, we make numerous assumptions about them that are not necessarily true. It is easy to fool our eyes by using the assumptions they make against them. For instance, read the phrase shown at bottom-left quickly, and write down what it says.

Your mind automatically takes shortcuts to make its job easier. That is one reason, for example, that proofreading requires concentration: You have to make sure you actually see what is on

> *The visible is how we orient ourselves. It remains our principal source of information about the world. Painting reminds us of what is absent. What we don't see anymore.*
>
> —SQUEAK CARNWATH

the page (two *the*'s) rather than what you expect to be on the page (one *the*).

When looking at images, it can be equally difficult actually to see everything, especially if what is there goes against your expectations. When reading an image, make sure your eyes look several times, and that they look with an open mind. All images contain a certain amount of ambiguity; the optical illusions reproduced in the middle and right illustrations below draw our attention to this fact. Read one way, they produce one picture; read another way, they produce a different one altogether. Try to look at them until you can see both pictures in each one.

In many ways, optical illusions are the visual equivalent of literary nonsense: their goal is to confuse us, to amuse us, and to make us notice why we are confused. Visual artists for thousands of years have been well aware of how important their viewers' perceptions are when

Think twice about what you see.

Two classic optical illusions.

creating meaning in their art. For example, the genre of painting known as **trompe l'oeil** (literally, "deceive the eye"), especially popular during the seventeenth century, makes a two-dimensional canvas or a flat wall appear as if it is three-dimensional (contemporary computer-generated animation does the same thing). A 1668 painting by the Dutch artist Cornelius Gijsbrechts (below) for instance, looks as if it is a bulletin board bulging with letters and mementos, half-covered by a black cloth.

The subject of Gijsbrechts' painting is a letter rack affixed with letters filled with words. When we read, we do not pay much attention to the physical page because we are too busy making sense of the words printed on it. When we see paintings, however, we assume that a flat canvas is a three-dimensional space, possessing depth as well as height and breadth. But Gijsbrechts' trompe l'oeil is so realistically three-dimensional that it makes us marvel at its illusion of depth rather than accepting it at face value. Just as writers create meaning by playing on our assumptions about words, so do artists create meaning by playing on our assumptions about images.

Trompe l'oeil today: Using a projection technique called *anamorphosis,* English chalk artist Julian Beever creates pavement art that is startlingly three-dimensional when viewed from the correct angle.

Cornelius Gijsbrechts, *Letter Rack with Christian V's Proclamation* (1671. Oil on canvas. Statens Museum for Kunst, Copenhagen). *Trompe l'oeil* makes flatness seem three-dimensional.

Writing a Summary of an Image

When working with images, as when working with literary texts, it can be extremely helpful to write a summary to organize your initial analysis. You can follow the same steps used when faced with a literary text:

- "Read" a visual text several times.
- Take note not only of the visual components that first strike your attention but also of its dimensions, its frame or borders, its medium, its genre, and the degree to which it is abstract or figurative.
- Reflect on and discuss the image, raising questions about it and considering the issues that arise with those questions.
- Summarize the image, just as you would a text: make a careful but concise description of the image and the events it depicts, note the point of view, and make a general statement about its main idea.

A Summary of *Letter Rack with Christian V's Proclamation* (1668)

by Alan Green

Painted in oil on canvas in 1671 by Cornelius Gijsbrechts, *Letter Rack with Christian V's Proclamation* is now in the collection of the Statens Museum for Kunst, Copenhagen. It is a trompe l'oeil painting in a realistic style of a bulletin board full of letters and mementos, partly covered by a black cloth. Each part of the painting is designed to make us see it as three-dimensional. The left two-thirds of the canvas depicts letters, mementos, seals, and writing instruments either hanging from the board or held to it by a grid of red ribbon. In the upper-right third of the frame, a black canvas cloth is pinned back, half uncovering the board. The frame of the painting reproduces the dimensions of the frame of the board.

WRITING EXERCISE: Summarizing *Letter Rack with Christian V's Proclamation*

1. Make a list of the strengths and weaknesses of Alan's summary. Has he included each required part of the summary? Has he included material that does not need to be there? How well has he observed the list of dos and don'ts?

2. Compare this summary with the summaries of literary texts earlier. How is it similar? How is it different?

3. Revise Alan's summary in light of your comments and evaluation of it.

WRITING EXERCISE: Summarizing a Visual Image

1. Choose an image, either black and white or color, from anywhere in this book, and write a paragraph summarizing it.

2. Write a paragraph reflecting on the process of summarizing a visual image. What was easiest about it? What was most difficult? What did you have to leave out? How was it different from summarizing a written text?

LOOKING BACK: A World of Meaning

- Literature challenges our expectations and makes the familiar strange to us. We first need to make *sense* of what we read before we start to think about one of the many ways of interpreting its meanings.

- Literature is based on the principle of comparison, and usually on unlikely comparisons. Literary images pose enigmas, or riddles, to the reader that can be resolved by close attention to details of the imagery of the comparison.

- We are able to understand the world of the imagination only because of the rules and constraints placed upon it. Literature is composed in a tension between imagination and nonsense on the one hand, and rules and constraints on the other.

- Thinking and writing about literature means being acutely aware of the different ways in which clarity and ambiguity interact with one another to create meaning.

- Reading critically means reading for what *does not* make sense. It includes being aware of expectations, reading carefully, and processing what you have read.

- The first step to take in understanding a difficult poem is to parse its sentences into their grammatical components, paying special attention to any ambiguities at the level of sentence structure. The first step in understanding a difficult short story, novel, or play is to perform a narrative segmentation, segment its action into distinct units.

- There are three principal types of sentence-level ambiguity: ambiguity of syntax, ambiguity of diction, and ambiguity of words. These are especially relevant when reading poetry. Ambiguity of situations, or ambiguities on the level of events, include ambiguity of event (*what* is taking place), of location (*where* a story is taking place), of time frame (*when* a story is taking place), of the relation of different events to one other (*how* a story is taking place), and of character motivation (*why* a story is taking place). These are particularly relevant when reading short stories, novels, and plays.

- The first step in writing formally about a literary text is the summary: a brief statement of its subject, form, and events.

- In addition to sentence-level ambiguity, a narrative can employ ambiguity of plot, a twist in the meaning of events that makes us modify or doubt our prior assessment of them.

- Essays will seldom employ ambiguity of language or event, but they will employ ambiguity of argument.

- An essay summary uses the same format as the summary of a literary work, except that it should begin with a statement of the essay's thesis and conclude with a statement about the demonstration of the thesis.

- Without even noticing, we are constantly making visual assumptions about what we see around us.

- Optical illusions make us aware of the visual assumptions that all artists use to create meaning.

- Images are summarized in the same way as texts, except that visual components take the place of language in the formal analysis.

ABSOLUT MANHATTAN.

CHAPTER 2

WRITING IN THE WORLD

ARGUMENT, CRITICAL THINKING, AND THE PROCESS OF WRITING

Chapter 1 began with an argument that illustrated how reading critically is a skill you can already apply to your everyday life; to learn to read literature critically you need only apply that familiar skill to a new context. In this chapter, you will extend the skill of reading critically into the three-step activity of critical thinking: reading, questioning, and writing. As the Renaissance philosopher and essayist Francis Bacon asserted (in an age long before gender-neutral language), these three steps are the foundation for success in the world: "Reading maketh a full man; conference a ready man; and writing an exact man" ("conference" is an old term for the process of reflection and discussion we call "questioning"). This is because we use the skills required for critical thinking all the time in our daily activities. After all, how many of us would not agree with the early twentieth-century American writer Gertrude Stein when she said that "Argument is to me the air I breathe"? Of course, the arguments you will make when writing for class will not always involve the red faces, shouting, and fisticuffs we often associate with the word "argument"; nevertheless, they will have the same goal: to persuade your audience. Rather than raising your voice or clenching your fist, however, you will be making arguments by using nothing but written words.

Knowing how to use words "fully, readily, and exactly" will enable you to make and win arguments in whatever world you happen to find yourself.

We begin with a detailed look at how to analyze the arguments of others and how to formulate persuasive arguments in your own writing, the primary goal of critical thinking. Next, we build on the reading skills introduced in Chapter 1 by using the mechanics of argument to work step by step through the stages of composing a paper using the process of critical thinking. We will study examples of the main types of finished writing you will be asked to produce in college: explication, analysis, argument, and comparison papers (we cover the research paper in Chapter 3). We conclude with an introduction to strategies for thinking critically about visual culture.

CRAFTING AN ARGUMENT

In Chapter 1 we focused on the most basic form of academic writing, the **summary.** Although the other types of paper-writing you will be producing for class vary in length, they all differ from the summary in one fundamental way: their success depends on how well you craft an argument; for the argument is the foundation of any critical paper.

Analyzing an Argumentative Essay

Our discussion here will begin with the **argumentative essay**—an essay, like those that you will be writing, whose primary purpose is to persuade us to agree with what it says. "The Rewards of Living a Solitary Life," by the Belgian-born American writer May Sarton (1912–1995), was first published in the *New York Times* in 1974. Sarton was author of novels, poems, and memoirs, a number of them with provocative sexual themes considered quite daring for their time, including *The Small Room* (1961) and *Mrs. Stevens Hears the Mermaids Singing* (1965). Late in her life, she wrote an influential

Truth springs from argument amongst friends.

—DAVID HUME

series of meditations on living alone. As you read her essay, notice the various strategies by which Sarton develops an argument that she has already summarized in the title of her essay. We have numbered the paragraphs for easy reference to the table on page 42.

MAY SARTON

THE REWARDS OF LIVING A SOLITARY LIFE

THE OTHER DAY AN ACQUAINTANCE OF MINE, a gregarious and charming man, told me he had found himself unexpectedly alone in New York for an hour or two between appointments. He went to the Whitney° and spent the "empty" time looking at things in solitary bliss. For him it proved to be a shock nearly as great as falling in love to discover that he could enjoy himself so much alone.

Whitney: The Whitney Museum of American Art, in Manhattan.

What had he been afraid of, I asked myself? That, suddenly alone, he would discover that he bored himself, or that there was, quite simply, no self there to meet? But having taken the plunge, he is now on the brink of adventure; he is about to be launched into his own inner space, space as immense, unexplored, and sometimes frightening as outer space to the astronaut.

His every perception will come to him with a new freshness and, for a time, seem startlingly original. For anyone who can see things for himself with a naked eye becomes, for a moment or two, something of a genius.

With another human being present vision becomes double vision, inevitably. We are busy wondering, what does my companion see or think of this, and what do I think of it? The original impact gets lost, or diffused.

5 "Music I heard with you was more than music."° Exactly. And therefore music *itself* can only be heard alone. Solitude is the salt of personhood. It brings out the authentic flavor of every experience.

"Alone one is never lonely: the spirit adventures, waking / In a quiet garden, in a cool house, abiding single there."

Music . . . : quoted from Conrad Aiken's poem, "Bread and Music" (1914).

Loneliness is most acutely felt with other people, for with others, even with a lover sometimes, we suffer from our differences of taste, temperament, mood. Human intercourse often demands that we soften the edge of perception, or withdraw at the very instant of personal truth for fear of hurting, or of being inappropriately present, which is to say naked, in a social situation. Alone we can afford to be wholly whatever we are, and to feel whatever we feel absolutely. That is a great luxury!

For me the most interesting thing about a solitary life, and mine has been that for the last twenty years, is that it becomes increasingly rewarding. When I can

---

The Rewards of Living a Solitary Life

By May Sarton

YORK, Me.—The other day an acquaintance of mine, a gregarious and charming man, told me he had found himself unexpectedly alone in New York for an hour or two between appointments. He went to the Whitney and spent the "empty" time looking at things in solitary bliss. For him it proved to be a shock nearly as great as falling in love to discover that he could enjoy himself so much alone.

What had he been afraid of, I asked myself? That, suddenly alone, he would discover that he bored himself, or that there was, quite simply, no self there to meet? But having taken the plunge, he is now on the brink of adventure; he is about to be launched into his own inner space, space as immense, unexplored and sometimes frightening as outer space to the astronaut.

His every perception will come to him with a new freshness and, for a time, seem startlingly original. For anyone who can see things for himself with a naked eye becomes, for a moment or two, something of a genius. With another human being present vision becomes double vision, inevitably. We are busy wondering, what does my companion see or think of this, and what do I think of it? The original impact gets lost, or diffused.

"Music I heard with you was more than music." Exactly. And therefore music *itself* can only be heard alone. Solitude is the salt of personhood. It brings out the authentic flavor of every experience.

"Alone one is never lonely: the spirit adventures, waking/In a quiet garden, in a cool house, abiding single there."

Loneliness is most acutely felt with other people, for with others, even with a lover sometimes, we suffer from our differences, differences of taste, temperament, mood. Human intercourse often demands that we soften

the edge of perception, or withdraw at the very instant of personal truth for fear of hurting, or of being inappropriately present, which is to say naked, in a social situation. Alone we can afford to be wholly whatever we are, and to feel whatever we feel absolutely. That is a great luxury!

For me the most interesting thing about a solitary life, and mine has been that for the last twenty years, is that it becomes increasingly rewarding. When I can wake up and watch the sun rise over the ocean, as I do most days, and know that I have an entire day ahead, uninterrupted, in which to write a few pages, take a walk with my dog, lie down in the afternoon for a long think, (why does one think better in a horizontal position?), read and listen to music, I am flooded with happiness.

I am lonely only when I am overtired, when I have worked too long without a break, when for the time being I feel empty and need filling up. And I am lonely sometimes when I come back home after a lecture trip, when I have seen a lot of people and talked a lot, and am full to the brim with experience that needs to be sorted out.

Then for a little while the house feels huge and empty, and I wonder where my self is hiding. It has to be recaptured slowly by watering the plants, perhaps, and looking again at each one as though it were a person, by feeding the two cats, by cooking a meal.

It takes a while, as I watch the surf blowing up in fountains at the end of the field, but the moment comes when the world falls away, and the self emerges again from the deep unconscious, bringing back all I have recently experienced to be explored and slowly understood, when I can converse again with my own hidden powers, and so grow, and so be renewed, till death do us part.

May Sarton, a poet and novelist, is author of "Journal of a Solitude."

Alan S. Orling

May Sarton's essay as it originally appeared in the *New York Times* on April 8, 1974.

wake up and watch the sun rise over the ocean, as I do most days, and know that I have an entire day ahead, uninterrupted, in which to write a few pages, take a walk with my dog, lie down in the afternoon for a long think (why does one think better in a horizontal position?), read and listen to music, I am flooded with happiness.

I am lonely only when I am overtired, when I have worked too long without a break, when for the time being I feel empty and need filling up. And I am lonely sometimes when I come back home after a lecture trip, when I have seen a lot of people and talked a lot, and am full to the brim with experience that needs to be sorted out.

10   Then for a little while the house feels huge and empty, and I wonder where my self is hiding. It has to be recaptured slowly by watering the plants, perhaps, and looking again at each one as though it were a person, by feeding the two cats, by cooking a meal.

It takes a while, as I watch the surf blowing up in fountains at the end of the field, but the moment comes when the world falls away, and the self emerges again from the deep unconscious, bringing back all I have recently experienced to be explored and slowly understood, when I converse again with my hidden powers, and so grow, and so be renewed, till death do us part.

[1974]

QUESTIONS FOR REFLECTION AND DISCUSSION

1. Summarize, in a single sentence, the main argument of the essay.

2. How, in her essay, does Sarton define "the solitary life"? What are its advantages? What are its disadvantages? Can you find any inconsistencies in her argument about the solitary life? Are there rewards to social life that she neglects to mention?

3. What do you think she means by the last sentence? What is the effect of her choice of concluding words, "till death do us part," on your understanding of the end of the essay?

4. Do you think the "gregarious and charming man" with whom Sarton begins her essay would be persuaded by her argument? Why or why not? Were you persuaded? Why or why not?

Sarton's title states her **leading argument:** a solitary life is rewarding. But if she can summarize her essay in the title, why does she need to do anything more to make her argument? Like any good argument, Sarton's is debatable; it is more likely we will disagree than agree with her leading argument. If her argument were self-evident enough to persuade merely by being stated, it would be a truism—a statement so obvious that it doesn't need demonstration ("Water wets"). We follow Sarton's essay step by step in the Writer's Guide on page 42 to watch how she develops her argument in order to persuade us of her provocative initial assertion. Analyzing an argument in this way helps us to see the different parts out of which this author has constructed her argument as a whole.

Sarton's two **narrative arguments** (¶ 1 and 8–11) help us to identify with the subject of the argument, first the acquaintance and then the narrator herself. Because her topic is subjective rather than factual, she relies heavily on **evaluation arguments** to persuade us that a situation we probably regarded negatively is actually something positive. The argument is persuasive because it first contradicts our expectations, and then tells us we can get what we want ("happiness") by the opposite of what we had thought. The **definition** that emerges from the evaluation arguments states that solitude is the remedy for "being alone" rather than its cause.

Breaking down an argumentative essay into its separate components is the best way either to evaluate it and explain it or to build a counter-argument, or rebuttal. What is at stake in her argument? Do we want the "rewards" that she wants? Do we accept her premise that loneliness is to be avoided? Are there other possible remedies for loneliness

that she has ignored? Are there counterarguments that she has failed to rebut? Are there possible contradictions in the construction of her argument? For example, if being with other people makes her lonely, why does she continue to do so (9)? A step-by-step analysis is helpful both for appreciating the strengths of an argument and for uncovering possible weaknesses.

Every good argument appeals to us both **objectively,** as rational observers, and **subjectively,** as passionate individuals. Distinguishing between objective and subjective components in an argument will help us analyze and evaluate it; it will also help us to determine its audience and purpose. Sarton's essay relies heavily on subjective arguments through **narrative** (because someone experienced it) and **evaluation** (because it is a good thing), although she also supports her case with objective

Types of Argument in Sarton's Essay

SUMMARY BY PARAGRAPH	COMMENTARY
¶ 1. Sarton tells the story of an acquaintance who unexpectedly spends a couple of hours alone, and enjoys it.	Sarton begins with a **narrative argument:** the story of someone like her assumed audience, who proves her assertion by his own experience.
¶ 2–4. She analyzes the episode: being alone is an exploration of one's self—new, exciting and intense.	She adds an **evaluation:** being alone is good because it is "new, exciting, intense."
¶ 5. Quoting a line of poetry, she refutes it with the evidence of her analysis above: we can only truly understand what we experience if we are alone; otherwise we are distracted.	Sarton quotes a line we think we agree with, and then refutes it with a **rebuttal.** She also adds to her evaluation with an **analogy:** Solitude is good because, like salt, it brings out the flavor of experience.
¶ 6. Two lines of poetry (her own, evidently) elaborate her prior definitions in paradoxical terms: "Alone is never lonely."	She continues with her **evaluation:** being alone is good because you are never lonely.
¶ 7. Conversely, we are most alone when with other people, because we cannot truly be ourselves.	The logical consequence of her evaluation is a **definitional argument:** solitude is the state in which we are most ourselves. This is also a **causal argument:** being alone is preferable *because* we can be ourselves.
¶ 8. As in (1), she argues from experience, this time her own, that the more time she spends alone, the more rewarding it becomes.	Sarton offers a second narrative argument: this is how being alone works for her; therefore it should also work for us.
¶ 9. Still, she concedes, there are circumstances under which she does get lonely.	She continues the narrative argument, while also rebutting a possible counterargument: she does get lonely, but it is not directly caused by being alone.
¶ 10. The best remedy for feeling lonely that she has found is more, not less, time alone.	The narrative argument extends her rebuttal: loneliness is *not* caused by solitude *nor* is it remedied by company.
¶ 11. With patience and enough time alone, she recovers from loneliness and is herself again; being oneself, for her, is the ultimate reward.	The narrative conclusion of her definition and evaluation: being alone is *good* because it *means* having your "self" to accompany you. (4)

arguments: **causal** (because these are its causes); **definitional** (because it has these qualities); **rebuttal** (because these assumptions about it are not true). In sum, "The Rewards of Living a Solitary Life" relies heavily on subjective arguments because Sarton is explaining her choices as an individual; she is more concerned with subjective states of mind such as happiness, loneliness, and experience than with objective criteria. In contrast, a fact-based argumentative essay such as Rosa Ehrenreich Brooks's "I Hate Trees" (p. 32) may also use narrative and evaluation arguments, but its primary arguments will be causal, definitional, and rebuttal, which appeal to us as rational observers more than as subjective individuals. The objectivity of an essay should be evaluated just as we should evaluate a subjective assumption about what makes us happy, but the criteria for evaluation are fact-based (are their sources reliable?) rather than value-based (do we agree with the values of the author?). In addition to rebutting what it considers to be faulty reasons, an argumentative essay will also take a **position** on its subject and make a **proposal** regarding what should be done to change the situation it is describing. These will usually be stated directly in a fact-based essay, but they may only be implied by a personal essay: Sarton takes a position on solitude and proposes that we embrace it, but that is not the main goal of her essay.

Key Points to Consider in Crafting an Argument

- *The type of assignment* given by your instructor. You may be encouraged to focus on a particular theme, a particular comparison, or a particular sort of analytical approach (rhetorical, historical, linguistic, biographical, aesthetic, political, feminist [see Appendix A for more on these approaches]). You may be asked to write a specific kind of argument paper—a personal argument, such as Sarton's; a rebuttal argument, such as Brooks's (p. 33); a proposal argument—or to incorporate arguments into an explication, an analysis, a comparison, or a research paper.

- *The type of text* you are writing about. Different texts respond better to different types of evidence. A sonnet by William Shakespeare or John Milton will derive much of its meaning from its rhythms and literary devices, so your argument will probably be based on textual analysis. Conversely, Michael Jackson's *Thriller* video will probably yield a better argument if you approach it historically or biographically, or if you compare it to other related songs.

- *The relevance of your argument.* You could certainly craft an argument regarding the quality of the artwork in the Whitney Museum, but that argument is unlikely to be relevant to an assignment to write about May Sarton's essay.

- *The amount and quality of evidence* you can find to support your argument. Don't choose an argument if you can't produce the evidence to back it up. To craft a persuasive argument that May Sarton prefers solitude because she had a miserable childhood, not only would you need biographical evidence that she *had* a miserable childhood, but you would also have to demonstrate a causal connection between having a miserable childhood and preferring solitude, and to persuade your reader that this causal connection was important to Sarton's argument.

Making Your Own Argument

Once you have analyzed and summarized the form of a text, as outlined in Chapter 1, and once you have categorized it in relation to other texts in terms of the conventions it uses and the expectations it raises in readers, you can begin to develop initial ideas for your own argument about it. The kind of paper you are asked to write will determine which type of argument you use. The Writer's Guide above outlines some of the criteria to consider in choosing an argument.

Argument versus Thesis

Think of your **thesis** as the summary of your **developed argument,** not just a restatement of the leading argument. Remember how Sarton uses her title to present the leading argument, which she then develops significantly within the body of her essay? Writing a literary essay, Sarton can use her first paragraph to establish a specific relationship with her audience. Writing an academic essay, you should do the same in your introductory paragraph, but you should also project a greater sense of

objectivity, describing each part of the argument that is to come. Your thesis, usually the final sentence of the first paragraph, should make an explicit argument about the relation between those parts. Sarton's first paragraph does do this ("For him it proved a shock nearly as great as falling in love to discover that he could enjoy himself so much alone"), but she establishes the relationship subjectively, through an image ("as great as falling in love") instead of

spelling it out objectively. In academic writing you have to spell it out; in literary writing, you do not.

Depending on the topic, a thesis may be more or less categorical, or unqualified, in its terms, but it should always be specific rather than general, and it should always summarize the terms of its argument. Take a look at the examples in the Writer's Guide below and note the differences between a leading argument and a thesis.

Argument versus Thesis

Leading Argument: "The solitary life is more rewarding than life with other people."

versus

Thesis: "The solitary life is more rewarding than life with other people for the following reasons: you are more yourself, you experience life more fully, and, paradoxically, you are less alone."

Leading Argument: "The rewards offered by the solitary life outweigh its drawbacks."

versus

Thesis: "The solitary life has drawbacks: you are especially vulnerable to fatigue, overwork, and letdown after social events. Nevertheless, the rewards outweigh the drawbacks: you are more yourself, you experience life more fully, and, paradoxically, you are less alone."

Each of the points enumerated in the two theses in the Writer's Guide requires demonstration in the body of the essay, but that is not the function of the thesis or the introductory paragraph.

If you are writing a paper on a factual topic—say, public transportation versus private transportation, or the history of detective novels—you should rely heavily on fact-based research that requires analysis, interpretation, and synthesis, as well as on careful investigation of social science documents, studies, and statistics. A paper based on the analysis of a literary text will generally call for a less categorical thesis, although it should still present an argument and include specific reasons supported by evidence drawn from close reading.

From Idea to Thesis

Read the following story by the award-winning Nigerian writer, Chinua Achebe, and work on formulating an argument about its meaning. Note the additional steps required to develop a thesis that is much more detailed than the ones we formulated about Sarton's essay.

Born in 1930 in Ogidi, Nigeria, Achebe published his first novel, the classic *Things Fall Apart,* in 1958. His many novels, short stories, and essays are primarily concerned with the clash between Igbo and European values. This clash is well evident in "Dead Men's Path," first published in 1972 and reprinted the following year in the collection *Girls at War and Other Stories.* As you read the story, set in rural Nigeria, annotate its pages with ideas and questions raised by your reading.

CHINUA ACHEBE
DEAD MEN'S PATH

MICHAEL OBI'S HOPES WERE FULFILLED MUCH earlier than he had expected. He was appointed headmaster of Ndume Central School in January 1949. It had always been an unprogressive school, so the Mission authorities decided to send a young and energetic man to run it. Obi accepted this responsibility with enthusiasm. He had many wonderful ideas and this was an opportunity to put them into practice. He had had sound secondary school education which designated him a "pivotal teacher" in the official records and set him apart from the other headmasters in the mission field. He was outspoken in his condemnation of the narrow views of these older and often less educated ones.

"We shall make a good job of it, shan't we?" he asked his young wife when they first heard the joyful news of his promotion.

"We shall do our best," she replied. "We shall have such beautiful gardens and everything will be just modern and delightful . . ." In their two years of married life she had become completely infected by his passion for "modern methods" and his denigration of "these old and superannuated people in the teaching field who would be better employed as traders in the Onitsha market." She began to see herself already as the admired wife of the young headmaster, the queen of the school.

The wives of the other teachers would envy her position. She would set the fashion in everything . . . Then, suddenly, it occurred to her that there might not be other wives. Wavering between hope and fear, she asked her husband, looking anxiously at him.

"All our colleagues are young and unmarried," he said with enthusiasm, which for once she did not share. "Which is a good thing," he continued.

"Why?"

"Why? They will give all their time and energy to the school."

Nancy was downcast. For a few minutes she became skeptical about the new school; but it was only for a few minutes. Her little personal misfortune could not blind her to her husband's happy prospects. She looked at him as he sat folded up in a chair. He was stoop-shouldered and looked frail. But he sometimes surprised people with sudden bursts of physical energy. In his present posture, however, all his bodily strength seemed to have retired behind his deepset eyes, giving them an extraordinary power of penetration. He was only twenty-six, but looked thirty or more. On the whole, he was not unhandsome.

"A penny for your thoughts, Mike," said Nancy after a while, imitating the woman's magazine she read.

"I was thinking what a grand opportunity we've got at last to show these people how a school should be run."

Ndume School was backward in every sense of the word. Mr. Obi put his whole life into the work, and his wife hers too. He had two aims. A high standard of teaching was insisted upon, and the school compound was to be turned into a place of beauty. Nancy's dream gardens came to life with the coming of the rains, and blossomed. Beautiful hibiscus and allamanda hedges in brilliant red and yellow marked out the carefully tended school compound from the rank neighborhood bushes.

One evening as Obi was admiring his work he was scandalized to see an old woman from the village hobble right across the compound, through a marigold flowerbed and the hedges. On going up there he found faint signs of an almost disused path from the village across the school compound to the bush on the other side.

"It amazes me," said Obi to one of his teachers who had been three years in the school, "that you people allowed the villagers to make use of this footpath. It is simply incredible." He shook his head.

"The path," said the teacher apologetically, "appears to be very important to them. Although it is hardly used, it connects the village shrine with their place of burial."

15 "And what has that got to do with the school?" asked the headmaster.

"Well, I don't know," replied the other with a shrug of the shoulders. "But I remember there was a big row some time ago when we attempted to close it."

"That was some time ago. But it will not be used now," said Obi as he walked away. "What will the Government Education Officer think of this when he comes to inspect the school next week? The villagers might, for all I know, decide to use the schoolroom for a pagan ritual during the inspection."

Heavy sticks were planted closely across the path at the two places where it entered and left the school premises. These were further strengthened with barbed wire.

Three days later the village priest of Ani called on the headmaster. He was an old man and walked with a slight stoop. He carried a stout walking stick which he usually tapped on the floor, by way of emphasis, each time he made a new point in his argument.

20 "I have heard," he said after the usual exchange of cordialities, "that our ancestral footpath has recently been closed. . . ."

"Yes," replied Mr. Obi. "We cannot allow people to make a highway of our school compound."

"Look here, my son," said the priest bringing down his walking stick, "this path was here before you were born and before your father was born. The whole life of this village depends on it. Our dead relatives depart by it and our ancestors visit us by it. But most important, it is the path of children coming in to be born. . . ."

Mr. Obi listened with a satisfied smile on his face.

"The whole purpose of our school," he said finally, "is to eradicate just such beliefs as that. Dead men do not require footpaths. The whole idea is just fantastic. Our duty is to teach your children to laugh at such ideas."

25 "What you say may be true," replied the priest, "but we follow the practices of our fathers. If you reopen the path we shall have nothing to quarrel about. What I always say is: let the hawk perch and let the eagle perch." He rose to go.

"I am sorry," said the young headmaster. "But the school compound cannot be a thoroughfare. It is

An Igbo masquerade illustrates the kind of traveler who would use the path in Achebe's story. The photograph was taken in Amuda village, Isu Ochi, Nigeria, in the 1930s by the district officer and later ethnographer G. I. Jones.

against our regulations. I would suggest your constructing another path, skirting our premises. We can even get our boys to help in building it. I don't suppose the ancestors will find the little detour too burdensome."

"I have no more words to say," said the old priest, already outside.

Two days later a young woman in the village died in childbed. A diviner was immediately consulted and he prescribed heavy sacrifices to propitiate ancestors insulted by the fence. Obi woke up next morning among the ruins of his work. The beautiful hedges were torn up not just near the path but right round the school, the flowers trampled to death and one of the school buildings pulled down. . . . That day, the white Supervisor came to inspect the school and wrote a nasty report on the state of the premises but more seriously about the "tribal war situation developing between the school and the village, arising in part from the misguided zeal of the new headmaster."

[1972]

QUESTIONS FOR REFLECTION AND DISCUSSION

1. What contrasts does the narrator establish between Michael Obi and the villagers?

2. What is the conflict in the use of space that arises? Why can the conflict not be resolved without a "tribal war situation"?

3. What types of argument does Michael Obi use? What types of argument does the village priest use?

4. With whom are we meant to identify in the story, and why?

The first step in formulating an argument, as for any encounter with a literary text, is to read it critically: pre-reading, reading, processing (see Chapter 1, p. 15). The work of processing is the beginning of **questioning** the text in order to generate possible arguments about it. Breaking down the steps in Sarton's argumentative essay helped us to distinguish and evaluate the different components of its arguments. As discussed in Chapter 1, **parsing,** or breaking down the grammatical structure of

WRITER'S GUIDE

Using Narrative Segments

SEGMENT	STUDENT'S SUMMARY	STUDENT'S COMMENTS AND ANALYSIS
¶ 1–10. ["Michael Obi's hopes . . . how a school should be run."]	In 1949, Michael Obi is appointed headmaster to reform and modernize a rural school in Nigeria.	Introduces Obi and his wife as main characters with an agenda.
¶ 11. ["Ndume Central School . . . neighborhood bushes."]	Obi arrives and dedicates himself to reforming the school; his wife cultivates an elaborate garden.	Brings Obi and his wife to the main scene of action and shows them executing their agenda.
¶ 12–18. ["One evening . . . barbed wire."]	Obi discovers a traditional footpath runs directly through the school garden; he has it blocked with heavy sticks and barbed wire.	Focuses the conflict on a key image—the path through the school—and Obi's reaction.
¶ 19–27. ["Three days later . . . already outside."]	The village priest visits Obi and explains to him the importance of the path to the spiritual life of the village, but Obi refuses to open it.	Introduces the second main character, the village priest, and his inability to persuade Obi of the villagers' point of view.
¶ 28. ["Two days later . . . headmaster."]	A woman dies in childbirth and in response the villagers vandalize the school and its gardens; Obi is censured by the colonial authorities for his "misguided zeal."	Presents the tragic results of the conflict; introduces a third point of view, the "white Supervisor," or colonial authority.

a poem, and **segmenting,** or dividing a narrative into parts, have the same function of questioning. To organize your thoughts about a story and begin formulating arguments about it, first segment its narrative, as in the Writer's Guide on page 46.

The observations that emerge from this segmentation can then be used to make an idea map like the one below, that will track the stages you will follow next: from grasping the story's primary image (the "dead men's path") to an argument about its meaning and then to a thesis.

This idea map began with a central image—the dead men's path—and, consequently, generated a thesis for a **textual analysis** of the story. The image is a good choice for an **explication,** which seeks to explain the central meaning of a text; it also works well for a textual analysis,

Student Idea Map for "Dead Men's Path"

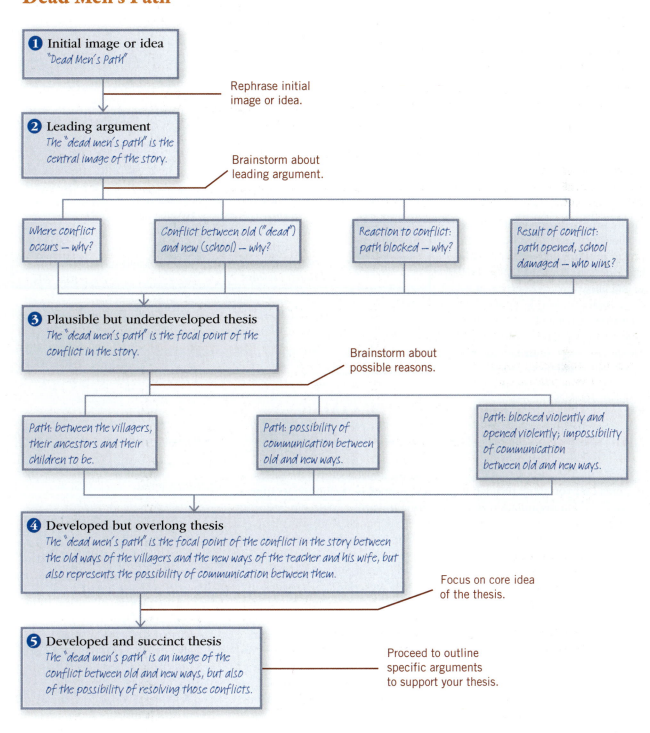

❶ Initial image or idea
"Dead Men's Path"

Rephrase initial image or idea.

❷ Leading argument
The "dead men's path" is the central image of the story.

Brainstorm about leading argument.

Where conflict occurs — why?

Conflict between old ("dead") and new (school) — why?

Reaction to conflict: path blocked — why?

Result of conflict: path opened, school damaged — who wins?

❸ Plausible but underdeveloped thesis
The "dead men's path" is the focal point of the conflict in the story.

Brainstorm about possible reasons.

Path: between the villagers, their ancestors and their children to be.

Path: possibility of communication between old and new ways.

Path: blocked violently and opened violently; impossibility of communication between old and new ways.

❹ Developed but overlong thesis
The "dead men's path" is the focal point of the conflict in the story between the old ways of the villagers and the new ways of the teacher and his wife, but also represents the possibility of communication between them.

Focus on core idea of the thesis.

❺ Developed and succinct thesis
The "dead men's path" is an image of the conflict between old and new ways, but also of the possibility of resolving those conflicts.

Proceed to outline specific arguments to support your thesis.

which can address any aspect of the form of a text. For an analysis paper, we could also have drawn an idea map for a less central image from the story, such as the garden; or focused on the characters of Obi and his wife or the village priest; or discussed with which character we are meant to identify in the story (we discuss further aspects of stories in Chapter 4). A textual analysis will draw primarily from your personal explication and analysis of the text, supplemented if necessary (or desired) by the reading of criticism or secondary sources. A **comparison paper** would generate a thesis comparing and contrasting your analysis of "Dead Men's Path" with one or more other texts. An **argumentative paper** would take a strong position on the issues brought out by the thesis you generated. A **research paper** would combine textual analysis with fact-based research. A thesis concerning the story's depiction of traditional religious beliefs or the nature of the power relations between Obi, the village priest, and the "white Supervisor" would likely involve research on these topics to provide a context for your close reading of the story. In the table above, we have summarized the different type of thesis required by the different types of paper.

Types of Papers and Their Theses

Type of Paper	Definition (with Thesis in Italics)	Student Examples of Paper
Descriptive	An objective description of a person, place, or thing providing a vivid impression of its defining characteristics.	page 186
Response	An initial reaction, including observations and questions.	page 196
Explication	A line-by-line analysis.	page 61
Textual analysis (or thesis-driven explication)	*The "dead men's path" is an image of the conflict between old and new ways, but also of the possibility of resolving those conflicts.*	page 66
Comparison	An analysis of similarities and differences between two or more texts. *The titles in Chinua Achebe's "Dead Men's Path" and Sherman Alexie's "This Is What It Means to Say Phoenix, Arizona" (p. 517) present images of the conflict between different ways of life, but also of the possibility of resolving those conflicts, although in different ways.*	pages 75, 161, 181
Argumentative	A paper that takes a strong position on issues brought out by its thesis. *"Dead Men's Path" presents an image of the conflict between old and new ways that can be resolved only through violence.*	page 207
Research	A paper that combines textual analysis with fact-based research. *"Dead Men's Path" presents an image of the conflict between old and new ways that occurred all over Africa in the years after World War II.*	pages 96, 105, APP B–5

CRITICAL THINKING: READING, QUESTIONING, WRITING

To write well about a subject requires that you think through its every facet and permutation; it also requires that you find other parts of your experience with which to compare it, the way Galway Kinnell discovers that ripe blackberries are like "many-lettered, one-syllabled lumps," words to be savored. Why spend so much time and so many words to describe something that you could experience simply by picking a ripe blackberry yourself, putting it in your mouth, and squinching it with your tongue? For starters, many readers may never have had the opportunity to pick

and eat a blackberry themselves, and Kinnell is attempting to approximate in words a replacement for the real experience. Moreover, many writers believe that carefully describing the simpler aspects of life can unravel the depths of life's complexities. To write literature successfully or to write successfully about literature, you need to be able to *think critically* about your subject and the process of writing about it. You have already been practicing the crucial skill of reading critically, as well as the key skill of formulating arguments and theses. In this section of the chapter, we fill in the

*. . . the ripest berries
fall almost unbidden to my tongue,
as words sometimes do, certain
peculiar words
like strengths or squinched,
many-lettered, one-syllabled lumps*

—GALWAY KINNELL,
"BLACKBERRY EATING"

rest of the process of critical thinking, with a particular focus on **revision,** an essential feature of effective writing that does not just refer to correcting mistakes. It literally means "to see again," to circle back and rethink, rework, and compare different sets of insights and approaches to a single text or group of texts.

CRITICAL THINKING FROM FIRST IMPRESSIONS TO FINISHED PAPER

Thinking critically about literature comprises three aspects: (1) reading; (2) questioning, or reflection and discussion; and (3) writing. We summarize the process below and will then follow a student step by step through the same process.

Critical Thinking Step by Step

Reading. To read literature critically is to think about the meaning of a text while you are reading it; to understand the possible meanings of every word and image in the text; to familiarize yourself with the context necessary to determine those meanings; to reread; and to develop questions about what you are reading. **Questioning.** To question literature means to reflect critically upon it by yourself and to discuss it critically with others. It means opening your mind to a variety of possible interpretations; probing and comparing those interpretations; testing arguments about specific words, images, and themes. **Writing.** To write critically about literature means to argue with it. This includes taking notes while you read; compiling those notes into a reading journal; synthesizing your journal entries into specific questions and arguments; using those questions and arguments to generate a thesis and structure a paper. You will not necessarily be able to do all of these things every time you read a work of literature, but the more of them you incorporate into your regular study habits the more you will appreciate what you read, and the better your formal writing for school and work will become.

Reading

Let's review our initial discussion about reading critically in Chapter 1 by looking again at the flowchart on page 15. When you approach a new work of literature, break down your reading into three stages.

1. Pre-Reading
2. Reading
3. Processing

Each stage builds on the previous one. Your **pre-reading** gives you a context against which to evaluate your initial reactions. Your **reading** tells you the key themes and concerns and what needs to be clarified and explained. **Processing** a text and its language lets you see each of its parts clearly so that you can begin raising questions about its form and meaning as a whole. Once you have laid this foundation of close reading, you are ready to move on to questioning and writing.

Pre-Reading and Reading. Your class has been assigned to read the poem "August," by the contemporary American poet Mary Oliver. How should you proceed during your initial reading?

- Reflect a minute about the title. What do you expect a poem entitled "August" to be about?
- Read the poem from beginning to end to get an initial impression. Since the selection is a poem, try reading it aloud.
  - Listen to the language and rhythms in your mind.
  - Don't worry about things you don't understand and don't try to figure out the poem all at once.
  - Concentrate: empty your mind of any external concerns or distractions. Savor what you're reading; don't skim or rush through it.
  - Focus on distinguishing between associations; those that

Mary Oliver

August

When the blackberries hang
swollen in the woods, in the brambles
nobody owns, I spend

all day among the high
branches, reaching   5
my ripped arms, thinking

of nothing, cramming
the black honey of summer
into my mouth; all day my body

accepts what it is. In the dark   10
creeks that run by there is
this thick paw of my life darting among

the black bells, the leaves; there is
this happy tongue.

                                                    [1983]

relate to what you are reading and those that indicate a wandering mind.

Always remember that each time you do a close reading of any type of text—whether it is a poem, short story, essay, or play—your path to understanding that text and making an argument about it will differ.

After completing your first reading of the poem, take a few minutes to write freely about it without censoring yourself. Jot down words, images, associations, and connections to your own experience and to other things you have read, in this class or elsewhere. Try not to evaluate what you are writing at this point. Sometimes your first impression will prove totally off the mark, and usually you will have to refine it with reflection and analysis later. More frequently, however, your first impression will end up proving rather insightful, and you'll find you can further develop those initial thoughts into a critical paper.

The following freewrite was done by Katherine Randall, a composition student, after her first reading of the poem:

why August

eating blackberries

not thinking

what is her body?

why the last lines which feel different (leaves)?

violent (ripped)?

but happy?

time

Compare your own freewrite with Katherine's. What similarities and/or differences do you see? What struck you that she does not mention, and what does she mention that you did not notice? Notice that Katherine's reactions take the form of questions, and that she recalls specific words from the poem as she writes. Sometimes we react very personally to what we read; sometimes we focus more on how it is written, its language and style. Try to do both at once, as Katherine does here when she wonders why the concluding lines "feel different." When you are tuned into your senses and your senses are concentrated on your reading, specific words and situations will raise questions and plant images in your mind that get your thoughts moving.

Now you are ready for your second reading, where you will focus on the process known as explication, from a Latin word meaning "to unfold." When you explicate a text, you determine the meaning of each part and the relationship between the parts, "unfolding" it to reveal the many different connections and associations that bind it together as a whole. How should you proceed when explicating a text?

- Focus your attention on comprehension.
- Stop every time you reach an unfamiliar word, or an image whose meaning is not perfectly clear.

- Parse the poem, dividing the sentences into grammatical units, as discussed in Chapter 1 (p. 21).
- Use your pencil to underline; make checks, stars, and notes in the margins; draw arrows to link up parallelisms; and circle key words and images.
  - Be consistent with the types of symbols you use; develop your own system of annotation, and you will be able to synthesize your notes in a glance.
  - If you expect to be doing a lot of writing in the margins— say for a writing assignment as opposed to regular class preparation—make a few photocopies of a poem or a very short story, and use one copy for each stage of the process of critical thinking.
- Make notes as you go along.
  - Identify any rhymes or rhyme schemes; note the number of stanzas, and the number of lines in each stanza, and try to recognize whether the poem takes on any particular type of form or genre. (For more about these technical elements, see Chapter 4.)
  - Look for parallels and connections between different parts of a poem, story, or essay: words and images that are repeated, or words and images that seem opposite or contradictory to each other.

Here is Oliver's "August" with the annotations made by Katherine Randall during her second reading. We have added comments on her annotations in boxes at the side.

A reaction comment
that characterizes the
language of the poem:
colloquial, not formal.

Written in everyday language: I know almost all of the words!

August*?*

A question
mark next to
the title—what
does it mean?

When the blackberries ✓ hang

swollen in the woods, in the brambles

"Swollen" is circled: a striking image. How does it fit?

nobody owns, I spend

Arrows between "nobody owns" and "I spend" to indicate
connection. "I spend" underlined because ambiguous:
does it go with "nobody owns" or with "all day"?

all day ✓ among the high

branches, reaching   5

my ripped arms, thinking   *violent*

A reaction note
describes the
imagery in stanza 2.

of nothing, cramming

the black ✓ honey of summer

into my mouth; all day ✓ my body   — *body (image pattern?)*

accepts what it is. In the dark   10

creeks that run by there is ✓

this thick paw of my life darting among

the black ✓ bells *?*, the leaves; there is ✓

"?" next to
"bells"—how
is a leaf like
a bell?

this happy tongue. ◄

Summary Comments
- **Enjambment** is when the sentence
  flows from one line to the next
  rather than ending (Katherine has
  marked lines 3–7).
- The word "body" with arrows to
  "swollen," "ripped arms," "thinking of nothing," "cramming . . .
  into my mouth," "my body,"
  "thick paw of my life," "happy
  tongue" discovers a key pattern
  of imagery in the poem.
- Katherine has placed checks
  next to "all day" and "there is,"
  because both are repeated.
- Katherine has placed a check
  next to the three occurrences of
  "black." Note that they come at
  the beginning, middle, and end
  of the poem.

Processing. As you process
the text, single out questions
arising from your notes and look
for ways to phrase those questions
in terms of the language and
form of the poem. The first step
Katherine took in processing
the poem was to clarify its
structure by parsing it. We have
drawn up the result, along with her
comments and ours, in the Writer's
Guide on page 52.

Parsing a Poem

"AUGUST"	GRAMMAR	KATHERINE'S COMMENTS	OUR COMMENTS
(a) When the blackberries hang swollen in the woods, (b) in the brambles nobody owns, (c) I spend all day among the high branches, (d) reaching my ripped arms, (e) thinking of nothing, (f) cramming the black honey of summer into my mouth; (g) all day my body accepts what it is.	(a) Adverbial clause + (b) adv. phrase + (c) independent clause + (d) adv. phrase + (e) adv. phrase + (f) adv. phrase + (g) independent clause	• *It's one long sentence!* • *It's perfectly grammatical. It's more ambiguous as a poem than as a sentence, because you don't have the line breaks.* • *Mostly adverbs, like lists— how and where – it's about a place and a time.* • *Semicolon: precedes (g). Important statement: "body"*	• The simple sentence structure reflects the everyday language. • Stresses importance of enjambment in the poem. • Emphasizes the importance of place and motivates Katherine's question about time in the title. • Parsing has reinforced Katherine's initial idea about "body" as a main image pattern. The break after "body" stresses its place at the heart of the poem.
(a) In the dark creeks that run by (b) there is this thick paw of my life darting among the black bells, the leaves; (c) there is this happy tongue.	(a) Adv. phrase + (b) independent clause + (c) independent clause.	• *Shorter, simpler sentences* • *Change of subject ("I" to "there is")—no longer personal.* • *Like (g), (c) is shorter, set off by semicolon, important statement, also about "body"–"tongue."*	• Starting over, the adverb again stresses "where" she is. • Katherine sees tone of new subject: "no longer personal"—but will have to question what that tone means. • Katherine notes a key parallel in the poem's structure.

Sometimes, as in Justin Schiel's parsing of "The Possessive" in Chapter 1 (p. 16), studying the grammatical structure of a poem will clarify your understanding by showing you ways you have misread it and revealing ambiguities in the language. Other times, as in Katherine's parsing here, your first observations will be strengthened and clarified.

Following her parsing, Katherine returned to the poem, developing her ideas and questions about images and parallels further.

Katherine's Third Reading Annotations

August   *time: summer vacation?*

When the blackberries hang   *blackberry* ←—→ *speaker?*
(swollen) in the woods, in the brambles
nobody owns, I spend

all day among the high
branches, reaching   5
my ripped arms, thinking

of nothing, cramming
the black honey of summer
into my mouth; all day my body   *human body*

accepts what it is. In the dark   10   *full stop*
creeks that run by there is
this (thick paw) of my life darting among   *speaker* ←—→ *animal*

the black bells, the leaves; there is   *bells?*   *two verses only*
this happy *?* tongue.   *full stop*
        last line shortest of the poem

Following her parsing, Katherine returned to the poem, further developing her ideas and questions about images and parallels. She worked to connect and synthesize her previous explication in terms of the poem as a whole. Here are the questions she focused on in her third reading and how her annotations responded to them:

- *What does the title have to do with the rest of the poem?*
Katherine refines an earlier vague question about time into a specific question ("time: summer vacation?") about what happens in the month of August.
- *Are the images of the body all similar in character and tone, or are some of them distinct?*
Based on her parsing, Katherine has broken down the general question about the body into three groups of imagery, one straightforward, the other two ambiguous. So, she has arrows leading from "arms," "mouth," and "tongue" to categorize them as a straightforward reference to the "human body." She signals ambiguity with a double arrow (← →): next to "swollen" because it can refer to either the speaker's body or the blackberry, and next to "thick paw" because it can refer either to an animal's or the speaker's own body.
- *What are some of the ways in which the ending differs from the rest of the poem?*
Katherine has focused on the final stanza by relating it back to a question she asked in her freewrite on p. 50 ("happy?"). She raises three questions about the form of the final stanza: 1) it has only two lines; 2) the last line is the shortest in the poem; 3) it includes one of two full stops, or periods, in the poem, emphasizing the parallel between "body" and "tongue" that her parsing had already revealed. She poses again

her question about the meaning of "bells," suggesting by association that its enigma may be related to the difference of the final stanza.

- *Are there any aspects of the last four stanzas that relate to line 3?*
No reading can account for all of the questions in a poem, and Katherine's focus has led her away from a direct focus on this question. Always note paths not taken, as they may prove important later in the reading process.

The key to critical thinking is figuring out which questions to ask and how to ask them most productively. Katherine's critical reading of the poem is not an attempt to "solve" it, or to look for the questions with the most straightforward answers. Instead, it demonstrates her steady

concentration of attention on a set of specific questions. Katherine's questions are simultaneously thematic and formal, and she has tied them closely to specific moments in the poem. She demonstrates that the more you can discover about the formal qualities of a text, the better the foundation of your argument about its meaning will be.

Questioning

After completing a close reading, you should now be ready to begin **questioning**—reflecting on and discussing the meanings of a text. Consider discussing it with your classmates or instructors; the more viewpoints you can take into account the better your final analysis will be. The first step is to turn your notes into open-ended questions that will prompt reflection and discussion. The Writer's Guide on page 53 contains a list of general questions to ask and some specific questions generated with them from Katherine Randall's notes and annotations.

Brainstorming Ideas about a Reading. When reflecting on your own, try **brainstorming.** Rather than limit yourself to one potential answer to your questions, try to come up with as many possibilities as you can, and in as much detail as possible. Imagine yourself in a discussion where various students are coming up with different ideas about a question, a word, an image. As you did during the first critical reading stage, resist the urge to censor any of your ideas; simply jot down everything that comes to mind into your reading journal. Remember that literature is built on ambiguity and multiple meanings; always ask yourself if the meaning you think of first is the only possibility. As a rule of thumb, if you are convinced after five minutes that you have nailed down the single definitive interpretation, chances are you have left out several important aspects of the text.

Think comparatively rather than exclusively. Work with the patterns and groups of images you have identified in your reading. Make lists of things that are similar and different. Here is how Katherine Randall began brainstorming about "August" based on her prior reading and annotation.

Body images:

1. Body parts: arms (6), mouth (9), tongue (14)—why these parts? Where are they in the poem? In lines about picking and eating blackberries

2. "Swollen"—refers to body as well as blackberry? Blackberry as body? Bruised, injured, like the ripped arm, or pregnant like a woman's body?

3. Body as a whole (9–10) + paw: body part of an animal (12)
   —"<u>all day</u> my body accepts what it is" related to "I spend <u>all day</u>"—is it also related to "thinking of nothing" b/c of just doing, accepting?

Is she a body, in the moment like an animal, eating blackberries? Or is she aware of what she is doing, where she is, what time it is?

"The thick paw of my life": this is a metaphor, not just a physical body. How is a life like a paw? Because it's in the moment, like an animal? Because it's part of the whole, so her body would be her whole life? Because she can't grasp it very well, like a hand could? Because it's ripped like her arms? What about the different subject in the second sentence? Is she watching herself here (there is this paw, this tongue)? Or is someone else watching?

Summarizing the Text. When you feel ready to make an argument about a text, you are then ready to move into writing critically. You have already been writing as an integral aspect of seeing and arguing: in the form of your reading journal, your notes, your questions, and your brainstorming, as well as class discussion on the blackboard. As we discussed in Chapter 1, a good first step in writing formally is the **summary.** A summary of a short poem like "August" should be only a few sentences, but it should still include the fundamentals of the summary as discussed in Chapter 1: a sentence stating the poem's main idea; a sentence on its form, genre, speaker, and point of view; and an account of the events described (see the full discussion and checklist, p. 23). Because it tries to be objective and stand back from any interpretation, a summary is a good way to take stock of where you are in your questioning of a text. Katherine used her summary to organize her developing ideas about the poem (see p. 56). But not everyone's questioning will have followed the same path, so we have also included two other summaries of "August," by Katherine's classmates. As you read these summaries, compare them with your own ideas and argument about the poem, and think about what works well and what is missing from each one.

A Summary of Mary Oliver's "August"

by Nora Torres

A woman speaks about reaching for blackberries as if she was reaching for the freedom in her life. She describes herself as an animal, very much like a bear, reaching for honey. She goes to a place that seems to be calling her, like "black bells." She reaches her goal even if it causes her to get ripped by the thorns, she doesn't even feel her wounds. When she claims her goal, and is finally in complete happiness, the world even stops for a moment as she enjoys it.

A Summary of "August"

by Katherine Randall

"August" is a poem in 14 lines composed of two sentences. A woman describes a late summer day spent picking and eating blackberries that absorbs her so completely she lives in the moment, in her body. The first three stanzas describe eating blackberries like an animal, not noticing anything else, not even cuts from the thorns. In the last two stanzas she accepts this life and is happy with it.

A Summary of "August"

by Batsheva Pollak

"August" is a poem about a girl happily eating blackberries in the wood. She cuts her arm on the thorns but this doesn't bother her. She compares herself to an animal "darting among the black bells." She feels as if she is a part of nature.

1. What are some of the assumptions that the three summaries make about the poem?

2. Compare the opening sentences: which of them seems to you a more accurate statement of the poem's main idea?

3. How would you characterize the different approach taken by each summary to the events it describes?

Which of them is more descriptive? Which of them pays more attention to the poem's use of language?

4. What has each of these students omitted from her summary? Are any of these omissions crucial to your own understanding of the poem?

Summarizing Your Reading and Reflection. Good writing about literature persuades because it manages to explain the complexities of a particular text, not because it manages to explain them away. It is often the places where a text eludes your explanation of it that can help most to deepen your reading, take it in a new direction, or reveal a subtlety you had not noticed before. Always stop after you have written a summary and ask yourself the four questions in the Writer's Guide at right, which also contains Katharine's responses with reference to "August."

Sometimes your review of your summary will make you want to rewrite it (Katherine decided to add a word, "wild"). At other times, it will help you notice things you want to use in your interpretation of the text, as you rethink your notes and insights for class discussion or in terms of a specific paper. We will look at two examples of papers in this chapter. We will first follow Katherine Randall as she uses her reading and questioning to write an explication of "August"; then we will study how to write a comparison paper on two stories, also about blackberries.

Writing

Of course, you have been writing all along: noting, annotating, parsing, summarizing. But you start "Writing" with a capital "W" when you focus on applying your reading and questioning to the task of a specific paper assignment. First things first: never forget to read the assignment carefully word for word. All successful

papers demonstrate clarity, conciseness, and errorless execution. But each paper will also have specific parameters set by your teacher that you will need to follow closely. If you have done a thorough job with the first two steps of critical thinking, you will be well on your way to organizing your ideas into an outline for a paper. The table on page 48 provides sample theses for the most common types of paper assignments and tells you where in the book to find examples of student work in each genre of paper. The process that Katherine used to write a line-by-line explication paper also serves as a useful first

step for a textual analysis or an argumentative or comparison paper.

Organizing Your Material. Katherine's assignment required her to write a 2–3 page line-by-line explication paper on "August." Although she was not yet required to generate a thesis, her sense of the main idea in the poem helped her to organize the material and choose where to focus attention. It is impossible to explicate every aspect of even a fourteen-line poem in two pages. The Writer's Guide on page 57 provides a list of steps to take, and Katherine's decision at each step.

WRITER'S GUIDE

Reviewing a Summary

1. What have I left out?

   Descriptions and images. I mention "body" but none of the details about it.

   "Swollen" and its two possible meanings

   The question about being versus thinking

2. Is anything I have left out something I had earlier identified as essential to the meaning of the text?

   I have a little bit about each. But I don't have anything about other images I wondered about, like the words about owning and the "black bells"— everything that describes the blackberries, in fact, and not the speaker.

3. Can I reconcile this aspect of the text with the aspects my summary did cover?

   What if I call them "wild blackberries"? That seems to summarize the blackberry images for me.

   I don't know if I can bring in my thoughts about "swollen" without interpreting them.

4. What have I assumed or added to what the text explicitly states?

   My last sentence feels a little like an interpretation. The two words I use ("accept" and "happy") are in the poem, but I am generalizing a bit about their meaning. But I think this is what the last two stanzas are about, and I'm not sure if I can summarize them without generalizing in some way.

Organizing Ideas

- *Choose a main idea, pattern of images, or organizational focus for the text that will structure your paper*. We have shown Katherine's work as notes, and also in an idea map, which can be very effective if you like to think visually. Reviewing your reading and questioning will usually provide initial ideas and patterns. If you still find yourself stuck, you have a number of options: reread the text, talk to classmates, go to your school's writing center for assistance, or ask your instructor for help.

Body images. How are the three different patterns related? How can thinking about the body images help me understand other questions about the poem? One pattern is about her body. One pattern connects her to the blackberries or to being pregnant. One pattern connects her to an animal. And I have to connect these images to the thinking/life part of the poem.

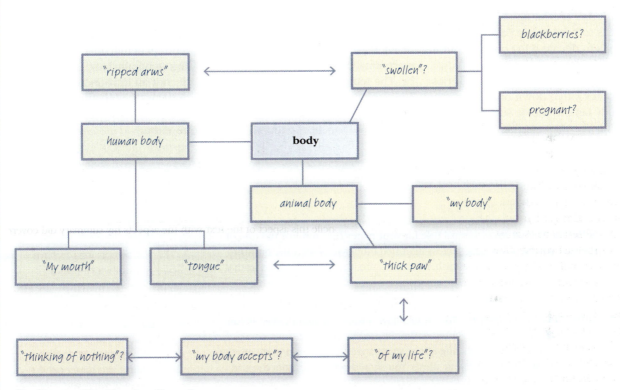

Idea Map: organizing ideas about "August"

- *Select the lines you will quote directly in your paper*. These may be a single word, part of a line, an entire line, or parts of several lines. Choose lines because they are key to the topic you want to discuss or because you do not understand them and still have questions about them. Note how Katherine has already used these quotes in her idea map.

Key to my topic: "When the blackberries hang / swollen in the woods"
 "my ripped arms" (6)
 "thinking / of nothing" (6–7)
 "cramming the black honey of summer into my mouth" (7–8)
 "all day my body / accepts what it is." (9–10)
 "there is / this thick paw of my life" (11–12)
 "there is / this happy tongue." (13–14)

Still have questions: "the brambles / nobody owns" (2–3)
 "I spend all day" (3–4)
 "the black bells, the leaves" (13)

- *Include consideration of the formal qualities of a text:* What kind of poem, story, play, or essay is it? Are there breaks in the pattern of its general structure? Does it use specific formal techniques, images, or literary devices? As in Katherine's case, your work of reading and questioning is likely to have provided material for this aspect of your paper. (We explore these topics in greater detail in Chapters 4 and 6 of this book.)

It's a fourteen-line poem in 5 stanzas. It could be a sonnet, but sonnets usually divide after line 8 or line 12. There is a break in the middle of line 9 ("all day my body"), and there is a shift in tone, as in a sonnet.

There are two sentences. The point of view changes in the second sentence.

The first four stanzas have three lines each. The last stanza has two. The last line is the shortest. There are no rhymes.

There are repetitions: "my"; "all day"; "there is"; "this"; "-ing" words (reaching, thinking, cramming, darting).

• ***Look for parallels and connections between the formal qualities and your ideas and the quotes you have chosen.***

I can connect the shift in the last two stanzas with the way a sonnet works. Which means in the end of the poem she's thinking about what she described happening to her in the first three stanzas (until "all day").

The repetitions of "my" "all day" and "-ing" reinforce the pattern of body images and of "being."

The repetitions of "there is" and "this" reinforce the difference of the end of the poem.

Katherine is clear about what she needs to have in her paper. Now, she needs to decide what order to put it in. This is the role of an **outline,** which can be anything from a series of notes jotted down on a napkin (many famous movie screenplays began like this) to a numbered and subdivided sentence-by-sentence plan. In general, the longer and more detailed the paper, the longer and more detailed the outline needs to be. The template in the Writer's Guide below follows the paragraph-by-paragraph organization we recommend for short papers.

Note that certain papers such as summaries and response papers do not generally follow this template (they generally have neither a formal title, nor an introductory paragraph, nor a conclusion), but, then, you do not usually need an outline to write one, either.

WRITER'S GUIDE

Outlining the Parts of a Paper

1. *Title.* You should have a formal title for your paper (i.e., not just the title of the text you are discussing) unless informed otherwise. Often the best title will come to you once you finish, but make sure it is in your outline so that you don't forget it.

   Title? The Speaker's Body in "August"?

   > It's a good idea to have a tentative title as a point of reference.

2. *Introductory paragraph.* You should have a topic paragraph even if you don't have a formal thesis. Here you should provide basic information about the text or texts you are writing about, summarize the different parts of your paper, and, of course, state your thesis. You should not quote from the text or include close reading.

   Main idea: the poem is organized around imagery of the body and it has an important break in lines 9 and 10.

   > Stating your thesis is all you have to do here unless you have specific ideas of what you want in your opening paragraph.

3. *Body paragraphs.* This is where you put the different parts of your argument, or the different parts of your explication, one paragraph for each. This is where you also put your quotes, close reading, and evidence (if there is a thesis). The body of a 2–3 page paper will have 2–4 paragraphs; a five-page paper will have 4–8.

   A. *Poem's title and opening description. "Swollen" and the body images*
   B. *The shift in the poem: lines 9 and 10*
   C. *The last two stanzas: "happy"*

   > In an argumentative paper, you might want more detail, but the key is that you include what you have to say and put it in the most effective order.

4. *Conclusion.* Your conclusion should summarize your argument and relate it back to your thesis. In a non-thesis-driven paper restate the main idea. You can also use your conclusion to bring up any loose ends that your argument couldn't account for, draw conclusions from your arguments, and make suggestions for further directions in which your arguments or your research might lead. You should not quote from the text or use close reading in the conclusion.

   I don't know yet what to put in my conclusion.

   > For a short paper, you don't usually need to outline your conclusion—you can figure it out along the way.

Putting the Words on the Page. You cannot start revising unless you have something to revise, so start writing! Use your outline to help you build the paper, sentence by sentence, paragraph by paragraph. Try to find a place to write where you are not likely to be interrupted and will not be easily distracted. Turn off your cell phone and disable your Internet connection. The more you can concentrate on what you are writing, the more cohesive your first draft will be, and the fewer revisions you will need to do later. Use a paper-writing checklist like the one that follows here to prevent yourself from making common mistakes.

Tips for Avoiding Common Paper-Writing Errors

A. Spelling and Word Choice

• Avoid the following common mistakes:

affect/effect: The light <u>affects</u> his eyes; they <u>effected</u> a clever settlement.

accept/except: He could not <u>accept</u> the consequences; <u>except</u> for us

two/too/to: <u>two</u> heads; <u>too</u> far; <u>to</u> the limit

rite/right: <u>rite</u> of passage; <u>right</u> turn; bill of <u>rights</u>

there/their/they're: <u>There</u> is only one explanation for <u>their</u> behavior: <u>they're</u> crazy.

where/were: <u>Where</u> <u>were</u> you?

loose/lose: <u>loose</u>-fitting; nothing to <u>lose</u>

lead/led: She <u>leads</u> now where once you <u>led</u>.

whose/who's: <u>Whose</u> fault is it? <u>Who's</u> there?

its/it's: <u>It's</u> not too late to save <u>its</u> life.

• *Prepositions:* Are you using the right ones?

• *Proper capitalization:* Capitalize at the beginning of a sentence and the beginning of a quotation. Check your dictionary for words, such as adjectives of nationality, that are always capitalized.

• *Names:* Refer to the *speaker* in a poem and the *narrator* in a story rather than using the author's name. Refer to characters in a film or television show by their proper names (not the actors'): you can find this information at imdb.com.

B. Syntax

• *Sentence fragments:* Does each of your sentences have a subject and a verb?

• *Run-on sentences:* Can you parse your sentences? Do all of the parts fit together grammatically?

• *Subject/verb agreement:* Is the subject singular or plural? "*One* of them *is* right but the *others are* wrong"

C. Diction

• *Punctuation:* Are your commas, semicolons, colons, and full stops necessary and in the right place? Remember, a colon introduces a list, and only a semicolon can join two independent clauses without a conjunction: "It was raining; I ran." "It was raining, but I ran." "It was a mess: hail, freezing rain, and sleet."

• *Word order:* Are the words in an order that actually says what you want to say?

• *Tenses:* Is the base tense for your critical writing in the present tense, not the past? "In this poem, a woman *is* eating blackberries."

• *Dangling modifiers:* Are your modifiers in the right place? Avoid sentences like this: "Running from the scene of the crime, the police arrested the suspect."

• *Awkward phrasing:* Have you written a sentence that may be grammatical, but that no one will be able to follow?

D. Structure

• *Thesis/topic sentence:* Is there one in the first paragraph? Do you know what your argument is?

• *Paragraphing:* Does each paragraph contain a topic sentence and argument?

• *Citations:* Do you analyze each passage you cite? Do you have at least one line of discussion for every line cited?

E. Style

- *Thesis and argument:* Is your thesis clear, engaging, and arguable? Do the arguments in the body of your paper relate to the claim your thesis makes? Do you produce concrete evidence to support your arguments?

- *Demonstration/critique/analysis versus assertion/opinion/evaluation:* Does your paper *show* how your thesis works through specific examples, comparisons, and detailed analysis, or does it merely *state* its conclusions as if they were self-evident?

- *Inconclusive/glosses over/closes down versus draws conclusions/interprets/raises questions:* Does your paper explore different approaches and/or aspects of a related set of issues (good), or does it reductively argue a single yes-or-no issue all the way (not good)?

- *Is your argument dictating your paper structure* or *are you just summarizing the plot?* If you are recounting events in the same order as the text you are writing about presents them, then you are not making an argument.

- *Adjectives (concrete versus abstract):* Do your adjectives impart useful information that helps visualize or imagine the nouns they modify (*tall, yellow, detailed*), or do they reflect value judgments and/or undefinable qualities (*great, bad, beautiful, ugly*)?

F. Apparatus

- *Text titles:* Have you italicized or underlined book and film titles? Titles of short texts (like poems and short stories) should be in quotation marks.

- *Citation:* Have you cited short excerpts (four lines or less) within the flow of text, double-spaced, and using quotation marks? Have you cited longer excerpts (more than four lines) separately: indented, double-spaced, and without quotation marks? (See Chapter 3 for further details on citation.)

- *Referencing and documentation:* Have you provided page references and bibliographical information for any source you have cited? Have you properly documented any idea, phrasing, or passage that you borrowed from another source? (See Chapter 3 for further details on documentation.)

- *Formatting:* Are you using a 12-point font and 1-inch margins? Are you following the length and formatting guidelines given in the assignment prompt? Is your paper as a whole doing what the assignment prompt asks you to do?

G. Process

- Have you rewritten your first draft at least once? Have you run the spell-check *and* proofread your writing?

- In a state of doubt or confusion?
  - Check a paper-writing handbook such as the *MLA Handbook for Writers of Research Papers.*
  - Ask a friend or classmate to read and comment on what you have so far.
  - Consult the helpful folk at your school's writing center.
  - Talk to your teacher during office hours.

As you read Katherine Randall's first draft on page 61, note that much of the paper borrows ideas and language from her reading and questioning of the poem. This is an excellent strategy, especially for a first draft.

Revising Your Initial Draft. Sometimes you will be required to submit a number of separate drafts as part of your formal assignment; at other times you will have an option to rewrite; at other times you will be required to revise on your own before submitting a final version for evaluation. Depending on the assignment, you may receive comments from your instructor, from a peer review by your classmates, or from both. Even if the assignment does not require you to rewrite, you should make every effort to do so before submitting your final draft. You can either rewrite on your own, with the help of peers, or with the help of tutors at your school's writing center. Katherine's paper was reviewed by her instructor for rewriting. Her instructor wrote marginal comments and noted problems that needed correcting, along with an evaluation of the paper with suggestions for revisions.

Katherine Randall
Professor Simon
English Composition II
3 March 2009

The Speaker's Body in "August"

In "August," a woman describes a late summer day spent picking and eating wild blackberries that absorbs her so completely she lives in the moment, in her body. The first three stanzas describe eating blackberries like an animal, not noticing anything else, not even cuts from the thorns. In the last two stanzas she accepts this life and is happy with it. The poem is organized around imagery of the body, but the meaning of this imagery changes in an important break in lines 9 and 10.

Although the poem is about blackberries, the title is "August." This tells us the time of year it takes place. The opening lines tell us what happens in August, "When the blackberries hang / swollen in the woods" (1-2). "Swollen" is an unusual word. It refers to the blackberries being very ripe, "swollen" with the juice that the speaker will soon taste. "Swollen" also relates to images of the body that soon appear in the poem, first in "my ripped arms" (6) and then in "cramming the black honey of summer / into my mouth" (7–8). "Summer" reminds us of the time period of the title, while "black honey" describes the juice of the ripe berries. The three "-ing" words that describe the speaker's actions ("reaching," "thinking of nothing," "cramming") make a pattern of action that show her body dominating her mind. She is doing nothing but hunting berries, and is not even paying enough attention to mind her ripped arms.

The poem has fourteen lines, like a sonnet. It does not rhyme, and is divided into four three-line stanzas and a two-line one, but there is a change in line 9, like you might find in a sonnet. The shift begins in the middle of line 9 and runs into line 10, where the first sentence in the poem ends, "; all day my body / accepts what it is." The poem uses

Good idea for a title, but can you rephrase it? "Speaker" is an awkward word choice here.

Make a new sentence from this.

Strong opening paragraph and succinct summary of main idea of your paper.

Can you rephrase this sentence to tell us why this information is important?

Avoid judgmental adjectives. Let your choice of words explain how it is unusual, rather than just saying that it is.

How is this meaning related to the previous one you stated, about blackberries?

Nice work. You're really focusing on the words here.

Just what a concluding sentence should do here: sum up the paragraph.

Good exposition, but can you rephrase the sentences so that they flow better?

a lot of enjambment, like here, making it move very quickly until this line. This line also changes the poem because it is telling us rather than showing us what is happening. Even though it is about only being her body, it is telling about it objectively instead of describing what it does, as it did in the previous lines. Like line 3 about "nobody owns, I spend," this line shows the speaker all on her own, and "accepting" it.

The last two stanzas are different from the first three, even though they are still about the speaker in the woods eating blackberries. Instead of using "I" she repeats the phrase "there is" (11, 13) and the word "this" (12, 14). Along with "thick" (12), all the "th-" sounds make these lines sound different, too. The image in line 12 is like the phrase in lines 9 and 10, and the parallel of "my body" and "my life" connects them. The phrase, "this thick paw of my life," makes her sound like an animal, except the paw is not hers but her life's. She is living like an animal, but in these lines she seems to be aware of it, which she wasn't in the first three stanzas. The final line is the shortest in the poem and seems to reinforce this conclusion, "this happy tongue." She is happy because her tongue is happy. Her tongue is happy because it is full of blackberry juice. There is still something ambiguous about this conclusion, though. The tongue could also be the speaker who is telling us about hunting blackberries. She understands how she is acting, but is not so sure that she likes it, even if her tongue is happy. Does she want to be like a blackberry, "swollen" with juice? Does she want to be like a bear, ripping its arm to satisfy its hunger? The strangest line is the next to last, "the black bells, the leaves." Black is the color of blackberries, but it seems negative here, like death, because of the bell. The poem is all about being in nature, and feeling her body, but it's not a completely comfortable feeling.

Margin comments:

Can you reorganize the paragraph? Your main argument should be stressed, while the details of the sonnet should support the argument, rather than leading it off.

Good topic sentence to begin the paragraph.

Nice attention to the sounds of the words. Especially important in a paper about poetry.

I'm not completely clear what you want to say here. Can you revise it?

Good idea to lead off the final paragraph by putting your argument in perspective. But I think you could say it more persuasively.

I like these sentences. Short and sweet.

It is an interesting point, but remember to avoid quoting or close reading in your concluding paragraph.

These are interesting ideas, and I like that you are being open about the possible meanings of the poem. But I still think you could phrase that opening more clearly. Don't just think aloud; guide your reader with your thoughts.

I wonder if this sentence might work well in the introductory paragraph. Often the end of the first draft gives you a good thesis or topic sentence for the next draft.

Work Cited

Oliver, Mary. "August." *Literature: A World of Writing*. Ed. David L. Pike

and Ana M. Acosta. New York: Pearson Longman, 2011.

49. Print.

Katherine, this is an excellent first draft. You are really working with the poem and thinking about its ideas and its use of language. This shows especially in the way you account for the meaning of all the words and images in the poem, as a good explication should do. You have a strong sense of the meaning of the poem as a whole. Your interpretation of "swollen" is suggestive, but I would like to see you produce more evidence that it is an image of pregnancy. What would motivate the poet's choice of this image? Is there anything in pregnancy that resembles the situation the speaker is describing here?

Your opening paragraph says clearly what you want to do. Each paragraph focuses on a different part of the poem, but each one makes an argument that works together. You note ambiguities in the structure of the poem, and pay attention to its form as well as its themes. Although your concluding paragraph doesn't have to decide on the issues it raises (whether the speaker is happy or not in nature), I do think you need to present the unease you have detected here in a clearer manner. Just because the speaker sounds unsure doesn't mean you have to sound unsure, too.

There are no major structural problems, but there is a lot to do to really make the paper click. I would like you to rework the third paragraph to clarify your argument, and the final paragraph, as I mentioned above. You followed your outline well, so each paragraph has what it needs to have in it. I'd like you to pay a lot of attention to your sentence structure and word choice when rewriting. Try to be sparing with words such as "like" that break up the flow of a sentence.

Katherine was pleased that her instructor had responded positively to several aspects of her essay; this helped her to assess its strengths and weaknesses. She took the following steps to prepare herself to rewrite:

- She read the instructor's comments carefully, and asked her about any questions she had.
- She read back through the Tips for Paper-writers (p. 59) for help in her revision.
  - She noted that her spelling and word choice (A) and her syntax (B) were in good order, but that the instructor wanted her to improve her diction (C).
- Her instructor had made several notes concerning structure (D) and style (E):

  Improve organization in paragraphs 3 and 5.
  Adapt thesis to include the final sentence of the paper.
  Demonstrate rather than assert.
  Choose informative rather than empty ("unusual") adjectives.

- Katherine made an outline of her rewriting, choosing the order in which to tackle her instructor's suggestions:

  - Rewrite paragraphs 2 and 5.
  - Rewrite other sentences needing work, not necessarily just those that instructor noted.
  - Read through entire paper to work on language and word order.
  - Choose a new title.
  - Proofread.

Here is the second version of Katherine's paper, annotated to indicate the key changes she made.

Randall 1

Katherine Randall
Professor Simon
English Composition II
10 March 2009

Happy about the Body in "August"?

In "August," a woman describes a late summer day spent picking and eating wild blackberries. The activity absorbs her so completely that she is living wholly in the moment, in her body. The poem is about the speaker's attitude toward being in nature, but it becomes clear in the second half of the poem that it is not a completely comfortable feeling.

The opening lines tell us about the end of the summer the title refers to, "When the blackberries hang / swollen in the woods" (1–2). "Swollen" mainly refers to the blackberries being very ripe, "swollen" with the juice that the speaker will soon taste. But "swollen" also makes us think of the speaker's body. Bodies are "swollen" when bruised and also when they are pregnant. The speaker mentions her "ripped arms" (6); she also uses several other images of the body, including "cramming the black honey of summer / into my mouth" (7–8). This image recalls the "blackberry" meaning of swollen, because of the "black honey" that bursts out. It recalls the "body" meaning because she is "cramming" the berries into her mouth. "Cramming" is the third of three present participles ("reaching," "thinking of nothing," "cramming") the speaker uses to make a pattern of action that shows her body dominating her mind. She is so focused on hunting berries, that she doesn't even mind her ripped arms.

The first three stanzas of the poem, up until the middle of line 9, describe what the body of the speaker does, "thinking of nothing." Images of the body continue in the final two stanzas, but the speaker's point of view changes after the middle of line 9, "all day my body / accepts what it is." The first sentence of the poem ends and the second sentence begins. This moment is like the shift that happens between the

K adapted her title to reflect the question of the discussion of the body.

When she wrote this new sentence, K also had to rewrite the language.

K cut her third sentence to make space for additions below.

K revised to condense and clarify her language.

K rephrased the last sentence of her paper to incorporate her idea about ambivalence into the opening paragraph.

K realized the sentence that was here didn't add to the paper, so she cut it.

K rephrased this sentence to make explicit the ambiguity she saw in the word "swollen."

Instead of replacing the adjective "unusual," K saw that the sentence had no essential information. So she cut it.

When she went to the Writing Center, K asked about the proper term for the "-ing" words she was discussing.

K revised for subject/verb agreement: "pattern . . . shows."

A new concluding sentence helps K wrap up the analysis in her second paragraph.

Note how K reworked the paragraph to focus on her argument about the shift: new topic and final sentences; material about sonnets in the body. She also cut material that distracted from her main discussion.

two parts of a sonnet, and the poem does have 14 lines like a sonnet. The speaker seems to be analyzing what she had only described in the first part of the poem. Instead of feeling the cuts on her arms and tasting the juice in her mouth, she tells us that her body "accepts what it is." Her attitude toward what she is doing does not appear to change, but she begins to discuss it rather than simply present it.

The last two stanzas are different from the first three, even though they are still about the speaker in the woods eating blackberries. Instead of using "I" she repeats the phrase "there is" (11, 13) and the word "this" (12, 14). Along with "thick" (12), all the "th-" sounds make these lines sound different, too. The image in line 12 is like the phrase in lines 9 and 10, and the parallel of "my body" and "my life" connects them. The phrase, "this thick paw of my life," suggests she is an animal, except the paw is not hers but her life's. In the first three stanzas she was stuffing herself like a wild animal. She hasn't stopped, but now her language tells us that she is also aware of what she is doing. The final line, "this happy tongue," is the shortest in the poem and seems to reinforce this conclusion. She is happy because her tongue is happy. Her tongue is happy because it is full of blackberry juice.

K has recast a problematic sentence into two in order to clarify her interpretation.

The image in the previous line, "the black bells, the leaves" (13), is not so happy. Black is the color of blackberries, but the bell makes us think of the color negatively, as connected to death. If this image can be interpreted figuratively, then the word "swollen" can also have two meanings in the poem. Like the speaker, the poem cannot make up its mind.

K moved the quotation and analysis out of the final paragraph and clarified their relation to her interpretation.

Even though her tongue is happy, there is still something ambiguous about the conclusion of "August." Does she want to be like a blackberry, "swollen" with juice? Does she want to be like a bear, ripping its arm to satisfy its hunger? This is like being pregnant, when you're full of

After moving the final sentence to her first paragraph, K reworked her conclusion to focus on tying together the different parts of the poem and the speaker's attitude toward them.

==something that's part of you but which you don't have any control over.==

==This ambivalence is the state of mind "August" wants its readers to feel.==

Randall 4

Work Cited

Oliver, Mary. "August." *Literature: A World of Writing.* Ed. David L. Pike

and Ana M. Acosta. New York: Pearson Longman, 2011.

49. Print.

Shifting Gears from One Type of Paper to Another. The final step of the assignment required Katherine to rewrite her explication as a thesis-driven paper, or textual analysis. Since she had already organized her paper around a main idea, and each paragraph around topic sentences, there were only four steps she needed to take:

1. *Draw a strong thesis out of the statement of the main idea of the poem.*
   My thesis: "August" uses a description of eating blackberries in the woods to portray the ambivalent feelings about the body that can arise during pregnancy.

2. *Briefly summarize the argument of each body paragraph within the introductory paragraph.*
   The poem begins with the speaker immersed in the act of eating blackberries, but in the second half she analyzes her situation. The concluding stanza depicts her ambivalence about the experience.

3. *Make sure each paragraph in the body states its argument clearly and provides textual evidence to support the argument.*
   Paragraph 2 topic sentence needs to express the argument that comes in the final sentence.

Paragraph 3 needs a topic sentence about the shift in the poem.
Paragraph 4 has a thesis sentence, I want it to be more precise.
Paragraph 5 also has a thesis sentence, but I want it to have more of the concluding sentence in it.

4. *Make sure that the concluding paragraph restates the thesis and clarifies any loose ends in the argument.*
   I like the conclusion. I think it does a good job summarizing and clarifying.

Here are the results of Katherine's rewrite of her line-by-line explication as a thesis-driven explication, with changes highlighted.

Randall 1

Katherine Randall

Professor Simon

English Composition II

17 March 2009

K changed her title to reflect her thesis.

==Ambivalence about the Pregnant Body in "August"==

In "August," a woman describes a late summer day spent picking

and eating wild blackberries. The activity absorbs her so completely that she is living wholly in the moment, in her body. The poem begins with the speaker immersed in the act of eating blackberries, but in the second half she begins to analyze her situation. The concluding stanza depicts her ambivalence about the experience. "August" uses a description of eating blackberries in the woods to portray the ambivalent feelings about the body that can arise during pregnancy.

K inserted the phrasing from her preparation, and replaced her previous topic sentence with her new thesis.

A new sentence to summarize the argument of the paragraph.

The first three stanzas show us the speaker consumed by the act of eating blackberries. The opening lines tell us about the end of the summer the title "August" refers to, "When the blackberries hang / swollen in the woods" (1–2). Swollen mainly refers to the blackberries being very ripe, "swollen" with the juice that the speaker will soon taste. But "swollen" also makes us think of the speaker's body. Bodies are "swollen" when bruised and also when they are pregnant. The speaker mentions her "ripped arms" (6); she also uses several other images of the body, including "cramming the black honey of summer / into my mouth" (7–8). This image recalls the "blackberry" meaning of swollen, because of the "black honey" that bursts out. It recalls the "body" meaning because she is "cramming" the berries into her mouth. "Cramming" is the third of three present participles ("reaching," "thinking of nothing," "cramming") the speaker uses to make a pattern of action that shows her body dominating her mind. She is so focused on hunting berries, that she doesn't even mind her ripped arms.

Because the paragraph already makes her argument, K made no revisions here.

A new topic sentence and a minor rewrite of the previous topic sentence focus the paragraph on K's argument.

A shift from experiencing her body eating to analyzing her experience occurs in the middle of line 9. Up to this point, the first three stanzas describe what the body of the speaker does, "thinking of nothing." Images of the body continue in the final two stanzas, but the speaker's point of view changes after the middle of line 9, "all day my body / accepts what it is." The first sentence of the poem ends and the second sentence begins. This moment is like the shift that happens between the two parts of a sonnet, and the poem does have 14 lines like a sonnet.

The speaker seems to be analyzing what she had only described in the first part of the poem. Instead of feeling the cuts on her arms and tasting the juice in her mouth, she tells us that her body "accepts what it is." Her attitude toward what she is doing does not appear to change, but she begins to reflect on it rather than simply present it.

Even though they are still about the speaker in the woods eating blackberries, changes in point of view and word choice and parallels with the first three stanzas suggest the change in focus. Instead of using "I" she repeats the phrase "there is" (11, 13) and the word "this" (12, 14). Along with "thick" (12), all the "th-" sounds make these lines sound different, too. The image in line 12 is like the phrase in lines 9 and 10, and the parallel of "my body" and "my life" connects them. The phrase, "this thick paw of my life" suggests she is an animal, except the paw is not hers but her life's. In the first three stanzas she was stuffing herself like a wild animal. She hasn't stopped, but now her language tells us that she is also aware of what she is doing.

The final line, "this happy tongue," is the shortest in the poem and seems to reinforce this conclusion. She is happy because her tongue is happy. Her tongue is happy because it is full of blackberry juice. The image in the previous line, "the black bells, the leaves" (13), however, is not so happy. Black is the color of blackberries, but the bell makes us think of the color negatively, as connected to death. Interpreted figuratively, this image reinforces the idea that the word "swollen" has two meanings in the poem. Because of the contrast between her "happy tongue," and the negative image of "black bells," the conclusion of "August" stresses the speaker's ambivalent feeling about her body.

The speaker knows what her body wants, but her mind is not so sure. Does she want to be like a blackberry, "swollen" with juice? Does she want to be like a bear, ripping its arm to satisfy its hunger? This ambivalence also

---

The new topic sentence retains the argument, but also summarizes the evidence K presents in the paragraph.

Because she needs the analysis of line 13 to contrast directly with the analysis of "happy" to prove her thesis, K combined paragraphs 4 and 5. She replaced her final sentence to restate the argument more directly.

K reworked the conclusion to summarize better her main argument and bring together the arguments of each paragraph in the body of the paper.

describes being pregnant, when you're full of something that's part of you but which you don't have any control over. The ambiguity of the imagery in the poem and the shift in focus between its two parts are there to make us feel the speaker's uncertain state of mind toward her body in "August."

Randall 5

Work Cited

Oliver, Mary. "August." *Literature: A World of Writing.* Ed. David L. Pike and Ana M. Acosta. New York: Pearson Longman, 2011. 49. Print.

Take a moment to look back at how Katherine's persuasive interpretation of "August" emerged from her initial questions and confusion over the poem's meaning. Her solid work in the first two steps of critical thinking meant that she had all the material at her disposal to adapt to the templates of the different assignments she was later asked to do.

WRITING EXERCISE: Explication Paper

1. Choose a poem, story, or essay in Part 2 or 3 of this book. Following the process of critical thinking used by Katherine Randall above (starting on page 49), write either a line-by-line or a thesis-driven explication of the text you chose.

2. Take a moment to reflect on the experience of writing the paper. What was the easiest part of the process? Which part was most difficult? Which part did you like the best? The least? What did you encounter in the process that you did not expect after working through Katherine's writing process?

Critical Thinking in a Comparison Paper

The blackberry has been a surprisingly fruitful topic for literature over the past few decades. What makes so many writers choose the blackberry as a subject? That is one of the questions a comparison paper is well-suited to address; for comparing and contrasting a number of related texts is a powerful tool for gaining insight on a particular subject. The assignment Cynthia Wilson completed below required her to write a comparison paper on two stories, both entitled "Blackberries." The first story was published in 1987 by the American writer Ellen Hunnicutt, who was born in Indiana and now lives in Wisconsin, where she has taught both piano and creative writing. She is the author of a collection of short stories, *In the Music Library* (1987), and a novel, *Suite for Calliope* (1987).

A nineteenth-century color engraving of a blackberry plant.

ELLEN HUNNICUTT
BLACKBERRIES

JUST BEFORE NOON THE HUSBAND CAME DOWN the near slope of the hill carrying his cap filled with blackberries. "They're ripe now. This week," he said to his wife. "We chose the right week to come." He was a tall man, slender-limbed but thickening now through the center of his body. He walked around the tent to where the canvas water bag hung, spilled the berries into an aluminum pan, and began to wash them gently.

"There isn't any milk left," his wife said. She was blond and fragile, still pretty in a certain light and with a careful arrangement of her features. "We finished the milk." She sat up from the blanket spread on the ground and laid aside the book she had been reading. "Albert and Mae went to New York," she said. "It's a tour. A theater tour."

"You told me that," he replied. "We can put these in cups. Cups will make fine berry bowls."

"There isn't any milk"

5 "I saw cattails," he said. "You'd think there would be too much woods for them. They need sun, but they're there. You can slice up cattail root and fry it. In butter. We have butter. It's good." He divided the berries into two cups and set one cup on the blanket beside his wife. He rummaged through the kitchen box and found a spoon, then began to eat his berries slowly and carefully, making them last.

"The tour covers everything," she said. "You only pay once. You pay one price."

"There aren't any bears here," he said, "nor dangerous snakes. It would be different if we were camped in a dangerous place. It's not like that here."

The woman smoothed the blanket she was sitting on with small, careful motions, as if making a bed. "It's going to be hot," she said. "There aren't any clouds, not even small ones."

"We can swim," he suggested, savoring his berries. "You always liked swimming. You're good at it."

10 "No, I'm not," she said. "I'm not good at it at all."

"You look great in a bathing suit. You always did. We have powdered milk."

"It has a funny taste."

"That green, silky bathing suit was the first one I ever saw you in."

"If we went down for milk we could go to the movie in the village. It's a musical. I looked when we drove through."

15 "They're probably only open on weekends," he said. "A little town like that. Powdered milk's okay."

"You don't like it at home. You told me you don't like powdered milk."

"I didn't say that," he replied. "Do you want me to go for the cattail root?"

"It's margarine," she said. "We have margarine, not butter."

"I'll fry them up."

20 "They're probably protected, like trillium."

"You can pick cattails," he said. "Nobody cares about cattails."

He went to the pile of fire logs and began splitting them, crouching, the hatchet working in clean, economical strokes. She watched him. He was good at splitting wood. The arc of arm and shoulder swung smoothly to aim each blow. "The summer's almost over," she said, taking one berry into her mouth. She mashed it with her tongue, chewed and swallowed. The sun passed its zenith and she saw a stripe of shadow appear on the grass beside her husband, a silhouette slim as a boy, tender as memory.

She began to eat the berries in twos and threes, picking them out with her fingers, forgoing a spoon. "It's almost September." He turned to look at her. "No it's not," he said. "It isn't, and it's scarcely noon. We have lots of time."

[1987]

QUESTIONS FOR REFLECTION AND DISCUSSION

1. Who narrates this story, and from what perspective?

2. How old are the man and wife in this story? What is the current state of their relationship? Where are they, and what are they doing? Support your assumptions with evidence from the language of the story.

3. Although there is no obviously figurative language in this story, there appears to be more going on than the narrator tells us. What is going on between the

lines of the conversation and how does Hunnicutt let us know it?

4. What do you think is the meaning of the story's ending?

5. Now that you have reflected on and discussed the story, summarize it in a paragraph: a general statement of what it is about (including narration and point of view) and a few sentences summarizing what happens in it.

The second story appeared in 1988 in a collection of short fiction by the Welsh writer Leslie Norris. Born in the coal-mining town of Merthyr Tydfil in Wales, Norris is the award-winning author of more than a dozen books of poetry, including two for children, two collections of short stories, and assorted nonfiction. He has taught in Wales and is currently professor emeritus at Brigham Young University in Utah.

LESLIE NORRIS

BLACKBERRIES

MR. FRENSHAM OPENED HIS SHOP AT EIGHT-THIRTY, but it was past nine when the woman and the child went in. The shop was empty and there were no foot-marks on the fresh sawdust shaken onto the floor. The child listened to the melancholy sound of the bell as the door closed behind him and he scuffed his feet in the yellow sawdust. Underneath, the boards were brown and worn, and dark knots stood up in them. He had never been in this shop before. He was going to have his hair cut for the first time in his life, except for the times when his mother had trimmed it gently behind his neck.

Mr. Frensham was sitting in a large chair, reading a newspaper. He could make the chair turn around, and he spun twice about in it before he put down his paper, smiled, and said, "Good morning."

He was old man, thin, with flat white hair. He wore a white coat.

"One gentleman," he said, "to have his locks shorn."

5   He put a board across the two arms of his chair, lifted the child, and sat him on it.

"How are you, my dear? And your father, is he well?" he said to the child's mother.

He took a sheet from a cupboard on the wall and wrapped it about the child's neck, tucking it into his collar. The sheet covered the child completely and hung almost to the floor. Cautiously the boy moved his hidden feet. He could see the bumps they made in the cloth. He moved his finger against the inner surface of the sheet and made a six with it, and then an eight. He liked those shapes.

"Snip snip," said Mr. Frensham, "and how much does the gentleman want off? All of it? All his lovely curls? I think not."

"Just an ordinary cut, please, Mr. Frensham," said the child's mother, "not too much off. I, my husband and I, we thought it was time for him to look like a little boy. His hair grows so quickly."

10   Mr. Frensham's hands were very cold. His hard fingers turned the boy's head first to one side and then to the other and the boy could hear the long scissors snapping away behind him, and above his

ears. He was quite frightened, but he liked watching the small tufts of his hair drop lightly on the sheet which covered him, and then roll an inch or two before they stopped. Some of the hair fell to the floor and by moving his hand surreptitiously he could make nearly all of it fall down. The hair fell without a sound. Tilting his head slightly, he could see the little bunches on the floor, not belonging to him any more.

"Easy to see who this boy is," Mr. Frensham said to the child's mother, "I won't get redder hair in the shop today. Your father had hair like this when he was young, very much this color. I've cut your father's hair for fifty years. He's keeping well, you say? There, I think that's enough. We don't want him to dislike coming to see me."

He took the sheet off the child and flourished it hard before folding it and putting it on a shelf. He swept the back of the child's neck with a small brush. Nodding his own old head in admiration, he looked at the child's hair for flaws in the cutting.

"Very handsome," he said.

The child saw his face in a mirror. It looked pale and large, but also much the same as always. When he felt the back of his neck, the new short hairs stood up sharp against his hand.

15   "We're off to do some shopping," his mother said to Mr. Frensham as she handed him the money.

They were going to buy the boy a cap, a round cap with a little button on top and a peak over his eyes, like his cousin Harry's cap. The boy wanted the cap very much. He walked seriously beside his mother and he was not impatient even when she met Mrs. Lewis and talked to her, and then took a long time at the fruiterer's buying apples and potatoes.

"This is the smallest size we have," the man in the clothes shop said. "It may be too large for him."

"He's just had his hair cut," said his mother. "That should make a difference."

The man put the cap on the boy's head and stood back to look. It was a beautiful cap. The badge in front was shaped like a shield and it was red and blue. It was not too big, although the man could put two fingers under it, at the side of the boy's head.

20   "On the other hand, we don't want it too tight," the man said. "We want something he can grow into, something that will last him a long time."

"Oh, I hope so," his mother said. "It's expensive enough."

The boy carried the cap himself, in a brown paper bag that had "Price, Clothiers, High Street" on it. He could read it all except "Clothiers" and his mother told him that. They put his cap, still in its bag, in a drawer when they got home.

His father came home late in the afternoon. The boy heard the firm clap of the closing door and his father's long step down the hall. He leaned against his father's knee while the man ate his dinner. The meal had been keeping warm in the oven and the plate was very hot. A small steam was rising from the potatoes, and the gravy had dried to a thin crust where it was shallow at the side of the plate. The man lifted the dry gravy with his knife and fed it to his son, very carefully lifting it into the boy's mouth, as if he were feeding a small bird. The boy loved this. He loved the hot savor of his father's dinner, the way his father cut away small delicacies for him and fed them to him slowly. He leaned drowsily against his father's leg.

Afterwards he put on his cap and stood before his father, certain of the man's approval. The man put his hand on the boy's head and looked at him without smiling.

25   "On Sunday," he said, "we'll go for a walk. Just you and I. We'll be men together."

Although it was late in September, the sun was warm and the paths dry. The man and his boy walked beside the disused canal and powdery white dust covered their shoes. The boy thought of the days before he had been born, when the canal had been busy. He thought of the long boats pulled by solid horses, gliding through the water. In his head he listened to the hushed, wet noises they would have made, the soft waves slapping the banks, and green tench° looking up as the barges moved above them, their water suddenly darkened. His grandfather had told him about that. But now the channel was filled with mud and tall reeds. Bullrush and water-grass grew in the damp passages. He borrowed his father's ashplant° and knocked the heads off a company of seeding dandelions, watching the tiny parachutes carry away their minute dark burdens.

"There they go," he said to himself. "There they go, sailing away to China."

"Come on," said his father, "or we'll never reach Fletcher's Woods."

Tench: a lakefish of the Carp family. Ashplant: a walking stick.

The boy hurried after his father. He had never been to Fletcher's Woods. Once his father had heard a nightingale there. It had been in the summer, long ago, and his father had gone with his friends, to hear the singing bird. They had stood under a tree and listened. Then the moon went down and his father, stumbling home, had fallen into a blackberry bush.

30　"Will there be blackberries?" he asked.

"There should be," his father said. "I'll pick some for you."

In Fletcher's Wood there was shade beneath the trees, and sunlight, thrown in yellow patches on to the grass, seemed to grow out of the ground rather than come from the sky. The boy stepped from sunlight to sunlight, in and out of shadow. His father showed him a tangle of bramble, hard with thorns, its leaves just beginning to color into autumn, its long runners dry and brittle on the grass. Clusters of purple fruit hung in the branches. His father reached up and chose a blackberry for him. Its skin was plump and shining, each of its purple globes held a point of reflected light.

"You can eat it," his father said.

The boy put the blackberry in his mouth. He rolled it with his tongue, feeling its irregularity, and crushed it against the roof of his mouth. Released juice, sweet and warm as summer, ran down his throat, hard seeds cracked between his teeth. When he laughed his father saw that his mouth was deeply stained. Together they picked and ate the dark berries, until their lips were purple and their hands marked and scratched.

35　"We should take some for your mother," the man said.

He reached with his stick and pulled down high canes where the choicest berries grew, picking them to take home. They had nothing to carry them in, so the boy put his new cap on the grass and they filled its hollow with berries. He held the cap by its edges and they went home.

"It was a stupid thing to do," his mother said, "utterly stupid. What were you thinking of?"

The young man did not answer.

"If we had the money, it would be different," his mother said. "Where do you think the money comes from?"

40　"I know where the money comes from," his father said. "I work hard enough for it."

"His new cap," his mother said. "How am I to get him another?"

The cap lay on the table and by standing on tiptoe the boy could see it. Inside it was wet with the sticky juice of blackberries. Small pieces of blackberry skins were stuck to it. The stains were dark and irregular.

"It will probably dry out all right," his father said.

His mother's face was red and distorted, her voice shrill.

45　"If you had anything like a job," she shouted, "and could buy caps by the dozen, then—"

She stopped and shook her head. His father turned away, his mouth hard.

"I do what I can," he said.

"That's not much!" his mother said. She was tight with scorn. "You don't do much!"

Appalled, the child watched the quarrel mount and spread. He began to cry quietly, to himself, knowing that it was a different weeping to any he had experienced before, that he was crying for a different pain. And the child began to understand that they were different people; his father, his mother, himself, and that he must learn sometimes to be alone.

[1988]

QUESTIONS FOR REFLECTION AND DISCUSSION

1. Who narrates the story and from what perspective? If you had to divide the story into segments, or scenes, how would you do so?

2. Whose father does the barber refer to? What role does the opening scene in the barber's shop play in the story as a whole?

3. Whose decision is it to put the blackberries in the boy's cap?

4. The boy understands "that he must learn sometimes to be alone." What does this mean?

5. In this text, blackberries do not play a dominant role in the events narrated. Why do you think Leslie Norris called it "Blackberries"? How would the meaning be changed if he had called it "The Haircut" or "The Cap"?

6. Now that you have reflected on and discussed the story, summarize it in a paragraph: a general statement of what it is about (including narration and point of view) and several sentences summarizing what happens in it.

Brainstorming a Comparison Paper It is impossible to compare two things that have nothing in common; every comparison begins with a resemblance. But it is also pointless to compare two things that are too much alike. All comparisons begin with a framework of similarity and then look for differences within that framework. It is the interaction of similarity and difference that creates meaning in a comparison. The best way to begin a comparison is by making lists. You can write your list either as an idea map or in columns (that's the route Cynthia Wilson chose below). The Writer's Guide below suggests some possible questions to ask and categories to use for generating lists.

Cynthia Wilson made the list on page 75 in preparation for writing a 2–3 page comparison paper on Hunnicutt's and Norris's short stories. The highlighted entries are the ones she used to summarize and analyze her findings.

Making Comparisons

Comparing Formal Qualities

- *Genre:* Are the texts poems, short stories, plays, or essays? Within each genre, are they a particular type (e.g., argumentative essay, explication, comparison)? Do the texts meet or not meet expectations about their genre?

- *Title:* What is the relation between the title and the text? Are titles of different texts similar or different?

- *Speaker/narrator:* Who is the speaker of the poem or the narrator of a story? Is there a first-person speaker (I) or a third person (he, she)? What information does the speaker present directly to us and what do we have to interpret?

- *Point of view:* Is the point of view limited to a single character, to several characters? Is it omniscient (unlimited)?

- *Time frame:* Is the text narrated as if it were happening as you are reading it, or in retrospect, looking back into the past? How much time passes?

- *Type of action:* Are the events described an isolated sequence occurring once, or a habitual activity?

- *Structure:* Parse poems; segment stories or essays. Are poems broken into stanzas? Do they rhyme? Are stories or essays divided into parts? Do plays have similar act and scene divisions?

- *Mood:* What is the mood (happy, melancholy, solitary, satisfied, dissatisfied, bored) of the text?

- *Language and imagery:* Do the texts use figurative language? Striking images?

Comparing Descriptive and Narrative Qualities

- *Setting:* What are the similarities and differences in setting?

- *Description:* What people, places, and things are described, and in what way?

- *Characterization:* Who are the characters? What are they like, how are they described?

- *Plot:* What events occur? What actions do the characters perform? Which characters do what?

Looking for Patterns, Themes, and Arguments

- Are there any repeating words, images or themes? Do they form any particular patterns? Are there any breaks in the pattern?

- What relationship does each text establish with the outside world? Do they connect to broad social themes (like the gender argument Cynthia Wilson identifies in her list on the next page?

From List to Thesis

- Summarize your findings as a list of patterns, or connections between, the similarities and differences in the texts you are comparing. Be selective: choose what seem to you to be the most significant rather than the most obvious patterns and topics.

- Analyze your list of patterns, looking for connections between them. Look for connections within each text, and connections between texts.

- Work with these connections to formulate an argument and thesis about what the texts share and what makes them different.

- Use your list of patterns to outline your argument paragraph by paragraph. There are two ways to structure the body of a comparison paper: you can discuss the texts one after the other, or you can discuss them together according to each aspect of your argument.

Next, we provide the first draft of the comparison paper Cynthia Wilson wrote as the result of her work with Hunnicutt's and Norris's stories. We have annotated the paper with comments about what already works well and comments about what still needs work.

Category	Similar?	Different?
Genre	Short stories	H is much shorter than N.
Title	"Blackberries"	N could have had other title; H is only blackberries.
Speaker or narrator	3rd person	N tells us everything; H does not.
Point of view		N is more omniscient, although mostly from child's pov; H is limited to the wife's pov.
Time frame	Told in past tense	More time passes in N, and more things happen.
Once or habitual?	Once, but we also see habits	"Once" is stronger in N; in H it feels like this kind of thing happens all the time.
Parse or segmentation		N has more events, more clearly separated; it's longer.
Mood	Both end a bit sad	H feels melancholy, but also a bit funny; N's mood varies— boy and father are happy picking berries, but ending is sad. In H husband is also happy picking blackberries.
Language and imagery	Blackberries mean more than just blackberries in both	N has other images, especially money and the cap, which relate to the blackberries.
Setting	Blackberry picking	H mostly takes place in the cabin; N is in house, town, and woods.
Description	People, picking	H tells us less about how things look; wife makes bed while talking to husband. N tells more and gives more detail.
Character	Husband and wife	N also has child and barber; H only the two people; you feel more about N's characters, especially the boy. Father and mother have good and bad things about them.
Events	Blackberry picking	In H, husband wants to pick, wife wants to go to town. N has lots more events, all involving the boy.
Patterns	Husband vs. wife Blackberries Don't communicate	Husband wife conflict about blackberries in both, but husband and wife argue about more things—and more concrete things—in N. Men pick blackberries, women stay home. Why? But only in H does wife eat them. Women don't approve of blackberries, but wife in N has a reason — dirty cap.
Outside world	Town	H's characters don't seem so real, more like types; the town just means not being in the woods—only blackberries are real. N's characters and the world around them seem real.

Wilson 1

Cynthia Wilson
Professor Franklin
English Composition 2
15 February 2009

Leave the Picking to the Boys

We are all aware of the so-called "gender roles" society expects from us. Women are to stay home, raise the children, and tend to the house. Little girls are to be clean, neat and play with dolls, all in preparation for becoming a wife and mother. Men, on the other hand, are to work outside the home, expect a warm meal when they come home, and often

Title and first five sentences give broad context of thesis nicely, but they need to be integrated better with argument and thesis of final two sentences, using more information from the stories.

have little responsibility for the children except to provide them with shelter, food, and clothing. Young boys are expected to play outside the home, and not mind getting dirty. When it comes to picking blackberries, it must be noted that they are found in the woods, and are extremely messy to gather. Using Leslie Norris's short story "Blackberries" and Ellen Hunnicutt's short story "Blackberries" as a base, it is clear that gender roles play a distinctive role in the appreciation of blackberry picking.

Leslie Norris's story "Blackberries" tells of a young boy going to Fletcher's Woods with his father to pick blackberries. Already a gender expectation is shown: the father takes the boy to the woods perhaps like his father did with him before. The father shows the son how to pick the berries, and before long their mouths are stained. The father suggests taking some berries home to the mother; however, they have nothing to carry them in except the boy's new cap. Without giving a second thought, they fill the cap with the messy berries. When they arrive home, the mother is furious with the father as well as the boy for ruining the cap. Gender roles are in full effect: the mother is at home, and fights with the father over money.

Ellen Hunnicutt's "Blackberries" presents us with a husband and wife on a camping trip. True to a male gender role, the husband finds enjoyment venturing off in the woods to pick blackberries. When the husband returns with his blackberries to share, the wife is looking for any way to escape the woods. She is obviously uncomfortable in the woods, perhaps in tune with the woman's role of being in the house. Perhaps the woods feel dirty to her and she finds them unentertaining. Furthermore, while conversing with her husband, both speaking about different things, she is noted as smoothing the sheet she is sitting on as if she was making a bed. This is another indication of a woman's role, expressing that maybe she wanted to be sitting on something more

Margin annotations (left):

Original and persuasive thesis with good foundation in the two stories . . .

One of several examples of awkward diction (roles/role)

Textual evidence to support thesis.

Good evidence from story to support thesis.

Good observation of detail nicely integrated into argument.

Margin annotations (right):

But, thesis is not focused enough on the two stories. Add summary of arguments to come.

Weak paragraph: argues by plot summary, not by example and analysis of specific detail relating to gender roles.

Good paragraph: argument through specific details and examples drawn from the story.

comfortable than the ground, like a bed she had just finished making. Unlike Norris, however, at the end of Hunnicutt, the wife finally eats one of the blackberries, enjoying its taste and relating to the husband's enjoyment. This isn't saying that women aren't supposed to eat blackberries because they are messy. It just proves that women are unlikely to pick the fruit themselves.

There have been many stories and poems written about blackberries, many by women. I feel that the actual picking of blackberries, as depicted in both short stories, is expressed as being done by men because of ties to gender roles. Perhaps the writers, both females, used males to pick the blackberries because the gender ties make the stories appeal to readers. Males might remember picking the blackberries, while a female might remember helping prepare the blackberries. Gender roles are beginning to change, however, and maybe more writers will place women in the messy, outside roles that have long belonged to men.

C concludes the paragraph with a key difference between the stories and relates this difference to the divergent tones of the ending and to a further remark about gender roles.

Always check the gender of your authors: Leslie is also a man's name!

C's conclusion develops the argument in new direction, using the paper's insights about gender roles to try to explain why they are used in the context of picking blackberries.

Conclusion raises interesting questions, but overstates its case. Limit conclusions to evidence and samples you have. C might ask what these two stories have in common that makes them divide gender roles this way (as opposed, for example, to "August," p. 49). C needs to refine and focus her argument.

Works Cited

Hunnicutt, Ellen. "Blackberries." *Literature: A World of Writing*. Ed.
    David L. Pike and Ana M. Acosta. New York: Pearson Longman,
    2011. 71. Print.

Norris, Leslie. "Blackberries." *Literature: A World of Writing*. Ed.
    David L. Pike and Ana M. Acosta. New York: Pearson Longman,
    2011. 73. Print.

Choose two or three poems, stories, plays, or essays elsewhere in this book that have something in common on which you can base a comparison. Following the process of critical thinking and the Writer's Guide for making comparisons, write a paper comparing and contrasting the texts you chose.

Or

Write a comparison paper using two or three poems about blackberries taken from the following list:

- Stephanie Bolster, "Many Have Written Poems About Blackberries" (http://www.library.utoronto.ca/ canpoetry/bolster/poem4.htm; *Two Bowls of Milk* [Toronto: McClelland & Stewart, 1999])
- Robert Hass, "Meditation at Lagunitas" (http://www.poetryfoundation.org/journal/ feature.html?id=178717; *Praise* [New York: Ecco, 1999])
- Robert Hass, "Picking Blackberries with a Friend Who Has Been Reading Jacques Lacan" (*Praise* [New York: Ecco, 1999])

- Seamus Heaney, "Blackberry-picking" http://www.npr.org/templates/story/ story.php?storyId=48189651966; *Opened Ground: Selected Poems 1966-1996* [New York: Farrar, Straus, Giroux, 1998])
- Galway Kinnell, "Blackberry Eating" (http://www.poetryarchive.org/poetryarchive/single Poem.do?poemId=2640; *A New Selected Poems* [New York: Houghton, Mifflin, 2000])
- Yusef Komunyakaa, "Blackberries" (http://www.ibiblio.org/ipa/poems/komunyakaa/ blackberries.php; *Pleasure Dome: New and Collected Poems* [Middletown, C.T.: Wesleyan UP, 2001])
- Sylvia Plath, "Blackberrying" (*The Collected Poems* [New York: Harper Perennial, 2008])

Take a moment to reflect on the experience of writing the paper. What was the easiest part of the process? Which part was most difficult? Which part did you like the best? The least? What did you encounter in the process that you did not expect after working through Cynthia Wilson's notes and paper?

THINKING CRITICALLY ABOUT VISUAL CULTURE

Because we spend our lives processing visual information, we often assume when we look at a visual text that it functions in the same way as any other object or phenomenon passing through our field of vision: that it is what we see. In fact, visual culture is as densely packed with carefully constructed meaning as literary texts, and seeing, as you know from the previous chapter, means more than just looking. Visual texts tend to be extremely attentive to the way shapes, colors, and lines are laid out within the frame of the picture, page, or screen. To get a sense of how visual texts present meaning to us, let's take another look at the topic of blackberries, but this time from a specifically visual perspective. Study carefully the illustration on page 79. It reproduces *Children Picking Blackberries,* by the British artist Myles Birket Foster, along with our annotations in numerical order clockwise around the painting.

Homo sapiens is the species that invents symbols in which to invest passion and authority, then forgets that symbols are inventions.

—JOYCE CAROL OATES

Thinking Critically about Signs

When thinking critically about visual culture, we distinguish between **things**—objects that are primarily what they appear to be—and **signs**—visual objects that signify, or mean something in addition to what they are as a thing. For example, as a thing, a traffic light is a metal frame encasing three colored lights that alternately turn on and off. As a sign, those lights inform drivers and pedestrians when they can proceed, when they must decide to hurry up or step on the brakes, and when they must stop. There is no fixed law determining when something is a sign and when it is just an object. Indeed, for many people, things are

always simply things, and the only signs are those, like traffic signals, that provide specific information necessary to get about in the world. This book is concerned less with signs in the world at large than with the signs of *visual culture,* created explicitly for the purpose of imparting meaning beyond their face value.

Many signs bear a resemblance to the meaning they signify—a *ristra,* or string of hot peppers hanging outside a Mexican restaurant, for example, tells us what to expect inside—but many other signs are arbitrary. There is no intrinsic reason that we use the Roman alphabet (ABC . . . XYZ) to spell the words we speak in English, or, for that matter, that we use the words we do to

2. The left-hand side forms a path leading deep into the distant hills. A border collie occupies the foreground of the path, while sheep graze on the green slope behind it.

3. The edge of the bramble neatly divides the top half of the picture, establishing a vertical line separating the girls and animals in the open half of the painting on the right from the boy and the bramble in the closed half on the left.

4. In contrast to the open fields, the dark bramble looms over the right half of the painting, blocking out the sky completely and visually swallowing up the boy's small figure.

1. The artist has posed his subjects, two girls and a younger boy, in front of the blackberry bramble, with several branches curling around them, especially the boy. Their faces are turned away from us, concentrated on the task of picking and collecting.

5. While the boy, clothing protected by a pinafore, is doing the main work of picking, the older girls stand back from the bramble. Like the sheep and the collie, they are static, although the younger of the two does reach out tentatively to pluck a berry.

6. It is unclear what narrative or symbolic meaning might lie behind the separation between the two sides of the painting; that is an issue of interpretation. Similarly ambiguous is the relationship between the two girls and the boy, and whether any of them is responsible for the sheep and the shepherd's dog. What we can summarize about the painting's main idea is that it portrays the two girls in the middle between the active boy in the wild bramble on the right and the stationary, domesticated animals in the cleared land to the left.

Children Picking Blackberries, Myles Birket Foster (1825–1899). The blackberry-picking scenario is familiar: the late summer weather, the rural setting, the apron brimming over with berries, the child berry-pickers. But note some significant differences: there is no trace of the scratches and stains left by berry-picking on the characters in the poem and stories you read, there are domestic animals in the picture, and the berry-picking occurs in a carefully drawn and detailed landscape.

refer to the things in our mind that we want to speak about. This is why as children we had to learn how to talk and to read just as we had to learn what such arbitrary signs as a traffic light, a clock, or a calendar mean. Because they have no basis in resemblance, symbolic signs, often just called **symbols,** can change radically from culture to culture and are prone to misunderstanding when taken out of context. Recognizing the arbitrary nature of many signs will help you to focus your interpretation on the aspects of a visual object of which you can be certain,

without making too many assumptions about the symbolic aspects you may have misunderstood through lack of a proper context.

Fighting over Symbols

Symbols can take on powerful meanings. Consider the example of the American flag. Although there is no intrinsic connection between the stars, the stripes, and the red, white and blue of the flag and the values for which they stand, the flag is one of the most powerful and widely recognized symbols in the world today. Its meaning has often been contested,

however, when soldiers defend an American flag or when protesters burn it, they are both making a statement not about the three-colored piece of cloth they see, but about what it symbolizes for them. When you look at and think about signs, be sure to distinguish between the qualities that are intrinsic to them as things, and the qualities that are attributed to them as symbols. Making a physical description before you begin to discuss symbolic qualities is a useful technique for seeing the thing before the symbol, especially if you can keep your

As a symbol, the flag can make a positive or a negative argument about America: (*Left*) The flag being raised at Iwo Jima during World War II. (*Right*) the flag being burned in protest against war in Iraq.

WRITING EXERCISE: A Symbolic Dispute: Parodying Ad

Choose a well-known symbolic sign (other than the flags discussed above), the meaning of which has been disputed. Print or copy a reproduction of it and place it in front of you.

1. Write a physical description of the object.

2. Outline the different types of symbolism attributed to that sign by the different parties in the dispute.
3. Conclude with a reflection on what qualities in this particular symbol may have given rise to argument.

description as free from value judgments and assumptions as possible. Here, as everywhere, the most persuasive argument is the one that argues from the facts first, and moves to the symbols second.

Signs in Advertising Probably the most complex use of symbolic signs occurs in the realm of advertising. Some of the most widely recognized symbols are those representing commercial brands; the golden arches of McDonald's restaurants and the Nike swoosh are familiar throughout the world. Contemporary advertising is almost exclusively focused on the strategy known as *branding:* creating a set of qualities that a company wants associated with its products in the minds of consumers. Because there is no intrinsic connection between the process of branding and what is being branded, if advertising is done effectively, it can persuade consumers that a product does whatever it says it does.

Let's look at an example of the way branding functions in adver-

tising. Like other symbols, a specific brand can generate widely divergent meanings based on the same basic identity. We have reproduced here a typical example of the award-winning

advertising campaign for Absolut Vodka, which began in 1980 and continues to this day, along with one of the many parodies of that campaign.

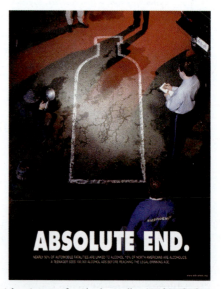

The power of branding: (*Left*) *Absolut Manhattan:* Advertisement for Absolut Vodka. (*Right*) *Absolute End,* a parody of the Absolut advertising campaign. The caption below the image reads: "Nearly 50% of automobile fatalities are linked to alcohol. 10% of North Americans are alcoholics. A teenager sees 100,000 alcohol ads before reaching the legal drinking age."

1. Write a summary of *Absolut Manhattan*. Based on this ad, what are the basic visual components of the Absolut advertising campaign? What qualities does it associate with the brand? What qualities does it not associate with the brand that you might have expected it to do? Is its argument persuasive? Why or why not?

2. What are some possible explanations for the extraordinary success of the campaign even among people who have no interest whatsoever in drinking the vodka the ads are supposed to be selling?

3. Write a summary of the mock ad, *Absolute End*. What argument does this ad make, and how does it use the brand symbolism differently than the original? Do you find it to be as effective as the positive ad? Why or why not?

WRITING EXERCISE: Subvertising: Parodying an Ad

1. Choose a familiar brand symbol and summarize the symbolic qualities associated with it through advertising.

2. Create a visual and/or written parody of the brand and its advertising campaign that uses the qualities associated to it but makes a different argument about those qualities, as in the example illustrated at the bottom of page 80.

3. Write an account of your thought process in planning and executing the parody and justify the reasons for your choices.

LOOKING BACK: Writing in the World

- An *argument* is an assertion whose primary purpose is to persuade us to agree with what it says. It is the foundation of most kinds of critical writing.

- *Subjective* forms of argument, such as *narrative* and *evaluation* appeal to our values and emotions.

- *Objective* forms of argument, such as *definitional*, *causal*, and *rebuttal*, appeal to objective criteria such as facts and logic.

- Most arguments combine subjective and objective forms, although in different proportions.

- A *thesis* is the *summary* of a *developed argument*, rather than only a restatement of the *leading*, or initial, *argument*.

- The most common types of academic papers are *descriptive, response, explication, textual analysis* (or *thesis-driven explication*), *comparison, argument*, and *research*.

- There are three steps to *thinking critically:* (1) *reading*, (2) *questioning*, and (3) *writing*.

- *Reading* includes three stages: (1) pre-reading, (2) reading, and (3) processing. Pre-reading gives you a context against which to evaluate your initial expectations and reactions. Your *reading* tells you the key themes and concerns and what needs to be clarified and explained. *Processing* a text and its language lets you see each of its parts clearly so that you can begin

raising questions about its form and meaning as a whole; it also includes *parsing* a poem or *segmenting* a story to clarify its structure.

- *Questioning* entails writing up your notes as specific questions, brainstorming about the various directions of inquiry opened up by those questions, and actively seeking connections and distinctions between images and events in different parts of the text.

- *Writing critically* begins with the notes you take while reading and the questions you compose while reflecting on and discussing what you have read. It continues when you synthesize your earlier writing into a *summary*, organize your ideas, make an outline, write a draft, and revise.

- Reading, questioning, and writing *comparatively* means to apply the same procedure to analyzing the patterns of similarity and difference between a number of texts related by a common genre, theme, character, image, setting, or other element.

- *Signs* are things that mean something in addition to what they are as a thing. *Symbolic signs* have no resemblance to the things or concepts to which they refer.

- Because its meaning was determined arbitrarily, the value of a symbolic sign is often emotionally weighted and subject to strong dispute.

- *Branding* in advertising uses signs to attribute a set of qualities to a product that has no intrinsic relation to those qualities.

CHAPTER 3

INVESTIGATING THE WORLD

PLANNING, WRITING, AND REVISING A RESEARCH PAPER

Perhaps more than any other form of writing you will do, the research paper is a process that involves many steps. The good news is that you have learned these steps already in the previous two chapters. To write a research paper, you just have to put those steps together. Follow each step carefully and thoroughly, and your paper will take shape before your eyes; skip a step and your paper risks tumbling down into a pile of rubble. In this chapter, we follow the research process of Lorraine Betesh pursuing a visual media research paper on photographs of the Brooklyn Bridge. We follow Lorraine through the various steps involved in building a research paper: choosing a topic; finding, evaluating, and summarizing sources in an annotated bibliography; moving from the annotated bibliography to the first draft; and the process of revision. In Appendix B (p. APP B–5), we include Rob Lanney's literary research paper on the setting of Elsinore in Shakespeare's *Hamlet*.

FINDING A TOPIC

The first step in writing a research paper is finding and limiting yourself to a specific and clearly defined paper topic. Make sure that you reserve plenty of time to think about your topic, and do some preliminary looking around, either in the library or on the Internet, in order to make sure that the subject fits the assignment, actually interests you, and will yield enough acceptable scholarly sources to work with. An ideal topic will usually be something unusual enough that not too much has been written about it, but not so unusual that you are unable to find any scholarly sources to use. Finding the perfect topic is a matter of matching your interests to the constraints of the research paper form, the instructor's requirements, and your course's particular focus.

Finding the right topic, like choosing the right title—as Cuban author Guillermo Cabrera Infante tells us—lets you get on with the business of the paper.

Once you have chosen a topic, you will then need to refine it. You will usually be asked to submit your topic as a written paragraph. Like a summary of the paper to come, your topic will reflect your initial, broad reading, and it will help you decide the specific direction to take once you begin research in earnest and start working on your annotated bibliography. Also like a summary, it will not yet have an argument or a thesis but if done right will help in synthesizing your initial thoughts in the direction of an argument.

Many first-time writers of research papers are tempted by what seems

Titles are not only important, they are essential for me. I cannot write without a title.

—GUILLERMO CABRERA INFANTE

the safe route of a purely historical topic—a biography of a writer, a study of a specific place or event. A college-level research paper is argument-based, however, and it is difficult to conceive a good thesis and sustain an original and cohesive argument if you are merely cutting and pasting other people's research on a topic. This was the problem Lorraine Betesh had when she originally formulated the topic for what would eventually become a research paper on drawings and photographs of the Brooklyn Bridge. Here is the first version, with our comments on the side and errors to be fixed highlighted.

> Overall, this paper topic is well written, without serious grammatical errors. Various mistakes, primarily of diction and style, have been circled in red, but not corrected here. Comments refer to text highlighted in yellow. Because it is only the first stage in writing the paper, it is not generally required to document sources for a paper topic paragraph; nevertheless, you should always use your own language and arguments.

Betesh 1

Manhattan Island and the borough of Brooklyn were once separate entities, divided by the East River. Although travel across the river was possible, the cold New York winters and tumultuous water conditions made it difficult to travel. When the New York Bridge Company was formed, the idea of a bridge to connect Manhattan and Brooklyn was devised and sixty years of political, financial, and technical discussions led to construction of the bridge to begin in 1869. The bridge was built over 14 years in the face of enormous difficulties. On May 24, 1883, the Brooklyn Bridge was opened. Since then, commerce and travel have never been the same. In this paper, I will discuss how the Brooklyn Bridge became a major thoroughfare for economic opportunities,

This sentence hints at a thesis, but one that would be so easy to demonstrate as not to be worth arguing.

These three sentences demonstrate Lorraine's excellent organization of her preliminary research, and her thorough assimilation of the arguments of her sources. But using this structure for her paper will only paraphrase her sources without an original thesis or compelling argument.

cultural growth, and socially connected the two boroughs. In addition, I will look at how the bridge was of incalculable value in a crowded commercial city; for now inhabitants of New York City could live outside the city, while at the same time, have the city at easy access. Finally, I will explore the various benefits of and examine the changes which were brought on with the construction of the Brooklyn Bridge.

In conference, Lorraine and her instructor discussed several possibilities for developing her topic: focusing on a particular detail of the bridge itself and the way it changed Brooklyn; analyzing literary writing about the Brooklyn Bridge; studying the use of the Bridge as a cinematic setting; examining illustrations and photographs of the Bridge. In her rewrite of the paper topic, Lorraine retained the historical background of the first half of her original paragraph (up to "the Brooklyn Bridge was opened"), and rewrote the second part to reflect her new focus:

This revision represents a big step forward. Lorraine has redefined her research to focus on critical thinking rather than recording facts. She is now presenting the Brooklyn Bridge as a phenomenon to be analyzed, interpreted, and argued about.

In this paper I will discuss how the Brooklyn Bridge was portrayed through photographs and illustrations from various times in history since its inception. I will provide analysis of the bridge's representation in photographs from times such as, but not limited to: the opening of the bridge to the general public, the centennial celebration, restoration period during the 1980s and 9/11. Additionally, I will report on the differences in depiction of the bridge on the various postcards, and the symbolic image these postcards create with a range of features attributed to the bridge.

A nice idea, but distinct enough from the previous focus to constitute a separate paper topic. In the end, Lorraine decided not to pursue this part of the research.

It is evident that Lorraine has done quite a bit of reading between the first and second paper topics, following the research direction that emerged from conferencing with her instructor. And, in fact, the same day that her rewrite of the paper topic was due, she was also required to hand in the first entry in her annotated bibliography of her paper sources.

FINDING, EVALUATING, AND SUMMARIZING YOUR SOURCES IN THE ANNOTATED BIBLIOGRAPHY

Perhaps the most important step in writing a successful research paper is choosing the correct sources. Good sources will inspire your thinking, push you in directions you had not yet thought of, and provide you with all the essential information you need to formulate a strong thesis and carry through a solid argument. If a source fulfills none of these needs, it probably will not be much help to you in writing your paper. Several key questions should be asked when evaluating a research source:

- Is the material relevant to your topic?
- Is the source well respected?
- Is the material accurate?
- Is the information current?
- Is the material from a primary source or a secondary source?

Your initial probing into a topic may or may not have led you directly to the sources you will need for your paper; in either case, once you start assembling material that will actually go into your paper, you need to do so with great care and careful organization. Proper documentation and note-taking at this stage will streamline the writing process and save you a lot of work later on, both for the paper itself and for the **annotated bibliography**—a

I spend eight months outlining and researching the novel before I begin to write a single word of the prose.

—JEFFREY DEAVER

summary and evaluation of your sources that you will likely be required to write beforehand.

The most important advice we can give you in writing a research paper is to follow carefully any guidelines your instructor has provided regarding the type of sources you are required to use and to consult with your instructor if you have any questions regarding those guidelines. In general, both the Internet and the printed volumes in your library can provide valid sources for a research paper, but you should always exercise critical judgment when choosing sources. One of the advantages of doing research in your college library is that trained librarians and other professionals have already sorted through the vast number of available sources and carefully chosen the ones that are best suited for academic use. There are also reference librarians readily available to help you in evaluating sources. The library should always be your first option when conducting research, just as its online portal should always be your first

option when doing research over the Internet (see the section below on beginning your research).

Primary Sources and Secondary Sources

Most research papers will include both **primary sources**—texts and documents from the time period of your topic or written by your subject—and **secondary sources**—history and criticism about your subject published within the last thirty years. It may be that your only primary source is the text you read in *Literature: A World of Writing* that provided the initial idea for your paper topic—as Shakespeare's tragedy *Hamlet* (p. 285) did for Rob Lanney. Or it may be further exploration of a theme introduced here, as Lorraine did with the unit "Living in the City" in Chapter 11.

Here are some examples of primary sources Lorraine considered and the secondary sources he would need to supplement them with in a research paper:

Primary Sources	Possible Secondary Sources	Questions to Ask
literary writing on the Brooklyn Bridge	biographies and critical interpretations of specific writers (Vladimir Mayakovksy, Hart Crane); crititical writing on the Brooklyn Bridge in literature	How do different writers respond to the Brooklyn Bridge? What meanings do they attribute to it? Are these meanings different in different historical moments?
responses to the Brooklyn Bridge when it opened and at important moments in its history	cultural histories of the Brooklyn Bridge and the public response to it	Was there any opposition to the bridge? Was there any negative reaction to its design?
movies using the Brooklyn Bridge as a setting	studies of New York as a cinematic setting	What actions tend to occur on the bridge? What meanings are associated with it?
historical documents on the ways in which the construction of the Brooklyn Bridge changed Brooklyn	histories of the city of Brooklyn and its relationship to Manhattan	What was the relationship of Brooklyn and Manhattan before the bridge? In what ways did that relationship change?

As you will see below, Lorraine's research incorporated both primary sources—photographs and illustrations of the Brooklyn Bridge—and secondary sources—histories of the bridge, a study of its history in pictures, and a guide to writing about photography. There will often be more sources available than you will either need or be able to read in the amount of time you have, so you must be focused and selective in your research. Know what you are looking for, be aware of the different critical genres—do you need history, biography, criticism, interpretation, and how much of each?—and of the different levels of critical writing—you do not necessarily want to slog through an intricate study of the Brooklyn Bridge written for specialized scholars, but you also do not want to waste your time with a book about the bridge written for junior high school students.

As is the case with textual sources, visual sources can be scholarly or nonscholarly. Visual sources to which you are most likely to refer include documentary films and photographic archives; you may also find yourself using visual material you find within written sources, such as photos, drawings, and diagrams. When using documentary films as primary sources, be sure to verify the degree to which the film aims toward an objective presentation of its subject matter; many contemporary documentaries, such as those of Michael Moore or Errol Morris, are strongly evaluative in their arguments. They may also present verifiable facts or persuasive interpretations, but you will need to distinguish in your paper whether you are presenting facts or interpretations. When citing visual materials or incorporating their arguments, be sure to take into account the ways that visual media present facts and data differently than written media.

Although it is tempting in today's multimedia world to include illustrations in your paper for aesthetic

appeal, the only place you should include an illustration for its own sake is on the title page. Within the body of your paper include an image only if you analyze it in detail within the text, as Lorraine Betesh does in her paper below. Do not include an image just because it is cool or just to show what someone looked like. Only if Rob had decided to focus on the production history of *Hamlet*, would he have been justified in including still photographs from a performance of the play in his paper (p. 000).

Working in the Library

You can begin your research from wherever you have access to the library's online catalog. Searching a catalog is a skill worth refining. For Lorraine's primary research, she had the option of searching by *author* for works about the Brooklyn Bridge by specific writers ("Crane, Hart"), by *keyword* ("Brooklyn" AND "Bridge"), or by *subject*—"Brooklyn Bridge" (New York, N.Y.)—with a number of possible subheadings (see below).

If you are researching for secondary sources on an established

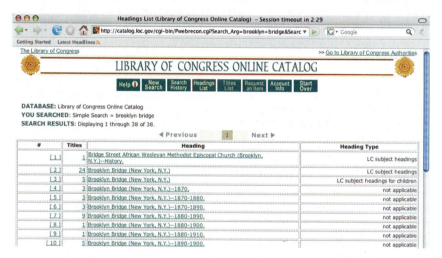

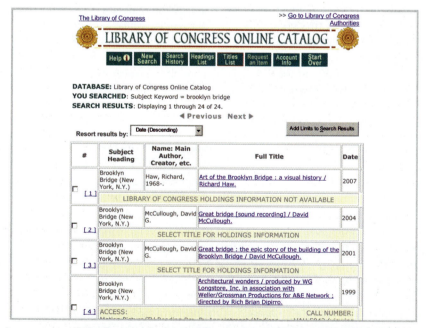

Screen captures of a headings page (top) and a titles page (bottom) found during a keyword search for "Brooklyn Bridge," in the Library of Congress online catalog.

author or topic—say, Emily Dickinson or William Shakespeare—a *subject* or *keyword* search may turn up more books than you can possibly handle. For a more recent author, you will find a more workable number ("Tan, Amy—Criticism and interpretation" lists five books on the author at the Library of Congress).

You can refine your search by adding the name of a specific work—"*Hamlet*" rather than "Shakespeare" (still more than you can read, but not in the hundreds)—or a specific topic—Ophelia. Most, if not all, of the sources you find will usually be located under a single **call number,** or location in the library stacks, or shelves, and you can go to the location and browse the different books to find out which are best suited to your research needs.

Books will provide a good introduction to your topic; they may also turn out to be either too broad or too detailed for what you are looking for. Most research papers use a combination of books and scholarly articles or essays. There are several ways to find the articles you need. The first is to use the bibliography of a book on the topic published within the last few years. Even better, if you are researching a literary topic, is the *MLA International Bibliography,* a compendium of references to scholarly writing on literature published annually by the Modern Language Association and available on CD-ROM and print versions in most libraries as well as online. The *MLA International Bibliography* indexes books, articles, and book chapters and can be searched by author, title of work, subject, keyword, or a combination of the four. Libraries also contain various databases and print guides for research on nonliterary topics such as visual media, or for primary research in newspapers and nonacademic serial publications (magazines). The *Readers' Guide to Periodical Literature* is available in both print and CD-ROM versions,

as are indexes to many different newspapers as well as specialized indexes for specific subjects. If you were looking for primary sources on performances of *Krapp's Last Tape,* you could consult a number of print indexes; you could also consult online or CD-ROM indexes such as the Arts and Humanities Citation Index and the International Index to the Performing Arts; and you could also consult full-text databases such as LexisNexis, which contains the texts of major newspapers and weeklies from around the world since 1985. The number of CD-ROMs and databases is growing annually; ask your reference librarian to help you to find the resources best suited to your research needs.

Working on the Internet

Many, although by no means all, of the sources available in libraries are also available online. If your library subscribes to them, academic databases will provide you with digitized versions of the same scholarly articles you would find in your library's collection of bound periodicals, and some that you would not. Many primary texts published before the 1920s—Shakespeare's plays and Walt Whitman's poetry, for example—are no longer in copyright and are legally available online from sites such as Project Gutenberg or the University of Toronto's *Representative Poetry Online.* Remember, however, that while the text itself may be out of copyright, any notes, annotations, or introductions remain the intellectual property of the Web site author and need to be properly documented. Similarly, whenever you cite a primary or secondary text from an online source, you must document that source as you would a print source. You may also choose to use an Internet search engine such as Google or Yahoo! to look for sources. You may find such a search useful in the early stages of your research to get a handle on your topic. But remember that there are very few topics on which no scholarly criti-

cism has been written and that many instructors will limit the number of purely Internet sources they allow, or will not allow them at all. Make sure that you are aware of these guidelines before you begin your research.

The Internet can be especially useful for working with visual media. While print sources provided the basis for her paper, Lorraine located several recent photographs of the Brooklyn Bridge on the Internet. She also used ArtLex, an online dictionary of art terms; PictureHistory, an Internet source of historical images; and an article on the Brooklyn Bridge from a Web site maintained by the American studies department of the University of Virginia.

Evaluating and Organizing Your Sources

As you begin assembling sources, and as the first sources you read point you toward further sources, you will find it helpful to compile a **working bibliography,** an evolving list of sources you have found, sources you have read, and sources that you will need. From your working bibliography, you will compose your annotated bibliography and the **works-cited list** for your research paper.

Before including any source in your working bibliography, assess its suitability for inclusion in a research paper. The first level of assessment is whether or not the source is suitably rigorous and scholarly. Regardless of whether you conduct your search on-site or online, you will encounter a wide variety of sources. We can categorize them as follows:

1. *Opinion-based sources: blogs, personal Web pages, op-ed pieces, unverifiable sources.* Because there are no objective guidelines in place to verify their accuracy, 95 percent of Internet sources (including Wikipedia) fall under the category of unacceptable sources for academic research. Consult with your instructor if you would like to request an exception to this rule. You should also avoid using

certain texts within your library as secondary sources, including fiction (suitable as a subject, but not as a research reference), editorial writing, and some work written before the current standards for academic writing were put into place. Consult with your instructor before using any secondary source written before 1980.

2. *Encyclopedia articles, general reference works, and university-based Web pages.* Peer-reviewed and held to an external set of standards, these sources can provide basic information and point you toward more in-depth sources. Due to their brevity and to their broad focus, however, they are not suitable as sources for a college paper except for brief biographical or factual information, such as the date of the construction of the Brooklyn Bridge.

3. *Newspapers and other general periodicals.* Accessed either in print form or through databases, newspapers of record such as the *New York Times* or the *Washington Post* are acceptable secondary sources, especially for current events or contemporary writers; other newspapers and popular periodicals are generally acceptable only as primary sources—reports of the opening of the Brooklyn Bridge, for example, that Lorraine might have used in her paper.

4. *General histories, surveys, and biographies.* Usually written for a nonspecialized audience by specialized scholars, these sources will reliably situate a topic within a broad context. Useful for background research, they are unlikely to give you the kind of detail and complexity you will need to develop a good thesis.

5. *Academic journals and monographs.* Because they are peer-reviewed by experts in the subject, academic journals

(collections of articles) and monographs (book-length studies) are held to a more rigorous set of standards than the sources listed above. Scholarly articles and monographs will be written by specialists on the topic, their arguments will be original, and their sources will be fully documented. Most, if not all, of the sources for the majority of the research paper should be drawn from academic journals and monographs. Your library's online portal will include a number of databases containing academic journals; your library may also provide access to online versions of certain academic monographs. Nearly all academic journals devoted to the study of literature are indexed by the Modern Language Association (MLA), which can be accessed through your library; some reliable and commonly available article databases are Project Muse, JSTOR, ProQuest Research Library, and Academic Search Premier (EBSCO).

The MLA Works-Cited List

As you compile your working bibliography, you should record each source according to the documentation format of the Modern Language Association (MLA) works-cited list, or bibliography, which you will be required to include at the end of your research paper. Detailed information on documenting sources is provided in Appendix B, and a full listing can be found in the *MLA Handbook for Writers of Research Papers,* 7th edition, by Joseph Gibaldi (New York: Modern Language Association, 2009) in your library. Works cited should be double-spaced and begin on a new page, each entry should be given a hanging indent of one half inch, and you should put a single space after all punctuation. The first author's name is always listed last name first; the list should

be alphabetized according to the author's last name. If the work is anonymous, alphabetize according to the first significant word of the title ("The Brooklyn Bridge" would go under "B" not "T"). Provide the medium of publication. For a book, this would be *Print;* other media include *CD, DVD, Performance,* etc. The medium for any source accessed online is *Web.* See Appendix B for more information about citing sources.

Once you have begun assembling your sources in the working bibliography, use the checklist on page 89 to process your research as effectively as possible when preparing to write a paper.

Plagiarism and How to Avoid It

Plagiarism is the use of someone else's work—words, ideas, or illustrations; published or unpublished—without giving the creator of that work sufficient credit. A serious breach of scholarly ethics, plagiarism can have severe consequences. Students risk a failing grade or disciplinary action ranging from suspension to expulsion. A record of such action can adversely affect professional opportunities in the future as well as graduate school admission.

Significance of Intellectual Honesty
Have you ever heard someone ask, "What's so terrible about copying someone else's work?" After all, many argue, in this age of the Internet and music downloads, information should be "free." It is in fact possible to preserve the free flow of information without plagiarizing. Actually, careful documentation of information sources helps ensure that information remains not only available, but reliable.

The issues around plagiarism touch two significant points—preserving intellectual honesty and giving credit for work done. The

Processing Research Sources

- *Selection.* Read through the sources quickly to determine whether they will be of any use.
- *Critical reading.* Read carefully all sources that pass the first cut, taking notes about anything related to your topic.
- *Documentation.* Always record the full bibliographical information of any source you consult, in case you end up citing it in your paper, and always record its location in the library or on the Internet, so that you can find it again if you need to.
- *Notetaking.* Once you have decided a source will be part of your paper, think about it critically: read it, reflect on it, and write about it. For a research paper, critical thinking will mean taking notes. It is imperative that you write down everything you might need for your paper, even for electronic sources. The more work you put into the note-taking stage, the more work you will save yourself when it comes time to write. When taking notes:
  - Summarize the entire text. These summaries will help keep you organized and you will be able to use them for your annotated bibliography.
  - Copy quotations *only* when there is a crucial idea or formulation that you know you will cite verbatim in your paper.
  - Be sure that you copy exactly what is in the text, mark it with quotation marks, and record the page numbers where it occurs.
  - Write down the rest of the material that you will need as paraphrase, translating the source's words and arguments into your own.
  - Always note the page number(s) to which your paraphrase corresponds, since you will need to document material you have paraphrased.
  - Use paraphrasing as the first step toward incorporating the information and arguments of others into the argument and structure of your own paper.
- *Summarizing.* Summarize each source as an entry in your annotated bibliography, a particular form of summary used to organize and present your research before you actually sit down to write your own paper.
  - Provide the full bibliographical reference as the title of each entry, in MLA style unless otherwise specified by your instructor (see Appendix B for a guide to MLA style).
  - Make each entry a substantial single-spaced paragraph, usually between half a page and a page long.
  - Summarize the part of the book or article that is relevant to your research in the same way as you learned to summarize an essay, beginning your summary with a statement of the text's argument. Sometimes your entry will summarize the entire text, sometimes only a part of it.
  - Conclude each entry by evaluating the source in terms of its applicability to your topic and outlining your next step in working with the source.
  - Bear in mind the following questions in preparing the entries of an annotated bibliography:
    - In what ways has this source altered my sense of where my paper is going?
    - What new ideas or approaches to my topic has it introduced?
    - What gaps in my knowledge of the topic has it filled in?
    - In what ways (if any) was it insufficient, and what questions (if any) did it leave unanswered?
    - What research still remains for me to do?

academic community relies upon the reciprocal exchange of ideas and information to further knowledge and research. Using material without acknowledging its source violates this expectation and consequently makes it hard for researchers to verify and build on others' results. It also cheats writers and researchers of the credit they deserve for their work and creativity.

Even with the writer's permission, presenting another's work as one's own is equivalent to lying; it's a form of dishonesty. Perhaps most importantly for students, plagiarizing damages their self-respect and negates the very reasons they are in college to begin with. A student who hands in a plagiarized paper has missed an opportunity for growth and learning.

Intentional Plagiarism

Suppose you are pressed for time on a deadline for a paper in your history class and a friend offers you a paper he wrote for a similar class the previous year. Handing in that paper as your own constitutes intentional plagiarism. In the same way, buying a paper from an Internet source—or taking one from a sorority or fraternity file—and handing it in, with or without minimal changes to wording, is plagiarism. Also, paying someone to write a paper that you then hand in as yours is plagiarism. Finally, handing in a paper of your own that someone else has heavily rewritten or revised is plagiarism.

Ethical considerations aside, it is extremely hard to get away with plagiarism. Experienced professors can easily tell when a paper is not written in a student's own style or is more professionally done than they would expect. In addition, online services now identify plagiarized papers for a fee, and academic institutions are increasingly subscribing to such services. The March 2, 2006, online edition of the *New York Sun* reported that more and more schools in New York City were requiring students to hand in papers through Turnitin.com, "a service that compares students' papers against everything on the Internet and a database of more than 15 million student papers." Clearly, students at these schools will have a hard time getting away with submitting nonoriginal papers.

Avoiding Unintentional Plagiarism
It can be difficult to tell when you have unintentionally plagiarized something. The legal doctrine of **fair use** allows writers to use a limited amount of another's work in their own papers and books. To make sure that you are not plagiarizing a work, however, you need to take care to credit accurately and clearly the source for *every* use as detailed above. To use documentation and avoid unintentionally plagiarizing from a source, you need to be sure that you have done the following:

- Identified sources and information that need to be documented.
- Documented sources in a works-cited list.
- Used material gathered from sources: summary, paraphrase, quotation.

- Created in-text references.
- Used correct grammar and punctuation to blend quotations with your writing.

Identifying Sources and Information That Need to Be Documented
Whenever you use information from **outside sources,** you need to identify the origin of that material. Virtually all the information you find in outside sources requires documentation. The one major exception to this guideline is that you do not have to document **common knowledge**—widely known information about current events, famous people, geographical facts, or familiar history. When in doubt, the safest strategy is to provide documentation.

Is It Plagiarism? Test Yourself on In-Text References
Read the excerpt below marked "Original Source." Can you spot the plagiarism in the examples that follow?

Original Source
Roebling's eighth wonder continued to be the most photographed bridge in the world. If most of these photographs were tourist snapshots or postcard images, banal in the extreme, all the more so did the bridge challenge the trained professional. How to avoid the clichés? Should one attempt to grasp the whole sweep of it, or capture its essence through intense fragments? How much of the surrounding city ought to enter the composition? Should one flatten the depth of field, collapse foreground into background . . . or emphasize the separation of visual planes? Where to situate oneself in order to take the best image? Above, below, to the side? How to capture a historical awareness of the bridge: the changes that Time—or our own mutating aesthetic perceptions—had wrought on it (Lopate, 19)?

Works-Cited Entry
Lopate, Philip. Introduction. *Bridge of Dreams: The Rebirth of the Brooklyn Bridge*. By Burhan Dogançay.

New York: Hudson Hills Press, 1999. 9–22. Print.

Plagiarism: Example 1
Because it is **the most photographed bridge in the world,** the Brooklyn Bridge makes it difficult even for **the trained professional** photographer to make an original image of it. As one recent critic suggested, there are so many choices to be made in deciding how to photograph the bridge. For example, should one try to get all of it in a single frame or find **its essence** in a **fragment**?

What's wrong? The source's name is not given, and there are no quotation marks around words taken directly from the source (boldfaced in the example).

Plagiarism: Example 2
Because it has been photographed so often, the Brooklyn Bridge is a difficult assignment for any photographer. As Lopate asks, "How to avoid the clichés? Should one attempt to grasp the whole sweep of it, or capture its essence through intense fragments?"

What's wrong? The page number of the source is missing. Parenthetical references should immediately follow the material being quoted, paraphrased, or summarized. You may omit a parenthetical reference only if the information that you have included in your attribution is sufficient to identify the source in your works-cited list and if no page number is needed.

Plagiarism: Example 3
Because it has been photographed so often, the Brooklyn Bridge **challenges** even **the trained professional.** How, for example, can one capture **a historical awareness of the bridge,** the ways our **perceptions** of it have changed since the time of its construction (Lopate, 19)?

What's wrong? A paraphrase should capture a specific idea

from a source but must not duplicate the writer's phrases and words (boldfaced in the example). In this example, the wording and sentence structure follow the source too closely.

The Annotated Bibliography

Here is the first annotated bibliography entry Lorraine wrote for her paper on the Brooklyn Bridge. The assignment also required her to cite four further sources she would include in the full annotated bibliography. The professor's comments and our annotations are in boxes linked to highlighted text. Text to be corrected is circled in red.

Lorraine Betesh
English Composition II
Professor Anderson
3 March 2009

Annotated Bibliography – Source #1

MLA format for annotated bibliography dictates a hanging indent, with the text continuing directly after the reference.

Shapiro, Mary J. *A Picture History of the Brooklyn Bridge*. Toronto: Dover Publications, Inc. 1983. Print. This book is a collection of photographs, illustrations, and engravings from many sources to document the achievement of the building of the Brooklyn Bridge in the 19th century.

Delete. (Use only primary name of publisher: Dover.)

Good: simple, direct opening statement.

Whereas the beginning of the book demonstrates mainly how the bridge was built and its technical components, the latter part of the book is most useful for my purposes, because it documents the Brooklyn Bridge from 1882 until 1982. From page 88, which illustrates the opening of the bridge, the photographs portray the bridge as a monumental and revered accomplishment in American history. This is especially seen in the photo of President Chester A. Arthur, on page 90, crossing the bridge, with his troops all carrying American flags held high and the scene of the fireworks that same evening. In addition, there is one picture of the disastrous tragedy on the bridge just six days after the bridge was opened. On May 30, 1883, due to overcrowding on the bridge and many people panicking, 12 people died. In this photograph, the bridge is portrayed in a negative sense as opposed to the beautiful, proud way it was portrayed merely six days before. Here, the bridge is frowned upon and is presented as unsafe, broken and unfinished. Moreover, the book continues and takes the reader further into the 1900s where the bridge and the way it is

Place page reference at end of the sentence as parenthetical documentation: (88). Rewrite sentence to accommodate the change.

Place page reference at end of the sentence as parenthetical documentation: (90).

Too much detail for a summary of a source. Condense considerably.

A good contrast that can be developed in the paper.

Awkward sentence: revise.

exposed changes during each time frame. This book provides essential information to the part of my paper which will analyze the representation of the bridge during the time of ⟨inception⟩ and in the early 1900s. It will also help me compare these photographs to those in other books, Internet sources and even postcards, and will enable me to come up with a consistent evaluation of the portrayal of the Brooklyn Bridge during each time period.

> In your conclusion, evaluate the usefulness of the source for your purpose. Please condense this evaluation when you rewrite.

Dogançay, Burhan. *Bridge of Dreams: The Rebirth of the Brooklyn Bridge.* New York: Hudson Hills Press, 1999. Print.

McCullough, David. *The Great Bridge.* 1972. New York: Simon, 2001. Print.

> Use MLA Short form: Simon.

St. George, Judith. *The Brooklyn Bridge: They Said It Couldn't Be Built.* Toronto: General Publishing, 1982. Print.

Trachtenberg, Alan. *Brooklyn Bridge: Fact and Symbol.* 1965. Chicago: U of Chicago P, 1979. Print.

> For a reprinted book, provide original date before new publisher information.

In addition to helping to organize your sources and refine your paper topic, a well-executed annotated bibliography can also provide the backbone of the paper itself. You will also need to summarize other people's arguments in the body of the paper. Moreover, if you can clarify the relationship between your argument and theirs, you will be well on the way toward an original thesis. Although overlong in her summary of her source, Lorraine is clearly moving toward the thesis of her paper: that there is a correlation between how a photograph depicts the bridge and the historical moment in which the photograph was taken.

FROM THE ANNOTATED BIBLIOGRAPHY TO THE FIRST DRAFT

Once you have completed your research and summarized each source you will be using in your annotated bibliography, you have probably formulated at least a provisional argument for your topic. Now is the time to formalize that argument and generate a thesis for your paper. (To review argument and thesis, see Chapter 2, pp. 41–48.) Once you have found your sources, read them, and summarized them as entries in your annotated bibliography, you are ready to begin transforming your paper topic into an argument.

In the process of comparing her historical sources on the Brooklyn Bridge, Lorraine decided to steer her thesis toward her own analysis of visual material.

Making an Outline

Having chosen the factual and historical material she needed to

There is no rule on how to write. Sometimes it comes easily and perfectly; sometimes it's like drilling rock and then blasting it out with charges.

—ERNEST HEMINGWAY

support her argument, and the photos she needed as evidence, Lorraine outlined her paper as follows:

The Brooklyn Bridge in Illustrations and Photographs—An Outline

1. Opening paragraph: Brooklyn Bridge in history

   1.1 Summary of historical sources

   1.2 Thesis: the Brooklyn Bridge has an ever-changing symbolic meaning depending on the time period in which the Bridge was photographed.

2. Body of paper:

   2.1 Summary of techniques for analyzing photographs and their use in my paper

   2.2 Photos of opening day 1883: a structure to be proud of

      2.2.1 Bridge on opening day (Figure 1): symbol of pride

      2.2.2 Bridge on opening day (Figure 2): bridge as unifying force

   2.3 Centennial celebration, 1983: reflecting on bridge's meaning

   2.4 9/11/2001: before and after: bridge as support of city

3. Conclusion: How much does each photo reflect its time?

[Annotation:] L chose to synthesize the historical material in her opening paragraph.

[Annotation:] L used her reference source on interpreting photography as the second focus of her second paragraph.

[Annotation:] 2.2 is the longest part of the paper, and the one L would revise the most. She still needs to clarify the different parts of the argument.

[Annotation:] L devoted the bulk of the paper (2.2–2.4) to her own analysis of a series of photographs in light of the historical context she had researched.

WRITER'S CHECKLIST

Generating an Argument and a Thesis

- *Reconsider initial assumptions.* You have probably begun your research with a set of expectations about your topic. In what way has your new research caused you to revise or refine your initial assumptions to account for new or different information or interpretations? The gap between your expectations and your results is fertile ground for generating a thesis.

- *Review and compare facts and analysis.* Consider ways to organize and bring together the information and analysis you have assembled from your different sources. Are there still gaps in your knowledge that will need to be filled in with further research? Look for a new source that can supplement what you already know. Make lists or an idea map to help organize your questioning process.

- *Review and compare arguments.* For each entry of your annotated bibliography, you summarized the argument of your source. Which aspects of each argument are persuasive? Which are not? Do all your sources agree about the topic? Points of disagreement can often provide a focus for your own argument.

- *Review and compare evaluations.* For each entry of your annotated bibliography, you evaluated your source. Now consider how your evaluation of each source affects the way you will use its information and argument.

- *Look back at your work.* Now that you are familiar with a body of knowledge about your topic, do you have a sense of what you want to say about it? If you don't yet, try reading another source to gain a different perspective.

- *Identify a clear goal for your research paper argument.* Seek the most effective way to organize your materials and to guide your reader through a comprehensive but pointed presentation of a specific topic. As opposed to a court case, a research paper will persuade your reader most effectively by addressing all aspects of the topic, not just the ones that support your own views, and by including different perspectives on each issue you raise.

Writing the First Draft

The better your first draft, the better your revisions will be, and the less work you will have in making those revisions. Here are some tips for producing a strong first draft.

- *Take advantage of your outline.*
  - *Do* use the outline to keep yourself on track and organize your material.
  - *Don't* follow it blindly: if you don't like how the paper is unfolding, revise your outline.
- *Use your annotated bibliography as your starting point.*
  - *Do* incorporate the analysis and language from your bibliography into your own argument in the final paper.
  - *Don't* just copy the argument of each source into your own paper.
- *Be selective in using your research.*
  - *Do* let your thesis dictate a logical sequence of argumentation and guide how you assemble your notes.
  - *Don't* include research and notes simply because you have done them already or you like them.
- *Be selective in choosing quotations.* Never take a quotation for granted.
  - *Do* make sure your analysis of each quote is at least as long as the quote.
  - *Don't* include long quotes without incorporating them into your argument with your own analysis.
  - *Do* use the quote as evidence to support the argument made in your analysis.
  - *Don't* use quotes as arguments on their own.
  - *Do* summarize or paraphrase the information that you want to incorporate into your own argument, followed by proper documentation.

- *Don't* use quotes to provide factual information; quote a secondary source only if you are going to analyze an argument it contains and quote a primary source only if you are going to perform a textual analysis.

MLA In-Text Citations   While compiling your annotated bibliography, you will also have compiled a works-cited list, which should begin a new page following the final page of the body of your paper. Your **in-text citations** will refer to this works-cited page; be sure that every source that you quote or document in your paper is included on this page. The purpose of in-text documentation is to give proper credit to the sources of facts and ideas that are not your own; to differentiate between other persons' ideas and your own; and to help your reader find out more about your topic by reading further. The MLA format uses in-text citations to document sources.

The following list provides examples of MLA in-text citation using a works-cited list. We have adapted these examples from student papers in Chapters 2 and 3. You can find further examples in Appendix B.

MLA Format for In-Text Citations

- Identify the source of a quotation, paraphrase, or summary with a brief parenthetical reference to an item in your works-cited list (no comma is required between author and page number):
  The Brooklyn Bridge was declared a national monument by Congress (Dogançay 18).
- The parentheses should enclose the minimum information necessary to make a clear reference to the correct source, ideally only the page number, omitting any abbreviation for "page":
  According to Trachtenberg, this was the moment the Brooklyn Bridge entered the national consciousness (80).

- If the author's name is not clear from the sentence you are documenting, include the author's name in the citation; if you are using more than one work by the same author, include a shortened version of the title. Here, you do need a comma between author and title:
  (Dogançay, *Bridge* 18).
- A general discussion can be cited simply by the author's name, but whenever possible provide a precise page reference, as Lorraine does in her paper below.
- If you cannot determine the author, cite by title only:
  In addition, color also sets the tone of the photo ("Tone").
- Poems can be cited by line number and plays by act, scene, and line number.
  - If your quotation is four lines or less, incorporate it into the main text, enclosed by double quotation marks. If quoting from a poem or play, indicate line break by a forward slash (/):
    The opening lines tell us what happens in August, "When the blackberries hang / swollen in the woods" (Oliver 1–2).
  - If a reference in the quotation needs to be explained or you need to change the syntax to make the quotation grammatically correct, signal the explanation or alteration by square brackets:
    The title of Mary Oliver's poem "August" refers to the season "[w]hen the blackberries hang / swollen in the woods" (1–2).
- When you incorporate quotations into the body of a sentence, make sure that the syntax and diction of the quotation agree with the syntax and diction of your own sentence:
  "Summer" (7) reminds us of the time period of Oliver's title, while "black honey" (7) describes the juice of the ripe berries.

- If your quotation is longer than four lines, you should set it off from the main text as a **block quotation** with a hard return, indenting the left margin:

A shift from experiencing her body eating to analyzing her experience occurs in the middle of line 9 of Oliver's "August":

> . . . cramming
> the black honey of summer
> into my mouth; . . . my body
>
> accepts what it is. In the dark
> creeks that run by there is
> this thick paw of my life . . . (7–12)

If you omit part of the passage you are quoting, indicate the omission with an ellipsis, three periods with spaces between them (. . .). Do not use the three dots at the beginning or end of a quotation of prose, but do use them if you have omitted part of a line of poetry or theatrical dialogue.

Reproduce the formatting of the original text, such as indenting, or the extra space here between "my body" and "accepts," in lines of poetry.

The speaker's point of view changes after the middle of line 9.

The works-cited list you would need for the examples here is included below.

Works Cited

Dogançay, Burhan. *Bridge of Dreams: The Rebirth of the Brooklyn Bridge*. New York: Hudson Hills Press, Inc., 1999. Print.

Oliver, Mary. "August." *Literature: A World of Writing*. Ed. David L. Pike and Ana M. Acosta. New York: Pearson Longman, 2011. 49. Print.

"Tone." *ArtLex Art Dictionary*. 2005. Ed. Michael Delahunt. Web. 1 March 2005.

Trachtenberg, Alan. *Brooklyn Bridge: Fact and Symbol*. 1965. Chicago: U of Chicago P, 1979. Print.

REVISING

Your instructor may require you to hand in one or more drafts before the final version of the research paper is due, or he or she may leave the number of drafts you write to your own discretion. No paper will be acceptable without at least one round of revisions, however; be sure to budget your time accordingly. Be sure also to allow time for someone else to read your first draft, whether your instructor, a writing center tutor, a friend or relative, or all of the above.

Revising the First Draft

A research paper can take many different forms depending on specific class requirements and choice of topic and materials. Lorraine's paper on the Brooklyn Bridge focuses on the changing meanings of the bridge between the time of its opening and the twenty-first century. For evidence, she uses photographs taken of the bridge at crucial moments in its history. Lorraine eventually completed three drafts of her paper. We include the initial version here, followed by a discussion on revising and the final version submitted by Lorraine. Mechanical problems and other material requiring revision are circled in red; highlighting indicates passages discussed in the margins by her teacher, Fred Anderson.

> *To finish a work? To finish a picture? What nonsense!*
>
> —PABLO PICASSO

Betesh 1

Lorraine Betesh
Professor Anderson
English Composition 2
2 April 2009

The Brooklyn Bridge

In the hustle and bustle of New York City, it is easy to get caught up in the flow of traffic. Often, we do not take the time to reflect and appreciate the amazing architecture that surrounds us or that we have access to on a continual basis. The ease in which we are able to reach each other is overshadowed by the few extra minutes that it may take because of heavy traffic. However, if one would pause for just a moment to consider how difficult it would be to get around without the use of roads and bridges, the picture that one would develop would be unfathomable. The Brooklyn Bridge is one particular structure that stands out among the others. Now the 45th longest suspension bridge in the world (McCullough 71), the Brooklyn Bridge has been declared a national monument by congress (Dogançay 18), and photographed and illustrated by countless photographers and artists. Captured by so many

Marginal comments:

- Can you select a title that gives a more specific sense of what the paper is about?

- Lorraine, this beginning feels awkward because I am not sure how it relates to your thesis or to the topic of the Brooklyn Bridge. Can you rewrite it to focus on introducing your thesis more directly?

- I like the way you are including your historical research, but I wonder if you can incorporate it more smoothly. Also, please give a specific date for this event. It's a single event, so you need a simple past ("was"). "Congress" should be capitalized.

- Are you sure this is the right source? See my comment in the works-cited list.

different people during a variety of time periods, the Brooklyn Bridge has an ever-changing symbolic meaning depending on the time period in which the Bridge was photographed. Throughout this paper, I have analyzed images of the Brooklyn Bridge from different time periods and perspectives to show a correlation of the photographs' portrayal to the specific time period it was photographed in. Photographs and illustrations analyzed are those from the bridge's opening, its centennial celebration, and pre and post the tragedy of 9/11.

> This is a good start for a thesis. Now I want you to make it much more specific. I like the use of specific examples in the final sentence about how you will develop your thesis. But I'm still missing the argument you will make about each one.

In order to fully understand the photographs and illustrations of the Brooklyn Bridge throughout the various times, one must first have cursory knowledge of artistic terms and tools of an artist. Only after understanding these tools can one understand the essence of the photograph. The use of color in a photograph is one that can highlight certain portions of a picture and bring to the forefront what a photographer wishes the viewer to notice (ArtLex, 2005). In addition, color also sets the tone of the photo. Besides color, the angle at which a landscape is shot is one of the most telling tools that an artist can use when capturing an image. The angle at which the photo is taken will alter the perspective of the viewer in regards to the object being shot. The angle will also alter the appearance of the image and allow a viewer to see beyond the image and see a concept greater than the bridge itself. Altering the appearance of an object through the picture can mean exaggerating the appearance of the object or a particular portion of the object, or downplaying certain aspects of the object (ArtLex, 2005). Both of these techniques have been used while photographing the bridge for very different reasons. The use of light, especially in photographs that lack color, has the same exaggerating effects of adding color as well as mood altering effects (ArtLex, 2005). Many of these techniques are used in conjunction with one another in some photographs, while in others, only one

> You need a reference at the end of this sentence.

> See my comment in the works-cited list.

technique is used. In any case, these methods undeniably make the photographs come to life and highlight how the Brooklyn Bridge has ever-changing significance throughout time.

> *Call it "Fig. 1" and refer to it here by that title.*

In the picture below depicting the opening day of the Brooklyn Bridge in 1883, there is clearly no use of a standard camera. Given the time period, a drawing was made that captured the moment of its opening. The use of color is nonexistent. However, the use of exaggeration is very evident. The bridge is clearly the center of the photograph. Though not that largest structure in terms of height if drawn to scale, the bridge here towers over all other structures in the photograph. There are ships passing along both sides of the bridge, almost forming a circle that creates the feeling that the bridge is the center of not only the photograph but also the entire city itself. Each of these techniques speaks

> *More specifically, perhaps, the greatness of the occasion.*

to the concept of greatness. Taking into account the momentous occasion that is depicted in this photograph, the bridge is definitely a structure that the city's inhabitants are proud of. The bridge is the encapsulation of greatness and strength. The bridge represents the greatness of and the magnificence of the people who created it and the feeling of pride in

> *Yes, but can you speak more closely about what "leaps off the picture": the fireworks?*

the bridge leaps off the picture right at the viewer.

In yet another photograph from the time around when the bridge was open, we see that the photographer placed a different significance around the creation of the bridge. Capturing the bridge from a head-on angle, the photographer uses the illusion of linear perspective (ArtLex, 2005). By shooting the photograph looking straight into the bridge, the narrowing parallel lines create the appearance that the bridge extends continuously for miles and miles, almost never ending. The purpose of the Brooklyn Bridge was to unify the boroughs of Brooklyn and Manhattan and this photograph emphasizes the unifying ability of the bridge. The continuous path of the bridge connects one path to another with ease. The crowd of people making use of the bridge seems to go on forever. The people themselves are walking happily, some hand-in-hand, but all to a different destination now made one due to the bridge. Though not in color, the use of light and lack of darkness creates a calming, tranquil tone to the picture. There is a sense of completion in this photograph, expressing the completion of New York itself with the creation of the bridge. Here, the Brooklyn bridge is represented as a unifying force.

> Good focus on specific detail to develop your argument.

> Nice observation. This suggests that the bridge makes its own space, as well as connecting two others.

> Dangling modifer

> This photo needs to be closer to the analysis of it on the previous page. And, like the others, it needs a numbered label and a caption.

Passing through time, the below image was taken by Bruce Cratsley at the centennial celebration of the Brooklyn Bridge in 1983. Though the bridge has not changed physically over the course of one hundred years, the imagery and tools used by the photographer gives a feeling as if the bridge has undergone a dramatic change. Still in black and white, the photographer took this picture from the under side of the bridge. Rather than focusing on the total length of the bridge as in the pictures of opening day, here we see the focus on the bridge's tower. Not only is the picture centered on the tower, but the burst of festive light given off from the fireworks in the background creating a spotlight effect (ArtLex, 2005), further centering the bridge. The fireworks are used as the main light source for this photograph, adding to the joyous feel of the photo while creating an awing effect. Rather than a feeling of unity that was depicted in the previous opening day photograph, here we have a feeling of pride and accomplishment. More than recognizing the function of the bridge, the photographer is calling upon us to reflect on the meaning of being able to build such a monument.

[Margin note: Replace this phrase with "Fig. 3."]

[Margin note: Dangling modifer]

[Margin note: The photographer is not literally beneath the bridge. How would you describe his perspective?]

[Margin note: This is a good idea, but to be persuasive, you need to present evidence that explains how and why.]

http://www.thebody.com/visualaids/web_gallery/2004/clamp/10.html

[Margin note: Replace URL with figure number and caption. See my end comment.]

The above photographs were all taken on joyous occasions. The next photographs were taken by Ronald C. Saari, before and after the horrific events of September 11th.

> Add the year.

[http://www.ronsaari.com/stockImages/nyc/brooklynBridgePost911-6MP.php].

The photo on the left is the image of the city prior to the incident, with the World Trade Center in the background. The picture to the right is the depiction after 9/11. Though practically the same image, the two are strikingly different. The use of sunlight in the former creates a feeling of warmth. Juxtaposed with the latter, there is undoubtedly a feeling of bleakness and sullenness, caused by the lack of warm colors. The place-ment of the bridge in these photos gives a much different feel than that of the aerial view in the opening day drawing. In these photos, the bridge is in the foreground and the other buildings proportionate to the bridge given their distance. Though still the focal point of the picture, the bridge is not the center because of any festive reason. Rather, the bridge can be viewed as the support of the city. The bridge encompasses the entirety of the city, wrapping around the buildings, seemingly hugging the metropolis. The bridge is a lifeline running throughout the city. Though a piece of the city is missing, there are other monuments that still remain. The life of the city cannot be destroyed and the city takes comfort in the bridge. This is the message of these photos when looked at together. It is interesting that the full effect of the photos cannot be felt without looking at them in conjunction with each other.

> Persuasive obser-vation and analy-sis. Can you choose another term to replace "sullenness"?

> Great interpretation!

Though each of the photographs analyzed was of the same historic monument, each of the photographs (vary) tremendously in the tools that are used by the photographer as well as the meaning of the pictures themselves. It is evident that the significance of the location photographed by each photographer is heavily correlated with the time period in which the picture was taken. However, some discrepancies remain, While art and expression are reflective of the time in which these mediums are found, the opposite holds true as well. Perhaps the reason why these feelings are conveyed in these photographs is because this is how the artist feels. Perhaps these emotions and meanings are not reflective of the people of the time in which these pictures were taken. Perhaps this is simply a minority view. As an onlooker who was not there for the opening of the bridge or the centennial of the bridge, maybe these feelings were not the true feelings of the majority of the people. Is it time that influences the emotions portrayed in art or is art merely the reflection of a single person's emotions at a specific point in time? This is the next question that needs to be answered in order to truly determine the truth of the analysis of these moments captured in time. Only by analyzing literature of a particular time in conjunction with art along with other mediums, can one truly find the answer.

> I like the way you suggest the questions raised by the analysis rather than simply restating the thesis. But it would be even stronger if you condensed the argument to avoid repetition.

Works Cited

> Use this entry as cross-reference for the specific articles you are citing.

ArtLex Art Dictionary. 2005. Michael Delahunt. Web. 1 March 2009. <http://www.artlex.com/>.

> Delete. Only add URL if necessary to locate the work cited.

Brooklyn Bridge, Opening Day. 1883. PictureHistory. Web. 2003. 1 March 2009. <http://www.picturehistory.com/find/p/1800/mcms.html>.

Cratsley, Bruce. *Brooklyn Bridge Centennial.* 1983. Visual Aids. Web.

1 March 2009. <http://www.thebody.com/visualaids/web_gallery/
2004/clamp/10.html>.

Dogançay, Burhan. *Bridge of Dreams: The Rebirth of the Brooklyn
Bridge.* New York: Hudson Hills Press, Inc., 1999. Print.

McCullough, David. *The Great Bridge.* New York: Simon & Schuster, 1972.
Print.

Pricola, Jennifer. "The People's Bridge." American Studies at the University
of Virginia. 6 Sept, 2004. Web. 1 March 2009. <http://xroads
.virginia.edu/~MA03/pricola/Bridge/peoples.html>.

Saari, Ronald C. *Brooklyn Bridge post-9/11.* Ron Saari Photography and
Video. Web. 1 March 2009. <http://www.ronsaari.com/slideShow.php
?gallery=nyc&image=brooklynBridgePost911-6MP.jpg>.

– – –. *Brooklyn Bridge pre-9/11.* Ron Saari Photography and Video. Web.
1 March 2009. <http://www.ronsaari.com/slideShow.php?gallery=
nyc&image=brooklynBridge.jpg&selectedImage=>.

Shapiro, Mary J. *A Picture History of the Brooklyn Bridge.* Toronto:
Dover Publications, Inc., 1983. Print.

St. George, Judith. *The Brooklyn Bridge: They Said It Couldn't Be Built.*
Toronto: General Publishing Co. Limited, 1982. Print.

Trachtenberg, Alan. *Brooklyn Bridge: Fact and Symbol.* 1965. Chicago:
U of Chicago P, 1979. Print.

Keep these URLs: you need them to find these page.

Revise reference to cite Philip Lopate's introduction to the book.

Provide the reference for the 2001 reprint edition you consulted here.

You don't need the full publisher's name in a works-cited list. Only give as much as is needed to identify the publisher.

Lorraine, this is an accomplished first draft, although it is still quite short (less than six pages of text). You have a solid working thesis at the end of the first paragraph, where it should be. This thesis does need to be much more specific (see my marginal comment on p. 1). You do an excellent job of analyzing the photos and incorporating information about visual art. I would like you to expand the paper, either with more context about the photos, or with more photos to analyze and bring into the argument, or both. I also want you to work on tightening up the argument and expanding discussion of the connections between the different photographs. For example, why not compare the use of fireworks in two of the photographs?

You will need to do a lot of corrections and revision of mechanics in your next draft as well. I have circled in red the most important elements that need to be fixed; a careful revision will always find more. Pay close attention to dangling modifiers.

There are also a couple of problems in the works-cited list and in-text citations. Rather than citing ArtLex as your source for the various information about analyzing photography, you should cite the individual articles (and without giving the date of publication in text). You can enter these using the MLA format for cross-referencing: give the article title and the title of the collection. Because it's a Web page, you don't need to give page numbers for each entry. The photographs you include should be labeled and referred to as "Figures" and numbered consecutively. I also want you to pay close attention to where you place them--you do not want a photo appearing a page after you were discussing it. You also need to change the entry for "Dogançay," since your reference is to the introduction by Philip Lopate rather than Dogançay's photographs (see p. APP B–3 for how to reference an introduction).

There's a lot here you're already doing right, and potential for a lot more. I'm looking forward to seeing what you do with the next draft!

WRITER'S GUIDE

Troubleshooting a First Draft

- *Remedy* all mechanical errors that you didn't catch the first time around—mistakes of grammar, awkward or improper diction, misspellings of words, problems of citation or documentation
  - *Refer* to the Tips for Avoiding Common Paper-Writing Errors in Chapter 2 (p. 59).
  - *Be proactive.* Often, your instructor will simply circle or highlight mechanical mistakes and you will be required to figure out what is wrong and to fix it. If you are not sure what the problem is, be sure to ask your instructor or a writing center tutor to clarify.

- *Find and clarify your thesis.* Sometimes you will have begun writing without having fully clarified your thesis to yourself; other times the process of writing may have led you to modify your thesis.
  - *Look in the conclusion.* This is where you will often discover that you have actually formulated what your paper is about.
  - *Analyze each paragraph.* What is the argument? How is it related to what came before and to what comes next?

- *Get the page count right.* Many first drafts are either too short or too long.
  - Do not include the title page and the works-cited page in your page count.
  - Do not think you will fool anyone by increasing or shrinking your font.
  - Do not count a paper that runs a couple of lines onto the eighth page as an eight-page paper.

- *Lengthen your paper the right way.* Lorraine's initial draft for an eight-page paper was just over six pages, and she used the following strategies to produce a stronger, and longer, second paper:
  - Expand the analysis of your examples.
  - Spell out your argument; many first drafts assume the argument is self-evident when it is not.
  - Introduce additional evidence in support of your argument.

- *Shorten your paper the right way.* Rob Lanney's initial draft for an eight-page paper (p. APP B–5) was already at eight pages, and his revision was bound to add to that length. Here are some strategies to trim the fat as you add in the meat.
  - Find redundant examples and delete or shorten overly long quotations. As you read through your paper, ask questions about every example and every quotation: What is it doing here? How does it relate to my thesis? How does it provide support to my argument? If you cannot answer these questions, delete the example and the quotation.
  - Keep a sharp eye out for repetition. Seldom do you need to say anything twice in a paper.
  - *Get help.* All of the strategies above will be more effective if you do them with the assistance of your instructor, the writing center at your school, a classmate, or a friend.

Revising the Initial Draft

A research paper can take many different forms depending on specific class requirements and choice of topic and materials. Lorraine's paper on the Brooklyn Bridge includes a certain amount of historical research but is focused on analysis of a series of specific illustrations and photographs. Another paper might examine various historical or social issues raised by the Brooklyn Bridge, such as the "restoration period" referred to in Lorraine's second paper topic.

A literary research paper might study literary responses to or depictions of the Brooklyn Bridge, incorporating secondary criticism on specific texts and writers. The approach you take will depend on your particular interests and skills, and the material you find. After completing the first draft, Lorraine worked hard at both tightening and unpacking her argument. After an intermediate draft, continued revisions resulted in the following final draft that she submitted for her class. We have added comments on Lorraine's process of revision; text referred to in our comments is highlighted in yellow.

Lorraine Betesh
Professor Anderson
English Composition 2
2 May 2009

The Brooklyn Bridge in Illustrations and Photographs

Time affects people and places in many ways. Just as a person matures over time, changing in appearance and personality, buildings and monuments change in similar ways. Buildings that performed certain functions at one point in time either outgrow their function or need to adapt to the changing times. The Brooklyn Bridge is a perfect example of this concept. Once a great necessity connecting the city of Manhattan to the borough of Brooklyn, the bridge no longer serves the same functional purpose that it did over one hundred years ago. There are many bridges and tunnels linking Brooklyn and Manhattan, and it is now only the 45th longest suspension bridge in the world (McCullough 71). Nevertheless, its symbolic value has only increased with time. The Brooklyn Bridge was declared a national monument by Congress in 1964 (Trachtenberg 79), and has been photographed and illustrated by countless photographers and artists. Captured by so many different people during a variety of time periods, the Brooklyn Bridge has an ever-changing symbolic meaning depending on the time period in which the Bridge was photographed (Lopate 19). In this paper, I analyze images of the Brooklyn Bridge from the bridge's opening, its centennial celebration, and before and after the tragedy of 9/11 to show a correlation of the photographs' portrayal to the specific time period it was photographed in. When it first opened, the bridge was a source of happiness and

> Lorraine's first draft began with an awkward description of traffic in New York City. She replaced it here with a much stronger opening that proposes the Brooklyn Bridge as a specific example of a general claim about how places change meaning over time.

> These sentences incorporate details from Lorraine's research, cited by author and page number, into the flow of her argument. She has corrected one source and added a citation.

> Lorraine has revised her thesis statement to include a brief summary of her argument about each photograph.

celebration. A hundred years later, pride and accomplish remain, but as a monument to reflect upon. After 9/11, this monument becomes a warm and embracing support for the inhabitants of the city.

In order to fully understand photographs and illustrations of the Brooklyn Bridge in various time periods, one must first have cursory knowledge of artistic terms and the tools of an artist. Only after understanding these tools can one understand the essence of the photograph. The use of color in a photograph can highlight certain portions of a picture and bring to the forefront what a photographer wishes the viewer to notice ("Highlight"). In addition, color also sets the tone of the photo ("Tone"). Besides color, the angles at which the photo is taken will alter the perspective of the viewer in regards to the object being shot. The angle will also alter the appearance of the image and allow a viewer to see beyond the image and see a concept greater than the bridge itself. Altering the appearance of an object through the picture can mean exaggerating the appearance of the object or a particular portion of the object, or downplaying certain aspects of the object ("Telephoto"). Both of these techniques have been used while photographing the bridge for very different reasons. The use of light, especially in photographs that lack color, has the same exaggerating effect ("Value").

Many of these techniques are used in conjunction with one another in some photographs, while in others, only one technique is used. These artistic methods give life to the photographs, allowing viewers to feel what the photographer felt while taking the pictures. These tools and techniques are comparable to descriptive words used by authors of fiction to help readers feel and picture a time or place. These techniques undeniably make the photographs come to life. Analyzing their use helps to highlight the changing significance of the Brooklyn Bridge over time while helping to differentiate between photographs of the same monument.

Here and below, Lorraine has corrected her citation of specific articles from *ArtLex*. Cite an anonymous page on a Web site by title only.

In this paragraph, added during revisions, Lorraine clarifies the purpose of her summary of photographic techniques and how they contribute to her argument about visual images of the bridge.

Lorraine has relocated the photographs to come before the paragraph(s) in which she discusses them. She has also followed proper format, as she did not do in her earlier draft. Label all types of illustrations (i.e., photographs, maps, graphs, charts, etc.) as figures underneath the corresponding figure, double-spaced and followed by an Arabic numeral and a title/caption.

Fig. 1 *Fireworks Light up the Bridge on Opening Night.* (Pricola)

In the picture above depicting the opening day of the Brooklyn Bridge in 1883 (Fig. 1), we find a printed illustration from a newspaper based on a photograph of the event. There is a very evident use of exaggeration to heighten the effect of the bridge. The bridge is clearly the center of the photograph. Although it would not be the largest structure in terms of height if drawn to scale, the bridge here towers over all other structures in the photograph. There are ships passing along both sides of the bridge, almost forming a circle that creates the feeling that the bridge is the center not only of the illustration but also of the entire city. Each of these techniques speaks to the greatness of the occasion, arguing that the bridge is a structure that the city's inhabitants are proud of. a feeling of pride in the bridge leaps off the picture right at the viewer. This feeling of pride leaps off the picture and right at the viewer through the use of the fireworks. If looked at carefully, one can see that the fireworks are not the conventional rockets that launched from the ground before exploding in the sky. The sparks of the fireworks are actually emanating directly from the towers of the bridge, bringing the bridge to life. The fireworks represent the happiness pouring out of the completion of the bridge.

A nice use of visual detail to introduce an argument about the bridge's significance.

Here, Lorraine's revision has condensed four repetitive sentences into a single argument.

The analysis of the fireworks, introduced in this draft, persuasively expands upon the previous claim of the status of the bridge. The final sentence correctly identifies the fireworks as a figurative image for the sentiments of the occasion.

Fig. 2 *Brooklyn Bridge, Opening Day.*

We find a slightly different significance attributed to the bridge in another photograph commemorating its opening (Fig. 2). ==Capturing the bridge from a head-on angle, the photographer uses the illusion of linear perspective ("Linear Perspective"). The narrowing parallel lines resulting from the head-on framing create the illusion that the bridge extends continuously for miles and miles, almost never ending.== The purpose of the Brooklyn Bridge was to unify the boroughs of Brooklyn and Manhattan, and this photograph emphasizes the unifying ability of the bridge. The continuous path of the bridge connects one place to another with ease. The crowd of people making use of the bridge seems to go on forever. The people themselves are walking happily, some hand-in-hand, but all to a different destination now made one due to the bridge. The photograph's use of light and lack of darkness provide the picture a calming, tranquil tone. There is a sense of completion of New York itself with the creation of the bridge. Though connecting two bodies of land,

> Rather than introducing this technique with the others earlier, Lorraine wisely chose to introduce it in the context of the interpretation that relies on it.

the bridge also seems to possess its own space. Neither part of Manhattan or part of Brooklyn, the bridge is a separate entity that people enjoy. Here, the Brooklyn Bridge is represented as a unifying force.

Fig. 3 Bruce Cratsley. *Brooklyn Bridge Centennial.*

The bridge changed very little physically over the course of its first hundred years, but a photograph taken by Bruce Cratsley at the centennial celebration in 1983 (Fig. 3) gives the feeling that the bridge has changed dramatically. Still working in black and white, the photographer took this picture looking up at the bridge from a low angle. Rather than focusing on the total length of the bridge as in the opening day pictures in Figs. 1 and 2, here the photographer has focused on the bridge's tower. Not only is the picture centered on the tower, but the burst of festive light given off from the fireworks in the background creates a spotlight effect ("Tenebrism"), further centering the bridge. The fireworks are used as the main light source for this photograph, adding to the joyous feeling of the photo but primarily creating an effect of awe. Rather than the feeling of unity that was depicted in Fig. 2, here we have a feeling of pride and accomplishment. It is interesting to note the difference between the use of the fireworks here and in Fig. 1, where they were clearly a sign of celebration and joy in completing the bridge. In Fig. 3, the fireworks are less festive here than dramatic. Each artist uses fireworks in a different way to convey a different message about the bridge.

Beyond just recognizing the function of the bridge, Cratsley is calling upon us to reflect on the meaning of being able to build such a monument and what that monument means to each individual. The purpose of the photo is well suited to the occasion it commemorates. The photograph was taken at the centennial of the bridge, the celebration of a past that still exists in the present. At such occasions, it is only appropriate to reflect on the meaning of the monument being celebrated. The photograph causes each reader to think back on the building of the bridge and the meaning the bridge has for the city and its inhabitants.

The photographs and illustrations discussed above all record joyous occasions. The next two photographs (Figs. 4 and 5) were taken by Ronald C. Saari before and after the horrific events of September 11, 2001.

Fig. 4 Ronald Saari. *Brooklyn Bridge pre-9/11.*   Fig. 5 Ronald Saari. *Brooklyn Bridge post-9/11.*

> In sentences added to the second draft, Lorraine plays off her new analysis of fireworks in Fig. 2 to draw an excellent comparison with Fig. 3 that strengthens her argument and ties together the different parts of her paper. When you revise, always look for new connections that might have emerged.

The photo on the left is the image of the city prior to the incident, with the World Trade Center in the background. The picture to the right is the depiction after 9/11. Although practically the same image, the two photographs are strikingly different. The use of sunlight in Fig. 4 creates a feeling of warmth. Especially in comparison with this image, the lack of warm colors in Fig. 5 produces a feeling bleakness and melancholy. The placement of the bridge in these photos gives a much different feel than that of the aerial view in the opening day illustration (Fig. 1). In Saari's photos, the bridge is in the foreground and the other buildings visible behind it, proportionate in size to the bridge. While it is still the focal point of the picture, the bridge is no longer the center because of any celebration. Rather, the bridge can be viewed as the support of the city. It encompasses the entirety of the city, wrapping around the buildings, seemingly hugging the metropolis. The bridge is a lifeline running through the city. Although a piece of the city is missing, there are other monuments that still remain. The life of the city cannot be destroyed and the city takes comfort in the bridge. This is the message of these photos when looked at together. It is interesting that the full effect of the photos cannot be felt without looking at each of them in connection to the other.

Although each of the photographs analyzed depicts the same historic monument, each of them varies tremendously in the tools used by the photographer as well as in the meaning of the pictures themselves. The significance of the location photographed by each photographer depends heavily on the moment in which the picture was taken. Art and expression are indeed reflective of the time in which these media are found, but it is difficult to determine in what degree. Perhaps the feelings conveyed in these photographs only express the feelings of the

A thoughtful way to conclude the paper, suggesting questions raised by the analysis rather than simply restating the thesis.

artist without necessarily representing the emotions and meanings of the majority of the people of the time in which the pictures were taken. Is it time that influences the emotions portrayed in art or is art merely the reflection of a single person's emotions at a specific point in time? This is the next question that needs to be answered in order to truly determine the truth of the analysis of these moments captured in time. Only by analyzing literature of a particular time in conjunction with art along with other media, can one truly find the answer.

Works Cited

ArtLex Art Dictionary. 2005. Michael Delahunt. Web. 1 March 2009.

Brooklyn Bridge, Opening Day. 1883. PictureHistory. 2003. Web. 1 March 2009.

Cratsley, Bruce. *Brooklyn Bridge Centennial.* 1983. Visual Aids. Web. 1 March 2009. <http://www.thebody.com/visualaids/web_gallery/2004/clamp/10.html>.

Lopate, Philip. Introduction. *Bridge of Dreams: The Rebirth of the Brooklyn Bridge.* By Burhan Dogançay. New York: Hudson Hills Press, 1999. 9–22. Print.

"Highlight." *ArtLex.*

McCullough, David. *The Great Bridge.* 1972. New York: Simon, 2001. Print.

Pricola, Jennifer. "The People's Bridge." American Studies at the University of Virginia. 6 Sept, 2004. Web. 1 March 2009. <http://xroads.virginia.edu/~MA03/pricola/Bridge/peoples.html>.

Main Web site entry for the five cross-referenced listings below.

Entry for a work of art reprinted on a Web site.

Revised entry to signal use of newer rather than original edition of a book.

Saari, Ronald C. *Brooklyn Bridge post-9/11*. Ron Saari Photography and
  Video. Web. 1 March 2009.

– – –. *Brooklyn Bridge pre-9/11*. Ron Saari Photography and Video.
  Web. 1 March 2009.

Shapiro, Mary J. *A Picture History of the Brooklyn Bridge*. Toronto:
  Dover, 1983. Print.

St. George, Judith. *The Brooklyn Bridge: They Said It Couldn't Be Built*.
  Toronto: General Publishing, 1982. Print.

"Telephoto, telephoto lens, telephoto shot." *ArtLex*.

"Tenebrism." *ArtLex*.

"Tone and tonality." *ArtLex*.

Trachtenberg, Alan. *Brooklyn Bridge: Fact and Symbol*. 1965. Chicago:
  U of Chicago P, 1979. Print.

"Value." *ArtLex*.

LOOKING BACK: Investigating the World

- A paper topic for a research paper is a like a summary of the paper that is to be written. It takes the form of a paragraph with specific and carefully defined parameters of research and argument.

- Primary sources are texts and documents from the time period of your topic or written by your subject; secondary sources are history and criticism written since 1980 about your subject.

- An annotated bibliography is a summary and evaluation of the usefulness of each source you have researched. Each summary, headed with a reference to the source in MLA format, constitutes one entry in an annotated bibliography.

- Visual media present facts and data differently than written media, but need to be evaluated and cited according to the same rules as written sources.

- A working bibliography organizes and assesses research sources before they are formally selected for inclusion in the annotated bibliography and works-cited list.

- The *MLA Handbook for Writers of Research Papers* is the standard reference for in-text citations and for the proper format of bibliographies and works-cited lists.

- Plagiarism is using someone else's work—words, ideas, or illustrations; published or unpublished—without giving the creator of that work sufficient credit. Unintentional plagiarism occurs any time writers do not credit accurately and clearly the source for *every* use they make of someone else's material in their own work.

ORGANIZING THE WORLD OF LITERATURE

THE CONVENTIONS OF GENRE

A typical family with typical tastes goes to the local multiplex. The kids go to the animated feature about singing rats. The teenage girl goes to see a teen romance; the teenage boy goes to a horror movie. The parents are tempted to go together to see a foreign movie they read about in the paper but decide it might be too depressing. So Dad goes instead to the action adventure with Bruce Willis and Mom goes to the romantic comedy with Hugh Grant. What do you notice about these choices? Each one represents a *type* of film, or *genre,* and each genre raises a certain set of expectations. For example, you expect a teen romance to be about struggling young lovers who in the end live happily ever after; you expect a horror movie to be full of shocks and gore. To take it a step further, a true teen romance aficionado would also maintain that there is a world of difference between a Miley Cyrus, a Hilary Duff, and a Vanessa Hudgens movie. And, the true lover of action and adventure films would understand the difference between Bruce Willis, the Rock, and Vin Diesel. When you know a genre inside out, you know the general conventions and all the variations within those conventions; you know the ones that play by all the rules, the ones that twist them a bit, and the ones that break the conventions completely.

These same rules hold true for just about every aspect of American culture: movies, music, video games, television shows, sports, comics, mysteries, science fiction—and, of course, literature. We *expect* genres to follow certain *conventions*. Conventions take many forms, depending on the genre and the medium (print, music, TV, film). The most common conventions are related to *plot, character,* and *iconography*. **Plot** refers to what types of events happen, the order in which they happen, and how they end up.

When you go to a comedy, you expect humorous situations and a happy ending. In this same comedy, when a series of terrible events begins to happen to the protagonist, you do not worry, because somehow you know it will work out all right in the end. Conversely, if you were watching a movie that you knew was a tragedy—*Titanic,* say—you would expect that when things start to go wrong they will just get worse.

Most comedies are built around comic *types,* or **characters** that maintain similar qualities and traits from movie to movie. Comic actors—think of Jim Carrey, Mike Myers, Chris Rock, Adam Sandler, or Cameron Diaz—always play basically the same character. Such characters possess particular costume pieces, ways of speaking, and physical gestures that are part of their identity. We refer to this feature of genres by the art-historical term **iconography,** which originally described the way in which visual features recur in particular genres of painting. You are probably familiar with the iconography of the traditional western, for example, where the good guys wear white, the bad guys wear black, and both of them ride horses and carry six-shooters in the middle of a one-street town.

We begin this chapter with a brief look at how genres both create and confound our expectations as readers. Then, we take a close look at the conventions and expectations of the forms of literature that include the four literary genres that you will encounter in this book: poetry, fiction, plays, and nonfiction. We conclude with a discussion of the conventions of visual media.

PLOT CONVENTIONS AND EXPECTATIONS

One of the arguments of "Happy Endings," the story by Margaret Atwood that you are about to read, is that genre conventions and expectations heavily influence the ways we respond to the narratives we read. "Happy Endings" teases us about our fondness for unrealistic plots and our desire for happy endings to structure the events of our life stories. The story also suggests that writers find themselves constrained by the expectations of the genres in which they are writing. No matter how much they want to be original, if new writers simply reject existing genres and conventions they will have little or no audience. Moreover, they will have a hard time telling a story: it is still possible to find a new twist to the old genres, but very difficult indeed after several millennia of storytelling to come up with something so different that it would constitute a wholly new genre. Born in Ontario, Canada, in 1939, Atwood has taught widely in Canada and the United States, and has been a leading figure in Canadian literature, as well as committed feminist and social activist, for decades. Her poetry, novels, and short stories have won numerous awards; among her best-known novels are *The Handmaid's*

With a genre like film noir, everyone has these assumptions and expectations. And once all of those things are in place, that's when you can really start to twist it about and mess around with it.

—WRITER AND DIRECTOR LARRY WACHOWSKI ON MAKING THE MOTION PICTURE, *BOUND*

Tale (1985) and *The Blind Assassin* (2000). "Happy Endings" was first published in Canada in the short story collection, *Murder in the Dark*.

MARGARET ATWOOD
HAPPY ENDINGS

John and Mary meet.

What happens next?

If you want a happy ending, try A.

A

John and Mary fall in love and get married. They both have worthwhile and remunerative jobs which they find stimulating and challenging. They buy a charming house. Real estate values go up. Eventually, when they can afford live-in help, they have two children, to whom they are devoted. The children turn out well. John and Mary have a stimulating and challenging sex life and worthwhile friends. They go on fun vacations together. They retire. They both have hobbies which they find stimulating and challenging. Eventually they die. This is the end of the story.

B

Mary falls in love with John but John doesn't fall in love with Mary. He merely uses her body for selfish pleasure and ego gratification of a tepid kind. He comes to her apartment twice a week and she cooks him dinner, you'll notice that he doesn't even consider her worth the price of a dinner out, and after he's eaten dinner he fucks her and after that he falls asleep, while she does the dishes so he won't think she's untidy, having all those dirty dishes lying around, and puts on fresh lipstick so she'll look good when he wakes up, but when he wakes up he doesn't even notice, he puts on his socks and his shorts and his pants and his shirt and his tie and his shoes, the reverse order from the one in which he took them off. He doesn't take off Mary's clothes, she takes them off herself, she acts as if she's dying for it every time, not because she likes sex exactly, she doesn't, but she wants John to think she does because if they do it often enough surely he'll get used to her, he'll come to depend on her and they will get married, but John goes out the door with hardly so much as a good-night and three days later he turns up at six o'clock and they do the whole thing over again.

Mary gets run-down. Crying is bad for your face, everyone knows that and so does Mary but she can't stop. People at work notice. Her friends tell her John is a rat, a pig, a dog, he isn't good enough for her, but she can't believe it. Inside John, she thinks, is another John, who is much nicer. This other John will emerge like a butterfly from a cocoon, a Jack from a box, a pit from a prune, if the first John is only squeezed enough.

One evening John complains about the food. He has never complained about her food before. Mary is hurt.

5   Her friends tell her they've seen him in a restaurant with another woman, whose name is Madge. It's not even Madge that finally gets to Mary: it's the restaurant. John has never taken Mary to a restaurant. Mary collects all the sleeping pills and aspirins she can find, and takes them and a half a bottle of sherry. You can see what kind of a woman she is by the fact that it's not even whiskey. She leaves a note for John. She hopes he'll discover her and get her to the hospital in time and repent and then they can get married, but this fails to happen and she dies.

John marries Madge and everything continues as in A.

C

John, who is an older man, falls in love with Mary, and Mary, who is only twenty-two, feels sorry for him because he's worried about his hair falling out. She sleeps with him even though she's not in love with him. She met him at work. She's in love with someone called James, who is twenty-two also and not yet ready to settle down.

John on the contrary settled down long ago: this is what is bothering him. John has a steady, respectable job and is getting ahead in his field, but Mary isn't impressed by him, she's impressed by James, who has a motorcycle and a fabulous record collection. But James is often away on his motorcycle, being free. Freedom isn't the same for girls, so in the meantime Mary spends Thursday evenings with John. Thursdays are the only days John can get away.

John is married to a woman called Madge and they have two children, a charming house which they bought just before the real estate values went up, and hobbies which they find stimulating and challenging, when they have the time. John tells Mary how important she is to him, but of course he can't leave his wife because a commitment is a commitment. He goes on about this more than is necessary and Mary finds it boring, but older men can keep it up longer so on the whole she has a fairly good time.

10   One day James breezes in on his motorcycle with some top-grade California hybrid and James and Mary get higher than you'd believe possible and they climb into bed. Everything becomes very underwater, but along comes John, who has a key to Mary's apartment. He finds them stoned and entwined. He's hardly in any position to be jealous, considering Madge, but nevertheless he's overcome with despair. Finally he's middle-aged, in two years he'll be as bald as an egg and he can't stand it. He purchases a handgun, saying he needs it for target practice—this is the thin part of the plot, but it can be dealt with later—and shoots the two of them and himself.

Madge, after a suitable period of mourning, marries an understanding man called Fred and everything continues as in A, but under different names.

D

Fred and Madge have no problems. They get along exceptionally well and are good at working out any little difficulties that may arise. But their charming house is by the seashore and one day a giant tidal wave approaches. Real estate values go down. The rest of the story is about what caused the tidal wave and how they escape from it. They do, though

thousands drown, but Fred and Madge are virtuous and grateful, and continue as in A.

E

Yes, but Fred has a bad heart. The rest of the story is about how kind and understanding they both are until Fred dies. Then Madge devotes herself to charity work until the end of A. If you like, it can be "Madge," "cancer," "guilty and confused," and "bird watching."

F

If you think this is all too bourgeois, make John a revolutionary and Mary a counterespionage agent and see how far that gets you. Remember, this is Canada. You'll still end up with A, though in between you may get a lustful brawling saga of passionate involvement, a chronicle of our times, sort of.

15   You'll have to face it, the endings are the same however you slice it. Don't be deluded by any other endings, they're all fake, either deliberately fake, with malicious intent to deceive, or just motivated by excessive optimism if not by downright sentimentality.

    The only authentic ending is the one provided here:

John and Mary die. John and Mary die. John and Mary die.

    So much for endings. Beginnings are always more fun. True connoisseurs, however, are known to favor the stretch in between, since it's the hardest to do anything with.

    That's about all that can be said for plots, which anyway are just one thing after another, a what and a what and a what.

    Now try How and Why.

[1983]

QUESTIONS FOR REFLECTION AND DISCUSSION

1. How would you summarize this story?

2. Each of the six possible plots presented in the story as letters A–F adapts the conventions of a different genre. Briefly outline the conventions of each plot, and ways in which Atwood thwarts our expectation in each example.

3. Why is there no other possible "authentic ending" than "John and Mary die"? Why is this a "happy ending" only in version A?

4. Atwood's conclusion suggests that the ending is the most conventional aspect of a story. Do you agree? Why or why not?

5. Does Atwood's story tell only "a what and a what and a what" or does it also suggest a "How and Why" about the subject she is discussing?

COMPARING GENRES

Margaret Atwood's story "Happy Endings" suggests that telling a story the conventional way makes it impossible to get at the "How and Why" of experience. In *The Way to Rainy Mountain,* a book on the oral tradition of the Kiowa Indians, N. Scott Momaday suggests that conventional ways of narrating history are unable to capture the unique culture of his father's ancestors. Instead, he structured his book in brief chapters, each composed of three distinct parts. Each part employs different generic conventions in order to approach a different aspect of the story Momaday wants to tell. Son of a Kiowa father and a mother of English and Cherokee descent, Momaday was born in Lawton, Oklahoma, in 1934, and raised in Arizona. He graduated from the University of New Mexico, and received a PhD in English literature from Stanford University in 1963. Momaday has taught American Indian studies at many universities, and published several works of criticism, as well as several volumes of poetry, a play, and a memoir, among other genres. *The Way to Rainy Mountain* is a reworking of his first novel, *House Made of Dawn* (1968), which was awarded the Pulitzer Prize for Fiction.

As you read the following excerpt from *The Way to Rainy Mountain,* consider the different expectations raised by each of the three genres it uses: a mythical narrative, an anthropological commentary, and an autobiographical memoir. Consider also the way in which they work together to produce a whole that is greater than the sum of its parts.

> *The Judas Strain: National Treasure* meets *Die Hard* meets James Bond meets *28 Days Later.*
> —AN ANONYMOUS REVIEWER IN TVTROPES.ORG DESCRIBING A RECENT THRILLER BY JAMES ROLLINS

N. SCOTT MOMADAY

FROM
THE WAY TO
RAINY MOUNTAIN

Chapter 4

They lived at first in the mountains. They did not yet know of Tai-me, but this is what they knew: There was a man and his wife. They had a beautiful child, a little girl whom they would not allow to go out of their sight. But one day a friend of the family came and asked if she might take the child outside to play. The mother guessed that would be all right, but she told the friend to leave the child in its cradle and to place the cradle in a tree. While the child was in the tree, a redbird came among the branches. It was not like any bird that you have seen; it was very beautiful, and it did not fly away. It kept still upon a limb, close to the child. After a while the child got out of its cradle and began to climb after the redbird. And at the same time the tree began to grow taller, and the child was borne up into the sky. She was then a woman, and she found herself in a strange place. Instead of a redbird, there was a young man standing before her. The man spoke to her and said: "I have been watching you for a long time, and I knew that I would find a way to bring you here. I have brought you here to be my wife." The woman looked all around: she saw that he was the only living man there. She saw that he was the sun.

There the land itself ascends into the sky. These mountains lie at the top of the continent, and they cast a long rain shadow on the sea of grasses to the east. They arise out of the last North American wilderness, and they have wilderness names: Wasatch, Bitterroot, Bighorn, Wind River.

I have walked in a mountain meadow bright with Indian paintbrush, lupine, and wild buckwheat, and I have seen high in the branches of a lodgepole pine the male pine grosbeak, round and rose-colored, its dark, striped wings nearly invisible in the soft, mottled light. And the uppermost branches of the tree seemed very slowly to ride across the blue sky.

Chapter 5

After that the woman grew lonely. She thought about her people, and she wondered how they were getting on. One day she had a quarrel with the sun, and the sun went away. In her anger she dug up the root of a bush which the sun had warned her never to go near. A piece of earth fell from the root, and she could see her people far below. By that time she had given birth; she had a child—a boy by the sun. She made a rope out of sinew and took her child upon her back; she climbed down upon the rope, but when she came to the end, her people were still a long way off, and there she waited with her child on her back. It was evening; the sun came home and found his woman gone. At once he thought of the bush and went to the place where it had grown. There he saw the woman and the child, hanging by the rope half way down to the earth. He was very angry, and he took up a ring, a gaming wheel, in his hand. He told the ring to follow the rope and strike the woman dead. Then he threw the ring and it did what he told it to do; it struck the woman and killed her, and then the sun's child was all alone.

The plant is said to have been the pomme blanche, or pomme de prairie, of the voyageurs, whose chronicles refer time and again to its use by the Indians. It grows on the high plains and has a farinaceous root that is turnip-like in taste and in shape. This root is a healthful food, and attempts have been made to cultivate the plant as a substitute for the potato.

The anthropologist Mooney wrote in 1896: "Unlike the neighboring Cheyenne and Arapaho, who yet remember that they once lived east of the Missouri and cultivated corn, the Kiowa have no tradition of ever having been an agricultural people or anything but a tribe of hunters."

Even now they are meateaters; I think it is not in them to be farmers. My grandfather, Mammedaty, worked hard to make wheat and cotton grow on his land, but it came to very little in the end. Once when I was a small boy I went across the creek to the house where the old woman Keahdinekeah lived. Some men and boys came in from the pasture, where a calf had just been killed and butchered. One of the boys held the calf's liver— still warm and wet with life—in his hand, eating of it with great relish. I have heard that the old hunters of the Plains prized the raw liver and tongue of the buffalo above all other delicacies.

Chapter 6

The sun's child was big enough to walk around on the earth, and he saw a camp nearby. He made his way to it and saw that a great spider—that which is called a grandmother—lived there. The spider spoke to the sun's child, and the child was afraid. The grandmother was full of resentment; she was jealous, you see, for the child had not yet been weaned from its mother's breasts. She wondered whether the child were a boy or a girl, and therefore she made two things, a pretty ball and a bow and arrows. These things she left alone with the child all the next day. When she returned, she saw that the ball was full of arrows, and she knew then that the child was a boy and that he would be hard to raise. Time and again the grandmother tried to capture the boy, but he always ran away. Then one day she made a snare out of rope. The boy was caught up in the snare, and he cried and cried, but the grandmother sang to him and at last he fell asleep.

> Go to sleep and do not cry.
> Your mother is dead, and still you feed
>   upon her breasts.
> Oo-oo-la-la-la-la, oo-oo.

"There are things in nature that engender an awful quiet in the heart of man; Devil's Tower is one of them."—N. Scott Momaday, *The Way to Rainy Mountain*.

In the autumn of 1874, the Kiowas were driven southward towards the Staked Plains. Columns of troops were converging upon them from all sides, and they were bone-weary and afraid. They camped on Elk Creek, and the next day it began to rain. It rained hard all that day, and the Kiowas waited on horseback for the weather to clear. Then, as evening came on, the earth was suddenly crawling with spiders, great black tarantulas, swarming on the flood.

I know of spiders. There are dirt roads in the Plains. You see them, and you wonder where and how far they go. They seem very old and untraveled, as if they all led away to deserted houses. But creatures cross these roads: dung beetles and grasshoppers, sidewinders and tortoises. Now and then there comes a tarantula, at evening, always larger than you imagine, dull and dark brown, covered with long, dusty hairs. There is something crochety about them; they stop and go and angle away.

Chapter 7

The years went by, and the boy still had the ring which killed his mother. The grandmother spider told him never to throw the ring into the sky, but one day he threw it up, and it fell squarely on top of his head and cut him in two. He looked around, and there was another boy, just like himself, his twin. The two of them laughed and laughed, and then they went to the grandmother spider. She nearly cried aloud when she saw them, for it had been hard enough to raise the one. Even so, she cared for them well and made them fine clothes to wear.

Mammedaty owned horses. And he could remember that it was essentially good to own horses, that it

was hard to be without horses. There was a day: Mammedaty got down from a horse for the last time. Of all the tribes of the Plains, the Kiowas owned the greatest number of horses per person.

On summer afternoons I went swimming in the Washita River. The current was slow, and the warm, brown water seemed to be standing still. It was a secret place. There in the deep shade, inclosed in the dense, overhanging growth of the banks, my mind fixed on the wings of a dragonfly or the flitting motion of a water strider, the great open land beyond was all but impossible to imagine. But it was there, a stone's throw away. Once, from the limb of a tree, I saw myself in the brown water; then a frog leaped from the bank, breaking the Image apart.

Chapter 8

Now each of the twins had a ring, and the grandmother spider told them never to throw the rings into the sky. But one day they threw them up into the high wind. The rings rolled over a hill, and the twins ran after them. They ran beyond the top of the hill and fell down into the mouth of a cave. There lived a giant and his wife. The giant had killed a lot of people in the past by building fires and filling the cave with smoke, so that the people could not breathe. Then the twins remembered something that the grandmother spider had told them: "If ever you get caught in the cave, say to yourselves the word *thain-mom*, 'above my eyes.'" When the giant began to set fires around, the twins repeated the word *thain-mom* over and over to themselves, and the smoke remained above their eyes. When the giant had made three great clouds of smoke, his wife saw that the twins sat without coughing or crying, and she became frightened. "Let them go," she said, "or something bad will happen to us." The twins took up their rings and returned to the grandmother spider. She was glad to see them.

A word has power in and of itself. It comes from nothing into sound and meaning; it gives origin to all things. By means of words can a man deal with the world on equal terms. And the word is sacred. A man's name is his own; he can keep it or give it away as he likes. Until recent times, the Kiowas would not speak the name of a dead man. To do so would have been disrespectful and dishonest. The dead take their names with them out of the world.

When Aho saw or heard or thought of something bad, she said the word zei-dl-bei, "frightful." It was the one word with which she confronted evil and the incomprehensible. I liked her to say it, for she screwed up her face in a wonderful look of displeasure and clicked her tongue. It was not an exclamation so much, I think, as it was a warding off, an exertion of language upon ignorance and disorder.

Chapter 9

The next thing that happened to the twins was this: They killed a great snake which they found in their tipi. When they told the grandmother spider what they had done, she cried and cried. They had killed their grandfather, she said. And after that the grandmother spider died. The twins wrapped her in a hide and covered her with leaves by the water. The twins lived on for a long time, and they were greatly honored among the Kiowas.

In another and perhaps older version of the story, it is a porcupine and not a redbird that is the representation of the sun. In that version, too, one of the twins is said to have walked into the waters of a lake and disappeared forever, while the other at last transformed

himself into ten portions of "medicine," thereby giving of his own body in eucharistic form to the Kiowas. The ten bundles of the talyi-da-i, "boy medicine" are, like the Tai-me, chief objects of religious veneration.

When he was a boy, my father went with his grandmother, Keahdinekeah, to the shrine of one of the talyi-da-i. The old woman made an offering of bright cloth, and she prayed. The shrine was a small, specially-made tipi; inside, suspended from the lashing of the poles, was the medicine itself. My father knew that it was very powerful, and the very sight of it filled him with wonder and regard. The holiness of such a thing can be imparted to the human-spirit, I believe, for I remember that it shone in the sightless eyes of Keahdinekeah. Once I was taken to see her at the old house on the other side of Rainy Mountain Creek. The room was dark, and her old age filled it like a substance. She was white-haired and blind, and, in that strange reversion that comes upon the very old, her skin was as soft as the skin of a baby. I remember the sound of her glad weeping and the water-like touch of her hand.

[1969]

QUESTIONS FOR REFLECTION AND DISCUSSION

1. How do the three parts of each chapter differ? What are some of the generic conventions you can identify for each part? What are some of the similarities and differences between the conventions of the legend of the twins and other myths with which you may be more familiar?

2. Read through the excerpt again, but this time read first the six parts of the legend of the twins, then the six anthropological parts, and finally the six autobiographical pieces. Now reflect: what would the effect of the book be if it were composed only of the legend, or only of the anthropological part, or only of the autobiography?

3. The legend of the twins is a good example of Margaret Atwood's description of plot as "a what and a what and a what." Do the other parts of the excerpt provide the "How and Why"? If so, what is the "how and why" of this myth? If not, what else do the other two parts add to the original myth?

4. Animals and the natural world play an important role in all three parts of *The Way to Rainy Mountain*. How is nature depicted in each part? What are the similarities and what are the differences?

WRITING EXERCISE: A Life in Three Genres

1. Choose an event or series of events in your life or the life of someone you know well, and describe the event(s) according to the conventions of three different genres. For example, what would they look like remade as an action-adventure movie or as a pop song, video game, diary entry, soap opera, comedy, summary, or essay?

2. Sit back and reflect on your three versions. Were you able to include everything in each version, or did conventions require you to omit something in one version? Which version does a better job at describing what happened, and which version does a better job of explaining the how and why? Which version would you prefer to live through again?

WHAT IS POETRY?

The most ancient forms of literature were oral rather than written, and they were poems. Songs are the oldest genre of literary creation, and poetry originated from songs of oral traditions around the world. Many consider poetry the most challenging of literary genres. Often, you have to "read between the lines" to find a poem's meaning and argument. As you wrestle with the pleasures and challenges of the poems in this book, imagine what it must have been like to live in a time when poetry was a primary means of expressing social and cultural meaning, and its rules and conventions were as familiar to audiences as those of pop music are today. Although poetry no longer holds such a central role in Western culture, readers still bring strong expectations to a poem—for many a poem must rhyme; for many others, a poem must *not* rhyme. While at odds with each other, both of these expectations define poetry in terms of **form**—the way its thoughts and words are organized. The fact is, many poems are rhymed, many are unrhymed, and many are both (see, for example, T. S. Eliot's "The Love Song of J. Alfred Prufrock" [p. 389]).

We can also attempt to define poetry in terms of its subject or **theme,** what it is about. For many poets and many readers, poetry should talk about love, and nothing else. And, indeed, there are more poems about love than about any other subject. Nevertheless, many of the earliest poems we have are **epics**—long poems that tell of heroes and the deeds that brought them fame, few of which involved love. Although love songs may dominate the ranks of poetry, there is not a topic, theme, or object in the world that has not had at least a few poems devoted to it at some point somewhere by somebody.

Poetry may also be defined in terms of its creator—that is, anything written by a *poet*. There was a time when poems were composed by bards and performed by minstrels who never wrote or performed anything else besides poetry because, for the most part, there were no other genres in which to write. Nowadays, and for a long time, it has been nearly impossible to make a living exclusively as a professional poet (most contemporary poets teach writing in universities) and nearly impossible to find a professional poet who does not also write in other genres: reviews, essays, stories, plays, novels.

As in most genres, there will always be exceptions to any general rules about poetry. We can say that poetry is not prose, although we will have to make an exception for prose poems (p. 131). We can say that poetry employs literary devices and rules of verse, although we will have to make an exception for poems written without literary devices, rhyme, or meter (p. 130). No poem will rhyme perfectly or use a single meter with absolute consistency; what makes each poem unique are the patterns of meaning it establishes and the specific moments in which it breaks each pattern. Free verse and prose poems emerged in the nineteenth century in rebellion against the constraints and conventions of metrical composition. Open forms dominated poetry of the twentieth century, although recent years have seen a return to stricter forms. Knowledge of literary devices, rhyme, and meter will allow you to recognize the patterns each poem establishes; careful reading and critical thinking will help you to recognize where and how these patterns are broken, and

> *I, too, dislike it.*
> *Reading it, however, with a perfect*
> *contempt for it, one discovers in*
> *it, after all, a place for the genuine.*
> —MARIANNE MOORE, "POETRY"

to generate arguments about the meaning of those breaks.

Prosody: An Introduction

At the heart of a poem is its rhythm, the patterns of sounds formed by its words and lines. The knowledge of poetic rhythm and the rhymes that often accompany it is known as **prosody.** The initial steps to analyzing poetry, then, are to *scan,* or identify the *meter* (or formal rhythm) of the lines; to identify the structure of the *stanzas,* or groupings of lines; to *parse* the sentences of the poem; and to *analyze* when and how the poem diverges from poetic convention.

Meter The word *meter* comes from the Greek verb "to measure," and there are various means by which to measure the meter of a line of poetry:

- **Quantitative:** measured according to the length of each vowel and consonant combination.
- **Syllabic:** measured according to the number of units in each word
- **Accentual:** measured according to the number of accented syllables only (as in *free* or *open form* verse)
- **Accentual-syllabic:** measured according to the number of stressed and unstressed syllables combined (as in most *formal,* or *closed verse*).

Poetic Feet

Number of Feet per Line	Name of Foot	Number of Feet per Line	Name of Foot
1	Monometer	5	Pentameter
2	Dimeter	6	Hexameter
3	Trimeter	7	Heptameter
4	Tetrameter	8	Octameter

Poets have never ceased to experiment with meter, and there is a wide variety of possibilities; we focus here on the general principles of **scansion**—the act of scanning a line of poetry. Each unit of stressed and unstressed syllables in accentual-syllabic verse is known as a **foot.** The meter of a poem is signaled by the type of foot it employs and the number of feet in each line; four, five, six, and seven are the most common lines.

The Romantic poet Samuel Taylor Coleridge (1772–1834) composed the poem at right to assist his sons in mastering the various types of metrical feet: the trochee, spondee, dactyl, iamb, anapest, amphibrachys, and amphimacer. Coleridge treats the names as they sound: like strange mythical creatures, each with a different gait on its different feet.

Scansion is most commonly indicated by graphic symbols:

˘	Unstressed syllable
´	Stressed syllable
/	A break between feet
//	A *caesura,* or pause near the middle of a line which usually comes between two-syllable feet and in the middle of three-syllable feet (as in lines 4, 6, 7, and 8 below)

Most poems employ a single meter throughout, with specific feet or a line here or there varied for a particular sort of emphasis. Coleridge's poem changes from line to line; the number of feet, however, remains constant (with one exception): each line is a tetrameter. Here it is again on the right, marked for scansion.

When dealing with meter, always consider its relation to other elements in the poem, both formal and thematic. Meter is a tool for creating patterns and breaking them: listen for the questions and arguments raised by both aspects of it as you read. Here are some good initial questions to ask about a poem's meter:

- Is the meter prominent, as often in nonsense verse or in poetry concerned with the stuff of poetry, such as Coleridge's poem above?

- Is it regular and highly rhythmic, as in popular music (hip-hop, for instance) and in narrative poems (such as ballads)?

- Is it subtler and subordinated to the patterns of speech, as in the blank verse of many of Shakespeare's plays?

Samuel Taylor Coleridge

from Metrical Feet— Lesson for a Boy

Trochee trips from long to short;
From long to long in solemn sort
Slow Spondee stalks, strong foot!, yet ill able
Ever to come up with Dactyl's trisyllable.
Iambics march from short to long.   5
With a leap and a bound the swift Anapests throng.
One syllable long, with one short at each side,
Amphibrachys hastes with a stately stride—
First and last being long, middle short, Amphimacer
Strikes his thundering hoofs like a proud high-bred Racer.   10

Trochee / trips // from / long to / short;

From long / to long // in sol / emn sort

Slow Spon / dee stalks, // strong foot!, / yet ill / able

Ever to / come up // with Dactyl's tri / syllable.

Iamb / ics march // from short / to long.   5

With a leap / and a bound // the swift An / apests throng.

One syllab / le long, // with / one short at / each side,

Amphibrac / hys hastes // with / a state/ ly stride–

First and last / being long, // middle short, / Amphimac / er

Strikes his thund / ering hoofs // like a proud / high-bred Rac / er.   10

1. Compose a six-line stanza (a *sestet*), with two lines of indeterminate length containing four stressed syllables, and four lines of tetrameter—one in iambs, one in trochees, one in dactyls, one in anapests. Don't worry about the meaning or profundity of the lines; focus only on the rhythm. And don't be intimidated because you've never thought about meter before. Your everyday speech has rhythms, so you just have to talk out loud and listen to the patterns it forms. Adapt a conversation, or a sportscast, or recount something that happened to you, or simply write six lines of utter nonsense—it doesn't matter as long as the rhythm is right.

2. Exchange sestets with a classmate, and read each others' verses out loud. Can you hear the difference between the lines? Can you agree on the rhythm of each foot? Remember, prosody can be very subjective, and context, accent, and tone can change the stress of a particular syllable.

Rhyme and Repetition The Greek and Latin verse of the classical era was based only on meter, and rhyme in Western poetry did not appear until the Middle Ages. Rhyme can be as varied as meter, although its rules are less fixed. **End-rhyme** is the form of rhyming we recognize most easily. We generally record a poem's rhyme with a sequence of italicized lowercase letters, each new rhyme identified by a new letter. For instance, Coleridge's poem "Metrical Feet—Lessons for a Boy" follows an *aabbcc* pattern, each pair of lines sharing a new end-rhyme.

There are other varieties of rhyme and related repetition of sounds and letters that complicate and vary the aural effect of a poem.

End-Rhymes		
Name	**Definition**	**Example**
Perfect or *exact rhyme*:	Sounds of final vowels and consonants are identical	
A. *Masculine rhyme*	Final syllables of an exact rhyme are stressed and identical	sh**ort**—s**ort** l**ong**—thr**ong** s**ide**—str**ide**
B. *Feminine* or *double rhyme*	Unstressed rhyming syllable of an exact rhyme follows stressed rhyming syllable	amphim**acer**—r**acer**
Triple rhyme	Final three syllables are all identical	m**errily**—v**erily** (**ill able**—s**yllable** *if* the rhyme were exact)
Half- or *off-rhyme*	Only final consonant rhymes exactly	ill a**ble**—sylla**ble**

Other Forms of Rhyme and Repetition		
Eye rhyme	Two words that look as if they rhyme but are pronounced differently	blow—plow
Internal rhyme	At least one of the rhyming words is within the line	"In coop and in c**omb** the fleece of his f**oam**" (Gerard Manley Hopkins, "Inversnaid," p. 658)
Alliteration	Repetition of initial sounds	**c**oop, **c**omb **f**leece, **f**oam
Assonance	Repetition of vowel sounds followed by different consonants	c**oo**p, c**o**mb, **o**f
Consonance	Repetition of consonant sound with different vowel sounds	"Co**m**e to **m**y ar**m**s, **m**y bea**m**ish boy!" (Lewis Carroll, "Jabberwocky")

Meter tends to have more of a subliminal effect on us, especially affecting our sense of the **tone**, or attitude of the poem's speaker toward the material of the poem. By contrast, rhyme and repetition are overt structuring devices, the first thing we hear (or don't hear) in a poem. They are extremely effective in oral and other poetry intended for performance because they hold the attention and guide the ear regardless of the content of the words. Rhyme and repetition are also vehicles of the more playful pleasures of poetry: end-rhymes in particular create powerful expectations in each line, and waiting for the ingenious rhyme to a difficult word can be immensely satisfying, as any aficionado of hip-hop can testify.

Rhyme and repetition help to establish associations and relationships between different words and parts of a poem. Here are the first verse and chorus of "The Dallas Blues," written by Hart Wand in 1912, with words added in 1918 by Lloyd Garrett:

When your money's gone, friends have turned you d**own**,
And you wander 'round just like a h**oun**' (a lonesome h**oun**')
Then you stop to say, "Let me go away from this old t**own** (this awful t**own**)."
There's a place I know folks won't pass me b**y**,
Dallas, Texas, that's the town I cr**y**! (oh hear me cr**y**!)   5
And I'm going back, going back to stay there till I d**ie** (until I d**ie**).

I've got the Dallas blues and the Main Street heart dis**ease** (it's buzzin' r**ound**)
I've got the Dallas Blues and the Main Street heart dis**ease** (it's buzzin' 'r**ound**)
Buzzin' 'round my head like a swarm of little honey b**ees** (of honey b**ees**).

As befits a blues song, the message is direct and the language simple. The lyrics employ masculine end-rhymes throughout, putting a stress on the final word of each line that is emphasized by the repeated phrase in lines 2, 3, 5, and 6. The two triplets of rhyme-words (*aaabbb*) create a question and answer pattern in the verse, with a strong downbeat on the final word, "die." The phrases at the end of the chorus recall the *a* rhyme ("r**ound**") before the final stress of the *c* rhyme of "b**ees**."

Similarly, listen to the way the quartet of masculine end-rhymes in the first four lines of this verse of Bob Dylan's classic 1965 rock song "Like a Rolling Stone" builds up a wave of rhythm that crashes down as the final line breaks the pattern and rhythm of the rhyme:

You said you'd never comprom**ise**
With the mystery tramp, but now you real**ize**
He's not selling any alib**is**
As you stare into the vacuum of his **eyes**
And ask him do you want to make a deal?   5

Even without the musical accompaniment, the rhymes bind together the diverse and obscure meaning of the lyrics into a coherent argument expressed by the desperation of the concluding question.

The rhythmic qualities of music make it well suited for rhyme and repetition, but they can also be used for powerful effect in more sparing media. The open form of W. H. Auden's 1940 elegy "In Memory of W. B. Yeats," using a sparse accentual meter only, drives home the desolation of the poet's death with a series of alliterations that make the word "dead" echo through the opening lines of the poem. The lack of any other meter or rhyme seems to occur in deference to the sad occasion of a famous poet's death, the wintry setting heightening the sense of loss:

The **d**ay of his **d**eath was a **d**ark cold **d**ay.

Whether employed liberally or sparingly, rhyme and rhythm create intricate and persuasive patterns of association and argument. Enjoy their sonorous pleasures and dissonant melodies as you read, then consider the arguments made through those pleasures and melodies.

Poetic Diction

Many poems, especially those that closely follow a particular metrical pattern, will shorten or lengthen a word to fit a particular rhythm, or to make a different sort of poetic argument. **Elision**—the dropping of letters and syllables—is marked by an apostrophe ('); when an end syllable, nearly always an *-ed,* must be pronounced, it is marked with an *accent grave:* "belov'd" has two syllables; "belovèd" has three. In William Blake's poem "London" (p. 175), the poet regularly elides syllables from his words: "I wander thro' each charter'd street." Written in prose, the line would read "I wander through each chartered street," but this could potentially make a ten-syllable rather than an octosyllabic line. Moreover, the elisions throughout the poem heighten the short, clipped effect of the iambic tetrameter (four iambic feet in each line).

Other aspects of poetic diction you will encounter frequently involve the poet changing **word order** to rhyme specific words and to emphasize the meaning of particular words or phrases. From Blake's "London" again: "How the Chimney-sweeper's cry / Every black'ning Church appalls." In plain prose, this would read "How the chimney-sweeper's cry appalls every blackening church." The most emphatic moments in a poem are end-stopped lines, where the end of a line and the end of a sentence coincide. Here, Blake has altered the natural word order to give extra weight to the word "appalls." Moreover, the enjambment after the first line, at the place where "appalls" would appear in plain prose, makes us wait for the verb our ear had expected to find until the end of the next line.

Word choice, too, is an important element of poetic diction. In prose, words are primarily chosen for their semantic, or dictionary, meaning. In poetry they are chosen for many different reasons: semantic meaning; *etymology,* or origin in another language; aural properties, or sound; rhythmic properties; symbolism; associations; appearance on the page; placement in a line. Consequently, when puzzled by word choice or by other aspects of poetic diction, be sure you have considered the full range of possibilities for the work it is doing in a poem. Remember, too, that there may be multiple reasons for the choices a poet has made in the search of the perfect line.

Different forms of diction create a different mood, tone, and style in a poem. We can find examples of **formal** or **high diction,** in the blank verse of Shakespeare and Milton. Only proper language will be used, only genteel subjects will be discussed, and sentence structure and phrasing will be elegant and well-balanced. By contrast, "Dallas Blues" and the poems included in the section on ballads (p. 128) provide examples of **low** or **informal diction,** which uses colloquial, everyday language to discuss topics that are not always suited for polite company. Diction can also be **concrete,** used to describe material things, such as the airport ashtrays and blue cloth in Mary Oliver's "Singapore" (p. 177); or **abstract,** used to describe phenomena such as emotions or philosophical concepts that cannot be perceived directly by the five senses, as in Emily Dickinson's "I felt a Funeral, in my Brain" (p. 460). Like all other aspects of poetry, diction can surprise our expectations, as when John Donne's love poem "The Flea" (p. 386) combines formal and abstract diction with an unconventional image to describe a very physical act of seduction. We sometimes think of poetry as rarefied and distant from our lives, but often it can be the most immediate and accessible of all forms of literature.

Poetic Forms

Of all genres, poetry has the most numerous and the most carefully defined forms. The two tables that follow here define and tell you when you can find examples in this book of the many forms taken by rhyme, repetition, and meter in poetry. We have divided the tables according to whether or not the poems use end-rhyme, and further organized them according to the language of origin of each form. Poetry is a global phenomenon, and the richness of English poetry derives in large part from the willingness of its poets to incorporate forms they have discovered by reading poetry from nearly every corner of the world.

Rhyme was synonymous with the composition of verse for nearly a millennium, from the twelfth century to the beginning of the twentieth, and it remains for many the essential component of poetry. This is true even for the myriad twentieth-century and contemporary poets who choose open forms; nearly always, they are consciously forgoing the conventions of rhyme and the associations they have with it.

Poetic form adapted to the visual media. Publicity poster for *The Ballad of Jack and Rose* (2005; see "Ballad," p. 128).

READER'S **GUIDE**

Rhymed Forms of Poetry

1. Forms Derived from the Italian: *Terza rima* and the *Sonnet*

A. *Terza rima* or "third rhyme"	• A rhymed form invented by the Florentine poet Dante Alighieri. • Terza rima is composed of an indeterminate number of tercets, or three-line stanzas. The first and third lines of each tercet always rhyme with each other, and the middle line rhymes with the first and third lines of the following tercet: *aba bcb cdc*. Each tercet is a complete unit on its own, but the middle rhyme anticipates and subtly links the thread of the poem from one tercet to the next. • Introduced to the English language in the 15th century by Geoffrey Chaucer, terza rima was popular among Romantic poets such as Shelley and Byron. • The form effectively combined personal and social themes in the space of a single long poem. • **Examples:** Opening lines of T. S. Eliot's "The Love Song of J. Alfred Prufrock" (p. 389) and Dante's *Divine Comedy.*
B. *Sonnet*	• The 14-line form was first employed by the medieval poets of Italy and southern France and later perfected by the Florentine poet Francesco Petrarch. • All sonnets break into two parts: the first presents two versions of the theme; the second either resolves the theme or suggests a new approach. • Sonnets provide a highly compressed and carefully structured form for the focused presentation of a single poetic theme.

(continued)

Rhymed Forms of Poetry (*continued*)

a. Petrarchan sonnet	• Composed of four stanzas in two parts—an opening octave in two quatrains with an *abba* rhyme scheme and a concluding sestet in two *tercets,* or three-line stanzas, with a varied scheme. • **Example:** John Donne, "Death, Be Not Proud" (p. 457).
b. Elizabethan or **Shakespearean sonnet**	• Composed of three quatrains, each with a different pair of interlocking (*abab*) rhymes and a distinct syntactical unit presenting a distinct argument, this form is followed by a rhyming couplet summing up the poem's theme. • **Example:** Shakespeare, Sonnets 29, 116, 128 (p. 384).
c. Miltonic sonnet	• John Milton expanded the sonnet's thematic scope from a focus on love to include politics, religion, and other concerns. • This form combines an octave with a sestet, one rhyme scheme for each part, but the break between the two parts is less marked than in the Petrarchan version. • Seldom used during the 18th century, the sonnet was revived during the 19th century by the Romantic poets, and remains a favored form to this day. • **Example:** Elizabeth Barrett Browning, "On Hiram Powers' Greek Slave" (p. 225).
d. Sonnet sequence	• Individual sonnets are linked together, each poem expressing a specific variation on a general theme, most often a trajectory of love. • **Example:** John Donne, "Death Be Not Proud" (p. 457), tenth of the *Holy Sonnets*.

2. Forms Derived from the Provençal and French

• Intricately rhyming medieval forms, especially apt for musical performance, love songs, and the exploration of sound patterns.
• Frequently, the repetition of the form will reflect the theme of the poem.

A. Villanelle	• Nineteen lines in total, the villanelle has five tercets and a concluding quatrain. • Only two rhymes may be used, in an *aba* pattern, with the quatrain ending *abaa* • The first and third lines of the first tercet form a refrain, or repeating line; they are used alternately as the final line of the subsequent tercets, and together as the concluding couplet of the quatrain. • **Example:** Dylan Thomas, "Do Not Go Gentle into That Good Night" (p. 458).
B. Sestina	• Thirty-nine lines in total, the sestina is composed of six sextets and a three-line envoi, or send-off. • The same six words end each stanza, reproduced in a different order in each stanza but always so that the word that concludes one stanza appears in the first line of the next; all six words appear once again in the envoi. • The end-words of a sestina may or may not rhyme with one another as well. • The primary effect is a spiraling repetition rather than the rhyming pattern of the villanelle.
C. Ballade	• Perfected in the 16th century by French poet and part-time criminal François Villon, the ballade is composed of three stanzas, usually eight lines each, and a four-line envoi, with a three-rhyme scheme, and a refrain repeated at the end of each stanza. • The medieval ballade was used for many subjects. The modern ballade is primarily a vehicle for light and playful verse.
a. Ballad (not from the French, and not to be confused with the *ballade*)	• Traditional narrative songs, ballads are usually recited aloud and tell a story of popular origin or legend, composed primarily of dialogue. • The traditional ballad stanza is a quatrain alternating iambic tetrameter with iambic trimeter, and rhyming in an *abcb* pattern. • Still used today in popular music, and often appears as a title in other genres, especially film, to denote an epic story of popular origin (see p. 127). • **Examples:** Billy Joel, "The Ballad of Billy The Kid," and *The Ballad of Jack and Rose* (film; see p. 127).

Rhymed Forms of Poetry (*continued*)

D. Rondeau	• The rondeau consists of between ten and fifteen lines of eight or ten syllables each in three stanzas of uneven length, with two rhymes throughout and the first lines repeated as a refrain in the later stanzas. • Developed in 13th-century France as a setting for song lyrics, the rondeau is used especially, although not exclusively, for light themes.
E. Roundel	• Devised by the Victorian poet Algernon Charles Swinburne, the roundel is closely related to the rondeau. • The refrain repeats the opening words of the first line.
F. Rondeau redoublé ("doubled rondeau")	• This form consists of five quatrains and a concluding quintain, or five-line stanza. • Using two rhymes throughout, the first quatrain introduces the four refrain lines that appear, one after the other, as the last lines of the next four quatrains; the concluding line of the poem repeats a phrase from the first refrain.
G. Triolet	• This is the shortest of the refrain-based forms. • The triolet contains an eight-line stanza using two rhymes and two refrains, repeating the first line as the fourth and seventh line, and the second line as the eighth.

3. Forms Derived from the Greek and Latin

- Originally unrhymed, the forms followed metrical rhythms only.
- The names of the feet of Greek and Latin verse provided the names of English meters (p. 122); however, they are based on the quantity, or length of the vowels in each syllable (long or short), rather than on whether a syllable is stressed or unstressed.
- As poets adapted these forms to the rhythms of English, often by translating poems from the classics, they preserved the themes specific to each, and sometimes the structure of the stanzas, but they generally created their own prosodic conventions to express those themes.

A. Ode	• The ode originated in the spoken choruses of ancient Greek tragedy (see *Antigone*, p. 465); it was also used as a long poetic form for passionate and mythological subjects. • The odes of the Roman poet Horace, briefer and ordered into quatrains, were more focused on philosophical and ethical concerns. • Both forms were imitated in English, the Pindaric ode in irregular stanzas, the Horatian ode in regular stanzas with often intricate rhyme scheme. • **Example:** John Keats, "Ode on a Grecian Urn" (p. 224).
B. Elegy	• The Greek and Latin elegy was defined in terms of its meter—alternating lines of dactylic hexameter and dactylic pentameter lines—and dealt with various subjects, usually presented in the first-person by a speaker in the persona of the poet: love, lamentations, meditations on fate and fortune. • Most frequently used to mourn a death, concluding in consolation, and composed in the *elegiac stanza*—an *abab* quatrain in iambic pentameter—the modern elegy is also sometimes used for other themes, and sometimes composed in elegiac couplets, in imitation of the classical meter. • **Example:** John Donne, *Elegies*.
C. Couplet	• The paired lines of the rhyming couplet were widely used during the Middle Ages to translate the vast legendary and historical material of the classical world into French, English, and other modern languages. • Couplets were a dominant form during the seventeenth and eighteenth centuries, composed in lines of rhyming iambic pentameter. • **Examples:** Geoffrey Chaucer, *The Canterbury Tales* and Robert Frost, "A Brook in the City" (p. 659).
a. Doggerel or singsong	• A verse form in rhyming couplets with unvaried rhyme and rhythm. • Doggerel is avoided in serious verse but is effective in nursery rhymes, song lyrics, and satire. • **Example:** "Humpty Dumpty" (p. 9).

WRITING EXERCISE: Working with Rhymed Forms

Choose one of the rhymed forms above and compose a poem following the conventions of the form as closely as possible. As preparation for the exercise, you may wish to look at some of the additional examples listed on a Web page, such as Representative Poetry Online.

- Prepare yourself the way working poets do: choose your topic and consider which form will be best suited to your topic.
- Choose your rhyme words (feel free to consult rhyming dictionaries on the Internet or in the library if you get stuck).

- Choose your refrains and other elements as required.
- Begin building your poem around the rhyme words and refrains and the different combinations formed by them. Take your time to experiment, and watch for the ways the constraints of the poem influence what you want to say while what you want to say presses against those constraints. Some enjoy the process; others feel unduly hampered by it. If you experience the latter sentiment, have a look at the Writing Exercise that follows the Reader's Guide for Unrhymed Forms below instead.

READER'S GUIDE

Unrhymed Forms

There are as many varieties of unrhymed forms as there are rhymed forms, but their conventions are less formalized. When reading unrhymed poetry, we can ask the following questions:
- What is their degree of metrical regularity?
- What other kinds of patterns—aural, visual, grammatical, or thematic—are present?
- What breaks in the patterns can you find?

1. **Blank verse,** also known as **unrhymed iambic pentameter,** and **heroic verse**	• This has long been the standard form for dramatic and epic verse in English. • Blank verse mirrors the patterns of natural speech in varying degree.	• Shakespeare, *Hamlet* (p. 286) • John Milton, *Paradise Lost*
2. **Haiku, Tanka, and Other Brief Forms from Japan**	• Lines in traditional Japanese poetry are determined solely by the number of syllables. • Patterns are based on sound, imagery, grammar, associations between words, and parallelisms within and between lines. • Japan does have longer forms, but it is the brief forms, especially the haiku, that have had the most influence on Western poetry. • With their sharp focus on the perception or mood of a moment, these short forms are purely lyric in intention, with no sense of narrative or time passing.	
A. **Tanka**	• Originating around 600 CE, the tanka consists of a single sentence presented in five lines of five, seven, five, seven, and seven syllables, for a total of thirty-one syllables.	• Ono no Komachi, "The flowers withered" (p. 383)
B. **Haiku**	• The haiku consists of a single sentence presented in three lines of five, seven, and five syllables, for a total of seventeen syllables. • The haiku is meant to be a concrete description without commentary or symbolism, and its third line should present a different phenomenon than the first two.	• Bashō, "Sleep on horse-back" (p. 652); Richard Wright, "In the falling snow" (p. 653)
3. **Free verse, or open form**	• A dominant poetic form of the 20th century. • In the absence of conventional constraints such as metrical rules, stanzaic structure, and rhyme schemes, writers of open form poetry face an enormous range of formal choices.	• Elizabeth Bishop, "The Fish" (p. 655)

| 4. Prose poem | • A prose poem does not have the visual appearance or prosody of poetry but it can have some of the other poetic aspects, such as dense imagery, prominent repetitions or sound patterns, and lyric description.
• Invented, or at least named, by the French poet Charles Baudelaire, the prose poem had its heyday during the period of modernism, from the late 19th century through the first decades of the 20th century. | |

WRITING EXERCISE: Working with Unrhymed Forms

1. Choose one of the unrhymed forms above and compose a poem following the conventions of the form (or lack thereof) as closely as possible.

2. Write a brief description of the form you followed and the constraints you did or did not impose on yourself.

3. If you also completed the previous Writing Exercise on rhymed forms (p. 130), write a paragraph comparing the two exercises. If you did not, write a paragraph discussing the experience of writing a poem in unrhymed form. What came easily? What was most difficult?

WHAT IS FICTION?

The word *fiction* comes from the past participle of the Latin verb *fingere,* which means "to form" or "to craft"—and in many ways a fiction is indeed something that has been crafted. Usually, however, we use the word to refer to something that is not true. Nevertheless, for most writers, *fiction* continues to mean something that one crafts, painstakingly, from a diverse selection of raw materials, with language. The raw material of fiction—the stories it tells, the characters who act in them, and the places where they act—may be drawn from real life, the author's imagination, or some combination of the two. No matter the origin, crafting materials into fiction transforms those materials into artifact—another word from the Latin, meaning "made by art." As horror maestro Stephen King puts it, "Fiction is the truth inside the lie."

Fiction and History

In the classical world, the genre of fiction was contrasted to the genre of history in terms of the order in which events both real and imagined were told rather than in terms of imagined versus real events. Today many critics argue that the primary distinction between fiction and non-fiction is not the degree of truth each genre contains but the conventions and expectations, the way the events are presented to us. It is certainly possible to distinguish between truth and fiction most of the time: there are newspapers and histories that are credible most of the time, and there are plenty of genres of fiction that are totally imaginary. Nevertheless, when you read a newspaper headline while waiting in a supermarket checkout line that reads "Elvis Dug Up & It Isn't Him," you are not likely to believe a word of it. When you

Fiction is like a spider's web, attached ever so slightly perhaps, but still attached to life at all four corners. Often the attachment is scarcely perceptible.

—VIRGINIA WOOLF

read a historical novel about the events of the French Revolution, by contrast, you will likely assume that most of the events described are true. And even in the most wildly speculative novel of science fiction, you may find that a particular character or detail strikes you as quite realistic—after all, much of science fiction, too, is drawn from the raw material of the world around us.

If we cannot judge fiction solely according to how much truth it contains, then how do we recognize it? As with all genres, we recognize it through a combination of its own presentation and self-labeling and our familiarity with generic conventions and expectations. The ancients assumed that history started at the beginning and recounted events in chronological order; fiction, by contrast, started wherever it believed the story could best be presented. These days, fiction often borrows the conventions of history and newspaper reporting, and history and reporting often borrow the conventions of fiction. Fiction is better at some things—character, psychology, suspense—while fact-based writing is better at others—recounting events, making broad historical connections, making its subject appear true-to-life—and writers in each genre use whatever tools work best for the story they have to tell.

Types of Fiction

There are two different ways to distinguish between types of fiction: in terms of genre (*romance, mystery, science fiction*) and in terms of the form of the text, which is usually determined according to length (*short story, novella, novel*).

In general, novels and novellas offer a much broader variety of formal and thematic combinations; short stories offer structural elegance and compression of effect. Because the majority of the fiction selections in this book are short stories, we outline the basic components of fiction through short story examples.

The Craft of Fiction

As an introduction to the craft of fiction, read the very short story by Padgett Powell that follows here. Born in 1952, Powell is the author of several novels, including *Edisto* and *Edisto Revisited,* and many short stories. He teaches creative writing at the University of Florida, Gainesville. Observe how "A Gentleman's C" manages to tell a moving story, develop two characters, and establish a setting in a scant 163 words.

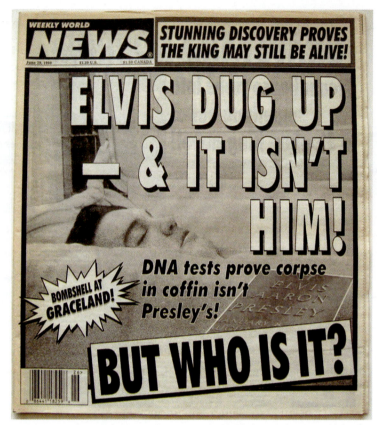

News as fiction: cover of the 29 June 1999 issue of the *Weekly World News,* a tabloid newspaper published between 1979 and 2007.

READER'S **GUIDE**

Common Forms of Fiction

Form	Conventional Features
Short story	• Length will range from a few sentences to a few dozen pages. • Text focuses on the events of the plot rather than on description and commentary; uses dialogue sparingly. • Narration covers a limited number of characters, settings, and situations. • There is little or no formal division between parts (although all short stories can be divided into segments, as in Chapter 1, p. 27). • Many short stories conclude with a final twist or revelation.
Novella	• Length will range somewhere between fifty and a hundred pages; often described as a "long" short story or a "little" novel. • Relative brevity allows for unity of structure and intensity of focus, while the length allows for depth and detail.
Novel	• Length may be described as a "longer" story, usually divided into formal segments: *chapters,* and sometimes the larger segments of *parts* and *books.* • The narration is greater in scope, either in breadth of events and chronology or in depth of characterization and detail of description. • There are multiple, usually intersecting, stories, with often detailed commentary on the events described.

WRITING EXERCISE: Fiction and History

Choose a short newspaper article and rewrite it as a story
or
Choose a brief story from elsewhere in this book and rewrite it according to the conventions of the newspaper article.

Based on your exercise, what are the primary differences between the conventions of fiction and the conventions of history?

PADGETT POWELL
A GENTLEMAN'S C

MY FATHER, TRYING TO FINALLY GRADUATE FROM college at sixty-two, came, by curious circumstance, to be enrolled in an English class I taught, and I was, perhaps, a bit tougher on him than I was on the others. Hadn't he been tougher on me than on other people's kids growing up? I gave him a hard, honest, low C. About what I felt he'd always given me.

We had a death in the family, and my mother and I traveled to the funeral. My father stayed put to complete his exams—it was his final term. On the way home we learned that he had received his grades, which were low enough in the aggregate to prevent him from graduating, and reading this news on the dowdy sofa inside the front door, he leaned over as if to rest and had a heart attack and died.

For years I had thought the old man's passing away would not affect me, but it did.

QUESTIONS FOR REFLECTION AND DISCUSSION

1. Who is the narrator of the story? What is his perspective on the events described?

2. Each paragraph narrates a different situation. What happens in each paragraph?

3. What has the author left out of the story in order to make it so short?

4. The author is in fact a professor of English and the events narrated may well be true, or they may be partially true, or they may be totally fabricated. What difference (if any) does the relation of the events to real life make in your attitude toward and understanding of the short story?

5. The final sentence is different in form and tone from the others. Characterize this difference and comment on the way it affects your understanding of the short story.

6. What is the meaning of the title and how does it relate to the story?

The Materials of Fiction

From what materials did Powell craft "A Gentleman's C"? The raw materials of any work of fiction can be categorized as follows: the *story,* the *character* or *characters,* the *setting,* and the *genre conventions* familiar to the writer. From these materials, the writer will begin to craft a fiction. The initial impetus to write can come from any one of these elements, or from all of them at once, but all four will be present in the finished text.

Story and Plot   The process of writing may begin with a **story,** a description of a set of *events.* The events we know for certain recount, in chronological order, a story:

1. A father is hard on his son (the narrator).
2. The father enrolls in his son's English class and receives a C.
3. A death in the family occurs while the father is completing the exams of his final semester.
4. The mother and son attend the funeral while the father has a heart attack on learning he will not be able to graduate.
5. The son reacts to his father's death.

The story also includes inferred events—events that we can logically assume to have occurred based on what we are told by the narrator but that are not actually recounted in the text itself. For example, we *infer* that the narrator must have attended school for years. The sum total of events that we infer or imagine in fiction is known as the **story world.** It can be helpful to characterize the degree to which the story world is established as *realistic* or *unrealistic,* but remember that this is a formal assessment rather than a value judgment. As we will see below, the conventions of realism are well suited for certain themes and topics, while the conventions of fantasy or antirealism are well suited for other themes and topics.

Sometimes our inference about story events turns out to be incorrect, and often the ending of a short story will cause us to reevaluate what we assume has happened. Choosing to omit or delay a crucial event in a story is one way that writers shape a narrative. We call the result of this shaping process a fiction's **plot.** That is, the story includes all of the events we are told about and infer, in chronological order; the plot includes only what we are told and the order in which we are told it. Comparing the plot of a text with what we can reconstruct of its story reveals its **structure**—the way it has been put together to create the illusion of a chain of story events in our minds as we read.

This is how the plot of "A Gentleman's C" orders the story events we presented above, beginning with the central element of the plot:

2. The narrator's father receives a C in the narrator's English class.
1. The narrator describes the events of his childhood with the suggestion that one event led to the next.
3. The father is facing his last semester.
4. The father dies when he learns he will not graduate.
5. The story describes the effect of the father's death on the narrator.

The plot tells most of the story in chronological sequence, but it interrupts this order to provide background information from the past. This is a common pattern in fiction; however, story events can be combined in any conceivable manner. Historical novels, for example, will often jump back and forth in time, putting dates at the head of each chapter to keep the reader from becoming disoriented.

When reading a narrative, pay close attention to how it establishes **temporal relations** between events.

• Are events recounted in chronological order?
• How much time passes between specific plot events?
• How clear is the temporal relation between each event recounted?

When the temporal relation between events is marked precisely, as in a historical novel, we tend to pay close attention to the plot and the sequence in which the events occur. When the temporal relation is less clear, we tend to focus more on character, setting, and other thematic aspects. The extreme brevity of "A Gentleman's C" does not provide the space to establish strongly the temporal relation between events. We neither know how much time passed between the "C" and the final semester, nor do we know if the final sentence refers to the period immediately following the father's death or to some later point. In contrast, the relation between the events in the second paragraph is extremely precise, because it is crucial for the meaning of the narrative that we know that the funeral and the heart attack occurred simultaneously.

Character   Every narrative includes at least one **character,** or actor, in its events; "A Gentleman's C" includes four: the narrator, the narrator's father and mother, and the relative who dies. We are provided no information about the latter two characters beyond the mere fact of

their existence. These two characters fulfill necessary plot functions: the funeral motivates the father's solitary death; the mother's existence establishes that the father is married rather than divorced or a widower. We call such figures **minor characters,** and while they are not always as underdeveloped as this pair, minor characters do usually fade in comparison to the **principal characters.** At the same time, however, they provide important information; here, for example, you can argue that the lack of attention they receive reveals to us how much the narrator's attention is fixed on the father. Minor characters often provide contrast that helps to define the principal characters, but often, as here, the contrast is implied by the way they are described rather than explicitly stated.

Short stories tend to develop character through action rather than description. This requires the reader to piece together the details, often with incomplete information, and "A Gentleman's C" is a good example of this tendency. We are provided almost no information about the narrator or the father either except for the specific circumstances of the "C," its origins, and its consequences. We are left to infer the father's character and motivation from what we are told. Sixty-two is an odd age to return to school. The likeliest possibility is that the father has taken early retirement, but there are other plausible explanations as well. That he is a "C" student is also a significant feature of this character, as is the fact that he has a heart attack when discovering he will not be able to graduate, but we do not have enough information to know what these facts mean, just as we do not know why he was hard on the young narrator.

When you are thinking critically about character, remember that meaning in literature is made less through what is said directly than what is done and what is said between the lines. When characters speak and act, note the context:

with whom are they speaking and with what possible motivations are they acting? If we view a character in a single context only, we must be especially conscious of how that context influences the presentation of that character—this is the case of the father in "A Gentleman's C." If we are provided multiple contexts—as in Flannery O'Connor's story "A Good Man Is Hard to Find" (p. 250)—or the objective presentation of an omniscient narrator—as in Kate Chopin's "The Story of the Hour" (p. 442)—we will have a stronger basis for a comparative assessment of the character.

Narration It is often the case that the character we are told the most about is not the main character, especially when a fiction is recounted by a **first-person narrator,** usually identified by the use of the pronoun *I.* By the end of "A Gentleman's C.," we in fact have learned far more about the narrator than we have about the father, even though he is the title character. This is not only because of the childhood memory in the first paragraph and the concession of the final sentence, but because every choice made in crafting this story has been made in terms of the person who is narrating it. If we reflect carefully on what is happening in the second paragraph, we realize that there is no way for the narrator to know what caused the father's heart attack, or to be able to reconstruct the death scene with the precision it is recounted in the short story. There is, for that matter, no objective reason for the narrator to feel that the father's "C" was the ultimate cause of his failure to graduate—there must have been plenty of other low grades as well that had nothing to do with him.

Because we have no perspective on the story events beyond what the narrator presents us, we cannot be certain what motivated his assumption of responsibility for his father's fate. What we can be certain of is what the plot does show: the

narrator has created a causal chain of events in his mind ("C"—failure to graduate—heart attack) that has no demonstrable basis in fact. From the basis of this argument, a textual analysis could then posit an interpretation about the narrator's motivation in creating this chain of events: guilt would be the most likely explanation, but others could be argued as well.

When a first-person narrator is also a primary character in the plot, the presentation of events will usually be affected by the narrator's subjectivity, or personality and motivations. Sometimes, as in Orhan Pamuk's "To Look Out the Window," the first-person narrator will be fairly objective; at other times, as in "A Gentleman's C," the first-person narrator will present personal conclusions as if they were facts. At other times, we find a **partially unreliable narrator,** one whose reliability we are never certain about, as in Charlotte Perkins Gilman's "The Yellow Wallpaper" (p. 541). We may also encounter a **wholly unreliable narrator,** as in Chuck Palahniuk's novel *Fight Club* (and the movie adapted from it), in which the relationship between the narrator and another major character turns out to be completely different than we had been led to believe. Faced with a first-person narrator who is a primary character, our first task will be to decide how much we should trust that character's version of events. We may also have to revise our initial assessment of a character after learning more about him or her later in the story, as in Ursula Le Guin's "The Wife's Story" (p. 29).

Fiction can also be narrated by a minor character that functions more as an observer than as a participant in the plot events; F. Scott Fitzgerald's novel *The Great Gatsby* is a famous example. Imagine, for example, how the relationship between the narrator and the father in "A Gentleman's C" might appear differently if the mother were narrating. Most of the time, the more a narrator participates in the plot, the more subjective the

narrator's point of view will be. Remember, however, that some fiction will play against our expectations: the narrator who portrays himself as a minor actor in a crime may turn out to be the perpetrator; the narrator who appears to be providing a wildly paranoid account of events may turn out to have been justified after all, like the child nobody believes until it is almost too late.

Every first-person narration implicitly addresses the reader; in **second-person narration,** the reader is addressed directly as "you." Because it is difficult to sustain the illusion of the story world when the narrator is directly addressing the reader in this way, such writing tends to be categorized as *self-conscious fiction.* In Margaret Atwood's "Happy Endings" (p. 116), for example, the narrator addresses the reader directly, making no effort to persuade us of the reality of the story world, for she is more concerned with how we tell stories and the ways in which story conventions affect our own lives than with persuading us to accept literary characters as real. By contrast, "The Chrysanthemums" (p. 375), a classic example of literary realism by the American writer John Steinbeck, treats the story world and the characters in it as if they actually existed in order to recount the complex personal history of a pair of middle-aged ladies. Gabriel García Márquez's story "The Handsomest Drowned Man in the World" falls in between these extremes, self-consciously presenting the conventions of storytelling but from within the broadly realistic framework of a third-person narrator.

Range and Depth of Narration
"The Chrysanthemums," like many fictions that stress the objective reality of their story world, is recounted by a **third-person narrator** from an **omniscient,** or all-knowing, point of view. Rather than a character in the story world, an omniscient narrator stands outside of it and is able to observe the actions and motivations

of every character within it. There are many degrees of omniscience available to the writer, and we can categorize them in terms of the **range of narration.** Many third-person narrators can be qualified as possessing *limited,* or *selective omniscience:* they may know a lot about some or all of the characters, but not everything, or they may limit their observations to only a single character, setting, or time. When analyzing a third-person narrative, it is important both to determine the range of omniscience attributed to the narrator and to define precisely the limits to the narrator's omniscience.

Point of view can also be characterized in terms of **depth of narration**—the degree to which the narration enters into the minds and motivations of its characters. Does it observe only the surface of events and characters' actions, as in Edgar Allan Poe's tale of horror, "The Cask of Amontillado" (p. 532), or does it delve more deeply into motivations and psychology, as in "The Chrysanthemums"? Depth of narration is distinct from range of narration. An omniscient narrator may primarily observe the story world or may comment at length upon its mechanisms and motivations. A selectively omniscient third-person narrator or first-person narrator may portray the world objectively or may be subject to the perceptions of a particular character. **Indirect free discourse** refers to a third-person narration that reproduces the inner thoughts and perceptions of a character or character primarily as narration rather than through dialogue, as in Sarah Orne Jewett's "The White Heron" (p. 641). When rendered in the first person, these inner thoughts and perceptions are known as **internal monologue,** as in Dorothy Parker's short story, "The Waltz" (p. 372), or, when closer to a representation of unformed thought processes, **stream-of-consciousness.**

Temporal Relations between the Narrator and Plot Events   In addition to range and depth, narration also includes the *temporal relation* of the narrator to the events being narrated. The most common temporal relation is *retrospective:* the narrator recounts events that occurred in the past. Looking back, the narrator presents his or her version of what happened. This is the situation in "A Gentleman's C"—every sentence records a past event or emotion in terms of the narrator's understanding of its significance. The other temporal relation we are likely to encounter is *simultaneous:* the narrator recounts events as they occur in the present—this is the situation in "The Yellow Wallpaper." Simultaneous temporal relations generally have the effect of increasing our sense of participation in the events as they unfold, and in decreasing our sense of the narrator's influence on their meaning.

Setting   The events of a story can take place anywhere—from the confinement of a single room to the streets of a metropolis to the expanse of outer space—and at any time from the present to the distant past to the future. **Setting** refers to the *when* and *where* of a story; basically, it includes whatever information does not fall under the purview of plot and character. Often given prominence in longer fiction where—as the nineteenth-century French novelist Honoré de Balzac maintained—the careful description of a room could tell you everything you needed to know about the character who inhabited it, setting is used more sparingly in the short story. Regardless of how sparingly it is used, however, setting provides essential context, atmosphere, and figurative meaning to any work of fiction.

Let's turn once again to "A Gentleman's C." Setting is filled in very broadly—the college classroom where father and narrator meet, the distant location of the funeral—with one exceptional detail: the "dowdy sofa inside the front door" on which the father is leaning as he suffers his fatal heart attack. What motivates this detail is a matter for interpretation; your initial analysis would single out its peculiarity in terms of the pattern established during the rest of the text (lack of precise setting). The singular appearance of this detail in the plot suggests a figurative meaning, associating the "dowdiness" of the sofa with some aspect of the father's character.

In other short stories you will find equally sparse settings; in others, you will find that setting plays a prominent role. In Toni Cade Bambara's "The Lesson" (p. 624), a famous New York toy shop provides crucial context for the characters' actions; T. C. Boyle considered the primary setting of "Greasy Lake" (p. 646) so important that he used its name for the story's title; the plot events of Julia Alvarez's "Snow" (p. 184) would be incomprehensible without the historical backdrop of the Cuban Missile Crisis. Whether setting takes center stage or appears only as carefully selected detail, you should never neglect it when constructing an argument about the meaning of a text.

Genre Conventions   The conventions of literary genres are a further raw material in any fiction. When "A Gentleman's C" begins with the words "My father" it immediately raises a set of expectations in the reader about the story that is to follow. When the advanced age of the father is introduced, the specter of death hovers over the story as well. And "A Gentleman's C" does indeed meet these expectations, although in its own way. We expect plots from first-person narrators to be different than those from third-person narrators, and different plots depending on the setting as well as the gender, age, race, and social class of the primary characters.

Genre expectations are an efficient and unobtrusive means of involving the reader immediately in the events of the fiction without the need for excessive exposition or introductory explanations. In contrast, look at the way in which the introductory sentence of Gabriel García Márquez's short story "The Very Old Man with Enormous Wings" (p. 674) raises expectations wholly at odds with the conventions of realism: "On the third day of rain they had killed so many crabs inside the house that Pelayo had to cross his drenched courtyard and throw them into the sea, because the newborn child had a temperature all night and they thought it was due to the stench." Going against convention, this sentence warns us to expect to be surprised, and the progress of the plot reinforces this first impression.

In addition to general conventions governing specific characters and situations, you should also be mindful of the more narrowly defined genres discussed above. A short story beginning with the description of a lone cowboy riding in the high plains will likely develop in one of the handful of directions governed by the western. But fictions can also raise expectations so as to confuse them—as occurs in Kazuo Ishiguro's short story, "A Family Supper" (p. 613)—or they can use genre expectations to fill in details around the story world they are describing. Whether general or specific, be attentive to the way a fictional text uses the raw material of genre conventions to guide and focus your responses.

The Tools of Fiction

Decisions about what materials to use and how to use them constitute the primary tool for writing a work of fiction: they provide the structure, the actors, the spatial context, and the social context. These are all decisions that can be made in the planning stages of a work of fiction; however, there are other tools that come into play during the actual process of writing. In order to craft a work of fiction, writers must use the tools of language to bring to life the images and ideas imagined in their head. To study the results of that transformation is the stuff of literary analysis.

Diction   As discussed above, **diction** is a matter of word choice and word order. Look again at the first sentence of "A Gentleman's C": "My father, trying finally to graduate from college at sixty-two, came, by curious circumstance, to be enrolled in an English class I taught, and I was, perhaps, a bit tougher on him than I was on the others." Like the placement of words in a line of poetry, the order of words in a sentence guides our attention. The opening words ("My father") are always the primary focus, while participial phrases ("trying finally to graduate from college at sixty-two"), prepositional phrases ("by curious circumstances"), and examples of *apposition,* or the addition of parallel terms separated by commas, channel our mind in various directions as we make our way through the sentence. Parallel constructions—notice how "by curious circumstances" in the first independent clause is mirrored by "perhaps" in the second independent clause—develop rhythmic patterns and associations.

Word choice is an equally significant tool for making meaning out of the raw materials of narrative. We commented above on the narrative function of the "dowdy sofa"; it is the choice of the adjective "dowdy" in a text extremely short on adjectives that makes the setting of the sofa stand out. Word choice creates patterns and associations just as word order does. Patterns and associations are formed both by the usual choices a text makes (lack of adjectives) and by the exceptions to those norms ("dowdy"). Once you notice the first exception to a pattern, start looking for parallel occurrences. Looking back, we can see that another noteworthy use of adjectives occurs in the phrase "hard, honest, low C," a phrase that echoes in the repetition of "low" in the third paragraph. So, the two moments the narrator judged worth elaborating through adjectives also turn out to be the two moments of the story in which the "C" plays a key role.

Imagery and Literary Devices

The patterns formed by diction provide the thematic backbone of a work of fiction, but that backbone is usually fleshed out by the use of **imagery** and **literary devices,** or **figures of speech.** Patterns of diction tend to focus our attention on the relation between characters and

---

WRITING EXERCISE: What's Your Point of View?

Retell the events of "A Gentleman's C" from one of the following points of view:

  • The father
  • The mother

• A student in the same class as the father who knows the events of the stories from hearsay only
• A third-person omniscient narrator
• A police detective who discovered the body when called to the father's house by a suspicious neighbor

events; imagery and literary devices establish **figurative meanings** that help us to interpret those characters and events. Figurative meanings are most commonly attributed to aspects of setting, especially objects, but they may also be attributed to particular characters and events. Whenever we can establish that some aspect of a fiction takes on significance in addition to its literal meaning, we say that it has a figurative meaning. The "C" in "A Gentleman's C" clearly means far more to the narrator than a letter on a page or even a grade for a class; it somehow encapsulates the meaning of the relationship with the father. Moreover, it imparts a particular quality to that relationship, a quality that changes through the telling of the story. It begins as the narrator had long conceived the relationship— "hard, honest, low"—but it ends with a less quantifiable sense of guilt presented to the reader in an image: the father dead on the sofa with the grade clutched in his hand. The fact that this image may exist only in the imagination of the narrator only makes it a more significant clue to his state of mind.

We use the term *imagery* to refer to any element of setting or character that takes on a figurative significance. Such imagery is usually signaled in a text through its diction, as in the adjectives in "A Gentleman's C," or through its apparent redundancy in terms of the plot information it supplies. Much of literary imagery is based in the patterned use of diction; the most common of these patterns and repetitions were described and categorized by the ancient Greeks and Romans as *rhetorical figures,* or literary devices. You will find a guide to the most important of these figures and a collection of examples in Chapter 6.

Figurative meaning is often referred to as **symbolism,** but this term can be confusing. A symbol is one type of literary device: an image whose meaning has become fixed by convention, such as the flag discussed in Chapter 2, a bald eagle, or a rose. When a symbol becomes so fixed in meaning that that it ceases to function figuratively and has only a literal meaning, writers call it a **cliché** and tend to avoid using it, preferring figures whose meaning they have more control over. Like the "Gentleman's C," the titular objects in John Steinbeck's "The Chrysanthemums" or Sarah Orne Jewett's "The White Heron" are emphasized to such a degree in the story that they take on as much significance as any of the characters. Nevertheless, it would be incorrect to call them symbols, because their meaning is wholly created and explained within the context of the plot rather than in reference to a previously existing definition. The meaning of imagery is primarily determined within the text through patterns of diction and narration. Raw materials will sometimes be used for their symbolic meaning— the early 1960s setting of the Cuban Missile Crisis in "Snow" is one such example—and your analysis of the text should incorporate the sense of that symbolism into the other textual patterns.

Style By **style,** we refer to the way a text brings its patterns and associations together into a cohesive whole. The lack of adjectives, of descriptive phrases, and of range and depth of narration characterizes "A Gentleman's C" as being written in an *objective style.* The choice of style can powerfully affect our understanding of character and events. Imagine, for example, if the narrator recounting the events of "A Gentleman's C" were hysterically wracked with grief over the father's death, rather than being tightly controlled in manner. Style is not identical with theme or argument, however; the breaks in stylistic patterns may suggest the opposite of what appears on the surface. To analyze style, use the tools of critical thinking:

1. Characterize the general style of a text or portion of text.

a. Does a text have a consistent style throughout—what is often referred to as a *voice*—or does the style vary?

b. Can you discover any likely motivation for variations in style?

c. Using analytical words such as "objective" or "subjective," list the patterns and characteristics of each style. Avoid evaluative words such as "brilliant," "flowery," and "boring," which can have a different meaning for each reader.

2. Look for breaks in the style you have identified, and try to identify possible thematic patterns established by these breaks.

There are many stylistic conventions in literature, and the style of many works of fiction may be wholly or partially influenced by these conventions. Particular narrative points of view are commonly associated with particular styles of writing. Objective forms of narration tend to employ a flat, rational style, as in Eudora Welty's "A Worn Path," while more subjective forms tend to employ a wider range of adjectives, imagery, and literary devices to reflect the greater subjectivity of the narrator as in T. C. Boyle's "Greasy Lake." But, again, other texts play with our expectations of style to surprise or momentarily to confuse us. Specific literary genres also have specific stylistic conventions just as they have conventions of plot, character, and point of view, and these conventions can create certain expectations that will be met, confounded, or confused.

The tools of fiction, like the raw materials crafted by them, can be used to recall the meanings conventionally associated with them, or to derive meaning from the ways they diverge from those conventions. The majority of fictions, like the majority of literary texts, employ a mix of both strategies. They use what is familiar to settle us into a particular story world, and they use what is unfamiliar or surprising to create the set of meanings unique to that world.

WHAT IS A PLAY?

Theater terminology is part of our everyday vocabulary. When a person behaves in an exaggerated and over-emotional manner, we say he or she is being *theatrical* or is acting like a *drama queen;* we may even accuse that person of *overacting.* We speak of *playing a role* or *performing* a duty, of *acting* appropriately or inappropriately, and of being *on stage.* We watch the *drama* of a news event *unfold* on the television, we refer to the *tragedy* of a war or a natural disaster, and we call a hopelessly muddled situation a *farce.* We often describe the world as if we are spectators in a theater, and we respond to its events as we would to a play, evaluating the tone and quality of the performances and measuring the degree to which its events live up to our expectations.

The conventions of drama may inform the world we inhabit, but when we read an individual play on the page we tend to forget that it was written to be performed, its lines of dialogue interpreted by actors, its events staged on a carefully constructed set for a live audience. This does not mean that plays should not be read, but it does mean that when reading a play we should always bear in mind the dramatic components that will be added to it when it is staged and the fact that unlike other literary forms—for example, poems, songs, and screenplays—the text, or **script,** of a play never constitutes the definitive version. Not only do set design, props, costume, and interpretation of the individual lines differ from one production to the next, but every individual performance differs from every other.

As a point of reference for learning about the elements and different types of drama, we begin by focusing on a short play by the American playwright Susan Glaspell (1882–1948). *Trifles* was first performed in 1916 by the Provincetown Players, a theatrical company founded by a group that included the play's author and her husband, the novelist George Cram Cook. Born in Iowa and educated at Drake University in Des Moines, Glaspell filled her play with both the atmosphere and dialect of the Midwest and the rising feminism of the Northeast. As you read the play, ask yourself why the author chose to cast these events in the form of a play rather than as a novel or short story (both of which she also wrote). Try to imagine each scene in your mind, and consider the different choices you would have to make if you were going to direct a performance of it on the stage.

> *All the world's a stage*
> *And all the men and women*
> *merely players.*
>
> —WILLIAM SHAKESPEARE,
> *AS YOU LIKE IT*

SUSAN GLASPELL

TRIFLES

SCENE: *The kitchen in the now abandoned farmhouse of John Wright, a gloomy kitchen, and left without having been put in order—unwashed pans under the sink, a loaf of bread outside the breadbox, a dish towel on the table—other signs of incompleted work. At the rear the outer door opens, and the Sheriff comes in, followed by the County Attorney and Hale. The Sheriff and Hale are men in middle life, the County Attorney is a young man; all are much bundled up and go at once to the stove. They are followed by* the two women—the Sheriff's Wife first; she is a slight wiry woman, a thin nervous face. Mrs. Hale is larger and would ordinarily be called more comfortable looking, but she is disturbed now and looks fearfully about as she enters. The women have come in slowly, and stand close together near the door.

County Attorney (*rubbing his hands*): This feels good. Come up to the fire, ladies.

Mrs. Peters (*after taking a step forward*): I'm not—cold.

Sheriff (*unbuttoning his overcoat and stepping away from the stove as if to the beginning of official business*): Now, Mr. Hale, before we move things about, you explain to Mr. Henderson just what you saw when you came here yesterday morning.

County Attorney: By the way, has anything been moved? Are things just as you left them yesterday?

Sheriff (*looking about*): It's just the same. When it dropped below zero last night, I thought I'd better send Frank out this morning to make a fire for us—no use getting pneumonia with a big case on, but I told him not to touch anything except the stove—and you know Frank.

County Attorney: Somebody should have been left here yesterday.

Sheriff: Oh—yesterday. When I had to send Frank to Morris Center for that man who went crazy—I want you to know I had my hands full yesterday. I knew you could get back from Omaha by today, and as long as I went over everything here myself—

County Attorney: Well, Mr. Hale, tell just what happened when you came here yesterday morning.

Hale: Harry and I had started to town with a load of potatoes. We came along the road from my place; and as I got here, I said, "I'm going to see if I can't get John Wright to go in with me on a party telephone." I spoke to Wright about it once before, and he put me off, saying folks talked too much anyway, and all he asked was peace and quiet—I guess you know about how much he talked himself; but I thought maybe if I went to the house and talked about it before his wife, though I said to Harry that I didn't know as what his wife wanted made much difference to John—

County Attorney: Let's talk about that later, Mr. Hale. I do want to talk about that, but tell now just what happened when you got to the house.

Hale: I didn't hear or see anything; I knocked at the door, and still it was all quiet inside. I knew they must be up, it was past eight o'clock. So I knocked again, and I thought I heard somebody say, "Come in." I wasn't sure, I'm not sure yet, but I opened the door—this door (*indicating the door by which the two women are still standing*) and there in that rocker—(*pointing to it*) sat Mrs. Wright. (*They all look at the rocker.*)

County Attorney: What—was she doing?

Hale: She was rockin' back and forth. She had her apron in her hand and was kind of—pleating it.

County Attorney: And how did she—look?

Hale: Well, she looked queer.

County Attorney: How do you mean—queer?

Hale: Well, as if she didn't know what she was going to do next. And kind of done up.

County Attorney: How did she seem to feel about your coming?

Hale: Why, I don't think she minded—one way or other. She didn't pay much attention. I said, "How do, Mrs. Wright, it's cold, ain't it?" And she said, "Is it?"—and went on kind of pleating at her apron. Well, I was surprised; she didn't ask me to come up to the stove, or to set down, but just sat there, not even looking at me, so I said, "I want to see John." And then she—laughed. I guess you would call it a laugh. I thought of Harry and the team outside, so I said a little sharp: "Can't I see John?" "No," she says, kind o' dull like. "Ain't he home?" says I. "Yes," says she, "he's home." "Then why can't I see him?" I asked her, out of patience. "'Cause he's dead," says she. "*Dead?*" says I. She just nodded her head, not getting a bit excited, but rockin' back and forth. "Why—where is he?" says I, not knowing what to say. She just pointed upstairs—like that (*himself pointing to the room above*). I got up, with the idea of going up there. I talked from there to here—then I says, "Why, what did he die of?" "He died of a rope around his neck," says she, and just went on pleatin' at her apron. Well, I went out and called Harry. I thought I might—need help. We went upstairs, and there he was lyin'—

County Attorney: I think I'd rather have you go into that upstairs, where you can point it all out. Just go on now with the rest of the story.

Hale: Well, my first thought was to get that rope off. I looked . . . (*Stops, his face twitches.*) . . . but Harry, he went up to him, and he said, "No, he's dead all right, and we'd better not touch anything." So we went back downstairs. She was still sitting that same way. "Has anybody been notified?" I asked. "No," says she, unconcerned. "Who did this, Mrs. Wright?" said Harry. He said it businesslike—and she stopped pleatin' of her apron. "I don't know," she says. "You don't know?" says Harry. "No," says she. "Weren't you sleepin' in the bed with him?" says Harry. "Yes," says she, "but I was on the inside." "Somebody slipped a rope round his neck and strangled him, and you didn't wake up?" says Harry. "I didn't wake up," she said after him. We must 'a looked as if we didn't see how that could be, for after a minute she said, "I sleep sound." Harry was going to ask her more questions, but I said maybe we ought to let her tell her story first to the coroner, or the sheriff, so Harry went fast as he could to Rivers' place, where there's a telephone.

County Attorney: And what did Mrs. Wright do when she knew that you had gone for the coroner?

Hale: She moved from that chair to this over here (*Pointing to a small chair in the corner*) and just sat there with her hands held together and looking down. I got a feeling that I ought to make some conversation, so I said I had come in to see if John wanted to put in a telephone, and at that she started to laugh, and then she stopped and looked at me—scared. (*The County Attorney, who has had his notebook out, makes a note.*) I dunno, maybe it wasn't scared. I wouldn't like to say it was. Soon Harry got back, and then Dr. Lloyd came, and you, Mr. Peters, and so I guess that's all I know that you don't.

County Attorney (*looking around*): I guess we'll go upstairs first—and then out to the barn and around there. (*To the Sheriff.*) You're convinced that there was nothing important here—nothing that would point to any motive?

Sheriff: Nothing here but kitchen things.

(*The County Attorney, after again looking around the kitchen, opens the door of a cupboard closet. He gets up on a chair and looks on a shelf. Pulls his hand away, sticky.*)

County Attorney: Here's a nice mess.

(*The women draw nearer.*)

Mrs. Peters (*to the other woman*): Oh, her fruit; it did freeze. (*To the Lawyer.*) She worried about that when it turned so cold. She said the fire'd go out and her jars would break.

Sheriff: Well, can you beat the women! Held for murder and worryin' about her preserves.

County Attorney: I guess before we're through she may have something more serious than preserves to worry about.

Hale: Well, women are used to worrying over trifles.

(*The two women move a little closer together.*)

County Attorney (*with the gallantry of a young politician*): And yet, for all their worries, what would we do without the ladies? (*The women do not unbend. He goes to the sink, takes a dipperful of water from the pail and, pouring it into a basin, washes his hands. Starts to wipe them on the roller towel, turns it for a cleaner place.*) Dirty towels! (*Kicks his foot against the pans under the sink.*) Not much of a housekeeper, would you say, ladies?

Mrs. Hale (*stiffly*): There's a great deal of work to be done on a farm.

County Attorney: To be sure. And yet (*With a little bow to her.*) I know there are some Dickson county farmhouses which do not have such roller towels. (*He gives it a pull to expose its full length again.*)

Mrs. Hale: Those towels get dirty awful quick. Men's hands aren't always as clean as they might be.

County Attorney: Ah, loyal to your sex, I see. But you and Mrs. Wright were neighbors. I suppose you were friends, too.

Mrs. Hale (*shaking her head*): I've not seen much of her of late years. I've not been in this house—it's more than a year.

County Attorney: And why was that? You didn't like her?

Mrs. Hale: I liked her all well enough. Farmers' wives have their hands full, Mr. Henderson. And then—

County Attorney: Yes—?

Mrs. Hale (*looking about*): It never seemed a very cheerful place.

County Attorney: No—it's not cheerful. I shouldn't say she had the homemaking instinct.

Mrs. Hale: Well, I don't know as Wright had, either.

County Attorney: You mean that they didn't get on very well?

Mrs. Hale: No, I don't mean anything. But I don't think a place'd be any cheerfuller for John Wright's being in it.

County Attorney: I'd like to talk more of that a little later. I want to get the lay of things upstairs now. (*He goes to the left, where three steps lead to a stair door.*)

Sheriff: I suppose anything Mrs. Peters does'll be all right. She was to take in some clothes for her, you know, and a few little things. We left in such a hurry yesterday.

County Attorney: Yes, but I would like to see what you take, Mrs. Peters, and keep an eye out for anything that might be of use to us.

Mrs. Peters: Yes, Mr. Henderson.

(*The women listen to the men's steps on the stairs, then look about the kitchen.*)

Mrs. Hale: I'd hate to have men coming into my kitchen, snooping around and criticizing. (*She arranges the pans under sink which the Lawyer had shoved out of place.*)

Mrs. Peters: Of course it's no more than their duty.

Mrs. Hale: Duty's all right, but I guess that deputy sheriff that came out to make the fire might have got a little of this on. (*Gives the roller towel a pull.*) Wish

I'd thought of that sooner. Seems mean to talk about her for not having things slicked up when she had to come away in such a hurry.

Mrs. Peters (*who has gone to a small table in the left rear corner of the room, and lifted one end of a towel that covers a pan*): She had bread set. (*Stands still.*)

Mrs. Hale (*eyes fixed on a loaf of bread beside the breadbox, which is on a low shelf at the other side of the room. Moves slowly toward it*): She was going to put this in there. (*Picks up loaf, then abruptly drops it. In a manner of returning to familiar things.*) It's a shame about her fruit. I wonder if it's all gone. (*Gets up on the chair and looks.*) I think there's some here that's all right, Mrs. Peters. Yes—here; (*Holding it toward the window.*) This is cherries, too. (*Looking again.*) I declare I believe that's the only one. (*Gets down, bottle in her hand. Goes to the sink and wipes it off on the outside.*) She'll feel awful bad after all her hard work in the hot weather. I remember the afternoon I put up my cherries last summer.

(*She puts the bottle on the big kitchen table, center of the room, front table. With a sigh, is about to sit down in the rocking chair. Before she is seated realizes what chair it is; with a slow look at it, steps back. The chair, which she has touched, rocks back and forth.*)

Mrs. Peters: Well, I must get those things from the front room closet. (*She goes to the door at the right, but after looking into the other room, steps back.*) You coming with me, Mrs. Hale? You could help me carry them.

(*They go into the other room; reappear, Mrs. Peters carrying a dress and skirt, Mrs. Hale following with a pair of shoes.*)

Mrs. Peters: My, it's cold in there. (*She puts the cloth on the big table, and hurries to the stove.*)

Mrs Hale (*examining the skirt*): Wright was close. I think maybe that's why she kept so much to herself. She didn't even belong to the Ladies' Aid. I suppose she felt she couldn't do her part, and then you don't enjoy things when you feel shabby. She used to wear pretty clothes and be lively, when she was Minnie Foster, one of the town girls singing in the choir. But that—oh, that was thirty years ago. This all you was to take in?

Mrs. Peters: She said she wanted an apron. Funny thing to want, for there isn't much to get you dirty in jail, goodness knows. But I suppose just to make her feel more natural. She said they was in the top drawer in this cupboard. Yes, here. And then her little shawl that always hung behind the door. (*Opens stair door and looks.*) Yes, here it is. (*Quickly shuts door leading upstairs.*)

Mrs. Hale (*abruptly moving toward her*): Mrs. Peters?

Mrs. Peters: Yes, Mrs. Hale?

Mrs. Hale: Do you think she did it?

Mrs. Peters (*in a frightened voice*): Oh, I don't know.

Mrs. Hale: Well, I don't think she did. Asking for an apron and her little shawl. Worrying about her fruit.

Mrs. Peters (*starts to speak, glances up, where footsteps are heard in the room above. In a low voice.*): Mr. Peters says it looks bad for her. Mr. Henderson is awful sarcastic in speech, and he'll make fun of her sayin' she didn't wake up.

Mrs. Hale: Well, I guess John Wright didn't wake when they was slipping that rope under his neck.

Mrs. Peters: No, it's strange. It must have been done awful crafty and still. They say it was such a—funny way to kill a man, rigging it all up like that.

Mrs. Hale: That's just what Mr. Hale said. There was a gun in the house. He says that's what he can't understand.

Mrs. Peters: Mr. Henderson said coming out that what was needed for the case was a motive; something to show anger or—sudden feeling.

Mrs. Hale (*who is standing by the table*): Well, I don't see any signs of anger around here. (*She puts her hand on the dish towel which lies on the table, stands looking down at the table, one half of which is clean, the other half messy.*) It's wiped here. (*Makes a move as if to finish work, then turns and looks at loaf of bread outside the breadbox. Drops towel. In that voice of coming back to familiar things.*) Wonder how they are finding things upstairs? I hope she had it a little more red-up° up there. You know, it seems kind of sneaking. Locking her up in town and then coming out here and trying to get her own house to turn against her!

Mrs. Peters: But, Mrs. Hale, the law is the law.

Mrs. Hale: I s'pose 'tis. (*Unbuttoning her coat.*) Better loosen up your things, Mrs. Peters. You won't feel them when you go out.

(*Mrs. Peters takes off her fur tippet, goes to hang it on hook at back of room, stands looking at the under part of the small corner table.*)

Mrs. Peters: She was piecing a quilt. (*She brings the large sewing basket, and they look at the bright pieces.*)

Mrs. Hale: It's a log cabin pattern. Pretty, isn't it? I wonder if she was goin' to quilt or just knot it?

red-up: readied up, ready to be seen

(*Footsteps have been heard coming down the stairs. The Sheriff enters, followed by Hale and the County Attorney.*)

Sheriff: They wonder if she was going to quilt it or just knot it. (*The men laugh, the women look abashed.*)

County Attorney (*rubbing his hands over the stove*): Frank's fire didn't do much up there, did it? Well, let's go out to the barn and get that cleared up.

(*The men go outside.*)

Mrs. Hale (*resentfully*): I don't know as there's anything so strange, our takin' up our time with little things while we're waiting for them to get the evidence. (*She sits down at the big table, smoothing out a block with decision.*) I don't see as it's anything to laugh about.

Mrs. Peters (*apologetically*): Of course they've got awful important things on their minds.

(*Pulls up a chair and joins Mrs. Hale at the table.*)

Mrs. Hale (*examining another block*): Mrs. Peters, look at this one. Here, this is the one she was working on, and look at the sewing! All the rest of it has been so nice and even. And look at this! It's all over the place! Why, it looks as if she didn't know what she was about!

(*After she has said this, they look at each other, then start to glance back at the door. After an instant Mrs. Hale has pulled at a knot and ripped the sewing.*)

Mrs. Peters: Oh, what are you doing, Mrs. Hale?

Mrs. Hale (*mildly*): Just pulling out a stitch or two that's not sewed very good. (*Threading a needle.*) Bad sewing always made me fidgety.

Mrs. Peters (*nervously*): I don't think we ought to touch things.

Mrs. Hale: I'll just finish up this end. (*Suddenly stopping and leaning forward.*) Mrs. Peters?

Mrs. Peters: Yes, Mrs. Hale?

Mrs. Hale: What do you suppose she was so nervous about?

Mrs. Peters: Oh—I don't know. I don't know as she was nervous. I sometimes sew awful queer when I'm just tired. (*Mrs. Hale starts to say something looks at Mrs. Peters, then goes on sewing.*) Well, I must get these things wrapped up. They may be through sooner than we think. (*Putting apron and other things together.*) I wonder where I can find a piece of paper, and string.

Mrs. Hale: In that cupboard, maybe.

Mrs. Peter: (*looking in cupboard*): Why, here's a bird-cage. (*Holds it up.*) Did she have a bird, Mrs. Hale?

Mrs. Hale: Why, I don't know whether she did or not— I've not been here for so long. There was a man around

last year selling canaries cheap, but I don't know as she took one; maybe she did. She used to sing real pretty herself.

Mrs. Peters (*glancing around*): Seems funny to think of a bird here. But she must have had one, or why should she have a cage? I wonder what happened to it?

Mrs. Hale: I s'pose maybe the cat got it.

Mrs. Peters: No, she didn't have a cat. She's got that feeling some people have about cats—being afraid of them. My cat got in her room, and she was real upset and asked me to take it out.

Mrs. Hale: My sister Bessie was like that. Queer, ain't it?

Mrs. Peters (*examining the cage*): Why, look at this door. It's broke. One hinge is pulled apart.

Mrs. Hale (*looking, too*): Looks as if someone must have been rough with it.

Mrs. Peters: Why, yes. (*She brings the cage forward and puts it on the table.*)

Mrs. Hale: I wish if they're going to find any evidence they'd be about it. I don't like this place.

Mrs. Peters: But I'm awful glad you came with me, Mrs. Hale. It would be lonesome for me sitting here alone.

Mrs. Hale: It would, wouldn't it? (*Dropping her sewing.*) But I tell you what I do wish, Mrs. Peters. I wish I had come over sometimes when *she* was here. I—(*Looking around the room.*)—wish I had.

Mrs. Peters: But of course you were awful busy, Mrs. Hale—your house and your children.

Mrs. Hale: I could've come. I stayed away because it weren't cheerful—and that's why I ought to have come. I—I've never liked this place. Maybe because it's down in a hollow, and you don't see the road. I dunno what it is, but it's a lonesome place and always was. I wish I had come over to see Minnie Foster some-times. I can see now—(*Shakes her head.*)

Mrs. Peters: Well, you mustn't reproach yourself, Mrs. Hale. Somehow we just don't see how it is with other folks until—something comes up.

Mrs. Hale: Not having children makes less work—but it makes a quiet house, and Wright out to work all day, and no company when he did come in. Did you know John Wright, Mrs. Peters?

Mrs. Peters: Not to know him; I've seen him in town. They say he was a good man.

Mrs. Hale: Yes—good; he didn't drink, and kept his word as well as most, I guess, and paid his debts. But he was a hard man, Mrs. Peters. Just to pass the time of day with him. (*Shivers.*) Like a raw wind that gets to the bone. (*Pauses, her eye falling on the cage.*) I should think she would 'a wanted a bird. But what do you suppose went with it?

Mrs. Peters: I don't know, unless it got sick and died. (*She reaches over and swings the broken door, swings it again; both women watch it.*)

Mrs. Hale: You weren't raised round here, were you? (*Mrs. Peters shakes her head.*) You didn't know—her?

Mrs. Peters: Not till they brought her yesterday.

Mrs. Hale: She—come to think of it, she was kind of like a bird herself—real sweet and pretty, but kind of timid and—fluttery. How—she—did—change. (*Silence; then as if struck by a happy thought and relieved to get back to everyday things.*) Tell you what, Mrs. Peters, why don't you take the quilt in with you? It might take up her mind.

Mrs. Peters: Why, I think that's a real nice idea, Mrs. Hale. There couldn't possibly be any objection to it, could there? Now, just what would I take? I wonder if her patches are in here—and her things. (*They look in the sewing basket.*)

Mrs. Hale: Here's some red. I expect this has got sewing things in it. (*Brings out a fancy box.*) What a pretty box. Looks like something somebody would give you. Maybe her scissors are in here. (*Opens box. Suddenly puts her hand to her nose.*) Why— (*Mrs. Peters bends nearer, then turns her face away.*) There's something wrapped up in this piece of silk.

Mrs. Peters: Why, this isn't her scissors.

Mrs. Hale (*lifting the silk*): Oh, Mrs. Peters—it's— (*Mrs. Peters bends closer.*)

Mrs. Peters: It's the bird.

Mrs. Hale (*jumping up*): But, Mrs. Peters—look at it. Its neck! Look at its neck! It's all—other side *to*.

Mrs. Peters: Somebody—wrung—its neck.

(*Their eyes meet. A look of growing comprehension of horror. Steps are heard outside. Mrs. Hale slips box under quilt pieces, and sinks into her chair. Enter Sheriff and County Attorney. Mrs. Peters rises.*)

County Attorney (*as one turning from serious thing to little pleasantries*): Well, ladies, have you decided whether she was going to quilt it or knot it?

Mrs. Peters: We think she was going to—knot it.

County Attorney: Well, that's interesting, I'm sure. (*Seeing the birdcage.*) Has the bird flown?

Mrs. Hale (*putting more quilt pieces over the box.*): We think the—cat got it.

County Attorney (*preoccupied*): Is there a cat?

(*Mrs. Hale glances in a quick covert way at Mrs. Peters.*

Mrs. Peters: Well, not now. They're superstitious, you know. They leave.

County Attorney (*to Sheriff Peters, continuing an interrupted conversation*): No sign at all of anyone having come from the outside. Their own rope. Now let's go up again and go over it piece by piece. (*They start upstairs.*) It would have to have been someone who knew just the—

(*Mrs. Peters sits down. The two women sit there not looking at one another, but as if peering into something and at the same time holding back. When they talk now, it is the manner of feeling their way over strange ground, as if afraid of what they are saying, but as if they cannot help saying it.*)

Mrs. Hale: She liked the bird. She was going to bury it in that pretty box.

Mrs. Peters (*in a whisper*): When I was a girl—my kitten—there was a boy took a hatchet, and before my eyes—and before I could get there—(*Covers her face an instant.*) If they hadn't held me back, I would have—(*Catches herself, looks upstairs, where steps are heard, falters weakly.*)—hurt him.

Mrs. Hale (*with a slow look around her*): I wonder how it would seem never to have had any children around. (*Pause.*) No, Wright wouldn't like the bird—a thing that sang. She used to sing. He killed that, too.

Mrs. Peters (*moving uneasily*): We don't know who killed the bird.

Mrs. Hale: I knew John Wright.

Mrs. Peters: It was an awful thing was done in this house that night, Mrs. Hale. Killing a man while he slept, slipping a rope around his neck that choked the life out of him.

Mrs. Hale: His neck. Choked the life out of him.

(*Her hand goes out and rests on the birdcage.*)

Mrs. Peters (*with a rising voice*): We don't know who killed him. We don't know.

Mrs. Hale (*her own feeling not interrupted*): If there'd been years and years of nothing, then a bird to sing to you, it would be awful—still, after the bird was still.

Mrs. Peters (*something within her speaking*): I know what stillness is. When we homesteaded in Dakota, and my first baby died—after he was two years old, and me with no other then—

Mrs. Hale (*moving*): How soon do you suppose they'll be through, looking for evidence?

Mrs. Peters: I know what stillness is. (*Pulling herself back.*) The law has got to punish crime, Mrs. Hale.

Mrs. Hale (*not as if answering that*): I wish you'd seen Minnie Foster when she wore a white dress with blue ribbons and stood up there in the choir and sang. (*A look around the room.*) Oh, I wish I'd come over here once in a while! That was a crime! That was a crime! Who's going to punish that?

Mrs. Peters (*looking upstairs*): We mustn't—take on.

Mrs. Hale: I might have known she needed help!

I know how things can be—for women. I tell you, it's queer, Mrs. Peters. We live close together and we live far apart. We all go through the same things—it's all just a different kind of the same thing. (*Brushes her eyes, noticing the bottle of fruit, reaches out for it.*) If I was you, I wouldn't tell her her fruit was gone. Tell her it ain't. Tell her it's all right. Take this in to prove it to her. She—she may never know whether it was broke or not.

Mrs. Peters (*takes the bottle, looks about for something to wrap it in; takes petticoat from the clothes brought from the other room, very nervously begins winding this around the bottle. In a false voice*): My, it's a good thing the men couldn't hear us. Wouldn't they just laugh! Getting all stirred up over a little thing like a—dead canary. As if that could have anything to do with—with—wouldn't they *laugh*!

(*The men are heard coming downstairs.*)

Mrs. Hale (*under her breath*): Maybe they would—maybe they wouldn't.

County Attorney: No, Peters, it's all perfectly clear except a reason for doing it. But you know juries when it comes to women. If there was some definite thing. Something to show—something to make a story about—a thing that would connect up with this strange way of doing it.

(*The women's eyes meet for an instant. Enter Hale from outer door.*)

Hale: Well, I've got the team around. Pretty cold out there.

County Attorney: I'm going to stay here awhile by myself (*To the Sheriff.*) You can send Frank out for me, can't you? I want to go over everything. I'm not satisfied that we can't do better.

Sheriff: Do you want to see what Mrs. Peters is going to take in?

(*The Lawyer goes to the table, picks up the apron, laughs.*)

County Attorney: Oh I guess they're not very dangerous things the ladies have picked up. (*Moves a few things about, disturbing the quilt pieces which cover the box. Steps back.*) No, Mrs. Peters doesn't need supervising. For that matter, a sheriff's wife is married to the law. Ever think of it that way, Mrs. Peters?

Mrs. Peters: Not—just that way.

Sheriff (*chuckling*): Married to the law. (*Moves toward the other room.*) I just want you to come in here a minute, George. We ought to take a look at these windows.

County Attorney (*scoffingly*): Oh, windows!

Sheriff: We'll be right out, Mr. Hale.

(*Hale goes outside. The Sheriff follows the County Attorney into the other room. Then Mrs. Hale rises, hands tight together, looking intensely at Mrs. Peters, whose eyes take a slow turn, finally meeting Mrs. Hale's. A moment Mrs. Hale holds her, then her own eyes point the way to where the box is concealed. Suddenly Mrs. Peters throws back quilt pieces and tries to put the box in the bag she is wearing. It is too big. She opens box, starts to take the bird out, cannot touch it, goes to pieces, stands there helpless. Sound of a knob turning in the other room. Mrs. Hale snatches the box and puts it in the pocket of her big coat. Enter County Attorney and Sheriff.*)

County Attorney (*facetiously*): Well, Henry, at least we found out that she was not going to quilt it. She was going to—what is it you call it, ladies!

Mrs. Hale (*her hand against her pocket*): We call it—knot it, Mr. Henderson.

CURTAIN

[1916]

QUESTIONS FOR REFLECTION AND DISCUSSION

1. The author was born in the Midwest, and uses the Nebraska setting effectively here. What are some of the ways the setting enters into the structure and themes of the play?

2. The opposition between "male" and "female" is an important pattern in *Trifles*. Make a list of the aspects of this opposition, both minor details and major themes, and both within the dialogue and in terms of the staging. What patterns can you observe among these opposites? Can you find any exceptions to this opposition in the play?

3. The bird cage and canary provide a central symbol to the play. How is the symbol introduced and developed through the play, what is its relation to the play's title, and how does it help to establish Mrs. Wright's motivation?

4. Discuss the other main props in the play. How are they related to the bird cage?

5. Explain the play on words in "knot it" in the final lines. How is this wordplay introduced into the play? Why do you think the author chose it as the play's final image?

Dramatic Structure

Plays are given their dramatic structure by being divided into parts that are based on changes of setting, which are dictated by the physical necessity of changing the **set,** or stage scenery, during performances. Major changes of setting, or breaks in temporal continuity, are called **acts,** and minor changes, often determined by a change in the number of characters on the stage, are known as **scenes.** Most plays are divided into one, three, or five acts. *Trifles* is a one-act play; that is, all of the action takes place during a single stretch of time in the single setting of John Wright's farmhouse kitchen. Note, however, that the *story world,* the imagined world in which the events take place, is much broader, including not only the rest of the house and the space surrounding it, but also the houses, quite distant, of neighbors such as Mrs. Hale, and the county jail where Mrs. Wright is imprisoned. Although not explicitly divided into scenes, the action of *Trifles* is segmented into seven parts by the entrance and exits of the male characters. Notice how the division of action between the apparently active, busy men and

the apparently inactive women stationed in the kitchen duplicates a major thematic division in the play between two different ways of gathering evidence and processing knowledge.

Dramatic Arc Each play has its own **dramatic arc**—the organization of story events into a plot. The standard arc rises as the action gathers to a climax and then falls again as the play reaches its conclusion. The conclusion is often called a **dénouement,** from a French word meaning *unknotting,* suggesting that the plot is composing of multiple strands that are knotted together into a climax and then separated into tidy resolutions in the conclusion. This term accurately describes the arc of *Trifles,* which begins with the gathering tension around the two women who reluctantly conclude from assembled evidence that Mrs. Wright has murdered her husband. Persuasive arguments could be made about the precise location of the climax, but the most likely moment is the discovery of the dead canary in the box about three-quarters of the way through the play. The final three segments of the play then dramatize the two

women's responses to this discovery and their final decision to hide the damning evidence of the bird.

Development of Theme through Action The arc of a play is central to our understanding and analysis of it more so than it is in narrated fiction because action in plays is dramatized rather than narrated. Plays are composed almost entirely of *action,* which can take the form either of *gesture* or *dialogue.* This means that we see what is happening as it happens, without the intermediary of a narrative voice, and we are meant to respond to it as if we were there. Nevertheless, there are many ways in which a play can frame and influence our reaction to what we see by what it chooses to show us on the stage. A convention of Greek tragedy, as in *Antigone* (p. 465), is for the most dramatic action— murder and suicide—to occur off-stage and be described by another character after it has occurred. Instead of the event itself, we observe the characters' reaction to it.

Trifles employs a variation of this convention when Hale describes his discovery of John Wright's body. Rather than the characters' reaction to the event, however, we observe their reactions as they discover the identity of the murderer. Glaspell uses several other strategies as well to direct our attention. The primary character in the drama, Mrs. Wright, never appears onstage. Consequently, everything we know about her is dependent on what the other characters do and say. Moreover, because the two women are onstage during the entire play, we tend to give more credence to their opinions and observations than to those of the men. This tendency is exacerbated by the way they help to create sympathy toward the situation Mrs. Wright faced, although it would certainly be possible to stage the play in such a way as to lessen this effect by instilling the actions and

A production of Susan Glaspell's *Trifles* at the University of Alaska, Fairbanks, in 2004.

words of the men with warmth and playing the female characters harshly. Some audience members might argue that such a staging would be contrary to the play's feminist theme; others might regard it as an interesting test of how we respond to gesture and delivery as opposed to the substance of the words.

The Three Unities

In an influential formulation, the Greek philosopher Aristotle argued that the most effective drama was one that observed three fundamental *unities:* of *place,* of *time,* and of *action.* In other words, there should be no change in setting, no breaks in time, and no distracting subplots or unmotivated actions. For Aristotle, theater should focus intensely on a character's immediate reaction to a crisis and the direct consequences of that reaction. The story world might be infinitely large, as it is in *Antigone,* but the plot should ideally unfold in *real time,* the time it takes for the play to be performed. Although many plays do not, *Trifles* strictly observes the three unities. The setting is confined to the kitchen, there are no temporal breaks in the plot, and the action is entirely focused on the discovery of Mrs. Wright's guilt and the decision to hide the evidence of it. The convention of the three unities is generally considered to provide the most *realistic* form of dramatic structure, and its assumptions equally influence such contemporary cultural forms as reality television and day-

time talk shows where audience members are confronted with a nasty surprise ("the stepmother who made her life hell," "deadbeat dads") with which they must come to terms in the action-packed minutes before the final commercial break. The three unities provide a highly effective tool for concentrating dramatic effect into a single moment. This is true of Creon's discovery of the devastating consequences of his actions in *Antigone,* and it is equally true of the reactions of the competitors in *Survivor* or *American Idol* as they learn of their fate at the end of each episode. *Antigone* and *Trifles* certainly raise far more pressing moral and ethical concerns than reality television, but they use an identical formal tool to mold their material into a form that rivets our attention and leaves us plenty to argue about afterward.

Realism tends to raise issues in stark contrasts—the men versus the women of *Trifles;* the winners and losers of reality television. For this reason, it is a highly effective vehicle for spurring debate, either in drama or in satirical comedy. When dramatists want to stress thematic uncertainty or ambiguity, however, they tend to break the convention of the three unities, an effect you can observe in *Krapp's Last Tape* (p. 189). The tragedies of Shakespeare, for example, while no less full of action than the examples above, flagrantly disregard the three unities, ranging widely in space and time, and including myriad subplots, such as

the famous play within a play in *Hamlet.* But, then, as is evident from Hamlet's famous soliloquy "To be or not to be," Shakespeare's plays are often more concerned with conflicting emotions than with the tragic decisiveness characteristic of Minnie Foster in *Trifles* or Creon and Antigone in Sophocles' play. As a long-time convention, the three unities continue to create dramatic expectations that specific plays either meet, or bend, or confound. Always note the degree to which a play structures time, space, and action. Use this knowledge not to judge a play, but to help you identify the way in which it presents its theme, and the type of argument it is making.

The Stage on the Page

When you read a play, the script will contain various information that would not be included in a performance. Different productions will place varying stress on divisions between scenes and acts; on the page these divisions will always be marked in the same way. The program you receive at the theater will probably provide you with setting— sometimes a simple notation of place, sometimes a detailed description, as in *Trifles*—and character information, including the names of the characters, and sometimes their occupations, their social standing, and their relationship to one another; you will usually find the same information listed on the first page of a printed play. The printed script will include **stage directions:** a description by the author of each scene, with suggestions about how the set should appear and how the actors should behave. These directions will sometimes give you a hint as to the author's intentions about a particular scene, but usually not enough to sustain an argument without evidence from the actual dialogue. Since there is no narration to guide it, the *tone* of a play can vary widely from one performance to the next. The famous soliloquy from *Hamlet,* for example, has been performed thousands of times, sometimes played for laughs, sometimes for tears, sometimes emphasizing the philosophical context, sometimes emphasizing the plot, sometimes implying that Hamlet is mad, other times implying that he is a schemer, other times that he is a fool. When reading a play script, always consider the different possible ways a particular speech or set of lines might be performed.

Characters

When speaking of short stories and novels, we used the terms *range* and *depth of narration* (p. 135) to specify the amount and type of information a narrator provides us about the characters. We can use the analogous expression *range of characterization* to refer to the number of characters included, and *depth of characterization* to specify how far we enter into the mind of a particular character in a play. The *principal characters* in a play will generally be portrayed in greater depth than the *secondary characters.* In some plays, such as those of Shakespeare, an important function of the secondary characters is to help to develop the principal characters, usually by contrast—such characters are referred to as **foils.** Sometimes, secondary characters will be used as **types,** their role defined in terms of their occupation or role in the plot—for example, the Messenger in *Antigone.* At other times, a character will present a combination of individual personality and social types—for example, the characters in Greek tragedy, who wore masks picturing stylized emotions but whose experiences nevertheless feel genuine to us.

Character Analysis   The absence of an overarching narration also means that in many plays each character presents a different point of view or perspective toward the story events. When you make an argument about a play, always consider the context of the character whose lines you quote as evidence for your argument. An important tool for understanding the context and perspective of a particular character is a version of the textual analysis known as the **character analysis.** In *Trifles,* for example, the two women eventually reach a tacit agreement to protect Mrs. Wright; however, their situations and motivations are quite distinct. An analysis of Mrs. Hale, for example, would examine her memory of Minnie Foster before she was married and her reluctance to visit her once Minnie had married John Wright. It would also consider the motivation of her presence in the scene: her situation as neighbor to the Wrights, accompanying her husband, who found the body, and helping Mrs. Peters gather what Mrs. Wright might need in prison. As a farmer's wife, Mrs. Hale is attentive to details with which Mrs. Peters, the sheriff's wife, might be less familiar. There are other ways in which Mrs. Peters' character differs, and which an analysis would bring out. She is not a local, and lives in town. She has had a difficult past, as the allusion to her experience as a homesteader in the Dakotas reveals to us. And, as the County Attorney observes near the end, as a sheriff's wife, she is "married to the law." Consequently, her decision to hide evidence has a different significance for her than it does for Mrs. Hale.

Another approach to the play can be made through the analysis of the two characters we never see:

Mr. and Mrs. Wright. Indeed, the plot of the play could be defined as a character analysis of Mrs. Wright. Note the conflicting images of the husband possessed by Mrs. Hale, who knew him personally, and Mrs. Peters, who knew him only by sight and hearsay. Consider the information about John Wright we can glean through Hale's description of his disinterest in a party, or shared, telephone line. This is character analysis as detective work, piecing together a portrait from the disparate sources of the different characters. The same can be said of Mrs. Wright, although the investigation and discussion by the two women provides much more evidence for an analysis, since it is central to the plot of the play. The author also uses language and imagery to reveal additional information about the murderer: the various objects associated with her and the two different names by which she is referred.

Analyzing different characters will provide you with different types of information about a play. The analyses of Mrs. Hale and Mrs. Peters, for example, bear directly on the central theme of the play: the division between men and women. The male characters—the County Attorney, the Sheriff, and Hale—provide far less material for an analysis, but each of them does have a different perspective on the situation, although their primary role is to act as foils for the development of the female characters. The evidence provided by Hale in the opening of the play is primarily used for plot development, but it also provides quite a lot of information about the life of a Midwestern farmer in the early twentieth century. A character analysis of Hale would draw out the details about his life revealed through his dialogue—the load of potatoes, the interest in a party line, the protocol of his visit, and the way Mrs. Wright violates it. This information is of limited importance to the central argument of the play, but it would be quite useful in a research paper analyzing Glaspell's depiction of the Midwest.

Conventions of Character   In some plays, it can be helpful to identify the **protagonist**—the main character of a play—and the **antagonist,** the character who opposes the protagonist. Both terms come from the Greek root, *agon,* or struggle: *pro-* means "for" and *ant-* means "against." Like the three unities, these terms help to define dramatic conventions and are a powerful tool for structuring story events for maximum contrast. The genre in which protagonists and antagonists appear most starkly contrasted is called **melodrama,** where they are known as the *hero* (or *heroine*) and the *villain,* respectively, and where the plot describes an endless and suspenseful struggle between good and evil. In most other dramatic forms, the convention of protagonist and antagonist is used more ambiguously. *Antigone,* for example, depicts a tragic struggle between Antigone and Creon in which the latter must be considered the antagonist of the former; however, the play provides Creon just enough legitimate arguments to support his actions that the balance of sympathy between the two characters is debatable rather than clear-cut. *Trifles* tweaks the convention in another way. Here, too, sympathy and right are more fully on the side of the woman than the man, but because both characters remain offstage for the duration of the play, we are unable to evaluate them directly.

WRITING EXERCISE: A Character Analysis

Choose one of the plays included in this book, preferably the same one you wrote about in the exercise on dramatic structure (p. 1), and write a character analysis of one of the secondary characters. Once you have assembled and organized all the information you can glean about the character, use that information to answer the following questions:

1. What motivates the presence of the character in the play? (Note that this question can be answered in terms of plot as well as in terms of theme.) How would the play be altered if this character were not included?

2. What particular perspective does this character bring to the actions of the principal character(s)?

3. Are there any secondary themes or other types of information introduced by this character that are not introduced elsewhere in the play?

Staging

Staging a play refers to the different aspects the director and theatrical company must consider in translating the text of a play onto the stage: the physical space of the theater itself; the *sets, lighting, sound* and *music; props, costume and makeup;* and *character speech* and *gesture.* We can also refer to the way the play's script uses *diction, imagery,* and *style* to stage its particular themes.

The Theatrical Space   The conventional nineteenth-century theater had what is known as a **proscenium arch** (see photo at right) which divides the space of the stage from the space of the audience as if it were a fourth wall or a movie screen. Because it allows the action to be presented as if the audience were gazing into a room, the proscenium stage is well suited for a realistic play such as *Trifles.* During the twentieth century, theatrical companies experimented with a number of different spaces, from theaters in the back rooms or floors above bars that seated a handful of spectators around a flat space in the room, to theaters in the round, with the stage wholly surrounded by the audience, to outdoor theaters. Greek tragedies were performed outdoors in vast amphitheaters to huge audiences, with actors wearing stylized masks to project their characters and

The Proscenium arch in the Grand Theatre in London, Ontario, opened in 1901.

emotions. Renaissance theaters in England ranged from a curtain hung over a wagon in a traveling show to the Globe Theatre of Shakespeare's later years, the stage of which jutted forth on three sides into an audience packed in steeply graded tiers of seats and a standing-room-only "pit" around it. The Globe Theatre was recently reconstructed near its original location in order to stage performances attempting to recreate the theatrical experience of Elizabethan London, different in many ways from our own expectations. It would be pointless to restrict the performance of plays to the conditions in which they were originally produced, but we should always be aware how the layout of the theater affects our experience of a play.

Setting and Set Design   Basic instructions about *set design* are often included in the stage directions, but they usually fall well short of complete, and many productions choose to alter the instructions to suit the constraints of the theater or a particular interpretation of the play. The most common strategy is to change the period of the setting. The plays of Shakespeare and other Renaissance playwrights are often performed in contemporary setting and costume, or in a particular historical period or location. In addition to providing a fresh look to a familiar play, a change in setting can also be used to bring out an aspect of a play considered to be particularly relevant to the present day. Because the title character in Shakespeare's *Othello* is a Moor among white Europeans in Venice, many stagings have chosen to focus on the resonances in this relationship with current concerns regarding race and religion.

The design of a set can range from the bare floor of a room filled with chairs for the spectators to a full-scale reproduction suitable for filming a Hollywood movie. A set design not only has to project the director's vision of the play; it also has to provide a way for the actors to be able to enter, exit, and move about the stage. Different styles of production will call for different types of sets. A realistic set for *Trifles* would strive to reproduce as precisely as possible the kitchen of a turn-of-the-century Midwestern farmhouse as in the production shown on page 146. The set designer would most likely base the design on photographs and descriptions of the time. The set would also provide doors in the **wings,** or sides, of the stage that would allow the actors to enter and exit the stage as if entering and leaving the kitchen. Such a production would focus our attention on the realism of the play, its depiction of credible characters in a credible set of circumstances. It is also possible to imagine a different production of *Trifles* by a director who wanted to focus our attention wholly on the language and symbolism of the play. A few chairs and a table would be enough to conjure up a kitchen; the actors would simply step in and out of the imaginary room around this furniture; key *props* such as the bird cage and the quilt could either be supplied or mimed by the actors. Such a production would not be realistic, but it would allow us to grasp the language and actions of the play with minimal distraction.

Lighting, Sound, and Music

Lighting began to play a prominent role in theater when it became possible to stage plays at night. Primarily used to focus our attention on different parts of the stage, usually on the character that is speaking, lighting can also be used for more expressive purposes. Special effects were already an important aspect of nineteenth-century theater, and continue to be used in many different theatrical settings today. Lighting is often also employed to enhance the atmosphere of a setting, especially in nocturnal or fantastical scenes, such as a journey to the underworld. *Sound effects* will often accompany lighting effects, as in the flash and bang that follow the firing of a gun, or the recreation of a thunderstorm. Sound effects can also create the illusion of space offstage.

Music, whether performed live or played on tape, can be either **diegetic,** belonging to the world of the play, as when it accompanies the performance of a song by one of the characters, or **nondiegetic,** played as background for the action on stage. The different qualities of the music can have a powerful effect on

A still from the 2001 film *O,* a modern interpretation of Shakespeare's *Othello* set in the present day. Mekhi Phifer plays O, the only black player on a boarding school basketball team. A teammate plays on his jealousy of his white girlfriend (Julia Stiles), with tragic consequences.

our attitude toward what we see on the stage. In *Antigone* and other Greek tragedies, the action of the characters is broken by long speeches by the chorus that would have been sung or chanted; in modern productions they have frequently been set to music. When you come across a song being performed in the text of a play (see, for example, the Gravedigger's Song in *Hamlet* 5.1, p. 285), imagine how the performance might look and sound, and how it would affect the mood and pacing of the action.

Props and Costume   An aspect of both the language of the play and its physical staging, a **prop** can be any object that plays a role in the action. Most props, such as the bird cage and quilt of *Trifles,* are written into the text of the play, but a certain production may introduce other props or alter the identity of the ones called for in the text. An Elizabethan play set in the present day might include guns rather than swords in the costumes of its soldiers, for example. Props can be purely practical—the notebook the County Attorney uses to take notes in *Trifles*—or heavily laden with figurative meaning—the bird cage and quilt. As you read a play, make a note of any props you encounter, and imagine how they would work onstage.

The most frequently added props are elements of *costume* and *makeup.* A director or actor might choose to give the "thin, nervous face" of Mrs. Peters a pair of glasses with which she could fidget to increase the impression of her nervousness. She might stare through them intently when faced with the

evidence of murder, and she might drop them when the County Attorney mentions that she is married to the law. Elements of costume, the clothes the characters wear, are usually designed to complement the time and place of the setting. They often also serve to emphasize character: the type and style of clothes denote social class; their degree of neatness and tidiness can also signify character; obtrusive makeup can change the appearance of a face. The film director Fritz Lang, criticized for being overly obsessive about stacking the dirty dishes in a sink in the background of a kitchen scene, claimed that everything about the character in the scene could be detected by the viewers if the dishes were stacked in just the right way. Judging by the detail with which Susan Glaspell describes the state of the Wright kitchen at the start of *Trifles,* she would have agreed with Mr. Lang.

Diction, Imagery, and Style
We tend to pay less attention to the details of language when watching a play, as our eyes will dominate our ears and focus on the action rather than the words. Reading the script of a play allows us to concentrate on the language, and it can be extremely rewarding to read a play just before viewing a performance in the theater or on a video recording. The same conventions of diction, imagery, and style apply to plays as to short stories and other works of fiction. When analyzing these conventions in terms of a play, however, we need to pay close attention to the way the language of the dialogue interacts with the

staging and action of the play. In *Trifles,* for example, the bird cage and canary take on figurative meaning from their use as props and because of their presence in the dialogue. The discovery of the physical birdcage prompts the discussion of the canary; the symbolism of the caged bird establishes the missing canary as a metaphor for Minnie Foster and builds a tension that increases until it reaches a climax in the discovery of the dead bird wrapped in silk. The physical objects introduce the imagery, but it is the diction, or choice of words, in the dialogue between the two women that allows us to understand the props as fully realized symbols.

The *style* of a specific play is usually closely related to its *genre,* but you may also use the term to refer to the ways in which it uses language. In generic terms, *Trifles* is realistic in style: it aims to create a time, place, and situation that we can accept without reservation as real. In terms of diction and imagery, it is densely symbolic, since it creates a strong pattern of figurative meaning with conventional imagery (birdcage and canary). This is not to say that its symbolism is unrealistic; precisely because it is conventional, its meaning is familiar and easy to accept as part of the story world. But it is certainly possible to imagine a similar set of events being staged without any figurative meaning. The theme might be altered, since it is the figurative meaning that underpins the dualisms of the play, but the events would be identical. In the same way, a play written without any overt meaning can be unrealistic in style—*Krapp's Last Tape,* for example (p. 189).

WRITING EXERCISE: An Analysis of Staging

Choose one of the plays in this book (see the Contents by Genre for a complete list), and write a proposal for a staging of the play at your school theater. Include ideas you have about each of the elements discussed above, and explain how they combine to form a particular argument about or interpretation of the play. Refer as much as possible to the stage directions in the script, and if you choose not to follow them, explain what principle you are using instead.

Form and Genre

The ancient Greeks and Romans recognized two primary forms of theater: tragedy and comedy. Aristotle distinguished them in terms of their structure: a tragedy begins well and ends poorly; a comedy begins poorly and ends well. He also characterized them in terms of their distinctive styles: tragedy employed a formal, elevated, and poetic style removed from the speech patterns of everyday life, while comedy reflected the language of the streets of Athens in a colloquial, "low" style of prose. The classical distinction in terms of form rather than content reflects the insight that comedy and tragedy both address truths about human experience, often the same ones. Their different approach to truth, however, means that each form offers different insights.

Many of the plays written through the nineteenth century observe the same formal distinction, although the specific conventions they associated with the structures of tragedy and comedy have changed. In the nineteenth century, the genre of realism, which regarded both comedy and tragedy as needlessly exaggerated in comparison to everyday life, came to dominate Western theater. More loosely defined than the classical forms, realism combines the catastrophic events of tragedy with the everyday language and absurd situations of comedy in varying proportions depending on the theme of a particular play.

Tragedy   We call an accident or disaster *tragic* when its scope exceeds our sense of proportion and when we feel it could have been prevented. Both senses of the word derive from the conventions of theatrical tragedy, in which larger-than-life characters—traditionally rulers and members of the nobility—experience larger-than-life emotions and suffer larger-than-life catastrophes. Tragedy magnifies and concentrates the personal sorrows

of death, betrayal, and broken taboos into earth-shattering events. Tragic dramas usually feature protagonists who transgress the limits of acceptable behavior: Antigone buries her brother when the king has forbidden it; Oedipus unknowingly murders his father and marries his mother; Hamlet slays his stepfather; Minnie Foster kills her husband because he killed her canary. Unlike the unmotivated crimes perpetrated by the villains of melodrama, the crimes portrayed in most tragedies are committed for reasons that the audience must, at least momentarily, consider as legitimate. In other words, tragedy poses a dilemma for its audience: unable either to dismiss the protagonists as criminals or to condone their acts unconditionally, we watch, as Aristotle phrased it, in a combination of pity and fear until the final resolution. Aristotle characterized this resolution as a **catharsis,** a combination of relief that we are not the ones who are suffering and pleasure in the knowledge we have gained from the experience.

Irony   Much of the pity and fear that we feel arises from our ability to see what the protagonist is unable to see before it is too late. We know whom Oedipus killed and whom he is married to; we know in *Antigone* that Creon is headed for disaster. This condition of knowledge is called **irony,** and it can refer either to actions—Creon hopes to save his city by punishing Antigone when he will instead accomplish its downfall—or to words. Early on in the play, Creon says this:

> Of course you cannot know a man
>   completely,
> his character, his principles, sense of
>   judgment,
> not till he's shown his colors, ruling
>   the people,
> making laws. Experience, there's
>   the test.

His assertion turns out to be true, but in the opposite sense from the

one he intended: rather than proving that he possesses them, he will show himself to be lacking in character, principles, and a sense of judgment. Be careful to distinguish **dramatic irony,** in which a character is unaware of the irony of his actions or words, from **verbal irony,** in which a character makes a consciously ironic statement. When Mrs. Hale concludes the action of *Trifles* with an answer to the County Attorney's facetious question about quilting with the words, "We call it—knot it, Mr. Henderson," she is quite aware of the significance of the word in associating the evidence in the quilt with the noose in the room above. Verbal irony is especially effective when its meaning is unknown to some of the characters. We and Mrs. Peters full well understand what she means, but we also full well understand that the men do not.

Because we watch a play as spectators unable to participate in the plot as it unfolds before our eyes, dramatic irony is a powerful tool for galvanizing our emotions and focusing our attention on the consequences of the sequence of actions being performed onstage. Noticing when and where dramatic irony is used in a play will often help us to identify the principal dramatic theme. In *Trifles,* for example, Glaspell repeatedly uses dramatically ironic speech by the male characters to draw out the irony of her title, as when Hale concludes, "Well, women are used to worrying over trifles." His words are perfectly true, but in the opposite sense from his intention: it is their worrying over trifles that allows the women to solve the crime. The use of irony underlines Glaspell's argument not only that women experience and gain knowledge of the world differently from men, but that only women are aware of this fact.

Tragic Themes   Tragedy has most frequently been defined in terms of character: the tragic hero whose downfall results from a *tragic flaw* or a *tragic error*. Focus on a particular character will bring out key issues within the play's theme, but it should not lead us to ignore the context in which the protagonist acts. Because it is enacted through the figures of society's leaders, traditional tragedy always has an ethical component, asking us to reflect on the basic values held by our society, and the conflicts that can arise between those values. The heights and depths of tragedy bring to light our deepest values and our greatest fears. When we read a tragedy, we must define the broad issues raised by the play's theme, and then observe the different perspective on that theme provided by each character, from the tragic hero to the lowly messenger.

Tragic Form   Rather than being divided into acts, **Greek tragedy** is structured as a series of intimate scenes between a small number of characters, usually two, separated by the dancing and the sung words of the chorus, known as the **ode** (p. 129), and divided into two parts, the *strophe* and the *antistrophe*. The chorus sometimes comments on the action, and sometimes refers to a mythological or historical context for the action taking place. Choral odes tend to be lyrical rather than plot-oriented, halting the action for reflection rather than moving it forward. All players wore stylized masks, all roles were played by male actors, and the often extreme violence was always described rather than depicted onstage. Performed a single time in an annual festival competition with a strong religious component, a Greek tragedy would have a one-time audience of up to 15,000 people seated in a giant semicircular outdoor amphitheater.

In contrast to the religious and ritualistic context of Greek tragedy, **Elizabethan tragedy** was a wholly secular product offered for a night's entertainment to whomever could afford a ticket. Rather than the condensed brevity of Greek tragedy, the tragedies of Shakespeare and his contemporaries were five acts long, and contained a great variety of action and characters around their central tragic protagonist and central theme, with something to appeal to every member of the audience, from the common "groundlings" in the pit to the nobility in their private boxes. As opposed to the high solemnity of Greek tragedy, Elizabethan tragedy often mixed styles, incorporating low comedy as well as the elevated language of the highborn characters.

The **realist drama** that developed in the eighteenth and nineteenth centuries incorporated many elements and conventions of the tragedy but adapted them to the characters and events of middle-class life, and, later, the poor. In realist drama, the scale of production is usually reduced along with the social class, but the dramatic arc of the plot remains quite similar. Moreover, a drama such as *Trifles* can play on our familiarity with the conventions of traditional tragedy, leading us to contrast the pitiful fate of Minnie Foster with the towering fall of an Oedipus or a Hamlet. Other realist plays, such as Henrik Ibsen's *A Doll's House* (p. 553), made different changes in the conventions, regarding the catastrophes of tragedy as exaggerations of real life, and redefining tragedy in a less absolute sense as someone being forced to live a life without the chance of growth or happiness.

Comedy   The common meaning of **comedy** is anything that is meant to elicit laughter. Comedy in this sense can run the gamut from pure **slapstick**—a man slips on a banana peel, as in *Krapp's Last Tape*—to **farce**—in which characters are trapped in ridiculous situations—to **satire**, a humorous and often vicious attack on a particular convention or social institution—to **romantic comedy,** in which a pair of lovers undergoes a series of trials and tribulations before being reunited to live happily ever after. Comic situations can appear in any dramatic form except classical tragedy; the men of Glaspell's drama find comedy in the women's continued concern with "trifles," although not everyone in the audience might do so. Comedy makes fun through the way it breaks conventions, whether those of society or those of language. Comedy makes us laugh when we know enough about those conventions to get the joke. This is one reason comic moments are notoriously difficult to translate: much depends on our knowledge of the context in which it takes place. Tragedy tends to deal in abstract ideas and values shared by many cultures; comedy tends to address those same values and ideas through the behavior and absurdities of everyday life, which vary widely from place to place and from time to time.

Comic Mechanisms   Because slang changes rapidly, *verbal humor* in a play written anytime before the last decade may require some work in recovering the meaning. Imagine what you will have to explain to the next generation in order to help them make sense of a Barack Obama or a George W. Bush joke. Because it functions visually instead of linguistically, *physical humor* requires much less effort to translate. Since time immemorial, a pie in the face has made audiences laugh the world over, but nobody has yet come up with a persuasive reason *why*. We all know that a pie in the face is not always funny. Timing and context are everything. *Comic timing,* whether verbal or physical, consists primarily in preparing the audience for the *punch line,* the final twist that makes the audience realize why the previous anecdote or the pie in the face that caps the building tension in a scene was so funny. Comedy establishes a pattern of repetition; it is the punch line that finally breaks the pattern. Timing, you could say, is the comic version of dramatic irony: the longer we see it coming, over and over again, and the longer the victim does not, the more effective—the funnier—it will be.

Why Analyze Comedy?   A cliché about jokes is that when you explain them you ruin them. Like all clichés, this one has a degree of truth to it: there is nothing more satisfying than the electric instant when a punch line connects directly to your funny bone and sends you into ripples of laughter that will not subside until you have tears running down your face. Nor is there anything better than hearing the same joke all over again. Why explain it then? First of all, there is nothing more perfect in form and structure than a good joke or its physical equivalent, a *gag*. One of the great pleasures of criticism is to succeed in breaking down a joke or gag into its different components and showing how they work together to make us laugh. As any writer and any actor will tell you, comedy is much harder than tragedy to create and to perform, because it must look as if it were the easiest and most natural thing in the world. Any slip in composition or execution will cause the entire structure to fall entirely flat—how many times have you tried unsuccessfully to recount a joke someone else told you, or an episode from a favorite comedy show? Analyzing comic moments helps us to figure out when they work and when they do not, and why.

A third reason to study comedy is that it is, like tragedy, an important vehicle for arguments about social norms and values. As another cliché has it, many a truth is said in jest, and we usually laugh at something precisely because it has touched a nerve or crossed a social boundary we would rather not have thought about. Jokes can expose our deepest fears and rawest nerves: if there is a joke about something, it means that it makes someone uncomfortable;

when a joke stops being funny, it means the issues it raises have no relevance anymore. Like the rest of literature, comedy is a question of conventions, and we also learn to laugh as we expand our knowledge of conventions. Kids recount jokes about sex that they have overheard because they know that they should not, even though they do not get the joke, although they may pretend that they do, and certainly wish they did. We recognize when something is supposed to be funny before we gain the knowledge required to actually laugh at it. Learn to recognize this intuition as you read, and use it to identify patterns of humor even if you are not quite sure what the conventions are behind them. The more you analyze and learn about humor, the more you will learn about its conventions, and the more things there will be in the world to make you laugh: this, in the end, is the best reason of all to study comedy.

Comic Form   Many students ask when first reading Dante's *Divine Comedy* why it is called a comedy when there is very little funny about a journey through hell or an ascent to heaven. Dante's contemporaries did not find it very funny either, but they did know the formal convention on which Dante based his title. The poem begins badly, with the protagonist stuck in hell, and ends well, in heaven. Moreover, it mixes styles, including moments of elevated, tragic rhetoric and moments of obscenity and slapstick. Unlike tragedy, the basic elements of which have remained fairly consistent, comedy has taken myriad forms, most of which are mixes of others. The table included on the next page describes some of the forms and genres you are most likely to encounter.

The Forms of Modern Drama

As in other literary forms, modern drama witnessed a flurry of experimentation during the twentieth century, often referred to collectively as *modernist* or *avant-garde theater*.

The realist drama remained the primary form, providing the conventions and expectations against which other forms of drama reacted, while the popular forms of comedy such as farce, satire, and parody provided a storehouse of theatrical techniques and conventions unconnected to realism. A shared feature of nearly all modern drama was its belief that instead of truthfully reflecting reality, the conventions of realism obscured some important feature of the human condition. Dramatic movements were often associated with artistic and philosophical movements. Two of the most influential movements during the middle of the twentieth century were the **theater of the absurd** and **epic** or **Brechtian theater.** Both forms sought ways of making the viewer aware of the conventions of realist theater and comparing the conventions of the theater to those of the real world. They used various strategies to foster *self-consciousness* or *self-reflexivity* in the audience. For practitioners of theater of the absurd, the stage reflected the meaninglessness and absurdity of existence. Consequently, their plays made ample use of nonsense in terms both of language and of plot, presenting a set of events with no apparent meaning or coherence. Epic or Brechtian theater, named after its inventor, the German playwright Bertolt Brecht, was more politically committed, arguing that the conventions of realist drama comforted the audience with a false picture of the world around them rather than showing it for what it really was, a place of oppression and injustice. For Brecht, theater was first and foremost a tool for teaching his audience the truth about the world. In Brechtian theater, actors step out of character to comment on the acts they have just committed; placards with captions explain what is about to happen on stage; and, of course, there are neither happy nor tragic endings.

Forms of Comedy

Form of Comedy	Definition	Examples
"Old" Greek Comedy	• Structure is loose, episodic, sketch-based. • Content is satirical. • Humor follows the "nothing sacred" approach.	• Plays of Aristophanes • *Monty Python, Saturday Night Live, The Simpsons*
"New" Greek Comedy	• Dramatic arc is clear. • Plot is unified, usually focused on romance. • As in tragedy, everything goes wrong but here it manages to go right again.	• Plays of the Greek dramatist Menander • Plays of the Roman dramatists Plautus and Terence • Much of romantic comedy and comic drama
Farce	• Structure is derived from mimed, or silent, Italian *commedia dell'arte*. • Comic moments are loosely assembled into a plot. • Plot seldom has direct social content of *satire* or formal conventions of *parody*. • Humor stresses verbal jokes and physical gags.	• Shakespeare's early comedies • Silent film comedies of Buster Keaton, Harold Lloyd, Charlie Chaplin, and Laurel and Hardy • Modern "gross-out" comedies
Shakespearean Comedy	• Structure is influenced by New Greek Comedy and farce, in five acts. • Plot is unified, romance-oriented. • Humor relies on coincidence and mistaken identity.	• *A Midsummer Night's Dream, Twelfth Night,* and other comedies by Shakespeare
Romantic Comedy	• Plot and structure are unified. • Plot events are based on realism. • Plot complications develop through character antipathy. • Coincidence in circumstances creates antipathy (e.g., competing jobs).	• Films such as *When Harry Met Sally, Shrek, Groundhog Day, There's Something about Mary, Bringing Up Baby, It Happened One Night*
Comic Drama	• Underlying structure is romantic, but main plot is unrelated to romance. • Plot is serious but ends well. • Love interest is not integrated into action until main plot is resolved.	• Films such as *Fight Club, Star Wars, The Lord of the Rings*
Comedy of Manners	• Minimal physical comedy, but plot structure resembles farce. • Language is used to satirize conventions of particular social class or set, usually a powerful one.	• Prominent in 17th-century France and England • Perfected by Oscar Wilde, most notably in *The Importance of Being Earnest* • Films such as *Rules of the Game*
Tragicomedy (also dark or black comedy)	• Structure follows various conventions of comedy and tragedy. • Plot is usually tragic but nevertheless ends happily. • In black comedy, bleakness of events is barely redeemed by the happy ending.	• Plays by Samuel Beckett and Tom Stoppard • Films such as *Life Is Beautiful, Fargo*
Satire	• Structure focuses on a comic moment within another form or a full-length form of its own. • Social and political conventions are attacked and distorted for comic effect.	• Plays of Molière • Editorial cartoons, late-night television • Films such as *Bob Roberts, Bullworth*
Parody	• Comic version of a particular genre or institution is executed using precise replicas of the conventions of the genre or institution. • The humor can be *deadpan* (requires expert identification) or *explicit* (obvious).	• Deadpan films such as *Best in Show, This Is Spinal Tap* • Explicit films such as *Scary Movie, Airplane!*

Often uncompromisingly extreme in their initial manifestations, the dramatic movements of modernism were eventually combined with the conventions of realism, which allowed audiences a certain comfort zone. As Shakespeare's theater combined the classical theater with medieval traditions to explore the new concerns of Elizabethan England, so contemporary playwrights and theatrical troupes combine the innovations of the avant-garde with the familiar conventions of realism to create forms capable of exploring the concerns of the contemporary world. The conventions of theater of absurd are a central feature of Samuel Beckett's one-act play, *Krapp's Last Tape* (p. 189). Throughout the century, playwrights were concerned with incorporating elements from theatrical traditions around the world: the Noh and Kabuki theater from Japan were an important influence on Brecht; we find the rituals and traditions of West-African cultures incorporated into the settings of modern African-American plays.

WHAT IS NONFICTION?

Much of our everyday experience with the written word comes from nonfiction forms and genres: billboards, letters, e-mail and text messages, junk mail and spam, Web pages, newspapers, magazines, textbooks. As the structure of the word informs us, **nonfiction** can be defined quite simply as anything written in prose that is *not* fiction. In some instances, we can usually tell when something is not factual or legitimate. For example, who among us has not received an e-mail stating, "You hav just one 5 thowsand dolars"? The faulty spelling tells us immediately that the message is not genuine. There are other forms of nonfiction, however, that require greater textual analysis and critical thinking skills to interpret. Such forms are the subject of this section, and in the pages that follow, we discuss various forms of literary nonfiction. We begin with the *essay*.

The Essay

A large category of form, the **essay** includes everything from the papers you write for class to the literary monument left us by Michel de Montaigne (1533–1592), the inventor of the form. Montaigne coined the term we still use today from the French word, *essayer,* which means "to attempt" or "to try," and his essays, written in an extremely personal voice, are "attempts" to get at the meaning of any number of chosen subjects. Since Montaigne's time, the meaning of the word has expanded to include numerous different approaches to a chosen subject in a nonfictional setting. Essays are written primarily to share knowledge about a particular subject matter, but there are many different ways in which a particular author may go about the process of sharing this knowledge.

A groundbreaking modernist novelist and short story writer, Virginia Woolf (1882–1941) was also an accomplished essayist. First published a year after the author's suicide, Woolf's essay "The Death of the Moth" offers a profound meditation on the experience of death and the immensity of nature within the tight confines of a brief description of a moth.

> *I write entirely to find out what I'm thinking, what I'm looking at, what I see and what it means.*
> —JOAN DIDION, "WHY I WRITE"

VIRGINIA WOOLF
THE DEATH OF THE MOTH

MOTHS THAT FLY BY DAY ARE NOT PROPERLY TO be called moths; they do not excite that pleasant sense of dark autumn nights and ivy-blossom which the commonest yellow-underwing asleep in the shadow of the curtain never fails to rouse in us. They are hybrid creatures, neither gay like butterflies nor sombre like their own species. Nevertheless the present specimen, with his narrow hay-coloured wings, fringed with a tassel of the same colour, seemed to be content with life. It was a pleasant morning, mid–September, mild, benignant, yet with a keener breath than that of the summer months. The plough was already scoring the field opposite the window, and where the share had been, the earth was pressed flat and gleamed with moisture. Such vigour came rolling in from the fields and the down beyond that it was difficult to keep the eyes strictly turned upon the book. The rooks too were keeping one of their annual festivities; soaring round the tree tops until it looked as if a vast net with thousands of black knots in it had been cast up into the air; which, after a few moments sank slowly down upon the trees until every twig seemed to have a knot at the end of it. Then, suddenly, the net would be thrown into the air again in a wider circle this time, with the utmost clamour and vociferation, as though to be thrown into the air and settle slowly down upon the tree tops were a tremendously exciting experience.

The same energy which inspired the rooks, the ploughmen, the horses, and even, it seemed, the lean bare-backed downs, sent the moth fluttering from side to side of his square of the window-pane. One could not help watching him. One was, indeed, conscious of a queer feeling of pity for him. The possibilities of pleasure seemed that morning so enormous and so various that to have only a moth's part in life, and a day moth's at that, appeared a hard fate, and his zest in enjoying his meagre opportunities to the full, pathetic. He flew vigorously to one corner of his compartment, and, after waiting there a second, flew across to the other. What remained for him but to fly to a third corner and then to a fourth? That was all he could do, in spite of the size of the downs, the width of the sky, the far-off smoke of houses, and the romantic voice, now and then, of a steamer out at sea. What he could do he did. Watching him, it seemed as if a fibre, very thin but pure, of the enormous energy of the world had been thrust into his frail and diminutive body. As often as he crossed the pane, I could fancy that a thread of vital light became visible. He was little or nothing but life.

Yet, because he was so small, and so simple a form of the energy that was rolling in at the open window and driving its way through so many narrow and intricate corridors in my own brain and in those of other human beings, there was something marvellous as well as pathetic about him. It was as if someone had taken a tiny bead of pure life and decking it as lightly as possible with down and feathers, had set it

dancing and zig-zagging to show us the true nature of life. Thus displayed one could not get over the strangeness of it. One is apt to forget all about life, seeing it humped and bossed and garnished and cumbered so that it has to move with the greatest circumspection and dignity. Again, the thought of all that life might have been had he been born in any other shape caused one to view his simple activities with a kind of pity.

After a time, tired by his dancing apparently, he settled on the window ledge in the sun, and, the queer spectacle being at an end, I forgot about him. Then, looking up, my eye was caught by him. He was trying to resume his dancing, but seemed either so stiff or so awkward that he could only flutter to the bottom of the window-pane; and when he tried to fly across it he failed. Being intent on other matters I watched these futile attempts for a time without thinking, unconsciously waiting for him to resume his flight, as one waits for a machine, that has stopped momentarily, to start again without considering the reason of its failure. After perhaps a seventh attempt he slipped from the wooden ledge and fell, fluttering his wings, on to his back on the window sill. The helplessness of his attitude roused me. It flashed upon me that he was in difficulties; he could no longer raise himself; his legs struggled vainly. But, as I stretched out a pencil, meaning to help him to right himself, it came over me that the failure and awkwardness were the approach of death. I laid the pencil down again.

5   The legs agitated themselves once more. I looked as if for the enemy against which he struggled. I looked out of doors. What had happened there? Presumably it was midday, and work in the fields had stopped. Stillness and quiet had replaced the previous animation. The birds had taken themselves off to feed in the brooks. The horses stood still. Yet the power was there all the same, massed outside indifferent, impersonal, not attending to anything in particular. Somehow it was opposed to the little hay-coloured moth. It was useless to try to do anything. One could only watch the extraordinary efforts made by those tiny legs against an oncoming doom which could, had it chosen, have submerged an entire city, not merely a city, but masses of human beings; nothing, I knew, had any chance against death. Nevertheless after a pause of exhaustion the legs fluttered again. It was superb this last protest,

and so frantic that he succeeded at last in righting himself. One's sympathies, of course, were all on the side of life. Also, when there was nobody to care or to know, this gigantic effort on the part of an insignificant little moth, against a power of such magnitude, to retain what no one else valued or desired to keep, moved one strangely. Again, somehow, one saw life, a pure bead. I lifted the pencil again, useless though I knew it to be. But even as I did so, the unmistakable tokens of death showed themselves. The body

relaxed, and instantly grew stiff. The struggle was over. The insignificant little creature now knew death. As I looked at the dead moth, this minute wayside triumph of so great a force over so mean an antagonist filled me with wonder. Just as life had been strange a few minutes before, so death was now as strange. The moth having righted himself now lay most decently and uncomplainingly composed. O yes, he seemed to say, death is stronger than I am.

[1942]

QUESTIONS FOR REFLECTION AND DISCUSSION

1. What is Woolf doing when the moth distracts her? How much time passes from the beginning of the essay until its end?

2. How would you characterize, point by point, the changes undergone in the author's attitude toward the moth?

3. Woolf uses the words "strange" and "strangely" three times in the final paragraph. What to her is "strange" about the experience she is describing?

4. The only other object described in the room with the author and the moth is the pencil, which appears several times. Given the evidence within the essay, would you attribute a figurative meaning to the pencil? Why or why not?

5. What, if anything, does the author claim to have learned from the death of the moth? What, if anything, does she want us to learn about it?

Essay, Short Story, and Poem

"The Death of the Moth" contains many elements we might expect to find in a short story. There is a plot composed of story events; there are characters; there are patterns of diction and imagery; there is a consistent writing style. It is, in other words, a work of literature. Nevertheless, all of these elements are put together differently than they would be in a short story. The plot involves a single human character and a moth, it lasts at most a couple of minutes, and almost nothing that we would normally characterize as action occurs. The scene is narrated, but the narrator is not developed as a literary character; rather, she speaks as if in her own voice, describing an event as if it happened in her own room while she was going about her regular life. When we read a short story, we expect the events to somehow stand out from the ordinary: the act of ordering events into a plot and narrating them to us gives them the weight of the extraordinary. Short stories tend to use their broad and

event-dominated form to arrive at subtle details of character. Conversely, from the "insignificant little moth" of her essay, Woolf experiences something so vast as the meaning of death.

In some ways, the essay is closest in form to the poem's condensed focus of attention, as, for example, in the close encounter described in Elizabeth Bishop's "The Fish," (p. 655). As in many poems, the essay's descriptions are usually channeled through the voice of a single speaker. The meaning is built through the interaction between the detailed description of a moment and the effect of that moment on the speaker. And the effect of that meaning is to achieve a broad insight from a focus on the narrow detail. Where the essay differs from the poem is that its description is *discursive*—made through logically constructed and causally related sentences—rather than image-based. Still, one could imagine a poem based on "The Death of the Moth" more easily than a short story. A poem would merely

need to cut, condense, and translate prose into verse; a short story would have to reframe and retell the events.

Like Woolf's essay, Annie Dillard's similarly titled "Death of a Moth" displays elements of both fiction and poetry. This is not surprising, as Dillard is a novelist and poet, as well as an acclaimed author of nonfiction. Born in 1945, she won the Pulitzer Prize for her book, *Pilgrim at Tinker Creek* (1982), a chronicle of nature walks near her Roanoke, Virginia, home. Honed down to book length from dozens of volumes of journals and stacks of note cards, *Tinker Creek* introduced Dillard's characteristic combination of the keen observation of nature with a wide-ranging sense of spirituality. Dillard currently teaches creative writing at Wesleyan University. First published in 1976, "Death of a Moth" takes the theme of Woolf's similarly named essay and gives it a wholly different context. As you read Dillard's essay, consider the differences from Woolf's essay and the effect they have on the experience of reading it.

ANNIE DILLARD
DEATH OF A MOTH

I LIVE ALONE WITH TWO CATS, WHO SLEEP ON MY legs. There is a yellow one, and a black one whose name is Small. In the morning, I joke to the black one, Do you remember last night? Do you remember? I throw them both out before breakfast, so I can eat.

There is a spider, too, in the bathroom, of uncertain lineage, bulbous at the abdomen and drab, whose six-inch mess of web works, works somehow, works miraculously, to keep her alive and me amazed. The web is in a corner behind the toilet, connecting tile wall to tile wall. The house is new, the bathroom is immaculate, save for the spider, her web, and the sixteen or so corpses tossed on the floor.

Today the earwig shines darkly, and gleams, what there is of him: a dorsal curve of thorax and abdomen, and a smooth pair of pincers by which I knew his name. Next week, if the other bodies are any indication, he'll be shrunk and gray, webbed to the floor with dust. The sow bugs beside him are curled and empty, fragile, a breath away from brittle fluff. The spiders lie on their sides, translucent and ragged, their legs drying in knots. The moths stagger against each other, headless, in a confusion of arcing strips of chitin like peeling varnish, like a jumble of buttresses for cathedral vaults, like nothing resembling moths, so that I would hesitate to call them moths, except that I have had some experience with the figure Moth reduced to a nub.

Two summers ago, I was camped alone in the Blue Ridge Mountains of Virginia. I had hauled myself and gear up there to read, among other things, *The Day on Fire,* by James Ullman, a novel about Rimbaud° that had made me want to be a writer when I was sixteen; I was hoping it would do it again. So I read every day sitting by a tree, while warblers sang in the leaves overhead and bristle worms trailed their inches over the twiggy dirt at my feet; and I read every night by candlelight, while barred owls called in the forest and pale moths seeking mates massed round my head in the clearing, where my light made a ring.

Rimbaud: The nineteenth-century French Symbolist poet Arthur Rimbaud began writing poetry at the age of sixteen and gave it up while still in his twenties.

5   Moths kept flying into the candle. They would hiss and recoil, reeling upside down in the shadows among my cooking pans. Or they would singe their wings and fall, and their hot wings, as if melted, would stick to the first thing they touched—a pan, a lid, a spoon—so that the snagged moths could struggle only in tiny arcs, unable to flutter free. These I could release by a quick flip with a stick; in the morning I would find my cooking stuff decorated with torn flecks of moth wings, ghostly triangles of shiny dust here and there on the aluminum. So I read the book, and boiled water, and replenished candles, and read on.

One night a moth flew into the candle, was caught, burnt dry, and held. I must have been staring at the candle, or maybe I looked up when the shadow crossed my page; at any rate, I saw it all. A golden female moth, a biggish one with a two-inch wing-spread, flapped into the fire, drooped abdomen into the wet wax, stuck, flamed, and frazzled in a second. Her moving wings ignited like tissue paper, like angels' wings, enlarging the circle of the darkness, the sudden blue sleeves of my sweater, the green leaves of jewel-weed by my side, the ragged red trunk of a pine; at once the light contracted again and the moth's wings vanished in a fine, foul smoke. At the same time, her six legs clawed, curled, blackened, and ceased, disappearing utterly. And her head jerked in spasms, making a spattering noise; her antennae crisped and burnt away and her heaving mouthparts cracked like pistol fire. When it was all over, her head was, so far as I could determine, gone, gone the long way of her wings and legs. Her head was a hole lost to time. All that was left was the glowing horn shell of her abdomen and thorax—a fraying, partially collapsed gold tube jammed upright in the candle's round pool.

And then this moth-essence, this spectacular skeleton, began to act as a wick. She kept burning. The wax rose in the moth's body from her soaking abdomen to her thorax to the shattered hole where her head should have been, and widened into a flame, a saffron-yellow flame that robed her to the ground like an immolating monk. That candle had two wicks, two winding flames of identical light, side by side. The moth's head was fire. She burned for two hours, until I blew her out.

She burned for two hours without changing, without swaying or kneeling—only glowing within, like a boiling fire glimpsed through silhouetted walls, like a hollow saint, like a flame-faced virgin gone to God, while I read by her light, kindled while Rimbaud in Paris burnt out his brain in a thousand poems, while night pooled wetly at my feet.

So. That is why I think those hollow shreds on the bathroom floor are moths. I believe I know what moths look like, in any state.

10   I have three candles here on the table which I disentangle from the plants and light when visitors come. The cats avoid them, though Small's tail caught fire once. I rubbed it out before she noticed. I don't mind living alone. I like eating alone and reading, I don't mind sleeping alone. The only time I mind being alone is when something is funny, when I am laughing at something funny, I wish someone were around. Sometimes I think it is pretty funny that I sleep alone.

[1976]

QUESTIONS FOR REFLECTION AND DISCUSSION

1. What is the function of the cats at the beginning and end of the essay?

2. What attitude does the speaker here take toward the death of the moth? What attitude does she take in Woolf's essay?

3. When Dillard reprinted the essay in book form, she cut out the final sentences from "I don't mind living alone" until the end. What do you think motivated the change? How does each ending affect our understanding of the essay as a whole?

4. Compare this essay to Woolf's essay. Beyond the similar titles, what else do they have in common? What are the most important differences between the two essays?.

WRITING EXERCISE: Comparing Moth Essays

In a response paper, compare your reaction to Woolf's and Dillard's essays.

- What struck you in each one, and why?
- Which essay appealed more to you, and why?

- Have you had an experience similar to the ones recorded in these essays?
- Which essay did the experience more closely resemble?

Analyzing an Essay

The first step in analyzing any literary essay is characterizing its *voice*. Most essayists develop a consistent voice in their writing, using it to bind together the material of the essay, guide us through it, and prepare us to accept its insights. Here are two key questions you should ask when beginning your analysis:

- What *tone* does the narrator take toward the essay's subject?
- How does the author use *diction* and *imagery* to create a voice?

Word choice and word order help to establish mood and tone, while imagery can be used to pattern the essay's meanings. There are no set rules for assembling an essay; the writer chooses the combination of segments that best suits the theme and materials at hand.

READING AND WRITING ESSAYS

The following textual analysis by Scott Nathanson studies the use of voice, style, and structure in Woolf's and Dillard's essays. Annotations provide additional suggestions on how to recognize voice, style, and structure, and how to use that analysis to formulate a thesis and argument.

Nathanson 1

Scott Nathanson
Professor Garcia
English Composition II
3 March 2009

The Meaning of Death

The essays "The Death of the Moth," by Virginia Woolf and "Death of a Moth" by Annie Dillard have almost the same title, but they are also very different from each other. In this paper, I will compare voice, style, and structure in the two essays to show how Woolf uses an ordinary observation to make a broad statement about life and Dillard uses an extraordinary sight to make a specific statement about an individual life.

Woolf's first sentence looks like it is objective because she uses "they" and "we," but it really tells us more about her own tastes: "Moths that fly by day are not properly to be called moths; they do not excite that pleasant sense of dark autumn nights and ivy–blossom which the commonest yellow–underwing asleep in the shadow of the curtain never fails to rouse in us" (156). By contrast, Dillard begins with a first-person singular observation about her own habits, "I live alone with two cats, who sleep on my legs. There is a yellow one, and a black one whose name is Small. In the morning, I joke to the black one, Do you remember last night? Do you remember? I throw them both out before breakfast, so I can eat" (159). Woolf describes what anyone might see if they looked at the nature around them. Dillard describes her relationship with her cats, creatures that belong to the world of nature.

Woolf and Dillard both speak to us in a friendly tone in these sentences. In Woolf's essay, the friendly tone of voice can be seen in the "us" that concludes the sentence. Dillard's voice is more informal and

---

The topic sentence combines the assignment prompt ("Compare the use of voice, style, and structure in Woolf's and Dillard's essays") with the thesis Scott formulated on the basis of his analysis.

It's good idea to begin with a close look at the opening sentences of the two essays. A topic sentence for the paragraph would have been a nice addition.

Scott's argument summarizes the differences between the two opening sentences in terms of the differences between the _personas_ used by the two authors.

Authorial _voice_ is characterized in terms of its _tone_. As Scott does here, use descriptive rather than evaluative or emotional terms to characterize voice and tone.

These two sentences would work better if put together (the second one is a sentence fragment).

suggests an intimate conversation, while Woolf could be speaking to a group of acquaintances around a dinner table. Woolf talks as if her observations are universally agreed-upon by the people listening to her. Whereas Dillard talks as if she can't take anything for granted about her readers. She has to explain a lot more. Each voice is well suited to the theme of each essay. Woolf describes a silent, easily overlooked struggle that takes place daily in the window of a room in her house. It is something that can be witnessed by anyone. Dillard, however, describes an unusual and extraordinary sight that provides knowledge and inspiration to her alone. While Woolf never changes setting or tone, Dillard's tone of voice shifts from the everyday observations of the scene in the bathroom that begins and ends the essay to the spectacular vision of the campfire.

Note how Scott connects the specifics of his analysis to the broader theme and argument of his essay and of the texts he is discussing.

Both authors write in long, flowing sentences full of specific description. Woolf uses everyday language to describe nature. She builds sentences that generalize based on her description. She uses the pronouns "we" and "one" to tell us how to understand her observations. Dillard uses technical, scientific language ("a dorsal curve of thorax," "chitin") and builds her sentences using "I" and personal detail. Woolf uses imagery that doesn't have any figurative meaning. Dillard's imagery, however, tells us that there is something symbolic about the burning moth, in particular when she says, "like a hollow saint, like a flame-faced virgin gone to God." Woolf wants to share the beauty and meaning we can find in everyday life. Dillard wants to share the once-in-a-lifetime experience that she still remembers as she goes about her life.

In this paragraph Scott focuses on *diction:* the way the words are put together to create the two different voices.

Scott gives specific evidence to back up his arguments.

The pencil is the only possible exception to this otherwise valid observation.

Here again, Scott's comparison distinguishes between the effects and aims of the different voices.

Woolf's essay, in other words, is unified in time, place, and action.

The events narrated in "The Death of the Moth" occur within the space of a few minutes, and Woolf rapidly zooms in from the general setting of a mid-September morning to a close-up of the struggling moth. She concentrates her attention on a single action ignored in the greater scheme of nature, whereas Dillard uses a flashback. Observing the insect corpses

In this paragraph Scott analyzes the different *structures* of the two essays.

By contrast, the events narrated in "Death of a Moth" have a more complex temporal and thematic relationship.

collected by the spider in her bathroom, she recalls the time two years before when she learned how to recognize a moth "in any state"(160). She remembers when she was younger and wanted to become a writer after reading about the life of Rimbaud, a French poet. Woolf's essay

Here Scott draws the essay's argument out of the analysis of its structure.

Noticing the nesting structure of Dillard's essay leads Scott to an argument about its theme.

tells us that the moth's death is just one of many similar observations she could have made. Because one observation makes her think about another one, Dillard's essay shows how important the moth's death was to her as an experience. She suggests that everything we see in nature has the ability to change our life if we look at it in the right way. Another difference is that whereas Woolf assumes that we agree with her, Dillard does not seem to assume that we share her view. She saw the moth and it changed her, but the cats couldn't care less, even though they are part of nature too.

As elsewhere in the essay, it would be clearer if Scott referred to Woolf's or Dillard's "voice" or "person." Don't assume the author is the same as the speaker in the essay.

Works Cited

Dillard, Annie. "Death of a Moth." *Literature: A World of Writing.* Ed. David L. Pike and Ana M. Acosta. New York: Pearson Longman, 2011. 159–60. Print.

Woolf, Virginia. "The Death of the Moth." *Literature: A World of Writing.* Ed. David L. Pike and Ana M. Acosta. New York: Pearson Longman, 2011. 156–58. Print.

┌─ WRITING EXERCISE: Analyzing an Essay ────────────

Select one of the essays in this book (see the Contents by Genre for a complete list) and write a textual analysis of it. Characterize its *voice* and *tone,* its *style,* and its *structure.*

Generate an argument relating the patterns you find in voice, tone, style, and structure to the theme or thesis of the essay.

Types of Essays

Literary, or **personal essays** are customarily broken down into five specific types: the *argumentative* or *persuasive* essay, the *reflective* or *meditative essay,* the *descriptive* essay, the *narrative* essay, and the *expository* essay. Many essays combine different aspects of these general types, but it is important to be able to identify the primary type being used. We have defined each type of essay in the table below, with references to examples of each type of essay elsewhere in the anthology.

Types of Essays

Type of Essay	Definition	Example
Argumentative or Persuasive	• The structure of this form generates a prominent argument, usually stated either in the title or in the opening paragraph, and aims to persuade its reader of the validity of that argument. • The kind of argument made can vary from a powerful dispute to an argument over the validity of several points of view. • This is the least subjective form of personal essay, but as a literary form it will often employ a personal voice.	• May Sarton, "The Rewards of Living a Solitary Life" (p. 39) • Louis D. Owens, "The American Indian Wilderness" (p. 661) • Student essays (pp. 66, 75, 96, 161, 181, 207, APP B–5)
Reflective, or Meditative	• The French Renaissance writer Michel de Montaigne named and perfected this form. • The essay begins with a topic and then follows it wherever it seems to lead. • The style is sometimes rambling and informal like a diary or journal, sometimes highly polished and focused. • An argument will often emerge, but not necessarily directly and not necessarily at the beginning of the essay.	• Sei Shonagon, *Hateful Things* (p. 392)
Descriptive	• The form is based on a detailed physical description of a particular object or event. • The essay is sometimes composed of pure description; often a broader argument is made through the vehicle of a description. • The basis for the description is usually autobiographical: the author describes something he or she has witnessed. • Always based on a physical phenomenon, whereas a reflective essay can have any topic.	• Student essay (p. 186)
Narrative	• The author narrates a sequence of events, usually also in the context of a reflective essay. • The form is usually autobiographical, but events may be narrated in terms of their autobiographical significance; or primarily as events reported by the observing author, as in a newspaper report; or as a combination of the two.	• Annie Dillard, "Death of a Moth" (p. 159) • Bill Buford, "Lions and Tigers and Bears" (p. 633)
Expository	• The primary goal of this form is *exposition,* or the presentation of information. • Many essays have moments of exposition. • Most academic writing and popular science writing can be characterized as expository.	• George Packer, "How Susie Bayer's T-Shirt Ended Up on Yusuf Mama's Back" (p. 200)

WHAT ARE VISUAL MEDIA?

Seeing is not always believing.

—MARTIN LUTHER KING JR.

Over the past few decades, visual media have superseded print media as the primary way that we distribute and obtain information and other kinds of meaning. In this section, we describe the main types of visual media and the ways of thinking critically that are specific to each one.

Still Images

A **still image** can be any sort of visual image whose meaning is self-contained—as opposed, that is, to the sequential images (such as comics), moving images, or hypertext images discussed below. A still image may be part of a sequence of images, but if you study and discuss it on its own terms, you should treat it as a still image.

Patterns of Form   There are many varieties of single-frame images. The most common are paintings, drawings, cartoons, and photographs. Although single-frame images can make abstract patterns, we focus here on figurative examples, or those that recognizably depict some aspect of the physical world.

When you look at an image, consider these basic questions:

- What medium is it?
- What is the quality of the image (sharply defined or grainy, visible or invisible brushstrokes, sharp or smudged lines)?
- Is it in color or black and white?
- What quality of color or black and white is it (high- or low-contrast, dark, bright, matte or glossy)?

Next, scan it for the major lines dividing it into sectors. We saw in Chapter 2 how the painting *Children Picking Blackberries* (p. 79) is divided into two halves by the dark blackberry bramble and the light path, and in Chapter 1 how the black velvet cloth in *Letter Rack with Christian V's Proclamation* (p. 35) similarly divides the canvas. The composition of *Campesinos* (Peasants, below), a photograph shot in

Mexico by the early twentieth-century Italian photographer Tina Modotti, is striking because it has no such divisions, although there is a straight line running from top to bottom of the frame just to the left of center that helps to stabilize the image. Instead, it is composed of the nearly uniform patterning created by the identical hats worn by the peasants.

Tina Modotti, *Campesinos* (1926). The photograph captures a workers' parade on May Day from a roof top in Mexico City.

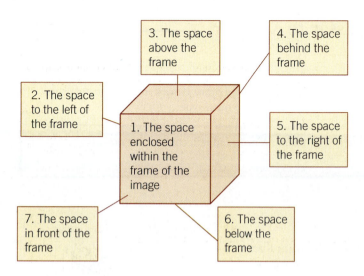

2. The space to the left of the frame

3. The space above the frame

4. The space behind the frame

1. The space enclosed within the frame of the image

5. The space to the right of the frame

7. The space in front of the frame

6. The space below the frame

You should now consider the image's use of space. The seven distinct spaces in any framed image are shown in the diagram above.

These spaces are illusory, of course, and framing can make us imagine any manner of exterior spaces around an image, in the same way that spaces in movies feel real to us even though the set may end just beyond the image framed in the camera. *Children Picking Blackberries* (p. 79), for example, makes strong use of the space to the right of the frame, where the children's eyes are focused, and where the blackberry bramble extends, and in front of and behind the frame, where the two ends of the path seem to disappear. In

contrast, *Letter Rack* (p. 35) is almost wholly self-contained because the frame of the letter rack exactly coincides with the frame of the painting.

In *Campesinos,* the space of the photograph has been carefully framed to create two key effects. First, a small gap in the crowd in the upper left-hand corner establishes a sense of movement as the figures stream out the top and back of the frame. Second, along with the sense of forward motion, the way the figures fill the frame except in the upper-left corner makes us feel that the crowd extends far beyond the confines of the photograph itself. We have no way of knowing the actual size of the crowd photographed by Modotti,

but we can comment on the way she chose to *represent* its size. Imagine how different the effect of the photograph would be if empty pavement were visible around the edges of the frame—we would feel as if there were merely an isolated group of some twenty men rather than the vast crowd conjured here.

Unlike *Children Picking Blackberries,* there is no individual story to be told here, and unlike *Letter Rack* there is no sense of an ordered and enclosed space. Instead, Modotti creates an image of numbers and dynamic movement. These peasants are going somewhere intently, and the sum of their members is more important than any one individual.

Patterns of Meaning   Pattern, framing, and form create harmonious images and establish the illusion of three-dimensional reality in a two-dimensional space. But they nearly always also underline the narrative and thematic meaning of the figures and spaces being depicted within the frame. Focusing on the way in which a still image manipulates the spaces within and around its frame raises questions that guide and deepen any analysis of the content of an image.

A famous image of the death of a soldier in the Spanish Civil War, this photograph made the Hungarian-born American war photographer Robert Capa world famous when first published in a French magazine. Consider the photo at left: so powerful is the sense that an instant of time has been captured that some scholars continue to debate whether the photograph was staged. The story of the moment wholly dominates our experience of this image as we grasp the suddenness and violence of death in battle: the rifle flying back, the legs buckling, the head jerked to the side by the impact of the bullet, the body falling backward. The photograph is so effective because the impact of its image duplicates the impact of the bullet on the soldier.

Robert Capa, *Falling Soldier. A loyalist militiaman is shown at the moment of death in Cerro Muriano, on September 5, 1936.*

1. Summarize either *Campesinos* or *Falling Soldier* in a few sentences.

2. Why, in *Campesinos,* has the photographer filled her frame completely? Why has the photographer in *Falling Soldier* chosen to include so much empty space in a photograph of a battle that must have been extremely full of fighting soldiers?

3. Which of these two photographs seems more real to you? What criteria did you use to decide what "real" means in answering this question?

4. Would it alter your understanding of either photograph if you were told that the event had been staged for the benefit of the photographer?

5. Compare the two photographs. List some of the ways in which they are wholly opposite to one another. What are some of the similarities between them, either in terms of form or thematically?

WRITING EXERCISE: Analyzing a Still Image

Choose any still image in this book not in Chapters 1–4 and analyze it as outlined above.

1. Describe the way the space of the frame is divided, and what is contained in each sector.

2. Discuss the way the image structures the spaces beyond the frame.

3. Discuss the questions raised by these formal qualities and their relation to the content and themes of the image.

Sequential Images

When a number of still images are placed together in some sort of meaningful relationship with each other, we call them **sequential images,** because they form a sequence of meaning.[1] For the most part, images are placed in sequence together because they tell stories. When we view sequential images, we generally read them one after another, looking for the story. When studying them, however, analyze them first individually, locate the key patterns and framings, and then put them together to see how the story unfolds.

Patterns and Framing in Sequential Images
Sequential images expand the initial seven distinct spaces we identified above to include **temporal space**—the time that passes from one frame to the next, which we fill in with our

[1]The term "sequential images" was coined by Will Eisner in *Comics and Sequential Art* (Tamarac, Fla.: Poorhouse Press, 1985) and elaborated by Scott McCloud in *Understanding Comics* (New York: HarperPerennial, 1994).

imagination. In effect, what we see in the final frame makes us reconstruct in our head a whole sequence of events leading up to it. Sequential images work by suggestion and implication. The eight-frame episode of Charles Schulz's classic comic strip, *Peanuts* (p. 168), tells a straightforward sequential narrative, but the shift in visual emphasis in the final frame duplicates the theme, or moral, of the strip. Linus's and Snoopy's attention, as well as our own, is focused on keeping his house of cards from falling down. Only too late do we realize that there was something else at stake as well. The tunnel vision of the strip's composition mirrors the tunnel vision of Linus and Snoopy that results in yet another mishap for the strip's eternal loser, Charlie Brown.

Storytelling in Sequential Images
A comic strip such as *Peanuts* provides a sketch of a story, just enough to set up the punch line at the end of a four-frame (daily) or eight-frame (Sunday) strip. Sequential images are also used to tell lengthy and complex stories. **Graphic novels** (comics bound together in book form) and **mangas** (Japanese graphic novels) can run to thousands of pages in length and involve hundreds of characters embroiled in epic plots. On page 169, we reproduce a full page from American comics artist Alison Bechdel's critically acclaimed 2006 memoir, *Fun Home*.

The space between the frames of sequential images is extremely versatile and it can manipulate time in various ways—freezing it, expanding it, or radically compressing it. A child can become an adult, generations can pass, and civilizations can fall to ruin in the space between one frame and the next. Consequently, when thinking critically about sequential images, pay close attention to the spatial and temporal relations between images and the various symbolic signs and visual conventions that allow you to understand those relations as if they were second nature.

Linus, Snoopy, and Charlie Brown in a Sunday comic strip from Charles Schulz's long-running (1950–2000) comic, *Peanuts*, collected in *Very Funny, Charlie Brown* (New York: Fawcett Crest, 1966).

QUESTIONS FOR REFLECTION AND DISCUSSION

1. In the *Peanuts* strip and the page from *Fun Home,* very little time passes between frames. What are the visual and narrative conventions that allow us to be certain of this fact?

2. Rather than being realistic in appearance, sequential images tend to be stylized in their depiction of characters. Examine the figures in the pages from *Peanuts* and *Fun Home.* What are some of the ways the artists have simplified and abstracted the appearance of the characters? What are the defining physical features of each one? How would we respond differently to these characters if they were realistically depicted?

3. Write a summary of the page from *Fun Home.* Why do you think the author chose the comics form to address a subject most people would consider inappropriate to depict in comics? What does the form of sequential images allow her to do that words would not? What does it not allow her to do?

WRITING EXERCISE: Stories in Pictures and Stories in Words

1. Compose dialogue appropriate to each frame of the comic strip from *Peanuts,* at least one line by each character in each frame.

   or

2. Compose additional text to accompany imagined frames that you would insert between at least three of the frames in the page from *Fun Home,* expanding the story as it appears here.

Once you are finished, compare your version with the original, told primarily through pictures. What do the words add to the *Peanuts* strip or the extra frames to *Fun Home*? Is there any way in which they detract? Why do you think Schulz chose to use only very few words and Bechdel a limited number of frames?

LIKE A MEDIUM CHANNELING LOST SOULS, THE FILAMENT OF A SPACE HEATER VIBRATED TUNELESSLY TO OUR FOOTFALLS.

JINNG
ZINNG

IT WASN'T THE SORT OF PLACE YOU WANTED TO BE ALONE IN.

WAIT FOR ME!

ON THE OTHER HAND, IT WAS NOT PARTICULARLY SCARY TO SPEND THE NIGHT IN THE FUNERAL HOME PROPER, EVEN WHEN WE HAD A DEAD PERSON.

MY BROTHERS AND I OFTEN SLEPT THERE WITH MY GRANDMOTHER.

PERMANENT GREASE STAIN FROM MY DEAD GRANDFATHER'S VITALIS

TO QUIET US DOWN, GRAMMY WOULD LET US SWEEP THE CEILING WITH THE BEAM OF HER FLASHLIGHT IN SEARCH OF BUGS.

THERE'S ONE!

PISS-ANT!

WHEN WE SPOTTED ONE, SHE WOULD DECLARE IT TO BE EITHER A "PISS-ANT" OR AN "ANTIE-MIRE"-- A TAXONOMIC DIFFERENTIATION I WAS NEVER CLEAR ON--AND SQUASH IT WITH A RAG ON THE END OF A BROOM.

Alison Bechdel, *Fun Home: A Family Tragicomic* (New York: Houghton Mifflin, 2006), p. 39. "Fun Home" is what the Bechdel children call the funeral home on Main Street run by their father's family. Their grandfather dies when Alison is three, but the grandmother still lives in the front of the building. This is where the page illustrated here takes place.

Moving Images

As the photographer Eadweard Muybridge documented in a series of photographs during the late nineteenth century, the naked eye is at times unable accurately to perceive rapid motion (see p. 170). Moving images take advantage of this perceptual confusion, flashing sequential images past our eyes faster than we can process them, and thus creating the illusion of movement. The reason we cannot perceive the gaps between the frames can be attributed to **persistence of vision,** a visual phenomenon that causes our brain to fill in the spaces. Televisions and computer screens create the illusion of motion with a different process. They are composed of minute pixels of visual information that our brains formulate into recognizable images.

The Shot The basic unit of meaning in moving images is called the **shot.** Individual shots are assembled by editors who splice them together; the gaps between shots are known as **cuts.** Sometimes cuts are noticeable, as in a music video composed of very brief shots cutting to different images, but usually we do not notice them at all unless we are paying close attention. We can ask the same questions about a shot as we did about a still image:

- What are its basic visual qualities: What are the major lines and patterns that divide up the frame? How does the image make use of and define the seven spaces around it (known in cinema studies as *offscreen space*)?
- How are the subjects or characters framed by the camera: Are they shown in *close-up* (just their head and shoulders) or in *long shot* (framed by their setting) or somewhere in between? Does the framing remain consistent, or does the camera move to change our perspective on the action?

Because our experience of moving images unfolds in time, our perception of that time and the way moving images can manipulate that perception is essential to our understanding of them. Consequently, we must take into account the temporal quality of moving images. A rapid pace of editing, a frenetic pace of action, a driving piece of music on the soundtrack, a dynamic visual composition are some of the ways moving pictures can intensify and speed up the pace of our experience: a music video, an action-adventure movie, a slapstick comedy. Conversely, a sequence of drawn-out shots, a deliberate pace of action with many lines of dialogue, contemplative music on the soundtrack, and a muted visual composition can slow down and draw out our

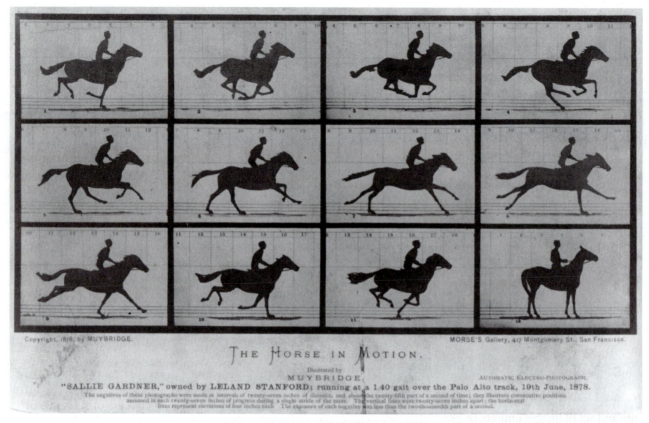

Eadweard Muybridge, *The Horse in Motion* (1879). Using a camera designed for capturing motion, Muybridge established what could not be seen with the naked eye: a running horse moves its right and left legs separately, and not together as previously thought.

experience of a concert film, a drama, or a comedy of manners.

The Scene   Once you have analyzed the visual qualities of specific shots, you are ready to consider them in terms of their effect on the larger shape of the film. Some types of moving images, such as music videos or short subjects, are best approached shot-by-shot, but feature-length films are better analyzed in terms of the stories they tell, through a narrative segmentation (p. 27). Individual shots combine to form specific **scenes,** defined with reference to the theater as a sequence of actions occurring in an unbroken stretch of time in a single locale. Sometimes a single shot coincides with a single scene, but more frequently there will be many shots per scene. When you are summarizing a movie or a sequence of moving images, the best way to start is by breaking it down into scenes, and listing the events that occur in each scene.

Scenes also raise questions related to staging and narrative:

- What are the styles of acting, costume, make-up?
- How are the events of the plot realized visually in the space created by the camera?

Consider how visual style illuminates narrative themes, and how narrative themes are affected by visual choices. The standard movie scene begins with an *establishing shot* to orient us to the setting, and then gradually cuts into medium close-ups of the principal characters in dialogue. But there are many other ways to stage action on film (see the photo, top of p. 171), and each of them will cause us to perceive the events portrayed in a somewhat different manner.

As viewers, we are accustomed to certain combinations of shots and certain ways of shooting certain scenes. Becoming aware of your expectations as a viewer and of ways in which visual media can meet or confound those expectations is the first step in thinking critically about them. For example, the opening scene of David Lynch's disturbing drama, *Blue Velvet* (1986), begins with what appears to be a standard establishing shot of a suburban neighborhood. Instead of gradually cutting into a conversation introducing the principal characters in their home, however, the camera zooms ever closer into an innocuous sector of the green lawn. Finally, reaching a degree of magnification reserved primarily for nature movie details of tiny creatures, the camera reveals, in extreme close-up, a severed ear lying in the grass (see p. 170). Where we had expected an ordinary scene, the camera has uncovered an unexpected and shocking object. As the director stated in an interview, "It had to be an ear because it's an opening. An ear is wide and you go down into it. It goes somewhere vast." Opening scenes frequently establish the tone of what is to come, the ways in which a film will meet or surprise our expectations.

Interactive Images

The rise of digital technology over the last few decades has introduced a new type of images which we can call **interactive images,** images without a fixed order and whose structure and meaning are often at least partly determined through choices taken by the viewer (see p. 172). *Video games, CD-ROMs,* and the *Internet* are important examples of this medium. We encounter still images and moving pictures in all of these media, but usually in the context of interactive images, particularly the Internet web-page, where images can nest within images, or transmute from one thing to another, or transport your screen to another site and set of images entirely, or present you with a cascading flurry of images simultaneously, with or without the click of a mouse. Internet technology is changing all the time, and is moving steadily toward an ever greater synthesis of sound, image, movement, and choice: multiple windows and menus on a single screen, screens within screens playing movies, music videos, games, or

A frame enlargement from a scene in the 2003 film *Crouching Tiger, Hidden Dragon.* A wide-angle lens allows an establishing shot of the street setting on the right-hand side of the frame while also framing the two principals on a balcony in medium long shot, or "American shot," a typical distance for exterior dialogue. Costume tells us this is a period drama, the actors' expressions suggest a tense drama, and the large number of armed extras promises spectacular action as well.

slide shows, and other types of spatial effects impossible to achieve on a printed page, a flat canvas, or a traditional reel of celluloid film.

Here are some pointers for thinking critically about interactive images and other new visual media:

• Always begin your critical thinking from the basis of the single image, just as with texts you work from the basic semantic unit of the line of verse or sentence of prose.

• Make a visual description of each component, one by one, rather than trying to encompass everything at once.

• If there are too many components to describe individually, describe only the key images. Address questions of form and style before those of plot and theme; the latter will follow naturally once your visual description comes together.

• Working out from the image, choose larger segments that make sense together.

• Base yourself on a menu or set of choices, on a Web page or on some other principle that fits the data in front of you.

• Seek the patterns behind the relationship between images or links: are they connected by a particular theme or topic, a visual motif, a plot element, a name, a place?

• Try to formulate the argument of the site or collection of interactive images, the principle that holds it together and that has led someone to invest the time and effort in constructing it.

Image of a single frame, or **frame enlargement,** from the movie *Blue Velvet* (1986).

Choose Your Own Carl - Section 1

COMPLETED NOVEMBER 1st, 1998

Click on any panel to see the winning suggestion and all other suggestions from that week.
(Note: The starter panel, "promise me...," and the grave panels came from the original Carl strip, so no suggestion lists for those.)

Scott McCloud, *Choose Your Own Carl* (1998–2001). Section 1 of 6 of "The Web's only *Fully Interactive, Multiple Path, Reader-Written, Death-Obsessed Comics Extravaganza.*" Like many of the comics and links on McCloud's Web site (http://www.scottmccloud.com/index.html), the style and form of *Choose Your Own Carl* are inseparable from the medium for which they were created. Our enjoyment of them, however, relies just as heavily on our familiarity with the age-old conventions of print narrative, set up by the premise of the initial frame: "Promise me you won't drink and drive, Carl."

Remember, what makes the new ways of navigating space presented by the Internet so exciting is not just what is new and unfamiliar about them. We enjoy the novel relationships of image and text because what is familiar about them—the conventions you have studied in the first four chapters of this book—gives us a context from which to process and appreciate what we have never seen before.

LOOKING BACK: Organizing the World of Literature

- Literary texts, movies, music, and many other forms of art are categorized by their creators and by their audience according to their type or *genre.*

- Genres have specific *conventions;* these conventions raise particular *expectations* in their audience that may or may not be fully met by a particular example of a genre.

- *Poetry* can be defined in terms of its *theme,* its *form,* or its *creator.*

- *Prosody* refers to the conventions of metrical composition in poetry. Most verse in English is either *accentual* or *accentual-syllabic.*

- Meter is measured according to the principles of *scansion,* which records the number of *feet* in a line. The primary feet used in English verse are: *iamb, trochee, spondee, dactyl,* and *anapest.*

- Varieties of rhyme and repetition in English verse include *end-rhymes,* which can be either *masculine* or *feminine* and can be *perfect, half-rhymes, off-rhymes,* or *eye rhymes. Internal rhymes* are closely related to other sound effects such as *alliteration, assonance,* and *consonance.*

- *Diction* refers to the choice of words, their spelling, and their arrangement in the poetic line or in prose.

- *Fiction* is categorized according to its form—the *short story,* the *novella,* the *novel*—and according to its genre.

- The materials of fiction writing include the following: *story events,* which are ordered and recounted as *plot; character; point of view,* which includes *mode,* or form of narration; *range* of narration; *depth* of narration; *temporal relations* between the narrator and the events being narrated; *setting; genre conventions.*

- The tools of fiction writing include: *diction; imagery* and *literary devices; style.*

- There is no definitive version of a *play.* We read the *script* of a play, but each production and each performance in that production presents a different version.

- The *story world* of a play is often vast, but most plays choose just a few events in that world to structure their *plot* in a *dramatic arc.*

- Plays are composed almost entirely of *action,* which can take the form either of *gesture* or *dialogue.*

- The Greek philosopher Aristotle defined three fundamental dramatic *unities:* of *place,* of *time,* and of *action.*

- *Stage directions* refer to everything in the script besides dialogue, and present the author's guidelines for staging the play.

- The terms *range of characterization* and *depth of characterization* define a play's use of characters. Conventions of character include *foils* and *types,* and the conflict between *protagonist* and *antagonist.*

- *Staging* a play encompasses three areas: (1) *sets, lighting, sound* and *music,* (2) *props, costume,* and *makeup,* and (3) *character speech* and *gesture.*

- We can also speak of *staging* to refer to the way the play's script uses *diction, imagery,* and *style* to render its *theme.*

- The conventions of *tragedy* include larger-than-life characters, emotions, and catastrophes; the use of *irony of action* or *of words;* and themes addressing conflicts between fundamental social values. The primary types of tragedy include Greek tragedy, Elizabethan tragedy, and realist drama.

- *Comedy* can refer either to *moments* in a variety of dramas or to particular types of comedy, including "Old" Greek Comedy, "New" Greek Comedy, Shakespearean comedy, romantic comedy, comedy of manners, tragicomedy (or dark comedy), farce, satire, and parody.

- The forms of *modern drama* include realist drama and a variety of experimental forms created in reaction against it, including theater of the absurd and epic, or Brechtian, drama.

- *Visual media* are texts that create meaning primarily through visual means. They include what are traditionally termed the *fine arts*—painting, printmaking, and sculpture—as well as media unique to the modern world such as photography, cinema, comics, and digital images.

- The analysis of images begins with patterns and framing. The image is divided into sectors and analyzed in conjunction with the six spaces around the frame.

- Images are generally placed in sequence together in order to tell a story. The spaces between the frames are crucial in defining the *temporal relationship* in the sequence.

- Moving images are composed of *shots* and *scenes.* Shots are best analyzed in terms of their visual qualities, scenes in terms of narrative qualities.

- Interactive images in the virtual space of the Internet can be approached with the same tools of critical thinking that are used to approach conventional images.

CHAPTER 5

READING THE WORLD

EXPLORING
THE FORMS OF
LITERATURE

The novelist E. L. Doctorow once said that "writing is a socially accepted form of schizophrenia." This is certainly true for the creative writer, who to succeed must be able persuasively to inhabit different characters and voices. But it is equally true for you as a critical writer, for each assignment you write will have a different organization, a different goal, and a different audience. Moreover, as the English novelist Angela Carter notes, each text you read elicits a different response and reaction: "Reading a book is like re-writing it for yourself. You bring to a novel, anything you read, all your experience of the world. You bring your history and you read it in your own terms." This process, too, in a minor way, is a kind of schizophrenia. Of course, there is a significant difference between writing as schizophrenia and schizophrenia as disease: the writer must remain in control of her multiple personalities and must be able to impart a coherent message to her audience. In this chapter, we work further with distinctions between genres and distinctions between the kinds of critical writing you may be called on to do in your academic and professional careers, focusing on poetry, fiction, plays, and nonfiction.

IMAGINING THE WORLD: POETRY

Just as meter, rhyme, and repetition are tools for the composition of poetry, so are they tools for critical thinking and writing about poetry. And just as aspiring poets must familiarize themselves with the tools of their craft in order to put them to creative use (or to decide to put them aside), so must we, as readers of poetry, be familiar enough with the tools of the genre to be able to discern the kinds of meaning and arguments made through them. The following three poems suggest the range of subjects available to the poet beyond the love poem, and the different formal means three poets have chosen to use to address their subject of the relationship between individuals in society, which range from poverty in a great metropolis to a nighttime journey, to an encounter in an airport bathroom.

> *Poetry is language at its most distilled and powerful.*
>
> —RITA DOVE

William Blake 1757–1827

One of the major poets of English Romanticism, William Blake is equally well-known as a print-maker and painter. Living all his life in London, Blake devoted himself to developing a printing technique able to express his complex personal mythology in a seamless blend of image and text. Among his works are *Songs of Innocence and Experience* (1794), *The Marriage of Heaven and Hell* (1793), *Jerusalem* (1804), and *Milton* (1804). He also produced series of watercolor illustrations to Dante's *Divine Comedy* and Milton's *Paradise Lost*.

London

I wander thro' each charter'd street,
Near where the charter'd Thames does flow,
And mark in every face I meet
Marks of weakness, marks of woe.

In every cry of every Man,   5
In every Infant's cry of fear,
In every voice, in every ban,
The mind-forg'd manacles I hear.

How the Chimney-sweeper's cry
Every black'ning Church appalls;   10
And the hapless Soldier's sigh
Runs in blood down Palace walls.

But most thro' midnight streets I hear
How the youthful Harlot's curse
Blasts the new born Infant's tear,   15
And blights with plagues the Marriage hearse.

[1794]

"London," as illustrated in William Blake's book *Songs of Innocence and Experience* (1794).

QUESTIONS FOR REFLECTION AND DISCUSSION

1. As part of processing your reading of the poem, look up the word "charter" in a dictionary. Blake's usage of the word is unusual here. What meaning or meanings do you think it has in this context? What is the effect of the repetition of the word in lines 1 and 2?

2. Discuss the meter and rhythm of line 4 in relation to the meter and rhythm of the first quatrain as a whole. Compare it with lines 8, 12, and 16.

3. What is the sense of "mind-forg'd manacles" and how does the alliteration affect the meaning of the line?

4. What is the relation between the speaker of the poem and his subject? What tone does he take toward it?

5. Study the illuminated version of the poem presented on page 175. Compare it with the poem in its plain-text version.

Robert Frost 1874–1963

Robert Frost, winner of four Pulitzer Prizes and considered by many the greatest American poet of the first half of the twentieth century, was born in San Francisco, California. Although educated at Dartmouth and Harvard, he would develop the poetic persona of a down-to-earth New England farmer. After establishing himself as a poet in England, he bought a farm in New Hampshire and taught as a professor at Amherst College from 1916 to 1938. "Stopping by Woods on a Snowy Evening" is one of Robert Frost's best-known poems. Composed, like "London," in four quatrains of iambic tetrameter, its use of the meter is quite distinct. As you read Frost's poem and compare it with "London," consider not only the effect of the radically different setting but the shift in the tone of the speaker.

Stopping by Woods on a Snowy Evening

Whose woods these are I think I know.
His house is in the village though;
He will not see me stopping here
To watch his woods fill up with snow.

My little horse must think it queer   5
To stop without a farmhouse near
Between the woods and frozen lake
The darkest evening of the year.

He gives his harness bells a shake
To ask if there is some mistake.   10
The only other sound's the sweep
Of easy wind and downy flake.

The woods are lovely, dark and deep.
But I have promises to keep,
And miles to go before I sleep,   15
And miles to go before I sleep.

[1923]

The home in Franconia, New Hampshire, purchased by Robert and Elinor Frost in 1915. They lived here until 1920, and summered in the house until 1938.

QUESTIONS FOR REFLECTION AND DISCUSSION

1. Part of the soothing effect of Frost's poem is its unusual rhyme scheme. What is this rhyme scheme, and how does it contribute to the poem's tone?

2. Unlike the meter in "London," the final lines of each quatrain do not break with the rhythm of the previous lines. What is the effect of keeping the meter regular throughout rather than breaking its pattern, as Blake does in "London"?

3. Both poems impart the mood of a wandering, solitary speaker. What is similar about the two speakers, and what is different?

4. Discuss the poetic means whereby one poem depicts the harsh life of the city, and another poem portrays the quiet of the country.

Mary Oliver

b. 1935

Born in Cleveland, Ohio, Mary Oliver attended Case Western University and Vassar College. She has taught poetry at a number of different schools, and has received several fellowships and awards, including a National Endowment for the Arts Fellowship and a Guggenheim Fellowship. Her first volume of poetry, *No Voyage and Other Poems,* appeared in 1963. Her collection *American Primitive,* which includes the poem "August" (p. 49), received the Pulitzer Prize in 1984. "Singapore" was published in Oliver's 1990 collection, *House of Light.* Like "Stopping by Woods on a Snowy Evening," "Singapore" tells the story of a traveler and her interaction with the world around her. Oliver chooses an open form—with no apparent meter, no rhymes, and few repetitions—to describe the speaker's unexpected encounter. As you read, compare the tone with the previous two poems, and try to specify the different effect on your reading caused by the lack of prosodic elements.

Singapore

In Singapore, in the airport,
a darkness was ripped from my eyes.
In the women's restroom, one compartment stood open.
A woman knelt there, washing something
    in the white bowl.   5

Disgust argued in my stomach
and I felt, in my pocket, for my ticket.

A poem should always have birds in it.
Kingfishers, say, with their bold eyes and gaudy wings.
Rivers are pleasant, and of course trees.   10
A waterfall, or if that's not possible, a fountain
    rising and falling.
A person wants to stand in a happy place, in a poem.

When the woman turned I could not answer her face.
Her beauty and her embarrassment struggled together, and   15
    neither could win.
She smiled and I smiled. What kind of nonsense is this?
Everybody needs a job.

Yes, a person wants to stand in a happy place, in a poem.
But first we must watch her as she stares down at her labor,   20
    which is dull enough.
She is washing the tops of the airport ashtrays, as big as
    hubcaps, with a blue rag.
Her small hands turn the metal, scrubbing and rinsing.
She does not work slowly, nor quickly, but like a river.   25
Her dark hair is like the wing of a bird.

I don't doubt for a moment that she loves her life.
And I want her to rise up from the crust and the slop
    and fly down to the river.
This probably won't happen.   30
But maybe it will.
If the world were only pain and logic, who would want it?

Of course, it isn't.
Neither do I mean anything miraculous, but only
the light that can shine out of a life. I mean   35
the way she unfolded and refolded the blue cloth,
The way her smile was only for my sake; I mean
the way this poem is filled with trees, and birds.

        [1990]

QUESTIONS FOR REFLECTION AND DISCUSSION

1. How do we know that we are reading a poem? Does the lack of prosodic devices make the poem seem more realistic than those of Blake and Frost? Less realistic? How and why?

2. What about the subject of the poem makes the speaker feel it to be inappropriate to put in a poem? Do the poems by Blake and Frost fit her criteria? Are they in "a happy place"? Do they have birds in them?

3. In what way is the speaker justified in concluding that her poem "is filled with trees, and birds"?

4. If you were going to write a poem emulating one of these three poems, or responding to it, which one would you choose, and why?

Orchids and tropical garden at Changi Airport, Singapore, an important global transportation hub frequently cited for its service excellence. First opened in 1981, the airport includes a number of flower gardens, along with a butterfly garden, a fish pond, and a waterfall. Does the actual presence of nature (some of it added since Oliver first wrote her poem "Singapore") within the airport strengthen or weaken the effect of the contrast made by the poem?

WRITING EXERCISE: A Social Response

Social poems are often meant to provoke a response in the reader; certainly this is the case of "London." Write a poem or a paragraph responding to the speaker of one of the three poems above. You might choose to imagine the point of view of the chimney sweep, the traveler's horse, or the cleaning woman; or you might choose to address the speaker as a friend or audience member who has just finished listening to the poem. Try as much as possible to respond using the same terms and imagery that appear in the poem.

THREE POEMS ABOUT SOCIAL RELATIONS

Melissa Pabon's writing assignment on the three poems you have just read was in two parts. First, she was asked to write summaries of "London," "Stopping by Woods on a Snowy Evening," and "Singapore." After completing the summaries, she was asked to use them as the basis for a comparison paper on the three poems.

Pabon 1

Melissa Pabon
English Composition 2
Professor Martin
22 September 2009

Summaries of "London," "Stopping by Woods
on a Snowy Evening," and "Singapore"

"London" (1794) by William Blake is about the corruption and disease that run rampant in the city for which the poem is named. The speaker expresses his disdain for the monarchy that has an oppressive control over the city but sheds a blind eye toward its citizens. Of these citizens, the speaker describes the plight of the chimney sweep, young children who cry both literally and figuratively about their jobs, and the soldier who risks life and limb for a country that will not grant him any recognition. The speaker also describes the prostitute who roams the streets, passing disease from bed to bed, contributing to the ever growing population of orphans in the city. By describing the problems of London, Blake shows the reader the obligation that the monarchy has to its people and the ever widening gap between the rich and the poor.

"Stopping by Woods on a Snowy Evening" (1923) by Robert Frost is a poem that is two-fold in meaning. At first glance the poem is about a man who, while riding his horse on "the darkest evening of the year," gets driven off the usual path and ends up in a secluded area of the woods. His horse notices the change en route and motions for his rider to get back on course. The speaker comes to the vital realization that even though the woods are lovely and inviting, he has much to do before his time is up. The repetition in the last two stanzas of the poem helps to reiterate for the speaker his promise to stay on the beaten track and not be distracted from the road of life.

In the poem "Singapore" (1990), Mary Oliver writes about the encounter with a cleaning lady in the restroom of a Singapore airport. The speaker walks into the restroom while the bathroom attendant is kneeling on the floor, busily wiping a toilet bowl. When the two women encounter each other, the attendant smiles to hide her embarrassment while the speaker is overcome with disgust. The speaker finds poetry in the encounter with the woman by comparing her dark hair to the "wing of a bird." Poetry is seeing beauty in everyday things and being able to extract a multitude of feelings and ideas from one little incident.

QUESTIONS FOR REFLECTION AND DISCUSSION

1. A summary should report the events of a poem without offering an interpretation of their meaning. How well has Melissa succeeded in each case in summarizing without interpreting?

2. A summary should analyze the formal elements of the poem as well as its events. How well has Melissa incorporated an analysis of formal elements in each summary?

3. In your opinion, which of the three summaries is more effective, and why? Which is less effective, and why?

WRITING EXERCISE: Revising a Summary

1. Choose one of Melissa Pabon's three summaries and revise it. Include material from your reflection and discussion in your summary.

2. Compare your summary with Melissa's. Are you pleased with the result? Have you responded to everything that you critiqued in her summary? Looking back, is there anything in her summary that you prefer to your own?

Here is the comparison paper Melissa wrote after completing her summaries of the three poems. As you read it, consider how well she has incorporated her work on the summaries into the paper. Annotate and comment on the paper as you would during a peer review. Consider the strengths and weaknesses of this draft, and how Melissa should revise it to clarify her argument and make her writing more effective.

Melissa Pabon
English Composition 2
Professor Martin
5 October 2009

The Importance of Everyday Occurrences in
"London," "Stopping by Woods on a Snowy Evening," and "Singapore"

"London" (1794) by William Blake, "Singapore" (1990) by Mary Oliver, and "Stopping by Woods on a Snowy Evening" (1923) by Robert Frost are three poems that are similar yet different in many ways. All three poems are comparable in that their subject matter is about everyday occurrences that contain hidden meanings and themes. In contrast, the structure and rhythm of each poem is totally different, ranging from free verse to traditional verse.

In Blake's poem "London," the speaker describes for the reader his daily encounters with the disease and rampant corruption that line London's "chartered" streets. As he depicts the plight of the city's inhabitants, from the figurative and literal cries of the chimney-sweep to the "harlot's curse," one cannot help but hear in each line the disdain for authority, the distance between the rich and the poor, and the excessiveness of corruption which are some of the themes that Blake addresses as problems that need to be reformed. Blake does this deliberately to shock people into action in order to make things better for the city. Mary Oliver's theme in her poem "Singapore" is apparent but is still kept slightly under wraps as not to be too blatant or in your face. She writes of an awkward encounter in a Singapore bathroom which is anything but sweet-smelling roses. She makes a social comment to the reader that beauty is in the eye of the beholder. Oliver breaks with the notion that all poems, or poetry itself, should be about a particular theme. In fact, she takes the discomfort and humiliation of the situation and goes beyond these emotions to discover an allure, charm, and elegance that are undetected by the naked eye.

Of the three poems, Robert Frost's "Stopping by Woods on a Snowy Evening" is the most ambiguous when it comes to theme and meaning. When reading it, he or she finds that the poem must be read more than once to come up with a clear idea of what is going on. At first glance, we get an account of a man who, while taking a leisurely ride down a familiar path, gets lost and comes across an unexplored woods. It is only when one digs down below the surface he or she hits on the theme of death and dying. The speaker alludes to the theme of the poem in the eighth line and in the repetition of the last two lines of the poem where he talks of "miles to go before I sleep."

The poems of Blake, Oliver, and Frost are distinct in form and style. "London" and "Stopping by Woods" are very much alike in that they are written in traditional verse. Both poems have a rhyme scheme, which is a habitual feature of poetry. In "London," Blake features four quatrains in an *abab, cdcd, efef, gdgd* scheme. Frost's poem also features four quatrains, but in an unusual *aaba, bbcb, ccdc, dddd* rhyme scheme. Another feature that is present in Frost's poem is the refrain. This is apparent in the last two verses of the poem. The refrain is used for dramatic effect as a reminder to the narrator of his urgency to keep on course and not fall off the beaten path. "Singapore" does not make use of traditional rhyming or meter. Oliver instead uses free verse in which there is no rhyme scheme or set form. Her poem is not conventional in any sense, even though there is style and function. "Singapore" was written as a break from conformity, which Oliver does with great passion and zeal. The commonplace use of rhyme in poetry would not make any difference and possibly detract from the essence of the poem. Oliver sends a message to all writers and poets saying that a good poem does not need to be convoluted or tainted, it just has to evoke a great deal of sentiment and emotion.

"London," "Singapore," and "Stopping by Woods" are three poems that are equally diverse as well as related in many ways. Each poem is similar in that they contain hidden meanings that are concealed in ordinary everyday occurrences. "London" is on the surface about a city wallowing in filth and corruption. The underlying theme is the narrator's yearning for reform as well as a call for action by the monarchy and possibly by the citizens of London. Mary Oliver takes the theme of beauty and allure from an awkward encounter in a Singapore bathroom. She breaks stereotypes by twisting preconceived notions of what traditional poetry should be about. "Stopping by Woods" is the most convoluted of the three poems when it comes to meaning. Readers often have to tackle the poem more than once to find out that its theme is death and dying. Each of the poems is different in form and style. Frost and Blake both use end rhyme. The major difference between the two is the rhyme scheme they use, and Frost's use of a refrain. "Singapore" uses free verse. Oliver's decision to use no rhyme scheme is deliberate. She greatly wants to break down barriers set up by conventional poetry.

Not all poetry has to abide by a set of rules written in stone. Poetry must be able to evoke an abundance of emotions that can range from the very high to the very low. Only then can it truly point us in the direction that the writer wants us to follow.

Works Cited

Blake, William. "London." Pike and Acosta 175.

Frost, Robert. "Stopping by Woods on a Snowy Evening." Pike and Acosta 176.

Pike, David L., and Ana M. Acosta, ed. *Literature: A World of Writing.* New York: Pearson Longman, 2011. Print.

Oliver, Mary. "Singapore." Pike and Acosta 177.

QUESTIONS FOR REFLECTION AND DISCUSSION

1. What is Melissa's argument? What is her thesis? Are they clearly expressed? How well does each paragraph support and develop her argument?

2. How has Melissa built on the work in her summaries?

3. What are the strengths of Melissa's draft? What are its weaknesses?

4. Go through Melissa's draft carefully, marking and commenting in terms of grammar and mechanics as well as style and argument. Using the guidelines for revision in Chapter 2 (p. 63), formulate a detailed plan for revisions.

WRITING EXERCISE: Revising a Comparison Paper

1. Write a revision of Melissa Pabon's comparison paper based on your review as outlined in the Questions for Reflection and Discussion above (#4). Detail her argument, add what you think needs to be added, expand what works in her draft, eliminate repetition, and rewrite or eliminate what does not work.

2. Review your own revision and evaluate its strengths and weaknesses. In what ways have you improved on Melissa's draft? In what ways could you revise your own draft to improve it further?

IMAGINING THE WORLD TOPICS FOR ESSAYS

1. Analyze the use of meter and/or rhyme in a poem included in this book.

2. Find an open form poem and analyze its formal components.

3. Compare a rhyming and a nonrhyming poem.

4. Compare two or three poems that use the same poetic form.

5. Compare two or three poems by the same poet, using either selections in this book or from another source.

6. Write an essay analyzing the use of rhyme in a contemporary musical genre such as hip-hop, show tunes, or rock.

7. Write an essay on the use of prosody in contemporary poetry.

DESCRIBING THE WORLD: STORIES

Unlike the other genres we study in this book, we categorize fiction according to the kinds of events (mystery, romance, science fiction) it narrates rather than the specific *forms* it takes. Moreover, within these broad categories, we find an enormous range of possible results of the writer's combination of the different materials and tools of fiction. As the American short-story writer John Cheever once said,

"Fiction is experimentation; when it ceases to be that, it ceases to be fiction." The stories in this book range in time over the last two centuries and in space around the world; collectively, they demonstrate how many different effects the fiction writer can achieve with the materials of plot, character, point of view, and setting, and the tools of diction, imagery, literary devices, and style. What all these stories share, as the

Good fiction reveals feeling, refines events, locates importance and, though its methods are as mysterious as they are varied, intensifies the experience of living our own lives.
—VINCENT CANBY

late contemporary American writer David Foster Wallace said about fiction in general, is that they're about "what it is to be a human being."

Julia Alvarez b. 1950

Born in New York City, Julia Alvarez spent her childhood in the Dominican Republic, returning to New York with her family as political refugees when she was ten. She completed her undergraduate education at Middlebury College and received an MFA from Syracuse University, and taught at various schools before returning to Middlebury, where she has been a professor of English since 1988. Alvarez began publishing poetry in the mid-1980s; her first novel, *How the Garcia Girls Lost Their Accents*, portrayed the lives of Dominican immigrants in New York, and incorporated the previously published story "Snow"; the continuing story of the main character is the subject of her third novel, *Yo!* As you read Julia Alvarez's "Snow," consider how she uses description to establish the setting and context of her very short story with consummate efficiency.

SNOW

OUR FIRST YEAR IN NEW YORK WE RENTED A small apartment with a Catholic school nearby, taught by the Sisters of Charity, hefty women in long black gowns and bonnets that made them look peculiar, like dolls in mourning. I liked them a lot, especially my grandmotherly fourth-grade teacher, Sister Zoe. I had a lovely name, she said, and she had me teach the whole class how to pronounce it. Yo-landa. As the only immigrant in my class, I was put in a special seat in the first row by the window, apart from the other children, so that Sister Zoe could tutor me without disturbing them. Slowly, she enunciated the new words I was to repeat: *laundromat, cornflakes, subway, snow*.

Soon I picked up enough English to understand holocaust was in the air. Sister Zoe explained to a wide-eyed classroom what was happening in Cuba.

Russian missiles were being assembled, trained supposedly on New York City. President Kennedy, looking worried too, was on the television at home, explaining we might have to go to war against the Communists. At school, we had air-raid drills: An ominous bell would go off and we'd file into the hall, fall to the floor, cover our heads with our coats, and imagine our hair falling out, the bones in our arms going soft. At home, Mami and my sisters and I said a rosary for world peace. I heard new vocabulary: *nuclear bomb, radioactive fallout, bomb shelter*. Sister Zoe explained how it would happen. She drew a picture of a mushroom on the blackboard and dotted a flurry of chalk marks for the dusty fallout that would kill us all.

The months grew cold, November, December. It was dark when I got up in the morning, frosty when I followed my breath to school. One morning, as I sat at my desk daydreaming out the window, I saw dots in the air like the ones Sister Zoe had drawn—random at first, then lots and lots. I shrieked, "Bomb! Bomb!" Sister Zoe jerked around, her full black skirt ballooning as she hurried to my side. A few girls began to cry.

But then Sister Zoe's shocked look faded. "Why, Yolanda dear, that's snow!" She laughed. "Snow."

5   "Snow," I repeated. I looked out the window warily. All my life I had heard about the white crystals that fell out of American skies in the winter. From my desk I watched the fine powder dust the sidewalk and parked cars below. Each flake was different, Sister Zoe said, like a person, irreplaceable and beautiful.

[1984]

QUESTIONS FOR REFLECTION AND DISCUSSION

1. What are the most important elements of description in the story? What is the function of each element within the story's form?

2. The words Yolanda learns are dense with the symbolism of American culture. Compare the two lists of English words she mentions. What motivates the choice of these words to stand for the immigrant's new culture?

3. The final paragraph marks a stylistic shift from the rest of the story and a change of tone from the prior narration. How would you characterize this change?

4. "Snow" is the title of the story; the figurative meaning of this image underlies the story and its themes of immigration and unfamiliarity with a new language and culture. Beyond the girl's literal misunderstanding of the falling snow, what figurative meaning is developed through this image?

5. We reproduce below a Sunday strip from the comic *Peanuts*, first published around the same time as "Snow" is set. Compare the use to which each text puts a child's confusion between snow and atomic fallout.

A 1960s comic strip from Charles Schulz's *Peanuts* based on the same misunderstanding described by Julia Alvarez in "Snow."

A DESCRIPTIVE ESSAY

Description is a fundamental tool of the fiction writer; it is also a key component of a number of different essays. To focus on the skill of description, Hashim Naseem's class was assigned a two-page descriptive essay. Without concern for narrative, the students were asked to describe a person, a setting, or a thing in such a way as to provide a vivid impression of its defining characteristics. As you read Hashim's essay, consider the choices he made in writing his description, and what choices you would have made given the same subject.

Naseem 1

Hashim Naseem
English Composition 2
Professor Frank
5 September 2009

The Motherland

I am sitting down outside of my grandmother's house by Ghizri Road in Karachi, Pakistan. I am observing the lifestyle of the people that live here so I can gain a better understanding of where I came from, where my parents lived most of their lives, and why they chose to leave our motherland to come to America.

There is no artificial cement or asphalt to cover the true beauty of Mother Nature. The ground consists of soft, powder-like sand the color of the desert with a few anomalies of dark brown patches amongst it. There are rocks emerging from the sand in absolute randomness with their rough and edgy texture, with the appearance of what seems to be a polished gray, almost silver-like surface. There is a calm that comes with the cool breeze, a sense of belonging, a sense of understanding. In the sky there is the blazing sun, a white circle surrounded by an intense ring of yellow which emits unbearable heat making it impossible to walk barefoot. The kids from the neighborhood have become immune to the heat. You can tell as they run around barefoot because they cannot afford shoes. I look down on my Jordans, disgusted by the fact that I spent over a hundred dollars, when the children out here have to adapt to the harsh conditions of poverty.

There are people, all of the same descent, walking around half naked with scars over their bodies and their ribcages exposed due to lack of proper nutrition. I wonder how life would have been had my parents not come to America. Would I have been among the men walking around, with scars over my body and my skeletal structure exposed due to hunger? My mind trembles even to consider it.

As I begin to feel sorrow and pity for the people who have had to endure this hardship, I am overwhelmed by the happiness of the children. You can sense the joy of the children in the air almost as if it had a texture and can be cut through with a knife. Some children are flying kites, others are playing "lattoo," a game where a pear-shaped piece of wood, with ridges on the surface and a nail sticking out from the bottom, is spun on the floor with a piece of white string as quickly as humanly possible.

The smell of the gutter is so intense that it seems like you were sitting inside of it. Up until this day, I would have squeezed my nostrils if I had smelled such an awful odor, but now I take in as much as I can to remind myself of the smell of the motherland. Regardless of the dirty water and the stench of the sewage system, which is the norm in most of the country, some people in Pakistan wouldn't trade living there for the world.

My parents decided to move, my father mainly. He thought we would live a better life in America. In terms of our financial situation, he was definitely right. I live in a three-bedroom and two-and-a-half bathroom apartment with just my parents. I have a 42" Sony television set with an Onkyo 6.1 surround sound system and a six-disc DVD player in my living room. Compared to my cousins in Pakistan, I am living large. I think it would have been better to move a few years later. That way I could have grown up in my country and would have had somewhere to call home. Pakistan is my home, but all I have really seen is the poverty for which it is famous. I realized that in America, money is the be all and end all of everything. In my country, money is just something you use to survive physically.

When someone dies in Pakistan, the entire neighborhood cooks for the family of the deceased to help ease the pain regardless of the financial situation of the giver. With love, one can survive the many struggles and obstacles life has in store for us. That is what I learned that day on the sand outside my grandmother's house.

QUESTIONS FOR REFLECTION AND DISCUSSION

1. What are the more successful elements of description in Hashim's essay? Why? What are the less successful elements? Why?

2. Conduct research on a short story that has been incorporated into a novel—Julia Alvarez's "Snow" is one possible choice; Tim O'Brien's "The Things They Carried" (p. 447) is another. Write an essay comparing the short story on its own and as a part of the larger text of a novel.

3. Are there elements in Hashim's essay that do not belong in a strictly descriptive essay? To what form of essay would they belong?

4. If you were going to revise this material as a short story, similar to Alvarez's "Snow," how would you do it? What would you take out? What would you add? How else would you change the essay?

Children playing at Karachi, Pakistan, in 2006. The largest port, financial center, and most populous city in Pakistan, Karachi has an arid hot climate. Like most world-class cities, it also has a sizeable under-class of its estimated 15 million inhabitants living in poverty.

WRITING EXERCISE: The Power of Description

1. Choose a person, place, or thing that you know extremely well, or that you can observe directly. In preparation for writing, make a list of the defining qualities of your subject: What makes it different from other people, places, or things? What makes it worth writing about? In 1 to 2 pages, write a detailed description of your chosen subject. Try to impart the defining qualities of your subject solely through a description, without relating any events involving it, and without overt commentary or analysis.

2. Reflect on the writing process. Which part was easiest? Which part was most difficult? How satisfied are you with your description? What works about it? What do you think requires further revision?

3. How would you revise your essay as a short story with the description as its primary setting? What would you take out? What would you add? How else would you have to change the essay?

DESCRIBING THE WORLD TOPICS FOR ESSAYS

1. Choose a short story in Part 3 of this book and analyze its use of description.

2. Compare the use of point of view in two or three stories included in this book.

3. Compare the use of setting in two or three stories included in this book.

4. Compare a short story and the novel into which it was expanded or in which it was included ("Snow" is one possible choice).

5. Compare a short story on its own to its place within a collection in which it was included.

6. Write an essay outlining the conventions of a specific genre of fiction and ways in which several stories employ those conventions.

STAGING THE WORLD: PLAYS

Working on theater, we reflect on its *active* quality, as the choreographer Martha Graham put it. Theater exists in many different forms simultaneously: the script on the page, different productions, different performances, and different media. In the Writer @ Work section, we discuss strategies for viewing and writing about a theatrical performance and examine Joshua Cohen's response to a filmed version of Samuel Beckett's play, *Krapp's Last Tape*.

> *Theater is a verb before it is a noun, an act before it is a place.*
> —MARTHA GRAHAM

Samuel Beckett 1906–1989

Born outside of Dublin, Ireland, to a middle-class, Anglo-Irish, Protestant family, Samuel Beckett studied French and Italian at local Trinity College before leaving for Paris in 1928 to teach English. In Paris, he met the Irish writer James Joyce (p. 355). After returning briefly to Ireland and traveling around Europe, Beckett settled in Paris for good in 1937. He joined the French resistance in 1941, and was arrested by the Germans the following year. Beckett began his writing career as a novelist, first in English and then after the war in French, the language in which he also wrote his two most famous plays, *Waiting for Godot* (first performed in 1953), and *Endgame*. With *Krapp's Last Tape*, Beckett returned to composing in his native English and continued to write mostly short plays and narratives for the rest of his life. He was awarded the Nobel Prize for Literature in 1969. First performed in 1958, *Krapp's Last Tape* is the portrait of an old man looking back on his life. What makes it unusual is that it is performed by a single actor listening to a tape recorder that holds recordings he made when he was a younger man (back in the 1950s, sound was recorded on spools of magnetic tape). As you read the play, imagine the effect of hearing a single actor's voice playing himself at three different ages. Note the extensive use of stage direction, for much of the action in the play is gesture and movement by Krapp rather than dialogue. Watch also for the moments of Beckett's trademark deadpan humor, not only in the business with the banana peel, but in Krapp's attitude toward his past. Consider the role humor plays here in the depiction of a lonely and bitter character obsessed with a single memory.

KRAPP'S LAST TAPE

A late evening in the future.

Krapp's den.

Front a small table, the two drawers of which open towards audience.

Sitting at the table, facing front, i.e. across from the drawers, a wearish old man: Krapp.

Rusty black narrow trousers too short for him. Rusty black sleeveless waistcoat, four capacious pockets. Heavy silver watch and chain. Grimy white shirt open at neck, no collar. Surprising pair of dirty white boots, size ten at least, very narrow and pointed.

White face. Purple nose. Disordered grey hair. Unshaven.

Very near-sighted (but unspectacled). Hard of hear'ng.

Cracked voice. Distinctive intonation.

Laborious walk.

On the table a tape-recorder with microphone and a number of cardboard boxes containing reels of recorded tapes.

Table and immediately adjacent area in strong white light. Rest of stage in darkness.

Krapp remains a moment motionless, heaves a great sigh, looks at his watch, fumbles in his pockets, takes out an envelope, puts it back, fumbles, takes out a small bunch of keys, raises it to his eyes, chooses a key, gets up and moves to front of table. He stoops, unlocks first drawer, peers into it, feels about inside it, takes out a reel of tape, peers at it, puts it back, locks drawer, unlocks second drawer, peers into it, feels about inside it, takes out a large banana, peers at it, locks drawer, puts keys back in his pocket. He turns, advances to edge of stage, halts, strokes banana, peels it, drops skin at his feet, puts end of banana in his mouth and remains motionless, staring vacuously before him. Finally he bites off the end, turns aside and begins pacing to and fro at edge of stage, in the light, i.e., not more than four or five paces either way, meditatively eating banana. He treads on skin, slips, nearly falls, recovers himself, stoops and peers at skin and finally pushes it, still stooping, with his foot over the edge of stage into pit. He resumes his pacing, finishes banana, returns to table, sits down, remains a moment motionless, heaves a great sigh, takes keys from his pockets, raises them to his eyes, chooses key, gets up and moves to front of table, unlocks second drawer, takes out a second large banana, peers at it, locks drawer, puts back keys in his pocket, turns, advances to the stage, halts, strokes banana, peels it, tosses skin into pit, puts end of banana in his mouth and remains motionless, staring vacuously before him. Finally he has an idea, puts banana in his waistcoat pocket, the end emerging, and goes with all the speed he can muster backstage into darkness. Ten seconds. Loud pop of cork. Fifteen seconds. He comes back into light carrying an old ledger and sits down at table. He lays ledger on table, wipes his mouth, wipes his hands on the front of his waistcoat, brings them smartly together and rubs them.

Krapp (*briskly*): Ah! (*He bends over ledger, turns the pages, finds the entry he wants, reads.*) Box . . . thrree . . . spool . . . five. (*He raises his head and stares front. With relish.*) Spool! (*Pause.*) Spoooool! (*Happy smile. Pause. He bends over table, starts peering and poking at the boxes.*) Box . . . thrree . . . thrree . . . four . . . two . . . (*with surprise*) nine! good God! . . . seven . . . ah! the little rascal! (*He takes up box, peers at it.*) Box thrree. (*He lays it on table, opens it and peers at spools inside.*) Spool . . . (*he peers at ledger*) . . . five . . . (*he peers at spools*) . . . five . . . five . . . ah! the little scoundrel! (*He takes out a spool, peers at it.*) Spool five. (*He lays it on table, closes box three, puts it back with the others, takes up the spool.*) Box thrree, spool five. (*He bends over the machine, looks up. With relish.*) Spooooool! (*Happy smile. He bends, loads spool on machine, rubs his hands.*) Ah! (*He peers at ledger, reads entry at foot of page.*) Mother at rest at last . . . Hm . . . The black ball . . . (*He raises his head, stares blankly front. Puzzled.*) Black ball? . . . (*He peers again at ledger, reads.*) The dark nurse . . . (*He raises his head, broods, peers again at ledger, reads.*) Slight improvement in bowel condition . . . Hm . . . Memorable . . . what? (*He peers closer.*) Equinox, memorable equinox. (*He raises his head, stares blankly front. Puzzled.*) Memorable equinox? . . . (*Pause. He shrugs his shoulders, peers again at ledger, reads.*) Farewell to—(*he turns the page*)—love.

He raises his head, broods, bends over machine, switches on and assumes listening posture, i.e. leaning forward, elbows on table, hand cupping ear towards machine, face front.

Tape (*strong voice, rather pompous, clearly Krapp's at a much earlier time*): Thirty-nine today, sound as a—(*Settling himself more comfortable he knocks one of the boxes off the table, curses, switches off, sweeps boxes and ledger violently to the ground, winds tape back to beginning, switches on, resumes posture.*) Thirty-nine today, sound as a bell, apart from my old weakness, and intellectually I have now every reason

to suspect at the . . . (*hesitates*) . . . crest of the wave—or thereabouts. Celebrated the awful occasion, as in recent years, quietly at the Winehouse. Not a soul. Sat before the fire with closed eyes, separating the grain from the husks. Jotted down a few notes, on the back on an envelope. Good to be back in my den, in my old rags. Have just eaten I regret to say three bananas and only with difficulty refrained from a fourth. Fatal things for a man with my condition. (*Vehemently.*) Cut 'em out! (*Pause.*) The new light above my table is a great improvement. With all this darkness round me I feel less alone. (*Pause.*) In a way. (*Pause.*) I love to get up and move about in it, then back here to . . . (*hesitates*) . . . me. (*Pause.*) Krapp.

Pause.

The grain, now what I wonder do I mean by that, I mean . . . (*hesitates*) . . . I suppose I mean those things worth having when all the dust has—when all *my* dust has settled. I close my eyes and try and imagine them.

Pause. Krapp closes his eyes briefly.

Extraordinary silence this evening, I strain my ears and do not hear a sound. Old Miss McGlome always sings at this hour. But not tonight. Songs of her girlhood, she says. Hard to think of her as a girl. Wonderful woman, though. Connaught,° I fancy. (*Pause.*) Shall I sing when I am her age, if I ever am? No. (*Pause.*) Did I sing as a boy? No. (*Pause.*) Did I ever sing? No.

Pause.

Just been listening to an old year, passages at random. I did not check in the book, but it must be at least ten or twelve years ago. At that time I think I was still living on and off with Bianca in Kedar Street. Well out of that, Jesus yes! Hopeless business. (*Pause.*) Not much about her, apart from a tribute to her eyes. Very warm. I suddenly saw them again. (*Pause.*) Incomparable! (*Pause.*) Ah well . . . (*Pause.*) These old P.M.s are gruesome, but I often find them—(*Krapp switches off, broods, switches on*)—a help before embarking on a new . . . (*hesitates*) . . . retrospect. Hard to believe I was ever that young whelp. The voice! Jesus! And the aspirations! (*Brief laugh in which Krapp joins.*) And the resolutions! (*Brief laugh in which Krapp joins.*) To drink less, in particular. (*Brief laugh of Krapp alone.*) Statistics. Seventeen hundred hours, out of the preceding eight thousand odd, consumed on licensed premises alone. More than 20%, say 40% of his waking

Connaught: Western Province of Ireland.

life. (*Pause.*) Plans for a less . . . (*hesitates*) . . . engrossing sexual life. Last illness of his father. Flagging pursuit of happiness. Unattainable laxation. Sneers at what he calls his youth and thanks to God that it's over. (*Pause.*) False ring there. (*Pause.*) Shadows of the opus . . . magnum. Closing with a —(*brief laugh*)— yelp to Providence. (*Prolonged laugh in which Krapp joins.*) What remains of all that misery? A girl in a shabby green coat, on a railway-station platform? No?

Pause.

When I look—

Krapp switches off, broods, looks at his watch, gets up, goes backstage into darkness. Ten seconds. Pop of cork. Ten seconds. Second cork. Ten seconds. Third cork. Ten seconds. Brief burst of quavering song.

Krapp (*sings*).

> Now the day is over,
> Night is drawing nigh-igh,
> Shadows—

Fit of coughing. He comes back into light, sits down, wipes his mouth, switches on, resumes his listening posture.

Tape—back on the year that is gone, with what I hope is perhaps a glint of the old eye to come, there is of course the house on the canal where mother lay a-dying, in the late autumn, after her long viduity (*Krapp gives a start*), and the—(*Krapp switches off, winds back tape a little, bends his ear closer to the machine, switches on*)—a-dying, after her long viduity, and the—

Krapp switches off, raises his head, stares blankly before him. His lips move in the syllables of "viduity." No sound. He gets up, goes backstage into darkness, comes back with an enormous dictionary, lays it on table, sits down and looks up the word.

Krapp (*reading from dictionary*): State—or condition of being—or remaining—a widow—or widower. (*Looks up. Puzzled.*) Being—or remaining? . . . (*Pause. He peers again at dictionary. Reading.*) "Deep weeds of viduity" . . . Also of an animal, especially a bird . . . the vidua or weaver bird . . . Black plumage of male . . . (*He looks up. With relish.*) The vidua-bird!

Pause. He closes dictionary, switches on, resumes listening posture.

Tape—bench by the weir from where I could see her window. There I sat, in the biting wind, wishing she were gone. (*Pause.*) Hardly a soul, just a few regulars, nursemaids, infants, old men, dogs. I got to know them quite well—oh by appearance of course I mean! One dark young beauty I recall particularly, all white and starch, incomparable bosom, with a big black hooded perambulator, most funereal thing. Whenever I looked in her direction she had her eyes on me. And yet when I was bold enough to speak to her—not having been introduced—she threatened to call a policeman. As if I had designs on her virtue! (*Laugh. Pause.*) The face she had! The eyes! Like . . . (*hesitates*) . . . chrysolite! (*Pause.*) Ah well . . . (*Pause.*) I was there when—(*Krapp switches off, broods, switches on again*)—the blind went down, one of those dirty brown roller affairs, throwing a ball for a little white dog, as chance would have it. I happened to look up and there it was. All over and done with, at last. I sat on for a few moments with the ball in my hand and the dog yelping and pawing at me. (*Pause.*) Moments. Her moments, my moments. (*Pause.*) The dog's moments. (*Pause.*) In the end I held it out to him and he took it in his mouth, gently, gently. A small, old, black, hard, solid rubber ball. (*Pause.*) I shall feel it, in my hand, until my dying day. (*Pause.*) I might have kept it. (*Pause.*) But I gave it to the dog.

Pause.

Ah well . . .

Pause.

Spiritually a year of profound gloom and indigence until that memorable night in March at the end of the jetty, in the howling wind, never to be forgotten, when suddenly I saw the whole thing. The vision, at last. This fancy is what I have chiefly to record this evening, against the day when my work will be done and perhaps no place left in my memory, warm or cold, for the miracle that . . . (*hesitates*) . . . for the fire that set it alight. What I suddenly saw then was this, that the belief I had been going on all my life, namely—(*Krapp switches off impatiently, winds tape forward, switches on again*)—great granite rocks the foam flying up in the light of the lighthouse and the wind-gauge spinning like a propeller, clear to me at last that the dark I have always struggled to keep under is in reality my most—(*Krapp curses, switches off, winds tape forward, switches on again*)—unshatterable association until my dissolution of storm and night with the light of the understanding and the fire—(*Krapp curses louder, switches off, winds tape forward, switches on again*)—my face in her breasts and my hand on her. We lay there without moving. But under us all moved, and moved us, gently, up and down, and from side to side.

Pause.

Past midnight. Never knew such silence. The earth might be uninhabited.

Pause.

Here I end—

Krapp switches off, winds tape back, switches on again.

—upper lake, with the punt, bathed off the bank, then pushed out into the stream and drifted. She lay stretched out on the floorboards with her hands under her head and her eyes closed. Sun blazing down, bit of a breeze, water nice and lively. I noticed a scratch on her thigh and asked her how she came by it. Picking gooseberries, she said. I said again I thought it was hopeless and no good going on, and she agreed, without opening her eyes. (*Pause.*) I asked her to look at me and after a few moments—(*pause*)—after a few moments she did, but the eyes just slits, because of the glare. I bent over her to get them in the shadow and they opened. (*Pause. Low.*) Let me in. (*Pause.*) We drifted in among the flags and stuck. The way they went down, sighing, before the stem! (*Pause.*) I lay down across her with my face in her breasts and my hand on her. We lay there without moving. But under us all moved, and moved us, gently, up and down, and from side to side.

Pause.

Past midnight. Never knew—

Krapp switches off, broods. Finally he fumbles in his pockets, encounters the banana, takes it out, peers at it, puts it back, fumbles, brings out the envelope, fumbles, puts back envelope, looks at his watch, gets up and goes backstage into darkness. Ten seconds. Sound of bottle against glass, then brief siphon. Ten seconds. Bottle against glass alone. Ten seconds. He comes back a little unsteadily into light, goes to front of table, takes out keys, raises them to his eyes, chooses key, unlocks first drawer, peers into it, feels about inside, takes out reel, peers at it, locks drawer, puts keys back in his pocket, goes and sits down, takes reel off machine, lays it on dictionary, loads virgin reel on machine, takes envelope from his pocket, consults back of it, lays it on table, switches on, clears his throat and begins to record.

Krapp: Just been listening to that stupid bastard I took myself for thirty years ago, hard to believe I was ever

as bad as that. Thank God that's all done with anyway. (*Pause.*) The eyes she had! (*Broods, realizes he is recording silence, switches off, broods. Finally.*) Everything there, everything, all the—(*Realizing this is not being recorded, switches on.*) Everything there, everything on this old muckball, all the light and dark and famine and feasting of … (*hesitates*) … the ages! (*In a shout.*) Yes! (*Pause.*) Let that go! Jesus! Take his mind off his homework! Jesus (*Pause. Weary.*) Ah well, maybe he was right. (*Broods. Realizes. Switches off. Consults envelope.*) Pah! (*Crumples it and throws it away. Broods. Switches on.*) Nothing to say, not a squeak. What's a year now? The sour cud and the iron stool. (*Pause.*) Revelled in the word spool. (*With relish.*) Spooool! Happiest moment of the past half million. (*Pause.*) Seventeen copies sold, of which eleven at trade price to free circulating libraries beyond the seas. Getting known. (*Pause.*) One pound six and something, eight I have little doubt. (*Pause.*) Crawled out once or twice, before the summer was cold. Sat shivering in the park, drowned in dreams and burning to be gone. Not a soul. (*Pause.*) Last fancies. (*Vehemently.*) Keep 'em under! (*Pause.*) Scalded the eyes out of me reading *Effie* again, a page a day, with tears again. Effie . . . (*Pause.*) Could have been happy with her, up there on the Baltic, and the pines, and the dunes. (*Pause.*) Could I? (*Pause.*) And she? (*Pause.*) Pah! (*Pause.*) Fanny came in a couple of times. Bony old ghost of a whore. Couldn't do much, but I suppose better than a kick in the crutch. The last time wasn't so bad. How do you manage it, she said, at your age? I told her I'd been saving up for her all my life. (*Pause.*) Went to Vespers once, like when I was in short trousers. (*Pause. Sings.*)

> Now the day is over,
> Night is drawing nigh-igh,
> Shadows—(*coughing, then almost inaudible*)—
>   of the evening
> Steal across the sky.

(*Gasping.*) Went to sleep and fell off the pew. (*Pause.*) Sometimes wondered in the night if a last effort mightn't—(*Pause.*) Ah finish your booze now and get to your bed. Go on with this drivel in the morning. Or leave it at that. (*Pause.*) Leave it at that. (*Pause.*) Lie propped up in the dark—and wander. Be again in the dingle° on a Christmas Eve, gathering holly, the red-berried. (*Pause.*) Be again on Croghan° on a Sunday

---

dingle: a small enclosed village.   **Croghan:** an extinct volcano in central Ireland, the highest point in the region.

Canadian actor Donald Davis in his Obie-winning performance as Krapp in the 1960 Provincetown Playhouse production of Samuel Beckett's *Krapp's Last Tape.*

morning, in the haze, with the bitch, stop and listen to the bells. (*Pause.*) And so on. (*Pause.*) Be again, be again. (*Pause.*) All that old misery. (*Pause.*) Once wasn't enough for you. (*Pause.*) Lie down across her.

Long pause. He suddenly bends over machine, switches off, wrenches off tape, throws it away, puts on the

other, winds it forward to the passage he wants, switches on, listens staring front.

Tape—gooseberries, she said. I said again I thought it was hopeless and no good going on, and she agreed, without opening her eyes. (*Pause.*) I asked her to look at me and after a few moments—(*pause*)—after a few moments she did, but the eyes just slits, because of the glare. I bent over her to get them in the shadow and they opened. (*Pause. Low.*) Let me in. (*Pause.*) We drifted in among the flags and stuck. The way they went down, sighing, before the stem! (*Pause.*) I lay down across her with my face in her breasts and my hand on her. We lay there without moving. But under us all moved, and moved us, gently, up and down, and from side to side.

Pause. Krapp's lips move. No sound.

Past midnight. Never knew such silence. The earth might be uninhabited.

Pause.

Here I end this reel. Box—(*pause*)—three, spool—(*pause*)—five. (*Pause.*) Perhaps my best years are gone. When there was a chance of happiness. But I wouldn't want them back. Not with the fire in me now. No, I wouldn't want them back.

Krapp motionless staring before him. The tape runs on in silence.

CURTAIN

[1958]

QUESTIONS FOR REFLECTION AND DISCUSSION

1. Take a brief moment to sort out the temporal relationship between the three versions of Krapp. At age sixty-nine, he is listening to a tape of himself made on his birthday thirty years before while listening to a tape made ten years before that. Write a character analysis for each of the three versions of Krapp. Why did the author choose these three moments to present Krapp's character?

2. There are two principal props in the play: the bananas and the tape recorder with its tapes. What is the role of each of these props in the action of the play? Why does Krapp eat bananas? Why does he listen to his old tapes?

3. Much of the effect of the play is based on repetition. Make a list of some of the actions, words, and images that are repeated. What is the role of repetition in the life of this

character? What makes him repeat the words he spoke on his birthday in his late twenties?

4. Why do you think Krapp chooses to record his thoughts and memories on tape rather than writing them down? Although it seems antique to us now, the reel-to-reel tape recorder was cutting-edge technology in the 1950s. Why do you think Beckett chose to use it as a prop for this play about a man who seems totally uninterested in the present?

5. If you were to stage *Krapp's Last Tape* today, would you choose to preserve the reel-to-reel machine, or would you replace it with a present-day machine for recording memories? What prop would you use, and for what reasons? How would changing the machine change our understanding of the play?

WRITING ABOUT A LIVE OR A TAPED PERFORMANCE

As part of your work on drama, we highly recommend that you watch (live or recorded) at least one theatrical performance, preferably several, and preferably performances of a play you will be working on as part of your writing for class.

There are two primary forms of filmed theater: recordings of live performances and cinematic adaptations. Make sure you are aware which one you are watching, since each form requires a different sort of attention. With a taped performance, focus on the interpretation of the script; with an adaptation, consider the film as a film and as an adaptation. If, for example, you are working on Shakespeare's *Hamlet* (p. 286), you could choose to watch any number of taped performances, but you might also choose to view Laurence Olivier's 1948 cinematic adaptation of the play, or the modern-day version made in 2000, among countless film and television versions of *Hamlet*. Viewing an adaptation is similar to

READER'S **GUIDE**

Watching a Performance

Preparation

Be sure that you have read the script of the play that you are going to see beforehand. This will permit you to focus your attention on aspects of staging and performance rather than having to spend your energy following the plot. As you read, make notes to yourself about particular points that raise interesting questions about staging: props, setting, costume, character speech, and movement. As you watch the play, pay close attention to how the director and the company have chosen to address these questions:

- *Compare* the set, props, costume, and makeup to those the stage directions called for and those you had imagined. Has anything been added or subtracted from the version you read?
- *Study* the actors and the way they recite their lines.
  - Do they look as you imagined the characters they are playing should look? What sort of acting style do they use: natural or stylized? If stylized, in what way?
  - Listen for key lines of dialogue. Is the delivery what you had expected? Does the meaning of a particular character change because of an especially striking performance?

At a Live Performance

- Arrive early to give yourself time to settle in to the experience and soak in the theater as a space in its own right. Imagine what it must have been like to go to the theater during the many centuries before film and television when it was a dominant form of public entertainment.
- Once the curtain goes up, focus on individual aspects, but also try to take in the experience as a whole. So many elements come together in a live performance, and so many things can go wrong.
  - Look for the sound technicians and lighting technicians, the musicians, the stagehands.
  - Study the set, and think about how it functions logistically, to arrange the characters around the stage in a particular fashion, and to facilitate their entries and exits.
    - Are there any particularly striking or ingenious features? Many sets will have a central feature that can provide a key to the director's interpretation of a play.
    - Does the set design or costume incorporate imagery from the text of the play?

Watching a Play on Video

Try to view a taped play in a location where you will be able to concentrate, and set aside a block of time long enough to watch it all the way through, or with an intermission, as would occur in a live performance. Remember, however, that a taped performance differs in several significant aspects from a live performance.

- Presence and concentration: at a theater you are immersed in a spectacle much larger than you are, surrounded by other equally concentrated spectators.
- Watching a television or computer screen you will be unable to grasp the totality of the performance.
- Even if the play is filmed from a static camera from the point of view of a spectator's seat, the scale of the scene will be different.
- Most filmed theater mimics the look of motion pictures, alternating longer shots with close ups.
  - You will be able closely to study makeup and facial expressions, which will aid in your analysis of character and styles of acting,
  - *But* you may have difficulty observing the interaction between characters.

doing a comparison of two different texts with a great deal of similarities. Ask yourself these questions:

- What has been omitted?
- What has been added?
- What has been changed?
- What are the consequences of these decisions for your understanding of the play and the film?
- What are possible motivations for the changes made?

At the end of the viewing or performance, jot down notes about everything you noticed, before you forget.

- Take a few notes while watching, especially if you can stop the tape, but resist doing too much or you will lose your sense of the whole.
- Focus your memories in terms of the questions you had to ask, but also try to recall everything that struck you during the performance.
- If you are watching on tape, review the tape to check your notes or look again at things you are not sure about.

As part of a classroom study of *Krapp's Last Tape*, Joshua Cohen viewed Canadian director Atom Egoyan's hour-long film version of the play, starring John Hurt. Here are the notes he made directly following

English actor John Hurt in Atom Egoyan's film of *Krapp's Last Tape* (2000).

the screening. Note how he incorporates his expectations about the film and reactions to it into his processing of the viewing, raising questions that he would address in his response paper.

Joshua Cohen, Screening Notes for *Krapp's Last Tape* (2000)

- Long extended shot of man staring out what appears to be a window.
- Seems to go on forever. Really get a feel for his loneliness and boredom.
- Sound is surprising. Voice wasn't what I expected.
- Shot still going on...
- Actor moved into medium close-up now, but shot still hasn't changed except for really slight movement.
- What is he doing? Actions are confusing.
- Can't tell whether I'm supposed to laugh or feel sorry. I just feel awkward.
- Sound/noise seems really exaggerated.
- Really effective use of lighting to set tone.
- Camera still hasn't changed positions—just slight movement.
- I don't know what to think about the character at this point.
- Camera has moved in closer—for what reason? Audience is already focusing solely on the character, what reason would there be to pull closer attention to character?
- 1st cut of the film
- Cut-away after he listens to the first tape and freaks out.
- Jarring effect since it hasn't cut until then. Used effectively to show anger, frustration, etc....
- I'm very confused.
- Character comments on darkness—seems to answer question that I'm thinking about right now.
- 2nd cut—close-up on tape player. Cut back.
- At this point, film definitely seems like nothing I've seen before. Unfamiliar on many levels, including movement of camera, editing, actions, and narrative plot.

- Film doesn't seem to raise any questions besides "what the heck is he doing?"
- Camera keeps going back and coming back in—seems to want to escape but not be able to, always drawn back for some reason.
- When he laughs, he sinks back into darkness—face hidden from light.
- Screen is now entirely dark—action is comprehended through use of sound.
- Seems as if the past him is treated like another whole character—refers to past self as "he."
- Black rubber ball—a reference to what he said earlier? What significance?
- Doesn't want to accept that the darkness is keeping him back?
- Very powerful in how much emotion he can display simply by lying there without moving or speaking.
- Is a picture of that girl in the locket he keeps looking at?
- Who exactly are these tapes for?
- He keeps assuming that he has reached a new stage in his life—keeps saying "thank god that's all done with."
- What is the earliest story event we hear about? Is it that he didn't sing as a boy? Does that count?
- Is this a completely restricted narration?
- Seems to disassociate himself from the past.
- Starting to drag on at this point... my mind is starting to wander.
- We've heard the same passage now 3 or 4 times?
- When 69—more single-minded in what he wants to remember.
- We never find out what he realized in the end. What we don't find out in this film seems to be just as important as what we do find out.

Organize your viewing notes into a *response paper*, focusing on your reaction to what you saw, and the degree to which it did or did not meet the expectations formed when reading the script of the play. Here is the response paper Joshua wrote based on his screening notes. Following Joshua's paper on page 199 is a list suggesting some additional ways in which to develop your notes and reactions to a viewed performance of a play into a more formal essay.

Cohen 1

Joshua Cohen
English Composition 2
Professor Sinclair
28 November 2009

Response Paper on *Krapp's Last Tape* (2000)

After watching Atom Egoyan's film of *Krapp's Last Tape*, I am able to realize that this is unlike anything I have ever seen in a film before, and as such, it helped me to see *why* it is different. It helped me to see the conventions of a Hollywood film, and I feel that seeing something different was refreshing.

The most obvious difference in *Last Tape* is evident right from the start: the incredibly slow pace. This is emphasized even further by the almost complete lack of editing or camera movement. I made special note any time the camera moved or cut because I knew that it would denote something important and significant to the narrative.

The narrative also differs from traditional film in how the character acts and what he is driven by. His motives are unclear, his actions are extremely unpredictable, and he never clearly expresses what he wants. I think that in a traditional Hollywood film, great pains would be taken to establish his back-story and how he got to the position he currently is in. As I was watching, I half-expected there to be a flashback or a narrator, or even an explanatory title card in the beginning. Instead, the film expresses an idea effectively as much in what it leaves out as what it shows. By not explaining who the character is, it leaves the audience to think about more than plot. It is slightly jarring for an audience that is not used to having to think while in the theater.

Another question that arose for me while watching this film is whether or not this represents a film that is completely restricted in its narration. Krapp is the only character that we see or hear from and the only one whom we learn anything about. The film, or at least Krapp, seems to treat the Krapp of thirty years ago as another character. He refers to himself as "he" several times in the film.

If a film treats the same character at two different periods of time as different characters, does that make them so? What if they have different outlooks on life? Clearly the 39-year-old and 69-year-old Krapp see life differently. The Krapp of the present is much more selective in what he wants to remember, as demonstrated by his unpredictable and violent reactions to things he doesn't want to hear. Yet the two Krapps are the same in many ways as well, even if he doesn't realize it. In the older tapes, Krapp expresses the fact that he can't believe how naïve the younger one sounds and how he's glad that he's past that and wiser now. Based on patterns of this throughout the film, you know that he's doomed to this cycle and that, if Krapp is still listening to his tapes in thirty years, he will feel the same way.

The title is misleading in this film. If it is to be believed, then this is his last entry, yet the plot gives no indication of this. There are no hints that suggest that this will be his last tape, or reasons why it might. In a traditional film, I feel like there would be much more closure to the narrative. This film is completely open-ended in that it introduces ideas and events that are never answered. Who is Krapp? Why does he leave these tapes to himself? Who is the girl that he was speaking about? What is the vision he saw, and what did he realize when he saw it? All of these questions are raised and yet the plot is not driven by them. They seem to be an aside to the character study of an eccentric and unbelievable man.

One question that was raised in class was how this film would be different on stage, since it was originally a play. I feel that it would be very different, because of the nature of what film offers that a stage doesn't. The film uses sound very effectively, to the point that they wouldn't be able to be conveyed in a live setting. All of the noises and effects in the film are greatly amplified, especially in the beginning. When Krapp opens drawers and even eats, the sounds seem louder than they would be in a natural setting. For me, this called attention to the fact that it is actually a film, and in some senses broke the "fourth wall." The film also offers a much more intimate experience than the stage would. There are close-ups in the movie that call attention to minute details, movements, and facial expressions that would be lost if one were sitting around a stage.

The lighting also carries a lot of weight in this film, although, if done right, it could also be accomplished for a live performance. Like the narrative, the lighting is very restricted and forces the audience to see only certain things.

QUESTIONS FOR REFLECTION AND DISCUSSION

1. What part of his notes has Joshua incorporated into his response paper? What has he left out? Has he added anything that was not in his notes? What criteria do you think motivated the choices he has made?

2. What are the strengths of Joshua's response paper? What are its weaknesses?

3. Do you think Joshua liked the film? How does his evaluation of the film affect his analysis of it in the response paper?

4. Go through Joshua's paper carefully, marking and commenting on grammar and mechanics as well as style and argument. Using the guidelines for revision in Chapter 2 (p. 63), formulate a detailed plan for revisions.

Types of Essays about Performance

Write a **review** of the production (1–2 pages), approaching it from the point of view of a drama critic or prospective spectator.

- Briefly introduce the play and provide factual details about the specific production: director, company, actors, theater.

- Describe the aspects unique to this production: sets, costumes, lighting, music, gesture, movement, and speech.

- Note any major alterations to the script, and any particular innovations you noticed.

- Choose a few key moments in the production and discuss how they epitomize what was successful and unsuccessful about it.

- Conclude your review with a recommendation—if that can be made to fit in with your style as a reviewer.

Write a **textual analysis** (4–5 pages), focusing in greater detail on the specific elements of the particular performance:

- Using your notes, and the questions you generated in preparation for the performance, look for patterns that will suggest the director's particular interpretation of the play.

- If it seems like a helpful idea, consult the program notes as well as reviews and newspaper features about the play. Be sure to reference your sources fully (p. APP B–4).

- If you find a consistent pattern, use it to generate a thesis about the production; if not, structure your analysis one element at a time.

Write a **comparison paper** (4–5 pages). This will be appropriate if the performance you viewed is sufficiently different from the original script, as in the example of the cinematic adaptations of *Hamlet* mentioned above, or Egoyan's film of *Krapp's Last Tape*.

- Review the discussion of writing a comparison paper in Chapter 2 (p. 74), and follow the directions there.

- Compare the text of the original script with the changes made to it.

Write a **research paper** (8–9 pages). You may incorporate your viewing of one or several different performances of a play into the broader context of research about its **production history**—an important branch of theater studies that traces the productions of a specific play from its première performance to the present day. Rather than the entire history, such a paper would synthesize reading in secondary sources on the history of the play and combine it with first-hand viewing of several different taped productions. If relevant, the paper might also compare theatrical productions of a play with cinematic adaptations. See Chapter 3 for additional information on research papers.

STAGING THE WORLD TOPICS FOR ESSAYS

In addition to the character analysis and the topics listed in the guidelines to writing about a live or taped performance, here are some additional topics for essays on plays.

1. Analyze the role of the chorus in *Antigone* (p. 465).

2. Analyze the use of repetition in *Krapp's Last Tape*.

3. Compare the depiction of gender roles in *Trifles* (p. 139), *Antigone* (p. 465), *Hamlet* (p. 286), and/or *A Doll's House* (p. 553).

4. Compare the use of story events not shown directly on stage in *Trifles* (p. 139), *Antigone* (p. 465), *Hamlet*, and/or *Krapp's Last Tape*.

5. Compare the use of the single-room setting in *Trifles* (p. 139) and *Krapp's Last Tape*.

6. Write an essay on the use of the conventions of tragedy in the news reporting of a recent catastrophe (either human-generated or natural).

7. Write an essay on the current forms of comedy in theater, in cinema, or on television.

EXPLAINING THE WORLD: ESSAYS

Chapter 4 introduced the broad principal categories of the essay (p. 164). You will find, however, in practice that the majority of essays, like Hashim Naseem's descriptive essay on page 186, tend to combine aspects of several different types in order to find the specific form that best fits their theme and the author's persona, or personal voice. As you read an essay, try first to determine the primary or dominant type it is using, and then look for aspects of other essay types. With each essay, try to identify the motivation behind the particular combination of qualities it comprises. Establish its attitude toward its material. Nonfiction, as the American naturalist and novelist Peter Matthiessen observes, is expected to tell the truth, but there are many ways of presenting material as true, and many ways of approaching the truth.

> *In nonfiction, you have that limitation, that constraint, of telling the truth.*
>
> —PETER MATTHIESSEN

George Packer b. 1960

Born and raised in San Francisco, and educated at Yale University, George Packer has been a staff writer for the *New Yorker* magazine since 2003. He has won awards for his coverage of war in Iraq and civil war in Sierra Leone, and has contributed articles, essays, and reviews on foreign affairs to *Dissent*, *Mother Jones*, *Harper's*, and the *New York Times Magazine*. In 2005, he published *The Assassins' Gate: America in Iraq*. First published in 2002, "How Susie Bayer's T-Shirt Ended Up on Yusuf Mama's Back" uses narrative as one of its tools, but its focus is the exposition of the web of economic forces that connect an African town with the rest of the world.

HOW SUSIE BAYER'S T-SHIRT ENDED UP ON YUSUF MAMA'S BACK

IF YOU'VE EVER LEFT A BAG OF CLOTHES OUTSIDE the Salvation Army or given to a local church drive, chances are the you've dressed an African. All over Africa, people are wearing what Americans once wore and no longer want. Visit the continent and you'll find faded remnants of secondhand clothing in the strangest of places. The LET'S HELP MAKE PHILADELPHIA THE FASHION CAPITAL OF THE WORLD T-shirt on a Malawian laborer. The white bathrobe on a Liberian rebel boy with his wig and automatic rifle. And the muddy orange sweatshirt on the skeleton of a small child, lying on its side in a Rwandan classroom that has become a genocide memorial.

A long chain of charity and commerce binds the world's richest and poorest people in accidental intimacy. It's a curious feature of the global age that hardly anyone on either end knows it.

A few years ago, Susie Bayer bought a T-shirt for her workouts with the personal trainer who comes regularly to her apartment on East 65th Street in Manhattan. It was a pale gray cotton shirt, size large, made in the U.S.A. by JanSport, with the red and black logo of the University of Pennsylvania on its front. Over time, it got a few stains on it, and Bayer, who is seventy two, needed more drawer space, so last fall she decided to get rid of the shirt. She sent it, along with a few other T-shirts and a couple of silk nightgowns, to the thrift shop that she has been donating her clothes to for the past forty years.

Americans buy clothes in disposable quantities—$165 billon worth last year. Then, like Susie Bayer, we run out of storage space, or we put on weight, or we get tired of the way we look in them, and so we pack the clothes in garbage bags and lug them off to thrift shops.

5 When I told Susie Bayer that I was hoping to follow her T-shirt to Africa, she cried, "I know exactly what you're doing!" As a girl, her favorite movie at the Loews on West 83rd was *Tales of Manhattan*—the story of a coat that passes from Charles Boyer

through a line of other people, including Charles Laughton and Edward G. Robinson, bringing tragedy or luck, before finally falling out of the sky with thousands of dollars in the pockets and landing on the dirt plot of a sharecropper played by Paul Robeson.

Bayer writes off about a thousand dollars a year in donations, and the idea that some of it ends up on the backs of Africans delights her. "Maybe our clothes change the lives of these people," she said. "This is Susie Bayer's statement. No one would agree with me, but maybe some of the vibrations are left over in the clothing. Maybe some of the good things about us can carry through." She went on: "I'd like us to be less selfish. Because we have been very greedy. Very greedy. Americans think they can buy happiness. They can't. The happiness comes in the giving, and that's why I love the thrift shop."

Twenty-four blocks north, up First Avenue, the Call Again Thrift Shop is run by two blunt-spoken women named Virginia Edelman and Marilyn Balk. They sit in their depressing back office, surrounded by malfunctioning TVs and used blenders and a rising sea of black garbage bags.

From a heap of clothing in front of her, Edelman extracts a baseball shirt that says YORKVILLE across its front. "Look at this. Who would want to buy something like this? It's just junk. Junky junky junk. This stuff bagged in a garbage bag, it's so wrinkled we don't even look at it. This is a Peter Pan costume or something—I don't know what the hell it is."

Edelman and Balk have been toiling at Call Again for two decades. Their dank little basement, crammed with last year's mildewing clothes, has no more space. The storage shed out back looks ready to explode. The women inspect every item that comes in, searching for any reason to get rid of it. Their shop space is limited, and their customers are relentlessly picky. This being the Upper East Side, the store displays a size-four Kenneth Cole leather woman's suit, worn once or not at all, that retails for six hundred dollars but is selling here for two hundred dollars.

10   Edelman and Balk sit neck-deep in the runoff of American prosperity, struggling to direct the flow and keep it from backing up and drowning them. "It's endless," Balk says. "Yesterday we got, I don't know, five donations. It's like seven maids and seven grooms trying to sweep the seas. Or Sisyphus, was it? Trying to roll the rock?"

One day a few years ago, relief came to them in the form of a young man named Eric Stubin, who runs Trans-Americas Trading Company, a textile recycling factory in Brooklyn. He said that he was willing to send a truck every Tuesday to haul away what the woman didn't want and that he would pay them three cents a pound for it. "You never heard two people happier to hear from someone in your life," Edelman says. Now every month 1,200 or 1,300 pounds of rejected donations are trucked to Brooklyn, and every three months Call Again gets a check for a hundred dollars or so, money that goes to charity.

Edelman estimates that more than a third of the donations that Call Again receives ends up in Trans-Americas' recycling factory. Goodwill Industries, which handles more than a billion pounds a year in North America, puts its figure at 50 percent. Some sources estimate that of the 2.5 billion pounds of clothes that Americans donate each year, as much as 80 percent gets trucked off to places like Trans-Americas.

Though the proceeds go to charity programs, these numbers are not readily publicized. Susie Bayer isn't the typical donor. "Everybody who gives us things thinks that it's the best thing in the world," Edelman says. "They feel as if they're doing a wonderful thing for charity. And they do it for themselves— for the tax write-off. Unfortunately, I don't think people know what charity is anymore. They would be horrified if they thought that they bought a suit at Barneys or Bergdorf's for eleven hundred dollars and we chucked it for three cents a pound because of a torn lining."

Susie Bayer's T-shirt goes straight into the reject pile. "we have a thousand of them," Virginia Edelman says. "Get it out of here."

15   This is where the trail grows tricky, for what had been charitable suddenly crosses a line that tax law and moral convention think inviolable—it turns commercial, and no one likes to talk very much about what happens next. A whiff of secrecy and even shame still clings to the used-clothing trade, left over from the days of shtetl Jews and Lower East Side rag dealers.

The used-clothing firms are mostly family-owned, and the general feeling seems to be that the less the public knows, the better.

The owners of Trans-Americas, Edward and Eric Stubin, father and son, are more open than most in the industry, though they wouldn't share their annual sales figures with me. In 2001, used clothing was one of America's major exports to Africa, with $61.7 million in sales. Latin America and Asia have formidable trade barriers. Some African countries—Nigeria, Eritrea, South Africa—ban used clothing in order to protect their own domestic textile industries, which creates a thriving and quite open black market. For years, Africa has been Trans-Americas' leading overseas market for used clothing, absorbing two-thirds of its exports.

"There'll always be demand for secondhand clothing," say Eric Stubin, who reads widely about Africa, "because unfortunately the world is becoming a poorer and poorer place. Used clothing is the only affordable means for these people to put quality clothing on their body."

Edward Stubin agrees. "I have a quote: 'We can deliver a garment to Africa for less than the cost of a stamp.'"

20   Trans-Americas' five-story brick building stands a block from the East River wharves in Greenpoint, Brooklyn. Inside, sixty thousand pounds of clothes a day pour down the slides from the top floor, hurry along conveyor belts where Hispanic women stand and fling pieces into this bin or down that chute, fall through openings from floor to floor and land in barrels and cages, where they are then pressure-packed into clear plastic four-foot-high bales and tied with metal strapping—but never washed. Whatever charming idiosyncrasy a pair of trousers might have once possessed is annihilated in the mass and crush. Not only does the clothing cease to be personal, it ceases to be clothing. Watching the process of sorting and grading feels a little like a visit to the slaughterhouse.

"We get the good, the bad and the ugly," Eric Stubin tells me as we tour the factory. "Ripped sweaters, the occasional sweater with something disgusting on it, the pair of underwear you don't want to talk about. We're getting what the thrifts can't sell." There are more than three hundred export categories at the factory, but the four essential classifications are "premium," "Africa A," "Africa B" and "Wiper Rag." "Premium" goes to Asia and Latin America. "Africa A"—a garment that has lost its brightness—goes to the better-off African countries like Kenya. "Africa B"—a stain or small hole—goes to the continent's disaster areas, its Congos and Angolas. By the time a shirt reaches Kisangani or Huambo, it has been discarded by its owner, rejected at the thrift shop and graded two steps down by the recycler.

Standing in Trans-Americas' office, with wooden airplane propellers hanging next to photographs from Africa, Eric Stubin casts a professional eye on Susie Bayer's T-shirt. In a week, a 54,000-pound container of used clothes will set sail on the steamship Claudia, destination Mombasa, Kenya. Stubin spots a pink stain on the belly of the T-shirt below the university logo and tosses the shirt aside. "Africa," he says.

But there are many Africas, and used clothing carries a different meaning in each of them. Christianity tenderized most of the continent for the foreign knife, but the societies of Muslim West Africa and Somalia are bits of gristle that have proved more resistant to Western clothes. In warlord-ridden, destitute Somalia, used clothing is called, rather contemptuously, *huudhaydh*—as in, "who died?" A woman in Kenya who once sold used dresses told me that not long ago Kenyans assumed the clothing was removed from dead people and washed it carefully to avoid skin diseases. In Togo, it is called "dead white man's clothing." In Sierra Leone, it's called "junks" and highly prized. In Rwanda, used clothing is known by the word for "choose," and in Uganda, it used to be called "Rwanda," which is where it came from illegally until Uganda opened its doors to what is now called *mivumba*.

At the vast Owino market in downtown Kampala, Uganda's capital, you can find every imaginable garment, all of it secondhand. Boys sit on hills of shoes, shining them to near-newness, hawkers shout prices, shoppers break a sweat bargaining, porters barge through with fresh bales on their heads. When the wire is cut and the bale bursts open like a piñata, a mob of retailers descends in a ferocious rugby scrum to fight over first pick. Between the humanity and the clothes there is hardly room to move. The used-clothing market is the densest, most electric section of Owino—the only place where ordinary Africans can join the frenetic international ranks of consumers.

25   I knew what this thrice-rejected clothing had gone through to get here, but somehow "Africa" looks much better in Africa—the colors brighter, the shapes shapelier. A dress that moved along a Brooklyn conveyor belt like a gutted chicken becomes a dress again when it has been charcoal-ironed and hangs sunlit in a Kampala vendor's stall,

The clothes section of Owino Market, in Kampala, Uganda: one link in the chain of global trade described in Packer's essay.

and a customer holds it to her chest with all the frowning interest of a Call Again donor shopping at Bergdorf-Goodman. Some of the stock looks so good that it gets passed off as new in the fashionable shops on Kampala Road. Government ministers, bodyguards in tow, are known to buy their suits at Owino. Once in Africa, the clothes undergo a transformation like inanimate objects coming to life in a fairy tale. Human effort and human desire work the necessary magic.

My guide through Owino is a radio-talk-show host named Anne Kizza, a sophisticated woman who knows what she wants in dance wear from reading South African fashion magazines. She always goes to the same vendors, whose merchandise and prices are to her liking; while I am with her, she buys a slim lime-green dress for the equivalent of sixty cents and a black skirt for thirty cents. Price tags are still stapled to some items—"Thrift Store, $3.99, ALL SALES FINAL"—but just as Americans don't know what happens beyond the thrift shop, Africans don't know the origin of the stuff. Most Ugandans assume that

the clothes were sold by the American owner. When I explain to a retailer named Fred Tumushabe, who specializes in men's cotton shirts, that the process starts with a piece of clothing that has been given away, he finds the whole business a monstrous injustice. "Then why are they selling to us?" he asks.

The big importers have their shops on Nakivubo Road, which is a hairy ten-minute walk through traffic from Owino. Trans-Americas' buyer in Kampala is a Pakistani named Hussein Ali Merchant. He is forty, with a beard and a paunch and a sad, gentle manner. A diabetic cigarette smoker, he seems to expect to die any day and extends the same good-natured fatalism to his business. "It's a big chain," he says, and all the links beyond Merchant are forged on credit. "Sometimes the people disappear, sometimes they die. Each year I'm getting the loss of at least thirty thousand dollars. Last year a customer died of yellow fever. His whole body was yellow. He died in Jinja. The money is gone. Forget about it, heh-heh-heh."

We drink tea in his dark shop among unsold bales stacked twenty feet high. Five or six years ago, when there were only a few clothing shops on Nakivubo Road, his annual profit was about $75,000. Today, with more than fifty stores, his profits are much lower. Merchant is one of Africa's rootless Asian capitalists. Before coming to Uganda in 1995, he twice lost all his money to looting soldiers in Zaire. Between disasters he went to Australia and pumped gas for three months, but he fled back to Africa before his visa expired. "I've been sitting like this for twenty years here. In America you have to work hard, no money, things are very expensive. Here, it's easy. I want to do hard work in America? For what?" Merchant has a frightening vision of himself squeezing price tags onto convenience store stock at midnight in Kentucky. As for Karachi, it terrifies him, and he goes back only once a year to see his family, his doctor and his tailor. "I'm a prince here," he says. "I'm a king here in Africa."

Merchant's warehouse—"my go down," he calls it in local slang—is in an industrial quarter of Kampala. On a Saturday afternoon in December, the truck carrying the Trans-Americas shipping container with Susie Bayer's T-shirt pulls in after its long drive from the port of Mombasa on the Kenyan coast. Seven customers—wholesalers from all over Uganda—anxiously wait along with Merchant. Among them is a heavy woman in her forties with a flapper's bob and a look of profound disgust on her fleshy face. Her name is Proscovia Batwaula, but everyone calls her Mama Prossy. As the bales start leaving the container on the heads of young porters, Mama Prossy literally throws her weight around to claim the ones she wants. Merchant, standing back from the flurry, murmurs that a week before, she bloodied another woman's nose in a scuffle over a bale of Canadian cotton skirts.

30 Eric Stubin has stenciled my initials on the bale containing Susie Bayer's T-shirt. But I never imagined 540 bales coming off the truck at a frantic clip, turned at all angles on young men's heads, amid the chaos of bellowing wholesalers in the glare of the afternoon sun. Finding the T-shirt suddenly seems impossible. When I try to explain my purpose to Mama Prossy, she answers without taking her eyes off the precious merchandise leaving the truck: "What gain will I have? Why should I accommodate you?" She scoffs at the idea of publicity benefits in New York, and as bales disappear into wholesalers' trucks, I start getting a bit desperate.

Then Mama Prossy learns that I teach in American universities. She badly wants her son to attend one; for the first time she takes an interest in me. Moments later, more good luck. Merchant spots my bale coming off the truck, the initials "GP" all of three inches high.

Mama Prossy insists on the right to tear it open and have a look. The used-clothing trade in Africa is fraught with suspicion and rumor and fear of bad bales. Wholesalers bribe the importers' laborers to give them first crack at the most promising stock, based on the look of things through clear plastic. But what Mama Prossy extracts from the top of my bale makes her lip curl in ever-deepening disgust. It is a pink woman's T-shirt. Women's clothes are not supposed to be mixed in with men's. "I will lose money," she announces, and pulls out another piece. "Is this for a fat child? Where are they in Africa? We don't have fat children here in Uganda."

She is angling for a price cut from Merchant, who reminds her that she still owes him fifty thousand Ugandan shillings (thirty dollars) from last week. She starts calling him "boss." After all, he is higher on the chain, and she needs him more than he needs her. They settle on the equivalent of sixty dollars for the bale, a price that amounts to nineteen cents a shirt. Merchant has paid Trans-Americas around thirteen

cents each, excluding freight charges; he will have little or no profit on the bale, which was graded "mixed," Africa A and B.

Mama Prossy turns to me. "You say this bale is best quality, better than the others?" It wasn't what I'd said, but I keep my mouth shut. "I doubt," says Mama Prossy, looking me over with quite naked contempt. "We shall see."

35 A Kampala journalist named Michael Wakabi told me that Kampala has become "a used culture." The cars are used—they arrive from Japan with broken power windows and air-conditioners, so Ugandan drivers bake in the sun. Used furniture from Europe lines the streets in Kampala. The Ugandan Army occupies part of neighboring Congo with used tanks and aircraft from Ukraine. And the traditional Ugandan dress made from local cotton, called gomesi, is as rare as the mountain gorilla. To dress African, Ugandans have to have money.

Twenty years ago, when I was a Peace Corps volunteer in Togo, all the village women wore printed cloth, and many of the men wore embroidered shirts of the same material. The village had at least half a dozen tailors. The mother of eight who lived next door dreamed of making clothes in her own market stall and asked me to help her buy a hand-cranked sewing machine. Used clothes were sold in limited and fairly expensive supply; a villager wore the same piece every day as it disintegrated on his body.

Then the floodgates opened. With the liberalization in Africa of the rules governing used-clothing imports in the past ten years, Africans, who keep getting poorer, can now afford to wear better than rags. Many told me that without used clothes they would go naked, which, as one pointed out, is not in their traditional culture. And yet they know that something precious has been lost.

"These secondhand clothes are a problem," a young driver named Robert Ssebunya told me. "Ugandan culture will be dead in ten years, because we are all looking to these Western things. Ugandan culture is dying even now. It is dead. Dead and buried." The ocean of used clothes that now covers the continent plays its part in telling Africans that their own things are worthless, that Africans can do nothing for themselves.

But the intensity of the used-clothing section in every market I entered suggests that if something called "Ugandan culture" is dying, something else is taking its place. The used clothes create a new culture here, one of furious commercial enterprise and local interpretation of foreign styles, cut-rate and imitative and vibrant.

40   For all this, Uganda is quite capable of mass-producing its own clothes. On the banks of the White Nile, at its source in Jinja on Lake Victoria, a textile company called Southern Range Nyanza uses local cotton, considered the second-best in the world after Egyptian, to manufacture 13 million yards of fabric a year. With the Africa Growth and Opportunity Act of 2000 opening the American market, Southern Range has begun exporting men's cotton shirts to New York—so shirts that begin in Uganda might make a double crossing of the ocean and end there as well.

Viren Thakkar, Southern Range's Indian managing director, insists that he can sell the same shirts in Uganda for three dollars—less than twice the cost of a used shirt—but the dumping of foreign clothes makes it impossible for him to break into the market. "The country has to decide what they want to do," he says, "whether they want to use secondhand clothes continually, or whether they want to bring industry and grow the economy." Globalization has helped to destroy Uganda's textile industry, but Ugandans simply don't believe that their own factory could make clothes as durable and stylish as the stuff that comes in bales from overseas.

In Jinja's market, Mama Prossy sits like a queen on her wooden storage bin and watches the morning trade. At her feet, half a dozen retailers poke through the innards of the Trans-Americas bale. "You see how you are picking very, very old material," she scolds me. "And you are mixing ladies'. My friend, why are you mixing ladies'? And too much is white."

"I told you," I say, "I don't work for them."

"But you put your initials on it."

45   She will lose money on my bale, Mama Prossy insists; she will never buy Trans-Americas again. But the entries she makes in her ledger book show a profit of ninety-eight dollars—more than 150 percent.

Her retailers sort the T-shirts by their own three-tier grading system. Susie Bayer's is rated second-class and goes for sixty cents to a slender, grave young man in slightly tattered maroon trousers who seems intimidated by the queen on her throne. His name is Philip Nandala, and he is the next-to-last link in the chain. Philip is an itinerant peddler of used clothes, the closest thing in Uganda to the nineteenth-century rag dealer with his horse-drawn cart—except that Philip transports his fifty-pound bag from market to market by minibus or on his own head, five days a week on the road. "If I stay at home," he says, "I can die of poverty."

His weekly odyssey begins in Kamu, a trading center on a plateau high above the plains that stretch north all the way to Sudan. I follow Philip and his bag of clothes through the market, watching him dive into one scrum after another as bales burst open. Out comes children's rummage, and Philip fights off several women for a handful of little T-shirts that go into his bag: "Ms. Y's Goofy Goof Troop," "2 Busy + 2 Smart for Tobacco = 4H" and "Future Harvard Freshman."

The sun beats down, and Scovia Kuloba, the woman who introduced Philip to the trade, sits under an umbrella among mounds of clothes. Her barker scolds at the market crowd: "People leave the clothes to buy fish! They let their children go naked! This white man brought the clothes with him— don't you want to buy?"

When I explain to Scovia Kuloba that her goods come from American charities, she stares in disbelief. "Sure? I thought maybe we Africans are the only ones who suffer. The people from there—I thought they were well off. I think they don't even work."

50   Her teenage daughter, Susan, whose braids and clothes look straight out of Brooklyn, adds: "I don't want to be poor, you just cry all the time. I hate the Sun. I hate Africans." She'll only marry a *mzungu*, she says, because she knows from movies like *Titanic* and *Why Do Fools Fall in Love* that white men are always faithful, unlike Africans.

Slowly, I become aware of the sound of amplified American voices nearby, along with gunshots and screeching tires. Next to the used-clothing market, an action flick plays on video, with speakers hooked up outside to attract customers. In a dark little room, two dozen adults and children, who have paid six cents apiece, sit riveted to *Storm Catcher*, starring Dolph Lundgren.

The end of the road is a small hilltop town, green and windswept, called Kapchorwa, about 110 miles northeast of Mama Prossy's stall in downtown Jinja. Clouds hide 14,000-foot Mt. Elgon and, beyond it, Kenya. Philip spreads his wares on a plastic sheet at the foot of a brick wall and works hard all day, a tape measure around his neck. Poor rural Ugandans, the chain's last links, crowd close, arguing and pleading, but Philip is now the one with power, and he barely stirs from his asking price. One young man comes back half a dozen times to try on the same gray hooded coat. It fits perfectly, and it has arrived just in time for the chilly season that is blowing in. But Phillip wants $4.70, and the customer only has $1.75.

"This coat is as thick as fish soup," Philip says. "The material lasts twenty years,"

"You are killing me," the customer says. "The money is killing me."

55 "I am not killing you. I bought it at a high price, I ask a high price."

The customer finally walks away, and Philip returns the coat to his pile. The thrift shop's price tag is still stapled to the back: "$1.00." At the sight of it, I suddenly feel sad. I think of Virginia Edelman and Marilyn Balk back on the Upper East Side, tossing out truckloads of the stuff, desperate to get rid of it. I remember the torrent pouring down the chutes at Trans-Americas' factory in Brooklyn. On balance, in spite of its problems, I have become a convert to used clothing. Africans want it. It gives them dignity and choice. But now that I have seen them prize so highly, and with such profound effects, what we

throw away without a thought, the trail of Susie Bayer's T-shirt only seems to tell one story, a very old one, about the unfairness of the world as it is.

The T-shirt is buried deep in Philip's pile. My flight back to New York is leaving in four days, and I am concerned about missing it. So I reach into the pile, wanting to position the T-shirt more advantageously. As soon as I touch it, the shirt flies out of my hand. An old man in an embroidered Muslim cap and djellaba, who is missing his lower front teeth, holds it up for inspection. Tracing with his finger, he puzzles out the words printed in red and black around an academic insignia: "University Pennsylvania," he says. He dances away, brandishing the shirt in his fist. Ninety cents is his first offer, but Philip won't budge from $1.20. Eventually, the old man pays. Yusuf Mama, seventy one, husband of four, father of thirty two, has found what he wants.

I ask him why, of all the shirts in the pile, he has chosen this one. "It can help me," he says vaguely. "I have only one shirt."

Later, when I tell the story to people back in Kampala, they shake their heads. Yusuf Mama wanted Susie Bayer's T-shirt, they say, because a *mzungu* had touched it.

[2002]

QUESTIONS FOR REFLECTION AND DISCUSSION

1. Summarize the information provided in this essay. Why do you think the author chose to structure the essay in terms of the links in a chain? Is there anything in the essay that does not belong to the chain? Was there anything the essay made you want to know that it did not tell you?

2. What are the arguments in favor of the used clothing business in Africa? What are the arguments against it? What is the author's attitude toward it? Does it change during the course of the essay?

3. How would the essay have been different if the author had written up his information as a purely expository essay without the narrative framework of following the t-shirt's journey?

4. What is the meaning of the final sentence of the essay? Do you think this is an accurate interpretation of Yusuf Mama's motivation in buying the T-shirt? Do you think the T-shirt's journey would have been different if George Packer had not been accompanying it? Why or why not?

ARGUING WITH AN ESSAY

Here is the prompt Jacquelynn Messina was given for her assignment:

Write a 2- to 3-page argumentative essay on the following topic:

Near the conclusion of his essay, Packer informs us that he has "become a convert to used clothing." Based on the information included in the essay, write an essay arguing a thesis in favor of or against this conclusion, or proposing some combination of the two.

Here is the essay Jacquelynn wrote in response to the prompt:

Messina 1

Jacquelynn Messina
English Composition 2
Professor Lang
14 November 2009

The Used Clothing Trade: Who Benefits?

Americans donate their clothes to charity because they have too much and want to feel good about themselves. Charities sell them because they have too many and no one wants them. People send them to Africa because that's where people want them. Who wins? After following one T-shirt from New York to Uganda, George Packer admits in his essay about globalization "How Susie Packer's T-Shirt Ended Up On Yusuf Mama's Back" that he has "become a convert to used clothing" (206), but he doesn't say exactly why. In this paper, I will argue that he becomes a convert because he sees that everybody is better off and nobody is worse off because of the used-clothing industry.

Susie Bayer donates a lot of clothes and saves money because she can deduct almost a thousand dollars every year from her taxes (201). She also likes the idea that giving away clothes makes her less selfish and that, "Maybe our clothes change the lives of these people" (201). Giving away clothes makes her feel better about herself and also helps her save on her taxes.

The Call Again Thrift Shop, where she has been donating clothes for forty years, cannot deal with the amount of clothes Americans want to get rid of and cannot sell them back to other Americans unless they are in perfect condition. They sell over a third of their clothes to Trans-Americas Trading Company in Brooklyn for about a hundred dollars a month (201). They are better off because they get to keep what they can sell and get money for the part they cannot sell that they can use to help run their charity. The used clothing business keeps them from throwing charity into the garbage.

It is obvious that Trans-Americas is better off from the business, since without it they wouldn't be in business. The man who runs the business, Eric Stubin, believes he is doing a service, he says that "Used clothing is the only affordable means for these people to put quality clothing on their body" (202). Packer thinks that a lot of people who give to charity would be offended if they knew clothes they gave away for nothing are being sold for a profit (202). He also says later on that some Africans are shocked to hear that people gave away the clothes they are buying (203). According to Packer, most Africans think that used clothes come from people who have died (202). Packer appears to think that business is business, and that we should not be bothered by the business.

The used clothing business provides jobs for people in Brooklyn and people in Africa. In Africa, Packer shows us the Owino market in Kampala, the capital of Uganda, where many people make a living: a buyer from Pakistan named Hussein Ali Merchant, a wholesaler named Mama Prossy, and a used-clothes seller named Philip Nandala (205). And Yusuf Mama, who buys Susie Bayer's T-shirt for $1.20 (206). Nobody in Africa has it easy, but because of the used clothing business, many people have jobs and Yusuf Mama has a new T-shirt in good condition.

However, there are some problems with this system due to globalization. Textile companies in Uganda cannot compete with the prices of used clothing from the United States, even though their clothes are good quality and local industry. "Africans simply don't believe that their own factory could make clothes as stylish and durable as the stuff that comes in bales from overseas" (205). Packer's conclusion seems to say that Yusuf Mama buys the T-shirt only because Packer, "*a mzungu*," touched it. He also says that his story is "a very old one, about the unfairness of the world as it is" (206). Will the T-shirt bring Yusuf Mama good luck even though Susie Bayer threw it away? Would Africans be better off if they could make their own T-shirts? Everybody benefits, but does it matter that the ones in America benefit more and the Africans benefit less? Are we asking the wrong questions about globalization?

Work Cited

Packer, George. "How Susie Bayer's T-Shirt Ended Up On Yusuf Mama's Back."
Literature: A World of Writing. Ed. David L. Pike and Ana M. Acosta.
New York: Pearson Longman, 2011. 200–06. Print.

QUESTIONS FOR REFLECTION AND DISCUSSION

1. What is Jacquelynn's argument? What is her thesis? Are they clearly expressed? How well does each paragraph support and develop her argument?

2. What types of argument (p. 41) does Jacquelynn employ in her essay? Are these the correct types of argument for this kind of paper? Why or why not?

3. What are the strengths of Jacquelynn's draft? What are its weaknesses? Has she left out any evidence that could strengthen her argument? Has she neglected to address any evidence that contradicts her argument?

4. Go through Jacquelynn's paper carefully, marking and commenting on grammar and mechanics as well as style and argument. Using the guidelines for revision in Chapter 2 (p. 63), formulate a detailed plan for revisions.

EXPLAINING THE WORLD TOPICS FOR ESSAYS

1. Analyze the imagery in either "The Death of the Moth" (p. 156) or "Death of a Moth" (p. 159).

2. Analyze the use of description in an essay included elsewhere in this book.

3. Choose a short story or poem included in Part 3 of this book and rewrite it as a specific form of essay.

4. Choose an essay included in Part 3 of this book and rewrite it as a poem or short story.

5. Compare the use of description in two or three of the essays in Part 3 of this book.

6. Compare the depiction of the relations between the developed and the developing world in "Susie Bayer's T-Shirt" and Binyavanga Wainaina's "How to Write about Africa" (p. 496).

7. Write an essay on the forms of nonfiction specific to the Internet.

8. Write a diary entry describing an episode in your childhood. Based on that entry, write a narrative essay that uses the episode to present an idea or an argument.

"Good news. The test results show it's a metaphor."

CHAPTER 6

WRITING THE WORLD

WORKING WITH LITERARY DEVICES

"Veni, vidi, vici"—the famous phrase Julius Caesar first spoke to the Roman Senate to announce his victory in battle—remains firmly implanted in our cultural memory more than two thousand years later because of its rhetorical brilliance: "I came, I saw, I conquered." You can find it on T-shirts ("Veni, vidi, veggie"), in pop songs ("Ooh, you came, you saw, you conquered all the love in me"), and in movies ("We came, we saw, we kicked some ass"). It works because rather than a detailed exposition of what Caesar had done, he summarized it in a phrase so authoritatively brief that he was accused of arrogance. If all he had said was a blunt, "I won," it is doubtful he would have gotten away with it; on the other hand, if he had give the customary unremarkable report of the events, he would not have been noticed. The announcement conveyed the news of his victory, but the form of that announcement conveyed far more to the members of the Senate: it characterized the victory the way Caesar wanted it characterized, and it distinguished Caesar the way he wanted to be distinguished. Caesar's sound—the density of repetition in "veni, vidi, vici"— the initial consonant "v," the end- and middle-vowel "i," the three nearly identical two-syllable verbs—echoes his meaning. His famous phrase thus neatly embodies the combination of brilliant planning and lightning-quick execution of the military campaign he had just completed.

In the classical world, the term **rhetoric** referred to the art of persuasion and was the specialty of politicians and public speakers, whose reputation depended on their ability to sway their audience with words, to make their words echo their meaning. The sound and rhythm of these techniques will be quite familiar to your ears, as they continue to be used by public speakers today. John F. Kennedy's "Ask not what your country can do for you; ask what you can do for your country"; Martin Luther King's "I have a dream" speech; Franklin Delano Roosevelt's "The only thing we have to fear is fear itself"; Abraham Lincoln's "Fourscore and seven years ago our fathers brought forth on this continent, a new nation": the enduring power of these and many other historic speeches derives in large part from their memorable use of figures of speech, or **literary devices.**

LITERARY DEVICES

Because so much of its meaning depends on form, poetry, like speechmaking, tends to use literary devices liberally, while in fiction and nonfiction these devices tend to be scattered sparingly, singling out and linking together key moments within the broader narrative. Because it depends so much on patterns of speech, drama can either be replete with literary devices, as in the speeches of Shakespeare's *Hamlet* (p. 286), or filled with dialogue that strives to achieve the effects of everyday speech, as in Susan Glaspell's *Trifles* (p. 139). Working with the devices in a literary text means not only noticing them and identifying them properly, but asking what function they serve in the text as a whole.

True ease in writing comes from art, not chance,
As those who move easiest have learned to dance.
—ALEXANDER POPE

Literary devices achieve their effect in two ways. They can change the expected *diction,* or word choice and word order, creating patterns of sound; or they can change or supplement the expected *meaning* of words, creating patterns of figurative meaning. The six Reader's Guides that follow here categorize the most common literary devices and provide brief examples of each, along with page references that will enable you to consult texts elsewhere in this book.

Patterns of Repetition

All speech is patterned and stressed to a certain degree, providing a wide range of raw material for rhetorical schemes to employ. Patterns in English range from the hard consonants that dominated Old English poetry to the softer repetition of vowel sounds inherited from French and other Romance languages. Rhetorical schemes can be subtle or prominent, harsh or melodious; they can enhance a metrical pattern or provide structure to free verse. In prose, drama, and speech, they can channel our attention, create associations, and emphasize the key moments in the narrative or argumentative structure. The most common patterns of repetition are **alliteration, assonance, consonance,** and **anaphora.**

WRITING EXERCISE: **Neutered Rhetoric 1**

1. "Neutered" speech, or speech free of rhetorical figures, is a technical term in linguistics; it is also a useful exercise in seeing how the presence of rhetorical figures works to create meaning. Choose a text in this book that uses alliteration, assonance, consonance, and/or anaphora, and rewrite it, retaining the original diction and meaning as much as possible but "neutering" it, removing any literary devices that you find in it. (For more on these devices, see p. 212.)

2. Write a paragraph comparing the original with your neutered version. How has the text changed in meaning as a result of your alteration?

Forms of Repetition

The sound must seem an echo to the sense.
—Alexander Pope

Literary Device	Definition	Example	Textual Examples
Alliteration	Repetition of initial consonant	<u>V</u>eni, <u>v</u>idi, <u>v</u>ici. (Julius Caesar)	• Emily Dickinson, "Tell All the Truth" (p. 462) • Gerald Manley Hopkins "Inversnaid" (p. 658)
Assonance	Repetition of a vowel sound	It w<u>a</u>s m<u>a</u>ny <u>a</u>nd m<u>a</u>ny <u>a</u> year <u>a</u>go (Edgar Allan Poe, "Annabel Lee")	• Elizabeth Bishop, "The Fish" (p. 655)
Consonance	Repetition of an internal consonant	The <u>m</u>oan of doves in i<u>mm</u>e<u>m</u>orial el<u>m</u>s And <u>m</u>ur<u>m</u>uring of innu<u>m</u>erable Bees. (Alfred Tennyson, "Come down, O Maid")	• Gerald Manley Hopkins "Inversnaid" (p. 658)
Anaphora	Repetition of same word or phrase to begin lines of poetry or sentences or clauses of prose	<u>Or</u> hand in hand with Plenty in the maize, <u>Or</u> red with spirted purple of the vats, <u>Or</u> foxlike in the vine; nor cares to walk (Alfred Tennyson, "Come down, O Maid")	• Langston Hughes, "The Negro Speaks of Rivers" (p. 657) • Martin Luther King, "I Have a Dream"

Patterns of Inversion

Alliteration, assonance, and consonance repeat individual letters; anaphora repeats words and phrases. The literary device known as **chiasmus** also repeats words and phrases, but its effect comes from the contrast in its repetition, as it inverts rather than maintains word order. Instead of strictly parallel, the repeated words and phrases are structured in an X, or crisscross pattern. Below is the scheme as applied to the opening lines of Emily Dickinson's poem, "Because I could not stop for Death" (p. 459).

Chiasmus (from the Greek letter *chi,* or X), can take a number of forms and be used for a variety of different effects; we list these in the Reader's Guide on page 213.

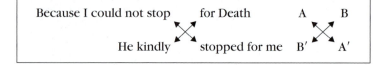

Patterns of Contradiction

Contradiction is a powerful tool for confounding expectations and provoking new ways of thinking about familiar topics. It is also frequently used to depict experiences that seem to contradict our assumptions about the rational structure of the universe: fierce passions such as love and hate; religious visions and inspirations; philosophical and social truths. **Antithesis** achieves its effect by combining contradictory words, phrases, or concepts in a parallel or a chiastic construction. When two

---

WRITING EXERCISE: Neutered Rhetoric 2

1. Choose one of the texts illustrating chiasmus, and rewrite it, retaining the original diction and meaning as much as possible but removing any rhetorical figures you find in it.

2. Write a paragraph comparing the original with your neutered version. How has the text changed in meaning as a result of your alteration?

Forms of Chiasmus

I realize the full significance of the singular fate which has led me to play with all the serious things of life and to deal seriously with all its plays.
—George Bernard Shaw

Form	Example	Source	Definition and Comments
Chiasmus as pattern of repetition without reversal of meaning	O le*t* **not** <u>T</u>ime deceive **you,** **You** <u>c</u>annot <u>c</u>onquer **Time.** A ("Time") B ("you") B′ ("you") A′ ("Time")	W. H. Auden, "As I Walked Out One Evening"	Uses *alliteration* (t, c) and *consonance* (*n, t*) to reinforce repetition of meaning and emphasize chiastic words.
Narrative chiasmus	Narrator and amphibian exchange positions midway through story	Julio Cortázar, "Axolotl" (p. 416)	Use of a chiastic pattern to structure a narrative. Many books of the Bible also use chiastic structure.
Palindrome: a letter-by-letter chiasmus	A man, a plan, a canal—Panama	Leigh Mercer, a London street artist (1893–1977)	A special pattern of repetition: reads the same from beginning to end as from end to beginning
Chiastic wordplay	It's not the *men* in my *life,* it's the *life* in my *men.*	Mae West, film actress	Changes meaning by reversing entire phrase
Chiastic wordplay	I'd rather have a *bottle* in *front of me* than a *frontal lobotomy.*	Most commonly attributed to writer Dorothy Parker (p. 372).	Changes meaning by reversing sounds in part of a word
Chiastic wordplay	Here's *champagne* to our *real friends,* and *real pain* to our *sham friends.*	Early twentieth-century English toast	Changes meaning by reversing two words and substituting homonyms (*sham* and *pain* for *champagne*)
Chiastic wordplay	*I wasted time,* and now doth *time waste me.*	Shakespeare, *Richard II* (5.5.49)	Reversal of order with double meaning (waste = "to squander" and = "to eat away")

Chiastic wordplay in the comic strip *Pearls Before Swine.*

antithetical words are combined more intimately as noun and adjective, we call the resulting device an **oxymoron.** Because there is no parallel structure to imply a comparison between two terms, an oxymoron, on the surface at least, is truly contradictory. Like the oxymoron, a **paradox** presents an apparently contradictory assertion that eventually resolves itself into a kind of truth, often a poetic or

Forms of Antithesis, Oxymoron, and Paradox

Contradiction is not a sign of falsity, nor the lack of contradiction a sign of truth.
—Blaise Pascal

Form of Contrast	Example	Source	Comments
Antithesis logically stating an opposition between ideas	It is better to *give* than to *receive.*	Proverb	Parallel construction contrasts antonyms (words with opposite meanings): *give* versus *receive.*
Antithesis logically stating an opposition between ideas	To err is *human,* to forgive *divine.*	Alexander Pope, *An Essay on Criticism*	Parallel construction assumes or establishes an opposite relation between words: *human* versus *divine.*
Antithesis logically stating an opposition between ideas in parallel construction	The inherent vice of capitalism is the unequal sharing of blessings; the inherent virtue of socialism is the equal sharing of misery.	Winston Churchill, British Prime Minister	Two pairs of antonyms (*vice/virtue; blessings/misery*) in a parallel construction establish an antithetical relationship between two abstract concepts (*capitalism/socialism*). Parallel construction stresses the antithetical relationship of the two systems and the flawed nature of both.
Antithesis logically stating an opposition between ideas in a chiastic construction	The inherent vice of capitalism is the unequal sharing of blessings; the equal sharing of misery is the inherent virtue of socialism.	Winston Churchill (rephrased for comparison)	Two pairs of antonyms in a chiastic construction stress the comparison between vice and virtue and blessings and misery.
Antithesis defining contradictions existing within a single idea	I hate and love.	Catullus, Poem 85 (p. 234)	The more compressed an antithesis, the closer it approaches a paradox.
Oxymoron in poetry: compressed antithesis: finds truth beneath an apparent contradiction	Darkness visible Serv'd onely to discover sights of woe	John Milton, *Paradise Lost,* Book 1. 64–65	Describes the unprecedented quality of illumination in hell. (1.65).
Oxymoron in humor, satire, and social commentary	Honest politicians; legal brief; military intelligence		Not antithetical by definition but labeled as oxymoron as an argument.
Oxymoron in everyday phrases	Jumbo shrimp; freezer burn; pretty ugly; true fiction		Antithetical by definition, but taken for granted through familiarity.
Paradox in a parallel antithetical construction	"*Heard* melodies are sweet, but those *unheard*/Are sweeter"	John Keats, "Ode on a Grecian Urn" (p. 224).	Parallel of antitheses "heard" and "unheard," stresses argument that those melodies we do not or cannot hear are "sweeter" than those we can.
Paradox in a chiastic antithetical construction	Fair is foul, and foul is fair.	The Witches in Shakespeare, *Macbeth,* 1.1.11.	Chiastic antitheses (*fair/foul*) stress mystery of paradox that unfolds only slowly through events of the tragic plot.

Forms of Antithesis, Oxymoron, and Paradox (*continued*)

Form of Contrast	Example	Source	Comments
Paradox with implied antithesis (often used satirically)	*Treason* doth never *prosper;* what's the reason? / For if it *prosper,* none dare call it *treason*	Sir John Harrington, "Of Treason" (1618)	Antithesis implied in repetition of *treason:* substituting the actual antithesis "it is called fidelity" for the final clause produces the same meaning.
Logical paradox (no antithesis)	All Cretans are liars.	Epimenides, 6th century BCE Cretan writer	Common in mathematics and logic: rather than producing a counterintuitive truth, the paradox appears to be impossible to resolve.

Software snafu: a feedback paradox created in 2006 by Microsoft's new instant messaging program. Lester Haines, a reader of the online newspaper *The Register,* explained the problem: "Basically the new MSN installer wants you to close the MSN installer to install the MSN installer that wants you to close the MSN installer that installs the MSN inst. . . ."

unexpected one. Rather than the oxymoron's compressed word pairing, however, the paradox is generally longer, composed of a clause or phrase. Whether pondering the meaning of a word or the meaning of life, the literary devices of contradiction use the tools of language to persuade us to reconsider something that we take for granted about the world in which we live.

Ambiguity and Double Meaning

It can be extremely unnerving to converse with people who say one thing and may mean another; we never know to what degree we can take what they are saying at face value. As opposed to patterns of repetition and contrast, literary devices based on ambiguity do not

---

WRITING EXERCISE: Rhetorical Rewriting

1. Rewrite the opening four words of Catullus's "Poem 85"—"I hate and love" (p. 234)—as an oxymoron rather than an antithesis.

2. Rewrite the proverb "To err is human, to forgive divine" as a paradox rather than an antithesis.

3. Rewrite the phrase "Fair is foul, and foul is fair" as a non-paradoxical antithesis.

4. Rewrite the phrase "Darkness visible" as an antithesis rather than an oxymoron.

Forms of Ambiguity

I look for ambiguity when I'm writing because life is ambiguous.
—Keith Richards

Name of Device	Form of Ambiguity	Definition	Example	Further Example Source
Hyperbole	Obvious	Exaggeration for effect	An hundred years should go to praise Thine eyes, and on thy forehead gaze; Two hundred to adore each breast, But thirty thousand to the rest;	Andrew Marvell, "To His Coy Mistress" (lines 13–16)
Litotes	Obvious	Understatement for effect	Coral is far more red than her lips' red	Shakespeare, Sonnet 130
Sarcasm	Obvious	Statement meaning the opposite of what is expected; meaning clear to everybody	"*Absurdity:* A statement or belief manifestly inconsistent with one's own opinion."	Ambrose Bierce, *The Devil's Dictionary*
Verbal irony	Some aware of it, others not	Statement meaning the opposite of what is expected; clear to speaker and audience but not to all characters	"We call it—knot it, Mr. Henderson."	Susan Glaspell, *Trifles* (p. 145)
Dramatic irony	Some aware of it, others not	Statement meaning the opposite of what is expected; clear to audience, but not to speaker	"Upon the murderer I invoke this curse . . . may he wear out his life in misery to miserable doom"	Oedipus, unknowing murderer of his own father, in Sophocles, *Oedipus the King*
Situational (or cosmic) irony	Some unaware of it	Unexpected and severe reversal of apparent outcome of events	The man Oedipus kills while trying to avoid killing his father turns out to have been his father.	Sophocles, *Oedipus the King*
"Isn't it ironic"	Common usage (not really irony)	Bad luck, bad timing, surprise—*not applicable to academic writing*	"It's a death row pardon two minutes too late."	Alanis Morissette, "Ironic"
Wordplay, or pun	Multiple meanings applicable to situation	A play on different meanings in a single word, or words with similar sounds, used either humorously or in a serious context.	"Ask for me tomorrow, and you shall find me a *grave* man."	Shakespeare, *Romeo and Juliet* (3.1.97–8)
Zeugma	Multiple meanings in grammatical construction	The use of a single verb to govern several objects or clauses, each in a different sense	"You held your breath and the door for me."	Alanis Morisette, "Head over Feet"

1. Recount (or imagine) one or several episodes that happened to you or a friend involving the misunderstanding of one of the above ambiguous figures: missing someone else's hyperbole or litotes; taking an ironic phrase at face-value; missing a pun or making an inadvertent pun. What were the consequences of the misunderstanding? How could it have been avoided?

or

2. Recount (or imagine) a perfect scenario for revenge involving the use of one of the ambiguous devices discussed above against someone who deserves its full rhetorical force. How would you set it up? What would the perfect retort sound like? Would you want the person to know it immediately (sarcasm, wordplay) or discover it only later, if at all (irony)?

"Good news. The test results show it's a metaphor."

Figurative versus literal meaning: Is it only an image?

An engraving illustrating some characters in John Bunyan's allegorical narrative *The Pilgrim's Progress*. The pilgrim Christian is armed by four noble ladies: Prudence, Discretion, Piety, and Charity. In other episodes, he will encounter male personifications of Pride, Arrogance, Self-Conceit, and Worldly Glory, enter the town of Vanity Fair, and get lost in the Slough of Despond. From an 1880 edition of *The Pilgrim's Progress*.

always call attention to their existence. To know whether a person is exaggerating (**hyperbole**), understating (**litotes**), using **sarcasm,** employing **irony,** using **wordplay,** or speaking ambiguously (**zeugma**), we must rely on our knowledge of that person and our assessment of the context. To recognize and establish the existence and interpretation of an ambiguous device in a literary text requires attention to diction and style and an awareness that words do not always mean only what they appear to mean. We can categorize these literary devices according to the degree of ambiguity or the level of multiple meanings they employ.

Imagery

When we think about what makes literature literary, the first thing we usually consider is its imagery: the symbols, the metaphors, the allegories, the figurative language that gives objects and events implied meaning, that is, meaning that is not always literal. As opposed to the way objects and events take on a figurative meaning simply through their repetition within a text (p. 212), the literary devices of **simile, synecdoche, metonymy, metaphor, symbol,** and **allegory** all require the reader to add something to them in order to reveal fully their figurative meaning.

Forms of Imagery

through metaphor to reconcile / the people and the stones.
—William Carlos Williams

Form of Imagery	Example	Source	Definition and Comments
Simile, or comparison	Without warning *as* a whirlwind swoops on an oak Love shakes my heart	Sappho, early 7th century BCE	Compares two distinct subjects, usually with *like* or *as*. Assumes strong resemblance between terms of comparison (*whirlwind/Love; oak/heart*)
Heroic, or Homeric, simile	he bowed his head *as* a garden poppy in full bloom	Homer, *Iliad*, Book 8	Uses everyday events to describe the distant and often unbelievable actions and characters of the heroic world of the epic.
Synecdoche (part for whole)	*Man* cannot live by bread alone.	Deuteronomy 8.33	The part (*man*) substituted for the whole (man and woman)
Synecdoche (whole for part)	*Brazil* wins the World Cup.	Sports headline	The whole (*Brazil*) substituted for part (the Brazilian soccer team)
Metonymy	The *pen* is mightier than the *sword*.	Proverb	One term (*pen, sword*) substituted for another (*writing, physical battle*) by association.
Metaphor	An *iron curtain* has descended across the *continent*.	Winston Churchill	Transfers the qualities of one thing (*iron curtain*) to another (*continent*) through an unexpected resemblance.
Dead, frozen, or conceptual metaphor	He *won* the argument by *beating* his opponent into *submission*.	George Lakoff, *Metaphors We Live By*	We accept metaphorical meaning (*argument*) without noticing literal meaning (*won, beating . . . into submission*) or its conceptual implication (*argument* as war).
Metaphor in slang	Ice, phat	Hip-hop slang	Slang words coined through metaphor: *ice* = diamonds; *phat* = rich like butter; any addictive musical beat or person
Symbol		American flag	Arbitrary association whose meaning is agreed upon by convention.
Allegory	The lion Aslan as Christ in the *Chronicles of Narnia*	C. S. Lewis	A narrative containing a figurative meaning distinct from and parallel to the explicit plot.
Emblem		The image on the back of the U.S. dollar bill	Allegorical narrative as visual puzzle: symbol of eagle surrounded by attributes, along with freemasonry symbol of the eye in the pyramid.

Forms of Imagery (continued)

Form of Imagery	Example	Source	Definition and Comments
Personification	My name is the Balkans. Hers, Europe.	Milorad Pavíc, "The Wedgwood Tea Set"	Places an abstract word or concept (*Balkans, Europe*) in a narrative context (protagonists of the story), gives it human qualities (*My name, hers*), and uses it to refer to a figurative level of meaning (relationship between Balkans and Europe).
Fable	*Animal Farm*	George Orwell	Meaning is clear and often spelled out in a moral at the end: pigs as dictators = Stalinism.
Parable	Let them alone: they be blind leaders of the blind. And if the blind lead the blind, both shall fall into the ditch.	Matthew 15.14	An allegory, often religious, whose meaning is not always perfectly clear and is often paradoxical (*blind leaders of the blind*).

Two famous images of the late 1960s and early '70s that became enduring symbols of the era: (*Left*) icons of the counter-culture enjoying the freedom of the open road and escape from the restrictions of regular life in Dennis Hopper's hit movie, *Easy Rider* (1969); (*Right*) the equally iconic, but shocking and heartrending 1972 photograph by Huỳnh Công Út (aka Nick Ut) of Kim Phuc and other victims of napalm.

WRITING EXERCISE: Symbols in Popular Culture: A Response Paper

Study the two images above and write a response paper that answers the questions that follow.

1. What qualities about the 1960s does each of these images symbolize? Do these two symbols have anything in common?

2. Once a symbol has been established, new images can use it to repeat the same meaning. For example, a recent soft drink commercial digitally added a middle-aged baby boomer riding on a third chopper next to the two anti-establishment icons. How did the commercial borrow the symbolism for its own purposes? How has the symbolism of the photograph of Kim Phuc been used since the photograph was originally taken?

3. Compare these two images with Maya Lin's Vietnam Veterans Memorial (p. 530). In what ways does Lin's memorial refuse the symbolism of both images? What meanings does it propose to replace them?

WRITING EXERCISE: Synecdoche, Metonymy, and Metaphor in Everyday Language

1. Make a list of all of the uses of synecdoche and metonymy in a newspaper or magazine article and explain each one. What is being equated or substituted? What is the relationship between the terms involved? Why is the literary device rather than the literal term being used? Be sure to attach a photocopy of the article you use. Exchange lists with a classmate and look for figures of speech your classmate might have missed. *Note:* Many uses of synecdoche and metonymy may be so familiar to you that you may not notice them (a pronouncement by *the Oval Office;* a *World Cup* victory for Brazil).

   or

2. Identify a conceptual or "dead" metaphor similar to the "argument is war" metaphor cited on page 218. List a number of examples of its usage, and discuss the consequences of the way the vehicle of the metaphor frames the meaning of its subject.

   or

3. Make a list of figurative words from slang or dialect with which you are familiar. Explain the etymology—the process by which it has come to mean what it means—of each term. What do the objects in your list suggest about the interests and concerns of the group that coined them?

The young prince Louis is pictured in the bow of the heavily laden vessel, looking for instruction to his powerful mother, Marie de Medici (Rubens's patron) on his left.

A personification of the nation of France perched high atop the ship of state.

The Virtue Temperance is lowering the sails as the ship enters into port.

The Virtue Fortitude is propelling the boat forward.

Guiding the ship are personifications of the virtues necessary in a ruler. Each of the virtues is identified and characterized by an emblematic shield, although, as with many emblems, experts do not agree about every specific meaning.

How to decode an allegorical picture. Peter Paul Rubens, *The Coming of Age of Louis XIII,* also known as *The Ship of State.*

1. Choose a short story from this book that contains at least one simile. Make a list of all of the similes (and possible similes, if there are some you are not sure about), and analyze each one. What are the two terms being compared? What is similar and what is different about them? What is a possible motivation for the choice of each simile?

2. In a substantial paragraph briefly analyze the relationship between similes. What, if anything, do they have in common? What patterns, if any, do they establish between them? Are they a prominent aspect of the story's style? How would the story be changed if instead of the similes simply the main term was used in each case?

The Coming of Age of Louis XIII (at left) is the sixteenth in a series of twenty-four paintings the Dutch artist Peter Paul Rubens created for his patron, Marie de Medici, Queen of France between 1621 and 1625, now in the Louvre Museum in Paris. It is an allegorical depiction of the moment in 1615 when the Queen Regent ceded power to her fifteen-year-old son. We have annotated the painting to suggest some of the information encoded in its allegorical emblems.

1. Write a summary of the painting.
2. Using your summary as a starting point, write a 1–2 page explication of the allegorical narrative proposed by the painting's use of the conventional image of the "Ship of State."

1. Choose a story or poem from this book and write an allegorical interpretation of it. Try to make your allegory match as closely as possible to the terms of the literal level of the story or poem.

2. Reflect on the process of making an allegorical reading. Have you illuminated any issues within the text you read, or simply added another layer of meaning to it? Are you persuaded by your reading? What does the text gain by being allegorized? What does it lose?

Referring to Other Texts

We use the term **reference** to describe any instance in which one text is used to elucidate the meaning of another text or situation. A bibliographical reference, for example, tells the reader that you have drawn evidence from another text. Bibliographical references should be as clear as possible about the relation between your sources and your own work, but when references are used as a literary device, the relationship will not always be so obvious. Sometimes a reference can have several meanings at once for different members of an audience—an inside joke by definition works when some people

Do you get the insider reference? In a scene from Luc Besson's 1985 film *Subway,* Fred (Christopher Lambert) wields a fluorescent light bulb beneath the streets of Paris as if it were a light saber.

Referring to Other Texts

Life itself is a quotation.
—Jorges Luis Borges

Type of Reference	Example	Source	Comments and Definitions
Explicit Allusion	"Greasy Lake"	Title of story by T. C. Boyle (p. 646)	Identifies allusion explicitly by epigraph to story quoting from Bruce Springsteen's song "Spirits in the Night."
Implicit Allusion	"Lion and Tigers and Bears"	Title of essay by Bill Buford (p. 633)	Makes implicit, or unstated, reference to song from movie *The Wizard of Oz.*
Contrafactum	"Gangsta's Paradise"	Song by Coolio	Gives new meaning to existing song (Stevie Wonder's "Pastime Paradise") by changing lyrics; knowledge of original music needed to understand the reference.
Visual parody		Parody of an Absolut Vodka advertisement (p. 80)	Reproduces key visual components of the original (the outline of the vodka bottle; the font and two words of the slogan) in a new context (death after drunk driving).
Aural parody	"Eat It"	"Weird Al" Yankovic	Copies music from Michael Jackson's hit single "Beat It"; lyrics copy the rhyme and rhythm of the original, but they are adapted to the comic context of food (a comic form of contrafactum).
Textual parody	*Hairy Pothead and the Marijuana Stone*	Dana Larsen	Based on the words of the book's original title (*Harry Potter and the Sorcerer's Stone*) as well as its characters, events, and conventions, while mocking them in a new context (drug culture) wholly opposed to the original.
Genre parody	*Scary Movie I–V*	Motion picture titles	Parodies the conventions of an entire genre (horror movies) rather than a particular text.
Satire by deflation of its subject	"If the Heat Doesn't Kill the Elderly, I Will"	Headline in *The Onion*	Uses conscious deadpan irony to call attention to a serious subject (death of elderly in heat wave) by understating its seriousness.
Satire by inflation of its subject	"Yacht Club Regatta Marred by Tragic Undergrilling of Mahi Mahi"	Headline in *The Onion*	Uses conscious deadpan irony to ridicule a subject (frivolous behavior of the wealthy) by overstating its importance.

get it and others don't. But even if you don't recognize a reference immediately, you can usually tell when it's happening: watch for the tone, the particular stress put on the words, and the sense that the literal meaning doesn't tell you everything about them. **Allusion** functions as shorthand for the immense contextual framework authors wish to incorporate into their texts; **contrafactum,** or changing the lyrics to an existing song, **parody,** and **satire** all work to create meaning out of the interaction between what we already know about a text or a situation and the new context in which the author places it.

WRITING EXERCISE: Spotting Allusions

1. List all of the allusions you can spot in a newspaper or magazine article. Track down the text, image, or object being alluded to, via the Internet or the library, and explain how it is being used in the article you chose.

2. Rewrite the article, replacing each allusion with a nonallusive synonym. How has the meaning or rhetorical effect of the article changed?

WRITING EXERCISE: Satire on the Internet

Using a search engine such as Google or Yahoo, locate a textual or visual example of each of the following types of satire:

1. A satire that achieves a comic effect by ironically deflating a serious subject.

2. A satire that achieves a comic effect by ironically inflating the importance of its subject.

3. A deadpan satire made with a serious intent at social change.

4. An overtly polemical satire made with a serious intent at social change.

Compare the means used by each satire to achieve its effect.

Word Pictures

How do you describe something you have seen to someone who has not seen it? Literature is full of written descriptions of physical objects, places, and works of art; we call such a description an **ecphrasis,** from a Greek word literally meaning to speak out, or call an object by name. Although it can refer to any physical description, ecphrasis is usually restricted to descriptions of works of art. Ecphrasis is a form of allusion (p. 222), because its meaning depends on the relationship it establishes to a prior work of art. Whenever you encounter a physical description in a literary text, ask yourself what functions it is serving. Is its primary purpose to establish a setting or character within the story world? Is it describing a natural object, place, or person or does it allude to an artistic representation of it? Is it describing something real or imagined? An ecphrasis within a longer text will often have a figurative meaning within the story world of that text; this is usually the case with *narrative ecphrasis* (see, for example, "The Kid's Guide to Divorce." [p. 352]). In contrast, *poetic ecphrasis* will generally explore more fully the relationship between a poem and the artwork it is describing; this is the case with the poems that follow here, on subjects ranging from ancient Greek sculpture to Akira Kurosawa's film, *The Seven Samurai.*

A drawing made by John Keats of the "Sosibios Vase," an ancient Greek urn in the Louvre Museum in Paris that depicts a religious procession similar to the one described in the fourth stanza of "Ode on a Grecian Urn."

John Keats 1795–1821

John Keats was the oldest of five children of a London stable keeper and the proprietor's daughter. Keats's father died when he was nine, and his mother died of tuberculosis six years later. He published his first book of poetry in 1817; around this time he made the acquaintance of other Romantic poets, including Percy Bysshe Shelley. Keats's second volume of poems, published in 1820, includes most of his major works, among them "Ode on a Grecian Urn." Suffering from tuberculosis for the last years of his life, Keats died in Rome at the age of twenty-five. The poem as a whole most likely describes an imagined urn composed of various designs viewed by Keats rather than a specifically identifiable object.

Ode on a Grecian Urn

Thou still unravish'd bride of quietness,
   Thou foster-child of silence and slow time,
Sylvan historian, who canst thus express
   A flowery tale more sweetly than our rhyme:
What leaf-fring'd legend haunts about thy shape 5
   Of deities or mortals, or of both,
      In Tempe or the dales of Arcady?°
What men or gods are these? What
      maidens loth?
What mad pursuit? What struggle to escape?
     What pipes and timbrels? What wild
      ecstasy?   10

Heard melodies are sweet, but those unheard
   Are sweeter; therefore, ye soft pipes, play on;
Not to the sensual ear, but, more endear'd,
   Pipe to the spirit ditties of no tone:
Fair youth, beneath the trees, thou canst not
      leave   15
   Thy song, nor ever can those trees be bare;
    Bold Lover, never, never canst thou kiss,
Though winning near the goal yet, do not grieve;
   She cannot fade, though thou hast not thy bliss,
    For ever wilt thou love, and she be fair!   20

Ah, happy, happy boughs! that cannot shed
   Your leaves, nor ever bid the Spring adieu;
And, happy melodist, unwearied,
   For ever piping songs for ever new;

More happy love! more happy, happy love!   25
   For ever warm and still to be enjoy'd,
    For ever panting, and for ever young;
All breathing human passion far above,
   That leaves a heart high-sorrowful and cloy'd,
    A burning forehead, and a parching
      tongue.   30

Who are these coming to the sacrifice?
   To what green altar, O mysterious priest,
Lead'st thou that heifer lowing at the skies,
   And all her silken flanks with garlands drest?
What little town by river or sea shore,   35
   Or mountain-built with peaceful citadel,
    Is emptied of this folk, this pious morn?
And, little town, thy streets for evermore
   Will silent be; and not a soul to tell
    Why thou art desolate, can e'er return.   40

O Attic shape! Fair attitude! with brede°
   Of marble men and maidens overwrought,
With forest branches and the trodden weed;
   Thou, silent form, dost tease us out of thought
As doth eternity: Cold Pastoral!   45
   When old age shall this generation waste,
    Thou shalt remain, in midst of other woe
Than ours, a friend to man, to whom thou say'st,
   "Beauty is truth, truth beauty,—that is all
    Ye know on earth, and all ye need to know." 50

[1820]

---

7 **Tempe . . . Arcady:** valleys in Greece associated with pastoral beauty.

41 **brede:** design.

1. What are the form, meter, and rhyme scheme of the poem? Are there any significant breaks in the pattern formed by the meter and rhyme?

2. Make a list of the objects, scenes, and human figures on the vase. Summarize each stanza. What can the speaker know about the vase? What can he not know about it?

3. Several times the speaker compares the vase and the poem. On what grounds does he make the comparison?

How do poem and vase remain different? What, if anything, is the vase able to express that the poem cannot? What, if anything, is the poem able to express that the vase cannot?

4. The message of the vase, according to the famous penultimate line, is "Beauty is truth, truth beauty." What is the beauty and truth the speaker finds in the vase? How is this idea expressed in the stanzas in the poem leading up to the final statement of the argument?

Elizabeth Barrett Browning 1806–1861

The Victorian poet Elizabeth Barrett Browning wrote her celebrated sequence of love poems, *Sonnets from the Portuguese,* during the two years of correspondence which concluded in 1846 in her marriage to the poet Robert Browning (p. 551). Browning had been prompted to write Barrett after reading the works collected in the two volumes of *Poems* (1844) that established Barrett's reputation, including a popular series of ballads. She is also remembered today for her long and controversial narrative poem on the "woman question," *Aurora Leigh* (1856); she also wrote occasional pieces, such as "On Hiram Powers' Greek Slave."

On Hiram Powers' Greek Slave

They say Ideal Beauty cannot enter
The house of anguish. On the threshold stands
An alien image with enshackled hands,
Called the Greek Slave! as if the artist meant her
(That passionless perfection which he lent her   5
Shadowed not darkened where the sill expands)
To so confront man's crimes in different lands
With man's ideal sense. Pierce to the center,
Art's fiery finger! and break up ere long
The serfdom of this world! appeal, fair stone,   10
From God's pure heights of beauty against man's
    wrong!
Catch up in the divine face, not alone
East griefs but West, and strike and shame the
    strong,
By thunders of white silence, overthrown.

[1851]

Hiram Powers, *The Greek Slave* (1843). Depicted nude with the chains granting her the barest scrap of modesty, the young woman, according to the sculptor, was a Greek captive stripped for sale in a Turkish slave market at the time of the Greek revolution earlier in the century. In Powers' view, she embodied Christian virtue. The work made him famous: after a blockbuster American tour, the statue was one of the hits of the Great Exhibition in London in 1851, where the poet Elizabeth Barrett Browning was so affected by it as to compose a sonnet on the occasion.

John Tenniel, *The Virginian Slave Intended as a Companion to Power's* [sic] *Greek Slave* (1851). Although no American critics noted any connection to the institution of slavery, this cartoon in the English humorous magazine *Punch* most certainly did: "We have the Greek captive in dead stone. Why not the Victorian slave in living ebony?"

THE VIRGINIAN SLAVE.

QUESTIONS FOR REFLECTION AND DISCUSSION

1. Explain the metaphor of the poem's opening lines. What is the "house of anguish" and why can the Greek Slave stand only on its threshold?

2. Where does the break occur in the sonnet? How does the focus shift in the sextet?

3. What attitude does the speaker take to the statue? Does she at any point allude to the issue of slavery in America as a satirical cartoon of the time (at left) did?

4. Compare Browning's use of the image of the silent artwork to Keats's "Grecian urn" (p. 224).

Pieter Brueghel the Elder, *Landscape with the Fall of Icarus* (c. 1558). The painting takes its subject from the classical myth of Daedalus and his son Icarus, who escaped from imprisonment on wings held together by wax. Ignoring his father's warning, Icarus flew too close to the sun, the wax melted, and he fell to his death in the sea. There have been nearly fifty poems written on the subject of Brueghel's painting, fourteen of them in English. Three of these poems are included here.

William Carlos Williams 1883–1963

William Carlos Williams was born and raised in Rutherford, New Jersey, and spent the rest of his life working there as a pediatrician. While a medical student at the University of Pennsylvania, he met the poets Ezra Pound (p. 234) and Hilda Dolittle (p. 654), with whom he remained friends for the rest of his life. The poems, novels, essays, and plays that he wrote during time away from his patients are noteworthy for the effort to create a natural language based on everyday American English and the focus on concrete description of objects without attributing figurative meaning to them. Williams published his first book, *The Tempers,* in 1913. He continued to publish poetry throughout the next few decades; however, he was known primarily as a writer of fiction until 1946, when he published *Paterson I,* the first volume of his epic poem about life in the industrial town of Paterson, New Jersey. In 1950, he received the National Book Award for *Selected Poems* and *Paterson III.* "Landscape with the Fall of Icarus" was published in 1962 in the volume *Pictures from Brueghel and Other Poems.*

Landscape with the Fall of Icarus

According to Brueghel
when Icarus fell
it was spring

a farmer was ploughing
his field   5
the whole pageantry

of the year was
awake tingling
near

the edge of the sea   10
concerned
with itself

sweating in the sun
that melted
the wings' wax   15

unsignificantly
off the coast
there was

a splash quite unnoticed
this was   20
Icarus drowning

[1962]

QUESTIONS FOR REFLECTION AND DISCUSSION

1. Why does Williams begin his poem with the line, "According to Brueghel"? How would the meaning be altered if this line were omitted?

2. Which elements of the painting does the speaker choose to describe? Which does he omit?

3. What is the antithesis introduced in lines 2 and 3? What does it tell us about the speaker's sense of the relationship between the landscape and the fall of Icarus?

W. H. Auden 1907–1973

Born in York, England, Wystan Hugh Auden was educated at Oxford and rose to prominence with the left-wing poetry he published during the turbulent years of the 1930s. After a brief and horrifying stint as an ambulance driver in the Spanish Civil War, Auden came to the United States in 1939 and became an American citizen in 1946. Widely considered the preeminent poet of the mid-twentieth century, Auden was equally comfortable with free verse and with conventional poetic forms, and he made innovative experiments with both. Auden wrote "Musée des Beaux Arts" in 1938 after a visit to the Musée des Beaux Arts museum in Brussels that houses Brueghel's painting. The term "Old Master" refers to the great European painters of the sixteenth through eighteenth centuries, the sort that would be housed in a fine arts museum.

Musée des Beaux Arts

About suffering they were never wrong,
The Old Masters; how well, they understood
Its human position; how it takes place
While someone else is eating or opening a
    window or just walking dully along;
How, when the aged are reverently, passionately
    waiting   5
For the miraculous birth, there always must be
Children who did not specially want it to
    happen, skating
On a pond at the edge of the wood:
They never forgot
That even the dreadful martyrdom must run
    its course   10
Anyhow in a corner, some untidy spot
Where the dogs go on with their doggy life and
    the torturer's horse

Scratches its innocent behind on a tree.

In Brueghel's *Icarus*, for instance: how
    everything turns away
Quite leisurely from the disaster; the ploughman
    may   15
Have heard the splash, the forsaken cry,
But for him it was not an important failure;
    the sun shone
As it had to on the white legs disappearing into
    the green
Water; and the expensive delicate ship that must
    have seen
Something amazing, a boy falling out of the sky,   20
Had somewhere to get to and sailed calmly on.

[1938]

QUESTIONS FOR REFLECTION AND DISCUSSION

1. What do the different titles of Williams's and Auden's poems suggest about the differences between their approaches to the description of Brueghel's painting?

2. Auden's speaker sees suffering in Brueghel's painting; Williams's does not mention it. Which interpretation of the poem do you find more persuasive, and why?

3. Both poems remark on the "unnoticed" splash of Icarus falling into the water, but only Auden's speaker comments on it. What is his explanation for the lack of attention paid to the "amazing" occurrence? Does Williams's speaker consider it an "amazing" occurrence?

Michael Hamburger 1924–2007

Michael Hamburger was born in Berlin; in 1933, his family emigrated to England, where he was educated at Christchurch, Oxford. In addition to his own compositions, Hamburger was a gifted translator of poetry. "Lines on Brueghel's Icarus" was published in *Ownerless Earth* (1973)

Lines on Brueghel's *Icarus*

The ploughman ploughs, the fisherman dreams
   of fish;
Aloft, the sailor, through a world of ropes
Guides tangled meditations, feverish
With memories of girls forsaken, hopes
Of brief reunions, new discoveries,   5
Past rum consumed, rum promised, rum potential.
Sheep crop the grass, lift up their heads and gaze
Into a sheepish present: the essential,
Illimitable juiciness of things,
Greens, yellows, browns are what they see.   10

Churlish and slow, the shepherd, hearing wings—
Perhaps an eagle's—gapes uncertainly;
Too late. The worst has happened: lost to man,
The angel, Icarus, for ever failed,
Fallen with melted wings when, near the sun   15
He scorned the ordering planet, which prevailed
And, jeering, now slinks off, to rise once more.
But he—his damaged purpose drags him down—
Too far from his half-brothers on the shore,
Hardly conceivable, is left to drown.   20

[1973]

QUESTIONS FOR REFLECTION AND DISCUSSION

1. What does Hamburger include that the other two poets do not?

2. Hamburger imports material not explicitly depicted in the painting, as does Auden. What is the relationship between this material and the physical description of what is in the painting?

3. Compare the meter and rhyme scheme (or lack thereof) in the three poems. To what degree do they reflect the different approach of each poem to Brueghel's painting?

4. Compare the three different descriptions of Icarus falling. How are they similar and how are they different from one another?

Robert Hass b. 1941

Born in San Francisco, Robert Hass teaches at the University of California at Berkeley and has published a number of volumes of poetry, translations, and essays. Hass was U.S Poet Laureate from 1995–1997; *Time and Materials* was awarded the 2008 Pulitzer Prize for Poetry. In 1997, Hass inaugurated the popular "Poet's Choice" newspaper column in the *Washington Post*. "Heroic Simile," published in *Praise* (1978), combines an opening ecphrasis of *The Seven Samurai* with an extended heroic simile (p. 218) in the Homeric style.

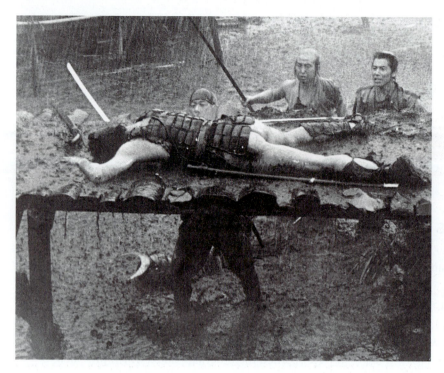

A frame enlargement from the celebrated Japanese director Akira Kurosawa's 1954 film *The Seven Samurai,* which tells the epic story of seven wandering samurai who agree to help a village defend itself from bandits. Toshiro Mifune plays a farmer masquerading as a samurai who in the end proves himself as a warrior but is killed in the decisive battle: his death is the subject of Robert Hass's poem.

Heroic Simile

When the swordsman fell in Kurosawa's *Seven*
   Samurai in the gray rain,
in Cinemascope and the Tokugawa dynasty,
he fell straight as a pine, he fell
as Ajax fell in Homer
in chanted dactyls and the tree was so huge   5
the woodsman returned for two days
to that lucky place before he was done with the
   sawing
and on the third day he brought his uncle.

They stacked logs in the resinous air,
hacking the small limbs off,   10
tying those bundles separately.
The slabs near the root
were quartered and still they were awkwardly large;
the logs from midtree they halved:
ten bundles and four great piles of fragrant
   wood,   15
moons and quarter moons and half moons
ridged by the saw's tooth.

The woodsman and the old man his uncle
are standing in midforest
on a floor of pine silt and spring mud.   20
They have stopped working

because they are tired and because
I have imagined no pack animal
or primitive wagon. They are too canny
to call in neighbors and come home   25
with a few logs after three days' work.
They are waiting for me to do something
or for the overseer of the Great Lord
to come and arrest them.

How patient they are!   30
The old man smokes a pipe and spits.
The young man is thinking he would be rich
if he were already rich and had a mule.
Ten days of hauling
and on the seventh day they'll probably   35
be caught, go home empty-handed
or worse. I don't know
whether they're Japanese or Mycenaean°
and there's nothing I can do.
The path from here to that village   40
is not translated. A hero, dying,
gives off stillness to the air.
A man and a woman walk from the movies
to the house in the silence of separate fidelities.
There are limits to imagination.   45

[1978]

38 Mycenaean: the ancient Greeks of Homer's epics.

QUESTIONS FOR REFLECTION AND DISCUSSION

1. Where does the simile begin and where does it end? What is its relation to the ecphrasis of the death of the warrior? Why do you think Hass chose to use a heroic simile to write about *The Seven Samurai?*

2. Why is the speaker confused about the identity of the woodcutters in lines 37–38? What does he mean when he says, "The path from here to the village is not translated"?

3. Compare the relationship between the woodcutters and the warrior in this poem with the relationship between Icarus and the peasants in Brueghel's painting and the poems about the painting above.

WRITING EXERCISE: A Word Picture

Choose a postcard, a reproduction in an art book, or an Internet image of a painting or other artwork.

1. Write a prose paragraph summarizing the object item by item.

2. Write a poem either describing it or developing the ideas it gives you.

3. Compare the paragraph and the poem. What did you leave out of the description to make your poem? What did you add? How has your understanding of the object you wrote about changed?

WRITING THE WORLD TOPICS FOR ESSAYS

1. Choose a text from elsewhere in this book, and analyze its use of forms of repetition.

2. Write an essay on the use of one or more patterns of repetition in contemporary political speechmaking.

3. Choose a text in this book and analyze its use of chiasmus.

4. Choose a text in in this book and analyze its use of antithesis, paradox, and/or oxymoron.

5. Choose a text in this book and analyze its use of devices of ambiguity.

6. Choose a text in this book and analyze its use of simile, synecdoche, metonymy, metaphor, symbolism, and/or allegory.

7. Write an essay comparing the use of literary devices of imagery, or of a particular type of imagery, in everyday language and popular culture versus the use of imagery in literary writing.

8. Choose a text in this book and analyze its use of allusion, contrafactum, parody, or satire.

9. Write an essay comparing a number of different editorial cartoons responding to a single recent political or historical event.

10. Write an essay on the use of satire or parody in popular culture versus its use in literature or the visual arts.

11. Choose a text in this book and analyze its use of word-pictures, or ecphrasis.

12. Read "The Shield of Achilles" from Book 18 of Homer's *Iliad* and compare it with the heroic simile of Hass's poem "Heroic Simile."

CHAPTER 7

TRANSLATING THE WORLD

READING
AND
WRITING
BETWEEN
LANGUAGES

It is reported that Charles V (1500–1558), the Holy Roman Emperor and ruler of Spain, was fond of boasting of his command of languages: "I speak Spanish to God, Italian with women, French with men, and German to my horse." While most of us use a smaller range of everyday languages than Charles did, we all work as translators in a broader sense: we speak one language at work, one with our family, one with our friends, one in the classroom—and this is just the tip of the iceberg. In its broadest sense, **translation** refers to all of the ways in which we switch from one context to another, and, of course, from one language to another. Translation is our means into the literature of the world; without it, our horizons would be severely shrunken. Moreover, most of the great works in the English language are heavily indebted to their authors' reading of literature written in language not their own: the Greek and Latin classics, the literature of continental Europe, and, in the twentieth century especially, the literatures of Africa, Asia, and the Americas. In this chapter, we survey the range of ways in which we can read and write between languages in a literary context: literary translation; translation as a topic within a literary text; literary writing in a dialect or in several languages simultaneously; and adaptation from one discipline to another.

I HATE AND LOVE: A CASEBOOK ON TRANSLATION

Translation is the lifeblood of poetry. The challenge of translating the harmonious combination of sound, rhythm, and meaning from one language to another has trained and exercised the skill of poets for millennia. Each language has its own structure and its own conceptual metaphors (p. 218). Consequently, not only is the translation invariably unfaithful to the original, but, as the Argentine poet Jorge Luis Borges paradoxically observed, "The original is unfaithful to the translation." Every translation creates a new work of literature independent of the original but related to it in the same way as the two subjects are related in literary devices such as allusion and metaphor. When reading a translation, you will seldom have the luxury of consulting the original language, but what you can do is observe the

tension created between the antithetical goals of the translator: to remain faithful to the source language and to remain faithful to the target language. A good translation will produce creative sparks and new meaning from this contradiction; a poor translation will surrender to one side or the other.

The casebook that follows focuses on a famous couplet by the first-century BCE Roman poet Catullus that poses a serious challenge for translators due to its extremely condensed form and the differences between Latin and English. Latin is a compact language because its verbs do not require pronouns and objects often do not require prepositions. Moreover, word order is highly flexible, and the original version had no punctuation, so words can be arranged for maximum effect. Don't

To have another language is to possess a second soul.

—CHARLEMAGNE

worry that you don't know any Latin; it is common practice in translation courses to work in unfamiliar languages. A brief look at the Latin original with a word-for-word translation above each line, followed by a fairly literal translation, will provide you with all the background you need to know to see what Catullus is doing and to evaluate the translations included here. These translations are followed by two far looser renderings of the couplet by Frank Bidart and a contemporary poem by Miriam Sagan about the pleasures of translating Catullus.

A pair of Roman lovers from the time of Catullus, portrayed in a fresco, or wall painting, preserved in a house in the southern Italian town of Herculaneum after it was buried by the eruption of Mount Vesuvius in 79 CE.

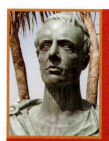

Catullus 84–54 BCE

Born into a well-to-do family in Verona, Gaius Valerius Catullus soon made his way to the capital city of Rome, where he moved among the pre-eminent political and literary figures of his day. He conducted a love affair with the powerful (and, according to Cicero, notorious) Clodia, half-sister of the tribune Publius Clodius Pulcher and wife of Quintus Caecilius Metellus, consul in the year 60. His depiction of love is central to Catullus's portrayal of life as a paradoxical mix of emotions, a heady brew both sweet and sour in which despair and joy are inseparable.

Poem 85

odi	*et*	*amo*	*quare*	*id*	*faciam*	*fortasse*	*requiris*
I hate	and	I love	why	it	I do	perhaps	you ask

nescio	*sed*	*fieri*	*sentio*	*et*
I do not know	but	being done	I feel it	and

excrucior.
I am tormented [literally "I am crucified"]

Translation of Poem 85

I hate and love. Perhaps you ask why I do it?
I do not know but I feel it being done and it is
    excruciating.

QUESTIONS FOR REFLECTION AND DISCUSSION

1. The couplet has a chiastic structure (p. 212): in addition to the opening antithesis the first two verbs and the last two verbs offer a contrast between active and passive constructions. Compare "odi et amo" with "fieri sentio et excrucior." How are the paired sentiments similar, and how are they different?

2. Do the final verbs represent a shift from the opening or simply a restatement?

3. Whom is the speaker addressing at the end of the first line?

As you read the following translations of Catullus's couplet, consider the choices each translator has made, and the consequences of those choices. What are the key decisions to be made in translating it? To what degree does each poem alter the form of the original? To what degree does each poem differently interpret the poem's theme?

I hate and love, wouldst thou
    the reason know?
I know not, but I burn and
    feel it so.

        Richard Lovelace
        (1618–1657)

I love and hate. Ah! never ask
    why so!
I hate and love—and that is all
    I know.
I see 'tis folly, but I feel 'tis
    woe.

        Walter Savage Landor
        (1775–1864)

I hate and love. Why? You ask
    me but
It beats me. I feel it done to
    me, and ache.

        Ezra Pound
        (1885–1972)

I hate and I love. And if you
    ask me how,
I do not know: I only feel it,
    and I'm torn in two.

        Peter Whigham
        (1925–1987)

I hate & love. And if you
    should ask how I can
    do both,
I couldn't say: but I feel it, and
    it shivers me.

        Charles Martin
        (b. 1942)

1. What effect does Landor achieve (or sacrifice) by expanding the couplet into a tercet?

2. How do the end-rhymes used by Lovelace and Landor affect their translations?

3. How has each poet chosen to translate the final word of Catullus's Latin ("excrucior")? What is it about this word

in particular that has led each poet to make a different choice? Which choice do you find more effective, and why?

4. Which translation feels closer to the original? Which feels more distant? Which do you think is the more effective translation, and why?

Frank Bidart b. 1939

Frank Bidart teaches at Wellesley College and is the author of five volumes of poetry characterized by their somber subject matter and troubled characters. Bidart has published two versions of "Poem 85," notable for their liberty with their source and for their difference from one another.

Catullus: Odi et Amo

I hate and love. Ignorant fish, who even
Wants the fly while writhing.

[1980]

Catullus: Excrucior

I hate and—love. The sleepless body hammering a nail
nails itself, hanging crucified.

[1997]

QUESTIONS FOR REFLECTION AND DISCUSSION

1. In each poem, what has Bidart preserved from Catullus and what has he added?

2. Summarize the changes made between the 1980 translation and the 1997 version. In "Catullus: Odi et Amo," who speaks the second sentence: the speaker of the first sentence or the person that sentence was addressed to? How does the identity of the speaker alter the meaning of the poem?

3. Compare the metaphors used in each poem. What do they have in common? How are they different? Do they have any source in Catullus's poem?

4. Bidart is the only one of the translators who literally translates the meaning of "excrucior." Do you think he is justified in making this word the focus of the poem? Why or why not?

Miriam Sagan b. 1954

Born in Manhattan and raised in New Jersey, Miriam Sagan holds degrees from Harvard University and Boston University. Author of twenty books of poetry, fiction, and nonfiction, and editor of *Santa Fe Poetry Broadside,* Sagan has lived in New Mexico for the past twenty years. Rather than a translation of "Odi et Amo," Sagan's poem "Translating Catullus" is about encountering the poet's writings and the meaning of translation to a New Jersey teenager.

Translating Catullus

At fifteen or sixteen I could
   translate lines
Of raw sex and rawer love
Straight out of the Latin
Like: that guy over there
Looks like a god   5
Just because he gets to sit next to
   you . . .

I went to girls' school where I wore
Plaid uniform skirt illegally rolled
Short above the thigh, and pink
   cummerbund
Also illegal, neatly tied   10
Around my fabric fat waist.

Catullus was not my first
Boyfriend, I'd already lost
That hindrance not worth clinging to
A cumbersome virginity.   15
I could also decline
Verbs in three languages.

Still, even I was shocked
Reading ahead, the lyric unassigned
Where the poet comes across a couple
   making love   20
Then did something I could barely
   visualize.

Hell, this was New Jersey, 1969
Everything was about to change
And I was itching
To riot in the street, throw a brick   25
Through a plate glass window . . .

Instead, I sat in my white man-tailored
Shirt and gray blazer
Following the track of dactyls, elegiacs
Knew when the poet said
   "passer"—sparrow   30
He meant something more personal.

He spoke to me—Catullus—
My second boyfriend.
The class set a modern dance to him
Floated with chiffon scarves   35
Beneath maple and elm
Coached someone's little brother
To stand still and drop a white flower
At the end to these words:
"Cut down by the plow."   40

Truly, I don't know
Any more now
Than I did then
Of hate and love
Of desire that consumes   45
And will consume
Whatever you may feed it.

[2002]

QUESTIONS FOR REFLECTION AND DISCUSSION

1. What, according to the speaker, is the appeal of translating Catullus? To what activities does she contrast the act of translation?

2. What does the speaker mean by applying the metaphor of "boyfriend" to Catullus?

3. The final stanza shortens the lengths of the lines to match the brevity of "Odi et Amo." In what other ways does this stanza differ from the previous ones?

WRITING EXERCISE: Translating "Odi et Amo"

1. Now that you have read and analyzed the translations above, try your hand at your own version. Before you begin, consider what your main priority will be: fidelity to the diction and rhetorical figures of the original; fidelity to the idea of the original; coherency in English; a loose adaptation to suit your own ideas, inspired by something in Catullus.

2. Once you have completed the translation, write a brief justification of each choice you made: what were the other options, and what motivated your final decision?

TRANSLATION AND BILINGUALISM

Very few, if any, living languages exist in a single, pure form. There may be an official language—the Queen's English or Standard American English—but the language as actually written and spoken diverges in myriad ways from that standard. As our culture becomes more and more global—more than 138 languages are currently spoken in the borough of Queens, New York, alone—so the cross-fertilization between languages and cultures becomes stronger and stronger. And, as is evident from Miriam Sagan's poem "Translating Catullus," translation is not only a literary activity, but an important literary theme in its own right. The theme of translation often serves as a metaphor for the relationship between cultures, as in the recent film *Lost in Translation* (see below).

When specific forms of a language possess their own pronunciation, vocabulary, and grammar, we call these languages **dialects.** Standard American and standard British English are both dialects; so are many traditional regional forms, such as Appalachian English, New York–New Jersey English, the dialect spoken by many African Americans (African American Vernacular English), and the dialect of the American West reproduced by Mark Twain in his stories. More recent immigrants have created their own dialects as well—Chicano English is often the only language spoken by Mexican Americans, although they may speak the dialect of Chicano Spanish as well; Nuyorican English is the only language of many Puerto Rican Americans in New York.

Many Americans are **bilingual** or **multilingual:** they speak fluently one or more non-English native languages or several dialects

> *Translation is an interestingly different way to be involved both with poetry and with the language that I've found myself living in much of the time. I think the two feed each other.*
>
> —MARILYN HACKER

Bob (Bill Murray) and Charlotte (Scarlett Johansson) explore the alien world of Tokyo in the 2003 film *Lost in Translation,* directed by Sofia Coppola. The language and culture of Tokyo provide a thematic backdrop for the difficulty experienced by the main characters in translating their confused desires into words and actions.

of English. Moreover, even many persons not technically bilingual are at ease in the many different variations on their single language required in different social and professional contexts. Our ability to shift, or translate, between languages, dialects, and situations— what the Chinese-American writer Amy Tan calls "All the Englishes I grew up with"—is known as **code switching.** The combination of English and Spanish known as *Spanglish* is a good example of code switching. Rather than an independent dialect, Spanglish works by inserting Spanish words into English or vice versa. As with all language use, code switching can be used fluently, as in "There Is No Word for Goodbye" by Mary TallMountain, or less fluently, as when the doctor in Roberto Fernández's short story "Wrong Channel" comments *"No bueno,"* exhausting no doubt his full repertoire of Spanish phrases (p. 7).

Wilfrid Owen 1893–1918

Born in the region of Shropshire near the Welsh border, Wilfrid Owen was educated at London University and was considering a career in the Anglican church before deciding in 1915 to enlist in the army. As lieutenant with the Lancashire Fusiliers, Owen was wounded in the French trenches in 1917, diagnosed with "shell shock," and sent for convalescence to a military hospital in Scotland. It was here that Owen wrote nearly all of his substantial contribution to the poetry of war, enclosing the poem included here, for example, in a letter to his mother. In 1918, he returned to the front, where he was killed a few days before the war ended. The words of Owen's title allude to Ode 2.13 of the ancient Roman poet Horace; the full line is quoted at the end of the poem: "Sweet and fitting it is to die for your fatherland."

Dulce et Decorum Est

Bent double, like old beggars under
    sacks,
Knock-kneed, coughing like hags, we
    cursed through sludge,
Till on the haunting flares we turned
    our backs
And towards our distant rest began to
    trudge.
Men marched asleep. Many had lost
    their boots   5
But limped on, blood-shod. All went
    lame; all blind;
Drunk with fatigue; deaf even to the hoots
Of tired, outstripped Five-Nines° that
    dropped behind.

Gas! Gas! Quick, boys!—An ecstasy of
    fumbling,
Fitting the clumsy helmets just in time;   10
But someone still was yelling out and
    stumbling
And floundering like a man in fire or lime.°—

8 **Five-Nines:** German artillery shells, so-called because they were 5.9 inches in diameter. **12 lime:** calcium oxide, or quick-lime, a chemical that strips the flesh off bones and was used to prevent disease in open burial sites.

Dim, through the misty panes and
    thick green light
As under a green sea, I saw him drowning.

In all my dreams, before my helpless sight,   15
He plunges at me, guttering, choking,
    drowning.

If in some smothering dreams you too
    could pace
Behind the wagon that we flung him in,
And watch the white eyes writhing in
    his face,
His hanging face, like a devil's sick of sin;   20
If you could hear, at every jolt,
    the blood

Come gargling from the froth-corrupted
    lungs,
Obscene as cancer, bitter as the cud
Of vile, incurable sores on innocent
    tongues,—
My friend, you would not tell with
    such high zest   25
To children ardent for some desperate
    glory,
The old Lie: Dulce et decorum est
Pro patria mori.

The first page of a draft manuscript of Wilfrid Owen's poem "Dulce et Decorum est." It is uncertain whether Owen made this draft in October 1917 at Craiglockhart in Scotland, at the hospital where he was recovering from shell-shock, or between January and March 1918, when he had returned to duty in Yorkshire. Much of the text matches the published version, but note several differences, especially the choice finally made for line 8.

QUESTIONS FOR REFLECTION AND DISCUSSION

1. The poem is twenty-eight lines, and the first fourteen are in sonnet form. To what degree does the theme of the first fourteen lines fit the traditional sonnet form (p. 127)? Why do you think Owen did not use the same form for the final fourteen lines?

2. What is the tone of the poem? What atmosphere do the images that Owen uses create? How is this atmosphere related to the "sweet and decorous" image of the title?

3. The final four lines explain the primary function of the poem's title. What is this function, and why is it important to it that the title be in Latin rather than English?

4. Study the changes visible in the manuscript page reproduced above. How would the poem be different if Owen had not made the revisions marked here? How do the later revisions change the meaning?

Mary TallMountain 1918–1997

Born in Nulato, a remote village on the Yukon River in Alaska, Mary TallMountain was adopted by a non-Native American couple when her mother (and many other villagers) contracted tuberculosis. Raised in Oregon, she trained as a legal secretary and moved to San Francisco, where she met the poet Paula Gunn Allen, who encouraged her to write about her native Alaskan heritage. TallMountain published seven collections of poems, and through her TallMountain Circle was an active supporter of young inner city and Native American writers. In "There Is No Word for Goodbye," TallMountain uses the different meanings between equivalent words in English and her native Athabaskan to meditate on the cultural differences expressed by these words.

There Is No Word for Goodbye

Sokoya, I said, looking through
   the net of wrinkles into
   wise black pools
   of her eyes.

What do you say in Athabaskan   5
   when you leave each other?
   What is the word
   For goodbye?

A shade of feeling rippled
   the wind-tanned skin.   10
   Ah, nothing, she said,
   watching the river flash.

She looked at me close.
   We just say, Tłaa. That means,
   See you.   15
   We never leave each other.
   When does your mouth
   Say goodbye to your heart?

She touched me light
   as a bluebell.   20

You forget when you leave us;
you're so small then.
We don't use that word.

We always think you're coming back,
   but if you don't,   25
   we'll see you some place else.
You understand.
There is no word for goodbye.

The cover illustration for Mary TallMountain's second collection of poetry (1980).

QUESTIONS FOR REFLECTION AND DISCUSSION

1. Why do you think TallMountain chose to begin the poem with the Athabaskan word *Sokoya* rather than the English equivalent *Auntie*?

2. Compare the conceptual metaphors that underlie the English word *goodbye* and the Athabaskan word *Tłaa*, which TallMountain translates as "see you." What simile does Sokoya use to explain the concept?

3. In the fifth stanza, why does Sokoya speak in the present tense about events that occurred in the past, when the speaker was a child?

4. In your assessment, is this poem based on a real or an imagined scene? Is there evidence in the text to support your conclusion? Is it important to the poem's meaning to decide one way or the other?

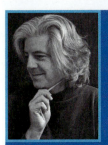

Michael Martone b. 1955

Born in Indiana, Michael Martone studied at Butler University, Indiana University, and Johns Hopkins University. He is director of the creative writing program at the University of Alabama and is the author of five collections of short fiction and an award-winning book of essays about the Midwest. The narrator of his very short story with a very long title reminds us of the most important role played by translation in the real world: the interpreter, or simultaneous translator, responsible for bridging the gap between two languages. Simultaneous translation tends to be used in occasions fraught with significance, whether court cases and diplomatic meetings or cross-cultural encounters such as the one recounted here.

THE MAYOR OF THE SISTER CITY SPEAKS TO THE CHAMBER OF COMMERCE IN KLAMATH FALLS, OREGON, ON A NIGHT IN DECEMBER IN 1976

"IT WAS AFTER THE RAID ON TOKYO. WE CHILDREN were told to collect scraps of cloth. Anything we could find. We picked over the countryside; we stripped the scarecrows. I remember this remnant from my sister's obi. Red silk suns bounced like balls. And these patches were quilted together by the women in the prefecture. The seams were waxed as if to make the stitches rainproof. Instead they held air, gases, and the rags billowed out into balloons, the heavy heads of chrysanthemums. The balloons bobbed as the soldiers attached the bombs. And then they rose up to the high wind, so many, like planets, heading into the rising sun and America. . . ."

I had stopped translating before he reached this point. I let his words fly away. It was a luncheon meeting. I looked down at the tables. The white napkins looked like mountain peaks of a range hung with clouds. We were high above them on the stage. I am yonsei, the fourth American generation. Four is an unlucky number in Japan. The old man, the mayor, was trying to say that the world was knit together with threads we could not see, that the wind was a bridge between people. It was a hot day. I told these

Japanese Americans in a dance at the Tule Lake internment camp thirty miles south of Klamath Falls, Oregon, during World War II.

beat businessmen about children long ago releasing the bright balloons, how they disappeared ages and ages ago. And all of them looked up as if to catch the first sight of the balloons returning to earth, a bright scrap of joy.

[1996]

QUESTIONS FOR REFLECTION AND DISCUSSION

1. What is the relationship between the title and the story?

2. The balloons are the central image of the story. What literary devices are used to characterize them? How does the meaning of that image change between the first and second paragraphs?

3. What motivates the narrator to provide us with biographical details? Why does the narrator stop translating the mayor's speech?

Have you or someone you know ever been involved in an episode involving simultaneous translation and/or mistranslation? What were the relevant languages?

What were the circumstances? Were they tragic, comic, or somewhere in between? What were the results?

Amy Tan b. 1952

Born in Oakland, California, to a middle-class family of first-generation Chinese immigrants, Amy Tan attended eight different colleges. She eventually received a master's degree in linguistics from San Jose State University. She held a wide variety of jobs before her semiautobiographical novel, *The Joy Luck Club*, became a bestseller in 1989, also winning the National Book Award. She has since published five additional novels. Tan lives with her husband in San Francisco. In her essay "Mother Tongue," published in *The Threepenny Review* in 1990, Tan discusses a life of code switching and how she came to incorporate the "different Englishes" she uses into the language of her fiction.

MOTHER TONGUE

I AM NOT A SCHOLAR OF ENGLISH OR LITERATURE. I cannot give you much more than personal opinions on the English language and its variations in this country or others. I am a writer. And by that definition, I am someone who has always loved language. I am fascinated by language in daily life. I spend a great deal of my time thinking about the power of language—the way it can evoke an emotion, a visual image, a complex idea, or a simple truth. Language is the tool of my trade. And I use them all—all the Englishes I grew up with.

Recently, I was made keenly aware of the different Englishes I do use. I was giving a talk to a large group of people, the same talk I had already given to half a dozen other groups. The nature of the talk was about my writing, my life, and my book, *The Joy Luck Club*. The talk was going along well enough, until I remembered one major difference that made the whole talk sound wrong. My mother was in the room. And it was perhaps the first time she had heard me give a lengthy speech, using the kind of English I have never used with her. I was saying things like, "The intersection of memory upon imagination" and "There is an aspect of my fiction that relates to thus-and-thus"—a speech filled with carefully wrought grammatical phrases, burdened, it suddenly seemed to me, with nominalized forms, past perfect tenses, conditional phrases, all the forms of standard English that I had learned in school and

Amy Tan and her mother Daisy strolling in San Francisco.

through books, the forms of English I did not use at home with my mother.

Just last week, I was walking down the street with my mother, and I again found myself conscious of the English I was using, the English I do use with her. We were talking about the price of new and used furniture and I heard myself saying this: "Not waste money that way." My husband was with us as well, and he didn't notice any switch in my English. And then I realized why. It's because over the twenty years we've been together I've often used the same kind of English with him, and sometimes he even uses it with me. It has become our language of intimacy, a different sort of English that relates to family talk, the language I grew up with.

So you'll have some idea of what this family talk I heard sounds like, I'll quote what my mother said during a recent conversation which I videotaped and then transcribed. During this conversation, my mother was talking about a political gangster in Shanghai who had the same last name as her family's, Du, and how the gangster in his early years wanted to be adopted by her family, which was rich by comparison. Later, the gangster became more powerful, far richer than my mother's family, and one day showed up at my mother's wedding to pay his respects. Here's what she said in part:

5   "Du Yusong having business like fruit stand. Like off the street kind. He is Du like Du Zong—but not Tsung-ming Island people. The local people call putong, the river east side, he belong to that side local people. That man want to ask Du Zong father take him in like become own family. Du Zong father wasn't look down on him, but didn't take seriously, until that man big like become a mafia. Now important person, very hard to inviting him. Chinese way, came only to show respect, don't stay for dinner. Respect for making big celebration, he shows up. Mean gives lots of respect. Chinese custom. Chinese social life that way. If too important won't have to stay too long. He come to my wedding. I didn't see, I heard it. I gone to boy's side, they have YMCA dinner. Chinese age I was nineteen."

You should know that my mother's expressive command of English belies how much she actually understands. She reads the Forbes report, listens to Wall Street Week, converses daily with her stockbroker, reads all of Shirley MacLaine's books with ease—all kinds of things I can't begin to understand. Yet some of my friends tell me they understand 50 percent of what my mother says. Some say they understand 80 to 90 percent. Some say they understand none of it, as if she were speaking pure Chinese. But to me, my mother's English is perfectly clear, perfectly natural. It's my mother tongue. Her language, as I hear it, is vivid, direct, full of observation and imagery. That was the language that helped shape the way I saw things, expressed things, made sense of the world.

Lately, I've been giving more thought to the kind of English my mother speaks. Like others, I have described it to people as "broken" or "fractured" English. But I wince when I say that. It has always bothered me that I can think of no way to describe it other than "broken," as if it were damaged and needed to be fixed, as if it lacked a certain wholeness and soundness. I've heard other terms used, "limited English," for example. But they seem just as bad, as if everything is limited, including people's perceptions of the limited English speaker.

I know this for a fact, because when I was growing up, my mother's "limited" English limited my perception of her. I was ashamed of her English. I believed that her English reflected the quality of what she had to say. That is, because she expressed them imperfectly her thoughts were imperfect. And I had plenty of empirical evidence to support me: the fact that people in department stores, at banks, and at restaurants did not take her seriously, did not give her good service, pretended not to understand her, or even acted as if they did not hear her.

My mother has long realized the limitations of her English as well. When I was fifteen, she used to have me call people on the phone to pretend I was she. In this guise, I was forced to ask for information or even to complain and yell at people who had been rude to her. One time it was a call to her stockbroker in New York. She had cashed out her small portfolio and it just so happened we were going to go to New York the next week, our very first trip outside California. I had to get on the phone and say in an adolescent voice that was not very convincing, "This is Mrs. Tan."

10   And my mother was standing in the back whispering loudly, "Why he don't send me check, already two weeks late. So mad he lie to me, losing me money."

And then I said in perfect English, "Yes, I'm getting rather concerned. You had agreed to send the check two weeks ago, but it hasn't arrived."

Then she began to talk more loudly. "What he want, I come to New York tell him front of his boss, you cheating me?" And I was trying to calm her down, make her be quiet, while telling the stockbroker, "I can't tolerate any more excuses. If I don't receive the check immediately, I am going to have to speak to your manager when I'm in New York next week." And sure enough, the following week there we were in front of this astonished stockbroker, and I was sitting there red-faced and quiet, and my mother, the real Mrs. Tan, was shouting at his boss in her impeccable broken English.

We used a similar routine just five days ago, for a situation that was far less humorous. My mother had gone to the hospital for an appointment, to find out about a benign brain tumor a CAT scan had revealed a month ago. She said she had spoken very good English, her best English, no mistakes. Still, she said, the hospital did not apologize when they said they had lost the CAT scan and she had come for nothing. She said they did not seem to have any sympathy when she told them she was anxious to know the exact diagnosis, since her husband and son had both died of brain tumors. She said they would not give her any more information until the next time and she would have to make another appointment for that. So she said she would not leave until the doctor called her daughter. She wouldn't budge. And when the doctor finally called her daughter, me, who spoke in perfect English—lo and behold—we had assurances the CAT scan would be found, promises that a conference call on Monday would be held, and apologies for any suffering my mother had gone through for a most regrettable mistake.

I think my mother's English almost had an effect on limiting my possibilities in life as well. Sociologists and linguists probably will tell you that a person's developing language skills are more influenced by peers. But I do think that the language spoken in the family, especially in immigrant families which are more insular, plays a large role in shaping the language of the child. And I believe that it affected my results on achievement tests, IQ tests, and the SAT. While my English skills were never judged as poor, compared to math, English could not be considered my strong suit. In grade school I did moderately well, getting perhaps B's, sometimes B-pluses, in English and scoring perhaps in the sixtieth or seventieth percentile on achievement tests. But those scores were not good enough to override the opinion that my true abilities lay in math and science, because in those areas I achieved A's and scored in the ninetieth percentile or higher.

15 This was understandable. Math is precise; there is only one correct answer. Whereas, for me at least, the answers on English tests were always a judgment call, a matter of opinion and personal experience. Those tests were constructed around items like fill-in-the-blank sentence completion, such as, "Even though Tom was _____ Mary thought he was _____." And the correct answer always seemed to be the most bland combinations of thoughts, for example, "Even though Tom was shy, Mary thought he was charming," with the grammatical structure "even though" limiting the correct answer to some sort of semantic opposites, so you wouldn't get

answers like, "Even though Tom was foolish, Mary thought he was ridiculous." Well, according to my mother, there were very few limitations as to what Tom could have been and what Mary might have thought of him. So I never did well on tests like that.

The same was true with word analogies, pairs of words in which you were supposed to find some sort of logical, semantic relationship—for example, "Sunset is to nightfall as _____ is to _____." And here you would be presented with a list of four possible pairs, one of which showed the same kind of relationship: red is to stoplight, bus is to arrival, chills is to fever, yawn is to boring. Well, I could never think that way. I knew what the tests were asking, but I could not block out of my mind the images already created by the first pair, "sunset is to nightfall"—and I would see a burst of colors against a darkening sky, the moon rising, the lowering of a curtain of stars. And all the other pairs of words—red, bus, stoplight, boring—just threw up a mass of confusing images, making it impossible for me to sort out something as logical as saying: "A sunset precedes nightfall" is the same as "a chill precedes a fever." The only way I would have gotten that answer right would have been to imagine an associative situation, for example, my being disobedient and staying out past sunset, catching a chill at night, which turns into feverish pneumonia as punishment, which indeed did happen to me.

I have been thinking about all this lately, about my mother's English, about achievement tests. Because lately I've been asked, as a writer, why there are not more Asian Americans represented in American literature. Why are there few Asian Americans enrolled in creative writing programs? Why do so many Chinese students go into engineering? Well, these are broad sociological questions I can't begin to answer. But I have noticed in surveys—in fact, just last week—that Asian students, as a whole, always do significantly better on math achievement tests than in English. And this makes me think that there are other Asian-American students whose English spoken in the home might also be described as "broken" or "limited." And perhaps they also have teachers who are steering them away from writing and into math and science, which is what happened to me.

Fortunately, I happen to be rebellious in nature and enjoy the challenge of disproving assumptions made about me. I became an English major my first year in college, after being enrolled as pre-med.

I started writing nonfiction as a freelancer the week after I was told by my former boss that writing was my worst skill and I should hone my talents toward account management.

But it wasn't until 1985 that I finally began to write fiction. And at first I wrote using what I thought to be wittily crafted sentences, sentences that would finally prove I had mastery over the English language. Here's an example from the first draft of a story that later made its way into *The Joy Luck Club,* but without this line: "That was my mental quandary in its nascent state." A terrible line, which I can barely pronounce.

20   Fortunately, for reasons I won't get into today, I later decided I should envision a reader for the stories I would write. And the reader I decided upon was my mother, because these were stories about mothers. So with this reader in mind—and in fact she did read my early drafts—I began to write stories using all the Englishes I grew up with: the English I spoke to my mother, which for lack of a better term might be described as "simple"; the English she used with me, which for lack of a better term might be described as "broken"; my translation of her Chinese, which could certainly be described as "watered down"; and what I imagined to be her translation of her Chinese if she could speak in perfect English, her internal language, and for that I sought to preserve the essence, but neither an English nor a Chinese structure. I wanted to capture what language ability tests can never reveal: her intent, her passion, her imagery, the rhythms of her speech and the nature of her thoughts.

Apart from what any critic had to say about my writing, I knew I had succeeded where it counted when my mother finished reading my book and gave me her verdict: "So easy to read."

[1990]

QUESTIONS FOR REFLECTION AND DISCUSSION

1. What are some of the examples Tan gives of code switching in her own life?

2. As she grows older, what changes in her attitude to the "different Englishes" in her life, and why?

3. What causes Tan to decide to incorporate a full range of languages in *The Joy Luck Club* rather than only standard English? In what dialect did Tan write this essay?

WRITING EXERCISE: Code Switching

Make a list of the different languages, dialects, and "Englishes" you use in your daily life. Provide an example of each one, and describe the contexts in which you use it. Which one have you spoken the longest? Which is the most recent? Which do you find easiest? Which do you find most challenging? Which is your favorite? Which is your least favorite? Are you comfortable code switching, or do you find it awkward? Why or why not?

TRANSLATING THE WORLD TOPICS FOR ESSAYS

1. Choose a translated text from elsewhere in this book and compare it with the original or with another translation of the same text.

2. Choose a text from elsewhere in this book and analyze its use of translation, multilingualism, dialect, or code switching.

3. Undertake your own translation of a text or group of texts. Keep a journal about the task of translation. Write up the journal as an essay about your translation, accompanied with the translation.

4. Compare the imagery of translation and multilingualism in a post-colonial context in the selections by TallMountain, Cronin (p. 501), and/or Hove (p. 502).

5. Compare the depiction of the life of immigrant and minority communities in TallMountain, Martone, Fernández (p. 7), Ali (p. 367), Soto (p. 368), and/or Tan.

6. Compare the use of translation in a humorous context in several of the texts mentioned in Question 5.

7. Write an essay on code switching in a specific popular culture medium (cinema, music video, television).

CHAPTER 8

THE WORLD CLOSEST TO US

ME AND YOU

The nineteenth-century American satirist Ambrose Bierce once defined the word intimacy as "A relation into which fools are providentially drawn for their mutual destruction." And it is certainly true that nothing produces extremes of emotion to the same degree as the intimacy we experience through family, childhood, adolescence, and love. And few topics have received such sustained attention from writers than these emotional extremes. The selections in this chapter will provoke hilarity, despair, and everything in between. In "Families," we explore the range of relationships within families and between generations. In "Children and Adolescents," we read texts that depict life before adulthood from the point of view of those living through it. And in "Lovers," we discover the many different ways of depicting what happens when two people come together. As you read these selections, consider the myriad literary and visual means writers and artists have used to make a seemingly universal experience into something singular and unique.

PHOTOGRAPHS FROM *THE FAMILY OF MAN*

The Family of Man was an exhibition curated by photographer Edward Steichen in 1955 for the Museum of Modern Art in New York. According to its curator, it was "a mirror of the essential oneness of mankind throughout the world"; it was also one of the most popular and successful art exhibitions ever. The 503 photographs on display, culled from an international pool of nearly two million submissions, included work by both amateur and established photographers, and aimed to depict the complete range of the human experience. The photos presented here are drawn from the bestselling book of the same title that accompanied the exhibition. They come from a section depicting families from around the world. As you study these three photographs, consider the assumptions they make about families and the relationships that emerge from the initial intimacy of the family circle. Reflect also on your own assumptions about family: what (if anything) is universal about a family and what (if anything) changes depending on variables such as time, place, economics, and values?

(Right) Postwar Japanese farming family posing with their tools in the field, 1948. Photo by Carl Mydans, originally published in *Life*.

(Below) A native bushman standing with his family in the arid Bechuanaland section of lower Africa, in the border area between Botswana and South Africa, 1947. Photo by Nat Farbman, originally published in *Life*.

(Bottom Right) Four generations of farmers in this Ozark family posing in front of a wall with portraits of their fifth generation, 1946. Photo by Nina Leen, originally published in *Life*.

1. What are some of the different ways in which the photographers have framed and defined their subjects? Which photographs are more successful and why? Which are less successful, and why?

2. Based on the evidence of the photographs and the captions, what can you hypothesize about the guiding beliefs and assumptions of Edward Steichen and the other curators of the exhibition regarding human experience? To what degree do you agree or disagree with these assumptions and beliefs, and why?

3. If you were going to design a similar exhibition today, how would you do it? What would you preserve of the exhibition from over fifty years ago, and what would you change?

FAMILIES

At its most basic, the family consists of the "community" satirically described by Ambrose Bierce at right. In itself, the married couple is complicated enough; throw in the relation between parents, children, and grandparents and you have the raw material for a writer's life work. And all this without even taking into account extended family or the many other permutations of the family unit to be found in contemporary society and around the world.

> *Marriage, n.* The state or condition of a community consisting of a master, a mistress and two slaves, making in all, two.
>
> —AMBROSE BIERCE,
> *THE DEVIL'S DICTIONARY*

FICTION

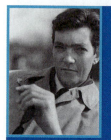

Julio Cortázar 1914–1984

The Argentine novelist, translator, and short-story writer Julio Cortázar emigrated to Paris, France, in 1951. He spent the rest of his life there, although he traveled widely. Leftist in his politics and ceaselessly experimenting with form in his novels, Cortázar was a central figure in the emergence of Latin American literature in the 1960s. Slyly humorous, ironic in their self-consciousness, and meditative in their subject matter, Cortázar's short stories are perhaps his greatest achievement. Both "Axolotl" (p. 416) and "The Tiger Lodgers" are slightly fantastic stories about the relationship between people and animals. "The Tiger Lodgers" is more explicitly humorous, and it describes a family at home rather than an individual in exile.

THE TIGER LODGERS

Translated by Paul Blackburn

LONG BEFORE BRINGING OUR IDEA TO THE LEVEL of actual practice, we knew that the lodging of tigers presented a double problem, sentimental and moral. The first aspect is not so much related to the lodging as to the tiger himself, insomuch as it is not particularly agreeable for these felines to be lodged and they summon all their energies, which are enormous, to resist being lodged. Is it fitting under those circumstances to defy the idiosyncrasy of the above-mentioned animals? But this question leads us directly to the moral level where any act can be the cause, or the effect, splendid or ignominious. At night, in our little house in Humboldt Street, we meditated over our bowls of rice and milk, forgetting to sprinkle the cinnamon and sugar on them. We were not really sure of our ability to lodge a tiger, and it was depressing.

It was decided finally that we would lodge just one for the sole purpose of seeing the mechanism at work in all its complexity; we could always evaluate the results later. I shall not speak here of the problem of coming by the first tiger: a delicate and troublesome job, a race past consulates, drugstores, a complex chain of tickets, air-mail letters, and work with the dictionary. One night my cousins came back covered with tincture of iodine: success. We drank so much chianti that my younger sister ended up having to clear the table with a rake. We were much younger in those days. Now that the experiment has yielded known results, I can supply the details of the lodging. The most difficult perhaps would be to describe everything related to the environment, since it requires a room with a minimum of furniture, a thing rather difficult to find in Humboldt Street. The layout is arranged in the center: two crossed planks, a complex of flexible withies,° and several earthenware bowls filled with milk and water. To lodge a tiger is really not too difficult; the operation can miscarry, however, and you've got everything to do over again. The real difficulty begins when, already lodged, the tiger recovers his liberty and chooses—in one of the many manners possible—to exercise it. At that stage, known as the intermediate stage, my family's reactions are pretty basic; everything depends on how my sisters behave, on the smartness with which my father manages to get the tiger lodged again, utilizing the natural propensities of the tiger to the maximum. The slightest mistake would be a catastrophe, the fuses burned

withy: a tough, flexible willow shoot used in thatching, weaving, and gardening.

out, the milk on the floor, the horror of those phosphorescent eyes shining through the utter darkness, warm spurts with every thud of the paw; I resist imagining what would follow since, up till now, we've managed to lodge a tiger without dangerous consequences. The layout, as well as the varying duties all of us must perforce perform, from the tiger down to my second cousins, are seemingly efficient and articulate harmoniously. The fact of lodging a tiger is not in itself important to us, rather that the ceremony be completed to the very end without a mistake. Either the tiger agrees to be lodged, or must be lodged in such a way that its acceptance or refusal is of no consequence. At these moments which one is tempted to call crucial—perhaps because of the two planks, perhaps because it's a mere commonplace expression—the family feels itself possessed by an extraordinary exaltation; my mother does not hide her tears, and my first cousins knit and unknit their fingers convulsively. Lodging a tiger has something of the total encounter, lining oneself up against an absolute; the balance depends upon so little and we pay so high a price, that these brief moments which follow the lodging and which confirm its perfection sweep us away from ourselves, annihilating both tigerness and humanity in a single motionless movement which is a dizziness, respite, and arrival. There's no tiger, no family, no lodging. Impossible to know what there is: a trembling that is not of this flesh, a centered time, a column of contact. And later we all go out to the covered patio, and our aunts bring out the soup as though something were singing or as if we were all at a baptism.

[1962]

QUESTIONS FOR REFLECTION AND DISCUSSION

1. Why is it important for the family to meditate about lodging the tiger before undertaking to do so? Why do they decide in the end to lodge just one?

2. What are the family's different roles in the endeavor? How have they managed to avoid "dangerous consequences"?

3. What is important to the family about lodging the tiger? What is the result of its achievement? Has your family ever experienced such a "brief moment" of perfection? Under what circumstances?

Flannery O'Connor 1925–1964

Born and raised in Georgia, Mary Flannery O'Connor received an MFA from the University of Iowa in 1946. In 1951, she was diagnosed with lupus, the disease that had killed her father ten years earlier, and she returned to her family farm in Milledgeville, where she raised all manner of birds, especially peacocks, and she focused on her writing. O'Connor's two novels and thirty-one short stories are among the wonders of American literature. "A Good Man Is Hard to Find" was the title story of her first collection of stories, published in 1955. It exhibits a characteristic blend of her wicked sense of humor, a knack for deadpan violence, and a deeply held Roman Catholic faith.

A GOOD MAN IS HARD TO FIND

THE GRANDMOTHER DIDN'T WANT TO GO TO Florida. She wanted to visit some of her connections in east Tennessee and she was seizing every chance to change Bailey's mind. Bailey was the son she lived with, her only boy. He was sitting on the edge of his chair at the table, bent over the orange sports section of the *Journal*. "Now look here, Bailey," she said, "see here, read this," and she stood with one hand on her thin hip and the other rattling the newspaper at his bald head. "Here this fellow that calls himself The Misfit is aloose from the Federal Pen and headed toward Florida and you read here what it says he did to these people. Just you read it. I wouldn't take my children in any direction with a criminal like that aloose in it. I couldn't answer to my conscience if I did."

Bailey didn't look up from his reading so she wheeled around then and faced the children's mother, a young woman in slacks, whose face was as broad and innocent as a cabbage and was tied around with a green headkerchief that had two points on the top like rabbit's ears. She was sitting on the sofa, feeding the baby his apricots out of a jar. "The children have been to Florida before," the old lady said. "You all ought to take them somewhere else for a change so they would see different parts of the world and be broad. They never have been to east Tennessee."

The children's mother didn't seem to hear her, but the eight-year-old boy, John Wesley, a stocky child with glasses, said, "If you don't want to go to Florida, why dontcha stay at home?" He and the little girl, June Star, were reading the funny papers on the floor.

"She wouldn't stay at home to be queen for a day," June Star said without raising her yellow head.

5 "Yes, and what would you do if this fellow, The Misfit, caught you?" the grandmother said.

"I'd smack his face," John Wesley said.

"She wouldn't stay at home for a million bucks," June Star said. "Afraid she'd miss something. She has to go everywhere we go."

"All right, Miss," the grandmother said. "Just remember that the next time you want me to curl your hair."

June Star said her hair was naturally curly.

10 The next morning the grandmother was the first one in the car, ready to go. She had her big black valise that looked like the head of a hippopotamus in one corner, and underneath it she was hiding a basket with Pitty Sing, the cat, in it. She didn't intend for the cat to be left alone in the house for three days because he would miss her too much and she was afraid he might brush against one of the gas burners and accidentally asphyxiate himself. Her son, Bailey, didn't like to arrive at a motel with a cat.

She sat in the middle of the back seat with John Wesley and June Star on either side of her. Bailey and the children's mother and the baby sat in front and they left Atlanta at eight forty-five with the mileage on the car at 55890. The grandmother wrote this down because she thought it would be interesting to say how many miles they had been when they got back. It took them twenty minutes to reach the outskirts of the city.

The old lady settled herself comfortably, removing her white cotton gloves and putting them up with her purse on the shelf in front of the back window.

The children's mother still had on slacks and still had her head tied up in a green kerchief, but the grandmother had on a navy blue straw sailor hat with a bunch of white violets on the brim and a navy blue dress with a small white dot in the print. Her collars and cuffs were white organdy trimmed with lace and at her neckline she had pinned a purple spray of cloth violets containing a sachet. In case of an accident, anyone seeing her dead on the highway would know at once that she was a lady.

She said she thought it was going to be a good day for driving, neither too hot nor too cold, and she cautioned Bailey that the speed limit was fifty-five miles an hour and that the patrolmen hid themselves behind bill-boards and small clumps of trees and sped out after you before you had a chance to slow down. She pointed out interesting details of the scenery: Stone Mountain; the blue granite that in some places came up to both sides of the highway; the brilliant red clay banks slightly streaked with purple; and the various crops that made rows of green lace-work on the ground. The trees were full of silver-white sunlight and the meanest of them sparkled. The children were reading comic magazines and their mother had gone back to sleep.

"Let's go through Georgia fast so we won't have to look at it much," John Wesley said.

15 "If I were a little boy," said the grandmother, "I wouldn't talk about my native state that way. Tennessee has the mountains and Georgia has the hills."

"Tennessee is just a hillbilly dumping ground," John Wesley said, "and Georgia is a lousy state too."

"You said it," June Star said.

"In my time," said the grandmother, folding her thin veined fingers, "children were more respectful of their native states and their parents and everything else. People did right then. Oh look at the cute little pickaninny!" she said and pointed to a Negro child standing in the door of a shack. "Wouldn't that make a picture, now?" she asked and they all turned and looked at the little Negro out of the back window. He waved.

"He didn't have any britches on," June Star said.

20 "He probably didn't have any," the grandmother explained. "Little niggers in the country don't have things like we do. If I could paint, I'd paint that picture," she said.

The children exchanged comic books.

The grandmother offered to hold the baby and the children's mother passed him over the front seat to her. She set him on her knee and bounced him and told him about the things they were passing. She rolled her eyes and screwed up her mouth and stuck her leathery thin face into his smooth bland one. Occasionally he gave her a faraway smile. They passed a large cotton field with five or six graves fenced in the middle of it, like a small island. "Look at the graveyard!" the grandmother said, pointing it out. "That was the old family burying ground. That belonged to the plantation."

"Where's the plantation?" John Wesley asked.

"Gone With the Wind," said the grandmother. "Ha. Ha."

25 When the children finished all the comic books they had brought, they opened the lunch and ate it. The grandmother ate a peanut butter sandwich and an olive and would not let the children throw the box and the paper napkins out the window. When there was nothing else to do they played a game by choosing a cloud and making the other two guess what shape it suggested. John Wesley took one the shape of a cow and June Star guessed a cow and John Wesley said, no, an automobile, and June Star said he didn't play fair, and they began to slap each other over the grandmother.

The grandmother said she would tell them a story if they would keep quiet. When she told a story, she rolled her eyes and waved her head and was very dramatic. She said once when she was a maiden lady she had been courted by a Mr. Edgar Atkins Teagarden from Jasper, Georgia. She said he was a very good-looking man and a gentleman and that he brought her a watermelon every Saturday afternoon with his initials cut in it, E. A. T. Well, one Saturday, she said, Mr. Teagarden brought the watermelon and there was nobody at home and he left it on the front porch and returned in his buggy to Jasper, but she never got the watermelon, she said, because a nigger boy ate it when he saw the initials, E. A. T.! This story tickled John Wesley's funny bone and he giggled and giggled but June Star didn't think it was any good. She said she wouldn't marry a man that just brought her a watermelon on Saturday. The grandmother said she would have done well to marry Mr. Teagarden because he was a gentleman and had bought Coca-Cola stock when it first came out and that he had died only a few years ago, a very wealthy man.

They stopped at The Tower for barbecued sandwiches. The Tower was a part-stucco and part-wood filling station and dance hall set in a clearing outside of Timothy. A fat man named Red Sammy Butts ran it and there were signs stuck here and there on the building and for miles up and down the highway saying, TRY RED SAMMY'S FAMOUS BARBECUE. NONE LIKE FAMOUS RED SAMMY'S! RED SAM! THE FAT BOY WITH THE HAPPY LAUGH. A VETERAN! RED SAMMY'S YOUR MAN!

Red Sammy was lying on the bare ground outside The Tower with his head under a truck while a gray monkey about a foot high, chained to a small chinaberry tree, chattered nearby. The monkey sprang back into the tree and got on the highest limb as soon as he saw the children jump out of the car and run toward him.

Inside, The Tower was a long dark room with a counter at one end and tables at the other and dancing space in the middle. They all sat down at a board table next to the nickelodeon and Red Sam's wife, a tall burnt-brown woman with hair and eyes lighter than her skin, came and took their order. The children's mother put a dime in the machine and played "The Tennessee Waltz," and the grandmother said that tune always made her want to dance. She asked Bailey if he would like to dance but he only glared at her. He didn't have a naturally sunny disposition like she did and trips made him nervous. The grandmother's brown eyes were very bright. She swayed her head from side to side and pretended she was dancing in her chair. June Star said play something she could tap to so the children's mother put in another dime and played a fast number and June Star stepped out onto the dance floor and did her tap routine.

30   "Ain't she cute?" Red Sam's wife said, leaning over the counter. "Would you like to come be my little girl?"

"No, I certainly wouldn't," June Star said. "I wouldn't live in a broken-down place like this for a million bucks!" and she ran back to the table.

"Ain't she cute?" the woman repeated, stretching her mouth politely.

"Aren't you ashamed?" hissed the grandmother.

Red Sam came in and told his wife to quit lounging on the counter and hurry with these people's order. His khaki trousers reached just to his hip

bones and his stomach hung over them like a sack of meal swaying under his shirt. He came over and sat down at a table nearby and let out a combination sigh and yodel. "You can't win," he said. "You can't win," and he wiped his sweating red face off with a gray handkerchief. "These days you don't know who to trust," he said. "Ain't that the truth?"

35   "People are certainly not nice like they used to be," said the grandmother.

"Two fellers come in here last week," Red Sammy said, "driving a Chrysler. It was an old beat-up car but it was a good one and these boys looked all right to me. Said they worked at the mill and you know I let them fellers charge the gas they bought? Now why did I do that?"

"Because you're a good man!" the grandmother said at once.

"Yes'm, I suppose so," Red Sam said as if he were struck with this answer.

His wife brought the orders, carrying the five plates all at once without a tray, two in each hand and one balanced on her arm. "It isn't a soul in this green world of God's that you can trust," she said. "And I don't count nobody out of that, not nobody," she repeated, looking at Red Sammy.

40   "Did you read about that criminal, The Misfit, that's escaped?" asked the grandmother.

"I wouldn't be a bit surprised if he didn't attack this place right here," said the woman. "If he hears about it being here, I wouldn't be none surprised to see him. If he hears it's two cent in the cash register, I wouldn't be a tall surprised if he . . ."

"That'll do," Red Sam said. "Go bring these people their Co'-Colas," and the woman went off to get the rest of the order.

"A good man is hard to find," Red Sammy said. "Everything is getting terrible. I remember the day you could go off and leave your screen door unlatched. Not no more."

He and the grandmother discussed better times. The old lady said that in her opinion Europe was entirely to blame for the way things were now. She said the way Europe acted you would think we were made of money and Red Sam said it was no use talking about it, she was exactly right. The children ran outside into the white sunlight and looked at the monkey in the lacy chinaberry tree. He was busy catching fleas on himself and biting each one carefully between his teeth as if it were a delicacy.

45   They drove off again into the hot afternoon. The grandmother took cat naps and woke up every five minutes with her own snoring. Outside of Toombsboro she woke up and recalled an old plantation that she had visited in this neighborhood once when she was a young lady. She said the house had six white columns across the front and that there was an avenue of oaks leading up to it and two little wooden trellis arbors on either side in front where you sat down with your suitor after a stroll in the garden. She recalled exactly which road to turn off to get to it. She knew that Bailey would not be willing to lose any time looking at an old house, but the more she talked about it, the more she wanted to see it once again and find out if the little twin arbors were still standing. "There was a secret panel in this house," she said craftily, not telling the truth but wishing that she were, "and the story went that all the family silver was hidden in it when Sherman came through but it was never found . . ."

    "Hey!" John Wesley said. "Let's go see it! We'll find it! We'll poke all the woodwork and find it! Who lives there? Where do you turn off at? Hey, Pop, can't we turn off there?"

    "We never have seen a house with a secret panel!" June Star shrieked. "Let's go to the house with the secret panel! Hey, Pop, can't we go see the house with the secret panel!"

    "It's not far from here, I know," the grandmother said. "It wouldn't take over twenty minutes."

    Bailey was looking straight ahead. His jaw was as rigid as a horseshoe. "No," he said.

50   The children began to yell and scream that they wanted to see the house with the secret panel. John Wesley kicked the back of the front seat and June Star hung over her mother's shoulder and whined desperately into her ear that they never had any fun even on their vacation, that they could never do what THEY wanted to do. The baby began to scream and John Wesley kicked the back of the seat so hard that his father could feel the blows in his kidney.

    "All right!" he shouted and drew the car to a stop at the side of the road. "Will you all shut up? Will you all just shut up for one second? If you don't shut up, we won't go anywhere."

    "It would be very educational for them," the grandmother murmured.

    "All right," Bailey said, "but get this. This is the only time we're going to stop for anything like this. This is the one and only time."

    "The dirt road that you have to turn down is about a mile back," the grandmother directed. "I marked it when we passed."

55   "A dirt road," Bailey groaned.

    After they had turned around and were headed toward the dirt road, the grandmother recalled other points about the house, the beautiful glass over the front doorway and the candlelamp in the hall. John Wesley said that the secret panel was probably in the fireplace.

    "You can't go inside this house," Bailey said. "You don't know who lives there."

    "While you all talk to the people in front, I'll run around behind and get in a window," John Wesley suggested.

    "We'll all stay in the car," his mother said.

60   They turned onto the dirt road and the car raced roughly along in a swirl of pink dust. The grandmother recalled the times when there were no paved roads and thirty miles was a day's journey. The dirt road was hilly and there were sudden washes in it and sharp curves on dangerous embankments. All at once they would be on a hill, looking down over the blue tops of trees for miles around, then the next minute, they would be in a red depression with the dust-coated trees looking down on them.

    "This place had better turn up in a minute," Bailey said, "or I'm going to turn around."

    The road looked as if no one had traveled on it in months.

    "It's not much farther," the grandmother said and just as she said it, a horrible thought came to her. The thought was so embarrassing that she turned red in the face and her eyes dilated and her feet jumped up, upsetting her valise in the corner. The instant the valise moved, the newspaper top she had over the basket under it rose with a snarl and Pitty Sing, the cat, sprang onto Bailey's shoulder.

    The children were thrown to the floor and their mother, clutching the baby, was thrown out the door onto the ground; the old lady was thrown into the front seat. The car turned over once and landed right-side-up in a gulch on the side of the road.

Bailey remained in the driver's seat with the cat—gray-striped with a broad white face and an orange nose—clinging to his neck like a caterpillar.

65 As soon as the children saw they could move their arms and legs, they scrambled out of the car, shouting, "We've had an ACCIDENT!" The grandmother was curled up under the dashboard, hoping she was injured so that Bailey's wrath would not come down on her all at once. The horrible thought she had had before the accident was that the house she had remembered so vividly was not in Georgia but in Tennessee.

Bailey removed the cat from his neck with both hands and flung it out the window against the side of a pine tree. Then he got out of the car and started looking for the children's mother. She was sitting against the side of the red gutted ditch, holding the screaming baby, but she only had a cut down her face and a broken shoulder. "We've had an ACCIDENT!" the children screamed in a frenzy of delight.

"But nobody's killed," June Star said with disappointment as the grandmother limped out of the car, her hat still pinned to her head but the broken front brim standing up at a jaunty angle and the violet spray hanging off the side. They all sat down in the ditch, except the children, to recover from the shock. They were all shaking.

"Maybe a car will come along," said the children's mother hoarsely.

"I believe I have injured an organ," said the grandmother, pressing her side, but no one answered her. Bailey's teeth were clattering. He had on a yellow sport shirt with bright blue parrots designed in it and his face was as yellow as the shirt. The grandmother decided that she would not mention that the house was in Tennessee.

70 The road was about ten feet above and they could see only the tops of the trees on the other side of it. Behind the ditch they were sitting in there were more woods, tall and dark and deep. In a few minutes they saw a car some distance away on top of a hill, coming slowly as if the occupants were watching them. The grandmother stood up and waved both arms dramatically to attract their attention. The car continued to come on slowly, disappeared around a bend and appeared again, moving even slower, on top of the hill they had gone over. It was a big black battered hearselike automobile. There were three men in it.

It came to a stop just over them and for some minutes, the driver looked down with a steady expressionless gaze to where they were sitting, and didn't speak. Then he turned his head and muttered something to the other two and they got out. One was a fat boy in black trousers and a red sweat shirt with a silver stallion embossed on the front of it. He moved around on the right side of them and stood staring, his mouth partly open in a kind of loose grin. The other had on khaki pants and a blue striped coat and a gray hat pulled down very low, hiding most of his face. He came around slowly on the left side. Neither spoke.

The driver got out of the car and stood by the side of it, looking down at them. He was an older man than the other two. His hair was just beginning to gray and he wore silver-rimmed spectacles that gave him a scholarly look. He had a long creased face and didn't have on any shirt or undershirt. He had on blue jeans that were too tight for him and was holding a black hat and a gun. The two boys also had guns.

"We've had an ACCIDENT!" the children screamed.

The grandmother had the peculiar feeling that the bespectacled man was someone she knew. His face was as familiar to her as if she had known him all her life but she could not recall who he was. He moved away from the car and began to come down the embankment, placing his feet carefully so that he wouldn't slip. He had on tan and white shoes and no socks, and his ankles were red and thin. "Good afternoon," he said. "I see you all had you a little spill."

75 "We turned over twice!" said the grandmother.

"Oncet," he corrected. "We seen it happen. Try their car and see will it run, Hiram," he said quietly to the boy with the gray hat.

"What you got that gun for?" John Wesley asked. "Whatcha gonna do with that gun?"

"Lady," the man said to the children's mother, "would you mind calling them children to sit down by you? Children make me nervous. I want all you to sit down right together there where you're at."

"What are you telling us what to do for?" June Star asked.

80 Behind them the line of woods gaped like a dark open mouth. "Come here," said their mother.

"Look here now," Bailey began suddenly, "we're in a predicament! We're in . . ."

The grandmother shrieked. She scrambled to her feet and stood staring. "You're The Misfit!" she said. "I recognized you at once!"

"Yes'm," the man said, smiling slightly as if he were pleased in spite of himself to be known, "but it would have been better for all of you, lady, if you hadn't of reckernized me."

Bailey turned his head sharply and said something to his mother that shocked even the children. The old lady began to cry and The Misfit reddened.

85 "Lady," he said, "don't you get upset. Sometimes a man says things he don't mean. I don't reckon he meant to talk to you thataway."

"You wouldn't shoot a lady, would you?" the grandmother said and removed a clean handkerchief from her cuff and began to slap at her eyes with it.

The Misfit pointed the toe of his shoe into the ground and made a little hole and then covered it up again. "I would hate to have to," he said.

"Listen," the grandmother almost screamed, "I know you're a good man. You don't look a bit like you have common blood. I know you must come from nice people!"

"Yes ma'm," he said, "finest people in the world." When he smiled he showed a row of strong white teeth. "God never made a finer woman than my mother and my daddy's heart was pure gold," he said. The boy with the red sweat shirt had come around behind them and was standing with his gun at his hip. The Misfit squatted down on the ground. "Watch them children, Bobby Lee," he said. "You know they make me nervous." He looked at the six of them huddled together in front of him and he seemed to be embarrassed as if he couldn't think of anything to say. "Ain't a cloud in the sky," he remarked, looking up at it. "Don't see no sun but don't see no cloud neither."

90 "Yes, it's a beautiful day," said the grandmother. "Listen," she said, "you shouldn't call yourself The Misfit because I know you're a good man at heart. I can just look at you and tell."

"Hush!" Bailey yelled. "Hush! Everybody shut up and let me handle this!" He was squatting in the position of a runner about to sprint forward but he didn't move.

"I pre-chate that, lady," The Misfit said and drew a little circle in the ground with the butt of his gun.

"It'll take a half a hour to fix this here car," Hiram called, looking over the raised hood of it.

"Well, first you and Bobby Lee get him and that little boy to step over yonder with you," The Misfit said, pointing to Bailey and John Wesley. "The boys want to ask you something," he said to Bailey. "Would you mind stepping back in them woods there with them?"

95 "Listen," Bailey began, "we're in a terrible predicament! Nobody realizes what this is," and his voice cracked. His eyes were as blue and intense as the parrots in his shirt and he remained perfectly still.

The grandmother reached up to adjust her hat brim as if she were going to the woods with him but it came off in her hand. She stood staring at it and after a second she let it fall on the ground. Hiram pulled Bailey up by the arm as if he were assisting an old man. John Wesley caught hold of his father's hand and Bobby Lee followed. They went off toward the woods and just as they reached the dark edge, Bailey turned and supporting himself against a gray naked pine trunk, he shouted, "I'll be back in a minute, Mamma, wait on me!"

"Come back this instant!" his mother shrilled but they all disappeared into the woods.

"Bailey Boy!" the grandmother called in a tragic voice but she found she was looking at The Misfit squatting on the ground in front of her. "I just know you're a good man," she said desperately. "You're not a bit common!"

"Nome, I ain't a good man," The Misfit said after a second as if he had considered her statement carefully, "but I ain't the worst in the world neither. My daddy said I was a different breed of dog from my brothers and sisters. 'You know,' Daddy said, 'it's some that can live their whole life without asking about it and it's others has to know why it is, and this boy is one of the latters. He's going to be into everything!'" He put on his black hat and looked up suddenly and then away deep into the woods as if he were embarrassed again. "I'm sorry I don't have on a shirt before you ladies," he said, hunching his shoulders slightly. "We buried our clothes that we had on when we escaped and we're just making do until we can get better. We borrowed these from some folks we met," he explained.

100 "That's perfectly all right," the grandmother said. "Maybe Bailey has an extra shirt in his suitcase."

"I'll look and see terrectly," The Misfit said.

"Where are they taking him?" the children's mother screamed.

"Daddy was a card himself," The Misfit said. "You couldn't put anything over on him. He never got in trouble with the Authorities though. Just had the knack of handling them."

"You could be honest too if you'd only try," said the grandmother. "Think how wonderful it would be to settle down and live a comfortable life and not have to think about somebody chasing you all the time."

105 The Misfit kept scratching in the ground with the butt of his gun as if he were thinking about it. "Yes'm, somebody is always after you," he murmured.

The grandmother noticed how thin his shoulder blades were just behind his hat because she was standing up looking down on him. "Do you ever pray?" she asked.

He shook his head. All she saw was the black hat wiggle between his shoulder blades. "Nome," he said.

There was a pistol shot from the woods, followed closely by another. Then silence. The old lady's head jerked around. She could hear the wind move through the tree tops like a long satisfied insuck of breath. "Bailey Boy!" she called.

"I was a gospel singer for a while," The Misfit said. "I been most everything. Been in the arm service, both land and sea, at home and abroad, been twict married, been an undertaker, been with the railroads, plowed Mother Earth, been in a tornado, seen a man burnt alive oncet," and he looked up at the children's mother and the little girl who were sitting close together, their faces white and their eyes glassy; "I even seen a woman flogged," he said.

110 "Pray, pray," the grandmother began, "pray, pray. . . ."

"I never was a bad boy that I remember of," The Misfit said in an almost dreamy voice, "but somewheres along the line I done something wrong and got sent to the penitentiary. I was buried alive," and he looked up and held her attention to him by a steady stare.

"That's when you should have started to pray," she said. "What did you do to get sent to the penitentiary that first time?"

"Turn to the right, it was a wall," The Misfit said, looking up again at the cloudless sky. "Turn to the left, it was a wall. Look up it was a ceiling, look down it was a floor. I forget what I done, lady. I set there

and set there, trying to remember what it was I done and I ain't recalled it to this day. Oncet in a while, I would think it was coming to me, but it never come."

"Maybe they put you in by mistake," the old lady said vaguely.

115 "Nome," he said. "It wasn't no mistake. They had the papers on me."

"You must have stolen something," she said.

The Misfit sneered slightly. "Nobody had nothing I wanted," he said. "It was a head-doctor at the penitentiary said what I had done was kill my daddy but I known that for a lie. " My daddy died in nineteen ought nineteen of the epidemic flu and I never had a thing to do with it. He was buried in the Mount Hopewell Baptist churchyard and you can go there and see for yourself."

"If you would pray," the old lady said, "Jesus would help you."

"That's right," The Misfit said.

120 "Well then, why don't you pray?" she asked trembling with delight suddenly.

"I don't want no hep," he said. "I'm doing all right by myself."

Bobby Lee and Hiram came ambling back from the woods. Bobby Lee was dragging a yellow shirt with bright blue parrots on it.

"Throw me that shirt, Bobby Lee," The Misfit said. The shirt came flying at him and landed on his shoulder and he put it on. The grandmother couldn't name what the shirt reminded her of. "No, lady," The Misfit said while he was buttoning it up, "I found out the crime don't matter. You can do one thing or you can do another, kill a man or take a tire off his car, because sooner or later you're going to forget what it was you done and just be punished for it."

The children's mother had begun to make heaving noises as if she couldn't get her breath. "Lady," he asked, "would you and that little girl like to step off yonder with Bobby Lee and Hiram and join your husband?"

125 "Yes, thank you," the mother said faintly. Her left arm dangled helplessly and she was holding the baby, who had gone to sleep, in the other. "Hep that lady up, Hiram," The Misfit said as she struggled to climb out of the ditch, "and Bobby Lee, you hold onto that little girl's hand."

"I don't want to hold hands with him," June Star said. "He reminds me of a pig."

The fat boy blushed and laughed and caught her by the arm and pulled her off into the woods after Hiram and her mother.

Alone with The Misfit, the grandmother found that she had lost her voice. There was not a cloud in the sky nor any sun. There was nothing around her but woods. She wanted to tell him that he must pray. She opened and closed her mouth several times before anything came out. Finally she found herself saying, "Jesus. Jesus," meaning, Jesus will help you, but the way she was saying it, it sounded as if she might be cursing.

"Yes'm," The Misfit said as if he agreed. "Jesus thown everything off balance. It was the same case with Him as with me except He hadn't committed any crime and they could prove I had committed one because they had the papers on me. Of course," he said, "they never shown me my papers. That's why I sign myself now. I said long ago, you get you a signature and sign everything you do and keep a copy of it. Then you'll know what you done and you can hold up the crime to the punishment and see do they match and in the end you'll have something to prove you ain't been treated right. I call myself The Misfit," he said, "because I can't make what all I done wrong fit what all I gone through in punishment."

130   There was a piercing scream from the woods, followed closely by a pistol report. "Does it seem right to you, lady, that one is punished a heap and another ain't punished at all?"

"Jesus!" the old lady cried. "You've got good blood! I know you wouldn't shoot a lady! I know you come from nice people! Pray! Jesus, you ought not to shoot a lady. I'll give you all the money I've got!"

"Lady," The Misfit said, looking beyond her far into the woods, "there never was a body that give the undertaker a tip."

There were two more pistol reports and the grandmother raised her head like a parched old turkey hen crying for water and called, "Bailey Boy, Bailey Boy!" as if her heart would break.

"Jesus was the only One that ever raised the dead," The Misfit continued, "and He shouldn't have done it. He thown everything off balance. If He did

what He said, then it's nothing for you to do but thow away everything and follow Him, and if He didn't, then it's nothing for you to do but enjoy the few minutes you got left the best way you can—by killing somebody or burning down his house or doing some other meanness to him. No pleasure but meanness," he said and his voice had become almost a snarl.

135   "Maybe He didn't raise the dead," the old lady mumbled, not knowing what she was saying and feeling so dizzy that she sank down in the ditch with her legs twisted under her.

"I wasn't there so I can't say He didn't," The Misfit said. "I wisht I had of been there," he said, hitting the ground with his fist. "It ain't right I wasn't there because if I had of been there I would of known. Listen lady," he said in a high voice, "if I had of been there I would of known and I wouldn't be like I am now." His voice seemed about to crack and the grandmother's head cleared for an instant. She saw the man's face twisted close to her own as if he were going to cry and she murmured, "Why you're one of my babies. You're one of my own children!" She reached out and touched him on the shoulder. The Misfit sprang back as if a snake had bitten him and shot her three times through the chest. Then he put his gun down on the ground and took off his glasses and began to clean them.

Hiram and Bobby Lee returned from the woods and stood over the ditch, looking down at the grandmother who half sat and half lay in a puddle of blood with her legs crossed under her like a child's and her face smiling up at the cloudless sky.

Without his glasses, The Misfit's eyes were red-rimmed and pale and defenseless-looking. "Take her off and thow her where you thown the others," he said, picking up the cat that was rubbing itself against his leg.

"She was a talker, wasn't she?" Bobby Lee said, sliding down the ditch with a yodel.

140   "She would of been a good woman," The Misfit said, "if it had been somebody there to shoot her every minute of her life."

"Some fun!" Bobby Lee said.

"Shut up, Bobby Lee," The Misfit said. "It's no real pleasure in life."

[1953]

1. What is the grandmother's place in her family? What is her relationship with the different family members?

2. Are O'Connor's characters realistic? Are they likeable? How does O'Connor make them funny?

3. How does O'Connor change the mood in the second half of the story?

4. What is the Misfit's place in his family? What do we know about his relationship with the different members of his family?

5. What is the Misfit's worry about Jesus? Why does he shoot the grandmother when he does? What is the meaning of the last two things he says?

James Baldwin 1924–1987

Born in Harlem, Baldwin followed in the footsteps of his stepfather, becoming a Pentecostal preacher at the age of fourteen. He moved to bohemian Greenwich Village in the 1940s, and published his first novel, *Go Tell It on the Mountain*, in 1953. From the late 1940s, he lived in the south of France, writing novels, stories, and essays concerned with race as well as with gay themes. "Sonny's Blues" was first published in 1957 and was reprinted in the collection, *Going to Meet the Man* (1965). Rather than a single jazz figure, Sonny's character is a composite of several giants of jazz, including saxophonist Charlie Parker (1920–1955), who killed himself with heroin and alcohol; saxophonist John Coltrane (1926–1967), who beat his habit but still died young; and pianist Thelonius Monk (1917–1982).

SONNY'S BLUES

I READ ABOUT IT IN THE PAPER, IN THE SUBWAY, on my way to work. I read it, and I couldn't believe it, and I read it again. Then perhaps I just stared at it, at the newsprint spelling out his name, spelling out the story. I stared at it in the swinging lights of the subway car, and in the faces and bodies of the people, and in my own face, trapped in the darkness which roared outside.

It was not to be believed and I kept telling myself that as I walked from the subway station to the high school. And at the same time I couldn't doubt it. I was scared, scared for Sonny. He became real to me again. A great block of ice got settled in my belly and kept melting there slowly all day long, while I taught my classes algebra. It was a special kind of ice. It kept melting, sending trickles of ice water all up and down my veins, but it never got less. Sometimes it hardened and seemed to expand until I felt my guts were going to come spilling out or that I was going to choke or scream. This would always be at a moment when I was remembering some specific thing Sonny had once said or done.

When he was about as old as the boys in my classes his face had been bright and open, there was a lot of copper in it; and he'd had wonderfully direct brown eyes, and great gentleness and privacy. I wondered what he looked like now. He had been picked up, the evening before, in a raid on an apartment downtown, for peddling and using heroin.

I couldn't believe it: but what I mean by that is that I couldn't find any room for it anywhere inside me. I had kept it outside me for a long time. I hadn't wanted to know. I had had suspicions, but I didn't name them, I kept putting them away. I told myself that Sonny was wild, but he wasn't crazy. And he'd always been a good boy, he hadn't ever turned hard or evil or disrespectful, the way kids can, so quick, so quick, especially in Harlem. I didn't want to believe that I'd ever see my brother going down, coming to nothing, all that light in his face gone out, in the condition I'd already seen so many others. Yet it had happened and here I was, talking about algebra to a lot of boys who might, every one of them for all I knew, be popping off needles every time they went to the head. Maybe it did more for them than algebra could.

5   I was sure that the first time Sonny had ever had horse, he couldn't have been much older than these boys were now. These boys, now, were living as we'd been living then, they were growing up with a rush and their heads bumped abruptly against the low ceiling of their actual possibilities. They were filled with rage. All they really knew were two darknesses, the darkness of their lives, which was now closing in on them, and the darkness of the movies, which had blinded them to that other darkness, and in which they now, vindictively, dreamed, at once more together than they were at any other time, and more alone.

When the last bell rang, the last class ended, I let out my breath. It seemed I'd been holding it for all that time. My clothes were wet—I may have looked as though I'd been sitting in a steam bath, all dressed up, all afternoon. I sat alone in the classroom a long time. I listened to the boys outside, downstairs, shouting and cursing and laughing. Their laughter struck me for perhaps the first time. It was not the joyous laughter which—God knows why—one associates with children. It was mocking and insular, its intent was to denigrate. It was disenchanted, and in this, also, lay the authority of their curses. Perhaps I was listening to them because I was thinking about my brother and in them I heard my brother. And myself.

One boy was whistling a tune, at once very complicated and very simple, it seemed to be pouring out of him as though he were a bird, and it sounded very cool and moving through all that harsh, bright air, only just holding its own through all those other sounds.

I stood up and walked over to the window and looked down into the courtyard. It was the beginning of the spring and the sap was rising in the boys. A teacher passed through them every now and again, quickly, as though he or she couldn't wait to get out of that courtyard, to get those boys out of their sight and off their minds. I started collecting my stuff. I thought I'd better get home and talk to Isabel.

The courtyard was almost deserted by the time I got downstairs. I saw this boy standing in the shadow of a doorway, looking just like Sonny. I almost called his name. Then I saw that it wasn't Sonny, but somebody we used to know, a boy from around our block. He'd been Sonny's friend. He'd never been mine, having been too young for me, and, anyway, I'd never liked him. And now, even though he was a grown-up man, he still hung around that block, still spent hours on the street corner, was always high and raggy. I used to run into him from time to time and he'd often work around to asking me for a quarter or fifty cents. He always had some real good excuse, too, and I always gave it to him, I don't know why.

10   But now, abruptly, I hated him. I couldn't stand the way he looked at me, partly like a dog, partly like a cunning child. I wanted to ask him what the hell he was doing in the school courtyard.

He sort of shuffled over to me, and he said, "I see you got the papers. So you already know about it."

"You mean about Sonny? Yes, I already know about it. How come they didn't get you?"

He grinned. It made him repulsive and it also brought to mind what he'd looked like as a kid. "I wasn't there. I stay away from them people."

"Good for you." I offered him a cigarette and I watched him through the smoke. "You come all the way down here just to tell me about Sonny?"

15   "That's right." He was sort of shaking his head and his eyes looked strange, as though they were about to cross. The bright sun deadened his damp dark brown skin and it made his eyes look yellow and showed up the dirt in his conked hair. He smelled funky. I moved a little away from him and I said, "Well, thanks. But I already know about it and I got to get home."

"I'll walk you a little ways," he said. We started walking. There were a couple of kids still loitering in the courtyard and one of them said good night to me and looked strangely at the boy beside me.

"What're you going to do?" he asked me. "I mean, about Sonny?"

"Look. I haven't seen Sonny for over a year. I'm not sure I'm going to do anything. Anyway, what the hell *can* I do?"

"That's right," he said quickly, "ain't nothing you can do. Can't much help old Sonny no more, I guess."

20   It was what I was thinking and so it seemed to me he had no right to say it.

"I'm surprised at Sonny, though," he went on—he had a funny way of talking, he looked straight ahead as though he were talking to himself—"I thought Sonny was a smart boy, I thought he was too smart to get hung."

"I guess he thought so too," I said sharply, "and that's how he got hung. And how about you? You're pretty goddamn smart, I bet."

Then he looked directly at me, just for a minute. "I ain't smart," he said. "If I was smart, I'd have reached for a pistol a long time ago."

"Look. Don't tell *me* your sad story, if it was up to me, I'd give you one." Then I felt guilty—guilty, probably, for never having supposed that the poor bastard *had* a story of his own, much less a sad one, and I asked, quickly, "What's going to happen to him now?"

25   He didn't answer this. He was off by himself some place. "Funny thing," he said, and from his tone we might have been discussing the quickest way to get to Brooklyn, "when I saw the papers this morning, the first thing I asked myself was if I had anything to do with it. I felt sort of responsible."

I began to listen more carefully. The subway station was on the corner, just before us, and I stopped. He stopped, too. We were in front of a bar and he ducked slightly, peering in, but whoever he was looking for didn't seem to be there. The juke box was blasting away with something black and bouncy and I half watched the barmaid as she danced her way from the juke box to her place behind the bar. And I watched her face as she laughingly responded to something someone said to her, still keeping time to the music. When she smiled one saw the little girl, one sensed the doomed, still-struggling woman beneath the battered face of the semi-whore.

"I never *give* Sonny nothing," the boy said finally, "but a long time ago I come to school high and Sonny asked me how it felt." He paused, I couldn't bear to watch him, I watched the barmaid, and I listened to the music which seemed to be causing the pavement to shake. "I told him it felt great." The music stopped, the barmaid paused and watched the juke box until the music began again. "It did."

All this was carrying me some place I didn't want to go. I certainly didn't want to know how it felt. It filled everything, the people, the houses, the music, the dark, quicksilver barmaid, with menace; and this menace was their reality.

"What's going to happen to him now?" I asked again.

30   "They'll send him away some place and they'll try to cure him." He shook his head. "Maybe he'll even think he's kicked the habit. Then they'll let him loose"—he gestured, throwing his cigarette into the gutter. "That's all."

"What do you mean, that's *all?*"

But I knew what he meant.

"I *mean,* that's *all.*" He turned his head and looked at me, pulling down the corners of his mouth. "Don't you know what I mean?" he asked, softly.

"How the hell *would* I know what you mean?" I almost whispered it, I don't know why.

35   "That's right," he said to the air, "how would *he* know what I mean?" He turned toward me again, patient and calm, and yet I somehow felt him shaking, shaking as though he were going to fall apart. I felt that ice in my guts again, the dread I'd felt all afternoon; and again I watched the barmaid, moving about the bar, washing glasses, and singing. "Listen. They'll let him out and then it'll just start all over again. That's what I mean."

"You mean—they'll let him out. And then he'll just start working his way back in again. You mean he'll never kick the habit. Is that what you mean?"

"That's right," he said, cheerfully. "*You* see what I mean."

"Tell me," I said at last, "why does he want to die? He must want to die, he's killing himself, why does he want to die?"

He looked at me in surprise. He licked his lips. "He don't want to die. He wants to live. Don't nobody want to die, ever."

40   Then I wanted to ask him—too many things. He could not have answered, or if he had, I could not have borne the answers. I started walking. "Well, I guess it's none of my business."

"It's going to be rough on old Sonny," he said. We reached the subway station. "This is your station?" he asked. I nodded. I took one step down. "Damn!" he said, suddenly. I looked up at him. He grinned again. "Damn if I didn't leave all my money home. You ain't got a dollar on you, have you? Just for a couple of days, is all."

All at once something inside gave and threatened to come pouring out of me. I didn't hate him any more. I felt that in another moment I'd start crying like a child.

"Sure," I said. "Don't sweat." I looked in my wallet and didn't have a dollar, I only had a five. "Here," I said. "That hold you?"

He didn't look at it—he didn't want to look at it. A terrible, closed look came over his face, as though he were keeping the number on the bill a secret from him and me. "Thanks," he said, and now he was dying to see me go. "Don't worry about Sonny. Maybe I'll write him or something."

45 "Sure," I said. "You do that. So long."

"Be seeing you," he said. I went on down the steps.

And I didn't write Sonny or send him anything for a long time. When I finally did, it was just after my little girl died, he wrote me back a letter which made me feel like a bastard.

Here's what he said:

Dear Brother,

You don't know how much I needed to hear from you. I wanted to write you many a time but I dug how much I must have hurt you and so I didn't write. But now I feel like a man who's been trying to climb up out of some deep, real deep and funky hole and just saw the sun up there, outside. I got to get outside.

I can't tell you much about how I got here. I mean I don't know how to tell you. I guess I was afraid of something or I was trying to escape from something and you know I have never been very strong in the head (smile). I'm glad Mama and Daddy are dead and can't see what's happened to their son and I swear if I'd known what I was doing I would never have hurt you so, you and a lot of other fine people who were nice to me and who believed in me.

I don't want you to think it had anything to do with me being a musician. It's more than that. Or maybe less than that. I can't get anything straight in my head down here and I try not to think about what's going to happen to me when I get outside again. Sometime I think I'm going to flip and *never* get outside and sometime I think I'll come straight back. I tell you one thing, though, I'd rather blow my brains out than go through this again. But that's what they all say, so they tell me. If I tell you when I'm coming to New York and if you could meet me, I sure would appreciate it. Give my love to Isabel and the kids and I was sorry to hear about little Gracie. I wish I could be like Mama and say the Lord's will be done, but I don't know it seems to me that trouble is the one thing that never does get stopped and I don't know what good it does to blame it on the Lord. But maybe it does some good if you believe it.

Your brother,
Sonny

Then I kept in constant touch with him and I sent him whatever I could and I went to meet him when he came back to New York. When I saw him many things I thought I had forgotten came flooding back to me. This was because I had begun, finally, to wonder about Sonny, about the life that Sonny lived inside. This life, whatever it was, had made him older and thinner and it had deepened the distant stillness in which he had always moved. He looked very unlike my baby brother. Yet, when he smiled, when we shook hands, the baby brother I'd never known looked out from the depths of his private life, like an animal waiting to be coaxed into the light.

50 "How you been keeping?" he asked me.

"All right. And you?"

"Just fine." He was smiling all over his face. "It's good to see you again."

"It's good to see you."

The seven years' difference in our ages lay between us like a chasm: I wondered if these years would ever operate between us as a bridge. I was remembering, and it made it hard to catch my breath, that I had been there when he was born; and I had heard the first words he had ever spoken. When he started to walk, he walked from our mother straight to me. I caught him just before he fell when he took the first steps he ever took in this world.

55 "How's Isabel?"

"Just fine. She's dying to see you."

"And the boys?"

"They're fine, too. They're anxious to see their uncle."

"Oh, come on. You know they don't remember me."

60 "Are you kidding? Of course they remember you."

He grinned again. We got into a taxi. We had a lot to say to each other, far too much to know how to begin.

As the taxi began to move, I asked, "You still want to go to India?"

He laughed. "You still remember that. Hell, no. This place is Indian enough for me."

"It used to belong to them," I said.

65 And he laughed again. "They damn sure knew what they were doing when they got rid of it."

Years ago, when he was around fourteen, he'd been all hipped on the idea of going to India. He read books about people sitting on rocks, naked, in all kinds of weather, but mostly bad, naturally, and walking barefoot through hot coals and arriving at wisdom. I used to say that it sounded to me as though they were getting away from wisdom as fast as they could. I think he sort of looked down on me for that.

"Do you mind," he asked, "if we have the driver drive alongside the park? On the west side—I haven't seen the city in so long."

"Of course not," I said. I was afraid that I might sound as though I were humoring him, but I hoped he wouldn't take it that way. . . .

So we drove along, between the green of the park and the stony, lifeless elegance of hotels and apartment buildings, toward the vivid, killing streets of our childhood. These streets hadn't changed, though housing projects jutted up out of them now like rocks in the middle of a boiling sea. Most of the houses in which we had grown up had vanished, as had the stores from which we had stolen, the basements in which we had first tried sex, the rooftops from which we had hurled tin cans and bricks. But houses exactly like the houses of our past yet dominated the landscape, boys exactly like the boys we once had been found themselves smothering in these houses, came down into the streets for light and air and found themselves encircled by disaster. Some escaped the trap, most didn't. Those who got out always left something of themselves behind, as some animals amputate a leg and leave it in the trap. It might be said, perhaps, that I had escaped, after all, I was a school teacher; or that Sonny had, he hadn't lived in Harlem for years. Yet, as the cab moved uptown through streets which seemed, with a rush, to darken with dark people, and as I covertly studied Sonny's face, it came to me that what we both were seeking through our separate cab windows was that part of ourselves which had been left behind. It's always at the hour of trouble and confrontation that the missing member aches.

70   We hit 110th Street and started rolling up Lenox Avenue. And I'd known this avenue all my life, but it seemed to me again, as it had seemed on the day I'd first heard about Sonny's trouble, filled with a hidden menace which was its very breath of life.

"We almost there," said Sonny.

"Almost." We were both too nervous to say anything more.

We live in a housing project. It hasn't been up long. A few days after it was up it seemed uninhabitably new, now, of course, it's already rundown.

It looks like a parody of the good, clean, faceless life— God knows the people who live in it do their best to make it a parody. The beat-looking grass lying around isn't enough to make their lives green, the hedges will never hold out the streets, and they know it. The big windows fool no one, they aren't big enough to make space out of no space. They don't bother with the windows, they watch the TV screen instead. The playground is most popular with the children who don't play at jacks, or skip rope, or roller skate, or swing, and they can be found in it after dark. We moved in partly because it's not too far from where I teach, and partly for the kids; but it's really just like the houses in which Sonny and I grew up. The same things happen, they'll have the same things to remember. The moment Sonny and I started into the house I had the feeling that I was simply bringing him back into the danger he had almost died trying to escape.

Sonny has never been talkative. So I don't know why I was sure he'd be dying to talk to me when supper was over the first night. Everything went fine, the oldest boy remembered him, and the youngest boy liked him, and Sonny had remembered to bring something for each of them; and Isabel, who is really much nicer than I am, more open and giving, had gone to a lot of trouble about dinner and was genuinely glad to see him. And she's always been able to tease Sonny in a way that I haven't. It was nice to see her face so vivid again and to hear her laugh and watch her make Sonny laugh. She wasn't, or, anyway, she didn't seem to be, at all uneasy or embarrassed. She chatted as though there were no subject which had to be avoided and she got Sonny past his first, faint stiffness. And thank God she was there, for I was filled with that icy dread again. Everything I did seemed awkward to me, and everything I said sounded freighted with hidden meaning. I was trying to remember everything I'd heard about dope addiction and I couldn't help watching Sonny for signs. I wasn't doing it out of malice. I was trying to find out something about my brother. I was dying to hear him tell me he was safe.

75   "Safe!" my father grunted, whenever Mama suggested trying to move to a neighborhood which might be safer for children. "Safe, hell! Ain't no place safe for kids, nor nobody."

He always went on like this, but he wasn't, ever, really as bad as he sounded, not even on weekends, when he got drunk. As a matter of fact, he was always on the lookout for "something a little better," but he died before he found it. He died suddenly, during a drunken weekend in the middle of the war, when Sonny was fifteen. He and Sonny hadn't ever got on too well. And this was partly because Sonny was the apple of his father's eye. It was because he loved Sonny so much and was frightened for him, that he was always fighting with him. It doesn't do any good to fight with Sonny. Sonny just moves back, inside himself, where he can't be reached. But the principal reason that they never hit it off is that they were so much alike. Daddy was big and rough and loud-talking, just the opposite of Sonny, but they both had—that same privacy.

Mama tried to tell me something about this, just after Daddy died. I was home on leave from the army.

This was the last time I ever saw my mother alive. Just the same, this picture gets all mixed up in my mind with pictures I had of her when she was younger. The way I always see her is the way she used to be on a Sunday afternoon, say, when the old folks were talking after the big Sunday dinner. I always see her wearing pale blue. She'd be sitting on the sofa. And my father would be sitting in the easy chair, not far from her. And the living room would be full of church folks and relatives. There they sit, in chairs all around the living room, and the night is creeping up outside, but nobody knows it yet. You can see the darkness growing against the window-panes and you hear the street noises every now and again, or maybe the jangling beat of a tambourine from one of the churches close by, but it's real quiet in the room. For a moment nobody's talking, but every face looks darkening, like the sky outside. And my mother rocks a little from the waist, and my father's eyes are closed. Everyone is looking at something a child can't see. For a minute they've forgotten the children. Maybe a kid is lying on the rug, half asleep. Maybe somebody's got a kid in his lap and is absent-mindedly stroking the kid's head. Maybe there's a kid, quiet and big-eyed, curled up in a big chair in the corner. The silence, the darkness coming, and the darkness in the faces frightens the child obscurely. He hopes that the hand which strokes his forehead will never stop—will never die. He hopes that there will never come a time when the old folks won't be sitting around the living room, talking about where they've come from, and what they've seen, and what's happened to them and their kinfolk.

But something deep and watchful in the child knows that this is bound to end, is already ending. In a moment someone will get up and turn on the light. Then the old folks will remember the children and they won't talk any more that day. And when light fills the room, the child is filled with darkness. He knows that everytime this happens he's moved just a little closer to that darkness outside. The darkness outside is what the old folks have been talking about. It's what they've come from. It's what they endure. The child knows that they won't talk any more because if he knows too much about what's happened to *them,* he'll know too much too soon, about what's going to happen to *him.*

80 The last time I talked to my mother, I remember I was restless. I wanted to get out and see Isabel. We weren't married then and we had a lot to straighten out between us.

There Mama sat, in black, by the window. She was humming an old church song, *Lord, you brought me from a long ways off.* Sonny was out somewhere. Mama kept watching the streets.

"I don't know," she said, "if I'll ever see you again, after you go off from here. But I hope you'll remember the things I tried to teach you."

"Don't talk like that," I said, and smiled. "You'll be here a long time yet."

She smiled, too, but she said nothing. She was quiet for a long time. And I said, "Mama, don't you worry about nothing. I'll be writing all the time, and you be getting the checks . . ." . . .

85 "I want to talk to you about your brother," she said, suddenly. "If anything happens to me he ain't going to have nobody to look out for him."

"Mama," I said, "ain't nothing going to happen to you *or* Sonny. Sonny's all right. He's a good boy and he's got good sense."

"It ain't a question of his being a good boy," Mama said, "nor of his having good sense. It ain't only the bad ones, nor yet the dumb ones that gets sucked under." She stopped, looking at me. "Your Daddy once had a brother," she said, and she smiled in a way that made me feel she was in pain. "You didn't never know that, did you?"

"No," I said, "I never knew that," and I watched her face.

"Oh, yes," she said, "your Daddy had a brother." She looked out of the window again. "I know you never saw your Daddy cry. But *I* did—many a time, through all these years."

90 I asked her, "What happened to his brother? How come nobody's ever talked about him?"

This was the first time I ever saw my mother look old.

"His brother got killed," she said, "when he was just a little younger than you are now. I knew him. He was a fine boy. He was maybe a little full of the devil, but he didn't mean nobody no harm."

Then she stopped and the room was silent, exactly as it had sometimes been on those Sunday afternoons. Mama kept looking out into the streets.

"He used to have a job in the mill," she said, "and, like all young folks, he just liked to perform on Saturday nights. Saturday nights, him and your father would drift around to different places, go to dances and things like that, or just sit around with people they knew, and your father's brother would sing, he had a fine voice, and play along with himself on his guitar. Well, this particular Saturday night, him and your father was coming home from some place, and they were both a little drunk and there was a moon that night, it was bright like day. Your father's brother was feeling kind of good, and he was whistling to himself, and he had his guitar slung over his shoulder. They was coming down a hill and beneath them was a road that turned off from the highway. Well, your father's brother, being always kind of frisky, decided to run down this hill, and he did, with that guitar banging and clanging behind him, and he ran across the road, and he was making water behind a tree. And your father was sort of amused at him and he was still coming down the hill, kind of slow. Then he heard a car motor and that same minute his brother stepped from behind the tree, into the road, in the moonlight. And he started to cross the road. And your father started to run down the hill, he says he don't know why. This car was full of white men. They was all drunk, and when they seen your father's brother they let out a great whoop and holler and they aimed the car straight at him. They was having fun, they just wanted to scare him, the way they do sometimes, you know. But they was drunk. And I guess the boy, being drunk, too, and scared, kind of lost his head. By the time he jumped

it was too late. Your father says he heard his brother scream when the car rolled over him, and he heard the wood of that guitar when it give, and he heard them strings go flying, and he heard them white men shouting, and the car kept on a-going and it ain't stopped till this day. And, time your father got down the hill, his brother weren't nothing but blood and pulp."

95 Tears were gleaming on my mother's face. There wasn't anything I could say.

"He never mentioned it," she said, "because I never let him mention it before you children. Your Daddy was like a crazy man that night and for many a night thereafter. He says he never in his life seen anything as dark as that road after the lights of that car had gone away. Weren't nothing, weren't nobody on that road, just your Daddy and his brother and that busted guitar. Oh, yes. Your Daddy never did really get right again. Till the day he died he weren't sure but that every white man he saw was the man that killed his brother."

She stopped and took out her handkerchief and dried her eyes and looked at me.

"I ain't telling you all this," she said, "to make you scared or bitter or to make you hate nobody. I'm telling you this because you got a brother. And the world ain't changed."

I guess I didn't want to believe this. I guess she saw this in my face. She turned away from me, toward the window again, searching those streets.

100 "But I praise my Redeemer," she said at last, "that He called your Daddy home before me. I ain't saying it to throw no flowers at myself, but, I declare, it keeps me from feeling too cast down to know I helped your father get safely through this world. Your father always acted like he was the roughest, strongest man on earth. And everybody took him to be like that. But if he hadn't had *me* there—to see his tears!"

She was crying again. Still, I couldn't move. I said, "Lord, Lord, Mama, I didn't know it was like that."

"Oh, honey," she said, "there's a lot that you don't know. But you are going to find it out." She stood up from the window and came over to me. "You got to hold on to your brother," she said, "and don't let him fall, no matter what it looks like is happening to him and no matter how evil you gets with him. You going to be evil with him many a time. But don't you forget what I told you, you hear?"

"I won't forget," I said. "Don't you worry, I won't forget. I won't let nothing happen to Sonny."

My mother smiled as though she were amused at something she saw in my face. Then, "You may not be able to stop nothing from happening. But you got to let him know you's *there*."

105   Two days later I was married, and then I was gone. And I had a lot of things on my mind and I pretty well forgot my promise to Mama until I got shipped home on a special furlough for her funeral.

And, after the funeral, with just Sonny and me alone in the empty kitchen, I tried to find out something about him.

"What do you want to do?" I asked him.

"I'm going to be a musician," he said.

For he had graduated, in the time I had been away, from dancing to the juke box to finding out who was playing what, and what they were doing with it, and he had bought himself a set of drums.

110   "You mean, you want to be a drummer?" I somehow had the feeling that being a drummer might be all right for other people but not for my brother Sonny.

"I don't think," he said, looking at me very gravely, "that I'll ever be a good drummer. But I think I can play a piano."

I frowned. I'd never played the role of the older brother quite so seriously before, had scarcely ever, in fact, *asked* Sonny a damn thing. I sensed myself in the presence of something I didn't really know how to handle, didn't understand. So I made my frown a little deeper as I asked: "What kind of musician do you want to be?"

He grinned. "How many kinds do you think there are?"

"Be *serious*," I said.

115   He laughed, throwing his head back, and then looked at me. "I *am* serious."

"Well, then, for Christ's sake, stop kidding around and answer a serious question. I mean, do you want to be a concert pianist, you want to play classical music and all that, or—or what?" Long before I finished he was laughing again. "For Christ's *sake*, Sonny!"

He sobered, but with difficulty. "I'm sorry. But you sound so—*scared!*" and he was off again.

"Well, you may think it's funny now, baby, but it's not going to be so funny when you have to make your living at it, let me tell you *that*." I was furious because I knew he was laughing at me and I didn't know why.

"No," he said, very sober now, and afraid, perhaps, that he'd hurt me, "I don't want to be a classical pianist. That isn't what interests me. I mean"—he paused, looking hard at me, as though his eyes would help me to understand, and then gestured helplessly, as though perhaps his hand would help—"I mean, I'll have a lot of studying to do, and I'll have to study *everything*, but I mean, I want to play *with*—jazz musicians." He stopped. "I want to play jazz," he said.

120   Well, the word had never before sounded as heavy, as real, as it sounded that afternoon in Sonny's mouth. I just looked at him and I was probably frowning a real frown by this time. I simply couldn't see why on earth he'd want to spend his time hanging around night clubs, clowning around on bandstands, while people pushed each other around a dance floor. It seemed—beneath him, somehow. I had never thought about it before, had never been forced to, but I suppose I had always put jazz musicians in a class with what Daddy called "good-time people."

"Are you *serious*?"

"Hell, *yes*, I'm serious."

He looked more helpless than ever, and annoyed, and deeply hurt.

I suggested, helpfully: "You mean—like Louis Armstrong?"

125   His face closed as though I'd struck him. "No. I'm not talking about none of that old-time, down home crap."

"Well, look, Sonny, I'm sorry, don't get mad. I just don't altogether get it, that's all. Name somebody—you know, a jazz musician you admire."

"Bird."

"Who?"

"Bird! Charlie Parker! Don't they teach you nothing in the goddamn army?"

130   I lit a cigarette. I was surprised and then a little amused to discover that I was trembling. "I've been out of touch," I said. "You'll have to be patient with me. Now. Who's this Parker character?"

"He's just one of the greatest jazz musicians alive," said Sonny, sullenly, his hands in his pockets, his back

JAMES BALDWIN   **265**

to me. "Maybe *the* greatest," he added, bitterly, "that's probably why *you* never heard of him."

"All right," I said, "I'm ignorant. I'm sorry. I'll go out and buy all the cat's records right away, all right?"

"It don't," said Sonny, with dignity, "make any difference to me. I don't care what you listen to. Don't do me no favors."

I was beginning to realize that I'd never seen him so upset before. With another part of my mind I was thinking that this would probably turn out to be one of those things kids go through and that I shouldn't make it seem important by pushing it too hard. Still, I didn't think it would do any harm to ask: "Doesn't all this take a lot of time? Can you make a living at it?"

135 He turned back to me and half leaned, half sat, on the kitchen table. "Everything takes time," he said, "and—well, yes, sure, I can make a living at it. But what I don't seem to be able to make you understand is that it's the only thing I want to do."

"Well, Sonny," I said, gently, "you know people can't always do exactly what they *want* to do—"

"*No,* I don't know that," said Sonny, surprising me. "I think people *ought* to do what they want to do, what else are they alive for?"

"You getting to be a big boy," I said desperately, "it's time you started thinking about your future."

"I'm thinking about my future," said Sonny, grimly. "I think about it all the time."

140 I gave up. I decided, if he didn't change his mind, that we could always talk about it later. "In the meantime," I said, "you got to finish school." We had already decided that he'd have to move in with Isabel and her folks. I knew this wasn't the ideal arrangement because Isabel's folks are inclined to be dicty and they hadn't especially wanted Isabel to marry me. But I didn't know what else to do. "And we have to get you fixed up at Isabel's."

There was a long silence. He moved from the kitchen table to the window. "That's a terrible idea. You know it yourself."

"Do you have a *better* idea?"

He just walked up and down the kitchen for a minute. He was as tall as I was. He had started to shave. I suddenly had the feeling that I didn't know him at all.

He stopped at the kitchen table and picked up my cigarettes. Looking at me with a kind of mocking, amused defiance, he put one between his lips. "You mind?"

145 "You smoking already?"

He lit the cigarette and nodded, watching me through the smoke. "I just wanted to see if I'd have the courage to smoke in front of you." He grinned and blew a great cloud of smoke to the ceiling. "It was easy." He looked at my face. "Come on, now. I bet you was smoking at my age, tell the truth."

I didn't say anything but the truth was on my face, and he laughed. But now there was something very strained in his laugh. "Sure. And I bet that ain't all you was doing."

He was frightening me a little. "Cut the crap," I said. "We already decided that you was going to go and live at Isabel's. Now what's got into you all of a sudden?"

"*You* decided it," he pointed out. "*I* didn't decide nothing." He stopped in front of me, leaning against the stove, arms loosely folded. "Look, brother. I don't want to stay in Harlem no more, I really don't." He was very earnest. He looked at me, then over toward the kitchen window. There was something in his eyes I'd never seen before, some thoughtfulness, some worry all his own. He rubbed the muscle of one arm. "It's time I was getting out of here."

150 "Where do you want to *go,* Sonny?"

"I want to join the army. Or the navy, I don't care. If I say I'm old enough, they'll believe me."

Then I got mad. It was because I was so scared. "You must be crazy. You goddamn fool, what the hell do you want to go and join the *army* for?"

"I just told you. To get out of Harlem."

"Sonny, you haven't even finished *school.* And if you really want to be a musician, how do you expect to study if you're in the *army?*"

155 He looked at me, trapped, and in anguish. "There's ways. I might be able to work out some kind of deal. Anyway, I'll have the G.I. Bill when I come out."

"*If* you come out." We stared at each other. "Sonny, please. Be reasonable. I know the setup is far from perfect. But we got to do the best we can."

"I ain't learning nothing in school," he said. "Even when I go." He turned away from me and opened the window and threw his cigarette out into the narrow alley. I watched his back. "At least, I ain't learning nothing you'd want me to learn." He slammed the window so hard I thought the glass would fly out, and turned back to me. "And I'm sick of the stink of these garbage cans!"

"Sonny," I said, "I know how you feel. But if you don't finish school now, you're going to be sorry later that you didn't." I grabbed him by the shoulders. "And you only got another year. It ain't so bad. And I'll come back and I swear I'll help you do *whatever* you want to do. Just try to put up with it till I come back. Will you please do that? For me?"

He didn't answer and he wouldn't look at me.

160 "Sonny. You hear me?"

He pulled away. "I hear you. But you never hear anything *I* say."

I didn't know what to say to that. He looked out of the window and then back at me. "OK," he said, and sighed. "I'll try."

Then I said, trying to cheer him up a little, "They got a piano at Isabel's. You can practice on it."

And as a matter of fact, it did cheer him up for a minute. "That's right," he said to himself. "I forgot that." His face relaxed a little. But the worry, the thoughtfulness, played on it still, the way shadows play on a face which is staring into the fire.

165 But I thought I'd never hear the end of that piano. At first, Isabel would write me, saying how nice it was that Sonny was so serious about his music and how, as soon as he came in from school, or wherever he had been when he was supposed to be at school, he went straight to that piano and stayed there until suppertime. And, after supper, he went back to that piano and stayed there until everybody went to bed. He was at the piano all day Saturday and all day Sunday. Then he bought a record player and started playing records. He'd play one record over and over again, all day long sometimes, and he'd improvise along with it on the piano. Or he'd play one section of the record, one chord, one change, one progression, then he'd do it on the piano. Then back to the record. Then back to the piano.

Well, I really don't know how they stood it. Isabel finally confessed that it wasn't like living with a person at all, it was like living with sound. And the sound didn't make any sense to her, didn't make any sense to any of them—naturally. They began, in a way, to be afflicted by this presence that was living in their home. It was as though Sonny were some sort of god, or monster. He moved in an atmosphere which wasn't like theirs at all. They fed him and he ate, he washed himself, he walked in and out of their door; he certainly wasn't nasty or unpleasant or rude, Sonny isn't any of those things; but it was as though he were all wrapped up in some cloud, some fire, some vision all his own; and there wasn't any way to reach him.

At the same time, he wasn't really a man yet, he was still a child, and they had to watch out for him in all kinds of ways. They certainly couldn't throw him out. Neither did they dare to make a great scene about that piano because even they dimly sensed, as I sensed, from so many thousands of miles away, that Sonny was at that piano playing for his life.

But he hadn't been going to school. One day a letter came from the school board and Isabel's mother got it—there had, apparently, been other letters but Sonny had torn them up. This day, when Sonny came in, Isabel's mother showed him the letter and asked where he'd been spending his time. And she finally got it out of him that he'd been down in Greenwich Village, with musicians and other characters, in a white girl's apartment. And this scared her and she started to scream at him and what came up, once she began—though she denies it to this day—was what sacrifices they were making to give Sonny a decent home and how little he appreciated it.

Sonny didn't play the piano that day. By evening, Isabel's mother had calmed down but then there was the old man to deal with, and Isabel herself. Isabel says she did her best to be calm but she broke down and started crying. She says she just watched Sonny's face. She could tell, by watching him, what was happening with him. And what was happening was that they penetrated his cloud, they had reached him. Even if their fingers had been a thousand times more gentle than human fingers ever are, he could hardly help feeling that they had stripped him naked and were spitting on that nakedness. For he also had to see that his presence, that music, which was life or death to him, had been torture for them and that they had endured it, not at all for his sake, but only for mine. And Sonny couldn't take that. He can take it a little better today than he could then but he's still not very good at it and, frankly, I don't know anybody who is.

170 The silence of the next few days must have been louder than the sound of all the music ever played

since time began. One morning, before she went to work, Isabel was in his room for something and she suddenly realized that all of his records were gone. And she knew for certain that he was gone. And he was. He went as far as the navy would carry him. He finally sent me a postcard from some place in Greece and that was the first I knew that Sonny was still alive. I didn't see him any more until we were both back in New York and the war had long been over.

He was a man by then, of course, but I wasn't willing to see it. He came by the house from time to time, but we fought almost every time we met. I didn't like the way he carried himself, loose and dreamlike all the time, and I didn't like his friends, and his music seemed to be merely an excuse for the life he led. It sounded just that weird and disordered.

Then we had a fight, a pretty awful fight, and I didn't see him for months. By and by I looked him up, where he was living, in a furnished room in the Village, and I tried to make it up. But there were lots of other people in the room and Sonny just lay on his bed, and he wouldn't come downstairs with me, and he treated these other people as though they were his family and I weren't. So I got mad and then he got mad, and then I told him that he might just as well be dead as live the way he was living. Then he stood up and he told me not to worry about him any more in life, that he *was* dead as far as I was concerned. Then he pushed me to the door and the other people looked on as though nothing were happening, and he slammed the door behind me. I stood in the hallway, staring at the door. I heard somebody laugh in the room and then the tears came to my eyes. I started down the steps, whistling to keep from crying, I kept whistling to myself, *You going to need me, baby, one of these cold, rainy days.*

I read about Sonny's trouble in the spring. Little Grace died in the fall. She was a beautiful little girl. But she only lived a little over two years. She died of polio and she suffered. She had a slight fever for a couple of days, but it didn't seem like anything and we just kept her in bed. And we would certainly have called the doctor, but the fever dropped, she seemed to be all right. So we thought it had just been a cold. Then, one day, she was up, playing, Isabel was in the kitchen fixing lunch for the two

boys when they'd come in from school, and she heard Grace fall down in the living room. When you have a lot of children you don't always start running when one of them falls, unless they start screaming or something. And, this time, Grace was quiet. Yet, Isabel says that when she heard that *thump* and then that silence, something happened in her to make her afraid. And she ran to the living room and there was little Grace on the floor, all twisted up and the reason she hadn't screamed was that she couldn't get her breath. And when she did scream, it was the worst sound, Isabel says, that she'd ever heard in all her life, and she still hears it sometimes in her dreams. Isabel will sometimes wake me up with a low, moaning, strangled sound and I have to be quick to awaken her and hold her to me and where Isabel is weeping against me seems a mortal wound.

I think I may have written Sonny the very day that little Grace was buried. I was sitting in the living room in the dark, by myself, and I suddenly thought of Sonny. My trouble made his real.

175   One Saturday afternoon, when Sonny had been living with us, or, anyway, been in our house, for nearly two weeks, I found myself wandering aimlessly about the living room, drinking from a can of beer, and trying to work up the courage to search Sonny's room. He was out, he was usually out whenever I was home, and Isabel had taken the children to see their grandparents. Suddenly I was standing still in front of the living room window, watching Seventh Avenue. The idea of searching Sonny's room made me still. I scarcely dared to admit to myself what I'd be searching for. I didn't know what I'd do if I found it. Or if I didn't.

On the sidewalk across from me, near the entrance to a barbecue joint, some people were holding an old-fashioned revival meeting. The barbecue cook, wearing a dirty white apron, his conked hair reddish and metallic in the pale sun, and a cigarette between his lips, stood in the doorway, watching them. Kids and older people paused in their errands and stood there, along with some older men and a couple of very tough-looking women who watched everything that happened on the avenue, as though they owned it, or were maybe owned by it. Well, they were watching this, too. The revival was being carried on by three sisters in black, and a brother. All they had were their voices and their Bibles and a tambourine. The brother was testifying and while he testified two of the sisters stood together, seeming to say, Amen, and the third sister walked around with the tambourine outstretched and a couple of people dropped coins into it. Then the brother's testimony ended and the sister who had been taking up the collection dumped the coins into her palm and transferred them to the pocket of her long black robe. Then she raised both hands, striking the tambourine against the air, and then against one hand, and she started to sing. And the two other sisters and the brother joined in.

It was strange, suddenly, to watch, though I had been seeing these street meetings all my life. So, of course, had everybody else down there. Yet, they paused and watched and listened and I stood still at the window. *"Tis the old ship of Zion,"* they sang, and the sister with the tambourine kept a steady, jangling beat, *"it has rescued many a thousand!"* Not a soul under the sound of their voices was hearing this song for the first time, not one of them had been rescued. Nor had they seen much in the way of rescue work being done around them. Neither did they especially believe in the holiness of the three sisters and the brother, they knew too much about them, knew where they lived, and how. The woman with the tambourine, whose voice dominated the air, whose face was bright with joy, was divided by very little from the woman who stood watching her, a cigarette between her heavy, chapped lips, her hair a cuckoo's nest, her face scarred and swollen from many beatings, and her black eyes glittering like coal. Perhaps they both knew this, which was why, when, as rarely, they addressed each other, they addressed each other as Sister. As the singing filled the air the watching, listening faces underwent a change, the eyes focusing on something within; the music seemed to soothe a poison out of them; and time seemed, nearly, to fall away from the sullen, belligerent, battered faces, as though they were fleeing back to their first condition, while dreaming of their last. The barbecue cook half shook his head and smiled, and dropped his cigarette and disappeared into his joint. A man fumbled in his pockets for change and stood holding it in his hand impatiently, as though he had just remembered a pressing appointment further up the avenue. He looked

furious. Then I saw Sonny, standing on the edge of the crowd. He was carrying a wide, flat notebook with a green cover, and it made him look, from where I was standing, almost like a schoolboy. The coppery sun brought out the copper in his skin, he was very faintly smiling, standing very still. Then the singing stopped, the tambourine turned into a collection plate again. The furious man dropped in his coins and vanished, so did a couple of the women, and Sonny dropped some change in the plate, looking directly at the woman with a little smile. He started across the avenue, toward the house. He has a slow, loping walk, something like the way Harlem hipsters walk, only he's imposed on this his own halfbeat. I had never really noticed it before.

I stayed at the window, both relieved and apprehensive. As Sonny disappeared from my sight, they began singing again. And they were still singing when his key turned in the lock.

"Hey," he said.

180 "Hey, yourself. You want some beer?"

"No. Well, maybe." But he came up to the window and stood beside me, looking out. "What a warm voice," he said.

They were singing *If I could only hear my mother pray again!*

"Yes," I said, "and she can sure beat that tambourine."

"But what a terrible song," he said, and laughed. He dropped his notebook on the sofa and disappeared into the kitchen. "Where's Isabel and the kids?"

185 "I think they went to see their grandparents. You hungry?"

"No." He came back into the living room with his can of beer. "You want to come some place with me tonight?"

I sensed, I don't know how, that I couldn't possibly say No. "Sure. Where?"

He sat down on the sofa and picked up his notebook and started leafing through it. "I'm going to sit in with some fellows in a joint in the Village."

"You mean, you're going to play, tonight?"

190 "That's right." He took a swallow of his beer and moved back to the window. He gave me a sidelong look. "If you can stand it."

"I'll try," I said.

He smiled to himself and we both watched as the meeting across the way broke up. The three sisters and the brother, heads bowed, were singing *God be with you till we meet again.* The faces around them were very quiet. Then the song ended. The small crowd dispersed. We watched the three women and the lone man walk slowly up the avenue.

"When she was singing before," said Sonny, abruptly, "her voice reminded me for a minute of what heroin feels like sometimes—when it's in your veins. It makes you feel sort of warm and cool at the same time. And distant. And—and sure." He sipped his beer, very deliberately not looking at me. I watched his face. "It makes you feel—in control. Sometimes you've got to have that feeling."

"Do you?" I sat down slowly in the easy chair.

195 "Sometimes." He went to the sofa and picked up his notebook again. "Some people do."

"In order," I asked, "to play?" And my voice was very ugly, full of contempt and anger.

"Well"—he looked at me with great, troubled eyes, as though, in fact, he hoped his eyes would tell me things he could never otherwise say—"they *think* so. And *if* they think so—!"

"And what do *you* think?" I asked.

He sat on the sofa and put his can of beer on the floor. "I don't know," he said, and I couldn't be sure if he were answering my question or pursuing his thoughts. His face didn't tell me. "It's not so much to *play.* It's to *stand* it, to be able to make it at all. On any level." He frowned and smiled: "In order to keep from shaking to pieces."

200 "But these friends of yours," I said, "they seem to shake themselves to pieces pretty goddamn fast."

"Maybe." He played with the notebook. And something told me that I should curb my tongue, that Sonny was doing his best to talk, that I should listen. "But of course you only know the ones that've gone to pieces. Some don't—or at least they haven't *yet* and that's just about all *any* of us can say." He paused. "And then there are some who just live, really, in hell, and they know it and they see what's happening and they go right on. I don't know." He sighed, dropped the notebook, folded his arms. "Some guys, you can tell from the way they play, they on something *all* the time. And you can see that, well, it makes something real for them. But of course," he picked up his beer from the floor and sipped it and put the can down again, "they *want* to, too, you've got to see that. Even some of them that say they don't—*some,* not all."

"And what about you?" I asked—I couldn't help it. "What about you? Do *you* want to?"

He stood up and walked to the window and remained silent for a long time. Then he sighed. "Me," he said. Then: "While I was downstairs before, on my way here, listening to that woman sing, it struck me all of a sudden how much suffering she must have had to go through—to sing like that. It's *repulsive* to think you have to suffer that much."

I said: "But there's no way not to suffer—is there, Sonny?"

205 "I believe not," he said and smiled, "but that's never stopped anyone from trying." He looked at me. "Has it?" I realized, with this mocking look, that there stood between us, forever, beyond the power of time or forgiveness, the fact that I had held silence—so long!—when he had needed human speech to help him. He turned back to the window. "No, there's no way not to suffer. But you try all kinds of ways to keep from drowning in it, to keep on top of it, and to make it seem—well, like *you.* Like you did something, all right, and now you're suffering for it. You know?" I said nothing. "Well you know," he said, impatiently, "why *do* people suffer? Maybe it's better to do something to give it a reason, *any* reason."

"But we just agreed," I said "that there's no way not to suffer. Isn't it better, then, just to—take it?"

"But nobody just takes it," Sonny cried, "that's what I'm telling you! *Everybody* tries not to. You're just hung up on the *way* some people try—it's not *your* way!"

The hair on my face began to itch, my face felt wet. "That's not true," I said, "that's not true. I don't give a damn what other people do, I don't even care how they suffer. I just care how *you* suffer." And he looked at me. "Please believe me," I said, "I don't want to see you—die—trying not to suffer."

"I won't," he said, flatly, "die trying not to suffer. At least, not any faster than anybody else."

210 "But there's no need," I said, trying to laugh, "is there? in killing yourself."

I wanted to say more, but I couldn't. I wanted to talk about will power and how life could be—well, beautiful. I wanted to say that it was all within; but was it? or, rather, wasn't that exactly the trouble? And I wanted to promise that I would never fail him again. But it would all have sounded—empty words and lies.

So I made the promise to myself and prayed that I would keep it.

"It's terrible sometimes, inside," he said, "that's what's the trouble. You walk these streets, black and funky and cold, and there's not really a living ass to talk to, and there's nothing shaking, and there's no way of getting it out—that storm inside. You can't talk it and you can't make love with it, and when you finally try to get with it and play it, you realize *nobody's* listening. So *you've* got to listen. You got to find a way to listen."

And then he walked away from the window and sat on the sofa again, as though all the wind had suddenly been knocked out of him. "Sometimes you'll do *anything* to play, even cut your mother's throat." He laughed and looked at me. "Or your brother's." Then he sobered. "Or your own." Then: "Don't worry. I'm all right now and I think I'll *be* all right. But I can't forget—where I've been. I don't mean just the physical place I've been, I mean where I've *been*. And *what* I've been."

215 "What have you been, Sonny?" I asked.

He smiled—but sat sideways on the sofa, his elbow resting on the back, his fingers playing with his mouth and chin, not looking at me. "I've been something I didn't recognize, didn't know I could be. Didn't know anybody could be." He stopped, looking inward, looking helplessly young, looking old. "I'm not talking about it now because I feel *guilty* or anything like that—maybe it would be better if I did, I don't know. Anyway, I can't really talk about it. Not to you, not to anybody," and now he turned and faced me. "Sometimes, you know, and it was actually when I was most *out* of the world, I felt that I was in it, that I was *with* it, really, and I could play or I didn't really have to *play*, it just came out of me, it was there. And I don't know how I played, thinking about it now, but I know I did awful things, those times, sometimes, to people. Or it wasn't that I *did* anything to them—it was that they weren't real." He picked up the beer can; it was empty; he rolled it between his palms: "And other times—well, I needed a fix, I needed to find a place to lean, I needed to clear a space to *listen*—and I couldn't find it, and I— went crazy, I did terrible things to *me*, I was terrible *for* me." He began pressing the beer can between his hands, I watched the metal begin to give. It glittered, as he played with it, like a knife, and I was afraid he would cut himself, but I said nothing. "Oh well. I can never tell you. I was all by myself at the bottom of something, stinking and sweating and crying and shaking, and I smelled it, you know? *my* stink, and I thought I'd die if I couldn't get away from it and yet, all the same, I knew that everything I was doing was just locking me in with it. And I didn't know," he paused, still flattening the beer can, "I didn't know, I still *don't* know, something kept telling me that maybe it was good to smell your own stink, but I didn't think that *that* was what I'd been trying to do—and—who can stand it?" and he abruptly dropped the ruined beer can, looking at me with a small, still smile, and then rose, walking to the window as though it were the lodestone rock. I watched his face, he watched the avenue. "I couldn't tell you when Mama died—but the reason I wanted to leave Harlem so bad was to get away from drugs. And then, when I ran away, that's what I was running from— really. When I came back, nothing had changed, *I* hadn't changed, I was just—older." And he stopped, drumming with his fingers on the windowpane. The sun had vanished, soon darkness would fall. I watched his face. "It can come again," he said, almost as though speaking to himself. Then he turned to me. "It can come again," he repeated. "I just want you to know that."

"All right," I said, at last. "So it can come again. All right."

He smiled, but the smile was sorrowful. "I had to try to tell you," he said.

"Yes," I said. "I understand that."

220 "You're my brother," he said, looking straight at me, and not smiling at all.

"Yes," I repeated, "yes. I understand that."

He turned back to the window, looking out. "All that hatred down there," he said, "all that hatred and misery and love. It's a wonder it doesn't blow the avenue apart."

We went to the only night club on a short, dark street, downtown. We squeezed through the narrow, chattering, jam-packed bar to the entrance of the big room, where the bandstand was. And we stood there for a moment, for the lights were very dim in this room and we couldn't see. Then, "Hello, boy," said a voice and an enormous black man, much older than Sonny or myself, erupted out of all that atmospheric lighting and put an arm around Sonny's shoulder. "I been sitting right here," he said, "waiting for you."

He had a big voice, too, and heads in the darkness turned toward us.

225   Sonny grinned and pulled a little away, and said, "Creole, this is my brother. I told you about him."

Creole shook my hand. "I'm glad to meet you, son," he said, and it was clear that he was glad to meet me *there*, for Sonny's sake. And he smiled, "You got a real musician in *your* family," and he took his arm from Sonny's shoulder and slapped him, lightly, affectionately, with the back of his hand.

"Well. Now I've heard it all," said a voice behind us. This was another musician, and a friend of Sonny's, a coal-black, cheerful-looking man, built close to the ground. He immediately began confiding to me, at the top of his lungs, the most terrible things about Sonny, his teeth gleaming like a lighthouse and his laugh coming up out of him like the beginning of an earthquake. And it turned out that everyone at the bar knew Sonny, or almost everyone; some were musicians, working there, or nearby, or not working, some were simply hangers-on, and some were there to hear Sonny play. I was introduced to all of them and they were all very polite to me. Yet, it was clear that, for them, I was only Sonny's brother. Here, I was in Sonny's world. Or, rather: his kingdom. Here, it was not even a question that his veins bore royal blood.

They were going to play soon and Creole installed me, by myself, at a table in a dark corner. Then I watched them, Creole, and the little black man, and Sonny, and the others, while they horsed around, standing just below the bandstand. The light from the bandstand spilled just a little short of them and, watching them laughing and gesturing and moving about, I had the feeling that they, nevertheless, were being most careful not to step into that circle of light too suddenly: that if they moved into the light too suddenly, without thinking, they would perish in flame. Then, while I watched, one of them, the small, black man, moved into the light and crossed the bandstand and started fooling around with his drums. Then—being funny and being, also, extremely ceremonious—Creole took Sonny by the arm and led him to the piano. A woman's voice called Sonny's name and a few hands started clapping. And Sonny, also being funny and being ceremonious, and so

touched, I think, that he could have cried, but neither hiding it nor showing it, riding it like a man, grinned, and put both hands to his heart and bowed from the waist.

Creole then went to the bass fiddle and a lean, very bright-skinned brown man jumped up on the bandstand and picked up his horn. So there they were, and the atmosphere on the bandstand and in the room began to change and tighten. Someone stepped up to the microphone and announced them. Then there were all kinds of murmurs. Some people at the bar shushed others. The waitress ran around, frantically getting in the last orders, guys and chicks got closer to each other, and the lights on the bandstand, on the quartet, turned to a kind of indigo. Then they all looked different there. Creole looked about him for the last time, as though he were making certain that all his chickens were in the coop, and then he— jumped and struck the fiddle. And there they were.

230   All I know about music is that not many people ever really hear it. And even then, on the rare occasions when something opens within, and the music enters, what we mainly hear, or hear corroborated, are personal, private, vanishing evocations. But the man who creates the music is hearing something else, is dealing with the roar rising from the void and imposing order on it as it hits the air. What is evoked in him, then, is of another order, more terrible because it has no words, and triumphant, too, for that same reason. And his triumph, when he triumphs, is ours. I just watched Sonny's face. His face was troubled, he was working hard, but he wasn't with it. And I had the feeling that, in a way, everyone on the bandstand was waiting for him, both waiting for him and pushing him along. But as I began to watch Creole, I realized that it was Creole who held them all back. He had them on a short rein. Up there, keeping the beat with his whole body, wailing on the fiddle, with his eyes half closed, he was listening to everything, but he was listening to Sonny. He was having a dialogue with Sonny. He wanted Sonny to leave the shore line and strike out for the deep water. He was Sonny's witness that deep water and drowning were not the same thing—he had been there, and he knew. And he wanted Sonny to know. He was waiting for Sonny to do the things on the keys which would let Creole know that Sonny was in the water.

And, while Creole listened, Sonny moved, deep within, exactly like someone in torment. I had never before thought of how awful the relationship must be between the musician and his instrument. He has to fill it, this instrument, with the breath of life, his own. He has to make it do what he wants it to do. And a piano is just a piano. It's made out of so much wood and wires and little hammers and big ones, and ivory. While there's only so much you can do with it, the only way to find this out is to try and make it do everything.

And Sonny hadn't been near a piano for over a year. And he wasn't on much better terms with his life, not the life that stretched before him now. He and the piano stammered, started one way, got scared, stopped; started another way, panicked, marked time, started again; then seemed to have found a direction, panicked again, got stuck. And the face I saw on Sonny I'd never seen before. Everything had been burned out of it, and, at the same time, things usually hidden were being burned in, by the fire and fury of the battle which was occurring in him up there.

Yet, watching Creole's face as they neared the end of the first set, I had the feeling that something had happened, something I hadn't heard. Then they finished, there was scattered applause, and then, without an instant's warning, Creole started into something else, it was almost sardonic, it was *Am I Blue*. And, as though he commanded, Sonny began to play. Something began to happen. And Creole let out the reins. The dry, low, black man said something awful on the drums, Creole answered, and the drums talked back. Then the horn insisted, sweet and high, slightly detached perhaps, and Creole listened, commenting now and then, dry, and driving, beautiful and calm and old. Then they all came together again, and Sonny was part of the family again. I could tell this from his face. He seemed to have found, right there beneath his fingers, a damn brand-new piano. It seemed that he couldn't get over it. Then, for awhile, just being happy with Sonny, they seemed to be agreeing with him that brand-new pianos certainly were a gas.

Then Creole stepped forward to remind them that what they were playing was the blues. He hit something in all of them, he hit something in me, myself, and the music tightened and deepened, apprehension began to beat the air. Creole began to tell us what the blues were all about. They were not about anything very new. He and his boys up there were keeping it new, at the risk of ruin, destruction, madness, and death, in order to find new ways to make us listen. For, while the tale of how we suffer, and how we are delighted, and how we may triumph is never new, it always must be heard. There isn't any other tale to tell, it's the only light we've got in all this darkness.

235   And this tale, according to that face, that body, those strong hands on those strings, has another aspect in every country, and a new depth in every generation. Listen, Creole seemed to be saying, listen. Now these are Sonny's blues. He made the little black man on the drums know it, and the bright, brown man on the horn. Creole wasn't trying any longer to get Sonny in the water. He was wishing him Godspeed. Then he stepped back, very slowly, filling the air with the immense suggestion that Sonny speak for himself.

Then they all gathered around Sonny and Sonny played. Every now and again one of them seemed to say, Amen. Sonny's fingers filled the air with life, his life. But that life contained so many others. And Sonny went all the way back, he really began with the spare, flat statement of the opening phrase of the song. Then he began to make it his. It was very beautiful because it wasn't hurried and it was no longer a lament. I seemed to hear with what burning he had made it his, with what burning we had yet to make it ours, how we could cease lamenting. Freedom lurked around us and I understood, at last, that he could help us to be free if we would listen, that he would never be free until we did. Yet, there was no battle in his face now. I heard what he had gone through, and would continue to go through until he came to rest in earth. He had made it his: that long line, of which we knew only Mama and Daddy. And he was giving it back, as everything must be given back, so that, passing through death, it can live forever. I saw my mother's face again, and felt, for the first time, how the stones of the road she had walked on must have bruised her feet. I saw the moon-lit road where my father's brother died. And it brought something else back to me, and carried me past it. I saw my little girl again and felt Isabel's tears again, and I felt my own tears begin to rise. And I was yet aware that this was only a moment, that the world waited outside, as hungry as a tiger, and that trouble stretched above us, longer than the sky.

Then it was over. Creole and Sonny let out their breath, both soaking wet, and grinning. There was a lot of applause and some of it was real. In the dark, the girl came by and I asked her to take drinks to the bandstand. There was a long pause, while they talked up there in the indigo light and after awhile

I saw the girl put a Scotch and milk on top of the piano for Sonny. He didn't seem to notice it, but just before they started playing again, he sipped from it and looked toward me, and nodded. Then he put it back on top of the piano. For me, then, as they began to play again, it glowed and shook above my brother's head like the very cup of trembling.

[1957]

QUESTIONS FOR REFLECTION AND DISCUSSION

1. Before Baldwin introduces Sonny as a musician, he introduces a number of other scenes punctuated by music or musical instruments. List these scenes. What is their function in the story as a whole?

2. What is the narrator's attitude toward jazz? Does it change as the story progresses?

3. What is the relationship between drugs and music in this story?

4. Why does the narrator accompany Sonny to the club to hear him play? Has he ever heard him play before? What does he hear?

5. Sonny's band is trying "to find new ways to make us listen." What does this mean?

Jonathan Safran Foer b. 1977

Jonathan Safran Foer was born in Washington, D.C., grew up in New York City, and attended Princeton University. A fictionalized version of his journey to Ukraine to research his grandfather's life was the focus of his first novel, *Everything Is Illuminated*, which was published to great acclaim and popular success in 2002. He published his second novel, *Extremely Loud and Incredibly Close*, in 2005. Like his novels, "A Primer for the Punctuation of Heart Disease," first published in the *New Yorker* in 2002, is formally experimental and simultaneously playful and deadly serious in its meditation on family relationships.

A PRIMER FOR THE PUNCTUATION OF HEART DISEASE

THE "SILENCE MARK" SIGNIFIES AN ABSENCE OF language, and there is at least one on every page of the story of my family life. Most often used in the conversations I have with my grandmother about her life in Europe during the war, and in conversations with my father about our family's history of heart disease—we have forty-one heart attacks between us, and counting—the silence mark is a staple of familial punctuation. Note the use of silence in the following brief exchange, when my father called me at college, the morning of his most recent angioplasty:

"Listen," he said, and then surrendered to a long pause, as if the pause were what I was supposed to listen to. "I'm sure everything's gonna be fine, but I just wanted to let you know—"

"I already know," I said.
"□"
"□"
"□"
"□"
"O.K.," he said.

5 "I'll talk to you tonight," I said, and I could hear, in the receiver, my own heartbeat.

He said, "Yup."

■ The "willed silence mark" signifies an intentional silence, the conversational equivalent of building a wall over which you can't climb, through which you can't see, against which you break the bones of your hands and wrists. I often inflict willed silences upon my mother when she asks about my relationships with girls. Perhaps this is because I never have *relationships* with girls—only *relations.* It depresses me to think that I've never had sex with anyone who really loved me. Sometimes I wonder if having sex with a girl who doesn't love me is like felling a tree, alone, in a forest: No one hears about it; it didn't happen.

?? The "insistent question mark" denotes one family member's refusal to yield to a willed silence, as in this conversation with my mother.

"Are you dating at all?"

"□"

"But you're seeing people, I'm *sure.* Right?"

"□"

"I don't get it. Are you ashamed of the girl? Are you ashamed of me?"

"■"

"??"

¡ As it visually suggests, the "unxclamation point" is the opposite of an exclamation point; it indicates a whisper.

The best example of this usage occurred when I was a boy. My grandmother was driving me to a piano lesson, and the Volvo's wipers only moved the rain around. She turned down the volume of the second side of the seventh tape of an audio version of *Shoah°* put her hand on my cheek, and said, "I hope that you never love anyone as much as I love you¡"

10 Why was she whispering? We were the only ones who could hear.

¡¡ Theoretically, the "extraunxclamation points" would be used to denote twice an unxclamation point, but in practice any whisper that quiet would not be heard. I take comfort in believing that at least some of the silences in my life were really extraunxclamation.

Shoah: Claude Lanzmann's nine-hour documentary film *Shoah* (1985) is composed entirely of interviews with persons involved in the Holocaust (to which *Shoah* refers in Hebrew).

!! The "extraexclamation points" are simply twice an exclamation point. I've never had a heated argument with any member of my family. We've never yelled at each other, or disagreed with any passion. In fact, I can't even remember a difference of opinion. There are those who would say that this is unhealthy. But, since it is the case, there exists only one instance of extraexclamation points in our family history, and they were uttered by a stranger who was vying with my father for a parking space in front of the National Zoo.

"Give it up, fucker!!" he hollered at my father, in front of my mother, my brothers, and me.

"Well, I'm sorry," my father said, pushing the bridge of his glasses up his nose, "but I think it's rather obvious that we arrived at this space first. You see, we were approaching from—"

15 "Give . . . it . . . up . . . fucker!!"

"Well, it's just that I think I'm in the right on this particu—"

"GIVE IT UP, FUCKER!!"

"Give it up, Dad¡" I said, suffering a minor coronary event as my fingers clenched his seat's headrest.

"Je-sus!" the man yelled, pounding his fist against the outside of his car door. "Giveitupfucker!!"

20 Ultimately, my father gave it up, and we found a spot several blocks away. Before we got out, he pushed in the cigarette lighter, and we waited, in silence, as it got hot. When it popped out, he pushed it back in. "It's never, ever worth it," he said, turning back to us, his hand against his heart.

~ Placed at the end of a sentence, the "pedal point" signifies a thought that dissolves into a suggestive silence. The pedal point is distinguished from the ellipsis and the dash in that the thought it follows is neither incomplete nor interrupted but an outstretched hand. My younger brother uses these a lot with me, probably because he, of all the members of my family, is the one most capable of telling me what he needs to tell me without having to say it. Or, rather, he's the one whose words I'm most convinced I don't need to hear. Very often he will say, "Jonathan" and I will say, "I know."

A few weeks ago, he was having problems with his heart. A visit to his university's health center to check out some chest pains became a trip to the

JONATHAN SAFRAN FOER   275

emergency room became a week in the intensive care unit. As it turns out, he's been having one long heart attack for the last six years. "It's nowhere near as bad as it sounds," the doctor told my parents, "but it's definitely something we want to take care of."

I called my brother that night and told him that he shouldn't worry. He said, "I know. But that doesn't mean there's nothing to worry about~"

"I know~" I said.

25 "I know~" he said.

"I~"

"I~"

"□"

Does my little brother have relationships with girls? I don't know.

30 ↓ Another commonly employed familial punctuation mark, the "low point," is used either in place—or for accentuation at the end—of such phrases as "This is terrible," "This is irremediable," "It couldn't possibly be worse."

> "It's good to have somebody, Jonathan. It's necessary."
> "□"
>
> "It pains me to think of you alone."
> "■↓"
> "??↓"

Interestingly, low points always come in pairs in my family. That is, the acknowledgment of whatever is terrible and irremediable becomes itself something terrible and irremediable—and often worse than the original referent. For example, my sadness makes my mother sadder than the cause of my sadness does. Of course, her sadness then makes me sad. Thus is created a "low-point chain": ↓↓↓↓↓. . .∞.

❄ The "snowflake" is used at the end of a unique familial phrase—that is, any sequence of words that has never, in the history of our family life, been assembled as such. For example, "I didn't die in the Holocaust, but all of my siblings did, so where does that leave me? ❄" Or, "My heart is no good, and I'm afraid of dying, and I'm also afraid of saying I love you. ❄"

☺ The "corroboration mark" is more or less what it looks like. But it would be a mistake to think that it simply stands in place of "I agree," or even

"Yes." Witness the subtle usage in this dialogue between my mother and my father:

> "Could you add orange juice to the grocery list, but remember to get the kind with reduced acid. Also some cottage cheese. And that bacon-substitute stuff. And a few Yahrzeit candles."
> "☺"
>
> "The car needs gas. I need tampons."
> "☺"
>
> "Is Jonathan dating anyone? I'm not prying, but I'm very interested."
> "☺"

My father has suffered twenty-two heart attacks—more than the rest of us combined. Once, in a moment of frankness after his nineteenth, he told me that his marriage to my mother had been successful because he had become a yes man early on.

35 "We've only had one fight," he said. "It was in our first week of marriage. I realized that it's never, ever worth it."

My father and I were pulling weeds one afternoon a few weeks ago. He was disobeying his cardiologist's order not to pull weeds. The problem, the doctor says, is not the physical exertion but the emotional stress that weeding inflicts on my father. He has dreams of weeds sprouting from his body, of having to pull them, at the roots, from his chest. He has also been told not to watch Orioles games and not to think about the current administration.

As we weeded, my father made a joke about how my older brother, who, barring a fatal heart attack, was to get married in a few weeks, had already become a yes man. Hearing this felt like having an elephant sit on my chest—my brother, whom I loved more than I loved myself, was surrendering.

"Your grandfather was a yes man," my father added, on his knees, his fingers pushing into the earth, "and your children will be yes men."

I've been thinking about that conversation ever since, and I've come to understand—with a straining heart—that I, too, am becoming a yes man, and that, like my father's and my brother's, my surrender has little to do with the people I say yes to, or with the existence of questions at all. It has to do with a fear of dying, with rehearsal and preparation.

40 ✂ 🕸 The "severed web" is a Barely Tolerable Substitute, whose meaning approximates "I love you," and which can be used in place of "I love you." Other Barely Tolerable Substitutes include, but are not limited to:

→ | ←, which approximates "I love you."
👂 □, which approximates "I love you."
🔒, which approximates "I love you."
✗ ✈, which approximates "I love you."

I don't know how many Barely Tolerable Substitutes there are, but often it feels as if they were everywhere, as if everything that is spoken and done—every "Yup," "Okay," and "I already know," every weed pulled from the lawn, every sexual act— were just Barely Tolerable.

● ● Unlike the colon, which is used to mark a major
● ● division in a sentence, and to indicate that what follows is an elaboration, summation, implication, etc., of what precedes, the "reversible colon" is used when what appears on either side elaborates, summates, implicates, etc., what's on the other side. In other words, the two halves of the sentence explain each other, as in the cases of "Mother::Me," and "Father::Death." Here are some examples of reversible sentences:

My eyes water when I speak about my family::
I don't like to speak about my family.
I've never felt loved by anyone outside of my family::my persistent depression.
1938 to 1945::□.
Sex::yes.
My grandmother's sadness::my mother's sadness::my sadness::the sadness that will come after me.
To be Jewish::to be Jewish.
Heart disease::yes.

← Familial communication always has to do with failures to communicate. It is common that in the course of a conversation one of the participants will not hear something that the other has said. It is also quite common that, one of the participants will not understand what the other has said. Somewhat less common is one participant's saying something whose words the other understands completely but whose meaning is not understood at all. This can happen with very simple sentences, like "I hope that you never love anyone as much as I love you¡"

But, in our best, least, depressing moments, we *try* to understand what we have failed to understand.

A "backup" is used: We start again at the beginning, we replay what was missed and make an effort to hear what was meant instead of what was said:

"It pains me to think of you alone."
"←It pains me to think of me without any grandchildren to love."

{ } A related set of marks, the "should-have brackets," signify words that were not spoken but should have been, as in this dialogue with my father:

"Are you hearing static?"
"{I'm crying into the phone.}"
"Jonathan?"
"□"
"Jonathan⁓"
"■"
"??"
"I::not myself⁓"
"{A child's sadness is a parent's sadness.}"
"(A parent's sadness is a child's sadness.)"
"←"
"I'm probably just tired¡"
"{I never told you this, because I thought it might hurt you, but in my dreams it was *you*. Not me, *You* were pulling the weeds from my chest.}"
"{I want to love and be loved.}"
"☺"
"☺"
"↓"
"↓"
"🔒"
"☺"
"□↔□↔□"
"↓"
"↓"
" ⏭ ○ ⏮"
"■+■→■"
"☺"
"👂□"
"⊠ ⊠"
"◎□❖◆○□◆⊙●"
"■"
"{I love you.}"
"{I love you, too. So much.}"

Of course, my sense of the should-have is unlikely to be the same as my brothers', or my mother's, or my father's. Sometimes—when I'm in the car, or having sex, or talking to one of them on the phone— I imagine their should-have versions. I sew them together into a new life, leaving out everything that actually happened and was said.

1. The "silence mark" is the central item in the story's system of punctuation. In what situations is this mark used, and why do these moments require its use rather than more conventional words and punctuation marks?

2. What does it mean in this story to be a "yes man"?

3. What is the function of the "should have" brackets ({}) in this story?

4. Foer's story uses punctuation marks to represent everything that is understood (at least by one of the speakers) in a family conversation but that has nothing to do with the words actually spoken. In an actual exchange, either face to face or by telephone, how would similar information be imparted?

5. Imagine rewriting the events of this story without using the invented punctuation marks. How would the story be changed?

6. Do you think any family is able to communicate without its own equivalent of what Foer represents via punctuation marks? If you were going to punctuate your own family's relationships, what punctuation marks would you choose?

Alice Walker b. 1944

Born in Eatonton, Georgia, Walker studied at Spelman College in Atlanta and received her BA from Sarah Lawrence College in New York. She worked in the civil rights movement in the South during the 1960s, and has remained an active supporter of a number of progressive causes. Author of some thirty novels, collections of stories, volumes of poetry, and essays, Walker won the Pulitzer Prize and the American Book Award for her best-known work, the novel *The Color Purple* (1982). "Everyday Use" was published in her first collection of short stories, *In Love and Trouble: Stories of a Black Woman,* in 1973.

EVERYDAY USE
For Your Grandmama

I WILL WAIT FOR HER IN THE YARD THAT MAGGIE and I made so clean and wavy yesterday afternoon. A yard like this is more comfortable than most people know. It is not just a yard. It is like an extended living room. When the hard clay is swept clean as a floor and the fine sand around the edges lined with tiny, irregular grooves anyone can come and sit and look up into the elm tree and wait for the breezes that never come inside the house.

Maggie will be nervous until after her sister goes: she will stand hopelessly in corners, homely and ashamed of the burn scars down her arms and legs, eyeing her sister with a mixture of envy and awe. She thinks her sister had held life always in the palm of one hand, that "no" is a word the world never learned to say to her.

You've no doubt seen those TV shows where the child who has "made it" is confronted, as a surprise, by her own mother and father, tottering in weakly from backstage. (A pleasant surprise, of course: What would they do if parent and child came on the show only to curse out and insult each other?) On TV mother and child embrace and smile into each other's faces. Sometimes the mother and father weep, the child wraps them in her arms and leans across the table to tell how she would not have made it without their help. I have seen these programs.

Sometimes I dream a dream in which Dee and I are suddenly brought together on a TV program of this sort. Out of a dark and soft-seated limousine I am ushered into a bright room filled with many people. There I meet a smiling, gray, sporty man like Johnny Carson who shakes my hand and tells me what a fine girl I have. Then we are on the stage and Dee is embracing me with tears in her eyes. She pins on my dress a large orchid, even though she has told me once that she thinks orchids are tacky flowers.

5   In real life I am a large, big-boned woman with rough, man-working hands. In the winter I wear flannel nightgowns to bed and overalls during the day. I can kill and clean a hog as mercilessly as a man. My fat keeps me hot in zero weather. I can work outside all day, breaking ice to get water for washing. I can eat pork liver cooked over the open fire minutes after it comes steaming from the hog. One winter I knocked a bull calf straight in the brain between the eyes with a sledge hammer and had the meat hung up to chill before nightfall. But of course all this does not show on television. I am the way my daughter would want me to be: a hundred pounds lighter, my skin like an uncooked barley pancake. My hair glistens in the hot bright lights. Johnny Carson has much to do to keep up with my quick and witty tongue.

But that is a mistake. I know even before I wake up. Who ever knew a Johnson with a quick tongue? Who can even imagine me looking a strange white man in the eye? It seems to me I have talked to them always with one foot raised in flight, with my head turned in whichever way is farthest from them. Dee, though. She would always look anyone in the eye. Hesitation was no part of her nature.

"How do I look, Mama?" Maggie says, showing just enough of her thin body enveloped in pink skirt and red blouse for me to know she's there, almost hidden by the door.

"Come out into the yard," I say.

Have you ever seen a lame animal, perhaps a dog run over by some careless person rich enough to own a car, sidle up to someone who is ignorant enough to be kind to him? That is the way my Maggie walks. She has been like this, chin on chest, eyes on ground, feet in shuffle, ever since the fire that burned the other house to the ground.

10   Dee is lighter than Maggie, with nicer hair and a fuller figure. She's a woman now, though sometimes I forget. How long ago was it that the other house burned? Ten, twelve years? Sometimes I can still hear the flames and feel Maggie's arms sticking to me, her hair smoking and her dress falling off her in little black papery flakes. Her eyes seemed stretched open, blazed open by the flames reflected in them. And Dee. I see her standing off under the sweet gum tree she used to dig gum out of; a look of

concentration on her face as she watched the last dingy gray board of the house fall in toward the red-hot brick chimney. Why don't you do a dance around the ashes? I'd wanted to ask her. She had hated the house that much.

I used to think she hated Maggie, too. But that was before we raised the money, the church and me, to send her to Augusta to school. She used to read to us without pity; forcing words, lies, other folks' habits, whole lives upon us two, sitting trapped and ignorant underneath her voice. She washed us in a river of make-believe, burned us with a lot of knowledge we didn't necessarily need to know. Pressed us to her with the serious way she read, to shove us away at just the moment, like dimwits, we seemed about to understand.

Dee wanted nice things. A yellow organdy dress to wear to her graduation from high school; black pumps to match a green suit she'd made from an old suit somebody gave me. She was determined to stare down any disaster in her efforts. Her eyelids would not flicker for minutes at a time. Often I fought off the temptation to shake her. At sixteen she had a style of her own: and knew what style was.

I never had an education myself. After second grade the school was closed down. Don't ask me why: in 1927 colored asked fewer questions than they do now. Sometimes Maggie reads to me. She stumbles along goodnaturedly but can't see well. She knows she is not bright. Like good looks and money, quickness passed her by. She will marry John Thomas (who has mossy teeth in an earnest face) and then I'll be free to sit here and I guess just sing church songs to myself. Although I never was a good singer. Never could carry a tune. I was always better at a man's job. I used to love to milk till I was hoofed in the side in '49. Cows are soothing and slow and don't bother you, unless you try to milk them the wrong way.

I have deliberately turned my back on the house. It is three rooms, just like the one that burned, except the roof is tin; they don't make shingle roofs any more. There are no real windows, just some holes cut in the sides, like the portholes in a ship, but not round and not square, with rawhide holding the shutters up on the outside. This house is in a pasture, too, like the other one. No doubt when Dee sees it she will want to tear it down. She wrote me once that no matter where we "choose" to live, she will manage to come see us. But she will never bring her friends. Maggie and I thought about this and Maggie asked me, "Mama, when did Dee ever *have* any friends?"

15 She had a few. Furtive boys in pink shirts hanging about on washday after school. Nervous girls who never laughed. Impressed with her they worshiped the well-turned phrase, the cute shape, the scalding humor that erupted like bubbles in lye. She read to them.

When she was courting Jimmy T she didn't have much time to pay to us, but turned all her faultfinding power on him. He *flew* to marry a cheap gal from a family of ignorant flashy people. She hardly had time to recompose herself.

When she comes I will meet—but there they are!

Maggie attempts to make a dash for the house, in her shuffling way, but I stay her with my hand. "Come back here," I say. And she stops and tries to dig a well in the sand with her toe.

It is hard to see them clearly through the strong sun. But even the first glimpse of leg out of the car tells me it is Dee. Her feet were always neat-looking, as if God himself had shaped them with a certain style. From the other side of the car comes a short, stocky man. Hair is all over his head a foot long and hanging from his chin like a kinky mule tail. I hear Maggie suck in her breath. "Uhnnnh," is what it sounds like. Like when you see the wriggling end of a snake just in front of your foot on the road. "Uhnnnh."

20 Dee next. A dress down to the ground, in this hot weather. A dress so loud it hurts my eyes. There are yellows and oranges enough to throw back the light of the sun. I feel my whole face warming from the heat waves it throws out. Earrings, too, gold and hanging down to her shoulders. Bracelets dangling and making noises when she moves her arm up to shake the folds of the dress out of her armpits. The dress is loose and flows, and as she walks closer, I like it. I hear Maggie go "Uhnnnh" again. It is her sister's hair. It stands straight up like the wool on a sheep. It is black as night and around the edges are two long pigtails that rope about like small lizards disappearing behind her ears.

"Wa-su-zo-Tean-o!" she says, coming on in that gliding way the dress makes her move. The short stocky fellow with the hair to his navel is all grinning and he follows up with "Asalamalakim, my mother and sister!" He moves to hug Maggie but she falls

back, right up against the back of my chair. I feel her trembling there and when I look up I see the perspiration falling off her chin.

"Don't get up," says Dee. Since I am stout it takes something of a push. You can see me trying to move a second or two before I make it. She turns, showing white heels through her sandals, and goes back to the car. Out she peeks next with a Polaroid. She stoops down quickly and lines up picture after picture of me sitting there in front of the house with Maggie cowering behind me. She never takes a shot without making sure the house is included. When a cow comes nibbling around the edge of the yard she snaps it and me and Maggie *and* the house. Then she puts the Polaroid in the back seat of the car, and comes up and kisses me on the forehead.

Meanwhile Asalamalakim is going through the motions with Maggie's hand. Maggie's hand is as limp as a fish, and probably as cold, despite the sweat, and she keeps trying to pull it back. It looks like Asalamalakim wants to shake hands but wants to do it fancy. Or maybe he don't know how people shake hands. Anyhow, he soon gives up on Maggie.

"Well," I say. "Dee."

25 "No, Mama," she says. "Not 'Dee,' Wangero Leewanika Kemanjo!"

"What happened to 'Dee'?" I wanted to know.

"She's dead," Wangero said. "I couldn't bear it any longer, being named after the people who oppress me."

"You know as well as me you was named after your aunt Dicie," I said. Dicie is my sister. She named Dee. We called her "Big Dee" after Dee was born.

"But who was *she* named after?" asked Wangero.

30 "I guess after Grandma Dee," I said.

"And who was she named after?" asked Wangero.

"Her mother," I said, and saw Wangero was getting tired. "That's about as far back as I can trace it," I said. Though, in fact, I probably could have carried it back beyond the Civil War through the branches.

"Well," said Asalamalakim, "there you are."

"Uhnnnh," I heard Maggie say.

35 "There I was not," I said, "before 'Dicie' cropped up in our family, so why should I try to trace it that far back?"

He just stood there grinning, looking down on me like somebody inspecting a Model A car. Every once in a while he and Wangero sent eye signals over my head.

"How do you pronounce this name?" I asked.

"You don't have to call me by it if you don't want to," said Wangero.

"Why shouldn't I?" I asked. "If that's what you want us to call you, we'll call you."

40   "I know it might sound awkward at first," said Wangero.

"I'll get used to it," I said. "Ream it out again."

Well, soon we got the name out of the way. Asalamalakim had a name twice as long and three times as hard. After I tripped over it two or three times he told me to just call him Hakim-a-barber. I wanted to ask him was he a barber, but I didn't really think he was, so I didn't ask.

"You must belong to those beef-cattle peoples down the road," I said. They said "Asalamalakim" when they met you, too, but they didn't shake hands. Always too busy: feeding the cattle, fixing the fences, putting up saltlick shelters, throwing down hay. When the white folks poisoned some of the herd the men stayed up all night with rifles in their hands. I walked a mile and a half just to see the sight.

Hakim-a-barber said, "I accept some of their doctrines, but farming and raising cattle is not my style." (They didn't tell me, and I didn't ask, whether Wangero (Dee) had really gone and married him.)

45   We sat down to eat and right away he said he didn't eat collards and pork was unclean. Wangero, though, went on through the chitlins and corn bread, the greens and everything else. She talked a blue streak over the sweet potatoes. Everything delighted her. Even the fact that we still used the benches her daddy made for the table when we couldn't afford to buy chairs.

"Oh, Mama!" she cried. Then turned to Hakim-a-barber. "I never knew how lovely these benches are. You can feel the rump prints," she said, running her hands underneath her and along the bench. Then she gave a sigh and her hand closed over Grandma Dee's butter dish. "That's it!" she said. "I knew there was something I wanted to ask you if I could have." She jumped up from the table and went over in the corner where the churn stood, the milk in it clabber by now. She looked at the churn and looked at it.

"This churn top is what I need," she said. "Didn't Uncle Buddy whittle it out of a tree you all used to have?"

"Yes," I said.

"Uh huh," she said happily. "And I want the dasher, too."

50   "Uncle Buddy whittle that, too?" asked the barber. Dee (Wangero) looked up at me.

"Aunt Dee's first husband whittled the dash," said Maggie so low you almost couldn't hear her. "His name was Henry, but they called him Stash."

"Maggie's brain is like an elephant's," Wangero said, laughing. "I can use the churn top as a centerpiece for the alcove table," she said, sliding a plate over the churn, "and I'll think of something artistic to do with the dasher."

When she finished wrapping the dasher the handle stuck out. I took it for a moment in my hands. You didn't even have to look close to see where hands pushing the dasher up and down to make butter had left a kind of sink in the wood. In fact, there were a lot of small sinks; you could see where thumbs and fingers had sunk into the wood. It was beautiful light yellow wood, from a tree that grew in the yard where Big Dee and Stash had lived.

55   After dinner Dee (Wangero) went to the trunk at the foot of my bed and started rifling through it. Maggie hung back in the kitchen over the dishpan. Out came Wangero with two quilts. They had been pieced by Grandma Dee and then Big Dee and me had hung them on the quilt frames on the front porch and quilted them. One was in the Lone Star pattern. The other was Walk Around the Mountain. In both of them were scraps of dresses Grandma Dee had worn fifty and more years ago. Bits and pieces of Grandpa Jarrell's paisley shirts. And one teeny faded blue piece, about the size of a penny matchbox, that was from Great Grandpa Ezra's uniform that he wore in the Civil War.

"Mama," Wangero said sweet as a bird. "Can I have these old quilts?"

I heard something fall in the kitchen, and a minute later the kitchen door slammed.

"Why don't you take one or two of the others?" I asked. "These old things was just done by me and Big Dee from some tops your grandma pieced before she died."

"No," said Wangero. "I don't want those. They are stitched around the borders by machine."

60   "That'll make them last better," I said.

"That's not the point," said Wangero. "These are all pieces of dresses Grandma used to wear. She did all this stitching by hand. Imagine!" She held the quilts securely in her arms, stroking them.

"Some of the pieces, like those lavender ones, come from old clothes her mother handed down to her,"

I said, moving up to touch the quilts. Dee (Wangero) moved back just enough so that I couldn't reach the quilts. They already belonged to her.

"Imagine!" she breathed again, clutching them closely to her bosom.

"The truth is," I said, "I promised to give them quilts to Maggie, for when she marries John Thomas."

65   She gasped like a bee had stung her.

"Maggie can't appreciate these quilts!" she said. "She'd probably be backward enough to put them to everyday use."

"I reckon she would," I said. "God knows I been saving 'em for long enough with nobody using 'em. I hope she will!" I didn't want to bring up how I had offered Dee (Wangero) a quilt when she went away to college. Then she had told me they were old-fashioned, out of style.

"But they're *priceless!*" she was saying now, furiously; for she has a temper. "Maggie would put them on the bed and in five years they'd be in rags. Less than that!"

"She can always make some more," I said. "Maggie knows how to quilt."

70   Dee (Wangero) looked at me with hatred. "You just will not understand. The point is these quilts, *these* quilts!"

"Well," I said, stumped. "What would *you* do with them?"

"Hang them," she said. As if that was the only thing you *could* do with quilts.

Maggie by now was standing in the door. I could almost hear the sound her feet made as they scraped over each other.

"She can have them, Mama," she said, like somebody used to never winning anything, or having anything reserved for her. "I can 'member Grandma Dee without the quilts."

75   I looked at her hard. She had filled her bottom lip with checkerberry snuff and it gave her face a kind of dopey, hangdog look. It was Grandma Dee and Big Dee who taught her how to quilt herself. She stood there with her scarred hands hidden in the folds of her skirt. She looked at her sister with something like fear but she wasn't mad at her. This was Maggie's portion. This was the way she knew God to work.

When I looked at her like that something hit me in the top of my head and ran down to the soles of my feet. Just like when I'm in church and the spirit of God touches me and I get happy and shout. I did something I never had done before: hugged Maggie to me, then dragged her on into the room, snatched the quilts out of Miss Wangero's hands and dumped them into Maggie's lap. Maggie just sat there on my bed with her mouth open.

"Take one or two of the others," I said to Dee.

But she turned without a word and went out to Hakim-a-barber.

"You just don't understand," she said, as Maggie and I came out to the car.

80   "What don't I understand?" I wanted to know.

"Your heritage," she said. And then she turned to Maggie, kissed her, and said, "You ought to try to make something of yourself, too, Maggie. It's really a new day for us. But from the way you and Mama still live you'd never know it."

She put on some sunglasses that hid everything above the tip of her nose and her chin.

Maggie smiled; maybe at the sunglasses. But a real smile, not scared. After we watched the car dust settle I asked Maggie to bring me a dip of snuff. And then the two of us sat there just enjoying, until it was time to go in the house and go to bed.

[1973]

QUESTIONS FOR REFLECTION AND DISCUSSION

1. What is the difference between family relationships as portrayed in the TV shows alluded to in the third paragraph and family relationships as portrayed in Walker's story?

2. What do we know about the narrator? What do we know about Maggie? What do we know about Dee?

3. What is Dee's relationship to her family and her ancestors? What is Maggie's relationship? What is the mother's? How does the story's title help to define this relationship?

4. What motivates the mother's gift of the quilts to Maggie? Were you surprised by Dee's reaction? With which character do you identify the most? Why?

5. What does the story's dedication mean? What is its relationship to the story?

POETRY

Robert Hayden 1913–1980

Raised by foster parents in Detroit, Robert Hayden studied at Detroit City College before joining the Federal Writers' Project, where he conducted research on black history and culture. He studied under the poet W. H. Auden while earning an M.A. at the University of Michigan. He taught over two decades at Fisk University, afterward returning to teach at Michigan. From 1976 to 1978, he was Consultant in Poetry to the Library of Congress (the post that would later be renamed Poet Laureate). Hayden published ten volumes of poetry between 1940 and the time of his death. "Those Winter Sundays" was published in *A Ballad of Remembrance* in 1962.

Those Winter Sundays

Sundays too my father got up early
And put his clothes on in the blueback cold,
then with cracked hands that ached
from labor in the weekday weather made   5
banked fires blaze. No one ever thanked him.

I'd wake and hear the cold splintering, breaking.
When the rooms were warm, he'd call,
and slowly I would rise and dress,
fearing the chronic angers of that house,

Speaking indifferently to him,   10
who had driven out the cold
and polished my good shoes as well.
What did I know, what did I know
of love's austere and lonely offices?

[1962]

QUESTIONS FOR REFLECTION AND DISCUSSION

1. In what ways can this fourteen-line poem be considered a sonnet (p. 127)? In what ways does it not resemble a traditional sonnet?

2. Why is it important that the poem is set on a Sunday?

3. How would you characterize the relationship between the speaker and his father? Has the speaker's sense of the relationship changed since the time in which the poem is set?

Lucille Clifton b. 1936

Born in Depew, New York, and raised in Buffalo, Thelma Lucille Sayres attended Howard University and Fredonia State Teachers College. Here, she met her future husband, Fred Clifton, a philosophy professor at the University of Buffalo, with whom she had six children. As a result of an award selected by Robert Hayden (above) she published her first poetry collection, *Good Times*, in 1969. Three of her poetry volumes have been nominated for the Pulitzer Prize; *Blessing the Boats: New and Selected Poems, 1988–2000* (2000) received a National Book Award. "wishes for sons" was published in the collection *Quilting* in 1991.

wishes for sons

i wish them cramps.
i wish them a strange town
and the last tampon.
i wish them no 7-11.

i wish them one week early   5
and wearing a white skirt.
i wish them one week late.

later i wish them hot flashes
and clots like you
wouldn't believe. let the
flashes come when they
meet someone special.
let the clots come
when they want to.

let them think they have accepted   15
arrogance in the universe,
then bring them to gynecologists
not unlike themselves.

[1990]

Kitty Tsui b. 1953

Kitty Tsui was born in Hong Kong, grew up there and in England, and moved to the United States with her family in 1968. One of the first writers to address directly the combined pressures of an Asian-American and a lesbian identity, Tsui is the author of several works of fiction and poetry, including the fittingly titled 1983 collection *The Words of a Woman Who Breathes Fire*, where "A Chinese Banquet" was published.

A Chinese Banquet

for the one who was not invited

it was not a very formal affair but
all the women over twelve
wore long gowns and a corsage
except for me.

it was not a very formal affair, just   5
the family getting together,
poa poa, kuw fu without *kuw mow*°
(her excuse this year is a headache).

aunts and uncles and cousins,
the grandson who is a dentist,   10
the one who drives a mercedes benz,
sitting down for shark's fin soup.

7 *Poa poa:* maternal grandmother. *kuw fuw:* uncle. *kuw mow:* aunt.

Conflicting traditions: A scene from Ang Lee's 1993 comedy-drama *The Wedding Banquet,* in which a gay Asian American man tries to placate his parents by staging a marriage with a mainland Chinese woman who needs a green card. Here, as the banquet gets raucous, the reluctant couple submits to an undignified and bawdy variation of bobbing for apples.

they talk about buying a house and
taking a two week vacation in Beijing.
i suck on shrimp and squab,   15
dreaming of the cloudscape in your eyes.

my mother, her voice beaded with sarcasm;
you're twenty-six and not getting younger.
it's about time you got a decent job.
she no longer asks when i'm getting married.   20

you're twenty-six and not getting younger.
what are you doing with your life?
you've got to make a living.
why don't you study computer programming?

she no longer asks when i'm getting married.   25
one day, wanting desperately to
bridge the boundaries that separate us,
wanting desperately to touch her,

tell her: mother, i'm gay,
mother i'm gay and so happy with her.   30
but she will not listen,
she shakes her head.

she sits across from me,
emotions invading her face.

her eyes are wet but   35
she will not let tears fall.

mother, i say,
you love a man.
i love a woman.
it is not what she wants to hear.   40

aunts and uncles and cousins,
very much a family affair.
but you are not invited,
being neither my husband nor my wife.

aunts and uncles and cousins
eating longevity noodles   45
fragrant with ham inquire:
sold that old car of yours yet?

i want to tell them: my back is healing,
i dream of dragons and water.   50
my home is in her arms,
our bedroom ceiling the wide open sky.

                                        [1983]

QUESTIONS FOR REFLECTION AND DISCUSSION

1. What are some of the reasons why Tsui might have chosen the scene of a wedding banquet as the setting for her poem?

2. What is the effect of using Chinese terms for family members in line 7? Does the poem give us any clues as to the real reason the aunt does not attend these banquets? What might have motivated Tsui to include this detail about the aunt?

3. Why do you think Tsui chose to focus the poem on the speaker's mother rather than on her father?

4. What imagery does the speaker use to characterize her family members at the banquet? What imagery does she use to characterize her family at "home"? Based on evidence in the poem, to what degree does she consider herself part of each of these families?

PLAY

William Shakespeare 1564–1616

Shakespeare's thirty-eight plays are the most performed pieces of theater in the world, and their characters, plots, and speeches are part of English-language culture. Written between 1599 and 1601, *Hamlet* belongs to the period of the other major tragedies. Like many of Shakespeare's plays, it borrows its plot from an earlier source, but completely transforms that source for the playwright's own purpose. *Hamlet* is among the most performed of Shakespeare's plays, and its language, situations, and themes profoundly influenced modern conceptions of literature and society.

HAMLET, PRINCE OF DENMARK

DRAMATIS PERSONAE

Ghost of Hamlet, the former King of Denmark
Claudius, King of Denmark, the former King's brother
Gertrude, Queen of Denmark, widow of the former
    King and now wife of Claudius
Hamlet, Prince of Denmark, son of the late King and of
    Gertrude

Polonius, councillor to the King
Laertes, his son
Ophelia, his daughter
Reynaldo, his servant

Horatio, Hamlet's friend and fellow student

Voltimand,
Cornelius,
Rosencrantz,
Guildenstern, } members of the Danish court
Osric,
A Gentleman,
A Lord,

Bernardo,
Francisco, } officers and soldiers on watch
Marcellus,

Fortinbras, Prince of Norway
Captain in his army

Three or Four PLAYERS, taking the roles of PROLOGUE,
    PLAYER KING, PLAYER QUEEN, and LUCIANUS
Two MESSENGERS
FIRST SAILOR
Two CLOWNS, a gravedigger and his companion
PRIEST
FIRST AMBASSADOR from England

Lords, Soldiers, Attendants, Guards, other Players,
    Followers of Laertes, other Sailors, another Ambassador
    or Ambassadors from England
Scene: Denmark

[1-1]

Enter Bernardo and Francisco, two sentinels, [meeting].

Bernardo: Who's there?

Francisco:

Nay, answer me. Stand and unfold yourself.   2

Bernardo: Long live the King!

Francisco: Bernardo?

Bernardo: He.

Francisco:

You come most carefully upon your hour.

Bernardo:

'Tis now struck twelve. Get thee to bed, Francisco.

Francisco:

For this relief much thanks. 'Tis bitter cold,

And I am sick at heart.

Bernardo: Have you had quiet guard?

Francisco: Not a mouse stirring.

Bernardo: Well, good night.

If you do meet Horatio and Marcellus,

The rivals of my watch, bid them make haste.   14

1-1 Location: Elsinore castle. A guard platform.
2 me (Francisco emphasizes that *he* is the sentry currently on watch.)
unfold yourself reveal your identity **14 rivals** partners

Enter Horatio and Marcellus.

Francisco:

I think I hear them.—Stand, ho! Who is there?

Vaneshran Arumugam as Hamlet and John Kani as the Ghost at the Swan
Theatre, Stratford-upon-Avon, May 2006.

Horatio: Friends to this ground. 16

Marcellus: And liegemen to the Dane. 17

Francisco: Give you good night. 18

Marcellus:

Oh, farewell, honest soldier. Who hath relieved you?

Francisco:

Bernardo hath my place. Give you good night.

Exit Francisco.

Marcellus: Holla! Bernardo!

Bernardo: Say, what, is Horatio there?

Horatio: A piece of him.

Bernardo:

Welcome, Horatio. Welcome, good Marcellus.

Horatio:

What, has this thing appeared again tonight?

Bernardo: I have seen nothing.

Marcellus:

Horatio says 'tis but our fantasy, 27

And will not let belief take hold of him

Touching this dreaded sight twice seen of us.

Therefore I have entreated him along 30

With us to watch the minutes of this night, 31

That if again this apparition come

He may approve our eyes and speak to it. 33

Horatio:

Tush, tush, 'twill not appear.

Bernardo: Sit down awhile

And let us once again assail your ears,

That are so fortified against our story,

What we have two nights seen.

Horatio: Well, sit we down,

And let us hear Bernardo speak of this.

Bernardo: Last night of all, 39

When yond same star that's westward from the pole 40

Had made his course t'illume that part of heaven 41

Where now it burns, Marcellus and myself,

The bell then beating one—

Enter Ghost.

Marcellus:

Peace, break thee off! Look where it comes again!

Bernardo:

In the same figure like the King that's dead.

Marcellus:

Thou art a scholar. Speak to it, Horatio. 46

Bernardo:

Looks 'a not like the King? Mark it, Horatio. 47

Horatio:

Most like. It harrows me with fear and wonder.

Bernardo:

It would be spoke to.

Marcellus: Speak to it, Horatio. 49

Horatio:

What art thou that usurp'st this time of night, 50

Together with that fair and warlike form

In which the majesty of buried Denmark 52

Did sometimes march? By heaven, I charge thee, speak! 53

Marcellus:

It is offended.

Bernardo: See, it stalks away.

Horatio:

Stay! Speak, speak! I charge thee, speak! *Exit Ghost.*

Marcellus: 'Tis gone and will not answer.

Bernardo:

How now, Horatio? You tremble and look pale.

Is not this something more than fantasy?

What think you on't? 59

Horatio:

Before my God, I might not this believe

Without the sensible and true avouch 61

Of mine own eyes.

Marcellus: Is it not like the King?

Horatio: As thou art to thyself.

Such was the very armor he had on

When he the ambitious Norway combated. 65

So frowned he once when, in an angry parle, 66

He smote the sledded Polacks on the ice. 67

'Tis strange.

Marcellus:

Thus twice before, and jump at this dead hour, 69

With martial stalk hath he gone by our watch. 70

Horatio:

In what particular thought to work I know not, 71

16 **ground** country, land 17 **liegemen to the Dane** men sworn to serve the Danish king 18 **Give** May God give 27 **fantasy** imagination 30 **along** to come along 31 **watch** keep watch during 33 **approve** corroborate 39 **Last . . . all** i.e., This *very* last night. (Emphatic.) 40 **pole** polestar, north star 41 **his** its. **t'illume** to illuminate

46 **scholar** one learned enough to know how to question a ghost properly 47 **'a** he 49 **It . . . to** (It was commonly believed that a ghost could not speak until spoken to.) 50 **usurp'st** wrongfully takes over 52 **buried Denmark** the buried King of Denmark 53 **sometimes** formerly 59 **on't** of it. 61 **sensible** confirmed by the senses. **avouch** warrant, evidence 65 **Norway** King of Norway 66 **parle** parley 67 **sledded** traveling on sleds. **Polacks** Poles 69 **jump** exactly 70 **stalk** stride 71 **to work** i.e., to collect my thoughts and try to understand this

But in the gross and scope of mine opinion 72

This bodes some strange eruption to our state.

Marcellus:

Good now, sit down, and tell me, he that knows, 74

Why this same strict and most observant watch

So nightly toils the subject of the land, 76

And why such daily cast of brazen cannon 77

And foreign mart for implements of war, 78

Why such impress of shipwrights, whose sore task 79

Does not divide the Sunday from the week.

What might be toward, that this sweaty haste 81

Doth make the night joint-laborer with the day?

Who is't that can inform me?

Horatio: That can I;

At least, the whisper goes so. Our last king,

Whose image even but now appeared to us,

Was, as you know, by Fortinbras of Norway,

Thereto pricked on by a most emulate pride, 87

Dared to the combat; in which our valiant Hamlet—

For so this side of our known world esteemed him— 89

Did slay this Fortinbras; who by a sealed compact 90

Well ratified by law and heraldry 91

Did forfeit, with his life, all those his lands

Which he stood seized of, to the conqueror; 93

Against the which a moiety competent 94

Was gagèd by our king, which had returned 95

To the inheritance of Fortinbras 96

Had he been vanquisher, as, by the same cov'nant 97

And carriage of the article designed, 98

His fell to Hamlet. Now, sir, young Fortinbras,

Of unimprovèd mettle hot and full, 100

Hath in the skirts of Norway here and there 101

Sharked up a list of lawless resolutes 102

For food and diet to some enterprise 103

That hath a stomach in't, which is no other— 104

As it doth well appear unto our state—

But to recover of us, by strong hand

And terms compulsatory, those foresaid lands

So by his father lost. And this, I take it,

Is the main motive of our preparations,

The source of this our watch, and the chief head 110

Of this posthaste and rummage in the land. 111

Bernardo:

I think it be no other but e'en so.

Well may it sort that this portentous figure 113

Comes armèd through our watch so like the King

That was and is the question of these wars. 115

Horatio:

A mote it is to trouble the mind's eye. 116

In the most high and palmy state of Rome, 117

A little ere the mightiest Julius fell, 118

The graves stood tenantless, and the sheeted dead 119

Did squeak and gibber in the Roman streets;

As stars with trains of fire and dews of blood, 121

Disasters in the sun; and the moist star 122

Upon whose influence Neptune's empire stands 123

Was sick almost to doomsday with eclipse. 124

And even the like precurse of feared events, 125

As harbingers preceding still the fates 126

And prologue to the omen coming on, 127

Have heaven and earth together demonstrated

Unto our climatures and countrymen. 129

Enter Ghost.

But soft, behold! Lo, where it comes again! 130

I'll cross it, though it blast me. (*It spreads his arms.*)

     Stay, illusion! 131

If thou hast any sound or use of voice,

Speak to me!

If there be any good thing to be done

That may to thee do ease and grace to me,

Speak to me!

If thou art privy to thy country's fate, 137

---

72 gross and scope general drift **74 Good now** (An expression denoting entreaty or expostulation.) **76 toils** causes to toil. **subject** subjects **77 cast** casting **78 mart** shopping **79 impress** impressment, conscription **81 toward** in preparation **87 Thereto ... pride** (Refers to old Fortinbras, not the Danish King.) **pricked on** incited. **emulate** emulous, ambitious **89 this ... world** i.e., all Europe, the Western world **90 sealed** certified, confirmed **91 heraldry** chivalry **93 seized** possessed **94 Against the** in return for. **moiety competent** corresponding portion **95 gagèd** engaged, pledged. **had returned** would have passed **96 inheritance** possession **97 cov'nant** i.e., the *sealed compact* of line 90 **98 carriage ... designed** purport of the article referred to **100 unimprovèd mettle** untried, undisciplined spirits **101 skirts** outlying regions, outskirts **102–4 Sharked ... in't** rounded up (as a shark scoops up fish) a troop of lawless desperadoes to feed and supply an enterprise of considerable daring

110 head source **111 posthaste and rummage** frenetic activity and bustle **113 Well ... sort** That would explain why **115 question** focus of contention **116 mote** speck of dust **117 palmy** flourishing **118 Julius** Julius Caesar **119 sheeted** shrouded **121 As** (This abrupt transition suggests that matter is possibly omitted between lines 120 and 121.) **trains** trails **122 Disasters** unfavorable signs or aspects. **moist star** i.e., moon, governing tides **123 Neptune's ... stands** the sea depends **124 Was ... eclipse** was eclipsed nearly to the cosmic darkness predicted for the second coming of Christ and the ending of the world. (See Matthew 24:29 and Revelation 6:12.) **125 precurse** heralding, foreshadowing **126 harbingers** forerunners. **still** always **127 omen** calamitous event **129 climatures** climes, regions **130 soft** i.e., enough, break off **131 cross** stand in its path, confront. **blast** wither, strike with a curse. **131 s.d.** *his* its **137 privy to** in on the secret of

Which, happily, foreknowing may avoid,   138

Oh, speak!

Or if thou hast uphoarded in thy life

Extorted treasure in the womb of earth,

For which, they say, you spirits oft walk in death,

Speak of it! *(The cock crows.)* Stay and speak!—Stop it,

Marcellus.

Marcellus:

Shall I strike at it with my partisan?   144

Horatio: Do, if it will not stand.   [*They strike at it.*]

Bernardo: 'Tis here!   146

Horatio: 'Tis here!   [*Exit Ghost.*] 147

Marcellus: 'Tis gone.

We do it wrong, being so majestical,

To offer it the show of violence,

For it is as the air invulnerable,

And our vain blows malicious mockery.

Bernardo:

It was about to speak when the cock crew.

Horatio:

And then it started like a guilty thing

Upon a fearful summons. I have heard

The cock, that is the trumpet to the morn,   156

Doth with his lofty and shrill-sounding throat

Awake the god of day, and at his warning,

Whether in sea or fire, in earth or air,

Th'extravagant and erring spirit hies   160

To his confine; and of the truth herein

This present object made probation.   162

Marcellus:

It faded on the crowing of the cock.

Some say that ever 'gainst that season comes   164

Wherein our Savior's birth is celebrated,

This bird of dawning singeth all night long,

And then, they say, no spirit dare stir abroad;

The nights are wholesome, then no planets strike,   168

No fairy takes, nor witch hath power to charm,   169

So hallowed and so gracious is that time.   170

Horatio:

So have I heard and do in part believe it.

But, look, the morn in russet mantle clad   172

Walks o'er the dew of yon high eastward hill.

Break we our watch up, and by my advice

Let us impart what we have seen tonight

Unto young Hamlet; for upon my life,

This spirit, dumb to us, will speak to him.

Do you consent we shall acquaint him with it,

As needful in our loves, fitting our duty?

Marcellus:

Let's do't, I pray, and I this morning know

Where we shall find him most conveniently.

> *Exeunt.*

[1-2]

Flourish. Enter Claudius, King of Denmark, Gertrude the Queen, [the] Council, as Polonius and his son Laertes, Hamlet, cum aliis [including Voltimand and Cornelius].

King:

Though yet of Hamlet our dear brother's death   1

The memory be green, and that it us befitted

To bear our hearts in grief and our whole kingdom

To be contracted in one brow of woe,

Yet so far hath discretion fought with nature

That we with wisest sorrow think on him

Together with remembrance of ourselves.

Therefore our sometime sister, now our queen,   8

Th'imperial jointress to this warlike state,   9

Have we, as 'twere with a defeated joy—

With an auspicious and a dropping eye,   11

With mirth in funeral and with dirge in marriage,

In equal scale weighing delight and dole—   13

Taken to wife. Nor have we herein barred

Your better wisdoms, which have freely gone

With this affair along. For all, our thanks.

Now follows that you know young Fortinbras,   17

Holding a weak supposal of our worth,   18

Or thinking by our late dear brother's death

Our state to be disjoint and out of frame,   20

Co-leaguèd with this dream of his advantage,   21

---

172 **russet** reddish brown
1-2 **Location:** The castle.
0.2 **as** i.e., such as, including. 0.3 *cum aliis* with others 1 **our** my. (The royal "we"; also in the following lines.) 8 **sometime** former
9 **jointress** woman possessing property with her husband 11 **With . . . eye** with one eye smiling and the other weeping 13 **dole** grief
17 **Now . . . know** Next, you need to be informed that 18 **weak supposal** low estimate 20 **disjoint . . . frame** in a state of total disorder
21 **Co-leaguèd . . . advantage** joined to his illusory sense of having the advantage over us and to his vision of future success

138 **happily** haply, perchance 144 **partisan** long-handled spear.
146–7 **'Tis Here! / 'Tis here!** (Perhaps they attempt to strike at the Ghost, but are baffled by its seeming ability to be here and there and nowhere.) 156 **trumpet** trumpeter 160 **extravagant and erring** wandering beyond bounds. (The words have similar meaning.) **hies** hastens 162 **probation** proof. 164 **'gainst** just before 168 **strike** destroy by evil influence 169 **takes** bewitches. **charm** cast a spell, control by enchantment 170 **gracious** full of grace

He hath not failed to pester us with message

Importing the surrender of those lands   23

Lost by his father, with all bonds of law,   24

To our most valiant brother. So much for him.

Now for ourself and for this time of meeting.

Thus much the business is: we have here writ

To Norway, uncle of young Fortinbras—

Who, impotent and bed-rid, scarcely hears   29

Of this his nephew's purpose—to suppress

His further gait herein, in that the levies,   31

The lists, and full proportions are all made   32

Out of his subject; and we here dispatch   33

You, good Cornelius, and you, Voltimand,

For bearers of this greeting to old Norway,

Giving to you no further personal power

To business with the King more than the scope

Of these dilated articles allow.   [*He gives a paper.*]   38

Farewell, and let your haste commend your duty.   39

Cornelius, Voltimand:

In that, and all things, will we show our duty.

King:

We doubt it nothing. Heartily farewell.   41

              [*Exeunt Voltimand and Cornelius.*]

And now, Laertes, what's the news with you?

You told us of some suit; what is't, Laertes?

You cannot speak of reason to the Dane   44

And lose your voice. What wouldst thou

   beg, Laertes,   45

That shall not be my offer, not thy asking?

The head is not more native to the heart,   47

The hand more instrumental to the mouth,   48

Than is the throne of Denmark to thy father.

What wouldst thou have, Laertes?

Laertes: My dread lord,

Your leave and favor to return to France,   51

From whence though willingly I came to Denmark

To show my duty in your coronation,

Yet now I must confess, that duty done,

My thoughts and wishes bend again toward France

And bow them to your gracious leave and pardon.   56

King:

Have you your father's leave? What says Polonius?

Polonius:

H'ath, my lord, wrung from me my slow leave   58

By laborsome petition, and at last

Upon his will I sealed my hard consent.   60

I do beseech you, give him leave to go.

King:

Take thy fair hour, Laertes. Time be thine,   62

And thy best graces spend it at thy will.   63

But now, my cousin Hamlet, and my son—   64

Hamlet:

A little more than kin, and less than kind.   65

King:

How is it that the clouds still hang on you?

Hamlet:

Not so, my lord. I am too much in the sun.   67

Queen:

Good Hamlet, cast thy nighted color off,   68

And let thine eye look like a friend on Denmark.   69

Do not forever with thy vailèd lids   70

Seek for thy noble father in the dust.

Thou know'st 'tis common, all that lives must die,   72

Passing through nature to eternity.

Hamlet:

Ay, madam, it is common.

Queen: If it be,

Why seems it so particular with thee?   75

Hamlet:

Seems, madam? Nay, it is. I know not "seems."

'Tis not alone my inky cloak, good mother,

Nor customary suits of solemn black,   78

Nor windy suspiration of forced breath,   79

No, nor the fruitful river in the eye,   80

Nor the dejected havior of the visage,   81

Together with all forms, moods, shapes of grief,   82

That can denote me truly. These indeed seem,

For they are actions that a man might play.

23 Importing having for its substance **24 with . . . law** (See 1.1.91, "Well ratified by law and heraldry.") **29 impotent** helpless **31 His** i.e., Fortinbras'. **gait** proceeding **31–3 in that . . . subject** since the levying of troops and supplies is drawn entirely from the King of Norway's own subjects **38 dilated** set out at length **39 let . . . duty** let your swift obeying of orders, rather than mere words, express your dutifulness. **41 nothing** not at all. **44 the Dane** the Danish king **45 lose your voice** waste your speech. **47 native** closely connected, related **48 instrumental** serviceable **51 leave and favor** kind permission **56 bow . . . pardon** entreatingly make a deep bow, asking your permission to depart.

58 H'ath He has **60 sealed** (as if sealing a legal document). **hard** reluctant **62 Take thy fair hour** Enjoy your time of youth **63 And . . . will** and may your time be spent in exercising your best qualities. **64 cousin** any kin not of the immediate family **65 A little . . . kind** Too close a blood relation, and yet we are less than kinsmen in that our relationship lacks affection and is indeed unnatural. (Hamlet plays on *kind* as [1] kindly [2] belonging to nature, suggesting that Claudius is not the same kind of being as the rest of humanity. The line is often delivered as an aside, though it need not be.) **67 the sun** i.e., the sunshine of the King's royal favor. (With pun on *son*.) **68 nighted color** (1) mourning garments of black (2) dark melancholy **69 Denmark** the King of Denmark. **70 vailèd lids** lowered eyes **72 common** of universal occurrence. (But Hamlet plays on the sense of "vulgar" in line 74.) **75 particular** personal **78 customary** customary to mourning **79 suspiration** sighing **80 fruitful** abundant **81 havior** expression **82 moods** outward expression of feeling

But I have that within which passes show;

These but the trappings and the suits of woe.

King:

'Tis sweet and commendable in your nature, Hamlet,

To give these mourning duties to your father.

But you must know your father lost a father,

That father lost, lost his, and the survivor bound

In filial obligation for some term

To do obsequious sorrow. But to persever   92

In obstinate condolement is a course   93

Of impious stubbornness. 'Tis unmanly grief.

It shows a will most incorrect to heaven,

A heart unfortified, a mind impatient,   96

An understanding simple and unschooled.   97

For what we know must be and is as common

As any the most vulgar thing to sense,   99

Why should we in our peevish opposition

Take it to heart? Fie, 'tis a fault to heaven,

A fault against the dead, a fault to nature,

To reason most absurd, whose common theme

Is death of fathers, and who still hath cried,   104

From the first corpse till he that died today,   105

"This must be so." We pray you, throw to earth

This unprevailing woe and think of us   107

As of a father; for let the world take note,

You are the most immediate to our throne,   109

And with no less nobility of love

Than that which dearest father bears his son

Do I impart toward you. For your intent   112

In going back to school in Wittenberg,   113

It is most retrograde to our desire,   114

And we beseech you bend you to remain   115

Here in the cheer and comfort of our eye,

Our chiefest courtier, cousin, and our son.

Queen:

Let not thy mother lose her prayers, Hamlet.

I pray thee, stay with us, go not to Wittenberg.

Hamlet:

I shall in all my best obey you, madam.   120

King:

Why, 'tis a loving and a fair reply.

Be as ourself in Denmark. Madam, come.

This gentle and unforced accord of Hamlet

Sits smiling to my heart, in grace whereof   124

No jocund health that Denmark drinks today   125

But the great cannon to the clouds shall tell,

And the King's rouse the heaven shall bruit again,   127

Respeaking earthly thunder. Come away.   128

Flourish. Exeunt all but Hamlet.

Hamlet:

Oh, that this too too sullied flesh would melt,   129

Thaw, and resolve itself into a dew!

Or that the Everlasting had not fixed

His canon 'gainst self-slaughter! Oh, God, God,   132

How weary, stale, flat, and unprofitable

Seem to me all the uses of this world!

Fie on't, ah, fie! 'Tis an unweeded garden

That grows to seed. Things rank and gross in nature

Possess it merely. That it should come to this!   137

But two months dead—nay, not so much, not two.

So excellent a king, that was to this   139

Hyperion to a satyr, so loving to my mother   140

That he might not beteem the winds of heaven   141

Visit her face too roughly. Heaven and earth,

Must I remember? Why, she would hang on him

As if increase of appetite had grown

By what it fed on, and yet within a month—

Let me not think on't; frailty, thy name is woman!—

A little month, or ere those shoes were old   147

With which she followed my poor father's body,

Like Niobe, all tears, why she, even she—   149

Oh, God, a beast, that wants discourse of reason,   150

Would have mourned longer—married with my uncle,

My father's brother, but no more like my father

Than I to Hercules. Within a month,

Ere yet the salt of most unrighteous tears

Had left the flushing in her gallèd eyes,   155

She married. Oh, most wicked speed, to post   156

124 to i.e., at. **grace** thanksgiving **125 jocund** merry **127 rouse** drinking of a draft of liquor. **bruit again** loudly echo **128 thunder** i.e., of trumpet and kettledrum, sounded when the King drinks; see 1.4.8-12. **129 sullied** defiled. (The early quartos read "sallied"; the Folio, "solid.") **132 canon** law **137 merely** completely. **139 to** in comparison to **140 Hyperion** Titan sun-god, father of Helios. **satyr** a lecherous creature of classical mythology, half-human but with a goat's legs, tail, ears, and horns **141 beteem** allow **147 or ere** even before **149 Niobe** Tantalus's daughter, Queen of Thebes, who boasted that she had more sons and daughters than Leto; for this, Apollo and Artemis, children of Leto, slew her fourteen children. She was turned by Zeus into a stone that continually dropped tears. **150 wants . . . reason** lacks the faculty of reason **155 gallèd** irritated, inflamed **156 post** hasten

92 obsequious suited to obsequies or funerals **93 condolement** sorrowing **96 unfortified** i.e., against adversity **97 simple** ignorant **99 As . . . sense** as the most ordinary experience **104 still** always **105 the first corpse** (Abel's) **107 unprevailing** unavailing, useless **109 most immediate** next in succession **112 impart toward** liberally bestow on. **For** As for **113 to school** i.e., to your studies. **Wittenberg** famous German university where Luther posted his 95 theses in 1517 **114 retrograde** contrary **115 bend you** incline yourself **120 in all my best** to the best of my ability

With such dexterity to incestuous sheets!   157

It is not, nor it cannot come to good.

But break, my heart, for I must hold my tongue.

Enter Horatio, Marcellus, and Bernardo.

Horatio:

Hail to Your Lordship!

Hamlet: I am glad to see you well.

Horatio!—or I do forget myself.

Horatio:

The same, my lord, and your poor servant ever.

Hamlet:

Sir, my good friend; I'll change that name with you.   163

And what make you from Wittenberg, Horatio?—   164

Marcellus.

Marcellus: My good lord.

Hamlet:

I am very glad to see you. [*To Bernardo*] Good even, sir.—

But what in faith make you from Wittenberg?

Horatio:

A truant disposition, good my lord.

Hamlet:

I would not hear your enemy say so,

Nor shall you do my ear that violence

To make it truster of your own report   172

Against yourself. I know you are no truant.

But what is your affair in Elsinore?

We'll teach you to drink deep ere you depart.

Horatio:

My lord, I came to see your father's funeral.

Hamlet:

I prithee, do not mock me, fellow student;

I think it was to see my mother's wedding.

Horatio:

Indeed, my lord, it followed hard upon.   179

Hamlet:

Thrift, thrift, Horatio! The funeral baked meats   180

Did coldly furnish forth the marriage tables.   181

Would I had met my dearest foe in heaven   182

Or ever I had seen that day, Horatio!   183

My father!—Methinks I see my father.

Horatio:

Where, my lord?

Hamlet: In my mind's eye, Horatio.

Horatio:

I saw him once. 'A was a goodly king.   186

Hamlet:

'A was a man. Take him for all in all,

I shall not look upon his like again.

Horatio:

My lord, I think I saw him yesternight.

Hamlet: Saw? Who?

Horatio: My lord, the King your father.

Hamlet: The King my father?

Horatio:

Season your admiration for a while   193

With an attent ear till I may deliver,   194

Upon the witness of these gentlemen,

This marvel to you.

Hamlet: For God's love, let me hear!

Horatio:

Two nights together had these gentlemen,

Marcellus and Bernardo, on their watch,

In the dead waste and middle of the night,   199

Been thus encountered. A figure like your father,

Armèd at point exactly, cap-à-pie,   201

Appears before them, and with solemn march

Goes slow and stately by them. Thrice he walked

By their oppressed and fear-surprisèd eyes

Within his truncheon's length, whilst they, distilled   205

Almost to jelly with the act of fear,   206

Stand dumb and speak not to him. This to me

In dreadful secrecy impart they did,   208

And I with them the third night kept the watch,

Where, as they had delivered, both in time,

Form of the thing, each word made true and good,

The apparition comes. I knew your father;

These hands are not more like.

Hamlet: But where was this?

Marcellus:

My lord, upon the platform where we watch.

Hamlet:

Did you not speak to it?

Horatio: My lord, I did,

But answer made it none. Yet once methought

It lifted up it head and did address   217

Itself to motion, like as it would speak;   218

157 **incestuous** (In Shakespeare's day, the marriage of a man like Claudius to his deceased brother's wife was considered incestuous.) 163 **change that name** i.e., give and receive reciprocally the name of "friend" rather than talk of "servant." Or Hamlet may be saying, "No, I am *your* servant." 164 **make you from** are you doing away from 172 **To . . . of** to make it trust 179 **hard** close 180 **baked meats** meat pies 181 **coldly** i.e., as cold leftovers 182 **dearest** closest (and therefore deadliest) 183 **Or ever** ere, before

186 **'A** He 193 **Season your admiration** Moderate your astonishment 194 **attent** attentive 199 **dead waste** desolate stillness 201 **at point** correctly in every detail. **cap-à-pie** from head to foot 205 **truncheon** officer's staff. **distilled** dissolved 206 **act** action, operation 208 **dreadful** full of dread 217 **it** its 217–18 **did . . . speak** prepared to move as though it was about to speak

But even then the morning cock crew loud,   219

And at the sound it shrunk in haste away

And vanished from our sight.

Hamlet: 'Tis very strange.

Horatio:

As I do live, my honored lord, 'tis true,

And we did think it writ down in our duty

To let you know of it.

Hamlet:

Indeed, indeed, sirs. But this troubles me.

Hold you the watch tonight?

All: We do, my lord.

Hamlet: Armed, say you?

All: Armed, my lord.

Hamlet: From top to toe?

All: My lord, from head to foot.

Hamlet: Then saw you not his face?

Horatio:

Oh, yes, my lord, he wore his beaver up.   232

Hamlet: What looked he, frowningly?   233

Horatio:

A countenance more in sorrow than in anger.

Hamlet: Pale or red?

Horatio: Nay, very pale.

Hamlet: And fixed his eyes upon you?

Horatio: Most constantly.

Hamlet: I would I had been there.

Horatio: It would have much amazed you.

Hamlet: Very like, very like. Stayed it long?

Horatio:

While one with moderate haste might tell a hundred.   242

Marcellus, Bernardo: Longer, longer.

Horatio: Not when I saw't.

Hamlet: His beard was grizzled—no?

Horatio:

It was, as I have seen it in his life,

A sable silvered.

Hamlet: I will watch tonight.

Perchance 'twill walk again.

Horatio: I warr'nt it will.

Hamlet:

If it assume my noble father's person,

I'll speak to it though hell itself should gape

And bid me hold my peace. I pray you all,

If you have hitherto concealed this sight,

Let it be tenable in your silence still,   253

And whatsomever else shall hap tonight,

Give it an understanding but no tongue.

I will requite your loves. So, fare you well.

Upon the platform twixt eleven and twelve

I'll visit you.

All: Our duty to Your Honor.

Hamlet:

Your loves, as mine to you. Farewell.   259

Exeunt [all but Hamlet].

My father's spirit in arms! All is not well.

I doubt some foul play. Would the night were come!   261

Till then sit still, my soul. Foul deeds will rise,

Though all the earth o'erwhelm them, to men's eyes.

Exit.

♣

[1-3]

Enter Laertes and Ophelia, his sister.

Laertes:

My necessaries are embarked. Farewell.

And, sister, as the winds give benefit

And convoy is assistant, do not sleep   3

But let me hear from you.

Ophelia: Do you doubt that?

Laertes:

For Hamlet, and the trifling of his favor,   5

Hold it a fashion and a toy in blood,   6

A violet in the youth of primy nature,   7

Forward, not permanent, sweet, not lasting,   8

The perfume and suppliance of a minute—   9

No more.

Ophelia: No more but so?

Laertes: Think it no more.

For nature crescent does not grow alone   11

In thews and bulk, but as this temple waxes   12

The inward service of the mind and soul   13

Grows wide withal. Perhaps he loves you now,   14

And now no soil nor cautel doth besmirch   15

The virtue of his will; but you must fear,   16

His greatness weighed, his will is not his own.   17

For he himself is subject to his birth.

259 **Your loves** i.e., Say "Your loves" to me, not just your "duty." **261
doubt** suspect **1-3 Location:** Polonius's chambers. **3 convoy is assistant**
means of conveyance are available **5 For** As for **6 toy in blood**
passing amorous fancy **7 primy** in its prime, springtime **8 Forward**
precocious **9 suppliance** pastime, something to fill the time **11–14
For nature . . . withal** For nature, as it ripens, does not grow only in
physical strength, but as the body matures the inner qualities of mind
and soul grow along with it. (Laertes warns Ophelia that the mature
Hamlet may not cling to his youthful interests.) **15 soil nor cautel**
blemish nor deceit **16 The . . . will** the purity of his desire **17 His
greatness weighed** taking into account his high fortune

219 **even then** at that very instant **232 beaver** visor on the helmet
233 What How **242 tell** count **253 tenable** held

He may not, as unvalued persons do,

Carve for himself, for on his choice depends   20

The safety and health of this whole state,

And therefore must his choice be circumscribed

Unto the voice and yielding of that body   23

Whereof he is the head. Then if he says he loves you,

It fits your wisdom so far to believe it

As he in his particular act and place   26

May give his saying deed, which is no further

Than the main voice of Denmark goes withal.   28

Then weigh what loss your honor may sustain

If with too credent ear you list his songs,   30

Or lose your heart, or your chaste treasure open

To his unmastered importunity.   32

Fear it, Ophelia, fear it, my dear sister,

And keep you in the rear of your affection,   34

Out of the shot and danger of desire.

The chariest maid is prodigal enough   36

If she unmask her beauty to the moon.   37

Virtue itself scapes not calumnious strokes.

The canker galls the infants of the spring   39

Too oft before their buttons be disclosed,   40

And in the morn and liquid dew of youth   41

Contagious blastments are most imminent.   42

Be wary then; best safety lies in fear.

Youth to itself rebels, though none else near.   44

Ophelia:

I shall the effect of this good lesson keep

As watchman to my heart. But, good my brother,

Do not, as some ungracious pastors do,   47

Show me the steep and thorny way to heaven,

Whiles like a puffed and reckless libertine   49

Himself the primrose path of dalliance treads,

And recks not his own rede.

Enter Polonius.

Laertes: Oh, fear me not.   51

I stay too long. But here my father comes.

A double blessing is a double grace;   53

Occasion smiles upon a second leave.   54

Polonius:

Yet here, Laertes? Aboard, aboard, for shame!

The wind sits in the shoulder of your sail,

And you are stayed for. There—my blessing with thee!

And these few precepts in thy memory

Look thou character. Give thy thoughts no tongue,   59

Nor any unproportioned thought his act.   60

Be thou familiar, but by no means vulgar.   61

Those friends thou hast, and their adoption tried,   62

Grapple them unto thy soul with hoops of steel,

But do not dull thy palm with entertainment   64

Of each new-hatched, unfledged courage. Beware   65

Of entrance to a quarrel, but being in,

Bear't that th'opposèd may beware of thee.   67

Give every man thy ear, but few thy voice;

Take each man's censure, but reserve thy judgment.   69

Costly thy habit as thy purse can buy,   70

But not expressed in fancy; rich, not gaudy,   71

For the apparel oft proclaims the man,

And they in France of the best rank and station

Are of a most select and generous chief in that.   74

Neither a borrower nor a lender be,

For loan oft loses both itself and friend,

And borrowing dulleth edge of husbandry.   77

This above all: to thine own self be true,

And it must follow, as the night the day,

Thou canst not then be false to any man.

Farewell. My blessing season this in thee!   81

Laertes:

Most humbly do I take my leave, my lord.

Polonius:

The time invests you. Go, your servants tend.   83

Laertes:

Farewell, Ophelia, and remember well

What I have said to you.

Ophelia: 'Tis in my memory locked,

And you yourself shall keep the key of it.

---

20 Carve i.e., choose **23 voice and yielding** assent, approval **26 in . . . place** in his particular restricted circumstances **28 main voice** general assent. **withal** along with. **30 credent** credulous. **list** listen to **32 unmastered** uncontrolled **34 keep . . . affection** don't advance as far as your affection might lead you. (A military metaphor.) **36 chariest** most scrupulously modest **37 If she unmask** if she does no more than show her beauty. **moon** (Symbol of chastity.) **39 canker galls** cankerworm destroys **40 buttons be disclosed** buds be opened **41 liquid dew** i.e., time when dew is fresh and bright **42 blastments** blights **44 Youth . . . rebels** Youth yields to the rebellion of the flesh **47 ungracious** ungodly **49 puffed** bloated, or swollen with pride **51 recks** heeds. **rede** counsel. **fear me not** don't worry on my account.

53–4 A double . . . leave The goddess Occasion or Opportunity smiles on the happy circumstance of being able to say good-bye twice and thus receive a second blessing. **59 Look thou character** see to it that you inscribe. **60 unproportioned** badly calculated, intemperate. **his** its **61 familiar** sociable. **vulgar** common. **62 and . . . tried** and their suitability to be your friends having been put to the test **64 dull thy palm** i.e., shake hands so often as to make the gesture meaningless **65 courage** swashbuckler. **67 Bear't that** manage it so that **69 censure** opinion, judgment **70 habit** clothing **71 fancy** excessive ornament, decadent fashion **74 Are . . . that** are of a most refined and well-bred preeminence in choosing what to wear. **77 husbandry** thrift. **81 season** mature **83 invests** besieges, presses upon. **tend** attend, wait.

Laertes: Farewell.   *Exit Laertes.*

Polonius:

What is't, Ophelia, he hath said to you?

Ophelia:

So please you, something touching the Lord Hamlet.

Polonius:

Marry, well bethought.   91

'Tis told me he hath very oft of late

Given private time to you, and you yourself

Have of your audience been most free and bounteous.

If it be so—as so 'tis put on me,   95

And that in way of caution—I must tell you

You do not understand yourself so clearly

As it behooves my daughter and your honor.   98

What is between you? Give me up the truth.

Ophelia:

He hath, my lord, of late made many tenders   100

Of his affection to me.

Polonius:

Affection? Pooh! You speak like a green girl,

Unsifted in such perilous circumstance.   103

Do you believe his tenders, as you call them?

Ophelia:

I do not know, my lord, what I should think.

Polonius:

Marry, I will teach you. Think yourself a baby

That you have ta'en these tenders for true pay

Which are not sterling. Tender yourself more dearly,   108

Or—not to crack the wind of the poor phrase,   109

Running it thus—you'll tender me a fool.   110

Ophelia:

My lord, he hath importuned me with love

In honorable fashion.

Polonius:

Ay, fashion you may call it. Go to, go to.   113

Ophelia:

And hath given countenance to his speech, my lord,   114

With almost all the holy vows of heaven.

Polonius:

Ay, springes to catch woodcocks. I do know,   116

When the blood burns, how prodigal the soul   117

Lends the tongue vows. These blazes, daughter,

Giving more light than heat, extinct in both

Even in their promise as it is a-making,   120

You must not take for fire. From this time

Be something scanter of your maiden presence.   122

Set your entreatments at a higher rate   123

Than a command to parle. For Lord Hamlet,   124

Believe so much in him that he is young,   125

And with a larger tether may he walk

Than may be given you. In few, Ophelia,   127

Do not believe his vows, for they are brokers,   128

Not of that dye which their investments show,   129

But mere implorators of unholy suits,   130

Breathing like sanctified and pious bawds,   131

The better to beguile. This is for all: 132

I would not, in plain terms, from this time forth

Have you so slander any moment leisure   134

As to give words or talk with the Lord Hamlet.

Look to't, I charge you. Come your ways.   136

Ophelia: I shall obey, my lord.   *Exeunt.*

❧

[1-4]

Enter Hamlet, Horatio, and Marcellus.

Hamlet:

The air bites shrewdly; it is very cold.   1

Horatio:

It is a nipping and an eager air.   2

Hamlet:

What hour now?

Horatio: I think it lacks of twelve.   3

Marcellus:

No, it is struck.

Horatio: Indeed? I heard it not.

It then draws near the season   5

Wherein the spirit held his wont to walk.   6

          A flourish of trumpets, and two pieces go off

                                                        [*within*].

What does this mean, my lord?

---

91 **Marry** i.e., By the Virgin Mary. (A mild oath.) 95 **put on** impressed on, told to 98 **behooves** befits 100 **tenders** offers 103 **Unsifted** i.e., untried 108 **sterling** legal currency. **Tender . . . dearly** (1) Bargain for your favors at a higher rate—i.e., hold out for marriage (2) Show greater care of yourself 109 **crack the wind** i.e., run it until it is broken-winded 110 **tender . . . fool** (1) make a fool of me (2) present me with a *fool* or baby. 113 **fashion** mere form, pretense. **Go to** (An expression of impatience.) 114 **countenance** credit, confirmation 116 **springes** snares. **woodcocks** birds easily caught; here used to connote gullibility. 117 **prodigal** prodigally

120 **it** i.e., the promise 122 **something** somewhat 123–4 **Set . . . parle** i.e., As defender of your chastity, negotiate for something better than a surrender simply because the besieger requests an interview. 124 **For** As for 125 **so . . . him** this much concerning him 127 **In few** Briefly 128 **brokers** go-betweens, procurers 129 **dye** color or sort. **investments** clothes. (The vows are not what they seem.) 130 **mere implorators** out-and-out solicitors 131 **Breathing** speaking 132 **for all** once for all, in sum 134 **slander** abuse, misuse. **moment** moment's 136 **Come your ways** Come along.
1-4 Location: The guard platform.
1 **shrewdly** keenly, sharply 2 **eager** biting 3 **lacks of** is just short of 5 **season** time 6 **held his wont** was accustomed 6.1 *pieces* i.e., of ordnance, cannon

Hamlet:

The King doth wake tonight and takes his rouse, 8

Keeps wassail, and the swagg'ring upspring reels; 9

And as he drains his drafts of Rhenish down, 10

The kettledrum and trumpet thus bray out

The triumph of his pledge.

Horatio: Is it a custom? 12

Hamlet: Ay, marry, is't,

But to my mind, though I am native here

And to the manner born, it is a custom 15

More honored in the breach than the observance. 16

This heavy-headed revel east and west 17

Makes us traduced and taxed of other nations. 18

They clepe us drunkards, and with swinish phrase 19

Soil our addition; and indeed it takes 20

From our achievements, though performed at height, 21

The pith and marrow of our attribute. 22

So, oft it chances in particular men,

That for some vicious mole of nature in them, 24

As in their birth—wherein they are not guilty,

Since nature cannot choose his origin— 26

By their o'ergrowth of some complexion, 27

Oft breaking down the pales and forts of reason, 28

Or by some habit that too much o'erleavens 29

The form of plausive manners, that these men, 30

Carrying, I say, the stamp of one defect,

Being nature's livery or fortune's star, 32

His virtues else, be they as pure as grace, 33

As infinite as man may undergo, 34

Shall in the general censure take corruption 35

From that particular fault. The dram of evil 36

Doth all the noble substance often dout 37

To his own scandal.

Enter Ghost.

Horatio: Look, my lord, it comes! 38

Hamlet:

Angels and ministers of grace defend us! 39

Be thou a spirit of health or goblin damned, 40

Bring with thee airs from heaven or blasts from hell, 41

Be thy intents wicked or charitable, 42

Thou com'st in such a questionable shape 43

That I will speak to thee. I'll call thee Hamlet,

King, father, royal Dane. Oh, answer me!

Let me not burst in ignorance, but tell

Why thy canonized bones, hearsèd in death, 47

Have burst their cerements; why the sepulcher 48

Wherein we saw thee quietly inurned 49

Hath oped his ponderous and marble jaws

To cast thee up again. What may this mean,

That thou, dead corpse, again in complete steel, 52

Revisits thus the glimpses of the moon, 53

Making night hideous, and we fools of nature 54

So horridly to shake our disposition 55

With thoughts beyond the reaches of our souls?

Say, why is this? Wherefore? What should we do?

                         [*The Ghost*] beckons [*Hamlet*].

Horatio:

It beckons you to go away with it,

As if it some impartment did desire 59

To you alone.

Marcellus: Look with what courteous action

It wafts you to a more removèd ground.

But do not go with it.

Horatio: No, by no means.

Hamlet:

It will not speak. Then I will follow it.

Horatio:

Do not, my lord!

Hamlet: Why, what should be the fear?

I do not set my life at a pin's fee, 65

And for my soul, what can it do to that, 66

Being a thing immortal as itself?

It waves me forth again. I'll follow it.

Horatio:

What if it tempt you toward the flood, my lord, 69

Or to the dreadful summit of the cliff

---

8 wake stay awake and hold revel. **takes his rouse** carouses **9 Keeps . . . reels** carouses, and riotously dances a German dance called the upspring **10 Rhenish** Rhine wine **12 The triumph . . . pledge** the celebration of his offering a toast. **15 manner** custom (of drinking) **16 More . . . observance** better neglected than followed. **17 east and west** i.e., everywhere **18 taxed of** censured by **19 clepe** call. **with swinish phrase** i.e., by calling us swine **20 addition** reputation **21 at height** outstandingly **22 The pith . . . attribute** the most essential part of the esteem that should be attributed to us. **24 for . . . mole** on account of some natural defect in their constitutions **26 his** its **27 their o'ergrowth . . . complexion** the excessive growth in individuals of some natural trait **28 pales** palings, fences (as of a fortification) **29–30 o'erleavens . . . manners** i.e., infects the way we should behave (much as bad yeast spoils the dough). *Plausive* means "pleasing." **32 Being . . . star** (that stamp of defect) being a sign identifying one as wearing the livery of, and hence being the servant to, nature (unfortunate inherited qualities) or fortune (mischance) **33 His virtues else** i.e., the other qualities of *these men* (line 30) **34 may undergo** can sustain **35 in . . . censure** in overall appraisal, in people's opinion generally **36-8 The dram . . . scandal** i.e., The small drop of evil blots out or works against the noble substance of the whole and brings it into disrepute. (To *dout* is to blot out. A famous crux.)

39 ministers of grace messengers of God **40 Be . . . health** Whether you are a good angel **41 Bring** whether you bring **42 Be thy intents** whether your intentions are **43 questionable** inviting question **47 canonized** buried according to the canons of the church. **hearsèd** coffined **48 cerements** grave clothes **49 inurned** entombed **52 complete steel** full armor **53 the glimpses . . . moon** i.e., the sublunary world, all that is beneath the moon **54 fools of nature** mere mortals, limited to natural knowledge and subject to nature **55 So . . . disposition** to distress our mental composure so violently **59 impartment** communication **65 fee** value **66 for** as for **69 flood** sea

That beetles o'er his base into the sea, 71

And there assume some other horrible form

Which might deprive your sovereignty of reason 73

And draw you into madness? Think of it.

The very place puts toys of desperation, 75

Without more motive, into every brain

That looks so many fathoms to the sea

And hears it roar beneath.

Hamlet:

It wafts me still.—Go on, I'll follow thee.

Marcellus:

You shall not go, my lord.   [*They try to stop him.*]

Hamlet: Hold off your hands!

Horatio:

Be ruled. You shall not go.

Hamlet: My fate cries out, 81

And makes each petty artery in this body 82

As hardy as the Nemean lion's nerve. 83

Still am I called. Unhand me, gentlemen.

By heaven, I'll make a ghost of him that lets me! 85

I say, away!—Go on, I'll follow thee.

                    Exeunt Ghost and Hamlet.

Horatio:

He waxes desperate with imagination.

Marcellus:

Let's follow. 'Tis not fit thus to obey him.

Horatio:

Have after. To what issue will this come? 89

Marcellus:

Something is rotten in the state of Denmark.

Horatio:

Heaven will direct it.

Marcellus: Nay, let's follow him.   *Exeunt.* 91

[1-5]

Enter Ghost and Hamlet.

Hamlet:

Whither wilt thou lead me? Speak. I'll go no further.

Ghost:

Mark me.

Hamlet: I will.

Ghost: My hour is almost come,

When I to sulf'rous and tormenting flames

Must render up myself.

Hamlet: Alas, poor ghost!

Ghost:

Pity me not, but lend thy serious hearing

To what I shall unfold.

Hamlet: Speak. I am bound to hear. 7

Ghost:

So art thou to revenge, when thou shalt hear.

Hamlet: What?

Ghost: I am thy father's spirit,

Doomed for a certain term to walk the night,

And for the day confined to fast in fires, 12

Till the foul crimes done in my days of nature 13

Are burnt and purged away. But that I am forbid 14

To tell the secrets of my prison house,

I could a tale unfold whose lightest word

Would harrow up thy soul, freeze thy young blood, 17

Make thy two eyes like stars start from their spheres, 18

Thy knotted and combinèd locks to part, 19

And each particular hair to stand on end

Like quills upon the fretful porcupine.

But this eternal blazon must not be 22

To ears of flesh and blood. List, list, oh, list!

If thou didst ever thy dear father love—

Hamlet: Oh, God!

Ghost:

Revenge his foul and most unnatural murder.

Hamlet: Murder?

Ghost:

Murder most foul, as in the best it is, 28

But this most foul, strange, and unnatural.

Hamlet:

Haste me to know't, that I, with wings as swift

As meditation or the thoughts of love,

May sweep to my revenge.

Ghost: I find thee apt;

And duller shouldst thou be than the fat weed 33

That roots itself in ease on Lethe wharf, 34

Wouldst thou not stir in this. Now, Hamlet, hear.

'Tis given out that, sleeping in my orchard, 36

---

71 beetles o'er overhangs threateningly (like bushy eyebrows). **his** its **73 deprive . . . reason** take away the rule of reason over your mind **75 toys of desperation** fancies of desperate acts, i.e., suicide **81 My fate cries out** My destiny summons me **82 petty** weak. **artery** blood vessel system through which the vital spirits were thought to have been conveyed **83 As . . . nerve** as a sinew of the huge lion slain by Hercules as the first of his twelve labors. **85 lets** hinders **89 Have after** Let's go after him. **issue** outcome **91 it** i.e., the outcome. **1-5 Location: The battlements of the castle.**

7 bound (1) ready (2) obligated by duty and fate. (The Ghost, in line 8, answers in the second sense.) **12 fast** do penance by fasting **13 crimes** sins. **of nature** as a mortal **14 But that** Were it not that **17 harrow up** lacerate, tear **18 spheres** i.e., eye-sockets, here compared to the orbits or transparent revolving spheres in which, according to Ptolemaic astronomy, the heavenly bodies were fixed **19 knotted . . . locks** hair neatly arranged and confined **22 eternal blazon** revelation of the secrets of eternity **28 in the best** even at best **33 shouldst thou be** you would have to be. **fat** torpid, lethargic **34 Lethe** the river of forgetfulness in Hades **36 orchard** garden

A serpent stung me. So the whole ear of Denmark

Is by a forgèd process of my death 38

Rankly abused. But know, thou noble youth, 39

The serpent that did sting thy father's life

Now wears his crown.

Hamlet: Oh, my prophetic soul! My uncle!

Ghost:

Ay, that incestuous, that adulterate beast, 43

With witchcraft of his wit, with traitorous gifts— 44

Oh, wicked wit and gifts, that have the power

So to seduce!—won to his shameful lust

The will of my most seeming-virtuous queen.

Oh, Hamlet, what a falling off was there!

From me, whose love was of that dignity

That it went hand in hand even with the vow 50

I made to her in marriage, and to decline

Upon a wretch whose natural gifts were poor

To those of mine! 53

But virtue, as it never will be moved, 54

Though lewdness court it in a shape of heaven, 55

So lust, though to a radiant angel linked,

Will sate itself in a celestial bed 57

And prey on garbage.

But soft, methinks I scent the morning air.

Brief let me be. Sleeping within my orchard,

My custom always of the afternoon,

Upon my secure hour thy uncle stole, 62

With juice of cursèd hebona in a vial, 63

And in the porches of my ears did pour 64

The leprous distillment, whose effect 65

Holds such an enmity with blood of man

That swift as quicksilver it courses through

The natural gates and alleys of the body, 68

And with a sudden vigor it doth posset 69

And curd, like eager droppings into milk, 70

The thin and wholesome blood. So did it mine,

And a most instant tetter barked about, 72

Most lazar-like, with vile and loathsome crust, 73

All my smooth body.

Thus was I, sleeping, by a brother's hand

Of life, of crown, of queen at once dispatched, 76

Cut off even in the blossoms of my sin,

Unhouseled, disappointed, unaneled, 78

No reck'ning made, but sent to my account 79

With all my imperfections on my head.

Oh, horrible! Oh, horrible, most horrible!

If thou hast nature in thee, bear it not. 82

Let not the royal bed of Denmark be

A couch for luxury and damnèd incest. 84

But, howsomever thou pursues this act,

Taint not thy mind nor let thy soul contrive

Against thy mother aught. Leave her to heaven

And to those thorns that in her bosom lodge,

To prick and sting her. Fare thee well at once.

The glowworm shows the matin to be near, 90

And 'gins to pale his uneffectual fire. 91

Adieu, adieu, adieu! Remember me.   [*Exit.*]

Hamlet:

O all you host of heaven! O earth! What else?

And shall I couple hell? Oh, fie! Hold, hold, my heart, 94

And you, my sinews, grow not instant old, 95

But bear me stiffly up. Remember thee?

Ay, thou poor ghost, whiles memory holds a seat

In this distracted globe. Remember thee? 98

Yea, from the table of my memory 99

I'll wipe away all trivial fond records, 100

All saws of books, all forms, all pressures past 101

That youth and observation copied there,

And thy commandment all alone shall live

Within the book and volume of my brain,

Unmixed with baser matter. Yes, by heaven!

Oh, most pernicious woman!

Oh, villain, villain, smiling, damnèd villain!

My tables—meet it is I set it down 108

That one may smile, and smile, and be a villain.

At least I am sure it may be so in Denmark.

So, uncle, there you are. Now to my word: 111

It is "Adieu, adieu! Remember me."

I have sworn't.

---

38 **forgèd process** falsified account 39 **abused** deceived. 43 **adulterate** adulterous 44 **gifts** (1) talents (2) presents 50 **even with the vow** with the very vow 53 **To** compared with 54 **virtue, as it** just as virtue 55 **shape of heaven** heavenly form 57 **sate . . . bed** gratify its lustful appetite to the point of revulsion or ennui, even in a virtuously lawful marriage 62 **secure hour** time of being free from worries 63 **hebona** a poison. (The word seems to be a form of *ebony*, though it is thought perhaps to be related to *henbane*, a poison, or to *ebenus*, "yew.") 64 **porches** gateways 65 **leprous distillment** distillation causing leprosylike disfigurement 68 **gates** entry ways 69–70 **posset . . . curd** coagulate and curdle 70 **eager** sour, acid 72 **tetter** eruption of scabs. **barked** covered with a rough covering, like bark on a tree 73 **lazar-like** leperlike

76 **dispatched** suddenly deprived 78 **Unhouseled . . . unaneled** without having received the Sacrament or other last rites including confession, absolution, and the holy oil of extreme unction 79 **reck'ning** settling of accounts 82 **nature** i.e., the promptings of a son 84 **luxury** lechery 90 **matin** morning 91 **his** its 94 **couple** add. **Hold** Hold together 95 **instant** instantly 98 **globe** (1) head (2) world (3) Globe Theater. 99 **table** tablet, slate 100 **fond** foolish 101 **All . . . past** all wise sayings, all shapes or images imprinted on the tablets of my memory, all past impressions 108 **My tables . . . down** (Editors often specify that Hamlet makes a note in his writing tablet, but he may simply mean that he is making a mental observation of lasting impression.) 111 **there you are** i.e., there, I've noted that against you.

Enter Horatio and Marcellus.

Horatio: My lord, my lord!

Marcellus: Lord Hamlet!

Horatio: Heavens secure him!   116

Hamlet: So be it.

Marcellus: Hillo, ho, ho, my lord!

Hamlet: Hillo, ho, ho, boy! Come, bird, come.   119

Marcellus: How is't, my noble lord?

Horatio: What news, my lord?

Hamlet: Oh, wonderful!

Horatio: Good my lord, tell it.

Hamlet: No, you will reveal it.

Horatio: Not I, my lord, by heaven.

Marcellus: Nor I, my lord.

Hamlet:

How say you, then, would heart of man once think it?   127

But you'll be secret?

Horatio, Marcellus: Ay, by heaven, my lord.

Hamlet:

There's never a villain dwelling in all Denmark

But he's an arrant knave.   130

Horatio: There needs no ghost, my lord, come from the grave

To tell us this.

Hamlet: Why, right, you are in the right.

And so, without more circumstance at all,   133

I hold it fit that we shake hands and part,

You as your business and desire shall point you—

For every man hath business and desire,

Such as it is—and for my own poor part,

Look you, I'll go pray.

Horatio:

These are but wild and whirling words, my lord.

Hamlet:

I am sorry they offend you, heartily;

Yes, faith, heartily.

Horatio: There's no offense, my lord.

Hamlet:

Yes, by Saint Patrick, but there is, Horatio,   142

And much offense too. Touching this vision here,   143

It is an honest ghost, that let me tell you.   144

For your desire to know what is between us,

O'ermaster't as you may. And now, good friends,

As you are friends, scholars, and soldiers,

Give me one poor request.

Horatio: What is't, my lord? We will.

Hamlet:

Never make known what you have seen tonight.

Horatio, Marcellus: My lord, we will not.

Hamlet: Nay, but swear't.

Horatio: In faith, my lord, not I.   153

Marcellus: Nor I, my lord, in faith.

Hamlet: Upon my sword. [*He holds out his sword.*]   155

Marcellus: We have sworn, my lord, already.   156

Hamlet: Indeed, upon my sword, indeed.

Ghost: (*cries under the stage*) Swear.

Hamlet:

Ha, ha, boy, say'st thou so? Art thou there, truepenny?   159

Come on, you hear this fellow in the cellarage.

Consent to swear.

Horatio: Propose the oath, my lord.

Hamlet:

Never to speak of this that you have seen,

Swear by my sword.

Ghost: [*beneath*] Swear.   [*They swear.*]   164

Hamlet:

Hic et ubique? Then we'll shift our ground.   165

[*He moves to another spot.*]

Come hither, gentlemen,

And lay your hands again upon my sword.

Swear by my sword

Never to speak of this that you have heard.

Ghost: [*beneath*] Swear by his sword. [*They swear.*]

Hamlet:

Well said, old mole. Canst work i'th'earth so fast?

A worthy pioneer!—Once more remove, good friends.   172

[*He moves again.*]

Horatio:

Oh, day and night, but this is wondrous strange!

Hamlet:

And therefore as a stranger give it welcome.   174

There are more things in heaven and earth, Horatio,

Than are dreamt of in your philosophy.   176

---

116 secure him keep him safe. **119 Hillo . . . come** (A falconer's call to a hawk in air. Hamlet mocks the hallooing as though it were a part of hawking.) **127 once** ever **130 But . . . knave** (Hamlet jokingly gives a self-evident answer: every villain is a thoroughgoing knave.) **133 circumstance** ceremony, elaboration **142 Saint Patrick** the keeper of Purgatory **143 offense** (Hamlet deliberately changes Horatio's "no offense taken" to "an offense against all decency.") **144 honest** genuine

153 In faith . . . I i.e., I swear not to tell what I have seen. (Horatio is not refusing to swear.) **155 sword** i.e., the hilt in the form of a cross. **156 We . . . already** i.e., We swore *in faith.* **159 truepenny** honest old fellow. **164 s.d.** *They swear* (Seemingly they swear here, and at lines 170 and 190, as they lay their hands on Hamlet's sword. Triple oaths would have particular force; these three oaths deal with what they have seen, what they have heard, and what they promise about Hamlet's *antic disposition.*) **165 Hic et ubique?** Here and everywhere? (Latin.) **172 pioneer** foot soldier assigned to dig tunnels and excavations. **174 as a stranger** i.e., needing your hospitality **176 your philosophy** this subject that is called "natural philosophy" or "science." (*Your* is not personal.)

But come;

Here, as before, never, so help you mercy,   178

How strange or odd some'er I bear myself—

As I perchance hereafter shall think meet

To put an antic disposition on—   181

That you, at such times seeing me, never shall,

With arms encumbered thus, or this headshake,   183

Or by pronouncing of some doubtful phrase

As "Well, we know," or "We could, an if we would,"   185

Or "If we list to speak," or "There be, an if they might,"   186

Or such ambiguous giving out, to note   187

That you know aught of me—this do swear,   188

So grace and mercy at your most need help you.

Ghost: [*beneath*] Swear.   [*They swear.*]

Hamlet:

Rest, rest, perturbèd spirit!—So, gentlemen,

With all my love I do commend me to you;   192

And what so poor a man as Hamlet is

May do t'express his love and friending to you,   194

God willing, shall not lack. Let us go in together,   195

And still your fingers on your lips, I pray.   196

The time is out of joint. Oh, cursèd spite   197

That ever I was born to set it right!

                    [*They wait for him to leave first.*]

Nay, come, let's go together.   *Exeunt*   199

♣

[2-1]

Enter old Polonius with his man [*Reynaldo*].

Polonius:

Give him this money and these notes, Reynaldo.

                    [*He gives money and papers.*]

Reynaldo: I will, my lord.

Polonius:

You shall do marvelous wisely, good Reynaldo,   3

Before you visit him, to make inquire   4

Of his behavior.

Reynaldo: My lord, I did intend it.

Polonius:

Marry, well said, very well said. Look you, sir,

Inquire me first what Danskers are in Paris,   7

Ethan Hawke as Hamlet in Miguel Almereyda's 2000 film: indecision moved from Denmark to the aisles of a Manhattan video store.

And how, and who, what means, and where they keep,   8

What company, at what expense; and finding

By this encompassment and drift of question   10

That they do know my son, come you more nearer   11

Than your particular demands will touch it.   12

Take you, as 'twere, some distant knowledge of him,   13

As thus, "I know his father and his friends,

And in part him." Do you mark this, Reynaldo?

Reynaldo: Ay, very well, my lord.

Polonius:

"And in part him, but," you may say, "not well.

But if't be he I mean, he's very wild,

Addicted so and so," and there put on him   19

What forgeries you please—marry, none so rank   20

As may dishonor him, take heed of that,

But, sir, such wanton, wild, and usual slips   22

As are companions noted and most known

To youth and liberty.

Reynaldo: As gaming, my lord.

Polonius: Ay, or drinking, fencing, swearing,

Quarreling, drabbing—you may go so far.   27

178 **so help you mercy** as you hope for God's mercy when you are judged 181 **antic** grotesque, strange 183 **encumbered** folded 185 **an if** if 186 **list** wished. **There . . . might** There are those who could talk if they were at liberty to do so 187 **note** indicate 188 **aught** anything 192 **commend . . . you** give you my best wishes 194 **friending** friendliness 195 **lack** be lacking. 196 **still** always 197 **out of joint** in utter disorder. 199 **let's go together** (Probably they wait for him to leave first, but he refuses this ceremoniousness.)
2-1 **Location:** Polonius's chambers.
3 **marvelous** marvelously 4 **inquire** inquiry 7 **Danskers** Danes

8 **what means** what wealth (they have). **keep** dwell 10 **encompassment . . . question** roundabout way of questioning 11-12 **come . . . it** you will find out more this way than by asking pointed questions (*particular demands*). 13 **Take you** Assume, pretend 19 **put on** impute to 20 **forgeries** invented tales. **rank** gross 22 **wanton** sportive, unrestrained 27 **drabbing** whoring

Reynaldo: My lord, that would dishonor him.

Polonius:

Faith, no, as you may season it in the charge. 29

You must not put another scandal on him

That he is open to incontinency; 31

That's not my meaning. But breathe his faults so quaintly 32

That they may seem the taints of liberty, 33

The flash and outbreak of a fiery mind,

A savageness in unreclaimèd blood, 35

Of general assault. 36

Reynaldo: But, my good lord—

Polonius: Wherefore should you do this?

Reynaldo: Ay, my lord, I would know that.

Polonius: Marry, sir, here's my drift,

And I believe it is a fetch of warrant. 41

You laying these slight sullies on my son,

As 'twere a thing a little soiled wi'th' working, 43

Mark you,

Your party in converse, him you would sound, 45

Having ever seen in the prenominate crimes 46

The youth you breathe of guilty, be assured 47

He closes with you in this consequence: 48

"Good sir," or so, or "friend," or "gentleman,"

According to the phrase or the addition 50

Of man and country.

Reynaldo: Very good, my lord.

Polonius: And then, sir, does 'a this—'a does—what was I about to

say? By the Mass, I was about to say something. Where did I leave?

Reynaldo: At "closes in the consequence."

Polonius:

At "closes in the consequence," ay, marry.

He closes thus: "I know the gentleman,

I saw him yesterday," or "th'other day,"

Or then, or then, with such or such, "and as you say,

There was 'a gaming," "there o'ertook in 's rouse," 60

"There falling out at tennis," or perchance 61

"I saw him enter such a house of sale,"

Videlicet a brothel, or so forth. See you now, 63

Your bait of falsehood takes this carp of truth; 64

And thus do we of wisdom and of reach, 65

With windlasses and with assays of bias, 66

By indirections find directions out. 67

So by my former lecture and advice 68

Shall you my son. You have me, have you not? 69

Reynaldo:

My lord, I have.

Polonius: God b'wi'ye; fare ye well.

Reynaldo: Good my lord.

Polonius:

Observe his inclination in yourself. 72

Reynaldo: I shall, my lord.

Polonius: And let him ply his music.

Reynaldo: Well, my lord.

Polonius:

Farewell.   *Exit Reynaldo.*

Enter Ophelia.

          How now, Ophelia, what's the matter?

Ophelia:

Oh, my lord, my lord, I have been so affrighted!

Polonius: With what, i'th' name of God?

Ophelia:

My lord, as I was sewing in my closet, 79

Lord Hamlet, with his doublet all unbraced, 80

No hat upon his head, his stockings fouled,

Ungartered, and down-gyvèd to his ankle, 82

Pale as his shirt, his knees knocking each other,

And with a look so piteous in purport 84

As if he had been loosèd out of hell

To speak of horrors—he comes before me.

Polonius:

Mad for thy love?

Ophelia: My lord, I do not know,

But truly I do fear it.

Polonius: What said he?

Ophelia:

He took me by the wrist and held me hard.

Then goes he to the length of all his arm,

And, with his other hand thus o'er his brow

He falls to such perusal of my face

As 'a would draw it. Long stayed he so. 93

At last, a little shaking of mine arm

---

29 season temper, soften **31 incontinency** habitual sexual excess
32 quaintly artfully, subtly **33 taints of liberty** faults resulting from
free living **35-6 A savageness . . . assault** a wildness in untamed youth
that assails all indiscriminately. **41 fetch of warrant** legitimate trick.
43 wi'th' working in the process of being made, i.e., in everyday experience **45 Your . . . converse** the person you are conversing with.
sound sound out **46 Having ever** if he has ever. **prenominate crimes**
aforenamed offenses **47 breathe** speak **48 closes . . . consequence** takes
you into his confidence as follows **50 addition** title **60 o'ertook in 's
rouse** overcome by drink **61 falling out** quarreling **63 Videlicet**
namely **64 carp** a fish **65 reach** capacity, ability

66 windlasses i.e., circuitous paths. (Literally, circuits made to head off
the game in hunting.) **assays of bias** attempts through indirection (like
the curving path of the bowling ball, which is biased or weighted to
one side) **67 directions** i.e., the way things really are **68 former lecture**
just-ended set of instructions **69 have** understand **72 in yourself** in
your own person (as well as by asking questions of others).
79 closet private chamber **80 doublet** close-fitting jacket. **unbraced**
unfastened **82 down-gyvèd** fallen to the ankles (like gyves or fetters)
84 in purport in what it expressed **93 As 'a** as if he

And thrice his head thus waving up and down,

He raised a sigh so piteous and profound

As it did seem to shatter all his bulk   97

And end his being. That done, he lets me go,

And with his head over his shoulder turned

He seemed to find his way without his eyes,

For out o' doors he went without their helps,

And to the last bended their light on me.

Polonius:

Come, go with me. I will go seek the King.

This is the very ecstasy of love,   104

Whose violent property fordoes itself   105

And leads the will to desperate undertakings

As oft as any passion under heaven

That does afflict our natures. I am sorry.

What, have you given him any hard words of late?

Ophelia:

No, my good lord, but as you did command

I did repel his letters and denied

His access to me.

Polonius: That hath made him mad.

I am sorry that with better heed and judgment

I had not quoted him. I feared he did but trifle   114

And meant to wrack thee. But beshrew my jealousy!   115

By heaven, it is as proper to our age   116

To cast beyond ourselves in our opinions   117

As it is common for the younger sort

To lack discretion. Come, go we to the King.

This must be known, which, being kept close, might move   120

More grief to hide than hate to utter love.   121

Come.   *Exeunt.*

[2-2]

Flourish. Enter King and Queen, Rosencrantz, and Guildenstern
[*with others*].

King:

Welcome, dear Rosencrantz and Guildenstern.

Moreover that we much did long to see you,   2

The need we have to use you did provoke

Our hasty sending. Something have you heard

Of Hamlet's transformation—so call it,

Sith nor th'exterior nor the inward man   6

Resembles that it was. What it should be,   7

More than his father's death, that thus hath put him

So much from th'understanding of himself,

I cannot dream of. I entreat you both

That, being of so young days brought up with him,   11

And sith so neighbored to his youth and havior,   12

That you vouchsafe your rest here in our court   13

Some little time, so by your companies

To draw him on to pleasures, and to gather

So much as from occasion you may glean,   16

Whether aught to us unknown afflicts him thus

That, opened, lies within our remedy.   18

Queen:

Good gentlemen, he hath much talked of you,

And sure I am two men there is not living

To whom he more adheres. If it will please you

To show us so much gentry and good will   22

As to expend your time with us awhile

For the supply and profit of our hope,   24

Your visitation shall receive such thanks

As fits a kings's remembrance.

Rosencrantz: Both Your Majesties   26

Might, by the sovereign power you have of us,   27

Put your dread pleasures more into command   28

Than to entreaty.

Guildenstern: But we both obey,

And here give up ourselves in the full bent   30

To lay our service freely at your feet,

To be commanded.

King:

Thanks, Rosencrantz and gentle Guildenstern.

Queen:

Thanks, Guildenstern and gentle Rosencrantz.

And I beseech you instantly to visit

My too much changèd son.—Go, some of you,

And bring these gentlemen where Hamlet is.

---

97 **As** that. **bulk** body **104 ecstasy** madness **105 property fordoes** nature destroys **114 quoted** observed **115 wrack** ruin, seduce. **beshrew my jealousy!** a plague upon my suspicious nature! **116 proper . . . age** characteristic of us (old) men **117 cast beyond** overshoot, miscalculate. (A metaphor from hunting.) **120 known** made known (to the King). **close** secret **120-1 might . . . love** i.e., might cause more grief (because of what Hamlet might do) by hiding the knowledge of Hamlet's strange behavior to Ophelia than unpleasantness by telling it.
2-2 Location: The castle.
2 Moreover that Besides the fact that

6 **Sith nor** since neither **7 that** what **11–12 That . . . havior** that, seeing as you were brought up with him from early youth (see 3.4.209, where Hamlet refers to Rosencrantz and Guildenstern as "my two schoolfellows"), and since you have been intimately acquainted with his youthful ways **13 vouchsafe your rest** consent to stay **16 occasion** opportunity **18 opened** being revealed **22 gentry** courtesy **24 supply . . . hope** aid and furtherance of what we hope for **26 As fits . . . remembrance** as would be a fitting gift of a king who rewards true service. **27 of** over **28 dread** inspiring awe **30 in . . . bent** to the utmost degree of our capacity. (An archery metaphor.)

Guildenstern:

Heavens make our presence and our practices   38

Pleasant and helpful to him!

Queen: Ay, amen!

Exeunt Rosencrantz and Guildenstern

[with some attendants].

Enter Polonius.

Polonius:

Th'ambassadors from Norway, my good lord,

Are joyfully returned.

King:

Thou still hast been the father of good news.   42

Polonius:

Have I, my lord? I assure my good liege

I hold my duty, as I hold my soul,

Both to my God and to my gracious king;

And I do think, or else this brain of mine

Hunts not the trail of policy so sure   47

As it hath used to do, that I have found

The very cause of Hamlet's lunacy.

King:

Oh, speak of that! That do I long to hear.

Polonius:

Give first admittance to th'ambassadors.

My news shall be the fruit to that great feast.   52

King:

Thyself do grace to them and bring them in.   53

[Exit Polonius.]

He tells me, my dear Gertrude, he hath found

The head and source of all your son's distemper.

Queen:

I doubt it is no other but the main,   56

His father's death and our o'erhasty marriage.

Enter Ambassadors [Voltimand and Cornelius,

with Polonius].

King:

Well, we shall sift him.—Welcome, my good friends!   58

Say, Voltimand, what from our brother Norway?   59

Voltimand:

Most fair return of greetings and desires.   60

Upon our first, he sent out to suppress   61

His nephew's levies, which to him appeared

To be a preparation 'gainst the Polack,

But, better looked into, he truly found

It was against Your Highness. Whereat grieved

That so his sickness, age, and impotence   66

Was falsely borne in hand, sends out arrests   67

On Fortinbras, which he, in brief, obeys,

Receives rebuke from Norway, and in fine   69

Makes vow before his uncle never more

To give th'assay of arms against Your Majesty.   71

Whereon old Norway, overcome with joy,

Gives him three thousand crowns in annual fee

And his commission to employ those soldiers,

So levied as before, against the Polack,

With an entreaty, herein further shown,

[giving a paper]

That it might please you to give quiet pass

Through your dominions for this enterprise

On such regards of safety and allowance   79

As therein are set down.

King: It likes us well,   80

And at our more considered time we'll read,   81

Answer, and think upon this business.

Meantime we thank you for your well-took labor.

Go to your rest; at night we'll feast together.

Most welcome home!   *Exeunt Ambassadors.*

Polonius: This business is well ended.

My liege, and madam, to expostulate   86

What majesty should be, what duty is,

Why day is day, night night, and time is time,

Were nothing but to waste night, day, and time.

Therefore, since brevity is the soul of wit,   90

And tediousness the limbs and outward flourishes,

I will be brief. Your noble son is mad.

Mad call I it, for, to define true madness,

What is't but to be nothing else but mad?

But let that go.

Queen: More matter, with less art.

Polonius:

Madam, I swear I use no art at all.

That he's mad, 'tis true; 'tis true 'tis pity,

And pity 'tis 'tis true—a foolish figure,   98

But farewell it, for I will use no art.

---

38 **practices** doings 42 **still** always 47 **policy** statecraft 52 **fruit** dessert
53 **grace** honor. (Punning on *grace* said before a *feast*, line 52.)
56 **doubt** fear, suspect 58 **sift him** question Polonius (or Hamlet)
closely. 59 **brother** fellow king 60 **desires** good wishes. 61 **Upon
our first** At our first words on the business

66 **impotence** weakness 67 **borne in hand** deluded, taken advantage
of. **arrests** orders to desist 69 **in fine** in conclusion 71 **give th'assay**
make trial of strength, challenge 79 **On . . . allowance** i.e., with such
considerations for the safety of Denmark and permission for
Fortinbras 80 **likes** pleases 81 **considered** suitable for deliberation 86
expostulate expound, inquire into 90 **wit** sense or judgment 98 **figure**
figure of speech

Mad let us grant him, then, and now remains

That we find out the cause of this effect,

Or rather say, the cause of this defect,

For this effect defective comes by cause. 103

Thus it remains, and the remainder thus.

Perpend. 105

I have a daughter—have while she is mine—

Who, in her duty and obedience, mark,

Hath given me this. Now gather and surmise. 108

[*He reads the letter.*] "To the celestial and my soul's

idol, the most beautified Ophelia"—

That's an ill phrase, a vile phrase; "beautified" is a

vile phrase. But you shall hear. Thus: [*He reads.*]

"In her excellent white bosom, these, etc." 113

Queen: Came this from Hamlet to her?

Polonius:

Good madam, stay awhile, I will be faithful. 115

[*He reads.*]

"Doubt thou the stars are fire,

Doubt that the sun doth move,

Doubt truth to be a liar, 118

But never doubt I love.

O dear Ophelia, I am ill at these numbers. I have not 120

art to reckon my groans. But that I love thee best, O 121

most best, believe it. Adieu.

Thine evermore, most dear lady, whilst this

machine is to him, Hamlet." 124

This in obedience hath my daughter shown me,

And, more above, hath his solicitings, 126

As they fell out by time, by means, and place, 127

All given to mine ear.

King: But how hath she 128

Received his love?

Polonius: What do you think of me?

King:

As of a man faithful and honorable.

Polonius:

I would fain prove so. But what might you think, 131

When I had seen this hot love on the wing—

As I perceived it, I must tell you that,

Before my daughter told me—what might you,

Or my dear Majesty your queen here, think,

If I had played the desk or table book, 136

Or given my heart a winking, mute and dumb, 137

Or looked upon this love with idle sight? 138

What might you think? No, I went round to work, 139

And my young mistress thus I did bespeak: 140

"Lord Hamlet is a prince out of thy star; 141

This must not be." And then I prescripts gave her, 142

That she should lock herself from his resort,

Admit no messengers, receive no tokens.

Which done, she took the fruits of my advice;

And he, repellèd—a short tale to make—

Fell into a sadness, then into a fast,

Thence to a watch, thence into a weakness, 148

Thence to a lightness, and by this declension 149

Into the madness wherein now he raves,

And all we mourn for.

King: [*to the Queen*]   Do you think 'tis this?

Queen: It may be, very like.

Polonius:

Hath there been such a time—I would fain know that—

That I have positively said "'Tis so,"

When it proved otherwise?

King: Not that I know.

Polonius:

Take this from this, if this be otherwise. 156

If circumstances lead me, I will find

Where truth is hid, though it were hid indeed

Within the center.

King: How may we try it further? 159

Polonius:

You know sometimes he walks four hours together

Here in the lobby.

Queen: So he does indeed.

Polonius:

At such a time I'll loose my daughter to him. 162

Be you and I behind an arras then. 163

Mark the encounter. If he love her not

And be not from his reason fall'n thereon, 165

---

103 **For . . . cause** i.e., for this defective behavior, this madness, must
have a cause. **105 Perpend** Consider. **108 gather and surmise** draw
your own conclusions. **113 "In . . . etc."** (The letter is poetically
addressed to her heart, where a letter would be kept by a young
lady.) **115 stay . . . faithful** i.e., hold on, I will do as you wish. **118
Doubt** suspect **120 ill . . . numbers** unskilled at writing verses.
121 reckon (1) count (2) number metrically, scan **124 machine** i.e.,
body **126–8 And . . . ear** and moreover she has told me when, how, and
where his solicitings of her occurred. **131 fain** gladly

136–7 If . . . dumb if I had acted as go-between, passing love notes, or if I
had refused to let my heart acknowledge what my eyes could see **138
with idle sight** complacently or incomprehendingly. **139 round** roundly,
plainly **140 bespeak** address **141 out of thy star** above your sphere, position **142 prescripts** orders **148 watch** state of sleeplessness **149 lightness**
lightheadedness. **declension** decline, deterioration. (With a pun on the
grammatical sense.) **156 Take this from this** (The actor probably gestures, indicating that he means his head from his shoulders, or his staff
of office or chain from his hands or neck, or something similar.)
159 center center of the earth, traditionally an extraordinarily inaccessible
place. **try** test **162 loose** (As one might release an animal that is being
mated.) **163 arras** hanging, tapestry **165 thereon** on that account

Let me be no assistant for a state,

But keep a farm and carters.

King: We will try it.   167

Enter Hamlet [reading on a book].

Queen:

But look where sadly the poor wretch comes reading.

Polonius:

Away, I do beseech you both, away.

I'll board him presently. Oh, give me leave.   170

                    Exeunt King and Queen [with attendants].

How does my good Lord Hamlet?

Hamlet: Well, God-a-mercy.   172

Polonius: Do you know me, my lord?

Hamlet: Excellent well. You are a fishmonger.   174

Polonius: Not I, my lord.

Hamlet: Then I would you were so honest a man.

Polonius: Honest, my lord?

Hamlet: Ay, sir. To be honest, as this world goes, is to be one man

picked out of ten thousand.

Polonius: That's very true, my lord.

Hamlet: For if the sun breed maggots in a dead dog,

being a good kissing carrion—Have you a daughter?   182

Polonius: I have, my lord.

Hamlet: Let her not walk i'th' sun. Conception is a   184

blessing, but as your daughter may conceive, friend,

look to't.

Polonius: [*aside*]   How say you by that? Still harping

on my daughter. Yet he knew me not at first; 'a said

I was a fishmonger. 'A is far gone. And truly in my

youth I suffered much extremity for love, very near

this. I'll speak to him again.—What do you read,

my lord?

Hamlet: Words, words, words.

Polonius: What is the matter, my lord?   194

Hamlet: Between who?

Polonius: I mean, the matter that you read, my lord.

Hamlet: Slanders, sir; for the satirical rogue says here

that old men have gray beards, that their faces are wrin-

kled, their eyes purging thick amber and plum-tree   199

gum, and that they have a plentiful lack of wit, to-   200

gether with most weak hams. All which, sir, though I

most powerfully and potently believe, yet I hold it not

honesty to have it thus set down, for yourself, sir, shall   203

grow old as I am, if like a crab you could go backward.   204

Polonius: [*aside*]   Though this be madness, yet there is

method in't.—Will you walk out of the air, my lord?   206

Hamlet: Into my grave.

Polonius: Indeed, that's out of the air. [*Aside*] How

pregnant sometimes his replies are! A happiness that   209

often madness hits on, which reason and sanity could

not so prosperously be delivered of. I will leave him   211

and suddenly contrive the means of meeting between   212

him and my daughter.—My honorable lord, I will

most humbly take my leave of you.

Hamlet: You cannot, sir, take from me anything that I

will more willingly part withal—except my life, except   216

my life, except my life.

Enter Guildenstern and Rosencrantz.

Polonius: Fare you well, my lord.

Hamlet: These tedious old fools!

Polonius: You go to seek the Lord Hamlet. There he is.

Rosencrantz: [*to Polonius*]   God save you, sir!

                              [*Exit Polonius.*]

Guildenstern: My honored lord!

Rosencrantz: My most dear lord!

Hamlet: My excellent good friends! How dost thou,

Guildenstern? Ah, Rosencrantz! Good lads, how do

you both?

Rosencrantz:

As the indifferent children of the earth.   227

Guildenstern:

Happy in that we are not overhappy.

On Fortune's cap we are not the very button.

Hamlet: Nor the soles of her shoe?

Rosencrantz: Neither, my lord.

Hamlet: Then you live about her waist, or in the mid-   232

dle of her favors?   233

Guildenstern: Faith, her privates we.   234

Hamlet: In the secret parts of Fortune? Oh, most true,

she is a strumpet. What news?   236

Rosencrantz: None, my lord, but the world's grown honest.

---

167 carters wagon drivers. **170 I'll . . . leave** I'll accost him at once. Please leave us alone; leave him to me. **172 God-a-mercy** God have mercy, i.e., thank you. **174 fishmonger** fish merchant. **182 a good kissing carrion** i.e., a good piece of flesh for kissing, or for the sun to kiss **184 i'th' sun** in public. (With additional implication of the sunshine of princely favors.) **Conception** (1) Understanding (2) Pregnancy **194 matter** substance. (But Hamlet plays on the sense of "basis for a dispute.") **199 purging** discharging. **amber** i.e., resin, like the resinous *plum-tree gum* **200 wit** understanding

203 honesty decency, decorum **204 old** as old **206 out of the air** (The open air was considered dangerous for sick people.) **209 pregnant** quick-witted, full of meaning. **happiness** felicity of expression **211 prosperously** successfully **212 suddenly** immediately **216 withal** with **227 indifferent** ordinary, at neither extreme of fortune or misfortune **232–3 the middle . . . favors** i.e., her genitals. **234 her privates we** (1) we dwell in her privates, her genitals, in the middle of her favors (2) we are her ordinary footsoldiers. **236 strumpet** (Fortune was proverbially thought of as fickle.)

Hamlet: Then is doomsday near. But your news is not true. Let me question more in particular. What have you, my good friends, deserved at the hands of Fortune that she sends you to prison hither?

Guildenstern: Prison, my lord?

Hamlet: Denmark's a prison.

Rosencrantz: Then is the world one.

Hamlet: A goodly one, in which there are many confines, wards, and dungeons, Denmark being one   247 o'th' worst.

Rosencrantz: We think not so, my lord.

Hamlet: Why then 'tis none to you, for there is nothing either good or bad but thinking makes it so. To me it is a prison.

Rosencrantz: Why then, your ambition makes it one. 'Tis too narrow for your mind.

Hamlet: Oh, God, I could be bounded in a nutshell and count myself a king of infinite space, were it not that I have bad dreams.

Guildenstern: Which dreams indeed are ambition, for the very substance of the ambitious is merely the   259 shadow of a dream.

Hamlet: A dream itself is but a shadow.

Rosencrantz: Truly, and I hold ambition of so airy and light a quality that it is but a shadow's shadow.

Hamlet: Then are our beggars bodies, and our mon-   264 archs and outstretched heroes the beggars' shadows.   265 Shall we to th' court? For, by my fay, I cannot reason.   266

Rosencrantz, Guildenstern: We'll wait upon you.   267

Hamlet: No such matter. I will not sort you with the   268 rest of my servants, for, to speak to you like an honest man, I am most dreadfully attended. But, in the   270 beaten way of friendship, what make you at Elsinore?   271

Rosencrantz: To visit you, my lord, no other occasion.

Hamlet: Beggar that I am, I am even poor in thanks; but I thank you, and sure, dear friends, my thanks are too dear a halfpenny. Were you not sent for? Is it your   275 own inclining? Is it a free visitation? Come, come, deal   276

justly with me. Come, come. Nay, speak.

Guildenstern: What should we say, my lord?

Hamlet: Anything but to th' purpose. You were sent   279 for, and there is a kind of confession in your looks which your modesties have not craft enough to color.   281 I know the good King and Queen have sent for you.

Rosencrantz: To what end, my lord?

Hamlet: That you must teach me. But let me conjure   284 you, by the rights of our fellowship, by the consonancy   285 of our youth, by the obligation of our ever-preserved   286 love, and by what more dear a better proposer   287 could charge you withal, be even and direct with me   288 whether you were sent for or no.

Rosencrantz: [*aside to Guildenstern*] What say you?

Hamlet: [*aside*] Nay, then, I have an eye of you.—If   291 you love me, hold not off.   292

Guildenstern: My lord, we were sent for.

Hamlet: I will tell you why; so shall my anticipation   294 prevent your discovery, and your secrecy to the King   295 and Queen molt no feather. I have of late—but   296 wherefore I know not—lost all my mirth, forgone all custom of exercises; and indeed it goes so heavily with my disposition that this goodly frame, the earth, seems to me a sterile promontory; this most excellent canopy, the air, look you, this brave o'erhanging   301 firmament, this majestical roof fretted with golden   302 fire, why, it appeareth nothing to me but a foul and pestilent congregation of vapors. What a piece of work   304 is a man! How noble in reason, how infinite in faculties, in form and moving how express and admirable, in   306 action how like an angel, in apprehension how like a   307 god! The beauty of the world, the paragon of animals! And yet, to me, what is this quintessence of dust?   309 Man delights not me—no, nor woman neither, though by your smiling you seem to say so.

Rosencrantz: My lord, there was no such stuff in my thoughts.

Hamlet: Why did you laugh, then, when I said man delights not me?

---

247 confines places of confinement **259 the very . . . ambitious** that seemingly very substantial thing that the ambitious pursue **264–5 Then . . . shadows** (Hamlet pursues their argument about ambition to its absurd extreme: if ambition is only a shadow of a shadow, then beggars, who are presumably without ambition, must be real, whereas monarchs and heroes are only their shadows—*outstretched* like elongated shadows, made to look bigger than they are.) **266 fay** faith **267 wait upon** accompany, attend. (But Hamlet uses the phrase in the sense of providing menial service.) **268 sort** class, categorize **270 dreadfully attended** waited upon in slovenly fashion. **271 beaten way** familiar path, tried-and-true course. **make** do **275 too dear a halfpenny** (1) too expensive at even a halfpenny, i.e., of little worth (2) too expensive by a halfpenny in return for worthless kindness. **276 free** voluntary

279 Anything but to th' purpose Anything except a straightforward answer. (Said ironically.) **281 color** disguise. **284 conjure** adjure, entreat **285–6 the consonancy of our youth** our closeness in our younger days **287 better** more skillful **288 charge** urge. **even** straight, honest **291 of** on **292 hold not off** don't hold back. **294–5 so . . . discovery** in that way my saying it first will spare you from having to reveal the truth **296 molt no feather** i.e., not diminish in the least. **301 brave** splendid **302 fretted** adorned (with fretwork, as in a vaulted ceiling) **304 congregation** mass. **piece of work** masterpiece **306 express** well-framed, exact, expressive **307 apprehension** power of comprehending **309 quintessence** very essence. (Literally, the fifth essence beyond earth, water, air, and fire, supposed to be extractable from them.)

Rosencrantz: To think, my lord, if you delight not in man, what Lenten entertainment the players shall receive from you. We coted them on the way, and hither are they coming to offer you service. 317 318

Hamlet: He that plays the king shall be welcome; His Majesty shall have tribute of me. The adventurous knight shall use his foil and target, the lover shall not sigh gratis, the humorous man shall end his part in peace, the clown shall make those laugh whose lungs are tickle o'th' sear, and the lady shall say her mind freely, or the blank verse shall halt for't. What players are they? 321 322 323 324 325 326

Rosencrantz: Even those you were wont to take such delight in, the tragedians of the city. 329

Hamlet: How chances it they travel? Their residence, both in reputation and profit, was better both ways. 330

Rosencrantz: I think their inhibition comes by the means of the late innovation. 332 333

Hamlet: Do they hold the same estimation they did when I was in the city? Are they so followed?

Rosencrantz: No, indeed are they not.

Hamlet: How comes it? Do they grow rusty? 337

Rosencrantz: Nay, their endeavor keeps in the wonted pace. But there is, sir, an aerie of children, little eyases, that cry out on the top of question and are most tyrannically clapped for't. These are now the fashion, and so berattle the common stages—so they call them— that many wearing rapiers are afraid of goose quills and dare scarce come thither. 338 339 340 341 342 343

Hamlet: What, are they children? Who maintains 'em? How are they escotted? Will they pursue the quality no longer than they can sing? Will they not say afterwards, 346 347

if they should grow themselves to common players—as it is most like, if their means are no better—their writers do them wrong to make them exclaim against their own succession? 348 349 350 351

Rosencrantz: Faith, there has been much to-do on both sides, and the nation holds it no sin to tar them to controversy. There was for a while no money bid for argument unless the poet and the player went to cuffs in the question. 352 353 354 355 356

Hamlet: Is't possible?

Guildenstern: Oh, there has been much throwing about of brains.

Hamlet: Do the boys carry it away? 360

Rosencrantz: Ay, that they do, my lord—Hercules and his load too. 361 362

Hamlet: It is not very strange; for my uncle is King of Denmark, and those that would make mouths at him while my father lived give twenty, forty, fifty, a hundred ducats apiece for his picture in little. 'Sblood, there is something in this more than natural, if philosophy could find it out. 364 366

A flourish [of trumpets within].

Guildenstern: There are the players.

Hamlet: Gentlemen, you are welcome to Elsinore. Your hands, come then. Th'appurtenance of welcome is fashion and ceremony. Let me comply with you in this garb, lest my extent to the players, which, I tell you, must show fairly outwards, should more appear like entertainment than yours. You are welcome. But my uncle-father and aunt-mother are deceived. 371 372 373 374 375

Guildenstern: In what, my dear lord?

Hamlet: I am but mad north-north-west. When the wind is southerly I know a hawk from a handsaw. 378 379

---

317 Lenten entertainment meager reception (appropriate to Lent) **318 coted** overtook and passed by **321 tribute** (1) applause (2) homage paid in money. **of** from **322 foil and target** sword and shield **323 gratis** for nothing. **humorous man** eccentric character, dominated by one trait or "humor" **323–4 in peace** i.e., with full license **325 tickle o'th' sear** hair trigger, ready to laugh easily. (A *sear* is part of a gun-lock.) **326 halt** limp **329 tragedians** actors **330 residence** remaining in their usual place, i.e., in the city **332 inhibition** formal prohibition (from acting plays in the city) **333 late innovation** i.e., recent new fashion in satirical plays performed by boy actors in the "private" theaters; or the Earl of Essex's abortive rebellion in 1601 against Elizabeth's government. (A much debated passage of seemingly topical reference.) **337 How . . . rusty?** Have they lost their polish, gone out of fashion? (This passage, through line 362, alludes to the rivalry between the children's companies and the adult actors, given strong impetus by the reopening of the Children of the Chapel at the Blackfriars Theater in late 1600.) **338 keeps . . . wonted** continues in the usual **339 aerie** nest. **eyases** young hawks **340 cry . . . question** speak shrilly, dominating the controversy (in decrying the public theaters) **340–1 tyrannically** vehemently **342 berattle . . . stages** clamor against the public theaters **343 many wearing rapiers** i.e., many men of fashion, afraid to patronize the common players for fear of being satirized by the poets writing for the boy actors. **goose quills** i.e., pens of satirists **346 escotted** maintained. **quality** (acting) profession **346–7 no longer . . . sing** i.e., only until their voices change.

348 common regular, adult **349 like** likely **349–50 if . . . better** if they find no better way to support themselves **351 succession** i.e., future careers. **352 to-do** ado **353 tar** incite (as in inciting dogs to attack a chained bear) **354–6 There . . . question** i.e., For a while, no money was offered by the acting companies to playwrights for the plot to a play unless the satirical poets who wrote for the boys and the adult actors came to blows in the play itself. **360 carry it away** i.e., win the day. **361–2 Hercules . . . load** (Thought to be an allusion to the sign of the Globe Theatre, which allegedly was Hercules bearing the world on his shoulders.) **364 mouths** faces **366 ducats** gold coins. **in little** in miniature. **'Sblood** By God's (Christ's) blood **371 Th'appurtenance** The proper accompaniment **372 comply** observe the formalities of courtesy **373 garb** i.e., manner. **my extent** that which I extend, i.e., my polite behavior **374 show fairly outwards** show every evidence of cordiality **375 entertainment** a (warm) reception **378 north-north-west** just off true north, only partly. **379 I . . . handsaw** (Speaking in his mad guise, Hamlet perhaps suggests that he can tell true from false. A *handsaw* may be a *hernshaw* or heron. Still, a supposedly mad disposition might compare hawks and handsaws.)

Enter Polonius.

Polonius: Well be with you, gentlemen!

Hamlet: Hark you, Guildenstern, and you too; at each
ear a hearer. That great baby you see there is not yet
out of his swaddling clouts. 383

Rosencrantz: Haply he is the second time come 384
to them, for they say an old man is twice a child.

Hamlet: I will prophesy he comes to tell me of the
players. Mark it.—You say right, sir, o' Monday 387
morning, 'twas then indeed. 388

Polonius: My lord, I have news to tell you.

Hamlet: My lord, I have news to tell you. When Roscius 390
was an actor in Rome—

Polonius: The actors are come hither, my lord.

Hamlet: Buzz, buzz! 393

Polonius: Upon my honor—

Hamlet: Then came each actor on his ass.

Polonius: The best actors in the world, either for
tragedy, comedy, history, pastoral, pastoral-comical,
historical-pastoral, tragical-historical, tragical-comical-
historical-pastoral, scene individable, or poem unlim- 399
ited. Seneca cannot be too heavy, nor Plautus too 400
light. For the law of writ and the liberty, these are the 401
only men.

Hamlet: O Jephthah, judge of Israel, what a 403
treasure hadst thou!

Polonius: What a treasure had he, my lord?

Hamlet: Why,

"One fair daughter, and no more,
The which he lovèd passing well." 408

Polonius: [*aside*]   Still on my daughter.

Hamlet: Am I not i'th' right, old Jephthah?

Polonius: If you call me Jephthah, my lord, I have
a daughter that I love passing well.

Hamlet: Nay, that follows not. 413

Polonius: What follows then, my lord? 414

Hamlet: Why,

"As by lot, God wot," 416

and then, you know,

"It came to pass, as most like it was"— 418
the first row of the pious chanson will show you 419
more, for look where my abridgment comes. 420

Enter the Players.

You are welcome, masters; welcome, all. I am glad to 421
see thee well. Welcome, good friends. Oh, old friend!
Why, thy face is valanced since I saw thee last. Com'st 423
thou to beard me in Denmark? What, my young lady 424
and mistress! By'r Lady, Your Ladyship is nearer to 425
heaven than when I saw you last, by the altitude of a 426
chopine. Pray God your voice, like a piece of uncur- 427
rent gold, be not cracked within the ring. Masters, you 428
are all welcome. We'll e'en to't like French falconers, 429
fly at anything we see. We'll have a speech straight. 430
Come, give us a taste of your quality. Come, a 431
passionate speech.

First Player: What speech, my good lord?

Hamlet: I heard thee speak me a speech once, but it
was never acted, or if it was, not above once, for the
play, I remember, pleased not the million; 'twas cav- 436
iar to the general. But it was—as I received it, and 437
others, whose judgments in such matters cried in the 438
top of mine—an excellent play, well digested in the 439
scenes, set down with as much modesty as cunning. I 440
remember one said there were no sallets in the lines to 441
make the matter savory, nor no matter in the phrase
that might indict the author of affectation, but called it 443
an honest method, as wholesome as sweet, and by very
much more handsome than fine. One speech in't I 445
chiefly loved: 'twas Aeneas' tale to Dido, and there-
about of it especially when he speaks of Priam's 447

383 swaddling clouts cloths in which to wrap a newborn baby. **384 Haply** Perhaps **387–8 You say . . . then indeed** (Said to impress upon Polonius the idea that Hamlet is in serious conversation with his friends.) **390 Roscius** a famous Roman actor who died in 62 B.C. **393 Buzz** (An interjection used to denote stale news.) **399–400 scene . . . unlimited** plays that are unclassifiable and all-inclusive. (An absurdly catchall conclusion to Polonius's pompous list of categories.) **400 Seneca** writer of Latin tragedies. **Plautus** writer of Latin comedies **401 law . . . liberty** dramatic composition both according to the rules and disregarding the rules. **these** i.e., the actors **403 Jephthah . . . Israel** (Jephthah had to sacrifice his daughter; see Judges 11. Hamlet goes on to quote from a ballad on the theme.) **408 passing** surpassingly **413 that follows not** i.e., just because you resemble Jephthah in having a daughter does not logically prove that you love her. **414 What . . . lord?** What does follow logically? (But Hamlet, pretending madness, answers with a fragment of a ballad, as if Polonius had asked, "What comes next?" See 419n.)

416 lot chance. **wot** knows **418 like** likely, probable **419 the first . . . more** the first stanza of this biblically based ballad will satisfy your stated desire to know *what follows* (line 414) **420 my abridgment** something that cuts short my conversation; also, a diversion **421 masters** good sirs **423 valanced** fringed (with a beard) **424 beard** confront, challenge. (With obvious pun.) **young lady** i.e., boy playing women's parts **425 By'r Lady** By Our Lady **425–6 nearer to heaven** i.e., taller **427 chopine** thick-soled shoe of Italian fashion. **427–8 uncurrent** not passable as lawful coinage **428 cracked . . . ring** i.e., changed from adolescent to male voice, no longer suitable for women's roles. (Coins featured rings enclosing the sovereign's head; if the coin was sufficiently clipped to invade within this ring, it was unfit for currency.) **429 e'en to't** go at it **430 straight** at once. **431 quality** professional skill. **436–7 caviar to the general** i.e., an expensive delicacy not generally palatable to uneducated tastes. **438–9 cried in the top of** i.e., spoke with greater authority than **439 digested** arranged, ordered **440 modesty** moderation, restraint. **cunning** skill. **441 sallets** i.e., something savory, spicy improprieties **443 indict** convict **445 handsome** well-proportioned. **fine** elaborately ornamented, showy. **447–8 Priam's slaughter** the slaying of the ruler of Troy, when the Greeks finally took the city.

slaughter. If it live in your memory, begin at this line: 448

let me see, let me see—

"The rugged Pyrrhus, like th' Hyrcanian beast"— 450

'Tis not so. It begins with Pyrrhus:

"The rugged Pyrrhus, he whose sable arms, 452

Black as his purpose, did the night resemble

When he lay couchèd in th' ominous horse, 454

Hath now this dread and black complexion
   smeared

With heraldry more dismal. Head to foot 456

Now is he total gules, horridly tricked 457

With blood of fathers, mothers, daughters, sons,

Baked and impasted with the parching streets, 459

That lend a tyrannous and a damnèd light 460

To their lord's murder. Roasted in wrath and fire, 461

And thus o'ersizèd with coagulate gore, 462

With eyes like carbuncles, the hellish Pyrrhus 463

Old grandsire Priam seeks."

So proceed you.

Polonius: 'Fore God, my lord, well spoken, with

good accent and good discretion.

First Player: "Anon he finds him

Striking too short at Greeks. His antique sword, 469

Rebellious to his arm, lies where it falls,

Repugnant to command. Unequal matched, 471

Pyrrhus at Priam drives, in rage strikes wide,

But with the whiff and wind of his fell sword 473

Th'unnervèd father falls. Then senseless Ilium, 474

Seeming to feel this blow, with flaming top

Stoops to his base, and with a hideous crash 476

Takes prisoner Pyrrhus' ear. For, lo! His sword,

Which was declining on the milky head 478

Of reverend Priam, seemed i'th'air to stick.

So as a painted tyrant Pyrrhus stood, 480

And, like a neutral to his will and matter, 481

Did nothing.

But as we often see against some storm 483

A silence in the heavens, the rack stand still, 484

The bold winds speechless, and the orb below 485

As hush as death, anon the dreadful thunder

Doth rend the region, so, after Pyrrhus' pause, 487

A rousèd vengeance sets him new a-work,

And never did the Cyclops' hammers fall 489

On Mars's armor forged for proof eterne 490

With less remorse than Pyrrhus' bleeding sword 491

Now falls on Priam.

Out, out, thou strumpet Fortune! All you gods

In general synod take away her power! 494

Break all the spokes and fellies from her wheel, 495

And bowl the round nave down the hill of heaven 496

As low as to the fiends!"

Polonius: This is too long.

Hamlet: It shall to the barber's with your beard.—

Prithee, say on. He's for a jig or a tale of bawdry, 500

or he sleeps. Say on; come to Hecuba. 501

First Player:

"But who, ah woe! had seen the moblèd queen"— 502

Hamlet: "The moblèd queen"?

Polonius: That's good. "Moblèd queen" is good.

First Player:

"Run barefoot up and down, threat'ning the flames 505

With bisson rheum, a clout upon that head 506

Where late the diadem stood, and, for a robe, 507

About her lank and all o'erteemèd loins 508

A blanket, in the alarm of fear caught up—

Who this had seen, with tongue in venom steeped,

'Gainst Fortune's state would treason have pronounced. 511

But if the gods themselves did see her then

When she saw Pyrrhus make malicious sport

In mincing with his sword her husband's limbs,

The instant burst of clamor that she made,

Unless things mortal move them not at all,

Would have made milch the burning eyes of heaven, 517

---

450 Pyrrhus a Greek hero in the Trojan War, also known as Neoptolemus, son of Achilles—another avenging son. **th' Hyrcanian beast** i.e., the tiger. (On the death of Priam, see Virgil, *Aeneid,* 2.506 ff.; compare the whole speech with Marlowe's *Dido Queen of Carthage,* 2.1.214 ff. On the *Hyrcanian* tiger, see *Aeneid,* 4.366-7. Hyrcania is on the Caspian Sea.) **452 rugged** shaggy, savage. **sable** black (for reasons of camouflage during the episode of the Trojan horse.) **454 couchèd** concealed. **ominous horse** fateful Trojan horse, by which the Greeks gained access to Troy **456 dismal** calamitous. **457 total gules** entirely red. (A heraldic term.) **tricked** spotted and smeared. (Heraldic.) **459 Baked . . . streets** roasted and encrusted, like a thick paste, by the parching heat of the streets (because of the fires everywhere) **460 tyrannous** cruel **461 their lord's** i.e., Priam's **462 o'ersizèd** covered as with size or glue **463 carbuncles** large fiery-red precious stones thought to emit their own light **469 antique** ancient, long-used **471 Repugnant** disobedient, resistant **473 fell** cruel **474 Th'unnervèd** the strengthless. **senseless Ilium** inanimate citadel of Troy **476 his** its **478 declining** descending. **milky** white-haired **480 painted** motionless, as in a painting

481 like . . . matter i.e., as though suspended between his intention and its fulfillment **483 against** just before **484 rack** mass of clouds **485 orb** globe, earth **487 region** sky **489 Cyclops'** The Cyclopes were giant armor makers in the smithy of Vulcan. **490 proof** proven or tested resistance to assault **491 remorse** pity **494 synod** assembly **495 fellies** pieces of wood forming the rim of a wheel **496 nave** hub. **hill of heaven** Mount Olympus **500 jig** comic song and dance often given at the end of a play **501 Hecuba** wife of Priam. **502 who . . . had** anyone who had. (Also in line 510.) **moblèd** muffled **505 threat'ning the flames** i.e., weeping hard enough to dampen the flames **506 bisson rheum** blinding tears. **clout** cloth **507 late** lately **508 all o'erteemèd** utterly worn out with bearing children **511 state** rule, managing. **pronounced** proclaimed. **517 milch** milky, moist with tears. **burning eyes of heaven** i.e., stars, heavenly bodies

---

HAMLET, PRINCE OF DENMARK: 2–2   **309**

And passion in the gods." 518

Polonius: Look whe'er he has not turned his color and 519
has tears in 's eyes. Prithee, no more.

Hamlet: 'Tis well; I'll have thee speak out the rest of
this soon.—Good my lord, will you see the players well
bestowed? Do you hear, let them be well used, for they 523
are the abstract and brief chronicles of the time. After 524
your death you were better have a bad epitaph than
their ill report while you live.

Polonius: My lord, I will use them according to their
desert.

Hamlet: God's bodikin, man, much better. Use every 529
man after his desert, and who shall scape whipping?
Use them after your own honor and dignity. The less 531
they deserve, the more merit is in your bounty. Take
them in.

Polonius: Come, sirs. [*Exit.*]

Hamlet: Follow him, friends. We'll hear a play tomorrow. [*As they
start to leave, Hamlet detains the First Player.*] Dost thou hear
me, old friend? Can you play *The Murder of Gonzago?*

First Player: Ay, my lord.

Hamlet: We'll ha 't tomorrow night. You could, for a 540
need, study a speech of some dozen or sixteen lines 541
which I would set down and insert in 't, could you not?

First Player: Ay, my lord.

Hamlet: Very well. Follow that lord, and look you mock him
not. *Exeunt players.*
My good friends, I'll leave you till night. You are welcome to
Elsinore.

Rosencrantz: Good my lord!

Exeunt [Rosencrantz and Guildenstern].

Hamlet:
Ay, so, goodbye to you.—Now I am alone.
Oh, what a rogue and peasant slave am I!
Is it not monstrous that this player here,
But in a fiction, in a dream of passion, 552
Could force his soul so to his own conceit 553
That from her working all his visage wanned, 554
Tears in his eyes, distraction in his aspect, 555
A broken voice, and his whole function suiting 556
With forms to his conceit? And all for nothing! 557

For Hecuba!
What's Hecuba to him, or he to Hecuba,
That he should weep for her? What would he do
Had he the motive and the cue for passion
That I have? He would drown the stage with tears
And cleave the general ear with horrid speech, 563
Make mad the guilty and appall the free, 564
Confound the ignorant, and amaze indeed 565
The very faculties of eyes and ears. Yet I,
A dull and muddy-mettled rascal, peak 567
Like John-a-dreams, unpregnant of my cause, 568
And can say nothing—no, not for a king
Upon whose property and most dear life 570
A damned defeat was made. Am I a coward? 571
Who calls me villain? Breaks my pate across? 572
Plucks off my beard and blows it in my face?
Tweaks me by the nose? Gives me the lie i'th' throat 574
As deep as to the lungs? Who does me this?
Ha, 'swounds, I should take it; for it cannot be 576
But I am pigeon-livered and lack gall 577
To make oppression bitter, or ere this 578
I should ha' fatted all the region kites 579
With this slave's offal. Bloody, bawdy villain! 580
Remorseless, treacherous, lecherous, kindless villain! 581
Oh, vengeance!
Why, what an ass am I! This is most brave, 583
That I, the son of a dear father murdered,
Prompted to my revenge by heaven and hell,
Must like a whore unpack my heart with words
And fall a-cursing, like a very drab, 587
A scullion! Fie upon 't, foh! About, my brains! 588
Hum, I have heard
That guilty creatures sitting at a play
Have by the very cunning of the scene 591
Been struck so to the soul that presently 592
They have proclaimed their malefactions;
For murder, though it have no tongue, will speak

---

518 passion overpowering emotion **519 whe'er** whether **523 bestowed** lodged. **524 abstract** summary account **529 God's bodikin** By God's (Christ's) little body, *bodykin.* (Not to be confused with *bodkin,* "dagger.") **531 after** according to **540 ha 't** have it **541 study** memorize **552 But** merely **553 force . . . conceit** bring his innermost being so entirely into accord with his conception (of the role) **554 from her working** as a result of, or in response to, his soul's activity. **wanned** grew pale **555 aspect** look, glance **556–7 his whole . . . conceit** all his bodily powers responding with actions to suit his thought.

563 the general ear everyone's ear. **horrid** horrible **564 appall** (Literally, make pale.) **free** innocent **565 Confound the ignorant** i.e., dumbfound those who know nothing of the crime that has been committed. **amaze** stun **567 muddy-mettled** dull-spirited **567–8 peak . . . cause** mope, like a dreaming idler, not quickened by my cause **570 property** person and function **571 damned defeat** damnable act of destruction **572 pate** head **574 Gives . . . throat** Calls me an out-and-out liar **576 'swounds** by his (Christ's) wounds **577 pigeon-livered** (The pigeon or dove was popularly supposed to be mild because it secreted no gall.) **578 To . . . bitter** to make things bitter for oppressors **579 region kites** kites (birds of prey) of the air **580 offal** entrails. **581 Remorseless** Pitiless. **kindless** unnatural **583 brave** fine, admirable. (Said ironically.) **587 drab** whore **588 scullion** menial kitchen servant. (Apt to be foul-mouthed.) **About** About it, to work **591 cunning** art, skill. **scene** dramatic presentation **592 presently** at once

With most miraculous organ. I'll have these players
Play something like the murder of my father
Before mine uncle. I'll observe his looks;
I'll tent him to the quick. If 'a do blench,   598
I know my course. The spirit that I have seen
May be the devil, and the devil hath power
T'assume a pleasing shape; yea, and perhaps,
Out of my weakness and my melancholy,
As he is very potent with such spirits,   603
Abuses me to damn me. I'll have grounds   604
More relative than this. The play's the thing   605
Wherein I'll catch the conscience of the King. *Exit.*

[3-1]

Enter King, Queen, Polonius, Ophelia,
Rosencrantz, Guildenstern, lords.

King:

And can you by no drift of conference
Get from him why he puts on this confusion,
Grating so harshly all his days of quiet
With turbulent and dangerous lunacy?

Rosencrantz:

He does confess he feels himself distracted,
But from what cause 'a will by no means speak.

Guildenstern:

Nor do we find him forward to be sounded,   7
But with a crafty madness keeps aloof
When we would bring him on to some confession
Of his true state.

Queen: Did he receive you well?

Rosencrantz: Most like a gentleman.

Guildenstern:

But with much forcing of his disposition.   12

Rosencrantz:

Niggard of question, but of our demands   13
Most free in his reply.

Queen: Did you assay him   14
To any pastime?

Rosencrantz:

Madam, it so fell out that certain players
We o'erraught on the way. Of these we told him,   17

Hamlet (Kenneth Branagh) and Ophelia (Kate Winslet) share a tense
moment in Branagh's four-hour, uncut film of *Hamlet* (1996).

And there did seem in him a kind of joy
To hear of it. They are here about the court,
And, as I think, they have already order
This night to play before him.

Polonius: 'Tis most true,
And he beseeched me to entreat Your Majesties
To hear and see the matter.

King:

With all my heart, and it doth much content me
To hear him so inclined.
Good gentlemen, give him a further edge   26
And drive his purpose into these delights.

Rosencrantz:

We shall, my lord.

                    Exeunt Rosencrantz and Guildenstern.

King: Sweet Gertrude, leave us too,
For we have closely sent for Hamlet hither,   29
That he, as 'twere by accident, may here
Affront Ophelia.   31
Her father and myself, lawful espials,   32
Will so bestow ourselves that seeing, unseen,
We may of their encounter frankly judge,
And gather by him, as he is behaved,
If't be th'affliction of his love or no
That thus he suffers for.

---

598 tent probe. **the quick** the tender part of a wound, the core. **blench**
quail, flinch **603 spirits** humors (of melancholy) **604 Abuses** deludes
605 relative cogent, pertinent
3-1 Location: The castle.
1 drift of conference course of talk **7 forward** willing. **sounded** questioned **12 disposition** inclination. **13 Niggard of question** Laconic.
demands questions **14 assay** try to win **17 o'erraught** overtook

26 edge incitement **29 closely** privately **31 Affront** confront, meet
32 espials spies

Queen: I shall obey you.

And for your part, Ophelia, I do wish

That your good beauties be the happy cause

Of Hamlet's wildness. So shall I hope your virtues

Will bring him to his wonted way again,

To both your honors.

Ophelia: Madam, I wish it may.

                                      [*Exit Queen.*]

Polonius:

Ophelia, walk you here.—Gracious, so please you,   43

We will bestow ourselves. [*To Ophelia*] Read

   on this book,   [*giving her a book*]   44

That show of such an exercise may color   45

Your loneliness. We are oft to blame in this—   46

'Tis too much proved—that with devotion's visage   47

And pious action we do sugar o'er

The devil himself.

King: [*aside*] Oh, 'tis too true!

How smart a lash that speech doth give my

   conscience!

The harlot's cheek, beautied with plast'ring art,

Is not more ugly to the thing that helps it   53

Than is my deed to my most painted word.   54

Oh, heavy burden!

Polonius:

I hear him coming. Let's withdraw, my lord.   56

           [*The King and Polonius withdraw.*]

      Enter Hamlet. [*Ophelia pretends to read a book.*]

Hamlet:

To be, or not to be, that is the question:

Whether 'tis nobler in the mind to suffer

The slings and arrows of outrageous fortune,

Or to take arms against a sea of troubles

And by opposing end them. To die, to sleep—

No more—and by a sleep to say we end

The heartache and the thousand natural shocks

That flesh is heir to. 'Tis a consummation

Devoutly to be wished. To die, to sleep;

To sleep, perchance to dream. Ay, there's the rub,   66

For in that sleep of death what dreams may come,

When we have shuffled off this mortal coil,   68

Must give us pause. There's the respect   69

That makes calamity of so long life.   70

For who would bear the whips and scorns of time,

Th'oppressor's wrong, the proud man's contumely,   72

The pangs of disprized love, the law's delay,   73

The insolence of office, and the spurns   74

That patient merit of th'unworthy takes,   75

When he himself might his quietus make   76

With a bare bodkin? Who would fardels bear,   77

To grunt and sweat under a weary life,

But that the dread of something after death,

The undiscovered country from whose bourn   80

No traveler returns, puzzles the will,

And makes us rather bear those ills we have

Than fly to others that we know not of?

Thus conscience does make cowards of us all;

And thus the native hue of resolution   85

Is sicklied o'er with the pale cast of thought,   86

And enterprises of great pitch and moment   87

With this regard their currents turn awry   88

And lose the name of action.—Soft you now,   89

The fair Ophelia.—Nymph, in thy orisons   90

Be all my sins remembered.

Ophelia: Good my lord,   91

How does Your Honor for this many a day?

Hamlet:

I humbly thank you; well, well, well.

Ophelia:

My lord, I have remembrances of yours,

That I have longèd long to redeliver.

I pray you, now receive them.   [*She offers tokens.*]

Hamlet:

No, not I, I never gave you aught.

Ophelia:

My honored lord, you know right well you did,

And with them words of so sweet breath composed

As made the things more rich. Their perfume lost,

Take these again, for to the noble mind

Rich gifts wax poor when givers prove unkind.

There, my lord.   [*She gives tokens.*]

---

43 **Gracious** Your Grace (i.e., the King) 44 **bestow** conceal 45 **exercise** religious exercise. (The book she reads is one of devotion.) **color** give a plausible appearance to 46 **loneliness** being alone. 47 **too much proved** too often shown to be true, too often practiced 53 **to . . . helps it** in comparison with the cosmetic that fashions the cheek's false beauty 54 **painted word** deceptive utterances. 56.1 **withdraw** (The King and Polonius may retire behind an arras. The stage directions specify that they "enter" again near the end of the scene.) 66 **rub** (Literally, an obstacle in the game of bowls.)

68 **shuffled** sloughed, cast. **coil** turmoil 69 **respect** consideration 70 **of . . . life** so long-lived, something we willingly endure for so long. (Also suggesting that long life is itself a calamity.) 72 **contumely** insolent abuse 73 **disprized** unvalued 74 **office** officialdom. **spurns** insults 75 **of . . . takes** receives from unworthy persons 76 **quietus** acquittance; here, death 77 **a bare bodkin** a mere dagger, unsheathed. **fardels** burdens 80 **bourn** frontier, boundary 85 **native hue** natural color, complexion 86 **cast** tinge, shade of color 87 **pitch** height (as of a falcon's flight). **moment** importance 88 **regard** respect, consideration. **currents** courses 89 **Soft you** i.e., Wait a minute, gently 90–1 **in . . . remembered** i.e., pray for me, sinner that I am.

Hamlet: Ha, ha! Are you honest? 104

Ophelia: My lord?

Hamlet: Are you fair? 106

Ophelia: What means Your Lordship?

Hamlet: That if you be honest and fair, your honesty 108
should admit no discourse to your beauty. 109

Ophelia: Could beauty, my lord, have better commerce 110
than with honesty?

Hamlet: Ay, truly, for the power of beauty will sooner
transform honesty from what it is to a bawd than the
force of honesty can translate beauty into his likeness. 114
This was sometime a paradox, but now the time gives 115
it proof. I did love you once. 116

Ophelia: Indeed, my lord, you made me believe so.

Hamlet: You should not have believed me, for virtue 118
cannot so inoculate our old stock but we shall relish of 119
it. I loved you not. 120

Ophelia: I was the more deceived.

Hamlet: Get thee to a nunnery. Why wouldst thou be a 122
breeder of sinners? I am myself indifferent honest, but 123
yet I could accuse me of such things that it were better
my mother had not borne me: I am very proud,
revengeful, ambitious, with more offenses at my beck 126
than I have thoughts to put them in, imagination to
give them shape, or time to act them in. What should
such fellows as I do crawling between earth and
heaven? We are arrant knaves all; believe none of us.
Go thy ways to a nunnery. Where's your father?

Ophelia: At home, my lord.

Hamlet: Let the doors be shut upon him, that he may play
the fool nowhere but in 's own house. Farewell.

Ophelia: Oh, help him, you sweet heavens!

Hamlet: If thou dost marry, I'll give thee this plague for
thy dowry: be thou as chaste as ice, as pure as snow,
thou shalt not escape calumny. Get thee to a nunnery,
farewell. Or, if thou wilt needs marry, marry a fool, for
wise men know well enough what monsters you 140
make of them. To a nunnery, go, and quickly too.
Farewell.

Ophelia: Heavenly powers, restore him!

Hamlet: I have heard of your paintings too, well 144
enough. God hath given you one face, and you make
yourselves another. You jig, you amble, and you 146
lisp, you nickname God's creatures, and make your 147
wantonness your ignorance. Go to, I'll no more on't; 148
it hath made me mad. I say we will have no more
marriage. Those that are married already—all but
one—shall live. The rest shall keep as they are. To a
nunnery, go.   *Exit.*

Ophelia:

Oh, what a noble mind is here o'erthrown!
The courtier's, soldier's, scholar's, eye, tongue, sword,
Th'expectancy and rose of the fair state, 155
The glass of fashion and the mold of form, 156
Th'observed of all observers, quite, quite down! 157
And I, of ladies most deject and wretched,
That sucked the honey of his music vows, 159
Now see that noble and most sovereign reason
Like sweet bells jangled out of tune and harsh,
That unmatched form and feature of blown youth 162
Blasted with ecstasy. Oh, woe is me, 163
T'have seen what I have seen, see what I see!

Enter King and Polonius.

King:

Love? His affections do not that way tend; 165
Nor what he spake, though it lacked form a little,
Was not like madness. There's something in his soul
O'er which his melancholy sits on brood, 168
And I do doubt the hatch and the disclose 169
Will be some danger; which for to prevent,
I have in quick determination
Thus set it down: he shall with speed to England 172
For the demand of our neglected tribute.
Haply the seas and countries different
With variable objects shall expel 175
This something-settled matter in his heart, 176

---

104 honest (1) truthful (2) chaste. **106 fair** (1) beautiful (2) just,
honorable. **108 your honesty** your chastity **109 discourse to** familiar
dealings with **110 commerce** dealings, intercourse **114 his** its
115–16 This . . . proof This was formerly an unfashionable view, but
now the present age confirms how true it is. **118–20 virtue . . . of it**
virtue cannot be grafted onto our sinful condition without our retaining some taste of the old stock. **122 nunnery** convent. (With an
awareness that the word was also used derisively to denote a brothel.)
123 indifferent honest reasonably virtuous **126 beck** command
140 monsters (An illusion to the horns of a cuckold.) **you** i.e., you
women

144 paintings use of cosmetics **146–8 You jig . . . ignorance** i.e., You
prance about frivolously and speak with affected coynesss, you put
new labels on God's creatures (by your use of cosmetics), and you
excuse your affectations on the grounds of pretended ignorance.
148 on't of it **155 Th'expectancy and rose** the hope and ornament
156 The glass . . . form the mirror of true self-fashioning and the pattern of courtly behavior **157 Th'observed . . . observers** i.e., the center
of attention and honor in the court **159 music** musical, sweetly
uttered **162 blown** blossoming **163 Blasted with ecstasy** blighted with
madness. **165 affections** emotions, feelings **168 sits on brood** sits like
a bird on a nest, about to *hatch* mischief (line 169) **169 doubt** suspect,
fear. **disclose** disclosure, hatching **172 set it down** resolved **175 variable objects** various sights and surroundings to divert him **176 This
something . . . heart** the strange matter settled in his heart

Whereon his brains still beating puts him thus   177
From fashion of himself. What think you on't?   178

Polonius:

It shall do well. But yet do I believe
The origin and commencement of his grief
Sprung from neglected love.—How now, Ophelia?
You need not tell us what Lord Hamlet said;
We heard it all.—My lord, do as you please,
But, if you hold it fit, after the play
Let his queen-mother all alone entreat him
To show his grief. Let her be round with him;   186
And I'll be placed, so please you, in the ear
Of all their conference. If she find him not,   188
To England send him, or confine him where
Your wisdom best shall think.

King: It shall be so.
Madness in great ones must not unwatched go.

Exeunt.

♣

[3-2]

Enter Hamlet and three of the Players.

Hamlet: Speak the speech, I pray you, as I pronounced
it to you, trippingly on the tongue. But if you mouth
it, as many of our players do, I had as lief the town crier   3
spoke my lines. Nor do not saw the air too much with
your hand, thus, but use all gently; for in the very
torrent, tempest, and, as I may say, whirlwind of your
passion, you must acquire and beget a temperance
that may give it smoothness. Oh, it offends me to the
soul to hear a robustious periwig-pated fellow tear a   9
passion to tatters, to very rags, to split the ears of the
groundlings, who for the most part are capable of   11
nothing but inexplicable dumb shows and noise. I   12
would have such a fellow whipped for o'erdoing Ter-   13
magant. It out-Herods Herod. Pray you, avoid it.   14

First Player: I warrant Your Honor.

Hamlet: Be not too tame neither, but let your own
discretion be your tutor. Suit the action to the word,

the word to the action, with this special observance,
that you o'erstep not the modesty of nature. For   19
anything so o'erdone is from the purpose of playing,   20
whose end, both at the first and now, was and is to
hold as 'twere the mirror up to nature, to show virtue
her feature, scorn her own image, and the very age   23
and body of the time his form and pressure. Now this   24
overdone or come tardy off, though it makes the   25
unskillful laugh, cannot but make the judicious grieve,   26
the censure of the which one must in your allowance   27
o'erweigh a whole theater of others. Oh, there be players that I have seen play, and heard others praise, and
that highly, not to speak it profanely, that, neither   30
having th'accent of Christians nor the gait of Chris-   31
tian, pagan, nor man, have so strutted and bellowed   32
that I have thought some of nature's journeymen had   33
made men and not made them well, they imitated
humanity so abominably.   35

First Player: I hope we have reformed that indifferently   36
with us, sir.

Hamlet: Oh, reform it altogether. And let those that play
your clowns speak no more than is set down for them;
for there be of them that will themselves laugh, to set   40
on some quantity of barren spectators to laugh too,   41
though in the meantime some necessary question of
the play be then to be considered. That's villainous,
and shows a most pitiful ambition in the fool that uses
it. Go make you ready.   [*Exeunt Players.*]

Enter Polonius, Guildenstern, and Rosencrantz.

How now, my lord, will the King hear this piece of work?

Polonius: And the Queen too, and that presently.   48

Hamlet: Bid the players make haste.   [*Exit Polonius.*]
Will you two help to hasten them?

Rosencrantz:

Ay, my lord.   Exeunt they two.

Hamlet: What ho, Horatio!

Enter Horatio.

Horatio: Here, sweet lord, at your service.

---

177 still continually **178 From . . . himself** out of his natural manner.
186 round blunt **188 find him not** fails to discover what is troubling him
3-2 Location: The castle.
3 our players players nowadays. **I had as lief** I would just as soon
9 robustious violent, boisterous. **periwig-pated** wearing a wig
11 groundlings spectators who paid least and stood in the yard of
the theater. **capable of** able to understand **12 dumb shows and noise**
noisy spectacle (rather than thoughtful drama). **13–14 Termagant**
a supposed deity of the Mohammedans, not found in any English
medieval play but elsewhere portrayed as violent and blustering.
14 Herod Herod of Jewry. (A character in *The Slaughter of the
Innocents* and other cycle plays. The part was played with great noise
and fury.)

19 modesty restraint, moderation **20 from** contrary to **23 scorn** i.e.,
something foolish and deserving of scorn **23–4 and the . . . pressure**
and the present state of affairs its likeness as seen in an impression,
such as wax. **25 come tardy off** falling short **25–6 the unskillful** those
lacking in judgment **27 the censure . . . one** the judgment of even one
of whom. **your allowance** your scale of values **30 not . . . profanely**
(Hamlet anticipates his idea in lines 33–4 that some men were not
made by God at all.) **31 Christians** i.e., ordinary decent folk **32 nor
man** i.e., nor any human being at all **33 journeymen** common work-
men **35 abominably** (Shakespeare's usual spelling, "abhominably,"
suggests a literal though etymologically incorrect meaning, "removed
from human nature.") **36 indifferently** tolerably **40 of them** some
among them **41 barren** i.e., of wit **48 presently** at once.

Hamlet:

Horatio, thou art e'en as just a man

As e'er my conversation coped withal.   54

Horatio:

Oh, my dear lord—

Hamlet: Nay, do not think I flatter,

For what advancement may I hope from thee

That no revenue hast but thy good spirits

To feed and clothe thee? Why should the poor be flattered?

No, let the candied tongue lick absurd pomp,   59

And crook the pregnant hinges of the knee   60

Where thrift may follow fawning. Dost thou hear?   61

Since my dear soul was mistress of her choice

And could of men distinguish her election,   63

Sh' hath sealed thee for herself, for thou hast been 64

As one, in suffering all, that suffers nothing,

A man that Fortune's buffets and rewards

Hast ta'en with equal thanks; and blest are those

Whose blood and judgment are so well commeddled   68

That they are not a pipe for Fortune's finger

To sound what stop she please. Give me that man   70

That is not passion's slave, and I will wear him

In my heart's core, ay, in my heart of heart,

As I do thee.—Something too much of this.—

There is a play tonight before the King.

One scene of it comes near the circumstance

Which I have told thee of my father's death.

I prithee, when thou see'st that act afoot,

Even with the very comment of thy soul   78

Observe my uncle. If his occulted guilt   79

Do not itself unkennel in one speech,   80

It is a damnèd ghost that we have seen,

And my imaginations are as foul

As Vulcan's stithy. Give him heedful note,   83

For I mine eyes will rivet to his face,

And after we will both our judgments join

In censure of his seeming.

Horatio: Well, my lord.   86

If 'a steal aught the whilst this play is playing   87

And scape detecting, I will pay the theft.

> [*Flourish.*] *Enter trumpets and kettledrums, King,*
> *Queen, Polonius, Ophelia, [Rosencrantz,*
> *Guildenstern, and other lords, with guards*
> *carrying torches*].

Hamlet: They are coming to the play. I must be idle.   89

Get you a place.

> [*The King, Queen, and courtiers sit.*]

King: How fares our cousin Hamlet?   91

Hamlet: Excellent, i'faith, of the chameleon's dish: I eat   92

the air, promise-crammed. You cannot feed capons so.   93

King: I have nothing with this answer, Hamlet. These   94

words are not mine.   95

Hamlet: No, nor mine now. [*To Polonius*] My lord, you   96

played once i'th'university, you say?

Polonius: That did I, my lord, and was accounted a good

actor.

Hamlet: What did you enact?

Polonius: I did enact Julius Caesar. I was killed i'th'   101

Capitol; Brutus killed me.   102

Hamlet: It was a brute part of him to kill so capital a   103

calf there.—Be the players ready?   104

Rosencrantz: Ay, my lord. They stay upon your   105

patience.

Queen: Come hither, my dear Hamlet, sit by me.

Hamlet: No, good mother, here's metal more

attractive.   108

Polonius: [*to the King*] Oho, do you mark that?

Hamlet: Lady, shall I lie in your lap?   110

> [*Lying down at Ophelia's feet.*]

Ophelia: No, my lord.

Hamlet: I mean, my head upon your lap?

Ophelia: Ay, my lord.

Hamlet: Do you think I meant country matters?   114

Ophelia: I think nothing, my lord.

Hamlet: That's a fair thought to lie between maids' legs.

---

54 my . . . withal my dealings encountered. **59 candied** sugared, flattering **60 pregnant** compliant **61 thrift** profit **63 could . . . election** could make distinguishing choices among persons **64 sealed thee** (Literally, as one would seal a legal document to mark possession.) **68 blood** passion. **commeddled** commingled **70 stop** hole in a wind instrument for controlling the sound **78 very . . . soul** your most penetrating observation and consideration **79 occulted** hidden **80 unkennel** (As one would say of a fox driven from its lair.) **83 Vulcan's stithy** the smithy, the place of stiths (anvils) of the Roman god of fire and metalworking. **86 censure of his seeming** judgment of his appearance or behavior. **87 If 'a steal aught** If he gets away with anything

89 idle (1) unoccupied (2) mad. **91 cousin** i.e., close relative **92 chameleon's dish** (Chameleons were supposed to feed on air. Hamlet deliberately misinterprets the King's *fares* as "feeds." By his phrase *eat the air* he also plays on the idea of feeding himself with the promise of succession, of being the *heir*.) **93 capons** roosters castrated and *crammed* with feed to make them succulent **94 have . . . with** make nothing of, or gain nothing from **95 are not mine** do not respond to what I asked. **96 nor mine now** (Once spoken, words are proverbially no longer the speaker's own—and hence should be uttered warily.) **101–2 i'th' Capitol** (where Caesar was assassinated, according to *Julius Caesar*, 3.1, but see 1.3.126n in that play) **103 brute** (The Latin meaning of *brutus,* "stupid," was often used punningly with the name Brutus.) **part** (1) deed (2) role **104 calf** fool **105 stay upon** await **108 metal** substance that is *attractive,* i.e., magnetic, but with suggestion also of *mettle,* "disposition" **110 Lady . . . lap?** Onstage, Hamlet often lies at Ophelia's feet, but he could instead offer to do this and continue to stand. **114 country matters** sexual intercourse. (With a bawdy pun on the first syllable of *country.*)

Ophelia: What is, my lord?

Hamlet: Nothing.   119

Ophelia: You are merry, my lord.

Hamlet: Who, I?

Ophelia: Ay, my lord.

Hamlet: Oh, God, your only jig maker. What should a   123
man do but be merry? For look you how cheerfully my
mother looks, and my father died within 's two hours.   125

Ophelia: Nay, 'tis twice two months, my lord.

Hamlet: So long? Nay then, let the devil wear black, for
I'll have a suit of sables. O heavens! Die two months   128
ago, and not forgotten yet? Then there's hope a great
man's memory may outlive his life half a year. But, by'r
Lady, 'a must build churches, then, or else shall 'a
suffer not thinking on, with the hobbyhorse, whose   132
epitaph is "For oh, for oh, the hobbyhorse is forgot."   133

The trumpets sound. Dumb show follows.

*Enter a King and a Queen [very lovingly]; the Queen
embracing him, and he her. [She kneels, and makes
show of protestation unto him.] He takes her up, and
declines his head upon her neck. He lies him down
upon a bank of flowers. She, seeing him asleep,
leaves him. Anon comes in another man, takes off his
crown, kisses it, pours poison in the sleeper's ears,
and leaves him. The Queen returns, finds the King
dead, makes passionate action. The Poisoner with
some three or four come in again, seem to condole
with her. The dead body is carried away. The Poisoner
woos the Queen with gifts; she seems harsh awhile,
but in the end accepts love.*

                                            [*Exeunt players.*]

Ophelia: What means this, my lord?

Hamlet: Marry, this' miching mallico; it means   135
mischief.

Ophelia: Belike this show imports the argument   137
of the play.

Enter Prologue.

Hamlet: We shall know by this fellow. The
players cannot keep counsel; they'll tell all.   140

Ophelia: Will 'a tell us what this show meant?

Hamlet: Ay, or any show that you will show him. Be   142
not you ashamed to show, he'll not shame to tell you   143
what it means.

Ophelia: You are naught, you are naught. I'll   145
mark the play.

Prologue:

For us, and for our tragedy,
Here stooping to your clemency,   148
We beg your hearing patiently.   [*Exit.*]

Hamlet: Is this a prologue, or the posy of a ring?   150

Ophelia: 'Tis brief, my lord.

Hamlet: As woman's love.

Enter [two Players as] King and Queen.

Player King:

Full thirty times hath Phoebus' cart gone round   153
Neptune's salt wash and Tellus' orbèd ground,   154
And thirty dozen moons with borrowed sheen   155
About the world have times twelve thirties been,
Since love our hearts and Hymen did our hands   157
Unite commutual in most sacred bands.   158

Player Queen:

So many journeys may the sun and moon
Make us again count o'er ere love be done!
But, woe is me, you are so sick of late,
So far from cheer and from your former state,
That I distrust you. Yet, though I distrust,   163
Discomfort you, my lord, it nothing must.   164
For women's fear and love hold quantity;   165
In neither aught, or in extremity.   166
Now, what my love is, proof hath made you know,   167
And as my love is sized, my fear is so.
Where love is great, the littlest doubts are fear;   169
Where little fears grow great, great love grows there.

Player King:

Faith, I must leave thee, love, and shortly too;

---

119 Nothing The figure zero or naught, suggesting the female sexual anatomy. (*Thing* not infrequently has a bawdy connotation of male or female anatomy, and the reference here could be male.) **123 only jig maker** very best composer of jigs, i.e., pointless merriment. (Hamlet replies sardonically to Ophelia's observation that he is merry by saying, "If you're looking for someone who is really merry, you've come to the right person.") **125 within 's** within this (i.e., these) **128 suit of sables** garments trimmed with the dark fur of the sable and hence suited for a person in mourning. **132 suffer . . . on** undergo oblivion **133 "For . . . forgot"** (Verse of a song occurring also in *Love's Labor's Lost*, 3.1.27–8. The hobbyhorse was a character made up to resemble a horse and rider, appearing in the morris dance and such May-game sports. This song laments the disappearance of such customs under pressure from the Puritans.) **133.12 *condole with*** offer sympathy to **135 this' miching mallico** this is sneaking mischief **137 Belike** Probably. **argument** plot

140 counsel secret **142–3 Be not you** Provided you are not **145 naught** indecent. (Ophelia is reacting to Hamlet's pointed remarks about not being ashamed to show all.) **148 stooping** bowing **150 posy . . . ring** brief motto in verse inscribed in a ring. **153 Phoebus' cart** the sun-god's chariot, making its yearly cycle **154 salt wash** the sea. **Tellus'** Tellus was goddess of the earth, of the *orbèd ground* **155 borrowed** i.e., reflected **157 Hymen** god of matrimony **158 commutual** mutually. **bands** bonds. **163 distrust** am anxious about **164 Discomfort . . . must** it must not distress you at all. **165 hold quantity** keep proportion with one another **166 In . . . extremity** (women feel) either no anxiety if they do not love or extreme anxiety if they do love. **167 proof** experience **169 the littlest** even the littlest

My operant powers their functions leave to do. 172

And thou shalt live in this fair world behind, 173

Honored, beloved; and haply one as kind

For husband shalt thou—

Player Queen: Oh, confound the rest!

Such love must needs be treason in my breast.

In second husband let me be accurst!

None wed the second but who killed the first. 178

Hamlet: Wormwood, wormwood. 179

Player Queen:

The instances that second marriage move 180

Are base respects of thrift, but none of love. 181

A second time I kill my husband dead

When second husband kisses me in bed.

Player King:

I do believe you think what now you speak,

But what we do determine oft we break.

Purpose is but the slave to memory, 186

Of violent birth, but poor validity, 187

Which now, like fruit unripe, sticks on the tree, 188

But fall unshaken when they mellow be.

Most necessary 'tis that we forget 190

To pay ourselves what to ourselves is debt. 191

What to ourselves in passion we propose,

The passion ending, doth the purpose lose.

The violence of either grief or joy

Their own enactures with themselves destroy. 195

Where joy most revels, grief doth most lament; 196

Grief joys, joy grieves, on slender accident. 197

This world is not for aye, nor 'tis not strange 198

That even our loves should with our fortunes

change;

For 'tis a question left us yet to prove,

Whether love lead fortune, or else fortune love.

The great man down, you mark his favorite flies; 202

The poor advanced makes friends of enemies. 203

And hitherto doth love on fortune tend; 204

For who not needs shall never lack a friend, 205

And who in want a hollow friend doth try 206

Directly seasons him his enemy. 207

But, orderly to end where I begun,

Our wills and fates do so contrary run 209

That our devices still are overthrown; 210

Our thoughts are ours, their ends none of our own. 211

So think thou wilt no second husband wed,

But die thy thoughts when thy first lord is dead.

Player Queen:

Nor earth to me give food, nor heaven light, 214

Sport and repose lock from me day and night, 215

To desperation turn my trust and hope,

An anchor's cheer in prison be my scope! 217

Each opposite that blanks the face of joy 218

Meet what I would have well and it destroy! 219

Both here and hence pursue me lasting strife 220

If, once a widow, ever I be wife!

Hamlet: If she should break it now!

Player King:

'Tis deeply sworn. Sweet, leave me here awhile;

My spirits grow dull, and fain I would beguile 224

The tedious day with sleep.

Player Queen: Sleep rock thy brain,

And never come mischance between us twain!

[He sleeps.] Exit [Player Queen].

Hamlet: Madam, how like you this play?

Queen: The lady doth protest too much, methinks. 228

Hamlet: Oh, but she'll keep her word.

King: Have you heard the argument? Is there no 230

offense in't?

Hamlet: No, no, they do but jest, poison in jest. 232

No offense i'th' world. 233

King: What do you call the play?

Hamlet: *The Mousetrap.* Marry, how? Tropically. 235

This play is the image of a murder done in Vienna.

Gonzago is the Duke's name, his wife, Baptista. You 237

shall see anon. 'Tis a knavish piece of work, but what

172 **My . . . to do** my vital functions are shutting down. 173 **behind** after I have gone 178 **None** (1) Let no woman; or (2) No woman does. **but who** except the one who 179 **Wormwood** i.e., How bitter. (Literally, a bitter-tasting plant.) 180 **instances** motives. **move** motivate 181 **base . . . thrift** ignoble considerations of material prosperity 186 **Purpose . . . memory** Our good intentions are subject to forgetfulness 187 **validity** strength, durability 188 **Which** i.e., purpose 190–1 **Most . . . debt** It's inevitable that in time we forget the obligations we have imposed on ourselves. 195 **enactures** fulfillments 196–7 **Where . . . accident** The capacity for extreme joy and grief go together, and often one extreme is instantly changed into its opposite on the slightest provocation. 198 **aye** ever 202 **down** fallen in fortune 203 **The poor . . . enemies** when one of humble station is promoted, you see his enemies suddenly becoming his friends. 204 **hitherto** up to this point in the argument, or, to this extent. **tend** attend 205 **who not needs** he who is not in need (of wealth)

206 **who in want** he who, being in need. **try** test (his generosity) 207 **seasons him** ripens him into 209 **Our . . . run** what we want and what we get go so contrarily 210 **devices** intentions. **still** continually 211 **ends** results 214 **Nor** Let neither 215 **Sport . . . night** may day deny me its pastimes and night its repose 217 **anchor's cheer** anchorite's or hermit's fare. **my scope** the extent of my happiness. 218–19 **Each . . . destroy!** May every adverse thing that causes the face of joy to turn pale meet and destroy everything that I desire to see prosper! 220 **hence** in the life hereafter 224 **spirits** vital spirits 228 **doth . . . much** makes too many promises and protestations 230 **argument** plot. 232 **jest** make believe. 232–3 **offense** crime, injury. (Hamlet playfully alters the King's use of the word in line 231 to mean "cause for objection.") 235 **Tropically** Figuratively. (The first quarto reading, "trapically," suggests a pun on *trap* in *Mousetrap.*) 237 **Duke's** i.e., King's. (An inconsistency that may be due to Shakespeare's possible acquaintance with a historical incident, the alleged murder of the Duke of Urbino by Luigi Gonzaga in 1538.)

of that? Your Majesty, and we that have free souls, it 239
touches us not. Let the galled jade wince, our withers 240
are unwrung. 241

Enter Lucianus.

This is one Lucianus, nephew to the King.

Ophelia: You are as good as a chorus, my lord. 243

Hamlet: I could interpret between you and your love, 244
if I could see the puppets dallying. 245

Ophelia: You are keen, my lord, you are keen. 246

Hamlet: It would cost you a groaning to take off
mine edge.

Ophelia: Still better, and worse. 249

Hamlet: So you mis-take your husbands.—Begin, mur- 250
derer; leave thy damnable faces and begin. Come, the
croaking raven doth bellow for revenge.

Lucianus:

Thoughts black, hands apt, drugs fit, and time agreeing,
Confederate season, else no creature seeing, 254
Thou mixture rank, of midnight weeds collected,
With Hecate's ban thrice blasted, thrice infected, 256
Thy natural magic and dire property 257
On wholesome life usurp immediately.

[He pours the poison into the sleeper's ear.]

Hamlet: 'A poisons him i'th' garden for his estate. His 259
name's Gonzago. The story is extant, and written in
very choice Italian. You shall see anon how the
murderer gets the love of Gonzago's wife.

[Claudius rises.]

Ophelia: The King rises.

Hamlet: What, frighted with false fire? 264

Queen: How fares my lord?

Polonius: Give o'er the play.

King: Give me some light. Away!

Polonius: Lights, lights, lights!

Exeunt all but Hamlet and Horatio.

Hamlet:

"Why, let the strucken deer go weep, 269
The hart ungallèd play. 270
For some must watch, while some must sleep; 271
Thus runs the world away." 272

Would not this, sir, and a forest of feathers—if the 273
rest of my fortunes turn Turk with me—with two 274
Provincial roses on my razed shoes, get me a fellow- 275
ship in a cry of players? 276

Horatio: Half a share.

Hamlet: A whole one, I.

"For thou dost know, O Damon dear, 279
This realm dismantled was 280
Of Jove himself, and now reigns here 281
A very, very—pajock." 282

Horatio: You might have rhymed.

Hamlet: Oh, good Horatio, I'll take the ghost's word for a
thousand pound. Didst perceive?

Horatio: Very well, my lord.

Hamlet: Upon the talk of the poisoning?

Horatio: I did very well note him.

Enter Rosencrantz and Guildenstern.

Hamlet: Aha! Come, some music! Come, the recorders.

"For if the King like not the comedy,
Why then, belike, he likes it not, perdy." 292

Come, some music.

Guildenstern: Good my lord, vouchsafe me a word with you.

Hamlet: Sir, a whole history.

Guildenstern: The King, sir—

Hamlet: Ay, sir, what of him?

Guildenstern: Is in his retirement marvelous 299
distempered. 300

Hamlet: With drink, sir?

Guildenstern: No, my lord, with choler. 302

---

239 free guiltless **240 galled jade** horse whose hide is rubbed by sad-dle or harness. **withers** the part between the horse's shoulder blades **241 unwrung** not rubbed sore. **243 chorus** (In many Elizabethan plays, the forthcoming action was explained by an actor known as the "chorus"; at a puppet show, the actor who spoke the dialogue was known as an "interpreter," as indicated by the lines following.) **244 interpret** (1) ventriloquize the dialogue, as in a puppet show (2) act as pander **245 puppets dallying** (With suggestion of sexual play, contin-ued in *keen*, "sexually aroused," *groaning*, "moaning in pregnancy," and *edge*, "sexual desire" or "impetuosity.") **246 keen** sharp, bitter **249 Still . . . worse** More keen, always *bettering* what other people say with witty wordplay, but at the same time more offensive. **250 So** Even thus (in marriage). **mis-take** take falseheartedly and cheat on. (The marriage vows say "for better, for worse.") **254 Confederate . . . seeing** the time and occasion conspiring (to assist me), and also no one seeing me **256 Hecate's ban** the curse of Hecate, the goddess of witchcraft **257 dire property** baleful quality **259 estate** i.e., the kingship. **His** i.e., the King's **264 false fire** the blank discharge of a gun loaded with powder but no shot.

269–72 Why . . . away (Perhaps from an old ballad, with allusion to the popular belief that a wounded deer retires to weep and die; compare with *As You Like It,* 2.1.33-66.) **270 ungallèd** unafflicted **271 watch** remain awake **272 Thus . . . away** Thus the world goes. **273 this** i.e., this success with the play I have just presented. **feathers** (Allusion to the plumes that Elizabethan actors were fond of wear-ing.) **274 turn Turk with** turn renegade against, go back on **275 Provincial roses** rosettes of ribbon, named for roses grown in a part of France. **razed** with ornamental slashing **275–6 fellowship . . . players** partnership in a theatrical company. **276 cry** pack (of hounds, etc.) **279 Damon** the friend of Pythias, as Horatio is friend of Hamlet; or, a traditional pastoral name **280–2 This realm . . . pajock** i.e., Jove, representing divine authority and justice, has abandoned this realm to its own devices, leaving in his stead only a peacock or vain pretender to virtue (though the rhyme-word expected in place of *pajock* or "peacock" suggests that the realm is now ruled over by an "ass"). **280 dismantled** stripped, divested **292 perdy** (A corruption of the French *par dieu,* "by God.") **299 retirement** withdrawal to his chambers **299–300 distempered** out of humor. (But Hamlet deliberately plays on the wider application to any illness of mind or body, as in lines 335-6, especially to drunkenness.) **302 choler** anger. (But Hamlet takes the word in its more basic humoral sense of "bilious disorder.")

Hamlet: Your wisdom should show itself more richer
to signify this to the doctor, for for me to put him to his
purgation would perhaps plunge him into more   305
choler.

Guildenstern: Good my lord, put your discourse into
some frame and start not so wildly from my affair.   308

Hamlet: I am tame, sir. Pronounce.

Guildenstern: The Queen, your mother, in most great
affliction of spirit, hath sent me to you.

Hamlet: You are welcome.

Guildenstern: Nay, good my lord, this courtesy is not
of the right breed. If it shall please you to make me a   314
wholesome answer, I will do your mother's commandment; if not, your pardon and my return shall be the   316
end of my business.

Hamlet: Sir, I cannot.

Rosencrantz: What, my lord?

Hamlet: Make you a wholesome answer; my wit's diseased. But, sir, such answer as I can make, you shall
command, or rather, as you say, my mother. Therefore
no more, but to the matter. My mother, you say—

Rosencrantz: Then thus she says: your behavior hath
struck her into amazement and admiration.   325

Hamlet: Oh, wonderful son, that can so 'stonish a mother!
But is there no sequel at the heels of
this mother's admiration? Impart.

Rosencrantz: She desires to speak with you in her
closet ere you go to bed.   330

Hamlet: We shall obey, were she ten times our mother.
Have you any further trade with us?

Rosencrantz: My lord, you once did love me.

Hamlet: And do still, by these pickers and stealers.   334

Rosencrantz: Good my lord, what is your cause of
distemper? You do surely bar the door upon your own
liberty if you deny your griefs to your friend.   337

Hamlet: Sir, I lack advancement.

Rosencrantz: How can that be, when you have the
voice of the King himself for your succession in
Denmark?

Hamlet: Ay, sir, but "While the grass grows"—the   342
proverb is something musty.   343

Enter the Players with recorders.

Oh, the recorders. Let me see one. [*He takes a
recorder.*]

To withdraw with you: why do you go about to recover   345
the wind of me, as if you would drive me into a toil?   346

Guildenstern: Oh, my lord, if my duty be too bold, my   347
love is too unmannerly.   348

Hamlet: I do not well understand that. Will you play   349
upon this pipe?

Guildenstern: My lord, I cannot.

Hamlet: I pray you.

Guildenstern: Believe me, I cannot.

Hamlet: I do beseech you.

Guildenstern: I know no touch of it, my lord.

Hamlet: It is as easy as lying. Govern these ventages   356
with your fingers and thumb, give it breath with your
mouth, and it will discourse most eloquent music.
Look you, these are the stops.

Guildenstern: But these cannot I command to any
utterance of harmony. I have not the skill.

Hamlet: Why, look you now, how unworthy a thing
you make of me! You would play upon me, you would
seem to know my stops, you would pluck out the heart
of my mystery, you would sound me from my lowest   365
note to the top of my compass, and there is much   366
music, excellent voice, in this little organ, yet cannot   367
you make it speak. 'Sblood, do you think I am easier
to be played on than a pipe? Call me what instrument
you will, though you can fret me, you cannot play   370
upon me.

Enter Polonius.

God bless you, sir!

Polonius: My lord, the Queen would speak with you,
and presently.   374

Hamlet: Do you see yonder cloud that's almost in
shape of a camel?

Polonius: By th' Mass, and 'tis, like a camel indeed.

Hamlet: Methinks it is like a weasel.

Polonius: It is backed like a weasel.

---

305 purgation (Hamlet hints at something going beyond medical treatment to bloodletting and the extraction of confession.) **308 frame**
order. **start** shy or jump away (like a horse; the opposite of *tame* in
line 309) **314 breed** (1) kind (2) breeding, manners. **316 pardon** permission to depart **325 admiration** bewilderment. **330 closet** private
chamber **334 pickers and stealers** i.e., hands. (So called from the catechism, "to keep my hands from picking and stealing.") **337 liberty** i.e.,
being freed from *distemper*, line 336; but perhaps with a veiled threat
as well. **deny** refuse to share **342 "While . . . grows"** (The rest of the
proverb is "the silly horse starves"; Hamlet implies that his hopes of
succession are distant in time at best.) **343 something** somewhat

343.1 *Players* actors **345 withdraw** speak privately **345–6 recover the
wind** get to the windward side (thus allowing the game to scent the
hunter and thereby be driven in the opposite direction into the *toil*
or net) **346 toil** snare. **347–8 if . . . unmannerly** if I am using an
unmannerly boldness, it is my love that occasions it. **349 I . . . that**
i.e., I don't understand how genuine love can be unmannerly. **356
ventages** finger-holes or *stops* (line 359) of the recorder **365 sound**
(1) fathom (2) produce sound in **366 compass** range (of voice)
367 organ musical instrument **370 fret** irritate. (With a quibble on the
frets or ridges on the fingerboard of some stringed instruments to
regulate the fingering.) **374 presently** at once.

Hamlet: Or like a whale.

Polonius: Very like a whale.

Hamlet: Then I will come to my mother by and by.

[*Aside*] They fool me to the top of my bent.—I will 383
come by and by.

Polonius: I will say so. [*Exit.*]

Hamlet: "By and by" is easily said. Leave me, friends.

[*Exeunt all but Hamlet.*]

'Tis now the very witching time of night, 387

When churchyards yawn and hell itself breathes out

Contagion to this world. Now could I drink hot blood

And do such bitter business as the day

Would quake to look on. Soft, now to my mother.

O heart, lose not thy nature! Let not ever 392

The soul of Nero enter this firm bosom. 393

Let me be cruel, not unnatural;

I will speak daggers to her, but use none.

My tongue and soul in this be hypocrites:

How in my words somever she be shent, 397

To give them seals never my soul consent! *Exit.* 398

[3-3]

Enter King, Rosencrantz, and Guildenstern.

King:

I like him not, nor stands it safe with us 1

To let his madness range. Therefore prepare you.

I your commission will forthwith dispatch, 3

And he to England shall along with you.

The terms of our estate may not endure 5

Hazard so near 's as doth hourly grow

Out of his brows.

Guildenstern: We will ourselves provide. 7

Most holy and religious fear it is 8

To keep those many many bodies safe

That live and feed upon Your Majesty.

Rosencrantz:

The single and peculiar life is bound 11

With all the strength and armor of the mind

To keep itself from noyance, but much more 13

That spirit upon whose weal depends and rests 14

The lives of many. The cess of majesty 15

Dies not alone, but like a gulf doth draw 16

What's near it with it; or it is a massy wheel 17

Fixed on the summit of the highest mount,

To whose huge spokes ten thousand lesser things

Are mortised and adjoined, which, when it falls, 20

Each small annexment, petty consequence, 21

Attends the boist'rous ruin. Never alone 22

Did the King sigh, but with a general groan.

King:

Arm you, I pray you, to this speedy voyage, 24

For we will fetters put about this fear,

Which now goes too free-footed.

Rosencrantz: We will haste us.

Exeunt gentlemen [Rosencrantz and Guildenstern].
Enter Polonius.

Polonius:

My lord, he's going to his mother's closet.

Behind the arras I'll convey myself 28

To hear the process. I'll warrant she'll tax him home, 29

And, as you said—and wisely was it said—

'Tis meet that some more audience than a mother, 31

Since nature makes them partial, should o'erhear

The speech of vantage. Fare you well, my liege. 33

I'll call upon you ere you go to bed

And tell you what I know.

King: Thanks, dear my lord.

Exit [Polonius].

Oh, my offense is rank! It smells to heaven.

It hath the primal eldest curse upon't, 37

A brother's murder. Pray can I not,

Though inclination be as sharp as will; 39

---

383 They fool . . . bent They humor my odd behavior to the limit of my ability or endurance. (Literally, the extent to which a bow may be bent.) **387 witching time** time when spells are cast and evil is abroad **392 nature** natural feeling. **393 Nero** (This infamous Roman emperor put to death his mother, Agrippina, who had murdered her husband, Claudius.) **397–8 How . . . consent!** however much she is to be rebuked by my words, may my soul never consent to ratify those words with deeds of violence!
3-3 Location: The castle.
1 him i.e., his behavior **3 dispatch** prepare, cause to be drawn up **5 terms of our estate** circumstances of my royal position **7 Out . . . brows** i.e., from his brain, in the form of plots and threats. **We . . . provide** We'll put ourselves in readiness. **8 religious fear** sacred concern

11 single and peculiar individual and private **13 noyance** harm **14 weal** well-being **15 cess** decease, cessation **16 gulf** whirlpool **17 massy** massive **20 mortised** fastened (as with a fitted joint). **when it falls** i.e., when it descends, like the wheel of Fortune, bringing a king down with it **21 Each . . . consequence** i.e., every hanger-on and unimportant person or thing connected with the King **22 Attends** participates in **24 Arm** Provide, prepare **28 arras** screen of tapestry placed around the walls of household apartments. (On the Elizabethan stage, the arras was presumably over a door or aperture in the tiring-house facade.) **29 process** proceedings. **tax him home** reprove him severely **31 meet** fitting **33 of vantage** from an advantageous place, or, in addition. **37 the primal eldest curse** the curse of Cain, the first murderer; he killed his brother Abel **39 Though . . . will** though my desire is as strong as my determination

My stronger guilt defeats my strong intent,

And like a man to double business bound   41

I stand in pause where I shall first begin,

And both neglect. What if this cursèd hand

Were thicker than itself with brother's blood,

Is there not rain enough in the sweet heavens

To wash it white as snow? Whereto serves mercy   46

But to confront the visage of offense?   47

And what's in prayer but this twofold force,

To be forestallèd ere we come to fall,   49

Or pardoned being down? Then I'll look up.

My fault is past. But oh, what form of prayer

Can serve my turn? "Forgive me my foul murder"?

That cannot be, since I am still possessed

Of those effects for which I did the murder:

My crown, mine own ambition, and my queen.

May one be pardoned and retain th'offense?   56

In the corrupted currents of this world   57

Offense's gilded hand may shove by justice,   58

And oft 'tis seen the wicked prize itself   59

Buys out the law. But 'tis not so above.

There is no shuffling, there the action lies   61

In his true nature, and we ourselves compelled,   62

Even to the teeth and forehead of our faults,   63

To give in evidence. What then? What rests?   64

Try what repentance can. What can it not?

Yet what can it, when one cannot repent?

O wretched state, O bosom black as death,

O limèd soul that, struggling to be free,   68

Art more engaged! Help, angels! Make assay.   69

Bow, stubborn knees, and heart with strings of steel,

Be soft as sinews of the newborn babe!

All may be well.   *[He kneels.]*

Enter Hamlet.

Hamlet:

Now might I do it pat, now 'a is a-praying;   73

And now I'll do't. *[He draws his sword.]* And so 'a goes to heaven,

And so am I revenged. That would be scanned: 75

A villain kills my father, and for that,

I, his sole son, do this same villain send

To heaven.

Why, this is hire and salary, not revenge.

'A took my father grossly, full of bread,   80

With all his crimes broad blown, as flush as May;   81

And how his audit stands who knows save heaven?   82

But in our circumstance and course of thought   83

'Tis heavy with him. And am I then revenged,

To take him in the purging of his soul,

When he is fit and seasoned for his passage?   86

No!

Up, sword, and know thou a more horrid hent.   88

            [He puts up his sword.]

When he is drunk asleep, or in his rage,   89

Or in th'incestuous pleasure of his bed,

At game, a-swearing, or about some act   91

That has no relish of salvation in't—   92

Then trip him, that his heels may kick at heaven,

And that his soul may be as damned and black

As hell, whereto it goes. My mother stays.   95

This physic but prolongs thy sickly days.   *Exit.*   96

King:

My words fly up, my thoughts remain below.

Words without thoughts never to heaven go.   *Exit.*

[3-4]

Enter [Queen] Gertrude and Polonius.

Polonius:

'A will come straight. Look you lay home to him.   1

Tell him his pranks have been too broad to bear with,   2

And that Your Grace hath screened and stood between

Much heat and him. I'll silence me even here.   4

Pray you, be round with him.   5

Hamlet: (*within*) Mother, mother, mother!

---

41 **bound** (1) destined (2) obliged. (The King wants to repent and still enjoy what he has gained.) 46–7 **Whereto . . . offense?** What function does mercy serve other than to meet sin face to face? 49 **forestallèd** prevented (from sinning) 56 **th'offense** the thing for which one offended. 57 **currents** courses of events 58 **gilded hand** hand offering gold as a bribe. **shove by** thrust aside 59 **wicked prize** prize won by wickedness 61 **There . . . lies** There in heaven can be no evasion, there the deed lies exposed to view 62 **his** its 63 **to the teeth and forehead** face to face, concealing nothing 64 **give in** provide. **rests** remains. 68 **limèd** caught as with birdlime, a sticky substance used to ensnare birds 69 **engaged** entangled. **assay** trial. (Said to himself, or to the angels to try him.) 73 **pat** opportunely 75 **would be scanned** needs to be looked into, or, would be interpreted as follows

80 **grossly, full of bread** i.e., enjoying his worldly pleasures rather than fasting. (See Ezekiel 16:49.) 81 **crimes broad blown** sins in full bloom. **flush** vigorous 82 **audit** account. **save** except for 83 **in . . . thought** as we see it from our mortal perspective 86 **seasoned** matured, readied 88 **know . . . hent** await to be grasped by me on a more horrid occasion. (*Hent* means "act of seizing.") 89 **drunk . . . rage** dead drunk, or in a fit of sexual passion 91 **game** gambling 92 **relish** trace, savor 95 **stays** awaits (me). 96 **physic** purging (by prayer), or, Hamlet's postponement of the killing
3-4 **Location:** The Queen's private chamber.
1 **lay . . . him** reprove him soundly. 2 **broad** unrestrained 4 **Much heat** i.e., the King's anger. **I'll silence me** I'll quietly conceal myself. (Ironic, since it is his crying out at line 24 that leads to his death. Some editors emend *silence* to "sconce." The first quarto's reading, "shroud," is attractive.) 5 **round** blunt

Queen: I'll warrant you, fear me not.

Withdraw, I hear him coming.

[*Polonius hides behind the arras.*]

Enter Hamlet.

Hamlet: Now, mother, what's the matter?

Queen:

Hamlet, thou hast thy father much offended. 10

Hamlet:

Mother, you have my father much offended.

Queen:

Come, come, you answer with an idle tongue. 12

Hamlet:

Go, go, you question with a wicked tongue.

Queen:

Why, how now, Hamlet?

Hamlet: What's the matter now?

Queen:

Have you forgot me?

Hamlet: No, by the rood, not so: 15

You are the Queen, your husband's brother's wife,

And—would it were not so!—you are my mother.

Queen:

Nay, then, I'll set those to you that can speak. 18

Hamlet:

Come, come, and sit you down; you shall not budge.

You go not till I set you up a glass

Where you may see the inmost part of you.

Queen:

What wilt thou do? Thou wilt not murder me?

Help, ho!

Polonius: [*behind the arras*] What ho! Help!

Hamlet: [*drawing*]

How now? A rat? Dead for a ducat, dead! 25

[*He thrusts his rapier through the arras.*]

Polonius: [*behind the arras*]

Oh, I am slain! [*He falls and dies.*]

Queen: Oh, me, what hast thou done?

Hamlet: Nay, I know not. Is it the King?

Queen:

Oh, what a rash and bloody deed is this!

Hamlet:

A bloody deed—almost as bad, good mother,

As kill a king, and marry with his brother.

Queen:

As kill a king!

Hamlet: Ay, lady, it was my word.

[*He parts the arras and discovers Polonius.*]

Thou wretched, rash, intruding fool, farewell!

I took thee for thy better. Take thy fortune.

Thou find'st to be too busy is some danger.— 34

Leave wringing of your hands. Peace, sit you down,

And let me wring your heart, for so I shall,

If it be made of penetrable stuff,

If damnèd custom have not brazed it so 38

That it be proof and bulwark against sense. 39

Queen:

What have I done, that thou dar'st wag thy tongue

In noise so rude against me?

Hamlet: Such an act

That blurs the grace and blush of modesty,

Calls virtue hypocrite, takes off the rose

From the fair forehead of an innocent love

And sets a blister there, makes marriage vows 45

As false as dicers' oaths. Oh, such a deed

As from the body of contraction plucks 47

The very soul, and sweet religion makes 48

A rhapsody of words. Heaven's face does glow 49

O'er this solidity and compound mass 50

With tristful visage, as against the doom, 51

Is thought-sick at the act.

Queen: Ay me, what act, 52

That roars so loud and thunders in the index? 53

Hamlet: [*showing her two likenesses*]

Look here upon this picture, and on this,

The counterfeit presentment of two brothers. 55

See what a grace was seated on this brow:

Hyperion's curls, the front of Jove himself, 57

An eye like Mars to threaten and command, 58

A station like the herald Mercury 59

New-lighted on a heaven-kissing hill— 60

A combination and a form indeed

Where every god did seem to set his seal 62

To give the world assurance of a man.

This was your husband. Look you now what follows:

Here is your husband, like a mildewed ear, 65

10 thy father i.e., your stepfather, Claudius **12 idle** foolish **15 forgot me** i.e., forgotten that I am your mother. **rood** cross of Christ **18 speak** i.e., speak to someone so rude. **25 Dead for a ducat** i.e., I bet a ducat he's dead; or, a ducat is his life's fee.

34 busy nosey **38 damnèd custom** habitual wickedness. **brazed** brazened, hardened **39 proof** impenetrable, like *proof* or tested armor. **sense** feeling. **45 sets a blister** i.e., brands as a harlot **47 contraction** the marriage contract **48 sweet religion makes** i.e., makes marriage vows **49 rhapsody** senseless string **49–52 Heaven's . . . act** Heaven's face blushes at this solid world compounded of the various elements, with sorrowful face as though the day of doom were near, and is sick with horror at the deed (i.e., Gertrude's marriage). **53 index** table of contents, prelude or preface. **55 counterfeit presentment** representation in portraiture **57 Hyperion's** the sun-god's. **front** brow **58 Mars** god of war **59 station** manner of standing. **Mercury** winged messenger of the gods **60 New-lighted** newly alighted. **heavenkissing** reaching to the sky **62 set his seal** i.e., affix his approval **65 ear** i.e., of grain

Blasting his wholesome brother. Have you eyes? 66
Could you on this fair mountain leave to feed 67
And batten on this moor? Ha, have you eyes? 68
You cannot call it love, for at your age
The heyday in the blood is tame, it's humble, 70
And waits upon the judgment, and what judgment
Would step from this to this? Sense, sure, you have, 72
Else could you not have motion, but sure that sense
Is apoplexed, for madness would not err, 74
Nor sense to ecstasy was ne'er so thralled, 75
But it reserved some quantity of choice 76
To serve in such a difference. What devil was't 77
That thus hath cozened you at hoodman-blind? 78
Eyes without feeling, feeling without sight,
Ears without hands or eyes, smelling sans all, 80
Or but a sickly part of one true sense
Could not so mope. O shame, where is thy blush? 82
Rebellious hell,
If thou canst mutine in a matron's bones, 84
To flaming youth let virtue be as wax 85
And melt in her own fire. Proclaim no shame 86
When the compulsive ardor gives the charge, 87
Since frost itself as actively doth burn, 88
And reason panders will. 89

Queen: Oh, Hamlet, speak no more!
Thou turn'st mine eyes into my very soul,
And there I see such black and grainèd spots 92
As will not leave their tinct.

Hamlet: Nay, but to live 93
In the rank sweat of an enseamèd bed, 94
Stewed in corruption, honeying and making love 95
Over the nasty sty! 96

Queen: Oh, speak to me no more!
These words like daggers enter in my ears.
No more, sweet Hamlet!

---

66 **Blasting** blighting 67 **leave** cease 68 **batten** gorge. **moor** barren or marshy ground. (Suggesting also "dark-skinned.") 70 **The heyday ... blood** (The blood was thought to be the source of sexual desire.) 72 **Sense** Perception through the five senses (the functions of the middle or sensible soul) 74 **apoplexed** paralyzed. **err** so err 75–7 **Nor ... difference** nor could your physical senses ever have been so enthralled to *ecstasy* or lunacy that they could not distinguish to some degree between Hamlet Senior and Claudius. 78 **cozened** cheated. **hoodman-blind** blindman's buff. (In this game, says Hamlet, the devil must have pushed Claudius toward Gertrude while she was blindfolded.) 80 **sans** without 82 **mope** be dazed, act aimlessly. 84 **mutine** mutiny 85–6 **To . . . fire** when it comes to sexually passionate youth, let virtue melt like a candle or stick of sealing wax held over a candle flame. (There's no point in hoping for self-restraint among young people when matronly women set such a bad example.) 86–9 **Proclaim ... will** Call it no shameful business when the compelling ardor of youth delivers the attack, i.e., commits lechery, since the *frost* of advanced age burns with as active a fire of lust and reason perverts itself by fomenting lust rather than restraining it. 92 **grainèd** ingrained, indelible 93 **leave their tinct** surrender their dark stain. 94 **enseamèd** saturated in the grease and filth of passionate lovemaking 95 **Stewed** soaked, bathed. (With a suggestion of "stew," brothel.) 96 **Over ... sty** (Like barnyard animals.)

Hamlet: A murderer and a villain,
A slave that is not twentieth part the tithe 100
Of your precedent lord, a vice of kings, 101
A cutpurse of the empire and the rule,
That from a shelf the precious diadem stole
And put it in his pocket! 105

Queen: No more!

Enter Ghost [in his nightgown].

Hamlet: A king of shreds and patches— 106
Save me, and hover o'er me with your wings,
You heavenly guards! What would your gracious figure?

Queen: Alas, he's mad!

Hamlet:
Do you not come your tardy son to chide,
That, lapsed in time and passion, lets go by 111
Th'important acting of your dread command? 112
Oh, say!

Ghost:
Do not forget. This visitation
Is but to whet thy almost blunted purpose. 115
But look, amazement on thy mother sits. 116
Oh, step between her and her fighting soul!
Conceit in weakest bodies strongest works. 118
Speak to her, Hamlet.

Hamlet: How is it with you, lady?

Queen: Alas, how is't with you,
That you do bend your eye on vacancy,
And with th'incorporal air do hold discourse? 122
Forth at your eyes your spirits wildly peep,
And, as the sleeping soldiers in th'alarm, 124
Your bedded hair, like life in excrements, 125
Start up and stand on end. O gentle son,
Upon the heat and flame of thy distemper 127
Sprinkle cool patience. Whereon do you look?

Hamlet:
On him, on him! Look you how pale he glares!
His form and cause conjoined, preaching to stones, 130
Would make them capable.—Do not look upon me, 131

---

100 **tithe** tenth part 101 **precedent lord** former husband. **vice** (From the morality plays, a model of iniquity and a buffoon.) 105.1 *nightgown* a robe for indoor wear. 106 **A king ... patches** i.e., a king whose splendor is all sham; a clown or fool dressed in motley 111 **lapsed ... passion** having let time and passion slip away 112 **Th'important** the importunate, urgent 115 **whet** sharpen 116 **amazement** distraction 118 **Conceit** Imagination 122 **th'incorporal** the immaterial 124 **as ... th'alarm** like soldiers called out of sleep by an alarum 125 **bedded** laid flat. **like life in excrements** i.e., as though hair, an outgrowth of the body, had a life of its own. (Hair was thought to be lifeless because it lacks sensation, and so its standing on end would be unnatural and ominous.) 127 **distemper** disorder 130 **His ... conjoined** His appearance joined to his cause for speaking 131 **capable** capable of feeling, receptive.

Lest with this piteous action you convert 132

My stern effects. Then what I have to do 133

Will want true color—tears perchance for blood. 134

Queen: To whom do you speak this?

Hamlet: Do you see nothing there?

Queen:

Nothing at all, yet all that is I see.

Hamlet: Nor did you nothing hear?

Queen: No, nothing but ourselves.

Hamlet:

Why, look you there, look how it steals away!

My father, in his habit as he lived! 141

Look where he goes even now out at the portal!

Exit Ghost.

Queen:

This is the very coinage of your brain. 143

This bodiless creation ecstasy 144

Is very cunning in. 145

Hamlet: Ecstasy?

My pulse as yours doth temperately keep time,

And makes as healthful music. It is not madness

That I have uttered. Bring me to the test,

And I the matter will reword, which madness 150

Would gambol from. Mother, for love of grace, 151

Lay not that flattering unction to your soul 152

That not your trespass but my madness speaks.

It will but skin and film the ulcerous place, 154

Whiles rank corruption, mining all within, 155

Infects unseen. Confess yourself to heaven,

Repent what's past, avoid what is to come,

And do not spread the compost on the weeds 158

To make them ranker. Forgive me this my virtue; 159

For in the fatness of these pursy times 160

Virtue itself of vice must pardon beg,

Yea, curb and woo for leave to do him good. 162

Queen:

Oh, Hamlet, thou hast cleft my heart in twain.

Hamlet:

Oh, throw away the worser part of it,

And live the purer with the other half.

Good night. But go not to my uncle's bed;

Assume a virtue, if you have it not.

That monster, custom, who all sense doth eat, 168

Of habits devil, is angel yet in this, 169

That to the use of actions fair and good

He likewise gives a frock or livery 171

That aptly is put on. Refrain tonight, 172

And that shall lend a kind of easiness

To the next abstinence; the next more easy;

For use almost can change the stamp of nature, 175

And either . . . the devil, or throw him out 176

With wondrous potency. Once more, good night;

And when you are desirous to be blest, 178

I'll blessing beg of you. For this same lord, 179

[*pointing to Polonius*]

I do repent; but heaven hath pleased it so

To punish me with this, and this with me, 181

That I must be their scourge and minister. 182

I will bestow him, and will answer well 183

The death I gave him. So, again, good night.

I must be cruel only to be kind.

This bad begins, and worse remains behind. 186

One word more, good lady.

Queen: What shall I do?

Hamlet:

Not this by no means that I bid you do:

Let the bloat king tempt you again to bed, 189

Pinch wanton on your cheek, call you his mouse, 190

And let him, for a pair of reechy kisses, 191

Or paddling in your neck with his damned fingers, 192

Make you to ravel all this matter out 193

That I essentially am not in madness,

But mad in craft. 'Twere good you let him know, 195

For who that's but a queen, fair, sober, wise,

Would from a paddock, from a bat, a gib, 197

Such dear concernings hide? Who would do so? 198

No, in despite of sense and secrecy, 199

132–3 **convert . . . effects** divert me from my stern duty. 134 **want . . . blood** lack plausibility so that (with a play on the normal sense of *color*) I shall shed colorless tears instead of blood. 141 **habit** clothes. **as** as when 143 **very** mere 144–5 **This . . . in** Madness is skillful in creating this kind of hallucination. 150 **reword** repeat word for word 151 **gambol** skip away 152 **unction** ointment 154 **skin** grow a skin over 155 **mining** working under the surface 158 **compost** manure 159 **this my virtue** my virtuous talk in reproving you 160 **fatness** grossness. **pursy** flabby, out of shape 162 **curb** bow, bend the knee. **leave** permission

168 **who . . . eat** which consumes and overwhelms the physical senses 169 **Of habits devil** devil-like in prompting evil habits 171 **livery** an outer appearance, a customary garb (and hence a predisposition easily assumed in time of stress) 172 **aptly** readily 175 **use** habit. **the stamp of nature** our inborn traits 176 **And either** (A defective line, often emended by inserting the word "master" after *either*, following the third quarto and early editors, or some other word such as "shame," "lodge," "curb," or "house.") 178–9 **when . . . you** i.e., when you are ready to be penitent and seek God's blessing, I will ask your blessing as a dutiful son should. 181 **To punish . . . with me** to seek retribution from me for killing Polonius, and from him through my means 182 **their scourge and minister** i.e., agent of heavenly retribution. 183 **bestow** stow, dispose of. **answer** account or pay for 186 **This** i.e., The killing of Polonius. **behind** to come. 189 **bloat** bloated 190 **Pinch wanton** i.e., leave his love pinches on your cheeks, branding you as wanton 191 **reechy** dirty, filthy 192 **paddling** fingering amorously 193 **ravel . . . out** unravel, disclose 195 **in craft** by cunning. **good** (Said sarcastically; also the following eight lines.) 197 **paddock** toad. **gib** tomcat 198 **dear concernings** important affairs 199 **sense and secrecy** secrecy that common sense requires

Ophelia's madness and suicide have long been a favorite topic for artists, especially in the nineteenth century. In his 1894 painting, *Ophelia*, John William Waterhouse imagines his subject just before her death, surrounded by the flowers of her final speech in act 4, scene 5.

Unpeg the basket on the house's top,   200

Let the birds fly, and like the famous ape,   201

To try conclusions, in the basket creep   202

And break your own neck down.   203

Queen:

Be thou assured, if words be made of breath,

And breath of life, I have no life to breathe

What thou hast said to me.

Hamlet:

I must to England. You know that?

Queen: Alack,

I had forgot. 'Tis so concluded on.

Hamlet:

There's letters sealed, and my two schoolfellows,

Whom I will trust as I will adders fanged,

They bear the mandate; they must sweep my way   211

And marshal me to knavery. Let it work.   212

For 'tis the sport to have the engineer   213

Hoist with his own petard, and 't shall go hard   214

---

200 Unpeg the basket open the cage, i.e., let out the secret **201 famous ape** (In a story now lost.) **202 try conclusions** test the outcome (in which the ape apparently enters a cage from which birds have been released and then tries to fly out of the cage as they have done, falling to its death) **203 down** in the fall. **211–12 sweep . . . knavery** sweep a path before me and conduct me to some *knavery* or treachery prepared for me. **212 work** proceed. **213 engineer** maker of *engines* of war **214 Hoist with** blown up by. **petard** an explosive used to blow in a door or make a breach **214–15 't shall . . . will** unless luck is against me, I will

---

But I will delve one yard below their mines   215

And blow them at the moon. Oh, 'tis most sweet

When in one line two crafts directly meet.   217

This man shall set me packing.   218

I'll lug the guts into the neighbor room.

Mother, good night indeed. This counselor

Is now most still, most secret, and most grave,

Who was in life a foolish prating knave.—

Come, sir, to draw toward an end with you.—   223

Good night, mother.

       Exeunt [separately, Hamlet dragging in Polonius].

❧

[4-1]

Enter King and Queen, with Rosencrantz and Guildenstern.

King:

There's matter in these sighs, these profound heaves.   1

You must translate; 'tis fit we understand them.

Where is your son?

Queen:

Bestow this place on us a little while.

       [Exeunt Rosencrantz and Guildenstern.]

Ah, mine own lord, what have I seen tonight!

King:

What, Gertrude? How does Hamlet?

Queen:

Mad as the sea and wind when both contend

Which is the mightier. In his lawless fit,

Behind the arras hearing something stir,

Whips out his rapier, cries, "A rat, a rat!"

And in this brainish apprehension kills   11

The unseen good old man.

---

215 mines tunnels used in warfare to undermine the enemy's emplacements; Hamlet will countermine by going under their mines **217 in one line** i.e., mines and countermines on a collision course, or the countermines directly below the mines. **crafts** acts of guile, plots **218 set me packing** set me to making schemes, and set me to lugging (him), and, also, send me off in a hurry. **223 draw . . . end** finish up. (With a pun on *draw*, "pull.")
4-1 Location: The castle.
0.1 *Enter . . . Queen* (Some editors argue that Gertrude does not in fact exit at the end of 3.4 and that the scene is continuous here. It is true that the Folio ends 3.4 with "*Exit Hamlet tugging in Polonius,*" not naming Gertrude, and opens 4.1 with "*Enter King.*" Yet the second quarto concludes 3.4 with a simple "*Exit,*" which often stands ambiguously for a single exit or an exeunt in early modern texts, and then starts 4.1 with "*Enter King, and Queene, with Rosencraus and Guyldensterne.*" The King's opening lines in 4.1 suggest that he has had time, during a brief intervening pause, to become aware of Gertrude's highly wrought emotional state. In line 35, the King refers to Gertrude's *closet* as though it were elsewhere. The differences between the second quarto and the Folio offer an alternative staging. In either case, 4.1 follows swiftly upon 3.4.) **1 matter** significance. **heaves** heavy sighs. **11 brainish apprehension** frenzied misapprehension

King: Oh, heavy deed! 12

It had been so with us, had we been there. 13

His liberty is full of threats to all—

To you yourself, to us, to everyone.

Alas, how shall this bloody deed be answered? 16

It will be laid to us, whose providence 17

Should have kept short, restrained, and out of haunt 18

This mad young man. But so much was our love,

We would not understand what was most fit,

But, like the owner of a foul disease,

To keep it from divulging, let it feed 22

Even on the pith of life. Where is he gone?

Queen:

To draw apart the body he hath killed,

O'er whom his very madness, like some ore 25

Among a mineral of metals base, 26

Shows itself pure: 'a weeps for what is done.

King: Oh, Gertrude, come away!

The sun no sooner shall the mountains touch

But we will ship him hence, and this vile deed

We must with all our majesty and skill

Both countenance and excuse.—Ho, Guildenstern! 32

Enter Rosencrantz and Guildenstern.

Friends both, go join you with some further aid.

Hamlet in madness hath Polonius slain,

And from his mother's closet hath he dragged him.

Go seek him out, speak fair, and bring the body 36

Into the chapel. I pray you, haste in this.

        [*Exeunt Rosencrantz and Guildenstern.*]

Come, Gertrude, we'll call up our wisest friends

And let them know both what we mean to do

And what's untimely done 40

Whose whisper o'er the world's diameter, 41

As level as the cannon to his blank, 42

Transports his poisoned shot, may miss our name

And hit the woundless air. Oh, come away! 44

My soul is full of discord and dismay.   *Exeunt.*

[4-2]

Enter Hamlet.

Hamlet: Safely stowed.

Rosencrantz, Guildenstern: (*within*) Hamlet! Lord
  Hamlet!

Hamlet: But soft, what noise? Who calls on Hamlet? Oh,
  here they come.

Enter Rosencrantz and Guildenstern.

Rosencrantz:

What have you done, my lord, with the dead body?

Hamlet:

Compounded it with dust, whereto 'tis kin.

Rosencrantz:

Tell us where 'tis, that we may take it thence

And bear it to the chapel.

Hamlet: Do not believe it.

Rosencrantz: Believe what?

Hamlet: That I can keep your counsel and not mine 12
  own. Besides, to be demanded of a sponge, what 13
  replication should be made by the son of a king? 14

Rosencrantz: Take you me for a sponge, my lord?

Hamlet:

Ay, sir, that soaks up the King's countenance, 16
  his rewards, his authorities. But such officers do the 17
  King best service in the end. He keeps them, like an
  ape, an apple, in the corner of his jaw, first mouthed
  to be last swallowed. When he needs what you have
  gleaned, it is but squeezing you, and, sponge, you
  shall be dry again.

Rosencrantz: I understand you not, my lord.

Hamlet: I am glad of it. A knavish speech sleeps in a 24
  foolish ear.

Rosencrantz: My lord, you must tell us where the
  body is and go with us to the King.

Hamlet: The body is with the King, but the King 28
  is not with the body. The King is a thing— 29

Guildenstern: A thing, my lord?

---

12 **heavy** grievous 13 **us** i.e., me. (The royal "we"; also in line 15.)
16 **answered** explained. 17 **providence** foresight 18 **short** i.e., on a
short tether. **out of haunt** secluded 22 **from divulging** from becoming
publicly known 25 **ore** vein of gold 26 **mineral** mine 32 **countenance**
put the best face on 36 **fair** gently, courteously 40 **And . . . done** (A
defective line; conjectures as to the missing words include "So, haply,
slander" [Capell and others]; "For, haply, slander" [Theobald and others];
and "So envious slander" [Jenkins].) 41 **diameter** extent from side to
side 42 **As level** with as direct aim. **his blank** its target at point-blank
range 44 **woundless** invulnerable

4-2 **Location:** The castle.
12–13 **That . . . own** i.e., Don't expect me to do as you bid me and not
follow my own counsel. 13 **demanded of** questioned by 13–14 **replication** reply 16 **countenance** favor 17 **authorities** delegated power,
influence. 24 **sleeps in** has no meaning to 28–9 **The . . . body**
(Perhaps alludes to the legal commonplace of "the king's two bodies,"
which drew a distinction between the sacred office of kingship and
the particular mortal who possessed it at any given time. Hence,
although Claudius's body is necessarily a part of him, true kingship is
not contained in it. Similarly, Claudius will have Polonius's body when
it is found, but there is no kingship in this business either.)

Hamlet: Of nothing. Bring me to him. Hide fox, and all   31
after!   32

Exeunt [running].

[4-3]

Enter King, and two or three.

King:

I have sent to seek him, and to find the body.
How dangerous is it that this man goes loose!
Yet must not we put the strong law on him.
He's loved of the distracted multitude,   4
Who like not in their judgment, but their eyes,   5
And where 'tis so, th'offender's scourge is weighed,   6
But never the offense. To bear all smooth and even,   7
This sudden sending him away must seem
Deliberate pause. Diseases desperate grown   9
By desperate appliance are relieved,   10
Or not at all.

*Enter Rosencrantz, [Guildenstern,]
and all the rest.*

       How now, what hath befall'n?

Rosencrantz:

Where the dead body is bestowed, my lord,
We cannot get from him.

King: But where is he?

Rosencrantz:

Without, my lord; guarded, to know your pleasure.   14

King:

Bring him before us.

Rosencrantz: [*calling*] Ho! Bring in the lord.

They enter [with Hamlet].

King: Now, Hamlet, where's Polonius?

Hamlet: At supper.

King: At supper? Where?

Hamlet: Not where he eats, but where 'a is eaten. A
certain convocation of politic worms are e'en at him.   20

Your worm is your only emperor for diet. We fat all   21
creatures else to fat us, and we fat ourselves for maggots. Your fat king and your lean beggar is but
variable service—two dishes, but to one table. That's   24
the end.

King: Alas, alas!

Hamlet: A man may fish with the worm that hath eat   27
of a king, and eat of the fish that hath fed of that
worm.

King: What dost thou mean by this?

Hamlet: Nothing but to show you how a king
may go a progress through the guts of a beggar.   32

King: Where is Polonius?

Hamlet: In heaven. Send thither to see. If your messenger find him not there, seek him i'th'other place yourself. But if indeed you find him not within this month,
you shall nose him as you go up the stairs into the   37
lobby.

King: [*to some attendants*] Go seek him there.

Hamlet: 'A will stay till you come. [*Exeunt attendants.*]

King:

Hamlet, this deed, for thine especial safety—
Which we do tender, as we dearly grieve   42
For that which thou hast done—must send thee hence
With fiery quickness. Therefore prepare thyself.
The bark is ready, and the wind at help,   45
Th'associates tend, and everything is bent   46
For England.

Hamlet: For England!

King: Ay, Hamlet.

Hamlet: Good.

King:

So is it, if thou knew'st our purposes.

Hamlet: I see a cherub that sees them. But come, for   52
England! Farewell, dear mother.

King: Thy loving father, Hamlet.

Hamlet: My mother. Father and mother is man and
wife, man and wife is one flesh, and so, my mother.
Come, for England!   *Exit.*

King:

Follow him at foot; tempt him with speed aboard.   58
Delay it not. I'll have him hence tonight.

---

31 Of nothing (1) Of no account (2) Lacking the essence of kingship, as in lines 28–9 and note. **31–2 Hide . . . after** (An old signal cry in the game of hide-and-seek, suggesting that Hamlet now runs away from them.)
4-3 Location: The castle.
4 of by. **distracted** fickle, unstable **5 Who . . . eyes** who choose not by judgment but by appearance **6–7 th'offender's . . . offense** i.e., the populace often takes umbrage at the severity of a punishment without taking into account the gravity of the crime. **7 To . . . even** To manage the business in an unprovocative way **9 Deliberate pause** carefully considered action. **10 appliance** remedies **14 Without** Outside **20 politic worms** crafty worms (suited to a master spy like Polonius). **e'en** even now

21 Your worm Your average worm. (Compare *your fat king and your lean beggar* in line 23.) **diet** food, eating. (With a punning reference to the Diet of Worms, a famous *convocation* held in 1521.) **24 service** food served at table. (Worms feed on kings and beggars alike.) **27 eat** eaten. (Pronounced *et.*) **32 progress** royal journey of state **37 nose** smell **42 tender** regard, hold dear. **dearly** intensely **45 bark** sailing vessel **46 tend** wait. **bent** in readiness **52 cherub** (Cherubim are angels of knowledge. Hamlet hints that both he and heaven are onto Claudius's tricks.) **58 at foot** close behind, at heel

Away! For everything is sealed and done

That else leans on th'affair. Pray you, make haste. 61

[*Exeunt all but the King.*]

And, England, if my love thou hold'st at aught— 62

As my great power thereof may give thee sense, 63

Since yet thy cicatrice looks raw and red 64

After the Danish sword, and thy free awe 65

Pays homage to us—thou mayst not coldly set 66

Our sovereign process, which imports at full, 67

By letters congruing to that effect, 68

The present death of Hamlet. Do it, England, 69

For like the hectic in my blood he rages, 70

And thou must cure me. Till I know 'tis done, 71

Howe'er my haps, my joys were ne'er begun. *Exit.* 72

♣

[4-4]

Enter Fortinbras with his army over the stage.

Fortinbras:

Go, Captain, from me greet the Danish king.

Tell him that by his license Fortinbras 2

Craves the conveyance of a promised march 3

Over his kingdom. You know the rendezvous.

If that His Majesty would aught with us,

We shall express our duty in his eye; 6

And let him know so.

Captain: I will do't, my lord.

Fortinbras: Go softly on. [*Exeunt all but the Captain.*] 9

Enter Hamlet, Rosencrantz, [Guildenstern,] etc.

Hamlet: Good sir, whose powers are these? 10

Captain: They are of Norway, sir.

Hamlet: How purposed, sir, I pray you?

Captain: Against some part of Poland.

Hamlet: Who commands them, sir?

Captain:

The nephew to old Norway, Fortinbras.

Hamlet:

Goes it against the main of Poland, sir, 16

Or for some frontier?

Captain:

Truly to speak, and with no addition, 18

We go to gain a little patch of ground

That hath in it no profit but the name.

To pay five ducats, five, I would not farm it; 21

Nor will it yield to Norway or the Pole

A ranker rate, should it be sold in fee. 23

Hamlet:

Why, then the Polack never will defend it.

Captain:

Yes, it is already garrisoned.

Hamlet:

Two thousand souls and twenty thousand ducats

Will not debate the question of this straw. 27

This is th'impostume of much wealth and peace, 28

That inward breaks, and shows no cause without 29

Why the man dies. I humbly thank you, sir.

Captain:

God b'wi'you, sir. [*Exit.*]

Rosencrantz: Will't please you go, my lord?

Hamlet:

I'll be with you straight. Go a little before.

[*Exeunt all except Hamlet.*]

How all occasions do inform against me 33

And spur my dull revenge! What is a man,

If his chief good and market of his time 35

Be but to sleep and feed? A beast, no more.

Sure he that made us with such large discourse, 37

Looking before and after, gave us not 38

That capability and godlike reason

To fust in us unused. Now, whether it be 40

Bestial oblivion, or some craven scruple 41

Of thinking too precisely on th'event— 42

A thought which, quartered, hath but one part wisdom

And ever three parts coward—I do not know

Why yet I live to say "This thing's to do,"

Sith I have cause, and will, and strength, and means 46

To do't. Examples gross as earth exhort me: 47

Witness this army of such mass and charge, 48

Led by a delicate and tender prince, 49

61 leans on bears upon, is related to **62 England** i.e., King of England. **at aught** at any value **63 As . . . sense** for so my great power may give you a just appreciation of the importance of valuing my love **64 cicatrice** scar **65 free awe** unconstrained show of respect **66 coldly set** regard with indifference **67 process** command. **imports at full** conveys specific directions for **68 congruing** agreeing **69 present** immediate **70 hectic** persistent fever **72 Howe'er . . . begun** whatever else happens, I cannot begin to be happy.
4-4 Location: The coast of Denmark.
2 license permission **3 conveyance** unhindered passage **6 We . . . eye** I will come pay my respects in person **9 softly** slowly, circumspectly **10 powers** forces **16 main** main part

18 addition exaggeration **21 To pay** i.e., For a yearly rental of. **farm it** take a lease of it **23 ranker** higher. **in fee** fee simple, outright. **27 debate . . . straw** argue about this trifling matter. **28 th'impostume** the abscess **29 inward breaks** festers within. **without** externally **33 inform against** denounce; take shape against **35 market of** profit of **37 discourse** power of reasoning **38 Looking before and after** able to review past events and anticipate the future **40 fust** grow moldy **41 oblivion** forgetfulness. **craven** cowardly **42 precisely** scrupulously. **th'event** the outcome **46 Sith** since **47 gross** obvious **48 charge** expense **49 delicate and tender** of fine and youthful qualities

Whose spirit with divine ambition puffed

Makes mouths at the invisible event, 51

Exposing what is mortal and unsure

To all that fortune, death, and danger dare, 53

Even for an eggshell. Rightly to be great 54

Is not to stir without great argument,

But greatly to find quarrel in a straw

When honor's at the stake. How stand I, then,

That have a father killed, a mother stained,

Excitements of my reason and my blood, 59

And let all sleep, while to my shame I see

The imminent death of twenty thousand men

That for a fantasy and trick of fame 62

Go to their graves like beds, fight for a plot 63

Whereon the numbers cannot try the cause, 64

Which is not tomb enough and continent 65

To hide the slain? Oh, from this time forth

My thoughts be bloody or be nothing worth!   *Exit.*

[4-5]

Enter Horatio, [Queen] Gertrude, and a Gentleman.

Queen:

I will not speak with her.

Gentleman: She is importunate,

Indeed distract. Her mood will needs be pitied. 2

Queen: What would she have?

Gentleman:

She speaks much of her father, says she hears

There's tricks i'th' world, and hems, and beats her heart, 5

Spurns enviously at straws, speaks things in doubt 6

That carry but half sense. Her speech is nothing,

Yet the unshapèd use of it doth move 8

The hearers to collection; they yawn at it, 9

And botch the words up fit to their own thoughts, 10

Which, as her winks and nods and gestures yield them, 11

Indeed would make one think there might be thought, 12

Though nothing sure, yet much unhappily. 13

51 Makes mouths makes scornful faces. **invisible event** unforeseeable outcome **53 dare** could do (to him) **54–7 Rightly . . . stake** True greatness is not a matter of being moved to action solely by a great cause; rather, it is to respond greatly to an apparently trivial cause when honor is at the stake. **59 blood** (The supposed seat of the passions.) **62 fantasy** fanciful caprice, illusion. **trick** trifle, deceit **63 plot** plot of ground **64 Whereon . . . cause** on which there is insufficient room for the soldiers needed to fight for it **65 continent** receptacle, container **4-5 Location: The castle.**
2 distract out of her mind. **5 tricks** deceptions. **hems** clears her throat, makes "hmm" sounds. **heart** i.e., breast **6 Spurns . . . straws** kicks spitefully, takes offense at trifles. **in doubt** of obscure meaning **8 unshapèd use** incoherent manner **9 collection** inference, a guess at some sort of meaning. **yawn** gape, wonder; grasp. (The Folio reading, "aim," is possible.) **10 botch** patch **11 Which** which words. **yield** deliver, represent **12–13 there might . . . unhappily** that a great deal could be guessed at of a most unfortunate nature, even if one couldn't be at all sure.

Horatio:

'Twere good she were spoken with, for she may strew

Dangerous conjectures in ill-breeding minds. 15

Queen: Let her come in.   *[Exit Gentleman.]*

[Aside] To my sick soul, as sin's true nature is,

Each toy seems prologue to some great amiss. 18

So full of artless jealousy is guilt, 19

It spills itself in fearing to be spilt. 20

Enter Ophelia [distracted].

Ophelia:

Where is the beauteous majesty of Denmark?

Queen: How now, Ophelia?

Ophelia: (*she sings*)

    "How should I your true love know

        From another one?

    By his cockle hat and staff, 25

        And his sandal shoon." 26

Queen: Alas, sweet lady, what imports this song?

Ophelia: Say you? Nay, pray you, mark.

    "He is dead and gone, lady,   (*Song.*)

        He is dead and gone;

    At his head a grass-green turf,

        At his heels a stone." 33

    Oho!

Queen: Nay, but Ophelia—

Ophelia: Pray you, mark.

    [*Sings*] "White his shroud as the mountain snow"—

Enter King.

Queen: Alas, look here, my lord.

Ophelia:

    "Larded with sweet flowers;   (*Song.*) 38

    Which bewept to the ground did not go

        With true-love showers." 40

King: How do you, pretty lady?

Ophelia: Well, God 'ild you! They say the owl was a 42

baker's daughter. Lord, we know what we are, but

know not what we may be. God be at your table!

King: Conceit upon her father. 45

Ophelia: Pray let's have no words of this; but when

they ask you what it means, say you this:

15 ill-breeding prone to suspect the worst and to make mischief **18 toy** trifle. **amiss** calamity. **19–20 So . . . spilt** Guilt is so burdened with conscience and guileless fear of detection that it reveals itself through apprehension of disaster. **20.1 Enter Ophelia** (In the first quarto, Ophelia enters "*playing on a lute, and her hair down, singing.*") **25 cockle hat** hat with cockleshell stuck in it as a sign that the wearer had been a pilgrim to the shrine of Saint James of Compostella in Spain **26 shoon** shoes. **33 Oho!** (Perhaps a sigh.) **38 Larded** strewn, bedecked **40 showers** i.e., tears. **42 God 'ild** God yield or reward. **owl** (Refers to a legend about a baker's daughter who was turned into an owl for being ungenerous when Jesus begged a loaf of bread.) **45 Conceit** Fancy, brooding

"Tomorrow is Saint Valentine's day,   (*Song.*)

    All in the morning betime,   49

And I a maid at your window,

    To be your Valentine.

Then up he rose, and donned his clothes,

    And dupped the chamber door,   53

Let in the maid, that out a maid

    Never departed more."

King: Pretty Ophelia—

Ophelia: Indeed, la, without an oath, I'll make an end

on't:

    [*Sings*]   "By Gis and by Saint Charity,   59

        Alack, and fie for shame!

    Young men will do't, if they come to't;

        By Cock, they are to blame.   62

    Quoth she, 'Before you tumbled me,

        You promised me to wed.'"

He answers:

      "'So would I ha' done, by yonder sun,

      An thou hadst not come to my bed.'"   67

King: How long hath she been thus?

Ophelia: I hope all will be well. We must be patient,

but I cannot choose but weep to think they would lay

him i'th' cold ground. My brother shall know of it.

And so I thank you for your good counsel. Come, my

coach! Good night, ladies, good night, sweet ladies,

good night, good night.   [*Exit.*]

King: [*to Horatio*]

Follow her close. Give her good watch, I pray you.

              [*Exit Horatio.*]

Oh, this is the poison of deep grief; it springs

All from her father's death—and now behold!

Oh, Gertrude, Gertrude,

When sorrows come, they come not single spies,   79

But in battalions. First, her father slain;

Next, your son gone, and he most violent author

Of his own just remove; the people muddied,   82

Thick and unwholesome in their thoughts and whispers

For good Polonius' death—and we have done but greenly,   84

In hugger-mugger to inter him; poor Ophelia   85

Divided from herself and her fair judgment,

Without the which we are pictures or mere beasts;

Last, and as much containing as all these,   88

Her brother is in secret come from France,

Feeds on this wonder, keeps himself in clouds,   90

And wants not buzzers to infect his ear   91

With pestilent speeches of his father's death,

Wherein necessity, of matter beggared,   93

Will nothing stick our person to arraign   94

In ear and ear. Oh, my dear Gertrude, this,   95

Like to a murd'ring piece, in many places   96

Gives me superfluous death.   *A noise within.*   97

Queen: Alack, what noise is this?

King: Attend!   99

Where is my Switzers? Let them guard the door.   100

Enter a Messenger.

What is the matter?

Messenger: Save yourself, my lord!

The ocean, overpeering of his list,   102

Eats not the flats with more impetuous haste   103

Than young Laertes, in a riotous head,   104

O'erbears your officers. The rabble call him lord,

And, as the world were now but to begin,   106

Antiquity forgot, custom not known,   107

The ratifiers and props of every word,   108

They cry, "Choose we! Laertes shall be king!"

Caps, hands, and tongues applaud it to the clouds,   110

"Laertes shall be king, Laertes king!"

Queen: How cheerfully on the false trail they cry!

           A noise within.

Oh, this is counter, you false Danish dogs!   113

Enter Laertes with others.

King: The doors are broke.

Laertes:

Where is this King?—Sirs, stand you all without.

All: No, let's come in.

Laertes: I pray you, give me leave.

All: We will, we will.

Laertes: I thank you. Keep the door. [*Exeunt followers.*]

                Oh, thou vile king,

Give me my father!

Queen: [*restraining him*] Calmly, good Laertes.

Laertes:

That drop of blood that's calm proclaims me bastard,

---

49 betime early **53 dupped** did up, opened **59 Gis** Jesus **62 Cock** (A perversion of "God" in oaths; here also with a quibble on the slang word for penis.) **67 An** if **79 spies** scouts sent in advance of the main force **82 remove** removal. **muddied** stirred up, confused **84 greenly** foolishly **85 hugger-mugger** secret haste **88 as much containing** as full of serious matter **90 Feeds . . . clouds** feeds his resentment on this whole shocking turn of events, keeps himself aloof and mysterious

91 wants lacks. **buzzers** gossipers, informers **93 necessity** i.e., the need to invent some plausible explanation. **of matter beggared** unprovided with facts **94–5 Will . . . ear** will not hesitate to accuse my (royal) person in everybody's ears. **96 murd'ring piece** cannon loaded so as to scatter its shot **97 Gives . . . death** kills me over and over. **99 Attend!** Guard me! **100 Switzers** Swiss guards, mercenaries. **102 overpeering of his list** overflowing its shore, boundary **103 flats** i.e., flatlands near shore. **impetuous** violent (perhaps also with the meaning of *impiteous* ["impitious," Q2], "pitiless") **104 riotous head** insurrectionary advance **106–8 And . . . word** and, as if the world were to be started all over afresh, utterly setting aside all ancient traditional customs that should confirm and underprop our every word and promise **110 Caps** (The caps are thrown in the air.) **113 counter** (A hunting term, meaning to follow the trail in a direction opposite to that which the game has taken.)

Cries cuckold to my father, brands the harlot

Even here between the chaste unsmirchèd brow 122

Of my true mother.

King: What is the cause, Laertes,

That thy rebellion looks so giantlike? 125

Let him go, Gertrude. Do not fear our person. 126

There's such divinity doth hedge a king 127

That treason can but peep to what it would, 128

Acts little of his will. Tell me, Laertes, 129

Why thou art thus incensed. Let him go, Gertrude.

Speak, man.

Laertes: Where is my father?

King: Dead.

Queen:

But not by him.

King: Let him demand his fill.

Laertes:

How came he dead? I'll not be juggled with. 133

To hell, allegiance! Vows, to the blackest devil!

Conscience and grace, to the profoundest pit!

I dare damnation. To this point I stand, 136

That both the worlds I give to negligence, 137

Let come what comes, only I'll be revenged

Most throughly for my father. 139

King: Who shall stay you?

Laertes: My will, not all the world's. 141

And for my means, I'll husband them so well 142

They shall go far with little.

King: Good Laertes,

If you desire to know the certainty

Of your dear father, is't writ in your revenge

That, swoopstake, you will draw both friend and foe, 146

Winner and loser?

Laertes: None but his enemies.

King: Will you know them, then?

Laertes:

To his good friends thus wide I'll ope my arms,

And like the kind life-rendering pelican 151

Repast them with my blood.

King: Why, now you speak 152

Like a good child and a true gentleman.

That I am guiltless of your father's death,

And am most sensibly in grief for it, 155

It shall as level to your judgment 'pear 156

As day does to your eye. *A noise within.*

Laertes: How now, what noise is that?

Enter Ophelia.

King: Let her come in.

Laertes:

O heat, dry up my brains! Tears seven times salt

Burn out the sense and virtue of mine eye! 160

By heaven, thy madness shall be paid with weight 161

Till our scale turn the beam. O rose of May! 162

Dear maid, kind sister, sweet Ophelia!

O heavens, is't possible a young maid's wits

Should be as mortal as an old man's life?

Nature is fine in love, and where 'tis fine 166

It sends some precious instance of itself 167

After the thing it loves. 168

Ophelia:

    "They bore him barefaced on the bier,   (*Song.*)

        Hey non nonny, nonny, hey nonny,

        And in his grave rained many a tear—"

Fare you well, my dove!

Laertes:

Hadst thou thy wits and didst persuade revenge,

It could not move thus.

Ophelia: You must sing "A-down a-down," and you 175

"call him a-down-a." Oh, how the wheel becomes it! It 176

is the false steward that stole his master's daughter. 177

Laertes: This nothing's more than matter. 178

Ophelia: There's rosemary, that's for remembrance; 179

pray you, love, remember. And there is pansies; 180

that's for thoughts.

Laertes: A document in madness, thoughts and 182

remembrance fitted.

Ophelia: There's fennel for you, and columbines. 184

155 **sensibly** feelingly 156 **level** plain 160 **virtue** faculty, power
161 **paid with weight** repaid, avenged equally or more 162 **beam** cross-bar of a balance. 166–8 **Nature . . . loves** Human nature is exquisitely sensitive in matters of love, and in cases of sudden loss it sends some precious part of itself after the lost object of that love. (In this case, Ophelia's sanity deserts her out of sorrow for her lost father and perhaps too out of her love for Hamlet.) 175–6 **You . . . a-down-a** (Ophelia assigns the singing of refrains, like her own "Hey non nonny," to others present.) 176 **wheel** spinning wheel as accompaniment to the song, or refrain 177 **false steward** (The story is unknown.) 178 **This . . . matter** This seeming nonsense is more eloquent than sane utterance. 179 **rosemary** (Used as a symbol of remembrance both at weddings and at funerals.) 180 **pansies** (Emblems of love and courtship; perhaps from French *pensèes*, "thoughts.") 182 **document** instruction, lesson 184 **There's fennel . . . columbines** (*Fennel* betokens flattery; *columbines*, unchastity or ingratitude. Throughout, Ophelia addresses her various listeners, giving one flower to one and another to another, perhaps with particular symbolic significance in each case.)

123 **between** amidst 125 **giantlike** (Recalling the rising of the giants of Greek mythology against Olympus.) 126 **fear our** fear for my 127 **hedge** protect, as with a surrounding barrier 128 **can . . . would** can only peep furtively, as through a barrier, at what it would intend 129 **Acts . . . will** (but) performs little of what it intends. 133 **juggled with** cheated, deceived. 136 **To . . . stand** I am resolved in this 137 **both . . . negligence** i.e., both this world and the next are of no consequence to me 139 **throughly** thoroughly 141 **My will . . . world's** I'll stop (*stay*) when my will is accomplished, not for anyone else's. 142 **for** as for 146 **swoopstake** i.e., indiscriminately. (Literally, taking all stakes on the gambling table at once. *Draw* is also a gambling term, meaning "take from.") 151 **pelican** (Refers to the belief that the female pelican fed its young with its own blood.) 152 **Repast** feed

There's rue for you, and here's some for me; we may 185

call it herb of grace o' Sundays. You must wear your

rue with a difference. There's a daisy. I would give 187

you some violets, but they withered all when my 188

father died. They say 'a made a good end—

[*Sings*] "For bonny sweet Robin is all my joy."

Laertes: Thought and affliction, passion, hell itself, 191

She turns to favor and to prettiness. 192

Ophelia:

"And will 'a not come again?   (*Song.*)

And will 'a not come again?

No, no, he is dead.

Go to thy deathbed,

He never will come again.

"His beard was as white as snow,

All flaxen was his poll. 199

He is gone, he is gone,

And we cast away moan.

God ha' mercy on his soul!"

And of all Christian souls, I pray God. God b'wi'you.

[*Exit, followed by Gertrude.*]

Laertes: Do you see this, O God?

King:

Laertes, I must commune with your grief,

Or you deny me right. Go but apart,

Make choice of whom your wisest friends you will, 207

And they shall hear and judge twixt you and me.

If by direct or by collateral hand 209

They find us touched, we will our kingdom give, 210

Our crown, our life, and all that we call ours

To you in satisfaction; but if not,

Be you content to lend your patience to us,

And we shall jointly labor with your soul

To give it due content.

Laertes: Let this be so.

His means of death, his obscure funeral—

No trophy, sword, nor hatchment o'er his bones, 217

No noble rite, nor formal ostentation— 218

Cry to be heard, as 'twere from heaven to earth,

That I must call't in question.

King: So you shall, 220

And where th'offense is, let the great ax fall.

I pray you, go with me.   *Exeunt.*

❖

[4-6]

Enter Horatio and others.

Horatio:

What are they that would speak with me?

Gentleman: Seafaring men, sir. They say they have

letters for you. 3

Horatio: Let them come in.   [*Exit Gentleman.*]

I do not know from what part of the world

I should be greeted, if not from Lord Hamlet.

Enter Sailors.

First Sailor: God bless you, sir.

Horatio: Let him bless thee too.

First Sailor: 'A shall, sir, an't please him. There's a 9

letter for you, sir—it came from th'ambassador that 10

was bound for England—if your name be Horatio,

as I am let to know it is.   [*He gives a letter.*]

Horatio: [*reads*] "Horatio, when thou shalt have over- 13

looked this, give these fellows some means to the King; 14

they have letters for him. Ere we were two days old at

sea, a pirate of very warlike appointment gave us 16

chase. Finding ourselves too slow of sail, we put on a

compelled valor, and in the grapple I boarded them.

On the instant they got clear of our ship, so I alone

became their prisoner. They have dealt with me like

thieves of mercy, but they knew what they did: I am to

do a good turn for them. Let the King have the letters 21

I have sent, and repair thou to me with as much speed

as thou wouldest fly death. I have words to speak in 23

thine ear will make thee dumb, yet are they much too

light for the bore of the matter. These good fellows will 26

bring thee where I am. Rosencrantz and Guildenstern

hold their course for England. Of them I have much to

tell thee. Farewell.

He that thou knowest thine, Hamlet."

Come, I will give you way for these your letters, 31

And do't the speedier that you may direct me

To him from whom you brought them.   *Exeunt.*

---

185 **rue** (Emblem of repentance—a signification that is evident in its popular name, *herb of grace.*) 187 **with a difference** (A device used in heraldry to distinguish one family from another on the coat of arms, here suggesting that Ophelia and the others have different causes of sorrow and repentance; perhaps with a play on *rue* in the sense of "ruth," "pity.") **daisy** (Emblem of love's victims and of faithlessness.) 188 **violets** (Emblems of faithfulness.) 191 **Thought** Melancholy. **passion** suffering 192 **favor** grace, beauty 199 **poll** head. 207 **whom** whichever of 209 **collateral hand** indirect agency 210 **us touched** me implicated 217 **trophy** memorial. **hatchment** tablet displaying the armorial bearings of a deceased person 218 **ostentation** ceremony

220 **That** so that. **call't in question** demand an explanation.
4-6 **Location:** The castle.
3 **letters** a letter 9 **an't** if it 10 **th'ambassador** (Hamlet's ostensible role; see 3.1.172-3.) 13–14 **overlooked** looked over 14 **means** means of access 16 **appointment** equipage 21 **thieves of mercy** merciful thieves 23 **repair** come 26 **bore** caliber, i.e., importance 31 **way** means of access

[4-7]

Enter King and Laertes.

King:

Now must your conscience my acquittance seal,   1

And you must put me in your heart for friend,

Sith you have heard, and with a knowing ear,   3

That he which hath your noble father slain

Pursued my life.

Laertes: It well appears. But tell me

Why you proceeded not against these feats   6

So crimeful and so capital in nature,   7

As by your safety, greatness, wisdom, all things else,

You mainly were stirred up.   9

King: Oh, for two special reasons,

Which may to you perhaps seem much unsinewed,   11

But yet to me they're strong. The Queen his mother

Lives almost by his looks, and for myself—

My virtue or my plague, be it either which—

She is so conjunctive to my life and soul   15

That, as the star moves not but in his sphere,   16

I could not but by her. The other motive

Why to a public count I might not go   18

Is the great love the general gender bear him,   19

Who, dipping all his faults in their affection,

Work like the spring that turneth wood to stone,   21

Convert his gyves to graces, so that my arrows,   22

Too slightly timbered for so loud a wind,   23

Would have reverted to my bow again

But not where I had aimed them.

Laertes:

And so have I a noble father lost,

A sister driven into desp'rate terms,   27

Whose worth, if praises may go back again,   28

Stood challenger on mount of all the age   29

For her perfections. But my revenge will come.

King:

Break not your sleeps for that. You must not think

That we are made of stuff so flat and dull

That we can let our beard be shook with danger

4-7 **Location: The castle.**
1 **my acquittance seal** confirm or acknowledge my innocence
3 **Sith** since 6 **feats** acts 7 **capital** punishable by death 9 **mainly** greatly
11 **unsinewed** weak 15 **conjunctive** closely united. (An astronomical metaphor.) 16 **his** its. **sphere** one of the hollow spheres in which, according to Ptolemaic astronomy, the planets were supposed to move 18 **count** account, reckoning, indictment 19 **general gender** common people 21 **Work** operate, act. **spring** i.e., a spring with such a concentration of lime that it coats a piece of wood with limestone, in effect gilding and petrifying it 22 **gyves** fetters (which, gilded by the people's praise, would look like badges of honor) 23 **Too . . . wind** with too light a shaft for so powerful a gust (of popular sentiment) 27 **terms** state, condition 28 **go back** recall what she was 29 **on mount** set up on high

And think it pastime. You shortly shall hear more.

I loved your father, and we love ourself;

And that, I hope, will teach you to imagine—

Enter a Messenger with letters.

How now? What news?

Messenger: Letters, my lord, from Hamlet:

This to Your Majesty, this to the Queen.

[He gives letters.]

King: From Hamlet? Who brought them?

Messenger:

Sailors, my lord, they say. I saw them not.

They were given me by Claudio. He received them

Of him that brought them.

King: Laertes, you shall hear them.—

Leave us.   *[Exit Messenger.]*

[He reads.] "High and mighty, you shall know I am set

naked on your kingdom. Tomorrow shall I beg leave   45

to see your kingly eyes, when I shall, first asking your

pardon, thereunto recount the occasion of my sudden   47

and more strange return.   Hamlet."

What should this mean? Are all the rest come back?

Or is it some abuse, and no such thing?   50

Laertes:

Know you the hand?

King: 'Tis Hamlet's character. "Naked!"   51

And in a postscript here he says "alone."

Can you devise me?   53

Laertes:

I am lost in it, my lord. But let him come.

It warms the very sickness in my heart

That I shall live and tell him to his teeth,

"Thus didst thou."

King: If it be so, Laertes—   57

As how should it be so? How otherwise?—   58

Will you be ruled by me?

Laertes: Ay, my lord,

So you will not o'errule me to a peace.   60

King: To thine own peace. If he be now returned,

As checking at his voyage, and that he means   62

No more to undertake it, I will work him

To an exploit, now ripe in my device,   64

Under the which he shall not choose but fall;

And for his death no wind of blame shall breathe,

45 **naked** destitute, unarmed, without following
47 **pardon** (for returning without authorization) 50 **abuse** deceit.
no such thing not what the letter says. 51 **character** handwriting.
53 **devise** explain to 57 **Thus didst thou** i.e., Here's for what you did to my father. 58 **As . . . otherwise?** how can this (Hamlet's return) be true? Yet how otherwise than true (since we have the evidence of his letter?) 60 **So** provided that 62 **checking at** i.e., turning aside from (like a falcon leaving the quarry to fly at a chance bird). **that** if
64 **device** devising, invention

But even his mother shall uncharge the practice 67
And call it accident.

Laertes: My lord, I will be ruled,

The rather if you could devise it so

That I might be the organ.

King: It falls right. 70

You have been talked of since your travel much,

And that in Hamlet's hearing, for a quality

Wherein they say you shine. Your sum of parts 73

Did not together pluck such envy from him

As did that one, and that, in my regard,

Of the unworthiest siege. 76

Laertes: What part is that, my lord?

King:

A very ribbon in the cap of youth,

Yet needful too, for youth no less becomes 79

The light and careless livery that it wears

Than settled age his sables and his weeds 81

Importing health and graveness. Two months since 82

Here was a gentleman of Normandy.

I have seen myself, and served against, the French,

And they can well on horseback, but this gallant 85

Had witchcraft in't; he grew unto his seat,

And to such wondrous doing brought his horse

As had he been incorpsed and demi-natured 88

With the brave beast. So far he topped my thought 89

That I in forgery of shapes and tricks 90

Come short of what he did.

Laertes: A Norman was't?

King: A Norman.

Laertes:

Upon my life, Lamord.

King: The very same.

Laertes:

I know him well. He is the brooch indeed 94

And gem of all the nation.

King: He made confession of you, 96

And gave you such a masterly report

For art and exercise in your defense, 98

And for your rapier most especial,

That he cried out 'twould be a sight indeed

If one could match you. Th'escrimers of their nation, 101

He swore, had neither motion, guard, nor eye

If you opposed them. Sir, this report of his

Did Hamlet so envenom with his envy

That he could nothing do but wish and beg

Your sudden coming o'er, to play with you. 106

Now, out of this—

Laertes: What out of this, my lord?

King:

Laertes, was your father dear to you?

Or are you like the painting of a sorrow,

A face without a heart?

Laertes: Why ask you this?

King:

Not that I think you did not love your father,

But that I know love is begun by time, 112

And that I see, in passages of proof, 113

Time qualifies the spark and fire of it. 114

There lives within the very flame of love

A kind of wick or snuff that will abate it, 116

And nothing is at a like goodness still, 117

For goodness, growing to a pleurisy, 118

Dies in his own too much. That we would do, 119

We should do when we would; for this "would" changes

And hath abatements and delays as many 121

As there are tongues, are hands, are accidents, 122

And then this "should" is like a spendthrift sigh, 123

That hurts by easing. But, to the quick o'th'ulcer: 124

Hamlet comes back. What would you undertake

To show yourself in deed your father's son

More than in words?

Laertes: To cut his throat i'th' church.

King:

No place, indeed, should murder sanctuarize; 128

Revenge should have no bounds. But good Laertes,

Will you do this, keep close within your chamber. 130

Hamlet returned shall know you are come home.

We'll put on those shall praise your excellence 132

And set a double varnish on the fame

The Frenchman gave you, bring you in fine together, 134

67 uncharge the practice acquit the stratagem of being a plot **70 organ** agent, instrument. **73 Your . . . parts** All your other virtues **76 unworthiest siege** least important rank. **79 no less becomes** is no less adorned by **81–2 his sables . . . graveness** its rich robes furred with sable and its garments denoting dignified well-being and seriousness. **85 can well** are skilled **88–9 As . . . beast** as if, centaurlike, he had been made into one body with the horse, possessing half its nature. **89 topped** surpassed **90 forgery** fabrication **94 brooch** ornament **96 confession** testimonial, admission of superiority **98 For . . . defense** with respect to your skill and practice with your weapon **101 Th'escrimers** The fencers

106 sudden immediate. **play** fence **112 begun by time** i.e., created by the right circumstance and hence subject to change **113 passages of proof** actual well-attested instances **114 qualifies** weakens, moderates **116 snuff** the charred part of a candlewick **117 nothing . . . still** nothing remains at a constant level of perfection **118 pleurisy** excess, plethora. (Literally, a chest inflammation.) **119 in . . . much** of its own excess. **That** That which **121 abatements** diminutions **122 As . . . accidents** as there are tongues to dissuade, hands to prevent, and chance events to intervene **123 spendthrift sigh** (An allusion to the belief that sighs draw blood from the heart.) **124 hurts by easing** i.e., costs the heart blood and wastes precious opportunity even while it affords emotional relief. **quick o'th'ulcer** i.e., heart of the matter **128 sanctuarize** protect from punishment. (Alludes to the right of sanctuary with which certain religious places were invested.) **130 Will you do this** if you wish to do this **132 put on those shall** arrange for some to **134 in fine** finally

And wager on your heads. He, being remiss, 135
Most generous, and free from all contriving, 136
Will not peruse the foils, so that with ease,
Or with a little shuffling, you may choose
A sword unbated, and in a pass of practice 139
Requite him for your father.

Laertes: I will do't,
And for that purpose I'll anoint my sword.
I bought an unction of a mountebank 142
So mortal that, but dip a knife in it,
Where it draws blood no cataplasm so rare, 144
Collected from all simples that have virtue 145
Under the moon, can save the thing from death 146
That is but scratched withal. I'll touch my point
With this contagion, that if I gall him slightly, 148
It may be death.

King: Let's further think of this,
Weigh what convenience both of time and means
May fit us to our shape. If this should fail, 151
And that our drift look through our bad performance, 152
'Twere better not assayed. Therefore this project
Should have a back or second, that might hold
If this did blast in proof. Soft, let me see. 155
We'll make a solemn wager on your cunnings— 156
I ha 't!
When in your motion you are hot and dry—
As make your bouts more violent to that end— 159
And that he calls for drink, I'll have prepared him
A chalice for the nonce, whereon but sipping, 161
If he by chance escape your venomed stuck, 162
Our purpose may hold there. [*A cry within.*] But stay,
   what noise?

Enter Queen.

Queen:
One woe doth tread upon another's heel,
So fast they follow. Your sister's drowned, Laertes.

Laertes: Drowned! Oh, where?

Queen:
There is a willow grows askant the brook, 167
That shows his hoar leaves in the glassy stream; 168

Therewith fantastic garlands did she make
Of crowflowers, nettles, daisies, and long purples, 170
That liberal shepherds give a grosser name, 171
But our cold maids do dead men's fingers call them. 172
There on the pendent boughs her crownet weeds 173
Clamb'ring to hang, an envious sliver broke, 174
When down her weedy trophies and herself 175
Fell in the weeping brook. Her clothes spread wide,
And mermaidlike awhile they bore her up,
Which time she chanted snatches of old lauds, 178
As one incapable of her own distress, 179
Or like a creature native and endued 180
Unto that element. But long it could not be
Till that her garments, heavy with their drink,
Pulled the poor wretch from her melodious lay 183
To muddy death.

Laertes: Alas, then she is drowned?

Queen: Drowned, drowned.

Laertes:
Too much of water hast thou, poor Ophelia,
And therefore I forbid my tears. But yet
It is our trick; nature her custom holds, 188
Let shame say what it will. [*He weeps.*] When these are gone, 189
The woman will be out. Adieu, my lord. 190
I have a speech of fire that fain would blaze,
But that this folly douts it.   *Exit.*

King: Let's follow, Gertrude. 192
How much I had to do to calm his rage!
Now fear I this will give it start again;
Therefore let's follow.   *Exeunt.*

♣

[5-1]

Enter two Clowns [with spades and mattocks].

First Clown: Is she to be buried in Christian burial, when she will-
   fully seeks her own salvation?   2

---

135 remiss negligently unsuspicious **136 generous** noble-minded
139 unbated not blunted, having no button. **pass of practice** treacherous thrust in an arranged bout **142 unction** ointment. **mountebank**
quack doctor **144 cataplasm** plaster or poultice **145 simples** herbs.
virtue potency **146 Under the moon** i.e., anywhere (with reference
perhaps to the belief that herbs gathered at night had a special
power) **148 gall** graze, wound **151 shape** part we propose to act.
152 drift . . . performance intention should be made visible by our
bungling **155 blast in proof** come to grief when put to the test.
156 cunnings respective skills **159 As** i.e., and you should **161 nonce**
occasion **162 stuck** thrust. (From *stoccado,* a fencing term.) **167 askant**
aslant **168 hoar leaves** white or gray undersides of the leaves

170 long purples early purple orchids **171 liberal** free-spoken.
a grosser name (The testicle-resembling tubers of the orchid, which
also in some cases resemble *dead men's fingers,* have earned various
slang names like "dogstones" and "cullions.") **172 cold** chaste
173 pendent overhanging. **crownet** made into a chaplet or coronet
174 envious sliver malicious branch **175 weedy** i.e., of plants **178 lauds**
hymns **179 incapable of** lacking capacity to apprehend **180 endued**
adapted by nature **183 lay** ballad, song **188 It is our trick** i.e., weeping is our natural way (when sad) **189–90 When . . . out** When my
tears are all shed, the woman in me will be expended, satisfied.
192 douts extinguishes. (The second quarto reads "drownes.")
5-1 Location: A churchyard.
0.1 Clowns rustics **2 salvation** (A blunder for "damnation," or perhaps
a suggestion that Ophelia was taking her own shortcut to heaven.)

Laurence Oliver as Hamlet with the skull of "poor Yorick," the court jester (act 5, scene 1, line 184), in the 1948 film of *Hamlet,* directed by Olivier, the preeminent Shakespearean actor of his day.

Second Clown: I tell thee she is; therefore make her
grave straight. The crowner hath sat on her, and finds   4
it Christian burial.   5

First Clown: How can that be, unless she drowned
herself in her own defense?

Second Clown: Why, 'tis found so.   8

First Clown: It must be *se offendendo,* it cannot be else.   9
For here lies the point: if I drown myself wittingly,
it argues an act, and an act hath three branches—it is
to act, to do, and to perform. Argal, she drowned   12
herself wittingly.

Second Clown: Nay, but hear you, goodman delver—   14

First Clown: Give me leave. Here lies the water; good.
Here stands the man; good. If the man go to this
water and drown himself, it is, will he, nill he, he
goes, mark you that. But if the water come to him and   17
drown him, he drowns not himself. Argal, he that is
not guilty of his own death shortens not his own life.

Second Clown: But is this law?

First Clown: Ay, marry, is't—crowner's quest law.   22

Second Clown: Will you ha' the truth on't? If this had
not been a gentlewoman, she should have been
buried out o' Christian burial.

First Clown: Why, there thou say'st. And the more   26
pity that great folk should have countenance in this   27
world to drown or hang themselves, more than their
even-Christian. Come, my spade. There is no ancient   29
gentlemen but gardeners, ditchers, and grave makers.
They hold up Adam's profession.   31

Second Clown: Was he a gentleman?

First Clown: 'A was the first that ever bore arms.   33

Second Clown: Why, he had none.

First Clown: What, art a heathen? How dost thou
understand the Scripture? The Scripture says Adam
digged. Could he dig without arms? I'll put another   37
question to thee. If thou answerest me not to the
purpose, confess thyself—   39

Second Clown: Go to.

First Clown: What is he that builds stronger than
either the mason, the shipwright, or the carpenter?

Second Clown: The gallows maker, for that frame   43
outlives a thousand tenants.

First Clown: I like thy wit well, in good faith. The
gallows does well. But how does it well? It does well to   46
those that do ill. Now thou dost ill to say the gallows
is built stronger than the church. Argal, the gallows
may do well to thee. To't again, come.

Second Clown: "Who builds stronger than a mason,
a shipwright, or a carpenter?"

First Clown: Ay, tell me that, and unyoke.   52

Second Clown: Marry, now I can tell.

First Clown: To't.

Second Clown: Mass, I cannot tell.   55

Enter Hamlet and Horatio [at a distance].

First Clown: Cudgel thy brains no more about it, for
your dull ass will not mend his pace with beating;
and when you are asked this question next, say "a
grave maker." The houses he makes lasts till doomsday.
Go get thee in and fetch me a stoup of liquor.   60

[Exit Second Clown. First Clown digs.]

Song.

4 **straight** straightway, immediately. (But with a pun on *strait,* "narrow.") **crowner** coroner. **sat on her** conducted an inquest on her case 4–5 **finds it** gives his official verdict that her means of death was consistent with 8 **found so** determined so in the coroner's verdict. 9 *se offendendo* (A comic mistake for *se defendendo,* a term used in verdicts of self-defense.) 12 **Argal** (Corruption of *ergo,* "therefore.") 14 **goodman** (An honorific title often used with the name of a profession or craft.) 17 **will he, nill he** whether he will or no, willy-nilly 22 **quest** inquest

26 **there thou say'st** i.e., that's right. 27 **countenance** privilege 29 **even-Christian** fellow Christians. **ancient** going back to ancient times 31 **hold up** maintain 33 **bore arms** (To be entitled to bear a coat of arms would make Adam a gentleman, but as one who bore a spade, our common ancestor was an ordinary delver in the earth.) 37 **arms** i.e., the arms of the body. 39 **confess thyself** (The saying continues, "and be hanged.") 43 **frame** (1) gallows (2) structure 46 **does well** (1) is an apt answer (2) does a good turn. 52 **unyoke** i.e., after this great effort, you may unharness the team of your wits. 55 **Mass** By the Mass 60 **stoup** two-quart measure

"In youth, when I did love, did love,

  Methought it was very sweet, 61

  To contract—oh—the time for—a—my behove, 63

  Oh, methought there—a—was nothing—a—meet." 64

Hamlet: Has this fellow no feeling of his business,

  'a sings in grave-making? 65

Horatio: Custom hath made it in him a property 67

  of easiness. 68

Hamlet: 'Tis e'en so. The hand of little employment

  hath the daintier sense. 70

First Clown: *Song.*

  "But age with his stealing steps

    Hath clawed me in his clutch,

  And hath shipped me into the land, 73

    As if I had never been such."

[*He throws up a skull.*]

Hamlet: That skull had a tongue in it and could sing

  once. How the knave jowls it to the ground, as if 76

  'twere Cain's jawbone, that did the first murder! This

  might be the pate of a politician, which this ass now 78

  o'erreaches, one that would circumvent God, might 79

  it not?

Horatio: It might, my lord.

Hamlet: Or of a courtier, which could say, "Good

  morrow, sweet lord! How dost thou, sweet lord?"

  This might be my Lord Such-a-one, that praised my

  Lord Such-a-one's horse when 'a meant to beg it,

  might it not?

Horatio: Ay, my lord.

Hamlet: Why, e'en so, and now my Lady Worm's,

  chapless, and knocked about the mazard with a sex- 89

  ton's spade. Here's fine revolution, an we had the trick 90

  to see't. Did these bones cost no more the breeding 91

  but to play at loggets with them? Mine ache to think 92

  on't.

First Clown: *Song.*

  "A pickax and a spade, a spade,

    For and a shrouding sheet; 95

Oh, a pit of clay for to be made

  For such a guest is meet."

[*He throws up another skull.*]

Hamlet: There's another. Why may not that be the skull

  of a lawyer? Where be his quiddities now, his quilli- 99

  ties, his cases, his tenures, and his tricks? Why does 100

  he suffer this mad knave now to knock him about the

  sconce with a dirty shovel, and will not tell him of his 102

  action of battery? Hum, this fellow might be in 's time 103

  a great buyer of land, with his statutes, his recogni- 104

  zances, his fines, his double vouchers, his recoveries. 105

  Is this the fine of his fines and the recovery of his 106

  recoveries, to have his fine pate full of fine dirt? Will 107

  his vouchers vouch him no more of his purchases, and 108

  double ones too, than the length and breadth of a 109

  pair of indentures? The very conveyances of his lands 110

  will scarcely lie in this box, and must th'inheritor 111

  himself have no more, ha?

Horatio: Not a jot more, my lord.

Hamlet: Is not parchment made of sheepskins?

Horatio: Ay, my lord, and of calves' skins too.

Hamlet: They are sheep and calves which seek out as- 116

  surance in that. I will speak to this fellow.—Whose 117

  grave's this, sirrah? 118

First Clown: Mine, sir.

[*Sings*] "Oh, pit of clay for to be made

    For such a guest is meet."

Hamlet: I think it be thine, indeed, for thou liest in't.

First Clown: You lie out on't, sir, and therefore 'tis not yours. For my

  part, I do not lie in't, yet it is mine.

Hamlet: Thou dost lie in't, to be in't and say it is

  thine. 'Tis for the dead, not for the quick; therefore 126

  thou liest.

First Clown: 'Tis a quick lie, sir; 'twill away again

  from me to you.

---

61 In . . . love (This and the two following stanzas, with nonsensical variations, are from a poem attributed to Lord Vaux and printed in *Tottel's Miscellany,* 1557. The *oh* and *a* [for "ah"] seemingly are the grunts of the digger.) **63 To contract . . . behove** i.e., to shorten the time for my own advantage. (Perhaps he means to *prolong* it.) **64 meet** suitable, i.e., more suitable. **65 'a** that he **67–8 property of easiness** something he can do easily and indifferently. **70 daintier sense** more delicate sense of feeling. **73 into the land** i.e., toward my grave (?) (But note the lack of rhyme in *steps, land.*) **76 jowls** dashes. (With a pun on *jowl,* "jawbone.") **78 politician** schemer, plotter **79 o'erreaches** circumvents, gets the better of **89 chapless** having no lower jaw. **mazard** i.e., head. (Literally, a drinking vessel.) **90 revolution** turn of Fortune's wheel, change. **trick** knack **91–2 cost . . . but** involve so little expense and care in upbringing that we may **92 loggets** a game in which pieces of hard wood shaped like Indian clubs or bowling pins are thrown to lie as near as possible to a stake **95 For and** and moreover

99–100 his quiddities . . . quillities his subtleties, his legal niceties **100 tenures** the holding of a piece of property or office, or the conditions or period of such holding **102 sconce** head **103 action of battery** lawsuit about physical assault. **104 his statutes** his legal documents acknowledging obligation of a debt **104–5 recognizances** bonds undertaking to repay debts **105 fines** procedures for converting entailed estates into "fee simple" or freehold. **double vouchers** vouchers signed by two signatories guaranteeing the legality of real estate titles. **recoveries** suits to obtain the authority of a court judgment for the holding of land. **106–7 Is this . . . dirt?** Is this the end of his legal maneuvers and profitable land deals, to have the skull of his elegant head filled full of minutely sifted dirt? (With multiple wordplay on *fine* and *fines.*) **107–10 Will . . . indentures?** Will his vouchers, even double ones, guarantee him no more land than is needed to bury him in, being no bigger than the deed of conveyance? (An *indenture* is literally a legal document drawn up in duplicate on a single sheet and then cut apart on a zigzag line so that each pair was uniquely matched.) **111 box** (1) deed box (2) coffin. **th'inheritor** the acquirer, owner **116–17 assurance in that** safety in legal parchments. **118 sirrah** (A term of address to inferiors.) **126 quick** living

Hamlet: What man dost thou dig it for?

First Clown: For no man, sir.

Hamlet: What woman, then?

First Clown: For none, neither.

Hamlet: Who is to be buried in't?

First Clown: One that was a woman, sir, but, rest her soul, she's dead.

Hamlet: How absolute the knave is! We must speak by 137
the card, or equivocation will undo us. By the Lord, 138
Horatio, this three years I have took note of it: the age 139
is grown so picked that the toe of the peasant comes so 140
near the heel of the courtier he galls his kibe.—How 141
long hast thou been grave maker?

First Clown: Of all the days i'th' year, I came to't
that day that our last king Hamlet overcame Fortinbras.

Hamlet: How long is that since?

First Clown: Cannot you tell that? Every fool can
tell that. It was that very day that young Hamlet
was born—he that is mad and sent into England.

Hamlet: Ay, marry, why was he sent into England?

First Clown: Why, because 'a was mad. 'A shall
recover his wits there, or if 'a do not, 'tis no great
matter there.

Hamlet: Why?

First Clown: 'Twill not be seen in him there. There
the men are as mad as he.

Hamlet: How came he mad?

First Clown: Very strangely, they say.

Hamlet: How strangely?

First Clown: Faith, e'en with losing his wits.

Hamlet: Upon what ground? 160

First Clown: Why, here in Denmark. I have been
sexton here, man and boy, thirty years.

Hamlet: How long will a man lie i'th'earth ere
he rot?

First Clown: Faith, if 'a be not rotten before 'a die—as
we have many pocky corpses nowadays, that will
scarce hold the laying in—'a will last you some eight 165
year or nine year. A tanner will last you nine year. 166

Hamlet: Why he more than another?

First Clown: Why, sir, his hide is so tanned with his
trade that 'a will keep out water a great while, and
your water is a sore decayer of your whoreson dead 171
body. [*He picks up a skull.*] Here's a skull now hath
lien you i'th'earth three-and-twenty years. 173

Hamlet: Whose was it?

First Clown: A whoreson mad fellow's it was.
Whose do you think it was?

Hamlet: Nay, I know not.

First Clown: A pestilence on him for a mad rogue! 'A
poured a flagon of Rhenish on my head once. This 179
same skull, sir, was, sir, Yorick's skull, the King's jester.

Hamlet: This?

First Clown: E'en that.

Hamlet: Let me see. [*He takes the skull.*] Alas, poor
Yorick! I knew him, Horatio, a fellow of infinite jest, of
most excellent fancy. He hath bore me on his back a 185
thousand times, and now how abhorred in my
imagination it is! My gorge rises at it. Here hung those 187
lips that I have kissed I know not how oft. Where be
your gibes now? Your gambols, your songs, your 189
flashes of merriment that were wont to set the table on
a roar? Not one now, to mock your own grinning? 192
Quite chopfallen? Now get you to my lady's chamber 193
and tell her, let her paint an inch thick, to this favor
she must come. Make her laugh at that. Prithee,
Horatio, tell me one thing.

Horatio: What's that, my lord?

Hamlet: Dost thou think Alexander looked o' this
fashion i'th'earth?

Horatio: E'en so.

Hamlet: And smelt so? Pah! [*He throws down the skull.*]

Horatio: E'en so, my lord.

Hamlet: To what base uses we may return, Horatio!
Why may not imagination trace the noble dust of
Alexander till 'a find it stopping a bunghole? 204

Horatio: 'Twere to consider too curiously to 205
consider so.

Hamlet: No, faith, not a jot, but to follow him thither
with modesty enough, and likelihood to lead it. As 208
thus: Alexander died, Alexander was buried, Alexander returneth to dust, the dust is earth, of earth we
make loam, and why of that loam whereto he was 211
converted might they not stop a beer barrel?

---

137 **absolute** strict, precise 137–8 **by the card** i.e., with precision.
(Literally, by the mariner's compass-card, on which the points of the
compass were marked.) 138 **equivocation** ambiguity in the use of terms
139 **took** taken 139–41 **the age . . . kibe** i.e., the age has grown so finical
and mannered that the lower classes ape their social betters, chafing at
their heels. (*Kibes* are chilblains on the heels.) 160 **ground** cause. (But, in
the next line, the gravedigger takes the word in the sense of "land," "country.") 165 **pocky** rotten, diseased. (Literally, with the pox, or syphilis.)
166 **hold the laying in** hold together long enough to be interred. **last you**
last. (*You* is used colloquially here and in the following lines.)

171 **sore** keen, veritable. **whoreson** (An expression of contemptuous
familiarity.) 173 **lien you** lain. (See the note at line 166.) 179 **Rhenish**
Rhine wine 185 **bore** borne 187 **My gorge rises** i.e., I feel nauseated
189 **gibes** taunts 192 **chopfallen** (1) lacking the lower jaw (2) dejected.
193 **favor** aspect, appearance 204 **bunghole** hole for filling or emptying a cask. 205 **curiously** minutely 208 **with . . . lead it** with moderation and plausibility. 211 **loam** a mixture of clay, straw, sand, etc. used
to mold bricks, or, in this case, bungs for a beer barrel

Imperious Caesar, dead and turned to clay, 213
Might stop a hole to keep the wind away.
Oh, that that earth which kept the world in awe
Should patch a wall t'expel the winter's flaw! 216

Enter King, Queen, Laertes, and the corpse [of Ophelia, in procession, with Priest, lords, etc.].

But soft, but soft awhile! Here comes the King, 217
The Queen, the courtiers. Who is this they follow?
And with such maimèd rites? This doth betoken 219
The corpse they follow did with desperate hand
Fordo it own life. 'Twas of some estate. 221
Couch we awhile and mark. 222

[He and Horatio conceal themselves. Ophelia's body is taken to the grave.]

Laertes: What ceremony else?

Hamlet: [*to Horatio*]
That is Laertes, a very noble youth. Mark.

Laertes: What ceremony else?

Priest:
Her obsequies have been as far enlarged
As we have warranty. Her death was doubtful, 227
And but that great command o'ersways the order 228
She should in ground unsanctified been lodged 229
Till the last trumpet. For charitable prayers, 230
Shards, flints, and pebbles should be thrown on her. 231
Yet here she is allowed her virgin crants, 232
Her maiden strewments, and the bringing home 233
Of bell and burial. 234

Laertes:
Must there no more be done?

Priest: No more be done.
We should profane the service of the dead
To sing a requiem and such rest to her 237
As to peace-parted souls.

Laertes: Lay her i'th'earth, 238
And from her fair and unpolluted flesh
May violets spring! I tell thee, churlish priest, 240
A ministering angel shall my sister be
When thou liest howling.

Hamlet: [*to Horatio*]   What, the fair Ophelia! 242

Queen: [*scattering flowers*] Sweets to the sweet! Farewell.

I hoped thou shouldst have been my Hamlet's wife.
I thought thy bride-bed to have decked, sweet maid,
And not t' have strewed thy grave.

Laertes: Oh, treble woe
Fall ten times treble on that cursèd head
Whose wicked deed thy most ingenious sense 248
Deprived thee of! Hold off the earth awhile,
Till I have caught her once more in mine arms.

[He leaps into the grave and embraces Ophelia.]

Now pile your dust upon the quick and dead,
Till of this flat a mountain you have made
T' o'ertop old Pelion or the skyish head 253
Of blue Olympus.

Hamlet: [*coming forward*] What is he whose grief
Bears such an emphasis, whose phrase of sorrow 255
Conjures the wandering stars and makes them stand 256
Like wonder-wounded hearers? This is I, 257
Hamlet the Dane. 258

Laertes: [*grappling with him*] The devil take thy soul! 259

Hamlet: Thou pray'st not well.
I prithee, take thy fingers from my throat,
For though I am not splenitive and rash, 262
Yet have I in me something dangerous,
Which let thy wisdom fear. Hold off thy hand.

King: Pluck them asunder.

Queen: Hamlet, Hamlet!

All: Gentlemen!

Horatio: Good my lord, be quiet.

[Hamlet and Laertes are parted.]

Hamlet:
Why, I will fight with him upon this theme
Until my eyelids will no longer wag. 270

Queen: Oh, my son, what theme?

Hamlet:
I loved Ophelia. Forty thousand brothers
Could not with all their quantity of love
Make up my sum. What wilt thou do for her?

---

248 ingenious sense a mind that is quick, alert, of fine qualities **253 Pelion** a mountain in northern Thessaly; compare *Olympus* and *Ossa* in lines 254 and 286. (In their rebellion against the Olympian gods, the giants attempted to heap Ossa on Pelion in order to scale Olympus.) **255 emphasis** i.e., rhetorical and florid emphasis. (*Phrase* has a similar rhetorical connotation.) **256 wandering stars** planets **257 wonder-wounded** struck with amazement **258 the Dane** (This title normally signifies the King; see 1.1.17 and note.) **259 s.d. grappling with him** The testimony of the first quarto that *"Hamlet leaps in after Laertes"* and of the ballad "Elegy on Burbage," published in *Gentleman's Magazine* in 1825 ("Oft have I seen him leap into a grave") seem to indicate one way in which this fight was staged; however, the difficulty of fitting two contenders and Ophelia's body into a confined space (probably the trapdoor) suggests to many editors the alternative, that Laertes jumps out of the grave to attack Hamlet.) **262 splenitive** quick-tempered **270 wag** move. (A fluttering eyelid is a conventional sign that life has not yet gone.)

213 Imperious Imperial **216 flaw** gust of wind. **217 soft** i.e., wait, be careful **219 maimèd** mutilated, incomplete **221 Fordo it** destroy its. **estate** rank. **222 Couch we** Let's hide, lie low **227 warranty** i.e., ecclesiastical authority. **228 order** (1) prescribed practice (2) religious order of clerics **229 She should . . . lodged** she should have been buried in unsanctified ground **230 For** In place of **231 Shards** broken bits of pottery **232 crants** garlands betokening maidenhood **233 strewments** flowers strewn on a coffin **233–4 bringing . . . burial** laying the body to rest, to the sound of the bell. **237 such rest** i.e., to pray for such rest **238 peace-parted souls** those who have died at peace with God. **240 violets** (See 4.5.188 and note.) **242 howling** i.e., in hell.

King: Oh, he is mad, Laertes.

Queen: For love of God, forbear him. 276

Hamlet:

'Swounds, show me what thou'lt do. 277

Woo't weep? Woo't fight? Woo't fast? Woo't tear thyself? 278

Woo't drink up eisel? Eat a crocodile? 279

I'll do't. Dost come here to whine?

To outface me with leaping in her grave?

Be buried quick with her, and so will I. 282

And if thou prate of mountains, let them throw

Millions of acres on us, till our ground,

Singeing his pate against the burning zone, 285

Make Ossa like a wart! Nay, an thou'lt mouth, 286

I'll rant as well as thou.

Queen: This is mere madness, 287

And thus awhile the fit will work on him;

Anon, as patient as the female dove

When that her golden couplets are disclosed, 290

His silence will sit drooping.

Hamlet: Hear you, sir.

What is the reason that you use me thus?

I loved you ever. But it is no matter.

Let Hercules himself do what he may, 294

The cat will mew, and dog will have his day. 295

Exit Hamlet.

King:

I pray thee, good Horatio, wait upon him.

[Exit] Horatio.

[*To Laertes*] Strengthen your patience in our last

night's speech; 297

We'll put the matter to the present push.— 298

Good Gertrude, set some watch over your son.—

This grave shall have a living monument. 300

An hour of quiet shortly shall we see; 301

Till then, in patience our proceeding be. *Exeunt.*

♣

276 **forbear him** leave him alone. 277 **'Swounds** By His (Christ's) wounds 278 **Woo't** Wilt thou 279 **Woo't . . . eisel?** Will you drink up a whole draft of vinegar? (An extremely self-punishing task as a way of expressing grief.) **crocodile** (Crocodiles were tough and dangerous, and were supposed to shed crocodile tears.) 282 **quick** alive 285 **his pate** its head, i.e., top. **burning zone** zone in the celestial sphere containing the sun's orbit, between the tropics of Cancer and Capricorn 286 **Ossa** (See 253n.) 287 **an thou'lt mouth** if you want to rant 287 **mere** utter 290 **golden couplets** two baby pigeons, covered with yellow down. **disclosed** hatched 294–5 **Let . . . day** i.e., (1) Even Hercules couldn't stop Laertes's theatrical rant (2) I, too, will have my turn; i.e., despite any blustering attempts at interference, every person will sooner or later do what he or she must do. 297 **in** i.e., by recalling 298 **present push** immediate test. 300 **living** lasting. (For Laertes' private understanding, Claudius also hints that Hamlet's death will serve as such a monument.) 301 **hour of quiet** time free of conflict

---

[5-2]

Enter Hamlet and Horatio.

Hamlet:

So much for this, sir; now shall you see the other. 1

You do remember all the circumstance?

Horatio: Remember it, my lord!

Hamlet:

Sir, in my heart there was a kind of fighting

That would not let me sleep. Methought I lay

Worse than the mutines in the bilboes. Rashly, 6

And praised be rashness for it—let us know 7

Our indiscretion sometime serves us well 8

When our deep plots do pall, and that should learn us 9

There's a divinity that shapes our ends,

Rough-hew them how we will—

Horatio: That is most certain. 11

Hamlet: Up from my cabin,

My sea-gown scarfed about me, in the dark 13

Groped I to find out them, had my desire, 14

Fingered their packet, and in fine withdrew 15

To mine own room again, making so bold,

My fears forgetting manners, to unseal

Their grand commission; where I found, Horatio—

Ah, royal knavery!—an exact command,

Larded with many several sorts of reasons 20

Importing Denmark's health and England's too, 21

With, ho! such bugs and goblins in my life, 22

That on the supervise, no leisure bated, 23

No, not to stay the grinding of the ax, 24

My head should be struck off.

Horatio: Is't possible?

Hamlet: [*giving a document*]

Here's the commission. Read it at more leisure.

But wilt thou hear now how I did proceed?

Horatio: I beseech you.

Hamlet:

Being thus benetted round with villainies—

Ere I could make a prologue to my brains, 30

They had begun the play—I sat me down, 31

5-2 **Location:** The castle.
1 **see the other** hear the other news. (See 4.6.24-6.) 6 **mutines** mutineers. **bilboes** shackles. **Rashly** On impulse. (This adverb goes with lines 12 ff.) 7 **know** acknowledge 8 **indiscretion** lack of foresight and judgment (not an indiscreet act) 9 **pall** fail, falter, go stale. **learn** teach 11 **Rough-hew** shape roughly 13 **sea-gown** seaman's coat. **scarfed** loosely wrapped 14 **them** i.e., Rosencrantz and Guildenstern 15 **Fingered** pilfered, pinched. **in fine** finally, in conclusion 20 **Larded** garnished. **several** different 21 **Importing** relating to 22 **With . . . life** i.e., with all sorts of warnings of imaginary dangers if I were allowed to continue living. (*Bugs* are bugbears, hobgoblins.) 23 **That . . . bated** that on the reading of this commission, no delay being allowed 24 **stay** await 30–1 **Ere . . . play** before I could consciously turn my brain to the matter, it had started working on a plan

Devised a new commission, wrote it fair. 32

I once did hold it, as our statists do, 33

A baseness to write fair, and labored much 34

How to forget that learning, but, sir, now

It did me yeoman's service. Wilt thou know

Th'effect of what I wrote?

Horatio: Ay, good my lord.

Hamlet:

An earnest conjuration from the King, 38

As England was his faithful tributary,

As love between them like the palm might flourish, 40

As peace should still her wheaten garland wear 41

And stand a comma 'tween their amities, 42

And many suchlike "as"es of great charge, 43

That on the view and knowing of these contents,

Without debatement further more or less,

He should those bearers put to sudden death,

Not shriving time allowed.

Horatio: How was this sealed? 47

Hamlet:

Why, even in that was heaven ordinant. 48

I had my father's signet in my purse, 49

Which was the model of that Danish seal; 50

Folded the writ up in the form of th'other, 51

Subscribed it, gave't th'impression, placed it safely, 52

The changeling never known. Now, the next day 53

Was our sea fight, and what to this was sequent 54

Thou knowest already.

Horatio:

So Guildenstern and Rosencrantz go to't.

Hamlet:

Why, man, they did make love to this

   employment.

They are not near my conscience. Their defeat 58

Does by their own insinuation grow. 59

'Tis dangerous when the baser nature comes 60

Between the pass and fell incensèd points 61

Of mighty opposites.

Horatio: Why, what a king is this!

Hamlet:

Does it not, think thee, stand me now upon— 63

He that hath killed my king and whored my mother,

Popped in between th'election and my hopes, 65

Thrown out his angle for my proper life, 66

And with such coz'nage—is't not perfect conscience 67

To quit him with this arm? And is't not to be damned 68

To let this canker of our nature come 69

In further evil? 70

Horatio:

It must be shortly known to him from England

What is the issue of the business there.

Hamlet:

It will be short. The interim is mine,

And a man's life's no more than to say "one." 74

But I am very sorry, good Horatio,

That to Laertes I forgot myself,

For by the image of my cause I see

The portraiture of his. I'll court his favors.

But, sure, the bravery of his grief did put me 79

Into a tow'ring passion.

Horatio: Peace, who comes here?

Enter a Courtier [Osric].

Osric: Your Lordship is right welcome back to Denmark.

Hamlet: I humbly thank you, sir. [*To Horatio*] Dost know
   this water fly?

Horatio: No, my good lord.

Hamlet: Thy state is the more gracious, for 'tis a vice to
   know him. He hath much land, and fertile. Let a beast 86
   be lord of beasts, and his crib shall stand at the King's 87
   mess. 'Tis a chuff, but, as I say, spacious in the 88
   possession of dirt.

Osric: Sweet lord, if Your Lordship were at leisure, I
   should impart a thing to you from His Majesty.

Hamlet: I will receive it, sir, with all diligence of spirit.
   Put your bonnet to his right use; 'tis for the head. 93

Osric: I thank Your Lordship, it is very hot.

Hamlet: No, believe me, 'tis very cold. The wind is northerly.

Osric: It is indifferent cold, my lord, indeed. 97

---

32 fair in a clear hand. **33 statists** politicians, men of public affairs
34 A baseness beneath my dignity **38 conjuration** entreaty **40 palm**
(An image of health; see Psalm 92:12.) **41 still** always. **wheaten garland**
(Symbolic of fruitful agriculture, of peace and plenty.) **42 comma**
(Indicating continuity, link.) **43 "as"es** (1) the "whereases" of a formal
document (2) asses. **charge** (1) import (2) burden (appropriate to
asses) **47 shriving time** time for confession and absolution **48 ordinant**
directing. **49 signet** small seal **50 model** replica **51 writ** writing **52**
Subscribed signed (with forged signature). **impression** i.e., with a wax
seal **53 changeling** i.e., substituted letter. (Literally, a fairy child substituted for a human one.) **54 was sequent** followed **58 defeat** destruction **59 insinuation** intrusive intervention, sticking their noses in my
business **60 baser** of lower social station **61 pass** thrust. **fell** fierce
62 opposites antagonists.

63 stand me now upon become incumbent on me now **65 th'election**
(The Danish monarch was "elected" by a small number of high-ranking
electors.) **66 angle** fishhook. **proper** very **67 coz'nage** trickery **68 quit**
requite, pay back **69 canker** ulcer **69–70 come In** grow into **74 a**
man's . . . "one" one's whole life occupies such a short time, only as
long as it takes to count to 1. **79 bravery** bravado **86–8 Let . . . mess**
i.e., If a man, no matter how beastlike, is as rich in livestock and possessions as Osric, he may eat at the King's table. **87 crib** manger
88 chuff boor, churl. (The second quarto spelling, "chough," is a variant
spelling that also suggests the meaning here of "chattering jackdaw.")
93 bonnet any kind of cap or hat. **his** its **97 indifferent** somewhat

Hamlet: But yet methinks it is very sultry and hot

for my complexion. 99

Osric: Exceedingly, my lord. It is very sultry, as

'twere—I cannot tell how. My lord, His Majesty

bade me signify to you that 'a has laid a great

wager on your head. Sir, this is the matter—

Hamlet: I beseech you, remember.

[Hamlet moves him to put on his hat.]

Osric: Nay, good my lord; for my ease, in good faith. 105

Sir, here is newly come to court Laertes—believe me,

an absolute gentleman, full of most excellent differ- 107

ences, of very soft society and great showing. Indeed, 108

to speak feelingly of him, he is the card or calendar of 109

gentry, for you shall find in him the continent of what 110

part a gentleman would see. 111

Hamlet: Sir, his definement suffers no perdition in 112

you, though I know to divide him inventorially would 113

dozy th'arithmetic of memory, and yet but yaw 114

neither in respect of his quick sail. But, in the verity of 115

extolment, I take him to be a soul of great article, and 116

his infusion of such dearth and rareness as, to make 117

true diction of him, his semblable is his mirror and 118

who else would trace him his umbrage, nothing 119

more. 120

Osric: Your Lordship speaks most infallibly of him.

Hamlet: The concernancy, sir? Why do we wrap 122

the gentleman in our more rawer breath? 123

Osric: Sir?

Horatio: Is't not possible to understand in another 125

tongue? You will do't, sir, really. 126

Hamlet: What imports the nomination of this 127

gentleman?

Osric: Of Laertes?

Horatio: *[to Hamlet]* His purse is empty already;

all 's golden words are spent.

Hamlet: Of him, sir.

Osric: I know you are not ignorant—

Hamlet: I would you did, sir. Yet in faith if you did, 134

it would not much approve me. Well, sir? 135

Osric: You are not ignorant of what excellence

Laertes is—

Hamlet: I dare not confess that, lest I should compare 138

with him in excellence. But to know a man well were 139

to know himself. 140

Osric: I mean, sir, for his weapon; but in the imputation 141

laid on him by them, in his meed he's unfellowed. 142

Hamlet: What's his weapon?

Osric: Rapier and dagger.

Hamlet: That's two of his weapons—but well. 145

Osric: The King, sir, hath wagered with him six Barbary

horses, against the which he has impawned, as I take 147

it, six French rapiers and poniards, with their assigns, 148

as girdle, hangers, and so. Three of the carriages, in 149

faith, are very dear to fancy, very responsive to the 150

hilts, most delicate carriages, and of very liberal con- 151

ceit. 152

Hamlet: What call you the carriages? 153

Horatio: *[to Hamlet]* I knew you must be edified

by the margent ere you had done. 155

Osric: The carriages, sir, are the hangers.

Hamlet: The phrase would be more germane to the

matter if we could carry a cannon by our sides; I would

it might be hangers till then. But, on: six Barbary horses

against six French swords, their assigns, and three lib-

eral-conceited carriages; that's the French bet against

the Danish. Why is this impawned, as you call it?

---

99 complexion constitution. **105 for my ease** (A conventional reply declining the invitation to put the hat back on.) **107 absolute** perfect **107–8 differences** special qualities **108 soft society** agreeable manners. **great showing** distinguished appearance. **109 feelingly** with just perception **109–10 the card . . . gentry** the model or paradigm (literally, a chart or directory) of good breeding **110–11 the continent . . . see** one who contains in himself all the qualities a gentleman would like to see. (A *continent* is that which contains.) **112–15 his definement . . . sail** the task of defining Laertes's excellences suffers no diminution in your description of him, though I know that to enumerate all his graces would stupify one's powers of memory, and even so could do no more than veer unsteadily off course in a vain attempt to keep up with his rapid forward motion. (Hamlet mocks Osric by parodying his jargon-filled speeches.) **115–20 But . . . more** But, in true praise of him, I take him to be a person of remarkable value, and his essence of such rarity and excellence as, to speak truly of him, none can compare with him other than his own mirror; anyone following in his footsteps can only hope to be the shadow to his substance, nothing more. **122 concernancy** import, relevance **123 rawer breath** unrefined speech that can only come short in praising him. **125–6 Is't . . . tongue?** i.e., Is it not possible for you, Osric, to understand and communicate in any other tongue than the overblown rhetoric you have used? (Alternatively, Horatio could be asking Hamlet to speak more plainly.) **126 You will do't** i.e., You can if you try, or, you may well have to try (to speak plainly).

127 nomination naming **134–5 I would . . . approve me** (Responding to Osric's incompleted sentence as though it were a complete statement, Hamlet says, with mock politeness, "I wish you did know me to be not ignorant [i.e., to be knowledgeable] about matters," and then turns this into an insult: "But if you did, your recommendation of me would be of little value in any case.") **138–40 I dare . . . himself** I dare not boast of knowing Laertes's excellence lest I seem to imply a comparable excellence in myself. Certainly, to know another person well, one must know oneself. **141–2 I mean . . . unfellowed** I mean his excellence with his rapier, not his general excellence; in the reputation he enjoys for use of his weapons, his merit is unequaled. **145 but well** but never mind. **147 he** i.e., Laertes. **impawned** staked, wagered **148 poniards** daggers. **assigns** appurtenances **149 hangers** straps on the sword belt (*girdle*), from which the sword hung. **and so** and so on. **149–52 Three . . . conceit** Three of the hangers, truly, are very pleasing to the fancy, decoratively matched with the hilts, delicate in workmanship, and made with elaborate ingenuity. **153 What call you** What do you refer to when you say **155 margent** margin of a book, place for explanatory notes

Osric: The King, sir, hath laid, sir, that in a dozen 163
passes between yourself and him, he shall not exceed 164
you three hits. He hath laid on twelve for nine, and it
would come to immediate trial, if Your Lordship would
vouchsafe the answer. 167

Hamlet: How if I answer no?

Osric: I mean, my lord, the opposition of your
person in trial.

Hamlet: Sir, I will walk here in the hall. If it please His
Majesty, it is the breathing time of day with me. Let 172
the foils be brought, the gentleman willing, and the
King hold his purpose, I will win for him an I can; if
not, I will gain nothing but my shame and the odd
hits.

Osric: Shall I deliver you so? 177

Hamlet: To this effect, sir—after what flourish
your nature will.

Osric: I commend my duty to Your Lordship. 180

Hamlet: Yours, yours.   *[Exit Osric.]*
'A does well to commend it himself; there are no
tongues else for 's turn. 183

Horatio: This lapwing runs away with the shell 184
on his head.

Hamlet: 'A did comply with his dug before 'a sucked 186
it. Thus has he—and many more of the same breed 187
that I know the drossy age dotes on—only got the 188
tune of the time, and, out of an habit of encounter, a 189
kind of yeasty collection, which carries them through 190
and through the most fanned and winnowed opin- 191
ions; and do but blow them to their trial, the bubbles 192
are out. 193

Enter a Lord.

Lord: My lord, His Majesty commended him to you by
young Osric, who brings back to him that you attend
him in the hall. He sends to know if your pleasure
hold to play with Laertes, or that you will take longer 197
time.

Hamlet: I am constant to my purposes; they follow the
King's pleasure. If his fitness speaks, mine is ready; 200
now or whensoever, provided I be so able as now.

Lord: The King and Queen and all are coming down.

Hamlet: In happy time. 203

Lord: The Queen desires you to use some gentle enter- 204
tainment to Laertes before you fall to play. 205

Hamlet: She well instructs me.   *[Exit Lord.]*

Horatio: You will lose, my lord.

Hamlet: I do not think so. Since he went into France, I
have been in continual practice; I shall win at the odds.
But thou wouldst not think how ill all's here about my
heart; but it is no matter.

Horatio: Nay, good my lord—

Hamlet: It is but foolery, but it is such a kind of gain- 213
giving as would perhaps trouble a woman. 214

Horatio: If your mind dislike anything, obey it. I will
forestall their repair hither and say you are not fit. 216

Hamlet: Not a whit, we defy augury. There is special 217
providence in the fall of a sparrow. If it be now, 'tis
not to come; if it be not to come, it will be now; if it
be not now; yet it will come. The readiness is all. Since 220
no man of aught he leaves knows, what is't to leave 221
betimes? Let be. 222

A table prepared. [Enter] trumpets, drums, and offi-
cers with cushions; King, Queen, [Osric,] and all the
state; foils, daggers, [and wine borne in;] and Laertes.

King:
Come, Hamlet, come and take this hand from me.
    [The King puts Laertes's hand into Hamlet's.]

Hamlet: *[to Laertes]*
Give me your pardon, sir. I have done you wrong,
But pardon't as you are a gentleman.
This presence knows, 226
And you must needs have heard, how I am punished 227
With a sore distraction. What I have done
That might your nature, honor, and exception 229

---

163 laid wagered **164 passes** bouts. (The odds of the betting are hard to explain. Possibly the King bets that Hamlet will win at least five out of twelve, at which point Laertes raises the odds against himself by betting he will win nine.) **167 vouchsafe the answer** be so good as to accept the challenge. (Hamlet deliberately takes the phrase in its literal sense of replying.) **172 breathing time** exercise period. **Let** i.e., If **177 deliver you** report what you say **180 commend** commit to your favor. (A conventional salutation, but Hamlet wryly uses a more literal meaning, "recommend," "praise," in line 182.) **183 for 's turn** for his purposes, i.e., to do it for him. **184 lapwing** (A proverbial type of youthful forwardness. Also, a bird that draws intruders away from its nest and was thought to run about with its head in the shell when newly hatched; a seeming reference to Osric's hat.) **186 comply . . . dug** observe ceremonious formality toward his nurse's or mother's teat **187–93 Thus . . . are out** Thus has he—and many like him of the sort our frivolous age dotes on—acquired the trendy manner of speech of the time, and, out of habitual conversation with courtiers of their own kind, have collected together a kind of frothy medley of current phrases, which enables such gallants to hold their own among persons of the most select and well-sifted views; and yet do but test them by merely blowing on them, and their bubbles burst.

197 play fence. **that** if **200 If . . . ready** If he declares his readiness, my convenience waits on his **203 In happy time** (A phrase of courtesy indicating that the time is convenient.) **204–5 entertainment** greeting **213–14 gaingiving** misgiving **216 repair** coming **217 augury** the attempt to read signs of future events in order to avoid predicted trouble. **220–2 Since . . . Let be** Since no one has knowledge of what he is leaving behind, what does an early death matter after all? Enough; forbear. **222.1 trumpets, drums** trumpeters, drummers **222.3 all the state** the entire court **226 presence** royal assembly **227 punished** afflicted **229 exception** disapproval

Roughly awake, I here proclaim was madness.
Was't Hamlet wronged Laertes? Never Hamlet.
If Hamlet from himself be ta'en away,
And when he's not himself does wrong Laertes,
Then Hamlet does it not, Hamlet denies it.
Who does it, then? His madness. If't be so,
Hamlet is of the faction that is wronged;   236
His madness is poor Hamlet's enemy.
Sir, in this audience
Let my disclaiming from a purposed evil
Free me so far in your most generous thoughts
That I have shot my arrow o'er the house
And hurt my brother.

Laertes: I am satisfied in nature,   242
Whose motive in this case should stir me most   243
To my revenge. But in my terms of honor
I stand aloof, and will no reconcilement
Till by some elder masters of known honor
I have a voice and precedent of peace   247
To keep my name ungored. But till that time   248
I do receive your offered love like love,
And will not wrong it.

Hamlet: I embrace it freely,
And will this brothers' wager frankly play.—   251
Give us the foils. Come on.

Laertes: Come, one for me.

Hamlet:
I'll be your foil, Laertes. In mine ignorance   253
  Your skill shall, like a star i'th' darkest night,
  Stick fiery off indeed.

Laertes: You mock me, sir.   255

Hamlet: No, by this hand.

King:
Give them the foils, young Osric. Cousin Hamlet,
You know the wager?

Hamlet: Very well, my lord.
Your Grace has laid the odds o'th' weaker side.   259

King:
I do not fear it; I have seen you both.
But since he is bettered, we have therefore odds.   261

Laertes:
This is too heavy. Let me see another.

[*He exchanges his foil for another.*]

Hamlet:
This likes me well. These foils have all a length?   263

[*They prepare to fence.*]

Osric: Ay, my good lord.

King:
Set me the stoups of wine upon that table.
If Hamlet give the first or second hit,
Or quit in answer of the third exchange,   267
Let all the battlements their ordnance fire.
The King shall drink to Hamlet's better breath,   269

And in the cup an union shall he throw   270
Richer than that which four successive kings
In Denmark's crown have worn. Give me the cups,
And let the kettle to the trumpet speak,   273
The trumpet to the cannoneer without,
The cannons to the heavens, the heaven to earth,
"Now the King drinks to Hamlet." Come, begin.

                         Trumpets the while.
And you, the judges, bear a wary eye.

Hamlet: Come on, sir.

Laertes: Come, my lord. [*They fence. Hamlet scores
a hit.*]

Hamlet: One.

Laertes: No.

Hamlet: Judgment.

Osric: A hit, a very palpable hit.   282

                    *Drum, trumpets, and shot. Flourish.
                         A piece goes off.*

Laertes: Well, again.

King:
Stay, give me drink. Hamlet, this pearl is thine.

                    [*He drinks, and throws a pearl
                              in Hamlet's cup.*]

Here's to thy health. Give him the cup.

Hamlet:
I'll play this bout first. Set it by awhile.
Come. [*They fence.*] Another hit; what say you?

Laertes: A touch, a touch, I do confess't.

King:
Our son shall win.

Queen: He's fat and scant of breath.   289
Here, Hamlet, take my napkin, rub thy brows.   290
The Queen carouses to thy fortune, Hamlet.   291

---

236 **faction** party 242 **in nature** i.e., as to my personal feelings 243
motive prompting 247 **voice** authoritative pronouncement. **of peace**
for reconciliation 248 **name ungored** reputation unwounded. 251
frankly without ill feeling or the burden of rancor 253 **foil** thin metal
background which sets a jewel off. (With pun on the blunted rapier
for fencing.) 255 **Stick fiery off** stand out brilliantly 259 **laid . . . side**
backed the weaker side. 261 **is bettered** is the odds-on favorite.
(Laertes's handicap is the "three hits" specified in line 165.)

263 **likes** pleases 267 **Or . . . exchange** or draws even with Laertes by
winning the third exchange 269 **better breath** improved vigor
270 **union** pearl. (So called, according to Pliny's *Natural History*, 9,
because pearls are *unique*, never identical.) 273 **kettle** kettledrum
282.2 *A piece* A cannon 289 **fat** not physically fit, out of training
290 **napkin** handkerchief 291 **carouses** drinks a toast

Hamlet: Good madam!

King: Gertrude, do not drink.

Queen:

I will, my lord, I pray you pardon me. [*She drinks.*]

King: [*aside*]

It is the poisoned cup. It is too late.

Hamlet:

I dare not drink yet, madam; by and by.

Queen: Come, let me wipe thy face.

Laertes: [*aside to the King*]

My lord, I'll hit him now.

King: I do not think't.

Laertes: [*aside*]

And yet it is almost against my conscience.

Hamlet:

Come, for the third, Laertes. You do but dally.

I pray you, pass with your best violence;   301

I am afeard you make a wanton of me.   302

Laertes: Say you so? Come on.   [*They fence.*]

Osric: Nothing neither way.

Laertes:

Have at you now!   305

[*Laertes wounds Hamlet; then, in scuffling, they change rapiers, and Hamlet wounds Laertes.*]

King: Part them! They are incensed.

Hamlet:

Nay, come, again.   [*The Queen falls.*]

Osric: Look to the Queen there, ho!

Horatio:

They bleed on both sides. How is it, my lord?

Osric: How is't, Laertes?

Laertes:

Why, as a woodcock to mine own springe, Osric;   309

I am justly killed with mine own treachery.

Hamlet:

How does the Queen?

King: She swoons to see them bleed.

Queen:

No, no, the drink, the drink—Oh, my dear Hamlet—

The drink, the drink! I am poisoned.   [*She dies.*]

Hamlet:

Oh, villainy! Ho, let the door be locked!

Treachery! Seek it out. [*Laertes falls. Exit Osric.*]

Laertes:

It is here, Hamlet. Hamlet, thou art slain.

No med'cine in the world can do thee good;

In thee there is not half an hour's life.

The treacherous instrument is in thy hand,

Unbated and envenomed. The foul practice   320

Hath turned itself on me. Lo, here I lie,

Never to rise again. Thy mother's poisoned.

I can no more. The King, the King's to blame.

Hamlet: The point envenomed too? Then, venom, to

thy work. [*He stabs the King.*]

All: Treason! Treason!

King: Oh, yet defend me, friends! I am but hurt.

Hamlet: [*forcing the King to drink*]

Here, thou incestuous, murderous, damnèd Dane,

Drink off this potion. Is thy union here?   328

Follow my mother.   [*The King dies.*]

Laertes: He is justly served.

It is a poison tempered by himself.   330

Exchange forgiveness with me, noble Hamlet.

Mine and my father's death come not upon thee,

Nor thine on me!   [*He dies.*]

Hamlet: Heaven make thee free of it! I follow thee.

I am dead, Horatio. Wretched Queen, adieu!

You that look pale and tremble at this chance,   336

That are but mutes or audience to this act,   337

Had I but time—as this fell sergeant, Death,   338

Is strict in his arrest—oh, I could tell you—   339

But let it be. Horatio, I am dead;

Thou livest. Report me and my cause aright

To the unsatisfied.

Horatio: Never believe it.

I am more an antique Roman than a Dane.   343

Here's yet some liquor left.

[*He attempts to drink from the poisoned cup.
Hamlet prevents him.*]

Hamlet: As thou'rt a man,

Give me the cup! Let go! By heaven, I'll ha 't.

Oh, God, Horatio, what a wounded name,

Things standing thus unknown, shall I leave behind me!

If thou didst ever hold me in thy heart,

Absent thee from felicity awhile,

And in this harsh world draw thy breath in pain

---

301 pass thrust **302 make . . . me** i.e., treat me like a spoiled child, trifle with me. **305.1–2** *in scuffling, they change rapiers* (This stage direction occurs in the Folio. According to a widespread stage tradition, Hamlet receives a scratch, realizes that Laertes's sword is unbated, and accordingly forces an exchange.) **309 woodcock** a bird, a type of stupidity or as a decoy. **springe** trap, snare

320 Unbated not blunted with a button. **practice** plot **328 union** pearl. (See line 270; with grim puns on the word's other meanings: marriage, shared death.) **330 tempered** mixed **336 chance** mischance **337 mutes** silent observers. (Literally, actors with nonspeaking parts.) **338 fell sergeant** remorseless arresting officer **339 strict** (1) severely just (2) unavoidable. **arrest** (1) taking into custody (2) stopping my speech **343 Roman** (Suicide was an honorable choice for many Romans as an alternative to a dishonorable life.)

To tell my story. *A march afar off [and a volley within]*.

What warlike noise is this?

Enter Osric.

Osric:

Young Fortinbras, with conquest come from Poland,

To th'ambassadors of England gives

This warlike volley.

Hamlet: Oh, I die, Horatio!

The potent poison quite o'ercrows my spirit.   355

I cannot live to hear the news from England,

But I do prophesy th'election lights

On Fortinbras. He has my dying voice.   358

So tell him, with th'occurrents more and less   359

Which have solicited. The rest is silence. [*He dies.*]   360

Horatio:

Now cracks a noble heart. Good night, sweet prince,

And flights of angels sing thee to thy rest!

[*March within.*]

Why does the drum come hither?

Enter Fortinbras, with the [English] Ambassadors [with drum, colors, and attendants].

Fortinbras:

Where is this sight?

Horatio: What is it you would see?

If aught of woe or wonder, cease your search.

Fortinbras:

This quarry cries on havoc. O proud Death,   366

What feast is toward in thine eternal cell,   367

That thou so many princes at a shot

So bloodily hast struck?

First Ambassador: The sight is dismal,

And our affairs from England come too late.

The ears are senseless that should give us hearing,

To tell him his commandment is fulfilled,

That Rosencrantz and Guildenstern are dead.

Where should we have our thanks?

Horatio: Not from his mouth,   374

Had it th'ability of life to thank you.

He never gave commandment for their death.

But since, so jump upon this bloody question,   377

You from the Polack wars and you from England

Are here arrived, give order that these bodies

High on a stage be placèd to the view,   380

And let me speak to th'yet unknowing world

How these things came about. So shall you hear

Of carnal, bloody, and unnatural acts,

Of accidental judgments, casual slaughters,   384

Of deaths put on by cunning and forced cause,   385

And, in this upshot, purposes mistook

Fall'n on th'inventors' heads. All this can I

Truly deliver.

Fortinbras: Let us haste to hear it,

And call the noblest to the audience.

For me, with sorrow I embrace my fortune.

I have some rights of memory in this kingdom,   391

Which now to claim my vantage doth invite me.   392

Horatio:

Of that I shall have also cause to speak,

And from his mouth whose voice will draw on more.   394

But let this same be presently performed,   395

Even while men's minds are wild, lest more mischance

On plots and errors happen.

Fortinbras: Let four captains   397

Bear Hamlet, like a soldier, to the stage,

For he was likely, had he been put on,   399

To have proved most royal; and for his passage,   400

The soldiers' music and the rite of war

Speak loudly for him.   402

Take up the bodies. Such a sight as this

Becomes the field, but here shows much amiss.   404

Go bid the soldiers shoot.

Exeunt [marching, bearing off the dead bodies; a peal of ordnance is shot off].

---

355 o'ercrows triumphs over (like the winner in a cockfight) **358 voice** vote. **359 th'occurrents** the events, incidents **360 solicited** moved, urged. (Hamlet doesn't finish saying what the events have prompted—presumably, his acts of vengeance, or his reporting of those events to Fortinbras.) **366 This . . . havoc** This heap of dead bodies loudly proclaims a general slaughter. **367 feast** i.e., Death feasting on those who have fallen. **toward** in preparation **374 his** Claudius's

377 so jump . . . question so hard on the heels of this bloody business **380 stage** platform **384 judgments** retributions. **casual** occurring by chance **385 put on** instigated. **forced cause** contrivance **391 of memory** traditional, remembered, unforgotten **392 vantage** favorable opportunity **394 voice . . . more** vote will influence still others. **395 presently** immediately **397 On** on top of **399 put on** i.e., invested in royal office and so put to the test **400 for his passage** to mark his passing **402 Speak** (let them) speak **404 Becomes the field** suits the field of battle

1. How does the very first line *of Hamlet* signal central themes and actions of the play?

2. Use the text to discuss whether the ghost of Hamlet Sr. is religiously neutral, Protestant, or Roman Catholic. Consider such words as "portent," "purgatory," and "hell"—as well as the symbolism of a cock crowing.

3. Look carefully at Prince Hamlet's advice to the professional players who visit Elsinore. Consider both his thoughts on "the purpose of playing" and his warning about clowns. Compare this to Shakespeare's own method of drama. Do *Hamlet* and Hamlet match up?

4. After seeing the ghost, Hamlet tells his friends he will pretend to be mad. Does he ever truly go mad? Defend your answer in the text.

5. Does Ophelia betray Hamlet when she cooperates with her father's plot to uncover the love that he thinks may cause the Prince's madness? Justify your answer using textual evidence.

6. Of what deeds can you *prove* Gertrude is guilty?

7. How old do you think Hamlet is? Why? In Act IV, how old does the play say Hamlet is? Why do the facts usually surprise people?

NONFICTION

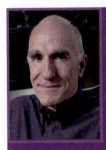

Scott Russell Sanders b. 1945

Author of nineteen books, Scott Russell Sanders is Distinguished Professor of English and Creative Writing at Indiana University. Born in Memphis, Tennessee, he spent his childhood in Ohio, attended Brown University, and received his PhD. from Cambridge University. Best-known for his highly personal writing about nature, Sanders has also written novels, children's books, and short stories. "Buckeye" was first published as the introduction to *In Buckeye Country,* a collection of photos and essays about Ohio.

BUCKEYE

YEARS AFTER MY FATHER'S HEART QUIT, I KEEP IN a wooden box on my desk the two buckeyes that were in his pocket when he died. Once the size of plums, the brown seeds are shriveled now, hollow, hard as pebbles, yet they still gleam from the polish of his hands. He used to reach for them in his overalls or suit pants and click them together, or he would draw them out, cupped in his palm, and twirl them with his blunt carpenter's fingers, all the while humming snatches of old tunes.

"Do you really believe buckeyes keep off arthritis?" I asked him more than once.

He would flex his hands and say, "I do so far."

My father never paid much heed to pain. Near the end, when his worn knee often slipped out of joint, he would pound it back in place with a rubber mallet. If a splinter worked into his flesh beyond the reach of tweezers, he would heat the blade of his knife over a cigarette lighter and slice through the skin. He sought to ward off arthritis not because he feared pain but because he lived through his hands, and he dreaded the swelling of knuckles, the stiffening of fingers. What use would he be if he could no longer hold a hammer or guide a plow? When he was a boy he had known farmers not yet forty years old whose hands had curled into claws, men so crippled up they could not tie their own shoes, could not sign their names.

5   "I mean to tickle my grandchildren when they come along," he told me, "and I mean to build doll houses and turn spindles for tiny chairs on my lathe."

So he fondled those buckeyes as if they were charms, carrying them with him when our family moved from Ohio at the end of my childhood, bearing them to new homes in Louisiana, then Oklahoma, Ontario, and Mississippi, carrying them still on his final day when pain a thousand times fiercer than arthritis gripped his heart.

The box where I keep the buckeyes also comes from Ohio, made by my father from a walnut plank he bought at a farm auction. I remember the auction,

A photograph of buckeyes, seeds of the buckeye tree, the state tree of Ohio and an image with deep associations for many Ohioans, including Scott Russell Sanders and his father, a Mississippi native who moved to the Buckeye State when his son was still a boy.

remember the sagging face of the widow whose home was being sold, remember my father telling her he would prize that walnut as if he had watched the tree grow from a sapling on his own land. He did not care for pewter or silver or gold, but he cherished wood. On the rare occasions when my mother coaxed him into a museum, he ignored the paintings or porcelain and studied the exhibit cases, the banisters, the moldings, the parquet floors.

I remember him planing that walnut board, sawing it, sanding it, joining piece to piece to make foot stools, picture frames, jewelry boxes. My own box, a bit larger than a soap dish, lined with red corduroy, was meant to hold earrings and pins, not buckeyes. The top is inlaid with pieces fitted so as to bring out the grain, four diagonal joints converging from the corners toward the center. If I stare long enough at those converging lines, they float free of the box and point to a center deeper than wood.

I learned to recognize buckeyes and beeches, sugar maples and shagbark hickories, wild cherries, walnuts, and dozens of other trees while tramping through the Ohio woods with my father. To his eyes, their shapes, their leaves, their bark, their winter buds were as distinctive as the set of a friend's shoulders. As with friends, he was partial to some, craving their company, so he would go out of his way to visit particular trees, walking in a circle around the splayed roots of a sycamore, laying his hand against the trunk of a white oak, ruffling the feathery green boughs of a cedar. "Trees breathe," he told me. "Listen."

10   I listened, and heard the stir of breath.

He was no botanist; the names and uses he taught me were those he had learned from country folks, not from books. Latin never crossed his lips. Only much later would I discover that the tree he called ironwood, its branches like muscular arms, good for ax handles, is known in books as hophornbeam; what he called tulip-tree or canoewood, ideal for log cabins, is officially the yellow poplar; what he called hoop ash, good for barrels and fence posts, appears in books as hackberry.

When he introduced me to the buckeye, he broke off a chunk of the gray bark and held it to my nose. I gagged.

"That's why the old-timers called it stinking buckeye," he told me. "They used it for cradles and feed troughs and peg legs.

"Why for peg legs?" I asked.

15   "Because it's light and hard to split, so it won't shatter when you're clumping around."

He showed me this tree in late summer, when the fruits had fallen and the ground was littered with prickly brown pods. He picked up one, as fat as a lemon, and peeled away the husk to reveal the shiny seed. He laid it in my palm and closed my fist around it so the seed peeped out from the circle formed by my index finger and thumb. "You see where it got the name?" he asked.

I saw: what gleamed in my hand was the bright eye of a deer. "It's beautiful," I said.

"It's beautiful," my father agreed, "but also poisonous. Nobody eats buckeyes, except maybe a fool squirrel."

I knew the gaze of deer from living in the Ravenna Arsenal,° in Portage County, up in the northeastern corner of Ohio. After supper we often drove the Arsenal's gravel roads, past the munitions bunkers, past acres of rusting tanks and wrecked bombers, into the far fields where we counted deer. One June evening, while mist rose from the ponds, we counted 311, our family record. We found deer in herds, in bunches, in amorous pairs. We came upon lone bucks, their antlers lifted against the sky like the bare branches of dogwood. If you were quiet, if your hands were empty, if you moved slowly, you could leave the car and steal to within a few paces of a grazing deer, close enough to see the delicate lips, the twitching nostrils, the glossy, fathomless eyes.

Arsenal: Ravenna Arsenal is a military base in northeastern Ohio. During and after the war, it was used as a military ammunition production facility for the U.S. Army. The facility is currently used for training the Ohio National Guard.

20   The wooden box on my desk holds these grazing deer, as it holds the buckeyes and the walnut plank and the farm auction and the munitions bunkers and the breathing forests and my father's hands. I could lose the box, I could lose the polished seeds, but if I were to lose the memories I would become a bush without roots, and every new breeze would toss me about.

  All those memories lead back to the northeastern corner of Ohio, where I learned to connect feelings with words. Much of the land I knew in that place as a child had been ravaged. The ponds in the Arsenal teemed with bluegill and beaver, but they were also laced with TNT from the making of bombs. Because the wolves and coyotes had long since been killed, some of the deer, so plump in the June grass, collapsed on the January snow, whittled by hunger to racks of bones. Outside the Arsenal's high barbed fences, many of the farms had failed, their barns caving in, their topsoil gone. Ravines were choked with swollen couches and junked washing machines and cars. Crossing fields, you had to be careful not to slice your feet on tin cans or shards of glass. Most of the rivers bad been dammed, turning fertile valleys into scummy playgrounds for boats.

  One free-flowing river, the Mahoning, ran past the small farm near the Arsenal where our family lived during my later years in Ohio. We owned just enough land to pasture three ponies and to grow vegetables for our table, but those few acres opened onto miles of woods and creeks and secret meadows. I walked that land in every season, every weather, following animal trails. But then the Mahoning, too, was doomed by a government decision; we were forced to sell our land, and a dam began to rise across the river.

  If enough people had spoken for the river, we might have saved it. If enough people had believed that our scarred country was worth defending, we might have dug in our heels and fought. Our attachments to the land were all private. We had no shared lore, no literature, no art to root us there, to give us courage, to help us stand our ground. The only maps we had were those issued by the state, showing a maze of numbered lines stretched over emptiness. The Ohio landscape never showed up on postcards or posters, never unfurled like tapestry in films, rarely filled even a paragraph in books. There were no mountains in that place, no waterfalls, no rocky gorges, no vistas. It was a country of low hills, cut over woods, scoured fields, villages that had lost their purpose, roads that had lost their way.

  "Let us love the country of here below," Simone Weil urged. "It is real; it offers resistance to love. It is this country that God has given us to love. He has willed that it should be difficult yet possible to love it." Which is the deeper truth about buckeyes, their poison or their beauty? I hold with the beauty; or rather, I am held by the beauty, without forgetting the poison. In my corner of Ohio the gullies were choked with trash, yet cedars flickered up like green flames from cracks in stone; in the evening bombs exploded at the ammunition dump, yet from the darkness came the mating cries of owls. I was saved from despair by knowing a few men and women who cared enough about the land to clean up trash, who planted walnuts and oaks that would long outlive them, who imagined a world that would have no call for bombs.

25   How could our hearts be large enough for heaven if they are not large enough for earth? The only country I am certain of is the one here below. The only paradise I know is the one lit by our everyday sun, this land of difficult love, shot through with shadow. The place where we learn this love, if we learn it at all, shimmers behind every new place we inhabit.

  A family move carried me away from Ohio thirty years ago; my schooling and marriage and job have kept me away ever since, except for occasional visits. I returned to the site of our farm one cold November day, when the trees were skeletons and the ground shone with the yellow of fallen leaves. From a previous trip I knew that our house had been bulldozed, our yard and pasture had grown up in thickets, and the reservoir had flooded the woods. On my earlier visit I had merely gazed from the car, too numb with loss to climb out. But on this November day, I parked the car, drew on my hat and gloves, opened the door, and walked.

  I was looking for some sign that we had lived there, some token of our affection for the place. All that I recognized, aside from the contours of the land, were two weeping willows that my father and I had planted near the road. They had been slips the length of my forearm when we set them out, and now their crowns rose higher than the telephone poles. When I touched them last, their trunks had been smooth and supple, as thin as my wrist and now they were furrowed and stout. I took off my gloves and laid my hands against the rough bark. Immediately I felt the wince of tears. "Hello, Father," I said, quietly at first, then louder and louder, as if only shouts could reach him through the bark and miles and years.

Surprised by sobs, I turned from the willows and stumbled away toward the drowned woods, calling to my father. I sensed that he was nearby. Even as I called, I was wary of grief's deceptions. I had never seen his body after he died. By the time I reached the place of his death, a furnace had reduced him to ashes. The need to see him, to let go of him, to let go of this land and time, was powerful enough to summon mirages; I knew that. But I also knew, stumbling toward the woods, that my father was here.

At the bottom of a slope where the creek used to run, I came to an expanse of gray stumps and withered grass. It was a bay of the reservoir from which the water had retreated, the level drawn down by engineers or drought. I stood at the edge of this desolate ground, willing it back to life, trying to recall the woods where my father had taught me the names of trees. No green shoots rose. I walked out among the stumps. The grass crackled under my boots, breath rasped in my throat, but otherwise the world was silent.

30   Then a cry broke overhead and I looked up to see a red-tailed hawk launching out from the top of an oak—a band of dark feathers across the creamy breast and the tail splayed like rosy fingers against the sun. It was a red-tailed hawk for sure; and it was also my father. Not a symbol of my father, not a reminder, not a ghost, but the man himself, right there, circling in the air above me. I knew this as clearly as I knew the sun burned in the sky. A calm poured though me. My chest quit heaving. My eyes dried.

Hawk and father wheeled above me, circle upon circle, wings barely moving, head still. My own head was still, looking up, knowing and being known. Time scattered like fog. At length, father and hawk stroked the air with those powerful wings, three beats, then vanished over a ridge.

The voice of my education told me then and tells me now that I did not meet my father, that I merely projected my longing onto a bird. My education may well be right; yet nothing I heard in school, nothing I've ever read, no lesson reached by logic has ever convinced me as utterly or stirred me as deeply as did that red-tailed hawk. Nothing in my education prepared me to love a piece of the earth, least of all a humble, battered country like northeastern Ohio; I learned from the land itself.

Before leaving the drowned woods, I looked around at the ashen stumps, the wilted grass, and for the first time since moving from this place I was able to let it go. This ground was lost; the flood would reclaim it. But other ground could be saved, must be saved, in every watershed, every neighborhood. For each home ground we need new maps, living maps, stories and poems, photographs and paintings, essays and songs. We need to know where we are so that we may dwell in our place with a full heart.

[1994]

QUESTIONS FOR REFLECTION AND DISCUSSION

1. What do the buckeyes mean to Sanders's father? What do they mean to Sanders? How do they feed his memory? What associations do they have?

2. What is important to Sanders about the land he describes?

3. What has changed between the time he remembers and the present of the essay?

4. How does Sanders understand the red-tailed hawk? What does it mean to "dwell in our place with a full heart"?

FAMILIES TOPICS FOR ESSAYS

1. Compare the depiction of mothers in several of the selections above. What do they have in common? How do they differ from one another?

2. Compare the depiction of fathers in several of the selections above. What do they have in common? How do they differ from one another?

3. Write an essay on the effect of death or illness in a family, based on examples from texts in this section of the chapter or those listed below.

4. Compose an argument essay about what, if anything, is universal about the family. Base your arguments on the readings in this section. Is there any quality that all of these texts share? What are some of the common patterns in the different stories, essays, and poems?

5. In a personal essay describe an experience in your own life that resembles an experience related in one of the texts above. Compare your experience with the one described in the literary text. How did you or your family members react differently and why?

Sherman Alexie, "This Is What It Means to Say Phoenix, Arizona" • Margaret Atwood, "Happy Endings" • Kate Chopin, "The Story of an Hour" • Charlotte Perkins Gilman, "The Yellow Wallpaper" • Susan Glaspell, *Trifles* • Ellen Hunnicutt, "Blackberries" • Jhumpa Lahiri, "When Mr. Pirzada Came to Dine" • Ursula Le Guin, "The Wife's Story" • Naguib Mahfouz, "Half a Day" • Leslie Norris, "Blackberries" • Sharon Olds, "The Possessive" • Orhan Pamuk, "My Father's Suitcase" and "To Look Out the Window" • Sylvia Plath, "Metaphors" • Padgett Powell, "A Gentleman's C" • John Steinbeck, "The Chrysanthemums" • Mary TallMountain, "There Is No Word for Goodbye" • Amy Tan, "Mother Tongue" • Dylan Thomas, "Do Not Go Gentle into That Good Night"

CHILDREN AND ADOLESCENTS

The previous section includes several texts presenting adult perspectives on the child's world. In this section, we examine some of the literary means used to depict the world of the child from the child's point of view and the world of the adolescent—"the folly of youth," as the cynical Ambrose Bierce would have it—from an adolescent point of view. When they are not worrying about their parents and their place in the adult world, what do children and adolescents think about and how do they think about it? When do children cease to think like children and begin to think and view the world as adults do? How do children think about the changes that take over their lives as they enter adolescence? As you ponder these questions in the readings below, consider also the formal and stylistic means used to present those questions to us persuasively. We have included several selections that view the world through a young child's eyes, a number of texts that capture the moment of transition when boys and girls find themselves torn between the different demands and desires of childhood and adolescence, and two stories that explore the complex

Childhood, n. *The period of human life intermediate between the idiocy of infancy and the folly of youth—two removes from the sin of manhood and three from the remorse of age.*

—AMBROSE BIERCE, *THE DEVIL'S DICTIONARY*

manifestations of the hormones that define adolescence and the conflicts, both comic and cruel, that they encounter with the world around them.

FICTION

Jamaica Kincaid b. 1949

Born in Saint John's on the island of Antigua, Elaine Cynthia Potter Richardson came to New York City to work as an au pair. She studied at the New School and at Franconia College, changing her name to Jamaica Kincaid at the request of her parents when she began writing. Often autobiographical, Kincaid's novels explore her relationship with her mother, the colonial experience of Antigua, and the immigrant experience in the United States. "Girl" was first published in the *New Yorker* and was later reprinted in her collection *At the Bottom of the River* (1983).

GIRL

WASH THE WHITE CLOTHES ON MONDAY AND put them on the stone heap; wash the color clothes on Tuesday and put them on the clothesline to dry; don't walk barehead in the hot sun; cook pumpkin fritters in very hot sweet oil; soak your little cloths right after you take them off; when buying cotton to make yourself a nice blouse, be sure that it doesn't have gum on it, because that way it won't hold up well after a wash; soak salt fish overnight before you cook it; is it true that you sing benna° in Sunday school?; always eat your food in such a way that it won't turn someone else's stomach; on Sundays try to walk like a lady and not like the slut you are so bent on becoming; don't sing benna in Sunday school; you mustn't speak to wharf-rat boys, not even to give directions; don't eat fruits on the street—flies will follow you; but I don't sing benna on Sundays at all and never in Sunday school; this is how

benna: an uptempo, often bawdy folk song, similar to calypso.

to sew on a button; this is how to make a button-hole for the button you have just sewed on; this is how to hem a dress when you see the hem coming down and so to prevent yourself from looking like the slut I know you are so bent on becoming; this is how you iron your father's khaki shirt so that it doesn't have a crease; this is how you iron your father's khaki pants so that they don't have a crease; this is how you grow okra—far from the house, because okra tree harbors red ants; when you are growing dasheen,° make sure it gets plenty of water or else it makes your throat itch when you are eating it; this is how you sweep a corner; this is how you sweep a whole house; this is how you sweep a yard; this is how you smile to someone you don't like too much; this is how you smile to someone you don't like at all; this is how you smile to someone you like completely; this is how you set a table for tea; this is how you set a table for dinner; this is how you set a table for dinner with an important guest; this is how you set a table for lunch; this is how you set a table for breakfast; this is how to behave in the presence of men who don't know you very well, and this way they won't recognize immediately the slut I have warned you against becoming; be sure to wash every day, even if it is with your own spit; don't squat down to play marbles—you are not a boy, you know; don't pick people's flowers—you might catch something; don't throw stones at blackbirds, because it might not be a blackbird at all; this is how to make a bread pudding; this is how to make doukona;° this is how to make pepper pot;° this is how to make a good medicine for a cold; this is how to make a good medicine to throw away a child before it even becomes a child; this is how to catch a fish; this is how to throw back a fish you don't like, and that way something bad won't fall on you; this is how to bully a man; this is how a man bullies you; this is how to love a man; and if this doesn't work there are other ways, and if they don't work don't feel too bad about giving up; this is how to spit up in the air if you feel like it, and this is how to move quick so that it doesn't fall on you; this is how to make ends meet; always squeeze bread to make sure it's fresh; but what if the baker won't let me feel the bread?; you mean to say that after all you are really going to be the kind of woman who the baker won't let near the bread?

[1978]

---

dasheen: taro, a starchy tuber similar to the potato; the edible leaves are known in the Caribbean as *callaloo*.

doukouna: a kind of pudding made from starchy roots, sweetened, spiced, and wrapped in plantain or banana leaves. **pepper pot:** also known as *callaloo*, a spicy soup of stew made with taro leaves and other variable ingredients.

QUESTIONS FOR REFLECTION AND DISCUSSION

1. Who is the narrator in the story? From whose point of view is the story told?

2. What do we know about the girl?

3. Why do you think Kincaid chose to structure her story in this way? How would its meaning be changed if it were narrated in the first person by the girl? In the third person by an objective narrator?

Lorrie Moore b. 1957

Born in Glens Falls, New York, Marie Lorena Moore attended Saint Lawrence University. After graduating, she completed an MFA at Cornell University, publishing her first collection of stories, *Self-Help*, in 1985, including "The Kid's Guide to Divorce." Author of two other story collections and three novels, Moore is the Delmore Schwartz Professor of Humanities at the University of Wisconsin, Madison.

THE KID'S GUIDE TO DIVORCE

PUT EXTRA SALT ON THE POPCORN BECAUSE YOUR mom'll say that she needs it because the part where Inger Berman almost dies and the camera does tricks to elongate her torso sure gets her every time.

Think: Geeze, here she goes again with the Kleenexes.

She will say thanks honey when you come slowly, slowly around the corner in your slippers and robe,

The climactic scene of the classic thriller *Notorious* (1946, Alfred Hitchcock), just before Cary Grant takes Ingrid Bergman away in the black car. T. R. Devlin (Grant), an American agent, has persuaded Alicia Huberman (Bergman) to marry and spy on secret Nazi agent Alexander Sebastian (Claude Rains) in South America. Sebastian has found her out and has been slowly poisoning her when Devlin bursts into the house to rescue her.

into the living room with Grandma's old used-to-be-salad-bowl piled high. I made it myself, remind her, and accidentally drop a few pieces on the floor. Mittens will bat them around with his paws.

Mmmmm, good to replenish those salts, she'll munch and smile soggily.

5   Tell her the school nurse said after a puberty movie once that salt is bad for people's hearts.

Phooey, she'll say. It just makes it thump, that's all. Thump, thump, thump—oh look! She will talk with her mouth full of popcorn. Cary Grant is getting her out of there. Did you unplug the popper?

Pretend you don't hear her. Watch Inger Berman look elongated; wonder what it means.

You'd better check, she'll say.

Groan. Make a little *tsk* noise with your tongue on the roof of your mouth. Run as fast as you can because the next commercial's going to be the end. Unplug the popper. Bring Mittens back in with you because he is mewing by the refrigerator. He'll leave hair on your bathrobe. Dump him in your mom's lap.

10   Hey baby, she'll coo at the cat, scratching his ears. Cuddle close to your mom and she'll reach around and scratch one of your ears too, kissing your cheek. Then she'll suddenly lean forward, reaching toward the bowl on the coffee table, carefully so as not to disturb the cat. I always think he's going to realize faster than he does, your mom will say between munches, hand to hand to mouth.

Men can be so dense and frustrating. She will wink at you.

Eye the tube suspiciously. All the bad guys will let Cary Grant take Inger Berman away in the black car. There will be a lot of old-fashioned music. Stand and pull your bathrobe up on the sides. Hang your tongue out and pretend to dance like a retarded person at a ball. Roll your eyes. Waltz across the living room with exaggerated side-to-side motions, banging into furniture. Your mother will pretend not to pay attention to you. She will finally say in a flat voice: How wonderful, gee, you really send me.

When the music is over, she will ask you what you want to watch now. She'll hand you the *TV Guide.* Look at it. Say: The Late, Late Chiller. She'll screw up one of her eyebrows at you, but say *please, please* in a soft voice and put your hands together like a prayer. She will smile back and sigh, okay.

Switch the channel and return to the sofa. Climb under the blue afghan with your mother. Tell her you like this beginning cartoon part best where the mummy comes out of the coffin and roars, *CHILLER!!* Get up on one of the arms of the sofa and do an imitation, your hands like claws, your elbows stiff, your head slumped to one side. Your mother will tell you to sit back down. Snuggle back under the blanket with her.

When she says, Which do you like better, the mummy or the werewolf, tell her the werewolf is scary because he goes out at night and does things that no one suspects because in the day he works in a bank and has no hair.

15   What about the mummy? she'll ask, petting Mittens.

Shrug your shoulders. Fold in your lips. Say: The mummy's just the mummy.

With the point of your tongue, loosen one of the chewed, pulpy kernels in your molars. Try to swallow it, but get it caught in your throat and begin to gasp and make horrible retching noises. It will scare the cat away.

Good god, be careful, your mother will say, thwacking you on the back. Here, drink this water.

Try groaning root beer, root beer, like a dying cowboy you saw on a commercial once, but drink the water anyway. When you are no longer choking, your face is less red, and you can breathe again, ask for a Coke. Your mom will say: I don't think so; Dr. Atwood said your teeth were atrocious.

20   Tell her Dr. Atwood is for the birds.

What do you mean by that? she will exclaim.

Look straight ahead. Say: I dunno.

The mummy will be knocking down telephone poles, lifting them up, and hurling them around like Lincoln Logs.

Wow, all wrapped up and no place to go, your mother will say.

25 Cuddle close to her and let out a long, low, admiring *Neato*.

The police will be in the cemetery looking for a monster. They won't know whether it's the mummy or the werewolf, but someone will have been hanging out there leaving little smoking piles of bones and flesh that even the police dogs get upset and whine at.

Say something like gross-out, and close your eyes.

Are you sure you want to watch this?

Insist that you are not scared.

30 There's a rock concert on Channel 7, you know.

Think about it. Decide to try Channel 7, just for your mom's sake. Somebody with greasy hair who looks like Uncle Jack will be saying something boring.

Your mother will agree that he does look like Uncle Jack. A little.

A band with black eyeshadow on will begin playing their guitars. Stand and bounce up and down like you saw Julie Steinman do once.

God, why do they always play them down at their crotches? your mom will ask.

35 Don't answer, simply imitate them, throwing your hair back and fidding bizarrely with the crotch of your pajama bottoms. Your mother will slap you and tell you you're being fresh.

Act hurt. Affect a slump. Pick up a magazine and pretend you're reading it. The cat will rejoin you. Look at the pictures of the food.

Your mom will try to pep you up. She'll say: Look! Pat Benatar! Let's dance.

Tell her you think Pat Benatar is stupid and cheap. Say nothing for five whole minutes.

When the B-52's come on, tell her you think *they're* okay.

40 Smile sheepishly. Then the two of you will get up and dance like wild maniacs around the coffee table until you are sweating, whooping to the oo-ah-oo's, jumping like pogo sticks, acting like space robots. Do razz-ma-tazz hands like your mom at either side of your head. During a commercial, ask for an orange soda.

Water or milk, she will say, slightly out of breath, sitting back down.

Say shit, and when she asks what did you say, sigh: Nothing.

Next is Rod Stewart singing on a roof somewhere. Your mom will say: He's sort of cute.

Tell her Julie Steinman saw him in a store once and said he looked really old.

45 Hmmmm, your mother will say.

Study Rod Stewart carefully. Wonder if you could make your legs go like that. Plan an imitation for Julie Steinman.

When the popcorn is all gone, yawn. Say: I'm going to bed now.

Your mother will look disappointed, but she'll say, okay, honey. She'll turn the TV off. By the way, she'll ask hesitantly like she always does. How did the last three days go?

Leave out the part about the lady and the part about the beer. Tell her they went all right, that he's got a new silver dartboard and that you went out to dinner and this guy named Hudson told a pretty funny story about peeing in the hamper. Ask for a 7-Up.

[1985]

QUESTIONS FOR REFLECTION AND DISCUSSION

1. What is the effect of the second-person narration? Whom is it addressed to? Who is the narrator? What do we know about the narrator?

2. How does each character react to each of the different programs they watch on television? What do their reactions tell us about their characters?

3. What do the final two paragraphs tell us that we didn't know already? How would the story be different without these paragraphs?

4. How would the effect and meaning of the story change if the narrator told it in the first person? How would they change if it were narrated in the third person?

James Joyce 1882–1941

One of the towering figures of European modernism, James Joyce was born in Dublin, Ireland, where he received a classical education and studied modern languages at University College. In 1914, Joyce published the short story collection *Dubliners*, which included the story "Araby"; the autobiographical novel *A Portrait of the Artist as a Young Man* appeared two years later. Like the hero of that novel, Joyce left Ireland at the age of twenty with his young wife, Nora; they spent the rest of their lives leading a financially precarious existence in Trieste, Zurich, and Paris, while Joyce wrote his two great experimental novels, *Ulysses* (1922) and *Finnegans Wake* (1939).

ARABY

NORTH RICHMOND STREET, BEING BLIND,° WAS a quiet street except at the hour when the Christian Brothers' School set the boys free. An uninhabited house of two storeys stood at the blind end, detached from its neighbours in a square ground. The other houses of the street, conscious of decent lives within them, gazed at one another with brown imperturbable faces.

The former tenant of our house, a priest, had died in the back drawing-room. Air, musty from having been long enclosed, hung in all the rooms, and the waste room behind the kitchen was littered with old useless papers. Among these I found a few paper-covered books, the pages of which were curled and damp: *The Abbot,* by Walter Scott, *The Devout Communicant* and *The Memoirs of Vidocq.*° I liked the last best because its leaves were yellow. The wild garden behind the house contained a central apple-tree and a few straggling bushes under one of which I found the late tenant's rusty bicycle-pump. He had been a very charitable priest; in his will he had left all his money to institutions and the furniture of his house to his sister.

When the short days of winter came dusk fell before we had well eaten our dinners. When we met in the street the houses had grown sombre. The space of sky above us was the colour of ever-changing violet and towards it the lamps of the street lifted their feeble lanterns. The cold air stung us and we played till our bodies glowed. Our shouts echoed in the silent street. The career of our play brought us through the dark muddy lanes behind the houses where we ran the gauntlet of the rough tribes from

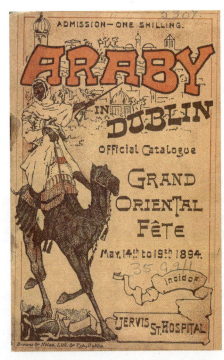

The official catalog of "Araby," a grand oriental fête at Ball's Bridge, Dublin, 1894, when Joyce would have been twelve.

the cottages, to the back doors of the dark dripping gardens where odours arose from the ashpits, to the dark odorous stables where a coachman smoothed and combed the horse or shook music from the buckled harness. When we returned to the street light from the kitchen windows had filled the areas. If my uncle was seen turning the corner we hid in the shadow until we had seen him safely housed. Or if Mangan's sister came out on the doorstep to call her brother in to his tea we watched her from our shadow peer up and down the street. We waited to see whether she would remain or go in and, if she remained, we left our shadow and walked up to

---

blind: a dead-end street. **The Abbot . . . :** three popular books from the early nineteenth-century.

Mangan's steps resignedly. She was waiting for us, her figure defined by the light from the half-opened door. Her brother always teased her before he obeyed and I stood by the railings looking at her. Her dress swung as she moved her body and the soft rope of her hair tossed from side to side.

Every morning I lay on the floor in the front parlour watching her door. The blind was pulled down to within an inch of the sash so that I could not be seen. When she came out on the doorstep my heart leaped. I ran to the hall, seized my books and followed her. I kept her brown figure always in my eye and, when we came near the point at which our ways diverged, I quickened my pace and passed her. This happened morning after morning. I had never spoken to her, except for a few casual words, and yet her name was like a summons to all my foolish blood.

5 Her image accompanied me even in places the most hostile to romance. On Saturday evenings when my aunt went marketing I had to go to carry some of the parcels. We walked through the flaring streets, jostled by drunken men and bargaining women, amid the curses of labourers, the shrill litanies of shop-boys who stood on guard by the barrels of pigs' cheeks, the nasal chanting of street-singers, who sang a *come-all-you* about O'Donovan Rossa, or a ballad about the troubles in our native land.° These noises converged in a single sensation of life for me: I imagined that I bore my chalice safely through a throng of foes. Her name sprang to my lips at moments in strange prayers and praises which I myself did not understand. My eyes were often full of tears (I could not tell why) and at times a flood from my heart seemed to pour itself out into my bosom. I thought little of the future. I did not know whether I would ever speak to her or not or, if I spoke to her, how I could tell her of my confused adoration. But my body was like a harp and her words and gestures were like fingers running upon the wires.

One evening I went into the back drawing-room in which the priest had died. It was a dark rainy evening and there was no sound in the house. Through one of the broken panes I heard the rain impinge upon the earth, the fine incessant needles of water playing in the sodden beds. Some distant lamp or lighted window gleamed below me. I was thankful that I could see so little. All my senses seemed to desire to veil themselves and, feeling that I was about to slip from them, I pressed the palms of my hands together until they trembled, murmuring: *O love! O love!* many times.

At last she spoke to me. When she addressed the first words to me I was so confused that I did not know what to answer. She asked me was I going to *Araby.* I forgot whether I answered yes or no. It would be a splendid bazaar, she said; she would love to go.

"And why can't you?" I asked.

While she spoke she turned a silver bracelet round and round her wrist. She could not go, she said, because there would be a retreat that week in her convent. Her brother and two other boys were fighting for their caps and I was alone at the railings. She held one of the spikes, bowing her head towards me. The light from the lamp opposite our door caught the white curve of her neck, lit up her hair that rested there and, falling, lit up the hand upon the railing. It fell over one side of her dress and caught the white border of a petticoat, just visible as she stood at ease.

10 "It's well for you," she said.

"If I go," I said, "I will bring you something."

What innumerable follies laid waste my waking and sleeping thoughts after that evening! I wished to annihilate the tedious intervening days. I chafed against the work of school. At night in my bedroom and by day in the classroom her image came between me and the page I strove to read. The syllables of the word *Araby* were called to me through the silence in which my soul luxuriated and cast an Eastern enchantment over me. I asked for leave to go to the bazaar on Saturday night. My aunt was surprised and hoped it was not some Freemason affair.° I answered few questions in class. I watched my master's face pass from amiability to sternness; he hoped I was not beginning to idle. I could not call my wandering thoughts together. I had hardly any patience with the serious work of life which, now that it stood between me and my desire, seemed to me child's play, ugly monotonous child's play.

---

come-all-you: a street song, or form of ballad, beginning "Come all you Irishmen . . ." Jeremiah O'Donovan was an Irish nationalist in American exile who urged violent revolution.

Freemason affair: Freemasonry was a secretive guild feared at the time by Roman Catholics as an enemy to their religion.

On Saturday morning I reminded my uncle that I wished to go to the bazaar in the evening. He was fussing at the hallstand, looking for the hat-brush, and answered me curtly:

"Yes, boy, I know."

15   As he was in the hall I could not go into the front parlour and lie at the window. I left the house in bad humour and walked slowly towards the school. The air was pitilessly raw and already my heart misgave me.

When I came home to dinner my uncle had not yet been home. Still it was early. I sat staring at the clock for some time and when its ticking began to irritate me, I left the room. I mounted the staircase and gained the upper part of the house. The high cold empty gloomy rooms liberated me and I went from room to room singing. From the front window I saw my companions playing below in the street. Their cries reached me weakened and indistinct and, leaning my forehead against the cool glass, I looked over at the dark house where she lived. I may have stood there for an hour, seeing nothing but the brown-clad figure cast by my imagination, touched discreetly by the lamplight at the curved neck, at the hand upon the railings and at the border below the dress.

When I came downstairs again I found Mrs. Mercer sitting at the fire. She was an old garrulous woman, a pawnbroker's widow, who collected used stamps for some pious purpose. I had to endure the gossip of the tea-table. The meal was prolonged beyond an hour and still my uncle did not come. Mrs. Mercer stood up to go: she was sorry she couldn't wait any longer, but it was after eight o'clock and she did not like to be out late as the night air was bad for her. When she had gone I began to walk up and down the room, clenching my fists. My aunt said:

"I'm afraid you may put off your bazaar for this night of Our Lord."

At nine o'clock I heard my uncle's latchkey in the halldoor. I heard him talking to himself and heard the hallstand rocking when it had received the weight of his overcoat. I could interpret these signs. When he was midway through his dinner I asked him to give me the money to go to the bazaar. He had forgotten.

20   "The people are in bed and after their first sleep now," he said.

I did not smile. My aunt said to him energetically:

"Can't you give him the money and let him go? You've kept him late enough as it is."

My uncle said he was very sorry he had forgotten. He said he believed in the old saying: *All work and no play makes Jack a dull boy.* He asked me where I was going and, when I had told him a second time he asked me did I know *The Arab's Farewell to his Steed.*° When I left the kitchen he was about to recite the opening lines of the piece to my aunt.

I held a florin tightly in my hand as I strode down Buckingham Street towards the station. The sight of the streets thronged with buyers and glaring with gas recalled to me the purpose of my journey. I took my seat in a third-class carriage of a deserted train. After an intolerable delay the train moved out of the station slowly. It crept onward among ruinous houses and over the twinkling river. At Westland Row Station a crowd of people pressed to the carriage doors; but the porters moved them back, saying that it was a special train for the bazaar. I remained alone in the bare carriage. In a few minutes the train drew up beside an improvised wooden platform. I passed out on to the road and saw by the lighted dial of a clock that it was ten minutes to ten. In front of me was a large building which displayed the magical name.

25   I could not find any sixpenny entrance and, fearing that the bazaar would be closed, I passed in quickly through a turnstile, handing a shilling to a weary-looking man. I found myself in a big hall girdled at half its height by a gallery. Nearly all the stalls were closed and the greater part of the hall was in darkness. I recognised a silence like that which pervades a church after a service. I walked into the centre of the bazaar timidly. A few people were gathered about the stalls which were still open. Before a curtain, over which the words *Café Chantant*° were written in coloured lamps, two men were counting money on a salver.° I listened to the fall of the coins.

Remembering with difficulty why I had come I went over to one of the stalls and examined porcelain vases and flowered tea-sets. At the door of the stall a young lady was talking and laughing with two young gentlemen. I remarked their English accents and listened vaguely to their conversation.

"O, I never said such a thing!"

The Arab's Farewell to his Steed: a popular poem by Caroline Norton (1808–1877) in the voice of an Arab boy who sells his beloved horse only to return the money at the last moment and retrieve his steed. *Café Chantant:* a French café with popular musical entertainment. **salver:** the plate that holds the chalice filled with communion wine for Catholic mass.

"O, but you did!"

"O, but I didn't!"

30 "Didn't she say that?"

"Yes. I heard her."

"O, there's a . . . fib!"

Observing me the young lady came over and asked me did I wish to buy anything. The tone of her voice was not encouraging; she seemed to have spoken to me out of a sense of duty. I looked humbly at the great jars that stood like eastern guards at either side of the dark entrance to the stall and murmured:

"No, thank you."

35 The young lady changed the position of one of the vases and went back to the two young men.

They began to talk of the same subject. Once or twice the young lady glanced at me over her shoulder.

I lingered before her stall, though I knew my stay was useless, to make my interest in her wares seem the more real. Then I turned away slowly and walked down the middle of the bazaar. I allowed the two pennies to fall against the sixpence in my pocket. I heard a voice call from one end of the gallery that the light was out. The upper part of the hall was now completely dark.

Gazing up into the darkness I saw myself as a creature driven and derided by vanity; and my eyes burned with anguish and anger.

[1914]

QUESTIONS FOR REFLECTION AND DISCUSSION

1. What is the narrator's relationship to Mangan's sister? How does this relationship guide his actions?

2. How does Araby become associated with Mangan's sister? What is the narrator's expectation about the bazaar?

3. What happens in the bazaar? Why does it cause the narrator to feel about himself as he does in the final sentence?

4. Using evidence from the story, characterize the narrator's attitude toward the events he is recounting. How much time do you think has passed since the events took place? How would the story change if narrated in the present tense? How would it change if narrated by an objective third-person narrator?

John Updike 1932–2009

One of America's most highly praised and prolific writers, Updike was born in Reading, Pennsylvania, and raised in Shillington. He attended Harvard University on a full scholarship and after graduation began working for the *New Yorker* magazine. Best-known for his realistic and often sexually explicit novels of suburban Massachusetts (where he lived from 1957), Updike has published more than two dozen novels, and numerous collections of stories and essays. Two of the volumes in his bestselling *Rabbit* series were awarded the Pulitzer Prize. "A & P" was first published in the *New Yorker* in 1961.

A & P

IN WALKS THESE THREE GIRLS IN NOTHING BUT bathing suits. I'm in the third checkout slot, with my back to the door, so I don't see them until they're over by the bread. The one that caught my eye first was the one in the plaid green two-piece. She was a chunky kid, with a good tan and a sweet broad soft-looking can with those two crescents of white just under it, where the sun never seems to hit, at the top of the backs of her legs. I stood there with my hand on a box of HiHo crackers trying to remember if I rang it up or not. I ring it up again and the customer starts giving me hell. She's one of these cash-register-watchers, a witch about fifty with rouge on her cheekbones and no eyebrows, and I know it made her day to trip me up. She'd been watching cash registers for fifty years and probably never seen a mistake before.

By the time I got her feathers smoothed and her goodies into a bag—she gives me a little snort in passing, if she'd been born at the right time they

The façade of an A&P supermarket, part of the biggest food retailing chain in the United States during the middle of the twentieth century.

would have burned her over in Salem—by the time I get her on her way the girls had circled around the bread and were coming back, without a pushcart, back my way along the counters, in the aisle between the check-outs and the Special bins. They didn't even have shoes on. There was this chunky one, with the two-piece—it was bright green and the seams on the bra were still sharp and her belly was still pretty pale so I guessed she just got it (the suit)—there was this one, with one of those chubby berry-faces, the lips all bunched together under her nose, this one, and a tall one, with black hair that hadn't quite frizzed right, and one of these sunburns right across under the eyes, and a chin that was too long—you know, the kind of girl other girls think is very "striking" and "attractive" but never quite makes it, as they very well know, which is why they like her so much—and then the third one, that wasn't quite so tall. She was the queen. She kind of led them, the other two peeking around and making their shoulders round. She didn't look around, not this queen, she just walked straight on slowly, on these long white prima-donna legs. She came down a little hard on her heels, as if she didn't walk in her bare feet that much, putting down her heels and then letting the weight move along to her toes as if she was testing the floor with every step, putting a little deliberate extra action into it. You never know for sure how girls' minds work (do you really think it's a mind in there or just a little buzz like a bee in a glass jar?) but

you got the idea she had talked the other two into coming in here with her, and now she was showing them how to do it, walk slow and hold yourself straight.

She had on a kind of dirty-pink—beige maybe, I don't know—bathing suit with a little nubble all over it and, what got me, the straps were down. They were off her shoulders looped loose around the cool tops of her arms, and I guess as a result the suit had slipped a little on her, so all around the top of the cloth there was this shining rim. If it hadn't been there you wouldn't have known there could have been anything whiter than those shoulders. With the straps pushed off, there was nothing between the top of the suit and the top of her head except just *her*, this clean bare plane of the top of her chest down from the shoulder bones like a dented sheet of metal tilted in the light. I mean, it was more than pretty.

She had sort of oaky hair that the sun and salt had bleached, done up in a bun that was unraveling, and a kind of prim face. Walking into the A & P with your straps down, I suppose it's the only kind of face you *can* have. She held her head so high her neck, coming up out of those white shoulders, looked kind of stretched, but I didn't mind. The longer her neck was, the more of her there was.

5   She must have felt in the corner of her eye me and over my shoulder Stokesie in the second slot watching, but she didn't tip. Not this queen. She kept her eyes moving across the racks, and stopped, and turned so slow it made my stomach rub the inside of my apron, and buzzed to the other two, who kind of huddled against her for relief, and they all three of them went up the cat-and-dog-food-breakfast-cereal-macaroni-rice-raisins-seasonings-spreads-spaghetti-soft-drinks-crackers-and-cookies aisle. From the third slot I look straight up this aisle to the meat counter, and I watched them all the way. The fat one with the tan sort of fumbled with the cookies, but on second thought she put the packages back. The sheep pushing their carts down the aisle—the girls were walking against the usual traffic (not that we have one-way signs or anything)—were pretty hilarious. You could see them, when Queenie's white shoulders dawned on them, kind of jerk, or hop, or hiccup, but their eyes snapped back to their own baskets and on they pushed. I bet you could set off dynamite in an A & P and the people would by and large keep reaching and checking oatmeal off their lists and muttering

"Let me see, there was a third thing, began with A, asparagus, no, ah, yes, applesauce!" or whatever it is they do mutter. But there was no doubt, this jiggled them. A few houseslaves in pin curlers even looked around after pushing their carts past to make sure what they had seen was correct.

You know, it's one thing to have a girl in a bathing suit down on the beach, where what with the glare nobody can look at each other much anyway, and another thing in the cool of the A & P, under the fluorescent lights, against all those stacked packages, with her feet padding along naked over our checker-board green-and-cream rubber-tile floor.

"Oh Daddy," Stokesie said beside me. "I feel so faint."

"Darling," I said. "Hold me tight." Stokesie's married, with two babies chalked up on his fuselage already, but as far as I can tell that's the only difference. He's twenty-two, and I was nineteen this April.

"Is it done?" he asks, the responsible married man finding his voice. I forgot to say he thinks he's going to be manager some sunny day, maybe in 1990 when it's called the Great Alexandrov and Petrooshki Tea Company or something.

10   What he meant was, our town is five miles from a beach, with a big summer colony out on the Point, but we're right in the middle of town, and the women generally put on a shirt or shorts or something before they get out of the car into the street. And anyway these are usually women with six children and varicose veins mapping their legs and nobody, including them, could care less. As I say, we're right in the middle of town, and if you stand at our front doors you can see two banks and the Congregational church and the newspaper store and three real-estate offices and about twenty-seven old freeloaders tearing up Central Street because the sewer broke again. It's not as if we're on the Cape; we're north of Boston and there's people in this town haven't seen the ocean for twenty years.

The girls had reached the meat counter and were asking McMahon something. He pointed, they pointed, and they shuffled out of sight behind a pyramid of Diet Delight peaches. All that was left for us to see was old McMahon patting his mouth and looking after them sizing up their joints. Poor kids, I began to feel sorry for them, they couldn't help it.

Now here comes the sad part of the story, at least my family says it's sad but I don't think it's sad

myself. The store's pretty empty, it being Thursday afternoon, so there was nothing much to do except lean on the register and wait for the girls to show up again. The whole store was like a pinball machine and I didn't know which tunnel they'd come out of. After a while they come around out of the far aisle, around the light bulbs, records at discount of the Caribbean Six or Tony Martin Sings or some such gunk you wonder they waste the wax on, six-packs of candy bars, and plastic toys done up in cellophane that fall apart when a kid looks at them anyway. Around they come, Queenie still leading the way, and holding a little gray jar in her hand. Slots Three through Seven are unmanned and I could see her wondering between Stokes and me, but Stokesie with his usual luck draws an old party in baggy gray pants who stumbles up with four giant cans of pineapple juice (what do these bums *do* with all that pineapple juice? I've often asked myself) so the girls come to me. Queenie puts down the jar and I take it into my fingers icy cold. Kingfish Fancy Herring Snacks in Pure Sour Cream: 49¢. Now her hands are empty, not a ring or a bracelet, bare as God made them, and I wonder where the money's coming from. Still with that prim look she lifts a folded dollar bill out of the hollow at the center of her nubbled pink top. The jar went heavy in my hand. Really, I thought that was so cute.

Then everybody's luck begins to run out. Lengel comes in from haggling with a truck full of cabbages on the lot and is about to scuttle into that door marked MANAGER behind which he hides all day when the girls touch his eye. Lengel's pretty dreary, teaches Sunday school and the rest, but he doesn't miss that much. He comes over and says, "Girls, this isn't the beach."

Queenie blushes, though maybe it's just a brush of sunburn I was noticing for the first time, now that she was so close. "My mother asked me to pick up a jar of herring snacks." Her voice kind of startled me, the way voices do when you see the people first, coming out so flat and dumb yet kind of tony, too, the way it ticked over "pick up" and "snacks." All of a sudden I slid right down her voice into her living room. Her father and the other men were standing around in ice-cream coats and bow ties and the women were in sandals picking up herring snacks on toothpicks off a big plate and they were all holding drinks the color of water with olives and sprigs of mint in them. When my parents have somebody over they get lemonade and if it's a real racy affair Schlitz in tall glasses with "They'll Do It Every Time" cartoons stencilled on.

15 "That's all right," Lengel said. "But this isn't the beach." His repeating this struck me as funny, as if it had just occurred to him, and he had been thinking all these years the A & P was a great big dune and he was the head lifeguard. He didn't like my smiling—as I say he doesn't miss much—but he concentrates on giving the girls that sad Sunday-school-superintendent stare.

Queenie's blush is no sunburn now, and the plump one in plaid, that I liked better from the back—a really sweet can—pipes up, "We weren't doing any shopping. We just came in for the one thing."

"That makes no difference," Lengel tells her, and I could see from the way his eyes went that he hadn't noticed she was wearing a two-piece before. "We want you decently dressed when you come in here."

"We *are* decent," Queenie says suddenly, her lower lip pushing, getting sore now that she remembers her place, a place from which the crowd that runs the A & P must look pretty crummy. Fancy Herring Snacks flashed in her very blue eyes.

"Girls, I don't want to argue with you. After this come in here with your shoulders covered. It's our policy." He turns his back. That's policy for you. Policy is what the kingpins want. What the others want is juvenile delinquency.

20 All this while, the customers had been showing up with their carts but, you know, sheep, seeing a scene, they had all bunched up on Stokesie, who shook open a paper bag as gently as peeling a peach, not wanting to miss a word. I could feel in the silence everybody getting nervous, most of all Lengel, who asks me, "Sammy, have you rung up this purchase?"

I thought and said "No" but it wasn't about that I was thinking. I go through the punches, 4, 9, GROC, TOT—it's more complicated than you think, and after you do it often enough, it begins to make a little song, that you hear words to, in my case "Hello (*bing*) there, you (*gung*) hap-py *pee*pul (*splat*)!"— the *splat* being the drawer flying out. I uncrease the bill, tenderly as you may imagine, it just having come from between the two smoothest scoops of vanilla I had ever known were there, and pass a half and a

penny into her narrow pink palm, and nestle the herrings in a bag and twist its neck and hand it over, all the time thinking.

The girls, and who'd blame them, are in a hurry to get out, so I say "I quit" to Lengel quick enough for them to hear, hoping they'll stop and watch me, their unsuspected hero. They keep right on going, into the electric eye; the door flies open and they flicker across the lot to their car, Queenie and Plaid and Big Tall Goony-Goony (not that as raw material she was so bad), leaving me with Lengel and a kink in his eyebrow.

"Did you say something, Sammy?"

"I said I quit."

"I thought you did."

25 "You didn't have to embarrass them."

"It was they who were embarrassing us."

I started to say something that came out "Fiddle-de-doo." It's a saying of my grandmother's, and I know she would have been pleased.

"I don't think you know what you're saying," Lengel said.

30 "I know you don't," I said. "But I do." I pull the bow at the back of my apron and start shrugging it off my shoulders. A couple customers that had been heading for my slot begin to knock against each other, like scared pigs in a chute.

Lengel sighs and begins to look very patient and old and gray. He's been a friend of my parents for years. "Sammy, you don't want to do this to your Mom and Dad," he tells me. It's true, I don't. But it seems to me that once you begin a gesture it's fatal not to go through with it. I fold the apron, "Sammy" stitched in red on the pocket, and put it on the counter, and drop the bow tie on top of it. The bow tie is theirs, if you've ever wondered. "You'll feel this for the rest of your life," Lengel says, and I know that's true, too, but remembering how he made that pretty girl blush makes me so scrunchy inside I punch the No Sale tab and the machine whirs "pee-pul" and the drawer splats out. One advantage to this scene taking place in summer, I can follow this up with a clean exit, there's no fumbling around getting your coat and galoshes, I just saunter into the electric eye in my white shirt that my mother ironed the night before, and the door heaves itself open, and outside the sunshine is skating around on the asphalt.

I look around for my girls, but they're gone, of course. There wasn't anybody but some young married screaming with her children about some candy they didn't get by the door of a powder-blue Falcon station wagon. Looking back in the big windows, over the bags of peat moss and aluminum lawn furniture stacked on the pavement, I could see Lengel in my place in the slot, checking the sheep through. His face was dark gray and his back stiff, as if he'd just had an injection of iron, and my stomach kind of fell as I felt how hard the world was going to be to me hereafter.

[1961]

QUESTIONS FOR REFLECTION AND DISCUSSION

1. How would you characterize the narrator's voice? What specific qualities does it have? What formal means does Updike use to create this voice?

2. Why are the three girls out of place in the A & P? How do the different persons in the shop react to them?

3. How does Updike inform us of the difference in social class between the clerk and the girls? What role does this difference play in the events and the meaning of the story?

4. What causes the grocery clerk to quit? Does he regret it? Using evidence from the text, explain why or why not.

POETRY

Elizabeth Bishop 1911–1979

Born in Massachusetts, as a child Elizabeth Bishop lost her father to death and her mother to a mental institution, and was raised in Nova Scotia by her grandparents. She graduated from Vassar College in 1934 and spent the next years traveling the world and writing poetry about what she saw. She lived for many years in Brazil, and her correspondence records her close friendship and professional relationship with other poets such as Marianne Moore and Robert Lowell. Bishop's poetry is known for its dazzling technique, precise observation, and innovative work in intricate forms such as the villanelle and the sestina as well as in free verse ("The Fish," p. 655). "In the Waiting Room," published in Bishop's last collection of poetry, *Geography III* (1976), is based on an experience, nearly sixty years before it was written, while the girl, for all practical purposes an orphan, was living with her aunt in Worcester, Massachusetts.

In the Waiting Room

In Worcester, Massachusetts,
I went with Aunt Consuelo
to keep her dentist's appointment
and sat and waited for her
in the dentist's waiting room.   5
It was winter. It got dark
early. The waiting room
was full of grown-up people,
arctics and overcoats,
lamps and magazines.   10
My aunt was inside
what seemed like a long time
and while I waited I read
the *National Geographic*
(I could read) and carefully   15
studied the photographs:
the inside of a volcano,
black, and full of ashes;
then it was spilling over
in rivulets of fire.   20
Osa and Martin Johnson
dressed in riding breeches,
laced boots, and pith helmets.
A dead man slung on a pole
—"Long Pig," the caption said.   25
Babies with pointed heads
wound round and round with string;
black, naked women with necks
wound round and round with wire

Part of Elizabeth Bishop's childhood memory: Osa and Martin Johnson on safari in the South Seas. A famous explorer couple, the Johnsons made the news in 1917 when rescued by a British gunboat from a Vanatu island tribe; a feature documentary of their expedition was released in 1918. The Johnsons were also famous for their photographs of "cannibals" and their "long pig," or human meat, and other sensational images from the remote islands of the South Seas.

like the necks of light bulbs.   30
Their breasts were horrifying.
I read it right straight through.
I was too shy to stop.
And then I looked at the cover:
the yellow margins, the date.   35
Suddenly, from inside,
came an *oh!* of pain
—Aunt Consuelo's voice—
not very loud or long.
I wasn't at all surprised;   40
even then I knew she was
a foolish, timid woman.
I might have been embarrassed,
but wasn't. What took me
completely by surprise   45
was that it was *me:*
my voice, in my mouth.
Without thinking at all
I was my foolish aunt,
I—we—were falling, falling,   50
our eyes glued to the cover
of the *National Geographic,*
February, 1918.

I said to myself: three days
and you'll be seven years old.   55

I was saying it to stop
the sensation of falling off
the round, turning world.
into cold, blue-black space.
But I felt: you are an I,   60
you are an *Elizabeth,*
you are one of *them.*
Why should you be one, too?
I scarcely dared to look
to see what it was I was.   65
I gave a sidelong glance
—I couldn't look any higher—
at shadowy gray knees,
trousers and skirts and boots
and different pairs of hands   70
lying under the lamps.
I knew that nothing stranger
had ever happened, that nothing
stranger could ever happen.

Why should I be my aunt,   75
or me, or anyone?
What similarities—
boots, hands, the family voice
I felt in my throat, or even
the *National Geographic*   80
and those awful hanging breasts—
held us all together
or made us all just one?
How—I didn't know any
word for it—how "unlikely". . .   85
How had I come to be here,
like them, and overhear
a cry of pain that could have
got loud and worse but hadn't?

The waiting room was bright   90
and too hot. It was sliding
beneath a big black wave,
another, and another.

Then I was back in it.
The War was on. Outside,   95
in Worcester, Massachusetts,
were night and slush and cold,
and it was still the fifth
of February, 1918.

[1976]

1. How, in the opening description, does Bishop capture the state of mind of a six-year-old in a waiting room?

2. What possible connections are there between the images Bishop includes here and the setting of the waiting room?

3. What happens to the speaker when she hears her aunt's cry of pain? How do her perceptions and her experience change?

4. What brings her "back in it"? Where was she?

5. Do you recall a similar experience as a child? How was it similar? How did it differ from the one Bishop describes? Why do you think Bishop still recalled this experience so vividly nearly sixty years later?

Anne Sexton   1928–1974

Born in Newton, Massachusetts, to a successful but dysfunctional family, Anne Sexton made her unhappy life the subject of her most successful poetry. She eloped from a finishing school at the age of nineteen, and worked as a fashion model while her husband served in the Korean War. After bearing two children and being in and out of therapy, Sexton began writing poetry in 1957, creating a confessional voice that drew on but transformed her experiences. Her success and recognition as a poet were at their height throughout the 1960s. She divorced her husband in 1973 and a year later committed suicide. "Red Riding Hood" was first published in *Transformations* (1971), a collection of seventeen poems revisiting and revising the tales of the Brothers Grimm.

Red Riding Hood

Many are the deceivers:

The suburban matron,
proper in the supermarket,
list in hand so she won't suddenly fly,
buying her Duz° and Chuck Wagon dog food,   5
meanwhile ascending from earth,
letting her stomach fill up with helium,
letting her arms go loose as kite tails,
getting ready to meet her lover
a mile down Apple Crest Road   10
in the Congregational Church parking lot.

Two seemingly respectable women
come up to an old Jenny
and show her an envelope
full of money   15
and promise to share the booty

if she'll give them ten thou
as an act of faith.
Her life savings are under the mattress
covered with rust stains   20
and counting.
They are as wrinkled as prunes
but negotiable.
The two women take the money and disappear.
Where is the moral?   25
Not all knives are for
stabbing the exposed belly.
Rock climbs on rock
and it only makes a seashore.
Old Jenny has lost her belief in mattresses   30
and now she has no wastebasket in which
to keep her youth.

The standup comic
on the "Tonight" show
who imitates the Vice President   35

5 **Duz:** a popular laundry soap.

Gustave Doré, *Little Red Riding Hood* (1862). In the original French folktale, the girl strips her clothing off piece by piece for the wolf waiting in bed; like Anne Sexton's and Agha Shahid Ali's poems, many modern versions equally stress the sexual tension between the innocent young girl and the predatory wolf.

and cracks up Johnny Carson°
and delays sleep for millions
of bedfellows watching between their feet,
slits his wrist the next morning
in the Algonquin's° old-fashioned bathroom,   40
the razor in his hand like a toothbrush,
wall as anonymous as a urinal,
the shower curtain his slack rubberman audience,
and then the slash
as simple as opening a letter   45
and the warm blood breaking out like a rose
upon the bathtub with its claw and ball feet.

And I. I too.
Quite collected at cocktail parties,
meanwhile in my head   50
I'm undergoing open-heart surgery.
The heart, poor fellow,
pounding on his little tin drum
with a faint death beat,
The heart, that eyeless beetle,   55
running panicked through his maze,
never stopping one foot after the other
one hour after the other
until he gags on an apple
and it's all over.   60

And I. I too again.
I built a summer house on Cape Ann.
A simple A-frame and this too was
a deception—nothing haunts a new house.
When I moved in with a bathing suit
   and tea bags   65
the ocean rumbled like a train backing up
and at each window secrets came in
like gas. My mother, that departed soul,
sat in my Eames chair and reproached me
for losing her keys to the old cottage.   70
Even in the electric kitchen there was
the smell of a journey. The ocean
was seeping through its frontiers
and laying me out on its wet rails.
The bed was stale with my childhood   75
and I could not move to another city
where the worthy make a new life.

Long ago
there was a strange deception: 80
a wolf dressed in frills,
a kind of transvestite.
But I get ahead of my story.
In the beginning
there was just little Red Riding Hood,   85
so called because her grandmother
made her a red cape and she was never
   without it.
It was her Linus blanket,° besides
it was red, as red as the Swiss flag,
yes it was red, as red as chicken blood,   90
But more than she loved her riding hood
she loved her grandmother who lived
far from the city in the big wood.

This one day her mother gave her
a basket of wine and cake   95
to take to her grandmother
because she was ill.
Wine and cake?
Where's the aspirin? The penicillin?
Where's the fruit juice?   100
Peter Rabbit got camomile tea.
But wine and cake it was.

On her way in the big wood
Red Riding Hood met the wolf.
Good day, Mr. Wolf, she said,   105
thinking him no more dangerous
than a streetcar or a panhandler.
He asked where she was going
and she obligingly told him
There among the roots and trunks   110
with the mushrooms pulsing inside the moss
he planned how to eat them both,
the grandmother an old carrot
and the child a shy budkin
in a red red hood.   115
He bade her to look at the bloodroot,
the small bunchberry and the dogtooth
and pick some for her grandmother.
And this she did.
Meanwhile he scampered off   120
to Grandmother's house and ate her up
as quick as a slap.
Then he put on her nightdress and cap
and snuggled down in to bed.
A deceptive fellow.   125

Red Riding Hood
knocked on the door and entered
with her flowers, her cake, her wine.
Grandmother looked strange,
a dark and hairy disease it seemed.   130
Oh Grandmother, what big ears you have,
ears, eyes, hands and then the teeth.
The better to eat you with my dear.
So the wolf gobbled Red Riding Hood down
like a gumdrop. Now he was fat.   135
He appeared to be in his ninth month
and Red Riding Hood and her grandmother
rode like two Jonahs up and down with
his every breath. One pigeon. One partridge.

He was fast asleep,   140
dreaming in his cap and gown,
wolfless.
Along came a huntsman who heard
the loud contented snores
and knew that was no grandmother.   145
He opened the door and said,
So it's you, old sinner.
He raised his gun to shoot him
when it occured to him that maybe
the wolf had eaten up the old lady.   150
So he took a knife and began cutting open
the sleeping wolf, a kind of caesarian section.

It was a carnal knife that let
Red Riding Hood out like a poppy,
quite alive from the kingdom of the belly.   155
And grandmother too
still waiting for cakes and wine.
The wolf, they decided, was too mean
to be simply shot so they filled his belly
with large stones and sewed him up.   160
He was as heavy as a cemetery
and when he woke up and tried to run off
he fell over dead. Killed by his own weight.
Many a deception ends on such a note.

The huntsman and the grandmother
    and Red Riding Hood   165
sat down by his corpse and had a meal of
    wine and cake.
Those two remembering
nothing naked and brutal
from that little death,
that little birth,   170
from their going down
and their lifting up.

[1971]

QUESTIONS FOR REFLECTION AND DISCUSSION

1. The poem is full of references to the popular culture of 1971 (for example, *The Tonight Show* and Linus's security blanket in the comic strip *Peanuts*). What is the effect of these references on the tone of the poem? How does it situate us as readers in relation to the stories it tells?

2. What is the relationship between the first part of the poem and the second, where the speaker retells the Little Red Riding Hood story?

3. What is the function of the imagery of childhood and adolescence within the context of the poem as a whole?

4. The final stanza emphasizes imagery of birth, sex, and death. How does this imagery function within the rest of the poem?

5. Compare the retelling of the story to the Brothers Grimm version on which it is based. How does the change in the voice of the narrator affect our understanding of the story? What is the narrator's attitude toward the material?

Agha Shahid Ali 1949–2001

Born in New Delhi, India, the Kashmiri-American poet and translator Agha Shahid Ali was raised in Kashmir. He taught at the University of Utah and a number of MFA programs, and was the author of four volumes of poetry, including *Rooms Are Never Finished* (2001), a finalist for the National Book Award, and *A Walk through the Yellow Pages* (1987), in which the following poem was published. Ali died of brain cancer in 2001.

The Wolf's Postscript to "Little Red Riding Hood"

First, grant me my sense of history:
I did it for posterity,
for kindergarten teachers
and a clear moral:
Little girls shouldn't wander off   5
in search of strange flowers,
and they mustn't speak to strangers.

And then grant me my generous sense of plot:
Couldn't I have gobbled her up
right there in the jungle?   10
Why did I ask her where her grandma lived?
As if I, a forest-dweller,
didn't know of the cottage
under the three oak trees
and the old woman who lived there   15
all alone?
As if I couldn't have swallowed her years before?

And you may call me the Big Bad Wolf,
now my only reputation.
But I was no child-molester   20
though you'll agree she was pretty.

And the huntsman:
Was I sleeping while he snipped
my thick black fur
and filled me with garbage and stones?   25
I ran with that weight and fell down,

Poster for Tex Avery, *Red Hot Riding Hood* (1943). The Tex Avery cartoon, "Red Hot Riding Hood," was censored when first released in 1943 (some of the cartoon transformations of the excited wolf referred a bit too directly to sexual arousal). Rather than an innocent girl, Avery's protagonist was designed as a pinup for the armed forces abroad. Similarly the pop group Sam the Sham and the Pharoahs had a hit single in 1966 with "Lil' Red Riding Hood," in which the singer half-mockingly, half-seriously salivates over the object of his lust as only a wolf can do.

simply so children could laugh
at the noise of the stones
cutting through my belly,
at the garbage spilling out   30
with a perfect sense of timing,
just when the tale
should have come to an end.

[1987]

QUESTIONS FOR REFLECTION AND DISCUSSION

1. Summarize the wolf's argument in each stanza. What character traits do these arguments attribute to the wolf? How do these traits differ from his conventional portrait?

2. Ali retells the same Brothers Grimm tale as Anne Sexton. What are some of the differences between the two retellings?

3. What do you think motivated Ali to write this poem? What evidence can you find for your conclusion in the poem itself?

Gary Soto b. 1952

Author of over twenty books of poetry and prose for adults and over two dozen for younger readers, Gary Soto was born in Fresno, California, to a family of laborers in the fields of nearby San Fernando Valley. When his father was killed in an accident working for the Sunmaid Raisin Company, Soto and two other children were raised by his mother in poverty, working in fields and factories from a young age. A struggling student, he discovered poetry while at college, graduated from California State, taught for sixteen years at the University of California, Berkeley, and is currently teaching at the University of California, Riverside. In 1978, he became the first Mexican-American to be nominated for the Pulitzer Prize. "Behind Grandma's House" appeared in his 1985 collection *Black Hair*.

Behind Grandma's House

At ten I wanted fame. I had a comb
And two Coke bottles, a tube of Bryl-creem.
I borrowed a dog, one with
Mismatched eyes and a happy tongue,
And wanted to prove I was tough   5
In the alley, kicking over trash cans,
A dull chime of tuna cans falling.
I hurled light bulbs like grenades
And men teachers held their heads,
Fingers of blood lengthening   10
On the ground. I flicked rocks at cats,

Their goofy faces spurred with foxtails.
I kicked fences. I shooed pigeons.
I broke a branch from a flowering peach
And frightened ants with a stream of spit.   15
I said "*Chale*,"° "In your face," and "No way
Daddy-O" to an imaginary priest
Until grandma came into the alley,
Her apron flapping in a breeze,
Her hair mussed, and said, "Let me help you,"   20
And punched me between the eyes.

[1985]

16 *Chale:* Mexican-American slang suggesting disagreement.

QUESTIONS FOR REFLECTION AND DISCUSSION

1. What is the attitude of the speaker toward himself at the age of ten? How would the tone of the poem change if he had taken a different attitude?

2. Who is the intended audience of the speaker's aspirations?

3. What is the surprise in the last four lines of the poem? What makes it surprising? How does it change the meaning of the poem?

4. Compare the grandmother in this poem with the grandmother in the poems by Anne Sexton and Agha Shahid Ali included here.

NONFICTION

Langston Hughes 1902–1967

Born in Joplin, Missouri, Langston Hughes spent most of his childhood with his grandmother in Lawrence, Kansas. Hughes studied for a year at Columbia University, but he left due to racial prejudice, shipping out as a crewman to West Africa and Europe. He lived in Paris as part of the African-American expatriate community, working as a nightclub bouncer. He eventually returned in 1924 to live and work in Washington, D.C., where he met poet Vachel Lindsay while working as a hotel busboy. Lindsay helped publicize Hughes's poetry, which he was about to collect into the volume, *The Weary Blues* (1926). Hughes moved to Harlem in the late 1920s and lived there until his death, an influential member of the literary movement known as the Harlem Renaissance. Hughes introduced popular musical rhythms into his poetry and created an unglamorous but realistic portrayal of African American lives.

SALVATION

I WAS SAVED FROM SIN WHEN I WAS GOING ON thirteen. But not really saved. It happened like this. There was a big revival at my Auntie Reed's church. Every night for weeks there had been much preaching, singing, praying, and shouting, and some very hardened sinners had been brought to Christ, and the membership of the church had grown by leaps and bounds. Then just before the revival ended, they held a special meeting for children, "to bring the young lambs to the fold." My aunt spoke of it for days ahead. That night I was escorted to the front row and placed on the mourners' bench with all the other young sinners, who had not yet been brought to Jesus.

My aunt told me that when you were saved you saw a light, and something happened to you inside! And Jesus came into your life! And God was with you from then on! She said you could see and hear and feel Jesus in your soul. I believed her. I had heard a great many old people say the same thing and it seemed to me they ought to know. So I sat there calmly in the hot, crowded church, waiting for Jesus to come to me.

The preacher preached a wonderful rhythmical sermon, all moans and shouts and lonely cries and dire pictures of hell, and then he sang a song about the ninety and nine safe in the fold, but one little lamb was left out in the cold. Then he said: "Won't you come? Won't you come to Jesus? Young lambs, won't you come?" And he held out his arms to all us

St. Luke African Methodist Episcopal Church, Lawrence, Kansas, built 1910. Hughes attended the church with his "Auntie" Reed and her husband, family friends with whom he lived after the death of his grandmother.

young sinners there on the mourners' bench. And the little girls cried. And some of them jumped up and went to Jesus right away. But most of us just sat there.

A great many old people came and knelt around us and prayed, old women with jet-black faces and braided hair, old men with work-gnarled hands. And the church sang a song about the lower lights are burning, some poor sinners to be saved. And the whole building rocked with prayer and song.

5   Still I kept waiting to *see* Jesus.

Finally all the young people had gone to the altar and were saved, but one boy and me. He was a rounder's° son named Westley. Westley and I were surrounded by sisters and deacons praying. It was very hot in the church, and getting late now. Finally Westley said to me in a whisper: "God damn! I'm tired o' sitting here. Let's get up and be saved." So he got up and was saved.

Then I was left all alone on the mourners' bench. My aunt came and knelt at my knees and cried, while prayers and song swirled all around me in the little church. The whole congregation prayed for me alone, in a mighty wail of moans and voices. And I kept waiting serenely for Jesus, waiting, waiting—but he didn't come. I wanted to see him, but nothing happened to me. Nothing! I wanted something to happen to me, but nothing happened.

I heard the songs and the minister saying: "Why don't you come? My dear child, why don't you come to Jesus? Jesus is waiting for you. He wants you. Why don't you come? Sister Reed, what is this child's name?"

"Langston," my aunt sobbed.

10   "Langston, why don't you come? Why don't you come and be saved? Oh, Lamb of God! Why don't you come?"

Now it was really getting late. I began to be ashamed of myself, holding everything up so long.

I began to wonder what God thought about Westley, who certainly hadn't seen Jesus either, but who was now sitting proudly on the platform, swinging his knickerbockered legs and grinning down at me, surrounded by deacons and old women on their knees praying. God had not struck Westley dead for taking his name in vain or for lying in the temple. So I decided that maybe to save further trouble, I'd better lie, too, and say that Jesus had come, and get up and be saved.

So I got up.

Suddenly the whole room broke into a sea of shouting, as they saw me rise. Waves of rejoicing swept the place. Women leaped in the air. My aunt threw her arms around me. The minister took me by the hand and led me to the platform.

When things quieted down, in a hushed silence, punctuated by a few ecstatic "Amens," all the new young lambs were blessed in the name of God. Then joyous singing filled the room.

15   That night, for the first time in my life but one—for I was a big boy twelve years old—I cried. I cried, in bed alone, and couldn't stop. I buried my head under the quilts, but my aunt heard me. She woke up and told my uncle I was crying because the Holy Ghost had come into my life, and because I had seen Jesus. But I was really crying because I couldn't bear to tell her that I had lied, that I had deceived everybody in the church, that I hadn't seen Jesus, and that now I didn't believe there was a Jesus anymore, since he didn't come to help me.

[1940]

rounders: a drunk or good-for-nothing.

QUESTIONS FOR REFLECTION AND DISCUSSION

1. What does the church look like through the eyes of a twelve-year-old boy? What is the boy's attitude to the events going on around him?

2. What is the difference between the narrator and the "rounder's son" Westley?

3. How does the meaning of Jesus change in the final paragraph?

CHILDREN AND ADOLESCENTS TOPICS FOR ESSAYS

1. What are some of the words of advice given to children and adolescents in these texts? Which are more effective? Which are less effective?

2. Write an essay on the difference between childhood and adolescence basing your argument on evidence from the texts in this section.

3. Choose one or more texts from this section and discuss how it would be different if written solely from an adult's point of view.

4. Compare the depiction of sexuality in several of the stories in this section. What role does it play in the plot? How is it understood by the narrator? How is it understood by the reader? How does it differ from adult sexuality?

5. Describe an experience you have had that resembles an experience described in one of these texts. Discuss the similarities and differences between these experiences.

CHILDREN AND ADOLESCENTS Further reading in *Literature: A World of Writing*

Julia Alvarez, "Snow" • Toni Cade Bambara, "The Lesson" • T. Coraghessan Boyle, "Greasy Lake" • Eleni Fourtouni, "Child's Memory" • Langston Hughes, "Theme for English B" • Sarah Orne Jewett, "A White Heron" • Leslie Norris, "Blackberries" • Orhan Pamuk, "To Look Out the Window" • Miriam Sagan, "Translating Catullus" • William Shakespeare, *Hamlet*

LOVERS

Notwithstanding general agreement that love is a universal experience, there are probably more different meanings attributed to the word *love* than just about any other in the English language. In this section, we limit ourselves to the sort of love that exists between lovers. Even here, you will find a wide range of ways to understand the love relationship, from passionate love lyric to corporeal pairings to love in the modern world, a frequently dysfunctional phenomenon—for writers, at least—already sharply diagnosed by Ambrose Bierce over a hundred years ago.

Love, n. *A temporary insanity curable by marriage or by removal of the patient from the influences under which he incurred the disorder. This disease, like* caries *and many other ailments, is prevalent only among civilized races living under artificial conditions; barbarous nations breathing pure air and eating simple food enjoy immunity from its ravages. It is sometimes fatal, but more frequently to the physician than to the patient.*

—AMBROSE BIERCE, *THE DEVIL'S DICTIONARY*

René Magritte, *The Lovers* (1928. Oil on canvas. Museum of Modern Art, New York). Like Magritte's painting *The Key to the Fields* (p. 14), *The Lovers* plays with our visual expectations in order to comment on our assumptions about reality and the subject of love. It may be that the painting echoes Ambrose Bierce's diagnosis of a disease that removes the sufferer's identity, as the cloths remove the identity of the two figures in the painting. Or perhaps the lovers are using the cloths to inoculate themselves from the spread of the disease. Or it may be that the cloths suggest their blissful isolation from the outside world. The ambiguity of meaning reflects the ambiguity of the painting's subject.

FICTION

Dorothy Parker 1893–1967

Born in New Jersey and raised in the Upper West Side of Manhattan, Dorothy Parker lost her mother and step-mother while still a girl, and her uncle and father before she was twenty. She soon began publishing poetry and working as an editor; she joined the board of the *New Yorker* magazine when it was founded in 1925. Her first volume of poetry, *Enough Rope,* appeared the following year, and became a bestseller. In 1919, Parker had co-founded the Algonquin Round Table, a group of writers including Harpo Marx and Edna Ferber, who lunched together at the Algonquin Hotel. Their scathing wit was also characteristic of Parker's own poetry and short stories. Parker later worked as a screenwriter in Hollywood. A socialist since 1927, she was also a staunch believer in civil rights, and left her literary estate to Martin Luther King, Jr., when she died. Like her poetry, Parker's short story "The Waltz," published in the *New Yorker* in 1933, takes a timeworn romantic convention and wittily turns it on its head.

THE WALTZ

WHY, THANK YOU SO MUCH. I'D ADORE TO.
I don't want to dance with him. I don't want to dance with anybody. And even if I did, it wouldn't be him. He'd be well down among the last ten. I've seen the way he dances; it looks like something you do on St. Walpurgis Night.° Just think, not a quarter of an hour ago, here I was sitting, feeling so sorry for the poor girl he was dancing with. And now *I'm* going to be the poor girl. Well, well. Isn't it a small world?

And a peach of a world, too. A true little corker. Its events are so fascinatingly unpredictable, are not they? Here I was, minding my own business, not doing a stitch of harm to any living soul. And then he comes into my life, all smiles and city manners, to sue me for the favor of one memorable mazurka. Why, he scarcely knows my name, let alone what it stands for. It stands for Despair, Bewilderment, Futility, Degradation, and Premeditated Murder, but little does he wot.° I don't wot his name, either; I haven't any idea what it is. Jukes,° would be my guess from the look in his eyes. How do you do,

Mr. Jukes? And how is that dear little brother of yours, with the two heads?

Ah, now why did he have to come around me, with his low requests? Why can't he let me lead my own life? I ask so little—just to be left alone in my quiet corner of the table, to do my evening brooding over all my sorrows. And he must come, with his bows and his scrapes and his may-I-have-this-ones. And I had to go and tell him that I'd adore to dance with him. I cannot understand why I wasn't struck right down dead. Yes, and being struck dead would look like a day in the country, compared to struggling out a dance with this boy. But what could I do? Everyone else at the table had got up to dance, except him and me. There I was, trapped. Trapped like a trap in a trap.

5   What can you say, when a man asks you to dance with him? I most certainly will *not* dance with you, I'll see you in hell first. Why, thank you, I'd like to awfully, but I'm having labor pains. Oh, yes, *do* let's dance together—it's so nice to meet a man who isn't a scaredy-cat about catching my beri-beri. No. There was nothing for me to do, but say I'd adore to. Well, we might as well get it over with. All right, Cannonball, let's run out on the field. You won the toss; you can lead.

St. Walpurgis Night: a pagan and Christian festival celebrating spring with carnivalesque activities. **wot:** an archaic form of "know." **Jukes:** a hillbilly.

Why, I think it's more of, a waltz, really. Isn't it? We might just listen to the music a second. Shall we? Oh, yes, it's a waltz. Mind? Why, I'm simply thrilled. I'd love to waltz with you.

I'd love to waltz with you. I'd love to waltz with you, I'd love to have my tonsils out, I'd love to be in a midnight fire at sea. Well, it's too late now. We're getting under way. *Oh.* Oh, dear. Oh, dear, dear, dear. Oh, this is even worse than I thought it would be. I suppose that's the one dependable law of life—everything is always worse than you thought it was going to be. Oh, if I had had any real grasp of what this dance would be like, I'd have held out for sitting it out. Well, it will probably amount to the same thing in the end. We'll be sitting it out on the floor in a minute, if he keeps this up.

I'm so glad I brought it to his attention that this is a waltz they're playing. Heaven knows what might have happened, if he had thought it was something fast; we'd have blown the sides right out of the building. Why does he always want to be somewhere that he isn't? Why can't we stay in one place just long enough to get acclimated? It's this constant rush, rush, rush, that's the curse of American life. That's the reason that we're all of us so—*Ow!* For God's sake, don't *kick,* you idiot; this is only second down. Oh, my shin. My poor, poor shin, that I've had ever since I was a little girl!

Oh, no, no, no. Goodness, no. It didn't hurt the least little bit. And anyway it was my fault. Really it was. Truly. Well, you're just being sweet, to say that. It really was all my fault.

10   I wonder what I'd better do—kill him this instant, with my naked hands, or wait and let him drop in his traces. Maybe it's best not to make a scene. I guess I'll just lie low, and watch the pace get him. He can't keep this up indefinitely—he's only flesh and blood. Die he must, and die he shall, for what he did to me. I don't want to be of the over-sensitive type, but you can't tell me that kick was unpremeditated. Freud says there are no accidents. I've led no cloistered life, I've known dancing partners who have spoiled my slippers and torn my dress; but when it comes to kicking, I am Outraged Womanhood. When you kick me in the shin, *smile.*

Maybe he didn't do it maliciously. Maybe it's just his way of showing his high spirits. I suppose I ought to be glad that one of us is having such a good time. I suppose I ought to think myself lucky if he brings me back alive. Maybe it's captious to demand of a practically strange man that he leave your shins as he found them. After all, the poor boy's doing the best he can. Probably he grew up in the hill country, and never had no larnin'. I bet they had to throw him on his back to get shoes on him.

Yes, it's lovely, isn't it? It's simply lovely. It's the loveliest waltz. Isn't it? Oh, I think it's lovely, too.

Why, I'm getting positively drawn to the Triple Threat here. He's my hero. He has the heart of a lion, and the sinews of a buffalo. Look at him—never a thought of the consequences, never afraid of his face, hurling himself into every scrimmage, eyes shining, cheeks ablaze. And shall it be said that I hung back? No, a thousand times no. What's it to me if I have to spend the next couple of years in a plaster cast? Come on, Butch, right through them! Who wants to live forever?

Oh. Oh, dear. Oh, he's all right, thank goodness. For a while I thought they'd have to carry him off the field. Ah, I couldn't bear to have anything happen to him. I love him. I love him better than anybody in the world. Look at the spirit he gets into a dreary, commonplace waltz; how effete the other dancers seem, beside him. He is youth and vigor and courage, he is strength and gayety and—*Ow!* Get off my instep, you hulking peasant! What do you think I am, anyway—a gangplank? *Ow!*

15   *No, of course it didn't hurt. Why, it didn't a bit. Honestly. And it was all my fault. You see, that little step of yours—well, it's perfectly lovely, but it's just a tiny bit tricky to follow at first. Oh, did you work it up yourself? You really did? Well, aren't you amazing! Oh, now I think I've got it. Oh, I think it's lovely. I was watching you do it when you were dancing before. It's awfully effective when you look at it.*

It's awfully effective when you look at it. I bet I'm awfully effective when you look at me. My hair is hanging along my cheeks, my skirt is swaddled about me, I can feel the cold damp of my brow. I must look like something out of "The Fall of the House of Usher." This sort of thing takes a fearful toll of a woman my age. And he worked up his little step himself, he with his degenerate cunning. And it was just a tiny bit tricky at first, but now I think I've got it. Two stumbles, slip, and a twenty-yard dash; yes, I've got it. I've got several other things, too, including a split shin and a bitter heart. I hate this creature I'm chained to. I hated him the moment I saw his leering, bestial face. And here I've been locked in his noxious embrace for the thirty-five years this waltz has lasted. Is that orchestra never going to stop playing? Or must this obscene travesty of a dance go on until hell burns out?

Oh, they're going to play another encore. Oh, goody. Oh, that's lovely. Tired? I should say I'm not tired. I'd like to go on like this forever.

I should say I'm not tired. I'm dead, that's all I am. Dead, and in what a cause! And the music is never going to stop playing, and we're going on like this, Double-Time Charlie and I, throughout eternity. I suppose I won't care any more, after the first hundred thousand years. I suppose nothing will matter then, not heat nor pain nor broken heart nor cruel, aching weariness. Well. It can't come too soon for me.

I wonder why I didn't tell him I was tired. I wonder why I didn't suggest going back to the table. I could have said let's just listen to the music. Yes, and if he would, that would be the first bit of attention he has given it all evening. George Jean Nathan° said that the lovely rhythms of the waltz should be listened to in stillness and not be accompanied by strange gyrations of the human body. I think that's what he said. I think it was George Jean Nathan. Anyhow, whatever he said and whoever he was and whatever he's doing now, he's better off than I am. That's safe. Anybody who isn't waltzing with this Mrs. O'Leary's cow°

George Jean Nathan: a famously learned and cynical drama critic of the first half of the twentieth century. **Mrs. O'Leary's cow:** a cow popularly blamed for starting the Chicago Fire of 1871.

I've got here is having a good time.

20   Still, if we were back at the table, I'd probably have to talk to him. Look at him—what could you say to a thing like that! Did you go to the circus this year, what's your favorite kind of ice cream, how do you spell cat? I guess I'm as well off here. As well off as if I were in a cement mixer in full action.

I'm past all feeling now. The only way I can tell when he steps on me is that I can hear the splintering of bones. And all the events of my life are passing before my eyes. There was the time I was in a hurricane in the West Indies, there was the day I got my head cut open in the taxi smash, there was the night the drunken lady threw a bronze ash-tray at her own true love and got me instead, there was that summer that the sailboat kept capsizing. Ah, what an easy, peaceful time was mine, until I fell in with Swifty, here. I didn't know what trouble was, before I got drawn into this *danse macabre*. I think my mind is beginning to wander. It almost seems to me as if the orchestra were stopping. It couldn't be, of course; it could never, never be. And yet in my ears there is a silence like the sound of angel voices. . . .

Oh, they've stopped, the mean things. They're not going to play any more. Oh, darn. Oh, do you think they would? Do you really think so, if you gave them fifty dollars? Oh, that would be lovely. And look, do tell them to play this same thing. I'd simply adore to go on waltzing.

[1933]

QUESTIONS FOR REFLECTION AND DISCUSSION

1. What is the difference between the two voices of the story?

2. Where does the word "love" appear in the story? What is its meaning?

3. What is the imagery the narrator associates with her dancing partner? What is the significance of her choice?

4. Who or what is the target of Parker's satire?

John Steinbeck 1902–1968

One of the preeminent chroniclers of working-class and migrant life, John Steinbeck made his name as a writer with his Depression-era novels *Of Mice and Men* (1937) and *The Grapes of Wrath* (1939), which was awarded the Pulitzer Prize. Born and raised in the agricultural Salinas Valley in central California, Steinbeck worked summers in local ranches; traveling the country during the 1920s solidified socialist leanings that he held for the rest of his life. One of the most popular writers of his era, Steinbeck also saw a number of his novels adapted to film. He received the Nobel Prize for Literature in 1962, but is best remembered for the sense of place and sensitivity to oppressed individuals of his great works of the 1930s.

THE CHRYSANTHEMUMS

THE HIGH GREY-FLANNEL FOG OF WINTER CLOSED off the Salinas Valley from the sky and from all the rest of the world. On every side it sat like a lid on the mountains and made of the great valley a closed pot. On the broad, level land floor the gang plows bit deep and left the black earth shining like metal where the shares had cut. On the foothill ranches across the Salinas River, the yellow stubble fields seemed to be bathed in pale cold sunshine, but there was no sunshine in the valley now in December. The thick willow scrub along the river flamed with sharp and positive yellow leaves.

It was a time of quiet and of waiting. The air was cold and tender. A light wind blew up from the southwest so that the farmers were mildly hopeful of a good rain before long; but fog and rain did not go together.

Across the river, on Henry Allen's foothill ranch there was little work to be done, for the hay was cut and stored and the orchards were plowed up to receive the rain deeply when it should come. The cattle on the higher slopes were becoming shaggy and rough-coated.

Elisa Allen, working in her flower garden, looked down across the yard and saw Henry, her husband, talking to two men in business suits. The three of them stood by the tractor shed, each man with one foot on the side of the little Fordson. They smoked cigarettes and studied the machine as they talked.

5   Elisa watched them for a moment and then went back to her work. She was thirty-five. Her face was lean and strong and her eyes were as clear as water. Her figure looked blocked and heavy in her gardening costume, a man's black hat pulled low down over her eyes, clod-hopper shoes, a figured print dress almost completely covered by a big corduroy apron with four big pockets to hold the snips, the trowel and scratcher, the seeds and the knife she worked with. She wore heavy leather gloves to protect her hands while she worked.

She was cutting down the old year's chrysanthemum stalks with a pair of short and powerful scissors. She looked down toward the men by the tractor shed now and then. Her face was eager and mature and handsome; even her work with the scissors was over-eager, over-powerful. The chrysanthemum stems seemed too small and easy for her energy.

She brushed a cloud of hair out of her eyes with the back of her glove, and left a smudge of earth on her cheek in doing it. Behind her stood the neat white farm house with red geraniums close-banked around it as high as the windows. It was a hard-swept looking little house, with hard-polished windows, and a clean mud-mat on the front steps.

Elisa cast another glance toward the tractor shed. The strangers were getting into their Ford coupe. She took off a glove and put her strong fingers down into the forest of new green chrysanthemum sprouts that were growing around the old roots. She spread the leaves and looked down among the close-growing stems. No aphids were there, no sowbugs or snails or cutworms. Her terrier fingers destroyed such pests before they could get started.

Elisa started at the sound of her husband's voice. He had come near quietly, and he leaned over the wire fence that protected her flower garden from cattle and dogs and chickens.

Yellow chrysanthemums. A popular fall flower, the genus *Chrysanthemum,* is a perennial plant first cultivated in China (the name is Chinese for "golden flower") and brought to Europe in the seventeenth century, and from there to the United States. Depending on the tradition, yellow chrysanthemums are associated with peace and tranquility and with death and funerals.

10   "At it again," he said. "You've got a strong new crop coming."

Elisa straightened her back and pulled on the gardening glove again. "Yes. They'll be strong this coming year." In her tone and on her face there was a little smugness.

"You've got a gift with things," Henry observed. "Some of those yellow chrysanthemums you had this year were ten inches across. I wish you'd work out in the orchard and raise some apples that big."

Her eyes sharpened. "Maybe I could do it, too. I've a gift with things, all right. My mother had it. She could stick anything in the ground and make it grow. She said it was having planters' hands that knew how to do it."

"Well, it sure works with flowers," he said.

15   "Henry, who were those men you were talking to?"

"Why, sure, that's what I came to tell you. They were from the Western Meat Company. I sold those thirty head of three-year-old steers. Got nearly my own price, too."

"Good," she said. "Good for you."

"And I thought," he continued, "I thought how it's Saturday afternoon, and we might go into Salinas for dinner at a restaurant, and then to a picture show— to celebrate, you see."

"Good," she repeated. "Oh, yes. That will be good."

20   Henry put on his joking tone. "There's fights tonight. How'd you like to go to the fights?"

"Oh, no," she said breathlessly. "No, I wouldn't like fights."

"Just fooling, Elisa. We'll go to a movie. Let's see. It's two now. I'm going to take Scotty and bring down those steers from the hill. It'll take us maybe two hours. We'll go in town about five and have dinner at the Cominos Hotel. Like that?"

"Of course I'll like it. It's good to eat away from home."

"All right, then. I'll go get up a couple of horses."

25   She said, "I'll have plenty of time to transplant some of these sets, I guess."

She heard her husband calling Scotty down by the barn. And a little later she saw the two men ride up the pale yellow hillside in search of the steers.

There was a little square sandy bed kept for rooting the chrysanthemums. With her trowel she turned the soil over and over, and smoothed it and patted it firm. Then she dug ten parallel trenches to receive the sets. Back at the chrysanthemum bed she pulled out the little crisp shoots, trimmed off the leaves of each one with her scissors and laid it on a small orderly pile.

A squeak of wheels and plod of hoofs came from the road. Elisa looked up. The country road ran along the dense bank of willows and cotton-woods that bordered the river, and up this road came a curious vehicle, curiously drawn. It was an old spring-wagon, with a round canvas top on it like the cover of a prairie schooner. It was drawn by an old bay horse and a little grey-and-white burro. A big stubble-bearded man sat between the cover flaps and drove the crawling team. Underneath the wagon, between the hind wheels, a lean and rangy mongrel dog walked sedately. Words were painted on the canvas in clumsy, crooked letters. "Pots, pans, knives, sisors, lawn mores, Fixed." Two rows of articles, and the triumphantly definitive "Fixed" below. The black paint had run down in little sharp points beneath each letter.

Elisa, squatting on the ground, watched to see the crazy, loose-jointed wagon pass by. But it didn't pass. It turned into the farm road in front of her house, crooked old wheels skirling and squeaking. The rangy dog darted from between the wheels and ran ahead. Instantly the two ranch shepherds flew out at him. Then all three stopped, and with stiff and quivering tails, with taut straight legs, with ambassadorial dignity, they slowly circled, sniffing daintily. The caravan pulled up to Elisa's wire fence and stopped. Now the newcomer dog, feeling outnumbered, lowered his tail and retired under the wagon with raised hackles and bared teeth.

30 The man on the wagon seat called out, "That's a bad dog in a fight when he gets started."

Elisa laughed. "I see he is. How soon does he generally get started?"

The man caught up her laughter and echoed it heartily. "Sometimes not for weeks and weeks," he said. He climbed stiffly down, over the wheel. The horse and the donkey drooped like unwatered flowers.

Elisa saw that he was a very big man. Although his hair and beard were graying, he did not look old. His worn black suit was wrinkled and spotted with grease. The laughter had disappeared from his face and eyes the moment his laughing voice ceased. His eyes were dark, and they were full of the brooding that gets in the eyes of teamsters and of sailors. The calloused hands he rested on the wire fence were cracked, and every crack was a black line.

He took off his battered hat.

35 "I'm off my general road, ma'am," he said. "Does this dirt road cut over across the river to the Los Angeles highway?"

Elisa stood up and shoved the thick scissors in her apron pocket. "Well, yes, it does, but it winds around and then fords the river. I don't think your team could pull through the sand."

He replied with some asperity, "It might surprise you what them beasts can pull through."

"When they get started?" she asked.

He smiled for a second. "Yes. When they get started."

40 "Well," said Elisa, "I think you'll save time if you go back to the Salinas road and pick up the highway there."

He drew a big finger down the chicken wire and made it sing. "I ain't in any hurry, ma'am. I go from Seattle to San Diego and back every year. Takes all my time. About six months each way. I aim to follow nice weather."

Elisa took off her gloves and stuffed them in the apron pocket with the scissors. She touched the under edge of her man's hat, searching for fugitive hairs. "That sounds like a nice kind of a way to live," she said.

He leaned confidentially over the fence. "Maybe you noticed the writing on my wagon. I mend pots and sharpen knives and scissors. You got any of them things to do?"

"Oh, no," she said quickly. "Nothing like that." Her eyes hardened with resistance.

45 "Scissors is the worst thing," he explained. "Most people just ruin scissors trying to sharpen 'em, but I know how. I got a special tool. It's a little bobbit kind of thing, and patented. But it sure does the trick."

"No. My scissors are all sharp."

"All right, then. Take a pot," he continued earnestly, "a bent pot, or a pot with a hole. I can make it like new so you don't have to buy no new ones. That's a saving for you.

"No," she said shortly. "I tell you I have nothing like that for you to do."

His face fell to an exaggerated sadness. His voice took on a whining undertone. "I ain't had a thing to do today. Maybe I won't have no supper tonight. You see I'm off my regular road. I know folks on the highway clear from Seattle to San Diego. They save their things for me to sharpen up because they know I do it so good and save them money.

50 "I'm sorry," Elisa said irritably. "I haven't anything for you to do."

His eyes left her face and fell to searching the ground. They roamed about until they came to the chrysanthemum bed where she had been working. "What's them plants, ma'am?"

The irritation and resistance melted from Elisa's face. "Oh, those are chrysanthemums, giant whites and yellows. I raise them every year, bigger than anybody around here."

"Kind of a long-stemmed flower? Looks like a quick puff of colored smoke?" he asked.

"That's it. What a nice way to describe them."

55 "They smell kind of nasty till you get used to them," he said.

"It's a good bitter smell," she retorted, "not nasty at all."

He changed his tone quickly. "I like the smell myself."

"I had ten-inch blooms this year," she said.

The man leaned farther over the fence. "Look. I know a lady down the road a piece, has got the nicest garden you ever seen. Got nearly every kind of flower but no chrysanthemums. Last time I was mending a copper-bottom washtub for her (that's a hard job but I do it good), she said to me, 'If you ever run acrost some nice chrysanthemums I wish you'd try to get me a few seeds.' That's what she told me."

60 Elisa's eyes grew alert and eager. "She couldn't have known much about chrysanthemums. You *can* raise them from seed, but it's much easier to root the little sprouts you see there."

"Oh," he said. "I s'pose I can't take none to her, then."

"Why yes you can," Elisa cried. "I can put some in damp sand, and you can carry them right along with you. They'll take root in the pot if you keep them damp. And then she can transplant them."

"She'd sure like to have some, ma'am. You say they're nice ones?"

"Beautiful," she said. "Oh, beautiful." Her eyes shone. She tore off the battered hat and shook out her dark pretty hair. "I'll put them in a flower pot, and you can take them right with you. Come into the yard."

65 While the man came through the picket fence Elisa ran excitedly along the geranium-bordered path to the back of the house. And she returned carrying a big red flower pot. The gloves were forgotten now. She kneeled on the ground by the starting bed and dug up the sandy soil with her fingers and scooped it into the bright new flower pot. Then she picked up the little pile of shoots she had prepared. With her strong fingers she pressed them into the sand and tamped around them with her knuckles. The man stood over her. "I'll tell you what to do," she said. "You remember so you can tell the lady."

"Yes, I'll try to remember."

"Well, look. These will take root in about a month. Then she must set them out, about a foot apart in good rich earth like this, see?" She lifted a handful of dark soil for him to look at. "They'll grow fast and tall. Now remember this. In July tell her to cut them down, about eight inches from the ground."

"Before they bloom?" he asked.

"Yes, before they bloom." Her face was tight with eagerness. "They'll grow right up again. About the last of September the buds will start."

70 She stopped and seemed perplexed. "It's the budding that takes the most care," she said hesitantly. "I don't know how to tell you." She looked deep into his eyes, searchingly. Her mouth opened a little, and she seemed to be listening. "I'll try to tell you," she said. "Did you ever hear of planting hands?"

"Can't say I have, ma'am."

"Well, I can only tell you what it feels like. It's when you're picking off the buds you don't want. Everything goes right down into your fingertips. You watch your fingers work. They do it themselves. You can feel how it is. They pick and pick the buds. They never make a mistake. They're with the plant. Do you see? Your fingers and the plant. You can feel that, right up your arm. They know. They never make a mistake. You can feel it. When you're like that you can't do anything wrong. Do you see that? Can you understand that?"

She was kneeling on the ground looking up at him. Her breast swelled passionately.

The man's eyes narrowed. He looked away self-consciously. "Maybe I know," he said. "Sometimes in the night in the wagon there—"

75 Elisa's voice grew husky. She broke in on him. "I've never lived as you do, but I know what you mean. When the night is dark—why, the stars are sharp-pointed, and there's quiet. Why, you rise up and up! Every pointed star gets driven into your body. It's like that. Hot and sharp and—lovely."

Kneeling there, her hand went out toward his legs in the greasy black trousers. Her hesitant fingers almost touched the cloth. Then her hand dropped to the ground. She crouched low like a fawning dog.

He said, "It's nice, just like you say. Only when you don't have no dinner, it ain't."

She stood up then, very straight, and her face was ashamed. She held the flower pot out to him and placed it gently in his arms. "Here. Put it in your wagon, on the seat, where you can watch it. Maybe I can find something for you to do."

At the back of the house she dug in the can pile and found two old and battered aluminum saucepans. She carried them back and gave them to him. "Here, maybe you can fix these."

80 His manner changed. He became professional. "Good as new I can fix them." At the back of his wagon he set a little anvil, and out of an oily tool box dug a small machine hammer. Elisa came through the gate to watch him while he pounded out the dents in the kettles. His mouth grew sure and knowing. At a difficult part of the work he sucked his under-lip.

"You sleep right in the wagon?" Elisa asked.

"Right in the wagon, ma'am. Rain or shine I'm dry as a cow in there."

"It must be nice," she said. "It must be very nice. I wish women could do such things."

"It ain't the right kind of a life for a woman."

85 Her upper lip raised a little, showing her teeth. "How do you know? How can you tell?" she said.

"I don't know, ma'am," he protested. "Of course I don't know. Now here's your kettles, done. You don't have to buy no new ones."

"How much?"

"Oh, fifty cents'll do. I keep my prices down and my work good. That's why I have all them satisfied customers up and down the highway."

Elisa brought him a fifty-cent piece from the house and dropped it in his hand. "You might be surprised to have a rival some time. I can sharpen scissors, too. And I can beat the dents out of little pots. I could show you what a woman might do."

90 He put his hammer back in the oily box and shoved the little anvil out of sight. "It would be a lonely life for a woman, ma'am, and a scarey life, too, with animals creeping under the wagon all night." He climbed over the singletree, steadying himself with a hand on the burro's white rump. He settled himself in the seat, picked up the lines. "Thank you kindly, ma'am," he said. "I'll do like you told me; I'll go back and catch the Salinas road."

"Mind," she called, "if you're long in getting there, keep the sand damp."

"Sand, ma'am? . . . Sand? Oh, sure. You mean around the chrysanthemums. Sure I will." He clucked his tongue. The beasts leaned luxuriously into their collars. The mongrel dog took his place between the back wheels. The wagon turned and crawled out the entrance road and back the way it had come, along the river.

Elisa stood in front of her wire fence watching the slow progress of the caravan. Her shoulders were straight, her head thrown back, her eyes half-closed, so that the scene came vaguely into them. Her lips moved silently, forming the words "Good-bye—good-bye." Then she whispered, "That's a bright direction. There's a glowing there." The sound of her whisper startled her. She shook herself free and looked about to see whether anyone had been listening. Only the dogs had heard. They lifted their heads toward her from their sleeping in the dust, and then stretched out their chins and settled asleep again. Elisa turned and ran hurriedly into the house.

In the kitchen she reached behind the stove and felt the water tank. It was full of hot water from the noonday cooking. In the bathroom she tore off her soiled clothes and flung them into the corner. And then she scrubbed herself with a little block of pumice, legs and thighs, loins and chest and arms, until her skin was scratched and red. When she had dried herself she stood in front of a mirror in her bedroom and looked at her body. She tightened her stomach and threw out her chest. She turned and looked over her shoulder at her back.

95 After a while she began to dress, slowly. She put on her newest underclothing and her nicest stockings and the dress which was the symbol of her prettiness. She worked carefully on her hair, pencilled her eyebrows and rouged her lips.

Before she was finished she heard the little thunder of hoofs and the shouts of Henry and his helper as they drove the red steers into the corral. She heard the gate bang shut and set herself for Henry's arrival.

His step sounded on the porch. He entered the house calling, "Elisa, where are you?"

"In my room, dressing. I'm not ready. There's hot water for your bath. Hurry up. It's getting late."

When she heard him splashing in the tub, Elisa laid his dark suit on the bed, and shirt and socks and tie beside it. She stood his polished shoes on the floor beside the bed. Then she went to the porch and sat primly and stiffly down. She looked toward the river road where the willow-line was still yellow with frosted leaves so that under the high grey fog they seemed a thin band of sunshine. This was the only color in the grey afternoon. She sat unmoving for a long time. Her eyes blinked rarely.

100 Henry came banging out of the door, shoving his tie inside his vest as he came. Elisa stiffened and her face grew tight. Henry stopped short and looked at her. "Why—why, Elisa. You look so nice!"

"Nice? You think I look nice? What do you mean by 'nice'?"

Henry blundered on. "I don't know. I mean you look different, strong and happy."

"I am strong? Yes, strong. What do you mean 'strong'?"

He looked bewildered. "You're playing some kind of a game," he said helplessly. "It's a kind of a play. You look strong enough to break a calf over your knee, happy enough to eat it like a watermelon."

105   For a second she lost her rigidity. "Henry! Don't talk like that. You didn't know what you said." She grew complete again. "I'm strong," she boasted. "I never knew before how strong."

Henry looked down toward the tractor shed, and when he brought his eyes back to her, they were his own again. "I'll get out the car. You can put on your coat while I'm starting."

Elisa went into the house. She heard him drive to the gate and idle down his motor, and then she took a long time to put on her hat. She pulled it here and pressed it there. When Henry turned the motor off she slipped into her coat and went out.

The little roadster bounced along on the dirt road by the river, raising the birds and driving the rabbits into the brush. Two cranes flapped heavily over the willow-line and dropped into the river-bed.

Far ahead on the road Elisa saw a dark speck. She knew.

110   She tried not to look as they passed it, but her eyes would not obey. She whispered to herself sadly, "He might have thrown them off the road. That wouldn't have been much trouble, not very much. But he kept the pot," she explained. "He had to keep the pot. That's why he couldn't get them off the road."

The roadster turned a bend and she saw the cara-van ahead. She swung full around toward her husband so she could not see the little covered wagon and the mismatched team as the car passed them.

In a moment it was over. The thing was done. She did not look back.

She said loudly, to be heard above the motor, "It will be good, tonight, a good dinner."

"Now you're changed again," Henry complained. He took one hand from the wheel and patted her knee. "I ought to take you in to dinner oftener. It would be good for both of us. We get so heavy out on the ranch."

115   "Henry," she asked, "could we have wine at dinner?"

"Sure we could. Say! That will be fine."

She was silent for a while; then she said, "Henry, at those prize fights, do the men hurt each other very much?"

"Sometimes a little, not often. Why?"

"Well, I've read how they break noses, and blood runs down their chests. I've read how the fighting gloves get heavy and soggy with blood."

120   He looked around at her. "What's the matter, Elisa? I didn't know you read things like that." He brought the car to a stop, then turned to the right over the Salinas River bridge.

"Do any women ever go to the fights?" she asked.

"Oh, sure, some. What's the matter, Elisa? Do you want to go? I don't think you'd like it, but I'll take you if you really want to go."

She relaxed limply in the seat. "Oh, no. No. I don't want to go. I'm sure I don't." Her face was turned away from him. "It will be enough if we can have wine. It will be plenty." She turned up her coat collar so he could not see that she was crying weakly—like an old woman.

[1938]

QUESTIONS FOR REFLECTION AND DISCUSSION

1. Describe the relationship between Elisa and Henry at the start of the story, citing examples from the text. Describe their relationship at the end, again citing examples from the text. What, if anything, has changed during the course of the story?

2. Compare the interaction between Elisa and her husband to her interaction with the traveling peddler. What is similar and what is different? How does she respond to each one, and why?

3. Why is the story called "The Chrysanthemums"? What is the function of the image in the story? What meanings get associated with it over the course of the story?

4. What are some of the ways the story draws distinctions about gender? Are there any moments when characters do not follow these distinctions?

Amanda Holzer

"Love and Other Catastrophes: A Mix Tape" was first published in *Story Quarterly* in 2002. Amanda Holzer also co-runs the record label not not fun.

LOVE AND OTHER CATASTROPHES: A MIX TAPE

ALL BY MYSELF, *ERIC CARMEN.* LOOKING FOR LOVE, *Lou Reed.* I Wanna Dance with Somebody, *Whitney Houston.* Let's Dance, *David Bowie.* Let's Kiss, *Beat Happening.* Let's Talk About Sex, *Salt 'n' Pepa.* Like a Virgin, *Madonna.* We've Only Just Begun, *The Carpenters.* I Wanna Be Your Boyfriend, *The Ramones.* I'll Tumble 4 Ya, *Culture Club.* Head Over Heels, *The Go-Go's.* Nothing Compares to You, *Sinead O'Connor.* My Girl, *The Temptations.* Could This Be Love? *Bob Marley.* Love and Marriage, *Frank Sinatra.* White Wedding, *Billy Idol.* Stuck in the Middle with You, *Steelers Wheel.* Tempted, *The Squeeze.* There Goes My Baby, *The Drifters.* What's Going On? *Marvin Gaye.* Where Did You Sleep Last Night? *Leadbelly.* Whose Bed Have Your Boots Been Under? *Shania Twain.* Jealous Guy, *John Lennon.* Your Cheatin' Heart, *Tammy Wynette.* Shot Through the Heart, *Bon Jovi.* Don't Go Breaking My Heart, *Elton John and Kiki Dee.* My Achy Breaky Heart, *Billy Ray Cyrus.* Heartbreak Hotel, *Elvis Presley.* Stop! In the Name of Love, *The Supremes.* Try a Little Tenderness, Otis *Redding.* Try (Just a Little Bit Harder), *Janis Joplin.* All Apologies, *Nirvana.* Hanging on the Telephone, *Blondie.* I Just Called to Say I Love You, *Stevie Wonder.* Love Will Keep Us Together, *Captain and Tennille.* Let's Stay Together, *Al Green.* It Ain't Over 'til It's Over, *Lenny Kravitz.* What's Love Got to Do with It? *Tina Turner.* You Don't Bring Me Flowers Anymore, *Barbra Streisand and Neil Diamond.* I Wish You Wouldn't Say That, *Talking Heads.* You're So Vain, *Carly Simon.* Love Is a Battlefield, *Pat Benatar.* Heaven Knows I'm Miserable Now, *The Smiths.* (Can't Get No) Satisfaction, *Rolling Stones.* Must Have Been Love (But It's Over Now), *Roxette.* Breaking Up is Hard to Do, *Neil Sedaka.* I Will Survive, *Gloria Gaynor.* Hit the Road, Jack, *Mary McCaslin and Jim Ringer.* These Boots Were Made for Walking, *Nancy Sinatra.* All Out of Love, *Air Supply.* All By Myself, *Eric Carmen.*

[2002]

QUESTIONS FOR REFLECTION AND DISCUSSION

1. Paraphrase the plot in regular sentences. What makes the story different than when the plot is told through song titles?

2. Does this story make an argument about love? If yes, what is the argument? If no, what argument does the story make?

3. What is the role of pop songs in the way we think about love?

POETRY

Uruttiran 2nd–3rd Century CE

"What She Said to Her Girl Friend" comes from a series of anthologies of some 2,400 poems composed nearly a thousand years ago in the Tamil language of South India. They were attributed to male and female poets associated with the Tamil royal courts in the south of the Indian subcontinent, but little to nothing biographical is known about individual poets.

What She Said to Her Girl Friend, and What Her Girl Friend Said in Reply

Translated by A. K. Ramanujan

"Friend,
like someone who gets drunk secretly
on hard liquor
till his body begins to ooze with it,
and goes on to brag shamelessly   5
till listeners shiver,
and then gets caught
with the stolen liquor in his hand,

Detail of a carving on the Parsvanatha Temple, Khajuraho, India (ninth century CE). Famous for the erotic sculpture that decorates portions of the exteriors in the temple complex, Khajuraho suggests a frank attitude toward sexuality akin to that of the ancient Tamil country farther south.

I too got caught
with my secret in my hands: 10

my goatherd lover's
string of jasmine
that I'd twined in my hair
fell before my foster-mother
as she loosened my hair   15
to smear it with butter,

and embarrassed her
before Father, Mother,
and others in the house.

And she   20
didn't ask a thing about it,
or get angry,
but like someone
shaking off a live coal
she shook it off   25
and moved into the backyard.

Then I
dried my hair perfumed with sandal,
knotted it,
and picking up the end   30
of my blue flower-border dress
    that comes down to the floor
I tiptoed in fear
and hid
in the thick of the forest."   35

"O you got scared because of that?
No fears. Even as you wore
your young man's garlands,
they too have conspired
to give you to him.   40

They'll pour soft sand
in the wide yard,
put curtains all around,
and make a wedding there
very soon.   45

Not only all day today
but all night yesterday,
we've been scheming
to do just that."

QUESTIONS FOR REFLECTION AND DISCUSSION

1. Locate the first simile of the poem and paraphrase the description it is making. What important element does the opening simile introduce that is lacking in the straightforward description of the speaker? In what way does the simile provide a motivation for the woman's recklessness in brazenly wearing her young man's garlands?

2. Locate the second simile of the poem and paraphrase the description it is making.

3. What do the girlfriend's responses reveal to us of the reliability of the first speaker's perceptions imparted through the two similes? What do these two similes tell us about the first speaker's character and state of mind?

Ono no Komachi 9th century

Ono no Komachi, who flourished around 850, is one of the major figures of the Classical, or Heian, period of Japanese literature (794–1185), even though only eighteen of her poems, all *tanka* (p. 000), have survived. As you read the three poems that follow, consider how the highly compressed form gives a sense of the sentiments of love that is different from the longer poems in this section.

Three *tanka*

Thinking about him
I slept, only to have him
Appear before me—
Had I known it was a dream
I should never have wakened.
                    Translated by Donald Keene

A thing which fades
With no outward sign

Is the flower
Of the heart of man
In this world!
                    Translated by Arthur Waley

The flowers withered
Their color faded away
While meaninglessly
I spent my days in the world
And the long rains were falling

                    *Translated by
                    Donald Keene*

QUESTIONS FOR REFLECTION AND DISCUSSION

1. Each poem shifts emphasis, either in the third or the fourth line. How are the two parts related in each poem?

2. What do these poems tell us about love? What do they not tell us about love?

3. What effect does the short line length and brief stanza have on these poems? What is left out that would be included in a longer poem? What themes and subject matter are best suited to such brevity?

Sara Teasdale 1884–1933

Born in St. Louis, Missouri, Sara Teasdale moved to New York after her marriage to businessman Ernest Filsinger. "The Look" was published in her fourth volume of poetry, *Love Songs* (1917), which won Teasdale popularity as well as the Poetry Society of America Prize and the Columbia University Poetry Society Prize (later called the Pulitzer Prize). She divorced in 1929, and died of an overdose of pills in 1933. The names in "The Look" are conventional names from the traditional genre of the pastoral.

The Look

Strephon kissed me in the spring,
   Robin in the fall,
But Colin only looked at me
   And never kissed at all.

Strephon's kiss was lost in jest,   5
   Robin's lost in play,
But the kiss in Colin's eyes
   Haunts me night and day.

[1917]

QUESTIONS FOR REFLECTION AND DISCUSSION

1. "The Look" is composed in a modified ballad stanza (p. 128). How does this form give it a singsong quality? What other formal aspects contribute to this quality? What is the effect of the singsong quality on our understanding of the poem?

2. How does the second stanza echo the first? How does it alter it?

3. What is the poem's underlying argument about love?

William Shakespeare 1564–1616

Generally considered to be the greatest writer in the English language, William Shakespeare had a fundamental influence on the development of theater as well as of lyric poetry. Although not all of the 154 sonnets that Shakespeare wrote (published in a 1609 collection) are love poems, the vast majority are, and masterfully so. The three sonnets included here give a sense of the range and subtlety of Shakespeare's use of lyrical imagery.

Sonnet 128

How oft, when thou, my music, music play'st,
Upon that blessed wood whose motion sounds
With thy sweet fingers, when thou gently sway'st
The wiry concord that mine ear confounds,
Do I envy those jacks° that nimble leap   5
To kiss the tender inward of thy hand,

5 jacks: keys

Whilst my poor lips, which should that harvest reap,
At the wood's boldness by thee blushing stand!
To be so tickled, they would change their state
And situation with those dancing chips,°   10
O'er whom thy fingers walk with gentle gait,
Making dead wood more blest than living lips.
Since saucy jacks so happy are in this,
Give them thy fingers, me thy lips to kiss.

10 chips: keys

1. Keys, hands, and lips are the three elements that interact within the space of the sonnet. Of what wholes are they the parts? What is the effect of the substitution on the theme of the poem?

2. What are the substitutions proposed by the speaker during the poem?

3. Basing yourself on evidence in the poem, what, for the speaker, is love?

Sonnet 116

Let me not to the marriage of true minds
Admit impediments. Love is not love
Which alters when it alteration finds,
Or bends with the remover to remove.
O no! it is an ever-fixed mark   5
That looks on tempests and is never shaken;

It is the star to every wand'ring bark,
Whose worth's unknown, although his height be taken.
Love's not Time's fool, though rosy lips and cheeks
Within his bending sickle's compass come;   10
Love alters not with his brief hours and weeks,
But bears it out even to the edge of doom.
If this be error and upon me prov'd,
I never writ, nor no man ever lov'd.

1. Summarize the sonnet in six sentences: one for the main idea, one for the form, meter, and rhyme, one for each quatrain, and one for the concluding couplet. You may first need to paraphrase for yourself the meaning of some of the key phrases, such as "marriage of true minds," "Or bends with the remover to remove," "although his height be taken," "even to the edge of doom."

2. Comment on the meter in line 12. How does the word "even" break the pattern of the previous lines, and why do you think Shakespeare chose to break the pattern here?

3. Reflect on and discuss the use of rhyme in the sonnet, and its relation to the theme of the poem.

4. What is the definition of love propounded in the poem? Compare the discussion of love here with its depiction in sonnets 128 and 29.

Sonnet 29

When, in disgrace with fortune and men's eyes,
I all alone beweep my outcast state
And trouble deaf heaven with my bootless cries
And look upon myself and curse my fate,
Wishing me like to one more rich in hope,   5
Featur'd like him, like him with friends possess'd,

Desiring this man's art and that man's scope,
With what I most enjoy contented least;
Yet in these thoughts myself almost despising,
Haply I think on thee, and then my state,   10
Like to the lark at break of day arising
From sullen earth, sings hymns at heaven's gate;
For thy sweet love remember'd such wealth brings
That then I scorn to change my state with kings.

John Donne 1572–1631

Born in London to a Roman-Catholic family and trained as a lawyer at Oxford and Cambridge, John Donne converted to Anglicanism in the mid-1590s, was ordained an Anglican priest in 1615, and finished his life as dean of Saint Paul's Cathedral in London. He wrote some twenty elegies during his years as a scholar, based on the dramatic and confessional mode of the Roman poet Ovid's elegies of love, rich in their dense imagery, and often ribald in content. Written in the late sixteenth century, Donne's masterful collection of love poems *Songs and Sonnets* includes "The Flea." He is equally celebrated for the *Divine Poems* and the *Holy Sonnets* (p. 457), intense and passionate in their exploration of the paradoxes of man's relationship with divinity.

The Flea

Mark but this flea, and mark in this,
How little that which thou deniest me is;
It suck'd me first, and now sucks thee,
And in this flea our two bloods mingled be.
Thou know'st that this cannot be said   5
A sin, nor shame, nor loss of maidenhead;
   Yet this enjoys before it woo,
   And pamper'd swells with one blood made of two;
   And this, alas! is more than we would do.

O stay, three lives in one flea spare,   10
Where we almost, yea, more than married are.
This flea is you and I, and this
Our marriage bed, and marriage temple is.
Though parents grudge, and you, we're met,
And cloister'd in these living walls of jet.   15
   Though use make you apt to kill me,
   Let not to that self-murder added be,
   And sacrilege, three sins in killing three.

Cruel and sudden, hast thou since
Purpled thy nail in blood of innocence?   20
Wherein could this flea guilty be,
Except in that drop which it suck'd from thee?
Yet thou triumph'st, and say'st that thou
Find'st not thyself nor me the weaker now.
'Tis true; then learn how false fears be;   25
Just so much honour, when thou yield'st to me,
Will waste, as this flea's death took life from thee.

[1633]

Jimmy Santiago Baca b. 1952

Born in Santa Fe, New Mexico, Chicano writer Jimmy Santiago Baca was abandoned by his parents and spent most of his childhood on the streets. He taught himself to read and write, and began composing poetry while in prison for drug possession. He has since published a number of collections of poetry, as well as memoirs and essays. Baca devotes much of his time to conducting poetry workshops in a wide variety of settings, from the university to the prison. Baca's poem "Spliced Wire" finds a contemporary metaphor for an age-old experience.

Spliced Wire

I filled your house with light.
There was warmth in all corners
of the house. My words I gave you
like soft warm toast in early morning.
I brewed your tongue   5
to a rich dark coffee, and drank
my fill. I turned on the music for you,
playing notes along the crest
of your heart, like birds,
eagles, ravens, owls on rims of red canyon.   10

I brought reception clear to you,
and made the phone ring at your request,
from Paris or South America,
you could talk to any of the people,
as my words gave them life,   15
from a child in a boat with his father,

to a prisoner in a concentration camp,
all at your bedside.

And then you turned away, wanted
a larger mansion. I said no. I left you.   20
The plug pulled out, the house blinked out,
into a quiet darkness, swallowing wind,
collecting autumn leaves like stamps
between its old boards where they stick.

You say, or carry the thought with you   25
to comfort you, that faraway somewhere,
lightning knocked down all the power lines.
But no my love, it was I,
pulling the plug. Others will come, plug in,
but often the lights will dim weakly   30
in storms, the music stop to a drawl,
the warmth shredded by cold drafts.

[1982]

QUESTIONS FOR REFLECTION AND DISCUSSION

1. Whom do you think the speaker is addressing in the poem? What events does the poem record? What is the speaker's attitude to these events?

2. When does the title metaphor first appear in the body of the poem? How does it develop through the poem? What qualities does the speaker attribute to "spliced wire"?

To what subject are these qualities transferred? What do these qualities tell you about that subject?

3. Make a list of the other imagery used by the speaker in the poem. What is the relation of this imagery to the title metaphor?

Edgar Allan Poe 1809–1849

Born to a pair of traveling actors who died before he was three, Edgar Allan Poe was raised in Richmond, Virginia, by the merchant John Allan. When Allan broke off Poe's engagement and refused to pay his gambling debts, the young man was obliged to enlist in the army, and, later, to enroll at West Point. Already a published poet, Poe eventually settled with an aunt in Baltimore, married her daughter, and began writing short stories and literary journalism to support himself. Famed for both his macabre short fiction (see "The Cask of Amontillado," p. 532) and his musical verse, Poe died at the age of forty of "congestion of the brain." "Annabel Lee," one of Poe's best-known poems, was written the year of his death. The repetitive form resembles the song-based villanelle and rhyming sestina. As you read this poem, listen to the way Poe uses assonance in particular to saturate the poem with the sounds in the name of the lost lover.

Annabel Lee

It was many and many a year ago,
　In a kingdom by the sea,
That a maiden there lived whom you may know
　By the name of Annabel Lee;—
And this maiden she lived with no other thought 5
　Than to love and be loved by me.

I was a child and *she* was a child,
　In this kingdom by the sea;
But we loved with a love that was more than love—
　I and my Annabel Lee— 10
With a love that the wingèd seraphs in Heaven
　Coveted her and me.

And this was the reason that, long ago,
　In this kingdom by the sea,
A wind blew out of a cloud, chilling 15
　My beautiful Annabel Lee;
So that her high-born kinsmen came
　And bore her away from me,
To shut her up in a sepulchre,
　In this kingdom by the sea. 20

The angels, not half so happy in Heaven,
　Went envying her and me—
Yes!—that was the reason (as all men know,
　In this kingdom by the sea)
That the wind came out of the cloud by night, 25
　Chilling and killing my Annabel Lee.

But our love it was stronger by far than the love
　Of those who were older than we—
　Of many far wiser than we—
And neither the angels in Heaven above; 30
　Nor the demons down under the sea,

Word inspires image: James Abbott McNeill Whistler, *Annabel Lee,* c. 1890. Pastel on brown paper. Freer Gallery of Art, Washington, D.C.

Can ever dissever my soul from the soul
　Of the beautiful Annabel Lee:—

For the moon never beams, without bringing me
　dreams
　Of the beautiful Annabel Lee; 35
And the stars never rise, but I feel the bright eyes
　Of the beautiful Annabel Lee:—
And so, all the night-tide, I lie down by the side
Of my darling—my darling—my life and my bride,
　In her sepulchre there by the sea— 40
　In her tomb by the sounding sea.

[1849]

1. Mark the poem for assonance, alliteration, and consonance (p. 212). What sounds repeat the most frequently? What patterns stand out?

2. Although written throughout in anapestic feet (p. 123), the lines are of varying length and the rhyme scheme is irregular. What is the basis of the rhyme, and why do you think Poe chose to forgo a more regular form, meter, and rhyme scheme?

3. Comment on the rhythm and sound of the word "chilling" in its first appearance in line 15 and when repeated in line 26.

4. In line 7 the speaker stresses the youthfulness of himself and Annabel Lee. What is the function of this stress in the poem's theme? In what ways is this youthfulness reflected in the form and tone of the poem?

T. S. Eliot 1888–1965

Considered the most important poet of the first half of the twentieth century and awarded the Nobel Prize for Literature in 1948, the poet, essayist, and dramatist Thomas Stearns Eliot was born in St. Louis, Missouri. After receiving his B.A. from Harvard, Eliot lived and studied in Paris for a year before returning to Harvard. He completed his doctoral thesis in philosophy, but never returned to defend it. He had settled in England in 1914 and lived the rest of his life there, marrying Vivienne Haigh-Wood in 1915. After working several years at Lloyds Bank in London, Eliot took a position as a director of the publishing house later known as Faber and Faber. Eliot was separated from his wife in 1935; she was institutionalized five years later, and he never saw her again. He remarried in 1957. "The Love Song of J. Alfred Prufrock" was published in *Poetry* magazine in 1915 on the recommendation of Ezra Pound (p. 234). Like Eliot's later masterpieces *The Waste Land* (1922) and *The Four Quartets* (1936–1942), "Prufrock" is a cornerstone of modernist literature and its rejection of the themes and forms of both romanticism and realism.

The Love Song of J. Alfred Prufrock

S' io credessi che mia risposta fosse
A persona che mai tornasse al mondo,
Questa fiamma staria senza più scosse.
Ma perciocchè giammai di questo fondo
Non tornò vivo alcum, s' i' odo il vero,
Senza tema d' infamia ti rispondo.[1]

Let us go then, you and I,
When the evening is spread out against the sky
Like a patient etherized upon a table;
Let us go, through certain half-deserted streets,
The muttering retreats   5
Of restless nights in one-night cheap hotels
And sawdust restaurants with oyster-shells:
Streets that follow like a tedious argument
Of insidious intent
To lead you to an overwhelming question . . .   10
Oh, do not ask, "What is it?"
Let us go and make our visit.

In the room the women come and go
Talking of Michelangelo.

The yellow fog that rubs its back upon the
    window-panes   15
The yellow smoke that rubs its muzzle on the
    window-panes
Licked its tongue into the corners of the evening,
Lingered upon the pools that stand in drains,
Let fall upon its back the soot that falls from chimneys,
Slipped by the terrace, made a sudden leap,   20
And seeing that it was a soft October night
Curled once about the house, and fell asleep.

And indeed there will be time
For the yellow smoke that slides along the street,
Rubbing its back upon the window-panes;   25
There will be time, there will be time
To prepare a face to meet the faces that you meet;

[1] Lines from canto 27 of Dante's *Inferno* spoken by a damned soul in hell: "If I did think, my answer were to one, / Who ever could return unto the world, / This flame should rest unshaken. But since ne'er, / If true be told me, any from this depth / Has found his upward way, I answer thee, / Nor fear lest infamy record the words."

There will be time to murder and create,
And time for all the works and days of hands
That lift and drop a question on your plate; 30
Time for you and time for me,
And time yet for a hundred indecisions
And for a hundred visions and revisions
Before the taking of a toast and tea.

In the room the women come and go 35
Talking of Michelangelo.

   And indeed there will be time
To wonder, "Do I dare?" and, "Do I dare?"
Time to turn back and descend the stair,
With a bald spot in the middle of my hair— 40
(They will say: "How his hair is growing thin!")
My morning coat, my collar mounting firmly to the chin,
My necktie rich and modest, but asserted by a
   simple pin—
(They will say: "But how his arms and legs are thin!")
Do I dare 45
Disturb the universe?
In a minute there is time
For decisions and revisions which a minute
   will reverse.

For I have known them all already, known them all;
Have known the evenings, mornings, afternoons, 50
I have measured out my life with coffee spoons;
I know the voices dying with a dying fall
Beneath the music from a farther room.
   So how should I presume?

And I have known the eyes already, known
   them all— 55
The eyes that fix you in a formulated phrase,
And when I am formulated, sprawling on a pin,
When I am pinned and wriggling on the wall,
Then how should I begin
To spit out all the butt-ends of my days
   and ways? 60
   And how should I presume?

And I have known the arms already, known
   them all—
Arms that are braceleted and white and bare
(But in the lamplight, downed with light brown hair!)
Is it perfume from a dress 65
That makes me so digress?

Arms that lie along a table, or wrap about a shawl.
   And should I then presume?
   And how should I begin?

. . .

Shall I say, I have gone at dusk through narrow
   streets 70
And watched the smoke that rises from the pipes
Of lonely men in shirt-sleeves, leaning out of
   windows? . . .

I should have been a pair of ragged claws
Scuttling across the floors of silent seas.

. . .

And the afternoon, the evening, sleeps so
   peacefully! 75
Smoothed by long fingers,
Asleep . . . tired . . . or it malingers,
Stretched on the floor, here beside you and me.
Should I, after tea and cakes and ices,
Have the strength to force the moment to its
   crisis? 80
But though I have wept and fasted, wept and prayed,
Though I have seen my head (grown slightly bald)
   brought in upon a platter,°
I am no prophet—and here's no great matter;
I have seen the moment of my greatness flicker,
And I have seen the eternal Footman hold my
   coat, and snicker, 85
And in short, I was afraid.

And would it have been worth it, after all,
After the cups, the marmalade, the tea,
Among the porcelain, among some talk of you and me,
Would it have been worth while, 90
To have bitten off the matter with a smile,
To have squeezed the universe into a ball
To roll it toward some overwhelming question,
To say: "I am Lazarus, come from the dead,
Come back to tell you all, I shall tell you all"° 95
If one, settling a pillow by her head,
   Should say, "That is not what I meant at all.
   That is not it, at all."

And would it have been worth it, after all,
Would it have been worth while, 100

82 platter: In the New Testament, the prophet John the Baptist is beheaded by King Herod, and at the bequest of his wife Herodias his head brought to her on a platter. **95** In the New Testament, Jesus raises Lazarus from the dead.

After the sunsets and the dooryards and the
    sprinkled streets,
After the novels, after the teacups, after the skirts that
    trail along the floor—
And this, and so much more?—
It is impossible to say just what I mean!
But as if a magic lantern° threw the nerves in patterns
    on a screen: 105
Would it have been worth while
If one, settling a pillow or throwing off a shawl,
And turning toward the window, should say:
    "That is not it at all,
    That is not what I meant, at all."   110
    . . .
No! I am not Prince Hamlet, nor was meant to be;
Am an attendant lord, one that will do
To swell a progress, start a scene or two
Advise the prince; no doubt, an easy tool,
Deferential, glad to be of use,   115
Politic, cautious, and meticulous;

Full of high sentence, but a bit obtuse;
At times, indeed, almost ridiculous—

Almost, at times, the Fool.
I grow old . . . I grow old . . .
I shall wear the bottoms of my trousers rolled.   120
Shall I part my hair behind? Do I dare to eat a peach?
I shall wear white flannel trousers, and walk upon
    the beach.
I have heard the mermaids singing, each to each.

I do not think they will sing to me.   125
I have seen them riding seaward on the waves
Combing the white hair of the waves blown back
When the wind blows the water white and black.

We have lingered in the chambers of the sea
By sea-girls wreathed with seaweed red and
    brown   130
Til human voices wake us, and we drown.
    . . .

        [1915]

105 magic lantern: an ancestor of the modern slide projector popular in the nineteenth century that would project images using candlelight.

NONFICTION

Sei Shonagon   c. 967–c. 1017

Daughter and granddaughter of poets, Sei Shonagon was married at sixteen and mother of two children before, divorced, she entered the service of the Emperor's consort while in her late twenties. *The Pillow Book,* her best-known work, was written in various drafts between 996 and 1000 while Shonagon was living in the women's chambers of the palace, and further revised after she left the palace. The book includes diary-like descriptions of daily events in the palace, many different lists, and meditations on nature and, especially, love, a primary activity of this, as of most, royal courts. Topics for lists include "Things That Especially Attract One's Attention on Some Occasions," "Things That Look Commonplace but That Become Impressive When Written in Chinese Characters," "Things That Give a Clean Feeling," "Things That Give an Unclean Feeling," and the list presented here, "Hateful Things."

FROM HATEFUL THINGS

Translated by Ivan Morris

ONE IS IN A HURRY TO LEAVE, BUT ONE'S VISITOR
keeps chattering away. If it is someone of no
importance, one can get rid of him by saying, "You
must tell me all about it next time"; but, should it
be the sort of visitor whose presence commands
one's best behavior, the situation is hateful
indeed. [. . .]

Someone has suddenly fallen ill and one summons
the exorcist. Since he is not at home, one has to send
messengers to look for him. After one has had a long
fretful wait, the exorcist finally arrives, and with a
sigh of relief one asks him to start his incantations.
But perhaps he has been exorcizing too many evil
spirits recently; for hardly has he installed himself
and begun praying when his voice becomes drowsy.
Oh, how hateful!

A man who has nothing in particular to recommend him discusses all sorts of subjects at random as
though he knew everything. [. . .]

To envy others and to complain about one's own
lot; to speak badly about people; to be inquisitive
about the most trivial matters and to resent and
abuse people for not telling one, or, if one does manage to worm out some facts, to inform everyone in
the most detailed fashion as if one had known all
from the beginning—oh, how hateful! [. . .]

An admirer has come on a clandestine visit, but a
dog catches sight of him and starts barking. One
feels like killing the beast.

One has been foolish enough to invite a man to
spend the night in an unsuitable place—and then he
starts snoring.

A gentleman has visited one secretly. Though he is
wearing a tall, lacquered hat, he nevertheless wants
no one to see him. He is so flurried, in fact, that
upon leaving he bangs into something with his hat.
Most hateful! [. . .]

One has gone to bed and is about to doze off
when a mosquito appears and announces itself in a
reedy voice. One can actually feel the wind made by
his wings and, slight though it is, one finds it hateful
in the extreme. [...]

One is in the middle of a story when someone
butts in and tries to show that he is the only clever

The Poet Sei Shonagon as a Courtesan, a nineteenth-century Japanese
woodblock print by Kikukawa Eizan.

person in the room. Such a person is hateful, and so,
indeed, is anyone, child or adult, who tries to push
himself forward.

One is telling a story about old times when
someone breaks in with a little detail that he happens to know, implying that one's own version
is inaccurate—disgusting behavior!

Very hateful is a mouse that scurries all over the
place. [...]

A certain gentleman whom one does not
want to see visits one at home or in the Palace, and
one pretends to be asleep. But a maid comes to
tell one and shakes one awake, with a look on
her face that says, "What a sleepyhead!" Very
hateful. [. . .]

Indeed, one's attachment to a man depends largely on the elegance of his leave-taking. When he jumps out of bed, scurries about the room, tightly fastens his trouser-sash, rolls up the sleeves of his Court cloak, over-robe, or hunting costume, stuffs his belongings into the breast of his robe and then briskly secures the outer sash—one really begins to hate him.

[Late 10th century]

QUESTIONS FOR REFLECTION AND DISCUSSION

1. The loose structure of the list makes Shonagon's writing similar in form to a journal entry. How does the list function to unite the diverse entries? What patterns of style emerge? What thematic patterns?

2. From the basis of evidence contained within this list, write a paragraph summarizing the routine of Shonagon's daily life. What aspects of it can we know from this list? What aspects of it does the list not address?

3. Judging from the items included in the list, how would Shonagon define the word "hateful"? How would she define love?

LOVERS TOPICS FOR ESSAYS

1. Write an essay comparing the depiction of intimacy in several of this section's texts.

2. Write an essay comparing the imagery used in several texts in this section to depict the relationship between lovers.

3. What is the difference between what people say about love and what they actually think about it or how they act? Use examples from this section's texts to support your argument.

4. Have ideas and definitions of love changed over the centuries or have they remained the same? Use examples from this section's texts to support your argument.

Lovers Further Readings in *Literature: A World of Writing*

Jane Evelyn Atwood, *Internal Visiting Space for Incarcerated Couples, France* • Robert Browning, "My Last Duchess" • Catullus, "I Hate and Love" • William Faulkner, "A Rose for Emily" • Nathaniel Hawthorne, "Young Goodman Brown" • Ernest Hemingway, "Hills Like White Elephants"

WORKING FURTHER WITH THE WORLD CLOSEST TO US

1. What makes human relationships comic? Use examples from this chapter's texts to support your argument.

2. What makes human relationships tragic? Use examples from this chapter's texts to support your argument.

3. What, if anything, is universal about human relationships? Use examples from this chapter's texts to support your argument.

4. Write a personal essay, a description essay, or an argument essay on an aspect of human relationships you feel has not been covered in the readings in this chapter.

-1

-1

Akureyri

Iceland

United Ki

Londonderr

Ireland

Dubl

Ma

Portugal ★

Lisbon

Casablanca

Morocco

Safi

Goulimine

Laayoune

tern Sahara

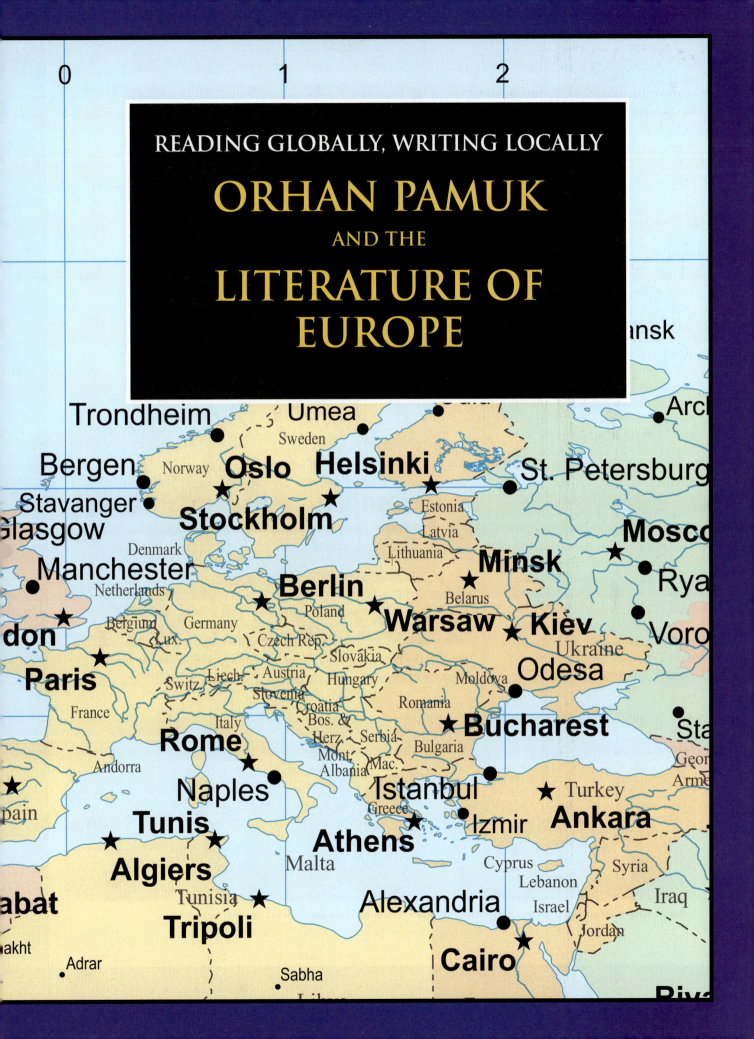

> Europe has what we do not have yet, a sense of the mysterious and inexorable limits of life, a sense, in a word, of tragedy. And we have what they sorely need: a sense of life's possibilities.
>
> — James Baldwin

The literature of Europe is the literature we are used to thinking about when we think of the classics: the great works of ancient Greece and Rome; the medieval and early modern masterpieces of Dante, Cervantes, and Shakespeare; the extraordinary nineteenth-century novels of England, Russia, and France; the stunning experiments of modernist writers from Virginia Woolf and James Joyce to Franz Kafka and Marcel Proust. Very little of what we read today was written outside of the influence of European literature. The "Old World," as it used to be called, transformed the "New World." In the thousand years since the first Viking expeditions, millions of immigrants brought ancient languages, lore, and literature along with their new sense of infinite possibility, as James Baldwin—born in Harlem, settled in France—put it.

What people actually mean when they speak of "Europe" has changed many times over. For the ancient Romans, they were barbarians to be subjugated, speaking foreign tongues and practicing strange religions, living and fighting in small bands rather than highly organized cities and armies. In the early centuries of the common era, the barbarians swept southward, converted to Christianity, and replaced the Romans at the head of their own empire. During the next thousand years or so, from around 400 to 1500, most of the institutions, languages, and nations we think of as Europe slowly

Detail of the Bayeux tapestry (eleventh century): Unloading the horses on arrival at Pevensey.

View of Acropolis and Parthenon, Lykavitos Hill and Odeum of Herodes Atticus, Athens, Greece.

A Moor and a Christian playing chess in a tent, 1282.

View of City Hall and Tower Bridge, London, England.

developed from the tattered remains of the Roman empire: cathedrals, castles, and cities; institutions of government and religion; codes of honor and chivalry; poems of love and tales of adventure. The great story of the next five hundred years was the spread of these institutions around the world in waves of commerce, colonization, and immigration both forced and voluntary. Europe has never been a peaceful place, and historians tend to wage fierce arguments about which period of its history has been the most turbulent and violent, but most agree that the Europe from which immigrants were fleeing in the twentieth century was a particularly difficult place to live. Two world wars ravaged the continent. Revolution shook the first two decades; totalitarian governments dominated the rest of the century.

Difficult to live in, but for that very reason a compelling place for making art—no wonder so many New World writers, from Ernest Hemingway and Gertrude Stein to James Baldwin, Richard Wright, and Julio Cortázar, were drawn to the continent. From the epics, tragedies, and philosophy of ancient Greece through the allegories, romances, and songs of the middle ages, the great discoveries of the Renaissance, and the rise of the novel in the eighteenth and nineteenth centuries to the rapid sequence of avant-garde movements known as modernism, Europe has long dominated the creation and production of literature. Even in the twentieth century, when writers and artists around the world began to create astonishing works outside of the bounds of European dominance, their creations were marked and inspired by opposition and response to European models and, often, European rule. This is not to say that Asia, Africa, and the Americas did not have ancient and important indigenous traditions, but for those traditions to reach a modern audience, and for those cultures to have an impact beyond their immediate context, they were compelled somehow to make sense of and come to terms with the European heritage everywhere around them as is evident from readings elsewhere in this book, this was neither an easy nor an unambivalent process either for Europeans or for their former subjects or adversaries. A hallmark of literature of the past hundred years has been to explore the legacy of Europe in all the complexity of its great peaks and barbarous valleys—and we have chosen our selections here to highlight a number of twentieth-century reckonings with this legacy.

Politically, Europe is now as divided as many Europeans had dreamed it would be since the Roman Empire collapsed more than 1,500 years ago. The transnational entity known as the European Union (EU) governs a common market stretching from Portugal to Turkey. Responsible for 30 percent of the world's gross domestic product (GDP), the EU remains culturally fragmented and rife with disagreement about its role in the lives of its members. Our featured author, the Turkish exile Orhan Pamuk, well dramatizes the fault lines of a contemporary Europe caught between a stubbornly enduring self-image as a homogeneous population of Caucasian Christians and a reality of enormous religious, ethnic, and racial diversity, haunted by its past and confronting a new future of expanding borders and vanishing boundaries.

Comic map of Europe by Frederick Rose, c. 1870.

ORHAN PAMUK B. 1952

> TO WRITE, TO READ, WAS LIKE LEAVING ONE WORLD TO FIND CONSOLATION IN THE OTHERNESS OF ANOTHER, IN THE STRANGE AND THE WONDROUS. I FELT THAT MY FATHER HAD READ NOVELS IN ORDER TO ESCAPE HIS LIFE AND FLEE TO THE WEST—JUST AS I DID LATER.
>
> —ORHAN PAMUK

Like the city of Istanbul he long called home, Orhan Pamuk straddles two cultures—the Christian tradition of Western Europe and the Muslim culture of Turkey and the empire it once was. But writers such as Pamuk also show that this is not an easy distinction to make. Christianity, Judaism, and Islam have coexisted and battled each other all over Europe for more than a millennium, and their fates and cultures are far more intertwined than any geographical divide could separate. Born and raised in Istanbul, Pamuk published his first novel, *Cevdet Bey and His Sons*, in 1982. He reached international prominence and popularity in the 1990s with a trio of formally complex and innovative novels, *The Black Book* (1990), *New Life* (1992), and *My Name Is Red* (2000). Pamuk also increasingly came into conflict with Turkish authorities for statements regarding the persecution of Armenian and Kurdish minorities. After criminal charges were brought against him, he went into exile and is currently a professor of comparative literature at Columbia University. His recent books, the novel *Snow* (2002) and the memoir *Istanbul: Memoirs of a City* (2003), continue his engagement with the complex relationship between value systems in his native city and country. In 2006, he became the first Turkish writer to be awarded the Nobel Prize in Literature; in "My Father's Suitcase," the lecture he gave at the award ceremony, Pamuk uses personal recollection to define the role of writers and literature in the twenty-first century. The short story "To Look Out the Window," which appears in his collection of writings, *Other Colours* (2006), evokes the author's childhood in Istanbul.

MY FATHER'S SUITCASE

The Nobel Prize Lecture

TWO YEARS BEFORE MY FATHER DIED, HE GAVE ME A SMALL suitcase filled with his manuscripts and notebooks. Assuming his usual jocular, mocking air, he told me that he wanted me to read them after he was gone, by which he meant after his death.

"Just take a look," he said, slightly embarrassed. "See if there's anything in there that you can use.

Maybe after I'm gone you can make a selection and publish it."

We were in my study, surrounded by books. My father was searching for a place to set down the suitcase, wandering around like a man who wished to rid himself of a painful burden. In the end, he deposited it quietly, unobtrusively, in a corner. It was a shaming moment that neither of us ever quite forgot, but once it had passed and we had gone back to our usual roles, taking life lightly, we relaxed. We talked as we always did—about trivial, everyday things, and Turkey's never-ending political troubles, and my father's mostly failed business ventures—without feeling too much sorrow.

For several days after that, I walked back and forth past the suitcase without ever actually touching it. I was already familiar with this small black leather case, with a lock and rounded corners. When I was a child, my father had taken it with him on short trips and had sometimes used it to carry documents to work. Whenever he came home from a trip, I'd rush to open this little suitcase and rummage through his things, savoring the scent of cologne and foreign countries. The suitcase was a friend, a powerful reminder of my past, but now I couldn't even touch it. Why? No doubt because of the mysterious weight of its contents.

5   I am now going to speak of the meaning of that weight: that weight is what a person creates when he shuts himself up in a room and sits down at a table or retires to a corner to express his thoughts—that is, the weight of literature.

When I did finally touch my father's suitcase, I still could not bring myself to open it. But I knew what was inside some of the notebooks it held. I had seen my father writing in them. My father had a large library. In his youth, in the late nineteen-forties, he had wanted to be an Istanbul poet, and had translated Valéry° into Turkish, but he had not wanted to live the sort of life that came with writing poetry in a poor country where there were few readers. My father's father—my grandfather—was a wealthy businessman, and my father had led a comfortable life as a child and a young man; he had no wish to endure hardship for the sake of literature, for writing. He loved life with all its beauties: this I understood.

The first thing that kept me away from my father's suitcase was, of course, a fear that I might not like what I read. Because my father understood this, too, he had taken the precaution of acting as if he did not take the contents of the case

seriously. By this time, I had been working as a writer for twenty-five years, and his failure to take literature seriously pained me. But that was not what worried me most: my real fear—the crucial thing that I did not wish to discover—was that my father might be a good writer. If true and great literature emerged from my father's suitcase, I would have to acknowledge that inside my father there existed a man who was entirely different from the one I knew. This was a frightening possibility. Even at my advanced age, I wanted my father to be my father and my father only—not a writer.

A writer is someone who spends years patiently trying to discover the second being inside him, and the world that makes him who he is. When I speak of writing, the image that comes first to my mind is not a novel, a poem, or a literary tradition; it is the person who shuts himself up in a room, sits down at a table, and, alone, turns inward. Amid his shadows, he builds a new world with words. This man—or this woman—may use a typewriter, or profit from the ease of a computer, or write with a pen on paper, as I do. As he writes, he may drink tea or coffee, or smoke cigarettes. From time to time, he may rise from his table to look out the window at the children playing in the street, or, if he is lucky, at trees and a view, or even at a blank wall. He may write poems, or plays, or novels, as I do. But all these differences arise only after the crucial task is complete—after he has sat down at the table and patiently turned inward. To write is to transform that inward gaze into words, to study the worlds into which we pass when we retire into ourselves, and to do so with patience, obstinacy, and joy.

As I sit at my table, for days, months, years, slowly adding words to empty pages, I feel as if I were bringing into being that other person inside me, in the same way that one might build a bridge or a dome, stone by stone. As we hold words in our hands, like stones, sensing the ways in which each is connected to the others, looking at them sometimes from afar, sometimes from very close, caressing them with our fingers and the tips of our pens, weighing them, moving them around, year in and year out, patiently and hopefully, we create new worlds.

Valéry: Paul Valéry (1871–1945), French Symbolist poet.

The writer's secret is not inspiration—for it is never clear where that comes from—but stubbornness, endurance. The lovely Turkish expression "to dig a well with a needle" seems to me to have been invented with writers in mind. In the old stories, I love the patience of Ferhat, who digs through mountains for his love—and I understand it, too. When I wrote, in my novel *My Name Is Red*, about the old Persian miniaturists who drew the same horse with the same passion for years and years, memorizing each stroke, until they could re-create that beautiful horse even with their eyes closed, I knew that I was talking about the writing profession, and about my own life. If a writer is to tell his own story— to tell it slowly, and as if it were a story about other people—if he is to feel the power of the story rise up inside him, if he is to sit down at a table and give himself over to this art, this craft, he must first be given some hope. The angel of inspiration (who pays regular visits to some and rarely calls on others) favors the hopeful and the confident, and it is when a writer feels most lonely, when he feels most doubtful about his efforts, his dreams, and the value of his writing, when he thinks that his story is only *his* story—it is at such moments that the angel chooses to reveal to him the images and dreams that will draw out the world he wishes to build. If I think back on the books to which I have devoted my life, I am most surprised by those moments when I felt as if the sentences and pages that made me ecstatically happy came not from my own imagination but from another power, which had found them and generously presented them to me.

I was afraid of opening my father's suitcase and reading his notebooks because I knew that he would never have tolerated the difficulties that I had tolerated, that it was not solitude he loved but mixing with friends, crowds, company. Still, later my thoughts took a different turn. These dreams of renunciation and patience, it occurred to me, were prejudices that I had derived from my own life and my own experience as a writer. There were plenty of brilliant writers who wrote amid crowds and family, in the glow of company and happy chatter. In addition, even my father had, at

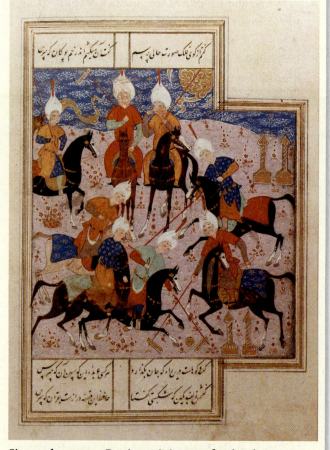

Sixteenth-century Persian miniature of polo players from Tabriz, Iran, demonstrating the beauty that comes from drawing "the same horse with the same passion for years, memorizing each stroke."

some point, tired of the monotony of family life and left for Paris, where—like so many writers— he had sat in a hotel room filling notebooks. I knew that some of those very notebooks were in the suitcase, because, during the years before he brought me the case, he had finally begun to talk about that period in his life. He had spoken about those years when I was a child, but he had never discussed his vulnerabilities, his dreams of becoming a writer, or the questions of identity that had plagued him in his Paris hotel room. He'd spoken instead of the times he'd seen Sartre° on the sidewalks of Paris, of the books he'd read and the films he'd gone to, all with the elated sincerity of someone imparting important news.

Sartre: Jean-Paul Sartre (1905–1980), Existentialist philosopher, critic, and political activist—probably the most influential European intellectual of the 1950s.

When I became a writer, I knew that it was partly thanks to the fact that I had a father who spoke of world writers much more than he ever spoke of pashas or great religious leaders. So perhaps, I told myself, I would have to read my father's notebooks with my gratitude in mind, remembering, too, how indebted I was to his large library. I would have to remember that, when he was living with us, my father, like me, enjoyed being alone with his books and his thoughts—and not pay too much attention to the literary quality of his writing. But as I gazed so anxiously at the suitcase he had bequeathed to me I also felt that this was the very thing I would not be able to do.

[. . .]

A writer talks of things that we all know but do not know that we know. To explore this knowledge, and to watch it grow, is a pleasurable thing; the reader visits a world that is at once familiar and miraculous. When a writer uses his secret wounds as his starting point, he is, whether he is aware of it or not, putting great faith in humanity. My confidence comes from the belief that all human beings resemble one another, that others carry wounds like mine—and that they will therefore understand. All true literature rises from this childish, hopeful certainty that we resemble one another. When a writer shuts himself up in a room for years on end, with this gesture he suggests a single humanity, a world without a center.

But, as can be seen from my father's suitcase and the pale colors of our lives in Istanbul, the world did have a center, and it was far away from us. I know from experience that the great majority of people on this earth live with the same feeling of inauthenticity and Chekhovian provinciality, and that many suffer from an even deeper sense of insufficiency, insecurity, and degradation than I do. Yes, the greatest dilemmas facing humanity are still landlessness, homelessness, and hunger . . . but today our televisions and newspapers tell us about these fundamental problems more quickly and more simply than literature ever could. What literature most needs to tell and to investigate now is humanity's basic fears: the fear of being left outside, the fear of counting for nothing, and the feeling of worthlessness that comes with

such fears—the collective humiliations, vulnerabilities, slights, grievances, sensitivities, and imagined insults, and the nationalist boasts and inflations that are their next of kin. . . . Whenever I am confronted by such sentiments, and by the irrational, overstated language in which they are usually expressed, I know that they touch on a darkness inside me. We have often witnessed peoples, societies, and nations outside the Western world—and I can identify with them easily—succumbing to fears that lead them to commit stupid acts. I also know that in the West—a world with which I can identify just as easily—nations and peoples that take an excessive pride in their wealth, and in their glory at having brought us the Renaissance, the Enlightenment, and modernism, have, from time to time, succumbed to a self-satisfaction that is almost as stupid.

15 So my father was not the only one: we all give too much importance to the idea of a world with a center. Whereas the impulse that compels us to shut ourselves up in our rooms to write for years on end is a faith in the opposite, the belief that one day our writings will be read and understood, because people the world over resemble one another. This, as I know from my own and my father's writing, is a troubled optimism, scarred by the anger of being consigned to the margins. The love and hate that Dostoyevsky° felt toward the West all his life—I have felt this, too, on many occasions. But if I have grasped an essential truth, if I have cause for optimism, it is because I have travelled with this great writer through his love-hate relationship with the West and I have beheld the world that he built on the other side.

All writers who have devoted their lives to their work know this reality: whatever our original purpose, the world that we create after years and years of hopeful writing will, in the end, take us to other, very different places. It will take us far from the table at which we have worked in sadness or in anger; it will take us to the other side of that sadness and anger, into another world. Could my father not have reached such a world himself? Like the

Dostoyevsky: Fyodor Dostoyevsky (1821–1881), Russian novelist and critic. One of the major figures of nineteenth-century literature, Dostoyevsky was a Slavophile, or nativist, but also profoundly influenced by the literature and culture of the West.

land that slowly begins to take shape, rising from the mist in its many colors like an island spied after a long sea journey, this other world enchants us. We are as beguiled as the Western travellers who voyaged from the south to behold Istanbul rising from the mist. At the end of a journey begun in hope and curiosity, there lies before us a city of mosques and minarets, a medley of houses, streets, hills, bridges, and slopes—an entire world. Seeing this world, we wish to enter it and lose ourselves in it, just as we might in a book. After sitting down to write because we felt provincial, excluded, marginalized, angry, or deeply melancholic, we have found an entire world beyond these sentiments.

What I feel now is the opposite of what I felt as a child and a young man: for me, the center of the world is Istanbul. This is not just because I have lived there all my life but because, for the past thirty-three years, I have been narrating its streets, its bridges, its people, its dogs, its houses, its mosques, its fountains, its strange heroes, its shops, its famous characters, its dark spots, its days, and its nights, making them a part of me, embracing them all. A point arrived when this world that I had made with my own hands, this world that existed only in my head, was more real to me than the city in which I actually lived. That was when all these people and streets, objects and buildings seemed to begin to talk among themselves, interacting in ways that I had not anticipated, as if they lived not just in my imagination or my books but for themselves. This world that I had created, like a man digging a well with a needle, then seemed truer than anything else.

As I gazed at my father's suitcase, it occurred to me that he might also have discovered this kind of happiness in the years he spent writing. I should not prejudge him. I was so grateful to him, after all. He had never been a commanding, forbidding, overpowering, punishing, ordinary father. He had always left me free, always showed me the utmost respect. I had often thought that if I had, from time to time, been able to draw on my imagination, whether in freedom or in childishness, it was because, unlike so many of my friends from childhood and youth, I had no fear of my father. On some deeper level, I was able to become a

The seventeenth-century Sultan Ahmed Mosque, known as the "Blue Mosque," seen through an Istanbul window.

writer because my father, in his youth, had also wished to be one. I would have to read him with tolerance—to seek to understand what he had written in those hotel rooms.

It was with these hopeful thoughts that I walked over to the suitcase, which was still sitting where my father had left it. Using all my will power, I read through a few manuscripts and notebooks. What had my father written about? I recall a few views from the windows of Paris hotels, a few poems, paradoxes, analyses. . . . As I write, I feel like someone who has just been in a traffic accident and is struggling to remember how it happened, while at the same time dreading the prospect of remembering too much. When I was a child, and my father and mother were on the brink of a quarrel—when they fell into one of their deadly silences—my father would turn on the radio, to change the mood, and the music would help us forget it all faster.

20   So let me change the mood with a few sweet words that will, I hope, serve as well as that music. The question we writers are asked most often, the favorite question, is: Why do you write? I write because I have an innate need to write. I write because I can't do normal work as other people do. I write because I want to read books like the ones I write. I write because I am angry at everyone. I write because I love sitting in a room all day writing. I write because I can partake of real life only by changing it. I write because I want others, the whole world, to know what sort of life we lived, and continue to live, in Istanbul, in Turkey. I write because I love the smell of paper,

pen, and ink. I write because I believe in literature, in the art of the novel, more than I believe in anything else. I write because it is a habit, a passion. I write because I am afraid of being forgotten. I write because I like the glory and interest that writing brings. I write to be alone. Perhaps I write because I hope to understand why I am so very, very angry at everyone. I write because I like to be read. I write because once I have begun a novel, an essay, a page I want to finish it. I write because everyone expects me to write. I write because I have a childish belief in the immortality of libraries, and in the way my books sit on the shelf. I write because it is exciting to turn all life's beauties and riches into words. I write not to tell a story but to compose a story. I write because I wish to escape from the foreboding that there is a place I must go but—as in a dream—can't quite get to. I write because I have never managed to be happy. I write to be happy.

A week after he came to my office and left me his suitcase, my father paid me another visit; as always, he brought me a bar of chocolate (he had forgotten that I was forty-eight years old). As always, we chatted and laughed about life, politics, and family gossip. A moment arrived when my father's gaze drifted to the corner where he had left his suitcase, and he saw that I had moved it. We looked each other in the eye. There followed a pressing silence. I did not tell him that I had opened the suitcase and tried to read its contents; instead, I looked away. But he understood. Just as I understood that he had understood. Just as he understood that I had understood that he had understood. But all this understanding went only as far as it could go in a few seconds. Because my father was a happy, easygoing man who had faith in himself, he smiled at me the way he always did. And, as he left the house, he repeated all the lovely and encouraging things he always said to me, like a father.

As always, I watched him leave, envying his happiness, his carefree and unflappable temperament. But I remember that on that day there was also a flash of joy inside me that made me ashamed. It was prompted by the thought that maybe I wasn't as comfortable in life as he was,

maybe I had not led as happy or footloose a life as he had, but at least I had devoted mine to writing. You understand . . . I was ashamed to be thinking such things at my father's expense—of all people, my father, who had never been a source of pain to me, who had left me free. All this should remind us that writing and literature are intimately linked to a void at the center of our lives, to our feelings of happiness and guilt.

But my story has a symmetry that immediately reminded me of something else that day, bringing with it an even deeper sense of guilt. Twenty-three years before my father left me his suitcase, and four years after I had decided, at the age of twenty-two, to become a novelist, and, abandoning all else, shut myself up in a room, I finished my first novel, *Cevdet Bey and His Sons*. With trembling hands, I gave my father a typescript of the still unpublished novel, so that he could read it and tell me what he thought. I did this not only because I had confidence in his taste and his intellect; his opinion was very important to me because, unlike my mother, he had not opposed my wish to become a writer. At that point, my father was not with us, but far away. I waited impatiently for his return. When he arrived, two weeks later, I ran to open the door. My father said nothing, but he immediately threw his arms around me in a way that told me he had liked the book very much. For a while, we were plunged into the sort of awkward silence that often accompanies moments of great emotion. Then, when we had calmed down and begun to talk, my father resorted to highly charged and exaggerated language to express his confidence in me and in my first novel: he told me that one day I would win the prize that I have now received with such great happiness. He said this not because he was trying to convince me of his good opinion or to set the prize as a goal; he said it like a Turkish father, supporting his son, encouraging him by saying, "One day you'll be a pasha!" For years, whenever he saw me, he would encourage me with the same words.

My father died in December, 2002.

[2006]

QUESTIONS FOR REFLECTION AND DISCUSSION

1. What is the history of the suitcase and what significance does it hold for Pamuk? What significance does the suitcase have for the father? Why does Pamuk describe the initial encounter between himself and his father concerning the suitcase as "shameful"?

2. What, for Pamuk, does it mean to be a writer? Why does it disturb him that his father might be a writer?

3. What, for Pamuk, is the difference between living in the "center of things" and living in the "provinces"? What is the relationship between this distinction and the "world without a center" (p. 401) of which he says the writer dreams?

4. What role do Europe and the West play in Pamuk's vision of the writer's place in society? What role do Turkey and "nations outside the Western world" play? What is the relationship between them? What should it be?

FICTION

TO LOOK OUT THE WINDOW

Orhan Pamuk

Translated by Maureen Freely

1.

IF THERE'S NOTHING TO WATCH AND NO STORIES TO listen to, life can get tedious. When I was a child, boredom was something we fought off by listening to the radio or looking out the window into neighboring apartments or at people passing in the street below. In those days, in 1958, there was still no television in Turkey. But we didn't like to admit it: We talked about television optimistically, just as we did the Hollywood adventure films that took four or five years to reach Istanbul's film theaters, saying it "had yet to arrive."

Looking out the window was such an important pastime that when television did finally come to Turkey, people acted the same way in front of their sets as they had in front of their windows. When my father, my uncles, and my grandmother watched television, they would argue without looking at one another, pausing now and again to report on what they'd just seen, just as they did while gazing out the window.

"If if keeps snowing like this, it's going to stick," my aunt would say, looking at the snow flakes swirling past.

"That man who sells *helva* is back on the Nişantaşı corner!" I would say, peering from the other window, which looked out over the avenue with the streetcar lines.

5   On Sundays, we'd go upstairs with my uncles and aunts and everyone else who lived in the downstairs apartments to have lunch with my grandmother. As I stood at the window, waiting for the food to arrive, I'd be so happy to be there with my mother, my father, my aunts, and my uncles that everything before me seemed to glow with the pale light of the crystal chandelier hanging over the long dining table. My grandmother's sitting room was dark, as were the downstairs sitting rooms, but to me it always seemed darker. Maybe this was because of the tulle curtains and the heavy drapes that hung at either side of the never-opened balcony doors, casting fearsome shadows. Or maybe it was the screens inlaid with mother-of-pearl, the massive tables, the chests, and

the baby grand piano, with all those framed photographs on top, or the general clutter of this airless room that always smelled of dust.

The meal was over, and my uncle was smoking in one of the dark adjoining rooms. "I have a ticket to a football match, but I'm not going," he'd say. "Your father is going to take you instead."

"Daddy, take us to the football match!" my older brother would cry from the other room.

"The children could use some fresh air," my mother would call from the sitting room.

"Then you take them out," my father said to my mother.

"I'm going to my mother's," my mother replied.

"We don't want to go to Granny's," said my brother.

"You can have the car," said my uncle.

"Please, Daddy!" said my brother.

There was a long, strange silence. It was as if everyone in the room was thinking certain thoughts about my mother, and as if my father could tell what those thoughts were.

"So you're giving me your car, are you?" my father asked my uncle.

Later, when we had gone downstairs, while my mother was helping us put on our pullovers and our thick checked woolen socks, my father paced up and down the corridor, smoking a cigarette. My uncle had parked his "elegant, cream colored" '52 Dodge in front of the Teşvikiye Mosque. My father allowed both of us to sit in the front seat and managed to get the motor started with one turn of the key.

There was no line at the stadium. "This ticket for the two of them," said my father to the man at the turnstile. "One is eight, and the other is ten." As we went through, we were afraid to look into the man's eyes. There were lots of empty seats in the stands, and we sat down at once.

The two teams had already come out to the muddy field, and I enjoyed watching the players run up and down in their dazzling white shorts to warm up. "Look, that's Little Mehmet," said my brother, pointing to one of them. "He's just come from the junior team."

"We know."

The match began, and for a long time we didn't speak. A while later my thoughts wandered from the match to other things. Why did footballers all wear the same strip when their names were all different? I imagined that there were no longer players running up and down the field, just names. Their shorts were getting dirtier and dirtier. A while later, I watched a ship with an interesting smokestack passing slowly down the Bosphorus, just behind the bleachers. No one had scored by halftime, and my father bought us each a cone of chickpeas and a cheese pita.

"Daddy, I can't finish this," I said, showing him what was left in my hand.

"Put it over there," he said. "No one will see you."

We got up and moved around to warm up, just like everyone else. Like our father, we had shoved our hands into the pockets of our woolen trousers and turned away from the field to look at the people sitting behind us, when someone in the crowd called out to my father. My father brought his hand to his ear, to indicate that he couldn't hear a thing with all the noise.

"I can't come," he said, as he pointed in our direction. "I have my children with me."

The man in the crowd was wearing a purple scarf. He fought his way to our row, pushing the seatbacks and shoving quite a few people to reach us.

"Are these your boys?" he asked, after he had embraced my father. "They're so big. I can hardly believe it."

My father said nothing.

"So when did these children appear?" said the man, looking at us admiringly. "Did you get married as soon as you finished school?"

"Yes," said my father, without looking him in his face. They spoke for a while longer. The man with the purple scarf turned to my brother and me and put an unshelled American peanut into each of our palms. When he left, my father sat down in his seat and for a long time said nothing.

Not long after the two teams had returned to the field in fresh shorts, my father said, "Come on, let's go home. You're getting cold."

"I'm not getting cold," said my brother.

"Yes, you are," said my father. "And Ali's cold. Come on, let's get going."

As we were making our way past the others in our row, jostling against knees and sometimes stepping on feet, we stepped on the cheese pita I'd left on the ground. As we walked down the stairs, we heard the referee blowing his whistle to signal the start of the second half.

35   "Were you getting cold?" my brother asked. "Why didn't you say you weren't cold?" I stayed quiet. "Idiot," said my brother.

"You can listen to the second half on the radio at home," said my father.

"This match is not on the radio," my brother said.

"Quiet, now," said my father. "I'm taking you through Taksim on our way back."

We stayed quiet. Driving across the square, my father stopped the car just before we got to the off-track betting shop—just as we'd guessed. "Don't open the door for anyone," he said. "I'll be back in a moment."

40   He got out of the car. Before he had a chance to lock the car from the outside, we'd pressed down on the buttons and locked it from the inside. But my father didn't go into the betting shop; he ran over to the other side of the cobblestone street. There was a shop over there that was decorated with posters of ships, big plastic airplanes, and sunny landscapes, and it was even open on Sundays, and that's where he went.

"Where did Daddy go?"

"Are we going to play upstairs or downstairs when we get home?" my brother asked.

When my father got back, my brother was playing with the accelerator. We drove back to Nişantaşı and parked again in front of the mosque. "Why don't I buy you something!" said my father. "But please, don't ask for that Famous People series again."

"Oh, please, Daddy!" we pleaded.

45   When we got to Alaaddin's shop, my father bought us each ten packs of chewing gum from the Famous People series. We went into our building; I was so excited by the time we got into the lift that I thought I might wet my pants. It was warm inside and my mother wasn't back yet. We ripped open the chewing gum, throwing the wrappers on the floor. The result:

I got two Field Marshal Fevzi Çakmaks; one each of Charlie Chaplin, the wrestler Hamit Kaplan, Gandhi, Mozart, and De Gaulle; two Atatürks, and one Greta Garbo—number 21— which my brother didn't have yet. With these I now had 173 pictures of Famous People, but I still needed another 27 to complete the series. My brother got four Field Marshal Fevzi Çakmaks, five Atatürks, and one Edison. We tossed the chewing gum into our mouths and began to read the writing on the backs of the cards.

Field Marshal Fevzi Çakmak
General in the War of Independence
(1876–1950)

MAMBO SWEETS CHEWING GUM, INC
A leather soccer ball will be awarded to the lucky person who collects all 100 famous people.

My brother was holding his stack of 165 cards. "Do you want to play Tops or Bottoms?"

"No."

"Would you give me your Greta Garbo for my twelve Fevzi Çakmaks?" he asked. "Then you'll have one hundred and eight-four cards."

50   "No."

"But now you have two Greta Garbos."

I said nothing.

"When they do our inoculations at school tomorrow, it's really going to hurt," he said. "Don't expect me to take care of you, okay?"

"I wouldn't anyway."

55   We ate supper in silence. When *World of Sports* came on the radio, we found out that the match had been a draw, 2–2, and then our mother came into our room to put us to bed. My brother started getting his bag ready for school, and I ran into the sitting room. My father was at the window, staring down at the street.

"Daddy, I don't want to go to school tomorrow."

"Now how can you say that?"

"They're giving us those inoculations tomorrow. I come down with a fever, and then I can hardly breathe. Ask Mummy."

He looked at me, saying nothing. I raced over to the drawer and got out a pen and a piece of paper.

60 "Does your mother know about this?" he asked, putting the paper down on the volume of Kierkegaard that he was always reading but never managed to finish. "You're going to school, but you won't have that injection," he said. "That's what I'll write."

He signed his name. I blew on the ink and then folded up the paper and put it in my pocket. Running back to the bedroom, I slipped it into my bag, and then I climbed up onto my bed and began to bounce on it.

"Calm down," said my mother. "It's time to go to sleep."

2.

I was at school, and it was just after lunch. The whole class was lined up two by two, and we were going back to that stinking cafeteria to have our inoculations. Some children were crying; others were waiting in nervous anticipation. When a whiff of iodine floated up the stairs, my heart began to race. I stepped out of line and went over to the teacher standing at the head of the stairs. The whole class passed us noisily.

"Yes?" said the teacher. "What is it?"

65 I took out the piece of paper my father had signed and gave it to the teacher. She read it with a frown. "Your father's not a doctor, you know," she said. She paused to think. "Go upstairs. Wait in Room 2-A."

There were six or seven children in 2-A who like me had been excused. One was staring in terror out the window. Cries of panic came floating down the corridor; a fat boy with glasses was munching on pumpkin seeds and reading a Kinova comic book. The door opened and in came thin, gaunt Deputy Headmaster Seyfi Bey.

"Probably some of you are genuinely ill, and if you are, we won't take you downstairs," he said. "But I have this to say to those of you who've lied to get excused. One day you will grow up, serve our country, and maybe even die for it. Today it's just an injection you're running away from—but if

you try something like this when you grow up, and if you don't have a genuine excuse, you'll be guilty of treason. Shame on you!"

There was a long silence. I looked at Atatürk's picture, and tears came to my eyes.

Later, we slipped unnoticed back to our classrooms. The children who'd had their inoculations started coming back: Some had their sleeves rolled up, some had tears in their eyes, some scuffled in with very long faces.

70 "Children living close by can go home," said the teacher. "Children with no one to pick them up must wait until the last bell. Don't punch one another on the arm! Tomorrow there's no school."

Everyone started shouting. Some were holding their arms as they left the building; others stopped to show the janitor, Hilmi Efendi, the iodine tracks on their arms.

When I got out to the street, I slung my bag over my shoulder and began to run. A horse cart had blocked traffic in front of Karabet's butcher shop, so I weaved between the cars to get to our building on the other side. I ran past Hayri's fabric shop and Salih's florist shop. Our janitor, Hazim Efendi, let me in.

"What are you doing here all alone at this hour?" he asked.

"They gave us our inoculations today. They let us out early."

75 "Where's your brother? Did you come back alone?"

"I crossed the streetcar lines by myself. Tomorrow we have the day off."

"Your mother's out," he said. "Go up to your grandmother's."

"I'm ill," I said. "I want to go to our house. Open the door for me."

He took a key off the wall and we got into the lift. By the time we had reached our floor, his cigarette had filled the whole cage with smoke that burned my eyes. He opened our door. "Don't play with the electrical sockets," he said, as he pulled the door closed.

80 There was no one at home, but I still shouted out, "Is anyone here, anyone home? Isn't there anyone home?" I threw down my bag, opened up my brother's drawer, and began to look at the film

ticket collection he'd never shown me. Then I had a good long look at the pictures of football matches that he'd cut out of newspapers and glued into a book. I could tell from the footsteps that it wasn't my mother coming in now, it was my father. I put my brother's tickets and his scrapbook back where they belonged, carefully, so he wouldn't know I'd been looking at them.

My father was in his bedroom; he'd opened up his wardrobe and was looking inside.

"You're home already, are you?"

"No, I'm in Paris," I said, the way they did at school.

"Didn't you go to school today?"

85 "Today they gave us our inoculations."

"Isn't your brother here?" he asked. "All right then, go to your room and show me how quiet you can be."

I did as he asked. I pressed my forehead against the window and looked outside. From the sounds coming from the hallway I could tell that my father had taken one of the suitcases out of the cupboard there. He went back into his room and began to take his jackets and his trousers out of the wardrobe; I could tell from the rattling of the hangers. He began to open and close the drawers where he kept his shirts, his socks, and his underpants. I listened to him put them all into the suitcase. He went into the bathroom and came out again. He snapped the suitcase latches shut and turned the lock. He came to join me in my room.

"So what have you been up to in here?"

"I've been looking out the window."

90 "Come here, let's look out the window together."

He took me on his lap, and for a long time we looked out the window together. The tips of the tall cypress tree that stood between us and the apartment building opposite began to sway in the wind. I liked the way my father smelled.

"I'm going far away," he said. He kissed me. "Don't tell your mother. I'll tell her myself later."

"Are you going by plane?"

"Yes," he said, "to Paris. Don't tell this to anyone either." He took a huge two-and-a-half-lira coin from his pocket and gave it to me, and then he kissed me again. "And don't say you saw me here."

95 I put the money right into my pocket. When my father had lifted me from his lap and picked up his suitcase, I said, "Don't go, Daddy." He kissed me one more time, and then he left.

I watched him from the window. He walked straight to Alaaddin's store, and then he stopped a passing taxi. Before he got in, he looked up at our apartment one more time and waved. I waved back, and he took off.

I looked at the empty avenue for a long, long time. A streetcar passed, and then the water seller's horse cart. I rang the bell and called Hazim Efendi.

"Did you ring the bell?" he said, when he got to the door. "Don't play with the bell."

"Take this two-and-a-half-lira coin," I said, "go to Alaaddin's shop, and buy me ten chewing gums from the Famous People series. Don't forget to bring back the fifty kuruş change."

100 "Did your father give you this money?" he asked. "Let's hope your mother doesn't get angry."

I said nothing, and he left, I stood at the window and watched him go into Alaaddin's shop. He came out a little later. On his way back, he ran into the janitor from the Marmara Apartments across the way, and they stopped to chat.

When he came back, he gave me the change. I immediately ripped open the chewing gum: three more Fevzi Çakmaks, one Atatürk, and one each of Leonardo da Vinci and Süleyman the Magnificent, Churchill, General Franco, and one more number 21, the Greta Garbo that my brother still didn't have. So now I had 183 pictures in all. But to complete the full set of 100, I still needed 26 more.

I was admiring my first 91, which showed the plane in which Lindbergh had crossed the Atlantic, when I heard a key in the door. My mother! I quickly gathered up the gum wrappers that I had thrown on the floor and put them in the bin.

"We had our inoculations today, so I came home early," I said. "Typhoid, typhus, tetanus."

105 "Where's your brother?"

"His class hadn't had their inoculations yet," I said. "They sent us home. I crossed the avenue all by myself."

"Does your arm hurt?"

I said nothing. A little later, my brother came home. His arm was hurting. He lay down on his bed, resting on his other arm, and looked miserable as he fell asleep. It was very dark out by the time he woke up. "Mummy, it hurts a lot," he said.

"You might have a fever later on," my mother said, as she was ironing in the other room. "Ali, is your arm hurting too? Lie down, keep still."

110 We went to bed and kept still. After sleeping for a little my brother woke up and began to read the sports page, and then he told me it was because of me that we'd left the match early yesterday, and because we'd left early our team had missed four goals.

"Even if we hadn't left, we might not have made those goals," I said.

"What?"

After dozing a little longer, my brother offered me six Fevzi Çakmaks, four Atatürks, and three other cards I already had in exchange for one Greta Garbo, and I turned him down.

"Shall we play Tops or Bottoms?" he asked me.

115 "Okay, let's play."

You press the whole stack between the palms of your hands. You ask, "Tops or Bottoms?" If he says Bottoms, you look at the bottom picture, let's say number 68, Rita Hayworth. Now let's say it's number 18, Dante the Poet, on top. If it is, then Bottoms wins and you give him the picture you like the least, the one you already have the most of. Field Marshal Fevzi Çakmak pictures passed back and forth between us until it was evening and time for supper.

"One of you go upstairs and take a look," said my mother. "Maybe your father's come back."

We both went upstairs. My uncle was sitting, smoking, with my grandmother; my father wasn't there. We listened to the news on the radio, we read the sports page. When my grandmother sat down to eat, we went downstairs.

"What kept you?" said my mother. "You didn't eat anything up there, did you? Why don't I give you your lentil soup now. You can eat it very slowly until your father gets home."

120 "Isn't there any toasted bread?" my brother asked.

While we were silently eating our soup, our mother watched us. From the way she held her head and the way her eyes darted away from us, I knew she was listening for the lift. When we finished our soup, she asked, "Would you like some more?" She glanced into the pot. "Why don't I have mine before it gets cold," she said. But instead she went to the window and looked down at Nişantaşı Square; she stood there looking for some time. Then she turned around, came back to the table, and began to eat her soup. My brother and I were discussing yesterday's match.

"Be quiet! Isn't that the lift?"

We fell quiet and listened carefully. It wasn't the lift. A streetcar broke the silence, shaking the table, the glasses, the pitcher, and the water inside it. When we were eating our oranges, we all definitely heard the lift. It came closer and closer, but it didn't stop at our floor; it went right up to my grandmother's. "It went all the way up," said my mother.

After we had finished eating, my mother said, "Take your plates to the kitchen. Leave your father's plate where it is." We cleared the table. My father's clean plate sat alone on the empty table for a long time.

125 My mother went over to the window that looked down at the police station; she stood there looking for a long time. Then suddenly she made up her mind. Gathering up my father's knife and fork and empty plate, she took them into the kitchen. "I'm going upstairs to your grandmother's," she said. "Please don't get into a fight while I'm gone."

My brother and I went back to our game of Tops or Bottoms.

"Tops," I said, for the first time.

He revealed the top card: number 34, Koca Yusuf, the world-famous wrestler. He pulled out the card from the bottom of the stack: number 50, Atatürk. "You lose. Give me a card."

We played for a long time and he kept on winning. Soon he had taken nineteen of my twenty Fevzi Çakmaks and two of my Atatürks.

130 "I'm not playing anymore," I said, getting angry. "I'm going upstairs. To Mummy."

"Mummy will get angry."

"Coward! Are you afraid of being home all alone?"

My grandmother's door was open as usual. Supper was over. Bekir, the cook, was washing the dishes; my uncle and my grandmother were sitting across from each other. My mother was at the window looking down on Nişantaşi Square.

"Come," she said, still looking out the window. I moved straight into the empty space that seemed to be reserved just for me. Leaning against her, I too looked down at Nişantaşi Square. My mother put her hand on my head and gently stroked my hair.

135 "Your father came home early this afternoon, I hear. You saw him."

"Yes."

"He took his suitcase and left. Hazim Efendi saw him."

"Yes."

"Did he tell you where he was going, darling?"

140 "No," I said. "He gave me two and a half lira."

Down in the street, everything—the dark stores along the avenue, the car lights, the little empty space in the middle where the traffic policemen stood, the wet cobblestones, the letters on the advertising boards that hung from the trees— everything was lonely and sad. It began to rain, and my mother passed her fingers slowly through my hair.

That was when I noticed that the radio that sat between my grandmother's chair and my uncle's—the radio that was always on—was silent. A chill passed through me.

"Don't stand there like that, my girl," my grandmother said then.

My brother had come upstairs.

145 "Go to the kitchen, you two," said my uncle. "Bekir!" he called. "Make these boys a ball; they can play football in the hallway."

In the kitchen, Bekir had finished the dishes. "Sit down over there," he said. He went out to the glass-enclosed balcony that my grandmother had turned into a greenhouse and brought back a pile of newspapers that he began to crumple into a ball. When it was as big as a fist, he asked, "Is this good enough?"

"Wrap a few more sheets around it," said my brother.

While Bekir was wrapping a few more sheets of newsprint around the ball, I looked through the doorway to watch my mother, my grandmother, and my uncle on the other side. With a rope he took from a drawer, Bekir bound the paper ball until it was as round as it could be. To soften its sharp edges, he wiped it lightly with a damp rag and then he compressed it again. My brother couldn't resist touching it.

"Wow. It's hard as a rock."

150 "Put your finger down there for me." My brother carefully placed his finger on the spot where the last knot was to be tied. Bekir tied the knot and the ball was done. He tossed it into the air and we began to kick it around.

"Play in the hallway," said Bekir. "If you play in here, you'll break something."

For a long time we gave our game everything we had. I was pretending to be Lefter from Fenerbahçe, and I twisted and turned like he did. Whenever I did a wall pass, I ran into my brother's bad arm. He hit me, too, but it didn't hurt. We were both perspiring, the ball was falling to pieces, and I was winning five to three when I hit his bad arm very hard. He threw himself down on the floor and began to cry.

"When my arm gets better I'm going to kill you!" he said, as he lay there.

He was angry because he'd lost. I left the hallway for the sitting room; my grandmother, my mother, and my uncle had all gone into the study. My grandmother was dialing the phone.

155 "Hello, my girl," she said then, in the same voice she used when she called my mother the same thing. "Is that Yeşilköy Airport? Listen, my girl, we want to make an inquiry about a passenger who flew out to Europe earlier today." She gave my father's name and twisted the phone cord around her finger while she waited. "Bring me my cigarettes," she said then to my uncle. When my uncle had left the room, she took the receiver away from her ear.

"Please, my girl, tell us," my grandmother said to my mother. "You would know. Is there another woman?"

I couldn't hear my mother's answer. My grandmother was looking at her as if she hadn't said a thing. Then the person at the other end of the line said something and she got angry. "They're not going to tell us," she said, when my uncle returned with a cigarette and an ashtray.

My mother saw my uncle looking at me, and that was when she noticed I was there. Taking me by the arm, she pulled me back into the hallway. When she'd felt my back and the nape of my neck, she saw how much I'd perspired, but she didn't get angry at me.

"Mummy, my arm hurts," said my brother.

160 "You two go downstairs now, I'll put you both to bed."

Downstairs on our floor, the three of us were silent for a long time. Before I went to bed I padded into the kitchen in my pajamas for a glass of water, and then I went into the sitting room. My mother was smoking in front of the window, and at first she didn't hear me.

"You'll catch cold in those bare feet," she said. "Is your brother in bed?"

"He's asleep. Mummy, I'm going to tell you something." I waited for my mother to make room for me at the window. When she had opened up that sweet space for me, I sidled into it. "Daddy went to Paris," I said. "And you know what suitcase he took?"

165 She said nothing. In the silence of the night, we watched the rainy street for a very long time.

3.

My other grandmother's house was next to Şişli Mosque and the end of the streetcar line. Now the square is full of minibus and municipal bus stops, and high ugly buildings and department stores plastered with signs, and offices whose workers spill out onto the pavements at lunchtime and look like ants, but in those days it was at the edge of the European city. It took us fifteen minutes to walk from our house to the wide cobblestone square, and as we walked hand in hand with my mother under the linden and mulberry trees, we felt as if we had come to the countryside.

My other grandmother lived in a four-story stone and concrete house that looked like a

matchbox turned on its side; it faced Istanbul to the west and in the back the mulberry groves in the hills. After her husband died and her three daughters were married, my grandmother had taken to living in a single room of this house, which was crammed with wardrobes, tables, trays, pianos, and other furniture. My aunt would cook her food and bring it over or pack it in a metal container and have her driver deliver it for her. It wasn't just that my grandmother would not leave her room to go two flights down to the kitchen to cook; she didn't even go into the other rooms of the house, which were covered with a thick blanket of dust and silky cobwebs. Like her own mother, who had spent her last years alone in a great wooden mansion, my grandmother had succumbed to a mysterious solitary disease and would not even permit a caretaker or a daily cleaner.

When we went to visit her, my mother would press down on the bell for a very long time and pound on the iron door, until my grandmother would at last open the rusty iron shutters on the second-floor window overlooking the mosque and peer down on us, and because she didn't trust her eyes—she could no longer see very far— she would ask us to wave at her.

"Come out of the doorway so your grandmother can see you, children," said my mother. Coming out into the middle of the pavement with us, she waved and cried, "Mother dear, it's me and the children; it's us, can you hear us?"

170 We understood from her sweet smile that she had recognized us. At once she drew back from the window, went into her room, took out the large key she kept under her pillow, and, after wrapping it in newsprint, threw it down. My brother and I pushed and shoved each other, struggling to catch it.

My brother's arm was still hurting, and that slowed him down, so I got to the key first, and I gave it to my mother. With some effort, my mother managed to unlock the great iron door. The door slowly yielded as the three of us pushed against it, and out from the darkness came that smell I would never come across again: decay, mold, dust, age, and stagnant air. On the coat rack next to the door—to make the frequent robbers think there was a man in the house—my grandmother had left my grandfather's felt hat and his fur-collared coat, and in the corner were the boots that always scared me so.

A little later, at the end of two straight flights of wooden stairs, far, far away, standing in a while light, we saw our grandmother. She looked like a ghost, standing perfectly still in the shadows with her cane, lit only by the light filtering through the frosted Art Deco doors.

As she walked up the creaking stairs, my mother said nothing to my grandmother. (Sometimes she would say, "How are you, darling Mother?" or "Mother dear, I've missed you; it's very cold out, dear Mother!") When I reached the top of the stairs, I kissed my grandmother's hand, trying not to look at her face, or the huge mole on her wrist. But still we were frightened by the lone tooth in her mouth, her long chin, and the whiskers on her face, so once we were in the room we huddled next to our mother. My grandmother went back to the bed, where she spent most of the day in her long nightgown and her woolen vest, and she smiled at us, giving us a look that said, All right, now entertain me.

"Your stove isn't working so well, Mother," said my mother. She took the poker and stirred the coals.

175 My grandmother waited for a while, and then she said, "Leave the stove alone now. Give me some news. What's going on in the world?"

"Nothing at all," said my mother, sitting at our side.

"You have nothing to tell me at all?"

"Nothing at all, Mother dear."

After a short silence, my grandmother asked, "Haven't you seen anyone?"

180 "You know that already, Mother dear."

"For God's sake, have you no news?"

There was a silence.

"Grandmother, we had our inoculations at school," I said.

"Is that so?" said my grandmother, opening up her large blue eyes as if she were surprised. "Did it hurt?"

185 "My arm still hurts," said my brother.

"Oh, dear," said my grandmother with a smile.

There was another long silence. My brother and I got up and looked out the window at the hills in the distance, the mulberry trees, and the empty old chicken coop in the back garden.

"Don't you have any stories for me at all?" pleaded my grandmother. "You go up to see the mother-in-law. Doesn't anyone else?"

"Dilruba Hamm came yesterday afternoon," said my mother. "They played bezique with the children's grandmother."

190 In a rejoicing voice, our grandmother then said what we'd expected: "That's the palace lady!"

We knew she was talking not about one of the cream-colored palaces we read so much about in fairy tales and newspapers in those years but about Dolmabahçe Palace; it was only much later I realized that my grandmother looked down on Dilruba Hamm—who had come from the last sultan's harem—because she had been a concubine before marrying a businessman, and that she also looked down on my grandmother for having befriended this woman. Then they moved to another subject that they discussed every time my mother visited: Once a week, my grandmother would go to Beyoğlu to lunch alone at a famous and expensive restaurant called Aptullah Efendi, and afterward she would complain at great length about everything she'd eaten. She opened the third ready-made topic by asking us this question: "Children, does your other grandmother make you eat parsley?"

We answered with one voice, saying what our mother told us to say. "No, Grandmother, she doesn't."

As always, our grandmother told us how she'd seen a cat peeing on parsley in a garden, and how it was highly likely that the same parsley had ended up barely washed in some idiot's food, and how she was still arguing about this with the greengrocers of Şişli and Nişantaşi.

"Mother dear," said my mother, "the children are getting bored; they want to take a look at the other rooms. I'm going to open up the room next door."

195 My grandmother locked all the rooms in the house from the outside, to keep any thief who might enter through a window from reaching any other room in the house. My mother opened up the large cold room that looked out on the avenue with the streetcar line, and for a moment

she stood there with us, looking at the armchairs and the divans under their dust covers, the rusty, dusty lamps, trays, and chairs, the bundles of old newspaper; at the worn saddle and the drooping handlebars of the creaky girl's bicycle listing in the corner. But she did not take anything out of the trunk to show us, as she had done on happier days. ("Your mother used to wear these sandals when she was little, children; look at your aunt's school uniform, children; would you like to see your mother's childhood piggy bank, children?")

"If you get cold, come and tell me," she said, and then she left.

My brother and I ran to the window to look at the mosque and the streetcar in the square. Then we read about old football matches in the newspapers. "I'm bored," I said. "Do you want to play Tops or Bottoms?"

"The defeated wrestler still wants to fight," said my brother, without looking up from his newspaper. "I'm reading the paper."

We'd played again that morning, and my brother had won again.

200   "Please."

"I have one condition: If I win, you have to give me two pictures, and, if you win, I only give you one."

"No, one."

"Then I'm not playing," said my brother. "As you can see, I'm reading the paper."

He held the paper just like the English detective in a black-and white film we'd seen recently at the Angel Theater. After looking out the window a little longer, I agreed to my brother's conditions. We took our Famous People cards from our pockets and began to play. First I won, but then I lost seventeen more cards.

205   "When we play this way, I always lose," I said. "I'm not playing anymore unless we go back to the old rules."

"Okay," said my brother, still imitating that detective. "I wanted to read those newspapers anyway."

For a while I looked out the window. I carefully counted my pictures: I had 121 left. When my father left the day before, I'd had 183! But I didn't want to think about it. I had agreed to my brother's conditions.

In the beginning, I'd been winning, but then he started winning again. Hiding his joy, he didn't smile when he took my cards and added them to his pack.

"If you want, we can play by some other rules," he said, a while later. "Whoever wins takes one card. If I win, I can choose which card I take from you. Because I don't have any of some of them, and you never give me those."

210   Thinking I would win, I agreed. I don't know how it happened. Three times in a row I lost my high card to his, and before I knew it I had lost both my Greta Garbos (21) and my only King Faruk (78). I wanted to take them all back at once, so the game got bigger: This was how a great many other cards I had and he didn't—Einstein (63), Rumi (3), Sarkis Nazaryan, the founder of Mambo Chewing Gum-Candied Fruit Company (100), and Cleopatra (51)—passed over to him in only two rounds.

I couldn't even swallow. Because I was afraid I might cry, I ran to the window and looked outside: How beautiful everything had seemed only five minutes earlier—the streetcar approaching the terminus, the apartment buildings visible in the distance through the branches that were losing their leaves, the dog lying on the cobblestones, scratching himself so lazily! If only time had stopped. If only we could go back five squares as we did when we played Horse Race Dice. I was never playing Tops or Bottoms with my brother again.

"Shall we play again?" I said, without taking my forehead off the windowpane.

"I'm not playing," said my brother. "You'll only cry."

"Cevat, I promise. I won't cry," I insisted, as I went to his side. "But we have to play the way we did at the beginning, by the old rules."

215   "I'm going to read my paper."

"Okay," I said. I shuffled my thinner-than-ever stack. "with the old rules. Tops or Bottoms?"

"No crying," he said. "Okay, high."

I won and he gave me one of his Field Marshal Fevzi Çakmaks. I wouldn't take it. "Can you please give me seventy-eight, King Faruk?"

"No," he said. "That isn't what we agreed."

220   We played two more rounds, and I lost. If only I hadn't played that third round: When I gave him my 49, Napoleon, my hand was shaking.

"I'm not playing anymore," said my brother.

I pleaded. We played two more rounds, and instead of giving him the pictures he asked for, I threw all the cards I had left at his head and into the air: the cards I had been collecting for two and a half months, thinking about each and every one of them every single day, hiding them and nervously accumulating them with care—number 28, Mae West, and 82, Jules Verne; 7, Mehmet the Conqueror, and 70, Queen Elizabeth; 41, Celal Salik the columnist, and 42, Voltaire—they went flying through the air to scatter all over the floor.

If only I was in a completely different place, in a completely different life. Before I went back into my grandmother's room, I crept quietly down the creaky stairs, thinking about a distant relative who had worked in insurance and committed suicide. My father's mother had told me that suicides stayed in a dark place underground and never went to Heaven. When I'd gone a long way down the stairs, I stopped to stand in the darkness. I turned around and went upstairs and sat on the last step, next to my grandmother's room.

"I'm not well off like your mother-in-law," I heard my grandmother say. "You are going to look after your children and wait."

225 "But please, Mother dear, I beg you. I want to come back here with the children," my mother said.

"You can't live here with two children, not with all this dust and ghosts and thieves," said my grandmother.

"Mother dear," said my mother, "don't you remember how happily we lived here, just the two of us, after my sisters got married and my father passed away?"

"My lovely Mebrure, all you did all day was to leaf through old issues of your father's *Illustrations*."

"If I lit the big stove downstairs, this house would be cosy and warm in the space of two days."

230 "I told you not to marry him, didn't I?" said my grandmother.

"If I bring in a maid, it will only take us two days to get rid of all this dust," said my mother.

"I'm not letting any of those thieving maids into this house," said my grandmother. "Anyway, it would take six months to sweep out all this dust

and cobwebs. By then your errant husband will be back home again."

"Is that you last word, Mother dear?" my mother asked.

"Mebrure, my lovely girl, if you came here with your two children what would we live on, the four of us?"

235 "Mother dear, how many times have I asked you—pleaded with you—to sell the lots in Bebek before they're expropriated?"

"I'm not going to the deeds office to give those dirty men my signature and my picture."

"Mother dear, please don't say this: My older sister and I brought a notary right to your door," said my mother, raising her voice.

"I've never trusted that notary," said my grandmother. "You can see from his face that he's a swindler. Maybe he isn't even a notary. And don't shout at me like that."

"All right, then, Mother dear, I won't!" said my mother. She called into the room for us. "Children, children, come on now, gather up your things; we're leaving."

240 "Slow down!" said my grandmother. "We haven't even said two words."

"You don't want us, Mother dear," my mother whispered.

"Take this, let the children have some Turkish delight."

"They shouldn't eat it before lunch," said my mother, and as she left the room she passed behind me to enter the room opposite. "Who threw these pictures all over the floor? Pick them up at once. And you help him," she said to my brother.

As we silently gathered the pictures, my mother lifted the lids of the old trunks and looked at the dresses from her childhood, her ballet costumes, the boxes. The dust underneath the black skeleton of the pedal sewing machine filled my nostrils, making my eyes water, filling my nose,

245 As we washed our hands in the little lavatory, my grandmother pleaded in a soft voice. "Mebrure dear, you take this teapot; you love it so much, you have a right to," she said. "My grandfather brought it for my dear mother when he was the governor

of Damascus. It came all the way from China. Please take it."

"Mother dear, from now on I don't want anything from you," my mother said. "And put that into your cupboard or you'll break it. Come, children, kiss your grandmother's hand."

"My little Mebrure, my lovely daughter, please don't be angry at your poor mother," said my grandmother, as she let us kiss her hand. "Please don't leave me here without any visitors, without anyone."

We raced down the stairs, and when the three of us had pushed open the heavy metal door, we were greeted by brilliant sunlight as we breathed in the clean air.

"Shut the door firmly behind you!" cried my grandmother. "Mebrure, you'll come to see me again this week, won't you?"

250   As we walked hand in hand with my mother, no one spoke. We listened in silence as the other passengers coughed and waited for the streetcar to leave. When finally we began to move, my brother and I moved to the next row, saying we wanted to watch the conductor, and began to play Tops or Bottoms. First I lost some cards, then I won a few back. When I upped the ante, he happily agreed, and I quickly began to lose again. When we had reached the Osmanbey stop, my brother said, "In exchange for all the pictures you have left, here is this Fifteen you want so much."

I played and lost. Without letting him see, I removed two cards from the stack before handing it to my brother. I went to the back row to sit with my mother. I wasn't crying. I looked sadly out the window as the streetcar moaned and slowly gathered speed, and I watched them pass us by, all those people and places that are gone forever: the little sewing shops, the bakeries, the pudding shops with their awnings, the Tan cinema where we saw those films about ancient Rome, the children standing along the wall next to the front selling used comics, the barber with the sharp scissors who scared me so, and the half-naked neighborhood madman, always standing in the barbershop door.

We got off at Harbiye. As we walked toward home, my brother's satisfied silence was driving me mad. I took out the Lindbergh, which I'd hidden in my pocket.

This was his first sight of it. "Ninety-one: Lindbergh!" he read in admiration. "With the plane he flew across the Atlantic! Where did you find this?"

"I didn't have my injection yesterday," I said. "I went home early, and I saw Daddy before he left. Daddy bought it for me."

255   "Then half is mine," he said. "In fact, when we played that last game, the deal was you'd give me all the pictures you had left." He tried to grab the picture from my hand, but he couldn't manage it. He caught my wrist, and he twisted it so badly that I kicked his leg. We laid into each other.

"Stop!" said my mother. "Stop! We're in the middle of the street!"

We stopped. A man in a suit and a woman wearing a hat passed us. I felt ashamed for having fought in the street. My brother took two steps and fell to the ground. "It hurts so much," he said, holding his leg.

"Stand up," whispered my mother. "Come on now, stand up. Everyone's watching."

My brother stood up and began to hop down the road like a wounded soldier in a film. I was afraid he was really hurt, but I was still glad to see him that way. After we had walked for some time in silence, he said, "Just you see what happens when we get home. Mummy, Ali didn't have his injection yesterday."

260   "I did too, Mummy!"

"Be quiet!" my mother shouted.

We were now just across from our house. We waited for the streetcar coming up from Maçka to pass before we crossed the street. After it came a truck, a clattering Beşiktaş bus spewing great clouds of exhaust, and, in the opposite direction, a light violet De Soto. That was when I saw my uncle looking down at the street from the window. He didn't see me; he was staring at the passing cars. For a long time, I watched him.

The road had long since cleared. I turned to my mother, wondering why she had not yet taken our hands and crossed us over to other side, and saw that she was silently crying.

[1999]

1. How would you characterize the boys' relationship to their father? To their mother? Who are the Famous People?

2. What is the Tops and Bottoms game?

3. What is the relationship between the world of the two boys and the events in the adult world around them?

4. Describe the differences between the mother's home, the paternal grandmother's apartment upstairs, and the maternal grandmother's house. Why won't the grandmother allow the mother to move back in with her?

5. Compare Pamuk's depiction of the father in this story with the depiction of his father in "My Father's Suitcase."

JULIO CORTÁZAR 1914–1984

European Jews were both part of and estranged from their own culture; exiles such as the Argentinean writer Julio Cortázar (for his biography, see p. 248), who lived the final three decades of his life in Paris, France, also had a highly ambivalent relationship to a land that, while it attracted and repelled them, could never replace the home they had left behind. As you read "Axolotl," consider the way Cortázar uses the image of a Mexican salamander to evoke the sense of estrangement of the exile.

AXOLOTL

Translated by Paul Blackburn

THERE WAS A TIME WHEN I THOUGHT A GREAT DEAL about the axolotls. I went to see them in the aquarium at the Jardin des Plantes and stayed for hours watching them, observing their immobility, their faint movements. Now I am an axolotl.

I got to them by chance one spring morning when Paris was spreading its peacock tail after a wintry Lent. I was heading down the boulevard Port-Royal, then I took Saint-Marcel and L' Hôpital and saw green among all that grey and remembered the lions. I was friend of the lions and panthers, but had never gone into the dark, humid building that was the aquarium. I left my bike against the gratings and went to look at the tulips. The lions were sad and ugly and my panther was asleep. I decided on the aquarium, looked obliquely at banal fish until, unexpectedly, I hit it off with the axolotls. I stayed watching them for an hour and left, unable to think of anything else.

In the library at Sainte-Geneviève, I consulted a dictionary and learned that axolotls are the larval stage (provided with gills) of a species of salamander of the genus Ambystoma. That they were Mexican I knew already by looking at them and their little pink Aztec faces and the placard at the top of the tank. I read that specimens of them had been found in Africa capable of living on dry land during the periods of drought, and continuing their life under water when the rainy season came. I found their Spanish name, *ajolote,* and the mention that they were edible, and that their oil was used (no longer used, it said) like cod-liver oil.

I didn't care to look up any of the specialized works, but the next day I went back to the Jardin des Plantes. I began to go every morning, morning and afternoon some days. The aquarium guard

Photograph of an Axolotl, a large (6–18 inches) species of salamander native to the lake now covered over by Mexico City. The larvae of the axolotl are neotenic, meaning that they are able to mature into adults without undergoing the metamorphosis from water-breathing to air-breathing form typical of amphibians.

smiled perplexedly taking my ticket. I would lean up against the iron bar in front of the tanks and set to watching them. There's nothing strange in this, because after the first minute I knew that we were linked, that something infinitely lost and distant kept pulling us together. It had been enough to detain me that first morning in front of the sheet of glass where some bubbles rose through the water. The axolotls huddled on the wretched narrow (only I can know how narrow and wretched) floor of moss and stone in the tank. There were nine specimens, and the majority pressed their heads against the glass, looking with their eyes of gold at whoever came near them. Disconcerted, almost ashamed, I felt it a lewdness to be peering at these silent and immobile figures heaped at the bottom of the tank. Mentally I isolated one, situated on the right and somewhat apart from the others, to study it better. I saw a rosy little body, translucent (I thought of those Chinese figurines of milky glass), looking like a small lizard about six inches long, ending in a fish's tail of extraordinary delicacy, the most sensitive part of our body. Along the back ran a transparent fin which joined with the tail, but what obsessed me was the feet, of the slenderest nicety, ending in tiny fingers with minutely human nails. And then I discovered its eyes, its face. Inexpressive features, with no other trait save the eyes, two orifices, like brooches, wholly of transparent gold, lacking any life but looking, letting themselves be penetrated by my look, which seemed to travel past the golden level and lose itself in a diaphanous interior mystery. A very slender black halo ringed the eye and etched it onto the pink flesh, on to the rosy stone of the head, vaguely triangular, but with curved and irregular sides which gave it a total likeness to a statuette corroded by time. The mouth was masked by the triangular plane of the face, its considerable size would be guessed only in profile; in front a delicate crevice barely slit the lifeless stone. On both sides of the head where the ears should have been, there grew three tiny sprigs red as coral, a vegetal outgrowth, the gills, I suppose. And they were the only thing quick about it; every ten or fifteen seconds the sprigs pricked up stiffly and again subsided. Once in a while a foot would barely move, I saw the diminutive toes poise mildly on the moss. It's that we don't enjoy moving a lot, and the tank is so cramped—we barely move in any direction and we're hitting one of the others with our tail or our head—difficulties arise, fights, tiredness. The time feels like it's less if we stay quietly.

5   It was their quietness that made me lean toward them fascinated the first time I saw the axolotls. Obscurely I seemed to understand their secret will, to abolish space and time with an indifferent immobility. I knew better later; the gill contraction, the tentative reckoning of the delicate feet on the stones, the abrupt swimming (some of them swim with a simple undulation of the body) proved to me that they were capable of escaping that mineral lethargy in which they spent whole hours. Above all else, their eyes obsessed me. In the standing tanks on either side of them, different fishes showed me the simple stupidity of their handsome eyes so similar to our own. The eyes of the axolotls spoke to me of the presence of a different life, of another way of seeing. Glueing my face to the glass (the guard would cough fussily once in a while), I tried to see better those diminutive golden points, that entrance to the infinitely slow and remote world of these rosy creatures. It was useless to tap with one finger on the glass directly in front of their faces: they never gave the least reaction. The golden eyes continued burning with their soft, terrible light; they continued looking at me from an unfathomable depth which made me dizzy.

And nevertheless they were close. I knew it before this, before being an axolotl. I learned it the day I came near them for the first time. The anthropomorphic features of a monkey reveal the reverse of what most people believe, the distance that is traveled from them to us. The absolute lack of similarity between axolotls and human beings proved to me that my recognition was valid, that I was not propping myself up with easy analogies. Only the little hands . . . But an eft, the common newt, has such hands also, and we are not at all alike. I think it was the axolotls' heads, that triangular pink shape with the tiny eyes of gold. That looked and knew. That laid the claim. They were not *animals.*

It would seem easy, almost obvious, to fall into mythology. I began seeing in the axolotls a metamorphosis which did not succeed in revoking a mysterious humanity. I imagined them aware, slaves of their bodies, condemned infinitely to the silence of the abyss, to a hopeless meditation. Their blind gaze, the diminutive gold disc without expression and nonetheless terribly shining, went through me like a message: "Save us, save us." I caught myself mumbling words of advice, conveying childish hopes. They continued to look at me, immobile; from time to time the rosy branches of the gills stiffened. In that instant I felt a muted pain; perhaps they were seeing me, attracting my strength to penetrate into the impenetrable thing of their lives. They were not human beings, but I had found in no animal such a profound relation with myself. The axolotls were like witnesses of something, and at times like horrible judges. I felt ignoble in front of them; there was such a terrifying purity in those transparent eyes. They were larvas, but larva means disguise and also phantom. Behind those Aztec faces, without expression but of an implacable cruelty, what semblance was awaiting its hour?

I was afraid of them. I think that had it not been for feeling the proximity of other visitors and the guard, I would not have been bold enough to remain alone with them. "You eat them alive with your eyes, hey," the guard said, laughing; he likely thought I was a little cracked. What he didn't notice was that it was they devouring me slowly with their eyes, in a cannibalism of gold. At any distance from the aquarium, I had only to think of them, it was as though I were being affected from a distance. It got to the point that I was going every day, and at night I thought of them immobile in the darkness, slowly putting a hand out which immediately encountered another. Perhaps their eyes could see in the dead of night, and for them the day continued indefinitely. The eyes of axolotls have no lids.

I know now that there was nothing strange, that that had to occur. Leaning over in front of the tank each morning, the recognition was greater. They were suffering, every fiber of my body reached toward that stifled pain, that stiff torment at the bottom of the tank. They were lying in wait for something, a remote dominion destroyed, an age of liberty when the world had been that of the axolotls. Not possible that such a terrible expression which attaining the overthrow of that forced blankness on their stone faces should carry any message other than one of pain, proof of that eternal sentence, of that liquid hell they were undergoing. Hopelessly, I wanted to prove to myself that my own sensibility was projecting a nonexistent consciousness upon the axolotls. They and I knew. So there was nothing strange in what happened. My face was pressed against the glass of the aquarium, my eyes were attempting once more to penetrate the mystery of those eyes of gold without iris, without pupil. I saw, from very close up the face of an axolotl immobile next to the glass. No transition and no surprise, I saw my face against the glass, I saw it on the outside of the tank, I saw it on the other side of the glass. Then my face drew back and I understood.

10   Only one thing was strange: to go on thinking as usual, to know. To realize that was, for the first moment, like the horror of a man buried alive awaking to his fate. Outside, my face came close to the glass again, I saw my mouth, the lips compressed with the effort of understanding the axolotls. I was an axolotl and now I knew instantly that no understanding was possible. He was outside the aquarium, his thinking was a thinking outside the tank. Recognizing him, being him himself, I was an axolotl and in my world.

The horror began—I learned in the same moment—of believing myself prisoner in the body of an axolotl, metamorphosed into him with my human mind intact, buried alive in an axolotl, condemned to move lucidly among unconscious creatures. But that stopped when a foot just grazed my face, when I moved just a little to one side and saw an axolotl next to me who was looking at me, and understood that he knew also, no communication possible, but very clearly. Or I was also in him, or all of us were thinking humanlike, incapable of expression, limited to the golden splendor of our eyes looking at the face of the man pressed against the aquarium.

He returned many times, but he comes less often now. Weeks pass without his showing up. I saw him yesterday, he looked at me for a long time and left briskly. It seemed to me that he was not so much interested in us any more, that he was coming out of habit. Since the only thing I do is think, I could think about him a lot. It occurs to me that at the beginning we continued to communicate, that he felt more than ever one with the mystery which was claiming him. But the bridges were broken between him and me, because what was his obsession is now an axolotl, alien to his human life. I think that at the beginning I was capable of returning to him in a certain way—ah, only in a certain way—and of keeping awake his desire to know us better. I am an axolotl for good now, and if I think like a man it's only because every axolotl thinks like a man inside his rosy stone semblance. I believe that all this succeeded in communicating something to him in those first days, when I was still he. And in this final solitude to which he no longer comes, I console myself by thinking that perhaps he is going to write a story about us, that, believing he's making up a story, he's going to write all this about axolotls.

[1956]

QUESTIONS FOR REFLECTION AND DISCUSSION

1. What fascinates the narrator about the axolotl? How does that fascination develop into an obsession?

2. How does the fact of the axolotl's Mexican origin develop into a key image as the story unfolds? What other themes and images become associated with it?

3. Describe the specific character of the narrator's transformation. What motivates it? How does it occur? As opposed to many literary transformations, the narrator remains present in body even as he is transformed into an axolotl. How does this double identity function within the context of the story? What is the relationship between the man and the axolotl? Which one is narrating the story?

4. What insight or new perspective does the narrator gain from his transformation? What does he lose?

POETRY

ELENI FOURTOUNI B. 1933

Issues of the past and of national identity haunt the poetry of Eleni Fourtouni and many other writers, like Czesław Miłosz, working through the scars that mark their countries. Born in a village in Laconia, the Greek province once home to Sparta, as a child Fourtouni lived through Nazi occupation and civil war. After attending school in Athens, she went to college in Maine and Connecticut, and now splits her time between New Haven and the Greek island of Aegina. In addition to her own poetry composed in English, she has edited and translated memoirs of women fighters in the resistance and contemporary poems by Greek women.

Child's Memory

Every time I think of it
there's a peculiar tickle
at my throat
especially when I clean fish—
the fish my blond son brings me   5
proud of his catch—
and I must cut off the heads

my hand holding the knife hesitates—
that peculiar tickle again—
I set the knife aside   10
furtively I scratch my throat

then I bring the knife down
on the thick scaly neck—
not much of a neck really—
just below the gills   15
I hack at the slippery
hulk of bass
my throat itches
my hands stink fish

they drip blood   20
my knife cuts through

the great head is off
I breathe

Once again the old image comes
into focus—   25
the proud blond soldier
his polished black boots
his spotless green uniform
his smile
the sack he lugs   30
into the schoolyards

the children gather
the soldier dips his hand inside
the sack
the children hold their breath
what is it what?   35
their ink-smudged hands fly to their eyes

but we're full of curiosity
between our spread fingers we see . . .

the soldier's laughter is loud
as he pulls out   40
the heads of two Greek partisans.

quickly I rinse the blood off my knife

[1978]

Europe in the twentieth century. Anticommunist
militiamen display the heads of their partisan victims
during the Greek Civil War. (1946–1949).

QUESTIONS FOR REFLECTION AND DISCUSSION

1. What is happening in the present of "Child's Memory"? What
   happened in the past?

2. In what way do the events of the present resemble the
   childhood memory described by the speaker? In what way
   are they different?

3. How is the poem punctuated? How does the punctuation
   reflect the movement and theme of the poem?

4. What does the poem tell us about memory? What does it tell
   us about the relationship between the past and the present
   in a broader sense?

CZESŁAW MIŁOSZ 1911–2004

Born in Lithuania, Czesław Miłosz was leader of an avant-garde poetry movement in the Polish language during the 1930s, and fought with the resistance in Warsaw during World War II. Following the war, he served as cultural attaché to the Communist government of Poland before defecting to the West in 1951. After a decade in Paris, he accepted a position at the University of California, Berkeley, where he lived for the rest of his life, splitting time with a home in Kraków after 1989. Author of fiction and nonfiction as well as being considered one of the greatest Polish poets of the century, Miłosz was awarded the Nobel Prize in Literature in 2001. In "My Faithful Mother Tongue," he examines the exile's ambivalence with his native tongue and the history and memories embedded within it, exhibiting Miłosz's gift of combining lyric observation with attention to individual experience and greater historical forces.

My Faithful Mother Tongue

Faithful mother tongue
I have been serving you.
Every night, I used to set before you
   little bowls of colors
so you could have your birch, your
   cricket, your finch
as preserved in my memory.   5

This lasted many years.
You were my native land; I lacked any other.
I believed that you would also be a messenger
between me and some good people
even if they were few, twenty, ten   10
or not born, as yet.

Now, I confess my doubt.
There are moments when it seems to me I
   have squandered my life.
For you are a tongue of the debased,
of the unreasonable, hating themselves   15
even more than they hate other nations,
a tongue of informers,
a tongue of the confused,
ill with their own innocence.

But without you, who am I?   20
Only a scholar in a distant country,
a success, without fears and humiliations.
Yes, who am I without you?
Just a philosopher, like everyone else.

I understand, this is meant as my education: 25
the glory of individuality is taken away,
Fortune spreads a red carpet
before the sinner in a morality play
while on the linen backdrop a magic lantern throws
images of human and divine torture.   30

Faithful mother tongue,
perhaps after all it's I who must try to save you.
So I will continue to set before you little bowls of
    colors bright and pure if possible,
for what is needed in misfortune is a little order and
    beauty.

                                    [1968]

QUESTIONS FOR REFLECTION AND DISCUSSION

1. In what ways does Miłosz draw out the figurative meaning of "mother" in the phrase "mother tongue"? How are the "little bowls of color" related to this meaning?

2. What, for the speaker, is the relationship between the mother tongue and the native land?

3. What is the paradox of the mother tongue that the speaker discusses in the third and fourth stanzas?

4. Compare the first and last stanzas. What has changed in the speaker's attitude? What remains the same?

WORKING FURTHER WITH THE LITERATURE OF EUROPE

1. Write an essay on the different images of identity (either personal or national) used in the selections in this casebook.

2. Write an essay comparing the role of memory in several of the readings in this casebook.

3. Choose one of the authors in this casebook, research his or her life, and write an essay comparing the facts of that life with the text you have read.

4. Write a research paper on a topic related to one of the readings in this casebook and how that topic is reflected in the reading.

5. Basing yourself on the selections in this casebook, write an argument essay on what it means (if anything) to be European.

THE LITERATURE OF EUROPE FURTHER READINGS IN *LITERATURE: A WORLD OF WRITING*

Henrik Ibsen, *A Doll's House* • Franz Kafka, "Before the Law" • Wisława Szymborska, "Lot's Wife" • Voltaire, "Plato's Dream"

CHAPTER 9

THE WORLDS AROUND US

BELIEFS
AND
ETHICS

A lthough we tend to consider gods and devils as antagonists in a battle between good and evil, in many religious traditions the gods are not entirely reliable and the devils can be helpful as often as deceitful. Even in the Christian tradition, we find the devil-figure Mephistopheles in Goethe's *Faust* describing himself as "part of that Power which would do evil constantly, and constantly does good." How we define what is good and what is evil also defines us as individuals and as members of a society; a primary way we make those definitions is through the gods and devils we profess to serve or choose to repudiate. Religions have always been especially concerned with the mystery of beginnings and endings, and this chapter includes readings and images depicting gods and humans of different religions performing their most important task— creation—and devils and humans of the world doing what they do best— destruction. As you read these selections, reflect on the way in which each reading approaches the problem of creation and destruction, and the relationship it suggests between good and evil in the world.

IMAGES OF GOOD AND EVIL IN THE WORLD

Artists in all cultures have long sought means of giving visual expression to the relationship between the different forces that appear to them to guide the world. We have included three images here that suggest three ways of thinking about the world in terms of opposing forces. As you study these images, consider the way in which each depiction of opposing forces suggests we approach our own lives and decisions.

THE LORD:

MEPHISTOPHELES:

Must you complain each time you come my way?
Is nothing right on your terrestrial scene?
No, sir! The earth's as bad as it has always been.
I really feel quite sorry for mankind;
Tormenting them myself's no fun, I find.

—J. W. GOETHE, *FAUST*

How do we know good from evil? The charismatic but murderous sham preacher Harry Powell (Robert Mitchum) shows off his paradoxical tattoos of "Love" and "Hate" in the 1955 film, *Night of the Hunter*.

Is it possible for the opposing forces that structure the world to harmonize with each other perfectly? This illustration presents a visual interpretation of the traditional balance of Yin and Yang in Asian religion and culture.

What is the relationship between creation, destruction, and the human imagination? The Netherlander artist Hieronymous Bosch's triptych (three-paneled painting), *The Garden of Earthly Delights* (1503–1504), depicts the biblical Garden of Eden, Hell, and a strange middle realm whose relation to the other two realms remains a matter of scholarly debate.

1. What, if anything, do the three images have in common?

2. In what different ways has each artist framed and defined opposite forces and the relationship between them?

3. How does each image suggest we approach the world around us and the way we live our lives?

BELIEFS: CREATION AND BEGINNINGS

Where we came from is a foundational question for individuals, societies, and the world itself. Although modern science has done its best to explain the origin of the universe, many would argue that religious documents have long provided a more satisfying, if often mysterious and unverifiable account of what happened. As you read the selections below reflect on what each account reveals about the culture to which it belongs: its hopes, its dreams, its fears, its philosophical concerns. You may find it helpful to consider these readings first as written texts and to analyze the arguments they are making and the rhetorical means they use to make those arguments. But remember also, no matter what your own faith (or lack thereof), that each of these texts has emerged from a context of profound belief. What is the nature of that belief and how has that belief affected the meaning of the text and the images within it? How does the meaning of that text change when read from outside the context of belief within which it was written?

> *In my end is my beginning.*
> —T. S. ELIOT, "EAST COKER"

SACRED TEXT

Genesis 1st millennium BCE

According to most biblical scholars today, Genesis was first written down during the time of King Solomon in the early tenth century BCE. Usually known as the Yahwist version, this is the source of the story of Adam and Eve in the garden of Eden in Chapters 2 and 3. Later writers revised this first version, adding the quite different vision of creation in Chapter 1. The text, as we have it today, appears to date from 500–450 BCE.

FROM GENESIS
King James Version

Chapter 1

In the beginning God created the heaven and the earth. And the earth was without form, and void; and darkness was upon the face of the deep. And the Spirit of God moved upon the face of the waters. And God said, "Let there be light." And there was light. And God saw the light, that it was good: and God divided the light from the darkness. And God called the light Day, and the darkness he called Night. And the evening and the morning were the first day. And God said, "Let there be a firmament in the midst of the waters, and let it divide the waters from the waters." And God made the firmament, and divided the waters which were under the firmament from the waters which were above the firmament: and it was so. And God called the firmament Heaven. And the evening and the morning were the second day. And God said, "Let the waters under the heaven be gathered together unto one place, and let the dry land appear." And it was so. And God called the dry land Earth; and the gathering together of the waters called he Seas: and God saw that it was good. And God said, "Let the earth bring forth grass, the herb yielding seed, and the fruit tree yielding fruit after his kind, whose seed is in itself, upon the earth." And it was so. And the earth brought forth grass, and herb yielding seed after his kind, and the tree yielding fruit, whose seed was in itself, after his kind: and God saw that it was good. And the evening and the morning were the third day. And God said, "Let there be lights in the firmament of the heaven to divide the day from the night; and let them be for signs, and for seasons, and for days, and years: And let them be for lights in the firmament of the heaven to give light upon the earth." And it was so. And God made two great lights; the greater light to rule the day, and the lesser light to rule the night: he made the stars also. And God set them in the firmament of the heaven to give light upon the earth, And to rule over the day and over the night, and to divide the light from the darkness: and God saw that it was good. And the evening and the morning were the fourth day. And God said, "Let the waters bring forth abundantly the moving creature that hath life, and fowl that may fly above the earth in the open firmament of heaven." And God created great whales, and every living creature that moveth, which the waters brought forth abundantly, after their kind, and every winged fowl after his kind: and God saw that it was good. And God blessed them, saying, "Be fruitful, and multiply, and fill the waters in the seas, and let fowl multiply in the earth." And the evening and the morning were the fifth day. And God said, "Let the earth bring forth the living creature after his kind, cattle, and creeping thing, and beast of the earth after his kind." And it was so. And God made the beast of the earth after his kind, and cattle after their kind, and every thing that creepeth upon the earth after his kind: and God saw that it was good.

And God said, "Let us make man in our image, after our likeness: and let them have dominion over the fish of the sea, and over the fowl of the air, and over the cattle, and over all the earth, and over every creeping thing that creepeth upon the earth."

So God created man in his own image,
in the image of God created he him;
male and female created he them.

And God blessed them, and God said unto them, "Be fruitful, and multiply, and replenish the earth, and subdue it: and have dominion over the fish of the sea, and over the fowl of the air, and over every living thing that moveth upon the earth." And God said, "Behold, I have given you every herb bearing seed, which is upon the face of all the earth, and every tree, in the which is the fruit of a tree yielding seed; to you it shall be for meat. And to every beast of the earth, and to every fowl of the air, and to every thing that creepeth upon the earth, wherein there is life, I have given every green herb for meat." And it was so. And God saw every thing that he had made, and, behold, it was very good. And the evening and the morning were the sixth day.

Chapter 2

Thus the heavens and the earth were finished, and all the host of them. And on the seventh day God ended his work which he had made; and he rested on the seventh day from all his work which he had made. And God blessed the seventh day, and sanctified it: because that in it he had rested from all his work which God created and made.

These are the generations of the heavens and of the earth when they were created, in the day that the LORD God made the earth and the heavens, And every plant of the field before it was in the earth, and every herb of the field before it grew: for the LORD God had not caused it to rain upon the earth, and there was not a man to till the ground. But there went up a mist from the earth, and watered the whole face of the ground. And the LORD God formed man of the dust of the ground, and breathed into his nostrils the breath of life; and man became a living soul. And the LORD God planted a garden eastward in Eden; and there he put the man whom he had formed. And out of the ground made the LORD God to grow every tree that is pleasant to the sight, and good for food; the tree of life also in the midst of the garden, and the tree of knowledge of good and evil. And a river went out of Eden to water the garden; and from thence it was parted, and became into four heads. The name of the first is Pison: that is it which compasseth the whole land of Havilah, where there is gold; And the gold of that land is good: there is bdellium and the onyx stone. And the name of the second river is Gihon: the same is it that compasseth the whole land of Ethiopia. And the name of the third river is Hiddekel: that is it which goeth toward the east of Assyria. And the fourth river is Euphrates. And the LORD God took the man, and put him into the garden of Eden to dress it and to keep it. And the LORD God commanded the man, saying, "Of every tree of the garden thou mayest freely eat: But of the tree of the knowledge of good and evil, thou shalt not eat of it: for in the day that thou eatest thereof thou shalt surely die."

5   And the LORD God said, "It is not good that the man should be alone; I will make him an help meet for him." And out of the ground the LORD God formed every beast of the field, and every fowl of the air; and brought them unto Adam to see what he would call them: and whatsoever Adam called every living creature, that was the name thereof. And Adam gave names to all cattle, and to the fowl of the air, and to every beast of the field; but for Adam there was not found an help meet for him. And the LORD God caused a deep sleep to fall upon Adam and he slept: and he took one of his ribs, and closed up the flesh instead thereof; And the rib, which the LORD God had taken from man, made he a woman, and brought her unto the man. And Adam said,

"This is now bone of my bones,
and flesh of my flesh:
she shall be called Woman,
because she was taken out of Man."

Therefore shall a man leave his father and his mother, and shall cleave unto his wife: and they shall be one flesh. And they were both naked, the man and his wife, and were not ashamed.

Chapter 3

Now the serpent was more subtile than any beast of the field which the LORD God had made. And he said unto the woman, "Yea, hath God said, Ye shall not eat of every tree of the garden?" And the woman said unto the serpent, "We may eat of the fruit of the trees of the garden: But of the fruit of the tree which is in the midst of the garden, God hath said, Ye shall not eat of it, neither shall ye touch it, lest ye die." And the serpent said unto the woman, "Ye shall not surely die: For God doth know that in the day ye eat thereof, then your eyes shall be opened, and ye shall be as gods, knowing good and evil." And when the woman saw that the tree was good for food, and that it was pleasant to the eyes, and a tree to be desired to make one wise, she took of the fruit thereof, and did eat, and gave also unto her husband with her; and he did eat. And the eyes of them both were opened, and they knew that they were naked; and they sewed fig leaves together, and made themselves aprons.

And they heard the voice of the LORD God walking in the garden in the cool of the day: and Adam and his wife hid themselves from the presence of the LORD God amongst the trees of the garden. And the LORD God called unto Adam, and said unto him, "Where art thou?" And he said, "I heard thy voice in the garden, and I was afraid, because I was naked; and I hid myself." And he said, "Who told thee that thou wast naked? Hast thou eaten of the tree, whereof I commanded thee that thou shouldest not eat?" And the man said, "The woman whom thou gavest to be with me, she gave me of the tree, and I did eat." And the LORD God said unto the woman, "What is this that thou hast done?" And the woman said, "The serpent beguiled me, and I did eat." And the LORD God said unto the serpent, "Because thou hast done this,

thou art cursed above all cattle,
and above every beast of the field;
upon thy belly shalt thou go,
and dust shalt thou eat all the days of thy
    life:
And I will put enmity between thee and the
    woman,
and between thy seed and her seed;
it shall bruise thy head,
and thou shalt bruise his heel."

Unto the woman he said,

"I will greatly multiply thy sorrow and thy
    conception;
in sorrow thou shalt bring forth children;
and thy desire shall be to thy husband,
and he shall rule over thee."

And unto Adam he said, "Because thou hast hearkened unto the voice of thy wife, and hast eaten of the tree, of which I commanded thee, saying, Thou shalt not eat of it:

cursed is the ground for thy sake;
in sorrow shalt thou eat of it all the days of
    thy life;
Thorns also and thistles shall it bring forth
    to thee;
and thou shalt eat the herb of the field;
In the sweat of thy face shalt thou eat bread,
till thou return unto the ground;
for out of it wast thou taken:
for dust thou art,
and unto dust shalt thou return."

And Adam called his wife's name Eve; because she was the mother of all living. Unto Adam also and to his wife did the LORD God make coats of skins, and clothed them. And the LORD God said, "Behold, the man is become as one of us, to know good and evil: and now, lest he put forth his hand, and take also of the tree of life, and eat, and live for ever." Therefore the LORD God sent him forth from the garden of Eden, to till the ground from whence he was taken. So he drove out the man; and he placed at the east of the garden of Eden Cherubims, and a flaming sword which turned every way, to keep the way of the tree of life.

[1st millennium BCE]

QUESTIONS FOR REFLECTION AND DISCUSSION

1. What natural phenomena and social conventions are based on the description of creation here?

2. What is the difference between the versions of the creation of Adam and Eve in Chapters 1 and 2 in Genesis? What are some possible functions of the repetition and the differences between the versions?

3. What are some of the qualities attributed to the Garden of Eden? What makes it paradise?

4. What causes Adam and Eve to eat the fruit? What are the consequences of their action?

SECULAR TEXTS

Voltaire 1694–1778

Self-described as a deist, or believer in God but not in organized religion, François-Marie Arouet, who published under the name Voltaire, was a major figure of the eighteenth-century Enlightenment. In "Plato's Dream," he holds the world as he saw it around him to the assertion in Genesis that "it was good," using as the basis of his satire the fifth-century BCE Greek philosopher, Plato, who held that the world was fundamentally perfect.

PLATO'S DREAM

IN ANCIENT TIMES, DREAMS WERE MUCH REVERED, and Plato was one of the greatest dreamers. His dream *The Republic* is deservedly famous, but the following little-known tale is perhaps his most amazing dream—or nightmare:

The great Demiurgos, the eternal geometer, having scattered throughout the immensity of space innumerable worlds, decided to test the knowledge of those lesser superbeings who were also his creations, and who had witnessed his works. He gave them each a small portion of matter to arrange, just as our own art teachers give their students a statue to carve, or a picture to paint, if we may compare small things to great.

Demogorgon received the lump of mold we call Earth, and having formed it as it now appears, thought he had created a masterpiece. He imagined he had silenced Envy herself, and expected to receive the highest praise, even from his brethren. How great was his surprise, when, at the presentation of his work, they hissed in disapploval!

One among them, more sarcastic than the rest, spoke:

5   "Truly you have performed mighty feats! You have divided your world into two parts; and, to prevent them from communicating with each other, placed a vast collection of waters between the two hemispheres. The inhabitants must perish with cold under

both your poles, and be scorched to death under the equator. You have, in your great prudence, formed immense deserts of sand, so all who travel over them may die with hunger and thirst. I have no fault to find with your cows, sheep, cocks, and hens; but can never be reconciled to your serpents and spiders. Your onions and artichokes are very good things, but I cannot conceive what induced you to scatter such a heap of poisonous plants over the face of the planet, unless it was to poison its inhabitants. Moreover, if I am not mistaken, you have created about 30 different kinds of monkeys, a still greater number of dogs, yet only four or five races of humans. It is true, indeed, you have bestowed on the latter of these animals a faculty you call Reason, but it is so poorly executed that you might better call it Folly. Besides, you do not seem to have shown any very great regard for this two-legged creature, seeing you have left him with so few means of defense; subjected him to so many disorders, and provided him with so few remedies; and formed him with such a multitude of passions, and so little wisdom and prudence to resist them. You certainly were not willing that there should remain any great number of these animals on Earth at once; for, over the course of a given year, smallpox will regularly carry off a tenth of the species, and sister maladies will taint the springs of life in the remainder; and then, as if this was not enough, you have so disposed things that half of those who survive are occupied in lawsuits, or cutting each other's throats. Yes, they must be infinitely grateful to you, and I must admit that you have executed a masterpiece."

Demogorgon blushed. He now realized there was much moral and physical evil in his work, but still believed it contained more good than ill.

"It is easy to find fault," he said; "but do you imagine it is so easy to form an animal, who, having the gift of reason and free will, shall not sometimes abuse his liberty? Do you think that, in rearing 10,000 plants, it is so easy to prevent some few from having noxious qualities? Do you suppose that, with a certain quantity of water, sand, and mud, you could make a globe without sea or desert?

"As for you, my sneering friend, I think you have just finished the planet Jupiter. Let us see now what figure you make with your great belts, and your long nights, with four moons to enlighten them. Let us examine your worlds, and see whether the inhabitants you have made are exempt from folly and disease."

Accordingly, his fellow entities examined the planet Jupiter, and were soon laughing at the laugher. He who had made Saturn did not escape without his share of censure, and his fellows, the makers of Mars, Mercury, and Venus, was each in his turn reproached.

10   They were in the midst of railing against and ridiculing each other, when the eternal Demiurgos thus imposed silence on them all:

"In your performances there is both good and bad, because you have a great share of understanding, but at the same time fall short of perfection. Your works will endure for only a few billion years, after which you will acquire more knowledge and perform much better. It belongs to me alone to create things perfect and immortal."

"Us, for example?" asked Demogorgon.

Demiurgos scowled, and with that Plato awoke.
Or did he?

[1756]

QUESTIONS FOR REFLECTION AND DISCUSSION

1. What are the main criticisms made of Demogorgon's creation by his fellows? To what degree, in your opinion, are they justified?

2. Is Demogorgon's response persuasive?

3. Explain the paradox of the concluding three sentences. What is the thrust of Demogorgon's response to Demiurgos? What would it mean if Plato had not awakened at the end of the tale?

Salman Rushdie b. 1947

Salman Rushdie's polemical essay on the place of religion in the contemporary world was written for an anthology of essays published on the occasion of the birth of the six billionth human inhabitant of the planet. According to the United Nations Population Fund, this occurred on January 25, 2006. Current estimates predict world population will reach nine billion in 2050.

IMAGINE THERE'S NO HEAVEN[1]
A LETTER TO THE SIX BILLIONTH WORLD CITIZEN

DEAR LITTLE SIX BILLIONTH LIVING PERSON,

As the newest member of a notoriously inquisitive species, you'll probably soon be asking the two sixty-four-thousand-dollar questions with which the other 5,999,999,999 of us have been wrestling for some time: How did we get here? And, now that we are here, how shall we live?

Oddly—as if six billion of us weren't enough to be going on with—it will almost certainly be suggested to you that the answer to the question of origins requires you to believe in the existence of a further, invisible, ineffable Being "somewhere up there," an omnipotent creator whom we poor limited creatures are unable even to perceive, much less to understand. That is, you will be strongly encouraged to imagine a heaven, with at least one god in residence. This sky-god, it's said, made the universe by churning its matter in a giant pot. Or, he danced. Or, he vomited Creation out of himself. Or, he simply called it into being, and lo, it Was. In some of the more interesting creation stories, the single mighty sky-god is subdivided into many lesser forces—junior deities, avatars, gigantic metamorphic "ancestors" whose adventures create the landscape, or the whimsical, wanton, meddling, cruel pantheons of the great polytheisms, whose wild doings will convince you that the real engine of creation was lust: for infinite power, for too easily broken human bodies, for clouds of glory. But it's only fair to add that there are also stories which offer the message that the primary creative impulse was, and is, love.

Many of these stories will strike you as extremely beautiful, and therefore seductive. Unfortunately, however, you will not be required to make a purely literary response to them. Only the stories of "dead" religions can be appreciated for their beauty. Living religions require much more of you. So you will be told that belief in "your" stories, and adherence to the rituals of worship that have grown up around them, must become a vital part of your life in the crowded world. They will be called the heart of your culture, even of your individual identity. It is possible that they may at some point come to feel inescapable, not in the way that the truth is inescapable but in the way that a jail is. They may at some point cease to feel like the texts in which human beings have tried to solve a great mystery and feel, instead, like the pretexts for other, properly anointed human beings to order you around. And it's true that human history is full of the public oppression wrought by the charioteers of the gods. In the opinion of religious people, however, the private comfort that religion brings more than compensates for the evil done in its name.

5   As human knowledge has grown, it has also become plain that every religious story ever told about how we got here is quite simply wrong. This, finally, is what all religions have in common. They didn't get it right. There was no celestial churning, no maker's dance, no vomiting of galaxies, no snake or kangaroo ancestors, no Valhalla, no Olympus, no six-day conjuring trick followed by a day of rest. Wrong, wrong, wrong. But here's something genuinely odd. The wrongness of the sacred tales hasn't lessened the zeal of the devout in the least. If anything, the sheer out-of-step zaniness of religion leads the religious to insist ever more stridently on the importance of blind faith.

As a result of this faith, by the way, it has proved impossible, in many parts of the world, to prevent the human race's numbers from swelling alarmingly.

---

[1]Rushdie takes his title from the first line of "Imagine," a song by John Lennon (1940–1980), a former member of the Beatles.

Blame the overcrowded planet at least partly on the misguidedness of the race's spiritual guides. In your own lifetime, you may well witness the arrival of the nine billionth world citizen. If you're Indian (and there's a one in six chance that you are) you will be alive when, thanks to the failure of family-planning schemes in that poor, God-ridden land, its population surges past China's. And if too many people are being born as a result, in part, of religious strictures against birth control, then too many people are also dying because religious culture, by refusing to face the facts of human sexuality, also refuses to fight against the spread of sexually transmitted diseases.

There are those who say that the great wars of the new century will once again be wars of religion, jihads and crusades, as they were in the Middle Ages. I don't believe them, or not in the way they mean it. Take a look at the Muslim world, or rather the *Islamist* world, to use the word coined to describe Islam's present-day "political arm." The divisions between its great powers (Afghanistan versus Iran versus Iraq versus Saudi Arabia versus Syria versus Egypt) are what strike you most forcefully. There's very little resembling a common purpose. Even after the non-Islamic NATO fought a war for the Muslim Kosovar Albanians, the Muslim world was slow in coming forward with much-needed humanitarian aid.

The real wars of religion are the wars religions unleash against ordinary citizens within their "spheres of influence." They are wars of the godly against the largely defenseless—American fundamentalists against pro-choice doctors, Iranian mullahs against their country's Jewish minority, the Taliban against the people of Afghanistan, Hindu fundamentalists in Bombay against that city's increasingly fearful Muslims.

The victors in that war must not be the closed-minded, marching into battle with, as ever, God on their side. To choose unbelief is to choose mind over dogma, to trust in our humanity instead of all these dangerous divinities. So, how did we get here? Don't look for the answer in storybooks. Imperfect human knowledge may be a bumpy, potholed street, but it's the only road to wisdom worth taking. Virgil, who believed that the apiarist Aristaeus could spontaneously generate new bees from the rotting carcass of a cow, was closer to a truth about origins than all the revered old books.

10   The ancient wisdoms are modern nonsenses. Live in your own time, use what we know, and as you grow up, perhaps the human race will finally grow up with you and put aside childish things.

As the song says, "It's easy if you try."

As for morality, the second great question—how to live? What is right action, and what wrong?—it comes down to your willingness to think for yourself. Only you can decide if you want to be handed down the law by priests, and accept that good and evil are somehow external to ourselves. To my mind religion, even at its most sophisticated, essentially infantilizes our ethical selves by setting infallible moral Arbiters and irredeemably immoral Tempters above us; the eternal parents, good and bad, light and dark, of the supernatural realm.

How, then, are we to make ethical choices without a divine rulebook or judge? Is unbelief just the first step on the long slide into the brain-death of cultural relativism, according to which many unbearable things—female circumcision, to name just one—can be excused on culturally specific grounds, and the universality of human rights, too, can be ignored? (This last piece of moral unmaking finds supporters in some of the world's most authoritarian regimes and also, unnervingly, on the op-ed pages of *The Daily Telegraph*.)

Well, no, it isn't, but the reasons for saying so aren't clear-cut. Only hard-line ideology is clear-cut. Freedom, which is the word I use for the secular-ethical position, is inevitably fuzzier. Yes, freedom is that space in which contradiction can reign, it is a never-ending debate. It is not in itself the answer to the question of morals but the conversation about that question.

15   And it is much more than mere relativism, because it is not merely a never-ending talk-shop, but a place in which choices are made, values defined and defended. Intellectual freedom, in European history, has mostly meant freedom from the restraints of the Church, not the State. This is the battle Voltaire° was fighting, and it's also what all six billion of us could do for ourselves, the revolution in which each of us could play our small, six-billionth part: once and for all we could refuse to allow priests, and the fictions on whose behalf they claim to speak, to be the policemen of our liberties and behavior. Once and for all we could put the stories back into the books, put the books back on the shelves, and see the world undogmatized and plain.

Imagine there's no heaven, my dear Six Billionth, and at once the sky's the limit.

[1997]

Voltaire: The pen name of François-Marie Arouet (1694–1778). See page 429.

1. According to Rushdie, what is good about religious accounts of creation? What is the problem with them? Is there any difference between them?

2. In what account of creation does Rushdie believe?

3. Summarize the argument he makes about religion and the evidence he presents to support his

argument. Do you agree with his argument? Why or why not?

4. The title of the essay and its eleventh paragraph allude to the famous John Lennon song, "Imagine." What is the function of this allusion in the essay's meaning?

K. C. Cole

A graduate of Barnard College, K.C. Cole began writing about science for the *Washington Post* in the 1970s. She has also written for the *New York Times*, the *New Yorker*, the *Smithsonian, Discover, Newsweek,* and *Newsday,* among others, and published seven books. Since 1994, she has covered science for the *Los Angeles Times,* for which she also writes the column "Mind over Matter," where "Murmurs" was first published.

MURMURS

WHEN THE UNIVERSE SPEAKS, ASTRONOMERS LISTEN. When it sings, they swoon.

That's roughly what happened recently when a group of astronomers published the most detailed analysis yet of the cosmos's primordial song: a low hum, deep in its throat, that preceded both atoms and stars.

It is a simple sound, like the mantra "Om." But hidden within its harmonics are details of the universe's shape, composition, and birth. So rich are these details that within hours of the paper's publication, new interpretations of the data had already appeared on the Los Alamos web server for new astrophysical papers.

5   "It's stirred up a hornet's nest of interest," said UCLA astronomer Ned Wright, who gave a talk to his colleagues on the paper—as did so many others—the very next week. So what is all the fuss about? Why are astronomers churning out paper after paper on what looks to a layperson like a puzzling set of wiggly peaks—graphic depictions of the sound, based on hours of mathematical analysis?

Because there's scientific gold in them there sinusoidal hills.

The peaks and valleys paint a visual picture of the sound the newborn universe made when it was still wet behind the ears, a mere 300,000 years after its birth in a big bang. Nothing existed but pure light,

An artist's rendering of the big bang.

sprinkled with a smattering of subatomic particles. Nothing happened, either, except that this light and matter fluid, as physicists call it, sloshed in and out of gravity wells, compressing the liquid in some places and spreading it out in others. Like banging on the head of a drum, the compression of the "liquid light" as it fell into gravity wells set up the "sound waves" that cosmologist Charles Lineweaver has called "the oldest music in the universe."

Then, suddenly, the sound fell silent. The universe had gotten cold enough that the particles, in effect, congealed, like salad dressing left in the fridge; the light separated and escaped, like the oil on top.

The rest is the history of the universe: The particles joined each other to form atoms, stars, and everything else, including people.

10 "The universe was very simple back then," said Caltech's Andrew Lange in one talk. "After that, we have atoms, chemistry, economics. Things go downhill very quickly."

As for the light, or radiation, it still pervades all space. In fact, it's part of the familiar "snow" that sometimes shows up on broadcast TV. But it's more than just noise: When the particles congealed, they left an imprint on the light.

Like children going after cookies, the patterns of sloshing particles left their sticky fingerprints all over the sky. The pattern of the sloshes tells you all you need to know about the very early universe: its shape, how much was made of matter, how much of something else.

The principle is familiar: Your child's voice sounds like no one else's because the resonant cavities within her throat create a unique voiceprint. The large, heavy wood of the cello creates a mellower sound than the high-strung violin. Just so, the sounds

coming from the early universe depend directly on the density of matter, and the shape of the cosmos itself.

Astronomers can't hear the sounds, of course. But they can read them on the walls of the universe like notes on a page. Compressed sound gets hot and produces hot splotches, like a pressure cooker. Expanded areas cool. Analyze the hot and cold patches and you get a picture of the sound: exactly how much falls on middle C or B-flat. What they've seen so far is both exciting and troubling. The sound suggests that the universe is a tad too heavy with ordinary matter to agree with standard cosmological theories; it resonates more like an oboe than a flute. Something's going on that can't be explained. The answers will come as even more sensitive cosmic stethoscopes listen in over the next few years.

15 Lest you think these sounds are music only for astronomers' ears, consider: The same wrinkles in space that created the gravity wells that gave rise to the sound also blew up to form clusters, galaxies, stars, planets, us.

Even Hare Krishnas murmuring Om.

[2000]

QUESTIONS FOR REFLECTION AND DISCUSSION

1. List the metaphors (p. 218) and similes (p. 218) Cole uses to describe the sounds made by the universe and its origin. Why do you think she uses so many of them? Which for you are more effective and which are less effective? Why?

2. In what ways is this account of creation according to modern science similar to the mythic and religious account in Genesis (p. 426)? In what ways is it different? Do you find it more or less persuasive as an explanation? Why? Do you find it more or less satisfying as an explanation? Why?

CREATION AND BEGINNINGS TOPICS FOR ESSAYS

1. Choose one of these accounts of creations and analyze it as an *etiological myth*—an account of how a currently existing phenomenon came to be. In what ways does the description cause us to think about the phenomena described?

2. Compare two or more of the accounts of creation. What similarities do they have? What differences? What are the consequences of these differences for our understanding of each account?

3. Several of these accounts include a *theodicy*—an explanation of the origin of evil in the world. Compare several of

these theodicies. How does each define evil differently, and with what consequences?

4. Compare the relationship between humans and gods in two or more of these accounts. What distinguishes one from the other? What is the relationship between them? Do other, intermediary forms, such as demigods, exist as well? What is their role?

5. Write an argument essay on modern scientific explanations of the origin of the universe, such as Cole's on the big bang theory. What do these theories explain that Genesis does not? What does Genesis explain that modern science does not?

ETHICS: DESTRUCTION AND ENDINGS

While gods tend to define themselves through their role in the creation of the world, devils are more frequently associated with death and destruction. In many religions, we find gods playing both roles—the story of the flood, for example, shared by many religions, addresses the ethical dilemma raised when a creative force somehow commits acts of terrible destruction. There are many ways to raise ethical questions. Sometimes they are implicit in the act of comparison, as in this simile from the midst of a scene of battle in the Trojan War from Book 8 of Homer's *Iliad,* in which a violent death is compared to a delicate flower.

As he spoke he aimed another arrow straight at Hector, for he was bent on hitting him; nevertheless he missed him, and the arrow hit Priam's brave son Gorgythion in the breast. His mother, fair Castianeira, lovely as a goddess, had been married from Aesyme, and now he bowed his head as a garden poppy in full bloom when it is weighed down by showers in spring—even thus heavy bowed his head beneath the weight of his helmet. (8:300-342; prose translation by Samuel Butter)

In Homer's world even death in war is simultaneously natural and horrible. Sometimes death is personified as an abstract and apparently amoral

Pleased to meet you, hope you guessed my name
But what's puzzling you is the nature of my game.
—MICK JAGGER AND KEITH RICHARDS, "SYMPATHY FOR THE DEVIL"

force, as in the poetry of John Donne and Emily Dickinson; sometimes it takes on the personality and individual character of Carolyn Forché's Colonel (p. 464) or Flannery O'Connor's Misfit (p. 250). At other times, death becomes the responsibility of a community or a social force, as in Tim O'Brien's "The Things They Carried." (p. 447).

FICTION

Nathaniel Hawthorne 1804–1864

Nathaniel Hawthorne was born in Salem, Massachusetts, to a family dating back to the days of the Puritans, and including in its lineage a judge who had persecuted Quakers and a judge involved in the Salem witch trials. Hawthorne graduated from Bowdoin College in 1825 and returned to Salem to write; the results included "Young Goodman Brown" (1835). He married in 1842, and settled in Concord, where he came to know Ralph Waldo Emerson and Henry David Thoreau. He published his two most famous novels, *The Scarlet Letter* and *The House of the Seven Gables,* in 1850 and 1851, respectively. Hawthorne's great theme, often expressed allegorically, was the relation of flawed individuals with the moral absolutism of the Puritan past. As you read "Young Goodman Brown," note the skill with which Hawthorne's fable combines the everyday trials of a young married couple in a small New England town with the metaphysical trials of Puritan Christianity.

YOUNG GOODMAN BROWN

YOUNG GOODMAN° BROWN CAME FORTH, AT sunset, into the street of Salem village,° but put his head back, after crossing the threshold, to exchange a parting kiss with his young wife. And Faith, as the wife was aptly named, thrust her own pretty head into the street, letting the wind play with the pink ribbons of her cap, while she called to Goodman Brown.

Goodman: Puritan title for a male head of a household. **Salem village:** a 17th-century settlement in England's Massachusetts Bay Colony.

"Dearest heart," whispered she, softly and rather sadly, when her lips were close to his ear, "pray thee, put off your journey until sunrise, and sleep in your own bed to-night. A lone woman is troubled with such dreams and such thoughts, that she's afraid of herself, sometimes. Pray, tarry with me this night, dear husband, of all nights in the year!"

"My love and my Faith," replied young Goodman Brown, "of all nights in the year, this one night must I tarry away from thee. My journey, as thou callest it, forth and back again, must needs be done 'twixt now and sunrise. What, my sweet, pretty wife, dost thou doubt me already, and we but three months married!"

"Then, God bless you!" said Faith, with the pink ribbons, "and may you find all well, when you come back."

5   "Amen!" cried Goodman Brown. "Say thy prayers, dear Faith, and go to bed at dusk, and no harm will come to thee."

So they parted; and the young man pursued his way, until, being about to turn the corner by the meeting-house, he looked back, and saw the head of Faith still peeping after him, with a melancholy air, in spite of her pink ribbons.

"Poor little Faith!" thought he, for his heart smote him. "What a wretch am I, to leave her on such an errand! She talks of dreams, too. Methought, as she spoke, there was trouble in her face, as if a dream had warned her what work is to be done to-night. But, no, no! 'twould kill her to think it. Well; she's a blessed angel on earth; and after this one night, I'll cling to her skirts and follow her to Heaven."

With this excellent resolve for the future, Goodman Brown felt himself justified in making more haste on his present evil purpose. He had taken a dreary road, darkened by all the gloomiest trees of the forest, which barely stood aside to let the narrow path creep through, and closed immediately behind. It was all as lonely as could be; and there is this peculiarity in such a solitude, that the traveller knows not who may be concealed by the innumerable trunks and the thick boughs overhead; so that, with lonely footsteps, he may yet be passing through an unseen multitude.

"There may be a devilish Indian behind every tree," said Goodman Brown, to himself; and he glanced fearfully behind him, as he added, "What if the devil himself should be at my very elbow!"

10   His head being turned back, he passed a crook of the road, and looking forward again, beheld the figure of a man, in grave and decent attire, seated at the foot of an old tree. He arose, at Goodman Brown's approach, and walked onward, side by side with him.

"You are late, Goodman Brown," said he. "The clock of the Old South was striking as I came through Boston; and that is full fifteen minutes agone."°

"Faith kept me back awhile," replied the young man, with a tremor in his voice, caused by the sudden appearance of his companion, though not wholly unexpected.

It was now deep dusk in the forest, and deepest in that part of it where these two were journeying. As nearly as could be discerned, the second traveller was about fifty years old, apparently in the same rank of life as Goodman Brown, and bearing a considerable resemblance to him, though perhaps more in expression than features. Still, they might have been taken for father and son. And yet, though the elder person was as simply clad as the younger, and as simple in manner too, he had an indescribable air of one who knew the world, and would not have felt abashed at the governor's dinner-table, or in King William's court,° were it possible that his affairs should call him thither. But the only thing about him, that could be fixed upon as remarkable, was his staff, which bore the likeness of a great black snake, so curiously wrought, that it might almost be seen to twist and wriggle itself, like a living serpent. This, of course, must have been an ocular deception, assisted by the uncertain light.

"Come, Goodman Brown!" cried his fellow-traveller, "this is dull pace for the beginning of a journey. Take my staff, if you are so soon weary."

15   "Friend," said the other, exchanging his slow pace for a full stop, "having kept covenant by meeting thee here, it is my purpose now to return whence I came. I have scruples, touching the matter thou wot'st° of."

"Sayest thou so?" replied he of the serpent, smiling apart. "Let us walk on, nevertheless, reasoning as we go, and if I convince thee not, thou shalt turn back. We are but a little way in the forest, yet."

"Too far, too far!" exclaimed the goodman, unconsciously resuming his walk. "My father never went into the woods on such an errand, nor his father before him. We have been a race of honest men and good Christians, since the days of the martyrs.° And shall I be the first of the name of Brown, that ever took this path, and kept—"

"Such company, thou wouldst say," observed the elder person, interpreting his pause. "Well said, Goodman Brown! I have been as well acquainted with your family as with ever a one among the Puritans; and that's no trifle to say. I helped your grandfather, the constable, when he lashed the Quaker woman so smartly through the streets of

---

full fifteen minutes agone: in other words, about a mile a minute, since the old South Church in Boston was some sixteen miles away.

King William's court: the court of King William of England (1689–1702). **wot'st:** know. **days of the martyrs:** the period when the Roman Catholic Mary I, queen of England from 1553 to 1558, undertook a campaign of persecution against Protestants.

Salem. And it was I that brought your father a pitch-pine knot, kindled at my own hearth, to set fire to an Indian village, in King Philip's war.° They were my good friends, both; and many a pleasant walk have we had along this path, and returned merrily after midnight. I would fain° be friends with you, for their sake."

"If it be as thou sayest," replied Goodman Brown, "I marvel they never spoke of these matters. Or, verily, I marvel not, seeing that the least rumor of the sort would have driven them from New England. We are a people of prayer, and good works, to boot, and abide no such wickedness."

20   "Wickedness or not," said the traveller with the twisted staff, "I have a very general acquaintance here in New England. The deacons of many a church have drunk the communion wine with me; the selectmen, of divers towns, make me their chairman; and a majority of the Great and General Court are firm supporters of my interest. The governor and I, too—but these are state-secrets."

"Can this be so!" cried Goodman Brown, with a stare of amazement at his undisturbed companion. "Howbeit, I have nothing to do with the governor and council; they have their own ways, and are no rule for a simple husbandman, like me. But, were I to go on with thee, how should I meet the eye of that good old man, our minister, at Salem village? Oh, his voice would make me tremble, both Sabbath-day and lecture-day!"°

Thus far, the elder traveller had listened with due gravity, but now burst into a fit of irrepressible mirth, shaking himself so violently, that his snake-like staff actually seemed to wriggle in sympathy.

"Ha! ha! ha!" shouted he, again and again; then composing himself, "Well, go on, Goodman Brown, go on; but pray thee, don't kill me with laughing!"

"Well, then, to end the matter at once," said Goodman Brown, considerably nettled, "there is my wife, Faith. It would break her dear little heart; and I'd rather break my own!"

25   "Nay, if that be the case," answered the other, "e'en go thy ways, Goodman Brown. I would not, for twenty old women like the one hobbling before us, that Faith should come to any harm."

As he spoke, he pointed his staff at a female figure on the path, in whom Goodman Brown recognized a very pious and exemplary dame, who had taught

him his catechism, in youth, and was still his moral and spiritual adviser, jointly with the minister and Deacon Gookin.

"A marvel, truly, that Goody° Cloyse should be so far in the wilderness, at night-fall!" said he. "But, with your leave, friend, I shall take a cut through the woods, until we have left this Christian woman behind. Being a stranger to you, she might ask whom I was consorting with, and whither I was going."

"Be it so," said his fellow-traveller. "Betake you to the woods, and let me keep the path."

Accordingly, the young man turned aside, but took care to watch his companion, who advanced softly along the road, until he had come within a staff's length of the old dame. She, meanwhile, was making the best of her way, with singular speed for so aged a woman, and mumbling some indistinct words, a prayer, doubtless, as she went. The traveller put forth his staff, and touched her withered neck with what seemed the serpent's tail.

30   "The devil!" screamed the pious old lady.

"Then Goody Cloyse knows her old friend?" observed the traveller, confronting her, and leaning on his writhing stick.

"Ah, forsooth, and is it your worship, indeed?" cried the good dame. "Yea, truly is it, and in the very image of my old gossip, Goodman Brown, the grandfather of the silly fellow that now is. But—would your worship believe it?—my broomstick hath strangely disappeared, stolen, as I suspect, by that unhanged witch, Goody Cory, and that, too, when I was all anointed with the juice of smallage and cinquefoil and wolf's bane—"°

"Mingled with fine wheat and the fat of a newborn babe," said the shape of old Goodman Brown.

"Ah, your worship knows the receipt,"° cried the old lady, cackling aloud. "So, as I was saying, being all ready for the meeting, and no horse to ride on, I made up my mind to foot it; for they tell me, there is a nice young man to be taken into communion to-night. But now your good worship will lend me your arm, and we shall be there in a twinkling."

35   "That can hardly be," answered her friend. "I may not spare you my arm, Goody Cloyse, but here is my staff, if you will."

So saying, he threw it down at her feet, where, perhaps, it assumed life, being one of the rods which its

---

King Philip's war: Metacomet, the chief of the Wampanoag Indians and leader of a violent uprising of New England tribes in the 1670s, was called "King Philip" by the English. **fain:** gladly. **lecture-day:** a required sermon or Bible-reading in church on a weekday.

Goody: short for Goodwife, ordinary title for a married woman. **Smallage and cinquefoil and wolf's bane:** wild plants associated with witch's brews. **receipt:** recipe.

owner had formerly lent to the Egyptian Magi.° Of this fact, however, Goodman Brown could not take cognizance. He had cast up his eyes in astonishment, and looking down again, beheld neither Goody Cloyse nor the serpentine staff, but his fellow-traveller alone, who waited for him as calmly as if nothing had happened.

"That old woman taught me my catechism!" said the young man; and there was a world of meaning in this simple comment.

They continued to walk onward, while the elder traveller exhorted his companion to make good speed and persevere in the path, discoursing so aptly, that his arguments seemed rather to spring up in the bosom of his auditor, than to be suggested by himself. As they went, he plucked a branch of maple, to serve for a walking-stick, and began to strip it of the twigs and little boughs, which were wet with evening dew. The moment his fingers touched them, they became strangely withered and dried up, as with a week's sunshine. Thus the pair proceeded, at a good free pace, until suddenly, in a gloomy hollow of the road, Goodman Brown sat himself down on the stump of a tree, and refused to go any farther.

"Friend," said he, stubbornly, "my mind is made up. Not another step will I budge on this errand. What if a wretched old woman do choose to go to the devil, when I thought she was going to Heaven! Is that any reason why I should quit my dear Faith, and go after her?"

40 "You will think better of this, by-and-by," said his acquaintance, composedly. "Sit here and rest yourself awhile; and when you feel like moving again, there is my staff to help you along."

Without more words, he threw his companion the maple stick, and was as speedily out of sight, as if he had vanished into the deepening gloom. The young man sat a few moments, by the road-side, applauding himself greatly, and thinking with how clear a conscience he should meet the minister, in his morning-walk, nor shrink from the eye of good old Deacon Gookin. And what calm sleep would be his, that very night, which was to have been spent so wickedly, but purely and sweetly now, in the arms of Faith! Amidst these pleasant and praiseworthy meditations, Goodman Brown heard the tramp of horses along the road, and deemed it advisable to conceal himself within the verge of the forest, conscious of the guilty purpose that had brought him thither, though now so happily turned from it.

On came the hoof-tramps and the voices of the riders, two grave old voices, conversing soberly as they drew near. These mingled sounds appeared to pass along the road, within a few yards of the young man's hiding-place; but owing, doubtless, to the depth of the gloom, at that particular spot, neither the travellers nor their steeds were visible. Though their figures brushed the small boughs by the wayside, it could not be seen that they intercepted, even for a moment, the faint gleam from the strip of bright sky, athwart which they must have passed. Goodman Brown alternately crouched and stood on tip-toe, pulling aside the branches, and thrusting forth his head as far as he durst, without discerning so much as a shadow. It vexed him the more, because he could have sworn, were such a thing possible, that he recognized the voices of the minister and Deacon Gookin, jogging along quietly, as they were wont to do, when bound to some ordination or ecclesiastical council. While yet within hearing, one of the riders stopped to pluck a switch.

"Of the two, reverend Sir," said the voice like the deacon's, "I had rather miss an ordination-dinner than to-night's meeting. They tell me that some of our community are to be here from Falmouth and beyond, and others from Connecticut and Rhode Island; besides several of the Indian powows,° who, after their fashion, know almost as much deviltry as the best of us. Moreover, there is a goodly young woman to be taken into communion."

"Mighty well, Deacon Gookin!" replied the solemn old tones of the minister. "Spur up, or we shall be late. Nothing can be done, you know, until I get on the ground."

45 The hoofs clattered again, and the voices, talking so strangely in the empty air, passed on through the forest, where no church had ever been gathered, nor solitary Christian prayed. Whither, then, could these holy men be journeying, so deep into the heathen wilderness? Young Goodman Brown caught hold of a tree, for support, being ready to sink down on the ground, faint and overburdened with the heavy sickness of his heart. He looked up to the sky, doubting whether there really was a Heaven above him. Yet, there was the blue arch, and the stars brightening in it.

"With Heaven above, and Faith below, I will yet stand firm against the devil!" cried Goodman Brown.

Egyptian Magi: In the story of Moses (Exodus 7.8–12), these were Pharoah's sorcerers, who were able to change their staffs into living serpents.

Powows: Indian "priests" or spiritual leaders.

While he still gazed upward, into the deep arch of the firmament, and had lifted his hands to pray, a cloud, though no wind was stirring, hurried across the zenith, and hid the brightening stars. The blue sky was still visible, except directly overhead, where this black mass of cloud was sweeping swiftly northward. Aloft in the air, as if from the depths of the cloud, came a confused and doubtful sound of voices. Once, the listener fancied that he could distinguish the accents of town's-people of his own, men and women, both pious and ungodly, many of whom he had met at the communion-table, and had seen others rioting at the tavern. The next moment, so indistinct were the sounds, he doubted whether he had heard aught but the murmur of the old forest, whispering without a wind. Then came a stronger swell of those familiar tones, heard daily in the sunshine, at Salem village, but never, until now, from a cloud of night. There was one voice, of a young woman, uttering lamentations, yet with an uncertain sorrow, and entreating for some favor, which, perhaps, it would grieve her to obtain. And all the unseen multitude, both saints and sinners, seemed to encourage her onward.

"Faith!" shouted Goodman Brown, in a voice of agony and desperation; and the echoes of the forest mocked him, crying—"Faith! Faith!" as if bewildered wretches were seeking her, all through the wilderness.

The cry of grief, rage, and terror, was yet piercing the night, when the unhappy husband held his breath for a response. There was a scream, drowned immediately in a louder murmur of voices, fading into far-off laughter, as the dark cloud swept away, leaving the clear and silent sky above Goodman Brown. But something fluttered lightly down through the air, and caught on the branch of a tree. The young man seized it, and beheld a pink ribbon.

50 "My Faith is gone!" cried he, after one stupefied moment. "There is no good on earth; and sin is but a name. Come, devil! for to thee is this world given."

And maddened with despair, so that he laughed loud and long, did Goodman Brown grasp his staff and set forth again, at such a rate, that he seemed to fly along the forest-path, rather than to walk or run. The road grew wilder and drearier, and more faintly traced, and vanished at length, leaving him in the heart of the dark wilderness, still rushing onward, with the instinct that guides mortal man to evil. The whole forest was peopled with frightful sounds; the creaking of the trees, the howling of wild beasts, and the yell of Indians; while, sometimes, the wind tolled like a distant church-bell, and sometimes gave a broad roar around the traveller, as if all Nature were laughing him to scorn. But he was himself the chief horror of the scene, and shrank not from its other horrors.

"Ha! ha! ha!" roared Goodman Brown, when the wind laughed at him. "Let us hear which will laugh loudest! Think not to frighten me with your deviltry! Come witch, come wizard, come Indian powow, come devil himself! and here comes Goodman Brown. You may as well fear him as he fear you!"

In truth, all through the haunted forest, there could be nothing more frightful than the figure of Goodman Brown. On he flew, among the black pines, brandishing his staff with frenzied gestures, now giving vent to an inspiration of horrid blasphemy, and now shouting forth such laughter, as set all the echoes of the forest laughing like demons around him. The fiend in his own shape is less hideous, than when he rages in the breast of man. Thus sped the demoniac on his course, until, quivering among the trees, he saw a red light before him, as when the felled trunks and branches of a clearing have been set on fire, and throw up their lurid blaze against the sky, at the hour of midnight. He paused, in a lull of the tempest that had driven him onward, and heard the swell of what seemed a hymn, rolling solemnly from a distance, with the weight of many voices. He knew the tune; it was a familiar one in the choir of the village meeting-house. The verse died heavily away, and was lengthened by a chorus, not of human voices, but of all the sounds of the benighted wilderness, pealing in awful harmony together. Goodman Brown cried out; and his cry was lost to his own ear, by its unison with the cry of the desert.

In the interval of silence, he stole forward, until the light glared full upon his eyes. At one extremity of an open space, hemmed in by the dark wall of the forest, arose a rock, bearing some rude, natural resemblance either to an altar or a pulpit, and surrounded by four blazing pines, their tops aflame, their stems untouched, like candles at an evening meeting. The mass of foliage, that had overgrown the summit of the rock, was all on fire, blazing high into the night, and fitfully illuminating the whole field. Each pendent twig and leafy festoon was in a blaze. As the red light arose and fell, a numerous congregation alternately shone forth, then disappeared in shadow, and again grew, as it were, out of the darkness, peopling the heart of the solitary woods at once.

55 "A grave and dark-clad company!" quoth Goodman Brown.

In truth, they were such. Among them, quivering to-and-fro, between gloom and splendor, appeared faces that would be seen, next day, at the council-board of the province, and others which, Sabbath after Sabbath, looked devoutly heavenward, and benignantly over the crowded pews, from the holiest pulpits in the land. Some affirm that the lady of the governor was there. At least, there were high dames well known to her, and wives of honored husbands, and widows, a great multitude, and ancient maidens, all of excellent repute, and fair young girls, who trembled, lest their mothers should espy them. Either the sudden gleams of light, flashing over the obscure field, bedazzled Goodman Brown, or he recognized a score of the church-members of Salem village, famous for their especial sanctity. Good old Deacon Gookin had arrived, and waited at the skirts of that venerable saint, his revered pastor. But, irreverently consorting with these grave, reputable, and pious people, these elders of the church, these chaste dames and dewy virgins, there were men of dissolute lives and women of spotted fame, wretches given over to all mean and filthy vice, and suspected even of horrid crimes. It was strange to see, that the good shrank not from the wicked, nor were the sinners abashed by the saints. Scattered, also, among their pale-faced enemies, were the Indian priests, or powows, who had often scared their native forest with more hideous incantations than any known to English witchcraft.

"But, where is Faith?" thought Goodman Brown; and, as hope came into his heart, he trembled.

Another verse of the hymn arose, a slow and mournful strain, such as the pious love, but joined to words which expressed all that our nature can conceive of sin, and darkly hinted at far more. Unfathomable to mere mortals is the lore of fiends. Verse after verse was sung, and still the chorus of the desert swelled between, like the deepest tone of a mighty organ. And, with the final peal of that dreadful anthem, there came a sound, as if the roaring wind, the rushing streams, the howling beasts, and every other voice of the unconverted wilderness, were mingling and according with the voice of guilty man, in homage to the prince of all. The four blazing pines threw up a loftier flame, and obscurely discovered shapes and visages of horror on the smoke-wreaths, above the impious assembly. At the same moment, the fire on the rock shot redly forth, and formed a glowing arch above its base, where now appeared a figure. With reverence be it spoken, the figure bore no slight similitude, both in garb and manner, to some grave divine of the New England churches.

"Bring forth the converts!" cried a voice, that echoed through the field and rolled into the forest.

60   At the word, Goodman Brown stepped forth from the shadow of the trees, and approached the congregation, with whom he felt a loathful brotherhood, by the sympathy of all that was wicked in his heart. He could have well nigh sworn, that the shape of his own dead father beckoned him to advance, looking downward from a smoke-wreath, while a woman, with dim features of despair, threw out her hand to warn him back. Was it his mother? But he had no power to retreat one step, nor to resist, even in thought, when the minister and good old Deacon Gookin seized his arms, and led him to the blazing rock. Thither came also the slender form of a veiled female, led between Goody Cloyse, that pious teacher of the catechism, and Martha Carrier, who had received the devil's promise to be queen of hell. A rampant hag was she! And there stood the proselytes,° beneath the canopy of fire.

"Welcome, my children," said the dark figure, "to the communion of your race! Ye have found, thus young, your nature and your destiny. My children, look behind you!"

They turned; and flashing forth, as it were, in a sheet of flame, the fiend-worshippers were seen; the smile of welcome gleamed darkly on every visage.

"There," resumed the sable form, "are all whom ye have reverenced from youth. Ye deemed them holier than yourselves, and shrank from your own sin, contrasting it with their lives of righteousness, and prayerful aspirations heavenward. Yet, here are they all, in my worshipping assembly! This night it shall be granted you to know their secret deeds; how hoary-bearded elders of the church have whispered wanton words to the young maids of their households; how many a woman, eager for widow's weeds, has given her husband a drink at bedtime, and let him sleep his last sleep in her bosom; how beardless youths have made haste to inherit their fathers' wealth; and how fair damsels—blush not, sweet ones!—have dug little graves in the garden, and bidden me, the sole guest, to an infant's funeral. By the sympathy of your human hearts for sin, ye shall scent out all the places—whether in church, bed-chamber, street, field, or forest—where crime has

proselytes: new converts.

been committed, and shall exult to behold the whole earth one stain of guilt, one mighty bloodspot. Far more than this! It shall be yours to penetrate, in every bosom, the deep mystery of sin, the fountain of all wicked arts, and which inexhaustibly supplies more evil impulses than human power—than my power, at its utmost!—can make manifest in deeds. And now, my children, look upon each other."

They did so; and, by the blaze of the hell-kindled torches, the wretched man beheld his Faith, and the wife her husband, trembling before that unhallowed altar.

65 "Lo! there ye stand, my children," said the figure, in a deep and solemn tone, almost sad, with its despairing awfulness, as if his once angelic nature could yet mourn for our miserable race. "Depending upon one another's hearts, ye had still hoped, that virtue were not all a dream. Now are ye undeceived! Evil is the nature of mankind. Evil must be your only happiness. Welcome, again, my children, to the communion of your race!"

"Welcome!" repeated the fiend-worshippers, in one cry of despair and triumph.

And there they stood, the only pair, as it seemed, who were yet hesitating on the verge of wickedness, in this dark world. A basin was hollowed, naturally, in the rock. Did it contain water, reddened by the lurid light? or was it blood? or, perchance, a liquid flame? Herein did the Shape of Evil dip his hand, and prepare to lay the mark of baptism upon their foreheads, that they might be partakers of the mystery of sin, more conscious of the secret guilt of others, both in deed and thought, than they could now be of their own. The husband cast one look at his pale wife, and Faith at him. What polluted wretches would the next glance show them to each other, shuddering alike at what they disclosed and what they saw!

"Faith! Faith!" cried the husband. "Look up to Heaven, and resist the Wicked one!"

Whether Faith obeyed, he knew not. Hardly had he spoken, when he found himself amid calm night and solitude, listening to a roar of the wind, which died heavily away through the forest. He staggered against the rock and felt it chill and damp, while a hanging twig, that had been all on fire, besprinkled his cheek with the coldest dew.

70 The next morning, young Goodman Brown came slowly into the street of Salem village, staring around him like a bewildered man. The good old minister was taking a walk along the grave-yard, to get an appetite for breakfast and meditate his sermon, and bestowed a blessing, as he passed, on Goodman Brown. He shrank from the venerable saint, as if to avoid an anathema.° Old Deacon Goodkin was at domestic worship, and the holy words of his prayer were heard through the open window. "What God doth the wizard pray to?" quoth Goodman Brown. Goody Cloyse, that excellent old Christian, stood in the early sunshine, at her own lattice, catechizing a little girl, who had brought her a pint of morning's milk. Goodman Brown snatched away the child, as from the grasp of the fiend himself. Turning the corner by the meeting-house, he spied the head of Faith, with the pink ribbons, gazing anxiously forth, and bursting into such joy at sight of him, that she skipt along the street, and almost kissed her husband before the whole village. But, Goodman Brown looked sternly and sadly into her face, and passed on without a greeting.

Had Goodman Brown fallen asleep in the forest, and only dreamed a wild dream of a witch-meeting?

Be it so, if you will. But, alas! it was a dream of evil omen for young Goodman Brown. A stern, a sad, a darkly meditative, a distrustful, if not a desperate man, did he become, from the night of that fearful dream. On the Sabbath-day, when the congregation were singing a holy psalm, he could not listen, because an anthem of sin rushed loudly upon his ear, and drowned all the blessed strain. When the minister spoke from the pulpit, with power and fervid eloquence, and, with his hand on the open Bible, of the sacred truths of our religion, and of saint-like lives and triumphant deaths, and of future bliss or misery unutterable, then did Goodman Brown turn pale, dreading, lest the roof should thunder down upon the gray blasphemer and his hearers. Often, awakening suddenly at midnight, he shrank from the bosom of Faith, and at morning or even-tide, when the family knelt down at prayer, he scowled, and muttered to himself, and gazed sternly at his wife, and turned away. And when he had lived long, and was borne to his grave, a hoary corpse, followed by Faith, an aged woman, and children and grandchildren, a goodly procession, besides neighbors, not a few, they carved no hopeful verse upon his tombstone; for his dying hour was gloom.

[1835]

anathema: an official curse, banishing its recipient from the church and its sacraments.

1. Why does the devil-figure first take the form of Goodman Brown's grandfather?

2. The name of Brown's wife identifies her as a personification (p. 219). The wordplay Hawthorne performs with her name emphasizes that identity, but in the second half of the story the fable becomes more difficult to sustain. Were you surprised when Faith appeared at the gathering in the wood? To what degree is it possible to interpret the later events in the story as an allegory about Brown and his faith, and to what extent is it primarily a story about the relationship between a married couple?

3. In a conventional fable about Christian faith, the sinful coven would be wholly distinct from the world the wavering soul was betraying. What is the effect in Hawthorne's fable of merging the sinful with the purportedly pious? How does the final section of the story, in town the next morning, reflect this shift in expectations?

4. Goodman Brown's name suggests that he also has an aspect of personification about him. Is there anything else allegorical about him besides his name?

5. Compare the depiction of religious faith in the context of a family in this story and in "A Good Man Is Hard to Find" (p. 250).

Kate Chopin 1851–1904

Born Katherine O'Flaherty in St. Louis, Missouri, Kate Chopin lived many years in New Orleans and on the Mississippi River plantation of her husband, Oscar Chopin. When her husband died of malaria in 1882, she returned with her six children to live with her mother, and began writing stories and novels. Controversial at the time for their depiction of women and frank attitude toward issues of race and sexuality, Chopin's fiction uses irony (p. 216) to dramatize the gap between convention and reality in her female characters. "The Story of an Hour" was first published in the collection *Bayou Folk* (1894).

THE STORY OF AN HOUR

KNOWING THAT MRS. MALLARD WAS AFFLICTED with a heart trouble, great care was taken to break to her as gently as possible the news of her husband's death.

It was her sister Josephine who told her, in broken sentences, veiled hints that revealed in half concealing. Her husband's friend Richards was there, too, near her. It was he who had been in the newspaper office when intelligence of the railroad disaster was received, with Brently Mallard's name leading the list of "killed." He had only taken the time to assure himself of its truth by a second telegram, and had hastened to forestall any less careful, less tender friend in bearing the sad message.

She did not hear the story as many women have heard the same, with a paralyzed inability to accept its significance. She wept at once, with sudden, wild abandonment, in her sister's arms. When the storm of grief had spent itself she went away to her room alone. She would have no one follow her.

There stood, facing the open window, a comfortable, roomy armchair. Into this she sank, pressed down by a physical exhaustion that haunted her body and seemed to reach into her soul.

5   She could see in the open square before her house the tops of trees that were all aquiver with the new spring life. The delicious breath of rain was in the air. In the street below a peddler was crying his wares. The notes of a distant song which some one was singing reached her faintly, and countless sparrows were twittering in the eaves.

There were patches of blue sky showing here and there through the clouds that had met and piled one above the other in the west facing her window.

She sat with her head thrown back upon the cushion of the chair, quite motionless, except when a sob came up into her throat and shook her, as a child who has cried itself to sleep continues to sob in its dreams.

She was young, with a fair, calm face, whose lines bespoke repression and even a certain strength. But now there was a dull stare in her eyes, whose gaze was fixed away off yonder on one of those patches of blue sky. It was not a glance of reflection, but rather indicated a suspension of intelligent thought.

There was something coming to her and she was waiting for it, fearfully. What was it? She did not know; it was too subtle and elusive to name. But she felt it, creeping out of the sky, reaching toward her through the sounds, the scents, the color that filled the air.

10 Now her bosom rose and fell tumultuously. She was beginning to recognize this thing that was approaching to possess her, and she was striving to beat it back with her will—as powerless as her two white slender hands would have been.

When she abandoned herself a little whispered word escaped her slightly parted lips. She said it over and over under her breath: "Free, free, free!" The vacant stare and the look of terror that had followed it went from her eyes. They stayed keen and bright. Her pulses beat fast, and the coursing blood warmed and relaxed every inch of her body.

She did not stop to ask if it were not a monstrous joy that held her. A clear and exalted perception enabled her to dismiss the suggestion as trivial.

She knew that she would weep again when she saw the kind, tender hands folded in death; the face that had never looked save with love upon her, fixed and gray and dead. But she saw beyond that bitter moment a long procession of years to come that would belong to her absolutely. And she opened and spread her arms out to them in welcome.

There would be no one to live for during those coming years; she would live for herself. There would be no powerful will bending her in that blind persistence with which men and women believe they have a right to impose a private will upon a fellow creature. A kind intention or a cruel intention made the act seem no less a crime as she looked upon it in that brief moment of illumination.

15 And yet she had loved him—sometimes. Often she had not. What did it matter! What could love, the unsolved mystery, count for in face of this possession of self-assertion which she suddenly recognized as the strongest impulse of her being.

"Free! Body and soul free!" she kept whispering.

Josephine was kneeling before the closed door with her lips to the keyhole, imploring for admission. "Louise, open the door! I beg; open the door—you will make yourself ill. What are you doing, Louise? For heaven's sake open the door."

"Go away. I am not making myself ill." No; she was drinking in a very elixir of life through that open window.

Her fancy was running riot along those days ahead of her. Spring days, and summer days, and all sorts of days that would be her own. She breathed a quick prayer that life might be long. It was only yesterday she had thought with a shudder that life might be long.

20 She arose at length and opened the door to her sister's importunities. There was a feverish triumph in her eyes, and she carried herself unwittingly like a goddess of Victory. She clasped her sister's waist, and together they descended the stairs. Richards stood waiting for them at the bottom.

Some one was opening the front door with a latchkey. It was Brently Mallard who entered, a little travel-stained, composedly carrying his gripsack and umbrella. He had been far from the scene of the accident, and did not even know there had been one. He stood amazed at Josephine's piercing cry; at Richards' quick motion to screen him from the view of his wife.

But Richards was too late.

When the doctors came they said she had died of heart disease—of joy that kills.

[1894]

QUESTIONS FOR REFLECTION AND DISCUSSION

1. There are two distinct types of irony (p. 216) used in the story. What are these two types of irony, how are they used, and what is the relationship between them in the story?

2. How would it change the story if Mrs. Mallard had been able to share her true feelings with her sister before she died? How would the story's ironies be altered, if at all?

3. Why has Mrs. Mallard realized her true state of feelings toward her husband only upon learning of his death? In your opinion, which emotional reaction kills her in the end of the story: relief, guilt, frustration, or some other?

4. Who or what is responsible for killing Mrs. Mallard?

Ernest Hemingway 1899–1961

Born in Illinois, Ernest Hemingway began working as a newspaper reporter after graduating from high school in 1917. Soon, however, he left for Europe as a volunteer ambulance driver in Italy. Hemingway settled in Paris in 1922, where his circle included Gertrude Stein, James Joyce, Ezra Pound, and the painters Miro and Picasso, and he began writing the stories and novels that made him one of the most important writers of his generation. He worked as a journalist during the Spanish Civil War and World War II. He was awarded the Nobel Prize in Literature in 1954. Depressed by his deteriorating health, Hemingway took his own life seven years later. First published in 1927 in the avant-garde literary journal *transition* and reprinted the same year in the collection *Men and Women*, "Hills Like White Elephants" demonstrates the characteristic sparseness and directness of Hemingway's prose and dialogue, even as the major plot event goes unstated.

HILLS LIKE WHITE ELEPHANTS

THE HILLS ACROSS THE VALLEY OF THE EBRO were long and white. On this side there was no shade and no trees and the station was between two lines of rails in the sun. Close against the side of the station there was the warm shadow of the building and a curtain, made of strings of bamboo beads, hung across the open door into the bar, to keep out flies. The American and the girl with him sat at a table in the shade, outside the building. It was very hot and the express from Barcelona would come in forty minutes. It stopped at this junction for two minutes and went on to Madrid.

"What should we drink?" the girl asked. She had taken off her hat and put it on the table.

"It's pretty hot," the man said.

"Let's drink beer."

5 "Dos cervezas," the man said into the curtain.

"Big ones?" a woman asked from the doorway.

"Yes. Two big ones."

The woman brought two glasses of beer and two felt pads. She put the felt pads and the beer glasses on the table and looked at the man and the girl. The girl was looking off at the line of hills. They were white in the sun and the country was brown and dry.

"They look like white elephants," she said.

10 "I've never seen one," the man drank his beer.

"No, you wouldn't have."

"I might have," the man said. "Just because you say I wouldn't have doesn't prove anything."

The girl looked at the bead curtain. "They've painted something on it," she said. "What does it say?"

"Anis del Toro. It's a drink."

15 "Could we try it?"

The man called "Listen" through the curtain. The woman came out from the bar.

"Four reales."

"We want two Anis del Toro."

"With water?"

20 "Do you want it with water?"

The church and village of Miravat overlooking the River Ebro in Tarragona, Catalonia, Spain. Spain's most important river, the Ebro, flows through the north of the country before draining in the Mediterranean Sea.

"I don't know," the girl said. "Is it good with water?"

"It's all right."

"You want them with water?" asked the woman.

"Yes, with water."

25 "It tastes like licorice," the girl said and put the glass down.

"That's the way with everything."

"Yes," said the girl. "Everything tastes of licorice. Especially all the things you've waited so long for, like absinthe."

"Oh, cut it out."

"You started it," the girl said. "I was being amused. I was having a fine time."

30 "Well, let's try and have a fine time."

"All right. I was trying. I said the mountains looked like white elephants. Wasn't that bright?"

"That was bright."

"I wanted to try this new drink. That's all we do, isn't it—look at things and try new drinks?"

"I guess so."

35 The girl looked across at the hills.

"They're lovely hills," she said. "They don't really look like white elephants. I just meant the coloring of their skin through the trees."

"Should we have another drink?"

"All right."

The warm wind blew the bead curtain against the table.

40 "The beer's nice and cool," the man said.

"It's lovely," the girl said.

"It's really an awfully simple operation, Jig," the man said. "It's not really an operation at all."

The girl looked at the ground the table legs rested on.

"I know you wouldn't mind it, Jig. It's really not anything. It's just to let the air in."

45 The girl did not say anything.

"I'll go with you and I'll stay with you all the time. They just let the air in and then it's all perfectly natural."

"Then what will we do afterward?"

"We'll be fine afterward. Just like we were before."

"What makes you think so?"

50 "That's the only thing that bothers us. It's the only thing that's made us unhappy."

The girl looked at the bead curtain, put her hand out and took hold of two of the strings of beads.

"And you think then we'll be all right and be happy."

"I know we will. You don't have to be afraid. I've known lots of people that have done it."

"So have I," said the girl. "And afterward they were all so happy."

55 "Well," the man said, "if you don't want to you don't have to. I wouldn't have you do it if you didn't want to. But I know it's perfectly simple."

"And you really want to?"

"I think it's the best thing to do. But I don't want you to do it if you don't really want to."

"And if I do it you'll be happy and things will be like they were and you'll love me?"

"I love you now. You know I love you."

60 "I know. But if I do it, then it will be nice again if I say things are like white elephants, and you'll like it?"

"I'll love it. I love it now but I just can't think about it. You know how I get when I worry."

"If I do it you won't ever worry?"

"I won't worry about that because it's perfectly simple."

"Then I'll do it. Because I don't care about me."

65 "What do you mean?"

"I don't care about me."

"Well, I care about you."

"Oh, yes. But I don't care about me. And I'll do it and then everything will be fine."

"I don't want you to do it if you feel that way."

70 The girl stood up and walked to the end of the station. Across, on the other side, were fields of grain and trees along the banks of the Ebro. Far away, beyond the river, were mountains. The shadow of a cloud moved across the field of grain and she saw the river through the trees.

"And we could have all this," she said. "And we could have everything and every day we make it more impossible."

"What did you say?"

"I said we could have everything."

"We can have everything."

75 "No, we can't."

"We can have the whole world."

"No, we can't."

"We can go everywhere."

"No, we can't. It isn't ours any more."

80 "It's ours."

"No, it isn't. And once they take it away, you never get it back."

"But they haven't taken it away."

"We'll wait and see."

"Come on back in the shade," he said. "You mustn't feel that way."

85 "I don't feel any way," the girl said. "I just know things."

"I don't want you to do anything that you don't want to do—"

"Nor that isn't good for me," she said. "I know. Could we have another beer?"

"All right. But you've got to realize—"

"I realize," the girl said. "Can't we maybe stop talking?"

90 They sat down at the table and the girl looked across at the hills on the dry side of the valley and the man looked at her and at the table.

"You've got to realize," he said, "that I don't want you to do it if you don't want to. I'm perfectly willing to go through with it if it means anything to you."

"Doesn't it mean anything to you? We could get along."

"Of course it does. But I don't want anybody but you. I don't want any one else. And I know it's perfectly simple."

"Yes, you know it's perfectly simple."

95 "It's all right for you to say that, but I do know it."

"Would you do something for me now?"

"I'd do anything for you."

"Would you please please please please please please please stop talking?"

He did not say anything but looked at the bags against the wall of the station. There were labels on them from all the hotels where they had spent nights.

100 "But I don't want you to," he said, "I don't care anything about it."

"I'll scream," the girl said.

The woman came out through the curtains with two glasses of beer and put them down on the damp felt pads. "The train comes in five minutes," she said.

"What did she say?" asked the girl.

"That the train is coming in five minutes."

105 The girl smiled brightly at the woman, to thank her.

"I'd better take the bags over to the other side of the station," the man said. She smiled at him.

"All right. Then come back and we'll finish the beer."

He picked up the two heavy bags and carried them around the station to the other tracks. He looked up the tracks but could not see the train. Coming back, he walked through the barroom, where people waiting for the train were drinking. He drank an Anis at the bar and looked at the people. They were all waiting reasonably for the train. He went out through the bead curtain. She was sitting at the table and smiled at him.

"Do you feel better?" he asked.

110 "I feel fine," she said. "There's nothing wrong with me. I feel fine."

[1927]

QUESTIONS FOR REFLECTION AND DISCUSSION

1. The events described in the story last about thirty-five minutes; what are the events that structure the conversation but are not mentioned? What has happened previously, what is happening now, and what is going to happen? Which events can we be certain about and which ones must we guess?

2. When the girl says "And we could have all this" to what do you think she is referring?

3. What role is played by the title in the story? To which character is it associated? Why is the color of the elephants important?

4. What are the possible attitudes we can take toward the decision the two characters are making and to the two characters?

Tim O'Brien b. 1946

Born in Minnesota, Tim O'Brien was drafted the year he graduated from Macalester College at the age of twenty-one. He served in the Vietnam War, receiving a Purple Heart, and since then has devoted himself to writing about the war in short stories, novels, and a memoir. "The Things They Carried" was first published in *Esquire* in 1986 and reprinted as the title story in O'Brien's 1990 collection. As you read this selection, consider the role of the insistent use of zeugma (p. 216) in structuring the story and developing its argument regarding the experience and ethics of warfare.

THE THINGS THEY CARRIED

FIRST LIEUTENANT JIMMY CROSS CARRIED letters from a girl named Martha, a junior at Mount Sebastian College in New Jersey. They were not love letters, but Lieutenant Cross was hoping, so he kept them folded in plastic at the bottom of his rucksack. In the late afternoon, after a day's march, he would dig his foxhole, wash his hands under a canteen, unwrap the letters, hold them with the tips of his fingers, and spend the last hour of light pretending. He would imagine romantic camping trips into the White Mountains in New Hampshire. He would sometimes taste the envelope flaps, knowing her tongue had been there. More than anything, he wanted Martha to love him as he loved her, but the letters were mostly chatty, elusive on the matter of love. She was a virgin, he was almost sure. She was an English major at Mount Sebastian, and she wrote beautifully about her professors and roommates and midterm exams, about her respect for Chaucer and her great affection for Virginia Woolf. She often quoted lines of poetry; she never mentioned the war, except to say, Jimmy, take care of yourself. The letters weighed 10 ounces. They were signed Love, Martha, but Lieutenant Cross understood that Love was only a way of signing and did not mean what he sometimes pretended it meant. At dusk, he would carefully return the letters to his rucksack. Slowly, a bit distracted, he would get up and move among his men, checking the perimeter, then at full dark he would return to his hole and watch the night and wonder if Martha was a virgin.

The things they carried were largely determined by necessity. Among the necessities or near-necessities were P-38 can openers, pocket knives, heat tabs, wrist watches, dog tags, mosquito repellent, chewing gum, candy, cigarettes, salt tablets, packets of Kool-Aid, lighters, matches, sewing kits, Military Payment Certificates, C rations, and two or three canteens of water. Together, these items weighed between 15 and 20 pounds, depending upon a man's habits or rate of metabolism. Henry Dobbins, who was a big man, carried extra rations; he was especially fond of canned peaches in heavy syrup over pound cake. Dave Jensen, who practiced field hygiene, carried a toothbrush, dental floss, and several hotel-sized bars of soap he'd stolen on R&R° in Sydney, Australia. Ted Lavender, who was scared, carried tranquilizers until he was shot in the head outside the village of Than Khe in mid-April. By necessity, and because it was SOP,° they all carried steel helmets that weighed 5 pounds including the liner and camouflage cover. They carried the standard fatigue jackets and trousers. Very few carried underwear. On their feet they carried jungle boots—2.1 pounds—and Dave Jensen carried three pairs of socks and a can of Dr. Scholl's foot powder as a precaution against trench foot. Until he was shot, Ted Lavender carried 6 or 7 ounces of premium dope, which for him was a necessity. Mitchell Sanders, the RTO,° carried condoms. Norman Bowker carried a diary. Rat Kiley carried comic books. Kiowa, a devout Baptist, carried an illustrated New Testament that had been presented to him by his father, who taught Sunday school in Oklahoma City, Oklahoma. As a hedge against bad

---

R&R: rest and rehabilitation leave. **SOP:** standard operating procedure. **RTO:** radio and telephone operator.

times, however, Kiowa also carried his grandmother's distrust of the white man, his grandfather's old hunting hatchet. Necessity dictated. Because the land was mined and booby-trapped, it was SOP for each man to carry a steel-centered, nylon-covered flak jacket, which weighed 6.7 pounds, but which on hot days seemed much heavier. Because you could die so quickly, each man carried at least one large compress bandage, usually in the helmet band for easy access. Because the nights were cold, and because the monsoons were wet, each carried a green plastic poncho that could be used as a raincoat or groundsheet or makeshift tent. With its quilted liner, the poncho weighed almost 2 pounds, but it was worth every ounce. In April, for instance, when Ted Lavender was shot, they used his poncho to wrap him up, then to carry him across the paddy, then to lift him into the chopper that took him away.

They were called legs or grunts.

To carry something was to hump it, as when Lieutenant Jimmy Cross humped his love for Martha up the hills and through the swamps. In its intransitive form, to hump meant to walk, or to march, but it implied burdens far beyond the intransitive.

5   Almost everyone humped photographs. In his wallet, Lieutenant Cross carried two photographs of Martha. The first was a Kodacolor snapshot signed Love, though he knew better. She stood against a brick wall. Her eyes were gray and neutral, her lips slightly open as she stared straight-on at the camera. At night, sometimes, Lieutenant Cross wondered who had taken the picture, because he knew she had boyfriends, because he loved her so much, and because he could see the shadow of the picture taker spreading out against the brick wall. The second photograph had been clipped from the 1968 Mount Sebastian yearbook. It was an action shot—women's volleyball—and Martha was bent horizontal to the floor, reaching, the palms of her hands in sharp focus, the tongue taut, the expression frank and competitive. There was no visible sweat. She wore white gym shorts. Her legs, he thought, were almost certainly the legs of a virgin, dry and without hair, the left knee cocked and carrying her entire weight, which was just over 100 pounds. Lieutenant Cross remembered touching that left knee. A dark theater, he remembered, and the movie was *Bonnie and Clyde,* and Martha wore a tweed skirt, and during the final scene, when he touched her knee, she turned and looked at him in a sad, sober way that made him pull his hand back, but he would always remember the feel of the tweed skirt and the knee beneath it and the sound of the gunfire that killed Bonnie and Clyde, how embarrassing it was, how slow and oppressive. He remembered kissing her goodnight at the dorm door. Right then, he thought, he should've done something brave. He should've carried her up the stairs to her room and tied her to the bed and touched that left knee all night long. He should've risked it. Whenever he looked at the photographs, he thought of new things he should've done.

What they carried was partly a function of rank, partly of field specialty.

As a first lieutenant and platoon leader, Jimmy Cross carried a compass, maps, code books, binoculars, and a .45-caliber pistol that weighed 2.9 pounds fully loaded. He carried a strobe light and the responsibility for the lives of his men.

As an RTO, Mitchell Sanders carried the PRC-25 radio, a killer, 26 pounds with its battery.

As a medic, Rat Kiley carried a canvas satchel filled with morphine and plasma and malaria tablets and surgical tape and comic books and all the things a medic must carry, including M&M's° for especially bad wounds, for a total weight of nearly 20 pounds.

10   As a big man, therefore a machine gunner, Henry Dobbins carried the M-60, which weighed 23 pounds unloaded, but which was almost always loaded. In addition, Dobbins carried between 10 and 15 pounds of ammunition draped in belts across his chest and shoulders.

As PFCs or Spec 4s, most of them were common grunts and carried the standard M-16 gas-operated assault rifle. The weapon weighed 7.5 pounds unloaded, 8.2 pounds with its full 20-round magazine. Depending on numerous factors, such as topography and psychology, the riflemen carried anywhere from 12 to 20 magazines, usually in cloth bandoliers, adding on another 8.4 pounds at minimum, 14 pounds at maximum. When it was available, they also carried M-16 maintenance gear—rods and steel brushes and swabs and tubes of LSA oil—all of which weighed about a pound. Among the grunts,

M&M: joking term for medical supplies.

some carried the M-79 grenade launcher, 5.9 pounds unloaded, a reasonably light weapon except for the ammunition, which was heavy. A single round weighed 10 ounces. The typical load was 25 rounds. But Ted Lavender, who was scared, carried 34 rounds when he was shot and killed outside Than Khe, and he went down under an exceptional burden, more than 20 pounds of ammunition, plus the flak jacket and helmet and rations and water and toilet paper and tranquilizers and all the rest, plus the unweighed fear. He was dead weight. There was no twitching or flopping. Kiowa, who saw it happen, said it was like watching a rock fall, or a big sandbag or something—just boom, then down—not like the movies where the dead guy rolls around and does fancy spins and goes ass over teakettle—not like that, Kiowa said, the poor bastard just flat-fuck fell. Boom. Down. Nothing else. It was a bright morning in mid-April. Lieutenant Cross felt the pain. He blamed himself. They stripped off Lavender's canteens and ammo, all the heavy things, and Rat Kiley said the obvious, the guy's dead, and Mitchell Sanders used his radio to report one U.S. KIA° and to request a chopper. Then they wrapped Lavender in his poncho. They carried him out to a dry paddy, established security, and sat smoking the dead man's dope until the chopper came. Lieutenant Cross kept to himself. He pictured Martha's smooth young face, thinking he loved her more than anything, more than his men, and now Ted Lavender was dead because he loved her so much and could not stop thinking about her. When the dustoff arrived, they carried Lavender aboard. Afterward they burned Than Khe. They marched until dusk, then dug their holes, and that night Kiowa kept explaining how you had to be there, how fast it was, how the poor guy just dropped like so much concrete. Boom-down, he said. Like cement.

In addition to the three standard weapons—the M-60, M-16, and M-79—they carried whatever presented itself, or whatever seemed appropriate as a means of killing or staying alive. They carried catch-as-catch-can. At various times, in various situations, they carried M-14s and CAR-15s and Swedish Ks and grease guns and captured AK-47s and Chi-Coms and RPGs and Simonov carbines and black market Uzis

KIA: killed in action.

and .38-caliber Smith & Wesson handguns and 66 mm LAWs and shotguns and silencers and blackjacks and bayonets and C-4 plastic explosives. Lee Strunk carried a slingshot; a weapon of last resort, he called it. Mitchell Sanders carried brass knuckles. Kiowa carried his grandfather's feathered hatchet. Every third or fourth man carried a Claymore antipersonnel mine—3.5 pounds with its firing device. They all carried fragmentation grenades—14 ounces each. They all carried at least one M-18 colored smoke grenade—24 ounces. Some carried CS or tear gas grenades. Some carried white phosphorus grenades. They carried all they could bear, and then some, including a silent awe for the terrible power of the things they carried.

In the first week of April, before Lavender died, Lieutenant Jimmy Cross received a good-luck charm from Martha. It was a simple pebble, an ounce at most. Smooth to the touch, it was a milky white color with flecks of orange and violet, oval-shaped, like a miniature egg. In the accompanying letter, Martha wrote that she had found the pebble on the Jersey shoreline, precisely where the land touched water at high tide, where things came together but also separated. It was this separate-but-together quality, she wrote, that had inspired her to pick up the pebble and to carry it in her breast pocket for several days, where it seemed weightless, and then to send it through the mail, by air, as a token of her truest feelings for him. Lieutenant Cross found this romantic. But he wondered what her truest feelings were, exactly, and what she meant by separate-but-together. He wondered how the tides and waves had come into play on that afternoon along the Jersey shoreline when Martha saw the pebble and bent down to rescue it from geology. He imagined bare feet. Martha was a poet, with the poet's sensibilities, and her feet would be brown and bare, the toenails unpainted, the eyes chilly and somber like the ocean in March, and though it was painful, he wondered who had been with her that afternoon. He imagined a pair of shadows moving along the strip of sand where things came together but also separated. It was phantom jealousy, he knew, but he couldn't help himself. He loved her so much. On the march, through the hot days of early April, he carried the pebble in his mouth, turning it with his tongue, tasting sea salt and moisture. His mind wandered.

He had difficulty keeping his attention on the war. On occasion he would yell at his men to spread out the column, to keep their eyes open, but then he would slip away into daydreams, just pretending, walking barefoot along the Jersey shore, with Martha, carrying nothing. He would feel himself rising. Sun and waves and gentle winds, all love and lightness.

What they carried varied by mission.

15   When a mission took them to the mountains, they carried mosquito netting, machetes, canvas tarps, and extra bug juice.

If a mission seemed especially hazardous, or if it involved a place they knew to be bad, they carried everything they could. In certain heavily mined AOs,° where the land was dense with Toe Poppers and Bouncing Betties, they took turns humping a 28-pound mine detector. With its headphones and big sensing plate, the equipment was a stress on the lower back and shoulders, awkward to handle, often useless because of the shrapnel in the earth, but they carried it anyway, partly for safety, partly for the illusion of safety.

On ambush, or other night missions, they carried peculiar little odds and ends. Kiowa always took along his New Testament and a pair of moccasins for silence. Dave Jensen carried night-sight vitamins high in carotene. Lee Strunk carried his slingshot; ammo, he claimed, would never be a problem. Rat Kiley carried brandy and M&M's candy. Until he was shot, Ted Lavender carried the starlight scope, which weighed 6.3 pounds with its aluminum carrying case. Henry Dobbins carried his girlfriend's pantyhose wrapped around his neck as a comforter. They all carried ghosts. When dark came, they would move out single file across the meadows and paddies to their ambush coordinates, where they would quietly set up the Claymores and lie down and spend the night waiting.

Other missions were more complicated and required special equipment. In mid-April, it was their mission to search out and destroy the elaborate tunnel complexes in the Than Khe area south of Chu Lai. To blow the tunnels, they carried one-pound blocks of pentrite high explosives, four blocks to a man, 68 pounds in all. They carried wiring, detonators, and battery-powdered clackers. Dave Jensen

carried earplugs. Most often, before blowing the tunnels, they were ordered by higher command to search them, which was considered bad news, but by and large they just shrugged and carried out orders. Because he was a big man, Henry Dobbins was excused from tunnel duty. The others would draw numbers. Before Lavender died there were 17 men in the platoon, and whoever drew the number 17 would strip off his gear and crawl in headfirst with a flashlight and Lieutenant Cross's .45-caliber pistol. The rest of them would fan out as security. They would sit down or kneel, not facing the hole, listening to the ground beneath them, imagining cobwebs and ghosts, whatever was down there— the tunnel walls squeezing in—how the flashlight seemed impossibly heavy in the hand and how it was tunnel vision in the very strictest sense, compression in all ways, even time, and how you had to wiggle in—ass and elbows—a swallowed-up feeling—and how you found yourself worrying about odd things: Will your flashlight go dead? Do rats carry rabies? If you screamed, how far would the sound carry? Would your buddies hear it? Would they have the courage to drag you out? In some respects, though not many, the waiting was worse than the tunnel itself. Imagination was a killer.

On April 16, when Lee Strunk drew the number 17, he laughed and muttered something and went down quickly. The morning was hot and very still. Not good, Kiowa said. He looked at the tunnel opening, then out across a dry paddy toward the village of Than Khe. Nothing moved. No clouds or birds or people. As they waited, the men smoked and drank Kool-Aid, not talking much, feeling sympathy for Lee Strunk but also feeling the luck of the draw. You win some, you lose some, said Mitchell Sanders, and sometimes you settle for a rain check. It was a tired line and no one laughed.

20   Henry Dobbins ate a tropical chocolate bar. Ted Lavender popped a tranquilizer and went off to pee.

After five minutes, Lieutenant Jimmy Cross moved to the tunnel, leaned down, and examined the darkness. Trouble, he thought—a cave-in maybe. And then suddenly, without willing it, he was thinking about Martha. The stresses and fractures, the quick collapse, the two of them buried alive under all that weight. Dense, crushing love. Kneeling, watching the hole, he tried to concentrate on Lee Strunk and the war, all the dangers, but his love was too much for

AOs: areas of operation.

him, he felt paralyzed, he wanted to sleep inside her lungs and breathe her blood and be smothered. He wanted her to be a virgin and not a virgin, all at once. He wanted to know her. Intimate secrets: Why poetry? Why so sad? Why that grayness in her eyes? Why so alone? Not lonely, just alone—riding her bike across campus or sitting off by herself in the cafeteria—even dancing, she danced alone—and it was the aloneness that filled him with love. He remembered telling her that one evening. How she nodded and looked away. And how, later, when he kissed her, she received the kiss without returning it, her eyes wide open, not afraid, not a virgin's eyes, just flat and uninvolved.

Lieutenant Cross gazed at the tunnel. But he was not there. He was buried with Martha under the white sand at the Jersey shore. They were pressed together, and the pebble in his mouth was her tongue. He was smiling. Vaguely, he was aware of how quiet the day was, the sullen paddies, yet he could not bring himself to worry about matters of security. He was beyond that. He was just a kid at war, in love. He was twenty-four years old. He couldn't help it.

A few moments later Lee Strunk crawled out of the tunnel. He came up grinning, filthy but alive. Lieutenant Cross nodded and closed his eyes while the others clapped Strunk on the back and made jokes about rising from the dead.

Worms, Rat Kiley said. Right out of the grave. Fuckin' zombie.

25   The men laughed. They all felt great relief.

Spook city, said Mitchell Sanders.

Lee Strunk made a funny ghost sound, a kind of moaning, yet very happy, and right then, when Strunk made that high happy moaning sound, when he went *Ahhooooo,* right then Ted Lavender was shot in the head on his way back from peeing. He lay with his mouth open. The teeth were broken. There was a swollen black bruise under his left eye. The cheekbone was gone. Oh shit, Rat Kiley said, the guy's dead. The guy's dead, he kept saying, which seemed profound—the guy's dead. I mean really.

The things they carried were determined to some extent by superstition. Lieutenant Cross carried his good-luck pebble. Dave Jensen carried a rabbit's foot. Norman Bowker, otherwise a very gentle person, carried a thumb that had been presented to him as a

gift by Mitchell Sanders. The thumb was dark brown, rubbery to the touch, and weighed 4 ounces at most. It had been cut from a VC corpse, a boy of fifteen or sixteen. They'd found him at the bottom of an irrigation ditch, badly burned, flies in his mouth and eyes. The boy wore black shorts and sandals. At the time of his death he had been carrying a pouch of rice, a rifle, and three magazines of ammunition.

You want my opinion, Mitchell Sanders said, there's a definite moral here.

30   He put his hand on the dead boy's wrist. He was quiet for a time, as if counting a pulse, then he patted the stomach, almost affectionately, and used Kiowa's hunting hatchet to remove the thumb.

Henry Dobbins asked what the moral was.

Moral?

You know. *Moral.*

Sanders wrapped the thumb in toilet paper and handed it across to Norman Bowker. There was no blood. Smiling, he kicked the boy's head, watched the flies scatter, and said, It's like with that old TV show—Paladin. Have gun, will travel.

35   Henry Dobbins thought about it.

Yeah, well, he finally said. I don't see no moral.

There it *is,* man.

Fuck off.

They carried USO stationery and pencils and pens. They carried Sterno, safety pins, trip flares, signal flares, spools of wire, razor blades, chewing tobacco, liberated joss sticks and statuettes of the smiling Buddha, candles, grease pencils, *The Stars and Stripes,* fingernail clippers, Psy Ops leaflets, bush hats, bolos, and much more. Twice a week, when the resupply choppers came in, they carried hot chow in green Mermite cans and large canvas bags filled with iced beer and soda pop. They carried plastic water containers, each with a 2-gallon capacity. Mitchell Sanders carried a set of starched tiger fatigues for special occasions. Henry Dobbins carried Black Flag insecticide. Dave Jensen carried empty sandbags that could be filled at night for added protection. Lee Strunk carried tanning lotion. Some things they carried in common. Taking turns, they carried the big PRC-77 scrambler radio, which weighed 30 pounds with its battery. They shared the weight of memory. They took up what others could no longer bear. Often, they carried each other, the wounded or weak. They carried infections. They carried chess sets, basketballs, Vietnamese-English dictionaries, insignia of rank, Bronze Stars and Purple Hearts, plastic cards imprinted with the Code of Conduct. They carried diseases, among them malaria and dysentery. They carried lice and ringworm and leeches and paddy algae and various rots and molds. They carried the land itself—Vietnam, the place, the soil—a powdery orange-red dust that covered their boots and fatigues and faces. They carried the sky. The whole atmosphere, they carried it, the humidity, the monsoons, the stink of fungus and decay, all of it, they carried gravity. They moved like mules. By daylight they took sniper fire, at night they were mortared, but it was not battle, it was just the endless march, village to village, without purpose, nothing won or lost. They marched for the sake of the march. They plodded along slowly, dumbly, leaning forward against the heat, unthinking, all blood and bone, simple grunts, soldiering with their legs, toiling up the hills and down into the paddies and across the rivers and up again and down, just humping, one step and then the next and then another, but no volition, no will, because it was automatic, it was anatomy, and the war was entirely a matter of posture and carriage, the hump was everything, a kind of inertia, a kind of emptiness, a dullness of desire and intellect and conscience and hope and human sensibility. Their principles were in their feet. Their calculations were biological. They had no sense of strategy or mission. They searched the villages without knowing what to look for, not caring, kicking over jars of rice, frisking children and old men, blowing tunnels, sometimes setting fires and sometimes not, then forming up and moving on to the next village, then other villages, where it would always be the same. They carried their own lives. The pressures were enormous. In the heat of early afternoon, they would remove their helmets and flak jackets, walking bare, which was dangerous but which helped ease the strain. They would often discard things along the route of march. Purely for comfort, they would throw away rations, blow their Claymores and grenades, no matter, because by nightfall the resupply choppers would arrive with more of the same, then a day or two later still more, fresh watermelons and crates of ammunition and sunglasses and woolen sweaters—the resources were stunning—sparklers

for the Fourth of July, colored eggs for Easter—it was the great American war chest—the fruits of science, the smoke stacks, the canneries, the arsenals at Hartford, the Minnesota forests, the machine shops, the vast fields of corn and wheat—they carried like freight trains; they carried it on their backs and shoulders—and for all the ambiguities of Vietnam, all the mysteries and unknowns, there was at least the single abiding certainty that they would never be at a loss for things to carry.

40   After the chopper took Lavender away, Lieutenant Jimmy Cross led his men into the village of Than Khe. They burned everything. They shot chickens and dogs, they trashed the village well, they called in artillery and watched the wreckage, then they marched for several hours through the hot afternoon, and then at dusk, while Kiowa explained how Lavender died, Lieutenant Cross found himself trembling.

He tried not to cry. With his entrenching tool, which weighed 5 pounds, he began digging a hole in the earth.

He felt shame. He hated himself. He had loved Martha more than his men, and as a consequence Lavender was now dead, and this was something he would have to carry like a stone in his stomach for the rest of the war.

All he could do was dig. He used his entrenching tool like an ax, slashing, feeling both love and hate, and then later, when it was full dark, he sat at the bottom of his foxhole and wept. It went on for a long while. In part, he was grieving for Ted Lavender, but mostly it was for Martha, and for himself, because she belonged to another world, which was not quite real, and because she was a junior at Mount Sebastian College in New Jersey, a poet and a virgin and uninvolved, and because he realized she did not love him and never would.

Like cement, Kiowa whispered in the dark. I swear to God—boom, down. Not a word.

45   I've heard this, said Norman Bowker.

A pisser, you know? Still zipping himself up. Zapped while zipping.

All right, fine. That's enough.

Yeah, but you had to see it, the guy just—

I *heard*, man. Cement. So why not shut the fuck *up?*

50 Kiowa shook his head sadly and glanced over at the hole where Lieutenant Jimmy Cross sat watching the night. The air was thick and wet. A warm dense fog had settled over the paddies and there was the stillness that precedes rain.

After a time Kiowa sighed.

One thing for sure, he said. The lieutenant's in some deep hurt. I mean that crying jag—the way he was carrying on—it wasn't fake or anything, it was real heavy-duty hurt. The man cares.

Sure, Norman Bowker said.

Say what you want, the man does care.

55 We all got problems.

Not Lavender.

No, I guess not, Bowker said. Do me a favor, though.

Shut up?

That's a smart Indian. Shut up.

60 Shrugging, Kiowa pulled off his boots. He wanted to say more, just to lighten up his sleep, but instead he opened his New Testament and arranged it beneath his head as a pillow. The fog made things seem hollow and unattached. He tried not to think about Ted Lavender, but then he was thinking how fast it was, no drama, down and dead, and how it was hard to feel anything except surprise. It seemed unchristian. He wished he could find some great sadness, or even anger, but the emotion wasn't there and he couldn't make it happen. Mostly he felt pleased to be alive. He liked the smell of the New Testament under his cheek, the leather and ink and paper and glue, whatever the chemicals were. He liked hearing the sounds of night. Even his fatigue, it felt fine, the stiff muscles and the prickly awareness of his own body, a floating feeling. He enjoyed not being dead. Lying there, Kiowa admired Lieutenant Jimmy Cross's capacity for grief. He wanted to share the man's pain, he wanted to care as Jimmy Cross cared. And yet when he closed his eyes, all he could think was Boom-down, and all he could feel was the pleasure of having his boots off and the fog curling in around him and the damp soil and the Bible smells and the plush comfort of night.

After a moment Norman Bowker sat up in the dark.

What the hell, he said. You want to talk, *talk*. Tell it to me.

Forget it.

No, man, go on. One thing I hate, it's a silent Indian.

65 For the most part they carried themselves with poise, a kind of dignity. Now and then, however, there were times of panic, when they squealed or wanted to squeal but couldn't, when they twitched and made moaning sounds and covered their heads and said Dear Jesus and flopped around on the earth and fired their weapons blindly and cringed and sobbed and begged for the noise to stop and went wild and made stupid promises to themselves and to God and to their mothers and fathers, hoping not to die. In different ways, it happened to all of them. Afterward, when the firing ended, they would blink and peek up. They would touch their bodies, feeling shame, then quickly hiding it. They would force themselves to stand. As if in slow motion, frame by frame, the world would take on the old logic—absolute silence, then the wind, then sunlight, then voices. It was the burden of being alive. Awkwardly, the men would reassemble themselves, first in private, then in groups, becoming soldiers again. They would repair the leaks in their eyes. They would check for casualties, call in dustoffs, light cigarettes, try to smile, clear their throats and spit and begin cleaning their weapons. After a time someone would shake his head and say, No lie, I almost shit my pants, and someone else would laugh, which meant it was bad, yes, but the guy had obviously not shit his pants, it wasn't that bad, and in any case nobody would ever do such a thing and then go ahead and talk about it. They would squint into the dense, oppressive sunlight. For a few moments, perhaps, they would fall silent, lighting a joint and tracking its passage from man to man, inhaling, holding in the humiliation. Scary stuff, one of them might say. But then someone else would grin or flick his eyebrows and say, Roger-dodger, almost cut me a new asshole, *almost.*

There were numerous such poses. Some carried themselves with a sort of wistful resignation, others with pride or stiff soldierly discipline or good humor or macho zeal. They were afraid of dying but they were even more afraid to show it.

They found jokes to tell.

They used a hard vocabulary to contain the terrible softness. *Greased* they'd say. *Offed, lit up, zapped while zipping.* It wasn't cruelty, just stage presence.

They were actors. When someone died, it wasn't quite dying, because in a curious way it seemed scripted, and because they had their lines mostly memorized, irony mixed with tragedy, and because they called it by other names, as if to encyst and destroy the reality of death itself. They kicked corpses. They cut off thumbs. They talked grunt lingo. They told stories about Ted Lavender's supply of tranquilizers, how the poor guy didn't feel a thing, how incredibly tranquil he was.

There's a moral here, said Mitchell Sanders.

70 They were waiting for Lavender's chopper, smoking the dead man's dope.

The moral's pretty obvious, Sanders said, and winked. Stay away from drugs. No joke, they'll ruin your day every time.

Cute, said Henry Dobbins.

Mind-blower, get it? Talk about wiggy. Nothing left, just blood and brains.

They made themselves laugh.

75 There it is, they'd say. Over and over—there it is, my friend, there it is—as if the repetition itself were an act of poise, a balance between crazy and almost crazy, knowing without going, there it is, which meant be cool, let it ride, because Oh yeah, man, you can't change what can't be changed, there it is, there it absolutely and positively and fucking well *is*.

They were tough.

They carried all the emotional baggage of men who might die. Grief, terror, love, longing—these were intangibles, but the intangibles had their own mass and specific gravity, they had tangible weight. They carried shameful memories. They carried the common secret of cowardice barely restrained, the instinct to run or freeze or hide, and in many respects this was the heaviest burden of all, for it could never be put down, it required perfect balance and perfect posture. They carried their reputations. They carried the soldier's greatest fear, which was the fear of blushing. Men killed, and died, because they were embarrassed not to. It was what had brought them to the war in the first place, nothing positive, no dreams of glory or honor, just to avoid the blush of dishonor. They died so as not to die of embarrassment. They crawled into tunnels and walked point and advanced under fire. Each morning, despite the unknowns, they made their legs move. They endured. They kept humping. They did not submit to the obvious

alternative, which was simply to close the eyes and fall. So easy, really. Go limp and tumble to the ground and let the muscles unwind and not speak and not budge until your buddies picked you up and lifted you into the chopper that would roar and dip its nose and carry you off to the world. A mere matter of falling, yet no one ever fell. It was not courage, exactly; the object was not valor. Rather, they were too frightened to be cowards.

By and large they carried these things inside, maintaining the masks of composure. They sneered at sick call. They spoke bitterly about guys who had found release by shooting off their own toes or fingers. Pussies, they'd say. Candy-asses. It was fierce, mocking talk, with only a trace of envy or awe, but even so the image played itself out behind their eyes.

They imagined the muzzle against flesh. So easy: squeeze the trigger and blow away a toe. They imagined it. They imagined the quick, sweet pain, then the evacuation to Japan, then a hospital with warm beds and cute geisha nurses.

80 And they dreamed of freedom birds.

At night, on guard, staring into the dark, they were carried away by jumbo jets. They felt the rush of takeoff. *Gone!* they yelled. And then velocity—wings and engines—a smiling stewardess—but it was more than a plane, it was a real bird, a big sleek silver bird with feathers and talons and high screeching. They were flying. The weights fell off; there was nothing to bear. They laughed and held on tight, feeling the cold slap of wind and altitude, soaring, thinking *It's over, I'm gone!* —they were naked, they were light and free—it was all lightness, bright and fast and buoyant, light as light, a helium buzz in the brain, a giddy bubbling in the lungs as they were taken up over the clouds and the war, beyond duty, beyond gravity and mortification and global entanglements— *Sin loi!°* they yelled, *I'm sorry, mother fuckers, but I'm out of it, I'm goofed, I'm on a space cruise, I'm gone!*—and it was a restful, unencumbered sensation, just riding the light waves, sailing that big silver freedom bird over the mountains and oceans, over America, over the farms and great sleeping cities and cemeteries and highways and the golden arches of McDonald's, it was flight, a kind of fleeing, a kind of falling, falling higher and higher, spinning off the

Sin loi: Sorry.

edge of the earth and beyond the sun and through the vast, silent vacuum where there were no burdens and where everything weighed exactly nothing—*Gone!* they screamed. *I'm sorry but I'm gone!*—and so at night, not quite dreaming, they gave themselves over to lightness, they were carried, they were purely borne.

On the morning after Ted Lavender died, First Lieutenant Jimmy Cross crouched at the bottom of his foxhole and burned Martha's letters. Then he burned the two photographs. There was a steady rain falling, which made it difficult, but he used heat tabs and Sterno to build a small fire, screening it with his body, holding the photographs over the tight blue flame with the tips of his fingers.

He realized it was only a gesture. Stupid, he thought. Sentimental, too, but mostly just stupid.

Lavender was dead. You couldn't burn the blame.

85 Besides, the letters were in his head. And even now, without photographs, Lieutenant Cross could see Martha playing volleyball in her white gym shorts and yellow T-shirt. He could see her moving in the rain.

When the fire died out, Lieutenant Cross pulled his poncho over his shoulders and ate breakfast from a can.

There was no great mystery, he decided.

In those burned letters Martha had never mentioned the war, except to say, Jimmy, take care of yourself. She wasn't involved. She signed the letters Love, but it wasn't love, and all the fine lines and technicalities did not matter. Virginity was no longer an issue. He hated her. Yes, he did. He hated her. Love, too, but it was a hard, hating kind of love.

The morning came up wet and blurry. Everything seemed part of everything else, the fog and Martha and the deepening rain.

90 He was a soldier, after all.

Half smiling, Lieutenant Jimmy Cross took out his maps. He shook his head hard, as if to clear it, then bent forward and began planning the day's march. In ten minutes, or maybe twenty, he would rouse the men and they would pack up and head west, where the maps showed the country to be green and inviting. They would do what they had always done. The rain might add some weight, but otherwise it would be one more day layered upon all the other days.

He was realistic about it. There was that new hardness in his stomach. He loved her but he hated her.

No more fantasies, he told himself.

Henceforth, when he thought about Martha, it would be only to think that she belonged elsewhere. He would shut down the daydreams. This was not Mount Sebastian, it was another world, where there were no pretty poems or midterm exams, a place where men died because of carelessness and gross stupidity. Kiowa was right. Boom-down, and you were dead, never partly dead.

95 Briefly, in the rain, Lieutenant Cross saw Martha's gray eyes gazing back at him.

He understood.

It was very sad, he thought. The things men carried inside. The things men did or felt they had to do.

He almost nodded at her, but didn't.

Instead he went back to his maps. He was now determined to perform his duties firmly and without negligence. It wouldn't help Lavender, he knew that, but from this point on he would comport himself as an officer. He would dispose of his good-luck pebble. Swallow it, maybe, or use Lee Strunk's slingshot, or just drop it along the trail. On the march he would impose strict field discipline. He would be careful to send out flank security, to prevent straggling or bunching up, to keep his troops moving at the proper pace and at the proper interval. He would insist on clean weapons. He would confiscate the remainder of Lavender's dope. Later in the day, perhaps, he would call the men together and speak to them plainly. He would accept the blame for what had happened to Ted Lavender. He would be a man about it. He would look them in the eyes, keeping his chin level, and he would issue the new SOPs in a calm, impersonal tone of voice, a lieutenant's voice, leaving no room for argument or discussion. Commencing immediately, he'd tell them, they would no longer abandon equipment along the route of march. They would police up their acts. They would get their shit together, and keep it together, and maintain it neatly and in good working order.

100 He would not tolerate laxity. He would show strength, distancing himself.

Among the men there would be grumbling, of course, and maybe worse, because their days would seem longer and their loads heavier, but Lieutenant Jimmy Cross reminded himself that his obligation was not to be loved but to lead. He would dispense with love; it was not now a factor. And if anyone quarreled or complained, he would simply tighten his lips and arrange his shoulders in the correct command posture. He might give a curt little nod. Or he might not. He might just shrug and say, Carry on, then they would saddle up and form into a column and move out toward the villages west of Than Khe.

[1986]

QUESTIONS FOR REFLECTION AND DISCUSSION

1. Much of the time, the repetition of "carried" is used for various enumerations. At which moments does the narrator shift to zeugma? What patterns of meaning are developed between these moments?

2. What is the primary event recounted in this short story? What is the effect on our understanding of the story of the author's choice to structure his story in terms of lists rather than as a more traditional event-centered narrative?

3. To what degree does "The Things They Carried" follow the conventions of war stories with which you are familiar? To what degree does it diverge from them?

4. What is the significance of the final variation on the story's central verb, "Carry on"? What is the relation of this ending to the rest of the story? How are we meant to evaluate Cross's actions and their result in Than Ke?

POETRY

William Carlos Williams 1883–1963

How do we measure the simple death of a cat or a collection of fleas faced with the vast scale of the world? How can we measure the emotions they conjure up from the surface observation of specific phenomena or acts? These are some of the questions William Carlos Williams asks us to consider with the hyperbolic (p. 216) title of his poem about the burial of (presumably) a pet. For a biography of Williams, see page 227.

Complete Destruction

It was an icy day.
We buried the cat,
then took her box
and set fire to it
in the back yard.   5
Those fleas that escaped
earth and fire
died by the cold.

[1921]

QUESTIONS FOR REFLECTION AND DISCUSSION

1. What is hyperbolic about the title in relation to the text of the poem? What is understated about the text of the poem in relation to its title?

2. How would the meaning of the poem change if its title reflected the tone of the text, as, for example, "The Burial of a Cat"?

3. It seems evident that neither the title nor the text on its own accurately captures the combination of emotions in the death of a pet. In what way does the combination of tones better capture these emotions?

Robert Frost 1874–1963

Like William Carlos Williams, Robert Frost uses the device of hyperbole to approach a sense of destruction and loss much more finite and difficult to describe than the end of the world. For a biography of Frost, see page 176.

Fire and Ice

Some say the world will end in fire,
Some say in ice.
From what I've tasted of desire
I hold with those who favor fire.
But if it had to perish twice,   5

I think I know enough of hate
To know that for destruction ice
Is also great
And would suffice.

[1923]

QUESTIONS FOR REFLECTION AND DISCUSSION

1. In this poem the hyperbole is implied in the imagery of destruction by fire, while the litotes is explicitly present in the concluding lines. What is the effect of associating hyperbole with one natural element and litotes with another? Would the poem work equally well if the association were switched? Why or why not?

2. In what way could the use of three lines of only four syllables each among the others of eight be characterized as a metrical understatement?

3. What is the argument of the poem? What phenomena do you think Frost is talking about through his imagery?

John Donne 1572–1631

Written by John Donne (p. 386) near the end of his life and published in his *Holy Sonnets*, "Death be not proud" directly confronts a personified Death and defies his power over the speaker's own life and in the world around him. For a biography of Donne, see page 386.

Death be not proud

Death be not proud, though some have called thee
Mighty and dreadful, for thou art not so;
For those whom thou think'st thou dost overthrow
Die not, poor death, nor yet canst thou kill me.
From rest and sleep, which but thy pictures be,   5
Much pleasure, then from thee much more must flow,
And soonest our best men with thee do go,
Rest of their bones, and soul's delivery.
Thou art slave to fate, chance, kings, and desperate men,
And dost with poison, war, and sickness dwell,   10
And poppy, or charms can make us sleep as well,
And better than thy stroke; why swell'st thou then?
One short sleep past, we wake eternally,
And death shall be no more; death, thou shalt die.

[1633]

1. Summarize the poem, one sentence for each of the three parts of the sonnet. What is the topic of each part?

2. Explain the use of paradox in lines 4 and 14. How does Donne use paradox to change the meaning of death?

3. What is the difference between Donne's personification of Death and the figure of the devil in Hawthorne's "Young Goodman Brown?" What do they share? How are they different?

Dylan Thomas 1914–1953

Born in Wales, Dylan Thomas dropped out of school at sixteen because he was unable to focus on any studies besides English. He published his first volume of poetry before the age of twenty. Thomas made a highly successful poetry-reading tour of America in 1950. His lyrical and emotional verse, combined with his hard-drinking and combative personal style, made his readings into theatrical events. Thomas died of the effects of alcoholism at the age of thirty-nine. First published in 1952, "Do Not Go Gentle into That Good Night" is addressed to the poet's dying father.

Do Not Go Gentle into That Good Night

Do not go gentle into that good night,
Old age should burn and rave at close of day;
Rage, rage against the dying of the light.

Though wise men at their end know dark is right,
Because their words had forked no lightning they   5
Do not go gentle into that good night.

Good men, the last wave by, crying how bright
Their frail deeds might have danced in a green bay,
Rage, rage against the dying of the light.

Wild men who caught and sang the sun in flight,   10
And learn, too late, they grieved it on its way,
Do not go gentle into that good night.

Grave men, near death, who see with blinding sight
Blind eyes could blaze like meteors and be gay,
Rage, rage against the dying of the light.   15

And you, my father, there on the sad height,
Curse, bless, me now with your fierce tears, I pray,
Do not go gentle into that good night.
Rage, rage against the dying of the light.

[1952]

1. Compare the two refrains. Is there any difference in the sentiment they express?

2. Discuss the function of the rhyme scheme. What is the relationship between the middle line of each of the tercets and the first and third lines?

3. Paraphrase the five tercets. What change in focus occurs in the final quatrain? In your mind, does it alter the meaning of the poem? If so, in what way? If not, how does it develop the earlier theme?

4. In form, the poem is a villanelle (p. 128). How, if at all, do the villanelle's conventions suit the poem's theme and development?

5. Compare the speaker's attitude toward death in this poem with the speaker's attitude in John Donne's "Death be not proud."

Emily Dickinson 1830–1886

Born in Amherst, Massachusetts, Emily Dickinson scarcely left this town for the rest of her life beyond a brief attendance at Mount Holyoke Seminary when she was seventeen. Dickinson compensated for the physical isolation of her life—there is little evidence that she even left her house during her last twenty years—by reading widely and corresponding actively. Although a few of her poems were published during her lifetime, the scale and brilliance of her poetic creation were discovered only after her death: she left behind 1,775 poems, most of them brief, many of them handwritten into hand-bound volumes. Heavily influenced by the Calvinist household in which she was raised, the Puritan atmosphere of New England, the religious poetry of seventeenth-century England, and her reading of the Book of Revelation in the Bible, Dickinson's verse is steeped in the imagery of inspiration and of death, sometimes personified, sometimes not.

I like a look of Agony

I like a look of Agony,
Because I know it's true –
Men do not sham Convulsion,
Nor simulate, a Throe –
The Eyes glaze once – and that is Death –   5
Impossible to feign
The Beads upon the Forehead
By homely Anguish strung.

QUESTIONS FOR REFLECTION AND DISCUSSION

1. Summarize the speaker's assertion regarding convulsions, throes, and death. Do you agree? Why or why not?

2. What is the meaning of the verb "like" in the first line? What attitude does it suggest we take toward the phenomenon of death?

3. What is the relationship the speaker establishes between death and truth? What are the consequences toward life if we accept this relationship?

Because I could not stop for Death

Because I could not stop for Death –
He kindly stopped for me –
The Carriage held but just Ourselves –
And Immortality.

We slowly drove – He knew no haste   5
And I had put away
My labor and my leisure too,
For His Civility –

We passed the School, where Children strove
At Recess – in the Ring –   10
We passed the Fields of Gazing Grain –
We passed the Setting Sun –

Or rather – He passed Us –
The Dews drew quivering and chill –
For only Gossamer, my Gown –   15
My Tippet° – only Tulle° –

We paused before a House that seemed
A Swelling of the Ground –

Carreta de la Muerte (Death Carriage), c. 1930–1940. Folk art made for a traditional Mexican Day of the Dead procession.

The Roof was scarcely visible –
The Cornice – in the Ground –   20

Since then – 'tis Centuries – and yet
Feels shorter than the Day
I first surmised the Horses' Heads
Were toward Eternity –

[1863]

16 Tippet: shawl. 16 Tulle: silk net.

1. Paraphrase each quatrain of the poem in a sentence. What event(s) is the speaker describing?

2. What is the difference between the speaker stopping for Death and Death stopping for the speaker? How does this opening scene depict Death? What are some of the other ways we might have expected Dickinson to portray

Death? Why do you think she chose to portray him this way?

3. How does it mold our perception of Death that he drives a carriage rather than walks or rides a horse? Would you attribute the same meaning to the carriage death drives in the Mexican *Carreta de la Muerte* (see p. 459)?

I felt a Funeral, in my Brain

I felt a Funeral, in my Brain,
And Mourners to and fro
Kept treading - treading - till it seemed
That Sense was breaking through -

And when they all were seated,   5
A Service, like a Drum -
Kept beating - beating - till I thought
My Mind was going numb -

And then I heard them lift a Box
And creak across my Soul   10

With those same Boots of Lead, again,
Then Space - began to toll,
As all the Heavens were a Bell,
And Being, but an Ear,
And I, and Silence, some strange Race   15
Wrecked, solitary, here -

And Then a Plank in Reason, broke,
And I dropped down, and down -
And hit a World, at every plunge,
And Finished knowing - then -   20

[1861]

1. List the main images of the poem and identify which literary devices (p. 211) they use. Do the images relate to one another or do they remain distinct?

2. What role is played by the different senses in the poem?

3. Does the poem describe the process of dying? Why or why not?

I heard a Fly buzz – when I died

I heard a Fly buzz - when I died -
The Stillness in the Room
Was like the Stillness in the Air -
Between the Heaves of Storm -

The Eyes around - had wrung them dry -   5
And Breaths were gathering firm
For that last Onset - when the King
Be witnessed - in the Room -

I willed my Keepsakes - Signed away
What portion of me be   10
Assignable - and then it was
There interposed a Fly -

With Blue - uncertain stumbling Buzz -
Between the light - and me -
And then the Windows failed - and then   15
I could not see to see -

[1862]

1. Rather than a literary device, this poem begins with a concrete description. How is the opening effect different from that of "I felt a Funeral in my Brain"? What literary devices does "I heard a Fly buzz" use after the opening line, and how do they alter the effect of the poem, if at all?

2. What remains after the speaker has "Signed away/ What Portion of me be/Assignable"?

It was not Death, for I stood up

It was not Death, for I stood up,
And all the Dead lie down –
It was not Night, for all the Bells
Put out their Tongues, for Noon.

It was not Frost, for on my Flesh   5
I felt Siroccos - crawl -
Nor Fire - for just my Marble feet
Could keep a Chancel, cool -

And yet it tasted like them all;
The Figures I have seen   10
Set orderly, for Burial,
Reminded me, of mine –

As if my life were shaven
And fitted to a frame,
And could not breathe without a key;   15
And 't was like Midnight, some -

When everything that ticked - has stopped -
And Space stares, all around -
Or Grisly frosts - first Autumn morns,
Repeal the Beating Ground -   20

But, most, like Chaos - Stopless - cool -
Without a Chance or Spar -
Or even a Report of Land -
To justify - Despair.

[1862]

1. What literary devices (p. 211) do the opening two stanzas of the poem employ? In what way do they introduce the main theme of the poem?

2. Three of the four stanzas use half-rhymes (p. 124). What is the effect of this choice on the poem's theme?

3. To what phenomena does the speaker compare her experience? Is she describing death, or something else?

A Toad, can die of Light

A Toad, can die of Light -
Death is the Common Right
Of Toads and Men -
Of Earl and Midge
The privilege -   5
Why swagger, then?
The Gnat's supremacy is large as Thine -

Life - is a different Thing -
So measure Wine -
Naked of Flask - Naked of Cask -   10
Bare Rhine -
Which Ruby's mine?

[1862]

1. Rather than describe the experience of death or a death-like experience, this poem reflects upon the meaning of death. What argument does it make about death?

2. Paraphrase the metaphor of wine in the second stanza. How does it relate to the first stanza?

3. Throughout her poems, Dickinson uses unconventional punctuation and capitalization. What is the effect of this usage on our understanding of the poems? How would they be different without it? In what way might this formal decision relate to the imagery and theme of the poetry?

Tell all the Truth but tell it slant

Tell all the Truth but tell it slant –
Success in Circuit lies
Too bright for our infirm Delight
The Truth's superb surprise

As Lightning to the Children eased   5
With explanation kind
The Truth must dazzle gradually
Or every man be blind –

[1868]

QUESTIONS FOR REFLECTION AND DISCUSSION

1. Why must poetry tell "all the Truth"? Why must it "tell it slant"? Compare this definition of truth with the one in "I like a look of Agony."

2. Paraphrase the simile, or comparison (p. 218), of the second stanza. What does this simile add to the first stanza?

3. How does Dickinson define poetry in this poem? To what degree does her definition of poetry apply to her other poems included here?

WORKING FURTHER WITH EMILY DICKINSON'S POETRY

1. Compare the different ways in which Emily Dickinson describes Death, the different images she associates with it or Him, and the different contexts in which Death appears in the poems you have read here. What patterns can you observe? What are the primary points of divergence in the different poems?

2. Does Death have an ethical dimension for Dickinson, or is it wholly individual?

3. Write a comparison paper about Dickinson's poems and one or two other selections in this chapter.

4. Find a collection of Dickinson's poetry and read a selection of poems *not* directly concerned with Death. What points of comparison can you find with the poems included here? How are the other poems different?

Lot's Wife

Translated by Stanislaw Barańczak and Clare Cavanagh.

They say I looked back out of curiosity.
But I could have had other reasons.
I looked back mourning my silver bowl.
Carelessly, while tying my sandal strap.
So I wouldn't have to keep staring at the
    righteous nape   5
of my husband Lot's neck.
From the sudden conviction that if I dropped dead
he wouldn't so much as hesitate.
From the disobedience of the meek.
Checking for pursuers.   10
Struck by the silence, hoping God had changed his
    mind.
Our two daughters were already vanishing over the
    hilltop.
I felt age within me. Distance.
The futility of wandering. Torpor.
I looked back setting my bundle down.   15
I looked back not knowing where to set my foot.
Serpents appeared on my path,
spiders, field mice, baby vultures.
They were neither good nor evil now—every living thing
was simply creeping or hopping along in the mass
    panic.   20
I looked back in desolation.
In shame because we had stolen away.
Wanting to cry out, to go home.
Or only when a sudden gust of wind
unbound my hair and lifted up my robe.   25
It seemed to me that they were watching from the
    walls of Sodom
and bursting into thunderous laughter again and again.
I looked back in anger.

Gustave Doré, *Lot's Flight from Sodom.* A nineteenth-century engraving of the episode of Genesis 19.14-26 in which Lot and his family flee from the destruction of Sodom and Gomorrah. Disregarding the angel's instructions not to look back, Lot's wife is turned into a pillar of salt.

To savor their terrible fate.
I looked back for all the reasons given above.   30
I looked back involuntarily.
It was only a rock that turned underfoot, growling at me.
It was a sudden crack that stopped me in my tracks.
A hamster on its hind paws tottered on the edge.
It was then we both glanced back.   35
No, no. I ran on,
I crept, I flew upward
until darkness fell from the heavens
and with it scorching gravel and dead birds.
I couldn't breathe and spun around and around.   40
Anyone who saw me must have thought I was dancing.
It's not inconceivable that my eyes were open.
It's possible I fell facing the city.

[1976]

1. What are some conventional explanations for Lot's wife looking back at the city of Sodom in Genesis 19? What reasons does the poem's speaker suggest? Does she say anything to suggest one of them is the true reason for her action?

2. Szymborska often includes animals in her poems. What do you think is the function of the hamster that appears in lines 34–35?

3. What is the meaning of the final line of the poem?

4. How does our understanding of the meaning of the episode change depending on which reason we accept for the wife's looking back? How does our understanding of the meaning of the episode change if we cannot decide on a single reason?

Carolyn Forché b. 1951

Born in Detroit, Carolyn Forché won the Yale Younger Poets Prize for her first volume of poetry. She subsequently was awarded a Guggenheim Fellowship, which she used to travel to El Salvador, on the advice of the nephew of the Salvadoran poet whose works she was translating. On the brink of a brutal civil war, the situation in El Salvador galvanized Forché as she traveled the country, documenting atrocities and transforming them into poetry. The resulting volume, *The Country Between Us* (1981) includes the prose poem "The Colonel." Forché has devoted her subsequent career to writing and collecting examples of what she terms "the poetry of witness." She currently teaches in the Department of English at Georgetown University.

THE COLONEL

What you have heard is true. I was in his house. His wife carried a tray of coffee and sugar. His daughter filed her nails, his son went out for the night. There were daily papers, pet dogs, a pistol on the cushion beside him. The moon swung bare on its black cord over the house. On the television was a cop show. It was in English. Broken bottles were embedded in the walls around the house to scoop the kneecaps from a man's legs or cut his hands to lace. On the windows there were gratings like those in liquor stores. We had dinner, rack of lamb, good wine, a gold bell was on the table for calling the maid. The maid brought green mangoes, salt, a type of bread. I was asked how I enjoyed the country. There was a brief commercial in Spanish. His wife took everything away. There was some talk then of how difficult it had become to govern. The parrot said hello on the terrace. The colonel told it to shut up, and pushed himself from the table. My friend said to me with his eyes: say nothing. The colonel returned with a sack used to bring groceries home. He spilled many human ears on the table. They were like dried peach halves. There is no other way to say this. He took one of them in his hands, shook it in our faces, dropped it into a water glass. It came alive there. I am tired of

Susan Meiselas, *Soldiers Searching Bus Passengers, Northern Highway, El Salvador, 1980*. A photojournalist best known for her work documenting civil war in El Salvador and Nicaragua, Meiselas took this photo near the beginning of a conflict that would last until the early 1990s.

fooling around he said. As for the rights of anyone, tell your people they can go fuck themselves. He swept the ears to the floor with his arm and held the last of his wine in the air. Something for your poetry, no? he said. Some of the ears on the floor caught this scrap of his voice. Some of the ears on the floor were pressed to the ground.

May 1978

[1981]

QUESTIONS FOR REFLECTION AND DISCUSSION

1. Can you imagine this poem written in verse rather than prose? Why or why not?

2. The first two-thirds of the poem are told without any rhetorical figures. At what point does this change? What motivates the shift?

3. The final sentences of the poem are different again from the rest of the poem. What makes these sentences a

synecdoche (or, perhaps, a metonymy, since they are no longer part of the bodies to which they belonged) while the previous description of them was not? How do you interpret the last three sentences?

4. What is the ethical dilemma Forché is posing through this poem?

PLAY

Sophocles 5th century BCE

The ancient Greek tragedian Sophocles was born in Colonus around 496 BCE and lived his entire life in nearby Athens, dying there at the age of 90. He first gained prominence in 468 when one of his tragedies defeated that of the great playwright Aeschylus in a competition. Although he is said to have written around 120 plays, only seven have survived. These include the three linked tragedies about the royal house of Thebes, of which *Antigonê* is the third; the other two are *Oedipus Rex* and *Oedipus at Colonus*. As you read *Antigonê*, consider the way its characters debate the principles that guide their decisions and balance the weight of the argument on both sides.

ANTIGONÊ

Translated by Dudley Fitts and Robert Fitzgerald

CHARACTERS

Antigonê
Ismenê
Eurydicê
Creon
Haimon
Teiresias
A Sentry
A Messenger
Chorus

SCENE: *Before the palace of Creon, King of Thebes. A central double door, and two lateral doors. A platform extends the length of the façade, and from this platform three steps lead down into the "orchestra," or chorus-ground.*

TIME: *Dawn of the day after the repulse of the Argive army from the assault on Thebes.*

PROLOGUE

Antigonê and Ismenê enter from the central door of the palace.

Antigonê: Ismenê, dear sister,
You would think that we had already suffered enough
For the curse on Oedipus:°
I cannot imagine any grief
That you and I have not gone through. And now—   5
Have they told you of the new decree of our
   King Creon?
Ismenê: I have heard nothing: I know
That two sisters lost two brothers, a double death
In a single hour; and I know that the Argive army

---

3 **the curse on Oedipus:** As Sophocles tells in *Oedipus the King*, the King of Thebes discovered that he had lived his life under a curse. Unknowingly, he had slain his father and married his mother. On realizing this terrible truth, Oedipus put out his own eyes and departed into exile. Now, years later, as *Antigonê* opens, Antigonê and Ismenê, daughters of Oedipus, are recalling how their two brothers died. After the abdication of their father, the brothers had ruled Thebes together. But they fell to quarreling. When Eteoclês expelled Polyneicês, the latter returned with an army and attacked the city. The two brothers killed each other in combat, leaving the throne to Creon. The new king of Thebes has buried Eteoclês with full honors, but, calling Polyneicês a traitor, has decreed that his body shall be left to the crows—an especially terrible decree, for a rotting corpse might offend Zeus; bring down plague, blight, and barrenness upon Thebes; and prevent the soul of a dead hero from entering the Elysian Fields, abode of those favored by the gods.

Antigone from "Antigone" by Sophocles (oil on canvas), by Marie Spartali Stillman (1844–1927), Simon Carter Gallery, Woodbridge, Suffolk, England.

Fled in the night; but beyond this, nothing.   10

Antigonê: I thought so. And that is why I wanted you

To come out here with me. There is something we
    must do.

Ismenê: Why do you speak so strangely?

Antigonê: Listen, Ismenê:

Creon buried our brother Eteoclês   15

With military honors, gave him a soldier's funeral,

And it was right that he should; but Polyneicês,

Who fought as bravely and died as miserably,—

They say that Creon has sworn

No one shall bury him, no one mourn for him,   20

But his body must lie in the fields, a sweet treasure

For carrion birds to find as they search for food.

That is what they say, and our good Creon is coming
    here

To announce it publicly; and the penalty—

Stoning to death in the public square!

                        There it is,   25

And now you can prove what you are:

A true sister, or a traitor to your family.

Ismenê: Antigonê, you are mad! What could I possibly
    do?

Antigonê: You must decide whether you will help me
    or not.

Ismenê: I do not understand you. Help you
    in what?   30

Antigonê: Ismenê, I am going to bury him. Will you
    come?

Ismenê: Bury him! You have just said the new law
    forbids it.

Antigonê: He is my brother. And he is your brother,
    too.

Ismenê: But think of the danger! Think what Creon
    will do!

Antigonê: Creon is not strong enough to stand
    in my way.   35

Ismenê: Ah sister!

Oedipus died, everyone hating him

For what his own search brought to light, his eyes

Ripped out by his own hand; and Iocastê died,

His mother and wife at once: she twisted
    the cords   40

That strangled her life; and our two brothers died,

Each killed by the other's sword. And we are left:

But oh, Antigonê,

Think how much more terrible than these

Our own death would be if we should go against
    Creon   45

And do what he has forbidden! We are only women,

We cannot fight with men, Antigonê!

The law is strong, we must give in to the law

In this thing, and in worse. I beg the Dead

To forgive me, but I am helpless: I must yield   50

To those in authority. And I think it is dangerous
    business

To be always meddling.

Antigonê: If that is what you think,

I should not want you, even if you asked to come.

You have made your choice, you can be what you
    want to be.

But I will bury him; and if I must die,   55

I say that this crime is holy: I shall lie down

With him in death, and I shall be as dear

To him as he to me.

                  It is the dead,

Not the living, who make the longest demands:

We die for ever . . .

                  You may do as you like,   60

Since apparently the laws of the gods mean nothing
    to you.

Ismenê: They mean a great deal to me; but I have no
    strength

To break laws that were made for the public good.

Antigonê: That must be your excuse, I suppose. But as
    for me,

I will bury the brother I love.

Ismenê: Antigonê,

I am so afraid for you!   65

Antigonê: You need not be:

You have yourself to consider, after all.

Ismenê: But no one must hear of this, you must tell

no one!

I will keep it a secret, I promise!

Antigonê: O tell it! Tell everyone!

Think how they'll hate you when it all comes out   70

If they learn that you knew about it all the time!

Ismenê: So fiery! You should be cold with fear.

Antigonê: Perhaps. But I am doing only what I must.

Ismenê: But you can do it? I say that you cannot.

Antigonê: Very well: when my strength gives out,

I shall do no more.   75

Ismenê: Impossible things should not be tried at all.

Antigonê: Go away, Ismenê:

I shall be hating you soon, and the dead will too,

For your words are hateful. Leave me my foolish plan:

I am not afraid of the danger; if it means death,   80

It will not be the worst of deaths—death without

honor.

Ismenê: Go then, if you feel that you must.

You are unwise,

But a loyal friend indeed to those who love you.

*Exit into the palace. Antigonê goes off, left. Enter the
Chorus.*

PÁRODOS°

Strophe° 1

Chorus: Now the long blade of the sun, lying

Level east to west, touches with glory

Thebes of the Seven Gates. Open, unlidded

Eye of golden day! O marching light

Across the eddy and rush of Dircê's stream,°   5

Striking the white shields of the enemy

Thrown headlong backward from the blaze of

morning!

Choragos:° Polyneicês their commander

Roused them with windy phrases,

Párodos a song sung by the chorus on first entering. **Strophe** (according to
scholarly theory) the part of the párodos sung while the chorus danced from
stage right to stage left. **5 Dircê's stream** river near Thebes. **8 Choragos**
leader of the Chorus and principal commentator on the play's action.

He the wild eagle screaming   10

Insults above our land,

His wings their shields of snow,

His crest their marshalled helms.

Antistrophe° 1

Chorus: Against our seven gates in a yawning ring

The famished spears came onward in the night;   15

But before his jaws were sated with our blood,

Or pinefire took the garland of our towers,

He was thrown back; and as he turned, great Thebes—

No tender victim for his noisy power—

Rose like a dragon behind him, shouting war.   20

Choragos: For God hates utterly

The bray of bragging tongues;

And when he beheld their smiling,

Their swagger of golden helms,

The frown of his thunder blasted   25

Their first man from our walls.

Strophe 2

Chorus: We heard his shout of triumph high in the air

Turn to a scream; far out in a flaming arc

He fell with his windy torch, and the earth struck him.

And others storming in fury no less than his   30

Found shock of death in the dusty joy of battle.

Choragos: Seven captains at seven gates

Yielded their clanging arms to the god

That bends the battle-line and breaks it.

These two only, brothers in blood,   35

Face to face in matchless rage,

Mirroring each the other's death,

Clashed in long combat.

Antistrophe 2

Chorus: But now in the beautiful morning of victory

Let Thebes of the many chariots sing for joy!   40

With hearts for dancing we'll take leave of war:

Our temples shall be sweet with hymns of praise,

And the long night shall echo with our chorus.

SCENE I

Choragos: But now at last our new King is coming:

Creon of Thebes, Menoikeus' son.

Antistrophe the part of the párodos sung while the chorus danced back
from stage left to stage right.

In this auspicious dawn of his reign
What are the new complexities
That shifting Fate has woven for him?   5
What is his counsel? Why has he summoned
The old men to hear him?

Enter Creon from the palace, center. He addresses the
Chorus from the top step.

Creon: Gentlemen: I have the honor to inform you
that our Ship of State, which recent storms have
threatened to destroy, has come safely to harbor at   10
last, guided by the merciful wisdom of Heaven. I
have summoned you here this morning because I
know that I can depend upon you: your devotion
to King Laïos was absolute; you never hesitated in
your duty to our late ruler Oedipus; and when   15
Oedipus died, your loyalty was transferred to his
children. Unfortunately, as you know, his two sons,
the princes Eteoclês and Polyneicês, have killed
each other in battle; and I, as the next in blood,
have succeeded to the full power of the throne.   20

I am aware, of course, that no Ruler can
expect complete loyalty from his subjects until he
has been tested in office. Nevertheless, I say to
you at the very outset that I have nothing but
contempt for the kind of Governor who is afraid,   25
for whatever reason, to follow the course that he
knows is best for the State; and as for the man
who sets private friendship above the public
welfare,—I have no use for him, either. I call God
to witness that if I saw my country headed for   30
ruin, I should not be afraid to speak out plainly;
and I need hardly remind you that I would never
have any dealings with an enemy of the people.
No one values friendship more highly than I; but
we must remember that friends made at the risk   35
of wrecking our Ship are not real friends at all.

These are my principles, at any rate, and that is
why I have made the following decision concerning the sons of Oedipus: Eteoclês, who died as a
man should die, fighting for his country, is to be   40
buried with full military honors, with all the ceremony that is usual when the greatest heroes die;
but his brother Polyneicês, who broke his exile to
come back with fire and sword against his native
city and the shrines of his fathers' gods, whose one   45
idea was to spill the blood of his blood and sell his
own people into slavery—Polyneicês, I say, is to

have no burial: no man is to touch him or say the
least prayer for him; he shall lie on the plain,
unburied; and the birds and the scavenging dogs   50
can do with him whatever they like.

This is my command, and you can see the wisdom behind it. As long as I am King, no traitor is
going to be honored with the loyal man. But whoever shows by word and deed that he is on the   55
side of the State,—he shall have my respect while
he is living, and my reverence when he is dead.

Choragos: If that is your will, Creon son of
Menoikeus,
You have the right to enforce it: we are yours.

Creon: That is my will. Take care that you do your   60
part.

Choragos: We are old men: let the younger ones
carry it out.

Creon: I do not mean that: the sentries have been
appointed.

Choragos: Then what is it that you would have
us do?

Creon: You will give no support to whoever breaks
this law.

Choragos: Only a crazy man is in love with death!   65

Creon: And death it is, yet money talks, and the
wisest
Have sometimes been known to count a few coins
too many.

Enter Sentry from left.

Sentry: I'll not say that I'm out of breath from running, King, because every time I stopped to think
about what I have to tell you, I felt like going   70
back. And all the time a voice kept saying, "You
fool, don't you know you're walking straight into
trouble?"; and then another voice: "Yes, but if you
let somebody else get the news to Creon first, it
will be even worse than that for you!" But good   75
sense won out, at least I hope it was good sense,
and here I am with a story that makes no sense at
all; but I'll tell it anyhow, because, as they say,
what's going to happen's going to happen and—

Creon: Come to the point. What have you to say?   80

Sentry: I did not do it. I did not see who did it. You
must not punish me for what someone else has done.

Creon: A comprehensive defense! More effective,
perhaps,
If I knew its purpose. Come: what is it?

Sentry: A dreadful thing ... I don't know how to
   put it—   85

Creon: Out with it!

Sentry: Well, then;
   The dead man—

                    Polyneicês—

Pause. The Sentry is overcome, fumbles for words.
Creon waits impassively.

                       out there—
                              someone,—
   New dust on the slimy flesh!

Pause. No sign from Creon.

   Someone has given it burial that way, and
   Gone ...   90

Long pause. Creon finally speaks with deadly
control.

Creon: And the man who dared do this?

Sentry: I swear I
   Do not know! You must believe me!

                         Listen:
   The ground was dry, not a sign of digging, no,
   Not a wheeltrack in the dust, no trace of anyone.
   It was when they relieved us this morning: and
     one of them,   95
   The corporal, pointed to it.

                    There it was,
   The strangest—

              Look:
   The body, just mounded over with light dust: you see?
   Not buried really, but as if they'd covered it
   Just enough for the ghost's peace. And no sign   100
   Of dogs or any wild animal that had been there.

   And then what a scene there was! Every man of us
   Accusing the other: we all proved the other man
    did it,
   We all had proof that we could not have done it.
   We were ready to take hot iron in our hands,   105
   Walk through fire, swear by all the gods,
   It was not I!
   I do not know who it was, but it was not I!

Creon's rage has been mounting steadily, but the
Sentry is too intent upon his story to notice it.

   And then, when this came to nothing, someone said
   A thing that silenced us and made us stare   110
   Down at the ground: you had to be told the news,

And one of us had to do it! We threw the dice,
And the bad luck fell to me. So here I am,
No happier to be here than you are to have me:
Nobody likes the man who brings bad news.   115

Choragos: I have been wondering, King: can it be
   that the gods have done this?

Creon (*furiously*)**:** Stop!
   Must you doddering wrecks
   Go out of your heads entirely? "The gods"!
   Intolerable!   120
   The gods favor this corpse? Why? How had he
    served them?
   Tried to loot their temples, burn their images,
   Yes, and the whole State, and its laws with it!
   Is it your senile opinion that the gods love to honor
    bad men?
   A pious thought!—

                       No, from the very beginning   125
   There have been those who have whispered together,
   Stiff-necked anarchists, putting their heads together,
   Scheming against me in alleys. These are the men,
   And they have bribed my own guard to do this thing.

(*Sententiously.*) Money!   130
   There's nothing in the world so demoralizing as
    money.
   Down go your cities,
   Homes gone, men gone, honest hearts corrupted,
   Crookedness of all kinds, and all for money!

(*To Sentry.*)   But you—!
   I swear by God and by the throne of God,   135
   The man who has done this thing shall pay for it!
   Find that man, bring him here to me, or your death
   Will be the least of your problems: I'll string you up
   Alive, and there will be certain ways to make you
   Discover your employer before you die;   140
   And the process may teach you a lesson you seem to
    have missed:
   The dearest profit is sometimes all too dear:
   That depends on the source. Do you understand me?
   A fortune won is often misfortune.

Sentry: King, may I speak?

Creon: Your very voice distresses me.

Sentry: Are you sure that it is my voice, and not your
   conscience?

Creon: By God, he wants to analyze me now!

Sentry: It is not what I say, but what has been done,
   that hurts you.

Creon: You talk too much.

Sentry: Maybe; but I've done nothing.

Creon: Sold your soul for some silver: that's all
  you've done.   150

Sentry: How dreadful it is when the right judge
  judges wrong!

Creon: Your figures of speech
  May entertain you now; but unless you bring me the
  man,
  You will get little profit from them in the end.

Exit Creon into the palace.

Sentry: "Bring me the man"—!   155
  I'd like nothing better than bringing him the man!
  But bring him or not, you have seen the last of me here.
  At any rate, I am safe!

Exit Sentry.

ODE I°

Strophe 1

Chorus: Numberless are the world's wonders, but none
  More wonderful than man; the stormgray sea
  Yields to his prows, the huge crests bear him high;
  Earth, holy and inexhaustible, is graven
  With shining furrows where his plows have gone   5
  Year after year, the timeless labor of stallions.

Antistrophe 1

  The lightboned birds and beasts that cling to cover,
  The lithe fish lighting their reaches of dim water,
  All are taken, tamed in the net of his mind;
  The lion on the hill, the wild horse windy-maned,   10
  Resign to him; and his blunt yoke has broken
  The sultry shoulders of the mountain bull.

Strophe 2

  Words also, and thought as rapid as air,
  He fashions to his good use; statecraft is his,
  And his the skill that deflects the arrows of snow,   15
  The spears of winter rain: from every wind
  He has made himself secure—from all but one:
  In the late wind of death he cannot stand.

Antistrophe 2

Ode I first song sung by the Chorus, who at the same time danced. Here
again, as in the *pàrodos, strophe* and *antistrophe* probably divide the song into
two movements of the dance: right to left, then left to right.

O clear intelligence, force beyond all measure!
O fate of man, working both good and evil!   20
When the laws are kept, how proudly his city stands!
When the laws are broken, what of his city then?
Never may the anárchic man find rest at my hearth,
Never be it said that my thoughts are his thoughts.

SCENE II

Re-enter Sentry leading Antigonê.

Choragos: What does this mean? Surely this captive
  woman
  Is the Princess, Antigonê. Why should she be taken?

Sentry: Here is the one who did it! We caught her
  In the very act of burying him.—Where is Creon?

Choragos: Just coming from the house.

Enter Creon, center.

Creon: What has happened?
  Why have you come back so soon?

Sentry (expansively):   O King,
  A man should never be too sure of anything:
  I would have sworn
  That you'd not see me here again: your anger
  Frightened me so, and the things you threatened
    me with;   10
  But how could I tell then
  That I'd be able to solve the case so soon?
  No dice-throwing this time: I was only too glad to come!

  Here is this woman. She is the guilty one:
  We found her trying to bury him.   15
  Take her, then; question her; judge her as you will.
  I am through with the whole thing now, and glad
    of it.

Creon: But this is Antigonê! Why have you brought her
  here?

Sentry: She was burying him, I tell you!

Creon *(severely):*   Is this the truth?

Sentry: I saw her with my own eyes. Can I say
  more?   20

Creon: The details: come, tell me quickly!

Sentry: It was like this:
  After those terrible threats of yours, King,
  We went back and brushed the dust away from the
    body.
  The flesh was soft by now, and stinking,

So we sat on a hill to windward and kept guard.   25
No napping this time! We kept each other awake.
But nothing happened until the white round sun
Whirled in the center of the round sky over us:
Then, suddenly,
A storm of dust roared up from the earth, and
  the sky   30
Went out, the plain vanished with all its trees
In the stinging dark. We closed our eyes and
  endured it.
The whirlwind lasted a long time, but it passed;
And then we looked, and there was Antigonê!
I have seen   35
A mother bird come back to a stripped nest, heard
Her crying bitterly a broken note or two
For the young ones stolen. Just so, when this girl
Found the bare corpse, and all her love's work wasted,
She wept, and cried on heaven to damn the hands   40
That had done this thing.
               And then she brought more dust
And sprinkled wine three times for her brother's
  ghost.
We ran and took her at once. She was not afraid,
Not even when we charged her with what she had
  done.
She denied nothing.
             And this was a comfort to me,   45
And some uneasiness: for it is a good thing
To escape from death, but it is no great pleasure
To bring death to a friend.
             Yet I always say
There is nothing so comfortable as your own safe
  skin!
Creon (*slowly, dangerously*): And you, Antigonê,   50
You with your head hanging,—do you confess this
  thing?
Antigonê: I do. I deny nothing.
Creon (*to Sentry*):   You may go.

Exit Sentry.

(*To Antigonê.*) Tell me, tell me briefly:
Had you heard my proclamation touching this
  matter?   55
Antigonê: It was public. Could I help hearing it?
Creon: And yet you dared defy the law.
Antigonê: I dared.
  It was not God's proclamation. That final Justice
  That rules the world below makes no such laws.

Your edict, King, was strong,
But all your strength is weakness itself against   60
The immortal unrecorded laws of God.
They are not merely now: they were, and shall be,
Operative for ever, beyond man utterly.

I knew I must die, even without your decree:
I am only mortal. And if I must die   65
Now, before it is my time to die,
Surely this is no hardship: can anyone
Living, as I live, with evil all about me,
Think Death less than a friend? This death of mine
Is of no importance; but if I had left my brother   70
Lying in death unburied, I should have suffered.
Now I do not.
         You smile at me. Ah Creon,
Think me a fool, if you like; but it may well be
That a fool convicts me of folly.
Choragos: Like father, like daughter: both headstrong,
  deaf to reason!   75
She has never learned to yield.
Creon: She has much to learn.
The inflexible heart breaks first, the toughest iron
Cracks first, and the wildest horses bend their necks
At the pull of the smallest curb.
             Pride? In a slave?
This girl is guilty of a double insolence,   80
Breaking the given laws and boasting of it.
Who is the man here,
She or I, if this crime goes unpunished?
Sister's child, or more than sister's child,
Or closer yet in blood—she and her sister   85
Win bitter death for this!
(*To Servants.*)   Go, some of you,
Arrest Ismenê. I accuse her equally.
Bring her: you will find her sniffling in the house there.

Her mind's a traitor: crimes kept in the dark
Cry for light, and the guardian brain shudders;   90
But how much worse than this
Is brazen boasting of barefaced anarchy!
Antigonê: Creon, what more do you want than
  my death?
Creon: Nothing.
  That gives me everything.
Antigonê: Then I beg you: kill me.
This talking is a great weariness: your words   95
Are distasteful to me, and I am sure that mine

Seem so to you. And yet they should not seem so:
I should have praise and honor for what I have done.
All these men here would praise me
Were their lips not frozen shut with fear of you.   100
(*Bitterly.*) Ah the good fortune of kings,
Licensed to say and do whatever they please!

Creon: You are alone here in that opinion.

Antigonê: No, they are with me. But they keep their
tongues in leash.

Creon: Maybe. But you are guilty, and they are not. 105

Antigonê: There is no guilt in reverence for the dead.

Creon: But Eteoclês—was he not your brother too?

Antigonê: My brother too.

Creon: And you insult his memory?

Antigonê (*softly*): The dead man would not say that
I insult it.

Creon: He would: for you honor a traitor as much
as him.   110

Antigonê: His own brother, traitor or not, and equal
in blood.

Creon: He made war on his country. Eteoclês
defended it.

Antigonê: Nevertheless, there are honors due all the
dead.

Creon: But not the same for the wicked as for the just.

Antigonê: Ah Creon, Creon,
Which of us can say what the gods hold wicked? 115

Creon: An enemy is an enemy, even dead.

Antigonê: It is my nature to join in love, not hate.

Creon (*finally losing patience*): Go join them, then;
if you must have your love,
Find it in hell!   120

Choragos: But see, Ismenê comes:

Enter Ismenê, guarded.

Those tears are sisterly, the cloud
That shadows her eyes rains down gentle sorrow.

Creon: You too, Ismenê,
Snake in my ordered house, sucking my blood   125
Stealthily—and all the time I never knew
That these two sisters were aiming at my throne!

                                                                          Ismenê,
Do you confess your share in this crime, or deny it?
Answer me.

Ismenê: Yes, if she will let me say so. I am guilty.   130

Antigonê (*coldly*): No, Ismenê. You have no right
to say so.
You would not help me, and I will not have you
help me.

Ismenê: But now I know what you meant; and
I am here
To join you, to take my share of punishment.

Antigonê:
The dead man and the gods who rule the dead   135
Know whose act this was. Words are not friends.

Ismenê: Do you refuse me, Antigonê? I want to die
with you:
I too have a duty that I must discharge to the dead.

Antigonê: You shall not lessen my death by
sharing it.

Ismenê: What do I care for life when you are dead? 140

Antigonê: Ask Creon. You're always hanging on his
opinions.

Ismenê: You are laughing at me. Why, Antigonê?

Antigonê: It's a joyless laughter, Ismenê.

Ismenê: But can I do nothing?

Antigonê: Yes. Save yourself. I shall not envy you.
There are those who will praise you; I shall have
honor, too.   145

Ismenê: But we are equally guilty!

Antigonê: No more, Ismenê.
You are alive, but I belong to Death.

Creon (*to the Chorus*): Gentlemen, I beg you to
observe these girls:
One has just now lost her mind; the other,
It seems, has never had a mind at all.   150

Ismenê: Grief teaches the steadiest minds to waver,
King.

Creon: Yours certainly did, when you assumed guilt
with the guilty!

Ismenê: But how could I go on living without her?

Creon: You are.
She is already dead.

Ismenê: But your own son's bride!

Creon: There are places enough for him to push his
plow.   155
I want no wicked women for my sons!

Ismenê: O dearest Haimon, how your father wrongs
you!

Creon: I've had enough of your childish talk of
marriage!

Choragos: Do you really intend to steal this girl from
your son?

Creon: No; Death will do that for me.

Choragos: Then she must die?

Creon (*ironically*): You dazzle me.
                                          —But enough of this talk!

(*To Guards.*) You, there, take them away and guard
   them well:
For they are but women, and even brave men run
When they see Death coming.

Exeunt Ismenê, Antigonê, and Guards.

ODE II

Chorus: Fortunate is the man who has never tasted
   God's vengeance!
Where once the anger of heaven has struck, that
   house is shaken
For ever: damnation rises behind each child
Like a wave cresting out of the black northeast,
When the long darkness under sea roars up   5
And bursts drumming death upon the windwhipped
   sand.

I have seen this gathering sorrow from time long past
Loom upon Oedipus' children: generation from
   generation
Takes the compulsive rage of the enemy god.
So lately this last flower of Oedipus' line   10
Drank the sunlight! but now a passionate word
And a handful of dust have closed up all its beauty.

   What mortal arrogance
   Transcends the wrath of Zeus?
Sleep cannot lull him nor the effortless long months 15
Of the timeless gods: but he is young for ever,
And his house is the shining day of high Olympos.
   All that is and shall be,
   And all the past, is his.
No pride on earth is free of the curse of heaven.   20

   The straying dreams of men
   May bring them ghosts of joy:
But as they drowse, the waking embers burn them;
Or they walk with fixed eyes, as blind men walk.
But the ancient wisdom speaks for our own time: 25
   Fate works most for woe
   With Folly's fairest show.
Man's little pleasure is the spring of sorrow.

SCENE III

Choragos: But here is Haimon, King, the last of all
   your sons.
  Is it grief for Antigonê that brings him here,
  And bitterness at being robbed of his bride?

Enter Haimon.

Creon: We shall soon see, and no need of diviners.
                          —Son,
  You have heard my final judgment on that girl: 5
  Have you come here hating me, or have you come
  With deference and with love, whatever I do?
Haimon: I am your son, father. You are my guide.
  You make things clear for me, and I obey you.
  No marriage means more to me than your
   continuing wisdom.   10
Creon: Good. That is the way to behave: subordinate
  Everything else, my son, to your father's will.
  This is what a man prays for, that he may get
  Sons attentive and dutiful in his house,
  Each one hating his father's enemies,   15
  Honoring his father's friends. But if his sons
  Fail him, if they turn out unprofitably,
  What has he fathered but trouble for himself
  And amusement for the malicious?
                        So you are right
  Not to lose your head over this woman.   20
  Your pleasure with her would soon grow cold, Haimon,
  And then you'd have a hellcat in bed and elsewhere.
  Let her find her husband in Hell!
  Of all the people in this city, only she
  Has had contempt for my law and broken it.   25

  Do you want me to show myself weak before the
   people?
  Or to break my sworn word? No, and I will not.
  The woman dies.
  I suppose she'll plead "family ties." Well, let her.
  If I permit my own family to rebel,   30
  How shall I earn the world's obedience?
  Show me the man who keeps his house in hand,
  He's fit for public authority.
                  I'll have no dealings
  With law-breakers, critics of the government:
  Whoever is chosen to govern should be obeyed—   35
  Must be obeyed, in all things, great and small,
  Just and unjust! O Haimon,

The man who knows how to obey, and that man only,
Knows how to give commands when the time comes.
You can depend on him, no matter how fast   40
The spears come: he's a good soldier, he'll stick it out.

Anarchy, anarchy! Show me a greater evil!
This is why cities tumble and the great houses rain down,
This is what scatters armies!

No, no: good lives are made so by discipline.   45
We keep the laws then, and the lawmakers,
And no woman shall seduce us. If we must lose,
Let's lose to a man, at least! Is a woman stronger than we?

Choragos: Unless time has rusted my wits,
What you say, King, is said with point and dignity.   50

Haimon (*boyishly earnest*)**:** Father:
Reason is God's crowning gift to man, and you are right
To warn me against losing mine. I cannot say—
I hope that I shall never want to say!—that you
Have reasoned badly. Yet there are other men   55
Who can reason, too; and their opinions might be helpful.
You are not in a position to know everything
That people say or do, or what they feel:
Your temper terrifies them—everyone
Will tell you only what you like to hear.   60
But I, at any rate, can listen; and I have heard them
Muttering and whispering in the dark about this girl.
They say no woman has ever, so unreasonably,
Died so shameful a death for a generous act:
"She covered her brother's body. Is this indecent?   65
She kept him from dogs and vultures. Is this a crime?
Death?—She should have all the honor that we can give her!"

This is the way they talk out there in the city.

You must believe me:
Nothing is closer to me than your happiness.   70
What could be closer? Must not any son
Value his father's fortune as his father does his?
I beg you, do not be unchangeable:
Do not believe that you alone can be right.
The man who thinks that,   75

The man who maintains that only he has the power
To reason correctly, the gift to speak, the soul—
A man like that, when you know him, turns out empty.
It is not reason never to yield to reason!

In flood time you can see how some trees bend,   80
And because they bend, even their twigs are safe,
While stubborn trees are torn up, roots and all.
And the same thing happens in sailing:
Make your sheet fast, never slacken,—and over you go,
Head over heels and under: and there's your voyage.   85
Forget you are angry! Let yourself be moved!
I know I am young; but please let me say this:
The ideal condition
Would be, I admit, that men should be right by instinct;
But since we are all too likely to go astray,   90
The reasonable thing is to learn from those who can teach.

Choragos: You will do well to listen to him, King,
If what he says is sensible. And you, Haimon,
Must listen to your father.—Both speak well.

Creon: You consider it right for a man of my years and experience   95
To go to school to a boy?

Haimon: It is not right,
If I am wrong. But if I am young, and right,
What does my age matter?

Creon: You think it right to stand up for an anarchist?

Haimon: Not at all. I pay no respect to criminals.   100

Creon: Then she is not a criminal?

Haimon: The City would deny it, to a man.

Creon: And the City proposes to teach me how to rule?

Haimon: Ah. Who is it that's talking like a boy now?

Creon: My voice is the one voice giving orders in this City!   105

Haimon: It is no City if it takes orders from one voice.

Creon: The State is the King!

Haimon: Yes, if the State is a desert.

Pause.

Creon: This boy, it seems, has sold out to a woman.

Haimon: If you are a woman: my concern is only for you.

Creon: So? Your "concern"! In a public brawl with your father!   110

Haimon: How about you, in a public brawl with justice?

Creon: With justice, when all that I do is within my rights?

Haimon: You have no right to trample on God's right.

Creon (*completely out of control*): Fool, adolescent fool! Taken in by a woman!

Haimon: You'll never see me taken in by anything vile.   115

Creon: Every word you say is for her!

Haimon (*quietly, darkly*):   And for you. And for me. And for the gods under the earth.

Creon: You'll never marry her while she lives.

Haimon: Then she must die.—But her death will cause another.

Creon: Another?   120
Have you lost your senses? Is this an open threat?

Haimon: There is no threat in speaking to emptiness.

Creon: I swear you'll regret this superior tone of yours!
You are the empty one!

Haimon: If you were not my father, I'd say you were perverse.   125

Creon: You girl-struck fool, don't play at words with me!

Haimon: I am sorry. You prefer silence.

Creon: Now, by God—!
I swear, by all the gods in heaven above us,
You'll watch it, I swear you shall!
(*To the Servants.*)   Bring her out!
Bring the woman out! Let her die before his eyes!   130
Here, this instant, with her bridegroom beside her!

Haimon: Not here, no; she will not die here, King.
And you will never see my face again.
Go on raving as long as you've a friend to endure you.

Exit Haimon.

Choragos: Gone, gone.   135
Creon, a young man in a rage is dangerous!

Creon: Let him do, or dream to do, more than a man can.
He shall not save these girls from death.

Choragos: These girls?
You have sentenced them both?

Creon: No, you are right.
I will not kill the one whose hands are clean.   140

Choragos: But Antigonê?

Creon (*somberly*):   I will carry her far away
Out there in the wilderness, and lock her
Living in a vault of stone. She shall have food,
As the custom is, to absolve the State of her death.
And there let her pray to the gods of hell: 145
They are her only gods:
Perhaps they will show her an escape from death,
Or she may learn,
                       though late,
That piety shown the dead is pity in vain.

Exit Creon.

ODE III

Strophe

Chorus: Love, unconquerable
Waster of rich men, keeper
Of warm lights and all-night vigil
In the soft face of a girl:
Sea-wanderer, forest-visitor!   5
Even the pure Immortals cannot escape you,
And mortal man, in his one day's dusk,
Trembles before your glory.

Antistrophe

Surely you swerve upon ruin
The just man's consenting heart,   10
As here you have made bright anger
Strike between father and son—
And none has conquered but Love!
A girl's glance working the will of heaven:
Pleasure to her alone who mocks us,   15
Merciless Aphroditê.°

SCENE IV

Choragos (*as Antigonê enters guarded*):
But I can no longer stand in awe of this,
Nor, seeing what I see, keep back my tears.
Here is Antigonê, passing to that chamber
Where all find sleep at last.

Strophe 1

Antigonê: Look upon me, friends, and pity me   5
Turning back at the night's edge to say
Good-by to the sun that shines for me no longer;
Now sleepy Death

16 **Aphroditê** goddess of love and beauty.

Summons me down to Acheron,° that cold shore:
There is no bridesong there, nor any music.   10

Chorus: Yet not unpraised, not without a kind of honor,
You walk at last into the underworld;
Untouched by sickness, broken by no sword.
What woman has ever found your way to death?

Antistrophe 1

Antigonê: How often I have heard the story of Niobê,°15
Tantalos' wretched daughter, how the stone
Clung fast about her, ivy-close: and they say
The rain falls endlessly
And sifting soft snow; her tears are never done.
I feel the loneliness of her death in mine.   20

Chorus: But she was born of heaven, and you
Are woman, woman-born. If her death is yours,
A mortal woman's, is this not for you
Glory in our world and in the world beyond?

Strophe 2

Antigonê: You laugh at me. Ah, friends, friends,   25
Can you not wait until I am dead? O Thebes,
O men many-charioted, in love with Fortune,
Dear springs of Dircê, sacred Theban grove,
Be witnesses for me, denied all pity,
Unjustly judged! and think a word of love   30
For her whose path turns
Under dark earth, where there are no more tears.

Chorus: You have passed beyond human daring and
come at last
Into a place of stone where Justice sits.
I cannot tell   35
What shape of your father's guilt appears in this.

Antistrophe 2

Antigonê: You have touched it at last: that bridal bed
Unspeakable, horror of son and mother mingling:
Their crime, infection of all our family!
O Oedipus, father and brother!   40
Your marriage strikes from the grave to murder mine.
I have been a stranger here in my own land:
All my life
The blasphemy of my birth has followed me.

Chorus: Reverence is a virtue, but strength   45
Lives in established law: that must prevail.

You have made your choice,
Your death is the doing of your conscious hand.

Epode°

Antigonê: Then let me go, since all your words are
bitter,
And the very light of the sun is cold to me.   50
Lead me to my vigil, where I must have
Neither love nor lamentation; no song, but silence.

Creon interrupts impatiently.

Creon: If dirges and planned lamentations could put
off death,
Men would be singing for ever.
(*To the Servants.*)   Take her, go!
You know your orders: take her to the vault   55
And leave her alone there. And if she lives or dies,
That's her affair, not ours: our hands are clean.

Antigonê: O tomb, vaulted bride-bed in eternal rock,
Soon I shall be with my own again
Where Persephonê° welcomes the thin ghosts
underground: 60
And I shall see my father again, and you, mother,
And dearest Polyneicês—
                          dearest indeed
To me, since it was my hand
That washed him clean and poured the ritual wine:
And my reward is death before my time!   65

And yet, as men's hearts know, I have done no wrong,
I have not sinned before God. Or if I have,
I shall know the truth in death. But if the guilt
Lies upon Creon who judged me, then, I pray,
May his punishment equal my own.

Choragos: O passionate heart,
Unyielding, tormented still by the same winds!

Creon: Her guards shall have good cause to regret
their delaying.

Antigonê: Ah! That voice is like the voice of death!

Creon: I can give you no reason to think you are
mistaken.

Antigonê: Thebes, and you my fathers' gods,   75
And rulers of Thebes, you see me now, the last

---

9 Acheron river in Hades, domain of the dead. **15 story of Niobê** a Theban queen whose fourteen children were slain. She wept so copiously she was transformed to a stone on Mount Sipylos, and her tears became the mountain's streams.

48 Epode the final section (after the strophe and antistrophe) of a lyric passage; whereas the earlier sections are symmetrical, it takes a different metrical form. **60 Persephonê** whom Pluto, god of the underworld, abducted to be his queen.

Unhappy daughter of a line of kings,
Your kings, led away to death. You will remember
What things I suffer, and at what men's hands,
Because I would not transgress the laws of heaven. 80
(*To the Guards, simply.*) Come: let us wait no longer.

Exit Antigonê, left, guarded.

ODE IV

Strophe 1

Chorus: All Danaê's beauty was locked away
In a brazen cell where the sunlight could not come:
A small room still as any grave, enclosed her.
Yet she was a princess too,
And Zeus in a rain of gold poured love upon her.° 5
O child, child,
No power in wealth or war
Or tough sea-blackened ships
Can prevail against untiring Destiny!

Antistrophe 1

And Dryas' son° also, that furious king, 10
Bore the god's prisoning anger for his pride:
Sealed up by Dionysos in deaf stone,
His madness died among echoes.
So at the last he learned what dreadful power
His tongue had mocked: 15
For he had profaned the revels,
And fired the wrath of the nine
Implacable Sisters° that love the sound of the flute.

Strophe 2

And old men tell a half-remembered tale
Of horror° where a dark ledge splits the sea 20
And a double surf beats on the gráy shóres:
How a king's new woman, sick
With hatred for the queen he had imprisoned,

Ripped out his two sons' eyes with her bloody
hands
While grinning Arês° watched the shuttle plunge 25
Four times: four blind wounds crying for revenge,

Antistrophe 2

Crying, tears and blood mingled.—Piteously born,
Those sons whose mother was of heavenly birth!
Her father was the god of the North Wind
And she was cradled by gales, 30
She raced with young colts on the glittering hills
And walked untrammeled in the open light:
But in her marriage deathless Fate found means
To build a tomb like yours for all her joy.

SCENE V

*Enter blind Teiresias, led by a boy. The opening
speeches of Teiresias should be in singsong contrast
to the realistic lines of Creon.*

Teiresias: This is the way the blind man comes,
Princes, Princes,
Lockstep, two heads lit by the eyes of one.
Creon: What new thing have you to tell us, old Teiresias?
Teiresias: I have much to tell you: listen to the
prophet, Creon.
Creon: I am not aware that I have ever failed to listen. 5
Teiresias: Then you have done wisely, King, and ruled
well.
Creon: I admit my debt to you. But what have you
to say?
Teiresias: This, Creon: you stand once more on the
edge of fate.
Creon: What do you mean? Your words are a kind of
dread.
Teiresias: Listen Creon: 10
I was sitting in my chair of augury, at the place
Where the birds gather about me. They were all
a-chatter,
As is their habit, when suddenly I heard
A strange note in their jangling, a scream, a
Whirring fury; I knew that they were fighting, 15
Tearing each other, dying
In a whirlwind of wings clashing. And I was afraid.
I began the rites of burnt-offering at the altar,
But Hephaistos° failed me: instead of bright flame,

1-5 All Danaê's beauty . . . poured love upon her In legend, when an oracle told Acrisius, king of Argos, that his daughter Danaê would bear a son who would grow up to slay him, he locked the princess into a chamber made of bronze, lest any man impregnate her. But Zeus, father of the gods, entered Danaê's prison in a shower of gold. The resultant child, the hero Perseus, was accidentally to fulfill the prophecy by killing Acrisius with an ill-aimed discus throw. **10 Dryas' son** King Lycurgus of Thrace, whom Dionysos, god of wine, caused to be stricken with madness. **18 Sisters** the Muses, nine sister goddesses who presided over poetry and music, arts and sciences.
19-20 a half-remembered tale of horror As the Chorus recalls in the rest of this song, the point of this tale is that being nobly born will not save one from disaster. King Phineas cast off his first wife, Cleopatra (not the later Egyptian queen, but the daughter of Boreas, god of the north wind) and imprisoned her in a cave. Out of hatred for Cleopatra, the cruel Eidothea, second wife of the king, blinded her stepsons.

25 Arês god of war, said to gloat over bloodshed. **19 Hephaistos** god of fire and the forge.

There was only the sputtering slime of the fat thigh-flesh 20
Melting: the entrails dissolved in gray smoke,
The bare bone burst from the welter. And no blaze!

This was a sign from heaven. My boy described it,
Seeing for me as I see for others. 25

I tell you, Creon, you yourself have brought
This new calamity upon us. Our hearths and altars
Are stained with the corruption of dogs and carrion birds
That glut themselves on the corpse of Oedipus' son.
The gods are deaf when we pray to them, their fire
Recoils from our offering, their birds of omen 30
Have no cry of comfort, for they are gorged
With the thick blood of the dead.
                     O my son,
These are no trifles! Think: all men make mistakes,
But a good man yields when he knows his course is wrong,
And repairs the evil. The only crime is pride. 35

Give in to the dead man, then: do not fight with a corpse—
What glory is it to kill a man who is dead?
Think, I beg you:
It is for your own good that I speak as I do.
You should be able to yield for your own good. 40

Creon: It seems that prophets have made me their especial province.
All my life long
I have been a kind of butt for the dull arrows
Of doddering fortune-tellers!
                   No, Teiresias:
If your birds—if the great eagles of God himself 45
Should carry him stinking bit by bit to heaven,
I would not yield. I am not afraid of pollution:
No man can defile the gods.
              Do what you will,
Go into business, make money, speculate
In India gold or that synthetic gold from Sardis, 50
Get rich otherwise than by my consent to bury him.
Teiresias, it is a sorry thing when a wise man
Sells his wisdom, lets out his words for hire!

Teiresias: Ah Creon! Is there no man left in the world—

Creon: To do what?—Come, let's have the aphorism! 55

Teiresias: No man who knows that wisdom outweighs any wealth?

Creon: As surely as bribes are baser than any baseness.

Teiresias: You are sick, Creon! You are deathly sick!

Creon: As you say: it is not my place to challenge a prophet.

Teiresias: Yet you have said my prophecy is for sale. 60

Creon: The generation of prophets has always loved gold.

Teiresias: The generation of kings has always loved brass.

Creon: You forget yourself! You are speaking to your King.

Teiresias: I know it. You are a king because of me.

Creon: You have a certain skill; but you have sold out. 65

Teiresias: King, you will drive me to words that—

Creon: Say them, say them!
Only remember: I will not pay you for them.

Teiresias: No, you will find them too costly.

Creon: No doubt. Speak:
Whatever you say, you will not change my will.

Teiresias: Then take this, and take it to heart! 70
The time is not far off when you shall pay back
Corpse for corpse, flesh of your own flesh.
You have thrust the child of this world into living night,
You have kept from the gods below the child that is theirs:
The one in a grave before her death, the other,
Dead, denied the grave. This is your crime: 75
And the Furies and the dark gods of Hell
Are swift with terrible punishment for you.

Do you want to buy me now, Creon?
                      Not many days,
And your house will be full of men and women weeping, 80
And curses will be hurled at you from far
Cities grieving for sons unburied, left to rot
Before the walls of Thebes.
These are my arrows, Creon: they are all for you.

(*To Boy.*) But come, child: lead me home. 85
Let him waste his fine anger upon younger men.
Maybe he will learn at last
To control a wiser tongue in a better head.

Exit Teiresias.

Choragos: The old man has gone, King, but his words
Remain to plague us. I am old, too,
But I cannot remember that he was ever false. 90

Creon: That is true. . . . It troubles me.
　Oh it is hard to give in! but it is worse
　To risk everything for stubborn pride.
Choragos: Creon: take my advice.
Creon: 　　　　　　　　　　　What shall I do?
Choragos: Go quickly: free Antigonê from her
　vault 　　　　　　　　　　　　　　　　95
　And build a tomb for the body of Polyneicês.
Creon: You would have me do this!
Choragos: 　　　　　　　　　　Creon, yes!
　And it must be done at once: God moves
　Swiftly to cancel the folly of stubborn men.
Creon: It is hard to deny the heart! But I 　　100
　Will do it: I will not fight with destiny.
Choragos: You must go yourself, you cannot leave it to
　others.
Creon: I will go.
　　　　　　—Bring axes, servants:
　Come with me to the tomb. I buried her, I
　Will set her free. 　　　　　　　　　105
　　　　　　　Oh quickly!
　My mind misgives—
　The laws of the gods are mighty, and a man must serve
　them
　To the last day of his life!

Exit Creon.

PAEAN°

Strophe 1

Choragos: God of many names
Chorus: 　　　　　　　　　O Iacchos
　　　　　　　　　　　　　son
　of Kadmeian Sémelê
　　　　　　　O born of the Thunder!
　Guardian of the West
　　　　　　　　　Regent
　of Eleusis' plain
　　　　　　　O Prince of maenad Thebes
　and the Dragon Field by rippling Ismenós:° 　　5

Antistrophe 1

Choragos: God of many names
Chorus: 　　　　　　　　　the flame of torches
　flares on our hills
　　　　　　　the nymphs of Iacchos
　dance at the spring of Castalia:°
　from the vine-close mountain
　　　　　　　　　come ah come in ivy:
　Evohé evohé!° sings through the streets of Thebes 　10

Strophe 2

Choragos: God of many names
Chorus: 　　　　　　　　　Iacchos of Thebes
　heavenly Child
　　　　　　　of Sémelê bride of the Thunderer!
　The shadow of plague is upon us:
　　　　　　　　　come
　with clement feet
　　　　　　　oh come from Parnasos
　down the long slopes
　　　　　　　across the lamenting water 　15

Antistrophe 2

Choragos: Iô° Fire! Chorister of the throbbing stars!
　O purest among the voices of the night!
　Thou son of God, blaze for us!
Chorus: Come with choric rapture of circling Maenads
　Who cry *Iô Iacche!*
　　　　　　God of many names! 　　20

ÉXODOS°

Enter Messenger from left.

Messenger: Men of the line of Kadmos, you who live
　Near Amphion's citadel:°
　　　　　　　I cannot say
　Of any condition of human life "This is fixed,
　This is clearly good, or bad." Fate raises up,
　And Fate casts down the happy and unhappy alike: 　5

Paean song of praise or prayer, here to Dionysos, god of wine. **1-5 God of many names . . . Dragon Field by rippling Ismenòs** Dionysos was also called Iacchos (or, by the Romans, Bacchus). He was the son of Zeus ("the Thunderer") and of Sémelê, daughter of Kadmos (or Cadmus), legendary founder of Thebes. "Regent of Eleusis' plain" is another name for Dionysos, honored in secret rites at Eleusis, a town northwest of Athens. "Prince of maenad Thebes" is yet another: the Maenads were women of Thebes said to worship Dionysos with wild orgiastic rites. Kadmos, so the story goes, sowed dragon's teeth in a field beside the river Ismenós. Up sprang a crop of fierce warriors who fought among themselves until only five remained. These victors became the first Thebans.

8 Castalia a spring on Mount Parnassus, named for a maiden who drowned herself in it to avoid rape by the god Apollo. She became a nymph, or nature spirit, dwelling in its waters. In the temple of Delphi, at the mountain's foot, priestesses of Dionysos (the "nymphs of Iacchos") used the spring's waters in rites of purification. **10 Evohé evohé!** cry of the Maenads in supplicating Dionysos: "Come forth, come forth!" **16 Iô** "Hail" or "Praise be to …" **Éxodos** the final scene, containing the play's resolution. **2 Amphion's citadel** a name for Thebes. Amphion, son of Zeus, had built a wall around the city by playing so beautifully on his lyre that the charmed stones leaped into their slots.

No man can foretell his Fate.

                                     Take the case of Creon:

Creon was happy once, as I count happiness:
Victorious in battle, sole governor of the land,
Fortunate father of children nobly born.
And now it has all gone from him! Who can say   10
That a man is still alive when his life's joy fails?
He is a walking dead man. Grant him rich,
Let him live like a king in his great house:
If his pleasure is gone, I would not give
  So much as the shadow of smoke for all he owns.   15

Choragos: Your words hint at sorrow: what is your
  news for us?

Messenger: They are dead. The living are guilty of
  their death.

Choragos: Who is guilty? Who is dead? Speak!

Messenger: Haimon.
  Haimon is dead; and the hand that killed him
  Is his own hand.

Choragos: His father's? or his own?   20

Messenger: His own, driven mad by the murder his
  father had done.

Choragos: Teiresias, Teiresias, how clearly you saw
  it all!

Messenger: This is my news: you must draw what
  conclusions you can from it.

Choragos: But look: Eurydicê, our Queen:
  Has she overheard us?   25

Enter Eurydicê from the palace, center.

Eurydicê: I have heard something, friends:
  As I was unlocking the gate of Pallas'° shrine,
  For I needed her help today, I heard a voice
  Telling of some new sorrow. And I fainted
  There at the temple with all my maidens about me.   30
  But speak again: whatever it is, I can bear it:
  Grief and I are no strangers.

Messenger: Dearest Lady.
  I will tell you plainly all that I have seen.
  I shall not try to comfort you: what is the use,
  Since comfort could lie only in what is not true?   35
  The truth is always best.

                        I went with Creon
To the outer plain where Polyneicês was lying,
No friend to pity him, his body shredded by dogs.

We made our prayers in that place to Hecatê
And Pluto,° that they would be merciful. And we
  bathed   40
The corpse with holy water, and we brought
Fresh-broken branches to burn what was left of it,
And upon the urn we heaped up a towering barrow
Of the earth of his own land.

                      When we were done, we ran
To the vault where Antigonê lay on her couch of
  stone.   45
One of the servants had gone ahead,
And while he was yet far off he heard a voice
Grieving within the chamber, and he came back
And told Creon. And as the King went closer,
The air was full of wailing, the words lost,   50
And he begged us to make all haste. "Am I a
  prophet?"
He said, weeping, "And must I walk this road,
The saddest of all that I have gone before?
My son's voice calls me on. Oh quickly, quickly!
Look through the crevice there, and tell me   55
If it is Haimon, or some deception of the gods!"

We obeyed; and in the cavern's farthest corner
We saw her lying:
She had made a noose of her fine linen veil
And hanged herself. Haimon lay beside her,   60
His arms about her waist, lamenting her,
His love lost under ground, crying out
That his father had stolen her away from him.

When Creon saw him the tears rushed to his eyes
And he called to him: "What have you done, child?
  Speak to me.   65
What are you thinking that makes your eyes so
  strange?
O my son, my son, I come to you on my knees!"
But Haimon spat in his face. He said not a word,
Staring—
                  And suddenly drew his sword
And lunged. Creon shrank back, the blade missed;
  and the boy,   70
Desperate against himself, drove it half its length
Into his own side, and fell. And as he died
He gathered Antigonê close in his arms again,
Choking, his blood bright red on her white cheek.

---

27 **Pallas** Pallas Athene, goddess of wisdom, and hence an excellent source
of advice.

39-40 **Hecatê and Pluto** two fearful divinities—the goddess of witchcraft
and sorcery and the king of Hades, underworld of the dead.

And now he lies dead with the dead, and she is his 75
At last, his bride in the houses of the dead.

Exit Eurydicê into the palace.

Choragos: She has left us without a word. What can this mean?
Messenger: It troubles me, too; yet she knows what is best,
Her grief is too great for public lamentation,
And doubtless she has gone to her chamber to weep 80
For her dead son, leading her maidens in his dirge.
Choragos: It may be so: but I fear this deep silence.
Pause.
Messenger: I will see what she is doing. I will go in.

Exit Messenger into the palace.
Enter Creon with attendants, bearing Haimon's body.

Choragos: But here is the king himself: oh look at him,
Bearing his own damnation in his arms. 85
Creon: Nothing you say can touch me any more.
My own blind heart has brought me
From darkness to final darkness. Here you see
The father murdering, the murdered son—
And all my civic wisdom! 90
Haimon my son, so young, so young to die,
I was the fool, not you; and you died for me.
Choragos: That is the truth; but you were late in learning it.
Creon: This truth is hard to bear. Surely a god
Has crushed me beneath the hugest weight of heaven, 95
And driven me headlong a barbaric way
To trample out the thing I held most dear.
The pains that men will take to come to pain!

Enter Messenger from the palace.

Messenger: The burden you carry in your hands is heavy,
But it is not all: you will find more in your house. 100
Creon: What burden worse than this shall I find there?
Messenger: The Queen is dead.

Creon: O port of death, deaf world,
Is there no pity for me? And you, Angel of evil,
I was dead, and your words are death again. 105
Is it true, boy? Can it be true?
Is my wife dead? Has death bred death?
Messenger: You can see for yourself.

The doors are opened and the body of Eurydicê is disclosed within.

Creon: Oh pity!
All true, all true, and more than I can bear! 110
O my wife, my son!
Messenger: She stood before the altar, and her heart
Welcomed the knife her own hand guided,
And a great cry burst from her lips for Megareus° dead,
And for Haimon dead, her sons; and her last breath 115
Was a curse for their father, the murderer of her sons.
And she fell, and the dark flowed in through her closing eyes.
Creon: O God, I am sick with fear.
Are there no swords here? Has no one a blow for me?
Messenger:
Her curse is upon you for the deaths of both. 120
Creon: It is right that it should be. I alone am guilty.
I know it, and I say it. Lead me in,
Quickly, friends.
I have neither life nor substance. Lead me in.
Choragos: You are right, if there can be right in so much wrong. 125
The briefest way is best in a world of sorrow.
Creon: Let it come,
Let death come quickly, and be kind to me.
I would not ever see the sun again.
Choragos: All that will come when it will; but we, meanwhile, 130
Have much to do. Leave the future to itself.
Creon: All my heart was in that prayer!
Choragos: Then do not pray any more: the sky is deaf.
Creon: Lead me away. I have been rash and foolish.
I have killed my son and my wife. 135
I look for comfort; my comfort lies here dead.
Whatever my hands have touched has come to nothing.
Fate has brought all my pride to a thought of dust.

114 Megareus Son of Creon and brother of Haimon, Megareus was slain in the unsuccessful attack upon Thebes.

As Creon is being led into the house, the Choragos advances and speaks directly to the audience.

Choragos: There is no happiness where there is no wisdom;

No wisdom but in submission to the gods.   140
Big words are always punished,
And proud men in old age learn to be wise.

[5th century BCE]

QUESTIONS FOR REFLECTION AND DISCUSSION

1. Summarize the plot of *Antigone*, paying close attention to the chain of cause and effect between actions. What is the familial relationship between the various members of the royal family? What is the earliest story event referred to within the plot? What is its relation in the chain of events to those that are depicted directly? Where in the chain of the events does the play begin? Why do you think Sophocles chose to begin here?

2. Now that you have analyzed the sequence of actions, summarize the arguments made by Antigone, Creon, Ismene, and Haimon to justify those actions. What must each character ignore in the arguments of the other characters in order for their own argument to be persuasive? Which argument(s) do you find more effective, and why?

3. Characterize in a sentence the conflicting social values at the heart of the dispute between the main characters.

4. Of the five members of the royal family, only Eurydice does not explain her reasons for acting. Based on evidence within the play, what are some possible explanations for this silence?

5. A central theme of *Antigone* is the different values held by men and by women. How does the play depict those values and how does it draw a distinction between male and female values in its society?

DESTRUCTION AND ENDINGS TOPICS FOR ESSAYS

1. A number of the texts in this section on ethics portray or discuss the role of a proactive figure of death in the lives of various individuals. Compare the different functions attributed to this figure and the different ways in which the characters or speakers react to him.

2. A number of the texts in this section on ethics depict death from the point of view of an individual. Compare several of these depictions and discuss the similarities and differences between the relationship established between death and the individual. To what degree do these texts also include a social context or make a broader statement about the role of death within society?

3. Several of these texts include Christian images of the after-life and the Last Judgment. Compare these images and the use made of them in each text.

4. Write an essay analyzing the representation of death as a natural phenomenon. You may either analyze it on its own terms or in comparison with the representation of death as a phenomenon of human culture.

5. Write an essay based on selections in this section discussing the role of gender. To what degree do the texts you selected argue for gender difference in attitudes toward death or toward the ethics of murder, killing, or execution?

6. Research contemporary arguments for and against capital punishment. Write an essay discussing the relationship between those arguments and one of the texts included here.

DESTRUCTION AND ENDINGS FURTHER READINGS IN LITERATURE: *A WORLD OF WRITING*

Chinua Achebe, "Dead Men's Path" • T. Coraghessan Boyle, "Greasy Lake" • Annie Dillard, "Death of a Moth" • William Faulkner, "A Rose for Emily" • Ursula K. Le Guin, "The Wife's Tale" • Naguib Mahfouz, "Zaabalawi" • Flannery O'Connor, "A Good Man Is Hard to Find" • Wilfred Owen, "Dulce et decorum est" • Salman Rushdie, "Imagine There's No Heaven" • William Shakespeare, *Hamlet* • Virginia Woolf, "The Death of the Moth"

WORKING FURTHER WITH THE WORLDS AROUND US

1. When we think of the words "gods" and "devils" or "good" and "evil," we tend to consider them as polar opposites. To what degree does this opposition apply to the readings in this chapter?

2. Similarly, we tend to draw a strong contrast between beginnings and endings or creation and destruction. To what degree does this contrast apply to the readings in this chapter?

3. Compare the depiction of gods and devils or good and evil, or life and death in Genesis with those in the second section. How are they similar? How are they different?

4. Make a list of the different belief systems represented in these selections. What can you extrapolate about these different belief systems based on the selections here? What are the similarities between them? What are the differences?

5. Compare the different ethics proposed by two or three of the selections in this chapter.

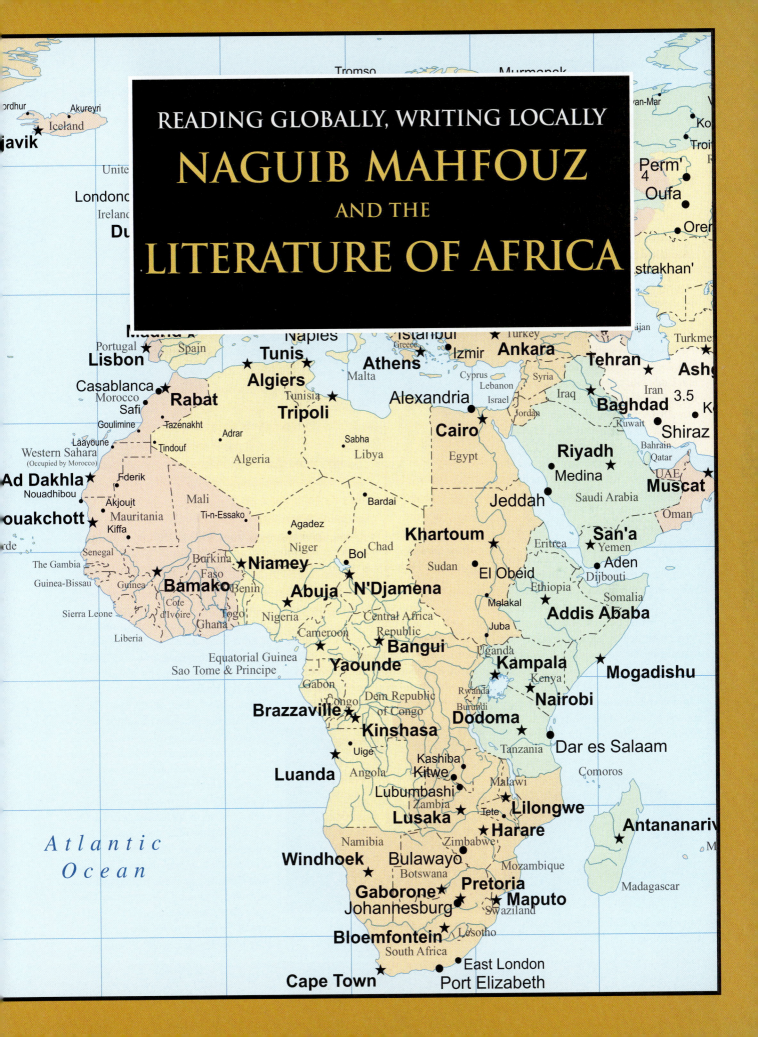

READING GLOBALLY, WRITING LOCALLY

NAGUIB MAHFOUZ

AND THE

LITERATURE OF AFRICA

The ties that bind Africa with the United States are as strong as those that bind it to Europe but even more tangled. There are the historical ties of the slave trade, as African-American writer Maya Angelou observes. Those first Africans brought with them a tradition of music, song, and storytelling that gave forth blues, jazz, gospel, poetry, plays, fiction, and nonfiction out of a history of suffering and oppression. The literature of Africa has had an equally complex history.

As part of the Ancient Near East 5,000 years ago, the kingdom of Egypt 5,000 years ago built some of the world's first great cities, devised one of the first writing systems, and composed some of its earliest literature. With the rise of Islam in the seventh century, the Arabic language and its poetic forms spread westward across North Africa, and then north across the Mediterranean into Spain and south through the Sahara desert. Thus, the Nobel-prizewinning Egyptian writer Naguib Mahfouz could describe himself as "the son of two civilizations that at a certain age in history have formed a happy marriage. The first of these, seven thousand years old, is the Pharaonic civilization; the second, one thousand four hundred years old, is the Islamic one." Moreover, the peoples of

Mode of Travelling in Africa. **Color engraving from William Hutton,** *A Voyage to Africa, including a narrative of an embassy to one of the interior Kingdoms in the year 1820.* **Hutton was the British consul to the Ashanti, in present-day Ghana.**

both northern and sub-Saharan Africa have had to reconcile a long tradition of oral storytelling with the written traditions of the nations that colonized their countries, especially English and French. Primarily a phenomenon of the second half of the twentieth century, modern African literature has seen an ongoing

debate over how to combine these traditions, over the choice of language, and over the best way to put into words the conflict between indigenous and colonizing cultures that has formed the history of the continent for many centuries.

In oral traditions, there is no single "authoritative" version of any text. The West African epic poem of warrior and sorcerer Son-Jara, legendary founder of the empire of Manden, or Old Mali, has been recounted by professional bards since the original events in the thirteenth century. In North Africa, written literature dates back to the hieroglyphs of ancient Egypt; in sub-Saharan Africa, the earliest written works date back to eighteenth-century contact with European traders. These are slave narratives, memoirs written by former slaves, including *The Interesting Life of the Slave Olaudah Equiano* (1789), victims of the four centuries of the Atlantic slave trade. The first fictional works by

Koran casket. Cairo, Egypt, ca. 1320–1330.

Detail of hand-woven Ashanti ceremonial cloth. Ghana, Africa.

Afro-pop singer Salif Keita (right), direct descendant of the lengendary Son-Jara, medieval founder of the Malian empire, performing in Abidjan, Côte d'Ivoire.

sub-Saharan Africans date from the late colonial period in the first half of the twentieth century. For North Africa, western-style novels began emerging from the long traditions of Arab writing at the end of the nineteenth century. Most important in West Africa were the poems anthologized by Senegalese poet (and later president) Léopold Sénar Senghor in 1948 and devoted to the concept of *négritude*, which rejected colonial discrimination and argued for a common black African identity. For the Arab world, the key figure was

A still from Ousmane Sembène's final film, *Faat-Kiné* (2000), a study of gender roles and politics in present-day Dakar centered around the title character (right), manager of a gas station.

Willem Blaeu's ornamental map of *Africa, Newly Described,* 1630.

Mahfouz, and his adoption of Western forms of novelistic realism to the problems and concerns of contemporary Egypt.

Most of the nations of Africa gained their independence from colonial rule during the 1950s and 1960s—even Egypt, which won a supposed freedom in 1922, was not fully independent from Britain until it nationalized the Suez Canal in 1956. This period also saw the rise of a postcolonial African literature written in colonial languages such as French, English, and Portuguese as well as in indigenous languages. This literature was devoted to issues arising from the clash of colonial and indigenous cultures as well as to those of newly independent nations struggling for a new identity that would also do justice to the many tribal traditions within new and often highly arbitrary national boundaries. In 1988, Mahfouz became the second African (after the Nigerian playwright Wole Soyinka in 1986) and the first Arab to be awarded the Nobel Prize in Literature. Written in English, the novels of Nigerian writer Chinua Achebe (p. 44) gained international recognition and remain the best-known writings of any African author. Other prominent writers include the Senegalese feminist Mariama Bâ (1929–1981) and the Kenyan novelist Ngugi wa Thiong'o (b. 1938), who began his career writing in English before switching to his native

Gĩkũyũ. For many African writers, the choice of language bore profoundly political as well as practical ramifications. Writing in English or French permitted a much broader and more international audience but risked betraying local ideas and conceptions. Writing in indigenous languages meant adapting them to Western generic conventions rather than oral tradition and limiting one's audience to an extremely local population. West Africa in particular has produced an important body of motion pictures since the 1960s, especially in the brilliant works of Senegalese Ousmane Sembène (1923–2007), an accomplished satirist and savage critic of corruption and hypocrisy in whatever form and whichever camp it may occur.

We begin this casebook with an author, Naguib Mahfouz, and two stories that probe the relationship between the everyday sights and sensations of contemporary urban life and eternal metaphysical questions. Looking back to the ethical and religious themes of Chapter 9, Mahfouz's stories explore the relationship between life and death, beginnings and endings. The three selections that conclude this casebook find different ways to probe the complex interactions and conflicts between white settlers and black peoples in sub-Saharan Africa, and the equally complex ways in which Africa is represented in the worlds beyond its shores.

NAGUIB MAHFOUZ 1911–2006

> I DEFEND BOTH THE FREEDOM OF EXPRESSION AND SOCIETY'S RIGHT TO COUNTER IT. I MUST PAY THE PRICE FOR DIFFERING. IT IS THE NATURAL WAY OF THINGS.
>
> —NAGUIB MAHFOUZ

Naguib Mahfouz was one of the first African novelists and a seminal figure in the development of modern Arabic fiction. A lifelong resident of Cairo, he was born into a devoutly Muslim lower-middle-class family. His love for his country and his immersion in the culture of Islam did not prevent him from being an outspoken critic of political and religious extremism. He barely survived an assassination attempt in 1994, after his public condemnation of the *fatwa* calling for the murder of novelist Salman Rushdie (p. 431) resulted in a similar judgment against his own person. Unlike Rushide, who had long ago settled in the West, Mahfouz remained in his home country. Cairo and its people, especially the struggles of its less privileged citizens, is the dominant subject of the 34 novels and 350 short stories he published during the course of his long life. The youngest of seven children of a civil servant, Mahfouz studied philosophy at the University of Cairo before turning to journalism. He spent most of his life in the civil service, however, first in the Ministry of Religious Affairs but primarily in the Ministry of Culture, where he held various posts related to the cinema before retiring in 1972. He began publishing in the 1930s, but following the war turned to the contemporary city and its historic neighborhoods, especially the Khan-el-Khalili, the medieval bazaar in the densely populated Gamaliya district of old Cairo where Mahfouz was born and lived much of his life. The largest city in Africa as well as in the Arab world, Cairo is also the setting of Mahfouz's most famous work, the *Cairo Trilogy* (1956–1957), the epic history of a middle-class family from the 1919 revolution that led to Egyptian independence in 1922 to the end of World War II. From the 1960s, Mahfouz began incorporating more elements of the fantastic into his fiction, explicitly invoking the great medieval story collection *The Thousand and One Nights* in his 1981 novel, *Arabian Nights and Days*. While still set on the teeming streets of Cairo, Mahfouz's later writings are often highly allegorical, using everyday situations to address indirectly both political and religious themes. This approach is evident in the two stories reproduced here, "Zaabalawi" (1963) and "Half a Day" (1989). In the latter story, the radical and fantastic telescoping of time transforms the simple childhood ritual of beginning school into a meditation on the passage of an entire life. In the longer "Zaabalawi," where a sick man undertakes a pilgrimage through the streets of Cairo in search of a saintly holy man whom he hopes will heal him. As in many writings of the late twentieth-century, it may be clear that there is a second level of meaning in these stories, but it is not so easy to pinpoint that meaning. As you read "Half a Day" and "Zaabalawi" consider the way they use the realistic, everyday elements of their setting in Cairo to ground their suggestive and enigmatic patterns of meaning.

FICTION

HALF A DAY

Translated by Denys Johnson-Davies

I PROCEEDED ALONGSIDE MY FATHER, CLUTCHING HIS right hand, running to keep up with the long strides he was taking. All my clothes were new: the black shoes, the green school uniform, and the red tarboosh.° My delight in my new clothes, however, was not altogether unmarred, for this was no feast day but the day on which I was to be cast into school for the first time.

My mother stood at the window watching our progress, and I would turn toward her from time to time, as though appealing for help. We walked along a street lined with gardens; on both sides were extensive fields planted with crops, prickly pears, henna trees, and a few date palms.

"Why school?" I challenged my father openly. "I shall never do anything to annoy you."

"I'm not punishing you," he said, laughing. "School's not a punishment. It's the factory that makes useful men out of boys. Don't you want to be like your father and brothers?"

5   I was not convinced. I did not believe there was really any good to be had in tearing me away from the intimacy of my home and throwing me into this building that stood at the end of the road like some huge, high-walled fortress, exceedingly stern and grim.

When we arrived at the gate we could see the courtyard, vast and crammed full of boys and girls. "Go in by yourself," said my father, "and join them. Put a smile on your face and be a good example to others."

I hesitated and clung to his hand, but he gently pushed me from him. "Be a man," he said. "Today

you truly begin life. You will find me waiting for you when it's time to leave."

I took a few steps, then stopped and looked but saw nothing. Then the faces of boys and girls came into view. I did not know a single one of them, and none of them knew me. I felt I was a stranger who had lost his way. But glances of curiosity were directed toward me, and one boy approached and asked, "Who brought you?"

"My father," I whispered.

10   "My father's dead," he said quite simply.

I did not know what to say. The gate was closed, letting out a pitiable screech. Some of the children burst into tears. The bell rang. A lady came along, followed by a group of men. The men began sorting us into ranks. We were formed into an intricate pattern in the great courtyard surrounded on three sides by high buildings of several floors; from each floor we were overlooked by a long balcony roofed in wood.

"This is your new home," said the woman. "Here too there are mothers and fathers. Here there is everything that is enjoyable and beneficial to knowledge and religion. Dry your tears and face life joyfully."

We submitted to the facts, and this submission brought a sort of contentment. Living beings were drawn to other living beings, and from the first moments my heart made friends with such boys as were to be my friends and fell in love with such girls as I was to be in love with, so that it seemed my misgivings had had no basis. I had never imagined school would have this rich variety. We played all sorts of different games: swings, the vaulting horse, ball games. In the music room we chanted our first songs. We also had our first introduction to language. We saw a globe of the

---

tarboosh: a tightly fitting, brimless felt or cloth hat with a flat top worn by Muslim men.

Earth, which revolved and showed the various continents and countries. We started learning the numbers. The story of the Creator of the universe was read to us, we were told of His present world and of His Hereafter, and we heard examples of what He said. We ate delicious food, took a little nap, and woke up to go on with friendship and love, play and learning.

As our path revealed itself to us, however, we did not find it as totally sweet and unclouded as we had presumed. Dust-laden winds and unexpected accidents came about suddenly, so we had to be watchful, at the ready, and very patient. It was not all a matter of playing and fooling around. Rivalries could bring about pain and hatred or give rise to fighting. And while the lady would sometimes smile, she would often scowl and scold. Even more frequently she would resort to physical punishment.

15 In addition, the time for changing one's mind was over and gone and there was no question of ever returning to the paradise of home. Nothing lay ahead of us but exertion, struggle, and perseverance. Those who were able took advantage of the opportunities for success and happiness that presented themselves amid the worries.

The bell rang announcing the passing of the day and the end of work. The throngs of children rushed toward the gate, which was opened again. I bade farewell to friends and sweethearts and passed through the gate. I peered around but found no trace of my father, who had promised to be there. I stepped aside to wait. When I had waited for a long time without avail, I decided to return home on my own. After I had taken a few steps, a middle-aged man passed by, and I realized at once that I knew him. He came toward me, smiling, and shook me by the hand, saying, "It's a long time since we last met—how are you?"

With a nod of my head, I agreed with him and in turn asked, "And you, how are you?"

"As you can see, not all that good, the Almighty be praised!"

Again he shook me by the hand and went off. I proceeded a few steps, then came to a startled halt. Good Lord! Where was the street lined with gardens? Where had it disappeared to? When did all these vehicles invade it? And when did all these hordes of humanity come to rest upon its surface? How did these hills of refuse come to cover its sides? And where were the fields that bordered it? High buildings had taken over, the street surged with children, and disturbing noises shook the air. At various points stood conjurers showing off their tricks and making snakes appear from baskets. Then there was a band announcing the opening of a circus, with clowns and weight lifters walking in front. A line of trucks carrying central security troops crawled majestically by. The siren of a fire engine shrieked, and it was not clear how the vehicle would cleave its way to reach the blazing fire. A battle raged between a taxi driver and his passenger, while the passenger's wife called out for help and no one answered. Good God! I was in a daze. My head spun. I almost went crazy. How could all this have happened in half a day, between early morning and sunset? I would find the answer at home with my father. But where was my home? I could see only tall buildings and hordes of people. I hastened on to the crossroads between the gardens and Abu Khoda. I had to cross Abu Khoda to reach my house, but the stream of cars would not let up. The fire engine's siren was shrieking at full pitch as it moved at a snail's pace, and I said to myself, "Let the fire take its pleasure in what it consumes." Extremely irritated, I wondered when I would be able to cross. I stood there a long time, until the young lad employed at the ironing shop on the corner came up to me. He stretched out his arm and said gallantly, "Grandpa, let me take you across."

[1989]

1. What purpose does the boy originally ascribe to the school? What purpose does his father ascribe to it? From the description of the activities that take place within it, what purpose do we ascribe to it?

2. What has changed between the time when the boy has entered the school and he leaves it? What are the first signs that something out of the ordinary has occurred during this time?

3. Based on evidence presented in the story, what are the possible meanings of the final paragraph? Which of these meanings do you think is most persuasive, and why?

The Khan-el-Khalili, a *souk,* or bazaar, dating back to medieval days, located in the Gamaliya neighborhood of Cairo, the setting of many of Mahfouz's stories and novels.

Zaabalawi

Naguib Mahfouz

Translated by Denys Johnson-Davies

Finally I became convinced that I had to find Sheikh Zaabalawi.°

The first time I had heard his name had been in a song:

> Oh what's become of the world, Zaabalawi?
> They've turned it upside down and taken
> away its taste.

Zaabalawi: the name of a popular Sufi saint. Sufism is an ascetic, mystical tradition within Islam.

It had been a popular song in my childhood, and one day it had occurred to me to demand of my father, in the way children have of asking endless questions:

"Who is Zaabalawi?"

5 He had looked at me hesitantly as though doubting my ability to understand the answer. However, he had replied, "May his blessing descend upon you, he's a true-saint of God, a remover of worries and troubles. Were it not for him I would have died miserably—"

In the years that followed, I heard my father many a time sing the praises of this good saint and speak of the miracles he performed. The days passed and brought with them many illnesses, for each one of which I was able, without too much trouble and at a cost I could afford, to find a cure, until I became afflicted with that illness for which no one possesses a remedy. When I had tried everything in vain and was overcome by despair, I remembered by chance what I had heard in my childhood: Why, I asked myself, should I not seek out Sheikh Zaabalawi? I recollected my father saying that he had made his acquaintance in Khan Gaafar at the house of Sheikh Qamar, one of those sheikhs who practiced law in the religious courts, and so I took myself off to his house. Wishing to make sure that he was still living there, I made inquiries of a vendor of beans whom I found in the lower part of the house.

"Sheikh Qamar!" he said, looking at me in amazement. "He left the quarter ages ago. They say he's now living in Garden City and has his office in al-Azhar Square."

I looked up the office address in the telephone book and immediately set off to the Chamber of Commerce Building, where it was located. On asking to see Sheikh Qamar, I was ushered into a room just as a beautiful woman with a most intoxicating perfume was leaving it. The man received me with a smile and motioned me toward a fine leather-upholstered chair. Despite the thick soles of my shoes, my feet were conscious of the lushness of the costly carpet. The man wore a lounge suit and was smoking a cigar; his manner of sitting was that of someone well satisfied both with himself and with his worldly possessions. The look of

warm welcome he gave me left no doubt in my mind that he thought me a prospective client, and I felt acutely embarrassed at encroaching upon his valuable time.

"Welcome!" he said, prompting me to speak.

10 "I am the son of your old friend Sheikh Ali al-Tatawi," I answered so as to put an end to my equivocal position.

A certain languor was apparent in the glance he cast at me; the languor was not total in that he had not as yet lost all hope in me.

"God rest his soul," he said. "He was a fine man."

The very pain that had driven me to go there now prevailed upon me to stay.

"He told me," I continued, "of a devout saint named Zaabalawi whom he met at Your Honor's. I am in need of him, sir, if he be still in the land of the living."

15 The languor became firmly entrenched in his eyes, and it would have come as no surprise if he had shown the door to both me and my father's memory.

"That," he said in the tone of one who has made up his mind to terminate the conversation, "was a very long time ago and I scarcely recall him now."

Rising to my feet so as to put his mind at rest regarding my intention of going, I asked, "Was he really a saint?"

"We used to regard him as a man of miracles."

"And where could I find him today?" I asked, making another move toward the door.

20 "To the best of my knowledge he was living in the Birgawi Residence in al-Azhar," and he applied himself to some papers on his desk with a resolute movement that indicated he would not open his mouth again. I bowed my head in thanks, apologized several times for disturbing him, and left the office, my head so buzzing with embarrassment that I was oblivious to all sounds around me.

I went to the Birgawi Residence, which was situated in a thickly populated quarter. I found that time had so eaten away at the building that nothing was left of it save an antiquated façade and a courtyard that, despite being supposedly in the charge of a caretaker, was being used as a rubbish dump. A small, insignificant fellow, a mere prologue to a man, was using the covered entrance as a place for the sale of old books on theology and mysticism.

When I asked him about Zaabalawi, he peered at me through narrow, inflamed eyes and said in amazement, "Zaabalawi! Good heavens, what a time ago that was! Certainly he used to live in this house when it was habitable. Many were the times he would sit with me talking of bygone days, and I would be blessed by his holy presence. Where, though, is Zaabalawi today?"

He shrugged his shoulders sorrowfully and soon left me, to attend to an approaching customer. I proceeded to make inquiries of many shopkeepers in the district. While I found that a large number of them had never even heard of Zaabalawi, some, though recalling nostalgically the pleasant times they had spent with him, were ignorant of his present whereabouts, while others openly made fun of him, labeled him a charlatan, and advised me to put myself in the hands of a doctor—as though I had not already done so. I therefore had no alternative but to return disconsolately home.

With the passing of days like motes in the air, my pains grew so severe that I was sure I would not be able to hold out much longer. Once again I fell to wondering about Zaabalawi and clutching at the hope his venerable name stirred within me. Then it occurred to me to seek the help of the local sheikh of the district; in fact, I was surprised I had not thought of this to begin with. His office was in the nature of a small shop, except that it contained a desk and a telephone, and I found him sitting at his desk, wearing a jacket over his striped galabeya. As he did not interrupt his conversation with a man sitting beside him, I stood waiting till the man had gone. The sheikh then looked up at me coldly. I told myself that I should win him over by the usual methods, and it was not long before I had him cheerfully inviting me to sit down.

25 "I'm in need of Sheikh Zaabalawi," I answered his inquiry as to the purpose of my visit.

He gazed at me with the same astonishment as that shown by those I had previously encountered.

"At least," he said, giving me a smile that revealed his gold teeth, "he is still alive. The devil of it is, though, he has no fixed abode. You might well bump into him as you go out of here, on the other hand you might spend days and months in fruitless searching."

"Even you can't find him!"

"Even I! He's a baffling man, but I thank the Lord that he's still alive!"

30 He gazed at me intently, and murmured, "It seems your condition is serious."

"Very."

"May God come to your aid! But why don't you go about it systematically?" He spread out a sheet of paper on the desk and drew on it with unexpected speed and skill until he had made a full plan of the district, showing all the various quarters, lanes, alleyways, and squares. He looked at it admiringly and said, "These are dwelling-houses, here is the Quarter of the Perfumers, here the Quarter of the Coppersmiths, the Mouski, the police and fire stations. The drawing is your best guide. Look carefully in the cafés, the places where the dervishes perform their rites,° the mosques and prayer-rooms, and the Green Gate,° for he may well be concealed among the beggars and be indistinguishable from them. Actually, I myself haven't seen him for years, having been somewhat preoccupied with the cares of the world, and was only brought back by your inquiry to those most exquisite times of my youth."

I gazed at the map in bewilderment. The telephone rang, and he took up the receiver.

"Take it," he told me, generously. "We're at your service."

35 Folding up the map, I left and wandered off through the quarter, from square to street to alleyway, making inquiries of everyone I felt was familiar with the place. At last the owner of a small establishment for ironing clothes told me, "Go to the calligrapher Hassanein in Umm al-Ghulam—they were friends."

I went to Umm al-Ghulam, where I found old Hassanein working in a deep, narrow shop full of

dervishes: a pious group of people interested primarily in worship. Their rite is a weekly evening concert that is open to the faithful.
Green Gate: one of the gates of the Mosque of al-Husain in old Cairo.

signboards and jars of color. A strange smell, a mixture of glue and perfume, permeated its every corner. Old Hassanein was squatting on a sheepskin rug in front of a board propped against the wall; in the middle of it he had inscribed the word "Allah" in silver lettering. He was engrossed in embellishing the letters with prodigious care. I stood behind him, fearful of disturbing him or breaking the inspiration that flowed to his masterly hand. When my concern at not interrupting him had lasted some time, he suddenly inquired with unaffected gentleness, "Yes?"

Realizing that he was aware of my presence, I introduced myself. "I've been told that Sheikh Zaabalawi is your friend; I'm looking for him," I said.

His hand came to a stop. He scrutinized me in astonishment. "Zaabalawi! God be praised!" he said with a sigh.

"He *is* a friend of yours, isn't he?" I asked eagerly.

40   "He was, once upon a time. A real man of mystery: he'd visit you so often that people would imagine he was your nearest and dearest, then would disappear as though he'd never existed. Yet saints are not to be blamed."

The spark of hope went out with the suddenness of a lamp snuffed by a power-cut.

"He was so constantly with me," said the man, "that I felt him to be a part of everything I drew. But where is he today?"

"Perhaps he is still alive?"

"He's alive, without a doubt. . . . He had impeccable taste, and it was due to him that I made my most beautiful drawings."

45   "God knows," I said, in a voice almost stifled by the dead ashes of hope, "how dire my need for him is, and no one knows better than you of the ailments in respect to which he is sought."

"Yes, yes. May God restore you to health. He is in truth, as is said of him, a man, and more. . . ."

Smiling broadly, he added, "And his face possesses an unforgettable beauty. But where is he?"

Reluctantly I rose to my feet, shook hands, and left. I continued wandering eastward and westward through the quarter, inquiring about

Zaabalawi from everyone who, by reason of age or experience, I felt might be likely to help me. Eventually I was informed by a vendor of lupine that he had met him a short while ago at the house of Sheikh Gad, the well-known composer. I went to the musician's house in Tabakshiyya, where I found him in a room tastefully furnished in the old style, its walls redolent with history. He was seated on a divan, his famous lute beside him, concealing within itself the most beautiful melodies of our age, while somewhere from within the house came the sound of pestle and mortar and the clamor of children. I immediately greeted him and introduced myself, and was put at my ease by the unaffected way in which he received me. He did not ask, either in words or gesture, what had brought me, and I did not feel that he even harbored any such curiosity. Amazed at his understanding and kindness, which boded well, I said, "O Sheikh Gad, I am an admirer of yours, having long been enchanted by the renderings of your songs."

"Thank you," he said with a smile.

50   "Please excuse my disturbing you," I continued timidly, "but I was told that Zaabalawi was your friend, and I am in urgent need of him."

"Zaabalawi!" he said, frowning in concentration. "You need him? God be with you, for who knows, O Zaabalawi, where you are."

"Doesn't he visit you?" I asked eagerly.

"He visited me some time ago. He might well come right now; on the other hand I mightn't see him till death!"

I gave an audible sigh and asked, "What made him like that?"

55   The musician took up his lute. "Such are saints or they would not be saints," he said, laughing.

"Do those who need him suffer as I do?"

"Such suffering is part of the cure!"

He took up the plectrum and began plucking soft strains from the strings. Lost in thought, I followed his movements. Then, as though addressing myself, I said, "So my visit has been in vain."

He smiled, laying his cheek against the side of the lute. "God forgive you," he said, "for saying such a thing of a visit that has caused me to know you and you me!"

60   I was much embarrassed and said apologetically, "Please forgive me; my feelings of defeat made me forget my manners."

    "Do not give in to defeat. This extraordinary man brings fatigue to all who seek him. It was easy enough with him in the old days, when his place of abode was known. Today, though, the world has changed, and after having enjoyed a position attained only by potentates, he is now pursued by the police on a charge of false pretenses. It is therefore no longer an easy matter to reach him, but have patience and be sure that you will do so."

    He raised his head from the lute and skillfully fingered the opening bars of a melody. Then he sang:

> *I make lavish mention, even though I blame*
> *   myself, of those I love,*
> *For the stories of the beloved are my wine.*

    With a heart that was weary and listless, I followed the beauty of the melody and the singing.

65   "I composed the music to this poem in a single night," he told me when he had finished. "I remember that it was the eve of the Lesser Bairam. Zaabalawi was my guest for the whole of that night, and the poem was of his choosing. He would sit for a while just where you are, then would get up and play with my children as though he were one of them. Whenever I was overcome by weariness or my inspiration failed me, he would punch me playfully in the chest and joke with me, and I would bubble over with melodies, and thus I continued working till I finished the most beautiful piece I have ever composed."

    "Does he know anything about music?"

    "He is the epitome of things musical. He has an extremely beautiful speaking voice, and you have only to hear him to want to burst into song and to be inspired to creativity. . . ."

    "How was it that he cured those diseases before which men are powerless?"

    "That is his secret. Maybe you will learn it when you meet him."

70   But when would that meeting occur? We relapsed into silence, and the hubbub of children once more filled the room.

    Again the sheikh began to sing. He went on repeating the words "and I have a memory of her" in different and beautiful variations until the very walls danced in ecstasy. I expressed my wholehearted admiration, and he gave me a smile of thanks. I then got up and asked permission to leave, and he accompanied me to the front door. As I shook him by the hand, he said, "I hear that nowadays he frequents the house of Hagg Wanas al-Damanhouri. Do you know him?"

    I shook my head, though a modicum of renewed hope crept into my heart.

    "He is a man of private means," the sheikh told me, "who from time to time visits Cairo, putting up at some hotel or other. Every evening, though, he spends at the Negma Bar° in Alfi Street."

    I waited for nightfall and went to the Negma Bar. I asked a waiter about Hagg Wanas, and he pointed to a corner that was semisecluded because of its position behind a large pillar with mirrors on all four sides. There I saw a man seated alone at a table with two bottles in front of him, one empty, the other two-thirds empty. There were no snacks or food to be seen,° and I was sure that I was in the presence of a hardened drinker. He was wearing a loosely flowing silk galabeya and a carefully wound turban; his legs were stretched out toward the base of the pillar, and as he gazed into the mirror in rapt contentment, the sides of his face, rounded and handsome despite the fact that he was approaching old age, were flushed with wine. I approached quietly till I stood but a few feet away from him. He did not turn toward me or give any indication that he was aware of my presence.

75   "Good evening, Mr. Wanas," I greeted him cordially.

Negma Bar: Mahfouz often links drinking in bars (something that is transgressive in the Muslim culture) to spirituality, and to Sufis.
no snacks or food: In Arabic culture, it is customary to have snacks with alcoholic drinks.

He turned toward me abruptly, as though my voice had roused him from slumber, and glared at me in disapproval. I was about to explain what had brought me when he interrupted in an almost imperative tone of voice that was nonetheless not devoid of an extraordinary gentleness, "First, please sit down, and second, please get drunk!"

I opened my mouth to make my excuses, but, stopping up his ears with his fingers, he said, "Not a word till you do what I say."

I realized I was in the presence of a capricious drunkard and told myself that I should at least humor him a bit. "Would you permit me to ask one question?" I said with a smile, sitting down.

Without removing his hands from his ears he indicated the bottle. "When engaged in a drinking bout like this, I do not allow any conversation between myself and another unless, like me, he is drunk, otherwise all propriety is lost and mutual comprehension is rendered impossible."

80 I made a sign indicating that I did not drink.

"That's your lookout," he said offhandedly. "And that's my condition!"

He filled me a glass, which I meekly took and drank. No sooner had the wine settled in my stomach than it seemed to ignite. I waited patiently till I had grown used to its ferocity, and said, "It's very strong, and I think the time has come for me to ask you about—"

Once again, however, he put his fingers in his ears. "I shan't listen to you until you're drunk!"

He filled up my glass for the second time. I glanced at it in trepidation; then, overcoming my inherent objection, I drank it down at a gulp. No sooner had the wine come to rest inside me than I lost all willpower. With the third glass, I lost my memory, and with the fourth the future vanished. The world turned round about me, and I forgot why I had gone there. The man leaned toward me attentively, but I saw him—saw everything—as a mere meaningless series of colored planes. I don't know how long it was before my head sank down onto the arm of the chair and I plunged into deep sleep. During it, I had a beautiful dream the like of which I had never experienced.

I dreamed that I was in an immense garden surrounded on all sides by luxuriant trees, and the sky was nothing but stars seen between the entwined branches, all enfolded in an atmosphere like that of sunset or a sky overcast with cloud. I was lying on a small hummock of jasmine petals, more of which fell upon me like rain, while the lucent spray of a fountain unceasingly sprinkled the crown of my head and my temples. I was in a state of deep contentedness, of ecstatic serenity. An orchestra of warbling and cooing played in my ear. There was an extraordinary sense of harmony between me and my inner self, and between the two of us and the world, everything being in its rightful place, without discord or distortion. In the whole world there was no single reason for speech or movement, for the universe moved in a rapture of ecstasy. This lasted but a short while. When I opened my eyes, consciousness struck at me like a policeman's fist, and I saw Wanas al-Damanhouri peering at me with concern. Only a few drowsy customers were left in the bar.

85 "You have slept deeply," said my companion. "You were obviously hungry for sleep."

I rested my heavy head in the palms of my hands. When I took them away in astonishment and looked down at them, I found that they glistened with drops of water.

"My head's wet," I protested.

"Yes, my friend tried to rouse you," he answered quietly.

"Somebody saw me in this state?"

90 "Don't worry, he is a good man. Have you not heard of Sheikh Zaabalawi?"

"Zaabalawi!" I exclaimed, jumping to my feet.

"Yes," he answered in surprise. "What's wrong?"

"Where is he?"

"I don't know where he is now. He was here and then he left."

95 I was about to run off in pursuit but found I was more exhausted than I had imagined. Collapsed over the table, I cried out in despair, "My sole reason for coming to you was to meet him! Help me to catch up with him or send someone after him."

The man called a vendor of prawns and asked him to seek out the sheikh and bring him back. Then he turned to me. "I didn't realize you were afflicted. I'm very sorry. . . ."

"You wouldn't let me speak," I said irritably.

"What a pity! He was sitting on this chair beside you the whole time. He was playing with a string of jasmine petals he had around his neck,° a gift from one of his admirers, then, taking pity on you, he began to sprinkle some water on your head to bring you around."

"Does he meet you here every night?" I asked, my eyes not leaving the doorway through which the vendor of prawns had left.

100 "He was with me tonight, last night, and the night before that, but before that I hadn't seen him for a month."

"Perhaps he will come tomorrow," I answered with a sigh.

"Perhaps."

"I am willing to give him any money he wants."

Wanas answered sympathetically, "The strange thing is that he is not open to such temptations, yet he will cure you if you meet him."

105 "Without charge?"

"Merely on sensing that you love him."

The vendor of prawns returned, having failed in his mission.

I recovered some of my energy and left the bar, albeit unsteadily. At every street corner I called out "Zaabalawi!" in the vague hope that I would be rewarded with an answering shout. The street boys turned contemptuous eyes on me till I sought refuge in the first available taxi.

The following evening I stayed up with Wanas al-Damanhouri till dawn, but the sheikh did not put in an appearance. Wanas informed me that he would be going away to the country and would not be returning to Cairo until he had sold the cotton crop.

110 I must wait, I told myself; I must train myself to be patient. Let me content myself with having made certain of the existence of Zaabalawi, and even of his affection for me, which encourages me to think that he will be prepared to cure me if a meeting takes place between us.

Sometimes, however, the long delay wearied me. I would become beset by despair and would try to persuade myself to dismiss him from my mind completely. How many weary people in this life know him not or regard him as a mere myth! Why, then, should I torture myself about him in this way?

No sooner, however, did my pains force themselves upon me than I would again begin to think about him, asking myself when I would be fortunate enough to meet him. The fact that I ceased to have any news of Wanas and was told he had gone to live abroad did not deflect me from my purpose; the truth of the matter was that I had become fully convinced that I had to find Zaabalawi.

Yes, I have to find Zaabalawi.

jasmine . . . neck: In Arabic culture, jasmine is a symbol of purity and innocence.

[1963]

QUESTIONS FOR REFLECTION AND DISCUSSION

1. List the people encountered by the narrator in his search for Zaabalawi. How is each person characterized? Are any patterns formed by the narrator's search?

2. How does the final encounter, with Mr. Wanas in the Negma Bar, differ from the previous ones?

3. What do we find out about Zaabalawi? What do we not find out about him?

4. Basing yourself on evidence in the story, does it have an allegorical meaning? If so, what possible meaning or meanings does it have?

NONFICTION

BINYAVANGA WAINAINA B. 1971

Born in Nakuru in Kenya, Binyavanga Wainaina attended the University of Transkei in South Africa, where he later worked as a food and travel writer. He won the Caine Prize for African Writing in 2002 and has worked since as an editor and writer, publishing in a wide variety of newspapers, magazines, and journals. He is currently writer-in-residence at Union College.

HOW TO WRITE ABOUT AFRICA

ALWAYS USE THE WORD "AFRICA" OR "DARKNESS" OR "Safari" in your title. Subtitles may include the words "Zanzibar," "Masai," "Zulu," "Zambezi," "Congo," "Nile," "Big," "Sky," "Shadow," "Drum," "Sun" or "Bygone." Also useful are words such as "Guerrillas," "Timeless," "Primordial" and "Tribal." Note that "People" means Africans who are not black, while "The People" means black Africans.

Never have a picture of a well-adjusted African on the cover of your book, or in it, unless that African has won the Nobel Prize. An AK-47, prominent ribs, naked breasts: use these. If you must include an African, make sure you get one in Masai or Zulu or Dogon dress.

In your text, treat Africa as if it were one country. It is hot and dusty with rolling grasslands and huge herds of animals and tall, thin people who are starving. Or it is hot and steamy with very short people who eat primates. Don't get bogged down with precise descriptions. Africa is big: fifty-four countries, 900 million people who are too busy starving and dying and warring and emigrating to read your book. The continent is full of deserts, jungles, highlands, savannahs and many other things, but your reader doesn't care about all that, so keep your descriptions romantic and evocative and unparticular.

Make sure you show how Africans have music and rhythm deep in their souls, and eat things no other humans eat. Do not mention rice and beef and wheat; monkey-brain is an African's cuisine of choice, along with goat, snake, worms and grubs and all manner of game meat. Make sure you show that you are able to eat such food without flinching, and describe how you learn to enjoy it—because you care.

5   Taboo subjects: ordinary domestic scenes, love between Africans (unless a death is involved), references to African writers or intellectuals, mention of school-going children who are not suffering from yaws or Ebola fever or female genital mutilation.

Throughout the book, adopt a *sotto* voice, in conspiracy with the reader, and a sad *I-expected-so-much* tone. Establish early on that your liberalism is impeccable, and mention near the beginning how much you love Africa, how you fell in love with the place and can't live without her. Africa is the only continent you can love—take advantage of this. If you are a man, thrust yourself into her warm virgin forests. If you are a woman, treat Africa as a man who wears a bush jacket and disappears off into the sunset. Africa is to be pitied, worshipped or dominated. Whichever angle you take, be sure to leave the strong impression that without your intervention and your important book, Africa is doomed.

Your African characters may include naked warriors, loyal servants, diviners and seers, ancient wise men living in hermitic splendour. Or corrupt politicians, inept polygamous travel-guides, and prostitutes you have slept with. The Loyal Servant always behaves like a seven-year-old and needs a firm hand; he is scared of snakes, good with children, and always involving you in his complex domestic dramas. The Ancient Wise Man always comes from a noble tribe (not the money-grubbing tribes like the Gikuyu, the Igbo or the Shona). He has rheumy eyes and is close to the Earth. The Modern African is a fat man who steals and works in the visa office, refusing to give work permits to qualified Westerners who really care about Africa. He is an enemy of development, always using his government job to make it difficult for pragmatic and good-hearted expats to set up NGOs or Legal Conservation Areas. Or he is an Oxford-educated intellectual turned serial-killing politician in a Savile Row suit. He is a cannibal who likes Cristal champagne, and his mother is a rich witch-doctor who really runs the country.

Among your characters you must always include The Starving African, who wanders the refugee camp nearly naked, and waits for the benevolence of the West. Her children have flies on their eyelids and pot bellies, and her breasts are flat and empty. She must look utterly helpless. She can have no past, no history; such diversions ruin the dramatic moment. Moans are good. She must never say anything about herself in the dialogue except to speak of her (unspeakable) suffering. Also be sure to include a warm and motherly woman who has a rolling laugh and who is concerned for your well-being. Just call her Mama. Her children are all delinquent. These characters should buzz around your main hero, making him look good. Your hero can teach them, bathe them, feed them; he carries lots of babies and has seen Death. Your hero is you (if reportage), or a beautiful, tragic international celebrity/aristocrat who now cares for animals (if fiction).

Bad Western Characters may include children of Tory cabinet ministers, Afrikaners, employees of the World Bank. When talking about exploitation by foreigners mention the Chinese and Indian traders. Blame the West for Africa's situation. But do not be too specific.

10   Broad brushstrokes throughout are good. Avoid having the African characters laugh, or struggle to educate their kids, or just make do in mundane circumstances. Have them illuminate something about Europe or America in Africa. African characters should be colourful, exotic, larger than life—but empty inside, with no dialogue, no conflicts or resolutions in their stories, no depth or quirks to confuse the cause.

Describe, in detail, naked breasts (young, old, conservative, recently raped, big, small) or mutilated genitals, or enhanced genitals. Or any kind of genitals. And dead bodies. Or, better, naked dead bodies. And especially rotting naked dead bodies. Remember, any work you submit in which people look filthy and miserable will be referred to as the "real Africa," and you want that on your dust jacket. Do not feel queasy about this: you are trying to help them to get aid from the West. The biggest taboo in writing about Africa is to describe or show dead or suffering white people.

Animals, on the other hand, must be treated as well rounded, complex characters. They speak (or grunt while tossing their manes proudly) and have names, ambitions and desires. They also have family values: *see how lions teach their children?* Elephants are caring, and are good feminists or dignified patriarchs. So are gorillas. Never, ever say anything negative about an elephant or a gorilla. Elephants may attack people's property, destroy their crops, and even kill them. Always take the side of the elephant. Big cats have public-school accents. Hyenas are fair game and have vaguely Middle Eastern accents. Any short Africans who live in the jungle or desert may be portrayed with good humour (unless they are in conflict with an elephant or chimpanzee or gorilla, in which case they are pure evil).

After celebrity activists and aid workers, conservationists are Africa's most important people. Do not offend them. You need them to invite you to their 30,000-acre game ranch or "conservation area," and this is the only way you will get to interview the celebrity activist. Often a book cover with a heroic-looking conservationist on it works magic for sales. Anybody white, tanned and wearing khaki who once had a pet antelope or a farm is a conservationist, one who is preserving Africa's rich heritage. When interviewing him or her, do not ask how much funding they have; do not ask how much money they make off their game. Never ask how much they pay their employees.

Readers will be put off if you don't mention the light in Africa. And sunsets, the African sunset is a must. It is always big and red. There is always a big sky. Wide empty spaces and game are critical—Africa is the Land of Wide Empty Spaces. When writing about the plight of flora and fauna, make sure you mention that Africa is overpopulated. When your main character is in a desert or jungle living with indigenous peoples (anybody short) it is okay to mention that Africa has been severely depopulated by Aids and War (use caps).

15   You'll also need a nightclub called Tropicana, where mercenaries, evil nouveau riche Africans and prostitutes and guerrillas and expats hang out.

Always end your book with Nelson Mandela saying something about rainbows or renaissances. Because you care.

[2005]

QUESTIONS FOR REFLECTION AND DISCUSSION

1. Make a list of the targets of Wainaina's satire. What are the "broad brushstrokes" with which Africa and Africans are generally painted?

2. How do non-Africans appear in Wainaina's essay? What, according to the essay, is their function in Africa?

3. What positive information does Wainaina include among his satirical targets? What is the function of this information?

4. How would the effect of the essay change if Wainaina had written it according to the title "How Not to Write about Africa"?

5. Based on evidence included in the essay, how does Wainaina think one *should* write about Africa?

POETRY

JEREMY CRONIN B. 1949

The son of a naval officer and an office worker, Jeremy Cronin studied philosophy at the University of Capetown, South Africa, and in Paris, France. A political activist and member of the African National Congress, Cronin was arrested in 1976 by the Apartheid government and charged with planning terrorist activities. He served a seven-year jail term, during which he began writing the poetry that was published in his collection *Inside* (1983). Cronin has continued to write poetry while also serving as a member of the post-Apartheid South African parliament. His poem "To learn how to speak" dramatizes the many different languages in which most Africans function on a day-to-day basis. Like most African countries, the nation of South Africa is a hodgepodge of tribes, ethnic groups, and settler peoples brought together for the convenience of a colonial government. In this poem, Cronin mixes the major languages of South Africa: English, Afrikaans, and a number of the nine different official indigenous languages.

To learn how to speak

To learn how to speak
With the voices of the land,
To parse the speech in its rivers,
To catch in the inarticulate grunt,
Stammer, call, cry, babble, tongue's knot   5
A sense of the stoneness of these stones
From which all words are cut.
To trace with the tongue wagon-trails
Saying the suffix of their aches in -kuil, -pan, -fontein,°
In watery names that confirm   10
The dryness of their ways.
To visit the places of occlusion, or the lick
in a vlei-bank dawn.
To bury my mouth in the pit of your arm,
In that planetarium,   15
Pectoral beginning to the nub of time
Down there close to the water-table, to feel
The full moon as it drums
At the back of my throat
Its cow-skinned vowel.   20
To write a poem with words like:
I'm telling you,
Stompie, stickfast, golovan,
Songololo, just boombang, just
To understand the least inflections,   25
To voice without swallowing
Syllables born in tin shacks, or catch
The 5.15 ikwata bust fife°
Chwannisberg° train, to reach
The low chant of the mine gang's   30
Mineral glow of our people's unbreakable resolve.

To learn how to speak
With the voices of this land.

[1983]

9 -kuil, -pan, - fontein: endings for place-names, all indicating
the presence of water. 28 ikwata bust fife: quarter past five.
29 Chwannisberg: Johannesburg.

QUESTIONS FOR REFLECTION AND DISCUSSION

1. In what sense can we say that a land has a voice? How, for the speaker of the poem, is that voice related to the languages spoken in South Africa?

2. What are some of the images of speech in the poem? How are they related to one another?

3. Why is it important to the speaker "to learn how to speak/ With the voices of the land"?

CHENJERAI HOVE B. 1956

The Zimbabwean poet, novelist, and essayist Chenjerai Hove was educated in Zimbabwe and South Africa. Living in political exile since 2001, he is currently International Writers Project Fellow in Residence at the Watson Institute of Brown University.

You Will Forget

If you stay in comfort too long
you will not know
the weight of a water pot
on the bald head of the village woman

You will forget   5
the weight of three bundles of thatch grass
on the sinewy neck of the woman
whose baby cries on her back
for a blade of grass in its eyes.

Sure, if you stay in comfort too long   10
you will not know the pain
of child birth without a nurse in white

You will forget
the thirst, the cracked dusty lips
of the woman in the valley   15
on her way to the headman who isn't there

You will forget
the pouring pain of a thorn prick
with a load on the head.
If you stay in comfort too long   20

You will forget
the wailing in the valley
of women losing a husband in the mines

You will forget
the rough handshake of coarse palms   25
full of teary sorrow at the funeral.

If you stay in comfort too long
You will not hear
the shrieky voice of old warriors sing
the songs of fresh stored battlefields.   30

You will forget
the unfeeling bare feet
gripping the warm soil turned by the plough

You will forget
the voice of the season talking to the oxen.   35

[1990]

Paul Weinberg, Magopa, Northwest Province, South Africa—return the land, 1991. Magopa was an area from which blacks had been forcibly removed. Compare the representation in this photo of the relationship between the subject and the land, and their relationship in the two poems above.

QUESTIONS FOR REFLECTION AND DISCUSSION

1. What are the things that the speaker is worried that "you" will forget? What qualities do these things share? Are they positive or negative?

2. In what way do the things listed by the speaker contrast with "comfort"? Why do you think the speaker does not enumerate the qualities of "comfort"? What would these qualities be?

3. Why is it important to the speaker that "you" not forgot? Is the speaker also in danger of forgetting?

4. To what degree are the things the speaker wants you not to forget specific to Zimbabwe? To the southern part of Africa? To the continent in general?

WORKING FURTHER WITH THE LITERATURE OF AFRICA

1. Write an essay analyzing the image of the land in Chenjerai Hove's and Jeremy Cronin's poems. How is it described? What function does it play in the selections you are analyzing?

2. Evaluate the selections in this casebook (and/or other writings from Africa included in this book) according to the criteria of Binyavanga Wainaina's essay "How to Write about Africa."

3. All of these readings make strong divisions. Some of the divisions are spatial, others are spiritual, others are racial,

others linguistic. Write an essay about the divisions in several of these selections. How are they similar? How are they different? Why is the image of division so important to these readings?

4. Read other writings of Naguib Mahfouz and write a paper on their principal themes.

5. Basing yourself on the selections in this casebook, write an argument essay on what it means (if anything) to be African.

THE LITERATURE OF AFRICA FURTHER READINGS IN *LITERATURE: A WORLD OF WRITING*

Chinua Achebe, "Dead Men's Path" • Elizabeth Bishop, "In the Waiting Room" • Langston Hughes, "The Negro Speaks of Rivers" • George Packer, "How Susie Bayer's T-Shirt Ended Up on Yusuf Mama's Back"

CHAPTER 10

THE WORLD WE LIVE IN
SPACES
AND
PLACES

As readers, we are fairly well accustomed to think critically about literature in terms of time: In what order do events take place? How much time passes between different events? How do characters change over time? But what happens if we think about a text in terms of space: In which places do events occur? In how many different spaces? How do characters change according to different places and settings? Some texts use setting to provide historical or biographical detail, others—such as Ibsen's play *A Doll's House* (p. 553)—use setting figuratively, and still others do both, as in the prison setting of *The Autobiography of Malcolm X* (p. 589). In this chapter we study how spaces and places structure our lives and influence the ways we think about the world around us. The chapter is divided into two sections focused on two different types of space. "In-Between Spaces" looks at the peculiar state of being between spaces, in transit between one place and another, and between one state of mind and another. "Confined Spaces" studies the varieties of physical and mental confinement, and the effect enclosed spaces have on our minds and bodies. As you read the texts in this chapter, pay special attention to their use of setting. What details do they include and what do they omit? What argument is being made by a specific choice of setting or detail? What relationships do the speakers, narrators, and characters have to the spaces in which they act? How do the authors of these texts use those relationships to define character and create meaning?

IMAGINING SPACES

To begin thinking about the ways we experience and imagine spaces, study the three images below, images of three very different kinds of space. What feelings does each image elicit and how does it elicit them?

Ansel Adams, *The Tetons and The Snake River* (1942). Grand Teton National Park, Wyoming. Records of the National Park Service.

Joseph Cornell. (1903-1972). *Untitled (Bébé Marie),* early 1940s. Papered and painted wood box with painted corrugated cardboard floor, containing doll in cloth dress and straw hat with cloth flowers, dried flowers, and twigs, flecked with paint, 23½ × 12⅜ × 5¼″ (59.7 × 31.5 × 13.3 cm).

Andreas Gursky, *Paris, Montparnasse,* 1993. Photograph on paper on perspex.

QUESTIONS FOR REFLECTION AND DISCUSSION

1. Describe the space depicted in each work of art. How big is it? What does it contain? What is its relationship to the scale of a human being?

2. Imagine yourself occupying each of these spaces? How would it feel to do so? Which space would you most like to be in, and why? Which space would you least like to be in, and why?

3. If you were in each of these spaces, how would you change it?

IN-BETWEEN SPACES

Anthropologists define a **liminal,** or threshold, moment as one in which normally accepted social conventions and hierarchies are temporarily suspended. In-between spaces are spaces that encourage such a transitional state. They can be natural spaces, like the seashore Rachel Carson describes in the essay that concludes this section; or they can be the result of human labor, like the highways of so many road trips; or they can be both, like the paths that predominate in the stories presented here. Journeys very often have a liminal quality to them; when we journey we are more open to chance encounters and unexpected occurrences, either within ourselves or with fellow passengers on a bus, train, or plane. In this section of readings about space, you will study a number of texts about journeys and paths. As you read them, pay close attention to the role played by the space of the journey—the pathway, the encounter—and by the way that space defines the starting point and endpoint of the journey.

> *Leaving the old, both worlds at once they view / That stand upon the threshold of the new.*
>
> —EDMUND WALLER

Robert Smithson, *Spiral Jetty* (1970). Famous for his site-specific "earthworks," Smithson was born in Passaic, New Jersey, and studied art in New York City. He experimented with various artistic media during the 1960s until he developed a fascination with land art and its relationship to decay and change. *Spiral Jetty* created a sensation in the art world in 1970. Using an earthmover, Smithson extended a 1,500 foot spiral-shaped jetty of rocks, earth, salt, and red algae into the Great Salt Lake of Utah, recording the construction on film and in photographs. Smithson died in a plane crash in Texas while inspecting sites for a new work entitled *Amarillo Ramp*.

QUESTIONS FOR REFLECTION AND DISCUSSION

1. In what ways does *Spiral Jetty* differ from a conventional jetty? If you encountered it in the Great Salt Lake, would you think it was natural or manmade?

2. What would it be like to walk or drive onto *Spiral Jetty*? How would this experience be different than looking at its photograph in this book or in an art gallery?

3. What do you think motivated Smithson to construct the artwork where he did and to make an artwork permanent enough that after four decades it is still intact?

4. In what ways does *Spiral Jetty* resemble a conventional work of art such as a painting? In what ways is it different?

FICTION

Eudora Welty 1909–2001

Born and raised in Jackson, Mississippi, Eudora Welty attended Mississippi State College for Women and the University of Wisconsin, Madison, and she spent a year studying business at Columbia University before her father's death in 1931 called her home. She lived in Jackson the rest of her life, taking photographs for the Works Progress Administration in rural Mississippi, and working in radio and newspapers. She began publishing her stories in 1936; her first collection, *A Curtain of Green*, which included "A Worn Path," appeared in 1941. Welty's writing takes a deceptively simple approach to what she identified as her true subject, human relationships. During her long life, Welty published five novels, five collections of short stories, several works of nonfiction, and two book of photographs; her 1970 novel *The Optimist's Daughter* won the Pulitzer Prize.

A WORN PATH

IT WAS DECEMBER—A BRIGHT FROZEN DAY IN the early morning. Far out in the country there was an old Negro woman with her head tied in a red rag, coming along a path through the pinewoods. Her name was Phoenix Jackson. She was very old and small and she walked slowly in the dark pine shadows, moving a little from side to side in her steps, with the balanced heaviness and lightness of a pendulum in a grandfather clock. She carried a thin, small cane made from an umbrella, and with this she kept tapping the frozen earth in front of her. This made a grave and persistent noise in the still air, that seemed meditative like the chirping of a solitary little bird.

She wore a dark striped dress reaching down to her shoe tops, and an equally long apron of bleached sugar sacks, with a full pocket: all neat and tidy, but every time she took a step she might have fallen over her shoelaces, which dragged from her unlaced shoes. She looked straight ahead. Her eyes were blue with age. Her skin had a pattern all its own of numberless branching wrinkles and as though a whole little tree stood in the middle of her forehead, but a golden color ran underneath, and the two knobs of her cheeks were illumined by a yellow burning under the dark. Under the red rag her hair came down on her neck in the frailest of ringlets, still black, and with an odor like copper.

Now and then there was a quivering in the thicket. Old Phoenix said, "Out of my way, all you foxes, owls, beetles, jack rabbits, coons and wild animals! . . . Keep out from under these feet, little bob-whites . . . . Keep the big wild hogs out of my path. Don't let none of those come running my direction. I got a long way." Under her small black-freckled hand her cane, limber as a buggy whip, would switch at the brush as if to rouse up any hiding things.

On she went. The woods were deep and still. The sun made the pine needles almost too bright to look at, up where the wind rocked. The cones dropped as light as feathers. Down in the hollow was the mourning dove—it was not too late for him.

5   The path ran up a hill. "Seem like there is chains about my feet, time I get this far," she said, in the voice of argument old people keep to use with themselves. "Something always take a hold of me on this hill—pleads I should stay."

After she got to the top she turned and gave a full, severe look behind her where she had come. "Up through pines," she said at length. "Now down through oaks."

Her eyes opened their widest, and she started down gently. But before she got to the bottom of the hill a bush caught her dress.

Her fingers were busy and intent, but her skirts were full and long, so that before she could pull them free in one place they were caught in another. It was not possible to allow the dress to tear. "I in the thorny bush," she said. "Thorns, you doing your appointed work. Never want to let folks pass, no sir. Old eyes thought you was a pretty little *green* bush."

Finally, trembling all over, she stood free, and after a moment dared to stoop for her cane.

10 "Sun so high!" she cried, leaning back and looking, while the thick tears went over her eyes. "The time getting all gone here."

At the foot of this hill was a place where a log was laid across the creek.

"Now comes the trial," said Phoenix.

Putting her right foot out, she mounted the log and shut her eyes. Lifting her skirt, leveling her cane fiercely before her, like a festival figure in some parade, she began to march across. Then she opened her eyes and she was safe on the other side.

"I wasn't as old as I thought," she said.

15 But she sat down to rest. She spread her skirts on the bank around her and folded her hands over her knees. Up above her was a tree in a pearly cloud of mistletoe. She did not dare to close her eyes, and when a little boy brought her a plate with a slice of marble-cake on it she spoke to him. "That would be acceptable," she said. But when she went to take it there was just her own hand in the air.

So she left that tree, and had to go through a barbed-wire fence. There she had to creep and crawl, spreading her knees and stretching her fingers like a baby trying to climb the steps. But she talked loudly to herself: she could not let her dress be torn now, so late in the day, and she could not pay for having her arm or her leg sawed off if she got caught fast where she was.

At last she was safe through the fence and risen up out in the clearing. Big dead trees, like black men with one arm, were standing in the purple stalks of the withered cotton field. There sat a buzzard.

"Who you watching?"

In the furrow she made her way along.

20 "Glad this not the season for bulls," she said, looking sideways, "and the good Lord made his snakes to curl up and sleep in the winter. A pleasure I don't see no two-headed snake coming around that tree, where it come once. It took a while to get by him, back in the summer."

She passed through the old cotton and went into a field of dead corn. It whispered and shook and was taller than her head. "Through the maze now," she said, for there was no path.

Then there was something tall, black, and skinny there, moving before her.

At first she took it for a man. It could have been a man dancing in the field. But she stood still and listened, and it did not make a sound. It was as silent as a ghost.

"Ghost," she said sharply, "who be you the ghost of? For I have heard of nary death close by."

25 But there was no answer—only the ragged dancing in the wind.

She shut her eyes, reached out her hand, and touched a sleeve. She found a coat and inside that an emptiness, cold as ice.

"You scarecrow," she said. Her face lighted. "I ought to be shut up for good," she said with laughter. "My senses is gone. I too old. I the oldest people I ever know. Dance, old scarecrow," she said, "while I dancing with you."

She kicked her foot over the furrow, and with mouth drawn down, shook her head once or twice in a little strutting way. Some husks blew down and whirled in streamers about her skirts.

Then she went on, parting her way from side to side with the cane, through the whispering field. At last she came to the end, to a wagon track where the silver grass blew between the red ruts. The quail were walking around like pullets, seeming all dainty and unseen.

30 "Walk pretty," she said. "This the easy place. This the easy going."

She followed the track, swaying through the quiet bare fields, through the little strings of trees silver in their dead leaves, past cabins silver from weather, with the doors and windows boarded shut, all like old women under a spell sitting there. "I walking in their sleep," she said, nodding her head vigorously.

In a ravine she went where a spring was silently flowing through a hollow log. Old Phoenix bent and drank. "Sweet-gum makes the water sweet," she said, and drank more. "Nobody know who made this well, for it was here when I was born."

The track crossed a swampy part where the moss hung as white as lace from every limb. "Sleep on, alligators, and blow your bubbles." Then the track went into the road.

Deep, deep the road went down between the high green-colored banks. Overhead the live-oaks met, and it was as dark as a cave.

35 A black dog with a lolling tongue came up out of the weeds by the ditch. She was meditating, and not

ready, and when he came at her she only hit him a little with her cane. Over she went in the ditch, like a little puff of milkweed.

Down there, her senses drifted away. A dream visited her, and she reached her hand up, but nothing reached down and gave her a pull. So she lay there and presently went to talking. "Old woman," she said to herself, "that black dog come up out of the weeds to stall you off, and now there he sitting on his fine tail, smiling at you."

A white man finally came along and found her— a hunter, a young man, with his dog on a chain.

"Well, Granny!" he laughed. "What are you doing there?"

"Lying on my back like a June-bug waiting to be turned over, mister," she said, reaching up her hand.

40　He lifted her up, gave her a swing in the air, and set her down. "Anything broken, Granny?"

"No sir, them old dead weeds is springy enough," said Phoenix, when she had got her breath. "I thank you for your trouble."

"Where do you live, Granny?" he asked, while the two dogs were growling at each other.

"Away back yonder, sir, behind the ridge. You can't even see it from here."

"On your way home?"

45　"No sir, I going to town."

"Why, that's too far! That's as far as I walk when I come out myself, and I get something for my trouble." He patted the stuffed bag he carried, and there hung down a little closed claw. It was one of the bob-whites, with its beak hooked bitterly to show it was dead. "Now you go on home, Granny!"

"I bound to go to town, mister," said Phoenix. "The time come around."

He gave another laugh, filling the whole landscape. "I know you old colored people! Wouldn't miss going to town to see Santa Claus!"

But something held old Phoenix very still. The deep lines in her face went into a fierce and different radiation. Without warning, she had seen with her own eyes a flashing nickel fall out of the man's pocket onto the ground.

50　"How old are you, Granny?" he was saying.

"There is no telling, mister," she said, "no telling."

Then she gave a little cry and clapped her hands and said, "Git on away from here, dog! Look! Look at that dog!" She laughed as if in admiration. "He ain't

scared of nobody. He a big black dog." She whispered, "Sic him!"

"Watch me get rid of that cur," said the man. "Sic him, Pete! Sic him!"

Phoenix heard the dogs fighting, and heard the man running and throwing sticks. She even heard a gunshot. But she was slowly bending forward by that time, further and further forward, the lids stretched down over her eyes, as if she were doing this in her sleep. Her chin was lowered almost to her knees. The yellow palm of her hand came out from the fold of her apron. Her fingers slid down and along the ground under the piece of money with the grace and care they would have in lifting an egg from under a setting hen. Then she slowly straightened up, she stood erect, and the nickel was in her apron pocket. A bird flew by. Her lips moved. "God watching me the whole time. I come to stealing."

55　The man came back, and his own dog panted about them. "Well, I scared him off that time," he said, and then he laughed and lifted his gun and pointed it at Phoenix.

She stood straight and faced him.

"Doesn't the gun scare you?" he said, still pointing it.

"No, sir, I seen plenty go off closer by, in my day, and for less than what I done," she said, holding utterly still.

He smiled, and shouldered the gun. "Well, Granny," he said, "you must be a hundred years old, and scared of nothing. I'd give you a dime if I had any money with me. But you take my advice and stay home, and nothing will happen to you."

60　"I bound to go on my way, mister," said Phoenix. She inclined her head in the red rag. Then they went in different directions, but she could hear the gun shooting again and again over the hill.

She walked on. The shadows hung from the oak trees to the road like curtains. Then she smelled wood-smoke, and smelled the river, and she saw a steeple and the cabins on their steep steps. Dozens of little black children whirled around her. There ahead was Natchez shining. Bells were ringing. She walked on.

In the paved city it was Christmas time. There were red and green electric lights strung and crisscrossed everywhere, and all turned on in the daytime. Old Phoenix would have been lost if she had not distrusted her eyesight and depended on her feet to know where to take her.

She paused quietly on the sidewalk where people were passing by. A lady came along in the crowd, carrying an armful of red-, green- and silver-wrapped presents; she gave off perfume like the red roses in hot summer, and Phoenix stopped her.

"Please, missy, will you lace up my shoe?" She held up her foot.

65 "What do you want, Grandma?"

"See my shoe," said Phoenix. "Do all right for out in the country, but wouldn't look right to go in a big building."

"Stand still then, Grandma," said the lady. She put her packages down on the sidewalk beside her and laced and tied both shoes tightly.

"Can't lace 'em with a cane," said Phoenix, "Thank you, missy. I doesn't mind asking a nice lady to tie up my shoe, when I gets out on the street."

Moving slowly and from side to side, she went into the big building, and into a tower of steps, where she walked up and around and around until her feet knew to stop.

70 She entered a door, and there she saw nailed up on the wall the document that had been stamped with the gold seal and framed in the gold frame, which matched the dream that was hung up in her head.

"Here I be," she said. There was a fixed and ceremonial stiffness over her body.

"A charity case, I suppose," said an attendant who sat at the desk before her.

But Phoenix only looked above her head. There was sweat on her face, the wrinkles in her skin shone like a bright net.

"Speak up, Grandma," the woman said. "What's your name? We must have your history, you know. Have you been here before? What seems to be the trouble with you?"

75 Old Phoenix only gave a twitch to her face as if a fly were bothering her.

"Are you deaf?" cried the attendant.

But then the nurse came in.

"Oh, that's just old Aunt Phoenix," she said. "She doesn't come for herself—she has a little grandson. She makes these trips just as regular as clockwork. She lives away back off the Old Natchez Trace." She bent down. "Well, Aunt Phoenix, why don't you just take a seat? We won't keep you standing after your long trip." She pointed.

The old woman sat down, bolt upright in the chair.

80 "Now, how is the boy?" asked the nurse.

Old Phoenix did not speak.

"I said, how is the boy?"

But Phoenix only waited and stared straight ahead, her face very solemn and withdrawn into rigidity.

"Is his throat any better?" asked the nurse. "Aunt Phoenix, don't you hear me? Is your grandson's throat any better since the last time you came for the medicine?"

85 With her hands on her knees, the old woman waited, silent, erect and motionless, just as if she were in armor.

"You mustn't take up our time this way, Aunt Phoenix," the nurse said. "Tell us quickly about your grandson, and get it over. He isn't dead, is he?"

At last there came a flicker and then a flame of comprehension across her face, and she spoke.

"My grandson. It was my memory had left me. There I sat and forgot why I made my long trip."

"Forgot?" The nurse frowned. "After you came so far?"

90 Then Phoenix was like an old woman begging a dignified forgiveness for waking up frightened in the night. "I never did go to school, I was too old at the Surrender," she said in a soft voice. "I'm an old woman without an education. It was my memory fail me. My little grandson, he is just the same, and I forgot it in the coming."

"Throat never heals, does it?" said the nurse, speaking in a loud, sure voice to old Phoenix. By now she had a card with something written on it, a little list. "Yes. Swallowed lye. When was it?—January—two-three years ago—"

Phoenix spoke unasked now. "No, missy, he not dead, he just the same. Every little while his throat begin to close up again, and he not able to swallow. He not get his breath. He not able to help himself. So the time come around, and I go on another trip for the soothing medicine."

"All right. The doctor said as long as you came to get it, you could have it," said the nurse. "But it's an obstinate case."

"My little grandson, he sit up there in the house all wrapped up, waiting by himself," Phoenix went on. "We is the only two left in the world. He suffer and it don't seem to put him back at all. He got a sweet look. He going to last. He wear a little patch quilt and peep out holding his mouth open like a little bird.

I remembers so plain now. I not going to forget him again, no, the whole enduring time. I could tell him from all the others in creation."

95   "All right." The nurse was trying to hush her now. She brought her a bottle of medicine. "Charity," she said, making a check mark in a book.

Old Phoenix held the bottle close to her eyes, and then carefully put it into her pocket.

"I thank you," she said.

"It's Christmas time, Grandma," said the attendant. "Could I give you a few pennies out of my purse?"

"Five pennies is a nickel," said Phoenix stiffly.

100   "Here's a nickel," said the attendant.

Phoenix rose carefully and held out her hand. She received the nickel and then fished the other nickel out of her pocket and laid it beside the new one. She stared at her palm closely, with her head on one side.

Then she gave a tap with her cane on the floor.

"This is what come to me to do," she said. "I going to the store and buy my child a little windmill they sells, made out of paper. He going to find it hard to believe there such a thing in the world. I'll march myself back where he waiting, holding it straight up in this hand."

She lifted her free hand, gave a little nod, turned around, and walked out of the doctor's office. Then her slow step began on the stairs, going down.

[1941]

QUESTIONS FOR REFLECTION AND DISCUSSION

1. How does the narrator signal to us that this is not the first time Phoenix has taken this path? Why is this information important to the story even before we find out about her grandson?

2. Why do you think Welty spends so much time telling us about the journey? Why does she include so many details about its different stages?

3. How is Phoenix different in the clinic than she is in the woods?

4. What evidence does the story provide that Phoenix is still alive? What in the story suggests that she might already be dead? What evidence does the story provide that her grandson is alive? What in the story suggests that he might be dead? How does each of these possibilities affect our understanding of the story?

5. What is the relationship between Phoenix and the white people she meets in the story?

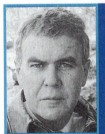

Raymond Carver 1938–1988

Son of an alcoholic lumber worker and a waitress, Raymond Carver grew up in working poverty. Married at nineteen, Carver juggled writing with various jobs. In 1977, he quit drinking and met the writer Tess Gallagher, who would become the companion of his last ten years of life. During the same period, Carver taught creative writing at Syracuse University. He died of lung cancer at the age of fifty. Carver published his first stories in the early 1960s. By mid-decade he had found his voice and style, an understated and brief but profound exploration of everyday lives. First published in 1981 in the *Atlantic Monthly,* "Cathedral" was reprinted in the collection of the same name in 1983.

CATHEDRAL

THIS BLIND MAN, AN OLD FRIEND OF MY WIFE'S, he was on his way to spend the night. His wife had died. So he was visiting the dead wife's relatives in Connecticut. He called my wife from his in-laws'. Arrangements were made. He would come by train, a five-hour trip, and my wife would meet him at the station. She hadn't seen him since she worked for him one summer in Seattle ten years ago. But she and the blind man had kept in touch. They made tapes and mailed them back and forth. I wasn't enthusiastic about his visit. He was no one I knew. And his being blind bothered me. My idea of blindness came from the movies. In the movies, the blind moved slowly and never laughed. Sometimes they were led by seeing-eye dogs. A blind man in my house was not something I looked forward to.

That summer in Seattle she had needed a job. She didn't have any money. The man she was going to marry at the end of the summer was in officers' training school. He didn't have any money, either. But she was in love with the guy, and he was in love with her, etc. She'd seen something in the paper: HELP WANTED—*Reading to Blind Man,* and a telephone number. She phoned and went over, was hired on the spot. She'd worked with this blind man all summer. She read stuff to him, case studies, reports, that sort of thing. She helped him organize his little office in the county social-service department. They'd become good friends, my wife and the blind man. How do I know these things? She told me. And she told me something else. On her last day in the office, the blind man asked if he could touch her face. She agreed to this. She told me he touched his fingers to every part of her face, her nose—even her neck! She never forgot it. She even tried to write a poem about it. She was always trying to write a poem. She wrote a poem or two every year, usually after something really important had happened to her.

When we first started going out together, she showed me the poem. In the poem, she recalled his fingers and the way they had moved around over her face. In the poem, she talked about what she had felt at the time, about what went through her mind when the blind man touched her nose and lips. I can remember I didn't think much of the poem. Of course, I didn't tell her that. Maybe I just don't understand poetry. I admit it's not the first thing I reach for when I pick up something to read.

Anyway, this man who'd first enjoyed her favors, the officer-to-be, he'd been her childhood sweetheart. So okay. I'm saying that at the end of the summer she let the blind man run his hands over her face, said good-bye to him, married her childhood etc., who was now a commissioned officer, and she moved away from Seattle. But they'd kept in touch, she and the blind man. She made the first contact after a year or so. She called him up one night from an Air Force base in Alabama. She wanted to talk. They talked. He asked her to send a tape and tell him about her life. She did this. She sent the tape. On the

tape, she told the blind man about her husband and about their life together in the military. She told the blind man she loved her husband but she didn't like it where they lived and she didn't like it that he was part of the military-industrial thing. She told the blind man she'd written a poem and he was in it. She told him that she was writing a poem about what it was like to be an Air Force officer's wife. The poem wasn't finished yet. She was still writing it. The blind man made a tape. He sent her the tape. She made a tape. This went on for years. My wife's officer was posted to one base and then another. She sent tapes from Moody AFB, McGuire, McConnell, and finally Travis, near Sacramento, where one night she got to feeling lonely and cut off from people she kept losing in that moving-around life. She got to feeling she couldn't go it another step. She went in and swallowed all the pills and capsules in the medicine chest and washed them down with a bottle of gin. Then she got into a hot bath and passed out.

5   But instead of dying, she got sick. She threw up. Her officer—why should he have a name? he was the childhood sweetheart, and what more does he want?—came home from somewhere, found her, and called the ambulance. In time, she put it all on a tape and sent the tape to the blind man. Over the years, she put all kinds of stuff on tapes and sent the tapes off lickety-split. Next to writing a poem every year, I think it was her chief means of recreation. On one tape, she told the blind man she'd decided to live away from her officer for a time. On another tape, she told him about her divorce. She and I began going out, and of course she told her blind man about it. She told him everything, or so it seemed to me. Once she asked me if I'd like to hear the latest tape from the blind man. This was a year ago. I was on the tape, she said. So I said okay, I'd listen to it. I got us drinks and we settled down in the living room. We made ready to listen. First she inserted the tape into the player and adjusted a couple of dials. Then she pushed a lever. The tape squeaked and someone began to talk in this loud voice. She lowered the volume. After a few minutes of harmless chitchat, I heard my own name in the mouth of this stranger, this blind man I didn't even know! And then this: "From all you've said about him, I can only conclude—" But we were interrupted, a knock at the door,

something, and we didn't ever get back to the tape. Maybe it was just as well. I'd heard all I wanted to.

Now this same blind man was coming to sleep in my house.

"Maybe I could take him bowling," I said to my wife. She was at the draining board doing scalloped potatoes. She put down the knife she was using and turned around.

"If you love me," she said, "you can do this for me. If you don't love me, okay. But if you had a friend, any friend, and the friend came to visit, I'd make him feel comfortable." She wiped her hands with the dish towel.

"I don't have any blind friends," I said.

10 "You don't have *any* friends," she said. "Period. Besides," she said, "goddamn it, his wife's just died! Don't you understand that? The man's lost his wife!"

I didn't answer. She'd told me a little about the blind man's wife. Her name was Beulah. Beulah! That's a name for a colored woman.

"Was his wife a Negro?" I asked.

"Are you crazy?" my wife said. "Have you just flipped or something?" She picked up a potato. I saw it hit the floor, then roll under the stove. "What's wrong with you?" she said. "Are you drunk?"

"I'm just asking," I said.

15 Right then my wife filled me in with more detail than I cared to know. I made a drink and sat at the kitchen table to listen. Pieces of the story began to fall into place.

Beulah had gone to work for the blind man the summer after my wife had stopped working for him. Pretty soon Beulah and the blind man had themselves a church wedding. It was a little wedding—who'd want to go to such a wedding in the first place?—just the two of them, plus the minister and the minister's wife. But it was a church wedding just the same. It was what Beulah had wanted, he'd said. But even then Beulah must have been carrying the cancer in her glands. After they had been inseparable for eight years—my wife's word, *inseparable*—Beulah's health went into a rapid decline. She died in a Seattle hospital room, the blind man sitting beside the bed and holding on to her hand. They'd married, lived and worked together, slept together—had sex, sure—and then the blind man had to bury her. All this without his having ever seen what the goddamned woman looked like. It was beyond my understanding. Hearing this, I felt sorry for the blind man for a little bit. And

then I found myself thinking what a pitiful life this woman must have led. Imagine a woman who could never see herself as she was seen in the eyes of her loved one. A woman who could go on day after day and never receive the smallest compliment from her beloved. A woman whose husband could never read the expression on her face, be it misery or something better. Someone who could wear makeup or not— what difference to him? She could, if she wanted, wear green eye-shadow around one eye, a straight pin in her nostril, yellow slacks, and purple shoes, no matter. And then to slip off into death, the blind man's hand on her hand, his blind eyes streaming tears— I'm imagining now—her last thought maybe this: that he never even knew what she looked like, and she on an express to the grave. Robert was left with a small insurance policy and a half of a twenty-peso Mexican coin. The other half of the coin went into the box with her. Pathetic.

So when the time rolled around, my wife went to the depot to pick him up. With nothing to do but wait—sure, I blamed him for that—I was having a drink and watching the TV when I heard the car pull into the drive. I got up from the sofa with my drink and went to the window to have a look.

I saw my wife laughing as she parked the car. I saw her get out of the car and shut the door. She was still wearing a smile. Just amazing. She went around to the other side of the car to where the blind man was already starting to get out. This blind man, feature this, he was wearing a full beard! A beard on a blind man! Too much, I say. The blind man reached into the backseat and dragged out a suitcase. My wife took his arm, shut the car door, and, talking all the way, moved him down the drive and then up the steps to the front porch. I turned off the TV. I finished my drink, rinsed the glass, dried my hands. Then I went to the door.

My wife said, "I want you to meet Robert. Robert, this is my husband. I've told you all about him." She was beaming. She had this blind man by his coat sleeve.

20 The blind man let go of his suitcase and up came his hand.

I took it. He squeezed hard, held my hand, and then he let it go.

"I feel like we've already met," he boomed.

"Likewise," I said. I didn't know what else to say. Then I said, "Welcome. I've heard a lot about you." We began to move then, a little group, from the porch into the living room, my wife guiding him by the arm. The blind man was carrying his suitcase in his other hand. My wife said things like, "To your left here, Robert. That's right. Now watch it, there's a chair. That's it. Sit down right here. This is the sofa. We just bought this sofa two weeks ago."

I started to say something about the old sofa. I'd liked that old sofa. But I didn't say anything. Then I wanted to say something else, small-talk, about the scenic ride along the Hudson. How going *to* New York, you should sit on the right-hand side of the train, and coming *from* New York, the left-hand side.

25 "Did you have a good train ride?" I said. "Which side of the train did you sit on, by the way?"

"What a question, which side!" my wife said. "What's it matter which side?" she said.

"I just asked," I said.

"Right side," the blind man said. "I hadn't been on a train in nearly forty years. Not since I was a kid. With my folks. That's been a long time. I'd nearly forgotten the sensation. I have winter in my beard now," he said. "So I've been told, anyway. Do I look distinguished, my dear?" the blind man said to my wife.

"You look distinguished, Robert," she said. "Robert," she said. "Robert, it's just so good to see you."

30 My wife finally took her eyes off the blind man and looked at me. I had the feeling she didn't like what she saw. I shrugged.

I've never met, or personally known, anyone who was blind. This blind man was late forties, a heavy-set, balding man with stooped shoulders, as if he carried a great weight there. He wore brown slacks, brown shoes, a light-brown shirt, a tie, a sports coat. Spiffy. He also had this full beard. But he didn't use a cane and he didn't wear dark glasses. I'd always thought dark glasses were a must for the blind. Fact was, I wished he had a pair. At first glance, his eyes looked like anyone else's eyes. But if you looked close, there was something different about them. Too much white in the iris, for one thing, and the pupils seemed to move around in the sockets without his knowing it or being able to stop it. Creepy. As I stared at his face, I saw the left pupil turn in toward his nose while the other made an effort to keep in one place. But it was only an effort, for that eye was on the roam without his knowing it or wanting it to be.

I said, "Let me get you a drink. What's your pleasure? We have a little of everything. It's one of our pastimes."

"Bub, I'm a Scotch man myself," he said fast enough in this big voice.

"Right," I said. Bub! "Sure you are. I knew it."

35 He let his fingers touch his suitcase, which was sitting alongside the sofa. He was taking his bearings. I didn't blame him for that.

"I'll move that up to your room," my wife said.

"No, that's fine," the blind man said loudly. "It can go up when I go up."

"A little water with the Scotch?" I said.

"Very little," he said.

40 "I knew it," I said.

He said, "Just a tad. The Irish actor, Barry Fitzgerald? I'm like that fellow. When I drink water, Fitzgerald said, I drink water. When I drink whiskey, I drink whiskey." My wife laughed. The blind man brought his hand up under his beard. He lifted his beard slowly and let it drop.

I did the drinks, three big glasses of Scotch with a splash of water in each. Then we made ourselves comfortable and talked about Robert's travels. First the long flight from the West Coast to Connecticut, we covered that. Then from Connecticut up here by train. We had another drink concerning that leg of the trip.

I remembered having read somewhere that the blind didn't smoke because, as speculation had it, they couldn't see the smoke they exhaled. I thought I knew that much and that much only about blind people. But this blind man smoked his cigarette down to the nubbin and then lit another one. This blind man filled his ashtray and my wife emptied it.

When we sat down at the table for dinner, we had another drink. My wife heaped Robert's plate with cube steak, scalloped potatoes, green beans. I buttered him up two slices of bread. I said, "Here's bread and butter for you." I swallowed some of my drink. "Now let us pray," I said, and the blind man lowered his head. My wife looked at me, her mouth agape. "Pray the phone won't ring and the food doesn't get cold," I said.

45 We dug in. We ate everything there was to eat on the table. We ate like there was no tomorrow. We didn't talk. We ate. We scarfed. We grazed that table. We were into serious eating. The blind man had

right away located his foods, he knew just where everything was on his plate. I watched with admiration as he used his knife and fork on the meat. He'd cut two pieces of meat, fork the meat into his mouth, and then go all out for the scalloped potatoes, the beans next, and then he'd tear off a hunk of buttered bread and eat that. He'd follow this up with a big drink of milk. It didn't seem to bother him to use his fingers once in a while, either.

We finished everything, including half a strawberry pie. For a few moments, we sat as if stunned. Sweat beaded on our faces. Finally, we got up from the table and left the dirty plates. We didn't look back. We took ourselves into the living room and sank into our places again. Robert and my wife sat on the sofa. I took the big chair. We had us two or three more drinks while they talked about the major things that had come to pass for them in the past ten years. For the most part, I just listened. Now and then I joined in. I didn't want him to think I'd left the room, and I didn't want her to think I was feeling left out. They talked of things that had happened to them—to them!—these past ten years. I waited in vain to hear my name on my wife's sweet lips: "And then my dear husband came into my life"—something like that. But I heard nothing of the sort. More talk of Robert. Robert had done a little of everything, it seemed, a regular blind jack-of-all-trades. But most recently he and his wife had had an Amway distributorship, from which, I gathered, they'd earned their living, such as it was. The blind man was also a ham radio operator. He talked in his loud voice about conversations he'd had with fellow operators in Guam, in the Philippines, in Alaska, and even in Tahiti. He said he'd have a lot of friends there if he ever wanted to go visit those places. From time to time, he'd turn his blind face toward me, put his hand under his beard, ask me something. How long had I been in my present position? (Three years.) Did I like my work? (I didn't.) Was I going to stay with it? (What were the options?) Finally, when I thought he was beginning to run down, I got up and turned on the TV.

My wife looked at me with irritation. She was heading toward a boil. Then she looked at the blind man and said, "Robert, do you have a TV?"

The blind man said, "My dear, I have two TVs. I have a color set and a black-and-white thing, an old relic. It's funny, but if I turn the TV on, and I'm always

turning it on, I turn on the color set. It's funny, don't you think?"

I didn't know what to say to that. I had absolutely nothing to say to that. No opinion. So I watched the news program and tried to listen to what the announcer was saying.

50 "This is a color TV," the blind man said. "Don't ask me how, but I can tell."

"We traded up a while ago," I said.

The blind man had another taste of his drink. He lifted his beard, sniffed it, and let it fall. He leaned forward on the sofa. He positioned his ashtray on the coffee table, then put the lighter to his cigarette. He leaned back on the sofa and crossed his legs at the ankles.

My wife covered her mouth, and then she yawned. She stretched. She said, "I think I'll go upstairs and put on my robe. I think I'll change into something else. Robert, you make yourself comfortable," she said.

"I'm comfortable," the blind man said.

55 "I want you to feel comfortable in this house," she said.

"I am comfortable," the blind man said.

After she'd left the room, he and I listened to the weather report and then to the sports roundup. By that time, she'd been gone so long I didn't know if she was going to come back. I thought she might have gone to bed. I wished she'd come back downstairs. I didn't want to be left alone with a blind man. I asked him if he wanted another drink, and he said sure. Then I asked if he wanted to smoke some dope with me. I said I'd just rolled a number. I hadn't, but I planned to do so in about two shakes.

"I'll try some with you," he said.

"Damm right," I said. "That's the stuff."

60 "I got our drinks and sat down on the sofa with him. Then I rolled us two fat numbers. I lit one and passed it. I brought it to his fingers. He took it and inhaled.

"Hold it as long as you can," I said. I could tell he didn't know the first thing.

My wife came back downstairs wearing her pink robe and her pink slippers.

"What do I smell?" she said.

"We thought we'd have us some cannabis," I said.

65 My wife gave me a savage look. Then she looked at the blind man and said, "Robert, I didn't know you smoked."

He said, "I do now, my dear. There's a first time for everything. But I don't feel anything yet."

"This stuff is pretty mellow," I said. "This stuff is mild. It's dope you can reason with," I said. "It doesn't mess you up."

"Not much it doesn't, bub," he said, and laughed.

My wife sat on the sofa between the blind man and me. I passed her the number. She took it and toked and then passed it back to me. "Which way is this going?" she said. Then she said, "I shouldn't be smoking this. I can hardly keep my eyes open as it is. That dinner did me in. I shouldn't have eaten so much."

70 "It was the strawberry pie," the blind man said. "That's what did it," he said, and he laughed his big laugh. Then he shook his head.

"There's more strawberry pie," I said.

"Do you want some more, Robert?" my wife said.

"Maybe in a little while," he said.

We gave our attention to the TV. My wife yawned again. She said, "Your bed is made up when you feel like going to bed, Robert. I know you must have had a long day. When you're ready to go to bed, say so." She pulled his arm. "Robert?"

75 He came to and said, "I've had a real nice time. This beats tapes, doesn't it?"

I said, "Coming at you," and I put the number between his fingers. He inhaled, held the smoke, and then let it go. It was like he'd been doing it since he was nine years old.

"Thanks, bub," he said. "But I think this is all for me. I think I'm beginning to feel it," he said. He held the burning roach out for my wife.

"Same here," she said. "Ditto. Me, too." She took the roach and passed it to me. "I may just sit here for a while between you two guys with my eyes closed. But don't let me bother you, okay? Either one of you. If it bothers you, say so. Otherwise, I may just sit here with my eyes closed until you're ready to go to bed," she said. "Your bed's made up, Robert, when you're ready. It's right next to our room at the top of the stairs. We'll show you up when you're ready. You wake me up now, you guys, if I fall asleep." She said that and then she closed her eyes and went to sleep.

The news program ended. I got up and changed the channel. I sat back down on the sofa. I wished my wife hadn't pooped out. Her head lay across the back of the sofa, her mouth open. She'd turned so that her robe slipped away from her legs, exposing a juicy thigh. I reached to draw her robe back over her, and it was then that I glanced at the blind man. What the hell! I flipped the robe open again.

80 "You say when you want some strawberry pie," I said.

"I will," he said.

I said, "Are you tired? Do you want me to take you up to your bed? Are you ready to hit the hay?"

"Not yet," he said. "No, I'll stay up with you, bub. If that's all right. I'll stay up until you're ready to turn in. We haven't had a chance to talk. Know what I mean? I feel like me and her monopolized the evening." He lifted his beard and he let it fall. He picked up his cigarettes and his lighter.

"That's all right," I said. Then I said, "I'm glad for the company."

85 And I guess I was. Every night I smoked dope and stayed up as long as I could before I fell asleep. My wife and I hardly ever went to bed at the same time. When I did go to sleep, I had these dreams. Sometimes I'd wake up from one of them, my heart going crazy.

Something about the church and the Middle Ages was on the TV. Not your run-of-the-mill TV fare. I wanted to watch something else. I turned to the other channels. But there was nothing on them, either. So I turned back to the first channel and apologized.

"Bub, it's all right," the blind man said. "It's fine with me. Whatever you want to watch is okay. I'm always learning something. Learning never ends. It won't hurt me to learn something tonight. I got ears," he said.

We didn't say anything for a time. He was leaning forward with his head turned at me, his right ear aimed in the direction of the set. Very disconcerting. Now and then his eyelids drooped and then they snapped open again. Now and then he put his fingers into his beard and tugged, like he was thinking about something he was hearing on the television.

On the screen, a group of men wearing cowls was being set upon and tormented by men dressed in skeleton costumes and men dressed as devils. The men dressed as devils wore devil masks, horns, and long tails. This pageant was part of a procession. The Englishman who was narrating the thing said it took place in Spain once a year. I tried to explain to the blind man what was happening.

90 "Skeletons," he said. "I know about skeletons," he said, and he nodded.

Rear view of Notre-Dame de Paris, showing the flying buttresses that support the South Tower of the cathedral. The narrator refers to it as "The famous one in Paris."

The TV showed this one cathedral. Then there was a long, slow look at another one. Finally, the picture switched to the famous one in Paris, with its flying buttresses and its spires reaching up to the clouds. The camera pulled away to show the whole of the cathedral rising above the skyline.

There were times when the Englishman who was telling the thing would shut up, would simply let the camera move around the cathedrals. Or else the camera would tour the countryside, men in fields walking behind oxen. I waited as long as I could. Then I felt I had to say something. I said, "They're showing the outside of this cathedral now. Gargoyles. Little statues carved to look like monsters. Now I guess they're in Italy. Yeah, they're in Italy. There's paintings on the walls of this one church."

"Are those fresco paintings, bub?" he asked, and he sipped from his drink.

I reached for my glass. But it was empty. I tried to remember what I could remember. "You're asking me are those frescoes?" I said. "That's a good question. I don't know."

95 The camera moved to a cathedral outside Lisbon. The differences in the Portuguese cathedral compared with the French and Italian were not that great. But they were there. Mostly the interior stuff. Then something occurred to me, and I said, "Something has occurred to me. Do you have any idea what a cathedral is? What they look like, that is? Do you follow me? If somebody says cathedral to you, do you have any notion what they're talking about? Do you know the difference between that and a Baptist church, say?"

He let the smoke dribble from his mouth. "I know they took hundreds of workers fifty or a hundred years to build," he said. "I just heard the man say that, of course. I know generations of the same families worked on a cathedral. I heard him say that, too. The men who began their life's work on them, they never lived to see the completion of their work. In that wise, bub, they're no different from the rest of us, right?" He laughed. Then his eyelids drooped again. His head nodded. He seemed to be snoozing. Maybe he was imagining himself in Portugal. The TV was showing another cathedral now. This one was in Germany. The Englishman's voice droned on. "Cathedrals," the blind man said. He sat up and rolled his head back and forth. "If you want the truth, bub, that's about all I know. What I just said. What I heard him say. But maybe you could describe one to me? I wish you'd do it. I'd like that. If you want to know, I really don't have a good idea."

I stared hard at the shot of the cathedral on the TV. How could I even begin to describe it? But say my life depended on it. Say my life was being threatened by an insane guy who said I had to do it or else.

I stared some more at the cathedral before the picture flipped off into the countryside. There was no use. I turned to the blind man and said, "To begin with, they're very tall." I was looking around the room for clues. "They reach way up. Up and up. Toward the sky. They're so big, some of them, they have to have these supports. To help hold them up, so to speak. These supports are called buttresses. They remind me of viaducts, for some reason. But maybe you don't know viaducts, either? Sometimes the cathedrals have devils and such carved into the front. Sometimes lords and ladies. Don't ask me why this is," I said.

He was nodding. The whole upper part of his body seemed to be moving back and forth.

100 "I'm not doing so good, am I?" I said.

He stopped nodding and leaned forward on the edge of the sofa. As he listened to me, he was running his fingers through his beard. I wasn't getting through to him, I could see that. But he waited for me to go on just the same. He nodded, like he was trying to encourage me. I tried to think what else to say. "They're really big," I said. "They're massive. They're built of stone. Marble, too, sometimes. In those olden days, when they built cathedrals, men wanted to be close to God. In those olden days, God was an important part of everyone's life. You could tell this from their cathedral-building. I'm sorry," I said, "but it looks like that's the best I can do for you. I'm just no good at it."

"That's all right, bub," the blind man said. "Hey, listen. I hope you don't mind my asking you. Can I ask you something? Let me ask you a simple question, yes or no. I'm just curious and there's no offense. You're my host. But let me ask if you are in any way religious? You don't mind my asking?"

I shook my head. He couldn't see that, though. A wink is the same as a nod to a blind man. "I guess I don't believe in it. In anything. Sometimes it's hard. You know what I'm saying?"

"Sure, I do," he said.

105   "Right," I said.

The Englishman was still holding forth. My wife sighed in her sleep. She drew a long breath and went on with her sleeping.

"You'll have to forgive me," I said. "But I can't tell you what a cathedral looks like. It just isn't in me to do it. I can't do any more than I've done."

The blind man sat very still, his head down, as he listened to me.

I said, "The truth is, cathedrals don't mean anything special to me. Nothing. Cathedrals. They're something to look at on late-night TV. That's all they are."

110   It was then that the blind man cleared his throat. He brought something up. He took a handkerchief from his back pocket. Then he said, "I get it, bub. It's okay. It happens. Don't worry about it," he said. "Hey, listen to me. Will you do me a favor? I got an idea. Why don't you find us some heavy paper? And a pen. We'll do something. We'll draw one together. Get us a pen and some heavy paper. Go on, bub, get the stuff," he said.

So I went upstairs. My legs felt like they didn't have any strength in them. They felt like they did after I'd done some running. In my wife's room I looked around. I found some ballpoints in a little basket on her table. And then I tried to think where to look for the kind of paper he was talking about.

Downstairs, in the kitchen, I found a shopping bag with onion skins in the bottom of the bag. I emptied the bag and shook it. I brought it into the living room and sat down with it near his legs. I moved some things, smoothed the wrinkles from the bag, spread it out on the coffee table.

The blind man got down from the sofa and sat next to me on the carpet.

He ran his fingers over the paper. He went up and down the sides of the paper. The edges, even the edges. He fingered the corners.

115   "All right," he said. "All right, let's do her."

He found my hand, the hand with the pen. He closed his hand over my hand. "Go ahead, bub, draw," he said. "Draw. You'll see. I'll follow along with you. It'll be okay. Just begin now like I'm telling you. You'll see. Draw," the blind man said.

So I began. First I drew a box that looked like a house. It could have been the house I lived in. Then I put a roof on it. At either end of the roof, I drew spires. Crazy.

"Swell," he said. "Terrific. You're doing fine," he said. "Never thought anything like this could happen in your lifetime, did you, bub? Well, it's a strange life, we all know that. Go on now. Keep it up."

I put in windows with arches. I drew flying buttresses. I hung great doors. I couldn't stop. The TV station went off the air. I put down the pen and closed and opened my fingers. The blind man felt around over the paper. He moved the tips of his fingers over the paper, all over what I had drawn, and he nodded.

120   "Doing fine," the blind man said.

I took up the pen again, and he found my hand. I kept at it. I'm no artist. But I kept drawing just the same.

My wife opened up her eyes and gazed at us. She sat up on the sofa, her robe hanging open. She said, "What are you doing? Tell me, I want to know."

I didn't answer her.

The blind man said, "We're drawing a cathedral. Me and him are working on it. Press hard," he said to me. "That's right. That's good," he said. "Sure. You got it, bub, I can tell. You didn't think you could. But you can, can't you? You're cooking with gas now. You know what I'm saying? We're going to really have us something here in a minute. How's the old arm?" he said. "Put some people in there now. What's a cathedral without people?"

125   My wife said, "What's going on? Robert, what are you doing? What's going on?"

    "It's all right," he said to her. "Close your eyes now," the blind man said to me.

    I did it. I closed them just like he said.

    "Are they closed?" he said. "Don't fudge."

    "They're closed," I said.

130   "Keep them that way," he said. He said, "Don't stop now. Draw."

    So we kept on with it. His fingers rode my fingers as my hand went over the paper. It was like nothing else in my life up to now.

    Then he said, "I think that's it. I think you got it," he said. "Take a look. What do you think?"

    But I had my eyes closed. I thought I'd keep them that way for a little longer. I thought it was something I ought to do.

    "Well?" he said. "Are you looking?"

135   My eyes were still closed. I was in my house. I knew that. But I didn't feel like I was inside anything.

    "It's really something," I said.

[1981]

QUESTIONS FOR REFLECTION AND DISCUSSION

1. How would you characterize the narrator's voice? What are the formal means Carver uses to create this voice? What attitude does this voice suggest we take toward the events it recounts?

2. What is the difference between the "blind man" of the movies and the blind man who comes to visit the narrator and his wife?

3. What is the meaning of the husband's "prayer" before supper? Support your conclusion with evidence from the story.

4. What is the relationship of the people on the television to the cathedral? What is the relationship of the narrator to the cathedral? What is the relationship of the blind man to the cathedral? What is the difference between the cathedral on television, the narrator's verbal description of the cathedral, and the version he draws with the blind man? What is the narrator's attitude to the events in the last paragraph of the story?

Sherman Alexie b. 1966

Born and raised on the Spokane Indian Reservation in Washington, Sherman Alexie attended Gonzaga University and Washington State University. Characterized by an unflinching depiction of modern reservation life, a keen sense of humor, and a sharp satirical edge, Alexie's writing includes novels, poetry, screenplays, and several collections of stories, including *The Lone Ranger and Tonto Fistfight in Heaven* (1993), in which "This Is What It Means to Say Phoenix, Arizona" was published. Alexie later adapted the story as the screenplay for the feature film *Smoke Signals* (1999).

THIS IS WHAT IT MEANS TO SAY PHOENIX, ARIZONA

JUST AFTER VICTOR LOST HIS JOB AT THE BUREAU of Indian Affairs,° he also found out that his father had died of a heart attack in Phoenix, Arizona. Victor hadn't seen his father in a few years, had only talked to him on the telephone once or twice, but there still was a genetic pain, which was as real and immediate as a broken bone. Victor didn't have any money. Who does have money on a reservation, except the cigarette and fireworks salespeople? His father had a savings account waiting to be claimed, but Victor needed to find a way to get from Spokane

Bureau of Indian Affairs: the division of the U.S. Department of the Interior that manages Native American matters; the bureau is operated by government officials, not tribal leaders.

to Phoenix. Victor's mother was just as poor as he was, and the rest of his family didn't have any use at all for him. So Victor called the tribal council.

"Listen," Victor said. "My father just died. I need some money to get to Phoenix to make arrangements."

"Now Victor," the council said, "you know we're having a difficult time financially.

"But I thought the council had special funds set aside for stuff like this."

5   "Now, Victor, we do have some money available for the proper return of tribal members' bodies. But I don't think we have enough to bring your father all the way back from Phoenix."

"Well," Victor said. "It ain't going to cost all that much. He had to be cremated. Things were kind of ugly. He died of a heart attack in his trailer and nobody found him for a week. It was really hot, too. You get the picture."

"Now, Victor, we're sorry for your loss and the circumstances. But we can really only afford to give you one hundred dollars."

"That's not even enough for a plane ticket."

"Well, you might consider driving down to Phoenix."

10   "I don't have a car. Besides, I was going to drive my father's pickup back up here."

"Now, Victor," the council said, "we're sure there is somebody who could drive you to Phoenix. Or could anybody lend you the rest of the money?"

"You know there ain't nobody around with that kind of money."

"Well, we're sorry, Victor, but that's the best we can do."

Victor accepted the tribal council's offer. What else could he do? So he signed the proper papers, picked up his check, and walked over to the Trading Post to cash it.

15   While Victor stood in line, he watched Thomas Builds-the-Fire standing near the magazine rack talking to himself. Like he always did. Thomas was a storyteller whom nobody wanted to listen to. That's like being a dentist in a town where everybody has false teeth.

Victor and Thomas Builds-the-Fire were the same age, had grown up and played in the dirt together. Ever since Victor could remember, it was Thomas who had always had something to say.

Once, when they were seven years old, when Victor's father still lived with the family, Thomas closed his eyes and told Victor this story: "Your father's heart is weak. He is afraid of his own family. He is afraid of you. Late at night, he sits in the dark. Watches the television until there's nothing but that white noise. Sometimes he feels like he wants to buy a motorcycle and ride away. He wants to run and hide. He doesn't want to be found."

Thomas Builds-the-Fire had known that Victor's father was going to leave, known it before anyone. Now Victor stood in the Trading Post with a one-hundred-dollar check in his hand, wondering if Thomas knew that Victor's father was dead, if he knew what was going to happen next.

Just then, Thomas looked at Victor, smiled, and walked over to him.

20   "Victor, I'm sorry about your father," Thomas said.

"How did you know about it?" Victor asked.

"I heard it on the wind. I heard it from the birds. I felt it in the sunlight. Also, your mother was just in here crying."

"Oh," Victor said and looked around the Trading Post. All the other Indians stared, surprised that Victor was even talking to Thomas. Nobody talked to Thomas anymore because he told the same damn stories over and over again. Victor was embarrassed, but he thought that Thomas might be able to help him. Victor felt a sudden need for tradition.

"I can lend you the money you need," Thomas said suddenly. "But you have to take me with you."

25   "I can't take your money," Victor said. "I mean, I haven't hardly talked to you in years. We're not really friends anymore."

"I didn't say we were friends. I said you had to take me with you."

"Let me think about it."

Victor went home with his one hundred dollars and sat at the kitchen table. He held his head in his hands and thought about Thomas Builds-the-Fire, remembered little details, tears and scars, the bicycle they shared for a summer, so many stories.

Thomas Builds-the-Fire sat on the bicycle, waiting in Victor's yard. He was ten years old and skinny. His hair was dirty because it was the Fourth of July.

30   "Victor," Thomas yelled. "Hurry up. We're going to miss the fireworks."

After a few minutes, Victor ran out of his family's house, vaulted over the porch railing, and landed gracefully on the sidewalk.

Thomas gave him the bike and they headed for the fireworks. It was nearly dark and the fireworks were about to start.

"You know," Thomas said, "it's strange how us Indians celebrate the Fourth of July. It ain't like it was our independence everybody was fighting for."

"You think about things too much," Victor said. "It's just supposed to be fun. Maybe Junior will be there."

35 "Which Junior? Everybody on this reservation is named Junior."

The fireworks were small, hardly more than a few bottle rockets and a fountain. But it was enough for two Indian boys. Years later, they would need much more.

Afterward, sitting in the dark, fighting off mosquitoes, Victor turned to Thomas Builds-the-Fire.

"Hey," Victor said. "Tell me a story."

Thomas closed his eyes and told this story: "There were these two Indian boys who wanted to be warriors. But it was too late to be warriors in the old way. All the horses were gone. So the two Indian boys stole a car and drove to the city. They parked the stolen car in the front of the police station and then hitchhiked back home to the reservation. When they got back, all their friends cheered and their parents' eyes shone with pride. 'You were very brave,' everybody said to the two Indian boys. 'Very brave.'"

40 "Ya-hey," Victor said. "That's a good one. I wish I could be a warrior."

"Me too," Thomas said.

Victor sat at his kitchen table. He counted his one hundred dollars again and again. He knew he needed more to make it to Phoenix and back. He knew he needed Thomas Builds-the-Fire. So he put his money in his wallet and opened the front door to find Thomas on the porch.

"Ya-hey, Victor," Thomas said. "I knew you'd call me."

Thomas walked into the living room and sat down in Victor's favorite chair.

45 "I've got some money saved up," Thomas said. "It's enough to get us down there, but you have to get us back."

"I've got this hundred dollars," Victor said. "And my dad had a savings account I'm going to claim."

"How much in your dad's account?"

"Enough. A few hundred."

"Sounds good. When we leaving?"

50 When they were fifteen and had long since stopped being friends, Victor and Thomas got into a fistfight. That is, Victor was really drunk and beat Thomas up for no reason at all. All the other Indian boys stood around and watched it happen. Junior was there and so were Lester, Seymour, and a lot of others.

The beating might have gone on until Thomas was dead if Norma Many Horses hadn't come along and stopped it.

"Hey, you boys," Norma yelled and jumped out of her car. "Leave him alone."

If it had been someone else, even another man, the Indian boys would've just ignored the warnings. But Norma was a warrior. She was powerful. She could have picked up any two of the boys and smashed their skulls together. But worse than that, she would have dragged them all over to some tepee and made them listen to some elder tell a dusty old story.

The Indian boys scattered, and Norma walked over to Thomas and picked him up.

55 "Hey, little man, are you O.K.?" she asked.

Thomas gave her a thumbs-up.

"Why they always picking on you?"

Thomas shook his head, closed his eyes, but no stories came to him, no words or music. He just wanted to go home, to lie in his bed and let his dreams tell the stories for him.

Thomas Builds-the-Fire and Victor sat next to each other in the airplane, coach section. A tiny white woman had the window seat. She was busy twisting her body into pretzels. She was flexible.

60 "I have to ask," Thomas said, and Victor closed his eyes in embarrassment.

"Don't," Victor said.

"Excuse me, miss," Thomas asked. "Are you a gymnast or something?"

"There's no something about it," she said. "I was first alternate on the 1980 Olympic team."

"Really?" Thomas asked.

65 "Really."

"I mean, you used to be a world-class athlete?" Thomas asked.

"My husband thinks I still am."

Thomas Builds-the-Fire smiled. She was a mental gymnast too. She pulled her leg straight up against her body so that she could've kissed her kneecap.

"I wish I could do that," Thomas said.

70 Victor was ready to jump out of the plane. Thomas, that crazy Indian story-teller with ratty old braids and broken teeth, was flirting with a beautiful Olympic gymnast. Nobody back home on the reservation would ever believe it.

"Well," the gymnast said. "It's easy. Try it."

Thomas grabbed at his leg and tried to pull it up into the same position as the gymnast's. He couldn't even come close, which made Victor and the gymnast laugh.

"Hey," she asked. "You two are Indian, right?"

"Full-blood," Victor said.

75 "Not me," Thomas said. "I'm half magician on my mother's side and half clown on my father's."

They all laughed.

"What are your names?" she asked.

"Victor and Thomas."

"Mine is Cathy. Pleased to meet you all."

80 The three of them talked for the duration of the flight. Cathy the gymnast complained about the government, how they screwed the 1980 Olympic team by boycotting the games.

"Sounds like you all got a lot in common with Indians," Thomas said.

Nobody laughed.

After the plane landed in Phoenix and they had all found their way to the terminal, Cathy the gymnast smiled and waved goodbye.

"She was really nice," Thomas said.

85 "Yeah, but everybody talks to everybody on airplanes," Victor said.

"You always used to tell me I think too much," Thomas said. "Now it sounds like you do."

"Maybe I caught it from you."

"Yeah."

Thomas and Victor rode in a taxi to the trailer where Victor's father had died.

90 "Listen," Victor said as they stopped in front of the trailer. "I never told you I was sorry for beating you up that time."

"Oh, it was nothing. We were just kids and you were drunk."

"Yeah, but I'm still sorry."

"That's all right."

Victor paid for the taxi, and the two of them stood in the hot Phoenix summer. They could smell the trailer.

95 "This ain't going to be nice," Victor said. "You don't have to go in."

"You're going to need help."

Victor walked to the front door and opened it. The stink rolled out and made them both gag. Victor's father had lain in that trailer for a week in hundred-degree temperatures before anyone had found him. And the only reason anyone found him was the smell. They needed dental records to identify him. That's exactly what the coroner said. They needed dental records.

"Oh, man," Victor said. "I don't know if I can do this."

"Well, then don't."

100 "But there might be something valuable in there."

"I thought his money was in the bank."

"It is: I was talking about pictures and letters and stuff like that."

"Oh," Thomas said as he held his breath and followed Victor into the trailer.

When Victor was twelve, he stepped into an underground wasps' nest. His foot was caught in the hole and no matter how hard he struggled, Victor couldn't pull free. He might have died there, stung a thousand times, if Thomas Builds-the-Fire had not come by.

105 "Run," Thomas yelled and pulled Victor's foot from the hole. They ran then, hard as they ever had, faster than Billy Mills, faster than Jim Thorpe,° faster than the wasps could fly.

Victor and Thomas ran until they couldn't breathe, ran until it was cold and dark outside, ran until they were lost and it took hours to find their way home. All the way back, Victor counted his stings.

"Seven," Victor said. "My lucky number."

Victor didn't find much to keep in the trailer. Only a photo album and a stereo. Everything else had that smell stuck in it or was useless anyway. "I guess this is all," Victor said. "It ain't much."

"Better than nothing," Thomas said.

110 "Yeah, and I do have the pickup," Victor said.

"Yeah," Thomas said. "It's in good shape."

"Dad was good about that stuff."

Billy Mills . . . Jim Thorpe: the second and first Native Americans to win gold metals at the Olympic Games.

"Yeah, I remember your dad."

"Really?" Victor asked. "What do you remember?"

Thomas Builds-the-Fire closed his eyes and told this story: "I remember when I had this dream that told me to go to Spokane, to stand by the falls in the middle of the city and wait for a sign. I knew I had to go there but I didn't have a car. Didn't have a license. I was only thirteen. So I walked all the way, took me all day, and I finally made it to the falls. I stood there for an hour waiting. Then your dad came walking up. 'What the hell are you doing here?' he asked me. I said, 'Waiting for a vision.' Then your father said, 'All you're going to get here is mugged.' So he drove me over to Denny's, bought me dinner, and then drove me home to the reservation. For a long time, I was mad because I thought my dreams had lied to me. But they hadn't. Your dad was my vision. *Take care of each other* is what my dreams were saying. *Take care of each other.*"

Victor was quiet for a long time. He searched his mind for memories of his father, found the good ones, found a few bad ones, added it all up, and smiled.

"My father never told me about finding you in Spokane," Victor said.

"He said he wouldn't tell anybody. Didn't want me to get in trouble. But he said I had to watch out for you as part of the deal."

"Really?"

"Really. Your father said you would need the help. He was right."

"That's why you came down here with me, isn't it?" Victor asked.

"I came because of your father."

Victor and Thomas climbed into the pickup, drove over to the bank, and claimed the three hundred dollars in the savings account.

Thomas Builds-the-Fire could fly.

Once, he jumped off the roof of the tribal school and flapped his arms like a crazy eagle. And he flew. For a second he hovered, suspended above all the other Indian boys, who were too smart or too scared to jump too.

"He's flying," Junior yelled, and Seymour was busy looking for the trick wires or mirrors. But it was real. As real as the dirt when Thomas lost altitude and crashed to the ground.

He broke his arm in two places.

"He broke his wing, he broke his wing, he broke his wing," all the Indian boys chanted as they ran off, flapping their wings, wishing they could fly too. They hated Thomas for his courage, his brief moment as a bird. Everybody has dreams about flying. Thomas flew.

One of his dreams came true for just a second, just enough to make it real.

Victor's father, his ashes, fit in one wooden box with enough left over to fill a cardboard box.

"He always was a big man," Thomas said.

Victor carried part of his father out to the pickup, and Thomas carried the rest. They set him down carefully behind the seats, put a cowboy hat on the wooden box and a Dodgers cap on the cardboard box. That was the way it was supposed to be.

"Ready to head back home?" Victor asked.

"It's going to be a long drive."

"Yeah, take a couple days, maybe."

"We can take turns," Thomas said.

"O.K.," Victor said, but they didn't take turns. Victor drove for sixteen hours straight north, made it halfway up Nevada toward home before he finally pulled over.

"Hey, Thomas," Victor said. "You got to drive for a while."

"O.K."

Thomas Builds-the-Fire slid behind the wheel and started off down the road. All through Nevada, Thomas and Victor had been amazed at the lack of animal life, at the absence of water, of movement.

"Where is everything?" Victor had asked more than once.

Now, when Thomas was finally driving, they saw the first animal, maybe the only animal in Nevada. It was a long-eared jackrabbit.

"Look," Victor yelled. "It's alive."

Thomas and Victor were busy congratulating themselves on their discovery when the jackrabbit darted out into the road and under the wheels of the pickup.

"Stop the goddamn car," Victor yelled, and Thomas did stop and backed the pickup to the dead jackrabbit.

"Oh, man, he's dead," Victor said as he looked at the squashed animal.

"Really dead."

"The only thing alive in this whole state and we just killed it."

"I don't know," Thomas said. "I think it was suicide."

150   Victor looked around the desert, sniffed the air, felt the emptiness and loneliness, and nodded his head.

"Yeah," Victor said. "It had to be suicide."

"I can't believe this," Thomas said. "You drive for a thousand miles and there ain't even any bugs smashed on the windshield. I drive for ten seconds and kill the only living thing in Nevada."

"Yeah," Victor said. "Maybe I should drive."

"Maybe you should."

Thomas Builds-the-Fire walked through the corridors of the tribal school by himself. Nobody wanted to be anywhere near him because of all those stories. Story after story.

Thomas closed his eyes and this story came to him: "We are all given one thing by which our lives are measured, one determination. Mine are the stories that can change or not change the world. It doesn't matter which, as long as I continue to tell the stories. My father, he died on Okinawa° in World War II, died fighting for this country, which had tried to kill him for years. My mother, she died giving birth to me, died while I was still inside her. She pushed me out into the world with her last breath. I have no brothers or sisters. I have only my stories, which came to me before I even had the words to speak. I learned a thousand stories before I took my first thousand steps. They are all I have. It's all I can do."

Thomas Builds-the-Fire told his stories to all those who would stop and listen. He kept telling them long after people had stopped listening.

Victor and Thomas made it back to the reservation just as the sun was rising. It was the beginning of a new day on earth, but the same old shit on the reservation.

"Good morning," Thomas said.

160   "Good morning."

The tribe was waking up, ready for work, eating breakfast, reading the newspaper, just like everybody else does. Willene LeBret was out in her garden,

wearing a bathrobe. She waved when Thomas and Victor drove by.

"Crazy Indians made it," she said to herself and went back to her roses.

Victor stopped the pickup in front of Thomas Builds-the-Fire's HUD° house. They both yawned, stretched a little, shook dust from their bodies.

"I'm tired," Victor said.

165   "Of everything," Thomas added.

They both searched for words to end the journey. Victor needed to thank Thomas for his help and for the money, and to make the promise to pay it all back.

"Don't worry about the money," Thomas said. "It don't make any difference anyhow."

"Probably not, enit?"

"Nope."

170   Victor knew that Thomas would remain the crazy storyteller who talked to dogs and cars, who listened to the wind and pine trees. Victor knew that he couldn't really be friends with Thomas, even after all that had happened. It was cruel but it was real. As real as the ash, as Victor's father, sitting behind the seats.

"I know how it is," Thomas said. "I know you ain't going to treat me any better than you did before. I know your friends would give you too much shit about it."

Victor was ashamed of himself. Whatever happened to the tribal ties, the sense of community? The only real thing he shared with anybody was a bottle and broken dreams. He owed Thomas something, anything.

"Listen," Victor said and handed Thomas the cardboard box that contained half of his father. "I want you to have this."

Thomas took the ashes and smiled, closed his eyes, and told this story: "I'm going to travel to Spokane Falls one last time and toss these ashes into the water. And your father will rise like a salmon, leap over the bridge, over me, and find his way home. It will be beautiful. His teeth will shine like silver, like a rainbow. He will rise, Victor, he will rise."

175   Victor smiled.

"I was planning on doing the same thing with my half," Victor said. "But I didn't imagine my

Okinawa: largest island of the Ryukyus, a chain of Japanese islands that was the scene of a large and deadly battle near the end of World War II.

HUD: the U.S. Department of Housing and Urban Development.

father looking anything like a salmon. I thought it'd be like cleaning the attic or something. Like letting things go after they've stopped having any use."

"Nothing stops, cousin," Thomas said. "Nothing stops."

Thomas Builds-the-Fire got out of the pickup and walked up his driveway. Victor started the pickup and began the drive home.

"Wait," Thomas yelled suddenly from his porch. "I just got to ask one favor."

180 Victor stopped the pickup, leaned out the window, and shouted back.

"What do you want?" he asked.

"Just one time when I'm telling a story somewhere, why don't you stop and listen?" Thomas asked.

"Just once?"

"Just once."

185 Victor waved his arms to let Thomas know that the deal was good. It was a fair trade. That's all Thomas had ever wanted from his whole life. So Victor drove his father's pickup toward home while Thomas went into his house, closed the door behind him, and heard a new story come to him in the silence afterward.

[1993]

QUESTIONS FOR REFLECTION AND DISCUSSION

1. What are some of the expectations about Native Americans and reservation life that Alexie uses in the story? Do the characters and situations meet these expectations?

2. Characterize Victor and Thomas Builds-the-Fire and describe their relationship. Has the relationship always been the same? Does it change over the course of the story? What role does Victor's father play in it?

3. What is the function of the plane flight in the story? How are the characters different in this space than elsewhere? How is it different from the drive home?

4. What sort of stories does Thomas tell? How are they related to his dreams? What is their function in "This Is What It Means to Say Phoenix, Arizona"?

POETRY

Robert Frost 1874–1963

In what ways does a wall produce an in-between space? In this famous poem by Robert Frost, the wall simultaneously brings together and separates the speaker and his neighbor. In what other ways does the wall also affect the space and people around it? For a biography of Frost, see page 176.

Mending Wall

Something there is that doesn't love a wall,
That sends the frozen-ground-swell under it,
And spills the upper boulders in the sun;
And makes gaps even two can pass abreast.
The work of hunters is another thing: 5
I have come after them and made repair
Where they have left not one stone on a stone,
But they would have the rabbit out of hiding,
To please the yelping dogs. The gaps I mean,
No one has seen them made or heard them made,   10
But at spring mending-time we find them there.
I let my neighbor know beyond the hill;
And on a day we meet to walk the line
And set the wall between us once again.

We keep the wall between us as we go.   15
To each the boulders that have fallen to each.
And some are loaves and some so nearly balls
We have to use a spell to make them balance:
"Stay where you are until our backs are turned!"
We wear our fingers rough with handling them.   20
Oh, just another kind of outdoor game,
One on a side. It comes to little more:
There where it is we do not need the wall:
He is all pine and I am apple orchard.
My apple trees will never get across   25
And eat the cones under his pines, I tell him.
He only says, "Good fences make good neighbors."
Spring is the mischief in me, and I wonder
If I could put a notion in his head:
"*Why* do they make good neighbors? Isn't it   30
Where there are cows? But here there are no cows.

Before I built a wall I'd ask to know
What I was walling in or walling out,
And to whom I was like to give offence.
Something there is that doesn't love a wall,   35
That wants it down." I could say "Elves" to him,
But it's not elves exactly, and I'd rather
He said it for himself. I see him there
Bringing a stone grasped firmly by the top
In each hand, like an old-stone savage armed.   40
He moves in darkness as it seems to me,
Not of woods only and the shade of trees.
He will not go behind his father's saying,
And he likes having thought of it so well
He says again, "Good fences make good
    neighbors."   45

                                                                  [1914]

James Wright 1927–1980

Born into a working-class Irish family in Martins Ferry, Ohio, James Wright attended Kenyon College on the G. I. Bill after serving in World War II. He earned a PhD at the University of Washington, and held a number of teaching posts while assembling an impressive body of poetry, including the Pulitzer Prize–winning *Collected Poems* (1971). "Lying in a Hammock" is characteristic in its strong emphasis on the image as vehicle for the expression of deep emotion.

Lying in a Hammock at William Duffy's Farm in Pine Island, Minnesota

Over my head, I see the bronze butterfly,
Asleep on the black trunk,
Blowing like a leaf in green shadow.
Down the ravine behind the empty house,
The cowbells follow one another   5

Into the distances of the afternoon.
To my right,
In a field of sunlight between two pines,
The droppings of last year's horses
Blaze up into golden stones.   10
I lean back, as the evening darkens and comes on.
A chicken hawk floats over, looking for home.
I have wasted my life.

                                                                  [1963]

1. How is the title related to the body of the poem? Why is it important that the speaker is in a hammock? How would the poem be changed with a different title?

2. What does the speaker see around him? What is the relationship between the different things and creatures that he sees?

3. How is the final line related to the previous twelve? Does it require us to change our understanding of those first twelve lines?

Henry Taylor b. 1942

Born in Loudoun County, Virginia, Henry Taylor attended the University of Virginia. Former professor of literature and co-director of the MFA Program in Creative Writing at American University, Taylor today lives in Bethesda, Maryland. He is the author of five volumes of poetry, a collection of essays, and a number of translations. "Landscape with Tractor" was published in *The Flying Change* (1985), which was awarded the Pulitzer Prize.

Landscape with Tractor

How would it be if you took yourself off
to a house set well back from a dirt road,
with, say, three acres of grass bounded
by road, driveway, and vegetable garden?

Spring and summer you would mow the field,   5
not down to lawn, but with a bushhog,
every six weeks or so, just often enough
to give grass a chance, and keep weeds down.

And one day—call it August, hot, a storm
recently past, things green and growing a bit,   10
and you're mowing, with half your mind
on something you'd rather be doing, or did once.

Three rounds, and then on the straight
alongside the road, maybe three swaths in
from where you are now, you glimpse it. People   15
will toss all kinds of crap from their cars.

It's a clothing-store dummy, for God's sake.
Another two rounds, and you'll have to stop,
contend with it, at least pull it off to one side.
You keep going. Two rounds more, then down   20

off the tractor, and Christ! Not a dummy, a corpse.
The field tilts, whirls, then steadies as you run.
Telephone. Sirens. Two local doctors use pitchforks
to turn the body, some four days dead, and ripening.

And the cause of death no mystery: two bullet holes   25
in the breast of a well-dressed black woman
in perhaps her mid-thirties. They wrap her,
take her away. You take the rest of the day off.

Next day, you go back to the field, having
to mow over the damp dent in the tall grass   30
where bluebottle flies are still swirling,
but the bushhog disperses them, and all traces.

Weeks pass. You hear at the post office
that no one comes forward to say who she was.
Brought out from the city, they guess, and dumped   35
like a bag of beer cans. She was someone,

and now is no one, buried or burned
or dissected; but gone. And I ask you
again, how would it be? To go on with your life,
putting gas in the tractor, keeping down thistles,   40

and seeing, each time you pass that spot,
the form in the grass, the bright yellow skirt,
black shoes, the thing not quite like a face
whose gaze blasted past you at nothing

when the doctors heaved her over? To wonder,   45
from now on, what dope deal, betrayal,
or innocent refusal, brought her here,
and to know she will stay in that field till you die?

[1985]

1. Why does the speaker address us directly? How would the poem be different if it simply described what had happened?

2. Why does it take the speaker so long to realize what he is seeing? Why does it take him so long to get down off of his tractor?

3. How does the landscape change once the speaker has found the body in it? Why doesn't the body disappear?

4. What is the relationship between this landscape and the city? What do you think is the speaker's relationship to this landscape? To the city?

Louise Erdrich b. 1954

Louise Erdrich was born in 1954 in Little Falls, Minnesota, and raised in North Dakota. Her German-born father and French Ojibwe, or Chippewa, mother both worked as teachers for the Bureau of Indian Affairs. Erdrich graduated from Dartmouth College in 1976 and taught poetry in North Dakota before returning east to Johns Hopkins University to complete a master's degree in creative writing. She was married to the author and anthropologist Michael Dorris (1945–1997), founder of the Native American Studies Program at Dartmouth College, with whom she collaborated on the novel, *The Crown of Columbus* (1991). Erdrich's acclaimed series of novels about contemporary Native American life, including *Love Medicine* (1984), *The Beet Queen* (1986), and *Tracks* (1988) among others, follows the lives of a continuing cast of characters. "Dear John Wayne" was published in her volume of poetry, *Jacklight* (1984). Erdrich uses an allusion to the career of Western movie icon John Wayne and the cultural context surrounding that career to ground the scene of her poem.

Dear John Wayne

August and the drive-in picture is packed.
We lounge on the hood of the Pontiac
surrounded by the slow-burning spirals they sell
at the window, to vanquish the hordes of mosquitoes.
Nothing works. They break through the smoke
    screen for blood.   5

Always the lookout spots the Indians first,
spread north to south, barring progress.
The Sioux or some other Plains bunch
in spectacular columns, ICBM missiles,°
feathers bristling in the meaningful sunset.   10

The drum breaks. There will be no parlance.
Only the arrows whining, a death-cloud of nerves
swarming down on the settlers
who die beautifully, tumbling like dust weeds

John Wayne (right, on horseback) as Civil War veteran cavalry Captain Kirby York in John Ford's western, *Fort Apache* (1948), filmed in Monument Valley, Utah. When his incompetent superior Owen Thursday (Henry Fonda) antagonizes the Apache and their leader, Cochise, they ride into battle, killing Thursday's regiment and sparing only York's troops. As the film ends, York is preparing to lead a new campaign against the Apache.

9 ICBM: Intercontinental ballistic missile, a rocket designed to deliver a nuclear warhead at an enormous distance.

into the history that brought us all here
together: this wide screen beneath the sign of
   the bear.°   15

The sky fills, acres of blue squint and eye
that the crowd cheers. His face moves over us,
a thick cloud of vengeance, pitted
like the land that was once flesh. Each rut,
each scar makes a promise: *It is*
not over, this fight, not as long as you resist.   20

Everything we see belongs to us.

A few laughing Indians fall over the hood
slipping in the hot spilled butter.
The eye sees a lot, John, but the heart is so blind.
Death makes us owners of nothing.   25
He smiles, a horizon of teeth
the credits reel over, and then the white fields

again blowing in the true-to-life dark.
The dark films over everything.
We get into the car   30
scratching our mosquito bites, speechless and small
as people are when the movie is done.
We are back in our skins.

How can we help but keep hearing his voice,
the flip side of the sound track, still playing: 35
Come on, boys, we got them
where we want them, drunk, running.
They'll give us what we want, what we need.
Even his disease° was the idea of taking
   everything.
Those cells, burning, doubling, splitting out of their
   skins.   40

[1984]

15 **the bear:** the constellation of the Great Bear in the night sky.

39 his disease: John Wayne (1907–1979) died of lung and stomach cancer after a long film career dominated by roles as heroes in westerns.

QUESTIONS FOR REFLECTION AND DISCUSSION

1. Describe the scene of the poem. What happens on the screen of the drive-in and what happens in the audience?

2. What is the attitude of the audience members toward what they see? How is this different from a conventional audience reaction, and why?

3. In the fourth stanza and again in lines 28–29, the speaker describes John Wayne's appearance on the movie screen.

How does this description reflect Wayne's relation to this audience?

4. How would you characterize the relationship of the audience in this poem to the movies? In what ways is this a conventional relationship? In what ways is it unconventional?

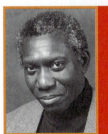

Yusef Komunyakaa b. 1947

Born in Bogalusa, Louisiana, Yusef Komunyakaa served in the U.S. Army in Vietnam, where he was also a correspondent for the military newspaper, *The Southern Cross*, which he later edited. Since 1977, he has published over a dozen collections of poetry, a collection of essays, interviews, and commentaries, and co-edited volumes of jazz poetry. He received the Pulitzer Prize in 1994 for *Neon Vernacular*, and is currently a professor of creative writing at Princeton University. "Facing It" is the concluding poem of Komunyakaa's collection, *Dien Cai Dau* (1988), which draws from his experiences in Vietnam.

Facing It

My black face fades,
hiding inside the black granite.
I said I wouldn't,

dammit: No tears.
I'm stone. I'm flesh.   5
My clouded reflection eyes me
like a bird of prey, the profile of night
slanted against morning. I turn

this way—the stone lets me go.
I turn that way—I'm inside
the Vietnam Veterans Memorial   10
again, depending on the light
to make a difference.
I go down the 58,022 names,
half-expecting to find   15
my own in letters like smoke.
I touch the name Andrew Johnson;
I see the booby trap's white flash.
Names shimmer on a woman's blouse
but when she walks away   20
the names stay on the wall.

Brushstrokes flash, a red bird's
wings cutting across my stare.
The sky. A plane in the sky.
A white vet's image floats   25
closer to me, then his pale eyes
look through mine. I'm a window.
He's lost his right arm
inside the stone. In the black mirror
a woman's trying to erase names: 30
No, she's brushing a boy's hair.

[1988]

Visitors look closely at the names inscribed on the Vietnam Veterans Memorial during ceremonies on November 7, 2007, to mark the wall's twenty-fifth anniversary on the National Mall in Washington, D.C. Organizers commemorated the anniversary with "The Reading of the Names," a four-day event during which the more than 58,000 names inscribed on the wall are read aloud.

QUESTIONS FOR REFLECTION AND DISCUSSION

1. What is the wordplay in the poem's title, and how is its meaning expressed within the body of the poem?

2. Paraphrase each event that occurs as the speaker gazes at the wall. What is the relation between the play of reflections and the main theme of the poem?

3. In what ways is the space described in "Facing It" a liminal space? In what way is it not?

4. The final sentence of the poem expresses a visual ambiguity. What is the significance of the speaker's initial confusion over the action he sees reflected in the wall?

5. "Facing It" has its origins in events in the poet's life. How does the depiction of that experience affect our understanding of the poem?

NONFICTION

Rachel Carson 1907–1964

A founder of the modern environmental movement, the marine biologist and zoologist Rachel Carson was born in Pittsburgh, Pennsylvania. She attended Pennsylvania College for Women, received a masters degree in zoology from Johns Hopkins University in 1932, and was hired by the U.S. Bureau of Fisheries in 1936. Her first book of nature writing appeared in 1941; her second, *The Sea around Us*, received the National Book Award in 1952 and was a national bestseller, as was the follow-up, *The Edge of the Sea* (1955), which included "The Marginal World." Carson had begun researching the danger of pesticides during the 1940s; she published her controversial findings in 1962 in *Silent Spring*, and spent the last years of her life fighting for a change in government policy.

THE MARGINAL WORLD

THE EDGE OF THE SEA IS A STRANGE AND beautiful place. All through the long history of Earth it has been an area of unrest where waves have broken heavily against the land, where the tides have pressed forward over the continents, receded, and then returned. For no two successive days is the shore line precisely the same. Not only do the tides advance and retreat in their eternal rhythms, but the level of the sea itself is never at rest. It rises or falls as the glaciers melt or grow, as the floor of the deep ocean basins shifts under its increasing load of sediments, or as the earth's crust along the continental margins warps up or down in adjustment to strain and tension. Today a little more land may belong to the sea, tomorrow a little less. Always the edge of the sea remains an elusive and indefinable boundary.

The shore has a dual nature, changing with the swing of the tides, belonging now to the land, now to the sea. On the ebb tide it knows the harsh extremes of the land world, being exposed to heat and cold, to wind, to rain and drying sun. On the flood tide it is a water world, returning briefly to the relative stability of the open sea.

Only the most hardy and adaptable can survive in a region so mutable, yet the area between the tide lines is crowded with plants and animals. In this difficult world of the shore, life displays its enormous toughness and vitality by occupying almost every conceivable niche. Visibly, it carpets the intertidal rocks; or half hidden, it descends into fissures and crevices, or hides under boulders, or

A harbor tidal pool in Matinicus Island, Maine.

lurks in the wet gloom of sea caves. Invisibly, where the casual observer would say there is no life, it lies deep in the sand, in burrows and tubes and passageways. It tunnels into solid rock and bores into peat and clay. It encrusts weeds or drifting spars or the hard, chitinous shell of a lobster. It exists minutely, as the film of bacteria that spreads over a rock surface or a wharf piling; as spheres of protozoa, small as pinpricks, sparkling at the surface of the sea; and as Lilliputian beings swimming through dark pools that lie between the grains of sand.

The shore is an ancient world, for as long as there has been an earth and sea there has been this place of the meeting of land and water. Yet it is a world that keeps alive the sense of continuing creation and of the relentless drive of life. Each time that I enter it, I gain some new awareness of its beauty and its deeper meanings, sensing that intricate fabric of life by which one creature is linked with another, and each with its surroundings.

5   In my thoughts of the shore, one place stands apart for its revelation of exquisite beauty. It is a pool hidden within a cave that one can visit only rarely and briefly when the lowest of the year's low tides fall below it, and perhaps from that very fact it acquires some of its special beauty. Choosing such a tide, I hoped for a glimpse of the pool. The ebb was to fall early in the morning. I knew that if the wind held from the north west and no interfering swell ran in from a distant storm the level of the sea should drop below the entrance to the pool. There had been sudden ominous showers in the night, with rain like handfuls of gravel flung on the roof. When I looked out into the early morning the sky was full of a gray dawn light but the sun had not yet risen. Water and air were pallid. Across the bay the moon was a luminous disc in the western sky, suspended above the dim line of distant shore—the full August moon, drawing the tide to the low, low levels of the threshold of the alien sea world. As I watched, a gull flew by, above the spruces. Its breast was rosy with the light of the unrisen sun. The day was, after all, to be fair.

Later, as I stood above the tide near the entrance to the pool, the promise of that rosy light was sustained. From the base of the steep wall of rock on which I stood, a moss-covered ledge jutted seaward into deep water. In the surge at the rim of the ledge the dark fronds of oarweeds swayed, smooth and gleaming as leather. The projecting ledge was the path to the small hidden cave and its pool. Occasionally a swell, stronger than the rest, rolled smoothly over the rim and broke in foam against the cliff. But the intervals between such swells were long enough to admit me to the ledge and long enough for a glimpse of that fairy pool, so seldom and so briefly exposed.

And so I knelt on the wet carpet of sea moss and looked back into the dark cavern that held the pool in a shallow basin. The floor of the cave was only a few inches below the roof, and a mirror had been created in which all that grew on the ceiling was reflected in the still water below.

Under water that was clear as glass the pool was carpeted with green sponge. Gray patches of sea squirts glistened on the ceiling and colonies of soft coral were a pale apricot color. In the moment when I looked into the cave a little elfin starfish hung down, suspended by the merest thread, perhaps by only a single tube foot. It reached down to touch its own reflection, so perfectly delineated that there might have been, not one starfish, but two. The beauty of the reflected images and of the limpid pool itself was the poignant beauty of things that are ephemeral, existing only until the sea should return to fill the little cave.

Whenever I go down into this magical zone of the low water of the spring tides, I look for the most delicately beautiful of all the shore's inhabitants— flowers that are not plant but animal, blooming on the threshold of the deeper sea. In that fairy cave I was not disappointed. Hanging from its roof were the pendent flowers of the hydroid Tubularia, pale pink, fringed and delicate as the wind flower. Here were creatures so exquisitely fashioned that they seemed unreal, their beauty too fragile to exist in a world of crushing force. Yet every detail was functionally useful, every stalk and hydranth and petal-like tentacle fashioned for dealing with the realities of existence. I knew that they were merely waiting, in that moment of the tide's ebbing, for the return of the sea. Then in the rush of water, in the surge of surf and the pressure of the incoming tide, the delicate flower heads would stir with life. They would sway on their slender stalks, and their long tentacles would sweep the returning water, finding in it all that they needed for life.

10   And so in that enchanted place on the threshold of the sea the realities that possessed my mind were far from those of the land world I had left an hour before. In a different way the same sense of remoteness and of a world apart came to me in a twilight hour on a great beach on the coast of Georgia. I had come down after sunset and walked far out over sands that lay wet and gleaming, to the very edge of the retreating sea. Looking back across that immense flat, crossed by winding, water-filled gullies and here and there holding shallow pools left by the tide, I was filled with awareness that this intertidal area, although abandoned briefly and rhythmically by the sea, is always reclaimed by the rising tide. There at

the edge of low water the beach with its reminders of the land seemed far away. The only sounds were those of the wind and the sea and the birds. There was one sound of wind moving over water, and another of water sliding over the sand and tumbling down the faces of its own wave forms. The flats were astir with birds, and the voice of the willet rang insistently. One of them stood at the edge of the water and gave its loud, urgent cry; an answer came from far up the beach and the two birds flew to join each other.

The flats took on a mysterious quality as dusk approached and the last evening light was reflected from the scattered pools and creeks. Then birds became only dark shadows, with no color discernible. Sanderlings scurried across the beach like little ghosts, and here and there the darker forms of the willets stood out. Often I could come very close to them before they would start up in alarm— the sanderlings running, the willets flying up, crying. Black skimmers flew along the ocean's edge silhouetted against the dull, metallic gleam, or they went flitting above the sand like large, dimly seen moths. Sometimes they "skimmed" the winding creeks of tidal water, where little spreading surface ripples marked the presence of small fish.

[. . .]

There is a common thread that links these scenes and memories—the spectacle of life in all its varied manifestations as it has appeared, evolved, and sometimes dies out. Underlying the beauty of the spectacle there is meaning and significance. It is the elusiveness of that meaning that haunts us, that sends us again and again into the natural world where the key to the riddle is hidden. It sends us back to the edge of the sea, where the drama of life played its first scene on earth and perhaps even its prelude; where the forces of evolution are at work today, as they have been since the appearance of what we know as life; and where the spectacle of living creatures faced by the cosmic realities of their world is crystal clear.

[1955]

QUESTIONS FOR REFLECTION AND DISCUSSION

1. What gives the edge of the sea its dual nature? Why is it an ancient world, and what can it tell us about the world of many millions of years ago?

2. Why for Carson is the pool within the cave a special place? What is unusual about the flowers that she finds there?

3. Why, for Carson, is this in-between space an image for life in general?

4. What is similar between this liminal space in nature and the liminal spaces created by humans in the other selections above? What is different?

IN-BETWEEN SPACES TOPICS FOR ESSAYS

1. Write an essay comparing the different images of in-between space in nature described in these texts.

2. Write an essay comparing the different images of pathways in these texts, focusing on their quality as liminal spaces and their effect on the characters around them.

3. Write an essay comparing different images of the journey and its meaning for the character that takes it.

4. Write an essay comparing different images of stasis and its meaning for the character that is static.

5. Write a personal essay describing your own experience with a liminal or in-between space. Did it have the same effect on you as the spaces described in this section? Why or why not?

IN-BETWEEN SPACES FURTHER READINGS IN *LITERATURE: A WORLD OF WRITING*

Chinua Achebe, "Dead Men's Path" • Elizabeth Bishop, "In the Waiting Room" • Robert Frost, "Stopping by Woods on a Snowy Evening" • Ernest Hemingway, "Hills Like White Elephants" • James Joyce, "Araby" • Franz Kafka, "Before the Law" • Naguib Mahfouz, "Half a Day" • Sharon Olds, "On the Subway" • Mary Oliver, "Singapore" • Ezra Pound, "In a Station of the Metro"

CONFINED SPACES

All human beings begin life in the confined space of their mother's womb, and for most children closed spaces such as closets, caves, and cribs have a comforting quality to them. Of course, as writer Edgar Allan Poe well knew, such spaces can easily become terrifying when one is trapped within them. As you read the texts in this section, take note of the degree of ambivalence that is attached to the confined space described, the degree to which it functions as a safe haven and the degree to which it functions as a prison. Whether literal or metaphorical or both simultaneously, confined spaces are a common literary image, especially, as you will see, in writing about female characters. In this section of the chapter, you will also look at texts and images concerned with the actual incarceration of prisoners, a fact of life for millions of the world's inhabitants. Just as in fictional texts you will evaluate the effect of the confined space on the characters, in these nonfiction texts consider the degree to which the space acts on the mind as well as the body of the prisoner.

Jane Evelyn Atwood, *Internal Visiting Space for Incarcerated Couples, France* (2000). In 1989, photojournalist Jane Evelyn Atwood began interviewing and photographing women in prisons in the United States, France, and elsewhere in Europe. She published a collection of these photographs in 2000 in *Too Much Time: Women in Prison*.

FICTION

Edgar Allan Poe 1809–1849

To be buried alive was, before modern medical techniques for ascertaining death, a realistic fear; in the stories of Edgar Allan Poe it is also a frequently used literary image for creating terror in the mind of the reader. Amontillado today refers to any dry sherry wine; during Poe's time it meant a specific sherry-type wine from Montilla, Spain. For a biography of Poe, see page 388.

THE CASK OF AMONTILLADO

THE THOUSAND INJURIES OF FORTUNATO I HAD borne as I best could, but when he ventured upon insult, I vowed revenge. You, who so well know the nature of my soul, will not suppose, however, that I gave utterance to a threat. *At length* I would be avenged; this was a point definitively settled—but the very definitiveness with which it was resolved precluded the idea of risk. I must not only punish, but punish with impunity. A wrong is unredressed when retribution overtakes its redresser. It is equally unredressed when the avenger fails to make himself felt as such to him who has done the wrong.

It must be understood that neither by word nor deed had I given Fortunato cause to doubt my good will. I continued as was my wont, to smile in his face, and he did not perceive that my smile *now* was at the thought of his immolation.

He had a weak point—this Fortunato—although in other regards he was a man to be respected and even feared. He prided himself on his connoisseurship in wine. Few Italians have the true virtuoso spirit. For the most part their enthusiasm is adopted to suit the time and opportunity to practise imposture upon the British and Austrian *millionaires*. In painting and gemmary, Fortunato, like his countrymen, was a quack, but in the matter of old wines he was sincere. In this respect I did not differ from him materially; I was skilful in the Italian vintages myself, and bought largely whenever I could.

It was about dusk, one evening during the supreme madness of the carnival season, that I encountered my friend. He accosted me with excessive warmth, for he had been drinking much. The man wore motley. He had on a tight-fitting parti-striped dress and his head was surmounted by the conical cap and bells. I was so pleased to see him, that I thought I should never have done wringing his hand.

5   I said to him—"My dear Fortunato, you are luckily met. How remarkably well you are looking to-day! But I have received a pipe° of what passes for Amontillado, and I have my doubts." "How?" said he, "Amontillado? A pipe? Impossible! And in the middle of the carnival?" "I have my doubts," I replied; "and I was silly enough to pay the full Amontillado price without consulting you in the matter. You were not to be found, and I was fearful of losing a bargain."

"Amontillado!"

"I have my doubts."

"Amontillado!"

"And I must satisfy them."

10   "Amontillado!"

"As you are engaged, I am on my way to Luchesi. If any one has a critical turn, it is he. He will tell me—"

"Luchesi cannot tell Amontillado from Sherry."

"And yet some fools will have it that his taste is a match for your own."

"Come let us go."

15   "Whither?"

"To your vaults."

"My friend, no; I will not impose upon your good nature. I perceive you have an engagement. Luchesi—"

"I have no engagement; come."

"My friend, no. It is not the engagement, but the severe cold with which I perceive you are afflicted. The vaults are insufferably damp. They are encrusted with nitre."

20   "Let us go, nevertheless. The cold is merely nothing. Amontillado! You have been imposed upon; and as for Luchesi, he cannot distinguish Sherry from Amontillado."

Thus speaking, Fortunato possessed himself of my arm. Putting on a mask of black silk and drawing a roquelaire° closely about my person, I suffered him to hurry me to my palazzo.

There were no attendants at home; they had absconded to make merry in honour of the time. I had told them that I should not return until the morning and had given them explicit orders not to stir from the house. These orders were sufficient, I well knew, to insure their immediate disappearance, one and all, as soon as my back was turned.

I took from their sconces two flambeaux, and giving one to Fortunato bowed him through several suites of rooms to the archway that led into the vaults. I passed down a long and winding staircase, requesting him to be cautious as he followed. We came at length to the foot of the descent, and stood together on the damp ground of the catacombs of the Montresors.

The gait of my friend was unsteady, and the bells upon his cap jingled as he strode.

25   "The pipe," said he.

"It is farther on," said I; "but observe the white webwork which gleams from these cavern walls."

He turned towards me and looked into my eyes with two filmy orbs that distilled the rheum of intoxication.

"Nitre?" he asked, at length.

"Nitre," I replied. "How long have you had that cough!"

---

pipe: a cask for storing wine or cider.

roquelaire: a knee-length cloak.

30 "Ugh! ugh! ugh!—ugh! ugh! ugh!—ugh! ugh!
ugh!—ugh! ugh! ugh!—ugh! ugh! ugh!"

My poor friend found it impossible to reply for
many minutes.

"It is nothing," he said, at last.

"Come," I said, with decision, we will go back; your
health is precious. You are rich, respected, admired,
beloved; you are happy as once I was. You are a man
to be missed. For me it is no matter. We will go back;
you will be ill and I cannot be responsible. Besides,
there is Luchesi—"

"Enough," he said; "the cough is a mere nothing; it
will not kill me. I shall not die of a cough."

35 "True—true," I replied; "and, indeed, I had no
intention of alarming you unnecessarily—but you
should use all proper caution. A draught of this
Medoc° will defend us from the damps."

Here I knocked off the neck of a bottle which I
drew from a long row of its fellows that lay upon the
mould.

"Drink," I said, presenting him the wine.

He raised it to his lips with a leer. He paused
and nodded to me familiarly, while his bells
jingled.

"I drink," he said, "to the buried that repose
around us."

40 "And I to your long life."

He again took my arm and we proceeded.

"These vaults," he said, "are extensive."

"The Montresors," I replied, "were a great and
numerous family."

"I forget your arms."

45 "A huge human foot d'or, in a field azure; the foot
crushes a serpent rampant whose fangs are
imbedded in the heel."

"And the motto?"

"*Nemo me impune lacessit.*"°

"Good!" he said.

The wine sparkled in his eyes and the bells
jingled. My own fancy grew warm with the Medoc.
We had passed through walls of piled bones, with
casks and puncheons° intermingling, into the inmost
recesses of the catacombs. I paused again, and this
time I made bold to seize Fortunato by an arm above
the elbow.

50 "The nitre!" I said: "see, it increases. It hangs like
moss upon the vaults. We are below the river's bed.
The drops of moisture trickle among the bones. Come,
we will go back ere it is too late. Your cough—"

"It is nothing" he said; "let us go on. But first,
another draught of the Medoc."

I broke and reached him a flagon of De Grave. He
emptied it at a breath. His eyes flashed with a fierce
light. He laughed and threw the bottle upwards
with a gesticulation I did not understand. I looked
at him in surprise. He repeated the movement—a
grotesque one.

"You do not comprehend?" he said.

"Not I," I replied.

55 "Then you are not of the brotherhood."

"How?"

"You are not of the masons."°

"Yes, yes," I said "yes! yes."

"You? Impossible! A mason?"

60 "A mason," I replied.

"A sign," he said.

"It is this," I answered, producing a trowel from
beneath the folds of my *roquelaire.*

"You jest," he exclaimed, recoiling a few paces.
"But let us proceed to the Amontillado."

"Be it so," I said, replacing the tool beneath the
cloak, and again offering him my arm. He leaned
upon it heavily. We continued our route in search of
the Amontillado. We passed through a range of low
arches, descended, passed on, and descending again,
arrived at a deep crypt, in which the foulness of the
air caused our flambeaux rather to glow than flame.

65 At the most remote end of the crypt there
appeared another less spacious. Its walls had been
lined with human remains piled to the vault
overhead, in the fashion of the great catacombs of
Paris. Three sides of this interior crypt were still
ornamented in this manner. From the fourth the
bones had been thrown down, and lay promiscuously
upon the earth, forming at one point a mound of
some size. Within the wall thus exposed by the
displacing of the bones, we perceived a still interior
recess, in depth about four feet, in width three, in
height six or seven. It seemed to have been
constructed for no especial use in itself, but formed
merely the interval between two of the colossal

Medoc: wine produced in the region of Médoc, France. *Nemo . . .*
lacessit: no one touches me with impunity; this is also the motto of the
kings of Scotland. **puncheons:** a large cask for liquid.

masons: the Freemasons, a secret society founded in the early eighteenth
century. The narrator plays on the primary meaning of the word: a
person who builds with stone and brick.

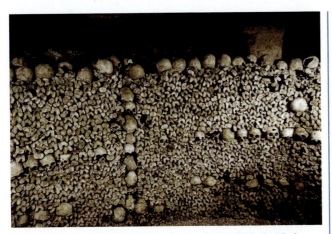

A wall of human remains in the Paris Catacombs. Established with the human remains removed from cemeteries in Paris that had become a health hazard, the Catacombs were a popular tourist attraction during the early nineteenth century. Poe may have visited them in 1832; he and his readers would have been familiar with their strange appearance from the many travel accounts published at the time.

supports of the roof of the catacombs, and was backed by one of their circumscribing walls of solid granite.

It was in vain that Fortunato, uplifting his dull torch, endeavoured to pry into the depths of the recess. Its termination the feeble light did not enable us to see.

"Proceed," I said; "herein is the Amontillado. As for Luchesi—"

"He is an ignoramus," interrupted my friend, as he stepped unsteadily forward, while I followed immediately at his heels. In an instant he had reached the extremity of the niche, and finding his progress arrested by the rock, stood stupidly bewildered. A moment more and I had fettered him to the granite. In its surface were two iron staples, distant from each other about two feet, horizontally. From one of these depended a short chain. from the other a padlock. Throwing the links about his waist, it was but the work of a few seconds to secure it. He was too much astounded to resist. Withdrawing the key I stepped back from the recess.

"Pass your hand," I said, "over the wall; you cannot help feeling the nitre. Indeed it is *very* damp. Once more let me *implore* you to return. No? Then I must positively leave you. But I must first render you all the little attentions in my power."

70 "The Amontillado!" ejaculated my friend, not yet recovered from his astonishment.

"True," I replied; "the Amontillado."

As I said these words I busied myself among the pile of bones of which I have before spoken. Throwing them aside, I soon uncovered a quantity of building stone and mortar. With these materials and with the aid of my trowel, I began vigorously to wall up the entrance of the niche. I had scarcely laid the first tier of my masonry when I discovered that the intoxication of Fortunato had in a great measure worn off. The earliest indication I had of this was a low moaning cry from the depth of the recess. It was *not* the cry of a drunken man. There was then a long and obstinate silence. I laid the second tier, and the third, and the fourth; and then I heard the furious vibrations of the chain. The noise lasted for several minutes, during which, that I might hearken to it with the more satisfaction, I ceased my labours and sat down upon the bones. When at last the clanking subsided, I resumed the trowel, and finished without interruption the fifth, the sixth, and the seventh tier. The wall was now nearly upon a level with my breast. I again paused, and holding the flambeaux over the mason-work, threw a few feeble rays upon the figure within.

A succession of loud and shrill screams, bursting suddenly from the throat of the chained form, seemed to thrust me violently back. For a brief moment I hesitated—I trembled. Unsheathing my rapier, I began to grope with it about the recess; but the thought of an instant reassured me. I placed my hand upon the solid fabric of the catacombs, and felt satisfied. I reapproached the wall. I replied to the yells of him who clamoured. I reechoed—I aided— I surpassed them in volume and in strength. I did this, and the clamorer grew still.

It was now midnight, and my task was drawing to a close. I had completed the eighth, the ninth, and the tenth tier. I had finished a portion of the last and the eleventh; there remained but a single stone to be fitted and plastered in. I struggled with its weight; I placed it partially in its destined position. But now there came from out the niche a low laugh that erected the hairs upon my head. It was succeeded by a sad voice, which I had difficulty in recognising as that of the noble Fortunato. The voice said—

75 "Ha! ha! ha!—he! he!—a very good joke indeed— an excellent jest. We will have many a rich laugh about it at the palazzo—he! he! he!—over our wine—he! he! he!"

"The Amontillado!" I said.

"He! he! he!—he! he! he!—yes, the Amontillado. But is it not getting late? Will not they be awaiting us at the palazzo, the Lady Fortunato and the rest? Let us be gone."

"Yes," I said "let us be gone."

"*For the love of god, Montresor!*"

80 "Yes," I said, "for the love of God!"

But to these words I hearkened in vain for a reply. I grew impatient. I called aloud—

"Fortunato!"

No answer. I called again-

"Fortunato!"

85 No answer still. I thrust a torch through the remaining aperture and let it fall within. There came forth in return only a jingling of the bells. My heart grew sick—on account of the dampness of the catacombs. I hastened to make an end of my labour. I forced the last stone into its position; I plastered it up. Against the new masonry I reerected the old rampart of bones. For the half of a century no mortal has disturbed them.

In pace requiescat!°

[1846]

In pace requiescat: May he rest in peace (Latin).

QUESTIONS FOR REFLECTION AND DISCUSSION

1. Why does Montresor never specify his motivation for revenging himself on Fortunato? How would the effect of the story be changed if he did?

2. What do we know about each character? What do we not know about them?

3. Why do you think Montresor has chosen this particular scheme for his revenge?

4. What qualities does the space of the catacombs have? What is particularly horrible about the death to which Montresor subjects Fortunato?

5. Is Montresor a reliable narrator? Why or why not?

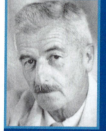

William Faulkner 1897–1962

The Nobel Prize–winning fiction writer William Faulkner was born in New Albany, Mississippi, and raised in nearby Oxford, Mississippi, where he lived most of this life. Like Eudora Welty (p. 505) and Flannery O'Connor (p. 250), his writing was imbued with the history and culture of the South. He set most of his stories and novels, including "A Rose for Emily," in fictional Yoknapatawpha County, which closely resembled the county of his hometown. Faulkner received a Pulitzer Prize and a National Book Award for his novel, *A Fable* (1954), and a National Book Award for his *Collected Stories* (1955); he was awarded the Nobel Prize in 1949. But he is best known for the formal innovation of his novels of the 1920s and 1930s, *The Sound and the Fury* (1929), *As I Lay Dying* (1930), *Light in August* (1932), and *Absalom, Absalom!* (1936).

A ROSE FOR EMILY

I

WHEN MISS EMILY GRIERSON DIED, OUR WHOLE town went to her funeral: the men through a sort of respectful affection for a fallen monument, the women mostly out of curiosity to see the inside of her house, which no one save an old manservant—a combined gardener and cook—had seen in at least ten years.

It was a big, squarish frame house that had once been white, decorated with cupolas and spires and scrolled balconies in the heavily lightsome style of the seventies, set on what had once been our most select street. But garages and cotton gins had encroached and obliterated even the august names of that neighborhood; only Miss Emily's house was left, lifting its stubborn and coquettish decay above the cotton wagons and the gasoline pumps—an eyesore among eyesores. And now Miss Emily had gone to join the representatives of those august names where they lay in the cedar-bemused cemetery among the ranked and anonymous graves of Union and Confederate soldiers who fell at the battle of Jefferson.

Alive, Miss Emily had been a tradition, a duty, and a care; a sort of hereditary obligation upon the town, dating from that day in 1894 when Colonel Sartoris, the mayor—he who fathered the edict that no Negro woman should appear on the streets without an apron—remitted her taxes, the dispensation dating from the death of her father on into perpetuity. Not that Miss Emily would have accepted charity. Colonel Sartoris invented an involved tale to the effect that Miss Emily's father had loaned money to the town, which the town, as a matter of business, preferred this way of repaying. Only a man of Colonel Sartoris' generation and thought could have invented it, and only a woman could have believed it.

When the next generation, with its more modern ideas, became mayors and aldermen, this arrangement created some little dissatisfaction. On the first of the year they mailed her a tax notice. February came, and there was no reply. They wrote her a formal letter, asking her to call at the sheriff's office at her convenience. A week later the mayor wrote her himself, offering to call or to send his car for her, and received in reply a note on paper of an archaic shape, in a thin, flowing calligraphy in faded ink, to the effect that she no longer went out at all. The tax notice was also enclosed, without comment.

5 They called a special meeting of the Board of Aldermen. A deputation waited upon her, knocked at the door through which no visitor had passed since she ceased giving china-painting lessons eight or ten years earlier. They were admitted by the old Negro into a dim hall from which a stairway mounted into still more shadow. It smelled of dust and disuse—a close, dank smell. The Negro led them into the parlor. It was furnished in heavy, leather-covered furniture. When the Negro opened the blinds of one window, they could see that the leather was cracked; and

when they sat down, a faint dust rose sluggishly about their thighs, spinning with slow motes in the single sunray. On a tarnished gilt easel before the fireplace stood a crayon portrait of Miss Emily's father.

They rose when she entered—a small, fat woman in black, with a thin gold chain descending to her waist and vanishing into her belt, leaning on an ebony cane with a tarnished gold head. Her skeleton was small and spare; perhaps that was why what would have been merely plumpness in another was obesity in her. She looked bloated, like a body long submerged in motionless water, and of that pallid hue. Her eyes, lost in the fatty ridges of her face, looked like two small pieces of coal pressed into a lump of dough as they moved from one face to another while the visitors stated their errand.

She did not ask them to sit. She just stood in the door and listened quietly until the spokesman came to a stumbling halt. Then they could hear the invisible watch ticking at the end of the gold chain.

Her voice was dry and cold. "I have no taxes in Jefferson. Colonel Sartoris explained it to me. Perhaps one of you can gain access to the city records and satisfy yourselves."

"But we have. We are the city authorities, Miss Emily. Didn't you get a notice from the sheriff, signed by him?"

10 "I received a paper, yes," Miss Emily said. "Perhaps he considers himself the sheriff. . . . I have no taxes in Jefferson."

"But there is nothing on the books to show that, you see. We must go by the—"

"See Colonel Sartoris. I have no taxes in Jefferson."

"But, Miss Emily—"

"See Colonel Sartoris." (Colonel Sartoris had been dead almost ten years.) "I have no taxes in Jefferson. Tobe!" The Negro appeared. "Show these gentlemen out."

II

15 So she vanquished them, horse and foot, just as she had vanquished their fathers thirty years before about the smell. That was two years after her father's death and a short time after her sweetheart—the one we believed would marry her—had deserted her. After her father's death she went out very little; after her sweetheart went away, people hardly saw her at

all. A few of the ladies had the temerity to call, but were not received, and the only sign of life about the place was the Negro man—a young man then—going in and out with a market basket.

"Just as if a man—any man—could keep a kitchen properly," the ladies said; so they were not surprised when the smell developed. It was another link between the gross, teeming world and the high and mighty Griersons.

A neighbor, a woman, complained to the mayor, Judge Stevens, eighty years old.

"But what will you have me do about it, madam?" he said.

"Why, send her word to stop it," the woman said. "Isn't there a law?"

20 "I'm sure that won't be necessary," Judge Stevens said. "It's probably just a snake or a rat that nigger of hers killed in the yard. I'll speak to him about it."

The next day he received two more complaints, one from a man who came in diffident deprecation. "We really must do something about it, Judge. I'd be the last one in the world to bother Miss Emily, but we've got to do something." That night the Board of Aldermen met—three graybeards and one younger man, a member of the rising generation.

"It's simple enough," he said. "Send her word to have her place cleaned up. Give her a certain time to do it in, and if she don't . . ."

"Dammit, sir," Judge Stevens said, "will you accuse a lady to her face of smelling bad?"

So the next night, after midnight, four men crossed Miss Emily's lawn and slunk about the house like burglars, sniffing along the base of the brickwork and at the cellar openings while one of them performed a regular sowing motion with his hand out of a sack slung from his shoulder. They broke open the cellar door and sprinkled lime there, and in all the out buildings. As they recrossed the lawn, a window that had been dark was lighted and Miss Emily sat in it, the light behind her, and her upright torso motionless as that of an idol. They crept quietly across the lawn and into the shadow of the locusts that lined the street. After a week or two the smell went away.

25 That was when people had begun to feel really sorry for her. People in our town, remembering how old lady Wyatt, her great-aunt, had gone completely crazy at last, believed that the Griersons held

themselves a little too high for what they really were. None of the young men were quite good enough for Miss Emily and such. We had long thought of them as a tableau; Miss Emily a slender figure in white in the background, her father a spraddled silhouette in the foreground, his back to her and clutching a horsewhip, the two of them framed by the back-flung front door. So when she got to be thirty and was still single, we were not pleased exactly, but vindicated; even with insanity in the family she wouldn't have turned down all of her chances if they had really materialized.

When her father died, it got about that the house was all that was left to her; and in a way, people were glad. At last they could pity Miss Emily. Being left alone, and a pauper, she had become humanized. Now she too would know the old thrill and the old despair of a penny more or less.

The day after his death all the ladies prepared to call at the house and offer condolence and aid, as is our custom. Miss Emily met them at the door, dressed as usual and with no trace of grief on her face. She told them that her father was not dead. She did that for three days, with the ministers calling on her, and the doctors, trying to persuade her to let them dispose of the body. Just as they were about to resort to law and force, she broke down, and they buried her father quickly.

We did not say she was crazy then. We believed she had to do that. We remembered all the young men her father had driven away, and we knew that with nothing left, she would have to cling to that which had robbed her, as people will.

III

She was sick for a long time. When we saw her again, her hair was cut short, making her look like a girl, with a vague resemblance to those angels in colored church windows—sort of tragic and serene.

30 The town had just let the contracts for paving the sidewalks, and in the summer after her father's death they began the work. The construction company came with niggers and mules and machinery, and a foreman named Homer Barron, a Yankee—a big, dark, ready man, with a big voice and eyes lighter than his face. The little boys would follow in groups to hear him cuss the niggers, and the niggers singing in time to the rise and fall of picks. Pretty soon he knew

everybody in town. Whenever you heard a lot of laughing anywhere about the square, Homer Barron would be in the center of the group. Presently we began to see him and Miss Emily on Sunday afternoons driving in the yellow-wheeled buggy and the matched team of bays from the livery stable.

At first we were glad that Miss Emily would have an interest, because the ladies all said, "Of course a Grierson would not think seriously of a Northerner, a day laborer." But there were still others, older people, who said that even grief could not cause a real lady to forget *noblesse oblige*—without calling it *noblesse oblige*. They just said, "Poor Emily. Her kinsfolk should come to her." She had some kin in Alabama; but years ago her father had fallen out with them over the estate of old lady Wyatt, the crazy woman, and there was no communication between the two families. They had not even been represented at the funeral.

And as soon as the old people said, "Poor Emily," the whispering began. "Do you suppose it's really so?" they said to one another. "Of course it is. . . ." This behind their hands; rustling of craned silk and satin behind jalousies closed upon the sun of Sunday afternoon as the thin, swift clop-clop-clop of the matched team passed: "Poor Emily."

She carried her head high enough—even when we believed that she was fallen. It was as if she demanded more than ever the recognition of her dignity as the last Grierson; as if it had wanted that touch of earthiness to reaffirm her imperviousness. Like when she bought the rat poison, the arsenic. That was over a year after they had begun to say "Poor Emily," and while the two female cousins were visiting her.

"I want some poison," she said to the druggist. She was over thirty then, still a slight woman, though thinner than usual, with cold, haughty black eyes in a face the flesh of which was strained across the temples and about the eyesockets as you imagine a lighthouse-keeper's face ought to look. "I want some poison," she said.

35   "Yes, Miss Emily. What kind? For rats and such? I'd recom—"

"I want the best you have. I don't care what kind."

The druggist named several. "They'll kill anything up to an elephant. But what you want is—"

"Arsenic," Miss Emily said. "Is that a good one?"

"Is . . . arsenic? Yes, ma'am. But what you want—"

40   "I want arsenic."

The druggist looked down at her. She looked back at him, erect, her face like a strained flag. "Why, of course," the druggist said. "If that's what you want. But the law requires you to tell what you are going to use it for."

Miss Emily just stared at him, her head tilted back in order to look him eye for eye, until he looked away and went and got the arsenic and wrapped it up. The Negro delivery boy brought her the package; the druggist didn't come back. When she opened the package at home there was written on the box, under the skull and bones: "For rats."

IV

So the next day we all said, "She will kill herself"; and we said it would be the best thing. When she had first begun to be seen with Homer Barron, we had said, "She will marry him." Then we said, "She will persuade him yet," because Homer himself had remarked—he liked men, and it was known that he drank with the younger men in the Elks' Club—that he was not a marrying man. Later we said, "Poor Emily," behind the jalousies as they passed on Sunday afternoon in the glittering buggy, Miss Emily with her head high and Homer Barron with his hat cocked and a cigar in his teeth, reins and whip in a yellow glove.

Then some of the ladies began to say that it was a disgrace to the town and a bad example to the young people. The men did not want to interfere, but at last the ladies forced the Baptist minister—Miss Emily's people were Episcopal—to call upon her. He would never divulge what happened during that interview, but he refused to go back again. The next Sunday they again drove about the streets, and the following day the minister's wife wrote to Miss Emily's relations in Alabama.

45   So she had blood-kin under her roof again and we sat back to watch developments. At first nothing happened. Then we were sure that they were to be married. We learned that Miss Emily had been to the jeweler's and ordered a man's toilet set in silver, with the letters H.B. on each piece. Two days later we learned that she had bought a complete outfit of men's clothing, including a nightshirt, and we said, "They are married." We were really glad. We were

glad because the two female cousins were even more Grierson than Miss Emily had ever been.

So we were not surprised when Homer Barron—the streets had been finished some time since—was gone. We were a little disappointed that there was not a public blowing-off, but we believed that he had gone on to prepare for Miss Emily's coming, or to give her a chance to get rid of the cousins. (By that time it was a cabal, and we were all Miss Emily's allies to help circumvent the cousins.) Sure enough, after another week they departed. And, as we had expected all along, within three days Homer Barron was back in town. A neighbor saw the Negro man admit him at the kitchen door at dusk one evening.

And that was the last we saw of Homer Barron. And of Miss Emily for some time. The Negro man went in and out with the market basket, but the front door remained closed. Now and then we would see her at a window for a moment, as the men did that night when they sprinkled the lime, but for almost six months she did not appear on the streets. Then we knew that this was to be expected too; as if that quality of her father which had thwarted her woman's life so many times had been too virulent and too furious to die.

When we next saw Miss Emily, she had grown fat and her hair was turning gray. During the next few years it grew grayer and grayer until it attained an even pepper-and-salt iron-gray, when it ceased turning. Up to the day of her death at seventy-four it was still that vigorous iron-gray, like the hair of an active man.

From that time on her front door remained closed, save for a period of six or seven years, when she was about forty, during which she gave lessons in china-painting. She fitted up a studio in one of the downstairs rooms, where the daughters and granddaughters of Colonel Sartoris' contemporaries were sent to her with the same regularity and in the same spirit that they were sent to church on Sundays with a twenty-five-cent piece for the collection plate. Meanwhile her taxes had been remitted.

50 Then the newer generation became the backbone and the spirit of the town, and the painting pupils grew up and fell away and did not send their children to her with boxes of color and tedious brushes and pictures cut from the ladies' magazines. The front door closed upon the last one and remained closed for good. When the town got free postal delivery, Miss Emily alone refused to let them fasten the metal numbers above her door and attach a mailbox to it. She would not listen to them.

Daily, monthly, yearly we watched the Negro grow grayer and more stooped, going in and out with the market basket. Each December we sent her a tax notice, which would be returned by the post office a week later, unclaimed. Now and then we would see her in one of the downstairs windows—she had evidently shut up the top floor of the house—like the carven torso of an idol in a niche, looking or not looking at us, we could never tell which. Thus she passed from generation to generation—dear, inescapable, impervious, tranquil, and perverse.

And so she died. Fell ill in the house filled with dust and shadows, with only a doddering Negro man to wait on her. We did not even know she was sick; we had long since given up trying to get any information from the Negro. He talked to no one, probably not even to her, for his voice had grown harsh and rusty, as if from disuse.

She died in one of the downstairs rooms, in a heavy walnut bed with a curtain, her gray head propped on a pillow yellow and moldy with age and lack of sunlight.

V

The Negro met the first of the ladies at the front door and let them in, with their hushed, sibilant voices and their quick, curious glances, and then he disappeared. He walked right through the house and out the back and was not seen again.

55 The two female cousins came at once. They held the funeral on the second day, with the town coming to look at Miss Emily beneath a mass of bought flowers, with the crayon face of her father musing profoundly above the bier and the ladies sibilant and macabre; and the very old men—some in their brushed Confederate uniforms—on the porch and the lawn, talking of Miss Emily as if she had been a contemporary of theirs, believing that they had danced with her and courted her perhaps, confusing time with its mathematical progression, as the old do, to whom all the past is not a diminishing road but, instead, a huge meadow which no winter ever quite touches, divided from them now by the narrow bottleneck of the most recent decade of years.

Already we knew that there was one room in that region above stairs which no one had seen in forty years, and which would have to be forced. They waited until Miss Emily was decently in the ground before they opened it.

The violence of breaking down the door seemed to fill this room with pervading dust. A thin, acrid pall as of the tomb seemed to lie everywhere upon this room decked and furnished as for a bridal: upon the valance curtains of faded rose color, upon the rose-shaded lights, upon the dressing table, upon the delicate array of crystal and the man's toilet things backed with tarnished silver, silver so tarnished that the monogram was obscured. Among them lay collar and tie, as if they had just been removed, which, lifted, left upon the surface a pale crescent in the dust. Upon a chair hung the suit, carefully folded; beneath it the two mute shoes and the discarded socks.

The man himself lay in the bed.

For a long while we just stood there, looking down at the profound and fleshless grin. The body had apparently once lain in the attitude of an embrace, but now the long sleep that outlasts love, that conquers even the grimace of love, had cuckolded him. What was left of him, rotted beneath what was left of the nightshirt, had become inextricable from the bed in which he lay; and upon him and upon the pillow beside him lay that even coating of the patient and biding dust.

60   Then we noticed that in the second pillow was the indentation of a head. One of us lifted something from it, and leaning forward, that faint and invisible dust dry and acrid in the nostrils, we saw a long strand of iron-gray hair.

[1930]

QUESTIONS FOR REFLECTION AND DISCUSSION

1. Who narrates the story? What is the narrator's attitude toward Emily?

2. Why is the house described in more detail than Emily at the beginning of the story? How does the role of the house change as the story unfolds? What is Emily's relationship to the house? Does it change, or does it remain the same?

3. With what senses and images is Homer Barron associated? What is his role in the story? What is his relationship with Emily?

4. What is left unsaid by the narrator? What do we deduce of the events of which we are not told directly? What is the meaning of the title?

Charlotte Perkins Gilman 1860–1935

Born in Hartford, Connecticut, Charlotte Perkins Gilman studied at the Rhode Island School of Design, and made a living designing greeting cards. She married the artist Charles Walter Stetson in 1884. They separated four years later, she divorced him in 1894, and he married her best friend. It was during this period that she wrote her penetrating analysis of marriage, "The Yellow Wallpaper." She married her first cousin, George Houghton Gilman, in 1900, and lived with him, in New York and in Hartford, until his death in 1934. She then moved to California and, suffering from inoperable breast cancer, took her own life in 1935. An active social reformer and feminist, Gilman published eight novels in her lifetime, including the utopian *Herland* (1915), and numerous short stories, poems, and works of nonfiction.

THE YELLOW WALLPAPER

IT IS VERY SELDOM THAT MERE ORDINARY PEOPLE like John and myself secure ancestral halls for the summer.

A colonial mansion, a hereditary estate, I would say a haunted house and reach the height of romantic felicity—but that would be asking too much of fate!

Still I will proudly declare that there is something queer about it.

Else, why should it be let so cheaply? And why have stood so long untenanted?

5 John laughs at me, of course, but one expects that.

John is practical in the extreme. He has no patience with faith, an intense horror of superstition, and he scoffs openly at any talk of things not to be felt and seen and put down in figures.

John is a physician, and *perhaps*—(I would not say it to a living soul, of course, but this is dead paper and a great relief to my mind)—*perhaps* that is one reason I do not get well faster.

You see, he does not believe I am sick! And what can one do?

If a physician of high standing, and one's own husband, assures friends and relatives that there is really nothing the matter with one but temporary nervous depression—a slight hysterical tendency—what is one to do?

10 My brother is also a physician, and also of high standing, and he says the same thing.

So I take phosphates or phosphites—whichever it is—and tonics, and air and exercise, and journeys, and am absolutely forbidden to "work" until I am well again.

Personally, I disagree with their ideas.

Personally, I believe that congenial work, with excitement and change, would do me good.

But what is one to do?

15 I did write for a while in spite of them; but it *does* exhaust me a good deal—having to be so sly about it, or else meet with heavy opposition.

I sometimes fancy that in my condition, if I had less opposition and more society and stimulus—but John says the very worst thing I can do is to think about my condition, and I confess it always makes me feel bad.

So I will let it alone and talk about the house.

The most beautiful place! It is quite alone, standing well back from the road, quite three miles from the village. It makes me think of English places that you read about, for there are hedges and walls and gates that lock, and lots of separate little houses for the gardeners and people.

There is a *delicious* garden! I never saw such a garden—large and shady, full of box-bordered paths, and lined with long grape-covered arbors with seats under them.

20 There were greenhouses, but they are all broken now.

There was some legal trouble, I believe, something about the heirs and co-heirs; anyhow, the place has been empty for years.

That spoils my ghostliness, I am afraid, but I don't care—there is something strange about the house— I can feel it.

I even said so to John one moonlight evening, but he said what I felt was a *draught,* and shut the window.

I get unreasonably angry with John sometimes. I'm sure I never used to be so sensitive. I think it is due to this nervous condition.

25 But John says if I feel so I shall neglect proper self-control; so I take pains to control myself—before him, at least, and that makes me very tired.

I don't like our room a bit. I wanted one downstairs that opened onto the piazza and had roses all over the window, and such pretty old-fashioned chintz hangings! But John would not hear of it.

He said there was only one window and not room for two beds, and no near room for him if he took another.

He is very careful and loving, and hardly lets me stir without special direction.

I have a schedule prescription for each hour in the day; he takes all care from me, and so I feel basely ungrateful not to value it more.

30 He said he came here solely on my account, that I was to have perfect rest and all the air I could get. "Your exercise depends on your strength, my dear," said he, "and your food somewhat on your appetite; but air you can absorb all the time." So we took the nursery at the top of the house.

It is a big, airy room, the whole floor nearly, with windows that look all ways, and air and sunshine galore. It was a nursery first, and then playroom and gymnasium, I should judge, for the windows are barred for little children, and there are rings and things in the walls.

The paint and paper look as if a boys' school had used it. It is stripped off—the paper—in great patches all around the head of my bed, about as far as I can reach, and in a great place on the other side of the room low down. I never saw a worse paper in my life. One of those sprawling, flamboyant patterns committing every artistic sin.

It is dull enough to confuse the eye in following, pronounced enough constantly to irritate and provoke study, and when you follow the lame uncertain curves for a little distance they suddenly commit suicide—plunge off at outrageous angles, destroy themselves in unheard-of contradictions.

The color is repellent, almost revolting: a smouldering unclean yellow, strangely faded by the slow-turning sunlight. It is a dull yet lurid orange in some places, a sickly sulphur tint in others.

35   No wonder the children hated it! I should hate it myself if I had to live in this room long.

There comes John, and I must put this away—he hates to have me write a word.

We have been here two weeks, and I haven't felt like writing before, since that first day.

I am sitting by the window now, up in this atrocious nursery, and there is nothing to hinder my writing as much as I please, save lack of strength.

John is away all day, and even some nights when his cases are serious.

40   I am glad my case is not serious!

But these nervous troubles are dreadfully depressing.

John does not know how much I really suffer. He knows there is no *reason* to suffer, and that satisfies him.

Of course it is only nervousness. It does weigh on me so not to do my duty in any way!

I meant to be such a help to John, such a real rest and comfort, and here I am a comparative burden already!

45   Nobody would believe what an effort it is to do what little I am able—to dress and entertain, and order things.

It is fortunate Mary is so good with the baby. Such a dear baby!

And yet I *cannot* be with him, it makes me so nervous.

I suppose John never was nervous in his life. He laughs at me so about this wallpaper!

At first he meant to repaper the room, but afterward he said that I was letting it get the better of me, and that nothing was worse for a nervous patient than to give way to such fancies.

50   He said that after the wallpaper was changed it would be the heavy bedstead, and then the barred windows, and then that gate at the head of the stairs, and so on.

"You know the place is doing you good," he said, "and really, dear, I don't care to renovate the house just for a three months' rental."

"Then do let us go downstairs," I said. "There are such pretty rooms there."

Then he took me in his arms and called me a blessed little goose, and said he would go down to the cellar, if I wished, and have it whitewashed into the bargain.

But he is right enough about the beds and windows and things.

55   It is as airy and comfortable a room as anyone need wish, and, of course, I would not be so silly as to make him uncomfortable just for a whim.

I'm really getting quite fond of the big room, all but that horrid paper.

Out of one window I can see the garden—those mysterious deep-shaded arbors, the riotous old-fashioned flowers, and bushes and gnarly trees.

Out of another I get a lovely view of the bay and a little private wharf belonging to the estate. There is a beautiful shaded lane that runs down there from the house. I always fancy I see people walking in these numerous paths and arbors, but John has cautioned me not to give way to fancy in the least. He says that with my imaginative power and habit of storymaking, a nervous weakness like mine is sure to lead to all manner of excited fancies, and that I ought to use my will and good sense to check the tendency. So I try.

I think sometimes that if I were only well enough to write a little it would relieve the press of ideas and rest me.

60   But I find I get pretty tired when I try.

It is so discouraging not to have any advice and companionship about my work. When I get really well, John says we will ask Cousin Henry and Julia down for a long visit; but he says he would as soon put fireworks in my pillow-case as to let me have those stimulating people about now.

I wish I could get well faster.

But I must not think about that. This paper looks to me as if it *knew* what a vicious influence it had!

There is a recurrent spot where the pattern lolls like a broken neck and two bulbous eyes stare at you upside down.

65 I get positively angry with the impertinence of it and the everlastingness. Up and down and sideways they crawl, and those absurd unblinking eyes are everywhere. There is one place where two breadths didn't match, and the eyes go all up and down the line, one a little higher than the other.

I never saw so much expression in an inanimate thing before, and we all know how much expression they have! I used to lie awake as a child and get more entertainment and terror out of blank walls and plain furniture than most children could find in a toy-store.

I remember what a kindly wink the knobs of our big old bureau used to have, and there was one chair that always seemed like a strong friend.

I used to feel that if any of the other things looked too fierce I could always hop into that chair and be safe.

The furniture in this room is no worse than inharmonious, however, for we had to bring it all from downstairs. I suppose when this was used as a playroom they had to take the nursery things out, and no wonder! I never saw such ravages as the children have made here.

70 The wallpaper, as I said before, is torn off in spots, and it sticketh closer than a brother—they must have had perseverance as well as hatred.

Then the floor is scratched and gouged and splintered, the plaster itself is dug out here and there, and this great heavy bed, which is all we found in the room, looks as if it had been through the wars.

But I don't mind it a bit—only the paper.

There comes John's sister. Such a dear girl as she is, and so careful of me! I must not let her find me writing.

She is a perfect and enthusiastic housekeeper, and hopes for no better profession. I verily believe she thinks it is the writing which made me sick!

75 But I can write when she is out, and see her a long way off from these windows.

There is one that commands the road, a lovely shaded winding road, and one that just looks off over the country. A lovely country, too, full of great elms and velvet meadows.

This wallpaper has a kind of subpattern in a different shade, a particularly irritating one, for you can only see it in certain lights, and not clearly then.

But in the places where it isn't faded and where the sun is just so—I can see a strange, provoking, formless sort of figure that seems to skulk about behind that silly and conspicuous front design.

There's sister on the stairs!

80 Well, the Fourth of July is over! The people are all gone, and I am tired out. John thought it might do me good to see a little company, so we just had Mother and Nellie and the children down for a week.

Of course I didn't do a thing. Jennie sees to everything now.

But it tired me all the same.

John says if I don't pick up faster he shall send me to Weir Mitchell° in the fall.

But I don't want to go there at all. I had a friend who was in his hands once, and she says he is just like John and my brother, only more so!

85 Besides, it is such an undertaking to go so far.

I don't feel as if it was worthwhile to turn my hand over for anything, and I'm getting dreadfully fretful and querulous.

I cry at nothing, and cry most of the time.

Of course I don't when John is here, or anybody else, but when I am alone.

And I am alone a good deal just now. John is kept in town very often by serious cases, and Jennie is good and lets me alone when I want her to.

90 So I walk a little in the garden or down that lovely lane, sit on the porch under the roses, and lie down up here a good deal.

I'm getting really fond of the room in spite of the wallpaper. Perhaps *because* of the wallpaper.

It dwells in my mind so!

I lie here on this great immovable bed—it is nailed down, I believe—and follow that pattern about by the hour. It is as good as gymnastics, I assure you. I start, we'll say, at the bottom, down in the corner over there where it has not been touched, and I determine for the thousandth time that I *will* follow that pointless pattern to some sort of a conclusion.

I know a little of the principle of design, and I know this thing was not arranged on any laws of radiation,° or alternation, or repetition, or symmetry, or anything else that I ever heard of.

Weir Mitchell: a physician (1829–1914) who specialized in nervous diseases of women. He was Gilman's doctor, and it is thought that his unsuccessful treatment of her with a "rest cure" provided the initial idea for "The Yellow Wallpaper." **laws of radiation:** a design principle arranging all elements in a circular pattern around a center.

95   It is repeated, of course, by the breadths, but not otherwise.

Looked at in one way, each breadth stands alone; the bloated curves and flourishes—a kind of "debased Romanesque" with *delirium tremens*—go waddling up and down in isolated columns of fatuity.

But, on the other hand, they connect diagonally, and the sprawling outlines run off in great slanting waves of optic horror, like a lot of wallowing sea-weeds in full chase.

The whole thing goes horizontally, too, at least it seems so, and I exhaust myself trying to distinguish the order of its going in that direction.

They have used a horizontal breadth for a frieze, and that adds wonderfully to the confusion.

100   There is one end of the room where it is almost intact, and there, when the crosslights fade and the low sun shines directly upon it, I can almost fancy radiation after all—the interminable grotesque seems to form around a common center and rush off in headlong plunges of equal distraction.

It makes me tired to follow it. I will take a nap, I guess.

I don't know why I should write this.

I don't want to.

I don't feel able.

105   And I know John would think it absurd. But I *must* say what I feel and think in some way—it is such a relief!

But the effort is getting to be greater than the relief.

Half the time now I am awfully lazy, and lie down ever so much. John says I mustn't lose my strength, and has me take cod liver oil and lots of tonics and things, to say nothing of ale and wines and rare meat.

Dear John! He loves me very dearly, and hates to have me sick. I tried to have a real earnest reasonable talk with him the other day, and tell him how I wish he would let me go and make a visit to Cousin Henry and Julia.

But he said I wasn't able to go, nor able to stand it after I got there; and I did not make out a very good case for myself, for I was crying before I had finished.

110   It is getting to be a great effort for me to think straight. Just this nervous weakness, I suppose.

And dear John gathered me up in his arms, and just carried me upstairs and laid me on the bed, and sat by me and read to me till it tired my head.

He said I was his darling and his comfort and all he had, and that I must take care of myself for his sake, and keep well.

He says no one but myself can help me out of it, that I must use my will and self-control and not let any silly fancies run away with me.

There's one comfort—the baby is well and happy, and does not have to occupy this nursery with the horrid wallpaper.

115   If we had not used it, that blessed child would have! What a fortunate escape! Why, I wouldn't have a child of mine, an impressionable little thing, live in such a room for worlds.

I never thought of it before, but it is lucky that John kept me here after all; I can stand it so much easier than a baby, you see.

Of course I never mention it to them any more—I am too wise—but I keep watch for it all the same.

There are things in the wallpaper that nobody knows about but me, or ever will.

Behind that outside pattern the dim shapes get clearer every day.

120   It is always the same shape, only very numerous.

And it is like a woman stooping down and creeping about behind that pattern. I don't like it a bit. I wonder—I begin to think—I wish John would take me away from here!

It is so hard to talk with John about my case, because he is so wise, and because he loves me so.

But I tried it last night.

It was moonlight. The moon shines in all around just as the sun does.

125   I hate to see it sometimes, it creeps so slowly, and always comes in by one window or another.

John was asleep and I hated to waken him, so I kept still and watched the moonlight on that undulating wallpaper till I felt creepy.

The faint figure behind seemed to shake the pattern, just as if she wanted to get out.

I got up softly and went to feel and see if the paper *did* move, and when I came back John was awake.

"What is it, little girl?" he said. "Don't go walking about like that—you'll get cold."

130   I thought it was a good time to talk, so I told him that I really was not gaining here, and that I wished he would take me away.

"Why, darling!" said he. "Our lease will be up in three weeks, and I can't see how to leave before.

"The repairs are not done at home, and I cannot possibly leave town just now. Of course, if you were in any danger, I could and would, but you really are better, dear, whether you can see it or not. I am a doctor, dear, and I know. You are gaining flesh and color, your appetite is better, I feel really much easier about you."

"I don't weigh a bit more," said I, "nor as much; and my appetite may be better in the evening when you are here but it is worse in the morning when you are away!"

"Bless her little heart!" said he with a big hug. "She shall be as sick as she pleases! But now let's improve the shining hours by going to sleep, and talk about it in the morning!"

135 "And you won't go away?" I asked gloomily.

"Why, how can I, dear? It is only three weeks more and then we will take a nice little trip for a few days while Jennie is getting the house ready. Really, dear, you are better!"

"Better in body perhaps—" I began, and stopped short, for he sat up straight and looked at me with such a stern, reproachful look that I could not say another word.

"My darling," said he, "I beg you, for my sake and for our child's sake, as well as for your own, that you will never for one instant let that idea enter your mind! There is nothing so dangerous, so fascinating, to a temperament like yours. It is a false and foolish fancy. Can you trust me as a physician when I tell you so?"

So of course I said no more on that score, and we went to sleep before long. He thought I was asleep first, but I wasn't, and lay there for hours trying to decide whether that front pattern and the back pattern really did move together or separately.

140 On a pattern like this, by daylight, there is a lack of sequence, a defiance of law, that is a constant irritant to a normal mind.

The color is hideous enough, and unreliable enough, and infuriating enough, but the pattern is torturing.

You think you have mastered it, but just as you get well under way in following, it turns a back-somersault and there you are. It slaps you in the face, knocks you down, and tramples upon you. It is like a bad dream.

The outside pattern is a florid arabesque,° reminding one of a fungus. If you can imagine a toadstool in joints, an interminable string of toadstools, budding and sprouting in endless convolutions—why, that is something like it.

That is, sometimes!

145 There is one marked peculiarity about this paper, a thing nobody seems to notice but myself, and that is that it changes as the light changes.

When the sun shoots in through the east window—I always watch for that first long, straight ray—it changes so quickly that I never can quite believe it.

That is why I watch it always.

By moonlight—the moon shines in all night when there is a moon—I wouldn't know it was the same paper.

At night in any kind of light, in twilight, candlelight, lamplight, and worst of all by moonlight, it becomes bars! The outside pattern, I mean, and the woman behind it is as plain as can be.

150 I didn't realize for a long time what the thing was that showed behind, that dim subpattern, but now I am quite sure it is a woman.

By daylight she is subdued, quiet. I fancy it is the pattern that keeps her so still. It is so puzzling. It keeps me quiet by the hour.

I lie down ever so much now. John says it is good for me, and to sleep all I can.

Indeed he started the habit by making me lie down for an hour after each meal.

It is a very bad habit, I am convinced, for you see, I don't sleep.

155 And that cultivates deceit, for I don't tell them I'm awake—oh, no!

The fact is I am getting a little afraid of John.

He seems very queer sometimes, and even Jennie has an inexplicable look.

It strikes me occasionally, just as a scientific hypothesis, that perhaps it is the paper!

I have watched John when he did not know I was looking, and come into the room suddenly on the most innocent excuses, and I've caught him several times *looking at the paper!* And Jennie too. I caught Jennie with her hand on it once.

arabesque: an ornamental style derived from the Arabic. It is based on repeated geometric forms in interlocking patterns usually derived from the shapes of plants and animals.

She didn't know I was in the room, and when I asked her in a quiet, a very quiet voice, with the most restrained manner possible, what she was doing with the paper, she turned around as if she had been caught stealing, and looked quite angry—asked me why I should frighten her so!

Then she said that the paper stained everything it touched, that she had found yellow smooches on all my clothes and John's and she wished we would be more careful!

Did not that sound innocent? But I know she was studying that pattern, and I am determined that nobody shall find it out but myself!

Life is very much more exciting now than it used to be. You see, I have something more to expect, to look forward to, to watch. I really do eat better, and am more quiet than I was.

John is so pleased to see me improve! He laughed a little the other day, and said I seemed to be flourishing in spite of my wallpaper.

I turned it off with a laugh. I had no intention of telling him it was *because* of the wallpaper—he would make fun of me. He might even want to take me away.

I don't want to leave now until I have found it out. There is a week more, and I think that will be enough.

I'm feeling so much better!

I don't sleep much at night, for it is so interesting to watch developments; but I sleep a good deal during the daytime.

In the daytime it is tiresome and perplexing.

There are always new shoots on the fungus, and new shades of yellow all over it. I cannot keep count of them, though I have tried conscientiously.

It is the strangest yellow, that wallpaper! It makes me think of all the yellow things I ever saw—not beautiful ones like buttercups, but old, foul, bad yellow things.

But there is something else about that paper—the smell! I noticed it the moment we came into the room, but with so much air and sun it was not bad. Now we have had a week of fog and rain, and whether the windows are open or not, the smell is here.

It creeps all over the house.

I find it hovering in the dining-room, skulking in the parlor, hiding in the hall, lying in wait for me on the stairs.

It gets into my hair.

Even when I go to ride, if I turn my head suddenly and surprise it—there is that smell!

Such a peculiar odor, too! I have spent hours in trying to analyze it, to find what it smelled like.

It is not bad—at first—and very gentle, but quite the subtlest, most enduring odor I ever met.

In this damp weather it is awful. I wake up in the night and find it hanging over me.

It used to disturb me at first. I thought seriously of burning the house—to reach the smell.

But now I am used to it. The only thing I can think of that it is like is the *color* of the paper! A yellow smell.

There is a very funny mark on this wall, low down, near the mopboard. A streak that runs round the room. It goes behind every piece of furniture, except the bed, a long, straight, even *smooch,* as if it had been rubbed over and over.

I wonder how it was done and who did it, and what they did it for. Round and round and round—round and round and round—it makes me dizzy!

I really have discovered something at last.

Through watching so much at night, when it changes so, I have finally found out.

The front pattern *does* move—and no wonder! The woman behind shakes it!

Sometimes I think there are a great many women behind, and sometimes only one, and she crawls around fast, and her crawling shakes it all over.

Then in the very bright spots she keeps still, and in the very shady spots she just takes hold of the bars and shakes them hard.

And she is all the time trying to climb through. But nobody could climb through that pattern—it strangles so; I think that is why it has so many heads.

They get through and then the pattern strangles them off and turns them upside down, and makes their eyes white!

If those heads were covered or taken off it would not be half so bad.

I think that woman gets out in the daytime!

And I'll tell you why—privately—I've seen her!

I can see her out of every one of my windows!

It is the same woman, I know, for she is always creeping, and most women do not creep by daylight.

I see her in that long shaded lane, creeping up and down. I see her in those dark grape arbors, creeping all round the garden.

I see her on that long road under the trees, creeping along, and when a carriage comes she hides under the blackberry vines.

I don't blame her a bit. It must be very humiliating to be caught creeping by daylight!

I always lock the door when I creep by daylight. I can't do it at night, for I know John would suspect something at once.

200 And John is so queer now that I don't want to irritate him. I wish he would take another room! Besides, I don't want anybody to get that woman out at night but myself.

I often wonder if I could see her out of all the windows at once.

But, turn as fast as I can, I can only see out of one at one time.

And though I always see her, she *may* be able to creep faster than I can turn! I have watched her sometimes away off in the open country, creeping as fast as a cloud shadow in a wind.

If only that top pattern could be gotten off from the under one! I mean to try it, little by little.

205 I have found out another funny thing, but I shan't tell it this time! It does not do to trust people too much.

There are only two more days to get this paper off, and I believe John is beginning to notice. I don't like the look in his eyes.

And I heard him ask Jennie a lot of professional questions about me. She had a very good report to give.

She said I slept a good deal in the daytime.

John knows I don't sleep very well at night, for all I'm so quiet!

210 He asked me all sorts of questions too, and pretended to be very loving and kind.

As if I couldn't see through him!

Still, I don't wonder he acts so, sleeping under this paper for three months.

It only interests me, but I feel sure John and Jennie are affected by it.

Hurrah! This is the last day, but it is enough. John is to stay in town over night, and won't be out until this evening.

215 Jennie wanted to sleep with me—the sly thing; but I told her I should undoubtedly rest better for a night all alone.

That was clever, for really I wasn't alone a bit! As soon as it was moonlight and that poor thing began to crawl and shake the pattern, I got up and ran to help her.

I pulled and she shook. I shook and she pulled, and before morning we had peeled off yards of that paper.

A strip about as high as my head and half around the room.

And then when the sun came and that awful pattern began to laugh at me, I declared I would finish it today!

220 We go away tomorrow, and they are moving all my furniture down again to leave things as they were before.

Jennie looked at the wall in amazement, but I told her merrily that I did it out of pure spite at the vicious thing.

She laughed and said she wouldn't mind doing it herself, but I must not get tired.

How she betrayed herself that time!

But I am here, and no person touches this paper but Me—not *alive!*

225 She tried to get me out of the room—it was too patent! But I said it was so quiet and empty and clean now that I believed I would lie down again and sleep all I could, and not to wake me even for dinner—I would call when I woke.

So now she is gone, and the servants are gone, and the things are gone, and there is nothing left but that great bedstead nailed down, with the canvas mattress we found on it.

We shall sleep downstairs tonight, and take the boat home tomorrow.

I quite enjoy the room, now it is bare again.

How those children did tear about here!

230 This bedstead is fairly gnawed!

But I must get to work.

I have locked the door and thrown the key down into the front path.

I don't want to go out, and I don't want to have anybody come in, till John comes.

I want to astonish him.

235 I've got a rope up here that even Jennie did not find. If that woman does get out, and tries to get away, I can tie her!

But I forgot I could not reach far without anything to stand on!

This bed will *not* move!

I tried to lift and push it until I was lame, and then I got so angry I bit off a little piece at one corner—but it hurt my teeth.

Then I peeled off all the paper I could reach standing on the floor. It sticks horribly and the pattern just enjoys it! All those strangled heads and bulbous eyes and waddling fungus growths just shriek with derision!

240 I am getting angry enough to do something desperate. To jump out of the window would be admirable exercise, but the bars are too strong even to try.

Besides I wouldn't do it. Of course not. I know well enough that a step like that is improper and might be misconstrued.

I don't like to *look* out of the windows even—there are so many of those creeping women, and they creep so fast.

I wonder if they all come out of that wallpaper as I did!

But I am securely fastened now by my well-hidden rope—you don't get *me* out in the road there!

245 I suppose I shall have to get back behind the pattern when it comes night, and that is hard!

It is so pleasant to be out in this great room and creep around as I please!

I don't want to go outside. I won't, even if Jennie asks me to.

For outside you have to creep on the ground, and everything is green instead of yellow.

But here I can creep smoothly on the floor, and my shoulder just fits in that long smooch around the wall, so I cannot lose my way.

250 Why, there's John at the door!

It is no use, young man, you can't open it!

How he does call and pound!

Now he's crying to Jennie for an axe.

It would be a shame to break down that beautiful door!

255 "John, dear!" said I in the gentlest voice. "The key is down by the front steps, under a plantain leaf!"

That silenced him for a few moments.

Then he said, very quietly indeed, "Open the door, my darling!"

"I can't," said I. "The key is down by the front door under a plantain leaf!" And then I said it again, several times, very gently and slowly, and said it so often that he had to go and see, and he got it of course, and came in. He stopped short by the door.

"What is the matter?" he cried. "For God's sake, what are you doing!"

260 I kept on creeping just the same, but I looked at him over my shoulder.

"I've got out at last," said I, "in spite of you and Jane. And I've pulled off most of the paper, so you can't put me back!"

Now why should that man have fainted? But he did, and right across my path by the wall, so that I had to creep over him every time!

[1892]

QUESTIONS FOR REFLECTION AND DISCUSSION

1. Describe the two main characters. How would you characterize their relationship to one another?

2. How does the first-person narration influence our understanding of events? Is the wife a reliable narrator? Why is it important that she is writing her narration rather than speaking it? How would the story change if it were narrated by her husband, John?

3. What is unusual about the room John chooses for the couple's bedroom? What are its positive qualities? What are its negative qualities? Why does John refuse to alter anything in it?

4. How does the narrator's attitude toward the wallpaper change? Why does it change? What is her relationship to the woman under the paper?

POETRY

Paul Laurence Dunbar 1872–1906

Paul Laurence Dunbar was born in Dayton, Ohio, to a couple of escaped slaves; his father was a Union veteran of the Civil War. Dunbar published his first volume of poetry when he was twenty; his second volume brought him the patronage he needed to move to Washington, D.C., to attend Howard University. Dunbar wrote a dozen volumes of poetry, in both dialect and standard English; he also published several novels and volumes of short stories, as well as a play. Dunbar died of tuberculosis at the age of thirty-three. Probably his best-known poem, "Sympathy" was published in 1899.

Sympathy

I know what the caged bird feels, alas!
  When the sun is bright on the upland slopes;
When the wind stirs soft through the springing
  grass,
And the river flows like a stream of glass;
  When the first bird sings and the first
    bud opes,
And the faint perfume from its chalice steals—   5
I know what the caged bird feels!

I know why the caged bird beats his wing
  Till its blood is red on the cruel bars;
For he must fly back to his perch and cling   10
When he fain would be on the bough a-swing;
  And a pain still throbs in the old, old scars
And they pulse again with a keener sting—
I know why he beats his wing!

I know why the caged bird sings, ah me,   15
  When his wing is bruised and his bosom sore,—
When he beats his bars and he would be free;
It is not a carol of joy or glee,
  But a prayer that he sends from his heart's deep
    core,
But a plea, that upward to Heaven he flings—   20
I know why the caged bird sings!

[1899]

QUESTIONS FOR REFLECTION AND DISCUSSION

1. What different assertion does the speaker make in each stanza? What is the difference between each assertion? What do the three assertions have in common?

2. What are the two possible explanations the speaker provides for why the caged bird sings? Which explanation does he choose, and why?

3. Why does the speaker know the answer to the questions he asks? Why does he repeat this assertion as a refrain throughout the poem?

Stevie Smith 1902–1971

The British poet and novelist Stevie Smith was raised in North London by her mother after her father ran off to sea when she was three. But she was brought up primarily by her feminist aunt Madge Spear, with whom she lived for most of the rest of her life. Developing tuberculosis at the age of five, Smith spent several years in a sanatorium. She attended Palmers Green High School and North London Collegiate School for Girls. She worked as a publisher's secretary for thirty years. She published three autobiographical novels and nine confessional and often dark volumes of poetry.

Not Waving but Drowning

Nobody heard him, the dead man,
But still he lay moaning:
I was much further out than you thought
And not waving but drowning.

Poor chap, he always loved larking   5
And now he's dead

It must have been too cold for him his heart gave way,
They said.

Oh, no no no, it was too cold always
(Still the dead one lay moaning)   10
I was much too far out all my life
And not waving but drowning.

[1957]

QUESTIONS FOR REFLECTION AND DISCUSSION

1. What is the relationship or association between the dead man and the speaker? How does the third stanza change the way we think about this relationship or association?

2. Why is it difficult to distinguish between waving and drowning?

3. What makes the space in which the dead man and the speaker both find themselves a confined space? How does this space differ from the confined spaces of the stories and poems above?

Robert Browning 1812–1889

Born in Camberwell, England, Robert Browning was educated primarily in the extensive library of his bank clerk father. An ardent admirer of the Romantic poets Byron and Shelley, Browning perfected the use of dramatic monologue in poetry and demonstrated a gift for verse narrative, well evident in "My Last Duchess." Browning initiated a correspondence with Elizabeth Barrett (p. 225) after reading a volume of her poetry; they were married two years later in 1846. Composed in the form of the dramatic monologue, a speech delivered by a single individual, "My Last Duchess" paints a vivid portrait of its speaker, Alfonso II, the fifteenth-century duke of the Italian city of Ferrara, and of the duke's young bride—she was fourteen years old when she married him.

My Last Duchess
Ferrara

That's my last Duchess painted on the wall,
Looking as if she were alive. I call

That piece a wonder, now; Frà Pandolf's hands
Worked busily a day, and there she stands.
Will't please you sit and look at her? I said   5
"Frà Pandolf" by design, for never read
Strangers like you that pictured countenance,

Portrait of Lucrezia de' Medici, Duchess of Ferrara, by Agnolo Bronzino, 16th century, Italy.

The depth and passion of its earnest glance,
But to myself they turned (since none puts by
The curtain I have drawn for you, but I)   10
And seemed as they would ask me, if they durst,
How such a glance came there; so, not the first
Are you to turn and ask thus. Sir, 'twas not
Her husband's presence only, called that spot
Of joy into the Duchess' cheek; perhaps   15
Frà Pandolf chanced to say, "Her mantle laps
Over my lady's wrist too much," or "Paint
Must never hope to reproduce the faint
Half-flush that dies along her throat." Such stuff
Was courtesy, she thought, and cause enough   20
For calling up that spot of joy. She had
A heart—how shall I say?—too soon made glad,
Too easily impressed; she liked whate'er
She looked on, and her looks went everywhere.

Sir, 'twas all one! My favor at her breast,   25
The dropping of the daylight in the West,
The bough of cherries some officious fool
Broke in the orchard for her, the white mule
She rode with round the terrace—all and each
Would draw from her alike the approving speech,   30
Or blush, at least. She thanked men,—good! but
    thanked
Somehow—I know not how—as if she ranked
My gift of a nine-hundred-years-old name
With anybody's gift. Who'd stoop to blame
This sort of trifling? Even had you skill   35
In speech—which I have not—to make your will
Quite clear to such an one, and say "Just this
Or that in you disgusts me; here you miss,
Or there exceed the mark"—and if she let
Herself be lessoned so, nor plainly set   40
Her wits to yours, forsooth, and made excuse—
E'en then would be some stooping; and I choose
Never to stoop. Oh, sir, she smiled, no doubt,
Whene'er I passed her; but who passed without
Much the same smile? This grew; I gave
    commands;   45
Then all smiles stopped together. There she stands
As if alive. Will't please you rise? We'll meet
The company below, then. I repeat,
The Count your master's known munificence
Is ample warrant that no just pretense   50
Of mine for dowry will be disallowed;
Though his fair daughter's self, as I avowed
At starting, is my object. Nay, we'll go
Together down, sir. Notice Neptune, though,
Taming a sea-horse, thought a rarity,   55
Which Claus of Innsbruck cast in bronze for me!

[1842]

1. What is the effect of composing the poem as a dramatic monologue spoken by the Duke? What can we deduce of the Duke from his words? What can we deduce of his wife? What can we deduce about their relationship?

2. What possible motivation does the Duke have for his speech? Is the Duke aware of what he is saying and of whom he is addressing?

3. What is the Duke's relationship to the portrait? Is it the same as his relationship to the Duchess herself or different?

4. What are some of the ways in the poem in which the Duchess has been confined?

5. Discuss the portrait as an example of a word picture, or ecphrasis (p. 223).

PLAY

Henrik Ibsen 1828–1906

One of the world's most performed and influential playwrights, Henrik Ibsen is generally regarded as the originator of the modern realistic drama. Born in the small Norwegian town of Skien to an eminent family that went bankrupt while he was a young child, Ibsen left home at fifteen to work as an apprentice pharmacist. He published his first play at the age of twenty-two, but his first success did not come until *Brand* (1866) and *Peer Gynt* (1867), at which point he was living in Italy. He moved to Germany the following year, and did not return to Norway until 1891. Published in 1879 and first performed in Denmark, *A Doll's House* was a scandalous success. It was followed by Ibsen's other great plays, which also tackled major social problems of the day: *Ghosts* (1881), *An Enemy of the People* (1882), *The Wild Duck* (1884), *Hedda Gabler* (1890), and *The Master Builder* (1892).

A DOLL'S HOUSE

Translated by R. Farquharson Sharps
Revised by Viktoria Michelsens

CHARACTERS

Torvald Helmer, a lawyer
Nora, his wife
Doctor Rank
Mrs. Kristine Linde
Nils Krogstad

The Helmers' three young children
Anne Marie, their nursemaid
Helene, the maid
A Porter

The action takes place in the Helmers' apartment.

ACT I

The scene is a room furnished comfortably and tastefully, but not extravagantly. At the back wall, a door to the right leads to the entrance hall. Another to the left leads to Helmer's study. Between the doors there is a piano. In the middle of the left-hand wall is a door, and beyond it a window. Near the window are a round table, armchairs, and a small sofa. In the right-hand wall, at the farther end, is another door, and on the same side, nearer the footlights, a stove, two easy chairs and a rocking chair. Between the stove and the door there is a small table. There are engravings on the walls, a cabinet

Photograph from the experimental and controversial 2007 Mabou Mines production of Ibsen's play, retitled *Dollhouse*. All sets and props were child-sized, the male roles all played by actors under four feet tall, and the female roles by average-height actresses. The production, said director Lee Breuer, was all about size.

with china and other small objects, and a small bookcase with expensively bound books. The floors are carpeted, and a fire burns in the stove. It is winter.

A bell rings in the hall. A moment later, we hear the door being opened. Enter Nora, humming a tune and in high spirits. She is wearing a hat and coat and carries a number of packages, which she puts down on the table to the right. She leaves the outer door open behind her. Through the door we see a porter who is carrying a Christmas tree and a basket, which he gives to the maid, who has opened the door.

Nora: Hide the Christmas tree carefully, Helene. Make sure the children don't see it till it's decorated this evening. (*To the Porter, taking out her purse.*) How much?

Porter: Fifty ore.

Nora: Here's a krone. No, keep the change.

(The Porter thanks her and goes out. Nora shuts the door. She is laughing to herself as she takes off her hat and coat. She takes a bag of macaroons from her pocket and eats one or two, then goes cautiously to the door of her husband's study and listens.)

Yes, he's there. (*Still humming, she goes to the table on the right.*)

Helmer (*calls out from his study*): Is that my little lark twittering out there?

Nora (*busy opening some of the packages*): Yes, it is!

Helmer: Is it my little squirrel bustling around?

Nora: Yes!

Helmer: When did my squirrel come home?

Nora: Just now. (*Puts the bag of macaroons into her pocket and wipes her mouth.*) Come in here, Torvald, and see what I bought.

Helmer: I'm very busy right now. (*A little later, he opens the door and looks into the room, pen in hand.*) Bought, did you say? All these things? Has my little spendthrift been wasting money again?

Nora: Yes, but, Torvald, this year we really can let ourselves go a little. This is the first Christmas that we don't have to watch every penny.

Helmer: Still, you know, we can't spend money recklessly.

Nora: Yes, Torvald, but we can be a little more reckless now, can't we? Just a tiny little bit! You're going to have a big salary and you'll be making lots and lots of money.

Helmer: Yes, after the New Year. But it'll still be a whole three months before the money starts coming in.

Nora: Pooh! We can borrow till then.

Helmer: Nora! (*Goes up to her and takes her playfully by the ear.*) The same little featherbrain! Just suppose that I borrowed a thousand kroner today, and you spent it all on Christmas, and then on New Year's Eve a roof tile fell on my head and killed me, and—

Nora (*putting her hand over his mouth*): Oh! Don't say such horrible things.

Helmer: Still, suppose that happened. What then?

Nora: If that happened, I don't suppose I'd care whether I owed anyone money or not.

Helmer: Yes, but what about the people who'd lent it to us?

Nora: Them? Who'd care about them? I wouldn't even know who they were.

Helmer: That's just like a woman! But seriously, Nora, you know how I feel about that. No debt, no borrowing. There can't be any freedom or beauty in a home life that depends on borrowing and debt. We two have managed to stay on the straight road so far, and we'll go on the same way for the short time that we still have to be careful.

Nora (*moving towards the stove*): As you wish, Torvald.

Helmer (*following her*): Now, now, my little skylark mustn't let her wings droop. What's the matter? Is my little squirrel sulking? (*Taking out his purse.*) Nora, what do you think I've got here?

Nora (*turning round quickly*): Money!

Helmer: There you are. (*Gives her some money.*) Do you think I don't know how much you need for the house at Christmastime?

Nora (*counting*): Ten, twenty, thirty, forty! Thank you, thank you, Torvald. That'll keep me going for a long time.

Helmer: It's going to have to.

Nora: Yes, yes, it will. But come here and let me show you what I bought. And all so cheap! Look, here's a new suit for Ivar, and a sword. And a horse and a trumpet for Bob. And a doll and doll's bed for Emmy. They're not the best, but she'll break them soon enough anyway. And here's dress material and handkerchiefs for the maids. Old Anne Marie really should have something nicer.

Helmer: And what's in this package?

Nora (*crying out*): No, no! You can't see that till this evening.

Helmer: If you say so. But now tell me, you extravagant little thing, what would you like for yourself?

Nora: For myself? Oh, I'm sure I don't want anything.

Helmer: But you must. Tell me something that you'd especially like to have—within reasonable limits.

Nora: No, I really can't think of anything. Unless, Torvald . . .

Helmer: Well?

Nora (*playing with his coat buttons, and without raising her eyes to his*): If you really want to give me something, you might . . . you might . . .

Helmer: Well, out with it!

Nora (*speaking quickly*): You might give me money, Torvald. Only just as much as you can afford. And then one of these days I'll buy something with it.

Helmer: But, Nora—

Nora: Oh, do! Dear Torvald, please, please do! Then I'll wrap it up in beautiful gold paper and hang it on the Christmas tree. Wouldn't that be fun?

Helmer: What do they call those little creatures that are always wasting money?

Nora: Spendthrifts. I know. Let's do as I suggest, Torvald, and then I'll have time to think about what I need most. That's a very sensible plan, isn't it?

Helmer (*smiling*): Yes, it is. That is, if you really did save some of the money I give you, and then really buy something for yourself. But if you spend it all on the housekeeping and all kinds of unnecessary things, then I just have to open my wallet all over again.

Nora: Oh, but, Torvald—

Helmer: You can't deny it, my dear little Nora. (*Puts his arm around her waist.*) She's a sweet little spendthrift, but she uses up a lot of money. One would hardly believe how expensive such little creatures are!

Nora: That's a terrible thing to say. I really do save all I can.

Helmer (*laughing*): That's true. All you can. But you can't save anything!

Nora (*smiling quietly and happily*): You have no idea how many bills skylarks and squirrels have, Torvald.

Helmer: You're an odd little soul. Just like your father. You always find some new way of wheedling money out of me, and, as soon as you've got it, it seems to melt in your hands. You never know where it's gone. Still, one has to take you as you are. It's in the blood. Because, you know, it's true that you can inherit these things, Nora.

Nora: Ah, I wish I'd inherited a lot of Papa's traits.

Helmer: And I wouldn't want you to be anything but just what you are, my sweet little skylark. But, you know, it seems to me that you look rather—how can I put it—rather uneasy today.

Nora: Do I?

Helmer: You do, really. Look straight at me.

Nora (*looks at him*): Well?

Helmer (*wagging his finger at her*): Has little Miss Sweet Tooth been breaking our rules in town today?

Nora: No, what makes you think that?

Helmer: Has she paid a visit to the bakery?

Nora: No, I assure you, Torvald—

Helmer: Not been nibbling pastries?

Nora: No, certainly not.

Helmer: Not even taken a bite of a macaroon or two?

Nora: No, Torvald, I assure you, really—

Helmer: Come on, you know I was only kidding.

Nora (*going to the table on the right*): I wouldn't dream of going against your wishes.

Helmer: No, I'm sure of that. Besides, you gave me your word. (*Going up to her.*) Keep your little Christmas secrets to yourself, my darling. They'll all be revealed tonight when the Christmas tree is lit, no doubt.

Nora: Did you remember to invite Doctor Rank?

Helmer: No. But there's no need. It goes without saying that he'll have dinner with us. All the same, I'll ask him when he comes over this morning. I've ordered some good wine. Nora, you have no idea how much I'm looking forward to this evening.

Nora: So am I! And how the children will enjoy themselves, Torvald!

Helmer: It's great to feel that you have a completely secure position and a big enough income. It's a delightful thought, isn't it?

Nora: It's wonderful!

Helmer: Do you remember last Christmas? For three whole weeks you hid yourself away every evening until long after midnight, making ornaments for the Christmas tree and all the other fine things that were going to be a surprise for us. It was the most boring three weeks I ever spent!

Nora: I wasn't bored.

Helmer (*smiling*): But there was precious little to show for it, Nora.

Nora: Oh, you're not going to tease me about that again. How could I help it that the cat went in and tore everything to pieces?

Helmer: Of course you couldn't, poor little girl. You had the best of intentions to make us all happy, and that's the main thing. But it's a good thing that our hard times are over.

Nora: Yes, it really is wonderful.

Helmer: This time I don't have to sit here and be bored all by myself, and you don't have to ruin your dear eyes and your pretty little hands—

Nora (*clapping her hands*): No, Torvald, I don't have to any more, do I! It's wonderfully lovely to hear you say so! (*Taking his arm.*) Now let me tell you how I've been thinking we should arrange things, Torvald. As soon as Christmas is over—(*A bell rings in the hall.*) There's the bell. (*She tidies the room a little.*) There's somebody at the door. What a nuisance!

Helmer: If someone's visiting, remember I'm not home.

Maid (*in the doorway*): A lady to see you, ma'am. A stranger.

Nora: Ask her to come in.

Maid (*to Helmer*): The doctor's here too, sir.

Helmer: Did he go straight into my study?

Maid: Yes, sir.

(*Helmer goes into his study. The maid ushers in Mrs. Linde, who is in traveling clothes, and shuts the door.*)

Mrs. Linde (*in a dejected and timid voice*): Hello, Nora.

Nora (*doubtfully*): Hello.

Mrs. Linde: You don't recognize me, I suppose.

Nora: No, I don't know . . . Yes, of course, I think so—(*Suddenly.*) Yes! Kristine! Is it really you?

Mrs. Linde: Yes, it is.

Nora: Kristine! Imagine my not recognizing you! And yet how could I— (*In a gentle voice.*) You've changed, Kristine!

Mrs. Linde: Yes, I certainly have. In nine, ten long years—

Nora: Is it that long since we've seen each other? I suppose it is. The last eight years have been a happy time for me, you know. And so now you've come to town, and you've taken this long trip in the winter. That was brave of you.

Mrs. Linde: I arrived by steamer this morning.

Nora: To have some fun at Christmastime, of course. How delightful! We'll have such fun together! But take off your things. You're not cold, I hope. (*Helps her.*) Now we'll sit down by the stove and be cozy. No, take this armchair. I'll sit here in the rocking chair. (*Takes her hands.*) Now you look like your old self again. It was only that first moment. You are a little paler, Kristine, and maybe a little thinner.

Mrs. Linde: And much, much older, Nora.

Nora: Maybe a little older. Very, very little. Surely not very much. (*Stops suddenly and speaks seriously.*) What a thoughtless thing I am, chattering away like this. My poor, dear Kristine, please forgive me.

Mrs. Linde: What do you mean, Nora?

Nora (*gently*): Poor Kristine, you're a widow.

Mrs. Linde: Yes. For three years now.

Nora: Yes, I knew. I saw it in the papers. I swear to you, Kristine, I kept meaning to write to you at the time, but I always put it off and something always came up.

Mrs. Linde: I understand completely, dear.

Nora: It was very bad of me, Kristine. Poor thing, how you must have suffered. And he left you nothing?

Mrs. Linde: No.

Nora: And no children?

Mrs. Linde: No.

Nora: Nothing at all, then?

Mrs. Linde: Not even any sorrow or grief to live on.

Nora (*looking at her in disbelief*): But, Kristine, is that possible?

Mrs. Linde (*smiles sadly and strokes Nora's hair*): It happens sometimes, Nora.

Nora: So you're completely alone. How terribly sad that must be. I have three beautiful children. You can't see them just now, because they're out with their nursemaid. But now you must tell me all about it.

Mrs. Linde: No, no, I want to hear about you.

Nora: No, you go first. I mustn't be selfish today. Today I should think only about you. But there is one thing I have to tell you. Do you know we've just had a fabulous piece of good luck?

Mrs. Linde: No, what is it?

Nora: Just imagine, my husband's been appointed manager of the bank!

Mrs. Linde: Your husband? That is good luck!

Nora: Yes, it's tremendous! A lawyer's life is so uncertain, especially if he won't take any cases that are the slightest bit shady, and of course Torvald has never been willing to do that, and I completely agree with him. You can imagine how delighted we are! He starts his job in the bank at New Year's, and then he'll have a big salary and lots of commissions. From now on we can live very differently. We can do just what we want. I feel so relieved and so happy, Kristine! It'll be wonderful to have heaps of money and not have to worry about anything, won't it?

Mrs. Linde: Yes. Anyway, I think it would be delightful to have what you need.

Nora: No, not only what you need, but heaps and heaps of money.

Mrs. Linde (*smiling*): Nora, Nora, haven't you learned any sense yet? Back in school you were a terrible spendthrift.

Nora (*laughing*): Yes, that's what Torvald says now. (*Wags her finger at her.*) But "Nora, Nora" isn't as silly as you think. We haven't been in a position for me to waste money. We've both had to work.

Mrs. Linde: You too?

Nora: Oh, yes, odds and ends, needlework, crocheting, embroidery, and that kind of thing. (*Dropping her voice.*) And other things too. You know Torvald left his government job when we got married? There was no chance of promotion, and he had to try to earn more money than he was making there. But in that first year he overworked himself terribly. You see, he had to make money any way he could, and he worked all hours, but he couldn't take it, and he got very sick, and the doctors said he had to go south, to a warmer climate.

Mrs. Linde: You spent a whole year in Italy, didn't you?

Nora: Yes. It wasn't easy to get away, I can tell you that. It was just after Ivar was born, but obviously we had to go. It was a wonderful, beautiful trip, and it saved Torvald's life. But it cost a tremendous amount of money, Kristine.

Mrs. Linde: I would imagine so.

Nora: It cost about four thousand, eight hundred kroner. That's a lot, isn't it?

Mrs. Linde: Yes, it is, and when you have an emergency like that it's lucky to have the money.

Nora: Well, the fact is, we got it from Papa.

Mrs. Linde: Oh, I see. It was just about that time that he died, wasn't it?

Nora: Yes, and, just think of it, I couldn't even go and take care of him. I was expecting little Ivar any day and I had my poor sick Torvald to look after. My dear, kind father. I never saw him again, Kristine. That was the worst experience I've gone through since we got married.

Mrs. Linde: I know how fond of him you were. And then you went off to Italy?

Nora: Yes. You see, we had money then, and the doctors insisted that we go, so we left a month later.

Mrs. Linde: And your husband came back completely recovered?

Nora: The picture of health!

Mrs. Linde: But . . . the doctor?

Nora: What doctor?

Mrs. Linde: Didn't your maid say that the gentleman who arrived here with me was the doctor?

Nora: Yes, that was Doctor Rank, but he doesn't come here professionally. He's our dearest friend, and he drops in at least once every day. No, Torvald hasn't been sick for an hour since then, and our children are strong and healthy, and so am I. (*Jumps up and claps her hands.*) Kristine! Kristine! It's good to be alive and happy! But how awful of me. I'm talking about nothing but myself. (*Sits on a nearby stool and rests her arms on her knees.*) Please don't be mad at me. Tell me, is it really true that you didn't love your husband? Why did you marry him?

Mrs. Linde: My mother was still alive then, and she was bedridden and helpless, and I had to provide for my two younger brothers, so I didn't think I had any right to turn him down.

Nora: No, maybe you did the right thing. So he was rich then?

Mrs. Linde: I believe he was quite well off. But his business wasn't very solid, and when he died, it all went to pieces and there was nothing left.

Nora: And then?

Mrs. Linde: Well, I had to turn my hand to anything I could find. First a small shop, then a small school, and so on. The last three years have seemed like one long workday, with no rest. Now it's over, Nora. My poor mother's gone and doesn't need me any more, and the boys don't need me, either. They've got jobs now and can manage for themselves.

Nora: What a relief it must be if—

Mrs. Linde: No, not at all. All I feel is an unbearable emptiness. No one to live for anymore. (*Gets up restlessly.*) That's why I couldn't stand it any longer in my little backwater. I hope it'll be easier to find something here that'll keep me busy and occupy my mind. If I could be lucky enough to find some regular work, office work of some kind—

Nora: But, Kristine, that's so awfully tiring, and you look tired out now. It'd be much better for you if you could get away to a resort.

Mrs. Linde (*walking to the window*): I don't have a father to give me money for a trip, Nora.

Nora (*rising*): Oh, don't be mad at me!

Mrs. Linde (*going up to her*): It's you who mustn't be mad at me, dear. The worst thing about a situation like mine is that it makes you so bitter. No one to work for, and yet you have to always be on the lookout for opportunities. You have to live, and so you grow selfish. When you told me about your good luck— you'll find this hard to believe—I was delighted less for you than for myself.

Nora: What do you mean? Oh, I understand. You mean that maybe Torvald could find you a job.

Mrs. Linde: Yes, that's what I was thinking.

Nora: He must, Kristine. Just leave it to me. I'll broach the subject very cleverly. I'll think of something that'll put him in a really good mood. It'll make me so happy to be of some use to you.

Mrs. Linde: How kind you are, Nora, to be so eager to help me! It's doubly kind of you, since you know so little of the burdens and troubles of life.

Nora: Me? I know so little of them?

Mrs. Linde (*smiling*): My dear! Small household cares and that sort of thing! You're a child, Nora.

Nora (*tosses her head and crosses the stage*): You shouldn't act so superior.

Mrs. Linde: No?

Nora: You're just like the others. They all think I'm incapable of anything really serious—

Mrs. Linde: Come on—

Nora: —that I haven't had to deal with any real problems in my life.

Mrs. Linde: But, my dear Nora, you've just told me all your troubles.

Nora: Pooh! That was nothing. (*Lowering her voice.*) I haven't told you the important thing.

Mrs. Linde: The important thing? What do you mean?

Nora: You really look down on me, Kristine, but you shouldn't. Aren't you proud of having worked so hard and so long for your mother?

Mrs. Linde: Believe me, I don't look down on anyone. But it's true, I'm proud and I'm glad that I had the privilege of making my mother's last days almost worry-free.

Nora: And you're proud of what you did for your brothers?

Mrs. Linde: I think I have the right to be.

Nora: I think so, too. But now, listen to this. I have something to be proud of and happy about too.

Mrs. Linde: I'm sure you do. But what do you mean?

Nora: Keep your voice down. If Torvald were to overhear! He can't find out, not under any circumstances. No one in the world must know, Kristine, except you.

Mrs. Linde: But what is it?

Nora: Come here. (*Pulls her down on the sofa beside her.*) Now I'll show you that I too have something to be proud and happy about. I'm the one who saved Torvald's life.

Mrs. Linde: Saved? How?

Nora: I told you about our trip to Italy. Torvald would never have recovered if he hadn't gone there—

Mrs. Linde: Yes, but your father gave you the money you needed.

Nora (*smiling*): Yes, that's what Torvald thinks, along with everybody else, but—

Mrs. Linde: But—

Nora: Papa didn't give us a penny. I was the one who raised the money.

Mrs. Linde: You? That huge amount?

Nora: That's right, four thousand, eight hundred kroner. What do you think of that?

Mrs. Linde: But, Nora, how could you possibly? Did you win the lottery?

Nora (*disdainfully*): The lottery? That wouldn't have been any accomplishment.

Mrs. Linde: But where did you get it from, then?

Nora (*humming and smiling with an air of mystery*): Hm, hm! Ha!

Mrs. Linde: Because you couldn't have borrowed it.

Nora: Couldn't I? Why not?

Mrs. Linde: No, a wife can't borrow money without her husband's consent.

Nora (*tossing her head*): Oh, if it's a wife with a head for business, a wife who has the brains to be a little clever—

Mrs. Linde: I don't understand this at all, Nora.

Nora: There's no reason why you should. I never said I'd borrowed the money. Maybe I got it some other way. (*Lies back on the sofa.*) Maybe I got it from an admirer. When a woman's as pretty as I am—

Mrs. Linde: You're crazy.

Nora: Now, you know you're dying of curiosity, Kristine.

Mrs. Linde: Listen to me, Nora dear. Have you done something rash?

Nora (*sits up straight*): Is it rash to save your husband's life?

Mrs. Linde: I think it's rash, without his knowledge, to—

Nora: But it was absolutely necessary that he not know! My goodness, can't you understand that? It was necessary he have no idea how sick he was. The doctors came to *me* and said his life was in danger and the only thing that could save him was to live in the south. Don't you think I tried first to get him to do it as if it was for me? I told him how much I would love to travel abroad like other young wives. I tried tears and pleading with him. I told him he should remember the condition I was in, and that he should be kind and indulgent to me. I even hinted that he might take out a loan. That almost made him mad, Kristine. He said I was thoughtless, and that it was his duty as my husband not to indulge me in my "whims and caprices," as I believe he called them. All right, I thought, you need to be saved. And that was how I came to think up a way out of the mess—

Mrs. Linde: And your husband never found out from your father that the money hadn't come from him?

Nora: No, never. Papa died just then. I'd meant to let him in on the secret and beg him never to reveal it. But he was so sick. Unfortunately, there never was any need to tell him.

Mrs. Linde: And since then you've never told your secret to your husband?

Nora: Good heavens, no! How could you think I would? A man with such strong opinions about these things! Besides, how painful and humiliating it would be for Torvald, with his masculine pride, to know that he owed me anything! It would completely upset the balance of our relationship. Our beautiful happy home would never be the same.

Mrs. Linde: Are you never going to tell him about it?

Nora (*meditatively, and with a half smile*): Yes, someday, maybe, in many years, when I'm not as pretty as I am now. Don't laugh at me! I mean, of course, when Torvald is no longer as devoted to me as he is now, when he's grown tired of my dancing and dressing up and reciting. Then it may be a good thing to have something in reserve—(*Breaking off.*) What nonsense! That time will never come. Now, what do you think of my great secret, Kristine? Do you still think I'm useless? And the fact is, this whole situation has caused me a lot of worry. It hasn't been easy for me to make my payments on time. I can tell you that there's something in business that's called quarterly interest, and something else called installment payments, and it's always so terribly difficult to keep up with them. I've had to save a little here and there, wherever I could, you understand. I haven't been able to put much aside from my housekeeping money, because Torvald has to live well. And I couldn't let my children be shabbily dressed. I feel I have to spend everything he gives me for them, the sweet little darlings!

Mrs. Linde: So it's all had to come out of your own allowance, poor Nora?

Nora: Of course. Besides, I was the one responsible for it. Whenever Torvald has given me money for new dresses and things like that, I've never spent more than half of it. I've always bought the simplest and cheapest things. Thank heaven, any clothes look good on me, and so Torvald's never noticed anything. But it was often very hard on me, Kristine, because it is delightful to be really well dressed, isn't it?

Mrs. Linde: I suppose so.

Nora: Well, then I've found other ways of earning money. Last winter I was lucky enough to get a lot of copying to do, so I locked myself up and sat writing every evening until late into the night. A lot of the time I was desperately tired, but all the same it was a tremendous pleasure to sit there working and earning money. It was like being a man.

Mrs. Linde: How much have you been able to pay off that way?

Nora: I can't tell you exactly. You see, it's very hard to keep a strict account of a business matter like that. I only know that I've paid out every penny I could scrape together. Many a time I was at my wits' end. (*Smiles.*) Then I used to sit here and imagine that a rich old gentleman had fallen in love with me—

Mrs. Linde: What! Who was it?

Nora: Oh, be quiet! That he had died, and that when his will was opened it said, in great big letters: "The lovely Mrs. Nora Helmer is to have everything I own paid over to her immediately in cash."

Mrs. Linde: But, my dear Nora, who could the man be?

Nora: Good gracious, can't you understand? There wasn't any old gentleman. It was only something that I used to sit here and imagine, when I couldn't think of any way of getting money. But it's all right now. The tiresome old gent can stay right where he is, as far as I'm concerned. I don't care about him or his will either, because now I'm worry-free. (*Jumps up.*) My goodness, it's delightful to think of, Kristine! Worry-free! To be able to have no worries, no worries at all! To be able to play and romp with the children! To be able to keep the house beautifully and have everything just the way Torvald likes it! And, just think of it, soon the spring will come and the big blue sky! Maybe we can take a little trip. Maybe I can see the sea again! Oh, it's a wonderful thing to be alive and happy.

(*A bell rings in the hall.*)

Mrs. Linde (*rising*): There's the bell. Perhaps I should be going.

Nora: No, don't go. No one will come in here. It's sure to be for Torvald.

Servant (*at the hall door*): Excuse me, ma'am. There's a gentleman to see the master, and as the doctor is still with him—

Nora: Who is it?

Krogstad (*at the door*): It's me, Mrs. Helmer.

(*Mrs. Linde starts, trembles, and turns toward the window.*)

Nora (*takes a step toward him, and speaks in a strained, low voice*): You? What is it? What do you want to see my husband for?

Krogstad: Bank business, in a way. I have a small position in the bank, and I hear your husband is going to be our boss now—

Nora: Then it's—

Krogstad: Nothing but dry business matters, Mrs. Helmer, that's all.

Nora: Then please go into the study.

(*She bows indifferently to him and shuts the door into the hall, then comes back and makes up the fire in the stove.*)

Mrs. Linde: Nora, who was that man?

Nora: A lawyer. His name is Krogstad.

Mrs. Linde: Then it really was him.

Nora: Do you know the man?

Mrs. Linde: I used to, many years ago. At one time he was a law clerk in our town.

Nora: That's right, he was.

Mrs. Linde: How much he's changed.

Nora: He had a very unhappy marriage.

Mrs. Linde: He's a widower now, isn't he?

Nora: With several children. There, now it's really caught. (*Shuts the door of the stove and moves the rocking chair aside.*)

Mrs. Linde: They say he's mixed up in a lot of questionable business.

Nora: Really? Maybe he is. I don't know anything about it. But let's not talk about business. It's so tiresome.

Doctor Rank (*comes out of Helmer's study. Before he shuts the door he calls to Helmer*): No, my dear fellow, I won't disturb you. I'd rather go in and talk to your wife for a little while.

(*Shuts the door and sees Mrs. Linde.*)

I beg your pardon. I'm afraid I'm in the way here too.

Nora: No, not at all. (*Introducing him*): Doctor Rank, Mrs. Linde.

Rank: I've often heard that name in this house. I think I passed you on the stairs when I arrived, Mrs. Linde?

Mrs. Linde: Yes, I take stairs very slowly. I can't manage them very well.

Rank: Oh, some small internal problem?

Mrs. Linde: No, it's just that I've been overworking myself.

Rank: Is that all? Then I suppose you've come to town to get some rest by sampling our social life.

Mrs. Linde: I've come to look for work.

Rank: Is that a good cure for overwork?

Mrs. Linde: One has to live, Doctor Rank.

Rank: Yes, that seems to be the general opinion.

Nora: Now, now, Doctor Rank, you know you want to live.

Rank: Of course I do. However miserable I may feel, I want to prolong the agony for as long as possible. All my patients are the same way. And so are those who are morally sick. In fact, one of them, and a bad case too, is at this very moment inside with Helmer—

Mrs. Linde (*sadly*): Ah!

Nora: Who are you talking about?

Rank: A lawyer by the name of Krogstad, a fellow you don't know at all. He's a completely worthless creature, Mrs. Helmer. But even he started out by saying, as if it were a matter of the utmost importance, that he has to live.

Nora: Did he? What did he want to talk to Torvald about?

Rank: I have no idea. All I heard was that it was something about the bank.

Nora: I didn't know this—what's his name—Krogstad had anything to do with the bank.

Rank: Yes, he has some kind of a position there. (*To Mrs. Linde.*) I don't know whether you find the same thing in your part of the world, that there are certain people who go around zealously looking to sniff out moral corruption, and, as soon as they find some, they put the person involved in some cushy job where they can keep an eye on him. Meanwhile, the morally healthy ones are left out in the cold.

Mrs. Linde: Still, I think it's the sick who are most in need of being taken care of.

Rank (*shrugging his shoulders*): Well, there you have it. That's the attitude that's turning society into a hospital.

(*Nora, who has been absorbed in her thoughts, breaks out into smothered laughter and claps her hands.*)

Rank: Why are you laughing at that? Do you have any idea what society really is?

Nora: What do I care about your boring society? I'm laughing at something else, something very funny. Tell me, Doctor Rank, are all the people who work in the bank dependent on Torvald now?

Rank: That's what's so funny?

Nora (*smiling and humming*): That's my business! (*Walking around the room.*) It's just wonderful to think that we have—that Torvald has—so much power over so many people. (*Takes the bag out of her pocket.*) Doctor Rank, what do you say to a macaroon?

Rank: Macaroons? I thought they were forbidden here.

Nora: Yes, but these are some Kristine gave me.

Mrs. Linde: What! Me?

Nora: Oh, well, don't be upset! How could you know that Torvald had forbidden them? I have to tell you, he's afraid they'll ruin my teeth. But so what? Once in a while, that's all right, isn't it, Doctor Rank? With your permission! (*Puts a macaroon into his mouth.*) You have to have one too, Kristine. And I'll have one, just a little one—or no more than two. (*Walking around.*) I am tremendously happy. There's just one thing in the world now that I would dearly love to do.

Rank: Well, what is it?

Nora: It's something I would dearly love to say, if Torvald could hear me.

Rank: Well, why can't you say it?

Nora: No, I don't dare. It's too shocking.

Mrs. Linde: Shocking?

Rank: Well then, I'd advise you not to say it. Still, in front of us you might risk it. What is it you'd so much like to say if Torvald could hear you?

Nora: I would just love to say—"Well, I'll be damned!"

Rank: Are you crazy?

Mrs. Linde: Nora, dear!

Rank: Here he is. Say it!

Nora (*hiding the bag*): Shh, shh, shh!

(*Helmer comes out of his room, with his coat over his arm and his hat in his hand.*)

Nora: Well, Torvald dear, did you get rid of him?

Helmer: Yes, he just left.

Nora: Let me introduce you. This is Kristine. She's just arrived in town.

Helmer: Kristine? I'm sorry, but I don't know any—

Nora: Mrs. Linde, dear, Kristine Linde.

Helmer: Oh, of course. A school friend of my wife's, I believe?

Mrs. Linde: Yes, we knew each other back then.

Nora: And just think, she's come all this way in order to see you.

Helmer: What do you mean?

Mrs. Linde: No, really, I—

Nora: Kristine is extremely good at bookkeeping, and she's very eager to work for some talented man, so she can perfect her skills—

Helmer: Very sensible, Mrs. Linde.

Nora: And when she heard that you'd been named manager of the bank—the news was sent by telegraph, you know—she traveled here as quickly as she could. Torvald, I'm sure you'll be able to do something for Kristine, for my sake, won't you?

Helmer: Well, it's not completely out of the question. I expect that you're a widow, Mrs. Linde?

Mrs. Linde: Yes.

Helmer: And you've had some bookkeeping experience?

Mrs. Linde: Yes, a fair amount.

Helmer: Ah! Well, there's a very good chance that I'll be able to find something for you—

Nora (*clapping her hands*)**:** What did I tell you? What did I tell you?

Helmer: You've just come at a lucky moment, Mrs. Linde.

Mrs. Linde: How can I thank you?

Helmer: There's no need. (*Puts on his coat.*) But now you must excuse me—

Rank: Wait a minute. I'll come with you. (*Brings his fur coat from the hall and warms it at the fire.*)

Nora: Don't be long, Torvald dear.

Helmer: About an hour, that's all.

Nora: Are you leaving too, Kristine?

Mrs. Linde (*putting on her cloak*)**:** Yes, I have to go and look for a place to stay.

Helmer: Oh, well then, we can walk down the street together.

Nora (*helping her*)**:** It's too bad we're so short of space here. I'm afraid it's impossible for us—

Mrs. Linde: Please don't even think of it! Goodbye, Nora dear, and many thanks.

Nora: Goodbye for now. Of course you'll come back this evening. And you too, Dr. Rank. What do you say? If you're feeling up to it? Oh, you have to be! Wrap yourself up warmly.

(*They go to the door all talking together. Children's voices are heard on the staircase.*)

Nora: There they are! There they are!

(*She runs to open the door. The nursemaid comes in with the children.*)

Come in! Come in! (*Stoops and kisses them.*) Oh, you sweet blessings! Look at them, Kristine! Aren't they darlings?

Rank: Let's not stand here in the draft.

Helmer: Come along, Mrs. Linde. Only a mother will be able to stand it in here now!

(*Rank, Helmer, and Mrs. Linde go downstairs. The Nursemaid comes forward with the children. Nora shuts the hall door.*)

Nora: How fresh and healthy you look! Cheeks as red as apples and roses. (*The children all talk at once while she speaks to them.*) Did you have a lot of fun? That's wonderful! What, you pulled Emmy and Bob on the sled? Both at once? That was really something. You *are* a clever boy, Ivar. Let me take her for a little, Anne Marie. My sweet little baby doll! (*Takes the baby from the maid and dances her up and down.*) Yes, yes, mother will dance with Bob too. What! Have you been throwing snowballs? I wish I'd been there too! No, no, I'll take their things off, Anne Marie, please let me do it, it's such fun. Go inside now, you look half frozen. There's some hot coffee for you on the stove.

(*The Nursemaid goes into the room on the left. Nora takes off the children's things and throws them around, while they all talk to her at once.*)

Nora: Really! Did a big dog run after you? But it didn't bite you? No, dogs don't bite nice little dolly children. You mustn't look at the packages, Ivar. What are they? Oh, I'll bet you'd like to know. No, no, it's something boring! Come on, let's play a game! What should we play? Hide and seek? Yes, we'll play hide and seek. Bob will hide first. You want me to hide? All right, I'll hide first.

(*She and the children laugh and shout, and romp in and out of the room. At last Nora hides under the table. The children rush in and out looking for her, but they don't see her. They hear her smothered laughter, run to the table, lift up the cloth and find her. Shouts of laughter. She crawls forward and pretends to scare them. More laughter. Meanwhile there has been a knock at the hall door, but none of*) *them has noticed it. The door is opened halfway and Krogstad appears. He waits for a little while. The game goes on.)*

Krogstad: Excuse me, Mrs. Helmer.

Nora (*with a stifled cry, turns round and gets up onto her knees*): Oh! What do you want?

Krogstad: Excuse me, the outside door was open. I suppose someone forgot to shut it.

Nora (*rising*): My husband is out, Mr. Krogstad.

Krogstad: I know that.

Nora: What do you want here, then?

Krogstad: A word with you.

Nora: With me? (*To the children, gently.*) Go inside to Anne Marie. What? No, the strange man won't hurt Mother. When he's gone we'll play another game. (*She takes the children into the room on the left, and shuts the door after them.*) You want to speak to me?

Krogstad: Yes, I do.

Nora: Today? It isn't the first of the month yet.

Krogstad: No, it's Christmas Eve, and it's up to you what kind of Christmas you're going to have.

Nora: What do you mean? Today it's absolutely impossible for me—

Krogstad: We won't talk about that until later on. This is something else. I presume you can spare me a moment?

Nora: Yes, yes, I can. Although . . .

Krogstad: Good. I was in Olsen's restaurant and I saw your husband going down the street—

Nora: Yes?

Krogstad: With a lady.

Nora: So?

Krogstad: May I be so bold as to ask if it was a Mrs. Linde?

Nora: It was.

Krogstad: Just arrived in town?

Nora: Yes, today.

Krogstad: She's a very good friend of yours, isn't she?

Nora: She is. But I don't see—

Krogstad: I knew her too, once upon a time.

Nora: I'm aware of that.

Krogstad: Are you? So you know all about it. I thought so. Then I can ask you, without beating around the bush. Is Mrs. Linde going to work in the bank?

Nora: What right do you have to question me, Mr. Krogstad? You're one of my husband's employees. But since you ask, I'll tell you. Yes, Mrs. Linde is going

to work in the bank. And I'm the one who spoke up for her, Mr. Krogstad. So now you know.

Krogstad: So I was right, then.

Nora (*walking up and down the stage*): Sometimes one has a tiny little bit of influence, I should hope. Just because I'm a woman, it doesn't necessarily follow that— You know, when somebody's in a subordinate position, Mr. Krogstad, they should really be careful to avoid offending anyone who—who—

Krogstad: Who has influence?

Nora: Exactly.

Krogstad (*changing his tone*): Mrs. Helmer, may I ask you to use *your* influence on my behalf?

Nora: What? What do you mean?

Krogstad: Will you be kind enough to see to it that I'm allowed to keep my subordinate position in the bank?

Nora: What do you mean by that? Who's threatening to take your job away from you?

Krogstad: Oh, there's no need to keep up the pretence of ignorance. I can understand that your friend isn't very anxious to expose herself to the chance of rubbing shoulders with me. And now I realize exactly who I have to thank for pushing me out.

Nora: But I swear to you—

Krogstad: Yes, yes. But, to get right to the point, there's still time to prevent it, and I would advise you to use your influence to do so.

Nora: But, Mr. Krogstad, I have no influence.

Krogstad: Oh no? Didn't you yourself just say—

Nora: Well, obviously, I didn't mean for you to take it that way. Me? What would make you think I have that kind of influence with my husband?

Krogstad: Oh, I've known your husband since our school days. I don't suppose he's any more unpersuadable than other husbands.

Nora: If you're going talk disrespectfully about my husband, I'll have to ask you to leave my house.

Krogstad: Bold talk, Mrs. Helmer.

Nora: I'm not afraid of you anymore. When the New Year comes, I'll soon be free of the whole thing.

Krogstad (*controlling himself*): Listen to me, Mrs. Helmer. If I have to, I'm ready to fight for my little job in the bank as if I were fighting for my life.

Nora: So it seems.

Krogstad: It's not just for the sake of the money. In fact, that matters the least to me. There's another reason. Well, I might as well tell you. Here's my situation.

I suppose, like everybody else, you know that many years ago I did something pretty foolish.

Nora: I think I heard something about it.

Krogstad: It never got as far as the courtroom, but every door seemed closed to me after that. So I got involved in the business that you know about. I had to do something, and, honestly, I think there are many worse than me. But now I have to get myself free of all that. My sons are growing up. For their sake I have to try to win back as much respect as I can in this town. The job in the bank was like the first step up for me, and now your husband is going to kick me downstairs back into the mud.

Nora: But you have to believe me, Mr. Krogstad, it's not in my power to help you at all.

Krogstad: Then it's because you don't want to. But I have ways of making you.

Nora: You don't mean you'll tell my husband I owe you money?

Krogstad: Hm! And what if I did tell him?

Nora: That would be a terrible thing for you to do. (*Sobbing.*) To think he would learn my secret, which has been my pride and joy, in such an ugly, clumsy way—that he would learn it from you! And it would put me in a horribly uncomfortable position—

Krogstad: Just uncomfortable?

Nora (*impetuously*)**:** Well, go ahead and do it, then! And it'll be so much the worse for you. My husband will see for himself how vile you are, and then you'll lose your job for sure.

Krogstad: I asked you if it's just an uncomfortable situation at home that you're afraid of.

Nora: If my husband does find out about it, of course he'll immediately pay you what I still owe, and then we'll be through with you once and for all.

Krogstad (*coming a step closer*)**:** Listen to me, Mrs. Helmer. Either you have a very bad memory or you don't know much about business. I can see I'm going to have to remind you of a few details.

Nora: What do you mean?

Krogstad: When your husband was sick, you came to me to borrow four thousand, eight hundred kroner.

Nora: I didn't know anyone else to go to.

Krogstad: I promised to get you that amount—

Nora: Yes, and you did so.

Krogstad: I promised to get you that amount, on certain conditions. You were so preoccupied with your husband's illness, and you were so anxious to get the money for your trip, that you seem to have paid no attention to the conditions of our bargain. So it won't be out of place for me to remind you of them. Now, I promised to get the money on the security of a note which I drew up.

Nora: Yes, and which I signed.

Krogstad: Good. But underneath your signature there were a few lines naming your father as a co-signer who guaranteed the repayment of the loan. Your father was supposed to sign that part.

Nora: Supposed to? He did sign it.

Krogstad: I had left the date blank. That was because your father was supposed to fill in the date when he signed the paper. Do you remember that?

Nora: Yes, I think I remember. . . .

Krogstad: Then I gave you the note to mail to your father. Isn't that so?

Nora: Yes.

Krogstad: And obviously you mailed it right away, because five or six days later you brought me the note with your father's signature. And then I gave you the money.

Nora: Well, haven't I been paying it back regularly?

Krogstad: Fairly regularly, yes. But, to get back to the point, that must have been a very difficult time for you, Mrs. Helmer.

Nora: Yes, it was.

Krogstad: Your father was very sick, wasn't he?

Nora: He was very near the end.

Krogstad: And he died soon after?

Nora: Yes.

Krogstad: Tell me, Mrs. Helmer, can you by any chance remember what day your father died? On what day of the month, I mean.

Nora: Papa died on the 29th of September.

Krogstad: That's right. I looked it up myself. And, since that is the case, there's something extremely peculiar (*taking a piece of paper from his pocket*) that I can't account for.

Nora: Peculiar in what way? I don't know—

Krogstad: The peculiar thing, Mrs. Helmer, is the fact that your father signed this note three days after he died.

Nora: What do you mean? I don't understand—

Krogstad: Your father died on the 29th of September. But, look here. Your father dated his signature the 2nd of October. It is mighty peculiar, isn't it? (*Nora is silent.*) Can you explain it to me? (*Nora is still silent.*) And what's just as peculiar is that the words "October 2," as well as the year, are not in your father's handwriting, but in someone else's, which I think I recognize. Well, of course it can all be explained. Your father might have forgotten to date his signature, and someone else might have filled in the date before they knew that he had died. There's no harm in that. It all depends on the signature, and that's genuine, isn't it, Mrs. Helmer? It was your father himself who signed his name here?

Nora (*after a short pause, lifts her head up and looks defiantly at him*): No, it wasn't. I'm the one who wrote Papa's name.

Krogstad: Are you aware that you're making a very serious confession?

Nora: How so? You'll get your money soon.

Krogstad: Let me ask you something. Why didn't you send the paper to your father?

Nora: It was out of the question. Papa was too sick. If I had asked him to sign something, I'd have had to tell him what the money was for, and when he was so sick himself I couldn't tell him that my husband's life was in danger. It was out of the question.

Krogstad: It would have been better for you if you'd given up your trip abroad.

Nora: No, that was impossible. That trip was to save my husband's life. I couldn't give that up.

Krogstad: But didn't it ever occur to you that you were committing a fraud against me?

Nora: I couldn't take that into account. I didn't trouble myself about you at all. I couldn't stand you, because you put so many heartless difficulties in my way, even though you knew how seriously ill my husband was.

Krogstad: Mrs. Helmer, you evidently don't realize clearly what you're guilty of. But, believe me, my one mistake, which cost me my whole reputation, was nothing more and nothing worse than what you did.

Nora: You? You expect me to believe that you were brave enough to take a risk to save your wife's life?

Krogstad: The law doesn't care about motives.

Nora: Then the law must be very stupid.

Krogstad: Stupid or not, it's the law that's going to judge you, if I produce this paper in court.

Nora: I don't believe it. Isn't a daughter allowed to spare her dying father anxiety and concern? Isn't a wife allowed to save her husband's life? I don't know much about the law, but I'm sure there must be provisions for things like that. Don't you know anything about such provisions? You seem like a very poor excuse for a lawyer, Mr. Krogstad.

Krogstad: That's as may be. But business, the kind of business you and I have done together—do you think I don't know about that? Fine. Do what you want. But I can assure you of this. If I lose everything all over again, this time you're going down with me. (*He bows, and goes out through the hall.*)

Nora (*appears buried in thought for a short time, then tosses her head*): Nonsense! He's just trying to scare me! I'm not as naive as he thinks I am. (*Begins to busy herself putting the children's things in order.*) And yet . . . ? No, it's impossible! I did it for love.

Children (*in the doorway on the left*): Mother, the strange man is gone. He went out through the gate.

Nora: Yes, dears, I know. But don't tell anyone about the strange man. Do you hear me? Not even Papa.

Children: No, Mother. But will you come and play with us again?

Nora: No, no, not just now.

Children: But, Mother, you promised us.

Nora: Yes, but I can't right now. Go inside. I have too much to do. Go inside, my sweet little darlings.

(*She gets them into the room bit by bit and shuts the door on them. Then she sits down on the sofa, takes up a piece of needlework and sews a few stitches, but soon stops.*)

No! (*Throws down the work, gets up, goes to the hall door and calls out.*) Helene! Bring the tree in. (*Goes to the table on the left, opens a drawer, and stops again.*) No, no! It's completely impossible!

Maid (*coming in with the tree*): Where should I put it, ma'am?

Nora: Here, in the middle of the floor.

Maid: Do you need anything else?

Nora: No, thank you. I have everything I want.

(*Exit Maid.*)

Nora (*begins decorating the tree*): A candle here, and flowers here. That horrible man! It's all nonsense, there's nothing wrong. The tree is going to be magnificent! I'll do everything I can think of to make you happy, Torvald! I'll sing for you, dance for you—

(*Helmer comes in with some papers under his arm.*)

Oh! You're back already?

Helmer: Yes. Has anyone been here?

Nora: Here? No.

Helmer: That's strange. I saw Krogstad going out the gate.

Nora: You did? Oh yes, I forgot, Krogstad was here for a moment.

Helmer: Nora, I can tell from the way you're acting that he was here begging you to put in a good word for him.

Nora: Yes, he was.

Helmer: And you were supposed to pretend it was all your idea and not tell me that he'd been here to see you. Didn't he beg you to do that too?

Nora: Yes, Torvald, but—

Helmer: Nora, Nora, to think that you'd be a party to that sort of thing! To have any kind of conversation with a man like that, and promise him anything at all? And to lie to me in the bargain?

Nora: Lie?

Helmer: Didn't you tell me no one had been here? (*Shakes his finger at her.*) My little songbird must never do that again. A songbird must have a clean beak to chirp with. No false notes! (*Puts his arm round her waist.*) That's true, isn't it? Yes, I'm sure it is. (*Lets her go.*) We won't mention this again. (*Sits down by the stove.*) How warm and cozy it is here! (*Turns over his papers.*)

Nora (*after a short pause, during which she busies herself with the Christmas tree.*): Torvald!

Helmer: Yes?

Nora: I'm really looking forward to the masquerade ball at the Stenborgs' the day after tomorrow.

Helmer: And I'm really curious to see what you're going to surprise me with.

Nora: Oh, it was very silly of me to want to do that.

Helmer: What do you mean?

Nora: I can't come up with anything good. Everything I think of seems so stupid and pointless.

Helmer: So my little Nora finally admits that?

Nora (*standing behind his chair with her arms on the back of it*): Are you very busy, Torvald?

Helmer: Well . . .

Nora: What are all those papers?

Helmer: Bank business.

Nora: Already?

Helmer: I've gotten the authority from the retiring manager to reorganize the work procedures and make the necessary personnel changes. I need to take care

of it during Christmas week, so as to have everything in place for the new year.

Nora: Then that was why this poor Krogstad—

Helmer: Hm!

Nora (*leans against the back of his chair and strokes his hair*): If you weren't so busy, I would have asked you for a huge favor, Torvald.

Helmer: What favor? Tell me.

Nora: No one has such good taste as you. And I really want to look nice at the fancy-dress ball. Torvald, couldn't you take me in hand and decide what I should go as and what kind of costume I should wear?

Helmer: Aha! So my obstinate little woman has to get someone to come to her rescue?

Nora: Yes, Torvald, I can't get along at all without your help.

Helmer: All right, I'll think it over. I'm sure we'll come up with something.

Nora: That's so nice of you. (*Goes to the Christmas tree. A short pause.*) How pretty the red flowers look. But, tell me, was it really something very bad that this Krogstad was guilty of?

Helmer: He forged someone's name. Do you have any idea what that means?

Nora: Isn't it possible that he was forced to do it by necessity?

Helmer: Yes. Or, the way it is in so many cases, by foolishness. I'm not so heartless that I'd absolutely condemn a man because of one mistake like that.

Nora: No, you wouldn't, would you, Torvald?

Helmer: Many a man has been able to rehabilitate himself, if he's openly admitted his guilt and taken his punishment.

Nora: Punishment?

Helmer: But Krogstad didn't do that. He wriggled out of it with lies and trickery, and that's what completely undermined his moral character.

Nora: But do you think that that would—

Helmer: Just think how a guilty man like that has to lie and act like a hypocrite with everyone, how he has to wear a mask in front of the people closest to him, even with his own wife and children. And the children. That's the most terrible part of it all, Nora.

Nora: How so?

Helmer: Because an atmosphere of lies infects and poisons the whole life of a home. Every breath the children take in a house like that is full of the germs of moral corruption.

Nora (*coming closer to him*): Are you sure of that?

Helmer: My dear, I've seen it many times in my legal career. Almost everyone who's gone wrong at a young age had a dishonest mother.

Nora: Why only the mother?

Helmer: It usually seems to be the mother's influence, though naturally a bad father would have the same result. Every lawyer knows this. This Krogstad, now, has been systematically poisoning his own children with lies and deceit. That's why I say he's lost all moral character. (*Holds out his hands to her.*) And that's why my sweet little Nora must promise me not to plead his cause. Give me your hand on it. Come now, what's this? Give me your hand. There, that's settled. Believe me, it would be impossible for me to work with him. It literally makes me feel physically ill to be around people like that.

Nora (*takes her hand out of his and goes to the opposite side of the Christmas tree*): How hot it is in here! And I have so much to do.

Helmer (*getting up and putting his papers in order*): Yes, and I have to try to read through some of these before dinner. And I have to think about your costume, too. And it's just possible I'll have something wrapped in gold paper to hang up on the tree. (*Puts his hand on her head.*) My precious little songbird! (*He goes into his study and closes the door behind him.*)

Nora (*after a pause, whispers*): No, no, it's not true. It's impossible. It has to be impossible.

(*The nursemaid opens the door on the left.*)

Nursemaid: The little ones are begging so hard to be allowed to come in to see Mama.

Nora: No, no, no! Don't let them come in to me! You stay with them, Anne Marie.

Nursemaid: Very well, ma'am. (*Shuts the door.*)

Nora (*pale with terror*): Corrupt my little children? Poison my home? (*A short pause. Then she tosses her head.*) It's not true. It can't possibly be true.

ACT II

The same scene. The Christmas tree is in the corner by the piano, stripped of its ornaments and with burnt-down candle-ends on its disheveled branches. Nora's coat and hat are lying on the sofa. She is alone in the room, walking around uneasily. She stops by the sofa and picks up her coat.

Nora (*drops her coat*): Someone's coming! (*Goes to the door and listens.*) No, there's no one there. Of course, no one will come today. It's Christmas Day. And not tomorrow either. But maybe . . . (*opens the door and looks out*) No, nothing in the mailbox. It's empty. (*Comes forward.*) What nonsense! Of course he can't be serious about it. A thing like that couldn't happen. It's impossible. I have three little children.

(*Enter the nursemaid Anne Marie from the room on the left, carrying a big cardboard box.*)

Nursemaid: I finally found the box with the costume.

Nora: Thank you. Put it on the table.

Nursemaid (*doing so*): But it really needs to be mended.

Nora: I'd like to tear it into a hundred thousand pieces.

Nursemaid: What an idea! It can easily be fixed up. All you need is a little patience.

Nora: Yes, I'll go get Mrs. Linde to come and help me with it.

Nursemaid: What, going out again? In this horrible weather? You'll catch cold, Miss Nora, and make yourself sick.

Nora: Well, worse things than that might happen. How are the children?

Nursemaid: The poor little ones are playing with their Christmas presents, but—

Nora: Do they ask for me much?

Nursemaid: You see, they're so used to having their Mama with them.

Nora: Yes, but, Anne Marie, I won't be able to spend as much time with them now as I did before.

Nursemaid: Oh well, young children quickly get used to anything.

Nora: Do you think so? Do you think they'd forget their mother if she went away for good?

Nursemaid: Good heavens! Went away for good?

Nora: Anne Marie, I want you to tell me something I've often wondered about. How could you have the heart to let your own child be raised by strangers?

Nursemaid: I had to, if I wanted to be little Nora's nursemaid.

Nora: Yes, but how could you agree to it?

Nursemaid: What, when I was going to get such a good situation out of it? A poor girl who's gotten herself in trouble should be glad to. Besides, that worthless man didn't do a single thing for me.

Nora: But I suppose your daughter has completely forgotten you.

Nursemaid: No, she hasn't, not at all. She wrote to me when she was confirmed, and again when she got married.

Nora (*putting her arms round her neck*): Dear old Anne Marie, you were such a good mother to me when I was little.

Nursemaid: Poor little Nora, you had no other mother but me.

Nora: And if my little ones had no other mother, I'm sure that you would— What nonsense I'm talking! (*Opens the box.*) Go in and see to them. Now I have to . . . You'll see how lovely I'll look tomorrow.

Nursemaid: I'm sure there'll be no one at the ball as lovely as you, Miss Nora.

(*Goes into the room on the left.*)

Nora (*begins to unpack the box, but soon pushes it away from her*): If only I dared to go out. If only no one would come. If only I could be sure nothing would happen here in the meantime. What nonsense! No one's going to come. I just have to stop thinking about it. This muff needs to be brushed. What beautiful, beautiful gloves! Stop thinking about it, stop thinking about it! One, two, three, four, five, six— (*Screams.*) Aaah! Somebody *is* coming— (*Makes a movement towards the door, but stands in hesitation.*)

(*Enter Mrs. Linde from the hall, where she has taken off her coat and hat.*)

Nora: Oh, it's you, Kristine. There's no one else out in the hall, is there? How good of you to come!

Mrs. Linde: I heard you came by asking for me.

Nora: Yes, I was passing by. As a matter of fact, it's something you could help me with. Let's sit down here on the sofa. Listen, tomorrow evening there's going to be a fancy-dress ball at the Stenborgs'—they live upstairs from us—and Torvald wants me to go as a Neapolitan fisher-girl and dance the tarantella. I learned it when we were at Capri.

Mrs. Linde: I see. You're going to give them the whole show.

Nora: Yes, Torvald wants me to. Look, here's the dress. Torvald had it made for me there, but now it's all so torn, and I don't have any idea—

Mrs. Linde: We can easily fix that. Some of the trim has just come loose here and there. Do you have a needle and thread? That's all we need.

Nora: This is so nice of you.

Mrs. Linde (*sewing*): So you're going to be dressed up tomorrow, Nora. I'll tell you what. I'll stop by for a moment so I can see you in your finery. Oh, meanwhile I've completely forgotten to thank you for a delightful evening last night.

Nora (*gets up, and crosses the stage*): Well, I didn't think last night was as pleasant as usual. You should have come to town a little earlier, Kristine. Torvald really knows how to make a home pleasant and attractive.

Mrs. Linde: And so do you, if you ask me. You're not your father's daughter for nothing. But tell me, is Doctor Rank always as depressed as he was yesterday?

Nora: No, yesterday it was especially noticeable. But you have to understand that he has a very serious disease. He has tuberculosis of the spine, poor creature. His father was a horrible man who always had mistresses, and that's why his son has been sickly since childhood, if you know what I mean.

Mrs. Linde (*dropping her sewing*): But, my dear Nora, how do you know anything about such things?

Nora (*walking around the room*): Pooh! When you have three children, you get visits now and then from—from married women, who know something about medical matters, and they talk about one thing and another.

Mrs. Linde (*goes on sewing. A short silence*): Does Doctor Rank come here every day?

Nora: Every day, like clockwork. He's Torvald's best friend, and a great friend of mine too. He's just like one of the family.

Mrs. Linde: But tell me, is he really sincere? I mean, isn't he the kind of man who tends to play up to people?

Nora: No, not at all. What makes you think that?

Mrs. Linde: When you introduced him to me yesterday, he told me he'd often heard my name mentioned in this house, but later I could see that your husband didn't have the slightest idea who I was. So how could Doctor Rank—?

Nora: That's true, Kristine. Torvald is so ridiculously fond of me that he wants me completely to himself, as he says. At first he used to seem almost jealous if I even mentioned any of my friends back home, so naturally

I stopped talking about them to him. But I often talk about things like that with Doctor Rank, because he likes hearing about them.

Mrs. Linde: Listen to me, Nora. You're still like a child in a lot of ways, and I'm older than you and more experienced. So pay attention. You'd better stop all this with Doctor Rank.

Nora: Stop all what?

Mrs. Linde: Two things, I think. Yesterday you talked some nonsense about a rich admirer who was going to leave you his money—

Nora: An admirer who doesn't exist, unfortunately! But so what?

Mrs. Linde: Is Doctor Rank a wealthy man?

Nora: Yes, he is.

Mrs. Linde: And he has no dependents?

Nora: No, no one. But—

Mrs. Linde: And he comes here every day?

Nora: Yes, I told you he does.

Mrs. Linde: But how can such a well-bred man be so tactless?

Nora: I don't understand what you mean.

Mrs. Linde: Don't try to play dumb, Nora. Do you think I didn't guess who lent you the four thousand, eight hundred kroner?

Nora: Are you out of your mind? How can you even think that? A friend of ours, who comes here every day! Don't you realize what an incredibly awkward position that would put me in?

Mrs. Linde: Then he's really not the one?

Nora: Absolutely not. It would never have come into my head for one second. Besides, he had nothing to lend back then. He inherited his money later on.

Mrs. Linde: Well, I think that was lucky for you, my dear Nora.

Nora: No, it would never have crossed my mind to ask Doctor Rank. Although I'm sure that if I had asked him—

Mrs. Linde: But of course you won't.

Nora: Of course not. I have no reason to think I could possibly need to. But I'm absolutely certain that if I told Doctor Rank—

Mrs. Linde: Behind your husband's back?

Nora: I have to finish up with the other one, and that'll be behind his back too. I've got to wash my hands of him.

Mrs. Linde: Yes, that's what I told you yesterday, but—

Nora (*walking up and down*): A man can take care of these things so much more easily than a woman.

Mrs. Linde: If he's your husband, yes.

Nora: Nonsense! (*Standing still.*) When you pay off a debt you get your note back, don't you?

Mrs. Linde: Yes, of course.

Nora: And you can tear it into a hundred thousand pieces and burn up the filthy, nasty piece of paper!

Mrs. Linde (*stares at her, puts down her sewing and gets up slowly*): Nora, you're hiding something from me.

Nora: You can tell by looking at me?

Mrs. Linde: Something's happened to you since yesterday morning. Nora, what is it?

Nora (*going nearer to her*): Kristine! (*Listens.*) Shh! I hear Torvald. He's come home. Would you mind going in to the children's room for a little while? Torvald can't stand to see all this sewing going on. You can get Anne Marie to help you.

Mrs. Linde (*gathering some of the things together*): All right, but I'm not leaving this house until we've talked this thing through.

(*She goes into the room on the left, as Helmer comes in from the hall.*)

Nora (*going up to Helmer*): I've missed you so much, Torvald dear.

Helmer: Was that the seamstress?

Nora: No, it was Kristine. She's helping me fix up my dress. You'll see how nice I'm going to look.

Helmer: Wasn't that a good idea of mine, now?

Nora: Wonderful! But don't you think it's nice of me, too, to do what you said?

Helmer: Nice, because you do what your husband tells you to? Go on, you silly little thing, I am sure you didn't mean it like that. But I'll stay out of your way. I imagine you'll be trying on your dress.

Nora: I suppose you're going to do some work.

Helmer: Yes. (*Shows her a stack of papers.*) Look at that. I've just been at the bank. (*Turns to go into his room.*)

Nora: Torvald.

Helmer: Yes?

Nora: If your little squirrel were to ask you for something in a very, very charming way—

Helmer: Well?

Nora: Would you do it?

Helmer: I'd have to know what it is, first.

Nora: Your squirrel would run around and do all her tricks if you would be really nice and do what she wants.

Helmer: Speak plainly.

Nora: Your skylark would chirp her beautiful song in every room—

Helmer: Well, my skylark does that anyhow.

Nora: I'd be a little elf and dance in the moonlight for you, Torvald.

Helmer: Nora, you can't be referring to what you talked about this morning.

Nora (*moving close to him*): Yes, Torvald, I'm really begging you—

Helmer: You really have the nerve to bring that up again?

Nora: Yes, dear, you have to do this for me. You have to let Krogstad keep his job in the bank.

Helmer: My dear Nora, his job is the one that I'm giving to Mrs. Linde.

Nora: Yes, you've been awfully sweet about that. But you could just as easily get rid of somebody else instead of Krogstad.

Helmer: This is just unbelievable stubbornness! Because you decided to foolishly promise that you'd speak up for him, you expect me to—

Nora: That's not the reason, Torvald. It's for your own sake. This man writes for the trashiest newspapers, you've told me so yourself. He can do you an incredible amount of harm. I'm scared to death of him—

Helmer: Oh, I see, it's bad memories that are making you afraid.

Nora: What do you mean?

Helmer: Obviously you're thinking about your father.

Nora: Yes. Yes, of course. You remember what those hateful creatures wrote in the papers about Papa, and how horribly they slandered him. I believe they'd have gotten him fired if the department hadn't sent you over to look into it, and if you hadn't been so kind and helpful to him.

Helmer: My little Nora, there's an important difference between your father and me. His reputation as a public official was not above suspicion. Mine is, and I hope it will continue to be for as long as I hold my office.

Nora: You never can tell what trouble these men might cause. We could be so well off, so snug and happy here in our peaceful home, without a care in the world, you and I and the children, Torvald! That's why I'm begging you to—

Helmer: And the more you plead for him, the more you make it impossible for me to keep him. They already

know at the bank that I'm going to fire Krogstad. Do you think I'm going to let them all say that the new manager has changed his mind because his wife said to—

Nora: And what if they did?

Helmer: Right! What does it matter, as long as this stubborn little creature gets her own way! Do you think I'm going to make myself look ridiculous in front of my whole staff, and let people think that I can be pushed around by all sorts of outside influence? That would soon come back to haunt me, you can be sure! And besides, there's one thing that makes it totally impossible for me to have Krogstad working in the bank as long as I'm the manager.

Nora: What's that?

Helmer: I might have been able to overlook his moral failings, if need be—

Nora: Yes, you could do that, couldn't you?

Helmer: And I hear he's a good worker, too. But I knew him when we were boys. It was one of those rash friendships that so often turn out to be a millstone around the neck later on. I might as well tell you straight out, we were very close friends at one time. But he has no tact and no self-restraint, especially when other people are around. He thinks he has the right to still call me by my first name, and every minute it's Torvald this and Torvald that. I don't mind telling you, I find it extremely annoying. He would make my position at the bank intolerable.

Nora: Torvald, I can't believe you're serious.

Helmer: Oh no? Why not?

Nora: Because it's so petty.

Helmer: What do you mean, petty? You think I'm petty?

Nora: No, just the opposite, dear, and that's why I can't—

Helmer: It's the same thing. You say my attitude's petty, so I must be petty too! Petty! Fine! Well, I'll put a stop to this once and for all. (*Goes to the hall door and calls.*) Helene!

Nora: What are you going to do?

Helmer (*looking among his papers*): Settle it.

(*Enter Maid.*)

Here, take this letter downstairs right now. Find a messenger and tell him to deliver it, and to be quick about it. The address is on it, and here's the money.

Maid: Yes, sir. (*Exits with the letter.*)

Helmer (*putting his papers together*): There, Little Pigheaded Miss.

Nora (*breathlessly*): Torvald, what was that letter?

Helmer: Krogstad's notice.

Nora: Call her back, Torvald! There's still time. Oh, Torvald, call her back! Do it for my sake—for your own sake—for the children's sake! Do you hear me, Torvald? Call her back! You don't know what that letter can do to us.

Helmer: It's too late.

Nora: Yes, it's too late.

Helmer: My dear Nora, I can forgive this anxiety of yours, even though it's insulting to me. It really is. Don't you think it's insulting to suggest that I should be afraid of retaliation from a grubby pen-pusher? But I forgive you anyway, because it's such a beautiful demonstration of how much you love me. (*Takes her in his arms.*) And that is as it should be, my own darling Nora. Come what may, you can rest assured that I'll have both courage and strength if necessary. You'll see that I'm man enough to take everything on myself.

Nora (*in a horror-stricken voice*): What do you mean by that?

Helmer: Everything, I say.

Nora (*recovering herself*): You'll never have to do that.

Helmer: That's right, we'll take it on together, Nora, as man and wife. That's just how it should be. (*Caressing her.*) Are you satisfied now? There, there! Don't look at me that way, like a frightened dove! This whole thing is just your imagination running away with you. Now you should go and run through the tarantella and practice your tambourine. I'll go into my study and shut the door so I can't hear anything. You can make all the noise you want. (*Turns back at the door.*) And when Rank comes, tell him where I am.

(*Nods to her, takes his papers and goes into his room, and shuts the door behind him.*)

Nora (*bewildered with anxiety, stands as if rooted to the spot and whispers*): He's capable of doing it. He's going to do it. He'll do it in spite of everything. No, not that! Never, never! Anything but that! Oh, for somebody to help me find some way out of this! (*The doorbell rings.*) Doctor Rank! Anything but that—anything, whatever it is!

(*She puts her hands over her face, pulls herself together, goes to the door and opens it. Rank is standing in the hall, hanging up his coat. During the following dialogue it starts to grow dark.*)

Nora: Hello, Doctor Rank. I recognized your ring. But you'd better not go in and see Torvald just now. I think he's busy with something.

Rank: And you?

Nora (*brings him in and shuts the door behind him*): Oh, you know perfectly well I always have time for you.

Rank: Thank you. I'll make use of it for as long as I can.

Nora: What does that mean, for as long as you can?

Rank: Why, does that frighten you?

Nora: It was such a strange way of putting it. Is something going to happen?

Rank: Nothing but what I've been expecting for a long time. But I never thought it would happen so soon.

Nora (*gripping him by the arm*): What have you found out? Doctor Rank, you must tell me.

Rank (*sitting down by the stove*): I'm done for. And there's nothing I can do about it.

Nora (*with a sigh of relief*): Oh—you're talking about yourself?

Rank: Who else? And there's no use lying to myself. I'm the sickest patient I have, Mrs. Helmer. Lately I've been adding up my internal account. Bankrupt! In a month I'll probably be rotting in the ground.

Nora: what a horrible thing to say!

Rank: The thing itself is horrible, and the worst of it is all the horrible things I'll have to go through before it's over. I'm going to examine myself just once more. When that's done, I'll be pretty sure when I'm going to start breaking down. There's something I want to say to you. Helmer's sensitive nature makes him completely unable to deal with anything ugly. I don't want him in my sickroom.

Nora: Oh, but, Doctor Rank—

Rank: I won't have him there, period. I'll lock the door to keep him out. As soon as I'm quite sure that the worst has come, I'll send you my card with a black cross on it, and that way you'll know that the final stage of the horror has started.

Nora: You're being really absurd today. And I so much wanted you to be in a good mood.

Rank: With death stalking me? Having to pay this price for another man's sins? Where's the justice in that? In every single family, in one way or another, some such unavoidable retribution is being imposed.

Nora (*putting her hands over her ears*): Nonsense! Can't you talk about something cheerful?

Rank: Oh, this *is* something cheerful. In fact, it's hilarious. My poor innocent spine has to suffer for my father's youthful self-indulgence.

Nora (*sitting at the table on the left*): Yes, he did love asparagus and *pâté de foie gras*, didn't he?

Rank: Yes, and truffles.

Nora: Truffles, yes. And oysters too, I suppose?

Rank: Oysters, of course. That goes without saying.

Nora: And oceans of port and champagne. Isn't it sad that all those delightful things should take their revenge on our bones?

Rank: Especially that they should take their revenge on the unlucky bones of people who haven't even had the satisfaction of enjoying them.

Nora: Yes, that's the saddest part of all.

Rank (*with a searching look at her*): Hm!

Nora (*after a short pause*): Why did you smile?

Rank: No, it was you who laughed.

Nora: No, it was you who smiled, Doctor Rank!

Rank (*rising*): You're even more of a tease than I thought you were.

Nora: I am in a crazy mood today.

Rank: Apparently so.

Nora (*putting her hands on his shoulders*): Dear, dear Doctor Rank, we can't let death take you away from Torvald and me.

Rank: It's a loss that you'll easily recover from. Those who are gone are soon forgotten.

Nora (*looking at him anxiously*): Do you really believe that?

Rank: People make new friends, and then—

Nora: Who'll make new friends?

Rank: Both you and Helmer, when I'm gone. You yourself are already well on the way to it, I think. What was that Mrs. Linde doing here last night?

Nora: Oho! You're not telling me that you're jealous of poor Kristine, are you?

Rank: Yes, I am. She'll be my successor in this house. When I'm six feet under, this woman will—

Nora: Shh! Don't talk so loud. She's in that room.

Rank: Again today. There, you see.

Nora: She's just come to sew my dress for me. Goodness, how unreasonable you are! (*Sits down on the sofa.*) Be nice now, Doctor Rank, and tomorrow you'll see how beautifully I'll dance, and you can pretend that I'm doing it just for you—and for Torvald too, of course. (*Takes various things out of the box.*) Doctor Rank, come and sit down here, and I'll show you something.

Rank (*sitting down*): What is it?

Nora: Just look at these!

Rank: Silk stockings.

Nora: Flesh-colored. Aren't they lovely? It's so dark here now, but tomorrow—No, no, no! You're only supposed to look at the feet. Oh well, you have my permission to look at the legs too.

Rank: Hm!

Nora: Why do you look so critical? Don't you think they'll fit me?

Rank: I have no basis for forming an opinion on that subject.

Nora (*looks at him for a moment*): Shame on you! (*Hits him lightly on the ear with the stockings.*) That's your punishment. (*Folds them up again.*)

Rank: And what other pretty things do I have your permission to look at?

Nora: Not one single thing. That's what you get for being so naughty. (*She looks among the things, humming to herself.*)

Rank (*after a short silence*): When I'm sitting here, talking to you so intimately this way, I can't imagine for a moment what would have become of me if I'd never come into this house.

Nora (*smiling*): I believe you really do feel completely at home with us.

Rank (*in a lower voice, looking straight in front of him*): And to have to leave it all—

Nora: Nonsense, you're not going to leave it.

Rank (*as before*): And not to be able to leave behind the slightest token of my gratitude, hardly even a fleeting regret. Nothing but an empty place to be filled by the first person who comes along.

Nora: And if I were to ask you now for a—No, never mind!

Rank: For a what?

Nora: For a great proof of your friendship—

Rank: Yes, yes!

Nora: I mean a tremendously huge favor—

Rank: Would you really make me so happy, just this once?

Nora: But you don't know what it is yet.

Rank: No, but tell me.

Nora: I really can't, Doctor Rank. It's too much to ask. It involves advice, and help, and a favor—

Rank: So much the better. I can't imagine what you mean. Tell me what it is. You do trust me, don't you?

Nora: More than anyone. I know that you're my best and truest friend, so I'll tell you what it is. Well, Doctor

Rank, it's something you have to help me prevent. You know how devoted Torvald is to me, how deeply he loves me. He wouldn't hesitate for a second to give his life for me.

Rank (*leaning towards her*): Nora, do you think that he's the only one—

Nora (*with a slight start*): The only one?

Rank: Who would gladly give his life for you.

Nora (*sadly*): Oh, is that it?

Rank: I'd made up my mind to tell you before I—I go away, and there'll never be a better opportunity than this. Now you know it, Nora. And now you know that you can trust me more than you can trust anyone else.

Nora (*rises, deliberately and quietly*): Let me by.

Rank (*makes room for her to pass him, but sits still*): Nora!

Nora (*at the hall door*): Helene, bring in the lamp. (*Goes over to the stove.*) Dear Doctor Rank, that was really horrible of you.

Rank: To love you just as much as somebody else does? Is that so horrible?

Nora: No, but to go and tell me like that. There was really no need—

Rank: What do you mean? Did you know—

(*Maid enters with lamp, puts it down on the table, and goes out.*)

Nora—Mrs. Helmer—tell me, did you have any idea I felt this way?

Nora: Oh, how do I know whether I did or I didn't? I really can't answer that. How could you be so clumsy, Doctor Rank? When we were getting along so nicely.

Rank: Well, at any rate, now you know that I'm yours to command, body and soul. So won't you tell me what it is?

Nora (*looking at him*): After what just happened?

Rank: I beg you to let me know what it is.

Nora: I can't tell you anything now.

Rank: Yes, yes. Please don't punish me that way. Give me permission to do anything for you that a man can do.

Nora: You can't do anything for me now. Besides, I really don't need any help at all. The whole thing is just my imagination. It really is. It has to be! (*Sits down in the rocking chair, and smiles at him.*) You're a nice man, Doctor Rank. Don't you feel ashamed of yourself, now that the lamp is lit?

Rank: Not a bit. But maybe it would be better if I left— and never came back?

Nora: No, no, you can't do that. You must keep coming here just as you always did. You know very well Torvald can't do without you.

Rank: But what about you?

Nora: Oh, I'm always extremely pleased to see you.

Rank: And that's just what gave me the wrong idea. You're a puzzle to me. I've often felt that you'd almost just as soon be in my company as in Helmer's.

Nora: Yes, you see, there are the people you love the most, and then there are the people whose company you enjoy the most.

Rank: Yes, there's something to that.

Nora: When I lived at home, of course I loved Papa best. But I always thought it was great fun to sneak down to the maids' room, because they never preached at me, and I loved listening to the way they talked to each other.

Rank: I see. So I'm their replacement.

Nora (*jumping up and going to him*): Oh, dear, sweet Doctor Rank, I didn't mean it that way. But surely you can understand that being with Torvald is a little like being with Papa—

(*Enter Maid from the hall.*)

Maid: Excuse me, ma'am. (*Whispers and hands her a card.*)

Nora (*glancing at the card*): Oh! (*Puts it in her pocket.*)

Rank: Is something wrong?

Nora: No, no, not at all. It's just—it's my new dress—

Rank: What? Your dress is lying right there.

Nora: Oh, yes, that one. But this is another one, one that I ordered. I don't want Torvald to find out about it—

Rank: Oh! So that was the big secret.

Nora: Yes, that's it. Why don't you just go inside and see him? He's in his study. Stay with him for as long as—

Rank: Put your mind at ease. I won't let him escape. (*Goes into Helmer's study.*)

Nora (*to the maid*): And he's waiting in the kitchen?

Maid: Yes, ma'am. He came up the back stairs.

Nora: Didn't you tell him no one was home?

Maid: Yes, but it didn't do any good.

Nora: He won't go away?

Maid: No, he says he won't leave until he sees you, ma'am.

Nora: Well, show him in, but quietly. Helene, I don't want you to say anything about this to anyone. It's a surprise for my husband.

Maid: Yes, ma'am. I understand. (*Exit.*)

Nora: This horrible thing is really going to happen! It's going to happen in spite of me! No, no, no, it can't happen! I can't let it happen!

(*She bolts the door of Helmer's study. The maid opens the hall door for Krogstad and closes it behind him. He is wearing a fur coat, high boots, and a fur cap.*)

Nora (*advancing towards him*): Speak quietly. My husband's home.

Krogstad: What do I care about that?

Nora: What do you want from me?

Krogstad: An explanation of something.

Nora: Be quick, then. What is it?

Krogstad: I suppose you're aware that I've been let go.

Nora: I couldn't prevent it, Mr. Krogstad. I fought for you as hard as I could, but it was no use.

Krogstad: Does your husband love you so little, then? He knows what I can expose you to, and he still goes ahead and—

Nora: How can you think that he knows any such thing?

Krogstad: I didn't think so for a moment. It wouldn't be at all like dear old Torvald Helmer to show that kind of courage—

Nora: Mr. Krogstad, a little respect for my husband, please.

Krogstad: Certainly—all the respect he deserves. But since you've kept everything so carefully to yourself, may I be bold enough to assume that you see a little more clearly than you did yesterday just what it is that you've done?

Nora: More than you could ever teach me.

Krogstad: Yes, such a poor excuse for a lawyer as I am.

Nora: What is it you want from me?

Krogstad: Only to see how you're doing, Mrs. Helmer. I've been thinking about you all day. A mere bill collector, a pen-pusher, a—well, a man like me—even he has a little of what people call feelings, you know.

Nora: Why don't you show some, then? Think about my little children.

Krogstad: Have you and your husband thought about mine? But never mind about that. I just wanted to tell you not to take this business too seriously. I won't make any accusations against you. Not for now, anyway.

Nora: No, of course not. I was sure you wouldn't.

Krogstad: The whole thing can be settled amicably. There's no need for anyone to know anything about it. It'll be our little secret, just the three of us.

Nora: My husband must never know anything about it.

Krogstad: How are you going to keep him from finding out? Are you telling me that you can pay off the whole balance?

Nora: No, not just yet.

Krogstad: Or that you have some other way of raising the money soon?

Nora: No way that I plan to make use of.

Krogstad: Well, in any case, it wouldn't be any use to you now even if you did. If you stood in front of me with a stack of bills in each hand, I still wouldn't give you back your note.

Nora: What are you planning to do with it?

Krogstad: I just want to hold onto it, just keep it in my possession. No one who isn't involved in the matter will ever know anything about it. So, if you've been thinking about doing something desperate—

Nora: I have.

Krogstad: If you've been thinking about running away—

Nora: I have.

Krogstad: Or doing something even worse—

Nora: How could you know that?

Krogstad: Stop thinking about it.

Nora: How did you know I'd thought of that?

Krogstad: Most of us think about that at first. I did, too. But I didn't have the courage.

Nora (*faintly*): Neither do I.

Krogstad (*in a tone of relief*): No, that's true, isn't it? You don't have the courage either?

Nora: No, I don't. I don't.

Krogstad: Besides, it would have been an incredibly stupid thing to do. Once the first storm at home blows over . . . I have a letter for your husband in my pocket.

Nora: Telling him everything?

Krogstad: As gently as possible.

Nora (*quickly*): He can't see that letter. Tear it up. I'll find some way of getting money.

Krogstad: Excuse me, Mrs. Helmer, but didn't I just tell you—

Nora: I'm not talking about what I owe you. Tell me how much you want from my husband, and I'll get the money.

Krogstad: I don't want any money from your husband.

Nora: Then what do you want?

Krogstad: I'll tell you what I want. I want a fresh start, Mrs. Helmer, and I want to move up in the world. And your husband's going to help me do it. I've steered clear of anything questionable for the last year and a half. In all that time I've been struggling along, pinching every penny. I was content to work my way up step by step. But now I've been fired, and it's not going to be enough just to get my job back, as if you people were doing me some huge favor. I want to move up, I tell you. I want to get back into the bank again, but with a promotion. Your husband's going to have find me a position—

Nora: He'll never do it!

Krogstad: Oh yes, he will. I know him. He won't dare object. And as soon as I'm back there with him, then you'll see! Inside of a year I'll be the manager's right-hand man. It'll be Nils Krogstad, not Torvald Helmer, who's running the bank.

Nora: That's never going to happen!

Krogstad: Do you mean that you'll—

Nora: I have enough courage for it now.

Krogstad: Oh, you can't scare me. An elegant, spoiled lady like you—

Nora: You'll see, you'll see.

Krogstad: Under the ice, maybe? Down in the cold, coal-black water? And then floating up to the surface in the spring, all horrible and unrecognizable, with your hair fallen out—

Nora: You can't scare me.

Krogstad: And you can't scare me. People don't do that kind of thing, Mrs. Helmer. Besides, what good would it do? I'd still have him completely in my power.

Nora: Even then? When I'm no longer—

Krogstad: Have you forgotten that your reputation is completely in my hands? *(Nora stands speechless, looking at him.)* Well, now I've warned you. Don't do anything foolish. I'll be expecting an answer from Helmer after he reads my letter. And remember, it's your husband himself who's forced me to act this way again. I'll never forgive him for that. Goodbye, Mrs. Helmer. *(Exits through the hall.)*

Nora *(goes to the hall door, opens it slightly and listens.)*: He's leaving. He isn't putting the letter in the box. Oh no, no! He couldn't! *(Opens the door little by little.)* What? He's standing out there. He's not going downstairs. He's hesitating? Is he?

(A letter drops into the box. Then Krogstad's footsteps are heard, until they die away as he goes downstairs.

Nora utters a stifled cry, and runs across the room to the table by the sofa. A short pause.)

Nora: In the mailbox. *(Steals across to the hall door.)* It's there! Torvald, Torvald, there's no hope for us now!

(Mrs. Linde comes in from the room on the left, carrying the dress.)

Mrs. Linde: There, I can't find anything more to mend. Would you like to try it on?

Nora *(in a hoarse whisper)*: Kristine, come here.

Mrs. Linde *(throwing the dress down on the sofa)*: What's the matter with you? You look so agitated!

Nora: Come here. Do you see that letter? There, look. You can see it through the glass in the mailbox.

Mrs. Linde: Yes, I see it.

Nora: That letter is from Krogstad.

Mrs. Linde: Nora! It was Krogstad who lent you the money!

Nora: Yes, and now Torvald will know all about it.

Mrs. Linde: Believe me, Nora, that's the best thing for both of you.

Nora: You don't know the whole story. I forged a name.

Mrs. Linde: My God!

Nora: There's something I want to say to you, Kristine. I need you to be my witness.

Mrs. Linde: Your witness? What do you mean? What am I supposed to—

Nora: If I should go out of my mind—and it could easily happen—

Mrs. Linde: Nora!

Nora: Or if anything else should happen to me—anything, for instance, that might keep me from being here—

Mrs. Linde: Nora! Nora! What's the matter with you?

Nora: And if it turned out that somebody wanted to take all the responsibility, all the blame, you understand what I mean—

Mrs. Linde: Yes, yes, but how can you imagine—

Nora: Then you must be my witness that it's not true, Kristine. I'm not out of my mind at all. I'm perfectly rational right now, and I'm telling you that no one else ever knew anything about it. I did the whole thing all by myself. Remember that.

Mrs. Linde: I will. But I don't understand all this.

Nora: How could you understand it? Or the miracle that's going to happen!

Mrs. Linde: A miracle?

Nora: Yes, a miracle! But it's so terrible, Kristine. I can't let it happen, not for the whole world.

Mrs. Linde: I'll go and see Krogstad right this minute.

Nora: No, don't. He'll do something to hurt you too.

Mrs. Linde: There was a time when he would have gladly done anything for my sake.

Nora: What?

Mrs. Linde: Where does he live?

Nora: How should I know? Yes (*feeling in her pocket*), here's his card. But the letter, the letter—

Helmer (*calls from his room, knocking at the door*): Nora!

Nora (*cries out anxiously*): What is it? What do you want?

Helmer: Don't be so afraid. We're not coming in. You've locked the door. Are you trying on your dress?

Nora: Yes, that's it. Oh, it's going to look so nice, Torvald.

Mrs. Linde (*who has read the card*): Look, he lives right around the corner.

Nora: But it's no use. It's all over. The letter's lying right there in the box.

Mrs. Linde: And your husband has the key?

Nora: Yes, always.

Mrs. Linde: Krogstad can ask for his letter back unread. He'll have to make up some reason—

Nora: But now is just about the time that Torvald usually—

Mrs. Linde: You have to prevent him. Go in and talk to him. I'll be back as soon as I can.

(*She hurries out through the hall door.*)

Nora (*goes to Helmer's door, opens it and peeps in*): Torvald!

Helmer (*from the inner room*): Well? May I finally come back into my own room? Come along, Rank, now you'll see— (*Stopping in the doorway.*) But what's this?

Nora: What's what, dear?

Helmer: Rank led me to expect an amazing transformation.

Rank (*in the doorway*): So I understood, but apparently I was mistaken.

Nora: Yes, nobody gets to admire me in my dress until tomorrow.

Helmer: But, my dear Nora, you look exhausted. Have you been practicing too much?

Nora: No, I haven't been practicing at all.

Helmer: But you'll have to—

Nora: Yes, of course I will, Torvald. But I can't get anywhere without you helping me. I've completely forgotten the whole thing.

Helmer: Oh, we'll soon get you back up to form again.

Nora: Yes, help me, Torvald. Promise that you will! I'm so nervous about it—all those people. I need you to devote yourself completely to me this evening. Not even the tiniest little bit of business. You can't even pick up a pen. Do you promise, Torvald dear?

Helmer: I promise. This evening I will be wholly and absolutely at your service, you helpless little creature. But first I'm just going to— (*Goes towards the hall door.*)

Nora: Just going to what?

Helmer: To see if there's any mail.

Nora: No, no! Don't do that, Torvald!

Helmer: Why not?

Nora: Torvald, please don't. There's nothing there.

Helmer: Well, let me look. (*Turns to go to the mailbox. Nora, at the piano, plays the first bars of the tarantella. Helmer stops in the doorway.*) Aha!

Nora: I can't dance tomorrow if I don't practice with you.

Helmer (*going up to her*): Are you really so worried about it, dear?

Nora: Yes, terribly worried about it. Let me practice right now. We have time before dinner. Sit down and play for me, Torvald dear. Criticize me and correct me, the way you always do.

Helmer: With great pleasure, if you want me to. (*Sits down at the piano.*)

Nora (*takes a tambourine and a long multicolored shawl out of the box. She hastily drapes the shawl around her. Then she bounds to the front of the stage and calls out*): Now play for me! I'm going to dance!

(*Helmer plays and Nora dances. Rank stands by the piano behind Helmer and watches.*)

Helmer (*as he plays*): Slower, slower!

Nora: I can't do it any other way.

Helmer: Not so violently, Nora!

Nora: This is the way.

Helmer (*stops playing*): No, no, that's not right at all.

Nora (*laughing and swinging the tambourine*): Didn't I tell you so?

Rank: Let me play for her.

Helmer (*getting up*): Good idea. I can correct her better that way.

(*Rank sits down at the piano and plays. Nora dances more and more wildly. Helmer has taken up a position beside the stove, and as she dances, he gives her frequent instructions. She doesn't seem to hear him. Her hair comes undone and falls over her shoulders. She pays no attention to it, but goes on dancing. Enter Mrs. Linde.*)

Mrs. Linde (*standing as if spellbound in the doorway*): Oh!

Nora (*as she dances*): What fun, Kristine!

Helmer: My dear darling Nora, you're dancing as if your life depended on it.

Nora: It does.

Helmer: Stop, Rank. This is insane! I said stop!

(*Rank stops playing, and Nora suddenly stands still. Helmer goes up to her.*)

I never would have believed it. You've forgotten everything I taught you.

Nora (*throwing the tambourine aside*): There, you see.

Helmer: You're going to need a lot of coaching.

Nora: Yes, you see how much I need it. You have to coach me right up to the last minute. Promise me you will, Torvald!

Helmer: You can depend on me.

Nora: You can't think about anything but me, today or tomorrow. Don't open a single letter. Don't even open the mailbox—

Helmer: You're still afraid of that man—

Nora: Yes, yes, I am.

Helmer: Nora, I can tell from your face that there's a letter from him in the box.

Nora: I don't know. I think there is. But you can't read anything like that now. Nothing nasty must come between us until this is all over.

Rank (*whispers to Helmer*): Don't contradict her.

Helmer (*taking her in his arms*): The child shall have her way. But tomorrow night, after you've danced—

Nora: Then you'll be free. (*The Maid appears in the doorway to the right.*)

Maid: Dinner is served, ma'am.

Nora: We'll have champagne, Helene.

Maid: Yes, ma'am. (*Exit.*)

Helmer: Oh, are we having a banquet?

Nora: Yes, a banquet. Champagne till dawn! (*Calls out.*) And a few macaroons, Helene. Lots of them, just this once!

Helmer: Come on, stop acting so wild and nervous. Be my own little skylark again.

Nora: Yes, dear, I will. But go inside now, and you too, Doctor Rank. Kristine, please help me do up my hair.

Rank (*whispers to Helmer as they go out*): There isn't anything—she's not expecting—?

Helmer: No, nothing like that. It's just this childish nervousness I was telling you about. (*They go into the right-hand room.*)

Nora: Well?

Mrs. Linde: Out of town.

Nora: I could tell from your face.

Mrs. Linde: He'll be back tomorrow evening. I wrote him a note.

Nora: You should have left it alone. Don't try to prevent anything. After all, it's exciting to be waiting for a miracle to happen.

Mrs. Linde: What is it that you're waiting for?

Nora: Oh, you wouldn't understand. Go inside with them, I'll be there in a moment.

(*Mrs. Linde goes into the dining room. Nora stands still for a little while, as if to compose herself. Then she looks at her watch.*)

Five o'clock. Seven hours till midnight, and another twenty-four hours till the next midnight. And then the tarantella will be over. Twenty-four plus seven? Thirty-one hours to live.

Helmer (*from the doorway on the right*): Where's my little skylark?

Nora (*going to him with her arms outstretched*): Here she is!

ACT III

The same scene. The table has been placed in the middle of the stage, with chairs around it. A lamp is burning on the table. The door into the hall stands open. Dance music is heard in the room above. Mrs. Linde is sitting at the table idly turning over the pages of a book. She tries to read, but she seems unable to concentrate. Every now and then she listens intently for a sound at the outer door.

Mrs. Linde (*looking at her watch*): Not yet—and the time's nearly up. If only he doesn't— (*Listens again.*) Ah, there he is. (*Goes into the hall and opens the outer door carefully. Light footsteps are heard on the stairs. She whispers.*) Come in. There's no one else here.

Krogstad (*in the doorway*): I found a note from you at home. What does this mean?

Mrs. Linde: It's absolutely necessary that I have a talk with you.

Krogstad: Really? And is it absolutely necessary that we have it here?

Mrs. Linde: It's impossible where I live. There's no private entrance to my apartment. Come in. We're all alone. The maid's asleep, and the Helmers are upstairs at a dance.

Krogstad (*coming into the room*): Are the Helmers really at a dance tonight?

Mrs. Linde: Yes. Why shouldn't they be?

Krogstad: Certainly—why not?

Mrs. Linde: Now, Nils, let's have a talk.

Krogstad: What can we two have to talk about?

Mrs. Linde: Quite a lot.

Krogstad: I wouldn't have thought so.

Mrs. Linde: Of course not. You've never really understood me.

Krogstad: What was there to understand, except what the whole world could see—a heartless woman drops a man when a better catch comes along?

Mrs. Linde: Do you think I'm really that heartless? And that I broke it off with you so lightly?

Krogstad: Didn't you?

Mrs. Linde: Nils, did you really think that?

Krogstad: If not, why did you write what you did to me?

Mrs. Linde: What else could I do? Since I had to break it off with you, I had an obligation to stamp out your feelings for me.

Krogstad (*wringing his hands*): So that was it. And all this just for the sake of money!

Mrs. Linde: Don't forget that I had an invalid mother and two little brothers. We couldn't wait for you, Nils. Success seemed a long way off for you back then.

Krogstad: That may be so, but you had no right to cast me aside for anyone else's sake.

Mrs. Linde: I don't know if I did or not. Many times I've asked myself if I had the right.

Krogstad (*more gently*): When I lost you, it was as if the earth crumbled under my feet. Look at me now— a shipwrecked man clinging to a bit of wreckage.

Mrs. Linde: But help may be on the way.

Krogstad: It *was* on the way, till you came along and blocked it.

Mrs. Linde: Without knowing it, Nils. It wasn't till today that I found out I'd be taking your job.

Krogstad: I believe you, if you say so. But now that you know it, are you going to step aside?

Mrs. Linde: No, because it wouldn't do you any good.

Krogstad: Good? *I* would quit whether it did any good or not.

Mrs. Linde: I've learned to be practical. Life and hard, bitter necessity have taught me that.

Krogstad: And life has taught me not to believe in fine speeches.

Mrs. Linde: Then life has taught you something very sensible. But surely you believe in actions?

Krogstad: What do you mean by that?

Mrs. Linde: You said you were like a shipwrecked man clinging to a piece of wreckage.

Krogstad: I had good reason to say so.

Mrs. Linde: Well, I'm like a shipwrecked woman clinging to a piece of wreckage, with no one to mourn for and no one to care for.

Krogstad: That was your own choice.

Mrs. Linde: I had no other choice—then.

Krogstad: Well, what about now?

Mrs. Linde: Nils, how would it be if we two shipwrecked people could reach out to each other?

Krogstad: What are you saying?

Mrs. Linde: Two people on the same piece of wreckage would stand a better chance than each one on their own.

Krogstad: Kristine, I . . .

Mrs. Linde: Why do you think I came to town?

Krogstad: You can't mean that you were thinking about me?

Mrs. Linde: Life is unendurable without work. I've worked all my life, for as long as I can remember, and it's been my greatest and my only pleasure. But now that I'm completely alone in the world, my life is so terribly empty and I feel so abandoned. There isn't the slightest pleasure in working only for yourself. Nils, give me someone and something to work for.

Krogstad: I don't trust this. It's just some romantic female impulse, a high-minded urge for self-sacrifice.

Mrs. Linde: Have you ever known me to be like that?

Krogstad: Could you really do it? Tell me, do you know all about my past?

Mrs. Linde: Yes.

Krogstad: And you know what they think of me around here?

Mrs. Linde: Didn't you imply that with me you might have been a very different person?

Krogstad: I'm sure I would have.

Mrs. Linde: Is it too late now?

Krogstad: Kristine, are you serious about all this? Yes, I'm sure you are. I can see it in your face. Do you really have the courage, then—

Mrs. Linde: I want to be a mother to someone, and your children need a mother. We two need each other. Nils, I have faith in your true nature. I can face anything together with you.

Krogstad (*grasps her hands*): Thank you, thank you, Kristine! Now I can find a way to clear myself in the eyes of the world. Ah, but I forgot—

Mrs. Linde (*listening*): Shh! The tarantella! You have to go!

Krogstad: Why? What's the matter?

Mrs. Linde: Do you hear them up there? They'll probably come home as soon as this dance is over.

Krogstad: Yes, yes, I'll go. But it won't make any difference. You don't know what I've done about my situation with the Helmers.

Mrs. Linde: Yes, I know all about that.

Krogstad: And in spite of that you still have the courage to—

Mrs. Linde: I understand completely what despair can drive a man like you to do.

Krogstad: If only I could undo it!

Mrs. Linde: You can't. Your letter's lying in the mailbox now.

Krogstad: Are you sure?

Mrs. Linde: Quite sure, but—

Krogstad (*with a searching look at her*): Is that what this is all about? That you want to save your friend, no matter what you have to do? Tell me the truth. Is that it?

Mrs. Linde: Nils, when a woman has sold herself for someone else's sake, she doesn't do it a second time.

Krogstad: I'll ask for my letter back.

Mrs. Linde: No, no.

Krogstad: Yes, of course I will. I'll wait here until Helmer comes home. I'll tell him he has to give me back my letter, that it's only about my being fired, that I don't want him to read it—

Mrs. Linde: No, Nils, don't ask for it back.

Krogstad: But wasn't that the reason why you asked me to meet you here?

Mrs. Linde: In my first moment of panic, it was. But twenty-four hours have gone by since then, and in the meantime I've seen some incredible things in this house. Helmer has to know all about it. This terrible secret has to come out. They have to have a complete understanding between them. It's time for all this lying and pretending to stop.

Krogstad: All right then, if you think it's worth the risk. But there's at least one thing I can do, and do right away—

Mrs. Linde (*listening*): You have to leave this instant! The dance is over. They could walk in here any minute.

Krogstad: I'll wait for you downstairs.

Mrs. Linde: Yes, please do. I want you to walk me home.

Krogstad: I've never been so happy in my entire life!

(*Goes out through the outer door. The door between the room and the hall remains open.*)

Mrs. Linde (*straightening up the room and getting her hat and coat ready*): How different things will be! Someone to work for and live for, a home to bring happiness into. I'm certainly going to try. I wish they'd hurry up and come home—(*Listens.*) Ah, here they are now. I'd better put on my things.

(*Picks up her hat and coat. Helmer's and Nora's voices are heard outside. A key is turned, and Helmer brings Nora into the hall almost by force. She is in an Italian peasant costume with a large black shawl wrapped around her. He is in formal wear and a black domino—a hooded cloak with an eye-mask—which is open.*)

Nora (*hanging back in the doorway and struggling with him*): No, no, no! Don't bring me inside. I want to go back upstairs. I don't want to leave so early.

Helmer: But, my dearest Nora—

Nora: Please, Torvald dear, please, please, only one more hour.

Helmer: Not one more minute, my sweet Nora. You know this is what we agreed on. Come inside. You'll catch cold standing out there.

(*He brings her gently into the room, in spite of her resistance.*)

Mrs. Linde: Good evening.

Nora: Kristine!

Helmer: What are you doing here so late, Mrs. Linde?

Mrs. Linde: You must excuse me. I was so anxious to see Nora in her dress.

Nora: Have you been sitting here waiting for me?

Mrs. Linde: Yes, unfortunately I came too late, you'd already gone upstairs. And I didn't want to go away again without seeing you.

Helmer (*taking off Nora's shawl*): Yes, take a good look at her. I think she's worth looking at. Isn't she charming, Mrs. Linde?

Mrs. Linde: Yes, indeed she is.

Helmer: Doesn't she look especially pretty? Everyone thought so at the dance. But this sweet little person is extremely stubborn. What are we going to do with her? Believe it or not, I almost had to drag her away by force.

Nora: Torvald, you'll be sorry you didn't let me stay, even if only for half an hour.

Helmer: Listen to her, Mrs. Linde! She danced her tarantella and it was a huge success, as it deserved to be, though maybe her performance was a tiny bit too realistic, a little more so than it might have been by strict artistic standards. But never mind about that! The main thing is, she was a success, a tremendous success. Do you think I was going to let her stay there after that, and spoil the effect? Not a chance! I took my charming little Capri girl—my capricious little Capri girl, I should say—I took her by the arm, one quick circle around the room, a curtsey to one and all, and, as they say in novels, the beautiful vision vanished. An exit should always make an effect, Mrs. Linde, but I can't make Nora understand that. Whew, this room is hot!

(*Throws his domino on a chair and opens the door to his study.*)

Why is it so dark in here? Oh, of course. Excuse me.

(*He goes in and lights some candles.*)

Nora (*in a hurried, breathless whisper*): Well?

Mrs. Linde (*in a low voice*): I talked to him.

Nora: And?

Mrs. Linde: Nora, you have to tell your husband the whole story.

Nora (*in an expressionless voice*): I knew it.

Mrs. Linde: You have nothing to fear from Krogstad, but you still have to tell him.

Nora: I'm not going to.

Mrs. Linde: Then the letter will.

Nora: Thank you, Kristine. Now I know what I have to do. Shh!

Helmer (*coming in again*): Well, Mrs. Linde, have you been admiring her?

Mrs. Linde: Yes, I have, and now I'll say goodnight.

Helmer: What, already? Is this your knitting?

Mrs. Linde (*taking it*): Yes, thank you, I'd almost forgotten it.

Helmer: So you knit?

Mrs. Linde: Yes, of course.

Helmer: You know, you ought to embroider.

Mrs. Linde: Really? Why?

Helmer: It's much more graceful-looking. Here, let me show you. You hold the embroidery this way in your left hand, and use the needle with your right, like this, with a long, easy sweep. Do you see?

Mrs. Linde: Yes, I suppose—

Helmer: But knitting, that can never be anything but awkward. Here, look. The arms close together, the knitting needles going up and down. It's sort of Chinese looking. That was really excellent champagne they gave us.

Mrs. Linde: Well, good night, Nora, and don't be stubborn anymore.

Helmer: That's right, Mrs. Linde.

Mrs. Linde: Good night, Mr. Helmer.

Helmer (*seeing her to the door*): Good night, good night. I hope you get home safely. I'd be very happy to—but you only have a short way to go. Good night, good night.

(*She goes out. He closes the door behind her, and comes in again.*)

Ah, rid of her at last! What a bore that woman is.

Nora: Aren't you tired, Torvald?

Helmer: No, not at all.

Nora: You're not sleepy?

Helmer: Not a bit. As a matter of fact, I feel very lively. And what about you? You really look tired *and* sleepy.

Nora: Yes, I am very tired. I want to go to sleep right away.

Helmer: So, you see how right I was not to let you stay there any longer.

Nora: You're always right, Torvald.

Helmer (*kissing her on the forehead*): Now my little skylark is talking sense. Did you notice what a good mood Rank was in this evening?

Nora: Really? Was he? I didn't talk to him at all.

Helmer: And I only talked to him for a little while, but it's a long time since I've seen him so cheerful. (*Looks at her for a while and then moves closer to her.*) It's delightful to be home again by ourselves, to be alone with you, you fascinating, charming little darling!

Nora: Don't look at me like that, Torvald.

Helmer: Why shouldn't I look at my dearest treasure? At all the beauty that is mine, all my very own?

Nora (*going to the other side of the table*): I wish you wouldn't talk that way to me tonight.

Helmer (*following her*): You've still got the tarantella in your blood, I see. And it makes you more captivating than ever. Listen, the guests are starting to leave now. (*In a lower voice.*) Nora, soon the whole house will be quiet.

Nora: Yes, I hope so.

Helmer: Yes, my own darling Nora. Do you know why, when we're out at a party like this, why I hardly talk to you, and keep away from you, and only steal a glance at you now and then? Do you know why I do that? It's because I'm pretending to myself that we're secretly in love, and we're secretly engaged, and no one suspects that there's anything between us.

Nora: Yes, yes, I know you're thinking about me every moment.

Helmer: And when we're leaving, and I'm putting the shawl over your beautiful young shoulders, on your lovely neck, then I imagine that you're my young bride and that we've just come from our wedding and I'm bringing you home for the first time, to be alone with you for the first time, all alone with my shy little darling! This whole night I've been longing for you alone. My blood was on fire watching you move when you danced the tarantella. I couldn't stand it any longer, and that's why I brought you home so early—

Nora: Stop it, Torvald! Let me go. I won't—

Helmer: What? You're not serious, Nora! You won't? You won't? I'm your husband—

(*There is a knock at the outer door.*)

Nora (*starting*): Did you hear—

Helmer (*going into the hall*): Who is it?

Rank (*outside*): It's me. May I come in for a moment?

Helmer (*in an irritated whisper*): What does he want now? (*Aloud.*) Wait a minute! (*Unlocks the door.*) Come in. It's good of you not to pass by our door without saying hello.

Rank: I thought I heard your voice, and I felt like dropping by. (*With a quick look around.*) Ah, yes, these dear familiar rooms. You two are very happy and cozy in here.

Helmer: You seemed to be making yourself pretty happy upstairs too.

Rank: Very much so. Why shouldn't I? Why shouldn't we enjoy everything in this world? At least as much as we can, for as long as we can. The wine was first-rate—

Helmer: Especially the champagne.

Rank: So you noticed that too? It's almost unbelievable how much of it I managed to put away!

Nora: Torvald drank a lot of champagne tonight too.

Rank: Did he?

Nora: Yes, and it always makes him so merry.

Rank: Well, why shouldn't a person have a merry evening after a well-spent day?

Helmer: Well-spent? I'm afraid I can't take credit for that.

Rank (*clapping him on the back*): But I can, you know!

Nora: Doctor Rank, you must have been busy with some scientific investigation today.

Rank: Exactly.

Helmer: Listen to this! Little Nora talking about scientific investigations!

Nora: And may I congratulate you on the result?

Rank: Indeed you may.

Nora: Was it favorable, then?

Rank: The best possible result, for both doctor and patient—certainty.

Nora (*quickly and searchingly*): Certainty?

Rank: Absolute certainty. So wasn't I entitled to make a merry evening of it after that?

Nora: Yes, you certainly were, Doctor Rank.

Helmer: I think so too, as long as you don't have to pay for it in the morning.

Rank: Oh well, you can't have anything in this life without paying for it.

Nora: Doctor Rank, are you fond of fancy-dress balls?

Rank: Yes, if there are a lot of pretty costumes.

Nora: Tell me, what should the two of us wear to the next one?

Helmer: Little featherbrain! You're thinking of the next one already?

Rank: The two of us? Yes, I can tell you. You'll go as a good-luck charm—

Helmer: Yes, but what would be the costume for that?

Rank: She just needs to dress the way she always does.

Helmer: That was very nicely put. But aren't you going to tell us what you'll be?

Rank: Yes, my dear friend, I've already made up my mind about that.

Helmer: Well?

Rank: At the next fancy-dress ball I'm going to be invisible.

Helmer: That's a good one!

Rank: There's a big black cap . . . Haven't you ever heard of the cap that makes you invisible? Once you put it on, no one can see you anymore.

Helmer (*suppressing a smile*): Yes, that's right.

Rank: But I'm clean forgetting what I came for. Helmer, give me a cigar. One of the dark Havanas.

Helmer: With the greatest pleasure. (*Offers him his case.*)

Rank (*takes a cigar and cuts off the end*): Thanks.

Nora (*striking a match*): Let me give you a light.

Rank: Thank you. (*She holds the match for him to light his cigar.*) And now goodbye!

Helmer: Goodbye, goodbye, my dear old friend.

Nora: Sleep well, Doctor Rank.

Rank: Thank you for that wish.

Nora: Wish me the same.

Rank: You? Well, if you want me to. Sleep well! And thanks for the light. (*He nods to them both and goes out.*)

Helmer (*in a subdued voice*): He's had too much to drink.

Nora (*absently*): Maybe.

(*Helmer takes a bunch of keys out of his pocket and goes into the hall.*)

Torvald! What are you going to do out there?

Helmer: Empty the mailbox. It's quite full. There won't be any room for the newspaper in the morning.

Nora: Are you going to work tonight?

Helmer: You know I'm not. What's this? Someone's been at the lock.

Nora: At the lock?

Helmer: Yes, it's been tampered with. What does this mean? I never would have thought the maid— Look, here's a broken hairpin. It's one of yours, Nora.

Nora (*quickly*): Then it must have been the children—

Helmer: Then you'd better break them of those habits. There, I've finally got it open.

(*Empties the mailbox and calls out to the kitchen.*)

Helene! Helene, put out the light over the front door.

(*Comes back into the room and shuts the door into the hall. He holds out his hand full of letters.*)

Look at that. Look what a pile of them there are. (*Turning them over.*) What's this?

Nora (*at the window*): The letter! No! Torvald, no!

Helmer: Two calling cards of Rank's.

Nora: Of Doctor Rank's?

Helmer (*looking at them*): Yes, Doctor Rank. They were on top. He must have put them in there when he left just now.

Nora: Is there anything written on them?

Helmer: There's a black cross over the name. Look. What a morbid thing to do! It looks as if he's announcing his own death.

Nora: That's exactly what he's doing.

Helmer: What? Do you know anything about it? Has he said anything to you?

Nora: Yes. He told me that when the cards came it would be his farewell to us. He means to close himself off and die.

Helmer: My poor old friend! Of course I knew we wouldn't have him for very long. But this soon! And he goes and hides himself away like a wounded animal.

Nora: If it has to happen, it's better that it be done without a word. Don't you think so, Torvald?

Helmer (*walking up and down*): He's become so much a part of our lives, I can't imagine him not being with us anymore. With his poor health and his loneliness, he was like a cloudy background to our sunlit happiness. Well, maybe it's all for the best. For him, anyway. (*Standing still.*) And maybe for us too, Nora. Now we have only each other to rely on. (*Puts his arms around her.*) My darling wife, I feel as though I can't possibly hold you tight enough. You know, Nora, I've often wished you were in some kind of serious danger, so that I could risk everything, even my own life, to save you.

Nora (*disengages herself from him, and says firmly and decidedly*): Now you must go and read your letters, Torvald.

Helmer: No, no, not tonight. I want to be with you, my darling wife.

Nora: With the thought of your friend's death—

Helmer: You're right, it has affected us both. Something ugly has come between us, the thought of the horrors of death. We have to try to put it out of our minds. Until we do, we'll each go to our own room.

Nora (*with her arms around his neck*): Good night, Torvald. Good night!

Helmer (*kissing her on the forehead*): Good night, my little songbird. Sleep well, Nora. Now I'll go read all my mail. (*He takes his letters and goes into his room, shutting the door behind him.*)

Nora (*gropes distractedly about, picks up Helmer's domino and wraps it around her, while she says in quick, hoarse, spasmodic whispers*): Never to see him again. Never! Never! (*Puts her shawl over her head.*) Never to see my children again either, never again. Never! Never! Oh, the icy, black water, the bottomless depths! If only it were over! He's got it now, now he's reading it. Goodbye, Torvald . . . children!

(*She is about to rush out through the hall when Helmer opens his door hurriedly and stands with an open letter in his hand.*)

Helmer: Nora!

Nora: Ah!

Helmer: What is this? Do you know what's in this letter?

Nora: Yes, I know. Let me go! Let me get out!

Helmer (*holding her back*): Where are you going?

Nora (*trying to get free*): You're not going to save me, Torvald!

Helmer (*reeling*): It's true? Is this true, what it says here? This is horrible! No, no, it can't possibly be true.

Nora: It is true. I've loved you more than anything else in the world.

Helmer: Don't start with your ridiculous excuses.

Nora (*taking a step towards him*): Torvald!

Helmer: You little fool, do you know what you've done?

Nora: Let me go. I won't let you suffer for my sake. You're not going to take it on yourself.

Helmer: Stop play-acting. (*Locks the hall door.*) You're going to stay right here and give me an explanation. Do you understand what you've done? Answer me! Do you understand what you've done?

Nora (*looks steadily at him and says with a growing look of coldness in her face*): Yes, I'm beginning to understand everything now.

Helmer (*walking around the room*): What a horrible awakening! The woman who was my pride and joy for eight years, a hypocrite, a liar, worse than that, much worse—a criminal! The unspeakable ugliness of it all! The shame of it! The shame!

(*Nora is silent and looks steadily at him. He stops in front of her.*)

I should have realized that something like this was bound to happen. I should have seen it coming. Your father's shifty nature—be quiet!—your father's shifty nature has come out in you. No religion, no morality, no sense of duty. This is my punishment for closing my eyes to what he did! I did it for your sake, and this is how you pay me back.

Nora: Yes, that's right.

Helmer: Now you've destroyed all my happiness. You've ruined my whole future. It's horrible to think about! I'm in the power of an unscrupulous man. He can do what he wants with me, ask me for anything he wants, give me any orders he wants, and I don't dare say no. And I have to sink to such miserable depths, all because of a feather-brained woman!

Nora: When I'm out of the way, you'll be free.

Helmer: Spare me the speeches. Your father had always plenty of those on hand, too. What good would it do me if you were out of the way, as you say? Not the slightest. He can tell everybody the whole story. And if he does, I could be wrongly suspected of having been in on it with you. People will probably think I was behind it all, that I put you up to it! And I have you to thank for all this, after I've cherished you the whole time we've been married. Do you understand what you've done to me?

Nora (*coldly and quietly*): Yes.

Helmer: It's so incredible that I can't take it all in. But we have to come to some understanding. Take off that shawl. Take it off, I said. I have to try to appease him some way or another. It has to be hushed up, no matter what it costs. And as for you and me, we have to make it look as if everything is just as it always was, but only for the sake of appearances, obviously. You'll stay here in my house, of course. But I won't let you bring up the children. I can't trust them to you. To think that I have to say these things to someone I've loved so dearly, and that I still—No, that's all over. From this moment on happiness is out of the question. All that matters now is to save the bits and pieces, to keep up the appearance—

(The front doorbell rings.)

Helmer (*with a start*): What's that? At this hour! Can the worst—Can he—Go and hide yourself, Nora. Say you don't feel well. (*Nora stands motionless. Helmer goes and unlocks the hall door.*)

Maid (*half-dressed, comes to the door*): A letter for Mrs. Helmer.

Helmer: Give it to me. (*Takes the letter, and shuts the door.*) Yes, it's from him. I'm not giving it to you. I'll read it myself.

Nora: Go ahead, read it.

Helmer (*standing by the lamp*): I barely have the courage to. It could mean ruin for both of us. No, I have to know. (*Tears open the letter, runs his eye over a few lines, looks at a piece of paper enclosed with it, and gives a shout of joy.*) Nora! (*She looks at him questioningly.*) Nora! No, I'd better read it again. Yes, it's true! I'm saved! Nora, I'm saved!

Nora: And what about me?

Helmer: You too, of course. We're both saved, you and I. Look, he's returned your note. He says he's sorry and he apologizes—that a happy change in his life—what difference does it make what he says! We're saved, Nora! Nobody can hurt you. Oh, Nora, Nora! No, first I have to destroy these horrible things. Let me see. . . . (*Glances at the note.*) No, no, I don't want to look at it. This whole business will be nothing but a bad dream to me.

(Tears up the note and both letters, throws them all into the stove, and watches them burn.)

There, now it doesn't exist anymore. He says that you've known since Christmas Eve. These must have been a horrible three days for you, Nora.

Nora: I fought a hard fight these three days.

Helmer: And suffered agonies, and saw no way out but—No, we won't dwell on any of those horrors. We'll just shout for joy and keep saying, "It's all over! It's all over!" Listen to me, Nora. You don't seem to realize that it's all over. What's this? Such a cold, hard face! My poor little Nora, I understand. You find it hard to believe that I've really forgiven you. But I swear that it's true, Nora. I forgive you for everything. I know that you did it all out of love for me.

Nora: That's true.

Helmer: You've loved me the way a wife ought to love her husband. You just didn't have the awareness to see what was wrong with the means you used. But do you think I love you any less because you don't understand how to deal with these things? No, of course not. I want you to lean on me. I'll advise you and guide you. I wouldn't be a man if this womanly helplessness didn't make you twice as attractive to me. Don't think anymore about the hard things I said when I was so upset at first, when I thought everything was going to crush me. I forgive you, Nora. I swear to you that I forgive you.

Nora: Thank you for your forgiveness. (*She goes out through the door to the right.*)

Helmer: No, don't go—(*Looks in.*) What are you doing in there?

Nora (*from within*): Taking off my costume.

Helmer (*standing at the open door*): Yes, do. Try to calm yourself, and ease your mind again, my frightened little songbird. I want you to rest and feel secure. I have wide wings for you to take shelter underneath. (*Walks up and down by the door.*) What a warm and cozy home we have, Nora: Here's a safe haven for you, and I'll protect you like a hunted dove that I've rescued from a hawk's claws. I'll calm your poor pounding heart. It will happen, little by little, Nora, believe me. In the morning you'll see it in a very different light. Soon everything will be exactly the way it was before. Before you know it, you won't need my reassurances that I've forgiven you. You'll know for certain that I have. You can't imagine that I'd ever consider rejecting you, or even blaming you? You have no idea what a man feels in his heart, Nora. A man finds it indescribably sweet and satisfying to know that he's forgiven his wife, freely and with all his heart. It's as if he's made her his own all over again. He's given her a new life, in a way, and she's become both wife and child to him. And from this moment on that's what you'll be to me, my little scared, helpless darling. Don't worry about anything, Nora. Just be honest and open with me, and I'll be your will and your conscience. What's this? You haven't gone to bed yet? Have you changed?

Nora (*in everyday dress*): Yes, Torvald, I've changed.

Helmer: But why—It's so late.

Nora: I'm not going to sleep tonight.

Helmer: But, my dear Nora—

Nora (*looking at her watch*): It's not that late. Sit down here, Torvald. You and I have a lot to talk about. (*She sits down at one side of the table.*)

Helmer: Nora, what is this? Why this cold, hard face?

Nora: Sit down. This is going to take a while. I have a lot to say to you.

Helmer (*sits down at the opposite side of the table*): You're making me nervous, Nora. And I don't understand you.

Nora: No, that's it exactly. You don't understand me, and I've never understood you either, until tonight. No, don't interrupt me. I want you to listen to what I have to say. Torvald, I'm settling accounts with you.

Helmer: What do you mean by that?

Nora (*after a short silence*): Doesn't anything strike you as odd about the way we're sitting here like this?

Helmer: No, what?

Nora: We've been married for eight years. Doesn't it occur to you that this is the first time the two of us, you and I, husband and wife, have had a serious conversation?

Helmer: What do you mean by serious?

Nora: In the whole eight years—longer than that, for the whole time we've known each other—we've never exchanged one word on any serious subject.

Helmer: Did you expect me to be constantly worrying you with problems that you weren't capable of helping me deal with?

Nora: I'm not talking about business. I mean we've never sat down together seriously to try to get to the bottom of anything.

Helmer: But, dearest Nora, what good would that have done you?

Nora: That's just it. You've never understood me. I've been treated badly, Torvald, first by Papa and then by you.

Helmer: What? The two people who've loved you more than anyone else?

Nora (*shaking her head*): You've never loved me. You just thought it was pleasant to be in love with me.

Helmer: Nora, what are you saying?

Nora: It's true, Torvald. When I lived at home with Papa, he gave me his opinion about everything, and so I had all the same opinions, and if I didn't, I kept my mouth shut, because he wouldn't have liked it. He used to call me his doll-child, and he played with me the way I played with my dolls. And when I came to live in your house—

Helmer: What kind of way is that to talk about our marriage?

Nora (*undisturbed*): I mean that I was just passed from Papa's hands to yours. You arranged everything according to your own taste, and so I had all the same

tastes as you. Or else I pretended to, I'm not really sure which. Sometimes I think it's one way and sometimes the other. When I look back, it's as if I've been living here like a beggar, from hand to mouth. I've supported myself by performing tricks for you, Torvald. But that's the way you wanted it. You and Papa have committed a terrible sin against me. It's your fault that I've done nothing with my life.

Helmer: This is so unfair and ungrateful of you, Nora! Haven't you been happy here?

Nora: No, I've never really been happy. I thought I was, but it wasn't true.

Helmer: Not—not happy!

Nora: No, just cheerful. You've always been very kind to me. But our home's been nothing but a playroom. I've been your doll-wife, the same way that I was papa's doll-child. And the children have been my dolls. I thought it was great fun when you played with me, the way they thought it was when I played with them. That's what our marriage has been, Torvald.

Helmer: There's some truth in what you're saying, even though your view of it is exaggerated and overwrought. But things will be different from now on. Playtime is over, and now it's lesson-time.

Nora: Whose lessons? Mine, or the children's?

Helmer: Both yours and the children's, my darling Nora.

Nora: I'm sorry, Torvald, but you're not the man to give me lessons on how to be a proper wife to you.

Helmer: How can you say that?

Nora: And as for me, who am I to be allowed to bring up the children?

Helmer: Nora!

Nora: Didn't you say so yourself a little while ago, that you don't dare trust them to me?

Helmer: That was in a moment of anger! Why can't you let it go?

Nora: Because you were absolutely right. I'm not fit for the job. There's another job I have to take on first. I have to try to educate myself. You're not the man to help me with that. I have to do that for myself. And that's why I'm going to leave you now.

Helmer (*jumping up*): What are you saying?

Nora: I have to stand completely on my own, if I'm going to understand myself and everything around me. That's why I can't stay here with you any longer.

Helmer: Nora, Nora!

Nora: I'm leaving right now. I'm sure Kristine will put me up for the night—

Helmer: You're out of your mind! I won't let you go! I forbid it!

Nora: It's no use forbidding me anything anymore. I'm taking only what belongs to me. I won't take anything from you, now or later.

Helmer: This is insanity!

Nora: Tomorrow I'm going home. Back to where I came from, I mean. It'll be easier for me to find something to do there.

Helmer: You're a blind, senseless woman!

Nora: Then I'd better try to get some sense, Torvald.

Helmer: But to desert your home, your husband, and your children! And aren't you concerned about what people will say?

Nora: I can't concern myself with that. I only know that this is what I have to do.

Helmer: This is outrageous! You're just going to walk away from your most sacred duties?

Nora: What do you consider to be my most sacred duties?

Helmer: Do you need me to tell you that? Aren't they your duties to your husband and your children?

Nora: I have other duties just as sacred.

Helmer: No, you do not. What could they be?

Nora: Duties to myself.

Helmer: First and foremost, you're a wife and a mother.

Nora: I don't believe that anymore. I believe that first and foremost I'm a human being, just as you are—or, at least, that I have to try to become one. I know very well, Torvald, that most people would agree with you, and that opinions like yours are in books, but I can't be satisfied anymore with what most people say, or with what's in books. I have to think things through for myself and come to understand them.

Helmer: Why can't you understand your place in your own home? Don't you have an infallible guide in matters like that? What about your religion?

Nora: Torvald, I'm afraid I'm not sure what religion is.

Helmer: What are you saying?

Nora: All I know is what Pastor Hansen said when I was confirmed. He told us that religion was this, that, and the other thing. When I'm away from all this and on my own, I'll look into that subject too. I'll see if what he said is true or not, or at least whether it's true for me.

Helmer: This is unheard of, coming from a young woman like you! But if religion doesn't guide you, let me appeal to your conscience. I assume you have some moral sense. Or do you have none? Answer me.

Nora: Torvald, that's not an easy question to answer. I really don't know. It's very confusing to me. I only know that you and I look at it in very different ways. I'm learning too that the law isn't at all what I thought it was, and I can't convince myself that the law is right. A woman has no right to spare her old dying father or to save her husband's life? I can't believe that.

Helmer: You talk like a child. You don't understand anything about the world you live in.

Nora: No, I don't. But I'm going to try. I'm going to see if I can figure out who's right, me or the world.

Helmer: You're sick, Nora. You're delirious. I'm half convinced that you're out of your mind.

Nora: I've never felt so clearheaded and sure of myself as I do tonight.

Helmer: Clearheaded and sure of yourself—and that's the spirit in which you forsake your husband and your children?

Nora: Yes, it is.

Helmer: Then there's only one possible explanation.

Nora: Which is?

Helmer: You don't love me anymore.

Nora: Exactly.

Helmer: Nora! How can you say that?

Nora: It's very painful for me to say it, Torvald, because you've always been so good to me, but I can't help it. I don't love you anymore.

Helmer (*regaining his composure*): Are you clearheaded and sure of yourself when you say that too?

Nora: Yes, totally clearheaded and sure of myself. That's why I can't stay here.

Helmer: Can you tell me what I did to make you stop loving me?

Nora: Yes, I can. It was tonight, when the miracle didn't happen. That's when I realized you're not the man I thought you were.

Helmer: Can you explain that more clearly? I don't understand you.

Nora: I've been waiting so patiently for the last eight years. Of course I knew that miracles don't happen every day. Then when I found myself in this horrible situation, I was sure that the miracle was about to happen at last. When Krogstad's letter was lying out there, never for a moment did I imagine that you would agree to his conditions. I was absolutely certain that you'd say to him: Go ahead, tell the whole world. And when he had—

Helmer: Yes, what then? After I'd exposed my wife to shame and disgrace?

Nora: When he had, I was absolutely certain you'd come forward and take the whole thing on yourself, and say: I'm the guilty one.

Helmer: Nora—!

Nora: You mean that I would never have let you make such a sacrifice for me? Of course I wouldn't. But who would have believed my word against yours? That was the miracle that I hoped for and dreaded. And it was to keep it from happening that made me want to kill myself.

Helmer: I'd gladly work night and day for you, Nora, and endure sorrow and poverty for your sake. But no man would sacrifice his honor for the one he loves.

Nora: Hundreds of thousands of women have done it.

Helmer: Oh, you think and talk like a thoughtless child.

Nora: Maybe so. But you don't think or talk like the man I want to be with for the rest of my life. As soon as your fear had passed—and it wasn't fear for what threatened me, but for what might happen to you—when the whole thing was past, as far as you were concerned it was just as if nothing at all had happened. I was still your little skylark, your doll, but now you'd handle me twice as gently and carefully as before, because I was so delicate and fragile. (*Getting up.*) Torvald, that's when it dawned on me that for eight years I'd been living here with a stranger and had borne him three children. Oh, I can't bear to think about it! I could tear myself into little pieces!

Helmer (*sadly*): I see, I see. An abyss has opened up between us. There's no denying it. But, Nora, can't we find some way to close it?

Nora: The way I am now, I'm no wife for you.

Helmer: I can find it in myself to become a different man.

Nora: Maybe so—if your doll is taken away from you.

Helmer: But to be apart!—to be apart from you! No, no, Nora, I can't conceive of it.

Nora (*going out to the right*): All the more reason why it has to be done.

(*She comes back with her coat and hat and a small suitcase which she puts on a chair by the table.*)

Helmer: Nora, Nora, not now! Wait till tomorrow.

Nora (*putting on her cloak*): I can't spend the night in a strange man's room.

Helmer: But couldn't we live here together like brother and sister?

Nora (*putting on her hat*): You know how long that would last. (*Puts the shawl around her.*) Goodbye, Torvald. I won't look in on the children. I know they're in better hands than mine. The way I am now, I'm no use to them.

Helmer: But someday, Nora, someday?

Nora: How can I tell? I have no idea what's going to become of me.

Helmer: But you're my wife, whatever becomes of you.

Nora: Listen, Torvald. I've heard that when a wife deserts her husband's house, the way I'm doing now, he's free of all legal obligations to her. In any event, I set you free from all your obligations. I don't want you to feel bound in the slightest, any more than I will. There has to be complete freedom on both sides. Look, here's your ring back. Give me mine.

Helmer: That too?

Nora: That too.

Helmer: Here it is.

Nora: Good. Now it's all over. I've left the keys here. The maids know all about how to run the house, much better than I do. Kristine will come by tomorrow after I leave her place and pack up my own things, the ones I brought with me from home. I'd like to have them sent to me.

Helmer: All over! All over! Nora, will you ever think about me again?

Nora: I know I'll often think about you, and the children, and this house.

Helmer: May I write to you, Nora?

Nora: No, never. You mustn't do that.

Helmer: But at least let me send you—

Nora: Nothing, nothing.

Helmer: Let me help you if you're in need.

Nora: No. I can't accept anything from a stranger.

Helmer: Nora . . . can't I ever be anything more than a stranger to you?

Nora (*picking up her bag*): Ah, Torvald, for that, the most wonderful miracle of all would have to happen.

Helmer: Tell me what that would be!

Nora: We'd both have to change so much that— Oh, Torvald, I've stopped believing in miracles.

Helmer: But I'll believe. Tell me! Change so much that . . . ?

Nora: That our life together would be a true marriage. Goodbye.

(*She goes out through the hall.*)

Helmer (*sinks down into a chair at the door and buries his face in his hands*): Nora! Nora! (*Looks around, and stands up.*) Empty. She's gone. (*A hope flashes across his mind.*) The most wonderful miracle of all . . . ?

(*The heavy sound of a closing door is heard from below.*)

1. What names does Torvald call Nora? How do these names reflect their relationship? How do Torvald and Nora use these names in conversation with one another?

2. How does Nora imagine her household to be? How does Torvald imagine his household to be? How does the play portray the household to be? How compatible are these three images of the household?

3. What is Nora's conception of her secret? What is Mrs. Linden's? What is Krogstadt's? What is Torvald's? How

would you characterize the conflict between these different conceptions?

4. What is the function of Mrs. Linden's character in the play? How do her choices reflect Nora's choices? Why have their lives turned out so differently?

5. In what way is the image of confinement associated with each of the characters in the play? Which of them manage to escape, and why?

NONFICTION

Malcolm X 1925–1965

Malcolm X, the militant black nationalist leader, was born Malcolm Little in Omaha, Nebraska, son of a Baptist preacher and a Grenadan woman. He grew up in Lansing, Michigan, where his house was burned down by members of the Ku Klux Klan; his father was murdered and his mother institutionalized. Drifting to Harlem, he became involved in petty crime and was sentenced to ten years for burglary. While in prison, he converted to the Nation of Islam, meeting its founder Elijah Muhammad on his release from prison and changing his surname to "X." A charismatic speaker, Malcolm X traveled the country on speaking tours and was assigned in the early 1960s to the Harlem mosque. He left the Nation of Islam in 1964, embraced conventional Islam, made the pilgrimage to Mecca, and softened his views on race relations. In 1965, he was assassinated in Harlem by followers of Elijah Muhammad. *The Autobiography of Malcolm X*, compiled by Alex Haley from extensive interviews, was published the same year as his death and remains the primary source for information about much of Malcolm X's life.

FROM THE AUTOBIOGRAPHY OF MALCOLM X

TODAY, WHEN EVERYTHING THAT I DO HAS AN urgency, I would not spend one hour in the preparation of a book which had the ambition to perhaps titillate some readers. But I am spending many hours because the full story is the best way that I know to have it seen, and understood, that I had sunk to the very bottom of the American white man's society when—soon now, in prison—I found Allah and the religion of Islam and it completely transformed my life.

[. . .]

Shorty didn't know what the word "concurrently" meant.

Somehow, Lansing-to-Boston bus fare had been scraped up by Shorty's old mother. "Son, read the

Book of Revelations and pray to God!" she had kept telling Shorty, visiting him and once me, while we awaited our sentencing. Shorty had read the Bible's Revelations pages; he had actually gotten down on his knees, praying like some Negro Baptist deacon.

Then we were looking up at the judge in Middlesex County Court. (Our, I think, fourteen counts of crime were committed in that county.) Shorty's mother was sitting, sobbing with her head bowing up and down to her Jesus, over near Ella and Reginald. Shorty was the first of us called to stand up.

5   "Count one, eight to ten years—

"Count two, eight to ten years—

"Count three . . ."

And, finally, "The sentences to run concurrently."

Shorty, sweating so hard that his black face looked as though it had been greased, and not understanding the word "concurrently," had counted in his head to probably over a hundred years; he cried out, he began slumping. The bailiffs had to catch and support him.

In eight to ten seconds, Shorty had turned as atheist as I had been to start with.

I got ten years.

The girls got one to five years, in the Women's Reformatory at Framingham, Massachusetts.

This was in February, 1946. I wasn't quite twenty-one. I had not even started shaving.

They took Shorty and me, handcuffed together, to the Charlestown State Prison.

I can't remember any of my prison numbers. That seems surprising, even after the dozen years since I have been out of prison. Because your number in prison became part of you. You never heard your name, only your number. On all of your clothing, every item, was your number, stenciled. It grew stenciled on your brain.

Any person who claims to have deep feeling for other human beings should think a long, long time before he votes to have other men kept behind bars—caged. I am not saying there shouldn't be prisons, but there shouldn't be bars. Behind bars, a man never reforms. He will never forget. He never will get completely over the memory of the bars.

After he gets out, his mind tries to erase the experience, but he can't. I've talked with numerous former convicts. It has been very interesting to me to find that all of our minds had blotted away many details of years in prison. But in every case, he will tell you that he can't forget those bars.

As a "fish" (prison slang for a new inmate) at Charlestown, I was physically miserable and as evil-tempered as a snake, being suddenly without drugs. The cells didn't have running water. The prison had been built in 1805—in Napoleon's day—and was even styled after the Bastille. In the dirty, cramped cell, I could lie on my cot and touch both walls. The toilet was a covered pail; I don't care how strong you are, you can't stand having to smell a whole cell row of defecation.

The prison psychologist interviewed me and he got called every filthy name I could think of, and the prison chaplain got called worse. My first letter, I remember, was from my religious brother Philbert in Detroit, telling me his "holiness" church was going to pray for me. I scrawled him a reply I'm ashamed to think of today.

Ella was my first visitor. I remember seeing her catch herself, then try to smile at me, now in the faded dungarees stenciled with my number. Neither of us could find much to say, until I wished she hadn't come at all. The guards with guns watched about fifty convicts and visitors. I have heard scores of new prisoners swearing back in their cells that when free their first act would be to waylay those visiting-room guards. Hatred often focused on them.

I first got high in Charlestown on nutmeg. My cellmate was among at least a hundred nutmeg men who, for money or cigarettes, bought from kitchen-worker inmates penny matchboxes full of stolen nutmeg. I grabbed a box as though it were a pound of heavy drugs. Stirred into a glass of cold water, a penny matchbox full of nutmeg had the kick of three or four reefers.

With some money sent by Ella, I was finally able to buy stuff for better highs from guards in the prison. I got reefers, Nembutal, and Benzedrine. Smuggling to prisoners was the guards' sideline; every prison's inmates know that's how guards make most of their living.

I served a total of seven years in prison. Now, when I try to separate that first year-plus that I spent at Charlestown, it runs all together in a memory of nutmeg and the other semi-drugs, of cursing guards, throwing things out of my cell, balking in the lines, dropping my tray in the dining hall, refusing to answer my number—claiming I forgot—and things like that.

I preferred the solitary that this behavior brought me. I would pace for hours like a caged leopard, viciously cursing aloud to myself. And my favorite targets were the Bible and God. But there was a legal limit to how much time one could be kept in solitary. Eventually, the men in the cellblock had a name for me: "Satan." Because of my antireligious attitude.

The first man I met in prison who made any positive impression on me whatever was a fellow inmate, "Bimbi." I met him in 1947, at Charlestown. He was a light, kind of red-complexioned Negro, as I was; about my height, and he had freckles. Bimbi, an old-time burglar, had been in many prisons. In the license plate shop where our gang worked, he operated the machine that stamped out the numbers. I was along the conveyor belt where the numbers were painted.

Bimbi was the first Negro convict I'd known who didn't respond to "What'cha know, Daddy?" Often, after we had done our day's license plate quota, we would sit around, perhaps fifteen of us, and listen to Bimbi. Normally, white prisoners wouldn't think of listening to Negro prisoners' opinions on anything, but guards, even, would wander over close to hear Bimbi on any subject.

He would have a cluster of people riveted, often on odd subjects you never would think of. He would prove to us, dipping into the science of human behavior, that the only difference between us and outside people was that we had been caught. He liked to talk about historical events and figures. When he talked about the history of Concord, where I was to be transferred later, you would have thought he was hired by the Chamber of Commerce, and I wasn't the first inmate who had never heard of Thoreau until Bimbi expounded upon him. Bimbi was known as the library's best customer. What fascinated me with him most of all was that he was the first man I had ever seen command total respect . . . with his words.

Bimbi seldom said much to me; he was gruff to individuals, but I sensed he liked me. What made me seek his friendship was when I heard him discuss religion. I considered myself beyond atheism—I was Satan. But Bimbi put the atheist philosophy in a framework, so to speak. That ended my vicious cursing attacks. My approach sounded so weak alongside his, and he never used a foul word.

Out of the blue one day, Bimbi told me flatly, as was his way, that I had some brains, if I'd use them. I had wanted his friendship, not that kind of advice. I might have cursed another convict, but nobody cursed Bimbi. He told me I should take advantage of the prison correspondence courses and the library.

30 When I had finished the eighth grade back in Mason, Michigan, that was the last time I'd thought of studying anything that didn't have some hustle purpose. And the streets had erased everything I'd ever learned in school; I didn't know a verb from a house. My sister Hilda had written a suggestion that,

Henri Cartier-Bresson, *Cell in a Model Prison, USA, 1975*. One of the most important photographers of the twentieth century, Cartier-Bresson (1908–2004) took this photo of an inmate in solitary confinement in a high-security cell in a prison in Leesburg, New Jersey.

if possible in prison, I should study English and penmanship; she had barely been able to read a couple of picture post cards I had sent her when I was selling reefers on the road.

So, feeling I had time on my hands, I did begin a correspondence course in English. When the mimeographed listings of available books passed from cell to cell, I would put my number next to titles that appealed to me which weren't already taken.

Through the correspondence exercises and lessons, some of the mechanics of grammar gradually began to come back to me.

After about a year, I guess, I could write a decent and legible letter. About then, too, influenced by having heard Bimbi often explain word derivations, I quietly started another correspondence course— in Latin.

Under Bimbi's tutelage, too, I had gotten myself some little cellblock swindles going. For packs of cigarettes, I beat just about anyone at dominoes. I always had several cartons of cigarettes in my cell; they were, in prison, nearly as valuable a medium of exchange as money. I booked cigarette and money bets on fights and ball games. I'll never forget the prison sensation created that day in April, 1947, when Jackie Robinson had, then, his most fanatic fan in me. When he played, my ear was glued to the radio, and no game ended without my refiguring his average up through his last turn at bat.

35   One day in 1948, after I had been transferred to Concord Prison, my brother Philbert, who was forever joining something, wrote me this time that he had discovered the "natural religion for the black man." He belonged now, he said, to something called "the Nation of Islam." He said I should "pray to Allah for deliverance." I wrote Philbert a letter which, although in improved English, was worse than my earlier reply to his news that I was being prayed for by his "holiness" church.

When a letter from Reginald arrived, I never dreamed of associating the two letters, although I knew that Reginald had been spending a lot of time with Wilfred, Hilda, and Philbert in Detroit. Reginald's letter was newsy, and also it contained this instruction: "Malcolm, don't eat any more pork, and don't smoke any more cigarettes. I'll show you how to get out of prison."

My automatic response was to think he had come upon some way I could work a hype on the penal authorities. I went to sleep—and woke up— trying to figure what kind of a hype it could be. Something psychological, such as my act with the New York draft board? Could I, after going without pork and smoking no cigarettes for a while, claim some physical trouble that could bring about my release?

"Get out of prison." The words hung in the air around me, I wanted out so badly.

I wanted, in the worst way, to consult with Bimbi about it. But something big, instinct said, you spilled to nobody.

40   Quitting cigarettes wasn't going to be too difficult. I had been conditioned by days in solitary without cigarettes. Whatever this chance was, I wasn't going to fluff it. After I read that letter, I finished the pack I then had open. I haven't smoked another cigarette to this day, since 1948.

It was about three or four days later when pork was served for the noon meal.

I wasn't even thinking about pork when I took my seat at the long table. Sit-grab-gobble-stand-file out; that was the Emily Post in prison eating. When the meat platter was passed to me, I didn't even know what the meat was; usually, you couldn't tell, anyway—but it was suddenly as though *don't eat any more pork* flashed on a screen before me.

I hesitated, with the platter in mid-air; then I passed it along to the inmate waiting next to me. He began serving himself: abruptly, he stopped. I remember him turning, looking surprised at me.

I said to him, "I don't eat pork."

45   The platter then kept on down the table.

It was the funniest thing, the reaction, and the way that it spread. In prison, where so little breaks the monotonous routine, the smallest thing causes a commotion of talk. It was being mentioned all over the cell block by night that Satan didn't eat pork.

It made me very proud, in some odd way. One of the universal images of the Negro, in prison and out, was that he couldn't do without pork. It made me feel good to see that my not eating it had especially startled the white convicts.

Later I would learn, when I had read and studied Islam a good deal, that, unconsciously, my first pre-Islamic submission had been manifested. I had experienced, for the first time, the Muslim teaching, "If you will take one step toward Allah—Allah will take two steps toward you."

My brothers and sisters in Detroit and Chicago had all become converted to what they were being taught was the "natural religion for the black man" of which Philbert had written to me. They all prayed for me to become converted while I was in prison. But after Philbert reported my vicious reply, they discussed what was the best thing to do. They had decided that Reginald, the latest convert, the one to whom I felt closest, would best know how to approach me, since he knew me so well in the street life.

50   Independently of all this, my sister Ella had been steadily working to get me transferred to the Norfolk, Massachusetts, Prison Colony, which was an

experimental rehabilitation jail. In other prisons, convicts often said that if you had the right money, or connections, you could get transferred to this Colony whose penal policies sounded almost too good to be true. Somehow, Ella's efforts in my behalf were successful in late 1948, and I was transferred to Norfolk.

The Colony was, comparatively, a heaven, in many respects. It had flushing toilets; there were no bars, only walls—and within the walls, you had far more freedom. There was plenty of fresh air to breathe; it was not in a city.

There were twenty-four "house" units, fifty men living in each unit, if memory serves me correctly. This would mean that the Colony had a total of around 1200 inmates. Each "house" had three floors and, greatest blessing of all, each inmate had his own room.

About fifteen percent of the inmates were Negroes, distributed about five to nine Negroes in each house.

Norfolk Prison Colony represented the most enlightened form of prison that I have ever heard of. In place of the atmosphere of malicious gossip, perversion, grafting, hateful guards, there was more relative "culture," as "culture" is interpreted in prisons. A high percentage of the Norfolk Prison Colony inmates went in for "intellectual" things, group discussions, debates, and such. Instructors for the educational rehabilitation programs came from Harvard, Boston University, and other educational institutions in the area. The visiting rules, far more lenient than other prisons', permitted visitors almost every day, and allowed them to stay two hours. You had your choice of sitting alongside your visitor, or facing each other.

55 Norfolk Prison Colony's library was one of its outstanding features. A millionaire named Parkhurst had willed his library there; he had probably been interested in the rehabilitation program. History and religions were his special interests. Thousands of his books were on the shelves, and in the back were boxes and crates full, for which there wasn't space on the shelves. At Norfolk, we could actually go into the library, with permission—walk up and down the shelves, pick books. There were hundreds of old volumes, some of them probably quite rare. I read aimlessly, until I learned to read selectively, with a purpose.

Malcolm X in the years following his release from prison.

I hadn't heard from Reginald in a good while after I got to Norfolk Prison Colony, But I had come in there not smoking cigarettes, or eating pork when it was served. That caused a bit of eyebrow-raising. Then a letter from Reginald telling me when he was coming to see me. By the time he came, I was really keyed up to hear the hype he was going to explain.

Reginald knew how my street-hustler mind operated. That's why his approach was so effective.

He had always dressed well, and now, when he came to visit, was carefully groomed. I was aching with wanting the "no pork and cigarettes" riddle answered. But he talked about the family, what was happening in Detroit, Harlem the last time he was there. I have never pushed anyone to tell me anything before he is ready. The offhand way Reginald talked and acted made me know that something big was coming.

He said, finally, as though it had just happened to come into his mind, "Malcolm, if a man knew every imaginable thing that there is to know, who would he be?"

60 Back in Harlem, he had often liked to get at something through this kind of indirection. It had often irritated me, because my way had always been direct. I looked at him. "Well, he would have to be some kind of a god—"

Reginald said, "There's a *man* who knows everything."

I asked, "Who is that?"

"God is a man," Reginald said. "His real name is Allah."

Allah. That word came back to me from Philbert's letter; it was my first hint of any connection. But Reginald went on. He said that God had 360 degrees of knowledge. He said that 360 degrees represented "the sum total of knowledge."

65 To say I was confused is an understatement. I don't have to remind you of the background against which I sat hearing my brother Reginald talk like this. I just listened, knowing he was taking his time in putting me onto something. And if somebody is trying to put you onto something, you need to listen.

"The devil has only thirty-three degrees of knowledge—known as Masonry," Reginald said. I can so specifically remember the exact phrases since, later, I was going to teach them so many times to others. "The devil uses his Masonry to rule other people."

He told me that this God had come to America, and that he had made himself known to a man named Elijah—"a black man, just like us." This God had let Elijah know, Reginald said, that the devil's "time was up."

I didn't know what to think. I just listened.

"The devil is also a man," Reginald said.

70 "What do you mean?"

With a slight movement of his head, Reginald indicated some white inmates and their visitors talking, as we were, across the room.

"Them," he said. "The white man is the devil."

He told me that all whites knew they were devils—"especially Masons."

I never will forget: my mind was involuntarily flashing across the entire spectrum of white people I had ever known; and for some reason it stopped upon Hymie, the Jew, who had been so good to me.

75 Reginald, a couple of times, had gone out with me to that Long Island bootlegging operation to buy and bottle up the bootleg liquor for Hymie.

I said, "Without any exception?"

"Without any exception."

"What about Hymie?"

"What is it if I let you make five hundred dollars to let me make ten thousand?"

80 After Reginald left, I thought. I thought. Thought.

I couldn't make of it head, or tail, or middle.

The white people I had known marched before my mind's eye. From the start of my life. The state white people always in our house after the other whites I didn't know had killed my father . . . the white people who kept calling my mother "crazy" to her face and before me and my brothers and sisters, until she finally was taken off by white people to the Kalamazoo asylum . . . the white judge and others who had split up the children . . . the Swerlins, the other whites around Mason . . . white youngsters I was in school there with, and the teachers—the one who told me in the eight grade to "be a carpenter" because thinking of being a lawyer was foolish for a Negro. . . .

My head swam with the parading faces of white people. The ones in Boston, in the white-only dances at the Roseland Ballroom where I shined their shoes . . . at the Parker House where I took their dirty plates back to the kitchen . . . the railroad crewmen and passengers . . . Sophia . . .

The whites in New York City—the cops, the white criminals I'd dealt with . . . the whites who piled into the Negro speakeasies for a taste of Negro *soul* . . . the white women who wanted Negro men . . . the men I'd steered to the black "specialty sex" they wanted. . . .

85 The fence back in Boston, and his ex-con representative . . . Beston cops . . . Sophia's husband's friend, and her husband, whom I'd never seen, but knew so much about . . . Sophia's sister . . . the Jew jeweler who'd helped trap me . . . the social workers . . . the Middlesex County Court people . . . the judge who gave me ten years . . . the prisoners I'd known, the guards and the officials . . . .

A celebrity among the Norfolk Prison Colony inmates was a rich, older fellow, a paralytic, called John. He had killed his baby, one of those "mercy" killings. He was a proud, bigshot type, always reminding everyone that he was a 33rd-degree Mason, and what powers Masons had—that only Masons ever had been U.S. Presidents, that Masons in distress could secretly signal to judges and other Masons in powerful positions.

I kept thinking about what Reginald had said. I wanted to test it with John. He worked in a soft job in the prison's school. I went over there.

"John," I said, "how many degrees in a circle?"

He said, "Three hundred and sixty."

90   I drew a square. "How many degrees in that?" He said three hundred and sixty.

I asked him was three hundred and sixty degrees, then the maximum of degrees in anything?

He said "Yes."

I said, "Well, why is it that Masons go only to thirty-three degrees?"

He had no satisfactory answer. But for me, the answer was that Masonry, actually, is only thirty-three degrees of the religion of Islam, which is the full projection, forever denied to Masons, although they know it exists.

95   Reginald, when he came to visit me again in a few days, could gauge from my attitude the effect that his talking had had upon me. He seemed very pleased. Then, very seriously, he talked for two solid hours about "the devil white man" and "the brainwashed black man."

When Reginald left, he left me rocking with some of the first serious thoughts I had ever had in my life: that the white man was fast losing his power to oppress and exploit the dark world: that the dark world was starting to rise to rule the world again, as it had before; that the white man's world was on the way down, it was on the way out.

"You don't even know who you are," Reginald had said. "You don't even know, the white devil has hidden it from you, that you are of a race of people of ancient civilizations, and riches in gold and kings. You don't even know your true family name, you wouldn't recognize your true language if you heard it. You have been cut off by the devil white man from all true knowledge of your own kind. You have been a victim of the evil of the devil white man ever since he murdered and raped and stole you from your native land in the seeds of your forefathers. . . ."

I began to receive at least two letters every day from my brothers and sisters in Detroit. My oldest brother, Wilfred, wrote, and his first wife, Bertha, the mother of his two children (since her death, Wilfred has met and married his present wife, Ruth). Philbert wrote, and my sister Hilda. And Reginald visited, staying in Boston awhile before he went back to Detroit, where he had been the most recent of them to be converted. They were all Muslims, followers of a man they described to me as "The Honorable Elijah Muhammad," a small, gentle man, whom they sometimes referred to as "The Messenger of Allah." He was, they said, "a black man, like us." He had been born in America on a farm in Georgia. He had moved with his family to Detroit, and there had met a Mr. Wallace D. Fard who he claimed was "God in person." Mr. Wallace D. Fard had given to Elijah Muhammad Allah's message for the black people who were "the Lost-Found Nation of Islam here in this wilderness of North America."

All of them urged me to "accept the teachings of the Honorable Elijah Muhammad." Reginald explained that pork was not eaten by those who worshiped in the religion of Islam, and not smoking cigarettes was a rule of the followers of The Honorable Elijah Muhammad, because they did not take injurious things such as narcotics, tobacco, or liquor into their bodies. Over and over, I read, and heard, "The key to a Muslim is submission, the attunement of one toward Allah."

100   And what they termed "the true knowledge of the black man" that was possessed by the followers of The Honorable Elijah Muhammad was given shape for me in their lengthy letters, sometimes containing printed literature.

[1965]

QUESTIONS FOR REFLECTION AND DISCUSSION

1. What distinction does Malcolm X draw between "prisons" and "bars"? How do bars change the experience of the space of confinement?

2. Why does Malcolm X respect Bimbi? What is Bimbi's attitude toward him?

3. How is the Norfolk prison different from the previous two prisons?

4. What do the library and Malcolm X's new religion contribute to freeing him from confinement? What effect do they have on him?

CONFINED SPACES TOPICS FOR ESSAYS

1. Write an essay comparing the image of the house in several of the texts in this section. What role does it play in each text?

2. Nearly all of the characters are ambivalent toward the confined space in which they find themselves. Write an essay analyzing how this ambivalence manifests itself in several different examples from this section.

3. Write an essay comparing physical confinement with psychological confinement using examples from the selections in this section.

4. Many of the confined characters in these selections are women. Using examples from the readings in this section, write an essay discussing the effect of gender on the way we experience or imagine space.

5. Write a personal essay describing your own experience with a confined space and analyzing the effect on you of that experience.

6. Compare Malcolm X's description of prison with the way prison life is depicted in the photographs on pages 534 and 592. How are they similar? In what ways are they different?

CONFINED SPACES FURTHER READINGS IN *LITERATURE: A WORLD OF WRITING*

James Baldwin, "Sonny's Blues" • Samuel Beckett, *Krapp's Last Tape* • William Blake, "London" • Kate Chopin, "The Story of an Hour" • Julio Cortázar, "Axolotl" • Salman Rushdie, "Imagine There's No Heaven" • William Shakespeare, *Hamlet, Prince of Denmark* • John Steinbeck, "The Chrysanthemums"

WORKING FURTHER WITH THE WORLD WE LIVE IN

1. Write an essay comparing the ability of a particular space to alter a person's life, basing your argument on examples from this chapter.

2. Write an essay comparing the role played by race in several of the texts in this chapter. How does race affect the experience of space? What spaces and images are associated with it?

3. Write an essay comparing the role played by gender in several of the texts in this chapter. How does gender affect the experience of space? What spaces and images are associated with it?

4. Write an essay on the way imagery of nature is used in the texts in this chapter. How are animals associated with particular spaces? Is their relationship to space different than that of humans in these texts? What makes the imagery of animals and nature an effective way to define human relationships to space?

5. Write a personal essay on your own experience of space. What are the most important spaces in your life? What do they have in common? How do they affect you?

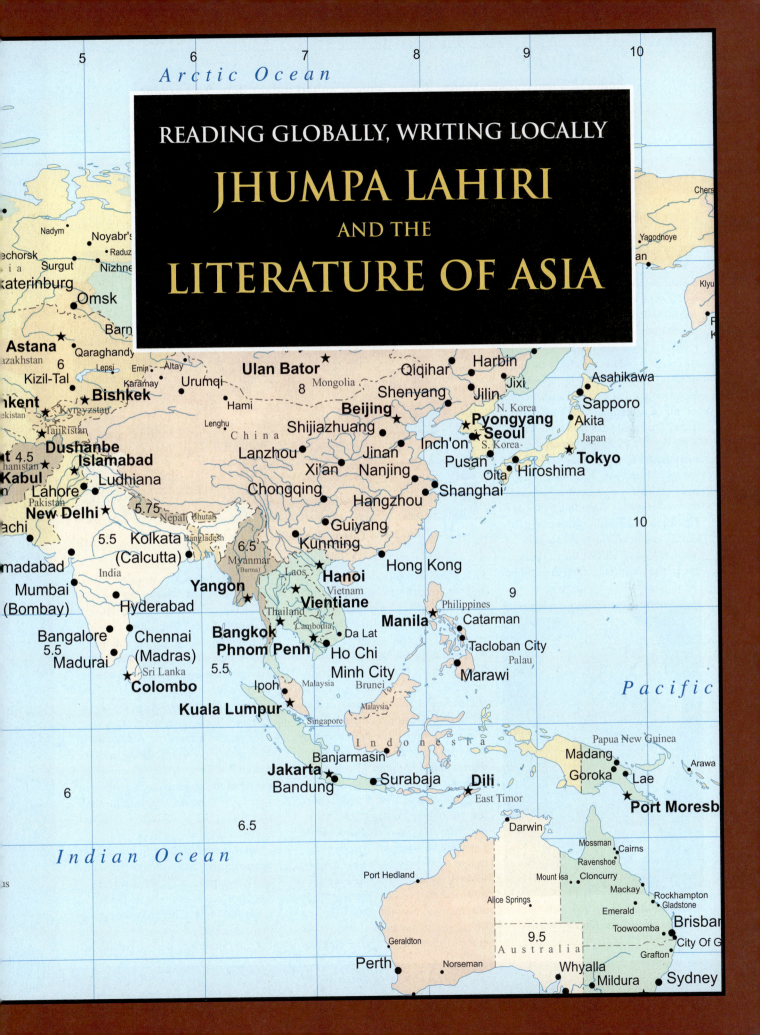

READING GLOBALLY, WRITING LOCALLY

JHUMPA LAHIRI

AND THE

LITERATURE OF ASIA

What Winston Churchill said over fifty years ago about India is even more the case with Asia as a whole. The largest of the world's continents, Asia also contains nearly sixty percent of the world's population, including India and China, the world's two most populous countries, and six of its top ten. And if we include the islands of the Indian and Pacific oceans within its conceptual limits, "Asia" becomes even broader and more varied. Long defined by simple opposition to everything "Western," the East in fact has its own ancient, illustrious, and complex history and cultures. In addition to being the origin and center of Hinduism and Buddhism, two of the world's largest religions, Asia is also home to more Muslims than anywhere else in the world, including the Middle

Wat Phra Keo Royal Palace, Bangkok, Thailand.

East. It has seen countless empires rise and fall, fought wars both within itself and with the West, and been both colonizing power and colonized, imperial power and imperial subject.

The longest continuing civilization in human history, China has a historical record dating back to the second century BCE, and an established literary tradition by the first millennium, including the *I Ching*, or *Book of Changes*, and various works attributed to the influential thinker and philosopher Confucius. The *Mahabharata* and the *Ramayana*, the two great epics of ancient South Asia (the region now known as the Indian subcontinent), date to the same period. The political organization of these regions under powerful ruling dynasties ensured a continuity of tradition able to withstand the myriad political struggles that also mark the history of India and China. In contrast to great ancient works of the Mediterranean such as the epics of

Homer or the ancient Mesopotamian *Epic of Gilgamesh*, which were lost or unread for many centuries, the classic texts of India and China have been a constant presence in the life and literature of the cultures from which they emerged. Moreover, they retain a currency in contemporary religion and philosophy quite different from the purely literary status of ancient Greek or Mesopotamian literature. Although somewhat more recent, dating from the first millennium CE, the great novels and poetry of the imperial court in medieval Japan have exerted a similar influence over the literature and culture that continues to this day.

In this casebook, we do not attempt to encompass the enormous temporal and geographic range of Asian literature; instead, we focus on its global reach and prominence in contemporary literature. Our feature author, Jhumpa Lahiri, was born to Bengali parents in

A tortoise shell inscribed with Chinese characters. Shang Dynasty (c. 1766–1122 BCE).

Rice paddy. Mie Prefecture, Japan.

Hand painting a Bollywood film poster. Mumbai, India, is home to the largest movie industry in the world.

London, and raised in Rhode Island. We include here a personal essay in which she discusses issues of identity that emerge from what she calls her "two lives." Like Lahiri, Garrett Hongo, a Hawaiian-born Japanese American, uses sensual memories, especially of food, to ground an identity formed out of multiple backgrounds and influences. The other writers included in this casebook have attained global prominence while remaining based in their native lands. Raised in England, fiction writer Kazuo Ishiguro has tackled both Japanese and English subjects; his best-known novel is told from the point of view of a country house butler. The Chinese poet Xu Gang uses forms of poetry dating back millennia to record a moment of natural beauty but also to address subtly the contemporary condition of his land.

Fractured identities and displacement around the globe characterize Asian literature perhaps more than other regions of the world, but what characterizes these texts even more is the depth of commitment they also show to retaining cultural identities that date back for millennia. This commitment is not without its ambivalence, however; as you read these selections, take special note of the tension between these identities, as also of the tensions between East and West, and between past and present.

The Dalai Lama, September 23, 2009, in Memphis, Tennessee.

Marco Polo's account of the Map of Asia, engraved by Jenkinson, 1562.

JHUMPA LAHIRI B. 1967

> IT'S EASY TO SET A STORY ANYWHERE IF YOU
> GET A GOOD GUIDEBOOK AND GET SOME
> BASIC STREET NAMES, AND SOME DESCRIPTIONS,
> BUT, FOR ME, YES, I AM INDEBTED TO MY TRAVELS
> TO INDIA FOR SEVERAL OF THE STORIES.
>
> —JHUMPA LAHIRI

Born in London and raised in Rhode Island, Jhumpa Lahiri creates fiction steeped in the transplanted cultures of exiles and immigrants. After graduating from Barnard College, Lahiri completed a handful of advanced degrees at Boston University, including a PhD in Renaissance Studies. She lives in Brooklyn, New York, with her husband and two children. Lahiri's first collection of stories, *Interpreter of Maladies,* won the Pulitzer Prize in 2000. In 2003 she published a novel *The Namesake* (adapted to film in 2006), and in 2008 a second collection of stories, *Unaccustomed Earth.* Focused on the lives of Indians and Indian Americans, Lahiri's fiction is universal in its attention to the complex and often unspoken emotions of its characters while also highly specific in the details of a unique community.

NONFICTION

MY TWO LIVES

I HAVE LIVED IN THE UNITED STATES for almost 37 years and anticipate growing old in this country. Therefore, with the exception of my first two years in London, "Indian-American" has been a constant way to describe me. Less constant is my relationship to the term. When I was growing up in Rhode Island in the 1970s I felt neither Indian nor American. Like many immigrant offspring I felt intense pressure to be two things, loyal to the old world and fluent in the new, approved of on either side of the hyphen. Looking back, I see that this was generally the case. But my perception as a young girl was that I fell short at both ends, shuttling between two dimensions that had nothing to do with one another.

At home I followed the customs of my parents, speaking Bengali and eating rice and dal with my fingers. These ordinary facts seemed part of a secret, utterly alien way of life, and I took pains to hide them from my American friends. For my parents, home was not our house in Rhode Island but Calcutta, where they were raised. I was aware that the things they lived for—the Nazrul songs they listened to on the reel-to-reel, the family they missed, the clothes my mother wore that were not available in any store in any mall—were at once as precious and as worthless as an outmoded currency.

I also entered a world my parents had little knowledge or control of: school, books, music,

Kazi Nazrul Islam (1899–1976), the national poet of Bangladesh. A revolutionary activist who championed the poor and rights for women, Nazrul was also a popular recording artist.

television, things that seeped in and became a fundamental aspect of who I am. I spoke English without an accent, comprehending the language in a way my parents still do not. And yet there was evidence that I was not entirely American. In addition to my distinguishing name and looks, I did not attend Sunday school, did not know how to ice-skate, and disappeared to India for months at a time. Many of these friends proudly called themselves Irish-American or Italian-American. But they were several generations removed from the frequently humiliating process of immigration, so that the ethnic roots they claimed had descended underground whereas mine were still tangled and green. According to my parents I was not American, nor would I ever be no matter how hard I tried. I felt doomed by their pronouncement, misunderstood and gradually defiant. In spite of the first lessons of arithmetic, one plus one did not equal two but zero, my conflicting selves always canceling each other out.

When I first started writing I was not conscious that my subject was the Indian-American experience. What drew me to my craft was the desire to force the two worlds I occupied to mingle on the page as I was not brave enough, or mature enough, to allow in life. My first book was published in 1999, and around then, on the cusp of a new century, the term "Indian-American" has become part of this country's vocabulary. I've heard it so often that these days, if asked about my background, I use the term myself, pleasantly surprised that I do not have to explain further. What a difference from my early life, when there was no such way to describe me, when the most I could do was to clumsily and ineffectually explain.

5   As I approach middle age, one plus one equals two, both in my work and in my daily existence. The traditions on either side of the hyphen dwell in me like siblings, still occasionally sparring, one outshining the other depending on the day. But like siblings they are intimately familiar with one another, forgiving and intertwined. When my husband and I were married five years ago in Calcutta we invited friends who had never been to India, and they came full of enthusiasm for a place I avoided talking about in my childhood, fearful of what people might say. Around non-Indian friends, I no longer feel compelled to hide the fact that I speak another language. I speak Bengali to my children, even though I lack the proficiency to teach them to read or write the language. As a child I sought perfection and so denied myself the claim to any identity. As an adult I accept that a bicultural upbringing is a rich but imperfect thing.

While I am American by virtue of the fact that I was raised in this country, I am Indian thanks to the efforts of two individuals. I feel Indian not because of the time I've spent in India or because of my genetic composition but rather because of my parents' steadfast presence in my life. They live three hours from my home; I speak to them daily and see them about once a month. Everything will change once they die. They will take certain things with them—conversations in another tongue, and perceptions about the difficulties of being foreign. Without them, the back-and-forth life my family leads, both literally and figuratively, will at last approach stillness. An anchor will drop, and a line of connection will be severed.

I have always believed that I lack the authority my parents bring to being Indian. But as long as they live they protect me from feeling like an impostor. Their passing will mark not only the loss of the people who created me but the loss of a singular way of life, a singular struggle. The immigrant's journey, no matter how ultimately rewarding, is founded on departure and deprivation, but it secures for the subsequent generation a sense of arrival and advantage. I can see a day coming when my American side, lacking the counterpoint India has until now maintained, begins to gain ascendancy and weight. It is in fiction that I will continue to interpret the term "Indian-American," calculating that shifting equation, whatever answers it may yield.

[2006]

QUESTIONS FOR REFLECTION AND DISCUSSION

1. How, according to Lahiri, does being Indian American differ from the experience of being Irish American or Italian American?

2. In what ways does Lahiri feel Indian? In what ways does she feel American?

3. How has the relationship between Lahiri's two "siblings" changed as she has grown older?

4. How does Lahiri expect this relationship to change after her parents die?

FICTION

WHEN MR. PIRZADA CAME TO DINE

Jhumpa Lahiri

IN THE AUTUMN OF 1971 A MAN USED TO COME TO OUR house, bearing confections in his pocket and hopes of ascertaining the life or death of his family. His name was Mr. Pirzada, and he came from Dacca, now the capital of Bangladesh, but then a part of Pakistan. That year Pakistan was engaged in civil war. The eastern frontier, where Dacca was located, was fighting for autonomy from the ruling regime in the west. In March, Dacca had been invaded, torched, and shelled by the Pakistani army. Teachers were dragged onto streets and shot, women dragged into barracks and raped. By the end of the summer, three hundred thousand people were said to have died. In Dacca Mr. Pirzada had a three-story home, a lectureship in botany at the university, a wife of twenty years, and seven daughters between the ages of six and sixteen whose names all began with the letter A. "Their mother's idea." he explained one day, producing from his wallet a black-and-white picture of seven girls at a picnic, their braids tied with ribbons, sitting cross-legged in a row, eating chicken curry off banana leaves. "How am I to distinguish? Ayesha, Amira, Amina, Aziza, you see the difficulty."

Each week Mr. Pirzada wrote letters to his wife, and sent comic books to each of his seven daughters, but the postal system, along with most everything else in Dacca, had collapsed, and he had not heard word of them in over six months. Mr. Pirzada, meanwhile, was in America for the year, for he had been awarded a grant from the government of Pakistan to study the foliage of New England. In spring and summer he had gathered data in Vermont and Maine, and in autumn he moved to a university north of Boston, where we lived, to write a short book about his discoveries. The grant was a great honor, but when converted into dollars it was not generous. As a result, Mr. Pirzada lived in a room in a graduate dormitory, and did not own a proper stove or a television set. And so he came to our house to eat dinner and watch the evening news.

At first I knew nothing of the reason for his visits. I was ten years old, and was not surprised that my parents, who were from India, and had a number of Indian acquaintances at the university, should ask Mr. Pirzada to share our meals. It was a small campus, with narrow brick walkways and white pillared buildings, located on the fringes of what seemed to be an even smaller town. The supermarket did not carry mustard oil, doctors did not make house calls, neighbors never dropped by without an invitation, and of these things, every so often, my parents complained. In search of compatriots, they used to trail their fingers, at the start of each new semester, through the columns of the university directory, circling surnames familiar to their part of the world. It was in this manner that they discovered Mr. Pirzada, and phoned him, and invited him to our home.

I have no memory of his first visit, or of his second or his third, but by the end of September I had grown so accustomed to Mr. Pirzada's presence in our living room that one evening, as I was dropping ice cubes into the water pitcher, I asked my mother to hand me a fourth glass from a cupboard still out of my reach. She was busy at the stove, presiding over a skillet of fried spinach with radishes, and could not hear me because of the drone of the exhaust fan and the fierce scrapes of her spatula. I turned to my father, who was leaning against the refrigerator, eating spiced cashews from a cupped fist.

5   "What is it, Lilia?"

"A glass for the Indian man."

"Mr. Pirzada won't be coming today. More importantly, Mr. Pirzada is no longer considered Indian," my father announced, brushing salt from the cashews out of his trim black beard. "Not since Partition. Our country was divided. 1947."

When I said I thought that was the date of India's independence from Britain, my father said, "That too. One moment we were free and then we were sliced up," he explained, drawing an X with his finger on the countertop, "like a pie. Hindus here, Muslims there. Dacca no longer belongs to us." He told me that during Partition Hindus and Muslims had set fire to each other's homes. For many, the idea of eating in the other's company was still unthinkable.

It made no sense to me. Mr. Pirzada and my parents spoke the same language, laughed at the same jokes, looked more or less the same. They ate pickled mangoes with their meals, ate rice every night for supper with their hands. Like my parents, Mr. Pirzada took off his shoes before entering a room, chewed fennel seeds after meals as a digestive, drank no alcohol, for dessert dipped austere biscuits into successive cups of tea. Nevertheless my father insisted that I understand the difference, and he led me to a map of the world taped to the wall over his desk. He seemed concerned that Mr. Pirzada might take offense if I accidentally referred to him as an Indian, though I could not really imagine Mr. Pirzada being offended by much of anything. "Mr. Pirzada is Bengali, but he is a Muslim," my father informed me. "Therefore he lives in East Pakistan, not India." His finger trailed across the Atlantic, through Europe, the Mediterranean, the Middle East, and finally to the sprawling orange diamond that my mother once told me resembled a woman wearing a sari with her left arm extended. Various cities had been circled with lines drawn between them to indicate my parents' travels, and the place of their birth, Calcutta, was signified by a small silver star. I had been there only once and had no memory of the trip. "As you see, Lilia, it is a different country, a different color," my father said. Pakistan was yellow, not orange. I noticed that there were two distinct parts to it, one much larger than the other, separated by an expanse of Indian territory; it was as if California and Connecticut constituted a nation apart from the U.S.

10   My father rapped his knuckles on top of my head. "You are, of course, aware of the current situation? Aware of East Pakistan's fight for sovereignty?"

I nodded, unaware of the situation.

We returned to the kitchen, where my mother was draining a pot of boiled rice into a colander. My father opened up the can on the counter and eyed me sharply over the frames of his glasses as he ate some more cashews. "What exactly do they teach you at school? Do you study history? Geography?"

"Lilia has plenty to learn at school," my mother said. "We live here now, she was born here." She seemed genuinely proud of the fact, as if it were a reflection of my character. In her estimation, I knew, I was assured a safe life, an easy life, a fine education, every opportunity. I would never have to eat rationed food, or obey curfews, or watch riots from my rooftop, or hide neighbors in water tanks to prevent them from being shot, as she and my father had. "Imagine having to place her in a decent school. Imagine her having to read during power failures by the light of kerosene lamps. Imagine the pressures, the tutors, the constant exams." She ran a hand through her hair, bobbed to a suitable length for her part-time job as a bank teller. "How can you possibly expect her to know about Partition? Put those nuts away."

"But what does she learn about the world?" My father rattled the cashew can in his hand. "What is she learning?"

15   We learned American history, of course, and American geography. That year, and every year, it seemed, we began by studying the Revolutionary War. We were taken in school buses on field trips to visit Plymouth Rock, and to walk the Freedom Trail, and to climb to the top of the Bunker Hill Monument. We made dioramas out of colored construction paper depicting George Washington crossing the choppy waters of the Delaware River, and we made puppets of King George wearing white tights and a black bow in his hair. During tests we were given blank maps of the thirteen colonies, and asked to fill in names, dates, capitals. I could do it with my eyes closed.

The next evening Mr. Pirzada arrived, as usual, at six o'clock. Though they were no longer strangers, upon first greeting each other, he and my father maintained the habit of shaking hands.

"Come in, sir. Lilia, Mr. Pirzada's coat, please."

He stepped into the foyer, impeccably suited and scarved, with a silk tie knotted at his collar. Each evening he appeared in ensembles of plums, olives, and chocolate browns. He was a compact man, and though his feet were perpetually splayed, and his belly slightly wide, he nevertheless maintained an efficient posture, as if balancing in either hand two suitcases of equal weight. His ears were insulated by tufts of graying hair that seemed to block out the unpleasant traffic of life. He had thickly lashed eyes shaded with a trace of camphor, a generous mustache that turned up playfully at the ends, and a mole shaped like a flattened raisin in the very center of his left cheek. On his head he wore a black fez made from the wool of Persian lambs, secured by bobby pins, without which I was never to see him. Though my father always offered to fetch him in our car, Mr. Pirzada preferred to walk from his dormitory to our neighborhood, a distance of about twenty minutes on foot, studying trees and shrubs on his way, and when he entered our house his knuckles were pink with the effects of crisp autumn air.

"Another refugee, I am afraid, on Indian territory."

20   "They are estimating nine million at the last count," my father said.

Mr. Pirzada handed me his coat, for it was my job to hang it on the rack at the bottom of the stairs. It was made of finely checkered gray-and-blue wool, with a striped lining and horn buttons, and carried in its weave the faint smell of limes. There were no recognizable tags inside, only a hand-stitched label with the phrase "Z. Sayeed, Suitors" embroidered on it in cursive with glossy black thread. On certain days a birch or maple leaf was tucked into a pocket. He unlaced his shoes and lined them against the baseboard; a golden paste clung to the toes and heels, the result of walking through our damp, unraked lawn. Relieved of his trappings, he grazed my throat with his short, restless fingers, the way a person feels for solidity behind a wall before driving in a nail. Then he followed my father to the living room, where the television was tuned to the local news. As soon as they were seated my mother appeared from the kitchen with a plate of mince-meat kebabs with coriander chutney. Mr. Pirzada popped one into his mouth.

"One can only hope," he said, reaching for another, "that Dacca's refugees are as heartily fed. Which reminds me." He reached into his suit pocket and gave me a small plastic egg filled with cinnamon hearts. "For the lady of the house," he said with an almost imperceptible splay-footed bow.

"Really, Mr. Pirzada," my mother protested. "Night after night. You spoil her."

"I only spoil children who are incapable of spoiling."

25   It was an awkward moment for me, one which I awaited in part with dread, in part with delight. I was charmed by the presence of Mr. Pirzada's rotund elegance, and flattered by the faint theatricality of his attentions, yet unsettled by the superb ease of his gestures, which made me feel, for an instant, like a stranger in my own home. It had become our ritual, and for several weeks, before we grew more comfortable with one another, it was the only time he spoke to me directly. I had no response, offered no comment, betrayed no visible reaction to the steady stream of honey-filled lozenges, the raspberry truffles, the slender rolls of sour pastilles. I could not even thank him, for once, when I did, for an especially spectacular peppermint lollipop wrapped in a spray of purple cellophane, he had demanded, "What is this thank-you? The lady at the bank thanks me, the cashier at the shop thanks me, the librarian thanks me when I return an overdue book, the overseas operator thanks me as she tries to connect me to Dacca and fails. If I am buried in this country I will be thanked, no doubt, at my funeral."

It was inappropriate, in my opinion, to consume the candy Mr. Pirzada gave me in a casual manner. I coveted each evening's treasure as I would a jewel, or a coin from a buried kingdom, and I would place it in a small keepsake box made of carved sandal-wood beside my bed, in which, long ago in India, my father's mother used to store the ground areca nuts she ate after her morning bath. It was my only memento of a grandmother I had never known, and until Mr. Pirzada came to our lives I could find nothing to put inside it. Every so often before brushing my teeth and laying out my clothes for school the next day, I opened the lid of the box and ate one of his treats.

That night, like every night, we did not eat at the dining table, because it did not provide an unobstructed view of the television set. Instead we huddled around the coffee table, without conversing, our plates perched on the edges of our knees. From the kitchen my mother brought forth the succession of dishes: lentils with fried onions, green beans with coconut, fish cooked with raisins in a yogurt sauce. I followed with the water glasses, and the plate of lemon wedges, and the chili peppers, purchased on monthly trips to Chinatown and stored by the pound in the freezer, which they liked to snap open and crush into their food.

Before eating Mr. Pirzada always did a curious thing. He took out a plain silver watch without a band, which he kept in his breast pocket, held it briefly to one of his tufted ears, and wound it with three swift flicks of his thumb and forefinger. Unlike the watch on his wrist, the pocket watch, he had explained to me, was set to the local time in Dacca, eleven hours ahead. For the duration of the meal the watch rested on his folded paper napkin on the coffee table. He never seemed to consult it.

Now that I had learned Mr. Pirzada was not an Indian, I began to study him with extra care, to try to figure out what made him different. I decided that the pocket watch was one of those things. When I saw it that night, as he wound it and arranged it on the coffee table, an uneasiness possessed me; life, I realized, was being lived in Dacca first. I imagined Mr. Pirzada's daughters rising from sleep, tying ribbons in their hair, anticipating breakfast, preparing for school. Our meals, our actions, were only a shadow of what had already happened there, a lagging ghost of where Mr. Pirzada really belonged.

30   At six thirty, which was when the national news began, my father raised the volume and adjusted the antennas. Usually I occupied myself

with a book, but that night my father insisted that I pay attention. On the screen I saw tanks rolling through dusty streets, and fallen buildings, and forests of unfamiliar trees into which East Pakistani refugees had fled, seeking safety over the Indian border. I saw boats with fan-shaped sails floating on wide coffee-colored rivers, a barricaded university, newspaper offices burnt to the ground. I turned to look at Mr Pirzada; the images flashed in miniature across his eyes. As he watched he had an immovable expression on his face, composed but alert, as if someone were giving him directions to an unknown destination.

During the commercials my mother went to the kitchen to get more rice, and my father and Mr. Pirzada deplored the policies of a general named Yahyah Khan. They discussed intrigues I did not know, a catastrophe I could not comprehend. "See, children your age, what they do to survive," my father said as he served me another piece of fish. But I could no longer eat. I could only steal glances at Mr. Pirzada, sitting beside me in his olive green jacket, calmly creating a well in his rice to make room for a second helping of lentils. He was not my notion of a man burdened by such grave concerns. I wondered if the reason he was always so smartly dressed was in preparation to endure with dignity whatever news assailed him, perhaps even to attend a funeral at a moment's notice. I wondered, too, what would happen if suddenly his seven daughters were to appear on television, smiling and waving and blowing kisses to Mr. Pirzada from a balcony. I imagined how relieved he would be. But this never happened.

That night when I placed the plastic egg filled with cinnamon hearts in the box beside my bed, I did not feel the ceremonious satisfaction I normally did. I tried not to think about Mr. Pirzada, in his lime-scented overcoat, connected to the unruly, sweltering world we had viewed a few hours ago in our bright, carpeted living room. And yet for several moments that was all I could think about. My stomach tightened as I worried whether his wife and seven daughters were now members of the drifting, clamoring crowd that had flashed at intervals on the screen. In an effort to banish the image I looked around my room, at the yellow canopied bed with matching flounced curtains, at framed class pictures mounted on white and violet papered walls, at the penciled inscriptions by the closet door where my father recorded my height on each of my birthdays. But the more I tried to distract myself, the more I began to convince myself that Mr. Pirzada's family was in all likelihood dead. Eventually I took a square of white chocolate out of the box, and unwrapped it, and then I did something I had never done before. I put the chocolate in my mouth, letting it soften until the last possible moment, and then as I chewed it slowly, I prayed that Mr. Pirzada's family was safe and sound. I had never prayed for anything before, had never been taught or told to, but I decided, given the circumstances, that it was something I should do. That night when I went to the bathroom I only pretended to brush my teeth, for I feared that I would somehow rinse the prayer out as well. I wet the brush and rearranged the tube of paste to prevent my parents from asking any questions, and fell asleep with sugar on my tongue.

No one at school talked about the war followed so faithfully in my living room. We continued to study the American Revolution, and learned about the injustices of taxation without representation, and memorized passages from the Declaration of Independence. During recess the boys would divide in two groups, chasing each other wildly around the swings and seesaws, Redcoats against the colonies. In the classroom our teacher, Mrs. Kenyon, pointed frequently to a map that emerged like a movie screen from the top of the chalkboard, charting the route of the *Mayflower*, or showing us the location of the Liberty Bell. Each week two members of the class gave a report on a particular aspect of the Revolution, and so one day I was sent to the school library with my friend Dora to learn about the surrender at Yorktown. Mrs. Kenyon handed us a slip of paper with the names of three books to look up in the card catalog. We found them right away, and sat down at a low round table to read and take notes. But I could not concentrate. I returned to the blond-wood shelves, to a section I had noticed labeled "Asia." I saw books about China, India, Indonesia, Korea. Eventually I found a book titled *Pakistan: A Land and Its People*. I sat on a footstool and opened the book. The laminated jacket crackled in my grip. I began turning the pages, filled with photos of rivers and rice fields and men in military uniforms. There was a chapter about Dacca, and I began to read about its rainfall, and its jute production. I was studying a population chart when Dora appeared in the aisle.

"What are you doing back here? Mrs. Kenyon's in the library. She came to check up on us."

35   I slammed the book shut, too loudly. Mrs. Kenyon emerged, the aroma of her perfume filling up the tiny aisle, and lifted the book by the tip of its spine as if it were a hair clinging to my sweater. She glanced at the cover, then at me.

"Is this book a part of your report, Lilia?"

"No, Mrs. Kenyon."

"Then I see no reason to consult it," she said, replacing it in the slim gap on the shelf. "Do you?"

As weeks passed it grew more and more rare to see any footage from Dacca on the news. The report came after the first set of commercials, sometimes the second. The press had been censored, removed, restricted, rerouted. Some days, many days, only a death toll was announced, prefaced by a reiteration of the general situation. More poets were executed, more villages set ablaze. In spite of it all, night after night, my parents and Mr. Pirzada enjoyed long, leisurely meals. After the television was shut off, and the dishes washed and dried, they joked, and told stories, and dipped biscuits in their tea. When they tired of discussing political matters they discussed, instead, the progress of Mr. Pirzada's book about the deciduous trees of New England, and my father's nomination for tenure, and the peculiar eating habits of my mother's American coworkers at the bank. Eventually I was sent upstairs to do my homework, but through the carpet I heard them as they drank more tea, and listened to cassettes of Kishore Kumar, and played Scrabble on the coffee table, laughing and arguing long into the night about the spellings of English words. I wanted

to join them, wanted, above all, to console Mr. Pirzada somehow. But apart from eating a piece of candy for the sake of his family and praying for their safety, there was nothing I could do. They played Scrabble until the eleven o'clock news, and then, sometime around midnight, Mr. Pirzada walked back to his dormitory. For this reason I never saw him leave, but each night as I drifted off to sleep I would hear them, anticipating the birth of a nation on the other side of the world.

40   One day in October Mr. Pirzada asked upon arrival, "What are these large orange vegetables on people's doorsteps? A type of squash?"

"Pumpkins," my mother replied. "Lilia, remind me to pick one up at the supermarket."

"And the purpose? It indicates what?"

"You make a jack-o'-lantern," I said, grinning ferociously. "Like this. To scare people away."

"I see," Mr. Pirzada said, grinning back. "Very useful."

45   The next day my mother bought a ten-pound pumpkin, fat and round, and placed it on the dining table. Before supper, while my father and Mr. Pirzada were watching the local news, she told me to decorate it with markers, but I wanted to carve it properly like others I had noticed in the neighborhood.

"Yes, let's carve it," Mr. Pirzada agreed, and rose from the sofa. "Hang the news tonight." Asking no questions, he walked into the kitchen, opened a drawer, and returned, bearing a long serrated knife. He glanced at me for approval. "Shall I?"

I nodded. For the first time we all gathered around the dining table, my mother, my father, Mr. Pirzada, and I. While the television aired unattended we covered the tabletop with newspapers. Mr. Pirzada draped his jacket over the chair behind him, removed a pair of opal cuff links, and rolled up the starched sleeves of his shirt.

"First go around the top, like this," I instructed, demonstrating with my index finger.

He made an initial incision and drew the knife around. When he had come full circle he lifted the cap by the stem; it loosened effortlessly, and Mr. Pirzada leaned over the pumpkin for a moment to inspect and inhale its contents. My mother gave him a long metal spoon with which he gutted the interior until the last bits of string and seeds were gone. My father, meanwhile, separated the seeds from the pulp and set them out to dry on a cookie sheet, so that we could roast them later on. I drew two triangles against the ridged surface for the eyes, which Mr. Pirzada dutifully carved, and crescents for eyebrows, and another triangle for the nose. The mouth was all that remained, and the teeth posed a challenge. I hesitated.

50   "Smile or frown?" I asked.

"You choose," Mr. Pirzada said.

As a compromise I drew a kind of grimace, straight across, neither mournful nor friendly. Mr. Pirzada began carving, without the least bit of intimidation, as if he had been carving jack-o'-lanterns his whole life. He had nearly finished when the national news began. The reporter mentioned Dacca, and we all turned to listen: An Indian official announced that unless the world helped to relieve the burden of East Pakistani refugees, India would have to go to war against Pakistan. The reporter's face dripped with sweat as he relayed the information. He did not wear a tie or a jacket, dressed instead as if he himself were about to take part in the battle. He shielded his scorched face as he hollered things to the cameraman. The knife slipped from Mr. Pirzada's hand and made a gash dipping toward the base of the pumpkin.

"Please forgive me." He raised a hand to one side of his face, as if someone had slapped him there, "I am—it is terrible. I will buy another. We will try again."

"Not at all, not at all," my father said. He took the knife from Mr. Pirzada, and carved around the gash, evening it out, dispensing altogether with the teeth I had drawn. What resulted was a disproportionately large hole the size of a lemon, so that our jack-o'-lantern wore an expression of placid astonishment, the eyebrows no longer fierce, floating in frozen surprise above a vacant, geometric gaze.

55   For Halloween I was a witch. Dora, my trick-or-treating partner, was a witch too. We wore black capes fashioned from dyed pillowcases and conical hats with wide cardboard brims. We shaded our faces green with a broken eye shadow that belonged to Dora's mother, and my mother gave us two burlap sacks that had once contained basmati rice, for collecting candy. That year our parents decided that we were old enough to roam the neighborhood unattended. Our plan was to walk from my house to Dora's, from where I was to call to say I had arrived safely, and then Dora's mother would drive me home. My father equipped us with flashlights, and I had to wear my watch and synchronize it with his. We were to return no later than nine o'clock.

When Mr. Pirzada arrived that evening he presented me with a box of chocolate-covered mints.

"In here," I told him, and opened up the burlap sack. "Trick or treat!"

"I understand that you don't really need my contribution this evening," he said, depositing the box. He gazed at my green face, and the hat secured by a string under my chin. Gingerly he lifted the hem of the cape, under which I was wearing a sweater and a zipped fleece jacket. "Will you be warm enough?"

I nodded, causing the hat to tip to one side.

60   He set it right. "Perhaps it is best to stand still."

The bottom of our staircase was lined with baskets of miniature candy, and when Mr. Pirzada removed his shoes he did not place them there as he normally did, but inside the closet instead. He began to unbutton his coat, and I waited to take it from him, but Dora called me from the bathroom to say that she needed my help drawing a mole on her chin. When we were finally ready my mother took a picture of us in front of the fireplace, and then I opened the front door to leave. Mr. Pirzada and my father, who had not gone into the living room yet, hovered in the foyer. Outside it was already dark. The air smelled of wet leaves, and our carved jack-o'-lantern flickered impressively against the shrubbery by the door. In the distance came the sounds of scampering feet, and the howls of the older boys who wore no costumes at all other than a rubber mask, and the rustling apparel of the youngest children, some so young that they were carried from door to door in the arms of their parents.

"Don't go into any of the houses you don't know," my father warned.

Mr. Pirzada knit his brows together. "Is there any danger?"

"No, no," my mother assured him. "All the children will be out. It's a tradition."

65 "Perhaps I should accompany them?" Mr. Pirzada suggested. He looked suddenly tired and small, standing there in his splayed, stockinged feet, and his eyes contained a panic I had never seen before. In spite of the cold I began to sweat inside my pillowcase.

"Really, Mr. Pirzada," my mother said, "Lilia will be perfectly safe with her friend."

"But if it rains? If they lose their way?"

"Don't worry," I said. It was the first time I had uttered those words to Mr. Pirzada, two simple words I had tried but failed to tell him for weeks, had said only in my prayers. It shamed me now that I had said them for my own sake.

He placed one of his stocky fingers on my cheek, then pressed it to the back of his own hand, leaving a faint green smear. "If the lady insists," he conceded, and offered a small bow.

70 We left, stumbling slightly in our black pointy thrift-store shoes, and when we turned at the end of the driveway to wave good-bye, Mr. Pirzada was standing in the frame of the doorway, a short figure between my parents, waving back.

"Why did that man want to come with us?" Dora asked.

"His daughters are missing." As soon as I said it, I wished I had not, I felt that my saying it made it true, that Mr. Pirzada's daughters really were missing, and that he would never see them again.

"You mean they were kidnapped?" Dora continued. "From a park or something?"

"I didn't mean they were missing. I meant, he misses them. They live in a different country, and he hasn't seen them in a while, that's all."

75 We went from house to house, walking along pathways and pressing doorbells. Some people had switched off all their lights for effect, or strung rubber bats in their windows. At the McIntyres' a coffin was placed in front of the door, and Mr. McIntyre rose from it in silence, his face covered with chalk, and deposited a fistful of candy corns into our sacks. Several people told me that they had never seen an Indian witch before. Others

performed the transaction without comment. As we paved our way with the parallel beams of our flashlights we saw eggs cracked in the middle of the road, and cars covered with shaving cream, and toilet paper garlanding the branches of trees. By the time we reached Dora's house our hands were chapped from carrying our bulging burlap bags, and our feet were sore and swollen. Her mother gave us bandages for our blisters and served us warm cider and caramel popcorn. She reminded me to call my parents to tell them I had arrived safely, and when I did I could hear the television in the background. My mother did not seem particularly relieved to hear from me. When I replaced the phone on the receiver it occurred to me that the television wasn't on at Dora's house at all. Her father was lying on the couch, reading a magazine, with a glass of wine on the coffee table, and there was saxophone music playing on the stereo.

After Dora and I had sorted through our plunder, and counted and sampled and traded until we were satisfied, her mother drove me back to my house. I thanked her for the ride, and she waited in the driveway until I made it to the door. In the glare of her headlights I saw that our pumpkin had been shattered, its thick shell strewn in chunks across the grass. I felt the sting of tears in my eyes, and a sudden pain in my throat, as if it had been stuffed with the sharp tiny pebbles that crunched with each step under my aching feet. I opened the door, expecting the three of them to be standing in the foyer, waiting to receive me, and to grieve for our ruined pumpkin, but there was no one. In the living room Mr. Pirzada, my father, and mother were sitting side by side on the sofa. The television was turned off, and Mr. Pirzada had his head in his hands.

What they heard that evening, and for many evenings after that, was that India and Pakistan were drawing closer and closer to war. Troops from both sides lined the border, and Dacca was insisting on nothing short of independence. The war was to be waged on East Pakistani soil. The United States was siding with West Pakistan, the Soviet Union with India and what was soon to be Bangladesh. War was declared officially on December 4, and twelve days later, the Pakistani army, weakened by having to fight three thousand miles from their source of supplies, surrendered in Dacca. All of these facts I know only now, for they are available to me in any history book, in any library. But then it remained, for the most part, a remote mystery with haphazard clues. What I remember during those twelve days of the war was that my father no longer asked me to watch the news with them, and that Mr. Pirzada stopped bringing me candy, and that my mother refused to serve anything other than boiled eggs with rice for dinner. I remember some nights helping my mother spread a sheet and blankets on the couch so that Mr. Pirzada could sleep there, and high-pitched voices hollering in the middle of the night when my parents called our relatives in Calcutta to learn more details about the situation. Most of all I remember the three of them operating during that time as if they were a single person, sharing a single meal, a single body, a single silence, and a single fear.

In January, Mr. Pirzada flew back to his three-story home in Dacca, to discover what was left of it. We did not see much of him in those final weeks of the year; he was busy finishing his manuscript, and we went to Philadelphia to spend Christmas with friends of my parents. Just as I have no memory of his first visit, I have no memory of his last. My father drove him to the airport one afternoon while I was at school. For a long time we did not hear from him. Our evenings went on as usual, with dinners in front of the news. The only difference was that Mr. Pirzada and his extra watch were not there to accompany us. According to reports Dacca was repairing itself slowly, with a newly formed parliamentary government. The new leader, Sheikh Mujib Rahman, recently released from prison, asked countries for building materials to replace more than one million houses that had been destroyed in the war. Countless refugees returned from India, greeted, we learned, by unemployment and the threat of famine. Every now and then I studied the map above my father's desk and pictured Mr. Pirzada on that small patch of yellow, perspiring heavily, I imagined, in one of his suits, searching for his family. Of course, the map was outdated by then.

Finally, several months later, we received a card from Mr. Pirzada commemorating the Muslim New Year, along with a short letter. He was reunited, he wrote, with his wife and children. All were well, having survived the events of the past year at an estate belonging to his wife's grandparents in the mountains of Shillong. His seven daughters were a bit taller, he wrote, but otherwise they were the same, and he still could not keep their names in order. At the end of the letter he thanked us for our hospitality, adding that although he now understood the meaning of the words "thank you" they still were not adequate to express his gratitude. To celebrate the good news my mother prepared a special dinner that evening, and when we sat down to eat at the coffee table we toasted our water glasses, but I did not feel like celebrating. Though I had not seen him for months, it was only then that I felt Mr. Pirzada's absence. It was only then, raising my water glass in his name, that I knew what it meant to miss someone who was so many miles and hours away, just as he had missed his wife and daughters for so many months. He had no reason to return to us, and my parents predicted, correctly, that we would never see him again. Since January, each night before bed, I had continued to eat, for the sake of Mr. Pirzada's family a piece of candy I had saved from Halloween. That night there was no need to. Eventually, I threw them away.

[1999]

QUESTIONS FOR REFLECTION AND DISCUSSION

1. What are some of the distinctions made in the story between life in Massachusetts and life in East Pakistan?

2. What are some possible reasons Lahiri chose to set a key episode of the story on Halloween? Suggest some connections between the events of Halloween and the events in East Pakistan.

3. How does the family's relationship with Mr. Pirzada change once he is back in Dacca?

4. Lahiri implies a number of parallels between the friendship with Mr. Pirzada and the war between Pakistan and India. What is the relationship between this friendship and the war? How are they similar and how are they different?

KAZUO ISHIGURO B. 1954

Kazuo Ishiguro's family moved from Nagasaki, Japan, to England when he was six years old. He attended school there, became an English citizen in 1982, and now lives in London. Ishiguro is ambiguous about his relation to Japanese literature, claiming in an interview to have been more influenced by Japanese films and to have little familiarity with the country. And, in fact, although his first two novels are set in Japan, others are set in Central Europe and in England. What is clear from "A Family Supper" is that Ishiguro is quite familiar with clichés about his native country. As you read the story, pay close attention to the way he manipulates expectations about how "Japanese" characters are supposed to act.

A FAMILY SUPPER

FUGU IS A FISH CAUGHT OFF THE PACIFIC SHORES OF Japan. The fish has held a special significance for me ever since my mother died through eating one. The poison resides in the sexual glands of the fish, inside two fragile bags. When preparing the fish, these bags must be removed with caution, for any clumsiness will result in the poison leaking into the veins. Regrettably, it is not easy to tell whether or not this operation has been carried out successfully. The proof is, as it were, in the eating.

Fugu poisoning is hideously painful and almost always fatal. If the fish has been eaten during the evening, the victim is usually overtaken by pain during his sleep. He rolls about in agony for a few hours and is dead by morning. The fish became extremely popular in Japan after the war. Until stricter regulations were imposed, it was all the rage to perform the hazardous gutting operation in one's own kitchen, then to invite neighbours and friends round for the feast.

At the time of my mother's death, I was living in California. My relationship with my parents had become somewhat strained around that period, and consequently I did not learn of the circumstances surrounding her death until I returned to Tokyo two years later. Apparently, my mother had always refused to eat fugu, but on this particular occasion she had made an exception, having been invited by an old schoolfriend whom she was anxious not to offend. It was my father who supplied me with the details as we drove from the

airport to his house in the Kamakura district. When we finally arrived, it was nearing the end of a sunny autumn day.

"Did you eat on the plane?" my father asked. We were sitting on the tatami floor of his tearoom.

5 "They gave me a light snack."

"You must be hungry. We'll eat as soon as Kikuko arrives."

My father was a formidable-looking man with a large stony jaw and furious black eyebrows. I think now in retrospect that he much resembled Chou En-lai, although he would not have cherished such a comparison, being particularly proud of the pure samurai blood that ran in the family. His general presence was not one which encouraged relaxed conversation; neither were things helped much by his odd way of stating each remark as if it were the concluding one. In fact, as I sat opposite him that afternoon, a boyhood memory came back to me of the time he had struck me several times around the head for "chattering like an old woman." Inevitably, our conversation since my arrival at the airport had been punctuated by long pauses.

"I'm sorry to hear about the firm," I said when neither of us had spoken for some time. He nodded gravely.

"In fact the story didn't end there," he said. "After the firm's collapse, Watanabe killed himself. He didn't wish to live with the disgrace."

10   "I see."

"We were partners for seventeen years. A man of principle and honour. I respected him very much."

"Will you go into business again?" I asked.

"I am—in retirement. I'm too old to involve myself in new ventures now. Business these days has become so different. Dealing with foreigners. Doing things their way. I don't understand how we've come to this. Neither did Watanabe." He sighed. "A fine man. A man of principle."

The tea-room looked out over the garden. From where I sat I could make out the ancient well which as a child I had believed haunted. It was just visible now through the thick foliage. The sun had sunk low and much of the garden had fallen into shadow.

15   "I'm glad in any case that you've decided to come back," my father said. "More than a short visit, I hope."

"I'm not sure what my plans will be."

"I for one am prepared to forget the past. Your mother too was always ready to welcome you back—upset as she was by your behaviour."

"I appreciate your sympathy. As I say, I'm not sure what my plans are."

"I've come to believe now that there were no evil intentions in your mind," my father continued. "You were swayed by certain—influences. Like so many others."

20   "Perhaps we should forget it, as you suggest."

"As you will. More tea?"

Just then a girl's voice came echoing through the house.

"At last." My father rose to his feet. "Kikuko has arrived."

Despite our difference in years, my sister and I had always been close. Seeing me again seemed to make her excessively excited and for a while she did nothing but giggle nervously. But she calmed down somewhat when my father started to question her about Osaka and her university. She answered him with short formal replies. She in turn asked me a few questions, but she seemed inhibited by the fear that her questions might lead to awkward topics. After a while, the conversation had become even sparser than prior to Kikuko's arrival. Then my father stood up, saying: "I must attend to

A fugu restaurant in Kyoto, Japan. The prominent model of a fugu over the restaurant entrance suggests the outsized status of the fish within Japanese culture, a status with which "A Family Supper" is also concerned.

the supper. Please excuse me for being burdened down by such matters. Kikuko will look after you."

25   My sister relaxed quite visibly once he had left the room. Within a few minutes, she was chatting freely about her friends in Osaka and about her classes at university. Then quite suddenly she decided we should walk in the garden and went striding out onto the veranda. We put on some straw sandals that had been left along the veranda rail and stepped out into the garden. The daylight had almost gone.

"I've been dying for a smoke for the last half-hour," she said, lighting a cigarette.

"Then why didn't you smoke?"

She made a furtive gesture back towards the house, then grinned mischievously.

"Oh I see," I said.

30 "Guess what? I've got a boyfriend now."

"Oh yes?"

"Except I'm wondering what to do. I haven't made up my mind yet."

"Quite understandable."

"You see, he's making plans to go to America. He wants me to go with him as soon as I finish studying."

35 "I see. And you want to go to America?"

"If we go, we're going to hitch-hike." Kikuko waved a thumb in front of my face. "People say it's dangerous, but I've done it in Osaka and it's fine."

"I see. So what is it you're unsure about?"

We were following a narrow path that wound through the shrubs and finished by the old well. As we walked, Kikuko persisted in taking unnecessarily theatrical puffs on her cigarette.

"Well. I've got lots of friends now in Osaka. I like it there. I'm not sure I want to leave them all behind just yet. And Suichi—I like him, but I'm not sure I want to spend so much time with him. Do you understand?"

40 "Oh perfectly."

She grinned again, then skipped on ahead of me until she had reached the well. "Do you remember," she said, as I came walking up to her, "how you used to say this well was haunted?"

"Yes, I remember."

We both peered over the side.

"Mother always told me it was the old woman from the vegetable store you'd seen that night," she said. "But I never believed her and never came out here alone."

45 "Mother used to tell me that too. She even told me once the old woman had confessed to being the ghost. Apparently she'd been taking a short cut through our garden. I imagine she had some trouble clambering over these walls."

Kikuko gave a giggle. She then turned her back to the well, casting her gaze about the garden.

"Mother never really blamed you, you know," she said, in a new voice. I remained silent. "She always used to say to me how it was their fault, hers and Father's, for not bringing you up correctly. She used to tell me how much more careful they'd been with me, and that's why I was so

good." She looked up and the mischievous grin had returned to her face. "Poor Mother," she said.

"Yes. Poor Mother."

"Are you going back to California?"

50 "I don't know. I'll have to see."

"What happened to—to her? To Vicki?"

"That's all finished with," I said. "There's nothing much left for me now in California."

"Do you think I ought to go there?"

"Why not? I don't know. You'll probably like it." "I glanced towards the house. "Perhaps we'd better go in soon. Father might need a hand with the supper."

55 But my sister was once more peering down into the well. "I can't see any ghosts," she said. Her voice echoed a little.

"Is Father very upset about his firm collapsing?"

"Don't know. You can never tell with Father." Then suddenly she straightened up and turned to me. "Did he tell you about old Watanabe? What he did?"

"I heard he committed suicide."

"Well, that wasn't all. He took his whole family with him. His wife and his two little girls."

60 "Oh yes?"

"Those two beautiful little girls. He turned on the gas while they were all asleep. Then he cut his stomach with a meat knife."

"Yes, Father was just telling me how Watanabe was a man of principle."

"Sick," My sister turned back to the well.

"Careful. You'll fall right in."

65 "I can't see any ghost," she said. "You were lying to me all that time."

"But I never said it lived down the well."

"Where is it, then?"

We both looked around at the trees and shrubs. The light in the garden had grown very dim. Eventually I pointed to a small clearing some ten yards away.

"Just there I saw it. Just there."

70 We stared at the spot.

"What did it look like?"

"I couldn't see very well. It was dark."

"But you must have seen something."

"It was an old woman. She was just standing there, watching me."

75 We kept staring at the spot as if mesmerized.

"She was wearing a white kimono," I said. "Some of her hair had come undone. It was blowing around a little."

Kikuko pushed her elbow against my arm. "Oh be quiet. You're trying to frighten me all over again." She trod on the remains of her cigarette, then for a brief moment stood regarding it with a perplexed expression. She kicked some pine needles over it, then once more displayed her grin. "Let's see if supper's ready," she said.

We found my father in the kitchen. He gave us a quick glance, then carried on with what he was doing.

"Father's become quite a chef since he's had to manage on his own," Kikuko said with a laugh. He turned and looked at my sister coldly.

80 "Hardly a skill I'm proud of," he said. "Kikuko, come here and help."

For some moments my sister did not move. Then she stepped forward and took an apron hanging from a drawer.

"Just these vegetables need cooking now," he said to her. "The rest just needs watching." Then he looked up and regarded me strangely for some seconds. "I expect you want to look around the house," he said eventually. He put down the chopsticks he had been holding. "It's a long time since you've seen it."

As we left the kitchen I glanced back towards Kikuko, but her back was turned.

"She's a good girl," my father said quietly.

85 I followed my father from room to room. I had forgotten how large the house was. A panel would slide open and another room would appear. But the rooms were all startlingly empty. In one of the rooms the lights did not come on, and we stared at the stark walls and tatami in the pale light that came from the windows.

"This house is too large for a man to live in alone," my father said. "I don't have much use for most of these rooms now."

But eventually my father opened the door to a room packed full of books and papers. There were flowers in vases and pictures on the walls. Then I noticed something on a low table in the corner of the room. I came nearer and saw it was a plastic model of a battleship, the kind constructed by children. It had been placed on some newspaper; scattered around it were assorted pieces of grey plastic.

My father gave a laugh. He came up to the table and picked up the model.

"Since the firm folded," he said, "I have a little more time on my hands." He laughed again, rather strangely. For a moment his face looked almost gentle. "A little more time."

90 "That seems odd," I said. "You were always so busy."

"Too busy perhaps." He looked at me with a small smile. "Perhaps I should have been a more attentive father."

I laughed. He went on contemplating his battleship. Then he looked up. "I hadn't meant to tell you this, but perhaps it's best that I do. It's my belief that your mother's death was no accident. She had many worries. And some disappointments."

We both gazed at the plastic battleship.

"Surely," I said eventually, "my mother didn't expect me to live here for ever."

95 "Obviously you don't see. You don't see how it is for some parents. Not only must they lose their children, they must lose them to things they don't understand." He spun the battleship in his fingers. "These little gunboats here could have been better glued, don't you think?"

"Perhaps. I think it looks fine."

"During the war I spent some time on a ship rather like this. But my ambition was always the air force. I figured it like this. If your ship was struck by the enemy, all you could do was struggle in the water hoping for a lifeline. But in an aeroplane—well—there was always the final weapon." He put the model back onto the table. "I don't suppose you believe in war."

"Not particularly."

He cast an eye around the room. "Supper should be ready by now," he said. "You must be hungry."

100 Supper was waiting in a dimly lit room next to the kitchen. The only source of light was a big lantern that hung over the table, casting the rest of the room into shadow. We bowed to each other before starting the meal.

There was little conversation. When I made some polite comment about the food, Kikuko giggled a little. Her earlier nervousness seemed to have returned to her. My father did not speak for several minutes. Finally he said:

"It must feel strange for you, being back in Japan."

"Yes, it is a little strange."

"Already, perhaps, you regret leaving America."

105 "A little. Not so much. I didn't leave behind much. Just some empty rooms."

"I see."

I glanced across the table. My father's face looked stony and forbidding in the half-light. We ate on in silence.

Then my eye caught something at the back of the room. At first I continued eating, then my hands became still. The others noticed and looked at me. I went on gazing into the darkness past my father's shoulder.

"Who is that? In that photograph there?"

110 "Which photograph?" My father turned slightly, trying to follow my gaze.

"The lowest one. The old woman in the white kimono."

My father put down his chopsticks. He looked first at the photograph, then at me.

"Your mother." His voice had become very hard. "Can't you recognize your own mother?"

"My mother. You see, it's dark. I can't see it very well."

115 No one spoke for a few seconds, then Kikuko rose to her feet. She took the photograph down from the wall, came back to the table and gave it to me.

"She looks a lot older," I said.

"It was taken shortly before her death," said my father.

"It was the dark. I couldn't see very well."

I looked up and noticed my father holding out a hand. I gave him the photograph. He looked at it intently, then held it towards Kikuko. Obediently, my sister rose to her feet once more and returned the picture to the wall.

120 There was a large pot left unopened at the centre of the table. When Kikuko had seated herself again, my father reached forward and lifted the lid. A cloud of steam rose up and curled towards the lantern. He pushed the pot a little towards me.

"You must be hungry," he said. One side of his face had fallen into shadow.

"Thank you." I reached forward with my chopsticks. The steam was almost scalding. "What is it?"

"Fish."

"It smells very good."

125 In amidst soup were strips of fish that had curled almost into balls. I picked one out and brought it to my bowl.

"Help yourself. There's plenty."

"Thank you." I took a little more, then pushed the pot towards my father. I watched him take several pieces to his bowl. Then we both watched as Kikuko served herself.

My father bowed slightly. "You must be hungry," he said again. He took some fish to his mouth and started to eat. Then I too chose a piece and put it in my mouth. It felt soft, quite fleshy against my tongue.

"Very good," I said. "What is it?"

130 "Just fish."

"It's very good."

The three of us ate on in silence. Several minutes went by.

"Some more?"

"Is there enough?"

135 "There's plenty for all of us." My father lifted the lid and once more steam rose up. We all reached forward and helped ourselves.

"Here," I said to my father, "you have this last piece."

"Thank you."

When we had finished the meal, my father stretched out his arms and yawned with an air of satisfaction. "Kikuko," he said. "Prepare a pot of tea, please."

My sister looked at him, then left the room without comment. My father stood up.

140 "Let's retire to the other room. It's rather warm in here."

I got to my feet and followed him into the tea-room. The large sliding windows had been left open, bringing in a breeze from the garden. For a while we sat in silence.

"Father," I said, finally.

"Yes?"

"Kikuko tells me Watanabe-San took his whole family with him."

145 My father lowered his eyes and nodded. For some moments he seemed deep in thought. "Watanabe was very devoted to his work," he said at last. "The collapse of the firm was a great blow to him. I fear it must have weakened his judgement."

"You think what he did—it was a mistake?"

"Why, of course. Do you see it otherwise?"

"No, no. Of course not."

"There are other things besides work."

150 "Yes."

We fell silent again. The sound of locusts came in from the garden. I looked out into the darkness. The well was no longer visible.

"What do you think you will do now?" my father asked. "Will you stay in Japan for a while?"

"To be honest, I hadn't thought that far ahead."

"If you wish to stay here, I mean here in this house, you would be very welcome. That is, if you don't mind living with an old man."

155 "Thank you. I'll have to think about it."

I gazed out once more into the darkness.

"But of course," said my father, "this house is so dreary now. You'll no doubt return to America before long."

"Perhaps. I don't know yet."

"No doubt you will."

160 For some time my father seemed to be studying the back of his hands. Then he looked up and sighed.

"Kikuko is due to complete her studies next spring," he said. "Perhaps she will want to come home then. She's a good girl."

"Perhaps she will."

"Things will improve then."

"Yes, I'm sure they will."

165 We fell silent once more, waiting for Kikuko to bring the tea.

[1982]

QUESTIONS FOR REFLECTION AND DISCUSSION

1. What kind of fish does the father serve his children at the end of the story? Why is it important to know? What is the effect of Ishiguro's decision to make the ending ambiguous?

2. Several other key events in the story are left either unexplained or insufficiently motivated. What can we be certain about in the story and what must we infer or speculate about?

3. The "ancient well" in the backyard provides a potent image in the story. With which characters and themes does it become associated, and how does it affect the meaning of those characters and themes?

4. Does the relationship between the father and son change during the course of the story? Base your answer on specific details in the text.

POETRY

GARRETT HONGO B. 1951

The Japanese American poet Garrett Hongo was born in Volcano, Hawaii, and graduated from Claremont College. He is professor of creative writing at the University of Oregon, and author of two volumes of poetry, *Yellow Light* (1982) and *The River of Heaven* (1989), a finalist for the Pulitzer Prize. His most recent book is *Volcano: A Memoir of Hawaii* (1995).

Who Among You Knows the Essence of Garlic?

Can your foreigner's nose smell mullets
roasting in a glaze of black bean paste
and sprinkled with novas of sea salt?

Can you hear my grandmother
chant the mushroom's sutra?   5

Can you hear the papayas crying
as they bleed in porcelain plates?

I'm telling you that the bamboo
slips the long pliant shoots
of its myriad soft tongues   10
into your mouth that is full of oranges.

I'm saying that the silver waterfalls
of bean threads will burst in hot oil
and stain your lips like zinc.

The marbled skin of the blue mackerel   15
works good for men. The purple oils
from its flesh perfume the tongues of women.

If you swallow them whole, the rice cakes
soaking in a broth of coconut milk and brown sugar
will never leave the bottom of your stomach.   20

Flukes of giant black mushrooms
leap from their murky tubs
and strangle the toes of young carrots.

Broiling chickens ooze grease,
yellow tears of fat collect   25
and spatter in the smoking pot.

Soft ripe pears, blushing
on the kitchen window sill,
kneel like plump women
taking a long luxurious shampoo,   30
and invite you to bite their hips.

Why not grab basketfuls of steaming noodles,
lush and slick as the hair of a fine lady,
and squeeze?

The shrimps, big as Portuguese thumbs,   35
stew among cut guavas, red onions,
ginger root, and rosemary in lemon juice,
the palm oil bubbling to the top,
breaking through layers and layers
of shredded coconut and sliced cashews.   40

Who among you knows the essence
of garlic and black lotus root,
of red and green peppers sizzling
among squads of oysters in the skillet,
of crushed ginger, fresh green onions   45
and pale-blue rice wine simmering
in the stomach of a big red fish?

[1982]

QUESTIONS FOR REFLECTION AND DISCUSSION

1. Who is the "you" that the speaker addresses in the poem?
   What distinction does he make between himself and "you"?

2. What effect do you think Hongo seeks to create with the
   detailed description of food?

3. Does the poem develop as it goes along, or is it structured
   primarily as an anaphora (p. 212)?

4. What is the function of the similes in stanzas 10 and 11?
   Do they create a different effect than the straight descriptions used elsewhere in the poem?

XU GANG B. 1945

Born in Shanghai, Xu Gang was drafted into the Army at the age of seventeen, and he wrote his first
poetry in support of the goals of the Cultural Revolution. After graduating from Beijing University in 1974,
he worked for the *People's Daily* newspaper for over a decade, becoming known for reporting on China's
ecological crisis. He participated in the democracy movement in 1989 and currently lives in Paris. Gang
has published and been given prizes for a number of volumes of poetry.

Red Azalea on the Cliff

Translated by Fang Dai, Dennis Ding, and Edward Morin

Red azalea, smiling
From the Cliffside at me,
You make my heart shudder with fear!
A body could smash and bones splinter in the canyon
Beauty, always looking on at disaster.   5

But red azalea on the cliff,
That you comb your twigs even in a mountain gale
Calms me down a bit.
Of course you're not wilfully courting danger,
Nor are you at ease with whatever happens to you.   10
You're merely telling me: beauty is nature.

Would anyone like to pick a flower
To give to his love
Or pin to his own lapel?
On the cliff there is no road   15
And no azalea grows where there is a road.
If someone actually reached that azalea,
Then an azalea would surely bloom in his heart.

Red azalea on the cliff,
You smile like the Yellow Mountains,   20
Whose sweetness encloses slyness,
Whose intimacy embraces distance.
You remind us all of our first love.
Sometimes the past years look
Just like the azalea on the cliff.   25

[1982]

QUESTIONS FOR REFLECTION AND DISCUSSION

1. What is surprising to the speaker about where he finds the red azalea? What contrast does he find in the situation?

2. What in the azalea leads the speaker to relate it to images of love in stanzas 3 and 4?

3. Is the final simile meant to explain the previous lines of the poem or to open up a new line of thought?

WORKING FURTHER WITH THE LITERATURE OF ASIA

1. Write an essay on the role of food in two or three of the readings in this casebook.

2. Write an essay on the depiction of life within two different cultures in two or three of the readings in this casebook.

3. Write an essay on the function of visual media and/or popular culture in two or three of the selections in this casebook.

4. Read other writings by Jhumpa Lahiri and write a paper on their principal themes.

5. Drawing from the selections in this casebook, write an argument essay on what it means (if anything) to be Asian.

THE LITERATURE OF ASIA FURTHER READINGS IN *LITERATURE: A WORLD OF WRITING*

Robert Hass, "Heroic Simile" • Michael Martone, "The Mayor of the Sister City Speaks to the Chamber of Commerce in Klamath Falls, Oregon, on a Night in December in 1976" • Ono no Komachi, three *tanka* • Salman Rushdie, "Imagine There's No Heaven" • Sei Shonagon, "Hateful Things" • Amy Tan, "Mother Tongue" • Kitty Tsui, "A Chinese Banquet" • Uruttiran, "What She Said to Her Girl Friend"

CHAPTER 11

THE WORLD WE SHARE

NATURE, CITIES, AND THE ENVIRONMENT

In a world inhabited by well over six billion people, we have become ever more conscious that the spaces around us are spaces we share with others. To be isolated in nature was a common experience for the majority of human beings until quite recently. Such solitude first became something to seek out a couple of hundred years ago. For the Romantics, nature was something that took you out of the world you knew, and transported you into another place and another, deeper state of mind. While it has become more and more difficult to find places remote enough to attempt a romantic communion with the natural world, it has also become ever easier to imagine nature as something that exists outside of ourselves and the lives that we live. We have become equally accustomed to regard the living world with which we share our planet as alien from us as well, easily forgetting that we, too, are animals, and that we, too, inhabit this earth. What is this world we inhabit and how do we live in it? The readings in this chapter find many ways to address these fundamental questions and many ways to address the cataclysmic transformations our world has undergone in the past two centuries. In the first section of the chapter, we collect readings that relate to the dominant spatial organization of the modern world, the city. In the section that follows, we collect readings concerned with the place of nature in that same world.

IMAGING CITY AND NATURE TOGETHER

In 1970, construction began in the Arizona desert on Arcosanti, a prototype town for 5,000 people designed according to the ecological principle of "arcology" developed by Italian architect Paolo Soleri. According to the Arcosanti webpage, "Arcology advocates cities designed to maximize the interaction and accessibility associated with an urban environment; minimize the use of energy, raw materials and land, reducing waste and environmental pollution; and allow interaction with the surrounding natural environment." We include here several photographs of the ongoing project as a way of introducing the issues that arise when we think about nature, about cities, and about the world shared by both.

Critical Mass is the first "major phase" of development of Arcosanti. It is planned to be a town of 500 to 600 people who will live and work, study, and/or visit. This will be the staging ground for the subsequent larger development of Paolo Soleri's most recent design for Arcosanti, Arcosanti 5000.

Arcosanti. Southern exposure. The Arcosanti site is located about 60 miles north of Phoenix. Since 1970 thousands of students and professionals have come to Arcosanti to participate in seminars, conferences, and workshops conducted by Paolo Soleri and his staff.

The Visitor's Center at Arcosanti.

QUESTIONS FOR REFLECTION AND DISCUSSION

1. What seems to you different in the relationship between city and nature in these photos than in a city or cities you are familiar with? What seems to you similar?

2. Would you like to live in a town like this? Why or why not?

LIVING IN THE CITY

The city is a fact in nature, like a cave, a run of mackerel or an ant-heap. But it is also a conscious work of art, and it holds within its communal framework many simpler and more personal forms of art. Mind takes form in the city; and in turn, urban forms condition mind.

—LEWIS MUMFORD

At the turn of the millennium, nearly half of the world's population lived in cities. In 1900, only 14 percent did so, and before the Industrial Revolution nearly every person in the world lived in the country. Such a radical change in global living patterns has taken a long time to assimilate, and much of modern literature has been devoted to making sense of the new forms of urban living and the transformation wrought in the countryside by the emptying out of its population. The city nurtured new art forms such as jazz and the movies. It also created new kinds of spaces and settings such as skyscrapers and subways for which the rural world has no equivalent. But perhaps the greatest shock to new city dwellers was the sheer density of population and the extraordinary experience of being lost in a crowd of strangers. This section of the chapter explores different aspects of the peculiarity of urban space and the different ways we experience cities. At the same time, it asks you to remember that the city, as Lewis Mumford has described it, is both part of nature and a human artifact. The selections in this section explore this paradox in a range of settings, but they focus on perhaps the ultimate twentieth-century city, New York. What all of the selections share is the search for defining the place of individual experience within the urban landscape, and the way that social categories such as gender, race, and class divisions play out in specific locations and situations within that landscape.

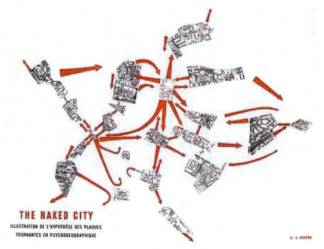

THE NAKED CITY
ILLUSTRATION DE L'HYPOTHÈSE DES PLAQUES
TOURNANTES EN PSYCHOGEOGRAPHIQUE

The Naked City, "psychogeographic" map by Guy Debord, 1957. In reaction to the rationalist city planning of the 1950s, Debord posited a "psychogeographic" map of Paris that would imagine a subjective, provisional, and unplanned experience of the city. How does this visual image of the clash between structure and individual compare to the imagery of the literary texts below?

FICTION

Toni Cade Bambara 1939–1995

Miltona Mirkin Cade grew up in Harlem and elsewhere in the New York City area, and attended Queens College. She received her MA in 1964 from the City College of New York, and began teaching there the following year. Politically radical and a social activist, Bambara saw writing as a means to transform society. In 1971, she edited *The Black Woman,* an influential anthology of nonfiction, fiction, and poetry. The following year, she published her first collection of stories, *Gorilla, My Love,* which includes "The Lesson." Her first novel, *The Salt Eaters,* appeared in 1978.

THE LESSON

BACK IN THE DAYS WHEN EVERYONE WAS OLD and stupid or young and foolish and me and Sugar were the only ones just right, this lady moved on our block with nappy hair and proper speech and no makeup. And quite naturally we laughed at her, laughed the way we did at the junk man who went about his business like he was some big-time president and his sorry-ass horse his secretary. And we kinda hated her too, hated the way we did the winos who cluttered up our parks and pissed on our handball walls and stank up our hallways and stairs so you couldn't halfway play hide-and-seek without a goddamn gas mask. Miss Moore was her name. The only woman on the block with no first name. And she was black as hell, cept for her feet, which were fish-white and spooky. And she was always planning these boring-ass things for us to do, us being my cousin, mostly, who lived on the block cause we all moved North the same time and to the same apartment then spread out gradual to breathe. And our parents would yank our heads into some kinda shape and crisp up our clothes so we'd be presentable for travel with Miss Moore, who always looked like she was going to church, though she never did. Which is just one of the things the grownups talked about when they talked behind her back like a dog. But when she came calling with some sachet she'd sewed up or some gingerbread she'd made or some book, why then they'd still be too embarrassed to turn her down and we'd get handed over all spruced up. She'd been to college and said it was only right that she should take responsibility for the young ones' education, and she not even related by marriage or blood. So they'd go for it. Specially Aunt Gretchen. She was the main gofer in the family. You got some ole dumb shit foolishness you want somebody to go for, you send for Aunt Gretchen. She been screwed into the go-along for so long, it's a blood-deep natural thing with her. Which is how she got saddled with me and Sugar and Junior in the first place while our mothers were in a la-de-da apartment up the block having a good ole time.

So this one day Miss Moore rounds us all up at the mailbox and it's puredee hot and she's knockin herself out about arithmetic. And school suppose to let up in summer I heard, but she don't never let up. And the starch in my pinafore scratching the shit outta me and I'm really hating this nappy-head bitch and her goddamn college degree. I'd much rather go to the pool or to the show where it's cool. So me and Sugar leaning on the mailbox being surly, which is a Miss Moore word. And Flyboy checking out what everybody brought for lunch. And Fat Butt already wasting his peanut-butter-and-jelly sandwich like the pig he is. And Junebug punchin on Q.T.'s arm for

potato chips. And Rosie Giraffe shifting from one hip to the other waiting for somebody to step on her foot or ask her if she from Georgia so she can kick ass, preferably Mercedes'. And Miss Moore asking us do we know what money is, like we a bunch of retards. I mean real money, she say, like it's only poker chips or monopoly papers we lay on the grocer. So right away I'm tired of this and say so. And would much rather snatch Sugar and go to the Sunset and terrorize the West Indian kids and take their hair ribbons and their money too. And Miss Moore files that remark away for next week's lesson on brotherhood, I can tell. And finally I say we oughta get to the subway cause it's cooler and besides we might meet some cute boys. Sugar done swiped her mama's lipstick, so we ready.

So we heading down the street and she's boring us silly about what things cost and what our parents make and how much goes for rent and how money ain't divided up right in this country. And then she gets to the part about we all poor and live in the slums, which I don't feature. And I'm ready to speak on that, but she steps out in the street and hails two cabs just like that. Then she hustles half the crew in with her and hands me a five-dollar bill and tells me to calculate 10 percent tip for the driver. And we're off. Me and Sugar and Junebug and Flyboy hangin out the window and hollering to everybody, putting lipstick on each other cause Flyboy a faggot anyway, and making farts with our sweaty armpits. But I'm mostly trying to figure how to spend this money. But they all fascinated with the meter ticking and Junebug starts laying bets to how much it'll read when Flyboy can't hold his breath no more. Then Sugar lays bets as to how much it'll be when we get there. So I'm stuck. Don't nobody want to go for my plan, which is to jump out at the next light and run off to the first bar-b-que we can find. Then the driver tells us to get the hell out cause we there already. And the meter reads eighty-five cents. And I'm stalling to figure out the tip and Sugar say give him a dime. And I decide he don't need it bad as I do, so later for him. But then he tries to take off with Junebug foot still in the door so we talk about his mama something ferocious. Then we check out that we on Fifth Avenue and everybody dressed up in stockings. One lady in a fur coat, hot as it is. White folks crazy.

"This is the place," Miss Moore say, presenting it to us in the voice she uses at the museum. "Let's look in the windows before we go in."

Giant stuffed animals in the grand entrance to the flagship FAO Schwartz toy store, which has been located on Fifth Avenue in New York City since 1931. Founded in 1862, the shop is known for the top-of-the-line children's toys and elaborate window and in-store displays admired by the children in "The Lesson."

5   "Can we steal?" Sugar asks very serious like she's getting the ground rules squared away before she plays. "I beg your pardon," say Miss Moore, and we fall out. So she leads us around the windows of the toy store and me and Sugar screamin, "This is mine, that's mine, I gotta have that, that was made for me, I was born for that," till Big Butt drowns us out.

"Hey, I'm going to buy that there."

"That there? You don't even know what it is, stupid."

"I do so," he say punchin on Rosie Giraffe. "It's a microscope."

"Whatcha gonna do with a microscope, fool?"

10   "Look at things."

"Like what, Ronald?" ask Miss Moore. And Big Butt ain't got the first notion. So here go Miss Moore gabbing about the thousands of bacteria in a drop of water and the somethin or other in a speck of blood and the million and one living things in the air around us is invisible to the naked eye. And what she say that for? Junebug go to town on that "naked" and we rolling. Then Miss Moore ask what it cost. So we all jam into the window smudgin it up and the price tag say $300. So then she ask how long'd take for Big Butt and Junebug to save up their allowances. "Too long," I say. "Yeh," adds Sugar, "outgrown it by that time." And, Miss Moore say no, you never outgrow learning instruments. "Why, even medical students and interns and," blah, blah, blah. And we ready to choke Big Butt for bringing it up in the first damn place.

"This here costs four hundred eighty dollars," say Rosie Giraffe. So we pile up all over her to see what she pointin out. My eyes tells me it's a chunk of glass cracked with something heavy, and different-color inks dripped into the splits, then the whole thing put into a oven or something. But for $480 it don't make sense.

"That's a paperweight made of semi-precious stones fused together under tremendous pressure," she explains slowly, with her hands doing the mining and all the factory work.

"So what's a paperweight?" asks Rosie Giraffe.

15   "To weigh paper with, dumbbell," say Flyboy, the wise man from the East.

"Not exactly," say Miss Moore, which is what she say when you warm or way off too. "It's to weigh paper down so it won't scatter and make your desk untidy." So right away me and Sugar curtsy to each other and then to Mercedes who is more the tidy type.

"We don't keep paper on top of the desk in my class," say Junebug, figuring Miss Moore crazy or lyin one.

"At home, then," she say. "Don't you have a calendar and a pencil case and a blotter and a letter-opener on your desk at home where you do your homework?" And she know damn well what our homes look like cause she nosys around in them every chance she gets.

"I don't even have a desk," say Junebug. "Do we?"

20   "No. And I don't get no homework neither," says Big Butt.

"And I don't even have a home," say Flyboy like he do at school to keep the white folks off his back and sorry for him. Send this poor kid to camp posters, is his specialty.

"I do," says Mercedes. "I have a box of stationery on my desk and a picture of my cat. My godmother bought the stationery and the desk. There's a big rose on each sheet and the envelopes smell like roses."

"Who wants to know about your smelly-ass stationery," say Rosie Giraffe fore I can get my two cents in.

"It's important to have a work area all your own so that . . ."

25 "Will you look at this sailboat, please," say Flyboy, cuttin her off and pointin to the thing like it was his. So once again we tumble all over each other to gaze at this magnificent thing in the toy store which is just big enough to maybe sail two kittens across the pond if you strap them to the posts tight. We all start reciting the price tag like we in assembly. "Hand-crafted sailboat of fiberglass at one thousand one hundred ninety-five dollars."

"Unbelievable," I hear myself say and am really stunned. I read it again for myself just in case the group recitation put me in a trance. Same thing. For some reason this pisses me off. We look at Miss Moore and she lookin at us, waiting for I dunno what.

"Who'd pay all that when you can buy a sailboat set for a quarter at Pop's, a tube of glue for a dime, and a ball of string for eight cents? It must have a motor and a whole lot else besides," I say. "My sailboat cost me about fifty cents."

"But will it take water?" say Mercedes with her smart ass.

"Took mine to Alley Pond Park once," say Flyboy. "String broke. Lost it. Pity."

30 "Sailed mine in Central Park and it keeled over and sank. Had to ask my father for another dollar."

"And you got the strap," laugh Big Butt. "The jerk didn't even have a string on it. My old man wailed on his behind."

Little Q.T. was staring hard at the sailboat and you could see he wanted it bad. But he too little and somebody'd just take it from him. So what the hell. "This boat for kids, Miss Moore?"

"Parents silly to buy something like that just to get all broke up," say Rosie Giraffe.

"That much money it should last forever," I figure.

35 "My father'd buy it for me if I wanted it."

"Your father, my ass," say Rosie Giraffe getting a chance to finally push Mercedes.

"Must be rich people shop here," say Q.T.

"You are a very bright boy," say Flyboy. "What was your first clue?" And he rap him on the head with the back of his knuckles, since Q.T. the only one he could get away with. Though Q.T. liable to come up behind you years later and get his licks in when you half expect it.

"What I want to know is," I says to Miss Moore though I never talk to her, I wouldn't give the bitch that satisfaction, "is how much a real boat costs? I figure a thousand'd get you a yacht any day."

40 "Why don't you check that out," she says, "and report back to the group?" Which really pains my ass. If you gonna mess up a perfectly good swim day least you could do is have some answers. "Let's go in," she say like she got something up her sleeve. Only she don't lead the way. So me and Sugar turn the corner to where the entrance is, but when we get there I kinda hang back. Not that I'm scared, what's there to be afraid of, just a toy store. But I feel funny, shame. But what I got to be shamed about? Got as much right to go in as anybody. But somehow I can't seem to get hold of the door, so I step away for Sugar to lead. But she hangs back too. And I look at her and she looks at me and this is ridiculous. I mean, damn, I have never ever been shy about doing nothing or going nowhere. But then Mercedes steps up and then Rosie Giraffe and Big Butt crowd in behind and shove, and next thing we all stuffed into the doorway with only Mercedes squeezing past us, smoothing out her jumper and walking right down the aisle. Then the rest of us tumble in like a glued-together jigsaw done all wrong. And people lookin at us. And it's like the time me and Sugar crashed into the Catholic church on a dare. But once we got in there and everything so hushed and holy and the candles and the bowin and the handkerchiefs on all the drooping heads, I just couldn't go through with the plan. Which was for me to run up to the altar and do a tap dance while Sugar played the nose flute and messed around in the holy water. And Sugar kept given me the elbow. Then later teased me so bad I tied her up in the shower and turned it on and locked her in. And she'd be there till this day if Aunt Gretchen hadn't finally figured I was lyin about the boarder takin a shower.

Same thing in the store. We all walkin on tiptoe and hardly touchin the games and puzzles and things. And I watched Miss Moore who is steady watchin us like she waitin for a sign. Like Mama Drewery watches the sky and sniffs the air and takes note of just how much slant is in the bird formation. Then me and Sugar bump smack into each other, so busy gazing at the toys, 'specially the sailboat. But we don't laugh and go into our fat-lady bump stomach routine. We just stare at that price tag. Then Sugar run a finger over the whole boat. And I'm jealous and want to hit her. Maybe not her, but I sure want to punch somebody in the mouth.

"Watcha bring us here for, Miss Moore?"

"You sound angry, Sylvia. Are you mad about something?" Givin me one of them grins like she tellin a grown-up joke that never turns out to be funny. And she's lookin very closely at me like maybe she plannin to do my portrait from memory. I'm mad, but I won't give her that satisfaction. So I slouch around the store bein very bored and say, "Let's go."

Me and Sugar at the back of the train watchin the tracks whizzin by large then small then gettin gobbled up in the dark. I'm thinkin about this tricky toy I saw in the store. A clown that somersaults on a bar then does chin-ups just cause you yank lightly at his leg. Cost $35. I could see me askin my mother for a $35 birthday clown. "You wanna who that costs what?" she'd say, cocking her head to the side to get a better view of the hole in my head. Thirty-five dollars could buy new bunk beds for Junior and Gretchen's boy. Thirty-five dollars and the whole household could go visit Granddaddy Nelson in the country. Thirty-five dollars would pay for the rent and the piano bill too. Who are these people that spend that much for performing clowns and $1000 for toy sailboats? What kinda work they do and how they live and how come we ain't in on it? Where we are is who we are, Miss Moore always pointin out. But it don't necessarily have to be that way, she always adds then waits for somebody to say that poor people have to wake up and demand their share of the pie and don't none of us know what kind of pie she talking about in the first damn place. But she ain't so smart cause I still got her four dollars from the taxi and she sure ain't gettin it. Messin up my day with this shit. Sugar nudges me in my pocket and winks.

45   Miss Moore lines us up in front of the mailbox where we started from, seem like years ago, and I got a headache for thinkin so hard. And we lean all over each other so we can hold up under the draggy-ass lecture she always finishes us off with at the end before we thank her for borin us to tears. But she just looks at us like she readin tea leaves. Finally she say, "Well, what did you think of F.A.O. Schwartz?"

Rosie Giraffe mumbles, "White folks crazy."

"I'd like to go there again when I get my birthday money," says Mercedes, and we shove her out the pack so she has to lean on the mailbox by herself.

"I'd like a shower. Tiring day," say Flyboy.

Then Sugar surprises me by sayin, "You know, Miss Moore, I don't think all of us here put together eat in a year what that sailboat costs." And Miss Moore lights up like somebody goosed her. "And?" she say, urging Sugar on. Only I'm standin on her foot so she don't continue.

50   "Imagine for a minute what kind of society it is in which some people can spend on a toy what it would cost to feed a family of six or seven. What do you think?"

"I think," say Sugar pushing me off her feet like she never done before, cause I whip her ass in a minute, "that this is not much of a democracy if you ask me. Equal chance to pursue happiness means an equal crack at the dough, don't it?" Miss Moore is besides herself and I am disgusted with Sugar's treachery. So I stand on her foot one more time to see if she'll shove me. She shuts up, and Miss Moore looks at me, sorrowfully I'm thinkin. And somethin weird is goin on, I can feel it in my chest.

"Anybody else learn anything today?" lookin dead at me. I walk away and Sugar has to run to catch up and don't even seem to notice when I shrug her arm off my shoulder.

"Well, we got four dollars anyway," she says.

"Uh hunh."

55   "We could go to Hascombs and get half a chocolate layer and then go to the Sunset and still have plenty money for potato chips and ice cream sodas."

"Uh hunh."

"Race you to Hascombs," she say.

We start down the block and she gets ahead which is O.K. by me cause I'm going to the West End and then over to the Drive to think this day through. She can run if she want to and even run faster. But ain't nobody gonna beat me at nuthin.

[1972]

QUESTIONS FOR REFLECTION AND DISCUSSION

1. Who narrates the story? How would you characterize her? How would the story be different if narrated by Miss Moore?

2. With whom is the reader meant to identify in the story, and why? Use evidence from the story to support your argument.

3. How do we know this toy store is a space to which the children have never been? What is their reaction to it? Why does Bambara use language that compares the store to a museum?

4. Why does Miss Moore take them to the toy store? Is her lesson the "lesson" of the title? Why or why not?

POETRY

Allen Ginsberg 1926–1997

Allen Ginsberg was born in Newark, New Jersey. His father was a poet and school teacher; his mother was a radical communist. Ginsberg attended Columbia University, where he met Jack Kerouac and William S. Burroughs, and discovered the poetry of William Blake (p. 175), Walt Whitman (p. 656), and William Carlos Williams (p. 227). In the early 1950s, Ginsberg moved to San Francisco and began working on the long landmark poem, "Howl," that made him a central figure in the 1960s counterculture. Published in *Howl and Other Poems* (1956) with an epigraph from Walt Whitman, "A Supermarket in California" imagines the nineteenth-century poet in the world of 1950s America. Ginsberg's other explicit allusion is to the surrealist Spanish poet Federico García Lorca, who attended Columbia University during the early 1930s, and was murdered by Nationalist partisans of General Franco shortly after the outbreak of the Spanish Civil War. His murder is attributed to both his politics and his homosexuality. The final lines allude to Charon, the boatman of classical mythology who ferried dead souls across the river Styx to the underworld.

A Supermarket in California

What thoughts I have of you tonight, Walt Whitman, for I walked down the sidestreets under the trees with a headache self-conscious looking at the full moon.

In my hungry fatigue, and shopping for images, I went into the neon fruit supermarket, dreaming of your enumerations!

What peaches and what penumbras! Whole families shopping at night! Aisles full of husbands! Wives in the avocados, babies in the tomatoes!—and you, García Lorca, what were you doing down by the watermelons?

I saw you, Walt Whitman, childless, lonely old grubber, poking among the meats in the refrigerator and eyeing the grocery boys.

5   I heard you asking questions of each: Who killed the pork chops? What price bananas? Are you my Angel?

I wandered in and out of the brilliant stacks of cans following you, and followed in my imagination by the store detective.

We strode down the open corridors together in our solitary fancy tasting artichokes, possessing every frozen delicacy, and never passing the cashier.

Where are we going, Walt Whitman? The doors close in an hour. Which way does your beard point tonight?

(I touch your book and dream of our odyssey in the supermarket and feel absurd.)

10   Will we walk all night through solitary streets? The trees add shade to shade, lights out in the houses, we'll both be lonely.

Will we stroll dreaming of the lost America of love past blue automobiles in driveways, home to our silent cottage?

Ah, dear father, graybeard, lonely old courage-teacher, what America did you have when Charon° quit poling his ferry and you got out on a smoking bank and stood watching the boat disappear on the black waters of Lethe?°

Berkeley, 1955

18 **Charon:** in classical mythology, the boatman who ferried dead souls across the river Styx to the underworld. 20 **Lethe:** in classical mythology, the river whose waters grant forgetfulness.

The supermarket was a novel phenomenon in the decade after World War II, and often used as an image of consumerism and alienation. In this still from the 1944 thriller *Double Indemnity,* Walter Neff and Phyllis Dietrichson meet surreptitiously in Jerry's Market in Los Angeles to plot her husband's murder. As in Ginsberg's poem, the improbable location establishes the mood of the scene.

1. Paraphrase the events recounted in the poem. What is the role of dreams in these events?

2. According to this poem, how has America changed since the days of Whitman? Is Whitman's poetry still a relevant model for depicting the new America?

3. How does Ginsberg describe the space of the supermarket? What in his language makes this a poem about living in the city? How does this space compare to the space we see in the movie still on page 629?

Ezra Pound 1885–1972

Born in Idaho, Ezra Pound studied at the University of Pennsylvania and at Hamilton College. He then traveled abroad, settling in London, where he became an important literary editor and continued writing his own poetry. A dominant force in poetic modernism, he was equally fascinated by the poetry of medieval Europe and East Asia, both of which he translated and both of which he incorporated into his own poetry. Pound moved to Italy in 1924, becoming embroiled in Fascist politics, until he was returned to the United States and put on trial for treason. Acquitted but declared mentally ill, he was institutionalized for over a decade before returning to Italy. His major poetic work is the massive *Cantos,* published in various parts between 1925 and 1972. "In a Station of the Metro" is Ezra Pound's version of a haiku. It is equally his major contribution to the poetic movement known as Imagism, which called for "clarity of expression" through the use of "precise visual images." The metro to which the title refers is the Paris Metro, or subway.

In a Station of the Metro

The apparition of these faces in the crowd:
Petals on a wet, black bough.

[1916]

QUESTIONS FOR REFLECTION AND DISCUSSION

1. Discuss the poem's image: in what way do faces in the crowd resemble "Petals on a wet, black bough"? In what way do they not resemble them?

2. What does the title contribute to the poem's meaning? How would its meaning change with a different title?

3. Why do you think Pound chose a natural image to describe a modern urban experience?

4. What attitude do you think the speaker expects us to take toward his subject?

Sharon Olds b. 1942

Born in San Francisco, Sharon Olds studied at Stanford University and earned her PhD in English from Columbia University in 1972, at which point she began writing poetry. She teaches creative writing at New York University. Author of eight volumes of poetry written in a personal voice with sometimes shockingly direct imagery, Olds published her first collection in 1980. "On the Subway" was published in *The Gold Cell* in 1987, as was her poem "The Possessive" (p. 16).

On the Subway

The boy and I face each other.
His feet are huge, in black sneakers
laced with white in a complex pattern like
a set of intentional scars. We are stuck on
opposite sides of the car, a couple of   5
molecules stuck in a rod of light
rapidly moving through darkness. He has the
casual cold look of a mugger,
alert under hooded lids. He is wearing
red, like the inside of the body   10
exposed. I am wearing dark fur, the
whole skin of an animal taken and
used. I look at his raw face,
he looks at my fur coat, and I don't
know if I am in his power—   15
he could take my coat so easily, my
briefcase, my life—
or if he is in my power, the way I am
living off his life, eating the steak
he does not eat, as if I am taking   20
the food from his mouth. And he is black
and I am white, and without meaning or
trying to I must profit from his darkness,
the way he absorbs the murderous beams of the
nation's head, as black cotton   25
absorbs the heat of the sun and holds it. There is
no way to know how easy this
white skin makes my life, this
life he could take so easily and
break across his knee like a stick the way his   30
own back is being broken, the
rod of his soul that at birth was dark and
fluid, rich as the head of a seedling
ready to thrust up into any available light.

[1987]

Photo from a production of Amiri Baraka's controversial 1964 play *Dutchman*. Like "On the Subway," *Dutchman* is concerned with a tense encounter between a white woman and a black man in a car on a New York subway train.

QUESTIONS FOR REFLECTION AND DISCUSSION

1. Paraphrase the initial scene as the speaker describes it. What imagery does Olds use to describe this scene? What is the effect of this imagery on our experience of the setting? How would the poem be different without these details?

2. What is the speaker's reaction to the encounter? Is this the reaction you expected? Why or why not?

3. Why do you think Olds chose an image from nature to conclude her poem?

4. What does the setting of the subway add to the poem? What is unique to a New York subway about the particular encounter described? How would the encounter change if it took place in a different setting?

Langston Hughes 1902–1967

Although born in Missouri rather than the North Carolina of the speaker in "Theme from English B," Langston Hughes did attend, for one year, Columbia University, "this college on the hill above Harlem" (for a biography of Hughes, see p. 369). As you read this poem, consider the effect Hughes achieves by combining the geographical situation of his setting with other themes equally specific to New York City.

Theme for English B

The instructor said,

> Go home and write
> a page tonight.
> And let that page come out of you—
> Then, it will be true.   5

I wonder if it's that simple?
I am twenty-two, colored, born in Winston-Salem.
I went to school there, then Durham, then here
to this college on the hill above Harlem.
I am the only colored student in my class.   10
The steps from the hill lead down into Harlem,
through a park, then I cross St. Nicholas,
Eighth Avenue, Seventh, and I come to the Y,
the Harlem Branch Y, where I take the elevator
up to my room, sit down, and write this page: 15
It's not easy to know what is true for you and me
at twenty-two, my age. But I guess I'm what
I feel and see and hear, Harlem, I hear you:
hear you, hear me—we two—you, me, talk on this page.
(I hear New York, too.) Me—who?   20
Well, I like to eat, sleep, drink, and be in love.

I like to work, read, learn, and understand life.
I like a pipe for a Christmas present,
or records—Bessie,° bop, or Bach.
I guess being colored doesn't make me *not* like   25
the same things other folks like who are other races.
So will my page be colored that I write?
Being me, it will not be white.
But it will be
a part of you, instructor.   30
You are white—
yet a part of me, as I am a part of you.
That's American.
Sometimes perhaps you don't want to be a part of me.
Nor do I often want to be a part of you.   35
But we are, that's true!
As I learn from you,
I guess you learn from me—
although you're older—and white—
and somewhat more free.   40

This is my page for English B.

[1949]

24 **Bessie:** blues singer Bessie Smith.

QUESTIONS FOR REFLECTION AND DISCUSSION

1. How does the speaker describe his experience at Columbia University? Why does he devote so much detail to the journey from the classroom to his room in the Y?

2. How does the speaker describe his relation to Harlem and to New York?

3. What is the speaker's concern about the page he will write? Will the instructor understand what the speaker writes?

4. What is the spatial relationship between Columbia and Harlem? How does Hughes make this relationship into a metaphor of the relationship between "white" and "colored"?

NONFICTION

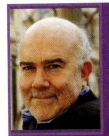

Bill Buford b. 1954

Former editor of the literary quarterly *Granta* and a staff writer and former fiction editor for the *New Yorker*, Bill Buford was born in Louisiana, raised in the San Fernando Valley in California, and attended Berkeley and Cambridge. He specializes in "total-immersion journalism"—in other words, he won't write about anything until he has done it himself. This approach is reflected in the title of his first book, *Among the Thugs* (1990), based on eight years of first-hand research about English football hooligans. His most recent book, *Heat* (2006), is about working in the kitchen of New York restaurateur Mario Batali. For the essay "Lions and Tigers and Bears," published in the *New Yorker* in 1999, Buford spent the night in New York's Central Park.

LIONS AND TIGERS AND BEARS

SO I THOUGHT I'D SPEND THE NIGHT IN CENTRAL Park, and, having stuffed my small rucksack with a sleeping bag, a big bottle of mineral water, a map, and a toothbrush, I arrived one heavy, muggy Friday evening in July to do just that: to walk around until I got so tired that I'd curl up under a tree and drop off to a peaceful, outdoorsy sleep. Of course, anybody who knows anything about New York knows the city's essential platitude—that you don't wander around Central Park at night—and in that, needless to say, was the appeal: it was the thing you don't do. And, from what I can tell, it has always been the thing you don't do, ever since the Park's founding commissioners, nearly a hundred and fifty years ago, decided that the place should be closed at night—a decision heartily endorsed by its coarchitect Frederick Law Olmsted, who said that once the Park was dark he'd "answer for no man's safety in it from bullies, garroters, or highway robbers." At the time, the commissioners were recovering from one of the Park's first fatalities: the result of a downtown lad's overturning his two-wheeler and snapping his neck in a brandy-inspired carriage race down the Mall. Most felons then were reckless carriage drivers. In modern times, they're distinctly more menacing, as Ogden Nash observed in 1961:

> If you should happen after dark
> To find yourself in Central Park,
> Ignore the paths that beckon you
> And hurry, hurry to the zoo,
> And creep into the tiger's lair.
> Frankly, you'll be safer there.

Even now, when every Park official, city administrator, and police officer tells us (correctly) that the Park is safe during the day, they all agree in this: only a fool goes there at night. Or a purse snatcher, loon, prostitute, drug dealer, homophobic gay basher, murderer—not to mention bully, garroter, highway robber.

I arrived at nine-fifteen and made for the only nocturnal spot I knew: the Delacorte Theatre. Tonight's show was *The Taming of the Shrew.* "Bonny Kate," Petruchio was saying, "she is my goods, my chattel . . . my horse, my ox, my ass, my any thing." Lights out, applause, and the audience began exiting through the tunnels at the bottom of the bleachers. So far, so normal, and this could have been an outdoor summer-stock Shakespeare production anywhere in America, except in one respect: a police car had pulled up just as Petruchio began his soliloquy and was now parked conspicuously in view, its roof light slowly rotating. The police were there to reassure the audience that it was being protected; the rotating red light was like a campfire in the wild, warning what's out there to stay away.

The Park has had its own police precinct since the end of the nineteenth century, and it is now staffed with what Police Commissioner Howard Safir, himself an evening-roller-blading Park enthusiast, describes as "people persons"—well-spoken, well-mannered policemen whose first task is to make visitors feel happy. And, on any normal visit, I, like anyone else, would actually be very happy to see one of the men in blue. But not tonight. It's against the law to spend the night in the Park, and at around eleven o'clock the police start their "sweep"—crisscrossing the place on foot and in unmarked cars, scooters, little three-wheeled vans, and helicopters.

5   During my first hour or so, I wandered around the Delacorte, reassured by the lights, the laughter, the lines of Shakespeare that drifted out into the summer night. I was feeling a certain exhilaration, the euphoria that comes from doing the thing you're not meant to be doing, climbing the steps of Belvedere Castle all alone, peeking through the windows of the Henry Luce Nature Observatory, identifying the herbs in the Shakespeare Garden, seeing no one, when, after turning this way and that, I was on a winding trail in impenetrable foliage, and, within minutes, I was lost.

There was a light ahead, and as I rounded the corner I came upon five men, all wearing white tank-top T-shirts, huddled around a bench. I walked past, avoiding eye contact, and turned down a path, a narrow one, black dark, going down a hill, getting darker, very dark. Is this a good idea? I asked myself, when, as if on cue, I heard a great shaking of the bushes beside me and froze. Animal? Mugger? Whatever I was hearing would surely stop making that noise, I thought. But it didn't. How can this be? I'm in the Park less than an hour and already I'm lost, on an unlighted path, facing an unknown thing shaking threateningly in the bushes. It was no small thing moving around in there, and, what's more, it was moving in my direction, and I thought, Shit! What *am* I doing here? And I bolted, not running, exactly, but no longer strolling—and certainly not looking back—turning left, turning right, all sense of direction obliterated, the crashing continuing behind me, louder even, *left,* another man in a tank-top T-shirt, *right,* another man, when finally I realized where I was—in the Ramble, stupid, where I'd been only once before (and got lost)—as I turned left again, and there was a lake, and the skyline of Central Park South, the Essex House Hotel, and the reassuring sign for A&E's *Biography,* announcing the temperature (eighty-two degrees), the time (ten-fifteen), and tonight's *Biography* special (William Shatner). I stopped. I breathed. Relax, I told myself. It's only darkness.

Map of Central Park, New York, New York, 2009.

About fifteen feet into the lake, there was a large boulder, with a heap of branches leading to it. I tiptoed across and sat, enjoying the picture of the city again, the very reassuring city. I looked around. There was a warm breeze, and heavy clouds overhead, but it was still hot, and I was sweating. Far out in the lake, there was a light—someone rowing a boat, a lantern suspended above the stern. I got my bearings—the twin towers of the San Remo in view, a penthouse all lit up, a party. I was on the West Side, around Seventy-seventh. People use the cross streets, imaginatively projecting them across the Park, like latitude lines, as a way of imposing a New York grid on this bit of New York gridlessness. The far side of the lake must be near Strawberry Fields, around Seventy-second. Just where that boat was now, I realized, was where, two years ago, the police had found the body of Michael McMorrow, a forty-four-year-old man (my age), who was stabbed thirty-four times by a fifteen-year-old. It was possible, the thought occurred to me, to chart my progress through the Park via its recent murders (I entered at East Seventy-second, where, two months ago, the police found the body of a publishing executive, inexplicably felled, the headphones of his Walkman still clamped to his ears, and later, as I headed for the Reservoir . . .), but no, this didn't seem like a fruitful way of organizing the evening. Even so, the menacing Central Park crime mystique lingered: the idea that here anything is possible. You enter the Park, you have sex in the bushes with a stranger, you leave. No memory, no trace. You find someone all alone, you rob him, you disappear. Unseen transgressions. After McMorrow was killed, he was disemboweled, his intestines ripped out so that his body would sink when rolled into the lake — a detail that I've compulsively reviewed in my mind since I first heard it. And then his killers, with time on their hands and no witnesses, just went home. Another feature of a Central Park crime: no one knows you're here.

One of the first events in the Park took place 140 years ago almost to the day: a band concert. The concert, pointedly, was held on a Saturday, still a working day, because the concert, like much of the Park then, was designed to keep the city's rougher elements out. The Park at night must have seemed luxurious and secluded — a giant evening garden party. There were no other entertainments. No rides, no playgrounds, no venders. The Park was to be strolled through, enjoyed as an aesthetic experience, like a walk inside a painting. George Templeton Strong, the indefatigable diarist, was an early Park user. On his first visit, on June 11, 1859, the place was a desolate landscape of mounds of compost and lakes without water. But even at that stage Strong recognized that the architects were building two different parks at once. One was the Romantic park, which included the Ramble, the thirty-seven-acre, carefully "designed" wilderness, wild nature re-created in the middle of the city, *rus in urbe,* an English notion—nature as surprising and unpredictable. The other, the southern end of the Park, was more French: ordered, and characterized by straight lines. Strong was unhappy with the straight lines, and could see that once the stunted elms were fully grown ("by A.D. 1950," he wrote) the place would look distinctly "Versailles-y." But by 1860 this section was tremendously popular, and paintings show a traffic jam of fancy carriages, all proceeding the wrong way up Fifth Avenue — "a broad torrent of vehicular gentility wherein profits shoddy and of petroleum were largely represented," Strong wrote in disgust.

I climbed back down from the rock. In the distance, I spotted a couple approaching. An uncomfortable thing: someone else in the Park. Your first thought is: nutcase? But then I noticed, even from a hundred feet, that the couple was panicking: the man was pulling the woman to the other side of him, so that he would be between her and me when we passed. The woman stopped, and the man jerked her forward authoritatively, and there was a muted exchange. I was surprised by how expressive their fear was—even in the way they were moving. As they got closer, I could see that he was tall and skinny, wearing a plaid shirt and black horn-rimmed glasses; she was a blonde, and looked determinedly at the ground, her face rigid. Both of them were now walking fast and stiffly. When they were within a few feet of me, he reached out and grabbed her arm. I couldn't resist: just as we were about to pass each other, I addressed them, forthrightly: "Hello, good people!" I said. "And how are you on this fine summer evening?" At first, silence, and then the woman started shrieking uncontrollably—"Oh, my God! Oh, my God!"—and they hurried away.

10   This was an interesting discovery. One of the most frightening things in the Park at night was a man on his own. One of the most frightening things tonight was me. I was emboldened by the realization, newly confident: I was no longer afraid; I was frightening. Another man approached, big and fat, wearing only shorts, with blubbery tits hanging over his swollen belly. Ah, well, I thought, someone who really is insane. No matter. I greeted him. He was very friendly. He had an aluminum container of food, and he was eating as he walked. He offered me some.

"What is it?" I asked.

"Pasta," he said. "Mmm, mmm. Would you like a bite?"

"No, thanks," I said. "I've eaten."

"You sure?" he said. "I got plenty."

15   "No, really," I said. "That's very kind, but I couldn't."

Not everyone likes the Park, but just about everyone feels he should. This was at the heart of Henry James's otherwise impressively incomprehensible observations when he visited the Park, in 1904. The Park, in James's eyes, was a failure. All the fake nature stuff, got up to be so many wild scenes, was not unlike "the effect of those old quaint prints which give in a single view the classic, gothic and other architectural wonders of the world." The Park was too narrow, and too short, and was overwhelmed by an obligation to "do." The most remarkable thing about it was simply that it existed, and any person who didn't, as James put it, "keep patting the Park on the back" was guilty of being seen as a social ingrate. By then, the Park's founders had died, and the Park, no longer the domain of the privileged, had been taken over by immigrants—a "polyglot Hebraic crowd of pedestrians," in James's inelegantly revealing phrase. In fact, between James's visit and the nineteen-thirties, the Park might well have been at its most popular, visited by more people than today, when current estimates put the number of visitors somewhere between ten and twenty million a year. The Park in fact was being destroyed by overuse, until 1934, when the legendary Robert Moses, genius urban impresario and civic fascist, was appointed parks commissioner. Moses was responsible for the third design element in the Park—neither English nor French, neither Romantic nor classical, but efficient, purposeful, and un-apologetically American. All that arty pretend-you're-in-a-painting-of-the-Hudson-River-School: he had no time for it. He wanted baseball diamonds, shuffleboard, volleyball, and swimming pools. He closed the Casino—originally the tea salon of the Park's other architect, Calvert Vaux, but by the nineteen-thirties a dubious if highly charismatic speakeasy of jazz, celebrities, and corrupt glamour—and replaced it, characteristically, with a playground. Even the Ramble became a target: Moses tried to chop it down and install a fourteen-acre senior citizens' recreation center. He was blocked by the protesting bird-watchers—one of the few times Moses was stopped. The irony was that by the end of the Moses era the Park—no longer a piece of nature but a piece of property, a venue for recreation, not conservation—was dangerous.

In my new confidence I set out for the northern end of the Park. Near the reservoir, a gang of kids on bicycles zoomed across the Eighty-fifth Street Transverse, hooting with a sense of ominous power. A little later, there was another gang, this one on foot—about a dozen black kids, moving eastward, just by the running track. I kept my head down and picked up my pace, but my mind involuntarily called up the memory of the 1989 "wilding" incident, in which a young investment banker was beaten and sexually assaulted by a group of kids on a rampage.

Around Ninety-fifth Street, I found a bench and stopped. I had taken one of the trails that run alongside the Park's West Drive, and the more northern apartments of Central Park West were in view. I sat as residents prepared for bed: someone watching television, a woman doing yoga, a man stepping into the shower. Who needs curtains when it's only the Park outside your window? Below me was the city, the top of the Empire State Building peeking over the skyline. George Templeton Strong discovered the beauty of Central Park at night on July 30, 1869, on a "starlit drive" with his wife. But what Strong saw was different from what I was looking at. The Park was darker then than now, genuinely empty, and something much closer to Olmsted's nature in the seeming wild. And, of course, you could see the stars. Tonight, even if it weren't clouding over, there'd be no stars. Too much glare. The Park is now framed, enveloped even, by the city in a way that Olmsted never imagined, but there was no escaping the recognition that this city—contrived, man-made, glaringly obtrusive, consuming wasteful and staggering quantities of electricity and water and energy—was very beautiful. I'm not sure why it should be so beautiful; I don't have the vocabulary to describe its appeal. But there it was: the city at night, viewed from what was meant to be an escape from it, shimmering.

Olmsted's son, also a landscape architect, was offended by the tall buildings that had begun crowding round his father's achievement. It was ruinous, the son said, "ugly, restless, and distressing," and there was talk of limiting the height of what greedy real estate developers could build. Young Olmsted did not understand the romance of what was taking form.

20   A policeman appeared. It was after midnight, and I thought that my visit was now terminated. But he could see that I was enjoying the view, so he found a bench not far away. He had a shaved head and a mild manner. He said nothing and took in the view himself. And that was what we did, sitting together, separated by twenty or thirty feet, in silence, for ten minutes, saying nothing, until finally I felt I could get up, and said good night, and resumed my journey.

I walked around the Harlem Meer, busy even at one in the morning—couples on benches, young men hunched over their girlfriends like question marks. From the hill of Fort Clinton, where the British drove Washington's troops north and took temporary possession of Manhattan, I watched a slow seduction. I walked and walked. Around one-thirty, I entered the North Woods, and made my way down to what my map would later tell me was a stream called the Loch. The stream was loud, sounding more like a river than a stream. And for the first time that night the city disappeared: no buildings, no lights, no sirens.

I was tired. I had been walking for a long time. I wanted to unroll my sleeping bag, out of view of the police, and fall asleep. I was looking forward to dawn and being awakened by birds.

I made my way down a ravine. A dirt trail appeared on my left. This looked promising. I followed it, and it wound its way down to the stream. I looked back: I couldn't see the trail; it was blocked by trees. This was good. Secluded. I walked on. It flattened out and I could put a sleeping bag here. This was good, too. Yes: good. There were fireflies, even at this hour, and the place was so dark and so densely shrouded by the trees overhead that the light of the fireflies was hugely magnified; their abdomens pulsed like great yellow flashlights. There was also a smell: a dampness, a kind of rotting fecundity. And the stream was very loud: this was the sound of nature, true, but it was all a bit too incongruous. Olmsted or not, I knew I was in Harlem.

I spotted a white article on the ground. I stared at it for a while before walking over to pick it up. It was a woman's blouse. Of course. A woman had simply left it behind. Fifty yards from here, a Brazilian jogger was killed—the murderer never found. (A week later, a woman would be murdered nearby, at the Blockhouse, at this very hour, her screams ignored by a resident who heard them. When I returned here, at midnight two nights after that killing, I, too, would hear a woman's screams—spooky, bleating screams, which I then reported to a policeman, startling him in the dark where I tracked him down.)

25   I eventually rolled out my sleeping bag atop a little rise beside the bridle path by the North Meadow, and then I sat, cross-legged, and asked myself questions: Why did I bring a little airline tube of toothpaste but no flashlight? Why didn't I bring a cell phone? Wouldn't a can of Mace have been prudent? I crawled inside my bag and closed my eyes. And then: *snap!* A tremendous cracking sound. I froze, then quickly whipped round to have a look: nothing. A forest is always full of noises. How did I manage to camp out as a kid? Finally, I fell asleep.

I know I fell asleep because I was awake again. Another branch snapping, but this sound was different—as if I could hear the tissue of the wood tearing. My eyes still closed, I was motionless. Another branch, and then a rustling of leaves. No doubt: someone was there. I could tell I was being stared at; I could feel the staring. I heard breathing.

I opened my eyes and was astonished by what I saw. I was surrounded by—what? Something. There were three of them, all within arm's reach. They looked very big. At first I didn't know what they were, except that they were animals. The only animal

I'd seen in the Park was a rat. These were not rats—that was my first thought. Actually, that was my second thought; my first was: This is not the police. Maybe they were bears, small ones. Then I realized; they were—what do you call them? Those animals that Daniel Boone made his hat out of.

They weren't moving; I wasn't moving. They just stared, brown eyes looking blankly into my own. They were obviously very perplexed to find me here. Suddenly, I was very perplexed to find me here, too. "Imagine this," one of them seemed to be saying. "A grown man sleeping out in Central Park!"

"Obviously, not from New York."

30   "Hi, guys," I muttered. I said this very softly.

My voice startled them and they scurried up the tree in front of me. But only ten feet up. Then they stopped and resumed staring. And then, very slowly, they inched a little farther up. What should I do? If I ignored them and fell asleep, I faced the prospect

of their coming down again. On the other hand, why would I want to frighten them? Besides, what if I frightened them and they *didn't* leave? After all, I was now in their way. They inched a little farther. They were about forty feet up, directly above me now, and the tree was swaying slightly with their weight.

It was starting to drizzle. I heard a helicopter, its searchlight criss-crossing the bridle path only ten feet away. So maybe there were bad guys.

I looked back at the raccoons. "Are there bad guys here?" I asked them. It was stupid to speak. My voice startled them and, directly overhead, one of them started peeing. And then, nature finding herself unable to resist, it started to pour.

But not for long. The rain stopped. The raccoons stared. And I fell asleep. I know I fell asleep because the next thing I heard was birds. A natural, naturally beautiful sound.

[1999]

QUESTIONS FOR REFLECTION AND DISCUSSION

1. What is the allusion of the title? What is its relevance to the essay?

2. What expectations does Buford bring with him to Central Park? What expectations do those he meets have of him?

3. To what degree are these expectations met?

4. What are the real dangers of Central Park that he encounters? To what degree is it a wild space? To what degree is it an urban space?

LIVING IN THE CITY TOPICS FOR ESSAYS

1. Write an essay on the role of memory in the experience of the city. Use examples from the readings in this section to argue your thesis.

2. Compare the ways several texts describe the space of a city street. What is its function? What are its specific qualities? What figurative role does it play in the text?

3. Write an essay on the role of strangers in urban space using examples from the texts in this section to argue your thesis.

4. What is the place of nature in the urban environment? Use examples from the texts in this section to argue your thesis.

5. Write an essay comparing the role of race in several of these texts. How does race affect the experience of urban space?

6. Write a personal essay describing your own experience with a specific urban space. Did it have the same effect on you as the spaces described in this section? Why or why not?

LIVING IN THE CITY FURTHER READINGS IN *LITERATURE: A WORLD OF WRITING*

James Baldwin, "Sonny's Blues" • William Blake, "London" • Robert Frost, "A Brook in the City" • James Joyce, "Araby" • Naguib Mahfouz, "Half a Day" and "Zaabalawi" • Mary Oliver, "Singapore" • George Packer, "How Susie Bayer's T-Shirt Ended Up on Yusuf Mama's Back • Orhan Pamuk, "My Father's Suitcase" and "To Look Out the Window" • May Sarton, "The Rewards of Living a Solitary Life"

LIVING IN NATURE

Science is a human invention to understand the world; *nature* is a descriptive term for everything that science has never quite been able to explain adequately. In the previous section, we explored life in an environment—the city—dominated by science and human creation and construction. In this section, we examine how literature approaches the relationship between humans and the natural world around them.

Two short stories use imagery of nature in startlingly different ways to make sense of the strange and sometimes perverse choices sometimes made by children and adolescents. A selection of poems focuses on the description of nature and considers the relationship between individuals and the natural world, and the ways in which the former change and are changed by the latter. In the essays that conclude this chapter we discover some approaches to thinking critically about the world we share and the effect our actions have on it.

We begin the section with a look at the epic projects of Christo and Jeanne-Claude, which equally prompt us to think critically about the world around us. Born on the same day in June in 1935, the Bulgarian-born and classically trained artist Christo Javacheff and the French socialite Jeanne-Claude met in the Paris art world at the end of the 1950s, and have never parted. They soon moved to New York City, where they have lived ever since, closely collaborating on a unique series of what one scholar has termed "ephemeral monuments." Beginning in the late 1960s, they began planning and executing large-scale public projects involving temporarily transforming natural landscapes and manmade structures by wrapping, enclosing, or otherwise changing their shape. Projects have included wrapping the Reichstag building in Berlin in 1 million square feet of silvery polypropylene fabric (a project that took twenty-four years to achieve) and the Pont Neuf, the oldest bridge in Paris, in

Surrounded Islands, Biscayne Bay, Greater Miami, Florida, 1980–83. In this project, eleven uninhabited islands off the coast of Florida were surrounded for two weeks by over 6.5 million square feet of bright pink nylon, a color deliberately chosen, according to the artists, to contrast as greatly as possible with the natural colors of the environment. Christo termed the work "a gigantic horizontal painting," his version of the Impressionist artist Claude Monet's famous series of water lily paintings.

champagne-colored polyamide fabric (a ten-year undertaking); *Valley Curtain* (1970–72), an orange nylon curtain stretched between two Colorado mountains; and *The Umbrellas* (1984–91), a joint project to erect over 3,000 giant colored umbrellas simultaneously in California and Japan. Each project is wholly funded by the proceeds from the sale of designs and drawings and other small-scale work by Christo and is completely dismantled after a defined timespan—usually around two weeks. All that remains of a Christo and Jeanne-Claude project after its completion

Running Fence, Sonoma and Marin Counties, California, 1973–76. A meandering twenty-four-and-a-half mile expanse of 2,000 sections of white nylon, eighteen feet high, suspended from cables slung between steel poles in northern California, *Running Fence* cost the artists $3.2 million to erect for two weeks in 1976. The photograph shows the final 600-foot stretch as the fence descends into the Pacific Ocean.

is a photographic record, a bureau-cratic trail (each project involves years, sometimes decades, of negoti-ating with public and private enti-ties for the required permissions), and the memories of those who have seen them. For the artists, the process is an integral element of the project, as is the vast number of people that become involved in their production and appreciation. Although completely rational in the painstaking planning they entail, the projects are absolutely irrational in having no practical purpose—not even permanency. "These pro-jects are richer than my imagina-tion," Christo has said. "They go beyond anything I had foreseen." We have included images from three of Christo and Jeanne-Claude's best-known projects over the past forty years. As you study these photographs, all by their official photographer Wolfgang Volz, consider especially the way they affect our perception and under-standing of the natural landscape in which they have temporarily been erected.

The art exhibit *The Gates*, Central Park, New York, 1979–2005 snakes around Central Park February 12, 2005, in New York City. Over twenty-five years in the making, this project entailed hanging 7,503 saffron-colored fabric panels from gate-like supports at twelve-foot intervals over twenty-three miles of walkways around New York's most famous park. *The Gates* was visited by an estimated four million people during the two mid-February weeks in which it was in existence.

QUESTIONS FOR REFLECTION AND DISCUSSION

1. In what way does each of these projects affect our experience of the site on which it has been created? How do the color and texture of the fabric and other materials used in each project contribute to this effect?

2. One critic wrote of *Running Fence* that an essential part of its effect was the impossibility of experiencing all of its more than twenty-four miles at the same time. How does the scale of the artists' projects contribute to our understanding of each of these works?

3. Christo has described his and his wife's projects as "conceived at the boundary between the possible and the impossible." What is "possible" about the projects documented in these photographs? What is "impossible" about them?

4. Although the artists commission environmental impact studies and contractually guarantee to restore the spaces of their project to their original condition, each major project has faced stiff resistance from environmental protection organizations as well as many civic groups. What are some of the arguments for objecting to these projects? What rebuttals can you offer to those arguments?

5. What argument or arguments do these three works of art make regarding the relationship between humans and nature?

FICTION

Sarah Orne Jewett 1849–1909

Maine native Sarah Orne Jewett was daughter of a country doctor, and continued to live at least part of every year in the pre-Revolutionary house that had belonged to her grandfather. Jewett published her first story at eighteen, and made her reputation as a regional chronicler of life in rural New England. "The White Heron" is the title story in Jewett's 1886 collection, published the same year the Audubon Society was formed to protect wild birds and their nesting sites.

A WHITE HERON

1

The woods were already filled with shadows one June evening, just before eight o'clock, though a bright sunset still glimmered faintly among the trunks of the trees. A little girl was driving home her cow, a plodding, dilatory, provoking creature in her behavior, but a valued companion for all that. They were going away from the western light, and striking deep into the dark woods, but their feet were familiar with the path, and it was no matter whether their eyes could see it or not.

There was hardly a night the summer through when the old cow could be found waiting at the pasture bars; on the contrary, it was her greatest pleasure to hide herself away among the high huckleberry bushes, and though she wore a loud bell she had made the discovery that if one stood perfectly still it would not ring. So Sylvia had to hunt for her until she found her, and call Co'! Co'! with never an answering Moo, until her childish patience was quite spent. If the creature had not given good milk and plenty of it, the case would have seemed very different to her owners. Besides, Sylvia had all the time there was, and very little use to make of it. Sometimes in pleasant weather it was a consolation to look upon the cow's pranks as an intelligent attempt to play hide and seek, and as the child had no playmates she lent herself to this amusement with a good deal of zest. Though this chase had been so long that the wary animal herself had given an unusual signal of her whereabouts, Sylvia had only laughed when she came upon Mistress Moolly at the swampside, and urged her affectionately homeward with a twig of birch leaves. The old cow was not inclined to wander farther, she even turned in the right direction for once as they left the pasture, and stepped along the road at a good pace. She was quite ready to be milked now, and seldom stopped to browse. Sylvia wondered what her grandmother would say because they were so late. It was a great while since she had left home at half past five o'clock, but everybody knew the difficulty of making this errand a short one. Mrs. Tilley had chased the horned torment too many summer evenings herself to blame any one else for lingering, and was only thankful as she waited that she had Sylvia, nowadays, to give such valuable assistance. The good woman suspected that Sylvia loitered occasionally on her own account; there never was such a child for straying about out-of-doors since the world was made! Everybody said that it was a good change for a little maid who had tried to grow for eight years in a crowded manufacturing town, but, as for Sylvia herself, it seemed as if she never had been alive at all before she came to live at the farm. She thought often with wistful compassion of a wretched dry geranium that belonged to a town neighbor.

"'Afraid of folks,'" old Mrs. Tilley said to herself, with a smile, after she had made the unlikely choice of Sylvia from her daughter's houseful of children, and was returning to the farm. "'Afraid of folks,' they said! I guess she won't be troubled no great with 'em up to the old place!" When they reached the door of the lonely house and stopped to unlock it, and the cat came to purr loudly, and rub against them, a deserted pussy, indeed, but fat with young robins, Sylvia whispered that this was a beautiful place to live in, and she never should wish to go home.

The companions followed the shady wood-road, the cow taking slow steps, and the child very fast ones. The cow stopped long at the brook to drink, as if the pasture were not half a swamp, and Sylvia stood still and waited, letting her bare feet cool themselves in the shoal water, while the great twilight moths struck softly against her. She waded on through the brook as the cow moved away, and listened to the thrushes with a heart that beat fast with pleasure. There was a stirring in the great boughs overhead. They were full of little birds and beasts that seemed to be wide-awake, and going about their world, or else saying good-night to each other in sleepy twitters. Sylvia herself felt sleepy as she walked along. However, it was not much farther to the house, and the air was soft and sweet. She was not often in the woods so late as this, and it made her feel as if she were a part of the gray shadows and the moving leaves. She was just thinking how long it seemed since she first came to the farm a year ago, and wondering if everything went on in the noisy town just the same as when she was there; the thought of the great red-faced boy who used to chase and frighten her made her hurry along the path to escape from the shadow of the trees.

5   Suddenly this little woods-girl is horror-stricken to hear a clear whistle not very far away. Not a bird's whistle, which would have a sort of friendliness, but a boy's whistle, determined, and somewhat aggressive. Sylvia left the cow to whatever sad fate might await her, and stepped discreetly aside into the bushes, but she was just too late. The enemy had discovered her, and called out in a very cheerful and persuasive tone, "Halloa, little girl, how far is it to the road?" and trembling Sylvia answered almost inaudibly, "A good ways."

She did not dare to look boldly at the tall young man, who carried a gun over his shoulder, but she came out of her bush and again followed the cow, while he walked alongside.

"I have been hunting for some birds," the stranger said kindly, "and I have lost my way, and need a friend very much. Don't be afraid," he added gallantly. "Speak up and tell me what your name is, and whether you think I can spend the night at your house, and go out gunning early in the morning."

Sylvia was more alarmed than before. Would not her grandmother consider her much to blame? But who could have foreseen such an accident as this? It did not appear to be her fault, and she hung her head as if the stem of it were broken, but managed to answer "Sylvy," with much effort when her companion again asked her name.

Mrs. Tilley was standing in the doorway when the trio came into view. The cow gave a loud moo by way of explanation.

10   "Yes, you'd better speak up for yourself, you old trial! Where'd she tucked herself away this time, Sylvy?" Sylvia kept an awed silence; she knew by instinct that her grandmother did not comprehend the gravity of the situation. She must be mistaking the stranger for one of the farmer-lads of the region.

The young man stood his gun beside the door, and dropped a heavy game-bag beside it; then he bade Mrs. Tilley good-evening, and repeated his wayfarer's story, and asked if he could have a night's lodging.

"Put me anywhere you like," he said. "I must be off early in the morning, before day; but I am very hungry, indeed. You can give me some milk at any rate, that's plain."

"Dear sakes, yes," responded the hostess, whose long slumbering hospitality seemed to be easily awakened. "You might fare better if you went out on the main road a mile or so, but you're welcome to what we've got. I'll milk right off, and you make yourself at home. You can sleep on husks or feathers," she proffered graciously. "I raised them all myself. There's good pasturing for geese just below here towards the ma'sh. Now step round and set a plate for the gentleman, Sylvy!" And Sylvia promptly stepped. She was glad to have something to do, and she was hungry herself.

It was a surprise to find so clean and comfortable a little dwelling in this New England wilderness. The young man had known the horrors of its most primitive housekeeping, and the dreary squalor of that level of society which does not rebel at the companionship of hens. This was the best thrift of an old-fashioned farmstead, though on such a small scale that it seemed like a hermitage. He listened eagerly to the old woman's quaint talk, he watched Sylvia's pale face and shining gray eyes with ever growing enthusiasm, and insisted that this was the best supper

A Great Egret, or White Heron, the bird of Jewett's title.

he had eaten for a month; then, afterward, the new-made friends sat down in the doorway together while the moon came up.

15   Soon it would be berry-time, and Sylvia was a great help at picking. The cow was a good milker, though a plaguy thing to keep track of, the hostess gossiped frankly, adding presently that she had buried four children, so that Sylvia's mother, and a son (who might be dead) in California were all the children she had left. "Dan, my boy, was a great hand to go gunning," she explained sadly. "I never wanted for pa'tridges or gray squer'ls while he was to home. He's been a great wand'rer, I expect, and he's no hand to write letters. There, I don't blame him, I'd ha' seen the world myself if it had been so I could.

"Sylvia takes after him," the grandmother continued affectionately, after a minute's pause. "There ain't a foot o' ground she don't know her way over, and the wild creatur's counts her one o' themselves. Squer'ls she'll tame to come an' feed right out o' her hands, and all sorts o' birds. Last winter she got the jay-birds to bangeing here, and I believe she'd 'a scanted herself of her own meals to have plenty to throw out amongst 'em, if I hadn't kep' watch. Anything but crows, I tell her, I'm willin' to help support,—though Dan he went an' tamed one o' them that did seem to have reason same as folks. It was round here a good spell after he went away. Dan an' his father they didn't hitch,—but he never held up his head ag'in after Dan had dared him an' gone off."

The guest did not notice this hint of family sorrows in his eager interest in something else.

"So Sylvy knows all about birds, does she?" he exclaimed, as he looked round at the little girl who sat, very demure but increasingly sleepy, in the moonlight. "I am making a collection of birds myself. I have been at it ever since I was a boy." (Mrs. Tilley smiled.) "There are two or three very rare ones I have been hunting for these five years. I mean to get them on my own ground if they can be found."

"Do you cage 'em up?" asked Mrs. Tilley doubtfully, in response to this enthusiastic announcement.

20   "Oh, no, they're stuffed and preserved, dozens and dozens of them," said the ornithologist, "and I have shot or snared every one myself. I caught a glimpse of a white heron three miles from here on Saturday, and I have followed it in this direction. They have never been found in this district at all. The little white heron, it is," and he turned again to look at Sylvia with the hope of discovering that the rare bird was one of her acquaintances.

But Sylvia was watching a hop-toad in the narrow footpath.

"You would know the heron if you saw it," the stranger continued eagerly. "A queer tall white bird with soft feathers and long thin legs. And it would have a nest perhaps in the top of a high tree, made of sticks, something like a hawk's nest."

Sylvia's heart gave a wild beat; she knew that strange white bird, and had once stolen softly near where it stood in some bright green swamp grass, away over at the other side of the woods. There was an open place where the sunshine always seemed strangely yellow and hot, where tall, nodding rushes grew, and her grandmother had warned her that she might sink in the soft black mud underneath and never be heard of more. Not far beyond were the salt marshes and beyond those was the sea, the sea which Sylvia wondered and dreamed about, but never had looked upon, though its great voice could often be heard above the noise of the woods on stormy nights.

"I can't think of anything I should like so much as to find that heron's nest," the handsome stranger was saying. "I would give ten dollars to anybody who could show it to me," he added desperately, "and I mean to spend my whole vacation hunting for it if need be. Perhaps it was only migrating, or had been chased out of its own region by some bird of prey."

25   Mrs. Tilley gave amazed attention to all this, but Sylvia still watched the toad, not divining, as she might have done at some calmer time, that the creature wished to get to its hole under the doorstep, and was much hindered by the unusual spectators at

that hour of the evening. No amount of thought, that night, could decide how many wished-for treasures the ten dollars, so lightly spoken of, would buy.

The next day the young sportsman hovered about the woods, and Sylvia kept him company, having lost her first fear of the friendly lad, who proved to be most kind and sympathetic. He told her many things about the birds and what they knew and where they lived and what they did with themselves. And he gave her a jack-knife, which she thought as great a treasure as if she were a desert-islander. All day long he did not once make her troubled or afraid except when he brought down some unsuspecting singing creature from its bough. Sylvia would have liked him vastly better without his gun; she could not understand why he killed the very birds he seemed to like so much. But as the day waned, Sylvia still watched the young man with loving admiration. She had never seen anybody so charming and delightful; the woman's heart, asleep in the child, was vaguely thrilled by a dream of love. Some premonition of that great power stirred and swayed these young foresters who traversed the solemn woodlands with soft-footed silent care. They stopped to listen to a bird's song; they pressed forward again eagerly, parting the branches,—speaking to each other rarely and in whispers; the young man going first and Sylvia following, fascinated, a few steps behind, with her gray eyes dark with excitement.

She grieved because the longed-for white heron was elusive, but she did not lead the guest, she only followed, and there was no such thing as speaking first. The sound of her own unquestioned voice would have terrified her,—it was hard enough to answer yes or no when there was need of that. At last evening began to fall, and they drove the cow home together, and Sylvia smiled with pleasure when they came to the place where she heard the whistle and was afraid only the night before.

2

Half a mile from home, at the farther edge of the woods, where the land was highest, a great pine-tree stood, the last of its generation. Whether it was left for a boundary mark, or for what reason, no one could say; the woodchoppers who had felled its mates were dead and gone long ago, and a whole forest of sturdy trees, pines and oaks and maples, had

grown again. But the stately head of this old pine towered above them all and made a landmark for sea and shore miles and miles away. Sylvia knew it well. She had always believed that whoever climbed to the top of it could see the ocean; and the little girl had often laid her hand on the great rough trunk and looked up wistfully at those dark boughs that the wind always stirred, no matter how hot and still the air might be below. Now she thought of the tree with a new excitement, for why, if one climbed it at break of day, could not one see all the world, and easily discover whence the white heron flew, and mark the place, and find the hidden nest?

What a spirit of adventure, what wild ambition! What fancied triumph and delight and glory for the later morning when she could make known the secret! It was almost too real and too great for the childish heart to bear.

All night the door of the little house stood open, and the whippoorwills came and sang upon the very step. The young sportsman and his old hostess were sound asleep, but Sylvia's great design kept her broad awake and watching. She forgot to think of sleep. The short summer night seemed as long as the winter darkness, and at last when the whippoorwills ceased, and she was afraid the morning would after all come too soon, she stole out of the house and followed the pasture path through the woods, hastening toward the open ground beyond, listening with a sense of comfort and companionship to the drowsy twitter of a half-awakened bird, whose perch she had jarred in passing. Alas, if the great wave of human interest which flooded for the first time this dull little life should sweep away the satisfactions of an existence heart to heart with nature and the dumb life of the forest!

There was the huge tree asleep yet in the paling moonlight, and small and hopeful Sylvia began with utmost bravery to mount to the top of it, with tingling, eager blood coursing the channels of her whole frame, with her bare feet and fingers, that pinched and held like bird's claws to the monstrous ladder reaching up, up, almost to the sky itself. First she must mount the white oak tree that grew alongside, where she was almost lost among the dark branches and the green leaves heavy and wet with dew; a bird fluttered off its nest, and a red squirrel ran to and fro and scolded pettishly at the harmless housebreaker. Sylvia felt her way easily. She had often climbed there, and knew that higher still one of the oak's upper branches chafed against the pine trunk, just where its lower boughs were set close together. There, when she made the dangerous pass from one tree to the other, the great enterprise would really begin.

She crept out along the swaying oak limb at last, and took the daring step across into the old pine-tree. The way was harder than she thought; she must reach far and hold fast, the sharp dry twigs caught and held her and scratched her like angry talons, the pitch made her thin little fingers clumsy and stiff as she went round and round the tree's great stem, higher and higher upward. The sparrows and robins in the woods below were beginning to wake and twitter to the dawn, yet it seemed much lighter there aloft in the pine-tree, and the child knew that she must hurry if her project were to be of any use.

The tree seemed to lengthen itself out as she went up, and to reach farther and farther upward. It was like a great main-mast to the voyaging earth; it must truly have been amazed that morning through all its ponderous frame as it felt this determined spark of human spirit creeping and climbing from higher branch to branch. Who knows how steadily the least twigs held themselves to advantage this light, weak creature on her way! The old pine must have loved his new dependent. More than all the hawks, and bats, and moths, and even the sweet-voiced thrushes, was the brave, beating heart of the solitary gray-eyed child. And the tree stood still and held away the winds that June morning while the dawn grew bright in the east.

Sylvia's face was like a pale star, if one had seen it from the ground, when the last thorny bough was past, and she stood trembling and tired but wholly triumphant, high in the tree-top. Yes, there was the sea with the dawning sun making a golden dazzle over it, and toward that glorious east flew two hawks with slow-moving pinions. How low they looked in the air from that height when before one had only seen them far up, and dark against the blue sky. Their gray feathers were as soft as moths; they seemed only a little way from the tree, and Sylvia felt as if she too could go flying away among the clouds. Westward, the woodlands and farms reached miles and miles into the distance; here and there were church steeples, and white villages; truly it was a vast and awesome world.

The birds sang louder and louder. At last the sun came up bewilderingly bright. Sylvia could see the white sails of ships out at sea, and the clouds that were purple and rose-colored and yellow at first began to fade away. Where was the white heron's nest in the sea of green branches, and was this wonderful sight and pageant of the world the only reward for having climbed to such a giddy height? Now look down again, Sylvia, where the green marsh is set among the shining birches and dark hemlocks; there where you saw the white heron once you will see him again; look, look! a white spot of him like a single floating feather comes up from the dead hemlock and grows larger, and rises, and comes close at last, and goes by the landmark pine with steady sweep of wing and outstretched slender neck and crested head. And wait! wait! do not move a foot or a finger, little girl, do not send an arrow of light and consciousness from your two eager eyes, for the heron has perched on a pine bough not far beyond yours, and cries back to his mate on the nest, and plumes his feathers for the new day!

The child gives a long sigh a minute later when a company of shouting cat-birds comes also to the tree, and vexed by their fluttering and lawlessness the solemn heron goes away. She knows his secret now, the wild, light, slender bird that floats and wavers, and goes back like an arrow presently to his home in the green world beneath. Then Sylvia, well satisfied, makes her perilous way down again, not daring to look far below the branch she stands on, ready to cry sometimes because her fingers ache and her lamed feet slip. Wondering over and over again what the stranger would say to her, and what he would think when she told him how to find his way straight to the heron's nest.

"Sylvy, Sylvy!" called the busy old grandmother again and again, but nobody answered, and the small husk bed was empty, and Sylvia had disappeared.

The guest waked from a dream, and remembering his day's pleasure hurried to dress himself that it might sooner begin. He was sure from the way the shy little girl looked once or twice yesterday that she had at least seen the white heron, and now she must really be persuaded to tell. Here she comes now, paler than ever, and her worn old frock is torn and tattered, and smeared with pine pitch. The grandmother and the sportsman stand in the door together and question her, and the splendid moment has come to speak of the dead hemlock-tree by the green marsh.

But Sylvia does not speak after all, though the old grandmother fretfully rebukes her, and the young man's kind appealing eyes are looking straight in her own. He can make them rich with money; he has promised it, and they are poor now. He is so well worth making happy, and he waits to hear the story she can tell.

No, she must keep silence! What is it that suddenly forbids her and makes her dumb? Has she been nine years growing, and now, when the great world for the first time puts out a hand to her, must she thrust it aside for a bird's sake? The murmur of the pine's green branches is in her ears, she remembers how the white heron came flying through the golden air and how they watched the sea and the morning together, and Sylvia cannot speak; she cannot tell the heron's secret and give its life away.

40 Dear loyalty, that suffered a sharp pang as the guest went away disappointed later in the day, that could have served and followed him and loved him as a dog loves! Many a night Sylvia heard the echo of his whistle haunting the pasture path as she came home with the loitering cow. She forgot even her sorrow at the sharp report of his gun and the piteous sight of thrushes and sparrows dropping silent to the ground, their songs hushed and their pretty feathers stained and wet with blood. Were the birds better friends than their hunter might have been,—who can tell? Whatever treasures were lost to her, woodlands and summer-time, remember! Bring your gifts and graces and tell your secrets to this lonely country child!

[1886]

QUESTIONS FOR REFLECTION AND DISCUSSION

1. What are the consequences of Jewett's decision to begin her story with Sylvia on her own with the cow in the woods?

2. Why is Sylvia tempted to help the stranger find the white heron?

3. The narrator writes that Sylvia "could not understand why he killed the very birds he seemed to like so much." What answer does the story give us to this question?

4. Why does Sylvia climb the tree? What effect does this journey have on her?

5. What choice does Sylvia make in the end? How does the narrator suggest we evaluate her choice?

T. Coraghessan Boyle b. 1948

The son of Irish immigrants, T. Coraghessan Boyle grew up in Peekskill, New York. He received his PhD from the University of Iowa Writers' Workshop and teaches writing at the University of Southern California. Boyle has published seven volumes of short stories and nine novels on a wide-ranging variety of unusual topics. Like "Greasy Lake," Boyle's fiction is boundary-pushing, both funny and horrifying, constantly surprising our expectations.

GREASY LAKE

It's about a mile down on the dark side of Route 88.
—Bruce Springsteen

There was a time when courtesy and winning ways went out of style, when it was good to be bad, when you cultivated decadence like a taste. We were all dangerous characters then. We wore torn-up leather jackets, slouched around with toothpicks in our mouths, sniffed glue and ether and what somebody claimed was cocaine. When we wheeled our parents' whining station wagons out onto the street we left a patch of rubber half a block long. We drank gin and grape juice, Tango, Thunderbird, and Bali Hai. We were nineteen. We were bad. We read André Gide° and struck elaborate poses to show that we didn't give a shit about anything. At night, we went up to Greasy Lake.

Through the center of town, up the strip, past the housing developments and shopping malls, street lights giving way to the thin streaming illumination of the headlights, trees crowding the asphalt in a black unbroken wall: that was the way out to Greasy Lake. The Indians had called it Wakan, a reference to the clarity of its waters. Now it was fetid and murky, the mud banks glittering with broken glass and strewn with beer cans and the charred remains of bonfires. There was a single ravaged island a hundred yards from shore, so stripped of vegetation it looked as if the air force had strafed it. We went up to the lake because everyone went there, because we wanted to snuff the rich scent of possibility on the breeze, watch a girl take off her clothes and plunge into the festering murk, drink beer, smoke pot, howl at the stars, savor the incongruous full-throated roar of rock and roll against the primeval susurrus of frogs and crickets. This was nature.

I was there one night, late, in the company of two dangerous characters. Digby wore a gold star in his right ear and allowed his father to pay his tuition at Cornell; Jeff was thinking of quitting school to become a painter/musician/head-shop proprietor. They were both expert in the social graces, quick with a sneer, able to manage a Ford with lousy shocks over a rutted and gutted blacktop road at eighty-five while rolling a joint as compact as a Tootsie Roll Pop stick. They could lounge against a bank of booming speakers and trade "man"s with the best of them or roll out across the dance floor as if their joints worked on bearings. They were slick and quick and they wore their mirror shades at breakfast and dinner, in the shower, in closets and caves. In short, they were bad.

I drove. Digby pounded the dashboard and shouted along with Toots & the Maytals while Jeff hung his head out the window and streaked the side of my mother's Bel Air with vomit. It was early June, the air soft as a hand on your cheek, the third night of summer vacation. The first two nights we'd been

out till dawn, looking for something we never found. On this, the third night, we'd cruised the strip sixty-seven times, been in and out of every bar and club we could think of in a twenty-mile radius, stopped twice for bucket chicken and forty-cent hamburgers, debated going to a party at the house of a girl Jeff's sister knew, and chucked two dozen raw eggs at mailboxes and hitchhikers. It was 2:00 A.M.; the bars were closing. There was nothing to do but take a bottle of lemon-flavored gin up to Greasy Lake.

5   The taillights of a single car winked at us as we swung into the dirt lot with its tufts of weed and washboard corrugations; '57 Chevy, mint, metallic blue. On the far side of the lot, like the exoskeleton of some gaunt chrome insect, a chopper leaned against its kickstand. And that was it for excitement: some junkie halfwit biker and a car freak pumping his girlfriend. Whatever it was we were looking for, we weren't about to find it at Greasy Lake. Not that night.

But then all of a sudden Digby was fighting for the wheel. "Hey, that's Tony Lovett's car! Hey!" he shouted, while I stabbed at the brake pedal and the Bel Air nosed up to the gleaming bumper of the parked Chevy. Digby leaned on the horn, laughing, and instructed me to put my brights on. I flicked on the brights. This was hilarious. A joke. Tony would experience premature withdrawal and expect to be confronted by grim-looking state troopers with flashlights. We hit the horn, strobed the lights, and then jumped out of the car to press our witty faces to Tony's windows; for all we knew we might even catch a glimpse of some little fox's tit, and then we could slap backs with red-faced Tony, roughhouse a little, and go on to new heights of adventure and daring.

The first mistake, the one that opened the whole floodgate, was losing my grip on the keys. In the excitement, leaping from the car with the gin in one hand and a roach clip in the other, I spilled them in the grass—in the dark, rank, mysterious nighttime grass of Greasy Lake. This was a tactical error, as damaging and irreversible in its way as Westmoreland's decision to dig in at Khe Sanh.° I felt it like a jab of intuition, and I stopped there by the open door, peering vaguely into the night that puddled up round my feet.

André Gide: controversial French writer (1869-1951) whose novels, including *The Counterfeiters* and *Lafcadio's Adventures,* often show individuals in conflict with accepted morality.

Westmoreland's decision . . . Khe Sanh: General William C. Westmoreland commanded U.S. troops in Vietnam (1964–68). In late 1967 the North Vietnamese and Viet Cong forces attacked Khe Sanh (or Khesanh) with a show of strength, causing Westmoreland to expend great effort to defend a plateau of relatively little tactical importance.

T. CORAGHESSAN BOYLE   **647**

The second mistake—and this was inextricably bound up with the first—was identifying the car as Tony Lovett's. Even before the very bad character in greasy jeans and engineer boots ripped out of the driver's door, I began to realize that this chrome blue was much lighter than the robin's-egg of Tony's car, and that Tony's car didn't have rear-mounted speakers. Judging from their expressions, Digby and Jeff were privately groping toward the same inevitable and unsettling conclusion as I was.

In any case, there was no reasoning with this bad greasy character—clearly he was a man of action. The first lusty Rockette° kick of his steel-toed boot caught me under the chin, chipped my favorite tooth, and left me sprawled in the dirt. Like a fool, I'd gone down on one knee to comb the stiff hacked grass for the keys, my mind making connections in the most dragged-out, testudineous° way, knowing that things had gone wrong, that I was in a lot of trouble, and that the lost ignition key was my grail and my salvation. The three or four succeeding blows were mainly absorbed by my right buttock and the tough piece of bone at the base of my spine.

10   Meanwhile, Digby vaulted the kissing bumpers and delivered a savage kung-fu blow to the greasy character's collarbone. Digby had just finished a course in martial arts for phys-ed credit and had spent the better part of the past two nights telling us apocryphal tales of Bruce Lee types and of the raw power invested in lightning blows shot from coiled wrists, ankles, and elbows. The greasy character was unimpressed. He merely backed off a step, his face like a Toltec mask, and laid Digby out with a single whistling roundhouse blow . . . but by now Jeff had got into the act, and I was beginning to extricate myself from the dirt, a tinny compound of shock, rage, and impotence wadded in my throat.

Jeff was on the guy's back, biting at his ear. Digby was on the ground, cursing. I went for the tire iron I kept under the driver's seat. I kept it there because bad characters always keep tire irons under the driver's seat, for just such an occasion as this. Never mind that I hadn't been involved in a fight since sixth grade, when a kid with a sleepy eye and two streams of mucus descending from his nostrils hit me in the

knee with a Louisville slugger,° never mind that I'd touched the tire iron exactly twice before, to change tires: it was there. And I went for it.

I was terrified. Blood was beating in my ears, my hands were shaking, my heart turning over like a dirtbike in the wrong gear. My antagonist was shirtless, and a single cord of muscle flashed across his chest as he bent forward to peel Jeff from his back like a wet overcoat. "Motherfucker," he spat, over and over, and I was aware in that instant that all four of us—Digby, Jeff, and myself included—were chanting "motherfucker, motherfucker," as if it were a battle cry. (What happened next? the detective asks the murderer from beneath the turned-down brim of his porkpie hat. I don't know, the murderer says, something came over me. Exactly.)

Digby poked the flat of his hand in the bad character's face and I came at him like a kamikaze, mindless, raging, stung with humiliation—the whole thing, from the initial boot in the chin to this murderous primal instant involving no more than sixty hyperventilating, gland-flooding seconds—I came at him and brought the tire iron down across his ear. The effect was instantaneous, astonishing. He was a stunt man and this was Hollywood, he was a big grimacing toothy balloon and I was a man with a straight pin. He collapsed. Wet his pants. Went loose in his boots.

A single second, big as a zeppelin, floated by. We were standing over him in a circle, gritting our teeth, jerking our necks, our limbs and hands and feet twitching with glandular discharges. No one said anything. We just stared down at the guy, the car freak, the lover, the bad greasy character laid low. Digby looked at me; so did Jeff. I was still holding the tire iron, a tuft of hair clinging to the crook like dandelion fluff, like down. Rattled, I dropped it in the dirt, already envisioning the headlines, the pitted faces of the police inquisitors, the gleam of handcuffs, clank of bars, the big black shadows rising from the back of the cell . . . when suddenly a raw torn shriek cut through me like all the juice in all the electric chairs in the country.

15   It was the fox. She was short, barefoot, dressed in panties and a man's shirt. "Animals!" she screamed, running at us with her fists clenched and wisps of blow-dried hair in her face. There was a silver chain

---

Rockette: member of a dance troupe in the stage show at Radio City Music Hall, New York, famous for its ability to kick fast and high with wonderful coordination.   Testudineous: at the pace of a tortoise.

Louisville slugger: a brand of baseball bat

round her ankle, and her toenails flashed in the glare of the headlights. I think it was the toenails that did it. Sure, the gin and the cannabis and even the Kentucky Fried may have had a hand in it, but it was the sight of those flaming toes that set us off—the toad emerging from the loaf in *Virgin Spring*,° lipstick smeared on a child; she was already tainted. We were on her like Bergman's deranged brothers—see no evil, hear none, speak none—panting, wheezing, tearing at her clothes, grabbing for flesh. We were bad characters, and we were scared and hot and three steps over the line—anything could have happened.

It didn't.

Before we could pin her to the hood of the car, our eyes masked with lust and greed and the purest primal badness, a pair of headlights swung into the lot. There we were, dirty, bloody, guilty, dissociated from humanity and civilization, the first of the Ur-crimes behind us, the second in progress, shreds of nylon panty and spandex brassiere dangling from our fingers, our flies open, lips licked—there we were, caught in the spotlight. Nailed.

We bolted. First for the car, and then, realizing we had no way of starting it, for the woods. I thought nothing. I thought escape. The headlights came at me like accusing fingers. I was gone.

Ram-bam-bam, across the parking lot, past the chopper and into the feculent undergrowth at the lake's edge, insects flying up in my face, weeds whipping, frogs and snakes and red-eyed turtles splashing off into the night: I was already ankle-deep in muck and tepid water and still going strong. Behind me, the girl's screams rose in intensity, disconsolate, incriminating, the screams of the Sabine women,° the Christian martyrs, Anne Frank° dragged from the garret. I kept going, pursued by those cries, imagining cops and bloodhounds. The water was up to my knees when I realized what I was doing: I was going to swim for it. Swim the breadth of Greasy Lake

and hide myself in the thick clot of woods on the far side. They'd never find me there.

20   I was breathing in sobs, in gasps. The water lapped at my waist as I looked out over the moon-burnished ripples, the mats of algae that clung to the surface like scabs. Digby and Jeff had vanished. I paused. Listened. The girl was quieter now, screams tapering to sobs, but there were male voices, angry, excited, and the high-pitched ticking of the second car's engine. I waded deeper, stealthy, hunted, the ooze sucking at my sneakers. As I was about to take the plunge—at the very instant I dropped my shoulder for the first slashing stroke—I blundered into something. Something unspeakable, obscene, something soft, wet, moss-grown. A patch of weed? A log? When I reached out to touch it, it gave like a rubber duck, it gave like flesh.

In one of those nasty little epiphanies for which we are prepared by films and TV and childhood visits to the funeral home to ponder the shrunken painted forms of dead grandparents, I understood what it was that bobbed there so inadmissibly in the dark. Understood, and stumbled back in horror and revulsion, my mind yanked in six different directions (I was nineteen, a mere child, an infant, and here in the space of five minutes I'd struck down one greasy character and blundered into the waterlogged carcass of a second), thinking, the keys, the keys, why did I have to go and lose the keys? I stumbled back, but the muck took hold of my feet—a sneaker snagged, balance lost—and suddenly I was pitching face forward into the buoyant black mass, throwing out my hands in desperation while simultaneously conjuring the image of reeking frogs and muskrats revolving in slicks of their own deliquescing juices. AAAAArrrgh! I shot from the water like a torpedo, the dead man rotating to expose a mossy beard and eyes cold as the moon. I must have shouted out, thrashing around in the weeds, because the voices behind me suddenly became animated.

"What was that?"

"It's them, it's them: they tried to, tried to . . . *rape* me!" Sobs.

A man's voice, flat Midwestern accent. "You sons a bitches, we'll kill you!"

25   Frogs, crickets.

Then another voice, harsh, *r*-less, Lower East Side: "Motherfucker!" I recognized the verbal virtuosity

Virgin Spring: film by Swedish director Ingmar Bergman (1960).
Sabine women: members of an ancient tribe in Italy, according to legend, forcibly carried off by the early Romans under Romulus to be their wives. The incident is depicted in a famous painting, *The Rape of the Sabine Women*, by seventeenth-century French artist Nicolas Poussin.
Anne Frank: German Jewish girl (1929–1945) whose diary written during the Nazi occupation of the Netherlands later became world-famous. She hid with her family in a secret attic in Amsterdam, but was caught by the Gestapo and sent to the concentration camp at Belsen, where she died.

of the bad greasy character in the engineer boots. Tooth chipped, sneakers gone, coated in mud and slime and worse, crouching breathless in the weeds waiting to have my ass thoroughly and definitively kicked and fresh from the hideous stinking embrace of a three-days-dead-corpse, I suddenly felt a rush of joy and vindication: the son of a bitch was alive! Just as quickly, my bowels turned to ice. "Come on out of there, you pansy mothers!" the bad greasy character was screaming. He shouted curses till he was out of breath.

The crickets started up again, then the frogs. I held my breath. All at once was a sound in the reeds, a swishing, a splash: thunk-a-thunk. They were throwing rocks. The frogs fell silent. I cradled my head. Swish, swish, thunk-a-thunk. A wedge of feldspar the size of a cue ball glanced off my knee. I bit my finger.

It was then that they turned to the car. I heard a door slam, a curse, and then the sound of the headlights shattering—almost a good-natured sound, celebratory, like corks popping from the necks of bottles. This was succeeded by the dull booming of the fenders, metal on metal, and then the icy crash of the windshield. I inched forward, elbows and knees, my belly pressed to the muck, thinking of guerrillas and commandos and *The Naked and the Dead.*° I parted the weeds and squinted the length of the parking lot.

The second car—it was a Trans-Am—was still running, its high beams washing the scene in a lurid stagy light. Tire iron flailing, the greasy bad character was laying into the side of my mother's Bel Air like an avenging demon, his shadow riding up the trunks of the trees. Whomp. Whomp. Whomp-whomp. The other two guys—blond types, in fraternity jackets—were helping out with tree branches and skull-sized boulders. One of them was gathering up bottles, rocks, muck, candy wrappers, used condoms, poptops, and other refuse and pitching it through the window on the driver's side. I could see the fox, a white bulb behind the windshield of the '57 Chevy. "Bobbie," she whined over the thumping, "come on." The greasy character paused a moment, took one good swipe at the left taillight, and then heaved the

The Naked and the Dead: novel (1948) by Norman Mailer, about U.S. Army life in World War II.

tire iron halfway across the lake. Then he fired up the '57 and was gone.

30 Blond head nodded at blond head. One said something to the other, too low for me to catch. They were no doubt thinking that in helping to annihilate my mother's car they'd committed a fairly rash act, and thinking too that there were three bad characters connected with that very car watching them from the woods. Perhaps other possibilities occurred to them as well—police, jail cells, justices of the peace, reparations, lawyers, irate parents, fraternal censure. Whatever they were thinking, they suddenly dropped branches, bottles, and rocks and sprang for their car in unison, as if they'd choreographed it. Five seconds. That's all it took. The engine shrieked, the tires squealed, a cloud of dust rose from the rutted lot and then settled back on darkness.

I don't know how long I lay there, the bad breath of decay all around me, my jacket heavy as a bear, the primordial ooze subtly reconstituting itself to accommodate my upper thighs and testicles. My jaws ached, my knee throbbed, my coccyx was on fire. I contemplated suicide, wondered if I'd need bridgework, scraped the recesses of my brain for some sort of excuse to give my parents—a tree had fallen on the car, I was blinded by a bread truck, hit and run, vandals had got to it while we were playing chess at Digby's. Then I thought of the dead man. He was probably the only person on the planet worse off than I was. I thought about him, fog on the lake, insects chirring eerily, and felt the tug of fear, felt the darkness opening up inside me like a set of jaws. Who was he, I wondered, this victim of time and circumstance bobbing sorrowfully in the lake at my back. The owner of the chopper, no doubt, a bad older character come to this. Shot during a murky drug deal, drowned while drunkenly frolicking in the lake. Another headline. My car was wrecked; he was dead.

When the eastern half of the sky went from black to cobalt and the trees began to separate themselves from the shadows, I pushed myself up from the mud and stepped out into the open. By now the birds had begun to take over for the crickets, and dew lay slick on the leaves. There was a smell in the air, raw and sweet at the same time, the smell of the sun firing buds and opening blossoms. I contemplated the car.

It lay there like a wreck along the highway, like a steel sculpture left over from a vanished civilization. Everything was still. This was nature.

I was circling the car, as dazed and bedraggled as the sole survivor of an air blitz, when Digby and Jeff emerged from the trees behind me. Digby's face was crosshatched with smears of dirt; Jeff's jacket was gone and his shirt was torn across the shoulder. They slouched across the lot, looking sheepish, and silently came up beside me to gape at the ravaged automobile. No one said a word. After a while Jeff swung open the driver's door and began to scoop the broken glass and garbage off the seat. I looked at Digby. He shrugged. "At least they didn't slash the tires," he said.

It was true: the tires were intact. There was no windshield, the headlights were staved in, and the body looked as if it had been sledge-hammered for a quarter a shot at the county fair, but the tires were inflated to regulation pressure. The car was drivable. In silence, all three of us bent to scrape the mud and shattered glass from the interior. I said nothing about the biker. When we were finished, I reached in my pocket for the keys, experienced a nasty stab of recollection, cursed myself, and turned to search the grass. I spotted them almost immediately, no more than five feet from the open door, glinting like jewels in the first tapering shaft of sunlight. There was no reason to get philosophical about it: I eased into the seat and turned the engine over.

35   It was at that precise moment that the silver Mustang with the flame decals rumbled into the lot. All three of us froze; then Digby and Jeff slid into the car and slammed the door. We watched as the Mustang rocked and bobbed across the ruts and finally jerked to a halt beside the forlorn chopper at the far end of the lot. "Let's go," Digby said. I hesitated, the Bel Air wheezing beneath me.

Two girls emerged from the Mustang. Tight jeans, stiletto heels, hair like frozen fur. They bent over the motorcycle, paced back and forth aimlessly, glanced once or twice at us, and then ambled over to where the reeds sprang up in a green fence round the perimeter of the lake. One of them cupped her hands to her mouth. "Al," she called. "Hey, Al!"

"Come on," Digby hissed. "Let's get out of here."

But it was too late. The second girl was picking her way across the lot, unsteady on her heels, looking up at us and then away. She was older—twenty-five or -six—and as she came closer we could see there was something wrong with her: she was stoned or drunk, lurching now and waving her arms for balance. I gripped the steering wheel as if it were the ejection lever of a flaming jet, and Digby spat out my name, twice, terse and impatient.

"Hi," the girl said.

40   We looked at her like zombies, like war veterans, like deaf-and-dumb pencil peddlers.

She smiled, her lips cracked and dry. "Listen," she said, bending from the waist to look in the window, "you guys seen Al?" Her pupils were pinpoints, her eyes glass. She jerked her neck. "That's his bike over there—Al's. You seen him?"

Al. I didn't know what to say. I wanted to get out of the car and retch, I wanted to go home to my parents' house and crawl into bed. Digby poked me in the ribs. "We haven't seen anybody," I said.

The girl seemed to consider this, reaching out a slim veiny arm to brace herself against the car. "No matter," she said, slurring the *t*'s, "he'll turn up." And then, as if she'd just taken stock of the whole scene—the ravaged car and our battered faces, the desolation of the place—she said: "Hey, you guys look like some pretty bad characters—been fightin', huh?" We stared straight ahead, rigid as catatonics. She was fumbling in her pocket and muttering something. Finally she held out a handful of tablets in glassine wrappers: "Hey, you want to party, you want to do some of these with me and Sarah?"

I just looked at her. I thought I was going to cry. Digby broke the silence. "No, thanks," he said, leaning over me. "Some other time."

45   I put the car in gear and it inched forward with a groan, shaking off pellets of glass like an old dog shedding water after a bath, heaving over the ruts on its worn springs, creeping toward the highway. There was a sheen of sun on the lake. I looked back. The girl was still standing there, watching us, her shoulders slumped, hand outstretched.

[1985]

1. What does the word "bad" mean in the context of the story? What does it mean to the three friends? How does the narrator feel about the term, and what attitude does he expect us to take toward it?

2. Why is the story called "Greasy Lake"? What is a "greasy" lake? What function does the setting play in the story and our understanding of the story? To what degree is this a "natural" place?

3. The story is replete with allusions, some of them to popular culture and history, and some of them to film and literature. What do these allusions tell us about the narrator? Are they consistent with his actions?

4. A number of the narrator's actions are of dubious morality, in particular the attempted gang rape of the "fox." How are we meant to react to these actions? How do they affect our judgment of the narrator?

5. Explain and discuss the situational irony (p. 216) of the ending.

POETRY

Bashō 1644–1694

A samurai until the age of twenty, Matsuo Munefusa from that point devoted himself to poetry, specifically the haiku. Highly influenced by the religion and philosophy of Zen Buddhism, he retreated from the world to Bashō, a hermitage from which he drew his pen name. Bashō also traveled widely, recording his journeys in diaries and in haiku. He made several compilations of poetry by himself and others; the most famous, *The Monkey's Raincoat*, was published in 1690.

Four haiku

Old pond
a frog jumps in
the sound of water

[1681–82]

With every gust of wind,
the butterfly changes its place
on the willow.

[1676]

The wind from Mt. Fuji
I put it on the fan.
Here, a souvenir from Edo.

[1676]

Sleep on horseback,
The far moon in my continuing dream,
Steam of roasting tea.

[1684]

1. These haiku split into two parts. Discuss the relationship between the two parts in each of Bashō's poems.

2. What does Bashō exclude from his poems? What does he include?

3. What attitude toward nature do these poems exhibit?

Richard Wright 1908–1960•

Born on a plantation in Mississippi, son of an illiterate sharecropper and a schoolteacher, Wright was raised in Jackson by his mother's family. He moved first to Chicago and then to New York, working as a writer and editor for various Communist newspapers and journals. He published his first and most famous novel, *Native Son,* in 1940, and settled in Paris in 1946. While confined to his bed in Paris near the end of his life, the novelist Richard Wright discovered the form of the haiku and composed nearly 4,000 of them.

Haiku

In the falling snow
A laughing boy holds out his palms
Until they are white

[1960]

Richard Wright in Paris, 1957.

QUESTIONS FOR REFLECTION AND DISCUSSION

1. Compare this haiku with the traditional ones by Bashō on the previous page. What is similar? What is different?

2. How does the meaning of the poem change when we take into account the race of its author?

William Carlos Williams 1883–1963

"so much depends," also known as "The Red Wheelbarrow," was heavily influenced by the movement known as "Imagism" and the Japanese haiku form (p. 130). The poem was first published in Williams's influential collection, *Spring and All* (1923). (For a biography of Williams, see p. 227.)

so much depends

so much depends
upon

a red wheel
barrow

glazed with rain   5
water

beside the white
chickens

[1923]

1. Where is the alliteration in the poem? What other patterns of poetic form does it contain? Would the poem be any different without these patterns? Explain.

2. The American writer and musician John Cage once wrote, "I have nothing to say / and I am saying it / and that is poetry / as I needed it." How can "so much depend" upon the words in Williams's poem, and how can Cage "need" poetry to say nothing? Do you think "so much depends" is saying nothing in poetry? If not, what do you think it is saying?

3. What attitude does the poem suggest we take toward the natural world?

H. D. (Hilda Doolittle) 1886–1961

Born in Pennsylvania, Hilda Doolittle was a classmate of poet Marianne Moore at Bryn Mawr College; she subsequently met Ezra Pound (p. 234) and William Carlos Williams (p. 227) at the University of Pennsylvania. She traveled to Europe in 1911 and remained abroad for the rest of her life, writing under the pen name H. D. Her poetry is characterized by intense imagery; in later works she incorporated an abiding interest in classical mythology. The first poem in *Sea Garden* (1916), H.D.'s first volume of poetry, "Sea Rose" plays against the conventional love symbolism of the rose. Known as "sea rose," the sea-wormwood (*Artemisia maritima*) has small, yellow and brownish heads. By contrast, the "spice-rose" to which the speaker refers in line 14 is a specific version of the conventional rose, whose fragrant petals are used to make a spice and a perfume.

Sea Rose

Rose, harsh rose,
marred and with stint of° petals,
meagre flower, thin,
sparse of leaf,

more precious   5
than a wet rose
single on a stem—
you are caught in the drift.

Stunted, with small leaf,
you are flung on the sand,   10
you are lifted
in the crisp sand
that drives in the wind.

Can the spice-rose
drip such acrid fragrance   15
hardened in a leaf?

20 Stint of: few   [1916]

Sea Wormwood

Engraving of a sea rose.

1. There are three distinct roses described in this poem. What characteristics does the speaker attribute to each one?

2. Compare the qualities this speaker prizes in the sea rose with those prized in the conventional rose. What makes the sea rose "more precious" than the conventional rose? What makes it compare favorably in the final stanza with the spice-rose?

Elizabeth Bishop 1911–1979

"The Fish" was inspired by an enormous Caribbean grouper caught by Elizabeth Bishop on a fishing expedition off Key West, Florida, where she was spending the winter of 1939–1940. Published in 1940 in the *Partisan Review,* it was a breakthrough poem for the young poet, and figured prominently in her prize-winning first book, *North & South: A Cold Spring* (1946). (For a biography of Bishop, see p. 362.)

The Fish

I caught a tremendous fish
and held him beside the boat
half out of water, with my hook
fast in a corner of his mouth.
He didn't fight.   5
He hadn't fought at all.
He hung a grunting weight,
battered and venerable
and homely. Here and there
his brown skin hung in strips   10
like ancient wall-paper,
and its pattern of darker brown
was like wall-paper:
shapes like full-blown roses
stained and lost through age.   15
He was speckled with barnacles,
fine rosettes of lime,
and infested
with tiny white sea-lice,
and underneath two or three   20
rags of green weed hung down.
While his gills were breathing in
the terrible oxygen
—the frightening gills,
fresh and crisp with blood,   25
that can cut so badly—
I thought of the coarse white flesh

packed in like feathers,
the big bones and the little bones,
the dramatic reds and blacks   30
of his shiny entrails,
and the pink swim-bladder
like a big peony.
I looked into his eyes
which were far larger than mine   35
but shallower, and yellowed,
the irises backed and packed
with tarnished tinfoil
seen through the lenses
of old scratched isinglass.°   40
They shifted a little, but not
to return my stare.
—It was more like the tipping
of an object toward the light.
I admired his sullen face,   45
the mechanism of his jaw,
and then I saw
that from his lower lip
—if you could call it a lip—
grim, wet, and weapon-like,   50
hung five old pieces of fish-line,
or four and a wire leader
with the swivel still attached,
with all their five big hooks

40 **isinglass:** a gelatin-like substance obtained from the swimbladders of fish, used in making beer as well as for repairing parchment, the use to which Bishop is referring here.

grown firmly in his mouth.   55
A green line, frayed at the end
where he broke it, two heavier lines,
and a fine black thread
still crimped from the strain and snap
when it broke and he got away.   60
Like medals with their ribbons
frayed and wavering,
a five-haired beard of wisdom
trailing from his aching jaw.
I stared and stared   65
and victory filled up

the little rented boat,
from the pool of bilge
where oil had spread a rainbow
around the rusted engine   70
to the bailer rusted orange,
the sun-cracked thwarts,
the oarlocks on their strings,
the gunnels—until everything
was rainbow, rainbow, rainbow!   75
And I let the fish go.

[1940]

QUESTIONS FOR REFLECTION AND DISCUSSION

1. Compare lines 5–9 with lines 45–67. How do we reconcile the "five-haired beard of wisdom" with the lack of fight emphasized at the beginning? What signals to us that the speaker's attitude has changed?

2. What motivates the speaker of the poem to provide such an extraordinarily detailed description of the fish? Notice that she uses similes, and metaphors quite sparingly. List them, and suggest what their role in her description might be.

3. Explain the relationship between the rainbow created by the spilled oil in the sunlight and the final line. Why not release the fish after line 64?

4. Do you think this poem is describing a specific episode, putting forth a philosophy about nature, or both? Use specific examples from the text to support your answer.

Walt Whitman 1819–1892

Born on Long Island and raised there and in Brooklyn, Walt Whitman was introduced to words and books through his work in the printing trade from the age of 12. After working as a teacher in a one-room schoolhouse on Long Island, he took up journalism full-time in 1841. In 1855, he published the first edition of *Leaves of Grass*, a collection of poems that he would expand and revise for the rest of his life. Whitman's use of free verse and his celebration of democracy and of physical sensation were groundbreaking and controversial. Strongly affected by the Civil War, Whitman nursed the wounded in Washington, D.C., while working as a government clerk. "When I Heard the Learn'd Astronomer" was published in 1865 in *Drum Taps*, a new volume in Whitman's ever-expanding masterpiece, *Leaves of Grass*.

When I Heard the Learn'd Astronomer

When I heard the learn'd astronomer,
When the proofs, the figures, were ranged in
    columns before me,
When I was shown the charts and diagrams, to add,
    divide, and measure them,
When I sitting heard the astronomer where he
    lectured with much applause in the lecture-room,

How soon unaccountable I became tired and sick,   5
Till rising and gliding out I wander'd off by myself,
In the mystical moist night-air, and from time
    to time,
Look'd up in perfect silence at the stars.

[1865]

1. How does Whitman use the device of anaphora (p. 212) to structure the two parts of the poem?

2. What is the distinction Whitman draws between the astronomer and the stars? What are the qualities he associates with each of them? What broader issues does he raise through this distinction?

Langston Hughes 1902–1967

Langston Hughes composed his first published poem, "The Negro Speaks of Rivers," in 1920, during the summer after he graduated from high school in Cleveland, Ohio. It was published the following year in the NAACP magazine *Crisis* and was included in Hughes's first book, *The Weary Blues* (1926). He dedicated the poem to the political activist and intellectual leader W. E. B. DuBois, cofounder of the NAACP and editor of *Crisis*. (For a biography of Hughes, see page 369.)

The Negro Speaks of Rivers

I've known rivers:
I've known rivers ancient as the world and older than
   the flow of human blood in human veins.
My soul has grown deep like the rivers.

I bathed in the Euphrates when dawns were young.
I built my hut near the Congo and it lulled me to
   sleep.   5

I looked upon the Nile and raised the pyramids above it.
I heard the singing of the Mississippi when Abe Lincoln
   went down to New Orleans, and I've seen its muddy
   bosom turn all golden in the sunset.

I've known rivers:
Ancient, dusky rivers.

My soul has grown deep like the rivers.   10

[1921]

1. Who is the speaker of the poem?

2. What motivates the speaker's choice of rivers to include in the poem?

3. What does it mean, in the context of the poem, to "know" a river? How is this "knowledge" related to the poem's refrain?

Gerard Manley Hopkins 1844–1889

Born in Stratford, Essex, Gerard Manley Hopkins read classics at Balliol College, Oxford. In 1866, he converted from Anglicanism to Catholicism, and the following year decided to become a Jesuit priest. He burned his early poems as unsuitable for his vocation, but some were preserved in friends' copies. Hopkins was ordained in 1877, serving in parishes all over England and Scotland as well as teaching. He was an innovator in poetic form, incorporating ancient Anglo-Saxon rhythms, Welsh forms, and dialect words into his verse. Few of Hopkins's poems were published in his lifetime. Written in 1881, "Inversnaid" was first published, along with Hopkins's other poems, in 1918.

Inversnaid

This darksome burn,° horseback brown,
His rollrock highroad roaring down,
In coop and in comb the fleece of his foam
Flutes and low to the lake falls home.

A windpuff-bonnet of fáwn-fróth   5
Turns and twindles over the broth
Of a pool so pitchblack, féll-frówning,
It rounds and rounds Despair to drowning.

Degged° with dew, dappled with dew
Are the groins° of the braes° that the brook treads
   through,   10
Wiry heathpacks, flitches of fern,
And the beadbonny ash° that sits over the burn.

What would the world be, once bereft
Of wet and of wildness? Let them be left,
O let them be left, wildness and wet;   15
Long live the weeds and the wilderness yet.

[1918]

1 **burn:** stream. 10 **Degged:** drizzled, sprinkled. 11 **groins:** deep trenches. **braes:** steep banks. 13 **beadbonny ash:** ash tree, full of berries.

A nineteenth-century engraving of the famous Falls of Inversnaid. Inversnaid is a scenic hamlet in the Scottish highlands on the shore of Loch Lomond, near the falls.

QUESTIONS FOR REFLECTION AND DISCUSSION

1. What are some of the literary devices Hopkins uses to reproduce the sound and movement of the stream? What is the effect of his use of dialect and combined words, such as "fawn-froth"? How do the formal techniques reflect the theme of the poem?

2. How does Hopkins define nature? What argument does the poem make about nature? Why do you think he chose the Falls of Inversnaid to make this argument?

Wendell Berry b. 1934

Poet, farmer, and nonfiction writer Wendell Berry was born in rural Kentucky, to which he returned after studying and teaching on both the West and the East coasts. Convinced of the importance of place, or "connectedness," in his life, he returned to Kentucky to work a farm and to write, which he has done, completing a large number of works. Berry is author of eight novels and several dozen short stories, all set in the same small Kentucky town. His *Collected Poems* were published in 1999, but he has not ceased to write in the new millennium.

Stay Home

I will wait here in the fields
to see how well the rain
brings on the grass.
In the labor of the fields
longer than a man's life   5
I am at home. Don't come with me.
You stay home too.

I will be standing in the woods
where the old trees
move only with the wind   10
and then with gravity.
In the stillness of the trees
I am at home. Don't come with me.
You stay home too.

[1980]

QUESTIONS FOR REFLECTION AND DISCUSSION

1. What does the speaker in the poem mean by "home"? What actions does he associate it with?

2. Why does he instruct his reader not to come with him?

3. What is the setting of each stanza of the poem? What is the relationship between them?

Robert Frost 1874–1963

Primarily associated with rural settings, Robert Frost's poetry also at times eloquently addressed the relationship between natural and urban settings, as in this poem from his Pulitzer Prize–winning volume, *New Hampshire* (1923). (For a biography of Frost, see page 176.)

A Brook in the City

The farmhouse lingers, though averse to square
With the new city street it has to wear
A number in. But what about the brook
That held the house as in an elbow-crook?
I ask as one who knew the brook, its strength   5
And impulse, having dipped a finger length
And made it leap my knuckle, having tossed
A flower to try its currents where they crossed.
The meadow grass could be cemented down
From growing under pavements of a town;   10
The apple trees be sent to a hearthstone flame.
Is water wood to serve a brook the same?
How else dispose of an immortal force
No longer needed? Staunch it at its source
With cinder loads dumped down? The brook was
    thrown   15

Deep in a sewer dungeon under stone
In fetid darkness still to live and run—
And all for nothing it had ever done,
Except forget to go in fear perhaps.
No one would know except for ancient maps   20
That such a brook ran water. But I wonder
If from its being kept forever under,
The thoughts may not have risen that so keep
This new-built city from both work and sleep.

[1923]

Minetta Street in Greenwich Village, New York City. The name and the curve in the street come from Minetta Brook, which in the nineteenth century flowed from 23rd Street to the Hudson River.

QUESTIONS FOR REFLECTION AND DISCUSSION

1. What happens to the rural world when the city arrives? How is the brook different?

2. Is the brook the same once in "sewer darkness" or is it changed?

3. Explain the last four lines of the poem. What is the speaker suggesting about the effect of nature in the city?

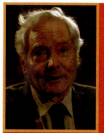

W. S. Merwin b. 1927

Author of numerous works of poetry and of plays and essays, and a brilliant translator, W. S. Merwin won the Pulitzer Prize in 1971 for his collection of poems, *The Carrier of Ladders*. Merwin was born in New York City and studied romance languages and medieval literature at Princeton University. Long a pacifist and ecological activist, Merwin moved in the early 1970s to the Hawaiian island of Maui. Deeply pessimistic in his outlook on history and highly concerned over the exploitation of land for profit, Merwin composed "Rain at Night" as part of his 1988 collection *The Rain in the Trees*.

Rain at Night

This is what I have heard

at last the wind in December
lashing the old trees with rain
unseen rain racing along the tiles
under the moon   5
wind rising and falling
wind with many clouds
trees in the night wind

after an age of leaves and feathers
someone dead   10
thought of this mountain as money
and cut the trees
that were here in the wind
in the rain at night
it is hard to say it   15
but they cut the sacred 'ōhi'as then
the sacred koas then
the sandalwood and the halas
holding aloft their green fires

and somebody dead turned cattle loose   20
among the stumps until killing time

but the trees have risen one more time
and the night wind makes them sound
like the sea that is yet unknown
the black clouds race over the moon   25
the rain is falling on the last place

[1988]

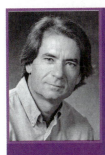

A young ʻōhiʻa tree, sacred to the Hawaiʻian goddess Pele, growing in a recent lava flow.

QUESTIONS FOR REFLECTION AND DISCUSSION

1. There are three different things that the speaker tells us of having heard. What are they, and what motivates the shift from one to the other?

2. What does the speaker mean when he refers to "someone dead" and "somebody dead" in lines 9 and 19?

3. Why is the poem named after the rain rather than the trees? How does this distinction help to explain the concluding line?

NONFICTION

Louis D. Owens 1948–2002

Born in Lompoc, California, Louis Owens is of Choctaw, Cherokee, and Irish American heritage. He earned his BA and MA from the University of California, Berkeley, and his PhD from the University of California, Davis, one of several universities where he taught as a professor of English, Native American Studies, and Creative Writing. Owens wrote short stories, essays, criticism, and novels, including the American Book Award-winning *Nightland* (1996). "The American Indian Wilderness" was first published in 1994 in the *American Nature Writing Newsletter*.

THE AMERICAN INDIAN WILDERNESS

IN THE CENTER OF THE GLACIER PEAK WILDERNESS in northern Washington, a magnificent, fully glaciated white volcano rises over a stunningly beautiful region of the North Cascades. On maps, the mountain is called Glacier Peak. To the Salishan people who have always lived in this part of the Cascades, however, the mountain is *Dakobed*, or the Great Mother, the place of emergence. For more than eighty years, a small, three-sided log shelter stood in a place called White Pass just below one shoulder of the great mountain, tucked securely into a meadow between thick stands of mountain hemlock and alpine fir.

In the early fall of seventy-six, while working as a seasonal ranger for the U.S. Forest Service, I drew the task of burning the White Pass shelter. After all those years, the shelter roof had collapsed like a broken bird wing under the weight of winter snow, and the time was right for fire and replanting. It was part of a Forest Service plan to remove all human-made objects from wilderness areas, a plan of which I heartily approved. So I backpacked eleven miles to the pass and set up camp, and for five days, while a bitter early storm sent snow driving horizontally out of the north, I dismantled the shelter and burned the old logs, piling and burning and piling and burning until nothing remained. The antique, hand-forged spikes that had held the shelter together I put into gunny sacks and cached to be packed out later by mule. I spaded up the earth beaten hard for nearly a century by boot and hoof, and transplanted plugs of vegetation from hidden spots on the nearby ridge.

At the end of those five days, not a trace of the shelter remained, and I felt good, very smug in fact, about returning the White Pass meadow to its "original" state. As I packed up my camp, the snowstorm had subsided to a few flurries and a chill that felt bone-deep with the promise of winter. My season was almost over, and as I started the steep hike down to the trailhead my mind was on the winter I was going to spend in sunny Arizona.

A half-mile from the pass I saw the two old women. At first they were dark, hunched forms far down on the last long switchback up the snowy ridge. But as we drew closer to one another, I began to feel a growing amazement that, by the time we were face-to-face, had become awe. Almost swallowed up in their baggy wool pants, heavy sweaters and parkas, silver braids hanging below thick wool caps, they seemed ancient, each weighted with at least seventy years as well as a small backpack. They paused every few steps to lean on their staffs and look out over the North Fork drainage below, a deep, heavily forested river valley that rose on the far side to the glaciers and sawtoothed black granite of the Monte Cristo Range. And they smiled hugely upon seeing me, clearly surprised and delighted to find another person in the mountains at such a time.

5   We stood and chatted for a moment, and as I did with all backpackers, I reluctantly asked them where

Glacier Peak Volcano, seventy miles northeast of Seattle, Washington.

they were going. The snow quickened a little, obscuring the view, as they told me that they were going to White Pass.

"Our father built a little house up here," one of them said, "when he worked for the Forest Service like you. Way back before we was born, before this century."

"We been coming up here each year since we was little," the other added. "Except last year when Sarah was not well enough."

"A long time ago, this was all our land," the one called Sarah said. "All Indi'n land everywhere you can see. Our people had houses up in the mountains, for gathering berries every year."

As they took turns speaking, the smiles never leaving their faces, I wanted to excuse myself, to edge around these elders and flee to the trailhead and my car, drive back to the district station and keep going south. I wanted to say, "I'm Indian too. Choctaw from Mississippi; Cherokee from Oklahoma"—as if mixed blood could pardon me for what I had done. Instead, I said, "The shelter is gone." Cravenly I added, "It was crushed by snow, so I was sent up to burn it. It's gone now."

10   I expected outrage, anger, sadness, but instead the sisters continued to smile at me, their smiles changing only slightly. They had a plastic tarp and would stay dry, they said, because a person always had to be prepared in the mountains. They would put up their tarp inside the hemlock grove above the meadow, and the scaly hemlock branches would turn back the snow. They forgave me without saying it—my ignorance and my part in the long pattern of loss which they knew so well.

Hiking out those eleven miles, as the snow of the high country became a drumming rain in the forests below, I had long hours to ponder my encounter with the sisters. Gradually, almost painfully, I began to understand that what I called "wilderness" was an absurdity, nothing more than a figment of the European imagination. Before the European invasion, there was no wilderness in North America; there was only the fertile continent where people lived in a hard-learned balance with the natural world. In embracing a philosophy that saw the White Pass shelter—and all traces of humanity—as a shameful stain upon the "pure" wilderness, I had succumbed to a five-hundred-year-old pattern of deadly thinking that separates us from the natural world. This is not to say that what we call wilderness today does not need careful safeguarding. I believe that White Pass really is better off now that the shelter doesn't serve as a magnet to backpackers and horsepackers who compact the soil, disturb and kill the wildlife, cut down centuries-old trees for firewood, and leave their litter strewn about. And I believe the man who built the shelter would agree. But despite this unfortunate reality, the global environmental crisis that sends species into extinction daily and threatens to destroy all life surely has its roots in the Western pattern of thought that sees humanity and "wilderness" as mutually exclusive.

In old-growth forests in the North Cascades, deep inside the official Wilderness Area, I have come upon faint traces of log shelters built by Suiattle and Upper Skagit people for berry harvesting a century or more ago—just as the sisters said. Those human-made structures were as natural a part of the Cascade ecosystem as the burrows of marmots in the steep scree slopes. Our Native ancestors all over this continent lived within a complex web of relations with the natural world, and in doing so they assumed a responsibility for their world that contemporary Americans cannot even imagine. Unless Americans, and all human beings, can learn to imagine themselves as intimately and inextricably related to every aspect of the world they inhabit, with the extraordinary responsibilities such relationship entails—unless they can learn what the indigenous peoples of the Americas knew and often still know—the earth simply will not survive. A few square miles of something called wilderness will become the sign of failure everywhere.

[1994]

QUESTIONS FOR REFLECTION AND DISCUSSION

1. What is the effect of structuring the essay around Owens's own learning experience? How does this structure affect our attitude toward the argument?

2. What, according to Owens, is the European conception of "wilderness"? What, for Owens, is wrong with this conception? What conception does he offer in its place?

3. How does Owens define the Native American relationship to the earth?

Donella Meadows 1941–2001

In 1972, the environmental scientist Donella Meadows coauthored a critical analysis of the international emphasis on economic growth, arguing that continued population expansion and overconsumption would lead to crisis. In 1992, the same authors updated their original argument with current numbers. In "Living Lightly and Inconsistently on the Land," first published as a newspaper column, Meadows describes the difference she sees between "sufficiency" and "abundance."

LIVING LIGHTLY AND INCONSISTENTLY ON THE LAND

I WAS RAISED IN ILLINOIS, AS A GOOD RED-BLOODED American kid, eating Jello, white bread, canned peas, and Midwestern steaks. I watched Howdy Doody and played softball and canasta. On my sixteenth birthday my father gave me a decrepit old car. I used it to drive to my summer job in a drugstore at a shopping mall. Everyone I knew lived just like me. I didn't know there was such a thing as a lifestyle. I went to college on a scholarship and developed tastes for things that went beyond my family's ken—artichokes and opera and Shakespeare. As a chemistry major I did a term paper on chemical additives in food, and for the first time I began to make consumer decisions that didn't come from habit. I read labels and tried to buy foods that were mainly composed of food.

Getting married and moving east didn't induce many changes until I started studying biochemistry. As I learned more about the body's chemical processes, I started putting more whole wheat flour in things I baked, using less sugar and fat, and serving more green vegetables. I eliminated the Jello and everything in cans and swore off soft drinks and coffee. All this was done for our own health, not from any sense of global responsibility.

The quantum leap in lifestyle came when my husband and I spent a year driving through Turkey, Iran, Afghanistan, Pakistan, and India (in those days Americans were welcome in all those countries). In India we became vegetarians because it was difficult to find meat. In the Muslim countries we couldn't buy alcohol. Our clothing had to be simple and practical. Hot showers became major luxuries. We were cut off from television, radio, and even newspapers for weeks at a time. Mostly we lived as the villagers around us did, and we discovered that we were perfectly happy to do so.

Coming home was a shock. Looking with Asian eyes, we couldn't believe how much *stuff* people had. We saw how little the stuff had to do with happiness. We also had strong memories of the poverty, the erosion, the deforestation, and the hunger we had seen. The world was very real to us. We resolved to live our lives in a way more consistent with the whole of it.

5   At first we had little desire for material things. That wore off, of course, and we became Americans again. But we kept our life simple. We continued to be vegetarians. We traveled by mass transit. We made our own clothes and bread and even furniture. We asked a long set of questions about everything we bought. Is this spinach organic or raised with pesticides? Were these bananas grown on an exploitive plantation or in a worker-owned cooperative? Is our electricity from a hydro dam or a nuclear power plant? If we buy plastic bags, how many nasty chemicals have we caused to be released somewhere? Can we get along without plastic bags?

We were the best global citizens we knew how to be. And we were a pain in the neck. We regarded most of the people around us as unaware, unconsciously wreaking planetary destruction for short-term gratification. We separated ourselves from them. It didn't occur to us that setting up us/them and right/wrong categories might be the surest way of all to wreak planetary destruction.

We moved to New Hampshire because we wanted to restore a beat-up farm to ecological health and to live more self-sufficiently. We ripped the house apart and put it back together with proper insulation. We added space so six or eight people could share the place without stifling one another, and since then we've lived communally. We heat the house and our water partly with wood, partly with oil. We cut the wood with a chain saw, split it with a hydraulic splitter attached to a tractor. We cook on a woodstove sometimes, but an electric stove mostly. Our electricity comes partially from a nuclear power plant.

We grow nearly all our vegetables, all our eggs, some fruit. We grow organically, of course. We've made the soil much better than it was when we came here. We dry, can, freeze, and pickle enough to get through the winter. We buy milk from another farm, grain from the co-op, and ice cream from the supermarket. We raise sheep for wool, some of which we sell, some of which we spin, dye, and knit ourselves. We sell the meat. We recycle organic garbage to the chickens, cans and bottles to a recycling center. We wash out and reuse plastic bags; we use old newspapers to start fires in the woodstoves. We put tons of junk mail out in the weekly garbage pickup, which goes to a trash-to-energy incinerator.

We bought a television when the Red Sox were in the World Series. It's hardly been on since, but classical music plays all day on a CD player. We have old-fashioned spinning wheels and modern computers, an energy-efficient Honda and a wildly inefficient Dodge pickup truck for farm work. We travel by jet all over the world to do environmental work, probably burning up 100 times as much fuel as any other family in our town.

10   I assume that the inconsistencies in this "lifestyle" are obvious to you. We try to live lightly on the land in a culture where that's impossible. But we have lightened up about our own compromises and those of others. We do our best, we're always willing to try to do better, and we're still major transgressors on the ecosystems and resources of the planet. We're a lot more tolerant of our fellow transgressors than we used to be.

As a child in the middle-class Midwest, I lived out of a subconscious sense of *abundance*. That sense permits security, innovation, generosity, and joy. But it can also harbor insensitivity, greed, and waste. After returning from India, I lived out of a sense of *scarcity*. That is fine when it fosters stewardship, simplicity, and frugality, but not when it leads to grimness, intolerance, and separation from one's fellows. Now I try to base my life on the idea of *sufficiency*—there is just enough of everything for everyone and not one bit more. There is enough for generosity but not waste, enough for security but not hoarding. Or, as Gandhi said, enough for everyone's need, but not for everyone's greed.

[1991]

QUESTIONS FOR REFLECTION AND DISCUSSION

1. What prompts Meadows's change in lifestyle?

2. What are some of the inconsistencies in her new lifestyle? What is her attitude toward these inconsistencies?

3. What does Meadows advise as a strategy for "Living Lightly"?

LIVING IN NATURE TOPICS FOR ESSAYS

1. Compare several of the poems in this section. How is their attitude toward nature similar? How is it different? How does the form of each poem relate to its theme?

2. Compare the image of wilderness or wild nature in several of the texts in this section.

3. Write an essay comparing the imagery of water in several selections in this section.

4. What different lands are described in these selections? What do they have in common? How are they different?

5. Write an essay comparing the depiction of death in several of this chapter's selections.

6. Write an essay discussing the relationship between gender and nature in several of the selections in this chapter.

7. Write an essay about current attitudes toward nature. Use the selections in this section as a starting point, but you will also want to do further research.

8. Write an essay comparing a scientific view of nature with the view of nature taken by one or two texts in this chapter.

LIVING IN NATURE FURTHER READINGS IN *LITERATURE: A WORLD OF WRITING*

Chinua Achebe, "Dead Men's Path" • William Blake, "The Tyger" • Bill Buford, "Lions and Tigers and Bears" • Rachel Carson, "The Marginal World" • K. C. Cole, "Murmurs" • Annie Dillard, "Death of a Moth • Rosa Ehrenreich, "I Hate Trees" • Robert Frost, "Mending Wall" and "Stopping by Woods on a Snowy Evening" • Xu Gang, "Red Azalea on the Cliff" • Ellen Hunnicutt, "Blackberries" • Leslie Norris, "Blackberries" • Mary Oliver, "August" • Scott Russell Sanders, "Buckeye" • John Steinbeck, "The Chrysanthemums" • Henry Taylor, "Landscape with Tractor" • Eudora Welty, "A Worn Path" • Virginia Woolf, "The Death of the Moth" • James Wright, "Lying in a Hammock at William Duffy's Farm in Pine Island, Minnesota"

WORKING FURTHER WITH THE WORLD WE SHARE

1. Write an essay analyzing the depiction of nature in the city in several texts in this chapter.

2. Write an essay comparing life in the city with life in wild nature, using selections from this chapter.

3. Write an essay comparing several personal essays in this chapter. How do they use voice? How autobiographical are they? What is their attitude toward memory?

4. Research a topic relating to nature in the city and write a paper about the results of your research.

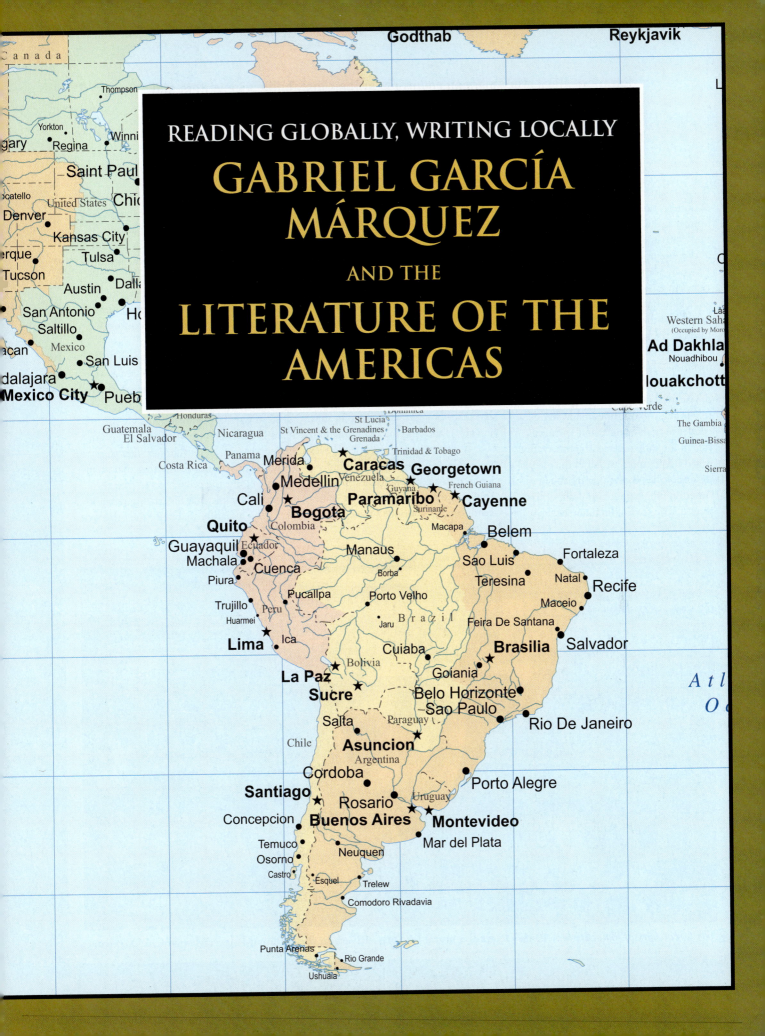

READING GLOBALLY, WRITING LOCALLY

GABRIEL GARCÍA MÁRQUEZ

AND THE

LITERATURE OF THE AMERICAS

Latin American literature first came to international notice during what is known as the "boom": the period during the 1960s and 1970s when writers such as the Argentinean Julio Cortázar, the Peruvian Mario Vargas Llosa, the Brazilian Clarice Lispector, and, above all, Colombian Gabriel García Márquez reinvented the form of the modern novel through the half-fantastic, half true-to-life form known as **magic realism.** This literature was inspired, as Argentinean boom writer Manuel Puig suggested, by the political instability that has been the rule in the two centuries following independence from Spanish and Portuguese rule in the early nineteenth century. But it had deeper roots as well in the oral traditions of the peoples that inhabited the Americas long before European settlers arrived. The ancient literature of the Americas has been preserved in two forms: as *codices*—pictograms depicting the myths of the Aztecs, the pre-Columbian Mesoamerican rulers of Mexico—and as oral traditions, preserving the myths of peoples ranging from the Inuits in the arctic north to the Yamana in Tierra del Fuego at the southern tip of South America. From the time of Columbus's first voyage to the Americas in 1492, these traditions were mixed and often submerged by the new influences of the colonial Europeans and the indigenous culture of the African slaves they brought with them. In the fifty years following the beginning of the U.S. War of Independence, nearly every country in the Americas gained independence from its colonial rulers. However, American writers throughout the nineteenth century continued to compose the literature of their new nations according to European models. During the twentieth century, instability dominated the politics as well as the aesthetics of most of the countries of Latin America, as indigenous peoples, freed slaves, and liberal- and radical-minded *criollos*, or descendants of Spanish settlers, asserted their presence in the life of their countries.

The term "magic realism" was coined to describe the fiction of Colombian writer Gabriel García Márquez, the featured author of this casebook. In magic realist writing, seemingly impossible events are related as if they were everyday, realistic occurrences. As García Márquez likes to say, however, it is not his writing that seems unreal, but the events of the country and its people that his writing recounts. This is a feature shared by the otherwise

The Great City of Tenochtitlan, 1945. Detail of a mural by Diego Rivera in the National Palace, Mexico City, Mexico.

Machu Picchu with Huayna Picchu peak in background, Peru.

enormously varied publications of the boom writers: each of them was struggling to find a way of writing literature that would accurately depict characters, lives, and events that were unarguably *different* from the European models that had determined the form literature had taken up to that point. American writers borrowed these models but then transformed them as a way of making sense of the experience of their own world. We can see that difference in the pair of strange and deceptively simple stories by García Márquez; and we can hear it in the powerful and mysterious language of Latin America's greatest poet, the Chilean Pablo Neruda.

Difference is also a linguistic issue. The first language of many Americans remains one of those spoken by the peoples that were here before the Europeans. The first language of more than half of Bolivia's residents is either Quechua (the language of the Incas, among others) or Aymara. Moreover, there are major Portuguese-, French-, and Dutch-speaking communities in South America and the Caribbean. But the primary spoken and literary language of the Americas is either Spanish or English, and the relationship between the two languages is a major theme of the contemporary literature of both Latin America and the various Latino communities within the United States, including Chicanos, or Mexican-Americans, probably the most politically vocal of these groups. We

Guatemalan Nobel Peace Prize Laureate Rigoberta Menchú, April, 2002.

include two poems by Chicano writers here. These selections give a sense of the literary range and thematic concerns of this important literary movement. As you read these selections, consider how the strategies these writers employ reflect the specific realities of life in the Americas.

Four young Mexicans atop the border fence in San Ysidro, California, 1998.

Antique map of the Americas, 1595.

GABRIEL GARCÍA MÁRQUEZ B. 1928

ULTIMATELY, LITERATURE IS NOTHING BUT
CARPENTRY. WITH BOTH YOU ARE WORKING
WITH REALITY, A MATERIAL JUST AS HARD
AS WOOD.   —GABRIEL GARCÍA MÁRQUEZ

Born in the small provincial town of Aracataca, Colombia, Gabriel García Márquez was two years old when his parents left him to be raised by his grandparents. After the death of his grandfather, a liberal veteran of the civil conflict known as the Thousand Days War, the eight-year-old García Márquez joined his parents in the port city of Baranquilla. After attending Jesuit boarding school in Baranquilla, García Márquez won a scholarship to study near the capital city of Bogotá. He then studied law at the National University in Bogotá, but eventually left his studies to write for a newspaper in Baranquilla. He worked at a number of jobs, including writing screenplays in Mexico City, and published fiction that went mostly unnoticed. In 1965, he began writing a novel in the completely matter-of-fact voice his grandmother had used while telling him the most fantastic stories. The resulting novel, *One Hundred Years of Solitude* (1967), introduced much of the world to Latin-American fiction and the style known as "magic realism." A master of close observation and character as well as a gifted storyteller, García Márquez was awarded the Nobel Prize for literature in 1982. We include here two of his best-known stories, both published in 1968, and both subtitled "A Tale for Children." As you read the stories, consider what exactly this subtitle might mean in this context.

FICTION

THE HANDSOMEST DROWNED MAN IN THE WORLD
A Tale for Children

Translated by Gregory Rabassa

THE FIRST CHILDREN WHO SAW THE DARK AND SLINKY bulge approaching through the sea let themselves think it was an empty ship. Then they saw it had no flags or masts and they thought it was a whale. But when it washed up on the beach, they removed the clumps of seaweed, the jellyfish tentacles, and the remains of fish and flotsam, and only then did they see that it was a drowned man.

They had been playing with him all afternoon, burying him in the sand and digging him up again, when someone chanced to see them and spread the alarm in the village. The men who carried him to the nearest house noticed that he weighed more than any dead man they had ever known, almost as much as a horse, and they said to each other that maybe he'd been floating too long and the water had got into his bones. When they laid him on the floor they said he'd been taller than all the other men because there was barely enough room for him in the house, but they thought that maybe the ability to keep on growing after death was part of the nature of certain drowned men. He had the smell of the sea about him and only his shape gave one to suppose that it was the corpse of a human being, because the skin was covered with a crust of mud and scales.

They did not even have to clean off his face to know that the dead man was a stranger. The village was made up of only twenty-odd wooden houses that had stone courtyards with no flowers and which were spread about on the end of a desertlike cape. There was so little land that mothers always went about with the fear that the wind would carry off their children and the few dead that the years had caused among them had to be thrown off the cliffs. But the sea was calm and bountiful and all the men fit into seven boats. So when they found the drowned man they simply had to look at one another to see that they were all there. That night they did not go out to work at sea. While the men went to find out if anyone was missing in neighboring villages, the women stayed behind to care for the drowned man. They took the mud off with grass swabs, they removed the underwater stones entangled in his hair, and they scraped the crust off with tools used for scaling fish. As they were doing that they noticed that the vegetation on him came from faraway oceans and deep water and that his clothes were in tatters, as if he had sailed through labyrinths of coral. They noticed too that he bore his death with pride, for he did not have the lonely look of other drowned men who came out of the sea or that haggard, needy look of men who drowned in rivers. But only when they finished cleaning him off did they become aware of the kind of man he was and it left them breathless. Not only was he the tallest, strongest, most virile, and best built man they had

ever seen, but even though they were looking at him there was no room for him in their imagination.

They could not find a bed in the village large enough to lay him on nor was there a table solid enough to use for his wake. The tallest men's holiday pants would not fit him, nor the fattest ones' Sunday shirts, nor the shoes of the one with the biggest feet. Fascinated by his huge size and his beauty, the women then decided to make him some pants from a large piece of sail and a shirt from some bridal brabant linen so that he could continue through his death with dignity. As they sewed, sitting in a circle and gazing at the corpse between stitches, it seemed to them that the wind had never been so steady nor the sea so restless as on that night and they supposed that the change had something to do with the dead man. They thought that if that magnificent man had lived in the village, his house would have had the widest doors, the highest ceiling, and the strongest floor, his bedstead would have been made from a midship frame held together by iron bolts, and his wife would have been the happiest woman. They thought that he would have had so much authority that he could have drawn fish out of the sea simply by calling their names and that he would have put so much work into his land that springs would have burst forth from among the rocks so that he would have been able to plant flowers on the cliffs. They secretly compared him to their own men, thinking that for all their lives theirs were incapable of doing what he could do in one night, and they ended up dismissing them deep in their hearts as the weakest, meanest, and most useless creatures on earth. They were wandering through the maze of fantasy when the oldest woman, who as the oldest had looked upon the drowned man with more compassion than passion, sighed:

"He has the face of someone called Esteban."

It was true. Most of them had only to take another look at him to see that he could not have any other name. The more stubborn among them, who were the youngest, still lived for a few hours with the illusion that when they put

5

his clothes on and he lay among the flowers in patent leather shoes his name might be Lautaro. But it was a vain illusion. There had not been enough canvas, the poorly cut and worse sewn pants were too tight, and the hidden strength of his heart popped the buttons on his shirt. After midnight the whistling of the wind died down and the sea fell into its Wednesday drowsiness. The silence put an end to any last doubts: he was Esteban. The women who had dressed him, who had combed his hair, had cut his nails and shaved him were unable to hold back a shudder of pity when they had to resign themselves to his being dragged along the ground. It was then that they understood how unhappy he must have been with that huge body since it bothered him even after death. They could see him in life, condemned to going through doors sideways, cracking his head on crossbeams, remaining on his feet during visits, not knowing what to do with his soft, pink, sea lion hands while the lady of the house looked for her most resistant chair and begged him, frightened to death, sit here, Esteban please, and he, leaning against the wall, smiling, don't bother, ma'am, I'm fine where I am, his heels raw and his back roasted from having done the same thing so many times whenever he paid a visit, don't bother, ma'am, I'm fine where I am, just to avoid the embarrassment of breaking up the chair, and never knowing perhaps that the ones who said don't go, Esteban, at least wait till the coffee's ready, were the ones who later on would whisper the big boob finally left, how nice, the handsome fool has gone. That was what the women were thinking beside the body a little before dawn. Later, when they covered his face with a handkerchief so that the light would not bother him, he looked so forever dead, so defenseless, so much like their men that the first furrows of tears opened in their hearts. It was one of the younger ones who began the weeping. The others, coming to, went from sighs to wails, and the more they sobbed the more they felt like weeping, because the drowned man was becoming all the more Esteban for them, and so they wept so much, for he was the most destitute, most peaceful, and

most obliging man on earth, poor Esteban. So when the men returned with the news that the drowned man was not from the neighboring villages either, the women felt an opening of jubilation in the midst of their tears.

"Praise the Lord," they sighed, "he's ours!"

The men thought the fuss was only womanish frivolity. Fatigued because of the difficult nighttime inquiries, all they wanted was to get rid of the bother of the newcomer once and for all before the sun grew strong on that arid, windless day. They improvised a litter with the remains of foremasts and gaffs, tying it together with rigging so that it would bear the weight of the body until they reached the cliffs. They wanted to tie the anchor from a cargo ship to him so that he would sink easily into the deepest waves, where fish are blind and divers die of nostalgia, and bad currents would not bring him back to shore, as had happened with other bodies. But the more they hurried, the more the women thought of ways to waste time. They walked about like startled hens, pecking with the sea charms on their breasts, some interfering on one side to put a scapular of the good wind on the drowned man, some on the other side to put a wrist compass on him, and after a great deal of *get away from there, woman, stay out of the way, look, you almost made me fall on top of the dead man,* the men began to feel mistrust in their livers and started grumbling about why so many main-altar decorations for a stranger, because no matter how many nails and holy-water jars he had on him, the sharks would chew him all the same, but the women kept piling on their junk relics, running back and forth, stumbling, while they released in sighs what they did not in tears, so that the men finally exploded with *since when has there ever been such a fuss over a drifting corpse, a drowned nobody, a piece of cold Wednesday meat.* One of the women, mortified by so much lack of care, then removed the handkerchief from the dead man's face and the men were left breathless too.

He was Esteban. It was not necessary to repeat it for them to recognize him. If they had been told Sir Walter Raleigh,° even they might have been impressed with his gringo accent, the macaw on his shoulder, his cannibal-killing blunderbuss, but there could be only one Esteban in the world and there he was, stretched out like a sperm whale, shoeless, wearing the pants of an undersized child, and with those stony nails that had to be cut with a knife. They only had to take the handkerchief off his face to see that he was ashamed, that it was not his fault that he was so big or so heavy or so handsome, and if he had known that this was going to happen, he would have looked for a more discreet place to drown in, seriously, I even would have tied the anchor off a galleon around my neck and staggered off a cliff like someone who doesn't like things in order not to be upsetting people now with this Wednesday dead body, as you people say, in order not to be bothering anyone with this filthy piece of cold meat that doesn't have anything to do with me. There was so much truth in his manner that even the most mistrustful men, the ones who felt the bitterness of endless nights at sea fearing that their women would tire of dreaming about them and begin to dream of drowned men, even they and others who were harder still shuddered in the marrow of their bones at Esteban's sincerity.

10   That was how they came to hold the most splendid funeral they could conceive of for an abandoned drowned man. Some women who had gone to get flowers in the neighboring villages returned with other women who could not believe what they had been told, and those women went back for more flowers when they saw the dead man, and they brought more and more until there were so many flowers and so many people that it was hard to walk about. At the final moment it pained them to return him to the waters as an orphan and they chose a father and mother from among the best people, and aunts and uncles and cousins, so that through him all the inhabitants of the village became kinsmen. Some sailors who heard weeping from a distance went off course and people heard of one who had himself tied to the mainmast, remembering ancient fables about sirens. While they fought for the privilege of carrying him on their shoulders along the steep escarpment by the cliffs, men and women became aware for the first time of the desolation of their streets, the dryness of their courtyards, the narrowness of their dreams as they faced the splendor and beauty of their drowned man. They let him go without an anchor so that he could come back if he wished and whenever he wished, and they all held their breath for the fraction of centuries the body took to fall into the abyss. They did not need to look at one another to realize that they were no longer all present, that they would never be. But they also knew that everything would be different from then on, that their houses would have wider doors, higher ceilings, and stronger floors so that Esteban's memory could go everywhere without bumping into beams and so that no one in the future would dare whisper the big boob finally died, too bad, the handsome fool has finally died, because they were going to paint their house fronts gay colors to make Esteban's memory eternal and they were going to break their backs digging for springs among the stones and planting flowers on the cliffs so that in future years at dawn the passengers on great liners would awaken, suffocated by the smell of gardens on the high seas, and the captain would have to come down from the bridge in his dress uniform, with his astrolabe, his pole star, and his row of war medals and, pointing to the promontory of roses on the horizon, he would say in fourteen languages, look there, where the wind is so peaceful now that it's gone to sleep beneath the beds, over there, where the sun's so bright that the sunflowers don't know which way to turn, yes, that's Esteban's village.

Sir Walter Raleigh: c. 1552–1618 English courtier, writer, and poet as well as a soldier and explorer who led two expeditions to colonize present-day Virginia and North Carolina, and two expeditions to what is now Venezuela, in search of El Dorado, the legendary city of gold.

[1968]

1. In what ways does this story resemble a fairy tale? In what ways does it not?

2. What is the immediate effect on the villagers of their discovery of the drowned man?

3. How does the villagers' relationship with the drowned man change after they name him?

4. Find the beginning of the final sentence of the story and read it again to the end. What has changed for the villagers? Is it a positive change or a negative change?

THE VERY OLD MAN WITH ENORMOUS WINGS
A Tale for Children

Gabriel García Márquez

Translated by Gregory Rabassa

ON THE THIRD DAY OF RAIN THEY HAD KILLED SO MANY crabs inside the house that Pelayo had to cross his drenched courtyard and throw them into the sea, because the newborn child had a temperature all night and they thought it was due to the stench. The world had been sad since Tuesday. Sea and sky were a single ash-gray thing and the sands of the beach, which on March nights glimmered like powdered light, had become a stew of mud and rotten shellfish. The light was so weak at noon that when Pelayo was coming back to the house after throwing away the crabs, it was hard for him to see what it was that was moving and groaning in the rear of the courtyard. He had to go very close to see that it was an old man, a very old man, lying face down in the mud, who, in spite of his tremendous efforts, couldn't get up, impeded by his enormous wings.

Frightened by that nightmare, Pelayo ran to get Elisenda, his wife, who was putting compresses on the sick child, and he took her to the rear of the courtyard. They both looked at the fallen body with mute stupor. He was dressed like a ragpicker. There were only a few faded hairs left on his bald skull and very few teeth in his mouth, and his pitiful condition of a drenched great-grandfather had taken away any sense of grandeur he might have had. His huge buzzard wings, dirty and half-plucked, were forever entangled in the mud. They looked at him so long and so closely that Pelayo and Elisenda very soon overcame their surprise and in the end found him familiar. Then they dared speak to him, and he answered in an incomprehensible dialect with a strong sailor's voice. That was how they skipped over the inconvenience of the wings and quite intelligently concluded that he was a lonely castaway from some foreign ship wrecked by the storm. And yet, they called in a neighbor woman who knew everything about life and death to see him, and all she needed was one look to show them their mistake.

"He's an angel," she told them. "He must have been coming for the child, but the poor fellow is so old that the rain knocked him down."

On the following day everyone knew that a flesh-and-blood angel was held captive in Pelayo's house. Against the judgment of the wise neighbor woman, for whom angels in those times were the fugitive survivors of a celestial conspiracy, they did not have the heart to club him to death. Pelayo watched over him all afternoon from the kitchen, armed with his bailiff's club, and before going to bed he dragged him out of the mud and locked him up with the hens in the wire chicken coop. In the middle of the night, when the rain stopped, Pelayo and Elisenda were still killing crabs. A short time afterward the child woke up without a fever and with a desire to eat. Then they felt magnanimous and decided to put the angel on a raft with fresh water and provisions for three days and leave him to his fate on the high seas. But when they went out into the courtyard with the first light of dawn, they found the whole neighborhood in front of the chicken coop having fun with the angel, without the slightest reverence, tossing him things to eat through the openings in the wire as if he weren't a supernatural creature but a circus animal.

5   Father Gonzaga arrived before seven o'clock, alarmed at the strange news. By that time onlookers less frivolous than those at dawn had already arrived and they were making all kinds of conjectures concerning the captive's future. The simplest among them thought that he should be named mayor of the world. Others of sterner mind felt that he should be promoted to the rank of five-star general in order to win all wars. Some visionaries hoped that he could be put to stud in order to implant on earth a race of winged wise men who could take charge of the universe. But Father Gonzaga, before becoming a priest, had been a robust woodcutter. Standing by the wire, he reviewed his catechism in an instant and asked them to open the door so that he could take a close look at that pitiful man who looked more like a huge decrepit hen among the fascinated chickens. He was lying in a corner drying his open wings in the sunlight among the fruit peels and breakfast leftovers that the early risers had thrown him. Alien to the impertinences of the world, he only lifted his antiquarian eyes and murmured something in his dialect when Father Gonzaga went into the chicken coop and said good morning to him in Latin. The parish priest had his first suspicion of an impostor when he saw that he did not understand the language of God or know how to greet His ministers. Then he noticed that seen close up he was much too human: he had an unbearable smell of the outdoors, the back side of his wings were strewn with parasites and his main feathers had been mistreated by terrestrial winds, and nothing about him measured up to the proud dignity of angels. Then he came out of the chicken coop and in a brief sermon warned the curious against the risks of being ingenuous. He reminded them that the devil had the bad habit of making use of carnival tricks in order to confuse the unwary. He argued that if wings were not the essential element in determining the difference between a hawk and an airplane, they were even less so in the recognition of angels. Nevertheless, he promised to write a letter to his bishop so that the latter would write to his primate so that the latter would write to the Supreme Pontiff in order to get the final verdict from the highest courts.

His prudence fell on sterile hearts. The news of a captive angel spread with such rapidity that after a few hours the courtyard had the bustle of a marketplace and they had to call in troops with fixed bayonets to disperse the mob that was about to knock the house down. Elisenda, her spine all twisted from sweeping up so much marketplace trash, then got the idea of fencing in the yard and charging five cents admission to see the angel.

The curious came from far away. A traveling carnival arrived with a flying acrobat who buzzed over the crowd several times, but no one paid any attention to him because his wings were not those of an angel but, rather, those of a sidereal bat. The most unfortunate invalids on earth came in search of health: a poor woman who since childhood had been counting her heartbeats and had run out of numbers; a Portuguese man who couldn't sleep because the noise of the stars disturbed him; a sleepwalker who got up at night to undo the things he had done while awake; and many others with less serious ailments. In the midst of that shipwreck disorder that made the earth tremble, Pelayo and Elisenda were happy with fatigue, for in less than a week they had crammed their rooms with money and the line of pilgrims waiting their turn to enter still reached beyond the horizon.

The angel was the only one who took no part in his own act. He spent his time trying to get comfortable in his borrowed nest, befuddled by the hellish heat of the oil lamps and sacramental candles that had been placed along the wire. At first they tried to make him eat some mothballs, which, according to the wisdom of the wise neighbor woman, were the food prescribed for angels. But he turned them down, just as he turned down the papal lunches that the penitents brought him, and they never found out whether it was because he was an angel or because he was an old man that in the end ate nothing but eggplant mush. His only supernatural virtue seemed to be patience. Especially during the first days, when the hens pecked at him, searching for the stellar parasites that proliferated in his wings, and the cripples pulled out feathers to touch their defective parts with, and even the most merciful threw stones at him, trying to get him to rise so they could see him standing. The only time they succeeded in arousing him was when they burned his side with an iron for branding steers, for he had been motionless for so many hours that they thought he was dead. He awoke with a start, ranting in his hermetic language and with tears in his eyes, and he flapped his wings a couple of times, which brought on a whirlwind of chicken dung and lunar dust and a gale of panic that did not seem to be of this world. Although many thought that his reaction had been one not of rage but of pain, from then on they were careful not to annoy him, because the majority understood that his passivity was not that of a hero taking his ease but that of a cataclysm in repose.

Father Gonzaga held back the crowd's frivolity with formulas of maidservant inspiration while awaiting the arrival of a final judgment on the nature of the captive. But the mail from Rome showed no sense of urgency. They spent their time finding out if the prisoner had a navel, if his dialect had any connection with Aramaic, how many times he could fit on the head of a pin, or whether he wasn't just a Norwegian with wings. Those meager letters might have come and gone until the end of time if a providential event had not put an end to the priest's tribulations.

10 It so happened that during those days, among so many other carnival attractions, there arrived in town the traveling show of the woman who had been changed into a spider for having disobeyed her parents. The admission to see her was not only less than the admission to see the angel, but people were permitted to ask her all manner of questions about her absurd state and to examine her up and down so that no one would ever doubt the truth of her horror. She was a frightful tarantula the size of a ram and with the head of a sad maiden. What was most heart-rending, however, was not her outlandish shape but the sincere affliction with which she recounted the details of her misfortune. While still practically a child she had sneaked out of her parents' house to go to a dance, and while she was coming back through the woods after having danced all night without permission, a fearful thunderclap rent the sky in two and through the crack came the lightning bolt of brimstone that changed her into a spider. Her only nourishment came from the meatballs that charitable souls chose to toss into her mouth. A spectacle like that, full of so much human truth and with such a fearful lesson, was bound to defeat without even trying that of a haughty angel who scarcely deigned to look at mortals. Besides, the few miracles attributed to the angel showed a certain mental disorder, like the blind man who didn't recover his sight but grew three new teeth, or the paralytic who didn't get to walk but almost won the lottery, and the leper whose sores sprouted sunflowers. Those consolation miracles, which were more like mocking fun, had already ruined the angel's reputation when the woman who had been changed into a spider finally crushed him completely. That was how Father Gonzaga was cured forever of his insomnia and Pelayo's courtyard went back to being as empty as during the time it had rained for three days and crabs walked through the bedrooms.

The owners of the house had no reason to lament. With the money they saved they built a two-story mansion with balconies and gardens and high netting so that crabs wouldn't get in during the winter, and with iron bars on the windows so that angels couldn't get in. Pelayo also set up a rabbit warren close to town and gave up his job as bailiff for good, and Elisenda bought some satin pumps with high heels and many dresses of iridescent silk, the kind worn on Sunday by the most desirable women in those times. The chicken coop was the only thing that didn't receive any attention. If they washed it down with creolin and burned tears of myrrh inside it every so often, it was not in homage to the angel but to drive away the dungheap stench that still hung everywhere like a ghost and was turning the new house into an old one. At first, when the child learned to walk, they were careful that he not get too close to the chicken coop. But then they began to lose their fears and got used to the smell,

and before the child got his second teeth he'd gone inside the chicken coop to play, where the wires were falling apart. The angel was no less stand-offish with him than with other mortals, but he tolerated the most ingenious infamies with the patience of a dog who had no illusions. They both came down with chicken pox at the same time. The doctor who took care of the child couldn't resist the temptation to listen to the angel's heart, and he found so much whistling in the heart and so many sounds in his kidneys that it seemed impossible for him to be alive. What surprised him most, however, was the logic of his wings. They seemed so natural on that completely human organism that he couldn't understand why other men didn't have them too.

When the child began school it had been some time since the sun and rain had caused the collapse of the chicken coop. The angel went dragging himself about here and there like a stray dying man. They would drive him out of the bedroom with a broom and a moment later find him in the kitchen. He seemed to be in so many places at the same time that they grew to think that he'd been duplicated, that he was reproducing himself all through the house, and the exasperated and unhinged Elisenda shouted that it was awful living in that hell full of angels. He could scarcely eat and his antiquarian eyes had also become so foggy that he went about bumping into posts. All he had left were the bare cannulae of his last feathers. Pelayo threw a blanket over him and extended him the charity of letting him sleep in the shed, and only then did they notice that he had a temperature at night, and was delirious with the tongue twisters of an old Norwegian. That was one of the few times they became alarmed, for they thought he was going to die and not even the wise neighbor woman had been able to tell them what to do with dead angles.

And yet he not only survived his worst winter, but seemed improved with the first sunny days. He remained motionless for several days in the farthest corner of the courtyard, where no one would see him, and at the beginning of December some large, stiff feathers began to grow on his wings, the feathers of a scarecrow, which looked more like another misfortune of decrepitude. But he must have known the reason for those changes, for he was quite careful that no one should notice them, that no one should hear the sea chanteys that he sometimes sang under the stars. One morning Elisenda was cutting some bunches of onions for lunch when a wind that seemed to come from the high seas blew into the kitchen. Then she went to the window and caught the angel in his first attempts at flight. They were so clumsy that his fingernails opened a furrow in the vegetable patch and he was on the point of knocking the shed down with the ungainly flapping that slipped on the light and couldn't get a grip on the air. But he did manage to gain altitude. Elisenda let out a sigh of relief, for herself and for him, when she saw him pass over the last houses, holding himself up in some way with the risky flapping of a senile vulture. She kept watching him even when she was through cutting the onions and she kept on watching until it was no longer possible for her to see him, because then he was no longer an annoyance in her life but an imaginary dot on the horizon of the sea.

[1968]

QUESTIONS FOR REFLECTION AND DISCUSSION

1. In what ways does this story resemble a fairy tale? In what ways does it not? Is it more or less like a fairy tale than "The Handsomest Drowned Man in the World"?

2. What is it about the old man that makes the villagers believe he is an angel? What is it that makes them doubt it?

3. Why do the villagers treat the old man as they do?

4. Compare the ending of this story with the ending of "The Handsomest Drowned Man in the World." How are they similar? How are they different?

POETRY

PABLO NERUDA 1904–1973

Born Ricardo Eliezer Neftali Reyes y Basoalto in the southern Chilean town of Parral to a railroad worker and his wife, who died when the boy was still young, Neruda spent his childhood in the small central-southern town of Temuco, surrounded by forests. His poetic gift was nurtured by Gabriel Mistral, a school head and poet who would herself be awarded the Nobel Prize for Literature in 1945. Neruda began publishing at the age of sixteen under the name Pablo Neruda; the following year, he went to the Chilean capital Santiago to study French literature. By the mid-1920s, he had published five volumes of poetry and established himself as a major figure in Chilean letters. Neruda's radical politics led to his forced exile, although he would later return. He published his major poetry collection, *Canto General*, or *General Song* in 1950, and was awarded the Nobel Prize for Literature in 1971. In "The Word," as in many of his poems, Neruda demonstrates his ability to use earthy and sensual imagery to speak both of language and of his love for the people of the Americas.

The Word
Translated by Stephen Mitchell

The word was born
in the blood,
it grew in the dark body, pulsing,
and took flight with the lips and mouth.

Farther away and nearer,   5
still, still it came
from dead fathers and from wandering races,
from territories that had become stone,
that had tired of their poor tribes,
because when grief set out on the road   10
the people went and arrived
and united new land and water
to sow their word once again.
And that's why the inheritance is this:
this is the air that connects us   15
with the buried man and with the dawn
of new beings that haven't yet arisen.

Still the atmosphere trembles
with the first word
produced   20
with panic and groaning.
It emerged

from the darkness
and even now there is no thunder
that thunders with the iron sound   25
of that word,
the first
word uttered:
perhaps it was just a whisper, a raindrop,
but its cascade still falls and falls.   30

Later on, meaning fills the word.
It stayed pregnant and was filled with lives,
everything was births and sounds:
affirmation, clarity, strength,
negation, destruction, death: 35
the name took on all the powers
and combined existence with essence
in its electric beauty.

Human word, syllable, flank
of long light and hard silver,   40
hereditary goblet that receives
the communications of the blood:
it is here that silence was formed by
the whole of the human word

and not to speak is to die among beings: 45
language extends out to the hair,
the mouth speaks without moving the lips:
suddenly the eyes are words.

I take the word and move
through it, as if it were   50
only a human form,
its lines delight me and I sail
in each resonance of language:
I utter and I am
and across the boundary of words,   55
without speaking, I approach silence.

I drink to the word, raising
a word or crystalline cup,

in it I drink
the wine of language   60
or unfathomable water,

maternal source of all words,
and cup and water and wine
give rise to my song
because the name is origin   65
and green life: it is blood,
the blood that expresses its substance,
and thus its unrolling is prepared:
words give crystal to the crystal,
blood to the blood,   70
and give life to life.

                                    [1970]

QUESTIONS FOR REFLECTION AND DISCUSSION

1. The speaker refers first to "the word," then to "the name," and later to "words." What subjects does he associate with each of these terms? What is the relation between the three terms?

2. Why do you think the poet chose this metaphorical way to address his subject? How would the meaning of the poem change if he had explicitly presented an argument about words or an argument about the subjects he associates with those words?

3. Do you think Neruda has a specific word in mind as "the word" of his title? Explain why or why not citing evidence from the poem.

JIMMY SANTIAGO BACA B. 1952

Published in 1979 in Baca's early collection of poetry, *Immigrants in Our Own Land*, "So Mexicans Are Taking Jobs from Americans" saw Baca finding a poetic voice to articulate a passionate engagement with his social identity and the place, or lack of place, for that identity within the American society of the time. (For a biography of Baca, see p. 387.)

So Mexicans Are Taking Jobs from Americans

O Yes? Do they come on horses
with rifles, and say,

   Ese gringo, gimmee your job?

And do you, gringo, take off your ring,
drop your wallet into a blanket   5
spread over the ground, and walk away?

I hear Mexicans are taking your jobs away.
Do they sneak into town at night,
and as you're walking home with a whore,
do they mug you, a knife at your throat,   10
saying, I want your job?

Even on TV, an asthmatic leader
crawls turtle heavy, leaning on an assistant,

and from a nest of wrinkles on his face,
a tongue paddles through flashing waves   15
of lightbulbs, of cameramen, rasping
"They're taking our jobs away."

Well, I've gone about trying to find them,
asking just where the hell are these fighters.
The rifles I hear sound in the night   20
are white farmers shooting blacks and browns
whose ribs I see jutting out
and starving children,
I see the poor marching for a little work,
I see small white farmers selling out   25
to clean-suited farmers living in New York,
who've never been on a farm,
don't know the look of a hoof or the smell
of a woman's body bending all day long in fields.

I see this, and I hear only a few people   30
got all the money in this world, the rest

count their pennies to buy bread and butter.

Below that cool green sea of money,
millions and millions of people fight to live,
search for pearls in the darkest depths   35
of their dreams, hold their breath for years
trying to cross poverty to just having something.

The children are dead already. We are killing them,
that is what America should be saying;
on TV, in the streets, in offices, should be saying,
"We aren't giving the children a chance to live."

Mexicans are taking our jobs, they say instead.
What they really say is, let them die,
and the children too.

                                                        [1977]

QUESTIONS FOR REFLECTION AND DISCUSSION

1. Judging from the title of the poem and the way the poem responds to that title, who is the intended audience?

2. How does the poem's speaker respond to the assertion of the poem's title? What manner of rebuttal does he produce?

3. What makes this text a poem rather than an argument essay? Why do you think Baca chose to write a poem rather than an essay?

TINO VILLANUEVA B. 1941

Born to a family of migrant field workers in the south-central Texas town of San Marcos, Tino Villanueva received a poor public school education and failed his college-entrance examination. Drafted by the U.S. Army in 1963, he spent two years in the Panama Canal Zone, where he encountered Spanish-language poetry for the first time. After the Army, he began studying and writing poetry at Southwest Texas State University. He received his BA in 1968 and was awarded a fellowship to study at the State University of New York at Buffalo, where he encountered the Chicano poetry movement; he soon became a significant figure within it. In 1972, he published his first collection of poems, *Hay Otra Voz,* containing Spanish, English, and bilingual poems. He edited the anthology *Chicanos* in 1980. He received a PhD in Spanish Literature from Boston University in 1981, and began teaching at Wellesley College. He now teaches at Boston University, and has published five additional books of poetry. "Variation on a Theme by William Carlos Williams" was published in 1984 in *Shaking off the Dark.*

Variation on a Theme by William Carlos Williams

I have eaten
the *tamales*
that were on
the stove heating

and which   5
you were probably
having for dinner

Perdóname
they were *riquísimos*
so juicy   10
and so steaming hot

[1984]

QUESTIONS FOR REFLECTION AND DISCUSSION

1. Villaneuva based his poem on William Carlos Williams,
   "This Is Just To Say," written in 1934:

   I have eaten
   the plums
   that were in
   the icebox

   and which   5
   you were probably
   saving
   for breakfast.

   Forgive me
   they were delicious   10

   so sweet
   and so cold.

   How has Villanueva altered the original? What is the effect
   of his changes?

2. One of the motivations for Villanueva's version of the poem is
   the fact, little remarked until recently, that Williams's mother
   was Puerto Rican. In what ways does this knowledge change
   your understanding of Williams's poem? In what ways does it
   change your understanding of Villanueva's poem?

3. Compare Villanueva's use of Spanish words within an
   English-language poem with Baca's use in "So Mexicans Are
   Taking Jobs from Americans."

WORKING FURTHER WITH THE LITERATURE OF THE AMERICAS

1. Write an essay on two or three selections in this casebook
   concerning ways in which the "reality" described in them
   differs from the "reality" of a middle-class resident of the
   United States.

2. Write an essay on the different languages used in two or
   three of the readings in this casebook and their relationship
   to the themes of the readings.

3. Write a research paper on a point of intersection between
   the two Americas.

4. Read further in the writings of Gabriel García Márquez and
   write a paper on their principal themes.

5. Basing yourself on the selections in this section, write an
   argument essay on what it means (if anything) to be an
   American in the sense it is used in this casebook.

THE LITERATURE OF THE AMERICAS FURTHER READINGS IN *LITERATURE: A WORLD OF WRITING*

Julia Alvarez, "Snow" • Jimmy Santiago Baca, "Spliced Wire" •
Julio Cortázar, "Axolotl" and "The Tiger Lodgers" • Roberto
Fernández, "Wrong Channel" • Carolyn Forché, "The Colonel"
• Gary Soto, "Behind Grandma's House"

THE WORLD OF LITERARY CRITICISM

If it is indeed the case that people approach literature with the desire to learn something about the world, and if it is indeed the case that the literary medium is not transparent, then a study of its non-transparency is crucial in order to deal with the desire one has to know something about the world by reading literature.

—IMRE SALUSINSZKY

If you think it so easy to be a critic, so difficult to be a poet or a painter, may I suggest you try both? You may discover why there are so few critics, and so many poets.

—PAULINE KAEL

All critical writing has at least one goal in common: to discover and to share knowledge. As you know from our discussion of critical thinking in Chapter 2, reading a text critically means being able to make an argument about it without necessarily passing judgment. There are many different ways of approaching a text critically, however; what is important to keep in mind is that even the most accomplished scholars (depending on their area of expertise) approach many texts with a certain level of naiveté. Consider, for example, the film critic who reads Homer for the first time in order to better inform her review of the blockbuster movie *Troy*; or the scholar of Elizabethan poetry who wants to know what hip-hop music is all about. Naive or not, readers who approach a new text with an open mind and a free-ranging curiosity will find themselves naturally exploring many paths of critical thinking.

Approaching Literary Criticism for the First Time

The scale of *literary criticism* can be daunting, as is evidenced by the thousands of articles published every year on the works of William Shakespeare alone and the online version of the Modern Language Association bibliography (p. 87), which comprises well over one million entries of scholarly books and articles. What never ceases to astound nonspecialists is that critics can still find anything to say. But they can, and there are several explanations for this fact. First, new works of literature are published all the time, all over the world. Second, scholars continue to unearth once-forgotten or underappreciated texts from the past. Third, the scope of criticism has widely expanded from a core canon of classics to include everything from film and music to popular fiction and graphic novels. And, finally, scholars are constantly developing new critical viewpoints that help them to discover new meaning in classic texts and better understand

the different meanings of contemporary and newly discovered texts. As Imre Salusinszky suggests, there is always more we can learn about the world; consequently, there is always a need for new ways to get at what literature has to tell us about the world.

If you are new to literary criticism and are approaching it for the first time, think of it as a tool for understanding and interpreting literature, much in the same way that literary devices and literary style are tools for creating literature. Literary criticism is conventionally divided into different *schools*, or approaches; this appendix will introduce you briefly to most of the major schools of criticism. Each school holds a set of beliefs about literature and offers unique analytical and interpretive strategies: these are their tools. No single school of criticism has yet provided a comprehensive account of how literature works, and none has yet been able to interpret a particular text comprehensively enough to preclude any further criticism—hence the various approaches. Always keep in mind that no single article, book, or critical school will provide you with all the answers you need about a text. Rather, expect each article you read to illuminate one aspect of a text while leaving you still curious about many others. Before applying any of the tools of literary criticism to a text, you should be certain that you have reached a solid understanding of its form and themes. In other words, you should always think critically on your own about a text before you start reading what others have said about it. (Note: in-text citations in the examples that follow refer to the Works-Cited list on p. APP A-9.)

Schools of Literary Criticism

This appendix divides the critical schools of literature into two broad categories. The first category, **expository approaches**, focuses on the exposition, or explanation, of the explicit workings of a text, such as genre, plot, character, setting, literary devices, and historical context. For instance, an expository approach to Shakespeare's *Hamlet* will likely begin with the assumption that Hamlet is innocent but hesitant to act, Claudius and Gertrude evil, and Ophelia the helpless victim of the action. These approaches will focus on the conventions and techniques by which the text presents these characters to us. The second category, **interpretive and ideological approaches**, devotes its energy to implicit or hidden aspects of a text—aspects that we are unlikely otherwise to have recognized. A feminist or psychoanalytic approach might agree that *Hamlet* depicts Claudius negatively and Ophelia as a helpless victim, but would be likely to reevaluate the character of Gertrude. These interpretive approaches, however, would set out to uncover the ideological attitude toward female sexuality underlying that contrast.

Expository Approaches to Literature   Most of the instructional material in this book is expository in nature—that is, it instructs you on how to think critically about literature, and it argues that in order to interpret a work of literature you first need to be able to explain what it is doing with language. The analytical tools put forth by the various schools of expository criticism provide the groundwork for understanding the workings of a text introduced to you in Parts 1 and 2 of *Literature: A World of Writing*. None of these approaches will exhaust the meaning of a text, but they will provide you with the necessary tools to make a persuasive argument about it.

Rhetorical Criticism   Dating back to classical times, **rhetorical criticism** focuses on the use of literary devices, or rhetorical figures (Chapter 6), and, more generally, on the role of the art of persuasion in making literary arguments. Poets and public speakers have long used rhetorical handbooks as guides for creating their texts, and critics have long used those same guides for analysis. More recent rhetorical critics such as Kenneth Burke have used the term "rhetoric" more broadly to describe any system of **symbols** (linguistic, visual, aural) and the forms of human communication it fosters. Knowledge of traditional rhetorical figures is extremely useful for analyzing most literary texts, and essential for many. More generally, rhetorical criticism draws our attention to the communicative intent of any text—that is, the ways in which it addresses an argument to an audience. In a more specialized sense, rhetorical criticism is especially suited for thinking critically about texts specifically designed to persuade. Such texts include not only speeches, sermons, declarations, manifestos, and pamphlets but also sacred texts.

Like the formalist approach described below, a rhetorical analysis of *Hamlet* would focus on its use of literary devices. Where a formalist approach would focus on the interrelationship between these different devices, a rhetorical analysis would analyze their effect on the audience. Kenneth Burke argued that Shakespeare's command of rhetoric—the way, for example, that Hamlet, Polonius, and Ophelia speak very differently from one another—persuades audiences to participate in making his characters matter to us as if they were real.

Formalist Criticism   In its broadest sense, **formalist criticism** simply means an attention to the ways in which the form of a work generates its meaning. For formalist critics, the fundamental act of criticism is the *close reading* of a text line by line, and the analysis of the formal relationship between these lines. Some formalist critics, such as those adhering to the influential mid-twentieth-century school of "New Criticism," argued that literature exists independently of any relation to the author, the audience, or the historical context. Today, formalist criticism is applied more as an analytical tool, a tool especially well suited to the condensed language of poetry. A New Critic, for example, would study Hamlet's speech "To be or not to be" in Act 3, Scene 1 (p. 312) in terms of its extraordinary imagery and would be likely to describe the power of this imagery to produce a complex mediation on morality. A contemporary formalist critic would apply the imagery of "the sleep of death" to the play as a whole and the power it wields over nearly every character.

Biographical Criticism   **Biographical criticism** refers both to the practice of using an author's life to provide information about his or her works and using these works to provide information about an author's life. Sources for biographical criticism include biographies and all of the documents used in writing biographies: diaries, memoirs, journals, and letters. Biographical criticism can be extremely helpful in understanding the atmosphere of a text, specific references it makes, or the sources of characters and events. It is useful to know that Dylan Thomas dedicated his poem "Do Not Go Gentle into That Good Night" to his father and that the characters of "The Things They Carried" are based on soldiers Tim O'Brien fought with in the Vietnam War. Such knowledge may help us to eliminate certain arguments we might otherwise have made and to evaluate the tone of the use a text makes of ambiguous figures such as irony (p. 216). Knowledge of Susan Glaspell's feminism and background as a journalist provides strong evidence of Mrs. Peters and Mrs. Hales' sympathy toward Mrs. Wright in her play, *Trifles,* thus confirming our suspicion of the irony of their statements toward the men investigating the case.

There is no doubt that biographical knowledge can strongly affect the emotional impact of our reading. We react differently to Sylvia Plath's poetry knowing that she suffered from mental illness and eventually committed suicide; we react differently to John Keats's poetry knowing that he would die young from tuberculosis, and to Wilfrid Owen's knowing that he would soon be killed in combat. Nevertheless, it is important not to let that emotional identification overwhelm our other impressions of a text when we are approaching it in an academic context. The very fact that writers chose to transform their experience into the formal constraints of a literary text should inform us that they had more in mind than channeling their own emotions. Certainly, it is fascinating that the protagonist of *Hamlet* is profoundly shaken by the need to revenge his father's ghost. It would be easy to assume (and it is quite possibly true) that the playwright himself suffered from many of the same emotions as his tragic protagonist. But one of the reasons that this interpretation of the play does not dominate critical writing on *Hamlet* is that biographical criticism is most effective when it works like an allusion. The resemblance between text and life establishes a common ground, while the difference between them adds an important level of meaning that most writers skillfully manipulate. Think of biography as another tool for critical thinking; rather than simply noting that it is there, ask what it is doing there and how it is helping to create meaning in the text as a whole.

Historical Criticism   **Historical criticism** can take several forms. The first is *textual*. Many works of literature, especially ancient ones such as the poems of Catullus (p. 234), exist only in copies made many centuries after an

original manuscript, now lost. Textual criticism aims to reconstruct an authoritative version of a text such as the Bible or the epics of Homer. In the case of more recent works, a certain text may exist in several different manuscript versions, or in several significantly different printed versions. There is strong disagreement, for example, about the textual status of Shakespeare's plays: how closely the printed versions reproduce the text of actual performances, and which printed version is more reliable. Even in the case of modern writers such as James Joyce, who constantly revised his novels, there is no consensus as to whether to prefer the original manuscript of *Ulysses*, the corrections Joyce made on the page proofs of the first edition, the first edition, or the later edition where Joyce corrected many mistakes made in the earlier one. Studying the different versions of a particular text can be a fascinating window into the process of artistic creation; knowledge of the choices an author eventually rejected can often provide insight into the meaning of the choices he or she finally did make.

Source or *influence studies* refers to the study of the sources used by a particular work of literature and the literary influences incorporated by the author into the work. Many of the plots of Shakespeare's plays were wholly or partially lifted from ancient, medieval, and contemporary sources. Comparing a text with its source or sources can clarify the text's argument and the author's choices; when a text itself alludes to that source, as in the case of Tino Villanueva's poem "Variation on a Theme by William Carlos Williams," such a comparison can be critical to understanding the text's meaning. Influence, too, provides important context: some familiarity with the Japanese haiku by Bashō (p. 652) and others that influenced Ezra Pound's "In a Station of the Metro" (p. 630) and Richard Wright's haiku (p. 653) adds enormously to the effect of the poems.

Historical criticism also refers to the study of a work within its historical context. This context can be something as specific as knowledge about the trench experience when reading Wilfrid Owen's "Dulce et decorum est" (p. 238) or attitudes toward slavery at the time Elizabeth Barrett Browning wrote "On Hiram Powers' *Greek Slave*." (p. 225). Historical context is an important tool for familiarizing ourselves with the world in which a text was created and the specific events in which the author would have participated, such as the Great Exhibition of 1851 attended by Browning. It cannot tell us how to interpret the transformation wrought by the literary text: whether or not historical context in a literary work is in tune with the majority opinion of the time and whether the author was faithful to the facts, misremembered them, or intentionally distorted them. When analyzing literature in the context of historical events or attitudes (or vice versa), always make a critical comparison rather than using one as a template for the other.

Reception history studies the changing ways in which a literary work has been read and interpreted. The reputations of certain authors rise and fall. Charles Dickens was regarded as a skilled but second-rate popular novelist until the mid-twentieth century, when he came to be regarded as the most important novelist in Victorian England; meanwhile, his contemporary Alfred Lord Tennyson, poet laureate and once considered one of the greatest of English poets, is now scarcely read outside of the classroom. The meaning of a text changes, too, as historical circumstances alter the way we view it. George Orwell's darkly satirical novel *1984* long seemed prophetic of the world to come; now that its titular year has receded into history, some of its forecasts have been accepted as standard practice (political "doublespeak" such as the "Department of Defense" or "collateral damage") while others have simply been forgotten. Reception history can trace reviews and critical writings concerning a specific text, as Rob Lanney does in his paper on *Hamlet*. It can study **production history**, the changing ways a particular play has been staged. It can study the **print history** of a particular book and the changing forms it took. For reception history, the changing attitude toward a particular work is an important tool for interpreting the meaning of that work.

Interdisciplinary Criticism   The term **interdisciplinarity** refers to the relationship among different academic disciplines. Although strictly applicable to the relationship between the humanities and the sciences, interdisciplinarity is generally used to describe any interaction between fields of inquiry, even such closely related fields as literature and film or art. Interdisciplinary criticism has several facets. The most traditional form is an aspect of historical criticism—the study of the influence of a nonliterary discipline on a literary text, such as jazz on James Baldwin's story "Sonny's Blues." When analyzing an interdisciplinary influence, the first step is to determine the depth of the influence. Is the writer simply importing an object or idea into a literary work, the way Beckett uses the reel-to-reel tape player in *Krapp's Last Tape*? Or is the writer speaking expertly enough about another discipline to be making a two-way comparison, as Tim O'Brien does about the science and tools of warfare in "The Things They Carried"?

The other primary form of interdisciplinary criticism concerns the practice of *adaptation*. What happens to a text created in one discipline when it is adapted to another discipline? The cinematic adaptation of literary texts is the most common form, but there are also examples of adaptations of scientific and medical literature, as for example the film version of Oliver Sacks's accounts of various neurological disorders, *The Man Who Mistook His Wife for a Hat*. *Hamlet* played a fundamental role in Sigmund Freud's and Ernest Jones's theories of psychoanalysis. Plays adapt fiction; operas are composed from historical events; dances are based on songs and poems. Moreover, as is evident from the section on ecphrasis in Chapter 6, many works of literature are based on visual texts. Approach an adaptation as you would any other comparison, but remember that the common ground is provided by the shared source, while the meaning-generating tension arises primarily from the different conventions of the two disciplines.

Interpretive and Ideological Approaches

The various schools of **interpretive** and **ideological criticism** are all concerned with the relationship between literary and cultural texts and the society in which they were produced or are being currently read. We use the term *ideology* to refer to a dominant set of ideas and values generally accepted as true in a particular society. Whether or not the ideology of a text is explicitly present—as it is, for example, in Langston Hughes's profession of faith in "Salvation" (p. 369)—the premise of interpretive and ideological criticism is that the primary meaning of a text is related to the way it reflects the ideas of its society. Diverse schools of criticism take different attitudes toward ideology and are concerned with various aspects of it. *Allegorical criticism* looks for hidden meanings that may be either positive or negative; *reader-response criticism* provides a wide range of meanings, both explicit and hidden. Adherents of *psychological and psychoanalytic criticism* and *structuralism* regard themselves primarily as descriptive—revealing an individual's or a society's underlying structures without explicitly evaluating them. *Marxism*, *new historicism*, *cultural studies*, *postcolonial criticism*, *feminism*, *gender studies*, *queer theory*, *African American studies*, and *ethnic studies* use ideological interpretation to reconsider social norms and assumptions. Finally, *deconstructive criticism* and *postmodernist criticism* argue that any concept of underlying meaning is deceptive and that any shared ideology is an illusion.

Allegorical Criticism

Allegorical reading, or finding a secret narrative hidden in the surface events of a literary text, is the most ancient form of interpretive criticism. Ancient allegorical reading tended to emphasize philosophical and religious ideas within texts with a sacred or near-sacred status: Homeric scholars found the ideas of Plato hidden in episodes of the *Odyssey*; scholars of Virgil's *Aeneid* found wisdom about the afterlife within the events of the poem. Many early Christian writings about the Hebrew Bible were concerned with discovering prophecies about the coming of Jesus. Some theorists of literature regard all interpretive criticism as fundamentally allegorical because it posits a meaning that is not explicitly present in the subject text. It is certainly true that most allegorical readings strongly reflect the ideology of the critic performing the reading. Nevertheless, there are varying degrees of allegorical reading. In order to read Hawthorne's story "Young Goodman Brown" (p. 435) as an allegory about evil, you would hardly need to do more than summarize its events and pay attention to the names of characters such as "Goodman" and "Faith." In contrast, you would have a difficult time persuading most people the red wheelbarrow in William Carlos Williams's poem "so much depends" (p. 653) is an allegory of the path toward enlightenment, "glazed" with the "rain water" of natural wisdom and accompanied by the "white chickens" of meritorious deeds. Most texts that will readily support an allegorical reading will provide explicit signals by using one of the various forms of allegory covered in Chapter 6 (p. 218).

If there are no such signals, you should avoid making an allegorical reading in the context of an academic paper.

Reader-Response Criticism

Reader-response criticism refers to a loose collection of theories of literature from the 1940s through the 1970s that share the belief that the primary meaning of a text is created not by the author but by the reader. There is seldom an absolute fit between the context and ideology of a text and those of a reader; rather, the encounter between the two includes both common ground and strong tension. Reader-response critics argue that the tension between text and reader generates a meaning at least partially independent of the text itself. This effect is certainly evident in the shift in performance conventions that now make it surprising when a Hamlet does not demonstrate some manner of repressed attraction to his mother, whereas before the theories of Sigmund Freud the opposite would have been the case. However much Shakespeare may have been aware of the mother/son tension he explored in the play, he could not have predicted the enormous change in attitude toward those dynamics among the twentieth-century readers and spectators.

Although some reader-response critics, such as Stanley Fish, have gone so far as to argue that there exists no literary text beyond the interpretation a reader makes of it, others argue that most texts presume an *informed reader*: a reader familiar with the codes and conventions of literature whose interpretation will usually fall within a fairly predictable range. In common with *reception history* (p. APP A-3), reader-response criticism has demonstrated that the meanings of a literary text change over time and between communities. This fact is less pressing if you for the most part share the historical context and ideology of the text you are studying; however, when you are analyzing a text from a different cultural or literary tradition, or when you find yourself disagreeing with or offended by a text you are reading, make an effort to identify the sources of tension and their effect on your reading. Your analysis will be the stronger for the effort.

Psychoanalytic Criticism

Psychoanalytic criticism, and the closely associated **psychological criticism** originated in the influential writings of the doctor and originator of psychoanalysis Sigmund Freud (1856–1939), who argued that the structure of Sophocles's play *Oedipus Rex*—in which Oedipus unknowingly kills his father and marries his mother—represents the hidden desire of all children. Freud argued that human behavior is heavily influenced by instinctive desires and our conscious efforts to reconcile those desires with the often contradictory demands of the individuals and society around us. The conflict between desires and the need to repress those desires motivates our behavior; sometimes it manifests itself in terms of psychological disorders (neurosis, paranoia, depression) and sometimes in terms of socially acceptable behavior. Psychoanalytic and psychological criticism can take many forms; they share the assumption that literary and cultural texts exhibit the psychological structures and disorders characteristic of the society and/or author that produced them.

Some critics focus on analyzing the unconscious motivations and behaviors of specific characters; others look for evidence of the author's psychology within his or her writings; still others believe such structures to be socially determined and psychoanalyze the disorders of a particular ideology. Both Freud and his disciple Ernest Jones explained Hamlet's apparently unmotivated procrastination of his revenge by arguing that, by killing his father and marrying his mother, Claudius had fulfilled the son's unconscious desire. They and others have further suggested that the situation of the play was influenced by Shakespeare's ambivalence toward his own recently deceased father. Others focus on the ways in which Ophelia's odd behavior and tragic fate disrupt the psychic framework of the primary characters in the play.

Freud believed that our dreams and our verbal and physical language provided evidence of unconscious desires. This is why slips of the tongue are also known as "Freudian slips": they are embarrassing because they reveal what you were really thinking rather than what you wanted to say. Consequently, psychoanalytic criticism often focuses on details of language to find evidence of hidden meaning and motivations. Wordplay and ambiguity provide insight into a mind at odds with itself, as in the multiple instances of Hamlet's sexual wordplay. Some critics view these as evidence of his unconscious desires, others of his need to displace, or surpress those desires. Many of the critical schools we discuss below borrow the interpretive techniques of psychoanalysis without necessarily agreeing with or applying the conclusions Frued and others drew from those techniques. Psychoanalytic criticism is a powerful tool for uncovering the most conflicted moments and issues in a literary text; how you interpret those moments is a different issue.

Structuralism

Most forms of psychoanalysis and psychological criticism assume an underlying psychic structure shared by most if not all members of the human race. The general tendency to view the world in terms of its shared deep structures is known, simply enough, as **structuralism**. Structuralism is most closely associated with the early-twentieth-century French linguist, Ferdinand de Saussure, who theorized the existence of a fundamental structure in language, and the mid–twentieth-century French anthropologist, Claude Lévi-Strauss, who argued that human communities share fundamental customs and taboos, such as incest. The term applies equally well to **archetypal criticism,** based on the theories of the Swiss psychiatrist Carl G. Jung, and **myth criticism,** whose proponents include Joseph Campbell and the Canadian literary critic Northrop Frye. According to Jung, we share a "collective unconscious" inherited through generations of universally shared experiences such as birth, love, and death. According to Campbell, all ancient mythologies share a large number of elements—the hero's journey to another world, for example. Frye adapted Campbell's argument to the task of identifying fundamental patterns and forms in literature. A structuralist reading of *Hamlet* might focus on its universal patterns: the tragic plot of betrayal and generational conflict; the problem of confronting evil when it occurs within one's own family, or even within oneself; the way Ophelia is bartered around like "tenders," or money, as her father Polonius terms her.

Structuralist thinking is an important tool for comparison and synthesis; it has been heavily criticized in recent years because it is also a universalizing theory. Structuralist critics are accused of a lack of interest in accounting for the individual qualities that make each text worth reading on its own terms. As with any comparison, a structuralist analysis is only as persuasive as the insights it derives from the differences between the subjects it compares. Such seemingly universal qualities as love or tragedy help draw us in to otherwise alien texts and cultures. It is only once we are drawn in, however, that we can begin to recognize everything that makes those texts distinct from our own experience.

Marxist Criticism

Marxist criticism combines a universal, structuralist account of history with a highly rooted examination of a particular moment in space and time. The political theorist Karl Marx (1818–1883) argued that history can be understood in terms of economic forces, and that each historical period is characterized by the relationship between its economic classes. In particular, Marx argued that every object and social relationship produced in recent centuries bore traces of the conflict between the workers that produced it and the factory owners, or capitalists, for whom it was produced. Consequently, Marxist criticism is dedicated to uncovering the hidden evidence of class conflict in literary and cultural texts. Marxist critics call their process of interpretation *dialectics,* a theory that assumes any text is the product of the capitalist system in general but also exhibits the specific characteristics of the space and time that produced it. No matter where the characters of Shakespeare's plays are set, for example, would depict the dominant ideology of Elizabethan England in their unquestioning assumption of the privileges of royalty and the inevitability of social inequality. At the same time, specific moments and details in the plays—the conflicted characters of the Jew Shylock in *A Merchant of Venice,* the Moor Othello in *Othello,* or the man-beast Caliban in *The Tempest,* or the young prince Hamlet—betray the limits to and contradictions in that ideology. The Marxist critic C. L. R. James, for example, argues that the core drama of *Hamlet* is political, because in it, "two ideas of society are directly confronted" (243).

Marxist critics share a belief that the world as it is does not match up to the world as it should be, and a belief that one role of criticism is to contribute in some manner to changing the world as it is. By the late twentieth century, Marxism as a social and political movement had by and large lost its impetus; since then Marxist criticism has shifted from a tool for the overthrow of capitalism to a more general tool for the critique of contemporary society. Dialectics is unrivaled as an interpretive tool for uncovering the ideological contradictions of a spoken, written, or visual text. Once critics have uncovered those contradictions, they must then decide how to interpret their meaning: they may choose to relate them in a structural manner to the workings of capitalism as a whole, or they may decide to apply them to understanding their role within the structure of a particular text, or they may decide on some combination of the two. We can observe some of the results of these choices in the critical schools below.

New Historicism

Called **new historicism** to distinguish it from traditional historicism, or historical criticism (p. APP A-3), this school of criticism originally developed in the United States during the 1980s among Renaissance scholars. New historicism argues that we should not view the past as an inevitable sequence leading naturally to the present state of events. For many new historicists, the celebration in 1992 of the 500th anniversary of Columbus's discovery of America was a perfect example of the tendency to idealize the past in terms of the present. Echoing a famous statement by the German Marxist critic Walter Benjamin (1892-1940) that "there is no document of civilization that is not also a document of barbarism," the new historicists demonstrated that literary texts can tell us as much about the negative effects of Western civilization and colonization as they can about the positive effects of progress.

New historicists place canonical texts such as Shakespeare's plays next to other, often forgotten, documents of the same period in order to study the ideological assumptions they share. A traditional historical critic would use such a comparison to explicate the surface events and characterizations of a text—showing, for example, that reactions to the appearance of Hamlet's father as a ghost reflect popular assumptions of the time about supernatural apparitions and their religious status. In contrast, a new historical critic would argue that Shakespeare's representation of the ghost is related to what critic Stephen Greenblatt calls a "discourse of power," a way of talking about and representing the world in which social oppression is a legitimate activity, and the ghost a possible challenge to that activity. For Greenblatt, the intense and equivocal status of the ghost derives from the ideological struggle between Catholicism and Protestantism over the conception of Purgatory and religious practices related to it. He argues that, "The psychological in Shakespeare's tragedy is constructed almost entirely out of the theological, and specifically out of the issue of remembrance" (229). While reminding us of the often disturbing role played by literature and culture in supporting policies and attitudes we now consider reprehensible, new historicism has also revealed to us the ways in which many texts have also worked to provide a critical assessment of those viewpoints.

Cultural Studies

Cultural studies is a blanket term for a number of contemporary critical concerns. As a field of criticism, it dates back to the 1930s, when scholars such as Walter Benjamin recognized the enormous potential behind reading conventional literature through the eye of popular culture. Benjamin studied newspapers, cartoons, architecture, and various forms of entertainment not simply as historical documents but as complex texts worthy of analysis and interpretation. During the 1960s, cultural studies critics began applying the tools of literary scholarship to popular music, youth subcultures, movies, television, and just about any other aspect of contemporary life. Cultural studies critics are for the most part opposed to the status quo. Their interpretation of popular culture generally falls into two camps: those who regard it as possessing aesthetic value of its own and those who regard it as an uncritical reflection of the economic forces of capitalism.

For the second camp, cultural studies consists primarily of demonstrating the ways in which popular culture functions as an oppressive force, implanting negative values in a passive consumer. A study of cinematic adaptations of *Hamlet* from this camp might argue, as Xianfeng Mou does, that the characterizations of the female characters in Franco Zeffirelli's film of *Hamlet* (1990) actually "strip [them] of power" (2) in comparison to Shakespeare's text, with the result of "consolidat[ing] the patriarchal society" (8). For the first camp, in contrast, cultural studies demonstrates the contradictory meanings possessed by any cultural product and evident in the ambivalent attitudes of consumers. A cultural study of recent *Hamlet* films from this perspective might argue, as Gulsen Teker does of Kenneth Branagh's film of *Hamlet* (1996), that his Ophelia "seems to be undermining those interpretations that read her suicide and death as signs of her defeat" (118). As a field, cultural studies has been instrumental in expanding the scope of academic criticism far beyond its origins in canonical, or classic, literature and into the analysis of culture in general.

Postcolonial Criticism

Postcolonial criticism combines elements of Marxism, new historicism, and cultural studies to address the unique circumstances of literary and cultural texts produced in former colonies of the European powers—that is, much of the world outside of Europe and parts of East Asia. Postcolonialism emerged from the influence of the Palestinian scholar Edward Said's seminal study, *Orientalism* (1978). Said argued that Western representations of Asia and the Middle East defined them simply as negative images of the West: exotic, decadent, pagan, and primitive. Said further argued that these representations, which he labeled "orientalism," helped to maintain colonial power, as it became extremely difficult for colonized peoples to create a national identity independent of the powerful images created of them by Western authors and artists. Since *Orientalism*, few scholars have been able to ignore the orientalist dimension of Western literature, in the same way that since the civil rights movement, they have been unable to ignore the implicit racism of a brilliant novel such as Mark Twain's *Huckleberry Finn*.

Postcolonial criticism has two primary focuses. The first follows directly from Said's work: uncovering the workings of orientalism in literature written during the colonial period, and expanding the sense of the term to include African and American peoples. Orientalist readings of *Hamlet* focus on its relationship to Freud's Oedipus conflict, which they view as a form of Eurocentrism rather than a universal model of subjectivity. The other focus of postcolonialism is on the literature and culture of the former colonies, especially in Africa and the Indian subcontinent. What are the consequences of writing in the language of colonial power versus an indigenous language? What are the consequences of using forms borrowed from canonical European literature versus the forms of one's own culture? Is it possible to distinguish between a colonial and an indigenous culture after decades or centuries of colonial rule? Many writers and critics have explored these issues with innovative and compelling results; some of those included in this anthology are Salman

Rushdie, Mary TallMountain, and many of the writers in the global casebooks on Africa, Asia, and the Americas.

Feminist Criticism and Gender Studies

As postcolonial criticism questions the portrayal of Asia and the Middle East by Western writers, **feminist criticism** questions the ways in which women have been defined through a literary tradition dominated by male authors and critics. Modern feminism can be traced to the woman's suffrage movements of the early twentieth century, and to authors like Susan Glaspell (p. 139), Charlotte Perkins Gilman (p. 543), and Virginia Woolf (p. 156), who argued that women would write as well as men if they had a room of their own and a sufficient income to live on. Contemporary feminist criticism grew out of the women's movements of the 1960s, especially in England, France, and the United States. English feminism had strong roots in Marxism and political activism; French feminism was primarily theoretical and based in language and literature; American feminism was fundamentally a social movement.

Feminist criticism developed three primary goals: (1) to recover the works of women writers from the past; (2) to provide a context for the creation and interpretation of new writing by women; and (3) to critique the representation of women in the literature of the past by men and by women. Many feminists argue that the forms and conventions of traditional literature allow only a certain type of female character to be portrayed, and that women as well as men are conditioned to respond in certain ways to those characters. Susan Glaspell's *Trifles* dramatizes this conflict: the men automatically condemn Mrs. Wright even though they are unable to understand her motive, while Mrs. Hale and Mrs. Peters are torn between their identification with patriarchal law and order and their sympathy for Mrs. Wright's dilemma.

Gender studies takes this critique a step further, arguing that gender identities have only a contingent relationship to one's physical sex. One may choose to identify oneself in any number of ways—heterosexual female, heterosexual male, bisexual, lesbian, gay, transgendered. **Lesbian** and **gay criticism**, also called **queer studies,** take a similar stance. Gender critics read literature for the ways in which it represents issues of gender and sexuality and to understand the ways in which it displaces or represses those issues. How do attitudes toward gender surface in different historical times and places? How did gay writers such as Walt Whitman or Allen Ginsberg negotiate this identity within their poetry? How did lesbian writers such as Elizabeth Bishop or bisexual writers such as Virginia Woolf negotiate their identities? For gender critics, as for many feminists, literary forms and conventions privilege certain ways of depicting sexual roles and identities, but writers have also found ways to appropriate those conventions for their own purposes. Just as irony says one thing to mean another, so have many writers used a conventional set of situations to make an unconventional argument.

A gender critic will tease out the assumptions underlying T. S. Eliot's unusual depiction of masculinity in "The Love Song of J. Alfred Prufrock" (p. 389) just as a feminist critic will reveal the feminist underpinnings of Charlotte Perkins Gilman's study of insanity, "The Yellow Wallpaper" (p. 543), and a queer studies critic might draw out the implications of Allen Ginsberg's allusions to Walt Whitman and Federico García Lorca in "A Supermarket in California" (p. 629). Much of gender criticism has a progressive or a radical social agenda, using its interpretations of literature to raise awareness of gender issues in mainstream culture and challenge the traditional invisibility of gender in a field long dominated by male readers.

African American Studies and Ethnic Studies

African American studies and **ethnic studies** place racial and ethnic identity at the center of their interpretive agenda. Scholars in African American studies argue that race lies at the heart of American culture; their interpretations of culture seek to reveal the impact of this fact. African American criticism traces the representation of race in both African American and white literature; indeed the newer field of **whiteness studies** seeks to define whites in terms of their race and ethnicity in the same manner that blacks and other minorities have always been defined. When studying a work of literature by an African American, many readers will be likely to consider the role played by race; African American criticism argues that we should do the same when reading literature written by whites. This is a valid point, but it is also true that we tend to consider such issues as race because they are raised within the text itself—Yusef Komunyakaa's poem "Facing It" (p. 529) and Richard Wright's haiku (p. 653), for example, both allude to the speaker's race. A careful reader will be attentive to any issue raised by a particular text, and it is the great contribution of recent interpretive theories to have increased our awareness of issues of race, ethnicity, and gender in the texts we read.

Ethnic studies is a blanket term encompassing all manner of American minority disciplines, including Native American studies, Asian American studies, and Latino/a or Chicano/a Studies. As their presence within literary tradition is less dominant than that of women, blacks, or colonial subjects, these fields tend to focus on recent literature and culture. These fields are also driven more by concern over defining ethnic identity and its role in literature and culture than with a critique of traditional literature. There are exceptions: Native American criticism is especially attuned to the movie genre of the western (see Louise Erdrich's "Dear John Wayne," p. 528) and with uncovering the whitewashing of the conquest of the West. Nevertheless, ethnic studies is more local than structuralist in its goals. By the same token, its insights are best applied to works specifically addressing its concerns.

Deconstructive Criticism

Derived from the philosophy of French theorist Jacques Derrida (1930-2004), the goal of **deconstructive criticism** is to question a fundamental assumption about language: that we mean what we say. Derrida argues that Western philosophy has persuaded us that words and concepts possess stable and unified meanings when—as most of us have in fact discovered intuitively from personal experience—they send mixed and often contradictory messages. Consequently, deconstructive critics argue that the meanings of literary texts are indeterminate rather than fixed. While strict deconstructionists are primarily interested in demonstrating the truth of their method by uncovering the contradictions hidden in any text, the various schools known as **poststructuralism** have borrowed the powerful analytical tools of deconstructive criticism for uncovering hidden social and cultural contradictions. The loose grouping of theorists and critics known as poststructuralism includes or has influenced many critics in cultural studies, psychoanalytic criticism, feminist, African American, and ethnic studies, postcolonial, and gender studies, all of whom use deconstructive techniques to demonstrate contradictions and inconsistencies in the ideology they oppose.

A strict deconstructionist would go much further than most poststructuralist critics, however, and would find contradictions in the concepts of identity, nationality, race, ethnicity, and gender that many regard as essential to approaches such as feminism, African American studies, and ethnic studies. One of the central debates in much of current literary criticism is how to reconcile the need of minority categories to define their field of inquiry and the need to deconstruct the broader categories of mainstream ideology that prevent them from doing so. It is one thing to use deconstructive analysis to show the contradictions in Hamlet's, Claudius's, and Gertrude's words and actions, as many critics of the play do, and uncover a hidden truth about the society in which they live, as many other critics do. A strict deconstructionist would feel obligated to demonstrate the contradictions in these hidden truths about society as well. The tendency today is to apply the tools of deconstructive criticism in specific contexts, as in the analysis of literary texts, while nevertheless accepting the provisional utility of certain structural categories. This may raise the hackles of hard-line deconstructive critics, but it is well suited to the current climate of criticism, which seems to be settling into a less doctrinaire, more pick-and-choose attitude toward the theories and tools of literary criticism after the bitterly fought "theory wars" of the 1980s and early 1990s.

Postmodernist Criticism   The back-and-forth movement between the desire for a categorical and unified theory of how literature, culture, and society function and the belief that such categories are always reductive and contradictory can be characterized as a tension between *modernity* and *postmodernity*. **Postmodernist criticism** derives from the latter category. Broadly speaking, modernity refers to the changes wrought in the world by industrialization during the nineteenth century, the grand theories such as Marxism and psychoanalysis, and the literary movement known as modernism that accompanied these changes. In this sense, *postmodernity* refers to the state of society following the collapse of social, political, and religious certainties of the nineteenth century and the shift in developed nations away from industrialization and toward a service economy and a culture dominated by mass media. Rather than organized in terms of nation-states, the postmodern world is global, dominated by multinational corporations, and divided between the wealthy consumer nations of the north and the impoverished producing nations of the south. Postmodernity is associated with an ironic

attitude toward any fundamental belief and a rejection of the notion of progress; the accompanying cultural texts are labeled *postmodern*, and are characterized by their rejection of the unified forms of modernism.

In literature, **postmodernism** refers to a style that arose in the 1960s as a rejection of what it saw as the restrictive rules of literary modernism and the social conformity of the 1950s. Literary postmodernists made frequent use of popular culture references—especially music and film—and told extravagantly fantastic and often episodic narratives that mocked the seriousness of conventional literature by calling attention to their own techniques of storytelling and narration. Literary postmodernism included not only American and English writers such as Thomas Pynchon, Don DeLillo, and Angela Carter, but also postcolonial writers such as Salman Rushdie (p. 431) and Gabriel García Márquez (p. 670). African American and other minority writers such as Ishmael Reed and Toni Morrison also appropriated postmodernist strategies as a way of addressing their marginal status in relation to mainstream American culture.

Postmodernist critics at the height of the movement in the 1980s primarily worked to analyze postmodernist motifs in specific literary and cultural texts that identified themselves as postmodern. More recently, critics have argued that modernism and postmodernism are not so much historical periods as contrasting attitudes that can be found in literature and culture from the early nineteenth century. Postmodernist criticism in this sense would examine a specific text for the form taken in it by the tension between modernist and postmodernist impulses: the way, for example, that Robert Hass shifts between the *Iliad* of Homer and Kurosawa's film, *The Seven Samurai,* in "Heroic Simile" (p. 229). While applicable only to texts produced during the past two centuries, the tools of postmodernist criticism can be an effective way of structuring the apparently contradictory assertions and allusions of many of these texts.

Choosing the Right Approach for the Right Text

Different critical approaches are more fruitful for some texts than for others. You would not have much use for biographical information when working with an anonymously composed sacred text such as Genesis (p. 426), but you would find information about Wilfrid Owen's life a well-nigh essential context for understanding "Dulce et decorum est" (p. 238). An approach based on prosody and rhetorical figures would be well suited to texts composed during periods in which such forms dominated—for example, in the late sixteenth-to early seventeenth-century poems of John Donne (p. 386), or in contemporary texts returning to those forms, but would have less to say about an open form prose poem such as Carolyn Forché's "The Colonel" (p. 464). Nevertheless, even the most straightforwardly polemical text will use the tools of the language in which it is written, and you should always begin any reading with a formal analysis. Rather than approaching any text with a specific interpretive approach, we recommend that you use an initial formal analysis to determine the primary concerns of a text and then match those concerns with the suitable critical approach or approaches.

Works Cited

Burke, Kenneth. *Kenneth Burke on Shakespeare.* Ed. Scott Newstok. West Lafayette, IN: Parlor P, 2007. Print.

Greenblatt, Stephen. *Hamlet in Purgatory.* Princeton: Princeton UP, 2001. Print.

James, C. L. R. "Notes on Hamlet." 1953. *The C. L. R. James Reader.* Ed. Anna Grimshaw. Oxford: Blackwell, 1992. 243–46. Print.

Mou, Xianfeng. "Cultural Anxiety and the Female Body in Zeffirelli's Hamlet." *CLCWeb: Comparative Literature and Culture* 6.1 (2004): 1-8. Web. 29 April 2009.

Said, Edward. *Orientalism.* New York: Vintage, 1978. Print.

Teker, Gulsen Sayin. "Empowered by Madness: Ophelia in the Films of Kozintsev, Zeffirelli, and Branagh." *Literature/Film Quarterly* 34:2 (2006): 113–19. Print.

LOOKING BACK: At the World of Literary Criticism

- All critical writing has at least one goal in common: to discover and to share knowledge about the object it is studying

- A *naive reader* approaches a text without consciousness of any particular attitudes or expectations, nor with any prior knowledge of it. Naive readers can be either open-minded and curious or closed-minded and dismissive.

- Literary criticism is a tool for the understanding of literature in the same way that rhetorical figures and style are tools in the creation of literature. Rather than an end in themselves, their goal is to give meaning to a text.

- Literary criticism is conventionally divided into different *schools*, or approaches to a literary text, each of which shares a set of beliefs about literature and analytical and interpretive strategies.

- We can divide schools of literary criticism into two primary types of approach: *expository approaches* and *interpretive and ideological approaches.*

- *Expository approaches* focus on what their adherents assume to be the exposition or explanation of the self-evident workings of a text.

- Expository approaches include *rhetorical criticism, formalist criticism, biographical criticism, historical criticism,* and *interdisciplinary criticism.*

- Forms of historical criticism include *textual criticism, source and influence studies,* the situation of a text in its historical context, and *reception history.*

- *Interpretive and ideological approaches* are devoted to uncovering aspects of a text assumed by its adherents *not* to be self-evident, or at least *not* to have been self-evident until a specific historical moment.

- *Ideology* is a set of ideas and values generally accepted as true by the dominant portion of a particular group or society.

- Interpretive and ideological approaches that provide a wide range of meanings and evaluations include *allegorical criticism* and *reader-response criticism.*

- Interpretive and ideological approaches that claim to reveal a society's underlying structures without evaluating them include *psychoanalytic and psychological criticism* and *structuralism,* including *archetypal* and *myth criticism.*

- Interpretive and ideological approaches that level a critique, or negative criticism, at the status quo include *Marxism, new historicism, cultural studies, postcolonial criticism, feminism, gender studies, African American studies,* and *ethnic studies.*

- Interpretive and ideological approaches that argue that any concept of underlying meaning is deceptive and that any shared ideology is illusory include *deconstructive criticism* and *postmodernist criticism.*

WORKING WITH MLA FORMATTING AND DOCUMENTATION

Part One of *Literature: A World of Writing* leads you step by step through nearly all of the elements of paper-writing in the context of the various skills introduced in each chapter. To make it easier to find these different elements in Chapters 1–4, we have listed relevant sections in the list below. Because we know that sometimes you just want a quick answer to a question, we have also provided new examples here for ready reference.

Getting Started

Because individual course directions may differ at times from MLA style, when in doubt, follow the specific prompt for your assignment, or check with your instructor.

Paper: 8½ by 11 inch, unlined, white paper.
Margins: Top, bottom, left, and right margins should all be 1 inch; unless instructed differently, *do not right justify the page.*
Line spacing: Double-space all parts of your paper should be *double-spaced.*
Page numbering: Number all pages in the top of the page. Type your name before the page number.
Title and heading: Unless told otherwise, you *do not need a title page* for your paper. Provide a heading with your name, your instructor's name, the title and number of the course, and the date in the top-left margin of the first page. Type the title, centered on the next line. Begin the text of the page on the next line, at the left margin, indented five spaces or ½ inch:

> Lanney 1
>
> Rob Lanney
> Ms. Franklin
> English Composition 101
> 15 March 2009
>
> Hamlet's Elsinore
> The setting of the court of Elsinore plays an important role in the action of Shakespeare's play. The historical

Works-cited list: Begin the works-cited list on a new page directly following the end of the body of the paper. If you have endnotes, the works-cited list should follow the endnotes on a new page (see Chapter 3, p. 00).

- List the works in alphabetical order.
- Double-space within and between entries.
- Begin the first line of each listing on the left-hand margin. Indent any additional lines five spaces.
- Include in the list only works that you have cited in the paper.

Citing Sources in Your Essay

1. **Paraphrasing source material:** Place the author's name and the page number in parentheses. For two authors, join the names with "and."

   Contrary to Hamlet's assumption that it is wholly corrupt, Elsinore has both the positive and the negative qualities of a royal court (Foakes 35).

2. **Using your own words with the author's name:** Place the page number in parentheses.

   Foakes argues that Hamlet believes the court to be corrupt, but the evidence of the play shows it in fact to have both positive and negative qualities (35).

3. **Quoting prose directly (less than five lines):** Use quotation marks and incorporate prose quotes of less than five lines into the text.

   According to Foakes, "The court of Elsinore . . . has a dual character" (35). **or** "The court of Elsinore . . . has a dual character" (Foakes 35).

4. **Quoting prose directly (five or more lines):** Separate passages from the main text as a double-spaced block quotation by starting it on a new line and indenting the entire passage 1 inch. Introduce with a colon. *Do not use quotation marks around a block quotation.*

   Anthony Davies summarizes well the decision facing a filmmaker with regards to the setting of Elsinore:

   > The most immediate challenge to any film maker who approaches *Hamlet* is the treatment of Elsinore. The castle offers the major spatial opportunities of the play and the film director has to decide whether Elsinore is essentially a place or a concept, and the extent to which it is subjectively or objectively seen. (20)

5. **Quoting poetry directly (less than three lines):** Place in quotation marks and incorporate into your own text. Mark line breaks with a forward slash (/) with a space on each side.

   The 19th-century poet George Castle Rankin makes the "halls of Elsinore" a metaphor for Hamlet's troubled mind: "The puzzle vast and complicate / Which ravels all the world's affairs, / The maze of love and pride and hate" (56)

6. **Quoting poetry directly (three or more lines):**

   The 19th-century poet George Castle Rankin makes the "halls of Elsinore" a metaphor for Hamlet's troubled mind:

   > The puzzle vast and complicate
   >   Which ravels all the world's affairs,
   > The maze of love and pride and hate,
   >   The conflict of beleaguering cares,
   > All are unsolved as much as when
   >   Thou hadst been wont to brood them o'er
   > Wand'ring apart from gayer men
   >   Among the halls of Elsinore. (56)

7. **Quoting drama directly:** When quoting dialogue between two or more characters, separate the extract as a block quotation. Introduce each character's dialogue with his or her name, in block capitals, indented 1 inch from left margin, and followed by a period. Indent any lines that follow an additional three spaces. If citing a play in verse, give act, scene, and line numbers in parentheses; if citing a play in prose, give page number in parentheses.

   Hamlet and Horatio employ the shared location of Elsinore to connect the father's death with the mother's remarriage:

   > HAMLET.   But what is your affair in Elsinore?
   >   We'll teach you to drink deep ere you depart.

HORATIO.   My lord, I came to see your father's funeral.
HAMLET.   I pray thee, do not mock me, fellow-student;
      I think it was to see my mother's wedding. (1.2.174–78)

Documenting Sources in the MLA Works-Cited List

We provide here examples of the sources you are most likely to need to document. If you find a source that does not fall into any of the categories below, you will need to consult a more comprehensive guide, such as Joseph Gibaldi's *MLA Handbook for Writers of Research Papers*, 7th ed., published by the Modern Language Association of America.

Books

1. A book with one author:

   Davies, Anthony. *Filming Shakespeare's Plays: The Adaptations of Laurence Olivier, Orson Welles, Peter Brook, Akira Kurosawa*. New York: Cambridge UP, 1988. Print.

2. Two or more books by the same author; list in alphabetical order by title:

   Greenblatt, Stephen. *Hamlet in Purgatory*. Princeton: Princeton UP, 2001. Print.

   ———. *Will in the World: How Shakespeare Became Shakespeare*. New York: Norton, 2004. Print.

3. A book with two authors:

   Gallagher, Catherine, and Stephen Greenblatt. *Practicing New Historicism*. Chicago: U of Chicago P, 2000.

4. A book with three authors:

   Barnes, Colin, Geof Mercer, and Tom Shakespeare. *Exploring Disability: A Sociological Introduction*. Oxford: Polity, 1999. Print.

5. A book with more than three authors:

   Kaufer, David, et al. *The Power of Words: Unveiling the Speaker and Writer's Hidden Craft*. London: Lawrence Erlbaum, 2004. Print.

6. A book with an editor and no author:

   Aasand, Hardin L., ed. *Stage Directions in Hamlet: New Essays and New Directions*. Madison, N.J.: Fairleigh Dickinson UP, 2003. Print.

7. A book with two editors and no author:

   Keller, James R., and Leslie Stratyner, eds. *Almost Shakespeare: Reinventing His Works for Cinema and Television*. Jefferson, NC: McFarland, 2004. Print.

8. A book with three editors and no author:

   Aebischer, Pascale, Edward J. Esche, and Nigel Wheale, eds. *Remaking Shakespeare: Performance across Media, Genres, and Cultures*. New York: Palgrave, 2003. Print.

9. A book with more than three editors and no author:

   Edens, Walter, et al., eds. *Teaching Shakespeare*. Princeton: Princeton UP, 1977. Print.

10. A later edition:

    Bradley, A. C. *Shakespearean Tragedy: Lectures on Hamlet, Othello, King Lear, Macbeth*. 4th ed. New York: Palgrave, 2007. Print.

11. A republished book:

    Van Doren, Mark. *Shakespeare*. 1939. New York: New York Review Books Classics, 2005. Print.

12. A multivolume work:

    Andrews, John F., ed. *William Shakespeare: His World, His Work, His Influence*. 3 vols. New York: Scribner, 1985. Print.

13. A translation:

    Bonnefoy, Yves. *Shakespeare and the French Poet*. Trans. John Naughton. Chicago: U of Chicago P, 2004. Print.

14. A selection from an anthology or a collection:

    Bertoldi, Andreas, "Shakespeare, Psychoanalysis, and the Colonial Encounter: The Case of Wulf Sachs's *Black Hamlet*." *Postcolonial Shakespeares*. Ed. Ania Loomba and Martin Orkin. New York: Routledge, 1998. 235-58. Print.

    Foakes, R. A. "Hamlet and the Court of Elsinore." *Shakespeare Survey 9: Hamlet*. Ed. Allardyce Nicoll. 1956. Cambridge: Cambridge UP, 2002. 35–44. Print.

15. A book with a corporate author:

    Encyclopaedia Britannica. *Shakespeare: The Essential Guide to the Life and Works of the Bard*. Hoboken, NJ: Wiley, 2007. Print.

16. A document that lacks publication information: Use "n.p." when no place of publication or publisher is given; use "n.d." when no date of publication is given:

    Know, I. Dont. *Who Really Wrote Shakespeare's Plays?* N.p.: n.p., n.d. Print.

17. A book in a series:

    McEvoy, Sean, ed. *William Shakespeare's Hamlet: A Sourcebook*. Routledge Guides to Literature. New York: Routledge, 2006. Print.

18. An introduction, preface, foreword, or afterword:

    Naughton, John. Introduction. *Shakespeare and the French Poet*. Trans. and ed. John Naughton. Chicago: U of Chicago P, 2004. vii-xviii. Print.

19. A government publication:

    Sustainable Development Unit, South Asia Region. *India: Rural Governments and Service Delivery*. New Delhi: World Bank, 2008. Print.

20. A signed article in a reference work

    Kutscher, E. Y. "Aramaic." *Encyclopaedia Judaica*. 1972. Print.

21. An unsigned article in a reference work:

    "Denmark." *Encylopædia Britannica*. 15th ed. 1992. Print.

Periodicals

22. An article from a periodical paginated continuously through the annual volume:

Floyd-Wilson, Mary. "Ophelia and Femininity in the Eighteenth Century: 'Dangerous conjectures in ill-breeding minds.'" *Women's Studies* 21 (1992): 397–409. Print.

23. An article from a periodical paginated by issue:

Sanchez, Reuben. "'Thou com'st in such a questionable shape': Interpreting the Textual and Contextual Ghost in *Hamlet*." *Hamlet Studies* 18.1–2 (Summer/Winter 1996): 65-84. Print.

24. A monthly periodical:

Bethell, Tom. "The Case for Oxford." *Atlantic Monthly* Oct. 1991: 45-61. Print.

25. A signed article in a weekly periodical:

Rosenbaum, Ron. "Shakespeare in Rewrite." *New Yorker* 13 May 2002: 68–77. Print.

26. An unsigned article in a weekly periodical:

"Remembering Bainbridge." *New Yorker* 30 Nov. 1992: 44. Print.

27. A signed article in a daily newspaper; include section of paper with page number:

Hesse, Monica. "It's Hannah Again. Should We Take This?" *Washington Post* 1 Aug. 2008: C1. Print.

28. An unsigned article in a daily newspaper:

"Your Last Chance for Fringe Fun." *Washington Post* 25 July 2008: WE43. Print.

29. A signed review, letter to the editor, or editorial:

Thomson, David. "I Act Therefore I Am." Rev. of *Olivier*, by Terry Coleman. *Nation* 5 Dec. 2004: 30-34. Print.

Samuelson, Robert J. "The Ownership Obsession." Editorial. *Washington Post* 30 July 2008: A15. Print.

Glitzenstein, Eric. "Valuing Animals Doesn't Devalue Us." Letter. *Washington Post* 1 Aug. 2008: A16. Print.

Internet and Other Electronic Sources

30. An entire Internet site for an online scholarly project or database:

An International Database of Shakespeare on Film, Television and Radio. Ed. Murray Weston et al. British Universities Film and Video Council. Web. 1 Aug. 2009.

31. A short work within a scholarly project:

Gray, Terry A. "A Shakespeare Timeline." *Mr. William Shakespeare and the Internet.* Web. 1 Aug. 2009.

32. A personal home page or professional site:

Leong, Virginia *The Hamlet Movie Page.* Web. 1 Aug. 2009. <http://www.geocities.com/Athens/ Parthenon/6261/hamlet.html>.

33. An online book:

Shakespeare, William. *The First Folios and Early Quartos of William Shakespeare.* Electronic Text Center. University of Virginia Library. Web. 1 Aug. 2009.

34. A part of an online book:

Shakespeare, William. *Hamlet (1623 First Folio Edition).* *The First Folios and Early Quartos of William Shakespeare.* Electronic Text Center. University of Virginia Library. Web. 1 Aug. 2009.

35. An article in a scholarly journal:

Worthen, W. B. "*Hamlet* at Ground Zero: The Wooster Group and the Archive of Performance." *Shakespeare Quarterly* 59.3 (Fall 2008): 303–22. Project Muse. Web. 29 Apr. 2009.

36. An unsigned article in a newspaper or on a newswire:

"World's oldest joke traced back to 1900 BC" *Reuters.* 31 July 2008. Web. 1 Aug. 2009.

37. A signed article in a newspaper or on a newswire:

Holden, Michael. "Man Held Over Theft of Rare Shakespeare Folio." *Reuters.* 11 July 2008. Web. 1 Aug. 2009.

38. An article in a magazine:

Rosenbaum, Ron. "Shakespeare in Rewrite." *New Yorker* 13 May 2002: 68–77. Web. 1 Aug. 2009.

39. A review:

Schillinger, Liesl. "Will I Am." Rev. of *My Name Is Will*, by Jess Winfield. *New York Times* 27 July 2008. Web. 1 Aug. 2009.

40. An editorial or a letter to the editor:

Hussey, Mark. "It's Why We Read, Online and Off." Letter. *New York Times.* 31 July 2008. Web. 1 Aug. 2009.

41. An abstract:

O'Brien, Dan. "Testimony and Lies." *Philosophical Quarterly* 57.227 (Feb. 2007): 225-38. Abstract. Web. 1 Aug. 2009.

42. Material from a periodically published database on CD-ROM:

Reed, William. "Whites and the Entertainment Industry." *Tennessee Tribune* 25 Dec. 1996: 28. CD-ROM. *Ethnic Newswatch.* Dataware Technologies. Feb. 1997.

43. Material from a nonperiodically published source on CD-ROM, diskette, or magnetic tape:

Shakespeare, William. *Hamlet. The Arden Shakespeare CD-ROM: Texts and Sources for Shakespeare Study.* Jonathan Bate, consultant ed. Version 1.0. Walton-on-Thames: Thomas Nelson [Arden Shakespeare], 1997. CD-ROM.

44. An e-mail communication:

Frederick, Simon. "Re: *Hamlet* and Elsinore." Message to Martha Randolph. 24 July 2009. E-mail.

Randolph, Martha. Message to the author. 25 July 2009. E-mail.

Other Print and Nonprint Sources

45. An interview conducted by the researcher:

McKellan, Ian. Personal interview. 14 April 2009.

46. A dissertation (abstracted in *Dissertation Abstracts International*):

Swindall, Lindsey R. "*Hamlet* in the Cinema." Diss. U of Oklahoma, 2007. *DAI* 68.01 (July 2008). Web. 1 Aug. 2009.

47. A lecture:

Greenblatt, Stephen. "Hamlet in Purgatory." Boston College. 31 Oct. 2001. Lecture.

48. A speech delivered at a professional conference:

Hodgkins, Christopher. "Claudius, Conviction, and Conversion: The Spiritual Failure of Playing in Hamlet." Conf. on Elizabethan Theatre. University of Waterloo, Ontario, Canada. 15 Nov. 1999. Speech.

49. A film:

Hamlet. Dir. Michael Almereyda. Perf. Ethan Hawke, Kyle MacLachlan, Sam Shephard, Bill Murray, Julia Stiles. Miramax. 2000. Film.

50. A recording of a television program or film:

Hamlet, Prince of Denmark. Dir. Rodney Bennett. Perf. Derek Jacobi, Claire Bloom, Patrick Stewart. 1980. Ambrose Video, 2002. DVD.

51. An audio recording:

Thomas, Ambroise. *Hamlet.* Cond. Antonio de Almeida. Perf. Thomas Hampson, June Anderson, Samuel Ramey. EMI Classics, 1995. CD.

52. Visual art:

Millais, John Everett. *Ophelia.* 1852. Painting. Tate Britain, London.

Sample Works-Cited Pages

See Chapter 3, p. 112; Appendix, p. APP A-9; and below, p. APP B-13.

Incorporating Your Research into a Paper

In Chapter 3, we follow Lorraine Betesh step by step through the process of researching, drafting, and revising a research paper on photographs of the Brooklyn Bridge. In this Appendix, we have included Rob Lanney's literary research paper on the setting of Elsinore in Shakespeare's *Hamlet*. Rob's research was the source for many of the examples given above. As is often the case, he did not end up using all of his research in the final paper. We reproduce here the final version Rob wrote for his class. We have annotated the paper to highlight in-text citation and the structure of the paper.

Lanney 1

Rob Lanney

Ms. Franklin

English Composition 101

15 March 2009

Hamlet's Elsinore

The setting of the court of Elsinore plays an important role in the action of Shakespeare's play. The historical Kronborg Castle, at Elsinore, in Denmark is the setting for the play. Critics like Hansen see details of this setting as "not very detailed or accurate" (109). But Foakes argues that it is "the focal point of all the action" (35). In this paper, I argue that the castle itself is an important image in the play. The way its spaces hide secrets emphasizes the play's theme of bringing evil-doing to light. First, I provide a short history of Kronborg castle.

[Rob's thesis]

These sentences detail the parts of the paper.

Then I look at the way Shakespeare uses Elsinore as an image in *Hamlet*. I include examples from a few productions of the play at the actual castle. I conclude the paper by analyzing the use of the setting in several specific productions and films of the play and ask why the setting is so important to *Hamlet* in particular?

Kronborg Castle is on the outskirts of the Danish town of Helsingor (the modern version of Elsinore). The castle is located on the water that separates the eastern coast of Denmark from Sweden, "protected by an imposing outer bastion wall, and on the landward side by a moat filled with water" (Jirik-Babb 65). It was built in the 1420s by Erik of Pomerania, but it was first called Krogan (Jirik-Babb 65). According to Jirik-Babb, Erik built it to be able to collect money from passing ships through a narrow point between Denmark and Sweden (65). He used the money he collected from tolls to pay for "the Krogan to be expanded over time to become a magnificent Renaissance edifice with festive towers and spires, renamed the Kronborg Castle in 1577" (Jirik-Babb 65). Shakespeare heard about the castle from members of his theater company, who had performed in it (Hansen 109). Jirik-Babb believes Shakespeare may have been led to set the play in Elsinore because King James of Scotland (later James I of England) had recently married the sister of Christian IV of Denmark (88). The play was in fact performed in front of the couple in 1603 (Jirik–Babb 88). It seems Kronborg was a famous castle at the time Shakespeare was writing and that there were connections between England and the court at Denmark. The castle was severely damaged by fire in 1629, but Christian IV had it rebuilt in the same style, using the parts that had survived the fire, meaning that "large portions of the ancient

Krogan form a part of the present-day Kronborg Castle" (Jirik–

Babb 65).

Throughout the years *Hamlet* has sometimes been performed at

the castle. Many directors have seen its walls as an image of the play.

When John Gielgud went to see the castle to think about the staging in

the 1939 version, this is what he said:

> When I saw the beautiful Courtyard of Kronborg Castle, I felt the
>
> play should be given there in a swift, concentrated
>
> production. . . . I decided after some thought that I preferred a
>
> more intimate stage, of which I might convey more easily that
>
> feeling of council chambers, passages and anterooms, where
>
> Hamlet walks, where his uncle father and aunt mother pass their
>
> days in feasting and debauchery, where Polonius and Rosencrantz
>
> and Guildenstern are ever lurking and spying, and where Ophelia
>
> is set on to trap the Prince whom she loves. (qtd. in Hansen 113)

For Gielgud, the best way to show the "lurking and spying" that is

actually going on in the "beautiful Courtyard" is to put a claustrophobic

set in the middle of it. In 1937, the play was performed at the castle,

starring Laurence Olivier and Vivien Leigh (Hansen 113). According to

Hansen, "the enclosing castle walls were felt to call to mind the

prison-like state of Denmark" (114). In both examples, the castle itself

was made to reflect the theme of the play.

A famous line in the play, "Something is rotten in the state of

Denmark" (1.4.90), implies that the foundations of the court are rotten.

As Horatio asks in the previous line, "To what issue will this come?" How

will the truth emerge? It comes out of the ground of the castle. As

Hamlet waits for his father ghost, he says, "Foul deeds will rise, /

Here, Rob makes the transition from the history of the castle to his analysis of the play by discussing a performance of the play at the actual castle.

In-text citation of more than four lines, separated from main text as a block quotation.

In-text citation for an indirect source ("qtd." abbreviates "quoted")

Begin each paragraph with a topic sentence summarizing the argument of the paragraph.

Cite plays by act, scene and line number.

Though all the earth o'erwhelm them, to men's eyes" (1.2.262–63). Hamlet's father, according to Horatio, is buried in Elsinore, and this father's ghost is the rotten "something" decomposing beneath its ground. For Foakes, the court is "cold and secretive . . . like a prison-house" (38). Hamlet is a prisoner above ground and his father is confined below, according to Greenblatt, "serving a prison term in Purgatory" (4). In his film of the play, Kenneth Branagh, Sheppard writes, "gets carried away with trapdoors in his Elsinore. He uses secret apertures no less than sixteen times" (37). The castle is a place of cells and mazes.

Conclude each paragraph with a sentence bringing together the different parts of the paragraph.

Working together, Hamlet and his father work to destroy the castle that is their prison. At the end of Act 1, as the ghost asks the witnesses of his appearance to swear secrecy, Hamlet, hearing him "*beneath*" (1.4.170), shouts out, "Well said, old mole. Canst work i'th'earth so fast?" (1.4.171). For Hamlet, the ghost is like a mole, digging under the soft foundation of the castle. But Hamlet also sees himself as ridding the castle of its pests, as the name of the play, "The Mousetrap," tells us (3.2.235). The 1937 play used platforms of different levels, "the highest of which was a kind of rostrum, a cube of about six by six by six feet, which towered above the rest of the set" (Hansen 113). The two biggest scenes in the play used this rostrum. In "The Mousetrap," "Claudius and Gertrude were seated up here during the play-within-the-play, which provided a strong focus for the King's horror and anger at being caught in the mousetrap" (Hansen 114).

The duel at the end of the play used the same rostrum, emphasizing the feeling of claustrophobia, that everything in the play is stacked on top of itself in the castle. Hansen writes that the duel ended with "the Queen's highly dramatic dying fall of fifteen feet" (114). After everybody has died of poison, Hamlet's friend Horatio orders that,

When you quote as part of the sentence, make sure the syntax of the quote matches the syntax of your own language.

"these bodies/High on a stage be placèd to the view" (5.2.379–80). By doing this, Horatio wants to show that the court that has concealed its secrets and betrayed each other is now all out in the open, and that there are no more secrets.

There is another part of the play where the different hidden levels of the castle are important. This is the story of Polonius, who is killed by Hamlet when he hides in the closet while Hamlet is talking to his mother. When the king asks where Polonius is, Hamlet answers,

> In heaven. Send thither to see. If your messenger find him not there, seek him i'th'other place yourself. But if indeed you find him not within this month, you shall nose him as you go up the stairs into the lobby. (4.4.34-38)

This block quote is too short. It should have been incorporated into the text.

Like Hamlet's father, Polonius has been buried beneath the floor of the castle. Hamlet's joke about "nosing him" reminds us of "something rotten in the state of Denmark." However, instead of being a metaphor, this is the real thing.

When she is dead, Ophelia, who goes crazy because she is upset about her father dying, plays a similar role to her father. In the scene in the churchyard that starts Act 5, the first clown tells a joke to the second clown that compares a grave to a house. The "grave maker," he says, makes the strongest house because "The houses he makes last till doomsday" (5.1.59). With Hamlet's father, Polonius, and Ophelia somehow buried beneath it, Elsinore is a grave and a house at the same time. This is even more so if we think of the end of the play, where the house of the royal family becomes the grave of Hamlet, Laertes, Claudius, and Gertrude. The pattern of jokes and accusations about the smell of rotting corpses and the smell of bad deeds emphasizes this connection.

According to Sheppard, in Branagh's movie of *Hamlet*, when Hamlet plans his play "The Mousetrap" he "punctuates his words by sending the king puppet to Hell through the trapdoor in his model Elizabethan theatre" (37). There are a few scenes in *Hamlet* that take place outside of the castle and its grounds. But the play feels like it is the whole world, or at least that it is to Hamlet. Like his joke about where to look for Polonius, Hamlet's "trapdoor to Hell" tells us that for him, Elsinore contains heaven and hell as well as his own world. Maybe this is why the bodies never leave, and the ghost of his father can't leave either.

In his article at one point, Hansen refers to plays set in Kronborg castle as "Hamlet comes home" (113). This seems to mean that the real place Shakespeare intended for the play draws people back to it. Hansen concludes his article on "the ten *Hamlets* at Kronborg" by asking "Why and when is it a good idea to play *Hamlet* at Kronborg?" (117) He divides the productions into two kinds, "the 'self-contained' set and the 'open' set" (117). Hansen concludes that the more the castle itself is involved the better it works, and so he decides that "open sets" are more effective, because the castle itself provides the setting (117).

Hansen's conclusion makes sense, but this also makes him not like John Gielgud's 1939 version as much as Laurence Olivier's 1937 play. But this seems like a value judgment, because Hansen seems to prefer Olivier's physical style of acting to Gielgud's focus on the words. I think the different platform layers in Olivier's play would give a very good sense of the way secrets come out in the play and would make you feel like they were coming out of the very walls of the castle. But I also think that a claustrophobic "self-contained" set inside the courtyard of the castle could be a strong image of the hidden spaces within the play, even though it might be a harder play to watch.

This paragraph introduces the final part of the paper, about specific productions.

Rob uses a question in one of his sources to reframe his original thesis.

Instead of merely citing his source, Rob demonstrates here that he has read it carefully enough to engage with its arguments.

The Canadian director Robert Lepage called his 1996 version of the play *Elsinore*, but he didn't stage it in Denmark, and he didn't show the whole play. It takes the idea of "self-contained" to an extreme. He cut lots of lines, making it less than two hours and twenty-three scenes (Wheale 124). It was a one-man show and Lepage played all the roles. The set designer Carl Fillion reduced the set to,

> a mobile cube construction which continuously (and silently) metamorphosed to create different kinds of playing space. A central plane with two side panels and top frame moved so as to alter the volume of the stage and selectively frame the action in a different way for each of the twenty three scenes; the central panel was a complex arrangement with a circular revolve including a rectangle which is used as a door, a grave-or viewing-slot as the action dictated. The combined effects of the design, Robert Caux's synthesized score, and video and slide-projection combined to powerfully envelop the audience. (Wheale 124)

Lepage's title tells us that he wants to emphasize the setting. In addition, he used different kinds of projection techniques to provide unique points of view, like the one from the point of view of the swords in the duel. When characters die, their images get "grabbed" and "frozen on the central panel" (Wheale 125). It is as if the entire play is taking place within the head of a person today, and that "Elsinore" is what Lepage calls that place.

Just as Foakes argued in 1956, the setting is still "the focal point of all the action" (35). This is because Elsinore as a place has an enormous influence on the way the characters feel and act. But it is also because the characters seem enormously influenced by the place they

Rob's conclusion recalls the quote from the beginning, but gives it a new context. Always try to conclude by raising a new question elicited by the development of your argument.

are in. Is this because in Shakespeare's play they are all living under the tragedy of the events that have happened, all the secrets hidden in the castle? Or is Shakespeare trying to tell us that all of us are affected this way by where we live?

Works Cited

Davies, Anthony. *Filming Shakespeare's Plays: The Adaptations of Laurence Olivier, Orson Welles, Peter Brook, Akira Kurosawa.* New York: Cambridge UP, 1988. Print.

Foakes, R. A. "Hamlet and the Court of Elsinore." *Shakespeare Survey 9: Hamlet.* Ed. Allardyce Nicoll. 1956. Cambridge: Cambridge UP, 2002. 35–44. Print.

Greenblatt, Stephen. *Hamlet in Purgatory.* Princeton: Princeton UP, 2001. Print.

Hansen, Niels B. "Gentlemen You Are Welcome to Elsinore: *Hamlet* in Performance at Kronborg Castle, Elsinore." *Shakespeare and his Contemporaries in Performance.* Ed. Edward J. Esche. Burlington, VT: Ashgate, 2000. 109–19. Print.

Jirik-Babb, Pauline. "Hamlet's Castle at Elsinore." *Shakespeare Newsletter* 53.3 (Fall 2000): 65, 88–89. Print.

Shakespeare, William. *Hamlet, Prince of Denmark. Literature: A World of Writing.* Ed. David L. Pike and Ana M. Acosta. New York: Pearson Longman, 2011. 286–347. Print.

Sheppard, Philippa. "The Castle of Elsinore: Gothic Aspects of Kenneth Branagh's *Hamlet.*" *Shakespeare Bulletin* 19.3 (Summer 2001): 36–39. Print.

Wheale, Nigel. "Culture Clustering, Gender Crossing: *Hamlet* Meets Globalization in Robert Lepage's *Elsinore.*" *Shakespeare and his Contemporaries in Performance.* Ed. Edward J. Esche. Burlington, VT: Ashgate, 2000. 121–33. Print.

Always include an entry for your primary source.

GLOSSARY OF LITERARY TERMS

Act The primary form of division in the structure of a play, usually determined by a major change of setting or a break in temporal continuity.

Allegory A narrative containing a **figurative meaning** distinct from and parallel to the explicit **plot**. See also **Emblem, Fable, Personification, Parable.**

Alliteration Repetition of the initial consonant in a series of words.

Allusion When one text refers to another text or situation whose meaning exists independently of the first text.

Ambiguity Uncertain or unclear meaning.

Ambiguity of argument Uncertainty arising from a change or surprise in the structure of an argument.

Ambiguity of diction Uncertainty regarding the way words are put together within a particular clause.

Ambiguity of plot Uncertainty arising from a change or surprise that causes us to modify or doubt our prior assessment of an event or series of events.

Ambiguity of situation Uncertainty regarding the basic meaning of what is happening in a narrative.

Ambiguity of syntax Uncertainty regarding the different grammatically possible readings of a specific sentence.

Ambiguity of words Uncertainty regarding multiple possible meanings of a particular word or group of words.

Analysis, textual The explanation of everything unambiguous within a text.

Anaphora Repetition of the same word or phrase to begin lines of poetry or sentences, clauses, or brief paragraphs of prose.

Antagonist A **character** who opposes the **protagonist** in a play or work of fiction.

Antistrophe The portion of the **ode** sung by the **chorus** in **Greek tragedy** while moving from west to east on the stage.

Antithesis The use of contrasting terms in a parallel construction or a **chiasmus.** See also **oxymoron** and **paradox.**

Antonyms Two words with opposite meanings.

Argument A statement intended to persuade.

Argument, causal Supports a claim based on a cause-and-effect relationship.

Argument, definitional Supports a claim because of certain qualities it possesses.

Argument, developed Elaborates and refines a central claim, or **leading argument.**

Argument, leading States the central claim of an argument.

Argument, narrative Supports a claim with recourse to individual experience.

Argument, objective A type of argument based on objective, or verifiable, criteria. See also **causal argument, definitional argument,** and **rebuttal.**

Argument, subjective A type of argument based on subjective, or individual criteria. See also **evaluation** and **narrative argument.**

Assonance Repetition of vowel sounds in a series of words.

Bibliography, annotated A full or partial selection from the **works-cited list** that includes a **summary** and **evaluation** of each source.

Bibliography, working An evolving list of sources from which the **annotated bibliography** and **works-cited list** will be drawn.

Bilingual Refers to an individual, group, or text that uses two languages. See also **multilingual.**

Body (1) The part of a letter between the salutation and the closing; (2) the paragraph of a summary following its title; (3) the part of an essay between the introduction and conclusion.

Brechtian theater See **epic theater.**

Call number A number indicating the location of a book in the library **stacks,** or shelves.

Catharsis According to classical theory of the experience of **Greek tragedy,** the combination of relief that we are not the ones who are suffering and pleasure in the knowledge we have gained from the experience.

CD-ROM Abbreviation for "compact disc read-only memory": an optical disk containing data that can be accessed but not altered or rewritten.

Character Actor within the events of a narrative.

Character, minor Actor within a narrative whose primary or sole purpose is to fulfill a function within the plot.

Character analysis A **textual analysis** with the goal of understanding the context and perspective of a particular **character** in a work of literature.

Chiasmus A pattern of repetition that reverses the order of the terms it repeats.

Chiasmus, narrative Refers to the use of a chiastic pattern to structure narrative events.

Chorus A group of characters in **Greek tragedy** and comedy who comment on or provide additional information about the events of the play, usually in song form.

Citation, in-text Citation in a text that refers to a primary or secondary source in the **works-cited list.**

Clause A syntactic construction containing a subject and predicate.

Clause, dependent A **clause** whose meaning is not complete in itself.

Clause, independent A **clause** whose meaning is complete in itself.

Closing The part of a letter that follows the body and introduces the signature.

Code switching To switch between languages, dialects, and situations.

Cognate A word that looks similar in two languages and has similar meanings.

Cognate, false A word that looks similar in two languages but has different meanings.

Comedy (1) In general, any text or situation that elicits laughter; (2) In specific, a form of drama meant to elicit laughter, or possessing an arc of events that begins badly and ends well.

Comedy, romantic A drama with the structure of a **comedy,** and where the main plot is concerned with a romantic relationship.

Comics A number of still images placed together in some sort of meaningful relationship with each other. See also **images, sequential.**

Common knowledge Widely known information about current events, famous people, geographical facts, and history.

Consonance The repetition of an internal consonant in a word or series of words.

Constraints The specific formal restrictions applied to a text or genre by the author or by **convention.**

Contrafactum The practice of writing new lyrics to the tune of a familiar song.

Conventions The spoken or unspoken rules regarding what is and is not permitted in a given genre or social situation.

Creator The person who creates a work of art.

Cut The gap between two **shots** in a movie or moving images.

Dénouement The action that follows the climax and concludes a drama or work of fiction.

Device, literary A recognized technique of literary style.

Dialect Refers to the specific form of a language, possessing its own pronunciation, vocabulary, and grammar.

Diction Refers to variation in word choice, word order, and expression within the general conventions of grammar.

Diegetic Belonging to the **story world** of a play or a narrative.

Drama, comic A drama possessing the structure of a **comedy,** with a main plot that is unrelated to a romantic relationship.

Drama, realist Adapts the plot structure of **tragedy** to the characters and events of middle-class life, or the life of the poor.

Dramatic arc The organization of story events into a plot where the action gathers to a climax and then falls again toward a conclusion.

Ecphrasis The verbal description of physical objects, places, and works of art.

Elision Refers to dropped letters and syllables in a word or phrase, especially in poetry.

Ellipsis Three periods with spaces between them (. . .), used to indicate an omission in a quotation.

Emblem An image presenting an allegorical narrative as a visual puzzle.

End-rhyme Rhyme occurring at the end of a line of poetry.

Enjambment Occurs when the end of a line of poetry does not coincide with a pause or end in the grammatical construction.

Epic A genre of poetry, usually long, that tells of heroes and the deeds that brought them fame.

Epic theater A form of modern theater that seeks to make its audience aware of dramatic conventions and the social structures related to them. Also known as **Brechtian theater.**

Essay A short form of literary nonfiction dealing with a single subject.

Essay, argumentative An essay whose primary purpose is to persuade us to agree with what it says.

Essay, descriptive An essay based on the detailed physical description of a particular object or event.

Essay, expository An essay whose primary purpose is the presentation of information.

Essay, narrative An essay that recounts a series of events in the form of a **narrative.**

Essay, reflective An essay that reflects or meditates on a specific topic without necessarily stating a thesis or reaching a conclusion.

Etiological myth A myth that explains the origin of a present-day phenomenon.

Evaluation (1) An argument supporting a claim by attributing value to it; (2) The part of an entry in an **annotated bibliography** that judges the value of a source for a specific project.

Explication A line-by-line explanation of the explicit, or unambiguous, meanings of a text.

Fable An **allegory** whose figurative meaning is clear and, often, spelled out in a moral at the end.

Fair use The legal doctrine allowing writers to cite a limited amount of a copyrighted work for certain non-commercial purposes, including scholarly argument.

Farce A **genre** of **comedy** in which characters are trapped in ridiculous situations.

Figure of speech The use of a word or phrase in a way different from or in addition to its literal meaning or standard usage.

Foil A secondary character, one of whose functions is to help develop the principal character(s), usually by contrast.

Foot A unit of stressed and unstressed syllables in verse written in accentual-syllabic **meter.**

Form The patterns and relationships formed by the different elements of a literary or artistic text.

Genre A type of literary, artistic, or cultural form.

Groundlings Spectators in the pit, or lowest level, of an Elizabethan theater.

Homograph Two words with the same spelling but different pronunciations and different meanings.

Homonym Two words with the same pronunciation but different meanings and, usually, spellings.

Homophone Two words with the same sound, but with different spellings and different meanings.

Hyperbole A **literary device** that employs exaggeration for dramatic effect.

Hypertext Texts that can be accessed in a single or variable sequence on a webpage.

Iconography Visual and other conventional elements that identify a **character** as belonging to a particular **type** or **genre.**

Image, still A single image whose visual information is self-contained and fixed in form.

Imagery Any element of setting or character in a work of art or literature that takes on significance beyond its literal meaning.

Images, sequential A number of still images placed together in some sort of meaningful relationship with each other. See also **comics.**

Interpretation An argument regarding the meaning of ambiguities in a text.

Introduction The opening paragraph of an essay, including its primary theme and, if required, its thesis and leading argument.

Irony A **literary device** that reverses the meaning of the statement or event to which it refers. Not to be confused with the common usage of the word to mean bad luck, bad timing, or surprise. See also specific forms of irony, below.

Irony, dramatic A statement meaning the opposite of what is expected; the meaning is clear to the audience or reader, but not to the speaker.

Irony, situational Occurs when the apparent outcome of events is reversed unexpectedly and severely.

Irony, verbal A statement meaning the opposite of what is expected; the meaning is clear to the speaker and the audience or reader, but not to all characters.

Liminal space A space in which normally accepted social conventions and hierarchies are temporarily suspended.

Literary form The way in which a writer has chosen to organize thoughts and words in a text.

Litotes A **literary device** that employs understatement for dramatic effect.

Magic realism A form of fiction which recounts seemingly impossible events as if they were everyday occurrences.

Manga Japanese comics, usually published serially.

Meaning, figurative Occurs when any aspect of a work of art or literature takes on significance in addition to its **literal meaning.**

Meaning, literal Consistent with the conventional meaning of specific words or images.

Melodrama A type of drama where protagonist and antagonist are starkly contrasted and the plot focuses on a protracted and suspenseful struggle between the forces of good and evil.

Metaphor A **literary device** that transfers the qualities of one thing to another through an unexpected resemblance.

Metaphor, dead A word whose metaphorical meaning is accepted in regular usage without reference to its literal meaning or its conceptual implications.

Meter The measure of a line of verse. Meter can be (1) **quantitative,** measured according to the length of each vowel and consonant combination; (2) **syllabic,** measured according to the number of units of pronunciation in each word; (3) **accentual,** measured according to the number of accented syllables only; or (4) **accentual-syllabic,** measured according to the number of stressed and unstressed syllables combined.

Metonymy A **literary device** in which one term is substituted for another by association.

Multilingual Refers to an individual, group, or text that uses two or more languages.

Multimedia web page A document on the World Wide Web that incorporates media beyond text into its mode of presentation.

Narration, depth of The degree to which a narrator enters into the minds and motivations of the characters in the **story world.**

Narration, first person A story told from the perspective of a single individual, usually referred to by the pronoun "I."

Narration, range of The degree to which a narrator's knowledge of the **story world** is restricted or unrestricted.

Narration, restricted A story in which knowledge of events is restricted to the point of view of a single character or selected characters.

Narration, second person A story told as a direct address to the reader.

Narration, third person A story told by an impersonal narrator using the third person pronoun.

Narration, unrestricted or omniscient A story in which the narrator, usually **third-person,** has access to all events and points of view.

Narrator The one who recounts, or narrates, the events of a story, or narrative.

Narrator, unreliable A narrator that causes readers to doubt the truthfulness of the facts and events being narrated.

Non-diegetic Appearing in a play or narrative but not belonging to its **story world.**

Nonfiction Any text written in prose that is not fiction, or that does not present itself as fiction.

Novel A long narrative, usually divided into smaller formal segments, such as chapters, usually exhibiting a breadth of events and chronology and/or a depth of characterization and detail of description.

Novel, graphic A **comic** bound together in book form that recounts an extended fictional narrative.

Novella A "long" story or a "little" novel, usually somewhere between fifty and a hundred pages long.

Ode (1) In Greek tragedy, refers to the dancing and sung words of the **chorus,** divided into **strophe** and **antistrophe;** (2) a classical and modern poetic form, either in irregular stanzas, or in regular stanzas with often intricate rhyme scheme.

Outline A schematic plan of the structure, thesis, arguments, and evidence of a paper.

Oxymoron A **literary device** that pairs words with opposite meanings.

Palindrome A form of **chiasmus** that repeats individual letters in reverse order.

Paper, argument A paper intended to persuade the reader of the validity of a specific thesis.

Paper, comparison A paper that compares two or more texts by establishing an initial resemblance and then analyzing the differences that occur within and around that resemblance.

Paper, research A longer, thesis-driven paper using evidence based on scholarly sources.

Parable A narrative with a moral at the end whose meaning is not always perfectly clear and is often **paradoxical.**

Paradox An **antithesis** whose meaning cannot be resolved logically but may produce a counterintuitive truth.

Paradox, logical A coherent but non-antithetical construction whose meaning cannot be logically resolved.

Parody A text written in the style of another text, or mimicking the **conventions** of a specific form or **genre.**

Parse To analyze a sentence according to its grammatical construction.

Persistence of vision A perceptual phenomenon in which the image of objects persists briefly in the brain after having been seen by the eye.

Personification Places an abstract word or concept in a narrative context, gives it human qualities, and uses it to refer to a figurative level of meaning.

Pit The audience area just in front of, and below, the stage in Elizabethan theater.

Plagiarism Using someone else's work—words, ideas, or illustrations; published or unpublished—without giving the creator of that work due credit.

Plot The events recounted in a narrative and the order in which they are recounted.

Position The view taken by an **argumentative essay** or an **argument paper** regarding its subject.

Pre-reading The assumptions and prior experience we have of a text before reading it.

Processing The third element of **reading critically,** after **pre-reading** and **reading.**

Production history The different productions of a specific play from its première performance to the present day; can also refer to the history of the making of a film.

Prop Any object which has a function in the action of a play or motion picture.

Proposal A statement about what should be done regarding the situation described in an **argumentative essay.**

Proscenium arch The arch dividing the space of a nineteenth-century stage from the space of the audience as if it were a fourth wall or a movie screen.

Prosody The conventions of metrical composition.

Protagonist The main character of a play or work of fiction.

Questioning The second step in the process of thinking critically about a text; includes the consideration of a variety of possible interpretations, probing and comparing those interpretations, and testing arguments about specific words, images, and themes.

Quotation, block A direct in-text citation longer than four lines, set off from the main text with a hard return and indented from the left margin.

Reading The first step in thinking critically about a text, involving three components: **pre-reading,** the act of reading, and **processing.**

Rebuttal An argument that persuades by proposing evidence contrary to the position it is opposing.

Review An **essay** that approaches a text or performance from the point of view of a critic writing for a prospective reader or spectator.

Revision A step in the process of writing that involves rethinking and reworking a prior draft of an essay or other piece of writing.

Rhetoric The art of persuasion through the power of words, either orally or in writing.

Salutation A formal sign or expression of greeting; the opening of a letter.

Sarcasm A statement meaning the opposite of what is expected; this meaning is clear to all concerned.

Satire A mode of writing that opposes the state of the world as it is by ridiculing its vices, pretensions, and absurd behavior.

Scansion The act of scanning a line of poetry to determine its **meter.**

Scene Secondary division in the structure of a play, often determined by a change in the number of characters on the stage. In film, refers to a group of **shots,** usually constituting a sequence of actions occurring in an unbroken stretch of time in a single setting.

Segmentation Division of a sequence of events into distinct and meaningful units.

Sentence, opening In a **summary,** expresses the main idea of the text being summarized.

Sentence, second In a **summary,** identifies the principal formal features of the text being summarized.

Set The décor of a stage play, representing the **setting** of the play's events.

Setting The locale or locales in which a poem, play, story, essay, or other text takes place.

Short story A brief narrative usually covering a limited number of characters, settings, and situations, with little or no formal divisions between parts, and often concluding with a final twist or revelation.

Shot The basic unit of meaning in moving images, defined as the images occurring between two **cuts.**

Sign A visual object that means something in addition to what it is as a thing.

Signature A person's name or initials placed at the conclusion of a letter or within an official document.

Simile A **literary device** that compares two distinct subjects, usually with "like" or "as," assuming a strong resemblance between the terms of comparison.

Simile, heroic or Homeric A **literary device** that uses everyday events to explain the distant and often unbelievable events and characters of the heroic world of the **epic.**

Slapstick Physical comedy.

Source, primary Texts and documents from the time period of a topic, or which were written by the subject of a paper.

Source, outside Anything that does not come from the original thoughts of a text's creator or **common knowledge,** and must, consequently, be properly documented.

Source, secondary History and criticism written in the present day about the subject of a paper.

Space, temporal Refers to the time that passes between one frame and the next in **sequential images.**

Speaker The voice or persona that speaks the words of a poem.

Stacks Refers to the shelves of books in a library, organized by **call number.**

Story The set of events, in chronological order, that make up the **plot** of a fictional narrative.

Story world The sum total of events that we infer or imagine in a fictional narrative.

Strophe The portion of the **ode** sung by the chorus in **Greek tragedy** while moving from east to west on the stage.

Structure The way a text is organized.

Style The way a text brings its patterns and associations together into a more or less cohesive whole.

Style, objective A set of formal choices and patterns that presents a narrative as the objective account of a sequence of events.

Style, subjective A set of formal choices and patterns that presents a narrative as the expression of the subjectivity of a specific character or characters.

Summary A brief statement of the subject, form, and events or substance of a specific text.

Symbol An arbitrary association between two terms whose meaning is agreed upon by **convention.**

Synecdoche A **literary device** in which a part is substituted for the whole, or the whole is substituted for a part.

Syntax The grammatical structure of a sentence.

Temporal relations Whether or not events in a narrative are recounted in chronological order, the amount of time that passes between specific plot events, and the relative clarity of the temporal relation between each event recounted.

Theater of the absurd Mid-twentieth century theater movement based on belief that the stage should reflect the meaninglessness and absurdity of human existence.

Theme Primary or secondary subject of a work of art or literature.

Theodicy An explanation for the existence of evil in the world.

Thesis The summary of the **developed argument** of an essay.

Title The name of a text; in a summary, the bibliographical reference for the text being summarized.

Tone The attitude of a poem's **speaker** or the **narrator** of a text toward the material of the poem or narrative.

Tragedy, Elizabethan A five-act play including a variety of action and characters around a central tragic protagonist, a central theme, and a dramatic arc that ends badly, usually written in a mixed style.

Tragedy, Greek A drama that begins well and ends badly, written in a formal, elevated, and poetic style, involving high-born characters who transgress the norms of their society, and a **chorus** that stands wholly or partly outside of the action.

Type A **character** identified in terms of an external situation—occupation, social status, plot function—rather than individual subjectivity.

Word choice Refers to the choice of words in a sentence or line of poetry, one element of its **diction.**

Word order Refers to the possible ways of ordering the words in a sentence or line of poetry, one element of the **diction** of a text.

Wordplay A **literary device** that plays on different meanings in a single word, or in words that resemble one another.

Works-cited list A list of all the sources consulted and cited in writing a paper, ordered alphabetically in MLA or another official style of documentation.

Zeugma A **literary device** that uses a single verb to govern several objects or clauses, each in a different sense of the verb.

CREDITS

TEXT CREDITS

Achebe, Chinua. "Dead Men's Path" from *Girls at War and Other Stories* by Chinua Achebe, copyright © 1972, 1973 by Chinua Achebe. Used by permission of Doubleday, a division of Random House, Inc. and The Wylie Agency LLC.

Alexie, Sherman. "This Is What it Means to Say Phoenix, Arizona" from *The Lone Ranger and Tonto Fistfight in Heaven*, copyright © 1993, 2005 by Sherman Alexie. Used by permission of Grove/Atlantic, Inc.

Ali, Agha Shahid. "The Wolf's Postscript to 'Little Red Riding Hood'" from *The Veiled Suite: The Collected Poems*. Copyright © 1987 by Agha Shadid Ali. Used by permission of W. W. Norton & Company, Inc.

Alvarez, Julia. "Snow" from *How the Garcia Girls Lost Their Accents*, copyright © 1991 by Julia Alvarez. Published by Plume, an imprint of The Penguin Group (USA), and originally in hardcover by Algonquin Books of Chapel Hill. Reprinted by permission of Susan Bergholz Literary Services, New York, NY and Lamy, NM. All rights reserved.

Atwood, Margaret. "Happy Endings" from *Good Bones and Simple Murders*, copyright © 1983, 1992, 1994 by O. W. Toad Ltd. A Nan A. Talese Book. Used by permission of Doubleday, a division of Random House, Inc. and McClelland & Stewart Ltd.

Auden, W. H. "Musée des Beaux Arts" copyright 1940 and renewed 1968 by W. H. Auden, from *Collected Poems* by W. H. Auden. Reprinted by permission of Random House, Inc.

Baca, Jimmy Santiago. "So Mexicans Are Taking Jobs from Americans" from *Immigrants in Our Own Land*, copyright © 1979 by Jimmy Santiago Baca. Reprinted by permission of New Directions Publishing Corp.

Baca, Jimmy Santiago. "Spliced Wire" from *Immigrants in our Own Land*, copyright © 1979 by Jimmy Santiago Baca. Reprinted by permission of New Directions Publishing Corp.

Baldwin, James. "Sonny's Blues," copyright © 1957 by James Baldwin. Originally published in *Partisan Review*. Copyright renewed. Collected in *Going to Meet the Man*, published by Vintage Books. Reprinted by arrangement with the James Baldwin Estate.

Bambara, Toni Cade. "The Lesson," copyright © 1972 by Toni Cade Bambara from *Gorilla, My Love* by Toni Cade Bambara. Used by permission of Random House, Inc.

Bashō, Matsuo. Selected Haiku from "The Narrow Road to the Deep North" translated by Haruo Shirane, from *Early Modern Japanese Literature: An Anthology, 1600-1900*, edited by Haruo Shirane. Copyright © 2002 by Columbian University Press.

Beckett, Samuel. *Krapp's Last Tape*, copyright © 1958 by the Estate of Samuel Beckett. Used by permission of Grove/Atlantic, Inc.

Berry, Wendell "Stay Home" from *The Selected Poems of Wendell Berry*. Copyright © 1999 by Wendell Berry. Reprinted by permission of Counterpoint.

Bishop, Elizabeth. "The Fish" from *The Complete Poems 1927-1979*. Copyright 1979, 1983 by Alice Helen Methfessel. Reprinted by permission of Farrar, Straus and Giroux, LLC.

Bishop, Elizabeth. "In the Waiting Room" from *The Complete Poems 1927-1979*, copyright © 1979, 1983 by Alice Helen Methfessel. Reprinted by permission of Farrar, Straus, and Giroux, LLC.

Boyle, T. Coraghessan. "Greasy Lake" from *Greasy Lake and Other Stories*, copyright © 1979, 1981, 1982, 1983, 1984, 1985 by T. Coraghessan Boyle. Used by permission of Viking Penguin, a division of Penguin Group (USA) Inc.

Brooks, Rosa Ehrenreich. "I Hate Trees", originally published in *Mademoiselle Magazine*. Reprinted by permission of the author.

Buford, Bill. "Lions and Tigers and Bears." Originally published in *The New Yorker*. Copyright © 1999 by Bill Buford. Reprinted by permission of The Wylie Agency LLC.

Carson, Rachel. "The Marginal World" from *The Edge of the Sea*. Copyright © 1955 by Rachel L. Carson, renewed 1983 by Roger Christie. Reprinted by permission of Houghton Mifflin Harcourt Publishing Company. All rights reserved.

Carver, Raymond. "Cathedral" from *Cathedral*, copyright © 1981, 1982, 1983 by Raymond Carver. Used by permission of Alfred A. Knopf, a division of Random House.

Catullus. "I hate and I love" (p. 197) from *The Poems of Catullus* translated with an introduction by Peter Whigham (Penguin Classics, 1966). Copyright © Penguin Books Ltd., 1966. Reproduced by permission of Penguin Books Ltd.

Clifton, Lucille. "wishes for sons" from *Quilting: Poems 1987-1990*, copyright © 1991 by Lucille Clifton. Reprinted with the permission of BOA Editions, Ltd., www.boaeditions.org.

Cole, K. C. "Murmurs" from *Mind Over Matter: Conversations with the Cosmos*, copyright © 2003 by K. C. Cole, reprinted by permission of Houghton Mifflin Harcourt Publishing Company.

Cortázar, Julio. "Axolotl" translated by Paul Blackburn from *End of the Game and Other Stories*, copyright © 1963, 1967 by Random House, Inc. Used by permission of Pantheon Books, a division of Random House.

Cortázar, Julio. "The Tiger Lodgers" translated by Paul Blackburn from *Cronopios and Famas*, copyright © 1962 by Julio Cortázar and the Heirs of Julio Cortázar. Translation copyright © 1969 by Random house, Inc. Reprinted by permission of New Directions Publishing and Agencia Literaria Carmen Balcells S. A.

Cronin, Jeremy. "To learn how to speak . . ." from *Inside and Out*, copyright © 1999 by Jeremy Cronin. Reprinted by permission of David Philip.

Dickinson, Emily. "Because I could not stop for death." Reprinted by permission of the publishers and the Trustees of Amherst College from *The Poems of Emily Dickinson*, Thomas H. Johnson, ed. Cambridge, Mass: The Belknap Press of Harvard University Press, copyright © 1951, 1955, 1979, 1983 by the President and Fellows of Harvard College.

Dickinson, Emily. "I felt a Funeral in my Brain." Reprinted by permission of the publishers and the Trustees of Amherst College from *The Poems of Emily Dickinson*, Thomas H. Johnson, ed. Cambridge, Mass: The Belknap Press of Harvard University Press, copyright © 1951, 1955, 1979, 1983 by the President and Fellows of Harvard College.

Dickinson, Emily. "I heard a Fly buzz - when I died." Reprinted by permission of the publishers and the Trustees of Amherst College from *The Poems of Emily Dickinson*, Thomas H. Johnson, ed. Cambridge, Mass: The Belknap Press of Harvard University Press, copyright © 1951, 1955, 1979, 1983 by the President and Fellows of Harvard College.

Dickinson, Emily. "I like a look of agony" Reprinted by permission of the publishers and the Trustees of Amherst College from *The Poems of Emily Dickinson*, Thomas H. Johnson, ed. Cambridge, Mass: The Belknap Press of Harvard University Press, copyright © 1951, 1955, 1979, 1983 by the President and Fellows of Harvard College.

Dickinson, Emily. "It was not Death for I stood up." Reprinted by permission of the publishers and the Trustees of Amherst College from *The Poems of Emily Dickinson*, Thomas H. Johnson, ed. Cambridge, Mass: The Belknap Press of Harvard University Press, copyright © 1951, 1955, 1979, 1983 by the President and Fellows of Harvard College.

Dickinson, Emily. "Tell the truth but tell it slant." Reprinted by permission of the publishers and the Trustees of Amherst College from *The Poems of Emily Dickinson*, Thomas H. Johnson, ed. Cambridge, Mass: The Belknap Press of Harvard University Press, copyright © 1951, 1955, 1979, 1983 by the President and Fellows of Harvard College.

Dickinson, Emily. "A toad can die of light - " Reprinted by permission of the publishers and the Trustees of Amherst College from *The Poems of Emily Dickinson*, Thomas H. Johnson, ed. Cambridge, Mass: The Belknap Press of Harvard University Press, copyright © 1951, 1955, 1979, 1983 by the President and Fellows of Harvard College.

Dillard, Annie. "The Death of a Moth" from *Holy the Firm*, copyright © 1977 by Annie Dillard. Reprinted by permission of HarperCollins Publishers.

Doolittle, Hilda. The "Sea Rose" from *Collected Poems 1912-1944*, copyright © 1982 by The Estate of Hilda Doolittle. Reprinted by permission of New Directions Publishing.

Dylan, Bob. Five lines from "Like a Rolling Stone," copyright © 1965; renewed 1993 Special Rider Music. All rights reserved. International copyright secured. Reprinted by permission.

Eliot, T. S. "The Love Song of J. Alfred Prufrock" from *Prufrock and Other Observations*. Reprinted by permission of Faber and Faber Ltd.

Erdrich, Louise. "Dear John Wayne" from *That's What She Said: A Collection of Contemporary Fiction and Poetry by Native American Women*. Copyright © 1984 by Louise Erdrich, reprinted with permission of The Wylie Agency, Inc.

Pamuk, Orhan. "My Father's Suitcase" Nobel Lecture given December 7, 2006. Copyright © The Nobel Foundation 2006. Reprinted with permission.

Pamuk, Orhan. "To Look out the Window" from *Other Colours: Essays and a Story* by Orhan Pamuk, translated by Maureen Freely, translation copyright © 2007 by Maureen Freely. Used by permission of Alfred A. Knopf, a division of Random House.

Parker, Dorothy. "The Waltz" copyright 1933, renewed © 1961 by Dorothy Parker, from *The Portable Dorothy Parker* by Dorothy Parker, edited by Marion Meade. Used by permission of Viking Penguin, a division of Penguin Group (USA) Inc.

Plath, Sylvia. "Metaphors" from *Crossing the Water* by Sylvia Plath. Copyright © 1960 by Ted Hughes. Reprinted by HarperCollins Publishers and Faber and Faber.

Pound, Ezra. "I hate and love" from *The Translations of Ezra Pound,* copyright © 1963 by Ezra Pound. Reprinted by permission of New Directions Publishing Corp.

Pound, Ezra. "In a Station of the Metro" from *Personae,* copyright 1926 by Ezra Pound. Reprinted by permission of New Directions Publishing.

Powell, Padgett. "A Gentleman's C" from *Typical* published by Farrar, Straus and Giroux, 1991. Reprinted by permission of the author.

Rushdie, Salman. "Imagine There's No Heaven" from *Step Across the Line* by Salman Rushdie, copyright © 2002 by Salman Rushdie. Reprinted by permission of Random House, Inc.

Sagan, Miriam. "Translating Catullus," 2002. Reprinted by permission of the author.

Sanders, Scott Russell. "Buckeye," copyright © 1995 by Scott Russell Sanders; first published in *Orion*; collected in the author's *Writing from the Center* (Indiana U.P., 1995). Reprinted by permission of the author.

Sarton, May. "The Rewards of Living a Solitary Life" from *The New York Times,* (April 8, 1974). Copyright © 1974 by The New York Times. All rights reserved. Used by permission and protected by the Copyright Laws of the United States. The printing, copying, redistribution, or transmission of the Material without express written permission is prohibited.

Sexton, Anne. "Red Riding Hood" from *Transformations.* Copyright © 1971 by Anne Sexton, renewed 1999 by Linda G. Sexton. Reprinted by permission of Houghton Mifflin Harcourt Publishing Company. All rights reserved.

Shakespeare, William. Notes to "Hamlet, Prince of Denmark" from *The Complete Works of Shakespeare,* 6th ed. by David Bevington, copyright © 2009 by Pearson Education. Reprinted by permission.

Shields, Carol. "Absence" from *Dressing Up for the Carnival,* copyright © 2000 by Carol Shields. Used by permission of Viking Penguin, a division of The Penguin Group (USA) Inc.

Shonagon, Sei. "Hateful Things" from *The Pillow Book of Sei Shonagon,* translated by Ivan Morris, 1967. Reprinted with permission of Columbia University Press and Oxford University Press.

Smith, Stevie. "Not Waving but Drowning" from *Collected Poems of Stevie Smith,* copyright © 1972 by Stevie Smith. Reprinted by permission of New Directions Publishing.

Sophocles. "Antigonê" from *Sophocles, The Oedipus Cycle: An English Version* by Dudley Fitts and Robert Fitzgerald, copyright 1939 by Harcourt, Inc. and renewed 1967 by Dudley Fitts and Robert Fitzgerald, reprinted by permission of the publisher. CAUTION: All rights, including professional, amateur, motion picture, recitation, lecturing, performance, public reading, radio broadcasting, and television are strictly reserved. Inquiries on all rights should be addressed to Houghton Mifflin Harcourt Publishing Company, Permissions Department, Orlando, FL 32887-6777.

Soto, Gary. "Behind Grandma's House" from *New and Selected Poems,* copyright © 1995 by Gary Soto. Used with permission of Chronicle Books LLC, San Francisco. Visit ChronicleBooks.com.

Steinbeck, John. "The Chrysanthemums," copyright 1937, renewed © 1965 by John Steinbeck. From *The Long Valley* by John Steinbeck. Used by permission of Viking Penguin, a division of Penguin Group (USA) Inc.

Szymborska, Wisława "Lot's Wife" from *View with a Grain of Sand* copyright © 1993 by Wisława Szymborska. English translation by Stanisław Barańczak and Clare Cavanagh copyright © 1993 by Houghton Mifflin Harcourt Publishing Company, reprinted with permission of the publisher.

TallMountain, Mary. "There Is No Word for Goodbye" from *There Is No Word for Goodbye,* copyright © TallMountain Literary Estate. Reprinted with permission.

Tan, Amy. From "Mother Tongue" copyright © 1989 by Amy Tan. First appeared in *The Threepenny Review.* Reprinted by permission of the author and the Sandra Dijkstra Literary Agency.

Taylor, Henry. "Landscape with Tractor" from *The Flying Change,* copyright © 1985 by Henry Taylor, Louisiana Paperback Editions. Reprinted with permission.

Thomas, Dylan. "Do Not Go Gentle into That Good Night" from *The Poems of Dylan Thomas,* copyright © 1952 by Dylan Thomas. Reprinted by permission of New Directions Publishing Corp.

Tsui, Kitty. "A Chinese Banquet" from *The Words of a Woman Who Breathes Fire* (Iowa City's Women's Press, 1983).

Updike, John. "A&P" from *Pigeon Feathers and Other Stories,* copyright © 1962 and renewed 1990 by John Updike. Used by permission of Alfred A. Knopf, a division of Random House, Inc.

Uruttiran. "What She Said to Her Girl Friend" from *Poems of Love and War: From the Eight Anthologies and the Ten Long Poems of Classical Tamil,* translated by A. K. Ramanujan. Published by Columbia University Press, 1985. Reprinted by permission.

Villaneueva, Tino. "Variations on a Theme by William Carlos Williams" from *Shaking Off the Dark* by Tino Villanueva. Copyright © 1998 by Bilingual Press/Editorial Bilingue. Originally published in 1984, re-published in 1998 by Bilingual Press/Editorial Bilingue, Arizona State University, Tempe AZ. Reprinted by permission of the publisher.

Wainaina, Binyavanaga. "How to Write about Africa" from *Granta* 92, Winter 2005. Reprinted with permission.

Walker, Alice. "Everyday Use" from *In Love and Trouble: Stories of Black Women,* copyright © 1973 by Alice Walker, reprinted by permission of Houghton Mifflin Harcourt Publishing Compay.

Welty, Eudora. "A Worm Path" from *A Curtain of Green and Other Stories,* copyright 1941 and renewed 1969 by Eudora Welty. Reprinted by permission of Houghton Mifflin Harcourt Publishing Company.

Williams, William Carlos. "Landscape with the Fall of Icarus" from *The Collected Poems: Volume II, 1939-1962,* copyright © 1962 by William Carlos Williams. Reprinted with permission of New Directions Publishing Corp.

Williams, William Carlos. "The Red Wheelbarrow" and "The Is Just to Say" from *Collected Poems: Volume I, 1909-1939,* copyright © 1938 by New Directions Publishing. Reprinted with permission of New Directions Publishing Corp.

Woolf, Virginia. "The Death of the Moth" from *The Death of the Moth and Other Essays,* copyright 1942 by Houghton Mifflin Harcourt Publishing Company and renewed 1970 by Marjorie T. Parsons, Executrix. Reprinted by permission of the publisher.

Wright, James. "Lying in a Hammock at William Duffy's Farm in Pine Island, Minnesota" from *Above the River: The Complete Poems,* © 1990 by Ann Wright and reprinted by permission of Wesleyan University Press.

Wright, Richard. Haiku #31 from *Haiku: This Other World,* copyright © 1998 by Richard Wright. Reprinted by permission of John Hawkins & Associates, Inc.

PHOTO CREDITS

Alaska Fairbanks Theater Department; Public Domain; p. 115, top to bottom: Archives of Ontario, F 4446-63-3; Excerpt from *Fun Home: A Family Tragicomic* by Alison Bechdel. Copyright © 2006 by Alison Bechdel. Reprinted by permission of Houghton Mifflin Harcourt; Library of Congress; p. 120: Creatas/Photolibrary; p. 127: IFC Films/Everett Digital; p. 132: Public Domain; p. 146: Kade Mendelowitz, University of Alaska Fairbanks Theater Department; p. 149: Archives of Ontario, F4446-63-3; p. 150: Everett Digital; p. 165: Public Domain; p. 166: Robert Capa/Magnum Photos; p. 168: Peanuts: © United Feature Syndicate, Inc.; p. 169: Excerpt from *Fun Home: A Family Tragicomic* by Alison Bechdel. Copyright © 2006 by Alison Bechdel. Reprinted by permission of Houghton Mifflin Harcourt Publishing Company. All rights reserved.; p. 170: Library of Congress; p. 171, top to bottom: Sony Pictures Classics/Everett Collection; De Laurentis Group/Everett Collection; p. 172: Scott McCloud. **Chapter 5** Page 174, counter-clockwise from top left: Rolf Muller/Wikipedia; Peanuts: © United Feature Syndicate, Inc.; Fitzwilliam Museum, University of Cambridge, UK/The Bridgeman Art Library; Photofest; Jessica Osborn; Photofest p. 175, top to bottom: Library of Congress; Fitzwilliam Museum, University of Cambridge, UK/The Bridgeman Art Library; p. 176, top to bottom: The Granger Collection; Rolf Muller/Wikipedia; p. 177: Miriam Berkley; p. 178: Liquid Light/Alamy; p. 184: Dorothy Alexander; p. 185: Peanuts: © United Feature Syndicate, Inc.; p. 188: Reza/Getty Images; p. 189: Hulton Archive/Getty Images; p. 193: Photofest; p. 195: Photofest; p. 200: Colin McPherson/Corbis; p. 203: Jessica Osborn. **Chapter 6** Page 210, top to bottom: The Gallery Collection/Corbis; © The New Yorker Collection 1999 Leo Cullum from cartoonbank.com. All Rights Reserved.; Columbia Pictures/Photofest; The Granger Collection; p. 211: Keats-Shelley House, Rome; p. 213: PEARLS BEFORE SWINE © Stephan Pastis/United Feature Syndicate, Inc.; p. 217, left to right: © The New Yorker Collection 1999 Leo Cullum from cartoonbank.com. All Rights Reserved.; The Granger Collection; p. 218, top to bottom: Big Stock Photo; iStockphoto; p. 219, left to right: Columbia Pictures/Photofest; AP Images/Nic Ut; p. 220: Reunion des Musees Nationaux/Art Resource, NY; p. 221: Films du Loups/TSF/Gaumont/The Kobal Collection; p. 222: Adbusters; p. 223: Keats-Shelley House, Rome; p. 224: National Portrait Library, London; p. 225, top to bottom: Michael Nicholson/Corbis; The Granger Collection; p. 226, top to bottom: Library of Congress; The Gallery Collection/Corbis; p. 227: Library of Congress; p. 228: Library of Congress; p. 229, top to bottom: Caroline Forbes; Miriam Berkley; p. 230: Toho/Cowboy/Photofest. **Chapter 7** Page 232, top to bottom: Focus Features/Everett Collection; Bancroft Library, University of California, Berkeley; Jim McHugh; p. 233: Scala/Art Resource, NY; p. 234: Stock Italia/Alamy; p. 235: Jerry Bauer; p. 236: Abigail Adler; p. 237: Focus Features/Everett Collection; p. 238: The Granger Collection; p. 239: The British Library; p. 240: Lance Woodruff; p. 241, top to bottom: Janine Crowley; Bancroft Library, University of California, Berkeley; p. 242, top to bottom: Frank Capri/Getty Images; Jim McHugh. **Chapter 8** Page 246, counter-clockwise from top: Everett Collection; University College Dublin; Everett Collection; Angers Museum, France/Superstock; Bibliotheque des Arts Decoratifs, Paris, France, Archives Charmet/The Bridgeman Art Library; blickwinkel/Alamy; p. 247: Time Life Pictures/Getty Images (3); p. 248: Rene Burri/Magnum Photos; p. 250: AP Image; p. 258: Library of Congress p. 274: Giulio Napolitano/Grazia Neri/Polaris; p. 278: Hulton Archive/Getty Images p. 283, top to bottom: Courtesy Robert Hayden; Miriam Berkley; p. 284, top to bottom: Jill Posener; Samuel Goldwyn/Everett Collection; p. 285: National Portrait Library, London; p. 286: Tristram Kenton/LeBrecht Photo Library; p. 300: Everett Collection; p. 311: Everett Collection; p. 325: Private Collection/Photo © Christie's Images/The Bridgeman Art Library; p. 336: Keystone/Eyedea/Everett Collection; p. 347: Steve Raymer; p. 348: blickwinkel/Alamy; p. 351: Sigrid Estrada; p. 352: Nancy Crampton; p. 353: Everett Collection; p. 355, top to bottom: The Granger Collection; Image taken from the original in Special Collections, University College Dublin Library; p. 358: Bettmann/Corbis; p. 359: Bettmann/Corbis; p. 362: Library of Congress; p. 363: Martin and Osa Johnson Safari Museum; p. 364: Bettmann/Corbis; p. 365: Bibliotheque des Arts Decoratifs, Paris, France, Archives Charmet/The Bridgeman Art Library; p. 367, top to bottom: Margaretta Mitchell; MGM/Photofest; p. 368: AP Images; p. 369, top to bottom: Nikolas Muray. Courtesy of George Eastman House, International Museum of Photography and Film; Denise and Tom Low; p. 371: Banques d'Images, ADAGP/Art Resource, NY; p. 372: The Granger Collection; p. 375: Bettmann/Corbis; p. 376: Oxford Scientific/Jupiter Images; p. 382: Hal Beral/Corbis; p. 383: Araldo de Luca/Corbis; p. 384, top to bottom: E.O. Hoppe/Corbis; National Portrait Library, London; p. 386: National Portrait Library, London; p. 387: AP Images/Frank Eyers; p. 388, top to bottom: Library of Congress; Freer Gallery of Art, Smithsonian Institution, Washington, DC: Gift of Charles Lang Greer, F1905.129a-b; p. 389: The Granger Collection; p. 391: Private Collection/Gianni Dagli Orti/The Art Archive; p. 392: Giraudon/The Bridgeman Art Library. **Europe Casebook** Page 394, top to bottom: Carsten Peter/National Geographic Stock; Nigel Hillier/Getty Images; Bridgeman-Giraudon/Art Resource, NY; p. 395: Map Resources; p. 396, top to bottom: The Granger Collection; Simeone Huber/Getty Images; p. 397, clockwise from top left: Biblioteca Monasterio del Escorial, Madrid, Spain, Index/The Bridgeman Art Library; Simon Crubellier/Getty Images; Comic map of Europe by Frederick Rose, c. 1879 (litho)/Private Collection/The Bridgeman Art Library; p. 398: Spencer Platt/Getty Images; p. 400: Bodleian Library/Oxford/The Art Archive; p. 402: Grant Faint/Getty Images; p. 417: Stephen Dalton/Photo Researchers; p. 421: Public Domain. **Chapter 9** Page 424, counter-clockwise from top left: The Granger Collection; Antonio M. Rosario/Getty Images; The Granger Collection; Smithsonian American Art Museum, Washington, DC; Simon Carter Gallery, Woodbridge, Suffolk, UK/The Bridgeman Art Library; Susan Meiselas/Magnum Photos; p. 425, clockwise from top left: Everett Collection; DeA Picture Library/Art Resource, NY; Public Domain; p. 429: Giraudon/The Bridgeman Art Library; p. 431: Ulf Andersen/Getty Images; p. 433, top to bottom: www.maggiesmith.com; Antonio M. Rosario/Getty Images; p. 435: Mark Sexton/Peabody Essex Museum; p. 442: Kate Chopin House, Cloutiersvile, LA; p. 444, top to bottom: Library of Congress; Ruth Tomlinson/Robert Harding Picture Library; p. 447: Peter Power/Toronto Star/Zuma Press; p. 456: The Granger Collection; p. 457, top to bottom: The Granger Collection; National Portrait Library, London; p. 458: The Granger Collection; p. 459, top to bottom: The Granger Collection; Smithsonian American Art Museum, Washington, DC/Art Resource, NY; p. 463, top to bottom: Jacek Bednarczyk/PAP/Corbis; Public Domain; p. 464, top to bottom: Christopher Felver/Corbis; Susan Meiselas/Getty Images; p. 465: The Bridgeman Art Gallery; p. 466: Simon Carter Library, Woodbridge, Suffolk, UK/The Bridgeman Art Library. **Africa Casebook** Page 484, top to bottom: The Granger Collection; DLILLC/Corbis; Remi Benali/Getty Images; p. 485: Map Resources; p. 486, clockwise from top: Private Collection/The Bridgeman Art Library; Ariadne Van Zandbergen/Getty Images; Bildarchiv Preussischer Kulturbesitz/Art Resource, NY; p. 487, clockwise from top left: Kampbel/AFP/Getty Images; The Granger Collection; New Yorker Films/Everett Collection; p. 488: Andersen/Sipa Press; p. 491: Adam Jones/Danita Delimont/Alamy; p. 503: Paul Weinberg. **Chapter 10** Page 504, counter-clockwise from top left: Dorling Kindersley Media Library; AP Image; Scott Smith/Corbis; North Carolina Museum of Art/Corbis; Nancy Santos; Digital Image © The Museum of Modern Art/Licensed by SCALA/Art Resource, NY; p. 505, clockwise from top left: National Archives; Digital Image © The Museum of Modern Art/Licensed by SCALA/Art Resource, NY; Tate, London/Art Resource, NY; p. 506, top to bottom: Jack Robinson/Hulton Archive/Getty Images; Scott Smith/Corbis; p. 507: AP Image; p. 511: Jerry Bauer; p. 517: Dorling Kindersley Media Library; p. 519: Marion Ettlinger; p. 525: E.O. Hoppe/Corbis; p. 526: AP Images/Nancy Crampton; p. 527: AP Images/Nancy Brown; p. 528, top to bottom: Nancy Crampton; RKO Radio Pictures/Photofest; p. 529: Nancy Crampton; p. 530: Chip Somodevilla/Getty Images; p. 531, top to bottom: Alfred Eisenstadt/Time Life Pictures/Getty Images; James C. Kuhn IV/takomabibelot; p. 534, top to bottom: Jane Evelyn Atwood/Agence Vu/Contact Press Images; Library of Congress; p. 537: Patrick Byrd/Getty Images; p. 538: Bern Keating/Black Star; p. 543: Corbis; p. 552: Library of Congress; p. 553, top to bottom: Evening Standard/Getty Images; Library of Congress; p. 554: North Carolina Museum of Art/Corbis; p. 555, top to bottom: Miriam and Ira D. Wallach Division of Arts, Prints and Photographs/New York Public Library; Nancy Santos; p. 590: The Granger Collection; p. 592: Henri Cartier-Bresson/Magnum Photos; p. 594: National Archives. **Asia Casebook** Page 598, top to bottom: The Granger Collection (2); Jill Gocher/Getty Images; p. 599: Map Resources; p. 600, top to bottom: Marco Simoni/Getty Images; The Granger Collection; p. 601, clockwise from top left: DAJ/Getty Images; Getty Images (2); British Library, London, UK/© British Library Board. All Rights Reserved/The Bridgeman Art Library; p. 602: Elena Seibert; p. 603: Habibullah Bahar; 614: F. Staud/www.phototravels.net. **Chapter 11** Page 622, counter-clockwise from top left: Harvey Lloyd/Getty Images; Wolfgang Volz/laif/Redux Pictures; Caleb Smith; Everett Collection; Dorling Kindersley Media Library; Mary Evans Picture Library; p. 623, top to bottom: Courtesy Arcosanti, Rendering: Young Soo Kim; Courtesy Arcosanti, Photo: Chris Ohlinger; Art on File/Corbis; p. 624, bottom: Annie Valva; p. 626: Ted Pink/Alamy p. 629, top to bottom: Library of Congress; Everett Collection; p. 630: Public Domain; p. 631, top to bottom: Nancy Crampton; Ferdinando Scianna/Magnum Photos; p. 632: Nikolas Muray. Courtesy of George Eastman House, International Museum of Photography and Film; p. 633: Ulf Andersen/Getty Images; p. 634: Shane Kelley/Kelley Graphics; p. 639: Wolfgang Volz/laif/Redux Pictures (2); p. 640: Wolfgang Volz/laif/Redux Pictures; p. 641: Bettmann/Corbis; p. 643: Dorling Kindersley Media Library; p. 646: Nancy Crampton; p. 652: Snark/Art Resource, NY; p. 653, top to bottom: Hulton Archive/Getty Images; Library of Congress; p. 654, top to bottom: Bettmann/Corbis; Mary Evans Picture Library; p. 655: Library of Congress; p. 656: Library of Congress; p. 657: Nikolas Muray. Courtesy of George Eastman House, International Museum of Photography and Film; p. 658, top to bottom: Private Collection/The Bridgeman Art Library; Mary Evans Picture Library/The Image Works; p. 659, top to bottom: Land Institute; The Granger Collection; p. 660, top to bottom: Caleb Smith; AP Image; p. 661, top to bottom: Don Smith/Getty Images; Don Harris/UCSC Photo Services; p. 662, Harvey Lloyd/Getty Images; p. 663: Courtesy Sustainer Institute: Stuart Bratesman, Dartmouth College, 1998. **Americas Casebook** Page 666, top to bottom: Rue des Archives/The Granger Collection; Chad Ehlers/Getty Images; Mingei International Museum/Art Resource, NY; p. 667: Map Resources; p. 668: The Granger Collection; p. 669, clockwise from top left: David Madison/Getty Images; AP Images/Gerald Lopez-Cepero; Biblioteca Universidad, Barcelona, Spain/© Paul Maeyaert/The Bridgeman Art Library; AP Images/Lenny Igneizi; p. 670: Rene Burri/Magnum Photos.

Cohen, Joshua, 195–198
Cole, K. C.
    Murmurs, 433–434
Coleridge, Samuel Taylor
    Metrical Feet—Lesson for a Boy, 123–124
The Colonel, 464, APP A-8
comedy, 153–154, G-2
comic drama, 155, G-2
comics, 164, G-2
The Coming of Age of Louis XIII, 220f
common knowledge, 90, G-2
comparison papers, 48, 70, 74–78, 199, G-3
Complete Destruction, 456
concrete diction, 127
consonance, 124, 211–212, G-2
constraints, 11, G-2
contradiction, 212
contrafactum, 222, G-2
conventions, 4, 10, G-2
Cortázar, Julio
    Axolotl, 5, 213, 416–419
    The Tiger Lodgers, 248–249
couplet, 129
creator, 88, 122, G-2
critical studies, APP A-6
critical thinking, 48–54, 70, 78–80
Cronin, Jeremy
    To learn how to speak, 500–501
cultural studies, APP A-6
cuts, 169, G-2

D

Dead Men's Path, 44–48
dead metaphor, 220, G-3
Dear John Wayne, 528–529, APP A-7
Death Be Not Proud, 128, 457
Death of a Moth, 158–164
The Death of the Moth, 156, 161–163
deconstructive criticism, APP A-7
definition, 41
definitional arguments, 42, G-1
dénouement, 146, G-2
dependent clauses, 20, G-1
depth of characterization, 148
depth of narration, 135, G-3
descriptive essays, 164, 186–189, G-2
developed arguments, 43, G-1
dialects, 237, G-2
Dickinson, Emily
    Because I Could Not Stop for Death, 212, 459
    I Felt a Funeral in My Brain, 127, 460
    I heard a Fly buzz - when I died-, 460
    I like a look of Agony, 459
    It was not Death, for I stood up, 461
    Tell All the Truth, 212, 462
    A Toad, can die of Light, 461
diction, 59, 126–127, 137
Didion, Joan, 156
diegetic music, 150, G-2
Dillard, Annie
    Death of a Moth, 158–164
doggerel, 129
A Doll's House, 153, 504, 555–589
Donne, John
    Death Be Not Proud, 128, 457
    The Flea, 127, 386
Do Not Go Gentle into That Good Night, 128,
    458, APP A-2

Doolittle, Hilda
    The Sea Rose, 654
drama. *See* Plays
dramatic arc, 146, G-2
dramatic irony, 152, G-3
Dulce et Decorum Est, 238–239, APP A-3,
    APP A-8
Dunbar, Paul Laurence
    Sympathy, 552
Dylan, Bob
    Like a Rolling Stone, 125

E

ecphrasis, 223, G-2
elegy, 129
Eliot, T. S.
    The Love Song of J. Alfred Prufrock, 122,
        127, 389–391, APP A-7
elision, 126, G-2
Elizabethan sonnet, 128
Elizabethan tragedy, 153, G-5
ellipsis, 95, G-2
emblem, 218, G-2
end-rhyme, 124, G-2
end-stopped lines, 126
enigma, 9
enjambment, 20, 51, G-2
epics, 122, G-2
epic theatre, 154, G-2
Erdrich, Louise
    Dear John Wayne, 528–529, APP A-7
essays, 156, 158, 160–161, 164, G-2
ethics, 435
ethnic studies, APP A-7
etiological myth, 434, G-2
European literature, 396–397
evaluation arguments, 41, 42, G-2
Everyday Use, 278–282
expectations, 11, G-2
explication, 47, G-2
expository approaches, APP A-1–APP A-3
expository essays, 164, G-2
eye rhyme, 124

F

fable, 219, G-2
Facing It, 529–530, APP A-7
fair use doctrine, 90, G-2
Falling Soldier, 166f
false cognates, 8, G-1
The Family of Man, 247
A Family Supper, 137, 613–618
farce, 153, G-2
Faulkner, William
    A Rose for Emily, 538–543
feminist criticism, APP A-7
Fernández, Roberto
    Wrong Channel, 7
fiction
    forms of, 132
    history and, 131–132
    materials of, 133–137
    tools of, 137–138
figurative meanings, 6, 138, G-3
figures of speech, 137–138, G-2
Fire and Ice, 457
First, grant me my sense of history, 367
first-person narrator, 135, G-3

The Fish, 130, 158, 655–656
The Flea, 127, 386
Foer, Jonathan Safran
    A Primer for the Punctuation of Heart
        Disease, 11, 274–278
foils, 148, G-2
foot, 122, G-2
Forché, Carolyn
    The Colonel, 464, APP A-8
form, 122, G-2
formal diction, 127
formalist criticism, APP A-2
Foster, Myles Birket
    Children Picking Blackberries, 79f,
        165–166
Four haiku, 652, APP A-3
Fourtouni, Eleni
    Child's Memory, 420–421
free verse, 130
Frost, Robert
    A Brook in the City, 129, 659–660
    Fire and Ice, 457
    Mending Wall, 525–526
    Stopping by Woods on a Snowy Evening,
        176, 179–183
Fun Home, 169f

G

Gang, Xu
    Red Azalea on the Cliff, 620–621
García Lorca, Federico
    Green how I want you green, 5–6
García Márquez, Gabriel
    The Handsomest Drowned Man in the
        World, 670–674
    The Very Old Man with Enormous Wings,
        137, 674–677
The Gates, 640
gender studies, APP A-7
Genesis, 426–429
genres. *See also* fiction; nonfiction; plays;
        poetry
    comparing, 118
    defined, G-2
    meaning and, 4
    plot conventions and expectations, 115
    storytelling and, 25
A Gentleman's C, 133–138
Gijsbrechts, Cornelius
    *Letter Rack with Christian V's
        Proclamation,* 35f, 165–166
Gilman, Charlotte Perkins
    The Yellow Wallpaper, 5, 136, 543–551,
        APP A-7
Ginsberg, Allen
    A Supermarket in California, 629, APP A-7
Girl, 351–352
Glaspell, Susan
    Trifles, 139–153, 211, 216, APP A-2,
        APP A-7
good and evil, 425
A Good Man is Hard to Find, 135
graphic novels, 167, G-3
Greasy Lake, 136, 138, 222, 646–651
The Greek Slave, 225
Greek tragedy, 153, G-5
Green how I want you green, 5
groundlings, 153, G-2

The Marginal World, 531–533
Mark but this flea, 386
Martin, Charles
    I hate & love, 234
Martone, Michael
    The Mayor of the Sister City Speaks to the
        Chamber of Commerce in Klamath Falls,
        Oregon, on a Night in December 1976, 241
Marxist criticsm, APP A-5
The Mayor of the Sister City Speaks to the
        Chamber of Commerce in Klamath Falls,
        Oregon, on a Night in December 1976, 241
McCloud, Scott
    Choose Your Own Carl, 172f
Meadows, Donella
    Living Lightly and Inconsistently on the
        Land, 663–665
meditative essays, 164
melodrama, 149, G-3
Mending Wall, 525–526
Merwin, W. S.
    Rain at Night, 660–661
metaphor, 9, 217, 218, G-3
Metaphors, 9–10, 14
meter, 122–123, G-3
metonymy, 217, 218, G-3
Metrical Feet—Lesson for a Boy, 123–124
Miłosz, Czesław
    My Faithful Mother Tongue, 421–422
Miltonic sonnet, 128
minor characters, 134, G-1
Modern Language Association (MLA), 87
Modotti, Tina
    Campesinos, 165–166
Momaday, Scott
    The Way to Rainy Mountain, 118–121
Moore, Lorrie
    The Kid's Guide to Divorce, 352–354
Mother Tongue, 242–245
multilingualism, 237, G-3
multimedia web page, 86, G-3
Murmurs, 433–434
Musée des Beaux Arts, 228
My black face fades, 529
My daughter—as if I owned her, 16
My Faithful Mother Tongue, 422
My Father's Suitcase, 398–403
My Last Duchess, 553–554
My Two Lives, 602–604

N

narrative arguments, 41, 42, G-1
narrative chiasmus, 213, G-1
narrative ecphrasis, 223
narrative essays, 164, G-2
nature writing, 638–640
The Negro Speaks of Rivers, 212, 657
Neruda, Pablo
    The Word, 678–679
new historicism, APP A-6
Nobody heard him, the dead man, 553
nondiegetic music, 150, G-3
nonfiction, 156, 158, 160–161, 164, G-3
Norris, Leslie
    Blackberries, 71–73
Not Waving but Drowning, 553
novel, 132, G-3
novella, 132, G-3

O

objective appeal, 41
objective arguments, 41, G-1
objective style, 138, G-5
O'Brien, Tim
    The Things They Carried, 447–456, APP A-2
O'Connor, Flannery
    A Good Man is Hard to Find, 135, 250–258
ode, 129, 153, G-3
Ode on a Grecian Urn, 129, 214, 224
Olds, Sharon
    On the Subway, 631
    The Possessive, 5, 16–21, 24
Oliver, Mary
    August, 49–58, 61–69
    Singapore, 127, 177–183
omniscient point of view, 135, G-3
On Hiram Powers' Greek Slave, 128,
        225–226, APP A-3
On the Subway, 631
opening sentence, 22, G-4
optical illusions, 34–35
organizing ideas, 56–58
outlines, 58, 92, G-3
outside sources, 90, G-4
Over my head, I see the bronze butterfly, 526
Owens, Louis D.
    The American Indian Wilderness, 164,
        661–663
Owen, Wilfred
    Dulce et Decorum Est, 238–239, APP A-3,
        APP A-8
oxymoron, 214, G-3
O Yes? Do they come on horses, 680

P

Packer, George
    How Susie Bayer's T-Shirt Ended Up on
        Yusuf Mama's Back, 164, 200–209
palindrome, 213, G-3
Pamuk, Orhan
    My Father's Suitcase, 398–403
    To Look Out the Window, 404–415
parable, 25, 219, G-3
paradox, 214–215, G-4
Parker, Dorothy
    The Waltz, 136, 372–374
parody, 80, G-4
parse, 20, 46, G-4
partially unreliable narrator, 135
Peanuts, 167, 168f, 185f
persistence of vision, 169, G-4
personal essays, 164
personification, 219, G-4
persuasive essays, 164. See also
        argumentative essays
Petrarchan sonnet, 128
The Pilgrim's Progress, 217f
The Pillow Book, 164
pit, 153, G-4
plagiarism, 88–90, G-4
Plath, Sylvia
    Metaphors, 9–10, 14
Plato's Dream, 429–430
plays
    characters, 148–149
    conventions of, 139
    dramatic structure, 146–148

form and genre, 152–156
    staging, 149–151
    writing about, 194–196, 199
plot, 114, 134, G-4
Poe, Edgar Allan
    Annabel Lee, 388
    The Cask of Amontillado, 136, 534–538
Poem 85, 214
poetic feet, 122
poetry
    comparison essay about, 179–183
    diction, 126–127
    forms, 127–131
    parsing, 52
    prosody, 122–126
position, 42, G-4
The Possessive, 5, 16–21, 24
postcolonial criticism, APP A-6
postmodernist criticism, APP A-8
poststructuralism, APP A-8
Pound, Ezra
    I hate and love, 234
    In a Station of the Metro, 630,
        APP A-3
Powell, Padgett
    A Gentleman's C, 133–138
Powers, Hiram
    The Greek Slave, 225
pre-reading, 15, 49
primary sources, 85, G-4
A Primer for the Punctuation of Heart
        Disease, 11, 274–278
principal characters, 134
print history, APP A-3
processing a text, 15, 49, 51, G-4
production history, 199, APP A-3, G-4
proposal, 42, G-4
props, 151
proscenium arch, 149, G-4
prose poem, 131
prosody, 122, G-4
protagonist, 149, G-4
psychoanalytic criticism, APP A-4
psychological criticism, APP A-4
punch line, 153

Q

quantitative meter, 122
queer studies, APP A-7
questioning the text, 46, 49, 53, G-4
quotations, 94

R

Rain at Night, 660–661
range of characterization, 148
range of narration, 136, G-3
reader-response criticism, APP A-4
reading critically, 6, 15, 49, G-4
realist drama, 153, G-2
rebuttal, 42, G-4
reception history, APP A-3, APP A-4
Red Azalea on the Cliff, 620–621
Red azalea, smiling, 620
Red Riding Hood, 364–366
reference, 221
reflection, 56
reflective essays, 164, G-2
repetition, 211